International Directory of
COMPANY
HISTORIES

International Directory of

COMPANY

HISTORIES

VOLUME 118

Editor

Jay P. Pederson

ST. JAMES PRESS
A part of Gale, Cengage Learning

GALE
CENGAGE Learning

Detroit • New York • San Francisco • New Haven, Conn • Waterville, Maine • London

International Directory of Company Histories, Volume 118

Jay P. Pederson, Editor

Project Editor: Miranda H. Ferrara

Editorial: Virgil Burton, Donna Craft, Peggy Geeseman, Julie Gough, Sonya Hill, Keith Jones, Matthew Miskelly, Lynn Pearce, Laura Peterson, Holly Selden

Production Technology Specialist: Mike Weaver

Imaging and Multimedia: John Watkins

Composition and Electronic Prepress: Gary Leach, Evi Seoud

Manufacturing: Rhonda Dover

Product Manager: Jenai Drouillard

Cover Photograph: Hughes Aircraft Company. Courtesy Library of Congress, Prints & Photographs Division, Historic American Buildings Survey.

For product information and technology assistance, contact us at **Gale Customer Support, 1-800-877-4253.**
For permission to use material from this text or product, submit all requests online at **www.cengage.com/permissions.**
Further permissions questions can be emailed to **permissionrequest@cengage.com**

Gale
27500 Drake Rd.
Farmington Hills, MI, 48331-3535

LIBRARY OF CONGRESS CATALOG NUMBER 89-190943
ISBN-13: 978-1-4144-4729-2
ISBN-10: 1-4144-4729-9

This title is also available as an e-book
ISBN-13: 978-1-55862-781-9 ISBN-10: 1-55862-781-2
Contact your Gale, a part of Cengage Learning sales representative for ordering information.

BRITISH LIBRARY CATALOGUING IN PUBLICATION DATA
International directory of company histories, Vol. 118
Jay P. Pederson
33.87409

Printed in Mexico
1 2 3 4 5 6 7 14 13 12 11 10

Contents

Preface

The St. James Press series *The International Directory of Company Histories* (*IDCH*) is intended for reference use by students, business people, librarians, historians, economists, investors, job candidates, and others who seek to learn more about the historical development of the world's most important companies. To date, *IDCH* has profiled more than 11,185 companies in 118 volumes.

INCLUSION CRITERIA

Most companies chosen for inclusion in *IDCH* have achieved a minimum of US$25 million in annual sales and are leading influences in their industries or geographical locations. Companies may be publicly held, private, or nonprofit. State-owned companies that are important in their industries and that may operate much like public or private companies also are included. Wholly owned subsidiaries and divisions are profiled if they meet the requirements for inclusion. Entries on companies that have had major changes since they were last profiled may be selected for updating.

The *IDCH* series highlights 25% private and nonprofit companies, and features updated entries on approximately 35 companies per volume.

ENTRY FORMAT

Each entry begins with the company's legal name; the address of its headquarters; its telephone, toll-free, and fax numbers; and its web site. A statement of public, private, state, or parent ownership follows. A company with a legal name in both English and the language of its headquarters country is listed by the English name, with the native-language name in parentheses.

The company's founding or earliest incorporation date, the number of employees, and the most recent available sales figures follow. Sales figures are given in local currencies with equivalents in U.S. dollars. For some private companies, sales figures are estimates and indicated by the abbreviation *est.* The entry lists the exchanges on which the company's stock is traded and its ticker symbol, as well as the company's NAICS codes.

Entries generally contain a *Company Perspectives* box which provides a short summary of the company's mission, goals, and ideals; a *Key Dates* box highlighting milestones in the company's history; lists of *Principal Subsidiaries, Principal Divisions, Principal Operating Units, Principal Competitors*; and articles for *Further Reading*.

American spelling is used throughout *IDCH*, and the word "billion" is used in its U.S. sense of one thousand million.

SOURCES

Entries have been compiled from publicly accessible sources both in print and on the Internet such as general and academic periodicals, books, and annual reports, as well as material supplied by the companies themselves.

CUMULATIVE INDEXES

IDCH contains three indexes: the **Cumulative Index to Companies**, which provides an alphabetical index to companies profiled in the *IDCH* series, the **Index to Industries**, which allows researchers to locate companies by their principal industry, and the **Geographic Index**, which lists companies alphabetically by the country of their headquarters. The indexes are cumulative and specific instructions for using them are found immediately preceding each index.

SPECIAL TO THIS VOLUME

This volume of *IDCH* contains an entry on K12 Inc., a leader in online education, and Woot, Inc., an online retailer with a unique marketing and sales strategy.

SUGGESTIONS WELCOME

Comments and suggestions from users of *IDCH* on any aspect of the product as well as suggestions for companies to be included or updated are cordially invited. Please write:

The Editor
International Directory of Company Histories
St. James Press
Gale, Cengage Learning
27500 Drake Rd.
Farmington Hills, Michigan 48331-3535

St. James Press does not endorse any of the companies or products mentioned in this series. Companies appearing in the *International Directory of Company Histories* were selected without reference to their wishes and have in no way endorsed their entries.

Notes on Contributors

M. L. Cohen
Novelist, business writer, and researcher living in Paris.

Jeffrey L. Covell
Seattle-based writer.

Ed Dinger
Writer and editor based in Bronx, New York.

Jodi Essey-Stapleton
Illinois-based writer specializing in business writing.

Paul R. Greenland
Illinois-based writer and researcher; author of two books and former senior editor of a national business magazine; contributor to *The Encyclopedia of Chicago History, The Encyclopedia of Religion,* and the *Encyclopedia of American Industries.*

Robert Halasz
Former editor in chief of *World Progress* and *Funk & Wagnalls New Encyclopedia Yearbook*; author, *The U.S. Marines* (Millbrook Press, 1993).

Frederick C. Ingram
Writer based in South Carolina.

Nelson Rhodes
Editor, writer, and consultant in the Chicago area.

Carrie Rothburd
Writer and editor specializing in corporate profiles, academic texts, and academic journal articles.

Roger Rouland
Writer and scholar specializing in company histories, literary criticism, literary essays, and poetry; freelance photographer specializing in nature photography.

Laura Rydberg
Minnesota-based writer specializing in company histories and creative nonfiction.

David E. Salamie
Part-owner of InfoWorks Development Group, a reference publication development and editorial services company.

Mary Tradii
Colorado-based writer.

Frank Uhle
Ann Arbor-based writer; movie projectionist, disc jockey, and staff member of *Psychotronic Video* magazine.

A. Woodward
Wisconsin-based writer.

List of Abbreviations

€ European euro
¥ Japanese yen
£ United Kingdom pound
$ United States dollar

A

AB Aktiebolag (Finland, Sweden)
AB Oy Aktiebolag Osakeyhtiot (Finland)
A.E. Anonimos Eteria (Greece)
AED Emirati dirham
AG Aktiengesellschaft (Austria, Germany, Switzerland, Liechtenstein)
aG auf Gegenseitigkeit (Austria, Germany)
A.m.b.a. Andelsselskab med begraenset ansvar (Denmark)
A.O. Anonim Ortaklari/Ortakligi (Turkey)
ApS Amparteselskab (Denmark)
ARS Argentine peso
A.S. Anonim Sirketi (Turkey)
A/S Aksjeselskap (Norway)
A/S Aktieselskab (Denmark, Sweden)
Ay Avoinyhtio (Finland)
ATS Austrian shilling
AUD Australian dollar
Ay Avoinyhtio (Finland)

B

B.A. Buttengewone Aansprakeiijkheid (Netherlands)
BEF Belgian franc

BHD Bahraini dinar
Bhd. Berhad (Malaysia, Brunei)
BND Brunei dollar
BRL Brazilian real
B.V. Besloten Vennootschap (Belgium, Netherlands)
BWP Botswana pula

C

C. de R.L. Compania de Responsabilidad Limitada (Spain)
C. por A. Compania por Acciones (Dominican Republic)
C.A. Compania Anonima (Ecuador, Venezuela)
C.V. Commanditaire Vennootschap (Netherlands, Belgium)
CAD Canadian dollar
CEO Chief Executive Officer
CFO Chief Financial Officer
CHF Swiss franc
Cia. Compagnia (Italy)
Cia. Companhia (Brazil, Portugal)
Cia. Compania (Latin America [except Brazil], Spain)
Cie. Compagnie (Belgium, France, Luxembourg, Netherlands)
CIO Chief Information Officer
CLP Chilean peso
CNY Chinese yuan
Co. Company
COO Chief Operating Officer
Coop. Cooperative

COP Colombian peso
Corp. Corporation
CPT Cuideachta Phoibi Theoranta (Republic of Ireland)
CRL Companhia a Responsabilidao Limitida (Portugal, Spain)
CZK Czech koruna

D

D&B Dunn & Bradstreet
DEM German deutsche mark (W. Germany to 1990; unified Germany to 2002)
Div. Division (United States)
DKK Danish krone
DZD Algerian dinar

E

E.P.E. Etema Pemorismenis Evthynis (Greece)
EC Exempt Company (Arab countries)
Edms. Bpk. Eiendoms Beperk (South Africa)
EEK Estonian Kroon
eG eingetragene Genossenschaft (Germany)
EGMBH Eingetragene Genossenschaft mit beschraenkter Haftung (Austria, Germany)
EGP Egyptian pound
Ek For Ekonomisk Forening (Sweden)
EP Empresa Portuguesa (Portugal)

ESOP Employee Stock Options and Ownership
ESP Spanish peseta
Et(s). Etablissement(s) (Belgium, France, Luxembourg)
eV eingetragener Verein (Germany)
EUR European euro

F
FIM Finnish markka
FRF French franc

G
G.I.E. Groupement d'Interet Economique (France)
gGmbH gemeinnutzige Gesellschaft mit beschraenkter Haftung (Austria, Germany, Switzerland)
GmbH Gesellschaft mit beschraenkter Haftung (Austria, Germany, Switzerland)
GRD Greek drachma
GWA Gewerbte Amt (Austria, Germany)

H
HB Handelsbolag (Sweden)
HF Hlutafelag (Iceland)
HKD Hong Kong dollar
HUF Hungarian forint

I
IDR Indonesian rupiah
IEP Irish pound
ILS Israeli shekel (new)
Inc. Incorporated (United States, Canada)
INR Indian rupee
IPO Initial Public Offering
I/S Interesentselskap (Norway)
I/S Interessentselskab (Denmark)
ISK Icelandic krona
ITL Italian lira

J
JMD Jamaican dollar
JOD Jordanian dinar

K
KB Kommanditbolag (Sweden)
KES Kenyan schilling
Kft Korlatolt Felelossegu Tarsasag (Hungary)
KG Kommanditgesellschaft (Austria, Germany, Switzerland)
KGaA Kommanditgesellschaft auf Aktien (Austria, Germany, Switzerland)
KK Kabushiki Kaisha (Japan)
KPW North Korean won
KRW South Korean won
K/S Kommanditselskab (Denmark)
K/S Kommandittselskap (Norway)
KWD Kuwaiti dinar
Ky Kommandiitiyhtio (Finland)

L
L.L.C. Limited Liability Company (Arab countries, Egypt, Greece, United States)
L.L.P. Limited Liability Partnership (United States)
L.P. Limited Partnership (Canada, South Africa, United Kingdom, United States)
LBO Leveraged Buyout
Lda. Limitada (Spain)
Ltd. Limited
Ltda. Limitada (Brazil, Portugal)
Ltee. Limitee (Canada, France)
LUF Luxembourg franc
LYD Libyan dinar

M
mbH mit beschraenkter Haftung (Austria, Germany)
Mij. Maatschappij (Netherlands)
MUR Mauritian rupee
MXN Mexican peso
MYR Malaysian ringgit

N
N.A. National Association (United States)
N.V. Naamloze Vennootschap (Belgium, Netherlands)
NGN Nigerian naira
NLG Netherlands guilder
NOK Norwegian krone
NZD New Zealand dollar

O
OAO Otkrytoe Aktsionernoe Obshchestve (Russia)
OHG Offene Handelsgesellschaft (Austria, Germany, Switzerland)
OMR Omani rial
OOO Obschestvo s Ogranichennoi Otvetstvennostiu (Russia)
OOUR Osnova Organizacija Udruzenog Rada (Yugoslavia)
Oy Osakeyhtiö (Finland)

P
P.C. Private Corp. (United States)
P.L.L.C. Professional Limited Liability Corporation (United States)
P.T. Perusahaan/Perseroan Terbatas (Indonesia)
PEN Peruvian Nuevo Sol
PHP Philippine peso
PKR Pakistani rupee
P/L Part Lag (Norway)
PLC Public Limited Co. (United Kingdom, Ireland)
PLN Polish zloty
PTE Portuguese escudo
Pte. Private (Singapore)
Pty. Proprietary (Australia, South Africa, United Kingdom)
Pvt. Private (India, Zimbabwe)
PVBA Personen Vennootschap met Beperkte Aansprakelijkheid (Belgium)
PYG Paraguay guarani

Q
QAR Qatar riyal

R
REIT Real Estate Investment Trust
RMB Chinese renminbi
Rt Reszvenytarsasag (Hungary)
RUB Russian ruble

S
S.A. Sociedad Anónima (Latin America [except Brazil], Spain, Mexico)
S.A. Sociedades Anônimas (Brazil, Portugal)
S.A. Société Anonyme (Arab countries, Belgium, France, Jordan, Luxembourg, Switzerland)
S.A. de C.V. Sociedad Anonima de Capital Variable (Mexico)
S.A.B. de C.V. Sociedad Anónima Bursátil de Capital Variable (Mexico)
S.A.C. Sociedad Anonima Comer-

cial (Latin America [except Brazil])

S.A.C.I. Sociedad Anonima Comercial e Industrial (Latin America [except Brazil])

S.A.C.I.y.F. Sociedad Anonima Comercial e Industrial y Financiera (Latin America [except Brazil])

S.A.R.L. Sociedade Anonima de Responsabilidade Limitada (Brazil, Portugal)

S.A.R.L. Société à Responsabilité Limitée (France, Belgium, Luxembourg)

S.A.S. Societe Anonyme Syrienne (Arab countries)

S.A.S. Societá in Accomandita Semplice (Italy)

S.C. Societe en Commandite (Belgium, France, Luxembourg)

S.C.A. Societe Cooperativa Agricole (France, Italy, Luxembourg)

S.C.I. Sociedad Cooperativa Ilimitada (Spain)

S.C.L. Sociedad Cooperativa Limitada (Spain)

S.C.R.L. Societe Cooperative a Responsabilite Limitee (Belgium)

S.E. Societas Europaea (European Union Member states

S.L. Sociedad Limitada (Latin America [except Brazil], Portugal, Spain)

S.N.C. Société en Nom Collectif (France)

S.p.A. Società per Azioni (Italy)

S.R.L. Sociedad de Responsabilidad Limitada (Spain, Mexico, Latin America [except Brazil])

S.R.L. Società a Responsabilità Limitata (Italy)

S.R.O. Spolecnost s Rucenim Omezenym (Czechoslovakia

S.S.K. Sherkate Sahami Khass (Iran)

S.V. Samemwerkende Vennootschap (Belgium)

S.Z.R.L. Societe Zairoise a Responsabilite Limitee (Zaire)

SAA Societe Anonyme Arabienne (Arab countries)

SAK Societe Anonyme Kuweitienne (Arab countries)

SAL Societe Anonyme Libanaise (Arab countries)

SAO Societe Anonyme Omanienne (Arab countries)

SAQ Societe Anonyme Qatarienne (Arab countries)

SAR Saudi riyal

Sdn. Bhd. Sendirian Berhad (Malaysia)

SEK Swedish krona

SGD Singapore dollar

S/L Salgslag (Norway)

Soc. Sociedad (Latin America [except Brazil], Spain)

Soc. Sociedade (Brazil, Portugal)

Soc. Societa (Italy)

Sp. z.o.o. Spólka z ograniczona odpowiedzialnoscia (Poland)

Ste. Societe (France, Belgium, Luxembourg, Switzerland)

Ste. Cve. Societe Cooperative (Belgium)

T

THB Thai baht

TND Tunisian dinar

TRL Turkish lira

TTD Trinidad and Tobago dollar

TWD Taiwan dollar (new)

U

U.A. Uitgesloten Aansporakeiijkheid (Netherlands)

u.p.a. utan personligt ansvar (Sweden)

V

V.O.f. Vennootschap onder firma (Netherlands)

VAG Verein der Arbeitgeber (Austria, Germany)

VEB Venezuelan bolivar

VERTR Vertriebs (Austria, Germany)

VND Vietnamese dong

VVAG Versicherungsverein auf Gegenseitigkeit (Austria, Germany)

W – Z

WA Wettelika Aansprakalikhaed (Netherlands)

WLL With Limited Liability (Bahrain, Kuwait, Qatar, Saudi Arabia)

YK Yugen Kaisha (Japan)

ZAO Zakrytoe Aktsionernoe Obshchestve (Russia)

ZAR South African rand

ZMK Zambian kwacha

ZWD Zimbabwean dollar

Advance America Cash Advance Centers, Inc.

———————— ■ ————————

135 North Church Street
Spartanburg, South Carolina 29306
U.S.A.
Telephone: (864) 342-5600
Fax: (864) 342-5612
Web site: http://www.advanceamerica.net

Public Company
Incorporated: 1997
Employees: 6,100
Sales: $647.68 million (2009)
Stock Exchanges: New York
Ticker Symbol: AEA
NAICS: 522291 Consumer Lending

■ ■ ■

Advance America Cash Advance Centers, Inc., is the largest nonbank provider of cash advance services in the United States, as measured by the number of its centers. These cash advances are for small amounts, with repayment, plus finance charges, due on the customer's next payday, typically in two weeks. In most cases the customer provides a postdated personal check for the amount due. Advance America operates more than 2,500 centers, or branch offices, in the United States. It also has a small presence in Canada and the United Kingdom.

QUICK RISE TO THE TOP: 1997–99

Advance America was started in South Carolina by William Webster IV, who, with his father, had made a fortune establishing and operating a fast-food restaurant chain. After working in the Clinton administration, he returned home to found another business. "Basically, I was looking for a consumer service business [that] was mom-and-pop dominated," he told Gary Rivlin for an article that appeared in *Bloomberg Business Week* in 2010. "I was looking for an industry that hadn't been professionalized."

Seeking a partner, Webster contacted George Dean Johnson Jr., a family friend who had struck it rich opening Blockbuster video rental outlets. According to Rivlin, Webster showed Johnson a graph with one line indicating the cost of a loan due on payday, while the other represented the rising cost of a bounced check or credit-card late fee. The payday lending industry had taken off, Webster said, when the latter line rose high enough to cross the former one.

With their histories of prior success, Webster and Johnson were able to borrow $40 million to $50 million from two banks to establish Advance America. It was a large-scale enterprise from the start. The company opened its first center in November 1997. By mid-1998, there were 243 centers in 10 states. By the end of 1999, there were 1,400 in 22 states, making Advance America the industry leader in this regard.

Advance America claimed to be seeking a middle-class clientele. The target customer was said to be 25 to 54 years old, with a household income ranging from

COMPANY PERSPECTIVES

Our goal is to attract customers by offering straightforward rapid access to short-term funding, while providing high-quality professional customer service. We believe that our products and services represent a competitive source of liquidity to the customer relative to other alternatives, which typically include overdraft privileges or bounced check protection, late bill payments, checks returned for insufficient funds, and short-term collateralized loans.

$25,000 to $45,000 a year. A company manager in the state of Washington described the average customer as a 34-year-old woman earning $26,000 a year. The company's branches were located in shopping centers rather than poor, run-down neighborhoods. To its detractors, however, Advance America, like its competitors, was preying on the working poor, charging desperate people unconscionable fees to meet one money crisis after another.

Although going back at least a century, payday lending never reached critical mass until the 1990s because many states adopted laws against so-called usury that barred interest rates seen as excessive. Between 1990 and 1998, however, legislators in 19 states exempted payday lenders from usury laws, often after being vigorously lobbied by industry personnel. The number of cash advancing firms and the size of the industry grew rapidly in the decade.

STATE AND FEDERAL RESTRICTIONS: 1999–2002

Advance America's ability to do business varied by jurisdiction. Thirteen states, at the beginning of 1999, allowed payday lending because small loans were not regulated. Nineteen had specific payday loan regulations establishing a maximum percentage fee and a maximum annual percentage rate (APR) of interest ranging from 261 percent to 625 percent for a 14-day loan. The remaining 18 states had usury laws on the books, without exemptions for payday lenders, that capped the APR at between 17 and 57.68 percent without regard for the limited 14-day life span of the loan.

Advance America's operations in the state of Washington were typical of its practices in the 19 states with specific payday loan regulations. The company charged the legal maximum fee of $15 for each $100

borrowed, for an APR of 391 percent. The law forbade cash advance companies to lend more than $500. This limitation sometimes led to rotating payday-to-payday loans that made it virtually impossible for borrowers ever to repay principal, but Advance America put a limit on 10 consecutive advances.

To qualify for the loan, a potential customer had to have a checking account. The applicant was also required to show two current pieces of identification, the most recent pay stub, and the most recent checking-account statement. As in most other states where Advance America was doing business, customers in Washington provided a personal check or an Automated Clearing House (ACH) authorization to cover the amount of the cash advance plus other charges.

In some states where Advance America and other payday lenders found it impossible to make loans directly, they negotiated partnerships with banks in which the bank actually extended the loan. In this "rent-a-bank" maneuver, the banks sought as partners were those operating under relatively permissive state laws that allowed them to establish a branch doing payday lending in a state with stricter laws. The federal Office of the Comptroller of the Currency began discouraging such arrangements involving national banks in 2002, and the Office of Thrift Supervision did the same for thrift institutions such as savings banks and savings and loan associations. State-chartered but federally insured banks, regulated by the Federal Deposit Insurance Corporation, found this agency's regulations to be less onerous.

FACING COMPETITION, GOING PUBLIC: 2003–04

By this time payday lenders were facing competition from the very banking industry that had formerly looked down its nose at the practice. Employing the genteel terms of "overdraft privilege," "courtesy overdraft," or "bounce protection," thousands of banks and other financial institutions were allowing their customers to indulge in the same transaction as payday lenders: short-term borrowing. Moreover, overdraft protection was said to generate higher fees for the banks than for the payday lenders.

Webster pointed out that payday lenders were required by law to treat the flat fee for a short-term loan as interest. Advance America was the first payday lending chain to state the cost of such a loan by APR, a decision Webster came to regret. The $15 fee per $100 borrowed over two weeks, which translated in annual terms into an interest rate of 391 percent, was a figure that Webster characterized to Rivlin as "a millstone

```
┌─────────────────────────────────────────────┐
│                                               │
│                 KEY DATES                     │
│                     ■                         │
│  ─────────────────────────────────────        │
│  1997:  Advance America is founded.           │
│  1999:  Company has more outlets than any other│
│         payday lender.                        │
│  2004:  Advance America makes its initial public of-│
│         fering of stock.                      │
│  2007:  Company enters the United Kingdom and │
│         Canada.                               │
│  2009:  Advance America ends the year with 2,553│
│         centers in 32 states.                 │
│                                               │
└─────────────────────────────────────────────┘
```

around our neck." However, the average bank bounced-check fee of $22 translated, in terms of a $100 loan, to 572 percent. According to Seth Lubove, author of a 2003 article in *Forbes*, Webster "relished the banks' dubious achievement of charging even more than he does."

Lubove described Advance America as one of the best-behaved companies in its field. Although 10 to 20 percent of its payday loans were said to be unrecoverable, the company eschewed the roughhouse tactics reported to be common in the payday lending business. "We don't threaten or use criminal prosecution, and we don't report to a credit bureau," Webster told Lubove.

Advance America issued its initial public offering (IPO) of stock in 2004, raising $322 million on the New York Stock Exchange. Investors bid up the $15-per-share offering 37 percent on the first day of trading.

STORM CLOUDS GATHER: 2005–08

At the high-water mark for the payday lending industry, in 2006, there were 24,000 outlets in the United States, according to one count: more than all McDonald's and Burger Kings combined. Nevertheless, by then there was a perceptible reaction against what was being regarded as excessive leniency toward an industry with a public relations problem. After Georgia passed a law banning the "rent-a-bank" model, Advance America suspended operations at its 86 centers in the state. Soon North Carolina also forbade the practice. Advance America, which had as many as 118 centers in the state before a law allowing payday loans expired in 2001, closed the remaining ones. Congress dealt the payday industry another blow in 2007, when it imposed an APR limit of 36 percent in charges on loans to members of the armed services.

Early that year, the Community Financial Services Association of America, a trade group representing a majority of payday lenders, announced that its members would offer an extended payment plan that would, once a year, grant borrowers an additional two to four months to repay a loan without having to pay more interest or fees. (Washington had given borrowers in the state the right to enter such a plan after four successive loans with a company.) The trade group also suggested that its members not advertise loans for such purposes as gambling, entertainment, or vacations and warn borrowers that payday advances be used for short-term financial needs only.

These measures failed to placate the opponents of payday lending. Advance America closed its 98 centers in Pennsylvania in 2007, after a state court ruled that its "choice line of credit" product violated the law by charging excessively high fees. This product allowed customers to borrow up to $500 by paying a $149.95 "participation fee" each month plus 5.98 percent interest.

Two months later, Oregon became the next state to close down payday lending. A new law specified that loans extend for at least 31 days and set the APR maximum for fees and interest at 154 percent. Advance America said it was no longer economically viable to operate in the state and closed its 45 centers. The company also left New Mexico in 2008 after the state legislature capped lending fees and prohibited immediate rollovers. Arkansas's attorney general sent letters to some 60 payday lenders in 2008, asking them to close their operations in the state immediately and void the debts of their customers or to accept the likelihood of lawsuits. The state constitution forbade lenders to charge an annual interest rate above 17 percent. Although a 1999 law exempted payday lenders by declaring that their fees "shall not be deemed interest," the state Supreme Court indicated that this law did not necessarily free such lenders from the constitutional prohibition. Advance America exited the state.

Legislation allowing cash advances in Arizona expired in 2008. An initiative sponsored by payday lenders and presented to the voters failed to win traction. Similarly, Ohio voters rejected a proposal to reverse the legislature's decision to cap the APR at 28 percent. Advance America shut down 63 of its 244 centers in Ohio but retained its presence in the state by offering other small loans and check-cashing services. It also remained in Arizona. The company withdrew from New Hampshire, however, after legislation adopted in 2008 effectively prohibited cash advances.

OFFERING OTHER FINANCIAL PRODUCTS: 2007–09

Advance America countered these adverse political trends by offering complementary products and services. In 2005, for example, it issued what it called a fee-based credit services package to assist customers in trying to improve their credit and in obtaining an extension of consumer credit through a third-party lender. In 2006 the company began offering installment loans directly to customers in Illinois and prepaid debit cards in most centers as an agent of a bank regulated by the U.S. Office of Thrift Supervision. In 2007 Advance America began selling money orders and providing money transfer services and bill payment services as an agent of a registered money transmitter. The following year it started offering small loans in Ohio. It also put into operation an online application process. The company expanded into the United Kingdom and Canada in 2007.

Advance America, in 2010, expressed its belief that the payday lending industry had largely stopped growing in the number of centers in the United States. The company's total assets peaked in 2006, followed by its revenues and number of centers in 2007. Net income fell in 2007 and 2008 but rose in 2009.

ADVANCE AMERICA: 2009–10

At the end of 2009 Advance America was operating 2,553 centers in 32 states of the United States, 21 centers in the United Kingdom, and 13 centers in Canada. These centers, all leased and typically about 1,500 square feet in size, were designed to resemble the branches of banks and other mainstream financial institutions. They were generally located in middle-income shopping areas with high retail activity. Some 122 centers operated under the brand National Cash Advance rather than Advance America.

Advance America maintained that it was focusing primarily on providing cash advance services to middle-income working individuals and that the median household annual income of a large sample of randomly selected customers across selected states averaged $50,000. The number of customers served in 2009 was nearly 1.32 million, and the number of cash advances originated, 10.86 million. The average amount of a cash advance was $361, and the average charge (excluding lines of credit and installment loans), $53.

Advance America invited customers to seek a cash advance by applying in person to one of its centers or by visiting its Web site. The applicant's identification, proof of income and/or employment, and proof of bank account were verified. After approval by the company or, where applicable, the third-party lender, the applicant provided a personal check or an ACH authorization (but this was not required in some states). An appointment was made to return on a specified due date, typically the next payday, to repay the cash advance and applicable charges. Payment was generally in person in cash at the center where the cash advance was authorized. If made over the Internet, the customer paid by ACH authorization.

Upon payment in full, the customer's check was returned. In the event that the customer did not repay the outstanding amount in full by the due date, Advance America sought to collect the outstanding amount and any applicable fee, such as a late fee. The company stated that it might deposit the customer's personal check or initiate the electronic payment from the customer's bank account. Repayment terms varied depending upon state law, the type of cash advance service offered, and whether the cash advance was completed online or in one of Advance America's centers.

Advance America maintained that its extended payment plans met the standards of the industry's trade group. It declared that customers could enter one of these plans for no additional fee once every 12 months or, in some states, more frequently. These plans called for scheduled payments coinciding with the customer's next four paydays. The company said it did not engage in collection efforts while a customer was enrolled in one of its extended payment plans.

In addition to cash advance services, Advance America was offering alternative products and services where permissible by law. In Ohio, for example, the company was offering check cashing services at rates authorized by the state. Advance America was also offering prepaid debit cards and money orders, money transmission, and bill-payment services through arrangements with third parties. A bank regulated by the federal Office of Thrift Supervision was issuing a prepaid Visa debit card with the Advance America brand. A licensed third-party money transmitter was using the company as an agent for money orders, money-transfer services, and bill-payment services.

Advance America's common stock fell as low in value as 80 cents a share in early 2009. The price was about $4 a share in mid-2010, well below the $15 a share of its IPO. Nevertheless, the company's net income of $54.2 million in 2009 was a healthy return on its revenues of $647.7 million, and it paid out its 21st consecutive quarterly dividend in early 2010.

Webster was chief executive officer of Advance America until 2005, when Kenneth E. Compton became president and CEO. Webster was chairman of the board between 2000 and 2004 and resumed the office in 2008. Johnson was chairman from 2004 to 2008. Johnson was also the principal shareholder in early 2010, with 10.7 percent of the company's common stock.

Robert Halasz

PRINCIPAL SUBSIDIARIES

NCA National Cash Advance (Canada), ULC.

PRINCIPAL COMPETITORS

ACE Cash Express, Inc.; Cash America International Inc.; Check into Cash; Check 'n Go; Dollar Financial Corp.; Rent-A-Center, Inc.

FURTHER READING

"Advance America Brings in Another 'Cash Advance' Store," *Wenatchee Business Journal*, January 2000, p. A5.

Conkey, Christopher, "Payday Lenders Strike a Defensive Pose," *Wall Street Journal*, February 21, 2007, p. A8.

Har, Janie, "Payday-Advance Firm Expands to Sacramento Area," *Sacramento Bee*, July 22, 1998, p. C1.

Hendren, John, "Exorbitant 'Payday Loans' Tide Over the Desperate," *Los Angeles Times*, January 24, 1999.

Jackson, Ben, "OCC Payday Purge Done; Lenders Eye State Banks," *American Banker*, February 3, 2003, pp. 1–2.

Lubove, Seth, "Race to the Bottom," *Forbes*, July 21, 2003, pp. 74–75.

Richardson, Karen, "Investors Rethink 'Payday Lending,'" *Wall Street Journal*, February 17, 2005, p. C3.

Rivlin, Gary, "Payday Nation," *Bloomberg Business Week*, May 24–30, 2010, pp. 56–59.

Advanced Energy
Industries, Inc.

1635 Sharp Point Drive
Fort Collins, Colorado 80525-4423
U.S.A.
Telephone: (970) 221-0108
Toll Free: (800) 446-9167
Fax: (970) 407-6550
Web site: http://www.advanced-energy.com

Public Company
Founded: 1981
Employees: 1,316
Sales: $186.4 million (2009)
Stock Exchanges: NASDAQ
Ticker Symbol: AEIS
NAICS: 334419 Other Electronic Component Manufacturing

∎∎∎

Advanced Energy Industries, Inc., specializes in the development and manufacture of high-technology tools used to deliver power and control processes in the manufacture of semiconductors, solar cells, flat-panel displays, data storage products, and architectural glass. The company is involved in the manufacture of power inversion products for the solar industry as well, including its award-winning Solaron brand. Advanced Energy Industries is a global company, with 17 service support and sales offices, including locations in Germany, England, China, Japan, South Korea, and Taiwan.

INNOVATIONS IN POWER CONVERSION DEVICES FOR SEMICONDUCTOR FABRICATION

Advanced Energy Industries, Inc. (AE), founded by Douglas Schatz and Brent Backman in 1981, originated as a small supplier of power conversion products serving the semiconductor industry. AE offered direct-current (DC) and radio-frequency (RF) power products used in precision manufacturing of semiconductors, especially silicon-based products used to conduct information and energy in the operation of modern electronics, such as computers, radios, and telephones. AE products provided a power source suitable for refined ion beam milling and etching in the fabrication of integrated circuit and thin-film products. As the inventor behind AE, Schatz created the company's first commercially viable product, the IT2500, the best power conversion product on the market at the time.

IBM and Motorola used AE power converters in research and development, and this early association put AE in the position to grow with the semiconductor industry as technology developed. For instance, when physical vapor deposition (PVD) replaced ion beam milling and etching, AE readily adapted to the change. When semiconductors became smaller, AE provided innovative DC power conversion products that met the needs of the industry. AE took semiconductor manufacturing to the next level with the magnetron drive (MDX) power converter, introduced in 1983. In addition to providing greater efficiency and reliability, the MDX was more than 10 times smaller than similar products available.

COMPANY PERSPECTIVES

Advanced Energy is a global leader in innovative power and flow solutions for emerging, renewable-energy and IT markets.

AE innovations attracted the attention of the industry. *Industrial Research and Development* magazine recognized the MDX on its annual "R&D 100" list of the most important inventions in the United States in 1983. AE found customers among prominent semiconductor manufacturers, such as Temescal Material Research, Varian Associates, and Applied Materials.

AE grew rapidly, especially as the success of the MDX propelled sales higher. Seagate Technology alone ordered 600 MDX power systems. Revenues rose from $4 million in 1985 to $22 million in 1992. International distribution contributed to the company's growth. AE opened offices in Japan in 1987, Germany in 1990, and the United Kingdom in 1993.

AE's leadership in the industry continued with the 1992 launch of the RFG, a 13.56 megahertz radio-frequency generator. The RFG became the primary power conversion device for such prominent semiconductor research and manufacturing companies as LAM Research, Hitachi, Leybold, Balzers, and Ulvac. Introduction of the RFG increased AE's market share in power conversion products for the semiconductor industry to about 39 percent.

1995 STOCK OFFERING

In order to fund continued growth AE decided to become a public company. In 1995 AE offered 2.5 million shares of stock at $10 per share, of which one million shares originated from the company and garnered gross proceeds of $10 million. Plans for expansion stalled, however, as a decline in the semiconductor industry led AE to implement cost-cutting measures in 1996. Nevertheless, product demand rebounded as the Internet economy exploded. Company sales rose from $99 million in 1996 to $141.9 million in 1997. The semiconductor equipment industry accounted for 59 percent sales, with Applied Materials and Lam Research accounting for 45 percent of sales.

In July 1998 AE introduced its Apex power conversion system, a 13.56 megahertz RF power system that offered consistent power and efficiency at lower cost. The company achieved these improvements by rearrang-ing the component configuration to reduce the number of parts and create immediate power amplification. The compact Apex system allowed AE to serve customers requiring smaller manufacturing tools, especially as they reduced the size of semiconductors to nanometers.

In May 1998 AE opened a new manufacturing plant in Austin, Texas, in order to fulfill renewal of a three-year contract for the manufacture of DC, RF, and mid-frequency power conversion systems as well as "matching network" technology, for effective, digital-based power modulation in PVD, CVD, and etch applications. The 7,000-square-foot facility employed 27 workers by the end of the year, and AE planned to add another 19,000 square feet of manufacturing space in early 1999.

In late 1998 AE entered into a series of acquisitions intended to expand the company's range of RF products. The acquisition of Fourth State Technology, Inc., of Austin, Texas, in September, added RF monitoring products, including data collection and analysis capabilities. In October AE acquired RF Power Products, a minor competitor based in Voorhees, New Jersey. In addition to expanding AE's global customer base, RF Power added capabilities in commercial coating, flat-panel display manufacturing, and analytical instrumentation.

LATE NINETIES: DIVERSIFICATION IN SEMICONDUCTOR MANUFACTURING TOOLS

In November 1998 AE raised $159 million as the company strived to expand its market base and to diversify its range of products used in semiconductor equipment manufacturing. The sale of convertible subordinated notes at 5.25 percent interest raised $120 million and an offering of one million shares of common stock raised $39 million. AE initiated plans to construct a 63,000-square-foot manufacturing plant at the company's global headquarters in Fort Collins, Colorado. Construction began in the spring of 2000.

Acquisitions contributed expertise in various aspects of semiconductor fabrication. AE acquired a majority interest in Litmas Corp. in August 1999. Litmas provided plasma abatement systems and high-density plasma for plasma-enhanced chemical vapor deposition. The Litmas Blue, a low-cost, water vapor-based tool, reduced PFC and HFC emissions during etching in the manufacture of semiconductors. In April 2000 AE purchased Noah Holdings, Inc., for $42 million, in a stock transaction. Through this pooling of interests, AE gained solid state temperature control system technology.

KEY DATES

1981: Company formation coincides with introduction of founder's groundbreaking power conversion technology.
1992: Revenues reach $22 million on strong sales of Advanced Energy Industries' (AE) magnetron drive (MDX) power converter.
1995: Initial public offering of stock raises funds for market expansion and diversification.
2008: Introduction of Solaron power inverter marks AE's prominence in the solar photovoltaic industry.

Other acquisitions contributed tools useful in the manufacture of semiconductors. The acquisition of Sekidenko, Inc., in August 2000, brought Optical Fiber Thermometers used in temperature control for silicon wafers during semiconductor manufacturing. In January 2001 AE acquired EMCO Engineering Measurements Company, which specialized in precision instruments used in liquid, steam, and gas flow control and measurement. AE complemented its strength in tools for integrated chip manufacturing by offering software for monitoring original equipment manufacturing productivity. In 2000 AE and Symphony began to collaborate on the development of network-based, open-architecture software. AE obtained the software technology from Symphony Systems in 2002.

Like most companies that flourished during the late 1990s then contracted in 2000, AE experienced a decline in sales activity that led to a retrenchment in operations. In 2001 AE implemented several cost-cutting measures. The company transferred assembly of some DC power products at its Austin facility to China. Outsourcing affected Voorhees, New Jersey, manufacturing as well. The company reduced its workforce by 26 percent between December 2000 and October 2001, cut spending on travel, and shut down operations on certain days.

2000–02: INTERNATIONAL ACTIVITIES

Through international expansion AE sought to develop a worldwide customer base as well as to diversify its technological capabilities. The company formed distribution partnerships and established its own distribution networks. New offices opened in Korea in 1996, in Taiwan in 1999, and China in 2000. Acquisitions met both criteria for expansion.

The March 2002 acquisition of Dressler HF Technik GmbH, of Stolberg, Germany, strengthened AE's market position in plasma-based applications, such as flat-panel equipment, data storage, and semiconductor markets. Moreover, the acquisition added laser and medical markets to AE's customer base. Dressler brought a positive reputation among European customers that would benefit AE as well. The $16.75 million acquisition expanded on an existing collaborative partnership in the field of RF power products for plasma-based applications. Dressler products included the Cesar power generator, sold primarily to semiconductor capital equipment and solar cell manufacturers, the VarioMatch matching network, the HPG high-power generator, and the LPPA linear amplifier.

In 2002 AE acquired Aera Japan Ltd. for $78 million. The leading worldwide supplier of mass flow controllers for plasma gas delivery systems, Aera brought additional expertise in the manufacture of semiconductor capital equipment.

AE INNOVATIONS: 2003–06

AE's expanded base of knowledge contributed to several product innovations. AE introduced its Xstream plasma-source platform in June 2003. Used in the manufacture of advanced semiconductors as well as flat-panel display, Xstream combined a remote plasma source with a highly efficient source of six- or eight-kilowatt power. Along with an active matching network, the product provided efficient gas delivery in a manner that prevented gas reactivity, thus improving manufacturing quality.

In 2004 AE introduced its most significant innovation in several years, the Ovation VHF (very high frequency) power system. The Ovation VHF provided refined power delivery for use in precision etching. Also, the company introduced the Litmas RPS 1501 in June. The product provided remote plasma for state-of-the-art, thin-film manufacturing applications.

In early 2005 AE launched a new series of DC power conversion and control systems under the Summit brand. The Summit products were designed to handle the refined manufacturing requirements of state-of-the art, Generation 7 and 8 flat-panel display and semiconductors at the sub-65 nanometer size. The Summit series incorporated AE's new Pulsar technology, a highly refined pulsing power control capability that reduced potential damage during the manufacturing process.

As semiconductors continued to be decrease in size and increase in complexity, AE continued to develop manufacturing equipment to meet the needs of these technological advances. In 2005 AE introduced a new Aera line of pressure-insensitive mass flow controllers. The Aera PI-980 provided constant, precise gas flow for etch, CVD, and PVD production. The Aera Transformer 780/7800 series offered similar qualities with digital-based mass flow controllers. Both products used a NeuralStep control technology, which provided quick, effective application of gas in manufacturing.

AE collaborated with original equipment manufacturers to develop the fabrication tools and power delivery required for their products. In 2007 AE launched the Paramount RF-power delivery system for etch and various deposition processes used in the manufacture of semiconductors, flat-panel display, solar photovoltaic panels, and microelectromechanical systems. The Paramount accommodated diverse manufacturing requirements, including the application of anti-reflective coatings for architectural glass, and hard masks, cap layers, and stop layers for tools and automotive parts.

SOLAR PHOTOVOLTAIC MANUFACTURING AND POWER CONVERSION INNOVATIONS

With the market for solar technology on the rise, AE applied its expertise in silicon manufacturing processes and power conversion to the solar industry. As the photovoltaic technology matured and renewable energy sources became of greater societal interest, AE's involvement in the solar industry became prominent.

A long-standing relationship with Energy Conversion Devices (ECD) expanded in April 2006, when ECD purchased Dressler's Cesar RF power generators, used for thin-film manufacturing, and VarioMatch matching networks, for the manufacture of 25 megawatts of photovoltaic (PV) equipment for United Solar Ovonic (Unisolar) PV roof shingles.

AE's Summit DC power systems supported the viability of the solar PV manufacturing. By improving the quality of thin-film manufacturing, the product reduced the amount of silicon material required for large scale thin-film solar cell manufacturing. Silicon sources were becoming scarce and expensive, and AE's RF and DC power-delivery systems for plasma-enhanced chemical vapor deposition (PECVD) and PVD reduced the cost of solar-cell manufacturing. In 2006, the quality of AE technology resulted in an order to sustain more than 65 megawatts of solar-cell production capacity.

AE's experience in power conversion led to the development of the Solaron PV inverter. The device transformed DC power generated by solar modules into alternating current (AC) electricity that could be used by independent power producers or utility customers through the power grid. The Solaron featured "transformerless," soft-switching technology that provided 97.5 percent energy efficiency, according to the California Energy Commission measurement standards. Energy retention contributed to a favorable cost-per-kilowatt-hour ratio and increased the return on investment gained from a solar power system, which tended to carry high purchase and installation costs.

AE designed the Solaron PV inverters for commercial and utility scale solar PV systems. The Solaron provided highly efficient and very reliable power inversion conducive to large-scale solar projects. SunPower Corp. installed Solaron PV inverters at two commercial solar installations in northern California in late summer 2007. Each generated 300 kilowatts of electricity.

Amid new developments in the solar industry, the global economic collapse of 2008 impacted AE and its customers dramatically. Sales at AE declined from $384.7 million in 2007 to $328.92 million in 2008. Sales to the company's largest customer, Applied Materials, declined from $69.3 million in 2008 to $37.2 million in 2009. The non-semiconductor market produced similar results. Overstock in the solar industry led to a 48.1 percent decline in sales to that market. Overall sales declined another 43.3 percent in 2009. However, the company remained profitable due to implementation of several cost-cutting measures, with $54.4 million in profits from sales of $186.4 million.

By late 2009 AE's solar operations began to rebound, as sales of the Solaron accelerated. In October SunEdison, LLC, placed an order for Solaron inverters for utility-scale solar energy projects. In November AE obtained a contract with Suntech Power Holdings to provide Solaron products, including PV power inverter and remote PV tie accessories. Suntech, the largest worldwide producer of crystalline-silicon solar modules, planned to use Solaron products in its Reliathon platform in the design and construction of utility-scale PV power generation systems. The multiyear agreement included AE's SafeGuard maintenance and support services, as well.

When Aeroject installed a six-megawatt solar plant at its corporate headquarters in Sacramento, California, Solaron inverters were chosen for the initial 3.6-megawatt project completed in November 2009. Sale of the product for an additional 2.4-megawatt project, completed in April 2010, followed. The Solaron was chosen for a five-megawatt solar plant constructed by Recurrent Energy for the City of San Francisco in 2010. AE also obtained a contract to provide support services for a two-megawatt PV solar power plant at Colorado

State University, in the company's home city of Fort Collins.

The growth of the solar energy industry and AE's success within it led the company to open a 250-megawatt grid-tie solar inverter production facility in Fort Collins. A $1.2 million federal green-job tax credit helped defray the costs of establishing the 48,000-square-foot manufacturing plant. The facility held capacity to produce the equivalent of one gigawatt of Solaron inverter and next-generation solar inverter equipment.

AE further expanded solar operations through the May 2010 acquisition of PV Powered, based in Bend, Oregon. A manufacturer of grid-tied PV inverters, the company brought innovation in a range of residential, commercial, and utility-scale power inversion products to AE. The transaction involved $35 million in cash, $15 million in stock, and a financial results-based cash payment of approximately $40 million. Shortly after the acquisition, PV Powered obtained a contract with Trinity Solar to provide inverters for a 429-kilowatt solar array at a mixed-use shopping center and housing development in Stafford Park, New Jersey. Also, installation was completed at a one-acre, 200-kilowatt, ground-mounted commercial solar project, located on a pecan farm in Arlington, Georgia, the largest in the state.

Mary Tradii

PRINCIPAL SUBSIDIARIES

PV Powered, Inc.

PRINCIPAL COMPETITORS

Brooks Instruments Company; Celerity, Inc.; Comdel, Inc.; Daihen Corporation; Huttinger Electronics, Inc.; KLA Tencor Corporation; MKS Instruments, Inc.; Schneider Electric SA; Siemens AG; SMA America, Inc.

FURTHER READING

"Advanced Energy Celebrates Its 25-Year Anniversary with New Product Launches," *PR Newswire*, May 2, 2006.

"Advanced Energy Industries Raises $159 Million in Public Offerings," *PR Newswire*, November 5, 1999, p. 8116.

Chappell, Jeff, "AE Achieves Critical Mass," *Electronic News*, 2001, p. 28.

Fasca, Chad, "Advanced Energy Industries," *Electronic News*, 1998, p. 34.

AIXTRON AG

———— ■ ————

Kaiserstr. 98
Herzogenrath, D-52134
Germany
Telephone: (+49 0241) 89 09 0
Fax: (+49 0241) 89 09 40
Web site: http://www.aixtron.com

Public Company
Founded: 1983
Employees: 655
Sales: EUR 302.9 million ($424.2 million) (2009)
Stock Exchanges: Frankfurt NASDAQ
Ticker Symbol: AIXG
NAICS: 334413 Semiconductor and Related Device
Manufacturing

■ ■ ■

AIXTRON AG (Aixtron) is the world's leading producer of MOCVD (Metallo-Organic Chemical Vapour Deposition) equipment, crucial for the production of compound semiconductors. Compound semiconductors, as opposed to silicon semiconductors, are composed of both metallic and organic materials, providing faster speeds and higher operating temperatures. Compound semiconductors can convert energy into light and light into energy, making them the basis for such applications as light-emitting diodes (LEDs) and lasers, on the one hand, and solar power panels on the other. Aixtron controls more than 50 percent of the world's MOCVD equipment market. Sales of this equipment represent 88 percent of the

group's revenues. Another 9 percent is generated by the group's Spare Parts and Service division. Silicon conductor equipment accounts for the remainder.

The LED market is the group's largest, accounting for 81 percent of its revenues. Most of the company's equipment orders come from Asian manufacturers, accounting for 82 percent of Aixtron's sales. Europe contributes 14 percent, while the United States, home to the company's largest rival, Veeco, adds 4 percent. Aixtron is listed on the Frankfurt Stock Exchange and is led by President and CEO Paul Hyland.

LED PIONEER IN 1983

In 1983, two doctoral students at Rheinisch-Westfälische Technische Hochschule (RWTH) in Aachen in the North Rhine Westphalia region of Germany joined together with a business partner to found a company based on their research in developing new types of compound semiconductors. The partners named the company Aixtron, combining the French name for Aachen, Aix La Chappelle, with the word *electron*. Aixtron became one of the first start-ups to take up residence at the newly created Technology Center Aachen (TZA). That center served as an incubator for Germany's high-technology sector. By the beginning of the 1990s, TZA had supported the launch of more than 60 companies.

Aixtron became one of the stars of TZA. The company focused on developing commercial equipment for Metallo-Organic Chemical Vapour Deposition (MOCVD) technology, which had been pioneered in the 1970s. As the name implies, the category of equip-

COMPANY PERSPECTIVES

As a technology company, active in an extremely dynamic and challenging market environment, it is essential for AIXTRON to proactively anticipate market developments and customer requirements ahead of time, in order to have the right products available when the market and customers demand them. AIXTRON has continuously pursued this forward-looking market-led strategy to enable the company to become and remain a significant and leading player in the targeted markets. AIXTRON has achieved market leadership through technology leadership.

ment combined various metals, such as gallium arsenide, and natural elements in a gaseous state, which allowed them to be deposited in ultra-thin layers. The resulting compound semiconductors offered a number of properties not available from the more common silicon-based semiconductors (used largely for memory type applications). Among these was a resistance to high temperature, faster processing speeds, and, especially for the nascent LED sector, the capability of converting energy to light, and light to energy.

By 1985, the company had succeeded in installing its first MOCVD machinery. The company's equipment typically sold for $1 million to $2 million. Other orders poured in, and by 1988 the company's success had been recognized with the German Finance Award for Innovation. The following year, the company expanded its technological base by acquiring the exclusive license for a planetary reactor developed by Philips. This technology allowed for the applications of precise and consistent layers, and by the following year, 1990, the company had introduced its first MOCVD multi-wafer reactor.

MARKET LEADER IN 1995

Aixtron's customer list expanded rapidly as well, with such leading international firms as AT&T Bell Labs, IBM, Motorola, Rockwell, and Siemens installing the company's equipment. In 1992, the company debuted a new reactor type, the AIX 200 SC. The new equipment incorporated such features as heated gas lines and a horizontal reaction chamber. This technology enabled the development of layers capable of sustaining high temperatures, particularly useful in laser applications.

Demand for MOCVD equipment came especially from the LED market, however. The highly energy-efficient LEDs boasted extremely long lifetimes, up to 100,000 hours compared to the 19,000 of a fluorescent bulb and just 8,000 for an incandescent light. LEDs also provided greater brightness with a reduced surface area and generated little heat. In addition to offering the potential as a replacement for traditional lightbulbs, LEDs also became a major component of the growing market for laptop computers, mobile telephones, and later televisions and other devices.

Aixtron emerged as the MOCVD leader into the middle of the decade. The company became the first to market equipment enabling the production of blue LEDs in 1994. By 1995, the company had claimed the lead in the MOCVD market. By the end of the decade, Aixtron's share of the market topped 35 percent. Its nearest competitor, Emcore, controlled just 25 percent, with several small Asian companies forming the rest. Aixtron found itself in a more or less secure position, due to the high cost of starting up a new MOCVD company. As a result, no MOCVD equipment manufacturer had been created since the early 1980s.

PUBLIC OFFERING IN 1997

Aixtron became one of the first of Germany's high-technology companies to list its shares on the newly created Neuer Markt of the Frankfurt Stock Exchange. Aixtron's shares initially sold for the equivalent of EUR 25. By the end of the decade, the company's share price had soared past EUR 320 per share. Helping to fuel investor confidence was the swift rise of the LED market, which had been growing by 30 percent per year in the late 1990s.

A notable company feature was its insistence on maintaining all of its manufacturing in Germany, and largely in the Aachen area. The company held firm to this commitment, despite the difficult recession years at the beginning of the decade. In order to keep to its commitment, Aixtron adapted its organization to reduce its costs. Under co-CEO Kim Schindelhauer, who had joined Aixtron from tire maker Continental in 1991, the company adopted an outsourcing model. This enabled the company to reduce its direct payroll to just 180 employees. At the same time, the company turned primarily to other manufacturers in the Aachen area for its component supplies. By 2000, the group's supplier network included some 650 firms supplying the more than 15,000 components required in a typical Aixtron machine.

The other half of Aixtron's leadership, Holger Jurgensen, continued to expand the company's research and technological base. In 1999, Aixtron completed its first acquisition, of Thomas Swan Scientific Equipment,

KEY DATES

1983: Aixtron is founded as an offshoot of Rheinisch-Westfälische Technische Hochschule (RWTH) in Aachen, Germany.

1997: Aixtron goes public with a listing on the Frankfurt Stock Exchange's Neuer Markt.

1999: Aixtron acquires Thomas Swan Scientific Equipment in the United Kingdom.

2005: Company acquires Genus, Inc., in California.

2007: Aixtron acquires Nanoinstruments Ltd. in Cambridge, England.

2009: Company posts its highest-ever revenues.

a division of U.K.-based Thomas Swan & Co. The new operation brought Aixtron Swan's patented "shower-head" gas distribution system, which set a new standard for the MOCVD industry.

Soon after the Swan purchase, Aixtron turned to Sweden. There, the company bought Epigress AG, a producer of Chemical Vapor Distribution (CVD) systems, used for the production of silicon-carbide and similar compound semiconductors. That company, renamed Aixtron AB, became the world leader in this category of equipment. These acquisitions helped fuel Aixtron's revenue growth, as sales topped EUR 85 million at the end of 2009. The company also distinguished itself from many of its high-technology counterparts by posting strong profits, of EUR 17 million that year. In the meantime, the company's share price continued to climb, and by mid-2000 Aixtron's market capitalization topped $4.3 billion.

U.S. ACQUISITION IN 2005

Aixtron's sales nearly doubled through 2000, reaching EUR 158 million. By the end of 2001, at the peak of the technology boom, Aixtron's revenues approached EUR 240 million. Aixtron was soon hit by the collapse of the technology market. Its sales dropped sharply, to EUR 152 million in 2002, and to just EUR 90 million in 2003. In that year, too, the company posted a loss of EUR 17.8 million. Amid these difficulties, the company brought in a new chairman and CEO, Paul Hyland.

The company's fortunes soon turned for the better, however. By 2004, the group's sales had once again climbed to EUR 140 million, for profits of over EUR 7 million. The company benefited especially from the boom in the LED market. LED lighting, including for street lamps and traffic lights, had grown increasingly common. At the same time, a new generation of LED-based devices, including digital cameras, MP3 and multimedia players, portable DVD players, cell phones, coupled with a boom in computer laptop sales, promised renewed demand for the company's equipment.

In the short turn, Aixtron continued to face a difficult market. While sales held steady through 2005, the company experienced a new loss, of EUR 53.5 million for the year. Nonetheless, the company had begun to put into place the elements of its future growth. In 2002, for example, the company added a service center in Shanghai, China, bringing it closer to one of its largest and fastest-growing client bases.

Next, in 2005, Aixtron completed the acquisition of California-based Genus Inc. This acquisition expanded the company's range of deposition technologies, adding Genus's Atomic Layer Deposition and Atomic Vapor Deposition systems, among others. This purchase also positioned the company to take advantage of a new trend in the semiconductor industry, which saw the convergence of both silicon and compound semiconductor production.

REVENUE RECORDS IN 2010

Aixtron also sought to position itself at the beginning of another promising new technology, carbon nanotubes. These microscopic tubular structures presented a new range of future semiconductor possibilities. In order to establish itself in this field, Aixtron acquired Cambridge, England's Nanoinstruments Ltd. in 2007. That company added its Plasma-Enhanced Chemical Vapor Deposition (PECVD) technology to Aixtron's own.

Aixtron's interest in nanotechnology also led it to form a partnership with IMEC, based in Leuven, Belgium. In 2008, that partnership succeeded in demonstrating a new technique for the wafers incorporating aluminum gallium nitride and gallium nitride. This technology promised still higher semiconductor performance at a lower production cost.

Aixtron's sales continued to build strongly through the end of the decade. By 2009, Aixtron's revenues had topped EUR 300 million ($420 million) for the first time, setting a new revenue record for the company. The company's growth had also resulted in the steady growth of its payroll, and by 2010 Aixtron employed nearly 700. By then, too, Aixtron had boosted its command over the world's MOCVD market to more than 50 percent.

Aixtron's success had not gone unnoticed by the investment community. During 2009, the company's share price rose by some 400 percent, placing the company among the highest-performance technology stocks in the world that year. Also in 2009, the company carried out a new rights issue, raising another EUR 160 million for future investment. In this way, Aixtron expected to remain the driving force behind the global MOCVD equipment market.

M. L. Cohen

PRINCIPAL SUBSIDIARIES

AIXTRON AB (Sweden); AIXTRON KK (Japan); AIX-TRON Korea Co. Ltd. (South Korea); AIXTRON Ltd. (UK); AIXTRON Taiwan Co. Ltd.; AIXTRON, Inc. (USA).

PRINCIPAL OPERATING UNITS

Compound Semiconductor Equipment and Other Equipment; Spare Parts & Service; Silicon Semiconductor Equipment.

PRINCIPAL COMPETITORS

Taiyo Nippon Sanso; Veeco Instruments Inc.

FURTHER READING

"Aixtron Aligns with Taiwanese Research Lab," *Electronic News*, November 26, 2001, p. 22.

"Aixtron Opens Service Center in Shanghai," *Electronic News*, September 23, 2002, p. 25.

"Aixtron's Future Looking Bright; Firm Makes Equipment for Booming LED Field," *Investor's Business Daily*, January 11, 2010, p. B02.

"German Aixtron Receives Production Deposition Systems Order in China," *ADP News Germany*, June 8, 2010.

"German Semiconductor Equipment Maker Aixtron Views the World High-Tech Business Climate This Year as Difficult," *Purchasing*, April 21, 2005, p. 5.

Marsh, Peter, "The Elements of Survival," *Financial Times*, September 17, 2001, p. 19.

Raval, Anjli, "Aixtron Shines on Strong Demand," *Financial Times*, March 11, 2010, p. 22.

"Why Is This Man Smiling?" *Fortune*, July 24, 2000, p. 182.

Alexander & Baldwin, Inc.

———————■———————

822 Bishop Street
P.O. Box 3440
Honolulu, Hawaii 96801-3440
U.S.A.
Telephone: (808) 525-6611
Fax: (808) 525-6652
Web site: http://www.alexanderbaldwin.com

Public Company
Incorporated: 1900 as Alexander & Baldwin, Limited
Employees: 2,110
Sales: $1.4 billion (2010)
Stock Exchanges: New York
Ticker Symbol: AXB
NAICS: 311311 Sugarcane Mills; 311312 Cane Sugar
Refining; 311920 Coffee and Tea Manufacturing;
483111 Deep Sea Freight Transportation; 483113
Coastal and Great Lakes Freight Transportation;
488310 Port and Harbor Operations; 488320
Marine Cargo Handling; 488510 Freight
Transportation Arrangement; 493110 General
Warehousing and Storage; 531120 Lessors of
Nonresidential Buildings (Except Miniwarehouses);
531312 Nonresidential Property Managers; 531390
Other Activities Related to Real Estate; 541614
Process, Physical Distribution, and Logistics
Consulting Services

■ ■ ■

Alexander & Baldwin, Inc., one of the original Big Five
Hawaiian companies, is a diversified corporation with

operations in ocean transportation, food products, and
property development and management. Matson's
transportation offerings span the globe, providing a vital
lifeline to the island economies of Hawaii, Guam, and
Micronesia, and delivering a wide range of multi-modal
services throughout North America and between the
United States and China. As one of the nation's top
logistics providers, it offers customers domestic and
international rail intermodal service, long haul and
regional highway brokerage, expedited/air freight
services and less-than-truckload transportation services,
as well as third-party logistics services that include
warehousing, distribution, and freight forwarding. A&B
Properties, Inc., is a diversified real estate commercial
and development company. A&B agribusiness units are
leading producers of raw sugar, specialty food-grade
sugars, and roasted and green coffee, using nearly
40,000 acres of A&B's historical lands.

SUGARCANE ROOTS

Although A&B was not incorporated until 1900, the
company was founded 30 years earlier by the two men
whose names it bears, Samuel T. Alexander and Henry
P. Baldwin, both sons of missionaries living in Hawaii.
Longtime friends, the two men began working together
in the mid-1860s, when Alexander hired the younger
Baldwin as his assistant in managing a sugar plantation
in Waihee on the island of Maui. In 1869 the pair
purchased 12 acres of land in central Maui. The following year, with an additional 559 acres, they established
their own sugarcane plantation, marketing sugar on the
mainland through such exporting firms as Castle &
Cooke. Alexander and Baldwin became in-laws that year

when Baldwin married Emily Alexander, his partner's sister.

By 1876, the volume of sugarcane growing on the plantation had increased so much that the readily available supply of water could not support it. To address this problem, Alexander devised a sophisticated irrigation plan that involved the construction of a gigantic ditch through rain forest terrain. The resulting Hamakua ditch, 17 miles long and capable of carrying 60 million gallons of water a day from the waters of East Maui, was completed in 1878 and served as the model for many other such irrigation projects throughout Hawaii.

The partnership of Alexander and Baldwin was incorporated in 1883 under the name Paia Plantation. That year, Alexander resigned as manager of the neighboring Haiku Sugar Company, a position he had held since before the opening of Paia, and moved to California, leaving Baldwin to manage both plantations. Over the next few years, Paia acquired controlling interest in Haiku, as the partners continued to acquire land and expand their sugar production.

In 1894, A&B launched its own sugar agency, based in San Francisco. The agency was headed by Alexander's son, Wallace, and Joseph P. Cooke, son of Castle & Cooke cofounder Amos S. Cooke. In its first year of operation, the Alexander & Baldwin agency turned a profit of $2,670. By 1899, A&B was serving as agent for a formidable collection of companies, including the Paia and Haiku plantations, the Hawaiian Sugar Company, and the Hawaiian Commercial & Sugar Company (HC&S) and its subsidiary, Kahului Railroad

Company. A&B had in fact purchased a controlling interest in HC&S in 1898.

EXPANDING IN THE EARLY 20TH CENTURY

By 1900, the company had outgrown its partnership structure, and a new corporation, Alexander & Baldwin, Limited, was formed. In addition to the company's Honolulu headquarters, a branch office was maintained in San Francisco. Baldwin served as president. That year, the corporation reported its first annual profit, $150,000. A&B went into the insurance business the following year, establishing a division overseen by Alexander's son-in-law, John Waterhouse. By 1920, the division was acting as agent for several established insurance companies, including Home Insurance Company, German Alliance Insurance Association, and the Commonwealth Insurance Company, all based in New York. The insurance division thrived for several decades before it was sold off in 1967.

Another new entity, the Maui Agricultural Company (MA Co.), was founded in 1903, in order to offset the effects of the Organic Act, which limited the amount of land a new corporation could hold to 1,000 acres. In response, A&B formed five companies with less than 1,000 acres each. These five companies were then combined with the Paia and Haiku plantations to form MA Co. Through MA Co. and HC&S, A&B now controlled the operations of two of Maui's most important plantations.

Samuel Alexander died in 1904. In 1906, Henry Baldwin was succeeded as manager of HC&S by his son Frank, and when Henry died five years later, Frank became HC&S president, a position he would retain until his death in 1960. Both MA Co. and HC&S prospered during the first part of the 20th century. In 1908, the two companies jointly formed the East Maui Irrigation Company (EMI) to manage the extensive system of irrigation ditches that was in development. In 1917, MA Co. built a distillery for producing alcohol from molasses, the first such facility in the United States. HC&S completed several other major projects during this time, including the construction of the new Waihee ditch and the modernization of its power plant and other equipment. Another plantation, Kihei, was merged into HC&S during this period as well.

A&B's cargo shipping business was developed to complement its sugar operations. In 1908 the company became a minority shareholder in Matson Navigation Company, which had been handling most of A&B's shipping between Hawaii and San Francisco for years. A&B continued to increase its investment in Matson,

KEY DATES

∎

1870: Samuel T. Alexander and Henry P. Baldwin establish a sugarcane plantation on the Hawaiian island of Maui.

1898: Company purchases controlling interest in Hawaiian Commercial & Sugar Company.

1900: Company is reorganized under a new corporation, Alexander & Baldwin, Limited (A&B).

1908: A&B acquires a minority interest in Matson Navigation Company, a cargo shipping firm.

1949: Company moves into property development with formation of a subsidiary called Kahului Development Co., Ltd.

1964: A&B acquires a 94 percent controlling interest in Matson.

1969: A&B increases its holding in Matson to 100 percent.

1987: Joint venture is formed with Hills Brothers to grow coffee on Kauai, a venture that will eventually be 100 percent owned by A&B and be called Kauai Coffee Company.

1993: A&B takes full control of California and Hawaiian Sugar Company, Inc. (C&H), the main purchaser and marketer of A&B's sugar.

1998: A&B sells a 64 percent stake in C&H to an investment group.

2008: A&B transfers trading of its shares to the New York Stock Exchange under the new ticker symbol "AXB."

and the company eventually became a wholly owned subsidiary of A&B in 1969.

Wallace Alexander served as CEO of A&B from 1918 to 1930. During this time, the company began marketing pineapples, EMI completed construction of the Wailoa ditch, its final major ditch project, and A&B's headquarters building in Honolulu was completed. The following year, John Waterhouse succeeded Wallace Alexander as company president.

The 1930s were a period of technological advancement in A&B's sugar operations. In 1932, the company completed construction on the Alexander Dam, one of the largest hydraulic fill earth dams in the world. The Alexander Dam, located at the company's McBryde plantation, cost over $360,000 to build and was the site of a 1930 mudslide that killed several people. Both

HC&S and MA Co. switched from steam plows to tractors around this time, and HC&S began mechanical harvesting on a large scale in 1937.

VENTURING INTO PROPERTY DEVELOPMENT IN THE FORTIES

A&B sold its Hawaiian Sugar Company plantation in 1941. Although this plantation remained productive and profitable, it was situated on leased land, and A&B was unable to negotiate favorable lease terms or a purchase agreement. In 1945 Waterhouse was replaced as president of A&B by J. Platt Cooke, who served for a year before turning over the office to Frank Baldwin. In 1948, the HC&S and MA Co. plantations merged, creating one large plantation operating under the HC&S name. The two plantations produced more than 100,000 tons of sugar during the first year of the merger. Soon thereafter, the plantation began to phase out its railroad distribution system in favor of trucking.

A&B began to move into property development in 1949, forming Kahului Development Co., Ltd., as a subsidiary of HC&S. In response to the complaints of plantation employees regarding the inadequate housing available to them, Kahului Development built a new residential community, which was opened in 1950 and became known as Dream City. This development gradually evolved into the city of Kahului, Maui's most populous community.

A&B operated several general stores on plantations and railroad sites. In 1950, its stores and equipment manufacturing concerns, as well as the lumberyard and mill operations of the Kahului Railroad Company, were organized under the A&B Commercial Company. The following year, A&B opened the first A&B Super Market, as well as the Kahului Store, Maui's first complete department store.

The company made several technological strides in its sugar operations during the 1950s. In 1951, HC&S's two factories combined to produce a record 151,000 tons of sugar. Several improvements in machinery for weed control and harvesting were introduced during this time, and, in 1957, HC&S put the world's largest bagasse (cane residue) burning boiler into operation at its Paia sugar factory.

TAKING FULL CONTROL OF HC&S AND MATSON IN THE SIXTIES

Up until the 1960s, A&B had remained essentially a sales agent that held substantial interest in the companies it represented. Its income came from agency fees and dividends on the stock it owned in its client companies. This began to change, however, as A&B started turning many of its clients into subsidiaries. Much of this shift took place under C. C. Cadagan, who was named president of A&B in 1960, becoming the first chief executive from outside the founding families. In 1962, HC&S was merged into A&B, becoming a division of the company. HC&S's three subsidiaries, Kahului Railroad Company (KRR), East Maui Irrigation Company, and Kahului Development Company, all became subsidiaries of A&B. A&B Commercial Company, which ran the HC&S plantation stores, was made a division. At the same time, the last word of the company's name was changed from Limited to Inc.

Using funds it had received from the liquidation of Honolulu Oil Corporation, a company in which it had initially invested in 1911, A&B acquired a 94 percent controlling interest in Matson Navigation Company in 1964. The following year, the company eliminated what remained of KRR's unprofitable railroad operations, and that subsidiary was later renamed Kahului Trucking & Storage, Inc. By the end of the decade, the company had terminated its pineapple business and had increased its holding in Matson to 100 percent. The McBryde and Kahuke plantations had become wholly owned subsidiaries as well.

SHIFTING PLANS, CHANGING MANAGEMENT

The 1970s were a frustrating period of stalled expansion plans for A&B. In 1970, Allen Wilcox was named CEO, replacing Stanley Powell, Cadagan's successor four years earlier. Under Wilcox, A&B abandoned its plans to expand its Far East shipping operations, choosing instead to concentrate on its business closer to home, such as developing some of its Maui land for resort use. Another change in leadership took place in 1972, when Lawrence Pricher was named CEO.

Under Pricher, the company launched another expansion push, which included investments in oil refiner Pacific Resources, Inc., and Teakwood Holdings Ltd. (a Hong Kong furniture company), the purchase of Rogers Brothers Co. (an Idaho potato business), and the formation of a consulting firm called A&B Agribusiness Corporation. None of these ventures proved particularly fruitful, and, at the same time, some earlier investments that also proved unprofitable were sold off, including Edward R. Bacon Company and Acme Fast Freight, Inc. With the price of sugar falling, and profits at Matson unimpressive, A&B's net income remained sluggish through the mid-1970s.

Another change in command took place in 1978, when Gilbert Cox left Amfac Inc., Hawaii's largest sugar producer, to assume the presidency of A&B. Cox's strategy for growth involved selling off most of Pricher's small acquisitions, such as the potato company, and using the money for a major acquisition. In 1979, an agreement was reached under which A&B would acquire the 80 percent of Pacific Resources it did not already own. This deal fell through, however, following opposition from a group of stockholders led by well-known investor Harry Weinberg.

The rapid succession of new presidents at A&B finally slowed in 1980 with the arrival of Robert Pfeiffer, formerly the CEO at Matson. An upward swing in sugar prices helped boost the company's profits that year. By 1983, sugar accounted for 21 percent of A&B's $395 million in sales. As the company again considered diversification, Harry Weinberg, Hawaii's largest individual landowner, increased his holding in A&B to 25 percent. In 1984, Weinberg forced a proxy battle for control of the company, arguing that A&B's land holdings were worth far more than its books indicated and that property development should be the company's top priority. Unlike most of his boardroom conflicts with large Hawaiian companies, however, this one ended with Weinberg and his associates forced off the A&B board of directors.

In January 1987, A&B got rid of its merchandising division, selling A&B Commercial Company to Monarch Building Supply, Inc., a Honolulu-based company. By this time, A&B had revenues of $655 million, the bulk of which was generated by Matson, which controlled about 75 percent of the container cargo shipping market between Hawaii and the West Coast. Between 1983 and 1987, profits more than doubled to $120 million, and about three-fourths of that total came from Matson. In 1987 A&B began preparing to grow coffee on Kauai through a joint venture between its McBryde subsidiary and Hills Brothers. Another development in 1987 was Matson's formation of a new subsidiary, Matson Intermodal System, Inc., whose specialty was arranging for the transport by rail and truck of cargo containers from Pacific Coast ports to destinations in the U.S. interior.

Several key events occurred in 1989. A&B sold off its remaining shares of Pacific Resources to Australia's Broken Hill Proprietary Company for $123 million, pocketing a substantial profit. The company made another tidy sum on the sale of the Wailea resort community on Maui to Shinwa Golf Group for about $198 million. A&B had been developing the beachfront resort since 1970. Some of the proceeds from these sales were used to purchase development property on the U.S.

mainland, most notably in California, Washington State, Colorado, and Texas. Matson formed another subsidiary in 1989 called Matson Leasing Company, Inc. Matson Leasing quickly grew into one of the largest lessors of marine cargo containers in the world, establishing 12 offices in the Americas, Europe, Asia, and Australia and operating from 98 depot locations across the globe.

A final key development in 1989 was a company restructuring in which there would be two main subsidiaries of A&B: Matson Navigation and the newly created A&B-Hawaii, Inc. (ABHI). The latter took over management of all of A&B's food products and property development and management subsidiaries and operations. A&B recorded net income of $199 million on revenue of $846 million in 1989. Two years later Pfeiffer passed the reins of the company to John C. Couch, who became president and CEO. Couch had served A&B for 15 years, initially with Matson Navigation Company.

CHALLENGES DURING THE NINETIES

A&B's revenues stagnated and net income slumped during the first part of the 1990s, as the Hawaiian economy was battered from both the recession in the United States and the bursting of the late 1980s bubble economy in Japan. With sales hovering around the $750 million mark from 1990 to 1992, company earnings dipped to under $19 million in 1992, the lowest level in over a decade. That figure included a $15.8 million charge to cover losses from Hurricane Iniki, which devastated Kauai in 1992. Nevertheless, A&B mounted a successful comeback the following year. The company reported major increases in both profit and revenue, up to $67 million and $979 million, respectively. Moreover, in June 1993, A&B's $63 million purchase of the 72 percent of California and Hawaiian Sugar Company, Inc., (C&H) that it did not already own helped bolster revenues and profits. For most of the 20th century, C&H had bought the bulk of the raw sugar produced by A&B and had been cooperatively owned by all of Hawaii's sugar producers. A&B took full control of C&H in order to fund needed improvements at the company's huge refinery in Crockett, California. C&H, which had annual revenues of about $500 million, was the leading brand of sugar west of the Mississippi. Also in 1993, Nestlé Beverage Co., successor to Hills Brothers, pulled out of the Kauai coffee joint venture following the devastation of Hurricane Iniki, leaving A&B in full control of what would eventually be called Kauai Coffee Company, Inc.

The takeover of C&H helped propel revenues past the $1 billion mark in 1994, to $1.14 billion. Earnings

grew only slightly, however, totaling $74.6 million. That year, Matson launched a Pacific Coast shipping service linking the ports of Los Angeles, Seattle, and Vancouver, British Columbia. This shuttle service offered shippers an alternative to rail and truck transport along the coast. In April of the following year, Pfeiffer retired and Couch was named to the additional post of chairman. Two months later A&B sold Matson Leasing for about $362 million to Xtra Corporation, a Boston-based transportation services firm that had approached A&B with an unsolicited offer.

A&B had built Matson Leasing into the world's seventh-largest marine container leasing company and would have needed to make additional investments in the subsidiary to maintain its rapid growth rate. Most analysts applauded the sale for both its timing and its price. Other developments in 1995 included a restructuring of C&H, which was operating in the red. About one-fourth of the jobs at C&H's refinery in Crockett, California, were eliminated. A&B also phased out its unprofitable sugar operations on Kauai.

In early 1996 came the start of a planned 10-year trans-Pacific shipping alliance between Matson Navigation and American President Lines, Ltd. (APL). The first step involved APL selling six container ships and some assets in Guam to Matson for $164 million. Matson would use five of the vessels on westbound voyages from the Pacific Coast to Hawaii and Guam. Then APL would charter the ships for excursions to the Far East. Meantime, A&B continued to battle the effects of the prolonged economic malaise afflicting Hawaii, managing in spite of this operating environment to post record revenues of $1.28 billion in 1997 and earnings of $81.4 million, the latter the company's best performance in six years.

Aiding in these positives were A&B's income-generating properties on the mainland, which by this time included three million square feet in six western states. Although the Maui sugar plantation performed poorly that year, Kauai Coffee produced a record harvest of more than four million pounds, a 70 percent increase over the previous year and a total that represented nearly 60 percent of the coffee grown in the entire United States. Unfortunately, the coffee subsidiary had yet to make a profit.

In July 1998 Couch took an indefinite medical leave after he began receiving treatment for liver cancer. Pfeiffer was brought back as chairman temporarily, with Charles M. Stockholm taking over as chairman in August 1999. In October 1998 W. Allen Doane was promoted from executive vice president to president and CEO of A&B, having joined the company in 1991 as executive vice president and COO of ABHI. A&B made a strategic shift in December 1998 when it sold a 64 percent stake in C&H to an investment group headed by Citicorp Venture Capital Ltd. The company received about $80 million in proceeds but still posted a nearly $20 million loss on the sale. In December 1999 A&B's subsidiary structure was altered when ABHI was eliminated through its merger into the parent company. The former subsidiaries of ABHI were now direct subsidiaries of A&B. Another significant change to the food operations came in 2000 when the company decided to close one of its two sugar mills on Maui.

JOINT VENTURES AND NEW INITIATIVES

On the transport side, Matson in September 1998 entered into a joint venture with Saltchuk Resources, Inc., and International Shipping Agency, Inc., to operate an ocean shipping service between Florida and Puerto Rico. Matson Logistics Solutions, Inc., was formed in 1998 to begin offering supply and distribution services. In July of the following year, Matson formed a joint venture with Stevedoring Services of America that combined the companies' terminal and cargo handling services operations in Los Angeles, Long Beach, Oakland, and Seattle.

At the same time, Matson Intermodal was being rapidly expanded, including through the acquisition in 2000 of Paragon Transportation Group, an intermodal marketing firm based in Dublin, California, that was particularly strong in the California, Nevada, Montana, Oklahoma, and Michigan markets and was therefore able to bolster Matson's national coverage. In late 2000 the Pacific Coast shuttle service that was launched by Matson in 1994 was replaced by regular rail and truck service between Los Angeles and Seattle operated by Matson Intermodal.

The Hawaiian economy finally appeared to be entering into at least a period of moderate growth by 2000, and A&B's results reflected the better times. Revenues increased 7 percent, while earnings before exceptional items increased 15 percent. With the sale of the majority interest in C&H, the ocean transportation operations dwarfed both the real estate and food sectors, having generated about 80 percent of 2000 revenues. A&B planned to continue to expand its transport operations and launched a $32 million program to substantially improve its main terminal in Honolulu at Sand Island. In real estate, a key initiative was the company's 1,045-acre residential-resort community in Poipu, Kauai, the plans of which called for more than 200 hotel rooms, 700 time-share vacation units, and as many as 3,000 residential units. A&B's troubled food operations received some good news in 2000 in the

form of the first year of profitability for Kauai Coffee. The company was also investing $11 million into a new plant where sugarcane bagasse would be made into environmentally friendly composite panelboard. A&B was the last of Hawaii's Big Five companies to remain independent and based on the islands. Its durability over more than 130 years of operation proved that a mainland address was not a prerequisite for long-term success.

A DECADE OF EXTREME HIGHS AND LOWS: 2000–10

In 2000, A&B's leaders recognized that it needed to expand its reach to meet its growth expectations. One avenue to this end was real estate. Although A&B owned a significant amount of land, it was unable to develop it to turn a quick profit because of Hawaii's zoning regulations. Eager to put A&B's real estate expertise to fuller use, management transformed its real estate strategy in 2000 with an aggressive acquisition program in Hawaii and abroad. The company transitioned from developing its historic land holdings (the lands the company had owned for over 100 years for agricultural purposes) to acquiring and developing non-company-owned lands.

Allen Doane, A&B's chief executive officer, and Stan Kuriyama, the head of its real estate subsidiary, were credited with the shift. In 2000 the company spent an additional $100 million on commercial, residential, and industrial land, doubling local holdings for A&B and expanding its reach outside the island for the first time. The company's goal was to make Hawaii 80 percent of its real estate holdings with the other 20 percent abroad.

From 2001 to 2002, A&B's earnings suffered due to the depressed economy worldwide. The downturn was also attributed to a slump in the domestic economy following the September 11, 2001, terrorist attacks on the United States. However, by 2003 the company's balance sheet had rebounded and A&B was eager to invest its earnings. Limited real estate opportunities in Hawaii compelled A&B's property arm to embark on the first of many real estate developments on the mainland. By March 2003, A&B Properties' portfolio was 45 percent retail, 30 percent office, and 25 percent industrial. It spent the next several years further expanding its holdings by purchasing a wide range of commercial properties, including shopping centers in California and Texas, and an industrial complex in Utah. The strategy paid off and by the end of 2003, A&B's gross sales had jumped to $1.23 billion. Executives credited the strong earnings to its real estate strategy.

A&B showed even stronger earnings in 2004 with first quarter profits jumping 54 percent from the previous year and second quarter profits up 30 percent. Leading the improvement were A&B real estate operations, while profits from Matson were in line with expectations. Income from sugar operations was up despite a drop in production. Total earnings for the company broke down as follows: Matson generated 60 percent of operating profit, 37 percent came from real estate, and three percent from food and agricultural products. At the time, Matson was the largest domestic ocean shipper from the West Coast to Hawaii, Guam, and mid-Pacific ports. The company anticipated that Matson would grow 8 to 10 percent over the next several years.

The year 2005 surpassed all expectations for A&B. During this benchmark year, the company pursued residential development in Hawaii and was also successful with commercial and retail properties. Additionally, it did well with office space in Southern California. Growth for the real estate segment overall was 13 to 15 percent. While sugar and coffee remained important aspects of A&B's business, this business segment did not show the growth potential of other company segments in 2005. With such strong earnings, the company was optimistic about the immediate future because the economic environment was incredibly strong both in Hawaii and on the mainland.

By early 2006, however, there were signs that the Hawaiian residential market was cooling. Additionally, A&B missed its earnings forecast as revenues for Matson were less than anticipated. To combat the slump and jump-start growth, Matson started a new shipping service to China. By the summer of 2007, business had picked up considerably, and Matson was reporting higher-than-expected profits with service to Long Beach and Oakland, California; Seattle, Washington; and Portland, Oregon, as well as China, Guam, and Micronesia.

Throughout 2008, Matson's China service continued to grow. As a result, A&B's net income surged 70 percent even though its shipping segment faced a challenging economic climate in Hawaii and elsewhere. That same year, A&B's real estate segment also expanded with a focus on acquisitions in the light warehousing, packaging, and distribution market segment. The company purchased an industrial park in Savannah, Georgia, and a few months later, acquired Pan Pacific American Services LLC, a warehousing and distribution space in Oakland, California, and Republic Distribution Center, located in Houston, Texas. These acquisitions extended the company's emerging investment strategy of purchasing logistics-oriented warehouse facilities in key domestic transportation nodes.

CUTTING COSTS, LOOKING TO THE FUTURE

In October 2008, A&B transferred trading of its shares to the New York Stock Exchange from the NASDAQ. The new ticker symbol was AXB. However, 2008 proved to be a poor-performance year due to the increasing economic turmoil that had begun enveloping the world economy. By the end of 2008, the company's net income had dropped 25 percent. A&B acted quickly to reduce costs. In January 2009, Matson reduced its workforce by almost 15 percent. The cuts were part of an expansion of ongoing cost-reduction initiatives in response to what A&B called an "expected continued slowdown in economic activity."

By May 2009, A&B's drop in profits was staggering. Revenue had sunk 93 percent compared to the previous year. In addition to real estate losses, there was an unprecedented decrease in shipments carried by Matson. According to Doane in a May 2009 *Journal of Commerce* article, the volume drop at Matson had "no modern parallel." He also stated: "Our financial performance for the first quarter of 2009 was negatively impacted by the deepening national and international economic contraction." To offset its losses, A&B began selling real estate holdings, and by the end of the year, proceeds from the sales topped $100 million.

One year later, things seemed to be looking up for the company. In July 2010, A&B had seen a surge in profit with a 129 percent gain in second-quarter profit. The surge was due to improved results from Matson's China service, which A&B planned to expand. The new service would double Matson's trade between China and California. "The China-to-U.S. trade is one of the world's most robust and is expected to grow over time," A&B's chief executive officer, Stanley Kuriyama, said in a July 2010 *Honolulu Star-Advertiser* article. With a strategic eye on the future, A&B positioned itself to weather the continuing economic storm.

Robert R. Jacobson
Updated, David E. Salamie; Carrie Rothburd

PRINCIPAL SUBSIDIARIES

A&B Development Company; A&B Properties, Inc.; East Maui Irrigation Company, Limited; Kahului Trucking & Storage, Inc.; Kauai Commercial Company, Inc.; Kukui'ula Development Company, Inc.; Matson Navigation Company, Inc.; Matson Global Distribution Services, Inc.; Pacific American Services, LLC; Matson

Integrated Logistics; Matson Terminals, Inc.; McBryde Sugar Company, Inc.; Kauai Coffee Company, Inc.; WDCI, Inc.

PRINCIPAL DIVISIONS

Hawaiian Commercial & Sugar Company.

PRINCIPAL COMPETITORS

American Crystal Sugar Company; APL Limited; Barnwell Industries, Inc.; C.H. Robinson Worldwide, Inc.; Crowley Maritime Corporation; Expeditors International of Washington, Inc.; Horizon Lines, Inc.; Hub Group, Inc.; Hutchison Port Holdings Limited; Mitsui O.S.K. Lines, Limited; Nippon Yusen Kabushiki Kaisha; UPS Supply Chain Solutions, Inc.

FURTHER READING

"A&B, Land & Sea: One Hundred and Twenty-Five Years Strong," *Ampersand* (special issue), Honolulu: Alexander & Baldwin, Inc., 1995.

Baldwin, Arthur D., *A Memoir of Henry Perrine Baldwin, 1842 to 1911*, Cleveland: [privately printed], 1915.

Beauchamp, Marc, "Hunkering Down Is No Strategy," *Forbes*, October 31, 1988, pp. 54–62.

"Can Alexander & Baldwin Do It Again?" *Financial World*, May 15, 1981, pp. 27–28.

Cieply, Michael, "East of Eden," *Forbes*, January 31, 1983, pp. 34–36.

Duchemin, John, "A&B's Challenge: Embrace Change or Get Passed By," *Pacific Business News*, March 24, 2000, p. 14.

Fuller, Larry, "Kauai Coffee Grows into Next Millennium," *Pacific Business News*, March 12, 1999, p. 3.

Gillis, Curtis, "Matson Makes Tracks," *American Shipper*, September 2000, p. 60.

Norton, Leslie P., "Growing Rich Returns in the Land of Aloha," *Barron's*, August 29, 2005, p. 18.

Roig, Suzanne, "Matson Sells Container Lease Firm," *Honolulu Advertiser*, May 3, 1995.

Stindt, Fred A., *Matson's Century of Ships*, Kelseyville, CA: F.A. Stindt, 1982, 319 p.

Trifonovitch, Kelli Abe, "Evolving with the Economy," *Hawaii Business*, June 1, 2004, p. 13.

———, "From Big Five to Top Five," *Hawaii Business*, August 2000, p. 36.

Whitehead, John S., "Western Progressives, Old South Planters, or Colonial Oppressors: The Enigma of Hawaii's 'Big Five,' 1898–1940," *Western Historical Quarterly*, Autumn 1999, pp. 295–326.

Worden, William L., *Cargoes: Matson's First Century in the Pacific*, Honolulu: University Press of Hawaii, 1981, 192 p.

Anglo American PLC

Anglo American PLC 25
20 Carlton House Terrace
London, SW1Y 5AN
United Kingdom
Telephone: (44 0 20) 7698 8888
Fax: (44 0 20) 7698 8500
Web site: http://www.angloamerican.co.uk

Public Company
Incorporated: 1999
Employees: 107,000
Sales: $24.63 billion (2009)
Stock Exchanges: London Johannesburg
Ticker Symbol: AAL
NAICS: 212234 Copper Ore and Nickel Ore Mining;
212231 Lead Ore and Zinc Ore Mining; 212210
Iron Ore Mining; 212111 Bituminous Coal and
Lignite Surface Mining; 212112 Bituminous Coal
Underground Mining; 212221 Gold Ore Mining;
421840 Diamonds Wholesaling (Except Industrial);
212299 All Other Metal Ore Mining

■ ■ ■

Anglo American PLC is one of the world's largest mining concerns, controlling diversified interests in platinum group metals, copper, nickel, iron ore, and coal. The company holds a major stake, 45 percent, in the world's largest diamond exploration company, De Beers S.A. Anglo American own mines and properties in Africa, South America, Australia, Europe, and North America.

FORMATION IN 1917

The roots of Anglo American can be traced back to 1902, when Ernest Oppenheimer arrived in Kimberley representing diamond merchants A. Dunkelsbuhler & Co., a member of the Diamond Syndicate, the cartel that attempted to maintain prices for South African diamonds by regulating production. Working for Dunkelsbuhler and on his own account, Oppenheimer also became interested in gold and coal mining, and in 1905 acquired the Consolidated Mines Selection Company (CMS), originally formed in 1887, with properties on the Far East Rand gold field. By 1916, when that field's true value was more widely appreciated, Oppenheimer/CMS was in a stronger position there than any of the other Transvaal mining-finance groups.

CMS had a large number of German shareholders and directors, causing it to be rather unpopular during World War I. Oppenheimer was a naturalized British subject who identified strongly throughout his life with South Africa's British, against its Dutch Afrikaner community. Oppenheimer was nevertheless attacked because of his German origins. These points, coupled with the war-imposed restrictions on British capital exports, led him to seek U.S. financing to develop the field. An American connection in CMS introduced him to Herbert Hoover, through whom Newmont Mining Corporation, J.P. Morgan & Co., and Guaranty Trust became involved. With their support, Anglo American Corporation of South Africa (AAC) was formed on December 25, 1917, with £2 million of authorized capital, half of which was issued. Various political reasons have been advanced for the decision to locate the company in South Africa rather than Britain, but the primary reason was to avoid the possibility of double taxation problems.

AAC joined the ranks of the mining-finance groups characteristic of South African mining. Cecil Rhodes and other early financiers concentrated ownership of individual mines in the hands of a few holding companies that provided basic financial, administrative, and technical services for the mines they owned. This process of concentration had begun with the diamond mines, initially because some claimholders had insufficient capital to continue exploitation as workings went deeper, and ultimately because ownership concentration meant more efficient production control. Gold mining did not face oversupply problems, but given gold's fixed price and the highly speculative nature of mining investment, concentration of ownership meant more efficient use of technical and administrative resources. It also focused wealth and power in the hands of the relative few who sought it and were able to command the necessary capital. A system of interlocking directorships developed, creating a close, interdependent network. A latecomer to the field, Oppenheimer soon showed that he was more than a match for his predecessors, as he set out to absorb much of what they had built, and took the concept of group control much further.

FROM GOLD TO DIAMONDS:
1922–29

With a strong base in gold and access to U.S. capital, Oppenheimer was able to challenge the Diamond Syndicate and De Beers, the dominant producer. He was helped by influential British and German connections, and by contacts between AAC Director H. C. Hull, former finance minister of the Union of South Africa, and his former political colleague, Prime Minister Jan Smuts. Oppenheimer acquired most of the diamond mines in Namibia, then known as South-West Africa, when the German companies operating them were encouraged to sell out to British interests. By the time De Beers and others learned of the negotiations, it was too late to prevent the sale to AAC, and they

initially welcomed the stability these acquisitions implied.

AAC's Namibian mines were quickly brought under centralized control in Consolidated Diamond Mines of South-West Africa (CDM). Initially, CDM cooperated with the Diamond Syndicate. In 1922, however, AAC and Barnato Bros reached a separate agreement for the purchase of the Belgian Congo's diamond output. In 1923 they acquired major interests in the Companhia de Diamantes de Angola, diamond mines in West Africa, and a share in British Guiana's diamond production. CDM subsequently became part of the De Beers group in 1930.

In 1924, AAC was given an 8 percent share in the Diamond Syndicate. The purchasing agreements AAC had with non-South African producers, including the right to take all of CDM's production, gave AAC apparent control over such producers. This control was more apparent than real, but led smaller South African producers to look to AAC as an alternative to the syndicate, with whom they were increasingly dissatisfied, owing to the prices they were offered. The principle of selling all of South Africa's diamonds through a single channel was seriously weakened. AAC was asked to leave the syndicate, and established a rival organization joined by Dunkelsbuhler, Barnato Bros., and Johannesburg Consolidated Investments Ltd. (JCI), a group originally established by Barnato, and subsequently absorbed into AAC's ambit.

The South African government was concerned about the implications for revenue of limited diamond production and a potentially disastrous price-cutting war between the two syndicates. The Diamond Control Act of 1925 gave the government sweeping powers to take over diamond production and distribution, and to prevent extreme behavior, namely price cutting. As a member of Parliament, Oppenheimer had been able to introduce an amendment that required the government, if it enforced any provisions of the law, to give preference to South African-registered diamond purchasers. AAC was the only one, while all the others were registered in London.

OPPENHEIMER HEADS DE BEERS:
1929

With AAC continuing to grow financially stronger in the face of declining world diamond demand, the new syndicate was able to outbid the old in an offer to South African producers. On July 30, 1925, the new syndicate's offer was accepted and the old syndicate collapsed. Having gained effective control of distribution, Oppenheimer moved to control production as

KEY DATES

1917: Sir Ernest Oppenheimer founds Anglo American Corporation of South Africa (AAC).

1929: AAC becomes the largest single shareholder in De Beers.

1993: Minorco acquires the non-African assets of AAC, excluding diamonds, while AAC acquires all the African assets of Minorco.

1998: AAC combines with Minorco to establish Anglo American PLC.

2001: Anglo American PLC eliminates its cross-holding with De Beers, increasing its interest in De Beers from 32 percent to 45 percent.

2006: Cynthia Carroll becomes the first non-South African to lead the company.

2009: Anglo American rejects a merger proposal from Xstrara PLC.

well. He became a De Beers director, while AAC further strengthened its position by buying properties in two new South African fields and by consolidating and expanding its links with outside producers. Resistance was strong. Oppenheimer's bid, first made in May 1927, to take control of De Beers, only succeeded in December 1929 with the support of the Rothschilds, introduced through Morgan Grenfell. Oppenheimer became chairman of De Beers, clearing the way for the consolidation of production and distribution functions in one organization, the Diamond Corporation, formed in February 1930 under De Beers' and Oppenheimer's effective control.

Negotiations with Sir Chester Beatty and Sir Edmund Davis, which had led to agreements for purchasing West African, Angolan, and Congolese diamonds, also led Oppenheimer to participate in the development of the Northern Rhodesian, later Zambian, copperbelt and that country's lead and zinc mines. Although these rich deposits had been known to exist for several decades at least, technological difficulties had prevented exploitation. Progress in the use of flotation techniques opened up new possibilities after World War I. AAC acted as engineering consultant to several companies formed to exploit these deposits, bringing some of them together in Rhodesian Anglo American Limited (Rhoanglo), formed in December 1928. American capital was also involved in this venture, as it was in the other

group operating on the copperbelt, Beatty's Rhodesian Selection Trust.

Oppenheimer wanted to combine Morgan Grenfell, Beatty, and others in a syndicate to develop the Mount Isa lead mine in northwest Queensland, Australia. Initial surveys were not promising, and AAC withdrew. AAC subsequently became involved in various Australian undertakings, ultimately establishing an Australian subsidiary. Overall, however, the group's direct involvement in Australia was limited.

DECENTRALIZED STRUCTURE TAKES SHAPE: 1930–45

The 1930s saw further expansion of AAC's holdings in the Far East Rand, in some cases in conjunction with New Consolidated Gold Fields. AAC also began to move into the Orange Free State gold fields. The areas it acquired initially were generally unpromising. It was only by purchasing a stake in European and African Investments Ltd. in 1943, and subsequently gaining full ownership by acquiring most of the shares of its parent company, Lewis and Marks, in 1945, that AAC laid the foundation for its subsequent domination of Free State gold mining. The 1930s and 1940s also saw the establishment of several subsidiary holding companies and the extension of the administration decentralization that characterized AAC. The precise extent to which effective Oppenheimer family control was maintained through E. Oppenheimer Sons, which absorbed A. Dunkelsbuhler & Co. in 1935, is unclear, but it is clear that personal influence remained strong. Anglo American Investment Trust took over AAC's diamond interests in 1936, while West Rand Investment Trust took responsibility for gold mines in the Far West Rand field that were opening up at this time.

The decentralized structure was intended to stimulate on-the-spot decision making, and to enable ideas to filter up from the people most directly involved in day-to-day operations. However, decentralization made it extremely difficult to trace the details of financial connections within the group as the constituent companies remained separately incorporated. Effective control, or at least coordination by central management, had not been sacrificed; information was constantly exchanged, both formally and informally. Interlocking directorships, and the power to appoint directors, were augmented by personal contacts based on friendship and, more importantly, by family connections. Members of the Oppenheimer family held important positions in many of the companies. On another level, AAC recruited people considered potentially high powered, including a substantial number of former Rhodes scholars.

As the group developed, acquiring or establishing companies in various fields, the decentralized structure remained. Some companies became subsidiaries, with at least 50 percent of their shares held by AAC. In other cases control mechanisms were more flexible, but just as effective. These included holding a greater number of shares than anyone else; the control of essential supplies, markets, or technology; and various financial links.

Between 1945 and 1960, AAC became the world's largest gold-mining group, owing to expansion in the Orange Free State as well as the richer mines in the Far West Rand and Klerksdorp fields. Capital requirements were high, in part because the Free State gold deposits lay at considerably deeper levels than the Rand's. The 1946 African miners' strike, although rapidly repressed, was evidence of considerable upward pressure on African wages. AAC decided to base Free State development on more capital-intensive techniques.

Building on its original financial concept, AAC went further afield in its search for capital, securing about 27 percent of the £370 million raised from British sources; 23 percent from Switzerland, Germany, elsewhere in Europe, and the United States; and 43 percent from within the AAC group itself. Most innovative, and significant in the longer term, was AAC's drawing on surplus capital and non-mining savings generated within South Africa itself for 7 percent. The greater availability of domestic capital was a particularly important development after World War II, forming the basis for a measure of domestic financing of development, which was associated in part with the expansion of Afrikaner, as opposed to British, capitalism. As internal savings increased over the following decades, they also laid the foundation for South Africa's ability to absorb a substantial portion of shares disposed of through disinvestment by foreign firms, although heavy reliance on foreign investment remained.

AAC'S STANCE TOWARD
APARTHEID: POST-WORLD WAR II

By 1960, AAC had taken over the leadership of the gold-mining industry. It was also making heavy inroads into the country's industrial and service sectors. The difficulties of importing manufactured goods from Europe during World War I had stimulated interest in domestic industrialization. Increasingly powerful Afrikaner politicians were wary of mining interests prepared to finance industrial development, partly because of an underlying antipathy to capitalists, and partly because of the politicians' foreign, particularly British, identity. This led in 1928 to the formation of the Iron and Steel Corporation as a nationalized basis for the country's iron and steel industry. As post-World War II mining develop-

ments generated more capital, pressure to create domestic investment opportunities led to increased, though often reluctant, cooperation between the government and the private sector which was increasingly dominated by AAC.

Social and political considerations also became important, particularly after 1948 when the rationale for the apartheid system included the expectation that industries would be established along the borders of homeland territories, providing employment for the Africans increasingly forced to inhabit them. While that hope was never fulfilled, antagonism between the British and Afrikaners began to diminish in the face of a perceived common threat from black Africans, and by the growth of Afrikaner involvement in business. The importance of Oppenheimer's and AAC's financial strength also diminished some of the specific antagonism toward them. Despite the fact that Harry Oppenheimer, who succeeded his father as head of the group after World War II, often criticized the apartheid regime, it was widely accepted that he did not intend to attempt to destroy it, was prepared to work within it, and was pressing for changes that would improve the position of Africans primarily because it made good business sense.

DIVERSIFICATION: 1961–69

Initially, most of AAC's industrial activity was directly related to mining. It had acquired African Explosive and Chemical Industries through its earlier investments in diamond interests. Its acquisition of Lewis and Marks brought it Union Steel and Vereeniging Refractories. In 1936, AAC established Boart and Hard Metals, concerned with the use of industrial diamonds in mining and other drilling applications. In 1961 it created the Highveld Steel and Vanadium Corporation which, along with Steel Ceilings and Aluminum Works, acquired in 1964, formed the basis of AAC's control of South African specialized steel production, as well as created a strong foundation for heavy engineering. The merging of three construction companies (Lewis Construction, James Thompson, and Anglo American Construction) into LTA Ltd. created a construction giant.

Diversification also led AAC into paper manufacturing (Mondi Paper Co., formed in 1967) and, through its 1960 takeover of Johannesburg Consolidated Investments, newspaper publishing (the Argus group and Times Media Limited). Building on motor vehicle distribution in the McCarthy group, it moved, by combining with Chrysler and then Ford, into automobile production as well. In freight services, in conjunction with Safmarine, it led the growth of containerized shipping in the country. Retail stores and large property holdings were also acquired.

An important merger involving AAC in the 1970s was between Rand Mines and Thomas Barlow. Rand Mines was a mining group that had not acquired interests in the Far West Rand and Orange Free State as its older Witwatersrand mines reached depletion. Seriously ailing, it came under AAC control in the 1960s, but AAC did little to revive it. Thomas Barlow had been a small engineering supply importer, which by 1970 controlled more than 70 companies manufacturing a wide variety of products. Barlow acquired all Rand Mines' issued shares in 1971. AAC held 10 percent of Barlow Rand's shares directly. By 1972, after reorganization and expansion, the merged group controlled 131 subsidiaries and associates in nine countries. Although executive control remained in the Barlow family hands, AAC was not without influence in the firm.

Although diamonds replaced gold as AAC's single most important source of profit in the 1980s, gold remained at the heart of the group's activities. A substantial holding in the U.S. precious metals refiners Engelhard Corporation, along with a stake in the United Kingdom's Johnson Matthey, gave AAC access to important sources of highly profitable information about the world's gold trade.

AAC's share in Engelhard was held by its subsidiary Minerals and Resources Corporation (Minorco), officially renamed Minorco in 1974. Minorco grew out of Rhoanglo. It was through Minorco that AAC attempted to take over Consolidated Gold Fields (Consgold) in 1988. AAC and Consgold had been closely associated, directly and indirectly, in many enterprises over the years, but relations between them were based at least as much on rivalry as on common interest, and the attempted takeover came as no surprise. AAC acquired about 25 percent of Consgold. This attempt came up against U.S. antitrust legislation and Consgold was bought by Hanson Trust instead.

AAC GRAPPLES WITH APARTHEID: 1980–89

AAC was at the center of political controversy in South Africa in the 1980s, not merely because of its economic strength, but because the Oppenheimers and the group itself took a public stand on the apartheid question. Politically active Ernest Oppenheimer and his son Harry were not in favor of black majority rule, but they did press for relaxation of certain aspects of the apartheid regime. Not surprisingly, they were particularly interested in decreasing dependence on migrant labor. A more settled, stable labor force was considered more

productive and efficient. Although some stabilization of labor did occur, relatively little could be done in the face of government opposition. In 1987, along with some other mining groups, AAC began to replace migrant workers' hostels with low-cost family accommodations. Like several other changes, this was seen by many as too little too late, and by others as merely a new method of social control. AAC was not prepared to raise African wages sufficiently to allow workers effective freedom of housing choice.

In 1985, AAC's chairman, Gavin Relly, and other senior AAC personnel met representatives of the African National Congress (ANC) in exile. In April 1990, AAC's Scenario Planning team published proposals for South Africa's constitutional development. These placed great emphasis on federalism and devolution of power. More dispersed state power, AAC argued, would facilitate accommodation of divergent interest groups. This, along with a massive image-building campaign in the U.K. press had been part of AAC's campaign to remain a major economic force in the country as its political structure changed inexorably.

UPHEAVAL: 1990–99

The rapid unraveling of the apartheid system in the early 1990s quickly changed forever the environment in which AAC operated and gave rise to much speculation about AAC's future, as well as a great deal of maneuvering by AAC to protect its interests. The major political events followed one after another. In 1990 the ban on the ANC was lifted and Nelson Mandela was released from prison. In 1991 the remaining apartheid laws were repealed. In 1992 an all-white referendum approved a new constitution that would lead to eventual free elections. Finally, in 1994, the first nationwide free elections were held and were won by the ANC, with Mandela elected president.

Meanwhile, the 1990s started for AAC with a change in leadership, as Julian Ogilvie Thompson, who at one time was Harry Oppenheimer's personal assistant, took over the chairmanship from the retiring Relly in 1990. At the same time, it was widely known that Oppenheimer's son Nicholas, then deputy chairman of AAC and the head of De Beers' London-based diamond sales operation, was being groomed as the next chairman. The new leadership faced the consequences of AAC's years of dealing with apartheid and the international boycotts and sanctions the system engendered. The company had been forced to reinvest its earnings within South Africa where it had no choice but to diversify in order to use all its excess cash.

By the early 1990s, AAC had created, no doubt aided by the apartheid system itself, a powerfully diversified company with admitted control of 25 percent of the South African stock market, a figure that outside observers placed as high as 40.5 percent. Threats to nationalize certain AAC assets, notably its mines, and to break up the AAC empire seemed quite real, although it eventually became apparent that Mandela had no intention of seizing the company's assets without compensation.

As part of a two-pronged defensive strategy, AAC first moved to protect some of its assets from nationalization by increasing its overseas investments and by transferring assets into the control of subsidiaries and affiliated companies located outside South Africa, with Luxembourg-based Minorco the key affiliate. Minorco expanded its North American mining operations by acquiring the U.S. firm Freeport-McMoRan Gold Company in 1990 (it was later renamed Independence Mining) and the Canadian-based Hudson Bay Mining & Smelting in 1991. In a 1993 $1.4 billion stock and asset swap, Minorco took over the South American, European, and Australian operations of both AAC and De Beers, which meant that all of AAC's non-African, non-diamond assets were now consolidated within Minorco and out of the reach of nationalization.

AAC's second strategy was a longer-term plan of making small concessions to the new political order over the course of several years, thus heading off the possibility that the country's new government of national unity would force AAC to make more dramatic changes. Essentially, this represented a revival of AAC's strategy of co-option, previously used successfully with the Afrikaners, being employed with the new group in power. AAC sought to spin off some of its vast holdings to black South Africans, such as in the 1994 deal in which African Life was bought by a group of black businesspeople.

DIVESTITURES: 1995–99

A more ambitious divestment began in 1995 when AAC divided its Johannesburg Consolidated Investment Company, Limited (Johnnies) subsidiary into three separate companies: AAC American Platinum Corporation Ltd. (Amplats), a trader of platinum and diamonds; JCI Ltd., an operator of gold, coal, ferro-chrome, and base metal mines; and Johnnies Industrial Corporation Ltd. (Johnnie), a holding company with industrial and real estate assets. AAC intended to hold onto its minority stake in Amplats, but to sell its stakes in JCI and Johnnie to black South Africans. As of mid-1996 neither of the stakes had been sold, but a serious bid was developing for Johnnie, whose lucrative holdings included a 13.7 percent stake in South Africa's largest brewing company, South African Breweries; 27.8

percent of a beverages group, Premier; 26.4 percent in an automobile maker, Toyota SA Marketing; and 43.2 percent of a newspaper and magazine publisher, Omni Media. Little interest had been apparent for the JCI stake, with the *Economist* speculating that black South Africans' business inexperience made running a holding company more attractive than the messy business of mining.

By the mid-1990s, AAC was slowly beginning to unbundle itself of its diverse and massive holdings in South Africa. The company's future was still clouded given the question of whether it was moving fast enough to suit those in the country wishing to see economic power transferred from white to black hands nearly as fast as political power had been transferred. While Mandela's government seemed content with a go-slow approach, the political situation was still unstable in the country, especially given Mandela's advanced age. Nevertheless, AAC's moves to shelter more of its assets offshore made it much less likely that possible future government intervention in its affairs would prove devastating.

REORGANIZATION: 1998

AAC undertook a major change in October 1998, when it announced a significant reorganization that would result in a name change and a new company headquarters in London. It was a complicated restructuring. AAC held considerable cross-holdings with De Beers, the South African company best known for its status in the world diamond industry. AAC also held 43 percent of Minorco, a Luxembourg-listed company that held assets outside South Africa with interests in similar industry sectors; and De Beers also owned 23 percent of Minorco.

AAC made a successful offer for the shares it did not already own in Minorco, priced at $2.3 billion; a bid for the minorities of Amcoal, South Africa's largest coal company, valued at $1.6 billion; the acquisition of Amic, another of South Africa's largest industrial companies; and the acquisition of several of De Beers's investments. Cross-holdings would remain between the two companies, but the result was one company, named Anglo American PLC. The company now held all the previous interests in gold, platinum, coal, and so on, and De Beers retained only diamond interests.

The combining of companies created several benefits. Anglo American became one of the world's largest mining and natural resources companies, with an array of interests in gold, platinum, and diamonds, and a central presence in coal, base and ferrous metals, industrial minerals, and forest products. The formation of Anglo American allowed the group to compete more effectively around the world and to exploit new business and growth opportunities, supported by improved access to international capital markets.

Before the closing of the public offer, Minorco divested itself of its gold interests and interests in Engelhard Corporation and Terra Industries. Based on the closing share price of AAC on October 14, 1998, and reflecting the terms of the share offer for Minorco, Anglo American had a market capitalization of nearly £6.1 billion, enough to be included in the FTSE 100 index. The company commenced trading shares on the London Stock Exchange in May 1999, with secondary listings on the Johannesburg Stock Exchange and Swiss Exchange SWX.

FOCUS ON CORE BUSINESSES AT THE MILLENNIUM

At the time of its listing, Anglo American announced shareholder value enhancement as its key objective. The company focused its efforts on strengthening its core portfolio of businesses and holdings. By early 2001, it had successfully accomplished a number of steps in this process, including significant growth in many divisions; major acquisitions in its Industrial Minerals, Coal and Forest Products divisions; the accelerated disposal of non-core industrial interests, which led to the sale of $840 million of assets in 2000; and the exchange of the major portion of its non-core holding in FirstRand in return for certain listed mining assets valued at around $730 million.

Rumors began to swirl in January 2001 that the long-standing marriage between Anglo American and De Beers was about to dissolve. The following month, Anglo American announced the creation of DB Investments (DBI), in conjunction with Central Holdings Limited and Debswana Diamond Company (Proprietary) Limited. The result of this deal was the elimination of the complicated cross-holding between De Beers and Anglo American, which had dampened the share price of both groups for some time. Anglo American's interest in De Beers rose from 32.2 percent to 45 percent.

The results of this move were overwhelmingly positive for Anglo American. It greatly simplified Anglo American's structure and with the removal of the cross-holding it brought an immediate cash inflow of $1.07 billion and $701 million on redemption of preference shares in DBI. It also increased the free float of Anglo American shares to approximately 90 percent.

Anglo American made financial news pages in March 2002 with the announcement by the mining group that it had taken a $488 million charge in 2001 to cover the cost of restructuring its base metals operations. Amid an extremely disappointing year for base metals, most of the exceptional costs resulted from the company's miscalculations of the dollar costs of its copper investments in Zambia. This led to the proposed closure of Konkola Copper Mines, which accounted for nearly two-thirds of Zambia's copper production. Anglo American had acquired the assumed low-cost assets two years prior, but its withdrawal from Zambia alone resulted in an exceptional charge of $353 million.

LEADERSHIP CHANGES AND REBUFFED MERGER: 2002–09

The first decade of the 21st century witnessed stagnant revenue growth, but the period saw profound changes on other fronts. Anglo American, which had been led by only four CEOs during more than 80 years of existence, anointed two new CEOs during a five-year period during the decade. Tony Trahar, an accountant by training who joined the company's finance division in 1974, became the fifth CEO in 2002. His relatively brief tenure involved selling Anglo American's non-mining assets as part of a strategic review undertaken by the company. Anglo American focused its efforts on mining during Trahar's time in charge, announcing in 2006 a $3.9 billion investment to increase its nickel production by 120 percent, its copper production by 60 percent, and its zinc production by 80. A greater emphasis was placed on shedding assets during Trahar's stint, divestitures that left his successor with $3 billion to facilitate financing for expansion.

Cynthia Carroll, a geologist who served as CEO and president of Alcan Inc.'s primary metal division, was announced as Anglo American's sixth CEO in 2006. Born in New Jersey, Carroll became the first non-South African to lead the company. "The company is on course to realize the next stage of its strategy of becoming a focused mining group and global leader in the metals and mining industry," she said in the October 26, 2006 issue of *American Metal Market*.

The price of Anglo American shares, which had languished during Trahar's stewardship, shot up 68 percent during Carroll's first year at the helm. Carroll doubled the budget for developing existing mining properties to $43 billion and acquired Brazilian iron ore properties for $6.7 billion. She also paid $403 million to the Peruvian government to exploit the Michiquillay copper mine, and orchestrated Anglo American's first U.S. deal, pledging $1.4 billion to a joint venture company to extract copper, gold, and molybdenum from the Pebble Mine in Alaska.

The global economic crisis at the end of the decade delivered a telling blow to Anglo American. Base metals prices plunged in late 2008, prompting the company to reduce its capital expenditure program for 2009 to $4.5 billion, 50 percent less than it had spent the previous year. "We've adjusted accordingly and have hunkered down," Sir Mark Moody-Stuart, Anglo American's chairman, said in the April 3, 2009 issue of the *America's Intelligence Wire*. As the company bided its time, Switzerland-based mining giant Xstrara PLC proposed a merger in mid-2009, but Anglo American's board of directors rejected the deal. The company appeared intent on weathering the economic storm and waiting for commodity prices to rebound, eschewing the trend toward industry consolidation that several of its largest rivals had embraced.

Simon Katzenellenbogen
Updated, David E. Salamie; Stacee Sledge; Jeffrey L. Covell

PRINCIPAL SUBSIDIARIES

Anglo Operations Limited; Anglo Platinum Limited (South Africa; 79.7%); Anglo American Sur SA (Chile); Anglo American Norte SA (Chile; 99.9%); Minera Quellaveco SA (Peru); De Beers S.A. (South Africa; 45%); Anglo American Brasil Limitada (Brazil); Minera Loma de Niquel, CA (Venezuela; 91.4%); Kumba Iron Ore Limited (South Africa; 62.8%); Anglo Ferrous Brazil SA; Anglo Ferrous Minas-Rio Mineracao SA (Brazil); Anglo Ferrous Amapa Mineracao Limitada (Brazil; 70%); Anglo Coal Holdings Australia Limited; Black Mountain Mining (Pty) Limited (South Africa; 74%); Ambase Exploration (Namibia) Proprietary Limited; Anglo American Lisheen Mining Limited (Ireland); Peace River Coal Partnership (Canada; 74.8%); Tarmac Group Limited; Tarmac France SA;

Lausitzer Grauwacke GmbH; WKSM SA (Poland); Tarmac CZ a.s. (Czech Republic); Tarmac SRL (Romania); Koca Beton Agrega Mining and Construction Industry and Trading Company Limited (Turkey); United Marine Holdings Limited.

PRINCIPAL COMPETITORS

BHP Billiton Limited; Impala Platinum Holdings Limited; Rio Tinto Limited.

FURTHER READING

Ball, Deborah, "Funds Will Reject Oppenheimer, Anglo American Bid for De Beers," *Wall Street Journal*, April 23, 2001, p. A16.

Block, Robert, "De Beers Owners Weigh Plan to Delist Diamond Giant," *Wall Street Journal*, February 2, 2001, p. A8.

———, "An $18.7 Billion Buyout of De Beers Appears Imminent," *Wall Street Journal*, May 18, 2001, p. A17.

Bradner, Tim, "Anglo Chairman Talks about the Future of Mining," *America's Intelligence Wire*, April 3, 2009.

Markram, Bianca, "Alcan's Carroll to Succeed Trahar as Anglo American Chief Executive," *American Metal Market*, October 26, 2006, p. 12.

Nevin, Tom, "Anglo, De Beers to Split?" *African Business*, January 2001, p. 30.

———, "'Think Again, Anglo,' Says Anderson Mazoka," *African Business*, March 2002, p. 40.

Pallister, David, Sarah Stewart, and Ian Lepper, *South Africa Inc.: The Oppenheimer Empire*, rev. ed., London: Simon & Schuster, 1987.

Stein, Nicholas, "The De Beers Story: A New Cut on an Old Monopoly," *Fortune*, February 19, 2001, pp. 186–206.

Williams, Stephen, "Shock as Anglo Pulls Out of Konkola," *African Business*, March 2002, p. 41.

Wright, Chris, "Now Anglo American Migrates to London," *Corporate Finance*, January 1999, p. 4.

API Group plc

Second Ave., Poynton Industrial Estate, Poynton
Stockport, Cheshire SK12 1ND
United Kingdom
Telephone: (44 01625) 858700
Fax: (44 01625) 858701
Web site: http://www.apigroup.com

Public Company
Incorporated: 1920 as Associated Paper Industries
Employees: 795
Sales: $146.4 million (2009)
Stock Exchanges: London
Ticker Symbol: API
NAICS: 322222 Coated and Laminated Paper Manufacturing

■ ■ ■

Based in the United Kingdom, API Group plc is a London Stock Exchange-listed company that manufactures specialized packaging foils, films, and laminates. Products include metallic foil, which in addition to packaging is used for decorative applications; cold foil, an alternative to hot stamping foil; decorative holographic foil, employed to produce eye-catching packaging; and pigment foil, the durability of which makes it ideal for date coding and other purposes that require a level of permanence.

API also produces laminated papers and boards, and security foils and films, as well as offering holographic services to help clients incorporate holographic images for security purposes, to maintain brand identity and

prevent counterfeiting or tampering. Some of those images can only be detected using a reading device or, in some cases, through laboratory analysis. End use markets for API products include packaging for cosmetics, perfumes, tobacco products, alcoholic beverages, specialty food products, health care products, greeting cards, book jackets, video cases, and printed plastics. Holographic images are incorporated into event tickets, identification cards, passports, and currency.

ORIGINS IN PAPER MANUFACTURING

API was founded in the United Kingdom as Associated Paper Industries in 1920 and two years later went public. The company was originally a paper manufacturer, operating a paper mill in Glasgow and a paper-coating facility in Cheshire. Because there was no ready supply of low-cost timber in the United Kingdom to produce paper in bulk, the company was heavily dependent on high tariffs imposed by the British government to ward off competition. As a result, API prospered for several decades, at its peak operating seven paper mills. Everything changed for English papermakers in the mid-1960s, however. The tariffs were abolished in 1967 and companies including API could no longer compete against paper manufacturers in Sweden and Finland that had massive supplies of timber at their disposal.

API did not adapt easily to the changing business conditions. One by one its mills closed, until only two remained by the late 1970s: Vale Board Mills in Scotland and Cooke and Nuttall in Yorkshire. A new managing director was hired and a new chairman installed in Charles Rawlinson, a merchant banker. Perhaps of more importance, API completed an acquisition that would help lead to a change in direction. Not only did the purchase of Peerless Gold Leaf Co., maker of stamping foils, provide some much needed diversity, it led to further investments and the eventual exit from paper manufacturing. In 1978 API acquired George Whiley, a public company that also produced stamping foils, but had fallen on hard times because of a poorly executed relocation from southeastern England to Scotland. Nevertheless, it was a well established stamping foil company and made a nice addition to Peerless. API was also coming off a strong year in 1977, but that all came to an end with a recession that resulted in a sharp decrease in profits in 1980.

EXITING THE BULK PAPER MARKET

In order to survive, API concluded that it had no choice but to exit the bulk paper business entirely and close its two remaining mills. The company was now left with two business segments: stamping foils and paper converting. The latter involved converting paper to other uses. The Garnett subsidiary produced advertising poster board, while Leonard Stace manufactured release papers, backings for such products as adhesive tapes and sticking plasters. Another unit, H and L Slater, made postage stamps for several countries and coated paperboard for gift packs, in particular whiskey packaging.

With the Whiley operation taking longer to turn around than hoped, API hired consultants to help the company diversify further. After reviewing a number of possibilities, API settled on filtration and purification products as the one area that offered the most promise. Through the Garnett subsidiary, it was already involved in the sector in a small way by fashioning artificial fibers into dry-formed webs that could be made into filters for deep-fat fryers, such as those it sold to the Kentucky Fried Chicken restaurant chains. They were also filled with activated carbon charcoal to make air fresheners. In 1982 the purification business was split off from Gar-

nett as an independent subsidiary.

To fund further growth through acquisitions, API made a stock offering that raised £2.7 million. After a year of research, management compiled a list of six companies it thought would make good acquisitions. They were all contacted, but only two expressed any interest. Both of them were acquired in 1983. They were Diffusion Radiator Co., a manufacturer of air conditioners and heating systems, and Airpel, which produced industrial filters.

While API held out hope for its new ventures, it was experiencing excellent growth in the stamping foil business. It became the fastest-growing source of income in the mid-1980s once the problems at Whiley had been rectified. A new factory for Peerless was also opened. The release paper business, on the other hand, began to falter, due to an influx of competition that led to overcapacity. To build on its foils business, APO paid $8.4 million for Rahway, New Jersey-based Dri-Print Foils, which made foil for use in luxury packaging, bookbinding, greeting cards, labels, and window coverings. With operations in both the United States and Canada, Dri-Print generated annual sales of $23 million and became available only because its parent company, Beatrice Chemical, was acquired and the foil business was not considered a good fit for the new owner.

CLOSING COATING AND CONVERTING OPERATIONS: 1989

In 1989 Associated Paper closed its coating and converting operations. Because the focus was no longer on the production of bulk paper, coating, or paper converting, the company decided to change its name in 1990, drawing on its longtime abbreviation to become API Group plc. The acronym had already been applied to its stamping foil unit, API Foils Limited, which had emerged as one of the world's largest producers of stamping foil. API was also a generic enough name to encompass the company's heating and ventilating systems business that remained a part of the mix in the early 1990s.

API found itself the subject of an unsolicited takeover bid in the summer of 1991 by another paper and packaging company, NMC, which offered 17 of its shares for 10 of API. The deal was worth £25.8 million, but API rejected the offer as it did a sweetened bid worth £30 million. Although NMC was warded off, API's chairman and management director resigned by the end of 1991, resulting in a period of vulnerability that the company successfully negotiated before it hired a new chief executive officer, Michael Smith. A graduate of Harvard University's School of Business, Smith had

KEY DATES

1920: Associated Paper Industries is founded.
1922: Company is taken public.
1967: Tariffs are lifted on foreign bulk paper, causing a change in focus for the company.
1990: Company changes name to API Group plc.
2000: Chromagem is acquired.

been with Avery since 1975 and eventually became group vice president of Avery's labeling and office products business outside of the Americas. He left in 1987 to become chief executive officer of Smurfit's print, packaging, and converting companies in the United Kingdom.

ACQUISITION OF GOLD IMPRESSIONS GROUP: 1992

Under Smith, API resumed expansion through acquisitions of its own in 1992. Its Dri-Print unit acquired the Gold Impressions Group of companies, a major U.S. distributor of foil products. At this stage, API was generating about $110 million in sales. Further acquisitions followed as the decade unfolded. Laminated board supplier J&J Makin Converting was added in 1995. API also became involved in the growing holographic design and products sector to pursue the premium packaging and security device business. In addition, API opened a manufacturing affiliate in China to produce its full range of products.

Michael Smith left API in 2000 at a time of deteriorating business conditions, but in the months just prior to his departure, the company completed a pair of significant acquisitions. In March of that year API paid $2.8 million for Ohio-based Chromagem, a company whose design capabilities filled in gaps in API's holographic portfolio. A month later, API acquired a Wales company, Van Leer Metallized Products Limited, for about £1 million. Van Leer mostly produced metallized paper for beer bottle labels and cigarette packet inner-liners. Following Smith's exit, Derek Ashley, former CEO of Applied Graphics Technologies Inc., took the reins at year's end.

A strategic review of API's operations was initiated, leading to a restructuring that included the 2001 closing of a laminates manufacturing facility in Rochdale. Other cost-cutting measures included the consolidation of metallized paper manufacturing and laminating operations, and the sourcing of low-cost product from the

Chinese unit. API also invested in holography for both decorative and security applications, markets that offered promising growth opportunities.

NEW CENTURY CHALLENGES

With growing competition from Eastern Europe and the Far East, conditions remained challenging in 2002 and 2003 as revenues fell to £176.2 million in 2003, reflecting a steady decline from the £188.8 million posted in 2000. A significant drag on API was its Converted Products business, which faced increasing competition in 2004. As a result, API's sales dipped to £169.5 million. Much of the decrease was due to the impact of discontinued businesses as API looked to divest money-losing non-core companies. In 2004 Learoy Packaging and Morris Plastics were sold. Although the market for Metallised Paper and Converted Products remained poor, the Foils and Laminates units performed well and enjoyed a 4.8 percent improvement in sales.

In 2005 API elected to sell its Metallised Paper and Converted Products divisions, receiving about £13 million for the assets. API even considered selling out to Illinois Tool Works, Inc., but the sale to the U.S. industrial conglomerate was never consummated. As a result of the divestitures, API's sales fell to £118.4 million in fiscal 2005 but operating profits improved.

Following several years of restructuring, API was now a company focused on its specialized foil and laminate products, but it continued to struggle. Sales from continuing operations in fiscal 2006 slipped another 3.4 percent to £102 million, due primarily to a poor performance in Europe. The company looked to spur growth by expanding its operations in China and bolstering its position in the United States. It also built up its U.S. and European sales operations.

SECONDARY STOCK OFFERING: 2008

Changes continued as the decade progressed. Operations in China were moved to a new location, allowing API to sell surplus property in China to help cut debt. The company was also able to refinance its debt, and in early 2008 API made a secondary stock offering that netted £7.2 million to provide the financial wherewithal to continue the reorganization of the company. While API made strides on some fronts, it still had to contend with a global recession in 2008. Business improvements in Europe were offset by difficulties in the United States and China. The following year produced similar results, modest gains in Europe combined with disappointment in China and the United States. By early 2010 business conditions began to improve significantly. After a challenging decade to start the new century, API had narrowed its focus, streamlined its operation, and was hopeful that better times lay ahead.

Ed Dinger

PRINCIPAL SUBSIDIARIES

API Laminates Limited; API Foils Holdings Limited; API Foils Limited; API Holographics Limited; API Overseas Holdings Limited.

PRINCIPAL COMPETITORS

Bemis Company, Inc.; Shorewood Packaging Corporation; Spectratek Technologies Inc.

FURTHER READING

"Battle between NMC and API Comes to a Head," *Financial Times*, August 9, 1991.

Hope, Christopher, "Rising Profits Put API in Bullish Mood," *Print Week*, May 16, 1997.

Jackson, Tony, "A Paper-Maker's Metamorphosis," *Financial Times*, March 22, 1985.

Marsh, Virginia, "API Forms Security Joint Venture in China," *Financial Times*, December 16, 1998, p. 27.

"Stamping Foil Growth Expands Associated Paper Profit by 55%," *Financial Times*, December 13, 1984, p. 25.

"Top Managers of the Future Are Coming Through—API Group," *Manchester Evening News*, July 25, 1996.

Atalanta Corporation

Atalanta Plaza
Elizabeth, New Jersey 07206
U.S.A.
Telephone: (908) 351-8000
Fax: (908) 351-1978
Web site: http://www.atalanta1.com

Private Company
Incorporated: 1945 as Atalanta Trading Corporation
Employees: 150
Sales: $350 million (2009 est.)
NAICS: 424410 General Line Grocery Merchant
Wholesalers; 424460 Fish and Seafood Merchant
Wholesalers; 424470 Meat and Meat Product
Merchant Wholesalers

■ ■ ■

Atalanta Corporation is a family-owned and -operated specialty food importer based in Elizabeth, New Jersey, that serves grocery stores, specialty food stores, restaurants, and other foodservice companies. Atalanta maintains offices across the United States, including Atlanta, Boston, Chicago, Dallas, Houston, Los Angeles, Miami, Oakland, and Tampa, as well as West Suffield, Connecticut, and Nashua, New Hampshire. Products include cheese from more than 30 countries; deli meats from several countries; specialty grocery items from around the world; pasta, rice, and grains from Chile, Italy, Israel, Spain, Thailand, and the United States; frozen lobster tails; a kosher food line; and a variety of

desserts, breads, and other baked goods from across the globe.

Brands include Arnaud, Atalanta, Casa Diva, Celebrity, Del Destino, Menu, and Martel. Subsidiary Atalanta International, operating out of Bucharest, Romania, imports furniture and such agricultural commodities as grains, oilseeds, sugar, and vegetable oils. It also owns equity partnerships in local trading companies around the world. Atalanta Corporation is part of Gellert Global Group, owned by Atalanta's chairman and CEO George Gellert.

POST-WORLD WAR II ORIGINS

Atalanta Corporation was cofounded in New York City as Atalanta Trading Corporation in 1945 by Herbert B. Moeller and Leon Rubin. Moeller was born in Brooklyn around 1898 and received meat-processing training in Europe. Rubin was born in St. Petersburg, Russia, in 1911. After studying languages at the University of London he came to the United States in 1936. He became a naturalized citizen five years later and subsequently served in the U.S. Army during World War II. With Moeller serving as president, the two men began Atalanta in Manhattan with just a rented desk in a downtown office building.

Atalanta's first major success was importing frozen frog legs and lobster tails from Cuba, the supply of which had been disrupted by World War II. Prior to the war Japan had been the primary supplier of frog legs to the United States as well as France. Lobster tails, on the other hand, had to be imported from South Africa following the war. With the advent of air shipments,

COMPANY PERSPECTIVES

■

Our Mission: To be the leading partner in the imported and specialty food business for our customers, suppliers, employees and community.

Atalanta was able to transport lobster tails and frog legs directly from a quick-freeze plant near Havana to New York's La Guardia Field in a DC-4 cargo plane. Packed in dry ice, they arrived in excellent condition and were quickly picked up by seafood distributors. As the supply increased in 1947, the lobster tails and frog legs became available in the frozen food section of New York City grocery stores as well.

POLISH HAM IMPORTS BEGIN: 1948

Atalanta made a bigger mark in 1948 when it forged a relationship with the Soviet Union satellite state of Poland and became the only importer of Polish hams to the United States. Rubin's cousins had been involved in pork production in Poland, and with the rise of the Communist government they had had their operations confiscated. The Polish government then contacted Rubin about serving as the U.S. agent for the ham and pork products. In 1952 Atalanta also began to import canned ham and pork by-products such as pork loins, pork sausage, and Canadian-style bacon from West Germany, which was still recovering from the war. While the country produced ample supplies of meat, it needed to import fats, lard, and oils to supplement the diet of the population. The lack of these items had a ripple effect on the economy. Coal production, for example, was hindered because fat shortages deprived workers of energy-producing foods and crippled their productivity. The funds received from the export of meat helped in the purchase of these necessary supplements to the diet.

Atalanta thrived as an importer of canned ham, lobster tails, and frozen shrimp. To keep pace with demand, the company in 1963 leased a 16-story refrigerated building lining the northern side of North Moore Street at the corner of Varick Street in what is now known as the Tribeca district of Manhattan. It had originally been constructed in 1924 as a refrigerated warehouse for Merchants Refrigerating Company and was ideally suited to handle Atalanta's frozen foods. It was renovated further to become one of the East Coast's largest receiving and distribution centers.

The Cold War hindered Atalanta's ability to expand further into Eastern Europe and threatened its Polish ham business. During the Korean War Poland supported North Korea, prompting some Americans to call for a boycott of Polish hams. In the early 1960s the right wing John Birch Society began leaving cards in supermarkets urging consumers to boycott hams and other products from Communist Poland. These efforts had the opposite of their intended effect, however. Atalanta's sales increased by raising awareness of Polish hams with U.S. consumers.

FURTHER EASTERN EUROPEAN BUSINESS

Atalanta entered a second Communist country, Hungary, in 1969, followed by Romania a year later. In the early 1970s the Soviet Union and the United States attempted to improve relations through what was known as détente, prompting other U.S. businesses to seek out opportunities in the Eastern Bloc. Because of its head start, Atalanta prospered further. By 1972 the company was generating $140 million in annual sales from imports from 42 countries. In addition to its Manhattan operation, it maintained 10 sales offices and 74 warehouses across the country as well as a fleet of trucks, refrigerated trailers, and even a fleet of trawlers to harvest shellfish.

Atalanta would also begin doing business with Communist China. In 1973 it reached a deal to import more than 100,000 pounds of frozen rabbit from the country. It was also in 1976, after nearly four decades of being the sole U.S. importer of Polish ham, that its exclusivity arrangement came to an end. Upon the expiration of a marketing and technical agreement at the end of 1976, Atalanta no longer received a commission on the sale of Polish hams and other products in the United States. It continued to import the products, but it was now just one of a dozen import partners.

By this time there had been a change in the top ranks of Atalanta. Moeller retired and then in April 1970 the 72-year-old was killed from smoke inhalation caused by a fire in his Greenwich Village apartment. Taking on an increasing amount of responsibility with the company was George Gellert, Rubin's son-in-law, who had been appointed vice president in 1969 and spearheaded the relationship with China, becoming only the second businessperson to be invited to the country to pursue a business venture. He had joined Atalanta in 1966. With a law degree as well as an M.B.A. from Cornell University, Gellert had previously worked as an attorney for the U.S. Securities and Exchange Commission and for the U.S. Army Materiel Command as a staff judge advocate.

KEY DATES

1945: Company is founded in New York City by Herbert B. Moeller and Leon Rubin.
1948: Atalanta begins importing Polish hams.
1980: George Gellert assumes majority ownership.
1988: Company moves to Elizabeth, New Jersey.
1999: Atalanta acquires two ConAgra subsidiaries.

Gellert succeeded Rubin as Atalanta's president in 1973 and soon became chairman of the American Stock Exchange-listed company. In the summer of 1979 he made a bid to take the company private along with a group of other Atalanta officers and directors. The deal was completed in 1980 and Gellert became majority owner of the company.

MOVE TO NEW JERSEY: 1988

The types of specialty and gourmet foods Atalanta offered grew increasingly popular in the 1980s, as supermarkets began to make shelf space available to compete with specialty stores in this sector. During the 1980s Atalanta's Tribeca neighborhood became trendy as well. Its industrial lofts were converted into residences by the affluent, many of them celebrities such as Robert De Niro, Bette Midler, Edward Albee, and Harvey Keitel, who brought even greater cachet to the area. As a result, it became increasingly difficult, and expensive, for Atalanta to do business there and in 1988 the company moved its operations across the Hudson River to Elizabeth, New Jersey, where it found a local government that was eager to accommodate its needs.

Atalanta moved into the former Singer manufacturing complex on the Elizabeth waterfront. The New Jersey Economic Development Authority helped to sell the company on the location by paying $7 million to purchase the site and spent a further $7 million to clean it up. Another attraction was the site's proximity to Port Newark, which received most of the area's containerized shipping, the primary way Atalanta's products were now transported. For its part, Atalanta invested $10 million in constructing its new headquarters-warehouse complex.

Atalanta continued to expand its offerings as it celebrated its 50th anniversary. In July 1995 the company acquired Finica Foods Specialties Limited. Founded in 1968, Finica distributed specialty cheese and gourmet items from around the world and made its name with the introduction of Finlandia "Lappi" cheese

from Finland. As the 1990s came to a close, Atalanta grew further with a pair of acquisitions from ConAgra Inc. The first deal, completed in May 1999, brought Camerican International, a Paramus, New Jersey-based company founded in 1916 that imported processed seafood, meats, fruits, and vegetables. Next, in September 1991, Atalanta acquired ConAgra's J.F. Braun & Sons, that added shelled nuts and dried fruit to Atalanta's portfolio of products and increased annual sales to the $500 million level. Founded in 1947, the Westbury, Long Island-based company also imported seeds and cocoa powder.

NEXT GENERATION JOINS COMPANY: 1984

The 1990s also brought a second generation of the Gellert family to Atalanta, when George Gellert's son, Thomas, joined the company in 1994. Like his father, the younger Gellert graduated from Cornell University. He spent two years with the company in Italy, exporting Italian food products, primarily cheese, to the United States as well as Europe. He then returned to Cornell to earn a law degree and an M.B.A., and spent some time working on Wall Street as an investment banker before returning to Atalanta. He would become vice president in charge of the cheese division and specialty food imports. His sister Amy would also become assistant general manager of Atalanta, and brother Andrew would head a unit of the company in Arlington, Texas.

As the new century dawned, Atalanta continued to grow despite changes in the marketplace. Importers had once been guarded about their sources of products, but with the advent of the Internet and other information venues, Atalanta's customers and suppliers were able to communicate directly. As a result, Atalanta positioned itself as more of a service company. Suppliers could perform the same role as Atalanta, but Atalanta remained viable because it could do the job better. Its expertise became even more valuable after the September 11, 2001, terrorist attacks on the United States brought increased security measures to ports.

Atalanta continued to add new products during the new millennium. In late 2002 the company forged a relationship with Spanish cheese producer Quesos Forlasa to import the Don Bernardo and Campobello brands to the United States. At the same time, Atalanta became the exclusive importer of Galbani Italian cheeses to the United States. To better serve the growing Hispanic population in the country, Atalanta expanded its offerings of products geared toward this market in 2005. In 2007, Gellert Global Group acquired De Medici Imports, Ltd., an importer of non-perishable specialty food brands, in particular the Castelas brand of olive oil from France. De Medici now joined Atalanta, Camerican International, J.F. Braun & Sons, Finica Food Specialties, Ltd., Swiss Chalet Fine Foods, and Ti-pico Products Co., Inc., in the stable of import companies owned by the Gellert family. To keep pace with growth, Atalanta expanded its warehouse in 2008. There was every reason to believe that Atalanta and its subsidiaries would enjoy continued prosperity in the years to come.

Ed Dinger

PRINCIPAL SUBSIDIARIES

Atalanta International (Romania).

PRINCIPAL COMPETITORS

DPI Specialty Foods, Inc.; European Imports, Ltd.; World Finer Foods Inc.

FURTHER READING

"Fire in 'Village' Flat Kills Retired Food Importer, 71," *New York Times*, April 2, 1970.

"Food Importer Sets Up Shop in New Home," *Journal of Commerce*, August 30, 1988, p. 4A.

"Frog Legs and Lobster Tails from Cuba Flown Here in Quantity for First Time," *New York Times*, January 25, 1947.

"Germany to Ship Canned Meat Here," *New York Times*, April 11, 1952.

"Merger Creates $385 Million Import 'Powerhouse,'" *Food Institute Report*, June 14, 1999.

Nagle, James J., "Eating and Drinking Our Way to Détente," *New York Times*, December 24, 1972.

"16-Story Building on Varick St. Sold," *New York Times*, August 16, 1963.

Atmos Energy Corporation

———■———

Three Lincoln Centre, Suite 1800
5430 LBJ Freeway
Dallas, Texas 75240
U.S.A.
Telephone: (972) 934-9277
Fax: (972) 855-3040
Web site: http://www.atmosenergy.com

Public Company
Incorporated: 1983
Employees: 4,891
Sales: $4.96 billion (2009)
Stock Exchanges: New York
Ticker Symbol: ATO
NAICS: 221210 Natural Gas Distribution

■ ■ ■

Atmos Energy Corporation is the largest natural-gas-only distributor in the United States. The company's regulated utility operations deliver natural gas to 3.2 million residential, commercial, industrial, and agricultural customers in 12 states. Atmos' non-regulated operations, which are conducted through Atmos Energy Holdings, market natural gas supplies to more than 1,000 industrial customers and municipalities in 22 states.

CONNECTING TO THE GREAT PANHANDLE GAS FIELD: 1906–23

Atmos traces its origins back to 1906, when brothers J. C. and Frank Storm of Kirksville, Missouri, got wind of the need for a gas plant in Amarillo, Texas. Although the Storms would later claim that Amarillo did not seem like a promising place to start a business, they decided to take a chance, hoping that Amarillo would grow into more than just a cattle trail junction. They formed Amarillo Gas Company and began laying pipe under the town's streets, not a terribly difficult task considering the fact that none of them was paved.

The Storms manufactured gas from coke and oil, unaware that Amarillo lay only 20 miles from one of the world's largest natural gas deposits, the great Panhandle gas field. The field was not discovered until 1918, when another predecessor of Atmos, the Amarillo Oil Company, began drilling there. Amarillo Gas made a pipeline connection to the field in 1920.

ACQUISITION BY SOUTHWESTERN DEVELOPMENT COMPANY: 1924

In 1924, Southwestern Development Company acquired both Amarillo Oil and Amarillo Gas. Southwestern also started other gas distribution companies. By 1927, in its search for new markets, it put a pipeline under construction to extend its service to west Texas, all the way to Midland and Odessa.

Despite having to contend with the economic problems caused by the Dust Bowl drought and the Great Depression, Southwestern Development continued to grow in the 1930s. In 1933, it was one of the country's first gas distributors to inject an odor additive to its gas, an important safety measure that in 1937 became mandatory throughout Texas.

COMPANY PERSPECTIVES

Our vision is for Atmos Energy to be one of the largest providers of gas distribution and related services. We will be recognized for excellent customer service, as an employer of choice and for achieving superior financial results. Our values reflect our vision and the culture of our organization. These values, as observed each day by our employees, have become the cornerstone for Atmos Energy to provide the excellence in customer service our customers have come to expect.

Through the war years of the early 1940s, Southwestern's customer base grew steadily. By 1945, it was serving about 53,000 people and businesses. At the war's end, a population boom started that by 1950 had nearly doubled the company's number of customers. With the start-up of new families, gas appliances became increasingly popular, encouraging home economists to provide such services as cooking demonstrations in "blue flame" kitchens in the company offices.

CONSOLIDATION AND EXPANSION: 1954–80

By 1954, Southwestern had consolidated all its diverse gas distribution businesses under the name Pioneer Natural Gas Company. The reorganized company faced excellent prospects for accelerated sales. For one thing, natural gas was a bargain commodity, and for another, its use was expanding. Notably, during the 1950s and 1960s, farmers in the Panhandle region of Texas, too often devastated by drought, turned to irrigation farming in increasing numbers. They used the inexpensive and readily available gas to power engines for pumping water from underground aquifers and circulating it through irrigation pipes and ditches. In those two decades, the farmers' need for gas greatly helped Pioneer's sales. Annually, during dry summer months, the company sold up to 50 billion cubic feet of natural gas, more than it sold for the winter heating of its customers' homes.

In 1958, Pioneer acquired Empire Southern Gas Company, again expanding its customer base. Then, during the 1960s, its success also prompted Pioneer to diversify beyond its production and utility operations. Among other things, it started coal and uranium mining, heavy machine production, and tire retreading

operations. In all, the parent company added 13 subsidiaries, some of which were closed down when they failed to operate at an acceptable profit margin. Included in these was Trans State Tire Company, which Pioneer bought in 1969 and sold off a year and a half later.

Pioneer's diversification continued into the 1970s. In 1973, it still owned and operated 10 subsidiaries. Notably, after the energy crunch that started in 1971, Pioneer began bolstering its exploration operations, and over the next 10 years, riding the oil boom, turned itself into a billion-dollar corporation.

SPIN-OFF OF ENERGAS: 1983

As part of a restructuring move, in 1981 Pioneer formed Energas Company, its natural gas distribution subsidiary, and two years later spun it off as an independent company, one that Pioneer's managers did not expect to survive on its own. Charles Vaughan, Energas' first president, had other expectations, however. He was determined to make the operation grow. Ironically, when the oil bubble burst in the mid-1980s, it was Pioneer that did not survive intact. It was absorbed in a merger, while Energas, despite the odds, not only survived but seemed to thrive on economic adversity.

In 1986, Energas began a period of significant expansion when it acquired the Trans Louisiana Gas Company (TransLa), a company originally formed in 1928 as Gulf Public Service Company.

Gulf Public had become part of a Louisiana utility company that had earlier started out in Alexandria, Louisiana, as an ice manufacturer and distributor. Through acquisitions and mergers, TransLa had increased the geographical range of its customer base to stretch from Monroe in the northern part of Louisiana to Franklin in the southern part.

Initially, Energas made history by attempting a hostile takeover of TransLa, the first such attempt in the industry. However, when TransLa was placed on the block by its own board, the buyout by Energas became amicable enough. Its acquisition added 69,000 Louisiana residents and businesses to Energas' customer base. The purchase also prompted the company to move its corporate headquarters to Dallas, a more centralized location.

In the following year, 1987, Energas acquired Western Kentucky Gas Company (WKG), an outfit that, in 1934, had begun providing natural gas for about 2,200 customers. At the time of its acquisition by Energas, WKG's customer base had grown to almost 150,000. It was serving Kentucky communities in the

KEY DATES

1906: J. C. and Frank Storm found Amarillo Gas Company, forerunner of Atmos Energy.

1924: Amarillo Gas Company and Amarillo Oil Company are acquired by Southwestern Development Company.

1954: Southwestern's various gas distribution businesses are consolidated as Pioneer Natural Gas Company.

1981: Pioneer Corporation names its natural gas distribution division Energas Company.

1983: Energas is spun off as an independent, publicly traded gas distribution company.

1988: Energas changes name to Atmos Energy and begins trading on the New York Stock Exchange.

1997: Atmos merges with United Cities Gas Company.

2004: After acquiring TXU Gas Company, Atmos becomes the largest pure natural gas distributor in the United States.

higher growth regions of the state. It also serviced a number of major industrial customers, including aluminum plants and food processors as well as the only Corvette plant in the world. The assets of WKG included those of two other companies: Western Kentucky Gas Resources and Dixie Irrigation. These became wholly owned subsidiaries of Energas.

ENERGAS BECOMES ATMOS ENERGY: 1988

In 1988, Energas changed its name to Atmos, a name selected on the strength of the fact that it came from a Greek word meaning "gases in the atmosphere." The name also seemed to connote energy. In any case, as Atmos Energy Corporation, the newly organized company began trading on the New York Stock Exchange. As part of the change, Energas Company was reorganized as an unincorporated division of Atmos. In the same year, Dixie Irrigation, which came to Energas with its acquisition of WKG, changed its name to WKI, Inc., but two years later was dissolved.

Atmos continued its dynamic growth into and through the 1990s. In 1993, it purchased Greeley Gas Company, then privately owned by the Schlessman family. Greeley had been founded in 1902 in Greeley,

Colorado. Like Amarillo Gas, until gas was piped in from the Texas Panhandle in the 1930s, it initially distributed manufactured gas for homes and such public conveniences as street lamps. In 1944, Gerald Schlessman acquired the company and began expanding its operations by purchasing several smaller companies. At the time of its transfer to Atmos, Greeley had almost 100,000 customers in Colorado, Kansas, and Missouri. Included in its customer base were residents and businesses in such fast-growing regions as Colorado's ski and resort areas surrounding Durango and Steamboat Springs.

In July 1997, Atmos reached a major milestone when it acquired its millionth customer. That mark came from its merger with United Cities Gas Company of Brentwood, Tennessee. United Cities was founded in 1929 as a butane air manufacturer and distributor, operating plants in 17 cities. It had grown through various acquisitions, eventually expanding its operations into 10 states. In 1996, the year before its purchase by Atmos, United Cities had revenues of $353.4 million and reported a net income of $17.2 million. As a division of Atmos, United Cities reduced its range to eight states, but by the decade's end it accounted for about 250,000 homes and businesses in Atmos' customer base, distributing natural gas in over 375 cities and towns in midwestern and southeastern states.

By 1998, Atmos had grown into the 12th-largest natural gas utility in the country, but not without some "painful side effects." Through 1996, the company's business strategy had been to operate each of its acquired companies, many of which lacked advanced technology, as separate business units. In time, that policy proved very inefficient, particularly when the company tried to link them in its expanding network. Many of the companies had incompatible computer systems that often made customer information retrieval difficult if not impossible. None of them even had identical billing systems.

INFRASTRUCTURE IMPROVEMENTS AND ACQUISITIONS: 1998–2000

To improve service and cut overhead, Atmos sought to create uniform and consistent procedures for conducting its business. Accordingly, it phased in some new programs, starting with a fresh customer service initiative (CSI). The CSI consisted of several projects, including the creation of a centralized customer support center, the implementation of handheld meter reading devices and mobile data terminals for in-field service, and the development of a new customer information system with the infrastructure to support it. The implementation of these new initiatives quickly cut operating expenses and increased Atmos' net earnings. Until Atmos created its centralized call center in Amarillo, it had relied on more than 100 unconnected local service offices to conduct its business, an inefficient system at best.

Atmos continued its growth into the start of the new century. In April 2000, it arranged to purchase two Louisiana natural gas local distribution companies (LDCs) from Citizens Utilities, paying approximately $365 million. The two companies, Louisiana Gas Service of Harvey, Louisiana, and LGS Natural Gas, its intrastate pipeline affiliate, added about 279,000 customers in the New Orleans and Monroe areas of the state.

Atmos' growth and consolidation strategies also involved some select divestitures and partnering agreements. Among other moves taken in 2000, Atmos sold the assets of a natural gas distribution system serving around 5,100 customers in the Gaffney, South Carolina, area to Piedmont Natural Gas.

However, the company's focus in 2000 was on growth. Besides its purchases in Louisiana, it acquired some smaller companies. Among others, it purchased the Missouri gas distribution assets of Southwestern Energy Co. The assets were part of Associated Natural Gas Co., a division of Arkansas Western Gas Co., Southwestern's utility subsidiary. The acquisition brought 48,000 additional residential, commercial, and industrial consumers into Atmos' customer base. In exchange for 1.4 million shares of its common stock, worth about $33.3 million, Atmos also purchased the remaining 55 percent interest in Houston-based Woodward Marketing L.L.C., a natural gas services company in which Atmos owned a 45 percent interest.

ACQUISITIONS FUEL GROWTH: 2001–04

Atmos entered the 21st century determined to become the largest, "pure" natural gas distributor in the country. The company had no intention of diversifying its business. It eschewed expanding into other areas of the energy sector. Instead, it focused wholly on becoming the premier natural-gas-distribution-only company in the United States. With CEO Robert W. Best at the helm throughout the decade ahead, Atmos chased its goal, reaching its objective quickly, enabling the company to tout itself as "America's Largest Natural Gas Only Utility."

Atmos leaped past its rivals by completing acquisitions, enjoying the immediate boost to its stature provided by acquiring operators in new markets. The

purchase of Louisiana Gas Service and LGS Natural Gas was completed in July 2001, a transaction that made Atmos the fifth-largest pure natural gas utility in the United States with 1.4 million customers in 11 states. Quickly, Best struck again, orchestrating another deal as summer turned to fall. In September 2001 he reached an agreement to acquire Mississippi Valley Gas Co., the state's largest natural gas utility. Based in Jackson, Mississippi, Mississippi Valley served 261,000 customers in 144 communities, boasting a 5,500-mile distribution system and 335 miles of transmission pipeline. The deal, subject to the approval of seven Public Service Commissions, took a year to complete, but once it was finalized, Atmos ranked as the third-largest pure natural gas distributor, trailing only Illinois-based Nicor Inc. and Georgia-based AGL Resources Inc.

The acquisition of Mississippi Valley meant that Atmos had doubled in size during a four-year period. Best and his management team wanted more, however, and they fulfilled their desires in October 2004. Atmos purchased the largest natural gas distributor in Texas, TXU Gas Company, and became the largest pure natural gas distributor in the country. The acquisition was immediately organized as the Mid-Tex Division, the company's seventh division, and ended its buying spree, representing the last purchase Atmos made in the decade.

In the wake of the TXU Gas acquisition, Atmos served 3.2 million customers in 1,500 communities in 12 states stretching from the Rocky Mountains in the west to the Blue Ridge Mountains in the east. Although the company withdrew from the acquisition front, evidence of its purchases was on display during the second half of the decade. Atmos entered the decade generating less than $1 billion in annual revenue. Its business volume peaked in 2008 when it recorded a staggering $7.2 billion in revenue, a total that slipped to $4.9 billion the following year as natural gas prices plunged. The company was financially sound, however, priding itself in 2009 on having accomplished its goal of increasing earnings per share by 4 to 6 percent for the ninth consecutive year. In the years ahead, Atmos promised to figure as a leader in the energy sector.

John W. Fiero
Updated, Jeffrey L. Covell

PRINCIPAL SUBSIDIARIES

Atmos Energy Holdings; Atmos Gathering Co.; Atmos Energy Marketing; Atmos Pipeline and Storage; Atmos Power Systems.

PRINCIPAL DIVISIONS

Atmos Energy Colorado-Kansas; Atmos Energy Kentucky/Mid-States; Atmos Energy Louisiana; Atmos Energy Mid-Tex; Atmos Energy Mississippi; Atmos Energy West Texas.

PRINCIPAL COMPETITORS

Energy Future Holdings Corp.; ONEOK, Inc.; Xcel Energy Inc.

FURTHER READING

"Energas to Change Name to Atmos Energy Corp.," *Wall Street Journal*, September 22, 1988, p. 10E.

Goodman, Charles, "Customer Service Initiatives Help Atmos Energy's Growth," *Pipeline & Gas Journal*, November 1998, p. 28.

Jeter, Lynne W., "Atmos: Smooth Sailing So Far on MS Valley Gas Deal," *Mississippi Business Journal*, April 15, 2002, p. 18.

Molis, Jim, "Dallas' Atmos Energy to Buy Tennessee's United Cities Gas Co.," *Knight-Ridder/Tribune Business News*, July 26, 1996.

Rohloff, Greg, "Atmos Energy Seeks More Acquisitions, CEO Says," *Knight-Ridder/Tribune Business News*, February 17, 1998.

———, "West Texas Gas Utility Requests 12.5 Percent Rate Hike," *Knight-Ridder/Tribune News*, August 11, 1999.

Shook, Barbara, "Atmos Energy Adds 2 LDCs to Network," *Oil Daily*, April 17, 2000.

Baker Hughes
Incorporated

2929 Allen Parkway, Suite 2100
Houston, Texas 77019-2118
U.S.A.
Telephone: (713) 439-8600
Fax: (713) 439-8699
Web site: http://www.bakerhughes.com

Public Company
Incorporated: 1987
Employees: 34,400
Sales: $9.66 billion (2009)
Stock Exchanges: New York Swiss
Ticker Symbol: BHI
NAICS: 213111 Drilling Oil and Gas Wells; 213112 Support Activities for Oil and Gas Operations; 333132 Oil and Gas Field Machinery and Equipment Manufacturing; 325998 All Other Miscellaneous Chemical Product and Preparation Manufacturing

■ ■ ■

Baker Hughes Incorporated is the product of the 1987 merger of two oilfield-services companies with surprisingly similar histories, Baker Oil Tools (later Baker International Corporation) and Hughes Tool Company. The company ranks as a leading provider of products and services to the world petroleum and continuous process industries. Its size and influence is not solely a result of the merger, but of a number of key post-1987 acquisitions. The largest of these deals was the $3.3 billion purchase of Western Atlas, Inc., completed in 1998,

and the $6.8 billion takeover of BJ Services Company, finalized in April 2010.

HISTORY OF HUGHES TOOL COMPANY

The invention of the first rotary drill bit, used to drill oil wells through rock, led to the creation of Sharp-Hughes Tool Company in 1909. Howard Hughes Sr. and Walter Sharp developed and manufactured the rotary drill bit, an invention so important to the fledgling oil industry of 1909 that variations of the same bit continued to be used in the early twenty-first century. When Sharp died in 1912, Hughes bought Sharp's share of the business. Hughes incorporated the business the following year, and in 1915 he dropped Sharp's name from the company. Armed with the exclusive patent to an essential product, Hughes brought his Houston-based company unrivaled market dominance for decades. Even after many key patents expired, during the 1930s and 1940s Hughes Tool was able to dominate the drill-bit business. During World War I Hughes developed a boring machine that could drill into enemy trenches. Explosives then could be dropped into the trenches. Although the secretary of war personally thanked Hughes for his contribution, the machine was never used because of the sudden shift, toward the end of the war, from trench warfare to active warfare.

If the market dominance of Hughes Tool was secured by the elder Howard Hughes before World War I, its tenor as an undiversified, closely held giant was set by the founder's son and namesake. The 19-year-old Howard Hughes Jr. inherited the company in 1924 fol-

COMPANY PERSPECTIVES

Baker Hughes' innovative technology, workflow and consultancy solutions enable our global customers to maximize recovery from their reservoirs and deliver sustainable energy.

In the process, we will enhance value for shareholders, customers and employees. For shareholders, this means differential earnings performance. For customers, it means helping them create more value from their oil and gas reservoirs through reduced risk, lower cost, and higher ultimate recovery. For employees, it means providing a challenging and rewarding working environment and creating opportunities for a diverse workforce that lead to the realization of both personal and professional potential.

lowing the death of his father. Under Hughes Jr., the oilfield-product company became a massive enterprise that he used largely to fund his various avocations. During World War II Hughes operated a gun plant and a strut-making facility for aircraft, in Dickinson, Texas.

Howard Hughes, who founded Hughes Aircraft Company, purchased over 78 percent of Trans World Airlines' stock, and held a substantial investment in RKO Pictures, remained the sole owner of Hughes Tool until 1972, when he put the company on the market. Hughes Tool became a publicly owned company, in a transaction reportedly valued at $150 million. Although successful, despite a general slump in the drilling industry from 1958 to 1972, Hughes Tool had remained undiversified, primarily because Howard Hughes wanted it that way. "Mr. Hughes, of course, felt he was personally diversified, so he never really considered diversifying the tool company," Raymond Holliday, a former Hughes chairman, told *Business Week* in October 1980. With public stockholders and a booming oil economy, especially after the Organization of Petroleum Exporting Countries (OPEC) oil embargo of the early 1970s, Hughes Tool made up for lost time.

Under the leadership of Chairman James Lesch the firm purchased the Byron Jackson oilfield-equipment division of Borg-Warner in 1974, for $46 million. In 1978 Hughes bought Brown Oil Tools, another family-owned business, whose founder had underutilized his 377 lucrative patents. With its massive expansion and the favorable oil-industry climate, Hughes Tool surged. By 1981, a peak year in the industry, new business

activities, which largely meant non-drill-bit products and services, accounted for 55 percent of the company's sales.

When the bottom fell out of the market in 1982, Hughes found itself a bloated, overextended, and debt-ridden concern. Under the guidance of William A. Kistler, an engineer who had come up through the core drill-bit division to become president, the company retrenched to its roots, concentrating on drill bits and shying away from services. For example, the company shut down 30 foreign offices and streamlined 11 divisions into one. In 1983 Hughes hired outside consultants Bain & Company to trim fat, laying off 36 percent of its workforce. The company still had one weapon neither world markets nor competitors could take away: a patented O-ring rock-bit seal. In 1986 Hughes won a $227 million patent-infringement judgment from Smith International, Inc., a California concern that had copied Hughes's drill seal too closely. In 1985 Hughes had been awarded $122 million from Dresser Industries, Inc., for patent violation. One rival that had innovated around Hughes's patent rather than copying it was Baker International.

Hughes Tool floundered through the mid-1980s. For the three years beginning in 1983, Hughes lost $200 million. Often cited as a potential takeover target, the company was faced with an offer it could not refuse when approached for a merger with Baker.

HISTORY OF BAKER INTERNATIONAL CORPORATION

Like Hughes Tool, Baker grew out of a single invention, the Baker Casing Shoe, a device to ensure the uninterrupted flow of oil through a well, developed in 1907 by Californian Reuben C. "Carl" Baker. Baker licensed his patents and incorporated the Baker Casing Shoe Company in 1913, mainly to protect his numerous patents on products that would soon become the industry standard. During World War I Baker was a member of the local draft board, although his company did not devote any of its production to goods to support the war effort. Baker lived off his royalties until the 1920s when he began manufacturing his own tools. In 1928, after successfully manufacturing tools in Huntington Park, California, for several years, Baker called the company Baker Oil Tools, Inc., a name it would carry for 40 years.

The Great Depression hit Baker hard, causing it to lay off numerous workers, but the late 1930s and 1940s were years of solid growth. During this period the company started offices in many states, including Texas, Wyoming, Illinois, Missouri, and Louisiana. During

```
┌─────────────────────────────────────────────┐
│                                               │
│              KEY DATES                        │
│                                               │
│  ━━━━━━━━━━━━━━━━━━━━■━━━━━━━━━━━━━━━━━━━━     │
│                                               │
│  1907:  Reuben C. "Carl" Baker develops the   │
│         Baker Casing Shoe, a device to        │
│         ensure the uninterrupted flow of      │
│         oil through a well.                   │
│  1909:  Invention of the first rotary drill   │
│         bit leads to the creation of          │
│         Sharp-Hughes Tool Company, led by     │
│         Howard Hughes Sr. and Walter Sharp.   │
│  1913:  Baker organizes Baker Casing Shoe     │
│         Company to hold and license his       │
│         patents.                              │
│  1915:  Sharp-Hughes is renamed Hughes Tool   │
│         Company.                              │
│  1928:  Baker Casing is renamed Baker Oil     │
│         Tools, Inc.                           │
│  1976:  Baker Oil Tools changes its name to   │
│         Baker International Corporation.      │
│  1987:  Hughes Tool and Baker International    │
│         merge to form Baker Hughes            │
│         Incorporated.                         │
│  1998:  Baker Hughes acquires Western Atlas    │
│         Inc.                                  │
│  2010:  BJ Services Company is acquired.      │
│                                               │
└─────────────────────────────────────────────┘
```

World War II Baker retooled to produce gun-recoil mechanisms. Following the war Baker prospered. In the 10 years after 1948 it opened 50 new offices in 16 states. In 1956 Carl Baker retired at age 85, leaving the company in the hands of Theodore Sutter, an executive who had joined the company in the early 1920s. Carl Baker died shortly after his retirement. Under Sutter the company began to expand globally, and it went public in 1961.

When E. H. "Hubie" Clark Jr. assumed control of Baker in 1965, the company developed into a global powerhouse. Clark, who had joined the company as a recent mechanical-engineering graduate from the California Institute of Technology in 1947, led Baker, now based in Orange, California, to new heights. Although Baker remained based in California, in 1965 the company's Houston operation was as large as the California operation. Clark acquired some 20 companies, the largest of which was Reed Tool Company, a drill-bit manufacturer purchased in 1975. Clark worked hard to predict trends in oil supply and demand. Baker operations were begun in Peru, Nigeria, Libya, Iran, and Australia, among other countries, and in 1976 the company changed its name to Baker International Corporation.

The company's reputation for quality and Clark's renown as a manager put Baker into the 1980s in solid shape. Even Baker could not avoid the downturn of petroleum-related business after 1981. Clark and James D. Woods, the company president, sought to improve efficiency in the slow-growing industry. The eventual answer was to merge with its Houston-based competitor, Hughes Tool. Both companies had been losing money, and they hoped to eliminate overproduction by merging.

MERGER OF BAKER AND HUGHES IN 1987

"This industry is plagued with overcapacity," said one Baker official, as he announced on October 22, 1986, that the two oil-services firms would merge. Wall Street immediately applauded the move, a complex stock swap that favored Baker stockholders by giving them one share of the new company for each share they owned, compared with an eight-tenths-of-a-share deal for Hughes shareholders. Reflecting the greater general strength of Baker, its executives were to be given the top posts. Clark was to be the new chairman and Woods the new president and CEO, while William Kistler, Hughes's chairman, would be named the merged company's vice chairman. The new company's home would be Houston, where Hughes was based, and where Baker had extensive operations. Baker's Orange, California, headquarters housed relatively few employees.

Wall Street showed its excitement over the merger by trading up the stock prices of both companies following the merger announcement, but the federal government frowned on the potential antitrust ramifications of combining two such powerful outfits. On January 25, 1987, the U.S. Justice Department announced that it would attempt to block the merger, citing reduced competition in markets for some oil-exploration machinery. As top executives worked out a consent agreement with the Justice Department, Hughes executives attempted to pull out of the merger. Baker responded in strong terms, threatening to sue Hughes for $1 billion if it failed to carry through with the agreement. After several delays Hughes capitulated. On April 3, 1987, Hughes agreed to the terms of the consent decree, which included the divestiture of the domestic operations of Reed Tool Company and some other units, and the merger was completed, creating an oil-services company second in size only to Schlumberger Limited.

POST-MERGER YEARS MARKED BY RESTRUCTURING, DIVESTMENTS, AND ACQUISITIONS

The consolidated company did not stop charging forward after the merger. Baker Hughes Incorporated outpaced its competition in the late 1980s. Part of its success was in realignment, as Woods slashed 6,000 jobs, closed several plants, and took a $1 billion write-off for restructuring expenses. The result was $90 million less in annual costs and impressive sales. The company was profitable by fiscal 1988. Woods added the chairmanship of Baker Hughes to his title in 1989.

Throughout the late 1980s and early 1990s, Baker Hughes did not hesitate to divest itself of unprofitable and/or noncore operations and to bolster the company through acquisition. In May 1989 its longtime money-losing mining equipment operation was sold to Tampella Ltd. of Finland for $155 million. In April 1990 Baker Hughes added the world's leading maker of directional and horizontal drilling equipment, Eastman Christensen Company, in a $550 million deal with Norton Co. The U.S. Department of Justice approved the deal, but only after Baker Hughes agreed to divest its own diamond drill business. In 1992 Eastman Christensen was merged with Hughes Tool Company to form a new division called Hughes Christensen Company.

In 1991 Baker Hughes divested Baker Hughes Tubular Services and also spun off to the public its profitable but lawsuit-plagued BJ Services Inc. pumping service unit. Parker & Parsley Petroleum Co. had filed suit against Baker Hughes and Dresser Industries (the two of which had originally jointly owned the predecessor of BJ Services), alleging that BJ Services had shortchanged Parker & Parsley on materials used to stimulate wells. A 1990 jury verdict awarding Parker & Parsley $185 million was later overturned, but in 1993 the three parties settled out of court for $115 million, with Baker Hughes and Dresser each responsible for half, or $57.5 million.

In 1992 Baker Hughes spent $350 million to buy Teleco Oilfield Services Inc. from Sonat Inc. Teleco was a pioneer in services for both directional and horizontal drilling. Later that year, Teleco and four other Baker Hughes companies specializing in drilling systems, Milpark Drilling Fluids, Baker Sand Control, Develco, and EXLOG, were combined into a new Baker Hughes INTEQ division, which enabled the company to offer comprehensive solutions for all phases of drilling projects.

Divestments continued in 1994 with the sales of EnviroTech Pumpsystems to the Weir Group of Scotland for $210 million and of EnviroTech Measurements & Controls to Thermo Electron Corporation for $134 million. In October 1995 Max L. Lukens, who had been with the company since 1981, was named president and COO, with Woods remaining chairman and CEO.

After enjoying its best post-merger year to date in fiscal 1996 (with $3.03 billion in revenues and profits of $176.4 million), Baker Hughes was busy in 1997 making acquisitions, three of which closed in July. Drilex International Inc., a provider of directional drilling services, was acquired for $108.8 million and was subsequently folded into Baker Hughes INTEQ. The company paid $751.2 million for Petrolite Corporation, thus augmenting its specialty chemical division, which was soon renamed Baker Petrolite and which became the leading provider to the oilfield chemical market. In the third July purchase, the Environmental Technology Division of German machinery maker Deutz AG was bought for $53 million. The division specialized in centrifuges and dryers and added to the existing centrifuge and filter product lines of the Baker Hughes Process Equipment Company.

Then in October a $31.5 million deal to purchase Oil Dynamics, Inc., from Franklin Electric Co., Inc., was completed. Oil Dynamics was a manufacturer of electric submersible pumps used to lift crude oil, and it was added to the company's Centrilift division. The year 1997 was also noteworthy for the retirement of Woods, who had not only made the Baker Hughes merger happen but had also focused and bolstered the company's product and service lines through more than 30 separate divestments and acquisitions. Woods was succeeded by Lukens.

THE 1998 WESTERN ATLAS MERGER

Consolidation in the oil-services industry continued in 1998, with the largest deal being the acquisition of Dresser Industries by Halliburton Company. Baker Hughes kept pace with its industry rivals, and maintained its number three position among oil-service firms (behind Halliburton and Schlumberger), by acquiring Western Atlas Inc. in August 1998 for $3.3 billion in stock and the assumption of $1.3 billion in debt. Western Atlas, which had been spun off from Litton Industries Inc. in 1994, was the industry's leading geoscience firm, specializing in seismic exploration, reservoir description, and field development services, as well as downhole data services. The acquired operations were placed within two new Baker Hughes divisions: Western Geophysical for the seismic services and Baker Atlas for the downhole services. Baker Hughes could now offer a full range of oilfield services, or "life-of-the-field" packages, from seismic surveys to drilling to production management. Following the merger, Lukens remained in charge of Baker Hughes as chairman and CEO.

As it was completing the Western Atlas merger, Baker Hughes began to feel the effects of another severe industry downturn. Demand for oilfield services declined sharply during the second half of 1998 as a result of the combined effects of the Asian economic crisis, tropical storms, and slumping oil prices. The company went into cost-cutting mode, slashing about 10,000 jobs from the payroll by the end of 1999 (about one-fourth of the total workforce), consolidating manufacturing facilities and field offices, and achieving nearly $1 billion in cost savings.

Charges for merger-related costs and restructuring expenses totaled more than $800 million for 1998, resulting in a net loss for the year of nearly $300 million. Baker Hughes also sold off some real estate to raise money to reduce its enlarged debt load, upgraded its information technology systems to improve the tracking of inventory and equipment, and created a new financial performance system in which a manager's performance would be tied to profits in the person's area.

Despite the new initiatives and restructuring efforts, as well as higher oil prices in the later months of the year, Baker Hughes's financial performance continued to suffer during 1999. In November the company warned that its fourth-quarter earnings would trail analysts' estimates. One month later the company announced that it had uncovered accounting irregularities at its IN-TEQ division amounting to $31 million.

The firm was subsequently forced to restate its earnings for the previous three years. In the wake of this debacle, INTEQ's president was replaced, and in February 2000 Lukens resigned under pressure. Joe B. Foster, a Baker Hughes outside director and head of Newfield Exploration Company, was named interim chairman and CEO. Wall Street was growing increasingly skeptical about the prospects for a turnaround, with Warburg Dillon Read analyst Byron Dunn telling the *Wall Street Journal* that the accounting snafu was "a symptom of a broader dysfunctional corporate culture."

DIVESTING NONCORE OPERATIONS

To further reduce the still burdensome debt load, Baker Hughes announced in February 2000 that it would sell its process systems unit, which had little relation to the core oil-services operations. Unable to sell it as a whole, the company divided the unit into three entities in 2001: BIRD Machine, EIMCO Process Equipment, and a newly formed joint venture, Petreco International, which was 49 percent owned by Baker Hughes. EIMCO was subsequently sold to Groupe Laperriere & Verreault, Inc., for about $50 million in November 2002. In the early months of 2004, Baker Hughes sold both BIRD

Machine and its interest in Petreco.

In the meantime, Baker Hughes and Schlumberger reached an agreement in June 2000 to combine their seismic units, Western Geophysical and Geco-Prakla, respectively, into a new joint venture firm called WesternGeco. Schlumberger paid Baker Hughes about $500 million to take a 70 percent stake in the venture, while Baker Hughes took the remaining 30 percent. Upon completion of the deal in November 2000, Baker Hughes used the proceeds to further reduce its debt.

In August 2000 Michael E. Wiley was hired to be the new chairman, president, and CEO of Baker Hughes. Wiley had been the president and COO of Atlantic Richfield Company from 1997 until May 2000, when that firm was acquired by BP Amoco. Baker Hughes continued to trim its operations under the new leader, announcing in October 2000 its intention to exit from the oil and gas exploration and production business. By early 2003 this exit had been completed through the sale of a 40 percent stake in a Nigerian oilfield.

ALLEGATIONS OF QUESTIONABLE BUSINESS PRACTICES

Although the company's financial performance improved in 2001 and 2002, concerns about the corporate culture at Baker Hughes once more came into the foreground. The Securities and Exchange Commission (SEC) charged that two high-ranking company officers, the CFO and the controller, authorized the payment of a $75,000 bribe to an Indonesian government official in March 1999. (The two officers both resigned later in 1999.) The bribe was allegedly made to induce the official to reduce the company's tax liability from $3.2 million to $270,000. Such an act constituted a violation of the Foreign Corrupt Practices Act (FCPA). The SEC further alleged that similar payoffs had been made in India and Brazil.

In September 2001 Baker Hughes reached a settlement with the SEC regarding these charges, without the firm admitting or denying the charges and without a fine being levied. Then in March 2002 a former Baker Hughes employee filed a civil lawsuit claiming that he had been fired in October 2001 for refusing to pay a bribe to a Nigerian oil official in order to secure a large drilling contract. In October 2003 the company settled this lawsuit out of court, with the terms not disclosed. Finally, in April 2007, federal investigations into the firm's alleged violations of the FCPA were concluded when Baker Hughes agreed to pay a record $44 million to settle charges of bribing oil-industry officials in Kazakhstan.

Having jettisoned the remainder of its process systems operations early in 2004, Baker Hughes in September of that year divested the last of its non-oilfield operations, Baker Hughes Mining Tools, which was sold to Atlas Copco AB for $31.5 million. In October 2004 Chad Deaton was brought onboard as Baker Hughes's new chairman and CEO, succeeding Wiley, who retired. Deaton had most recently served as CEO of Hanover Compressor Company, although he had spent most of his career at Schlumberger Oilfield Services, where he rose to executive vice president.

BOOM TIMES IN THE EARLY 21ST CENTURY

Deaton took over at an auspicious time as sharply rising energy prices prompted oil companies to boost production, which in turn ratcheted up demand for oilfield services. In 2005, for example, Baker Hughes enjoyed record revenues and net income of $7.19 billion and $878.4 million, respectively. Late in the year, Baker Hughes acquired Zeroth Technology Limited, a Scottish firm specializing in expandable metal-to-metal sealing technology for well intervention applications. Early the following year, Baker Hughes spent $55.4 million for Nova Technology Corporation, a firm based in Broussard, Louisiana, that supplied monitoring, chemical injection systems, and multiline services for offshore oil and gas well operations.

In addition to its pursuit of acquisitions, Baker Hughes remained active on the product development front. In 2006 new products accounted for 21 percent of the company's record revenues of $9.03 billion. Among the innovations that year was TruTrak, an automated drilling device for land-based directional drilling that included as one of its features a measurement-while-drilling system. Also in 2006 the company elected to cash out of its minority stake in WesternGeco, selling its 30 percent interest to majority owner Schlumberger for $2.4 billion in cash. The bulk of the net proceeds went toward Baker Hughes's stock buyback program.

The boom times for the oil and gas industry continued until mid-2008, when crude oil prices peaked at $145 per barrel. During the second half of the year, the financial crisis and a slowing global economy precipitated a sharp drop in oil prices (down to below $40 a barrel by late 2008) and the most dramatic downturn in upstream activity since the mid-1980s. Nevertheless, momentum from the first half of the year enabled Baker Hughes to report its sixth straight year of record revenues, a 14 percent increase to $11.86 billion. Net income increased as well, amounting to $1.64 billion.

ACQUIRING BJ SERVICES IN 2010

By early 2009, the deep recession forced Baker Hughes to retrench, and it announced plans to cut its 40,000-strong workforce by 3,000. In September of that year, the company took advantage of the downturn by reaching an agreement to acquire BJ Services Company. This deal, which was valued at $6.8 billion in stock and cash on its completion in April 2010, amounted to a reunion as this was the same BJ Services that Baker Hughes had spun off in 1991. Acquiring BJ Services filled a key hole in Baker Hughes's product line, adding pressure-pumping equipment and services commonly used in natural gas fields in North America and in increasingly high demand overseas. A more complete line of products and services was expected to aid the company in securing large contracts in international markets. The two companies' combined 2009 revenues of $13.6 billion situated Baker Hughes as the third-largest oilfield services company, well behind Schlumberger but just behind Halliburton and just ahead of National Oilwell Varco, Inc.

Adam Lashinsky
Updated, David E. Salamie

PRINCIPAL SUBSIDIARIES

Baker Hughes Financing Company; BJ Services Company; Western Atlas Inc.; Baker Hughes Limited (UK); Baker Hughes Canada Company; Baker Hughes Norge A/S (Norway).

PRINCIPAL DIVISIONS

Baker Atlas; Baker Hughes Drilling Fluids; Baker Oil Tools; Baker Petrolite; Centrilift; Hughes Christensen; INTEQ.

PRINCIPAL COMPETITORS

Champion Technologies, Inc.; Halliburton Company; Nalco Holding Company; National Oilwell Varco, Inc.; Newpark Resources, Inc.; Schlumberger Limited; Smith International, Inc.; Weatherford International Ltd.

FURTHER READING

Antosh, Nelson, "CEO Hunt Ends with Local Pick," *Houston Chronicle*, October 5, 2004.

"Baker Hughes: 100 Years of Service," spec. issue, *InDepth*, July 2007, Houston: Baker Hughes Inc., 91 p.

"Baker Hughes, Western Atlas Agree to Merge," *Oil and Gas Journal*, May 18, 1998, p. 30.

The Baker Story, Houston: Baker International Inc., 1979.

Casselman, Ben, and Angel Gonzalez, "Baker Hughes to Create Oilfield Giant: Deal for BJ Services, Valued at $5.5 Billion, Would Create Challenger to Industry Rivals," *Wall Street Journal*, September 1, 2009, p. B1.

Gold, Russell, "Baker Hughes Drills Deep for High-Stress Bits," *Wall Street Journal*, December 8, 2009, p. B8.

"Hughes Tool: Once Unleashed, It Grows into a Very Profitable Giant," *Business Week*, October 13, 1980, pp. 106+.

Ivey, Mark, "Baker Hughes: It Pays to Be a Big Spender," *Business Week*, March 12, 1990, p. 81.

Miller, William H., "A Merger That's Worked: Jim Woods Is Piloting Baker Hughes Inc. to Profit," *Industry Week*, April 15, 1991, pp. 21–23.

Norman, James R., "Cloud over Baker," *Forbes*, May 11, 1992, p. 220.

———, "Hot Potato?" *Forbes*, July 9, 1990, pp. 38–39.

Patel, Purva, and Tom Fowler, "Baker Hughes Ends Bribe Case," *Houston Chronicle*, April 27, 2007.

Tejada, Carlos, "Baker Hughes Names Foster Interim CEO," *Wall Street Journal*, February 1, 2000, p. A3.

———, "Oil-Services Firm Tries to Find Footing, Calm Holders," *Wall Street Journal*, October 14, 1999, p. B4.

Ballet Theatre
Foundation, Inc.

890 Broadway
New York, New York 10003
U.S.A.
Telephone: (212) 477-3030
Fax: (212) 254-5938
Web site: http://www.abt.org

Nonprofit Organization
Incorporated: 1940 as Ballet Theatre
Employees: 209
Operating Revenues: $20 million (2010 est.)
NAICS: 711120 Dance Companies

■ ■ ■

Ballet Theatre Foundation, Inc., better known as American Ballet Theatre (ABT), headquartered in New York City, is widely regarded as one of the preeminent ballet companies in the world. Known for showcasing dancers with flawless technique, ABT also prides itself on presenting a balanced repertoire of both classical ballets and contemporary dances. ABT also trains its own students at its Jacqueline Kennedy Onassis School, runs a prestigious summer intensive for students from around the world, and culls talented young artists for its apprentice company, ABT II.

FORMATION

In 1939, Lucia Chase, a wealthy dancer with the Mordkin Ballet, and Richard Pleasant, general manager of Mordkin, collaborated to create Ballet Theatre. Miss

Chase, as she was henceforth known, aimed at creating a company that "would be a showcase for the best ballets of the classical tradition and a forum for emerging modern American choreography," according to John Fraser's book *Private View*. The company, which performed for the first time on January 11, 1940, was already large, consisting of 85 dancers, 11 choreographers, and a repertoire of 21 ballets, 6 of which were world premieres.

Ballet Theatre quickly developed a reputation for superstar dancers and an "eclectic" repertoire, as Fraser noted, in spite of its numerous financial constraints. In 1945, Oliver Smith replaced Richard Pleasant as co-director with Chase. In 1957, the name was changed to American Ballet Theatre in order to reflect the precise identity which the company sought to convey: a company that was quintessentially *American*. Chase, who headed the company until 1980, had made her dream into a reality.

In 1980 Mikhail Baryshnikov became artistic director while also continuing to perform with the company. Baryshnikov had defected from the Soviet Union in 1974 while on tour in Canada with the Kirov Ballet, a Soviet ballet troupe. Upon his arrival at ABT, he immediately became a star and an enormous asset for the company. When a knee injury in 1982 forced his retirement, he took up the post of the company's artistic director full time. During his time as artistic director, Baryshnikov stressed a "strong, cohesive, and unified dancing ensemble" that featured "trimmed-down, cool versions of the [ballet] classics," according to Fraser.

COMPANY PERSPECTIVES

■

American Ballet Theatre is a collaborative effort of dedicated, passionate people who are committed to ensuring that the best in dance and movement is upheld and available to all who seek it.

Jane Hermann and Oliver Smith succeeded Baryshnikov as artistic directors in 1990, and worked to further solidify ABT's reputation for mastery of both classic and contemporary dance. However, money troubles were far from over for the company. According to an article in *Crain's New York Business*, ABT "was the poster child of how not to run an arts organization," and often "scrambled to make payroll." Funds for the company were given by the board of directors, which led to a flurry of negative press.

It was not until Kevin McKenzie, a former principal dancer with the company, was named artistic director in 1992 that fiscal concerns began to take a turn for the better. By 2006, the company was debt free, and received the prestigious $5 million challenge grant from the Andrew W. Mellon Foundation, the largest grant ever given to an arts organization. Corporate and individual sponsors also increased, securing a firm fiscal future for the company.

A VISION MANIFESTED

According to a June 1997 *Dance Magazine* article, Ballet Theatre founder Richard Pleasant once remarked that Ballet Theatre was to be "a museum of dance." The original vision for the company's performances was a highly arranged program of dance: a Russian wing, an American wing, and a British wing, which would allow the company to bring both classicism and modernism into its repertoire. Although this arrangement evaporated after World War II, the wide variety in choreography that grew carried Ballet Theatre for decades to come.

Such artistic freedom inspired many of the great 20th-century choreographers to work for the company, creating works of enduring appeal. In 1944, Jerome Robbins created *Fancy Free*, a tale of three U.S. sailors on leave. The ballet, which was considered to be quintessentially American, combined the music of Leonard Bernstein with a new mixture of classical and modern movement. The ballet was eventually adapted for the screen, and starred Gene Kelly.

In 1947 artistic director Lucia Chase commissioned a piece from George Balanchine, which culminated in *Theme and Variations*. This ballet, which sought to evoke the majesty of prerevolutionary Russia, was to become a trademark piece of ABT. The company's early years also brought such masterpieces as Agnes de Mille's *Fall River Legend*, and Anthony Tudor's *Jardin aux Lilies* (created in 1936; performed by Ballet Theatre in 1940).

The company became increasingly creative and experimental throughout the 1960s and 1970s, culminating in Twyla Tharp's *Push Comes to Shove* (1976). Tharp's ballet combined classical and vernacular music and dance, and used dancers from the ranks of the corps de ballet as well as the principals. Its first production starred ABT gem Baryshnikov. Famous choreographers who worked with the company also included Eliot Feld, Alvin Ailey, and Clark Tippet.

A number of ballet stars also reached their peaks while performing with ABT. These dancers included Alicia Alonso, Gelsey Kirkland, Cynthia Harvey, Julie Kent, Baryshnikov, Kevin McKenzie, and Ethan Stiefel.

TRAINING FOR THE FUTURE

In 2004, the school was renamed the Jacqueline Kennedy Onassis (JKO) School of American Ballet Theatre, in honor of one of its more famous members of the board of trustees (Onassis served on the ABT board for 25 years; her daughter Caroline Kennedy Schlossberg also served as an honorary chairman). The school began training dancers at a preprofessional level from the ages of 12 through 18. In 2009 they also began admitting dancers as young as nine. Also in 2009, the children's dance program was renamed the Children's Division of the JKO School. The program was designed for students ages 5 through 12. Franco de Vita acted as president of both divisions.

Both schools trained students in the elements of classical ballet and were dedicated to producing ballet dancers of the highest caliber. As students matured, they were exposed also to work in character, pas de deux (partnering), modern, and pointe. The preprofessional division was a competitive division, open to students by audition only. As de Vita noted on the company Web site, this division of the JKO School "strives to produce dancers who have no technical limitations … dancers who are strong, supple, and without affectation." Dancers in this division went on to join ABT's apprentice program (ABT II) as well as other ballet companies around the world.

Summer gave ABT another chance to display its prowess for developing extraordinary dancers. Each year, ABT hosted a ballet summer intensive for dancers from

KEY DATES

1939: Ballet Theatre begins as a collaboration between Lucia Chase and Richard Pleasant.
1957: Name is changed to American Ballet Theatre.
1980: Mikhail Baryshnikov assumes post of artistic director.
1990: Jane Hermann and Oliver Smith succeed Baryshnikov as joint artistic directors.
1992: Kevin McKenzie is named artistic director.
1996: ABT II, the company's apprentice program, is formed.

around the nation. Dancers, ages 12 to 17, selected via audition only, received a minimum of four classes each day, as well as exposure to ABT, its company, and history. A small number of scholarships were awarded for this highly prestigious summer intensive. ABT also hosted summer intensives for college-level students and young dancers (9 to 11 years of age).

Furthermore, ABT's dedication to dance education did not stop at simply schooling young students. In 2007, ABT introduced the National Training Curriculum. Devised by de Vita and Raymond Luekens, in collaboration with the medical board of ABT, the National Training Curriculum was a focused program of ballet technique merged with child development and dancer health. In 2009, the program expanded beyond New York as ABT invited dance educators from across the nation to participate in teacher training intensives. Dance educators who participated in the program become registered ABT teachers. ABT, partnering with New York University, also offered a master's degree in ballet pedagogy.

In 1996, American Ballet Theatre established ABT II. The program was devoted to serving as "a bridge between ballet training and professional performance," according to the company's Web site. Thus, the handpicked group of dancers train for one to two years before proceeding to join ABT or other leading dance companies. The dancers are given opportunities to work with burgeoning young choreographers as well as participate in large-scale ABT productions such as *Romeo and Juliet* and *Swan Lake*. On a smaller scale, ABT II placed a special emphasis on community outreach, as ABT II often performed demonstrations for schoolchildren across the nation. The program was sponsored by Moët-Hennessy Louis Vuitton.

OUTREACH AND INTERNATIONAL EXPOSURE

The company was dedicated to making available the best of dance. Therefore, it did not confine its purview to New York theaters or its own dance classrooms. Instead, it reached out to expose public and private schoolchildren to ballet. Through programs such as The Young People's Ballet Workshop and the Peter Jay Sharp Introduction for Dance, schoolchildren in both public and private schools were given performances, lectures, and demonstrations of ballet that they might otherwise never encounter. Make a Ballet was another successful venture of ABT outreach. This program encouraged and enabled students to construct, choreograph, produce, and perform an original piece of their own design. The program, which began at The Frederick Douglass Academy in central Harlem in 1997, grew to accommodate several different schools in New York City, as well as in Washington, D.C.; Connecticut; New Jersey; and Los Angeles and Orange County, California.

Since its inception, ABT had traveled to over 126 cities in 42 different countries, as well as all 50 U.S. states. Its overseas ventures began in 1946 with an eight-week trip to Covent Garden in England. In 1960, it became the first U.S. dance company to travel to the Soviet Union, and in 2000, traveled to China for the first time.

CONSTRUCTIVE CRITICISM FOR THE FUTURE

One criticism of ABT appeared unique to the company alone. In an article by Jennifer Homans, published in the *New Republic*, ABT was deemed to be at the forefront of the "ballet crisis" in New York. Homans, writing about the 2002 ABT season, noted that audiences were "wowed, but rarely moved; impressed, but almost never inspired." Homans blamed this "colorless monotony" on the "spiritual impoverishment" suffered by dancers who were absorbed in perfecting their technique, rather than mastering their art: "They can do anything," Homans wrote, "but what do they believe in?" Despite this complaint, American Ballet Theatre remained a driving force in the popularization of ballet, and continued to earn recognition worldwide for its devotion to artistry and excellence.

Laura Rydberg

PRINCIPAL DIVISIONS

Principals; Soloists; Corps de Ballet; Artistic Staff; Company Management; Production; Development;

Marketing and Communications; Education and Training.

FURTHER READING

Fraser, John, *Private View: Inside Baryshnikov's American Ballet Theatre*, Toronto: Bantam Books, 1988.

Homans, Jennifer, "Steps, Steps, Steps," *New Republic*, February 18, 2002, pp. 26–32.

Hunt, Marilyn, "American Ballet Theatre: A Living Museum of Dance," *Dance Magazine*, June 1997.

Souccar, Miriam Krennin, "ABT Takes a Big Leap," *Crain's New York Business*, April 10, 2006.

Bass Pro Shops, Inc.

2500 East Kearney
Springfield, Missouri 65898
U.S.A.
Telephone: (417) 873-5000
Toll Free: (800) 227-7776
Fax: (417) 873-4672
Web site: http://www.basspro.com

Private Company
Incorporated: 1971
Employees: 16,000
Sales: $3.4 billion (2009)
NAICS: 451110 Sporting Goods Stores; 454110 Mail-
Order Houses; 336612 Boat Building; 454113
Mail-Order Houses; 721110 Hotels (Except Casino
Hotels) and Motels

■ ■ ■

Bass Pro Shops, Inc., is a sporting goods retailer with a
special emphasis on fishing, hunting, and camping. The
company operates more than 50 stores in roughly 25
states and in two Canadian provinces. The stores average
100,000 square feet, with the largest unit, the
company's flagship Springfield, Missouri, store, measuring 300,000 square feet. Bass Pro Shop stores feature
gun and archery ranges, massive freshwater fish tanks,
restaurants, and amusement attractions. Bass Pro Shops
also sells its merchandise through a mail-order business
and on the Internet. The company operates a wholesale
business through American Rod & Gun and it
manufactures boats through Tracker Marine. Bass Pro

Shops also owns Big Cedar Lodge in Ridgedale, Missouri, which features more than 200 rooms, restaurants,
a nine-hole golf course, and numerous amenities.

FORMATION OF BASS PRO
SHOPS: 1971

The founder of Bass Pro Shops, John L. Morris, grew
up in Springfield, and as a boy fished with his father
and uncles in the Ozark area lakes, which featured some
of the best bass fishing in the world. While earning a
business degree from local Drury College he competed
in one of the early tournaments of the fledgling pro bass
fishing tour. He learned that the specialized lures used
by the top pros, as well as high-tech tackle, were not
available in stores. He asked a local retailer, Gibsons
Discount Store, which boasted the area's largest fishing
department, to stock some of these items, but the
manager refused.

In addition to a love for fishing, Morris also gained
an entrepreneurial spirit from his father. The elder Morris had started out running a service station and
restaurant in Springfield, and later operated a number of
Brown Derby Liquor stores and some dry cleaning
shops. Rebuffed by Gibsons, Morris turned to his father
and asked if he could have space in one of the Brown
Derby liquor stores in order to sell fishing merchandise.
Despite the fact that his father had already tried selling
bait out of the stores, and still had boxes of lures stored
in the basement to remind him of the failed attempt,
Morris finally received permission. His father also co-
signed a $10,000 inventory loan.

COMPANY PERSPECTIVES

Bass Pro Shops has become one of America's premier outdoor retailers with destination outdoor retail stores across America and Canada, serving over 75 million sportsmen a year. Each store is unique and offers a truly unforgettable shopping experience—as close to the Great Outdoors as you can get indoors!

After graduating from college in 1971 Morris took to the road with a trailer, buying up regional fishing lures until he ran out of cash. With eight feet of shelf space in one of his father's Brown Derby liquor stores, he then began to sell his lures to local fishermen. Because his focus was providing gear for bass fishermen, he named his business Bass Pro Shops. Morris knew his market because he was an avid bass fisherman himself and had talked to his customers about what they wanted. He also traveled the tournament fishing circuit to keep tabs on the kinds of lures the winners were using.

Although selling beer and spirits remained the primary business of the liquor store, Morris continued to add to his supply of baits and lures. Business expanded by word of mouth, and soon customers were calling to buy over the telephone, asking if he could send his products to them by United Parcel Service. This development prompted Morris to enter the mail-order business. He bought mailing lists of potential customers and then compiled a catalog that featured some 1,500 items in 180 pages. In 1974 he mailed his catalog to 10,000 names in 20 states. Using the basement of his father's warehouse as a distribution center, Morris's mail-order business took off. The catalog grew in size and increased in distribution, soon gaining a reputation as the bass fisherman's Bible. It would one day exceed 400 pages in length and be mailed to some four million people throughout the world. In later years a hunting catalog, RedHead Hunting, would be added. More than 500 customer service representatives would eventually be hired to accept orders 24 hours a day, 365 days a year.

MORRIS EXPANDS AND DIVERSIFIES: 1975–88

Morris was fortunate that bass fishing was surging in popularity, but he was also smart enough to let his business evolve naturally. Because he had a catalog business, he could arrange to have a large number of products manufactured as exclusives. To meet the demand for these products, in 1975 Morris set up the American Rod & Gun wholesale operation to distribute Bass Pro brand merchandise to independent sporting goods stores. Against all advice, Morris also began to sell boats through his catalog, which led to his entry into the boat building business. He found a niche in boats because, again, he knew what his customer wanted. From personal experience he understood how difficult it was to buy a complete fishing rig. After buying the boat the customer had to then pick out an appropriate motor and trailer. Anything beyond that, like a trolling motor or electronic fish finder, had to be purchased separately. Morris had a simple but elegant insight: sell an entire boat package that included the boat, motor, and trailer, as well as extras such as trolling motor, fish finders, built-in coolers, and padded seats. Overall the package offered the kind of value the customers were looking for. The marketing concept was simple but effective: "Just add water."

Morris named his new business Tracker Marine. The first aluminum boats he offered in 1978 were made by a Louisiana company. Meanwhile, his Trailstar Trailers were constructed in Springfield until a trailer plant opened in Nixa, Missouri, in 1980. As business picked up he opened his own boat manufacturing plant in Lebanon, Missouri, in 1982. Tracker rapidly added to its product mix. The first pontoon boat package was introduced in 1983, the first fiberglass boat package in 1985. Tracker expanded beyond fresh water vessels in 1987 when it acquired the SeaCraft saltwater boat line. In 1988 it acquired the Nitro performance bass boat line, then two years later offered Nitro boat packages on a nationwide basis. In the 1990s Tracker would also become involved in the houseboat business, acquiring Myacht Houseboats. Although precise sales figures were not available from the privately held company, in the early 1990s analysts ranked Tracker among the top 10 boat builders in the United States.

GENESIS OF OUTDOOR WORLD: 1981

Morris involved two of his sisters in the Bass Pro Shops business. Carol did advertising work for the company through an agency she headed, while Susie became an executive vice president. Susie, in fact, was with Morris when he received a major dose of the inspiration that would lead to the creation of Outdoor World. Although the catalog business was thriving in the late 1970s, Morris still felt the need for a showroom where customers could actually handle the merchandise. He and several employees began to scout retail operations in preparation of building a Bass Pro Shops store. He and Susie

KEY DATES

1971: John L. Morris establishes Bass Pro Shops; first catalog is mailed three years later.
1975: American Rod & Gun wholesale operation is launched.
1981: Outdoor World opens.
1988: Big Cedar Lodge Resort, located near Branson, Missouri, opens.
1995: First Bass Pro store outside of Missouri opens.
2005: A 280,000-square-foot store in Clarksville, Indiana, is the company's largest store in more than 20 years.
2007: Bass Pro Shops opens its first store in California.
2010: Bass Pro Shop chain exceeds 50 units.

were especially impressed by their visit to the hugely popular L.L. Bean store in Freeport, Maine. "I said, heck, if they can draw all those people to the middle of nowhere," Morris told the press, "we can do that in Springfield."

Adjacent to the Bass Pro Shops catalog operations in Springfield, Outdoor World opened in 1981. Although the focus of the superstore in the beginning was its breadth of selection and ability to service a range of needs, Outdoor World began to offer more and more entertainment features (as it also continued to expand in size), eventually taking up nearly 300,000 square feet. Again, it was a matter of paying attention to what the customers wanted. Morris used an old storage tank to create a fishing pond that could also be used for fish-feeding shows, something he first witnessed at Chicago's Shedd Aquarium. He added a pistol and rifle range, which he knew were features in German and Swedish sporting goods stores. Outdoor World became an extension of Morris's desire for his customers to have fun, as well as to sell them the equipment they wanted. In addition to fishing gear, Outdoor World offered hunting equipment, camping supplies, boats, and golf and general sporting equipment. It also featured service departments, book and gift stores, a cutlery shop, and a wildlife art gallery.

Outdoor World essentially grew into a sportsman's version of Disneyland, featuring a four-story high waterfall, a two-story indoor cabin, a 100-yard-long indoor rifle range, 25-yard ranges for handguns and archery, a taxidermy shop, countless stuffed animals and mounted fish adorning the interior, a trout stream that

meandered through the store, a barber shop, and a 250-seat auditorium and conference room. Promoted in the Bass Pro Shops catalog, Outdoor World began to attract visitors from around the world, eclipsing even St. Louis's better-known Gateway Arch as a tourist destination.

OPENING OF BIG CEDAR LODGE RESORT: 1988

The megastore concept was clearly a winner, but it would also be an expensive gamble to open other units, so Morris was cautious about expansion. First, he became involved in the resort business. In 1988 Bass Pro Shops opened Big Cedar Lodge Resort located by Table Rock Lake in the Ozark Mountains. The property had originally been the vacation retreat in the early 1920s of two wealthy Missouri businessmen who were both friends and sportsmen: Jude Simmons, who made his money in real estate and manufacturing, and Harry Worman, onetime president of Frisco Railroad. On 300 acres of land they both built log mansions that would now be put to other uses.

Simmons's home became the Devil's Pool restaurant, while Worman's home became the resort's registration building and gift shop. Simmons's garage was large enough to be converted into the Truman Smokehouse, a casual eatery. Big Cedar Lodge would encompass almost three times as much property as the original site and feature three lodges, as well as 81 private cabins. In addition to fishing, the resort offered water skiing, hiking, trail rides, cave explorations, and miniature golf. Big Cedar was expensive, with some cabins approaching $1,000 a night during the peak summer season, and attracted many celebrity guests, especially the country music stars who performed at nearby Branson.

To spread some of the risk in growing Bass Pro Shops, Morris began to form strategic partnerships, raising cash while keeping the company private. In 1992 Brunswick Corporation paid $25 million for a minority interest in Tracker Marine and thereby became the exclusive provider of engines, trolling motors, and other equipment for Tracker boats. In 1993 Morris sold a minority stake in Bass Pro Shops to Gaylord Entertainment Company for $60 million. A country music giant, Gaylord owned Country Music Television and The Nashville Network (TNN, which was later renamed The National Network to broaden its appeal). Through Gaylord, the company would be able to produce a syndicated radio show called *Bass Pro Shops Outdoor World*, which was not only heard in the United States, but throughout the world over more than 400 radio stations on the Armed Forces Radio Network. With Gaylord, Bass Pro Shops was able to produce hunting and fishing television shows. Morris also aligned his company with Mills Corporation, a Virginia mall developer, in anticipation of spreading the Outdoor World concept. In a similar vein, he also began to work with a Springfield-based hotel operator, John Q. Hammons, to combine Outdoor World outlets with Embassy Suite hotels.

RETAIL PRESENCE BROADENS: 1995–99

The first retail venture outside of Springfield came in 1995 when Bass Pro Shops opened the 90,000-square-foot Sportsman's Warehouse in Duluth, Georgia. Morris also purchased an adjacent property with plans to open an Outdoor World should the initial property prove to be successful. That same year Bass Pro Shops purchased the 27,000-square-foot World Wide Sportsman store in Islamorada in the Florida Keys. The second true Outdoor World megastore, a 125,000-square-foot mall anchor, opened in the fall of 1997 outside of Chicago in Gurnee, Illinois. It was followed by a 160,000-square-foot Outdoor World located near Fort Lauderdale, Florida. In 1999 an Outdoor World opened in the Dallas/Fort Worth area, located across from a Mills mall and connected to an Embassy Suites hotel. At 200,000 square feet, the Texas store was still significantly smaller than the Springfield Outdoor World, yet it stocked almost the same number of items. Also in 1999 a Detroit-area Outdoor World opened, again serving as a mall anchor.

Late in 1999 Bass Pro Shops decided to sell the land across from its Duluth, Georgia, Sportsman's Warehouse, electing to build a new and larger Outdoor World as part of a Mills mall under development in the area. From Mills's point of view, a Bass Pro Shop was a desired part of every new mall project. Although rollout of the concept was gathering momentum, Morris remained careful about not extending Bass Pro Shop too far, too quickly. Essentially he was expanding to prime fishing areas. In 2001 Bass Pro Shops opened an Outdoor World in Nashville, Tennessee, in conjunction with both of its partners, Mills and Gaylord. It also expanded to Charlotte, North Carolina; Cincinnati, Ohio; and the Maryland/Washington, D.C., area. In addition, a second Missouri store was added, located in the Mark Twain Center in St. Charles, Missouri.

With 15 showrooms, Bass Pro Shops was still looking to pursue judicious expansion. Many of the locations had become local tourist attractions, although not to the extent of the Springfield original, which remained by far the company's largest showroom. Morris seemed intent on maintaining the allure of the original site. He

bolstered its appeal by opening a nearby Wildlife Museum in 1993. The museum was also a reflection of his personal commitment to the conservation of the outdoors. He created Dogwood Canyon, a 10,000-acre wilderness area located near Big Cedar Lodge. Bass Pro Shops also contributed millions of dollars to a number of nonprofit wildlife conservation organizations, earning Morris a number of honors. At the same time, Bass Pro Shops continued to grow its varied business interests. In 1998 Tracker Marine introduce a full line of RVs, travel trailers, slide-in pickup truck campers, and minimotorhomes. In 2000 it signed an agreement with Bluegreen Corp., which planned to build a timeshare resort adjacent to Big Cedar Lodge, with some 300 vacation homes. Bass Pro Shops also looked to become a major Internet retailer, leveraging its brand to sell merchandise online.

RETAIL NETWORK EXPANDS: 2001–10

In the first decade of the 21st century, Bass Pro Shops fully developed its presence on the Internet, but its most notable advances occurred along more traditional lines. The company began opening new stores at a pace unprecedented in its history, emboldened by the continued success of its flagship Springfield store. The store attracted more than four million visitors annually, ranking as the most popular tourist destination in Missouri. The company's other retail locations demonstrated enviable strength as well, distinguishing Bass Pro Shops as a rare breed of retailer. The average Bass Pro Shop customer drove two hours to reach a store and spent more than three hours shopping. Other retailers typically averaged 15-minute drives and 30-minute visits. Morris and his management team, aware of their brick-and-mortar might, took advantage of the opportunity before them and began opening new stores in earnest.

During the first half of the decade, the company opened stores in a variety of sizes. A 78,000-square-foot store in St. Louis in 2001, the company's 13th store, became its second Sportsman's Warehouse store. During the next three years, Bass Pro Shops opened eight more stores, extending its geographic reach from Texas to Maryland. Annual sales eclipsed $1 billion, as the company shouldered past competitors to become the fifth-largest sporting goods retailer in the country.

Bass Pro Shops' pace of expansion became decidedly quicker beginning in 2005. The year marked the first time it opened a store that came close to rivaling the stature of its Springfield complex. Located in Clarksville, Indiana, the River Falls Mall store measured 280,000 square feet, featuring the same comprehensive displays, exhibits, and merchandise showcased at the Springfield store.

The opening of the Clarksville store coincided with a concerted effort to expand the Bass Pro Shop chain. There were 25 stores operating by 2005, pushing annual sales beyond $1.6 billion. During the next five years, the size of the chain more than doubled, as Morris and his executives extended the company's reach from coast to coast, opening the first store in California in 2007. By the end of the decade, there were more than 50 stores operating in two dozen states, as well as Canadian stores in Alberta and Ontario. Bass Pro Shops stood as a retail phenomenon as it neared its 40th anniversary, exuding a level of strength that distinguished it from nearly all rivals and made it one of the premier sporting goods retailers in the world.

Ed Dinger
Updated, Jeffrey L. Covell

PRINCIPAL SUBSIDIARIES

BPS Direct, LLC; Tracker Marine Group; American Rod & Gun; Big Cedar Lodge.

PRINCIPAL COMPETITORS

Academy, Ltd.; Cabela's Inc.; L.L. Bean, Inc.; Marine-Max, Inc.

FURTHER READING

Backover, Andrew, "Bass Pro Shops Ready to Open Huge Outdoor World Store in Grapevine, Texas," *Fort Worth Star-Telegram*, March 23, 1999.

Bridges, Toby, "Bass Pro: A Transcendental Marketer," *Direct Marketing*, October 1992, p. 20.

Childress, William, "Bass Pro Shops Reeling in the Customers," *St. Louis Post-Dispatch*, February 20, 1993, p. 3D.

Fass, Allison, "A Joint Venture Hopes to Tie the Product to the Entertainment and Create a Shopping Experience," *New York Times*, June 1, 2001, p. C7.

Kempner, Matt, "Sporting Goods Entrepreneur Turned Hobby into a Business," *Atlanta Constitution*, September 25, 1994, p. G9.

McDowell, Edwin, "A Successful Outfitter Ranges beyond Its Territory," *New York Times*, March 20, 1999, p. 1.

Mitchell, Rick, "A Showroom as Big as the Great Outdoors," *Houston Chronicle*, June 14, 1992, p. 1.

Ryan, Thomas J., "Ready to Rumble: Hyper Expansion by Outdoor Chains Rattles the Industry," *Sporting Goods Business*, February 2006, p. 7.

Bayer AG

———◼———

Werk Leverkusen, Postfach
Leverkusen, D-51368
Germany
Telephone: (+49) 214 30 1
Fax: (+49) 214 30 663 28
Web site: http://www.bayer-ag.de

Public Company
Incorporated: 1863 as Farbenfabriken vorm. Friedr. Bayer & Co.
Employees: 108,400
Sales: EUR 31.2 billion ($43.68 billion) (2009)
Stock Exchanges: Frankfurt London
Ticker Symbol: BAY
NAICS: 325412 Pharmaceutical Preparation Manufacturing; 325131 Inorganic Dye and Pigment Manufacturing; 325192 Cyclic Crude and Intermediate Manufacturing; 325211 Plastics Material and Resin Manufacturing; 325212 Synthetic Rubber Manufacturing; 325320 Pesticide and Other Agricultural Chemical Manufacturing; 325411 Medicinal and Botanical Manufacturing; 325998 All Other Miscellaneous Chemical Product Manufacturing; 541710 Research and Development in the Physical Sciences and Engineering Sciences; 551112 Offices of Other Holding Companies

◼ ◼ ◼

Bayer AG is one of the world's leading chemicals and pharmaceuticals companies. Based in Leverkusen, Germany, Bayer has more than 300 subsidiaries and nearly 109,000 employees throughout the world. The company's combined operations generated revenues of EUR 31.2 billion ($43.7 billion) in 2009. Bayer AG operates as the holding company for three independently operating subgroups and three service companies. These include Bayer HealthCare, Bayer CropScience, and Bayer MaterialScience, as well as the services companies Bayer Business Services and Bayer Technological Services, and chemical industry services supplier Currenta. Each of these businesses is led by its own executive board and management team. Altogether, Bayer markets more than 5,000 products. Bayer is listed on the Frankfurt and London stock exchanges. Group Chairman Werner Wenning announced his intention to retire at the end of September 2010, to be replaced by Marijn Dekkers.

BEGINNINGS AS DYESTUFFS FACTORY IN 1863

Bayer traces its history to the 1863 founding of a dyestuffs factory in Barmen, Germany, a region that later became part of the industrial city of Wuppertal on the Rhine River in West Germany. The factory was set up by Friedrich Bayer and Johan Friedrich Weskott, a master dyer. Only two years later, the men commenced global operations of sorts, acquiring a share in a U.S. coal tar dye factory and exporting the product. Subsequent expansion included a new factory in Moscow. By 1881, the growing company was being run by heirs of Bayer and Weskott, and they reorganized the concern as Farbenfabriken vorm. Friedr. Bayer & Co., a joint-stock company. A plant in northern France was

COMPANY PERSPECTIVES

Mission Statement: Working to Create Value through Innovation and Growth. Bayer is a global enterprise with core competencies in the fields of health care, nutrition and high-tech materials. Our products and services are designed to benefit people and improve their quality of life. At the same time we aim to create value through innovation, growth and high earning power.

established in 1883 and others throughout the homeland of Germany followed.

In 1884, chemist Carl Duisberg joined the company. He would oversee a period of remarkable innovation at Bayer. Expanding beyond the development and manufacture of dyestuffs, the company established a pharmaceutical department in 1888. Although Bayer became a world leader in dyestuffs, its place in the history of early 20th-century chemistry was secured by its contributions to pharmacology. Specifically, a Bayer chemist, Felix Hoffman, became the first to synthesize acetylsalicylic acid into a usable form. The result, Aspirin, was patented in 1899 and went on to become the most popular pain reliever worldwide.

Moreover, in 1908 the basic compound for sulfa drugs was synthesized in Bayer laboratories. The immediate application of the compound was a reddish orange dye, which was soon discovered to be effective against pneumonia, a major health hazard of the early 20th century. Despite the lives that could have been saved if the sulfa drug had been released throughout Europe immediately, Bayer held onto the formula. Frustrated French chemists were forced to duplicate the drug in their own laboratories in order to introduce it to the market. In 1912, Bayer moved its headquarters to Leverkusen, where they would remain into the 21st century.

UNIFYING UNDER THE GERMAN GOVERNMENT FROM THE TWENTIES

Bayer chemists regularly tested dye compounds for their effectiveness against bacteria. In 1921, they discovered a cure for African sleeping sickness, an infectious disease that had made parts of Africa uninhabitable. Aware of the political as well as pharmacological implications of its compound, Bayer offered the British the formula to the drug, known as Germanin, in exchange for African colonies. Britain declined the offer and noncooperation continued. During World War I Bayer deprived the Allies of drugs and anesthetics whenever possible. In 1925, Duisberg, who had become president of Bayer, organized a merger of the major German chemical companies into a single entity known as the Interessen Gemeinschaft Farbenwerke, or I.G. Farben. From their inception, the German chemical companies had been organized into a series of progressively more powerful trusts, but with I.G. Farben, the last vestiges of competition in the chemical industry were extinguished. Other industries, such as steel, were undergoing a similar process in Germany.

In addition to setting quotas and pooling profits, I.G. Farben pursued political aims, working to prevent any possibility of a leftist uprising that would establish worker control over industry. In order to prevent such an uprising, I.G. Farben financed right-wing politicians and attempted to influence domestic policy in secret meetings with German leaders. The trust also exercised its influence abroad, with Bayer and other companies contributing an estimated 10 million marks to Nazi Party associations in other countries. Money was also designated for propaganda. In 1938, Bayer forced a U.S. affiliate, Sterling Drug, to write its advertising contracts in such a way that they would be immediately canceled if the publication in which the advertising appeared presented Germany in an unflattering light.

PROFITING FROM THE NAZI ERA

Bayer and I.G. Farben profited handsomely from their support of Adolf Hitler. By 1942, I.G. Farben was making a yearly profit of 800 million marks more than its entire combined capitalization in 1925, the year the cartel was formalized. Not only was I.G. Farben given possession of chemical companies in foreign lands (it had control of Czechoslovakian dye works a week after the Nazi invasion of that country), but the captured lands provided its factories in Germany with slave labor. In order to take full advantage of slave labor, I.G. Farben plants were built next to Maidanek and Auschwitz.

Many of the I.G. Farben plants contracted during the war were built in remote areas, often with camouflage. Thus, these factories did not sustain much physical damage, in contrast to the many German cities that were completely destroyed. By I.G. Farben's account, only 15 percent of its productive capacity was destroyed by the Allies. The worst damage was sustained by the extensive BASF works and factories in eastern Germany, which were destroyed by I.G. Farben employees so that the buildings would not fall under Russian control.

KEY DATES

1863: Friedrich Bayer establishes a dyestuffs factory.
1888: Pharmaceutical department of the firm is created.
1899: Aspirin trademark is registered.
1925: Merger of the major German chemical companies results in the Interessen Gemeinschaft Farbenwerke, or I.G. Farben.
1972: Firm officially adopts the name Bayer A.G.
1978: Miles Laboratories is acquired.
1994: Bayer purchases the North American operations of Sterling Drug for $1 billion.
2003: Bayer regroups into three legally independent businesses: Bayer HealthCare, Bayer Material-Science, and Bayer CropScience.
2006: Bayer pays $19.6 billion for control of Schering.

Immediately after the war many members of I.G. Farben's Vorstand, or board of directors, were arrested and indicted for war crimes. I.G. Farben executives were in the habit of keeping copious records, not only of meetings and phone calls, but also of their private thoughts on I.G. Farben's dealings with the government. As a result, there was extensive written evidence incriminating the Vorstand. Despite this evidence and testimony from concentration camp survivors, the Vorstand was dealt with leniently by the judges at Nuremberg. Journalists covering the 1947 proceedings attributed the light sentences, none of which was longer than four years, to the fact that all the sentences handed down at the end of the trials tended to be less severe, as well as to the judges' unwillingness to expand their definition of war criminals to include businessmen.

BAYER INDEPENDENCE FROM
I.G. FARBEN IN THE FIFTIES

I.G. Farben plants operated under Allied supervision from 1947 until 1951, when the organization was dismantled in the interests of peace and democracy. The division of I.G. Farben generally adhered to the boundaries of the original companies. For example, the works at Leverkusen and Elberfeld reverted to Bayer. Bayer also received the Agfa photographic works.

In the first five years of its independence from I.G. Farben, Bayer concentrated on replacing outdated equipment and on supplying Germany's need for chemicals. By 1957, Bayer had developed new

insecticides and fibers, as well as new raw and plastic finished materials. Bayer's resiliency in recovering from the war impressed U.S. investors, who held 12 percent of the company's stock.

During the late 1950s, Bayer began to expand overseas and by 1962 was manufacturing chemicals in eight countries, including India and Pakistan. Most of the work done abroad was final stage processing, whereby active ingredients were sent from Germany and mixed with locally obtained inert ingredients that would be expensive to transport overseas. Final stage processing arrangements allowed Bayer to manufacture products, mostly farm chemicals and drugs, in developing countries more profitably.

High U.S. tariffs and high labor costs in Germany also provided incentives for Bayer to acquire production facilities in the United States. In 1954, Bayer and Monsanto formed a chemical company known as Mobay to manufacture engineering plastics and dyestuffs. Because Bayer did not have sufficient funds to build a plant in the United States, it provided technical expertise while Monsanto provided financial resources. Although Bayer had part, and eventually full, interest in Mobay, its promotional material was never allowed to mention Bayer's name, because the U.S. rights to the Bayer trademark had been given to Sterling Drug after World War I in retaliation for Bayer's suppression of U.S. dye companies during the early years of the 20th century.

Realizing that West Germany offered only limited opportunity for growth, Bayer worked to develop products for the U.S. chemical market, emphasizing value-added products for which Bayer held the patents, including pesticides, polyurethane, dyestuffs, and engineering plastics. Technical innovations that allowed Bayer to penetrate the U.S. market included the urethane compound that forms the familiar "crust" on urethane used in auto dashboards. Before Bayer's discovery, the porous quality of urethane limited its usefulness. During this period Bayer consolidated and slowly expanded its international operations, especially in the United States. Overall, the 1960s was a good decade for Bayer as domestic production increased 350 percent while foreign production increased 700 percent.

U.S. EXPANSION IN THE
SEVENTIES

In 1972 the firm officially adopted the name Bayer A.G. During this same period, Bayer began to increase its already substantial investment in the United States. Between 1973 and 1977, its investment rose from $300 million to $500 million, which went to expand production capacity and develop its product line, which included dyes, drugs, plastics, and synthetic rubber. Although all patents held by Bayer before 1952 had been taken away as war retribution, by the mid-1970s Bayer had expanded its product line to include 6,000 items, many of them patented by the company.

Bayer increased its capacity by expanding existing plants and purchasing new ones. In 1974, Bayer purchased Cutter Laboratories, a manufacturer of nutritional products and ethical drugs, which had financial difficulties until 1977. Later, Allied Chemical sold its organic pigments division to Bayer. In 1977, a U.S. antitrust suit forced Bayer to buy Monsanto's share of Mobay, which generated $540 million in sales. The following year Bayer purchased Miles Laboratories, manufacturers of Alka-Seltzer antacid and Flintstones vitamins.

Bayer had strong incentives to expand its U.S. operations. Due to the prevalence of strikes in Europe, which interrupted product shipments, U.S. retailers were wary of contracting with European suppliers who did not have large stockpiles of their products in the United States. Lower energy and labor costs made the United States even more attractive to Bayer. U.S. holdings also cushioned the negative effects of the strong deutsche mark on imports into the United States. By the mid-1970s, 65 percent of Bayer's sales came from outside of Germany, making it critical that Bayer protect itself against currency fluctuations.

RESTRUCTURING AND COST-CUTTING IN THE EIGHTIES

In the early 1980s, Bayer's worldwide holdings had expanded such that its corporate structure needed streamlining. German law mandated a two-tier structure for corporations, with a management board similar in function to the board of directors of a U.S. corporation reporting to a supervisory board made up of major stockholders, labor representatives, and outside interests. This board served in a supervisory capacity, approved major decisions, and appointed board members. In 1982, Bayer created a third tier below the management board. This board consisted of senior managers and corporate staff members who took over management of specific product lines that had previously been the responsibility of board members.

The late 1980s and early 1990s were a time of stagnant revenues, cost containment efforts, and an increasing emphasis on non-European markets for Bayer. From 1988 through 1993, sales fluctuated between DEM 40 billion and DEM 43.3 billion, while profits leveled off. Business was affected by a serious recession

in Western Europe, political changes in Eastern Europe, a cyclical downturn in the chemical industry, and government reforms in health care and agriculture. In 1993, Bayer's sales of pharmaceuticals in Germany fell 20 percent as a result of government efforts to cut expenditures on pharmaceuticals. Doctors, facing reduced drug budgets, began to prescribe more generic drugs in place of the expensive, proprietary drugs developed by Bayer. Agrochemical sales were dampened by the Common Agricultural Policy reform effort that reduced the amount of farmland in Europe and the amount of chemicals used in farming.

Part of Bayer's response to this crisis was to drastically cut costs: $1.6 billion in expenditures were eliminated between 1991 and early 1995. Its worldwide workforce was slashed by 14 percent, and unprofitable operations were shed, including its polyphenylene sulfide unit. In 1992, Bayer integrated all of its U.S. holdings under its Miles Inc. subsidiary, based in Pittsburgh. The following year, under the leadership of a new chairman of the board of management, Manfred Schneider, Bayer committed to enlarging its Asian and North American operations in order to reduce its dependence on the European market. In Asia, Bayer focused its expansion efforts on joint ventures with firms in Japan, Hong Kong, Taiwan, and China. In 1993, Bayer signed an agreement with the Eisai Company of Japan to sell nonprescription drugs, and the following year several joint ventures were signed in China to set up Bayer and Agfa-Gevaert production operations there.

(RE)ACQUIRING THE BAYER NAME IN 1994

In North America, Bayer began a drive not only to bolster its operations but also to fully regain the use of its name. After securing the rights to the Bayer name in the United States after World War I, Sterling Drug went on to establish Bayer aspirin as a household name. In 1986, for $25 million, Bayer secured from Sterling partial rights to use its name in North America outside the pharmaceutical area. In 1994, Eastman Kodak sold Sterling to the British firm SmithKline Beecham PLC, and only a few weeks later SmithKline sold the North American side of Sterling to Bayer for $1 billion. With the purchase, Bayer not only won back the full rights to its name in North America, but also gained Sterling's $366 million North American over-the-counter (OTC) drug business. In addition to the Bayer aspirin line, the Sterling acquisition included such familiar products as Midol analgesics and NeoSynephrine decongestant. The acquisition pushed Bayer into the top five producers of OTC products worldwide.

After the purchase of Sterling, Bayer changed the name of its Miles Inc. subsidiary to Bayer Corporation. The OTC operations of Miles and Sterling were then integrated into a single Bayer Corporation consumer care division. Another strategic step in North America, and one that brought added diversification to Bayer's health care operations, was the 1994 purchase of a 29.3 percent stake in Denver-based Schein Pharmaceutical Inc., a maker of generic drugs. Bayer planned to expand Schein's operations outside North America.

Bayer also beefed up its research and development (R&D) budget, particularly in health care. Its drug research efforts were beginning to pay off in the mid-1990s, especially in North America. Bayer's anti-infective drug Ciprobay had generated $1.3 billion in sales by early 1995, with the firm's patent in effect until 2002. In 1993, Bayer introduced a hemophilia treatment called Kogenate, the company's first genetically engineered drug. Other major drugs under development included a cholesterol reducer and treatments for asthma and Alzheimer's disease.

As a result of its increasing diversification within its core businesses and its aggressive program of worldwide expansion, Bayer operated as a leading chemical and pharmaceutical company in the mid-1990s. Net income increased by 20 percent to DEM 2.4 billion in 1995, the highest level the company had recorded in its history. The company's chemical business played a large role in securing such an increase. However, results for the firm's health care interests and its Agfa group were dim in comparison due to exchange rates, a decrease in demand, and increased pressure on prices.

NEW RESTRUCTURING IN 1995

The firm once again looked to restructure and control costs in order to maintain income levels. The financial success in 1995 was overshadowed by 3,800 job cuts and additional cuts were expected into the late 1990s. Underperforming assets and non-core assets were divested including the dental care and consumer businesses. As the German economy faltered, Bayer management continued to focus on cost-efficient operations. Chairman Schneider stated in an April 1996 *Chemistry and Industry* article, "if our German operations are to remain competitive, we must at least stop costs rising any further and actually start to reduce them again." In order to do just that, the firm's bulk chemical plants in Leverkusen, Dormagen, and Uerdingen, underwent a major restructuring in 1997 after recording a 79 percent decline in operating profits.

At the same time, Bayer looked for strategic alliances to secure top positions in niches of the industry.

In March 1996, the firm acquired the styrenics business of Monsanto Company for $580 million. The deal doubled Bayer's North American plastics operations and secured its position as the second-largest producer of engineering resins just behind GE Plastics. The firm also pledged to increase Asian business, which in 1996 secured 14 percent of company sales. Moreover, in September 1998, Bayer acquired U.S.-based Chiron Corporation's Diagnostics business for DEM 1.9 billion. The deal gave Bayer the number one spot in the diagnostic systems industry and also increased its international customer base as well as its research operations.

Bayer teamed with Millennium Pharmaceuticals Inc., a genome research company, to form a discovery alliance related to drug testing for cardiovascular disease, cancer, osteoporosis, liver fibrosis, and viral infections. Bayer also teamed up with General Electric to form GE Bayer Silicones GmbH & Co. KG, a unit dedicated to developing the silicon business. The firm also partnered with Japanese firm Fujisawa to prevent worms in pets and livestock, and also began work in China on crop protection and household insecticides.

Aspirin marked its centennial in March 1999. Bayer celebrated by tenting its corporate headquarters in an Aspirin box while 50,000 spectators looked on. Amid the festivities, the firm continued to strengthen its core businesses and spun off 70 million shares of its Agfa-Gevaert business in order to raise capital for other operations. At the same time, the firm continued to face increased competition, consolidation in the pharmaceutical industry, and difficult market conditions in the agrochemical field as well as in the chemicals segment. Strategic alliances remained a focus, and deals for the year included the purchase of the polycarbonate and polyester sheet business of Dutch-based DSM; the acquisition of Laserlite, an Australian plastic sheeting company; and Home & Garden Ltd, a plant protection and fertilizer manufacturer. Having spent the 1990s restructuring and selling off non-core assets, Bayer's key business segments included Health Care, Agriculture, Polymers, and Chemicals at the close of the 20th century.

ALLIANCES FOR THE NEW MILLENNIUM

Bayer entered the new millennium on solid ground, despite weakening market conditions in several of its business segments. The company's strategy of strengthening its portfolio continued, and in April 2000 the firm acquired the polyols business of U.S.-based Lyondell Chemical Company for $2.5 billion. Bayer stood as the world's largest polyurethane raw materials supplier after the deal.

Bayer also forged several key partnerships that were related to the firm's drive for research and development as well as product innovation. A deal with Incyte Pharmaceuticals gave Bayer access to the U.S.-based company's database of over 480 patented human genes that could be used for research. The company also partnered with LION Bioscience AG to do research in the life sciences including pharmaceuticals and diagnostics. In February 2001, Bayer teamed up with CuraGen Corporation to research, develop, and market pharmaceuticals related to metabolic disease. Bayer received the President's Service Award and the Presidential Green Chemistry Challenge Award in 2000 due to its long-standing commitment to research and development.

Although overall sales for 2000 were impressive, the Chemicals segment of the business continued to struggle, and restructuring continued. Bayer's focus on the future included expanding its research and technology operations, as well as continuing to shed unprofitable business. For example, in May 2001 the company ceded its 50 percent interest in EC Erdoelchemie to BP Energy in a deal valued at $500 million.

During this time, Tweedy Browne & Co., a large shareholder, called for Bayer to split into three segments: chemicals, pharmaceuticals, and agchems. In response to the proposed split, Chairman Schneider stated in a *Chemical Week* article, "we are sure such a move would not increase Bayer's value in the long term. Our current structure facilitates the running of the business, enables us to capitalize on existing synergies, and gives us scope to respond swiftly should acquisition opportunities arise in the life science sector." Shareholders voted down the proposal overwhelmingly.

BAYCOL DISASTER IN 2001

Nonetheless, Bayer announced a new four-year reorganization plan in 2001, aimed at saving up to $1.3 billion by the middle of the decade. As Werner Wenning took over as the company's CEO in 2002, Bayer also announced plans to focus on expanding its pharmaceuticals and agrochemicals businesses, while reducing its chemicals operations to just 10 percent of its overall revenues. Toward this end, the company completed a new major acquisition, of Aventis CropScience, for $6.6 billion in 2001. As a result, the company's health care and crop science divisions combined to account for 55 percent of the group's total revenues. By the middle of the decade, Bayer CropScience grew to become the world's leading crop sciences company.

Bayer's health care business hit a major setback in 2001, however, when its popular Baycol cholesterol-lowering drug was implicated in the deaths of more than 100 people. The company was forced to pull the product, losing more than $600 million in sales in the United States alone. The Baycol recall effectively wiped out all of Bayer's health care profits for that year.

The failure of Baycol was especially disastrous for the company as it represented one of the few promising new drugs in an increasingly meager pipeline. Bayer, like much of the global pharmaceuticals industry, had found it increasingly difficult to identify and develop new molecules. Another Bayer best seller, the antibiotic Cipro, was slated to lose its patent by 2003. Instead, Bayer pinned its pharmaceuticals hopes on vardenafil, an erectile dysfunction treatment similar to the global blockbuster Viagra. Bayer planned to market the drug as Nuviva or Levitra, depending on the market, in partnership with GlaxoSmithKline.

RESTRUCTURING IN 2003

Bayer continued working on its restructuring in the early part of the decade. In 2003, Bayer reorganized itself as a holding company overseeing three legally independent businesses: Bayer HealthCare, Bayer CropScience, and Bayer MaterialScience. The company also spun off parts of its chemicals businesses, as well as its rubber operations, selling these in 2005. The company sold another component of its chemicals businesses, Wolff Walsrode, to Dow Chemical for $726.2 million in 2007.

Bayer completed two significant acquisitions in 2004. The company boosted its CropScience business by buying out its partner in Gustafson, a seed treatment company, for $124 million. Bayer also expanded its HealthCare OTC business by acquiring the OTC division of Roche Holding AG. Bayer then became the largest OTC player in the European market.

Bayer also sought a means to revive its flagging prescription drugs operations. This led the company to launch the largest takeover in its history, paying $19.6 billion to gain control of Schering AG. That purchase provided Bayer with a new array of drugs, including the popular Yaz birth control pills and a number of best-selling cancer and multiple sclerosis treatments. Bayer bought out Schering's minority shareholders in 2008, taking full control of the company. Bayer then integrated its own pharmaceuticals operations into Schering, which became Bayer Schering Pharma, one of the four Bayer HealthCare subdivisions in 2009.

Bayer completed a number of other acquisitions through the end of the decade. In 2006, the company acquired Metrika, based in California, which developed diabetes metering devices. At the same time, Bayer expanded its presence in China, investing $1.9 billion to build a new chemical factory in Shanghai, and paying $136 million to the OTC business of Topsun Science and Technology in Qidong. In 2008, Bayer bought Possis Medical, a maker of cardiovascular diagnostic systems based in Minneapolis, for $361 million.

Bayer was one of the few remaining European companies to combine both pharmaceuticals and chemicals operations in the 21st century. Nonetheless, this diversity helped cushion parts of the effects of the global economic recession at the end of the decade. Despite the collapse of a number of major markets, notably in the chemicals industry, Bayer was able to limit the effects of the recession on its own sales. As a result, the company's revenues slipped back just 5 percent, to EUR 31.2 billion in 2009.

The next decade started out more hopefully for Bayer. In June 2010, the company announced that it had received approval to market a new erectile dysfunction treatment in the United States. Called Staxyn, the new treatment represented a reformulation of the group's vardenafil (marketed as Levitra in the United States). This new formulation became the first erectile dysfunction treatment available in an orodispersible form (the tablet disperses on the tongue without the need of water or other liquids). With a history approaching 150 years, Bayer looked forward to remaining one of the world's best known pharmaceutical and chemical names.

Updated, David E. Salamie; Christina M. Stansell;
M. L. Cohen

PRINCIPAL SUBSIDIARIES

Bayer HealthCare AG; Bayer CropScience AG; Bayer MaterialScience AG.

PRINCIPAL DIVISIONS

Bayer Business Services GmbH; Bayer Technology Services GmbH; Currenta GmbH & Co. OHG.

PRINCIPAL OPERATING UNITS

Bayer Schering Pharma; Animal Health, Consumer Care, Medical Care; Crop Protection; Environmental Science; BioScience; Polycarbonates; Polyurethanes; Coatings, Adhesives, Specialties.

PRINCIPAL COMPETITORS

Dhanalakshmi Drugs Ltd.; GlaxoSmithKline; Johnson and Johnson; Mano Pharmaceuticals; McKesson Corporation; Nanjing No 2 Pharmaceutical Factory; Novartis International AG; Pfizer Inc.; Roche Holding AG; Sanofi-Aventis; Stedman Pharmaceuticals Private Ltd.

FURTHER READING

Alperowicz, Natasha, "Bayer Posts Its Best Annual Results, but Idles PC Plants," *Chemical Week*, March 9, 2009, p. 13.

"Bayer Bids to Be No. 1 in Polycarbonate," *Plastics Technology*, February 2000, p. 69.

"Bayer Continues Restructuring Plans," *Chemical Week*, January 13, 1999, p. 6.

"Bayer Mobilizes Resources to Counter Crisis at Home," *Chemical Week*, April 21, 1993, pp. 24–31.

"Bayer Prepares Bulk Chemicals Restructuring," *Chemical Market Reporter*, March 24, 1997, p. 8.

"Bayer under Pressure," *Chemical Week*, March 24, 1993, p. 19.

"Bayer's Bid Wins Roche's OTC Arm," *ECN–European Chemical News*, July 26, 2004, p. 9.

Brown, Stuart F., "Growing Drugs Is a Tricky Business," *Fortune*, November 25, 2002, p. 176.

"Can Bayer Cure Its Own Headache," *Business Week*, January 28, 2002, p. 36.

Capell, Kerry, "Bayer's Big Headache," *Business Week*, May 6, 2002, p. 30.

Davis, Brian, "Bayer in China," *Chemical Week*, August 27, 2003, p. 28.

Esposito, Frank, "Bayer Reorganization Finds Less Is More," *Plastics News*, May 12, 2003, p. 18.

Hayes, Peter, *Industry and Ideology: IG Farben in the Nazi Era*, New York: Cambridge University Press, 1987, 411 p.

Hume, Claudia, "Bayer Rejects Call for Split," *Chemical Week*, March 21, 2001, p. 7.

Jackson, Debbie, "Bayer: Deals in the Pipeline as Decline Continues," *Chemical Week*, December 8, 1993, p. 18.

Jackson, Debbie, and Emma Chynoweth, "Recession Reaches German Majors: Turnaround in 1991 Is Still Elusive," *Chemical Week*, April 15, 1992, pp. 22–23.

"Job Losses Follow Best Year Ever," *Chemistry and Industry*, April 1, 1996, p. 237.

Johnson, Miles, and Emmanuelle Smith, "Bayer Stung by Drug Concerns," *Financial Times*, March 18, 2009, p. 24.

Mann, Charles C., and Mark L. Plummer, *The Aspirin Wars: Money, Medicine, and 100 Years of Rampant Competition*, New York: Alfred A. Knopf, 1991, 420 p.

O'Driscoll, Cath, "The Pick of the Crop," *ECN–European Chemical News*, June 20, 2005, p. 23.

Orr, Deborah, Susan Kitchens, and Stephane Fitch, "Another Look: Bayer Backs Down," *Forbes Global*, December 23, 2002, p. 12.

"Schering's White Knight," *Business Week*, April 10, 2006, p. 28.

Weintraub, Arlene, and Naomi Kresge, "Diabetes Is No Fun—But It Can Be a Game," *Business Week*, April 19, 2010, p. 62.

The Biltmore Company

1 North Pack Square
Asheville, North Carolina 28801
U.S.A.
Telephone: (828) 225-1333
Toll Free: (800) 411-3812
Web site: http://www.biltmore.com

Private Company
Incorporated: 1979
Employees: 1,200
Sales: $130 million (2006 est.)
NAICS: 712120 Historical Sites

■ ■ ■

The Biltmore Company is a family-owned company whose mission is the preservation of the Biltmore Estate in Asheville, North Carolina, without relying on government or foundation aid or tax-exempt status. The limestone and marble Biltmore mansion with its 250 rooms is the largest private residence in the United States and is a National Historic Landmark. It is surrounded by hundreds of acres of gardens and thousands of acres of natural habitat that include many miles of woodland trails. In addition to tours, the estate is available for weddings and corporate events, and has been used as a setting for feature films.

The Biltmore Company also operates restaurants, an off-site luxury hotel, an exclusive on-site cottage, retail shops, an equestrian center, and a winery, which since 2010 has been part of Biltmore's Antler Hill Village. Antler Hill is a pedestrian-friendly village that

includes an exhibition space dedicated to the Biltmore Estate and the interests of the Vanderbilt family, a tavern, creamery, bandstand, and outdoor adventure center that takes advantage of the estate's 8,000 acres. Further revenues come from catering and the licensing of the Biltmore name to dressings and marinades, as well as a variety of home décor products.

CORNELIUS VANDERBILT BUILDS 19TH-CENTURY FORTUNE

George Vanderbilt was a grandson of Cornelius Vanderbilt, who in the early decades of the 1800s launched his entrepreneurial career in shipping and by mid-century became involved in railroads. By the time he died in 1877 he had amassed a fortune of $100 million, 95 percent of which he left to his eldest son, William Henry, the father of George Vanderbilt. Born in 1862, George Vanderbilt was the youngest of eight children and the only one uninterested in finance or fashionable society. Extremely close to his mother, he grew up taciturn and intellectual and from an early age traveled widely, often accompanied by tutors. He spoke eight languages and was a connoisseur of art, but he was also an outdoorsman. In 1888 he spent a vacation in Asheville, North Carolina, fell in love with the Blue Ridge Mountains, and an idea took root of building an estate with a view of Mount Pisgah.

Vanderbilt began acquiring land south of Asheville in 1888 for $5 to $25 per acre, and by the time he was through, he owned 125,000 acres, including all of Mount Pisgah. In 1889 he hired famed architect Richard Morris Hunt, who had designed many of

Manhattan's finest mansions, the façade and Great Hall of the Metropolitan Museum of Art, and the pedestal of the Statue of Liberty. For a landscaper, Vanderbilt hired the genius behind Manhattan's Central Park, Frederick Law Olmsted. It was Hunt, according to most experts, who inspired Vanderbilt to pursue a grand vision. The two men traveled to Europe together to view English manors and French chateaux, and a vision for what would become Biltmore Estate took shape. The result was a French Renaissance-style mansion poised on a hill overlooking a river with a view of the Blue Ridge Mountains as a backdrop.

Construction on Biltmore began in late 1889. To transport the Indiana limestone used in construction, a railroad was built. Marble was imported from Italy. A kiln was also constructed on-site to produce 32,000 bricks a day. A Viennese sculptor, Karl Bitter, supplied the stone and wood carvings, while a forester and horti- culturalist were hired to carve out gardens and woodlands, and import millions of plants. During his travels, Vanderbilt purchased an abundance of treasures, including hundreds of carpets, 16th-century Flemish tapestries, Ming dynasty goldfish bowls, woodcuts by Albrecht Dürer, and Renoir paintings. He also commis- sioned work from renowned painters, including personal friends John Singer Sargent and James Abbott McNeill Whistler. The final cost of the estate, according to the *New York Times*, was more than $3 million and Vander- bilt was reported to have spent another $7 million on improvements to the estate.

ESTATE FINALLY OPENS: 1895

Vanderbilt choose Biltmore for the name of his estate in 1890 when construction began. When it was formally opened to friends and family on Christmas Eve in 1895, it included a host of modern conveniences and pleasures, including complete electricity, central heating, bowling alleys, a basement swimming pool, and a telephone. Vanderbilt went to a great deal of trouble to build a bachelor's residence, but in 1898 he married American socialite Edith Stuyvesant Dresser. When they were not traveling, they lived in Biltmore and in 1900 their only child, Cornelia, was born there.

During his ownership of the estate, Vanderbilt established the Biltmore Forest School, the country's first forestry school, in 1898 and in 1901 he and his wife launched Biltmore Industries, an apprentice program to train local youths in basketry, weaving, and woodworking. Two years later his wife organized the School for Domestic Science, a housekeeping training program. Vanderbilt also built a model village for the 2,000 employees of the estate, comprising cottages he built patterned after homes in Cheshire, England. He imposed his own laws, forbidding dogs, hen roosts, and live-in servants, all of which he believed were at the root of most domestic quarrels. Additionally, he became a model farmer and built an elaborate hunting lodge on his North Carolina property.

In 1911 Vanderbilt purchased a K Street residence in Washington, D.C., the former home of U.S. Senator Matthew Quay of Pennsylvania. It was here in 1914 that Vanderbilt died suddenly from heart failure. His wife continued to live at Biltmore, but after the death of her husband she sold more than 80,000 acres of the land he had acquired to the U.S. Department of Agriculture, forming the basis of Pisgah National Forest. In 1924 Edith Vanderbilt married John Francis Amherst Cecil, a British diplomat. Together they had two sons, William and George. Edith and John Cecil also began opening parts of their home to the public in 1930, at the behest of Asheville leaders who were looking to bring business to the town hard hit by the Depression. The couple divorced in the early 1930s and Edith took the boys to England where they were educated.

WORLD WAR II: ESTATE CLOSES TO PUBLIC

During World War II Biltmore was closed to the public and its remote locale was put to use by the National Gallery in Washington to store the nation's art treasures. The estate was reopened in 1946 but it was expensive to maintain, and despite the number of visitors it attracted, Biltmore was a money-losing proposition that drained the family's fortune. By the end of the 1950s it was los- ing $250,000 a year, despite drawing 50,000 visitors each year.

In 1960 William (Bill) and George Cecil returned to Asheville to run the estate. The eldest, George, took charge of the Biltmore dairy, which had remained a profitable concern over the years, while Bill Cecil was saddled with the task of making the house pay, taking over the management responsibilities that for some years had been handled by an aging family friend and judge. The 32-year-old Cecil was well suited for the task at hand. He had studied business at Harvard and was a

KEY DATES

1895: George Washington Vanderbilt opens Biltmore Estate in Asheville, North Carolina.
1914: George Vanderbilt dies.
1930: Biltmore first opens to the public.
1960: William Cecil takes over Biltmore's management.
1979: The Biltmore Company is established.

vice president for Chase Manhattan Bank when he moved his family to Asheville in an effort to save the family estate. They lived in town and he very much treated the property as a business, albeit the job was a labor of love and one that his friends told him was impossible.

When Bill Cecil took charge, the Biltmore house had grown shabby. He updated the plumbing and electricity and opened the second and third floors. He also upgraded the estate's marketing, which in the past had been limited to a one-page advertisement in the annual agriculture and travel issue of the *Asheville Citizen-Times*. Cecil spread the word about the Biltmore Estate through far-flung advertisements and billboards. He also added some panache in 1963 by having Biltmore Estate listed on the National Register of Historic Places. Moreover, he opened a restaurant and gift shop and courted hotel owners and tour operators. Cecil's efforts began to pay off and in 1968 the Biltmore Estate attracted 200,000 visitors and turned a profit of $16.34. Although a minuscule amount, it marked a turning point in the fortunes of the Biltmore Estate.

With the oil crisis of the early 1970s, Cecil became concerned that tourists would be less willing to drive to the Blue Ridge Mountains to pay visits to Biltmore. He began looking for new sources of income. A farm operation raised cattle and grew hay, corn, potatoes, and carrots. To pursue the possibility of opening a winery, he planted an experimental vineyard in 1972, initially relying on French-American hybrids. Pleased with the results, Cecil hired a French winemaster and in 1979 the dairy barn was converted into a winery. It was also in 1979 that Bill and George Cecil, whose mother had died three years earlier, decided to split their inheritance. George received the money he needed to start a real estate business, while Cecil received the mansion and 8,000 acres. The estate was now operated by The Biltmore Company, with Bill Cecil serving as president.

DAIRY BECOMES WINERY: 1984

While the winemaster planted new varieties of grapes and the vineyards came into maturity, Biltmore in 1984 invested $10 million to preserve the old dairy complex as well as convert it into a winery that opened to the public a year later. A frost devastated the vineyard in 1985, but the winery carried on while the vineyard recovered by importing juice from California. In charge of the winery was Cecil's 27-year-old son, William Cecil Jr. In a few short years, the Biltmore Winery, located a mile and a half from the Biltmore house, would attract about 500,000 visitors, making it the most popular winery in the United States.

At the start of the 1990s Cecil continued to restore the estate, opening more and more of the mansion to the public. In 1990 the butler's pantry, servants' quarters, and other portions of the house became available in the "Behind the Scene Tours." By this time, a long-term effort had been launched to preserve the estate's many tapestries. Biltmore also took advantage of the expertise it had developed to launch a restoration business. In addition, Biltmore sought to leverage the value of the Biltmore brand in 1990 with the start of a licensing operation, introduced in April of that year at High Point Furniture Market. Over the next 20 years, the Biltmore name would be licensed to scores of partners for Biltmore-inspired home and garden products.

Biltmore was generating more than $50 million in annual sales by the end of the 1990s. As the decade came to a close, the Biltmore Company was reorganized, an effort that resulted in a new business group: Biltmore Estate Brands. The new unit looked to extend the Biltmore name to reproductions and adaptations of the estate's collection along with new wines and agricultural products.

LUXURY HOTEL OPENS: 2001

Biltmore continued to expand in the new century. A $32 million, 213-room luxury hotel opened in 2001, a project that had been in development for 20 years. The rooms' designs were in keeping with the Biltmore estate, but they were not on the grounds. In 2006 the Cottage on Biltmore Estate was opened to give people a chance to reside on the premises. The cost for four adults to spend a night at the former home of the gardener was $2,800, but it included a butler and a chef.

New Biltmore products were added, and additional parts of the estate were renovated and opened to the public, including the servants' quarters of the fourth floor, rooms that since the 1950s had been used to store furniture. In 2009 Biltmore also began working with Bell Leadership Institute to offer corporate executive retreats and other leadership programs at Biltmore Estate. In 2010, Biltmore opened a major new attraction, the pedestrian-friendly Antler Hill Village, which became part of the daily admission to Biltmore. The Biltmore Company, now led by William Cecil Jr., did not appear close to exhausting its commercial potential.

Ed Dinger

PRINCIPAL SUBSIDIARIES

Biltmore Estate Wine Company Inc.; The Biltmore Village Company.

PRINCIPAL COMPETITORS

Broadmoor Hotel, Inc.; Grand Heritage Hotel Group LLC; Pinehurst, LLC.

FURTHER READING

"Biltmore More Than a Mountain Estate," *Lumberton (NC) Robesonian*, January 7, 2007, p. C6.

"G. W. Vanderbilt Dies Suddenly," *New York Times*, March 17, 1914.

Hechlinger, John, "Biltmore at 100: Will It Survive?" *Charlotte Observer*, January 1, 1995, p. 1A.

Lamme, Robert, "Biltmore: Capitalism at Work," *Greensboro News & Record*, December 28, 1998, p. A1.

Lione, Louise, "Biltmore, in 190 Years, Family Has Learned to Make Profit from Experience," *Charlotte Observer*, December 22, 1985, p. 1E.

Miller, Mary E., "Thirty Years Ago, Bill Cecil Fought to Save the Majestic Biltmore House," *News & Observer*, August 16, 1992, p. E1.

Myerson, Allen R., "William Amherst Vanderbilt Cecil; Opening His Door to 700,000 Visitors," *New York Times*, December 13, 1992.

Nowell, Paul, "Biltmore Gets Ritzy New Inn," *Durham (NC) Herald-Sun*, March 14, 2001, p. B1.

Patterson, Donald W., "Biltmore's Visionary Still a Mystery," *Greensboro News & Record*, October 8, 1995, p. D1.

Bose Corporation

The Mountain
Framingham, Massachusetts 01701-9168
U.S.A.
Telephone: (508) 879-7330
Toll Free: (800) 999-2673
Fax: (508) 872-6541
Web site: http://www.bose.com

Private Company
Founded: 1964
Employees: 8,000
Sales: $1.8 billion (2009 est.)
NAICS: 334310 Audio and Video Equipment Manufacturing; 443112 Radio, Television, and Other Electronics Stores; 334220 Radio and Television Broadcasting and Wireless Communications Equipment Manufacturing; 336399 All Other Motor Vehicle Parts Manufacturing

∎ ∎ ∎

Bose Corporation is one of the world's largest manufacturers of speakers for the automotive and home entertainment markets. The company also serves the professional market, designing and selling loudspeakers, amplifiers, and other equipment for musicians. For the home entertainment market, Bose sells a full line of equipment ranging from the $299 SoundDock Digital Music System to the $3,299 Lifestyle V-Class Home Entertainment System. For the automotive market, the company makes complete car stereo systems, including a suspension system that uses a linear electromagnetic mo-

tor to provide a smoother ride. Bose sell its products through affiliated retailers and through more than 100 factory and showcase stores. The company maintains operations in North America, Europe, Australia, Asia, and South America.

ORIGINS

Bose Corporation's founder, Dr. Amar G. Bose, was born in 1929 to a political refugee from India and his wife, a Philadelphia schoolteacher. Bose would later suggest, in an interview in *USA Today*, that defending himself as a young boy in a racially prejudiced nation equipped him with the fighting spirit important to his success. When his father's import business suffered during World War II, the teenaged Amar Bose persuaded his father to begin a radio repair facility in the family business. There, the self-taught Amar did the repair work. Following this early experience in the electronics field, Bose attended the Massachusetts Institute of Technology (MIT), where he earned a doctoral degree in electrical engineering in 1956.

Bose Corporation arose in part from Dr. Bose's dissatisfaction when he attempted to buy speakers for his home stereo system in 1956. As an engineer, he had expected that laboratory measurements would indicate sound quality. To his dismay, however, he realized that measured sound and perceived sound differed. Dr. Bose directed his research efforts into psychoacoustics, the study of sound as humans perceive it, and psychophysics, the study of the relationship between measurement and perception. His research led to numerous patents and the creation of Bose Corporation in 1964 to develop and market products using those patents. Despite the later financial success of his company, Dr. Bose, professor of electrical engineering and computer science, remained on the staff at MIT, teaching acoustics and mentoring undergraduate and graduate thesis students.

Bose started his company at the suggestion of MIT professor Y. W. Lee, who provided Bose with $10,000 in start-up capital. That investment would later be worth an estimated $250,000, when the company repurchased Lee's stock in 1972. So that he could continue his teaching career, Bose hired one of his students, Sherwin Greenblatt, to help develop and market a product. During their first year of business, according to a company publication, Greenblatt was the company's only employee, and "Bose, who was [still] teaching, was paying Greenblatt more than he, himself, was earning as a professor at MIT." Greenblatt would later become president of the company.

A TECHNOLOGICAL
BREAKTHROUGH: 1968

Bose produced its first 901 direct/reflecting loudspeaker in 1968, and its first customers were secured through contracts with the military and NASA. The 901 was based on Bose's earlier research, which indicated that in excess of 80 percent of what audiences heard at a concert, for example, was reflected sound. Sound bouncing off walls, floors, and ceilings apparently contributed to the quality of the listening experience. Bose determined that his disappointment in speakers then on the market resulted from the fact that speakers directed sound only straight forward. To achieve a better spatial distribution of sound, therefore, Bose developed the

901, which aimed eight of the nine transducers in the speaker to the rear of the speaker where the sound could bounce before it reached the listener. The 901 employed an active equalizer to allow the speaker to reproduce the audio spectrum.

Bose's 901 series was not an immediate success. *Consumer Reports* dismissed the product in 1970, alleging that "individual instruments heard through the 901 ... tended to wander about the room." Wounded by such criticism, Dr. Bose filed a lawsuit against the magazine, claiming that it had unfairly disparaged his speaker system. Litigation continued for nearly 13 years, and although Dr. Bose ultimately lost his case at the U.S. Supreme Court level in 1983, the 901 series had long since gained a reputation as one of the finer products on the market.

Critical to Bose's success was the company philosophy, itself a reflection of its founder. Company literature stated: "Bose believes that audio products exist to provide music for everyone, everywhere—that music, not equipment, is the ultimate benefit. The Bose goal is to create products that combine high technology with simplicity and small size, to create the best possible sound systems that are easy to use and accessible to all consumers."

From the beginning, Bose directed all profits back into research and development, avowing a greater interest in producing excellent speakers than in money, and keeping his company privately held, and therefore not responsible to stockholders. Dr. Bose and company officials also stressed the importance of creativity at the company. In *Operations* magazine, for example, Greenblatt stated "Our challenge is to prod people into being innovative and using their creativity to do something that's better. In the long run, this is the source of sustainable advantage over our competition."

Since its introduction in 1968, the 901 speaker series underwent several revisions in which sound quality was improved and the speakers were made suitable for the digital age. Bose also applied the direct/reflecting concept to lower priced speakers in the company line and began marketing speakers to the general public for use in home stereo systems.

CAR STEREOS AND JAPANESE
EXPANSION: 1971–79

In 1972 Bose Corporation began selling loudspeakers for professional musicians. Later in the decade, Dr. Bose became interested in developing sound reproduction systems for automobiles, having noted that consumers, dissatisfied with the stereo equipment then standard in U.S. cars, were purchasing Japanese systems for

KEY DATES

1964: Amar G. Bose founds Bose Corporation.
1972: Bose begins selling loudspeakers for professional musicians.
1984: Acoustic Wave Music System is introduced.
1990: Lifestyle speaker systems are introduced.
1993: Bose Wave radio makes its debut.
2004: Bose collaborates with Apple to develop the SoundDock Digital Music System.
2010: Bose introduces the Lifestyle V-Class and T-Class home entertainment systems.

installation. The project seemed to present particular challenges given the glass, upholstery, and plastic surfaces in a car's interior. Bose, however, was optimistic, later recalling in a 1990 *Electronic Business* article: "I thought I could actually create better sound in a car than in a room, [since] we can control where the sound goes in a car."

Bose's auto sound system ideas were presented to General Motors Corporation (GM) in 1979, and a verbal agreement was reached between Dr. Bose and Edward Czapor, GM's Delco Electronics president, which resulted in four years of Bose research at an estimated $13 million to adapt car audio systems to the acoustic environment of the automobile. At the conclusion of the successful research, Bose formed a joint venture with GM to design and manufacture car audio systems for certain Cadillac, Buick, and Oldsmobile models.

Although initially slow to realize profits, Bose's car stereos and the Original Equipment Manufacturer (OEM) division they necessitated at the company, eventually became highly successful, leading to Bose partnerships with Honda, Acura, Nissan, Infiniti, Audi, Mercedes Benz, and Mazda. In many cases, Bose was able to design products not only for a specific model of car but also for specific options packages offered by the automakers. Bose was even able to meet Honda's requirement that product failure rate not exceed 30 parts per million, an exacting standard. By 1995, Bose's car audio systems represented about one-fourth of its total sales.

Also in the 1970s, Bose began efforts to introduce its products to the Japanese consumer audio market, an effort begun with much frustration. Bose's initial efforts in the Japanese market were failures and the company lost money its first eight years in Japan. Then, Dr. Bose

recognized the problem as one in which Bose market representatives had neglected to establish close personal relationships with Japanese distributors. Bose decided to hire a native Japanese to head the company's sales efforts in Japan. After interviewing several unsuitable U.S. candidates, Bose made a few trips to Japan, during which he established social and business contacts. Eventually he hired someone who would have great success introducing Bose products to Japan and would later become a vice president in the corporation.

ACOUSTIC WAVEGUIDE AND OTHER INNOVATIONS: 1984–89

Further Bose innovations involved acoustic waveguide technology, through which Bose engineers eventually developed smaller, portable speakers and sound systems capable of producing "big sound." Specifically, acoustic waveguide technology showed that bass notes could be reproduced through a small tube or pipe, similar to that employed in a pipe organ, instead of the much larger "moving cones" used by traditional stereo manufacturers. Amplifying the bass notes via an 80-inch tube folded into less than one cubic foot of space, Bose's Acoustic Wave Music System was introduced in 1984. The stereo system won praise for its compact, simple design as well as sound that many reviewers found rivaled that of larger and more costly stereo speakers and components.

In 1985 Bose began investigating the market for its products in television. As he had with GM, Dr. Bose approached a major television manufacturer, Zenith Electronics Corporation, and proposed that his engineers design a sound system, incorporating their acoustic waveguide technology to produce high-fidelity sound in Zenith televisions. Zenith agreed, and the two companies entered into a joint venture that resulted in the deluxe Zenith/Bose television, a set that featured rich sound, and that, since its tube was folded inside, was only about an inch larger than Zenith's earlier 27-inch screen model.

Company innovation continued in 1986 with the introduction of Acoustimass speaker technology. Proving that bigger is not always better, the line featured compact yet high-quality speakers, some of which were so small they could fit in the palm of one's hand.

During the late 1980s, Bose introduced its Acoustic Noise Canceling headset, a sealed headset designed to cancel out unwanted sound. Remarking on the need for the headset, one writer for *New Scientist* magazine quoted Dr. Bose: "The US government pays out $200 million a year in compensation for hearing loss caused by military service. ... Hearing loss is a common reason for early retirement of pilots, second only to psychological stress." The headset proved valuable in military use, particularly among pilots and tank drivers. The headset also had civilian applications and could be used by small aircraft and helicopter pilots. Bose donated two of these headsets to Dick Rutan and Jeana Yeager, who piloted their light plane the *Voyager* on a nonstop around the world flight in 1986. Moreover, the technology Bose developed could be tailored to cancel out noise in several environments, such as airline passenger compartments or city streets.

By 1989 Bose's sales were estimated at $300 million, a figure that some analysts suggested was conservative. At the same time, nearly half of Bose's sales were derived from foreign markets; indeed, Bose speakers were outselling all other brands in Japan, including those of the Japanese manufacturers. The early 1990s saw steady gains for Bose, with net revenues increasing to $424 million by 1992.

NEW TECHNOLOGIES: 1992–94

The acoustiwave technology in Bose speakers and stereo systems made Bose products popular in the 1990s at concerts, theaters, and nightclubs. A Bose loudspeaker was even used at the 1992 Winter Olympics in Albertville, France. On the consumer front, the decade began with the introduction of a new line of speaker systems called Lifestyle. Featuring an integrated design, the Lifestyle system provided high-quality sound while offering ease of use for both home music systems and the burgeoning market for home theater systems.

In 1993 consumers were introduced to the Bose Wave radio, a small remote-controlled clock radio suited for use in the home. The Wave boasted rich, full sound not found in other portable radios and could also be hooked up to a television or CD player, enhancing the sound capabilities of the user's existing stereo components. Expensive for a radio and featuring an unusual design, the Wave befuddled retailers, leading the company to sell the product directly to consumers via direct mail and newspaper and magazine advertisements. It went on to be a huge success. By 1998 the company was able to boast sales of 200,000 Waves in a single year.

At its manufacturing facilities, Bose became a subscriber to the total quality management concept (TQM) introduced by W. Edwards Deming. Toward that end, Bose assembly line workers were cross-trained and promoted based on performance. Moreover, Bose sought to build teams based upon mutual trust and respect, operating according to principles of responsibility and quality consciousness. Describing the company's

management style in a 1993 *Production* article, Bose's vice president of manufacturing, Tom Beeson, asserted: "Communicate. Spend a lot of time on the factory floor. Micromanage every aspect. Involve all of the people. Foolproof the system so mistakes can't be made. Find the root cause of problems. Operate manufacturing with the fundamental principle: Do it right the first time."

In 1994 Bose unveiled the Auditioner audio demonstrator, a computer system that enabled builders, architects, and facility managers to hear the acoustics of a building's proposed sound system, working from as little input as the building's blueprints. This technology was under development for 10 years, and became reality only after computer technology caught up with the imagination of Bose engineers.

PHYSICAL EXPANSION: 1995–99

The mid-1990s also saw Bose undertake a $150 million expansion of its corporate headquarters in Framingham, Massachusetts, known as The Mountain for its commanding view of the countryside. The expansion included construction of a new six-story, all-glass-facade, ultramodern headquarters building, which had room for 800 employees and was completed in 1997. At the same time, the company phased out its factory in nearby Westboro, Massachusetts, citing the high cost of manufacturing in that state. (The company did continue to maintain a small manufacturing operation at the Framingham campus.) The production at Westboro was transferred to facilities in Hillsdale, Michigan, and Columbia, South Carolina. By the late 1990s, Bose had eight manufacturing sites, including the three aforementioned along with sites in Yuma, Arizona; Sainte Marie, Quebec, Canada; San Luis Rio Colorado and Tijuana, Mexico; and Carrickmacross, Ireland.

Starting with the company's long legal battle with *Consumer Reports*, Bose gained a reputation for litigiousness. In the mid- to late 1990s the company was involved in a number of lawsuits with Cambridge SoundWorks, Inc. (CSW), which was based in nearby Newton, Massachusetts. In 1994 Bose sued CSW after the latter claimed that its speakers were "better than Bose at half the price." After that suit was settled, Bose soon filed another lawsuit against CSW alleging patent violations. In early 1999 CSW filed a countersuit alleging that Bose had made false advertising claims when it stated that its Wave radio was the best reviewed product of its kind on the market.

Other developments in the late 1990s included the expansion of the company's car audio business in 1998 to include more popular and lower-priced vehicles, such as the Chevrolet Blazer and the Oldsmobile Intrigue; the launch of online sales of Bose products at the company Web site the following year; and the introduction of a new version of the Wave radio that included a built-in CD player. According to research firm NPD, the Bose brand at decade's end was the number one speaker brand in the United States, with a market share of 20 percent, while the company's closest rival, Harman International Industries, Inc., claimed only 13 percent with its two top brands, JBL and Infinity, combined. Bose also held the number one position worldwide in speakers, with a 25 percent share of that market. For the fiscal year ending in March 1999, Bose had estimated operating profits of $170 million on sales of nearly $1 billion. The company reported its sales for the following year at more than $1.1 billion.

NEW PRODUCT
INTRODUCTIONS: 2004–10

Bose entered the 21st century occupying an enviable position. The company's brand strength held it aloft, putting it in rarified air. A survey by Forrester Research conducted midway through the decade found Bose to be the most trusted consumer brand in the country, beating out 22 marquee brands such as Apple, Dell, Intel, and Sony. An estimated 17.5 million households planned to buy Bose products, the survey revealed, by far eclipsing the seven million households planning to purchase Apple products.

Propped up by widespread esteem, Bose took advantage of the opportunity before it. Amar Bose remained at the helm, his tenure stretching into its fifth decade, and he continued to observe his practice of investing all of the company's profits into research and development projects. The financial commitment paid dividends, resulting in the release of new products that demonstrated the skill of Bose designers and engineers.

The company completed work on a decade-long project to develop a suspension system for automobiles to smooth a vehicle's ride, introducing a system that used a linear electromagnetic motor and power amplifiers at each wheel. Bose released the SoundDock Digital Music System in 2004 after collaborating with Apple. In 2009 the company introduced SoundLink, a wireless music system that streamed music from a personal computer's music library to wireless speakers. In 2010 Bose unveiled the Lifestyle V-Class and T-Class home theater systems, high-end products that offered consumers a comprehensive system for managing and playing all formats of entertainment content.

Bose neared its 50th anniversary holding sway as a prestigious market leader. One uncertainty facing the company in the years ahead was the inevitable prospect of conducting its business without the leadership of its founder. Amar Bose turned 80 years old in 2010. He still presided over the company but was nearing the end of his leadership tenure. Bose Corporation was expected to continue to shine after its founder's departure, however. The company's dominance appeared ensured given Amar Bose's legacy of a total commitment to research and development.

Terry W. Hughes
Updated, David E. Salamie; Jeffrey L. Covell

PRINCIPAL SUBSIDIARIES

Bose Gesellschaft mit Beschrankter Haftung (Germany); Bose Corporation India Private Limited; Bose Instal Kinga Koscinska (Poland); Bose Automotive GmbH (Germany); Bose SP Z.o.o. (Poland).

PRINCIPAL COMPETITORS

Cambridge SoundWorks, Inc.; Harman International Industries, Incorporated; Klipsch, LLC.

FURTHER READING

Beam, Alex, "Bose's High-Decibel Litigation," *Boston Globe*, May 14, 1999, p. C1.

"Bose Unveils New Lifestyle Home Entertainment Systems," *Wireless News*, May 27, 2010.

Bulkeley, William M., "Sound Program Lets User Mimic Site's Acoustics," *Wall Street Journal*, October 19, 1994, p. B1.

Donker, Peter P., "Bose Corp. Unveils Its Latest Wave: New Corporate Center Dedicated," *Worcester (MA) Telegram and Gazette*, September 13, 1997, p. B8.

Hirsch, Julian, "Bose Lifestyle 12 Home Theater System," *Stereo Review*, March 1995, pp. 34–38.

Kharif, Olga, "Selling Sound: Bose Knows," *Business Week Online*, May 15, 2006.

Kiley, David, "Can Bose Tame Rhythms of the Road?" *Business Week Online*, July 23, 2004.

La Franco, Robert, "Loudspeaker Envy," *Forbes*, August 9, 1999, p. 68.

Lander, Kathleen, "HPR Interview: Amar Bose," *HPR: High Performance Review*, June 2, 1994, pp. 51–53.

Vasilash, Gary, "Bose Manufacturing Audiophiles Extraordinaire," *Production*, September 1993, pp. 64–67.

"Vox Populi," *Economist*, January 15, 2000, p. 71.

Wallack, Todd, "It's a Sound Strategy: Bose Knows Investment in Research Pays Off," *Boston Herald*, June 21, 1999, p. 27.

Bradley Corporation

W142 N9101 Fountain Boulevard
Menomonee Falls, Wisconsin 53051
U.S.A.
Telephone: (262) 251-6000
Toll Free: (800) 272-3537
Fax: (262) 251-5817
Web site: http://www.bradleycorp.com

Private Company
Incorporated: 1921 as Bradley Washfountain Company
Employees: 600
NAICS: 332913 Plumbing Fixture Fitting and Trim
   Manufacturing

■ ■ ■

Family owned and managed, Bradley Corporation is a major manufacturer of commercial plumbing fixtures and washroom accessories. The company also sells washroom partitions and solid plastic locker systems. Bradley maintains its headquarters in Menomonee Falls, Wisconsin, which is also the home of the fixture division. The washroom accessories division is located in a plant in Milwaukee; partitions are produced in a facility in Upper Sandusky, Ohio; and partitions and lockers are manufactured in a Marion, Ohio, plant. In addition, Bradley operates a distribution facility in Ontario, California, to serve the western United States. Inventory centers are maintained in Atlanta, Houston, and Kansas City. Bradley products are also distributed in Canada and about 140 other countries. Bradley is owned and

led by the fourth and fifth generations of the Mullett family.

INVENTION OF WASHFOUNTAIN: 1917

The man behind the Bradley name, Harry Bradley, was never directly involved in the Bradley Corporation. Rather, he invented the product on which the company was built: the washfountain. Bradley, along with his brother Lynde Bradley and financial backer Dr. Stanton Allen, had founded a company called the Compression Rheostate Company in 1903. Six years later it moved to Milwaukee and was renamed the Allen-Bradley Company. The manufacturer enjoyed strong growth but by 1917 Harry Bradley became frustrated with how much time and shop space was being lost to the simple task of the employees washing their hands. Banks of sinks took up an excessive amount of space and still required employees to line up to use them.

A man at home in the shop, Bradley sought a solution to the problem and in 1918 he developed a prototype for a "washfountain," a large circular basin with multiple streams of water that allowed several people to simultaneously wash their hands. He built and installed a few of the fixtures for his employees and patented the idea in 1919, but he had no interest in manufacturing washfountains. He instead sold the rights to Louis Schlesinger.

In August 1921, Schlesinger formed a company to manufacture and sell the washfountain with partners Gustav Grossenbach and Howard A. Mullett. An insurance executive, Grossenbach was Mullett's father-in-law.

For a corporate name they chose Bradley Washfountain Company. Schlesinger served as the company's initial president. In the first year, Bradley sold 15 washfountains. That number increased to 94 units in 1922. The units were hand operated, but improvements soon followed. The first foot-operated models were introduced in 1925, as was the first semicircular design.

MULLETT BUYS OUT PARTNER: 1928

Schlesinger served as president until 1928, when Mullett bought him out and took charge of the company. Born in Louisville, Kentucky, in 1880, Mullett was mostly raised in Kansas City, Missouri. He earned a degree in electrical engineering in 1904 from the Rose Polytechnic Institute in Terre Haute, Indiana, and furthered his education by completing the student course at Westinghouse Manufacturing Company in Pittsburgh, Pennsylvania. He came to Milwaukee in 1906 to take a position with Milwaukee Electric Railway & Light Company and three years later married Grossenbach's daughter, Lydia. Although a partner in Bradley Corporation, he moved to Chicago in 1925 to become vice president of Yellow Cab Co., followed by a stint as president of Minneapolis Street Car Co. He returned to Milwaukee to become secretary for Bradley and a short time later bought out Schlesinger, and took over as general manager and president.

Bradley continued to grow under Mullett. The washfountains were redesigned in the early 1930s. The original units sprayed water upward from the base, but all too often users were soaked by water surges. To correct this problem, the new washfountains employed a downward-pointing sprayhead. The early units were also single pieces. To make them easier to ship and install they were redesigned as two-piece units in the 1930s. Bradley also added a new product, introducing its first group shower fixture in 1931. The first column shower followed in 1940.

Howard Mullett served as Bradley's president until his death in February 1942 at the age of 61. The *Milwaukee Journal* reported that he "was found dead of carbon monoxide poisoning Friday in the garage in the rear of his home," but offered no further explanation.

He was succeeded as president by Elizabeth S. Wetherell, one of Milwaukee's first women executives. She was well familiar with the operation, having originally been hired by Schlesinger as a stenographer when he was president. She was actually only looking for part-time work, primarily to keep her occupied while her husband, a civil engineer, was away on assignment for a Milwaukee road contractor. She turned down Schlesinger's offer of a full-time job before finally relenting. After his departure, she stayed on at Bradley as a secretary but carved out an important role in sales by serving as the home office contact for the manufacturers' agents who sold the Bradley products. She became so knowledgeable about the company and its products that she was named vice president in 1941 and deemed the best person to succeed Mullett as president.

SECOND MULLETT TAKES CHARGE: 1953

Howard A. Mullett's son, Howard G. Mullett, was also employed by Bradley and became Wetherell's vice president. Only when she retired at the end of 1953, after 29 years with the company, did he become the second member of the Mullett family to assume the presidency. Under his leadership, Bradley moved to Menomonee Falls, where in 1964 the company opened a new 117,000-square-foot factory and office building, twice the size of the old Milwaukee site. The company also maintained plants in Moorestown, New Jersey; Ogden, Utah; and Plano and Somonauk, Illinois. The extra production capacity allowed the company to further diversify its product offerings into faucets, vanity tops, and washroom accessories. To reflect this shift, Bradley Washfountain changed its name in 1972 to Bradley Corporation.

The early 1970s proved to be a challenging time for Bradley. Its washfountains were being removed by architectural clients, primarily in California, because handicapped users were unable to trigger the footpedals. As a result, Bradley designed a new series of "barrier-free" bathroom devices. Later, when other parts of the country followed California's lead and became more responsive to the needs of the handicapped, Bradley held an advantage over its competitors. Bradley developed another product line during this period. In 1972 it introduced its first bright yellow safety shower and eyewash units. Other emergency fixtures designed to meet specific safety needs would follow in the years to come.

By 1980 Howard G. Mullett's son, Donald Mullett, had become president of Bradley and would eventually succeed John L. Palmer as chairman and chief executive officer. The company also entered another difficult

KEY DATES

1921: Bradley Washfountain Company is founded in Milwaukee.

1928: Howard A. Mullett buys out partner to become president.

1964: Company moves to new headquarters in Menomonee Falls.

1972: Bradley Corporation name is adopted.

2010: Fifth generation of Mullett family ascends to presidency.

period due to poor economic conditions, forcing Bradley to seek out new opportunities. In the early 1980s Bradley began producing a washing system for Middle Eastern Muslims, who were required to wash their hands and feet before prayer. To deal with the scarcity of water, Bradley designed a mosque washing system that made use of an "ablution panel," which used a metered faucet to dispense a requisite amount of water to the worshiper.

BRADLEY ENTERS PRISON MARKET: 1987

Bradley found a plentiful source of revenues in the United States in the correctional institution market. In 1982 it acquired the patents, engineering data, tooling, and inventory of a California company and began producing security plumbing fixtures and related equipment. The lavatories and waterclosets produced for this market also included metered faucets that supplied a measured amount of water and provided guards with greater control of inmates. Annual revenues for Bradley at this stage were reported to be more than $25 million.

To keep pace with customer demand, Bradley constructed a 120,000-square-foot addition to its Menomonee Falls facility. In 1990 the company introduced its plastic locker concept. Bradley also began to focus on light commercial washroom products. This work led to the 1993 introduction of the Express Lavatory System, an adjustable setup that consolidated space and was ideal for schools, cinemas, and other locations. While Bradley invested heavily in research and development, it also added to its capabilities through acquisitions.

In late 1997 Bradley acquired Upper Sandusky, Ohio-based Mills Co., maker of public restroom partitions. The following year Bradley acquired Lenoxville, Pennsylvania-based Lenox Locker Company, which produced plastic lockers for washrooms, athletic facili-

ties, airports, and amusement parks. The addition of the products of these acquired companies helped Bradley to become more of a one-stop shop for commercial washroom customers. The 1990s also brought a fifth generation of the Mullett family. Donald Mullett's son, Bryan Mullett, joined the company in 1997 and would be joined by brothers Erik and Christopher.

The new century saw more innovative products from Bradley as well as improvements to the manufacturing process, as the company embraced lean manufacturing techniques. In 2003 Bradley introduced the multi-height lavatory system. The OneStep bottled eyewash system followed a year later. With the rising cost of energy, Bradley developed ndite technology, which led to the 2005 introduction of the first lavatory system to be powered by room lighting. It employed photovoltaic cells in the top of the Express Lavatory System that turned normal restroom lighting into electricity, which in turn powered the sensors and valves of the handwashing stations. As a result, these advanced systems were easy to install, and were more environmentally friendly because they did not make use of batteries that in time would have to be discarded.

INTRODUCTION OF ADVOCATE LAVATORY SYSTEM: 2009

In 2008 Bradley introduced the first adjustable-speed hand dryer in the United States. The different speed settings allowed facility managers to use fast-drying settings that were beneficial in high-traffic conditions such as schools, sports centers, and amusement parks. In libraries, museums, and other venues where quiet operations are more appropriate, the managers could select a slower, quieter setting. In addition, the new Aerix hand dryer used much less electricity than other popular units on the market. In 2009 Bradley incorporated many of its advances to create the Advocate Lavatory system that placed water, soap, and hand drying capabilities within a user's individual space.

Bradley did not generally reveal annual sales figures. According to *BizTimes Milwaukee,* however, the company posted revenues of $113 million in 2005. It was a number that was certain to increase in the years to come, especially with Bradley's growing success in overseas markets. In 2010 the company was named Exporter of the Year by ThinkGlobal Inc., publisher of *Commercial News USA,* a magazine published by the U.S. Commerce Department. Also in 2010, Bryan Mullett was named president of the company, the fifth generation of his family to hold that post. With two other brothers committed to family ownership, the future of Bradley Corporation appeared secure.

Ed Dinger

PRINCIPAL SUBSIDIARIES

Bradley's Government Sales Division; Bradley—Washroom Accessories Division; Bradley—Mills Partitions; Bradley—Lenox Lockers/Mills Partitions.

PRINCIPAL COMPETITORS

Grohe AG; Moen Incorporated; Price Pfister, Inc.

FURTHER READING

Decker, Eric, "Bathing in Blue Oceans," *BizTimes Milwaukee,* April 14, 2006.

History of Milwaukee, Chicago and Milwaukee: The S.J. Clarke Publishing Company, 1922.

"Lady President Retires in Fountain of Praise," *Milwaukee Sentinel,* December 24, 1953, p. 18.

Lank, Avrum D., "Jails May Hold the Key to Bradley's Future," *Milwaukee Sentinel,* December 7, 1982, p. 48.

Martin, Mary Jo, "Bradley Corp. Is Committed to Green Manufacturing and Products," *Wholesaler,* March 2009.

"Mullett Rites Set Monday," *Milwaukee Journal,* February 28, 1942, p. 8.

"Officers Trace Half Century of Falls Firm," *Milwaukee Sentinel,* October 25, 1971, p. 20.

BRIDGESTONE

Bridgestone Corporation

1-10-1 Kyobashi
Chuo-ku
Tokyo, 104-8340
Japan
Telephone: (+81-3) 3563-6811
Fax: (+81-3) 3567-4615
Web site: http://www.bridgestone.co.jp

Public Company
Incorporated: 1931 as Bridgestone Ltd.
Employees: 137,135
Sales: ¥2.6 trillion ($28.2 billion) (2009)
Stock Exchanges: Tokyo Nagoya Osaka Fukuoka
Ticker Symbol: 5108
NAICS: 326211 Tire Manufacturing (Except Retreading); 314992 Tire Cord and Tire Fabric Mills; 325182 Carbon Black Manufacturing; 325212 Synthetic Rubber Manufacturing; 326212 Tire Retreading; 326220 Rubber and Plastics Hoses and Belting Manufacturing; 326291 Rubber Product Manufacturing for Mechanical Use; 336399 All Other Motor Vehicle Parts Manufacturing; 336991 Motorcycle, Bicycle, and Parts Manufacturing; 339920 Sporting and Athletic Goods Manufacturing; 441320 Tire Dealers

∎ ∎ ∎

Bridgestone Corporation is the world's leading manufacturer of tires and is led by its flagship Bridgestone and Firestone brands. In addition to its core tire manufacturing operations, which generate about 80 percent of overall sales, Bridgestone makes the raw materials that go into tires and maintains an extensive network of company-owned tire retail outlets, including about 2,200 in the United States and several hundred in Japan. The company's tires are also sold through thousands of independent retailers operating in more than 150 countries around the world.

Nontire products, which account for about 20 percent of sales, include automotive components, particularly vibration- and noise-isolating parts; industrial products, such as polyurethane foam, conveyor belts, and rubber tracks for crawler tractors; construction and civil engineering materials; sporting goods, including golf balls and clubs; and bicycles. Bridgestone products are made within about 75 tire manufacturing and retreading plants and around 110 nontire plants on six continents. Geographically, sales break down as follows: 43 percent from North and South America, 26 percent from Japan, 14 percent from Europe, and the remaining 17 percent from elsewhere (Africa and the Asia-Pacific region outside of Japan).

ORIGINS OF PIONEERING JAPANESE TIRE MAKER

Bridgestone was founded by Shojiro Ishibashi, whose name means "stone bridge." Prior to founding the company, Ishibashi, along with his brother, had led the family clothing business, which produced *tabi*, Japanese workers' footwear. Ishibashi made a fortune by adding rubber soles. Deciding that his future lay in the rubber business, he began intensive research and development in 1929, founding Bridgestone Ltd. two years later in

Kurume, Japan, as the first local tire supplier for the nascent Japanese automotive industry. Headquarters were moved to Tokyo in 1937. In 1942 the company changed its name to Nippon Tire Co., Ltd., but was renamed Bridgestone Tire Co., Ltd., in 1951 and became Bridgestone Corporation in 1984.

Ishibashi was an aggressive businessman with strong marketing skills whose main business principle was to expand during recessionary periods. He also thrived on business connections made through his children's marriages. It was said in Japan that his family connections to government officials allowed Bridgestone to secure orders during the Korean War of the 1950s, helping the company to gain its strong position in the domestic market. Meantime, production of nontire products began early on, with golf balls added to the portfolio in the 1930s and bicycles in 1946.

Before World War II, Bridgestone's business, like that of other major Japanese industrial concerns, was focused on supplying military requirements. At the same time, Bridgestone tires also supplied the growing Japanese automobile industry. Production was based at two plants, one in Kurume, the other in Yokohama. Growth after the war was rapid, with the establishment of four new production facilities in the 1960s and six during the 1970s. Bridgestone's first overseas factory was established in Singapore in 1963, with further factories built in Thailand in 1967 and Indonesia in 1973. Bridgestone Singapore ceased operations in 1980 following the Singapore government's lifting of tariff protection for locally made tires. In 1976 Bridgestone set up a sales company in Hamburg, Germany, in partnership with Mitsui. This new company, named Bridgestone Reifen G.m.b.H., was intended to increase tire sales in the important West German market. In 1990 Bridgestone set up a new subsidiary in London, Bridgestone Industrial, to handle industrial rubber products throughout Europe.

EXPANSION VIA ACQUISITIONS

Since the 1980s Bridgestone's most significant expansion occurred by acquisition, acquiring majority interests in Uniroyal Holdings Ltd. (UHL), the South Australian tire manufacturer, in 1980 and a Taiwanese company in 1986. In 1983 Bridgestone gained its first U.S. production base by purchasing a plant in LaVergne, Tennessee, belonging to the Firestone Tire & Rubber Company. This proved to be the first step toward Bridgestone's acquisition of that U.S. company in 1988, for a total of $2.65 billion.

Before acquiring Firestone, Bridgestone had first approached Goodyear in 1987, with proposals for a merger that would have created the world's largest tire manufacturer. Talks in Hawaii, however, failed to reach agreement as Bridgestone would not accept the high value that Goodyear had placed on its loss-making Trans-American oil pipeline. Bridgestone then turned to Firestone as a U.S. production base for the manufacture of heavy-duty radial truck tires. They were encouraged in this by the acquisition of an ailing Firestone plant in LaVergne, in 1983, which Bridgestone had turned into a success. Bridgestone originally agreed to buy Firestone's tire operations for $1.25 billion. However, Italian manufacturer Pirelli intervened with a rival bid, forcing the Japanese company to increase the offer. Bridgestone finally paid $2.65 billion for the whole company, with 54,000 employees and two headquarters, in 1988. The following year Bridgestone's North American operations were integrated with those of Firestone under the Bridgestone/Firestone, Inc., subsidiary. One year later, Bridgestone/Firestone Europe S.A. was created to manage European operations.

The Firestone deal gave Bridgestone its sought-after foothold in the United States and strengthened its posias wheels, as well as tires. The 200th Cockpit shop opened in the spring of 1990.

KEY DATES

1931: Shojiro Ishibashi founds Bridgestone Ltd. in Kurume, Japan, as the first local tire supplier for the nascent Japanese automotive industry.
1937: Headquarters are relocated to Tokyo.
1942: Company's name is changed to Nippon Tire Co., Ltd.
1951: Company is renamed Bridgestone Tire Co., Ltd.
1983: Bridgestone gains a U.S. production base through the purchase of a plant in LaVergne, Tennessee, belonging to the Firestone Tire & Rubber Company.
1984: Bridgestone Corporation is adopted as the new company name.
1988: Bridgestone acquires Firestone for $2.65 billion.
1994: Long and bitter strike begins at five Bridgestone/Firestone plants in the United States.
2000: Spate of rollover accidents, some fatal, involving Firestone tires and Ford Explorer vehicles leads to the recall of 6.5 million Firestone tires.
2007: Through a U.S. unit, Bridgestone acquires Bandag, Incorporated, a major global player in the retread tire sector.

MAJOR MODERNIZATION PROGRAM

Within six months of the Firestone purchase, Bridgestone announced a $1.5 billion modernization program. Firestone's auxiliary head office in Chicago and Bridgestone's own U.S. base in Nashville were closed to concentrate operations in Akron, and Firestone's management was reduced through a voluntary early retirement scheme. The investment in Firestone coincided with a slowdown in North American and European car production, however, heralding a period of much tougher competition in tire markets. The renovation of Firestone turned out to be more expensive and time-consuming than expected.

Other problems included weak markets in Latin America and the Middle East and intense competition in European markets. Fortunately for Bridgestone, not all of the massive investment came from borrowings but in part from Bridgestone's hidden assets, including land, buildings, and securities, purchases made decades earlier. Company founder Ishibashi had also invested heavily in art, mostly Western, opening the Bridgestone Museum of Art in 1952.

Bridgestone continued to retain its position in Asia, where Bridgestone and Firestone brands maintained the largest share of the market. This region promised to display rapid growth in the world's tire markets over the next decade, and Bridgestone was positioned to remain in a strong position to capitalize on this with local production operations and large market shares, particularly in Thailand, Indonesia, and Taiwan.

NONTIRE ACTIVITIES

Bridgestone's production, however, was not limited to tires. Its technical research and development laboratories worked on the development of rubber and nonrubber items. Rubber technology featured prominently with such items as conveyor belts, inflatable rubber dams, and marine fenders. Multi-rubber bearings were produced for use in the construction of buildings in areas prone to earthquakes as the rubber element in the construction enabled the buildings to vibrate with the earth's movement. Bridgestone's other innovative ideas included rubber "muscles" for robots and grease-free conveyor belts. Bridgestone became a Japanese leader in vibration-isolating components for automobiles and through Bridgestone/Firestone gained a large share of the North American market for rubberized roofing

tion in Europe, as Firestone also owned plants in Portugal, Spain, France, and Italy. In addition, it gave Bridgestone instant access to high-quality manufacturing facilities, with an extensive national marketing system for replacement tires, as well as large research and development laboratories. The Firestone name and sales network gave the Japanese company access to Detroit carmakers for original equipment sales and for the sale of Firestone brand tires for the two million cars a year produced by Japanese automobile firms.

In North America, Bridgestone's sales in the replacement market were through independent dealers and through their MasterCare network of more than 1,500 tire and service centers. These independent dealers also strengthened sales in the United States and Canada, and the company's marketing strategy widened further in the early 1990s through mass merchandisers such as Sears and Kmart. Another highlight of its international sales network was the chain of Cockpit retail outlets, which offered car audio equipment and accessories such

materials. It was also a major supplier in the United States of air springs for trucks, automobiles, trailers, and other vehicles.

In 1988 Bridgestone Cycle Co., Ltd., gave cyclists the first opportunity to design their own machines. Cyclists were able to choose, from a list of standard parts, the shape, color, and materials for the frame, brakes, handlebars, and seat, to make their own unique "mix and match" bicycle. Bridgestone's advance in metallurgy made it possible to produce bicycles that were lighter than ever in weight. The Radac line of racing, touring, and recreational bicycles was introduced in 1990, with a model that featured the world's lightest frame, thanks to an aluminum-ceramic composite, the first ceramic material ever to be used on a bicycle. Non-rubber products included items from special batteries for electronic equipment to weighing systems for aircraft.

Bridgestone was also a leading supplier of golf balls and clubs, tennis rackets, and other sporting goods. The Bridgestone Sports Co., Ltd., was established in 1972 and subsequently won many awards, including one from the Japanese Ministry for International Trade and Industry for a line of windsurfing boards. In 1987 the company introduced the Science Eye system, which gave a high-speed photographic analysis of a golfer's swing, for use in department stores and professional shops. Bridgestone also operated swimming schools and health clubs.

Although Bridgestone Corporation entered the 1990s with the ability to compete on equal terms with the industry's two other giants, Goodyear of the United States and Michelin of France, its international expansion came late. Bridgestone had concentrated on the domestic market while other Japanese companies were developing production plants and overseas markets. Japanese customers bought whatever Bridgestone sold, which did little to encourage Bridgestone to develop new products. In addition, Bridgestone's production of radial tires came late by Western standards. Japanese manufacturers were reluctant to import European or American tires in the 1960s and 1970s, even though foreign tires were considered superior to Bridgestone's. These factors conspired to give the company a commanding share of the Japanese market, 46 percent in 1990, while exports were 50 percent.

DIFFICULTIES WITH U.S. OPERATIONS

By 1991, Bridgestone's acquisition of Firestone generally was being called a huge blunder. Bridgestone, not wishing to step on American toes, was slow to push for changes that were needed at a Firestone bloated with

bureaucracy. Bridgestone even waited until late 1991 to integrate the U.S. headquarters of Bridgestone and Firestone into one location (which turned out to be Nashville, not Akron, where Firestone had resided). Bridgestone also had difficulty with the size of its new foreign subsidiary, finding it hard to manage from Japan. Finally, in March 1991 Yoichiro Kaizaki, who spoke little English and had a background in the company's nontire operations, was sent to the United States to head Bridgestone/Firestone, the first Japanese person to do so. Meanwhile, Bridgestone/Firestone had lost $1 billion in the United States from 1990 to 1992. Bridgestone's profits consequently suffered, totaling only ¥4.5 billion in 1990 and ¥7.47 billion in 1991 before rebounding slightly to ¥28.4 billion in 1992.

Kaizaki immediately began to turn around the company's U.S. operations. In addition to consolidating headquarters in Nashville, he also tightened the management structure by setting up 21 operating divisions at Bridgestone/Firestone, each with its own president whose pay was tied to his or her division's performance. Money was pumped in from Japan to raise productivity at the plants and to improve the quality of the tires produced there. After two years of improving the U.S. operation, Kaizaki returned to Japan as president of Bridgestone Corporation. Kaizaki appointed Masatoshi Ono, a trusted lieutenant, to lead Bridgestone/Firestone.

Bridgestone executives believed that its U.S. plants would not be profitable until the wages of its workers were cut and the workers agreed to operate the plants 24 hours a day. With labor and management on a collision course, United Rubber Workers (URW) contracts with major tire makers expired in April 1994. Goodyear was chosen that year as the target company, and it reached an agreement in June with the URW. Bridgestone, however, refused to accept the "pattern" agreement.

The union rejected the company's contract proposal, and on July 12, more than 4,000 URW workers at five Bridgestone/Firestone plants went on strike. In January 1995 Bridgestone hired more than 2,000 permanent "replacement workers," bringing criticism from both Robert Reich, the U.S. secretary of labor, and President Bill Clinton and much negative publicity for Bridgestone/Firestone. In May the URW called off the 10-month-old strike, with the workers agreeing to return to work without a contract. Nevertheless, not all of the workers were rehired immediately. In July 1995 the URW was absorbed into the United Steelworkers of America.

In September 1996 Bridgestone/Firestone recalled almost all of the workers it had replaced, and a little more than a month later, in early November, a three-year agreement was reached, which both the Steelworkers and Bridgestone claimed as victory. Among the provisions favoring the workers were the 4.4 percent wage hike and the rehiring of all workers dismissed during the long conflict. Bridgestone won the key concession on operating the factories around the clock.

U.S.-STYLE RESTRUCTURING INITIATIVES

In the midst of this labor strife, Bridgestone/Firestone managed to turn a 1996 profit of $180 million in part because it had unilaterally imposed an around-the-clock schedule. Back in Japan, meanwhile, Kaizaki was trimming domestic operations to contain costs, cutting the workforce 14 percent from 1993 to 1996. The company was also in the midst of building new tire plants in central Europe and China, as well as a plant in India through a joint venture with Tata Industries. In addition, despite its difficulties in the United States, Bridgestone spent $430 million in 1997 and 1998 to upgrade existing U.S. plants and announced in mid-1997 that it would build its eighth U.S. tire factory, a $435 million plant scheduled to open in Aiken, South Carolina, in early 1999. The new factory would manufacture about 25,000 car and light-truck tires at its peak, and reach full employment of 800 workers by 2000. The company needed the new plants to satisfy the increasing demand for its tires. The U.S. plant was also designed specifically to reduce the need to import tires from Japan. Tire sales had increased nearly 19 percent in 1996, a year in which Bridgestone earned a record ¥70.34 billion ($645.28 million) on a record ¥1.96 trillion ($17.96 billion) in sales.

Despite slumping sales of automobiles in Japan and other Asian nations because of the Asian economic crisis of 1997–98, Bridgestone closed out the decade strongly. The results for 1998 set new records: ¥104.63 billion ($921 million) in profits on ¥2.24 trillion ($19.69 billion) in revenues. The company was aided by its more efficient and productive U.S. operations, which showed steadily increasing profits in the late 1990s, reaching $300 million by 1999. The balance sheet of the U.S. subsidiary was also bolstered through a 1999 infusion of cash from the parent company aimed at reining in Bridgestone/Firestone, Inc.'s $3 billion debt.

On the negative side, Kaizaki had received much criticism in Japan for his aggressive, U.S.-style restructuring initiatives, including the launch of an early retirement program in the early 1990s. Such moves were, in large part, still considered anathema in Japan. The criticism of Kaizaki came to a head in March 1999. That month a Bridgestone manager who had agreed to take early retirement went into Kaizaki's office to demand that the company's personnel policies be changed. When Kaizaki refused to change course, the manager took out a knife and committed harakiri. The resulting firestorm of negative publicity was only heightened by Kaizaki's failure to speak publicly about the incident for four months. When he did break his silence during a meeting with reporters, the company president came off as defiant and unfeeling.

SURVIVING A POTENTIALLY DEVASTATING TIRE RECALL

In mid-2000 Kaizaki found himself embroiled in another crisis when reports began surfacing of possible defects in several Firestone tire models. Some of the tires, many of which had been used as the original tires on Ford Explorer sport-utility vehicles, were shredding on the highway, leading to rollover accidents and more than 200 deaths and some 800 injuries, according to investigators with the U.S. National Highway Traffic Safety Administration. In August 2000 Bridgestone announced that its U.S. subsidiary would recall 6.5 million Firestone-brand ATX, ATX II, and Wilderness AT tires and replace them at the cost of hundreds of millions of dollars. Bridgestone's stock nosedived, and the company was once again hurt by missteps on the public relations front. Kaizaki, as he had in the prior crisis, maintained a long public silence over the issue, and Ono, the head of the U.S. subsidiary, made a belated public apology that was further marred by the suggestion that the drivers were to blame for the accidents because they had failed to keep their tires properly inflated.

Bridgestone gained control over the crisis soon after new executives were installed. In October 2000 Ono was replaced by John Lampe, who had been marketing chief for Bridgestone/Firestone. In early 2001 Shigeo Watanabe, a senior vice president, took over the helm at Bridgestone, replacing Kaizaki. One of Watanabe's key early moves was to give Lampe more authority to make autonomous decisions concerning the crisis without constantly needing to gain approval from the Tokyo headquarters.

As an American, Lampe was better able to communicate the Bridgestone/Firestone line. While acknowledging that the company had made some bad tires, and after expressing regret for the tragic accidents, Lampe was aggressive in contending that the design of the Ford Explorer had played a key role in the rollover accidents. In addition, when Ford Motor Company announced in May 2001 that it would spend $3 billion to replace an additional 13 million Firestone tires on Ford vehicles, Lampe made the stunning announcement that the Bridgestone/Firestone unit would end its 95-year relationship with Ford, at least in North and South America. (The two companies had more than just a business relationship: William Clay Ford Jr., chairman of Ford, was the great-grandson of the founder of Firestone, Harvey Firestone.) While dramatic, cutting ties with Ford represented the loss of only 4 percent of Bridgestone's total revenues.

To escape the bankruptcy of the U.S. unit that many observers were predicting at the height of the crisis, Lampe engineered other moves. He took to the airwaves, starring in television commercials that had the theme "Making It Right" to begin repairing the damaged Firestone image. To the surprise of a number of analysts, the Firestone brand was not jettisoned but was instead retained as a mass-market brand in the United States, though repositioned slightly down-market, while the Bridgestone brand received greater emphasis as a premium brand. Lampe worked hard to keep Bridgestone/Firestone dealers onboard in particular by picking up the costs of the recall. He also launched a cost-cutting initiative to stem the unit's sea of red ink. Most notably, the company's plant in Decatur, Illinois, where many of the recalled tires had been made, was shut down at the end of 2001, costing about 1,500 workers their jobs.

Recall-related costs led to a $511 million loss at Bridgestone/Firestone in 2000, and the following year the unit lost $1.7 billion thanks not only to recall and restructuring costs but also to $285 million paid out to settle lawsuits filed in connection with the rollover accidents. The crisis meantime had a major impact on the company's U.S. market share, cutting its portion of the replacement-tire market from 10.5 percent in 1999 to 7.5 percent in 2001, while its share of the new-car market fell in the same period from 25 percent to 22 percent. To shore up the finances at Bridgestone/Firestone, the parent company injected it with $1.3 billion in January 2002. Despite the retention of the Firestone brand, Bridgestone began dropping the name from its subsidiaries, with the U.S. unit renamed Bridgestone Americas Holding, Inc., at the beginning of 2003 and the company's European holding company renamed Bridgestone Europe N.V./S.A. This rebranding was part of an effort to build a global corporate identity under the Bridgestone name.

POST-CRISIS EXPANSION

The remarkable turnaround at Bridgestone was evident in its results for 2002, which included a 5 percent increase in revenues, a 161 percent jump in profits, and the return of the U.S.-based subsidiary to profitability. Growing ever-more confident that the crisis was over, Bridgestone announced late in 2002 that it was earmarking ¥56 billion ($467 million) for an expansion of its global passenger tire production capacity at plants in Japan, Poland, Thailand, Indonesia, China, Costa Rica, and Mexico. An additional ¥27 billion ($225 million) was set aside to increase production capacity at plants in Thailand, China, and Spain, where truck and bus tires were made.

In March 2003 Bridgestone bolstered its European operations by purchasing an 18.9 percent interest in Finnish tire manufacturer Nokian Tyres plc for ¥78.3 million. Nokian was the largest tire producer in the Nordic region with sales of ¥479 million in 2002. Also in 2003, a fire at Bridgestone's Tochigi plant, located north of Tokyo, destroyed the facility's rubber-mixing shop and reduced the firm's domestic tire production for months to come. The fire and its after-effects shaved about ¥10 billion ($94 million) off Bridgestone's profits for 2003, but the company still recorded a near doubling of its net income for the year thanks to a strong performance in Europe and a continued recovery of its U.S. operations.

By 2005, Bridgestone had regained its position as the world's largest tire maker, after Michelin had reigned as number one for four straight years. The year was also notable for the return to profitability of the company's North American tire unit. On a global basis, Bridgestone enjoyed its best year ever, with record profits of ¥180.8 billion ($1.53 billion) on record sales of ¥2.69 trillion ($22.79 billion). Significantly higher costs for natural rubber and oil used in tire production were successfully offset through price increases. One of the pending legal hangovers from the Firestone tire recall was resolved in 2005 when Bridgestone agreed to pay Ford Motor $240 million to settle all outstanding financial claims arising out of the recall. At this time, Bridgestone was in the midst of another major expansion of its global tire production operations, including new tire plants in Hungary, Mexico, Brazil, and China. The Chinese plant would be the company's fourth in that nation.

A leadership change at the top occurred in the early months of 2006 when Watanabe stepped down from his positions as chairman, president, and CEO. His successor was Shoshi Arakawa, who had been an executive vice president. Later in the year, the Bridgestone Americas Holding unit agreed to acquire Bandag, Incorporated for $1.05 billion. The deal, which closed in May 2007, made Bridgestone a major global player in the retread tire sector. Bandag, based in Muscatine, Iowa, was a manufacturer of retreading materials and equipment for a network of more than 900 franchised dealers in 90 countries that produced and marketed retread tires and offered tire management services, particularly for commercial truck fleets. The company had production facilities in the United States, Mexico, Brazil, and Belgium.

REACTING TO GLOBAL ECONOMIC DOWNTURN

The major global tire makers were hit hard by the significant economic downturn that began in the later months of 2008. The downturn was marked by a decline in worldwide auto production and a sluggish replacement tire market. Bridgestone's net sales total for 2009 of ¥2.6 trillion ($28.2 billion) represented a sharp decline from its record 2007 total of ¥3.39 trillion ($29.7 billion). The company barely stayed in the black in 2009, reporting profits of just ¥1.04 billion ($11.3 million). During 2009 and into 2010, Bridgestone implemented a number of cost-containment initiatives, including the closure of two high-cost tire manufacturing plants in Australia and New Zealand. The company realigned its steel cord business by selling two steel cord production facilities located in Italy and China.

As it worked to maintain its position as the world's leading tire maker, Bridgestone positioned itself for future growth through a strategy aimed at differentiating its product offerings from those of the competition. The company placed increased emphasis on specialty tires, such as "run-flat" tires, which could be used for limited distances after losing air pressure, and ultra-high-performance replacement tires. Bridgestone was also pursuing the development of environmentally focused products. In its tire operation, this strategy included the launch of the ECOPIA tire line, which offered reduced rolling resistance without compromising the tire's safety profile in terms of handling and traction on wet surfaces. In its nontire operations, Bridgestone was also pursuing "green" growth opportunities, such as building on its position as a major producer of ethylene vinyl acetate (EVA) adhesive film, which was used to fasten solar cells to the glass bases of solar modules.

Lois Glass
Updated, David E. Salamie

PRINCIPAL SUBSIDIARIES

Bridgestone Chemitech Co., Ltd.; Bridgestone Cycle Co., Ltd.; Bridgestone Flowtech Corporation; Bridgestone Elastech Co., Ltd.; Bridgestone Sports Co., Ltd.; Asahi Carbon Co., Ltd. (99.4%); Bridgestone Finance Corporation; Bridgestone Argentina S.A.I.C.; Bridgestone Australia Ltd.; Bridgestone Earthmover Tyres Pty. Ltd. (Australia); Bridgestone Europe NV/SA (Belgium); Bridgestone Aircraft Tire (Europe) S.A. (Belgium);

Bridgestone do Brasil Industria e Comercio Ltda. (Brazil); Bridgestone Canada Inc.; Bridgestone Off-the-Road Tire Latin America S.A. (Chile; 75%); Bridgestone (China) Investment Co., Ltd.; Bridgestone (Tianjin) Tire Co., Ltd. (China; 94.5%); Bridgestone (Shenyang) Tire Co., Ltd.; Bridgestone Aircraft Tire Company (China) Ltd.; Bridgestone Aircraft Tire Company (Asia) Ltd. (China); Bridgestone de Costa Rica, S.A. (98.6%); Bridgestone France S.A.S.; Bridgestone Deutschland GmbH (Germany); Bridgestone Tatabanya Termelo Kft. (Hungary); Bridgestone India Private Ltd.; P.T. Bridgestone Tire Indonesia (54.3%); Bridgestone Italia S.p.A. (Italy); Bridgestone de Mexico, S.A. de C.V.; Bridgestone Finance Europe B.V. (Netherlands); Bridgestone New Zealand Ltd.; Bridgestone Poznan Sp. zo.o. (Poland); Bridgestone Stargard Sp. zo.o. (Poland); Limited Liability Company "Bridgestone C.I.S." (Russia); Bridgestone Singapore Pte Ltd; Bridgestone Asia Pacific Pte. Ltd. (Singapore); Bridgestone South Africa Holdings (Pty) Ltd.; Bridgestone Hispania S.A. (Spain; 99.7%); Bridgestone Taiwan Co., Ltd. (80%); Thai Bridgestone Co., Ltd. (Thailand; 69.2%); Bridgestone Tire Manufacturing (Thailand) Co., Ltd.; Bridgestone Natural Rubber (Thailand) Co., Ltd.; Brisa Bridgestone Sabanci Lastik Sanayi ve Ticaret A.S. (Turkey; 43.6%); Bridgestone U.K. Ltd.; Bridgestone Industrial Ltd. (UK); Bridgestone Middle East & Africa FZE (United Arab Emirates); Bridgestone Americas, Inc. (USA); Bridgestone Bandag, LLC (USA); Bridgestone Americas Tire Operations, LLC (USA); Bridgestone Retail Operations, LLC (USA); Firestone Diversified Products, LLC (USA); Morgan Tire & Auto, LLC (USA); Bridgestone APM Company (USA); Bridgestone Aircraft Tire (USA), Inc.; Bridgestone Firestone Venezolana, C.A. (Venezuela).

PRINCIPAL COMPETITORS

Compagnie Générale des Établissements Michelin; Continental AG; Cooper Tire & Rubber Company; The Goodyear Tire & Rubber Company; Hankook Tire Co., Ltd.; Kumho Tire Co., Inc.; Sumitomo Rubber Industries, Ltd.; Toyo Tire & Rubber Co., Ltd.; The Yokohama Rubber Company, Limited.

FURTHER READING

Aeppel, Timothy, Norihiko Shirouzo, and Michael Williams, "Pit Crew: Firestone Team Faces Challenge of Steering Company Past Crisis," *Wall Street Journal*, October 11, 2000, pp. A1+.

Belson, Ken, and Micheline Maynard, "Big Recall behind It, Tire Maker Regains Its Footing," *New York Times*, August 10, 2002, p. C1.

Chappell, Lindsay, "Bridgestone Waxes as Firestone Wanes," *Tire Business*, November 19, 2001, p. 20.

Davis, Bruce, "Bridgestone Sees Big Opportunities," *Tire Business*, August 29, 2005, p. 3.

———, "Bridgestone to Enhance Firestone Lines," *Tire Business*, March 15, 2010, p. 17.

Fahey, Jonathan, "Flats Fixed," *Forbes*, May 27, 2002, pp. 40–41.

Linsalata, Vera, "Bridgestone Americas to Buy Bandag," *Tire Business*, December 18, 2006, p. 3.

Lundegaard, Karen, and Timothy Aeppel, "Bridgestone, Ford Reach Recall Deal," *Wall Street Journal*, October 13, 2005, p. A3.

Nelson, Emily, "Anatomy of a Long, Bitter Labor Fight," *Wall Street Journal*, November 6, 1996, pp. B1, B4.

Welch, David, "Firestone: Is This Brand beyond Repair?" *Business Week*, June 11, 2001, p. 48.

Zaun, Todd, "A Blowout Blindsides Bridgestone," *Wall Street Journal*, August 7, 2000, p. A8.

Chemed Corporation

2600 Chemed Center
255 East Fifth Street
Cincinnati, Ohio 45202
U.S.A.
Telephone: (513) 762-6900
Fax: (513) 762-6919
Web site: http://www.chemed.com

Public Company
Incorporated: 1970 as DuBois Chemicals, Inc.
Employees: 12,308
Sales: $1.19 billion (2009)
Stock Exchanges: New York
Ticker Symbol: CHE
NAICS: 621610 Home Health Care Services; 424690 Other Chemical and Allied Products Merchant Wholesalers

■ ■ ■

Chemed Corporation operates through two businesses, Roto-Rooter and Vitas Healthcare. Roto-Rooter provides plumbing and drain services to residential and business customers in 90 percent of the United States and parts of Canada. There are 600 branch offices of Roto-Rooter in operation, 500 of which are franchise locations. Vitas Healthcare is the largest hospice company in the United States, providing end-of-life care to patients in 15 states.

ROOTS STRETCH TO DUBOIS SOAP COMPANY: 1920–64

Chemed Corporation's long history dates back to the founding of DuBois Soap Company. In June 1920 a confident and ambitious salesman named T. V. DuBois decided to open his own business. DuBois established DuBois Soap Company in a rented building, a small, four-story structure adjacent to the Ohio River. The fledgling operation made soap chips and powders for the city's growing restaurant trade. Within a few short years, the firm was selling its products all over the state. As revenues increased, additional employees were added to the payroll.

DuBois Soap Company survived the bleak years of the Great Depression in good financial condition. During the late 1930s and early 1940s the company expanded its restaurant dishwashing product line to encompass a whole range of different items, including industrial cleaning and maintenance products for other industries. Soon DuBois was servicing restaurants, steel companies, heavy manufacturing firms, and food processing plants. With the rapid expansion of its product line, the company decided to increase the amount of space for its administrative and manufacturing facilities in Cincinnati. By the end of World War II, the company was producing a huge variety of cleaning and maintenance products and had developed a reputation as one of the leaders in the specialty chemical industry.

W.R. GRACE ACQUIRES DUBOIS: 1964

During the late 1940s and throughout the 1950s, DuBois developed its sales network and expanded its manufacturing plants. Three new facilities were built in California, New Jersey, and Texas. As DuBois's revenues

KEY DATES

1920: DuBois Soap Company is formed.
1964: W.R. Grace acquires DuBois.
1971: W.R. Grace organizes its specialty chemicals group as Chemed Corporation.
1980: Chemed acquires Roto-Rooter, Inc.
1990: Chemed sells DuBois.
1993: Chemed acquires Patient Care, Inc., a home health care provider.
2004: After selling Patient Care, company acquires Vitas Healthcare, the largest hospice company in the country.

increased, the company came to the attention of W.R. Grace, a large conglomerate with holdings in the chemical, manufacturing, retail, fertilizer, food products, and restaurant industries. In 1964 Grace acquired DuBois and incorporated the company into its Specialty Products Group, renaming the firm the DuBois Chemicals Division.

In 1971 Grace management transformed its specialty chemicals group, which included the DuBois Chemicals Division, into Chemed Corporation. DuBois Chemicals developed and manufactured professional cleaning and maintenance chemicals, dispensing equipment, and processing compounds. It served as the single largest area of operation within Chemed. While Grace maintained ownership of the majority of Chemed stock, the company was given autonomy to develop its own products.

Another firm that remained an important part of Chemed Corporation in the mid-1990s was the National Sanitary Supply Company. Founded in 1929, National developed in much the same manner as DuBois. The company offered a variety of chemical products used to clean and maintain industrial, commercial, and institutional facilities. Goods produced by National over the years included floor finishes, trash liners, mops, buckets, brushes, paper and packaging products, and cleaning chemicals and equipment. By the time the company was purchased by Chemed in 1983, National had become the largest distributor of sanitary maintenance supplies in the United States.

The third major company to shape Chemed Corporation was Roto-Rooter, Inc. Founded in 1936, Roto-Rooter provided sewer and drain cleaning services. After a time it expanded its range of service to include plumbing repair and maintenance. The firm grew at

such a rapid pace that management decided to establish a network of independent franchises that could conduct business throughout the United States. By the time Chemed purchased the company in 1980, Roto-Rooter had become the leading supplier of sewer and drain cleaning services across the country. The company, which claimed that it had serviced more than two million customers, boasted that it had cleaned one out of every six clogged drains or sewers in the United States.

Armed with the thriving DuBois and Roto-Rooter businesses, and with plans to acquire National Sanitary Supply in motion, Chemed management decided to buy the remainder of W.R. Grace's 16.7 million shares of Chemed stock. This transaction allowed Chemed to become a totally autonomous, independent corporation. It was listed on the New York Stock Exchange in 1982.

CHEMED EXPANDS: 1981–89

Even as Chemed developed into a successful independent organization, DuBois remained the cornerstone of its operations. Throughout the 1980s, Chemed grew as DuBois grew. DuBois manufactured and marketed hundreds of specialty chemical products (including paint strippers, cutting fluids, specialty lubricants, sanitation chemicals, and water treatment chemicals) for use as industrial cleaning and maintenance compounds. The company sold its product line to customers in a number of diverse industries. Public utilities, mining organizations, airlines, meat packers, breweries, dairy plants, railroads, metal finishers, publishing companies, hospitals, and retail establishments all purchased materials from DuBois.

In the mid-1980s the company expanded its services to include laundry and linen supplies and uniform rentals. During this time DuBois expanded its product line to major overseas markets. By the end of the 1980s, the company had opened offices in Australia, England, France, Germany, Holland, Japan, Mexico, Saudi Arabia, Singapore, South Africa, Sweden, and Venezuela.

Chemed also established several new businesses during the 1980s. In 1981 Chemed formed Omnicare, Inc., a company designed to supply pharmacy management services and distribute dental and medical supplies. Omnicare was divided into two operating divisions, the Sequoia Pharmacy Group and the Veratex Group. Sequoia provided services for more than 200 nursing homes, and by 1990 it represented over 20 percent of Omnicare revenues. The Veratex Group, a supplier of medical and dental products, grew even more rapidly. By 1990 the Veratex Group ranked third in the U.S. dressings and sponge market on the strength of its sales of over 800 different kinds of proprietary disposable paper, gauze, and cotton products to professionals working in the veterinary, medical, and dental fields.

National Sanitary Supply Company and Roto-Rooter also helped Chemed increase its revenues during the 1980s. By the early 1990s, National reported over 150,000 standing accounts across the country, with 22 distribution centers in 14 states. The performance of Roto-Rooter was even better. In 1990, a year when revenues from the company's plumbing services increased 26 percent, the firm introduced a revolutionary drain and sewer cleaning product that broke down organic waste by biological means and converted it into water and harmless carbon dioxide. Roto-Rooter also made significant inroads toward expanding its base of operations through a franchising agreement that allowed the company to distribute products in Japan.

DIVESTITURE AND RESTRUCTURING: 1990–99

In the early 1990s, management at Chemed decided to concentrate on marketing and service-oriented businesses, rather than capital or production-intensive manufacturing. Although DuBois was the largest revenue and profit-generating division within Chemed, with sales of $275 million in 1990 and 2,800 employees, management thought it best to sell its flagship operation in order to refocus the company's priorities. As a result, DuBois was sold for $243 million to Molson Companies, Ltd., the largest brewery in Canada and the sixth-leading beer maker in the United States. Molson immediately combined DuBois with its Diversey Corporation subsidiary.

Chemed implemented a comprehensive restructuring program with the money garnered from the sale of DuBois. The revenue was immediately reinvested in the company's growing health care business. Money was also funneled into Chemed's appliance repair service interests. Chemed sold off Omnicare as well, but retained its highly profitable Veratex Group. Sales for Veratex amounted to over $95 million in 1994, but growing competition and significant changes in the health care industry forced Veratex Group to reduce its workforce and cut operating expenses. One development of interest in the industry, for example, was the decision by Tidi Wholesale, a leader in the manufacture of disposable medical and dental products, to merge its product line with Erving Healthcare, a producer of environmentally safe, recycled paper products.

National Sanitary Supply Company had offices in 71 locations across the United States in the mid-1990s. The company, which touted itself as a "one-stop shop"

for its customers, was one of the largest distributors of sanitary maintenance supply products in the country. In 1995 the company offered more than 10,000 products used to clean and maintain all types of commercial, industrial, and institutional facilities.

Roto-Rooter was the largest supplier of drain cleaning and plumbing services in the United States. The company also maintained the country's largest service contract business for the appliance, heating, and air conditioning repair markets. Roto-Rooter increased its overseas operations as well. Entering the mid-1990s the company was an industry leader in Canada and operated 17 franchises in Japan. In 1994 the company expanded the number of its service technicians by 15 percent. All this activity contributed to greater revenues for Roto-Rooter. From 1993 to 1994, the company reported a 20 percent growth in plumbing revenues. Roto-Rooter had enjoyed steady growth for a number of years. From 1984 to 1994, revenues advanced from $28.2 million to $171.9 million.

FORAY INTO HOME HEALTH CARE: 1993

In addition to the Veratex Group, National Sanitary Supply Company, and Roto-Rooter, Chemed had one other major subsidiary in the mid-1990s: Patient Care, Inc. Founded in 1974 to provide comprehensive home health care services in the New York, New Jersey, and Connecticut areas, Patient Care was acquired by Chemed in 1993. In the mid-1990s Patient Care's workforce included more than 4,500 nurses, home health care aides, speech therapists, physical therapists, occupational therapists, medical social workers, nutritionists, and other health care workers. Regarded by many as one of the anticipated solutions to the ever increasing cost of in-patient health services, the $20 billion home care industry had grown rapidly in the 1990s.

Mindful that the home care market was extremely fragmented, Patient Care claimed that its own comprehensive line of health care services offered better resources and was more cost-effective than smaller home health agencies. In its first year with Chemed, Patient Care proved to be a valuable acquisition. From 1993 to 1994 Patient Care's revenues grew from $53.5 million to $69 million.

Kevin J. McNamara, Chemed's vice president since the mid-1980s, was named president of the company in 1994 and appointed as CEO in 2001, posts he would hold throughout the first decade of the 21st century. The steady presence of McNamara was the one constant in a period of profound change that characterized his leadership tenure. Under his direction, Chemed transformed itself, becoming a far different company than the $500-million-in-sales holding company that existed in the mid-1990s.

TRANSFORMATION: 1997–2004

The McNamara era of sweeping change began in 1997 with divestitures. In September the company sold National Sanitary Supply and Omnia Group, giving it $185 million to invest in its three remaining businesses, Roto-Rooter, Patient Care, and Service America. McNamara used $85 million of the proceeds to buy as many Roto-Rooter franchises as he could purchase. He launched the campaign in 1999 and continued spending into 2000, allowing Chemed to prosper from the vibrant growth of the Roto-Rooter chain. "There's a huge change," an analyst said in the July 28, 2000 issue of *Business Courier*, referring to the actions taken by McNamara. "They've gone from a holding company to an operational company. They've got a good plan in place right now. The only thing they have to do now is to exit Patient Care and emphasize the Roto-Rooter business. That would make them a very attractive pure play."

McNamara heeded the advice coming from Wall Street, but not to the full extent of making Chemed a "pure play." He divested Patient Care, selling the company in October 2002 to an investor group that included Schroder Ventures Life Sciences Group. The sale of the home health care provider left Chemed reliant on Roto-Rooter for 80 percent of its annual revenues, which prompted a change in the company's corporate title in 2003 from Chemed Corporation to Roto-Rooter, Inc. The name change lasted only a year, however. The Chemed banner flew again, its return triggered by a massive acquisition orchestrated by McNamara.

In February 2004 McNamara acquired Vitas Healthcare Corporation, the largest hospice company in the United States. McNamara paid $406 million to acquire Vitas, and in return he gained assets that accounted for 60 percent of his company's annual revenues. To reflect the diminished importance of Roto-Rooter to its business volume, the company changed its name back to Chemed Corporation shortly after completing the transaction.

The addition of Vitas had an immediate impact on Chemed's balance sheet. After years of stagnant or decreasing financial totals, the company began to record vibrant revenue growth. Service America was sold in 2005, leaving the company supported by two businesses, Roto-Rooter and Vitas, as it progressed through the decade. By the end of the decade, Chemed stood as a $1.1-billion-in-sales company generating more than $70 million in annual earnings. With McNamara still at the helm, the company looked to Vitas as its primary engine for future growth, but Roto-Rooter, long an important contributor to the company's fortunes, remained an integral facet of Chemed's business.

Thomas Derdak
Updated, Jeffrey L. Covell

PRINCIPAL SUBSIDIARIES

Chemed RT, Inc.; Comfort Care Holdings Co.; Consolidated HVAC, Inc.; Jet Resource, Inc.; Roto-Rooter Canada, Ltd.; Roto-Rooter Corporation; Roto-Rooter Group, Inc.; Roto-Rooter Services Company; VITAS Care Solutions, Inc.; VITAS Healthcare Corporation; VITAS Hospice Services, L.L.C.; VITAS Holdings Corporation; VITAS Solutions, Inc.; Hospice Care Incorporated.

PRINCIPAL COMPETITORS

Amedisys, Inc.; American Residential Services L.L.C.; Odyssey HealthCare, Inc.

FURTHER READING

Bastian, Lisa, and Jeffrey Waddle, "Corporate Profiles," in *Cincinnati: City of Charm*, by Nick Clooney, Memphis, TN: Towery, 1991, pp. 308–09.

"Chemed Shifts Its Focus to End-of-Life Care," *America's Intelligence Wire*, November 9, 2004.

Frazier, Mya, "Chemed Sticks with Roto-Rooter Expansion Plans," *Business Courier*, July 28, 2000, p. 28.

"Roto-Rooter Parent Sells Health-Care Unit," *Plumbing & Mechanical*, July 2002, p. 20.

Sekhri, Rajiv, "Roto-Rooter Growth Spurred by Acquisition Binge," *Business Courier*, July 23, 1999, p. 29.

The China National Offshore Oil Corp.

———— ■ ————

Box 4705, 25 Chao Yangmen N Street
Dongcheng District
Beijing, 100010
China
Telephone: (+86 010) 8452 1010
Fax: (+86 010) 6460 2600
Web site: http://www.cnooc.com.cn

Government-Owned Company
Founded: 1982
Incorporated: 1999
Employees: 65,800
Sales: RMB 209.6 billion (2009)
NAICS: 213112 Support Activities for Oil and Gas
    Operations

■ ■ ■

The China National Offshore Oil Corp. (CNOOC) is, alongside Sinopec and China National Petroleum Corp., one of China's leading oil and gas producers. Wholly owned by the Chinese government, CNOOC holds the exclusive rights to govern China's offshore oil exploration and production, through its own subsidiaries and through the allocation of drilling rights to foreign companies. CNOOC's main production subsidiary is CNOOC Ltd., a public company with listings on the Hong Kong and New York stock exchanges. CNOOC operates as an integrated energy company, with operations spanning the upstream (oil and gas exploration, production, and sales), as well as downstream (including the production of petrochemicals, and fertilizers, as well

as refinery operations and gas and power supply). Through another publicly listed subsidiary, China Oilfield Services Ltd., CNOOC also provides technical services to the oil and gas industries, including oilfield and offshore engineering, construction, and other services.

The company's international holdings span operations in 11 countries, including in Australia, Myanmar, the Philippines, Indonesia, Kazakhstan, and, since May 2010, Iraq. In 2009, CNOOC's total oil and gas production neared 48 million tons (or 194.2 million barrels of oil equivalent). The company also produced 32 million tons of refinery and chemical products. The company employs 65,800 people, and generated revenues of nearly RMB 210 billion in 2009. CNOOC is led by Fu Chengyu.

CHINESE OFFSHORE EXPLORATION BEGINNING IN THE FIFTIES

China National Offshore Oil Corp., or CNOOC, was founded in 1982 as part of the Chinese government's economic reform policies. The creation of CNOOC formed a key element in the government's decision to attract foreign investment in order to stimulate the country's economic growth. The arrival of foreign corporations also promised to provide the country with a technology boost, replacing China's homegrown but often out-of-date and inefficient technologies. CNOOC was given the monopoly for overseeing the development of China's offshore oil exploration and production efforts.

COMPANY PERSPECTIVES

CNOOC has maintained rapid growth and a reputation for quality since its incorporation. It has evolved from an upstream company into an integrated energy company, possessing high performance core business and other related businesses along the value chain.

China's efforts to achieve self-sufficiency in energy production had formed a central element in the country's economic policies since the early years of Communist rule under Chairman Mao in the 1950s. During that decade, the country launched numerous oil exploration operations, both onshore and offshore. The country's earliest offshore operations started in 1957, with the initial exploration of the South China Sea. While this effort got underway, the country achieved a major triumph, with the discovery of the massive Daqing oilfields in the former Manchuria in 1959. This discovery alone enabled the country not only to achieve self-sufficiency, but to become an oil exporter.

By the mid-1960s, the country had made its first oilfield discoveries in the South China Sea, drilling its first test well in Bohai Gulf in 1967. This well, supported by the country's own somewhat crude platform technology, produced just 35 cubic meters per day. Nonetheless, it signaled the start of China's entry into the ranks of oil-producing nations.

China also widened its oil exploration effort to the northern Bohai Bay starting in 1966. By 1972, the country operated four offshore drilling platforms, and had drilled a total of 14 wells. The company's exploration of Bohai Bay had also resulted in some success, with the discovery of three oil-rich fields.

By then, following China's break with the Soviet Union, and then the collapse of the Maoist government, the Chinese government began turning to the West for technological support. As a result, the government carried out a major upgrade of its offshore exploration and production effort, including the addition of a fleet of support vessels, including jackup ships and geophysical survey vessels. The company stepped up its drilling program, including drilling its first wells in Bohai Bay from 1979. As a result, China, which remained a largely agrarian economy at the time, achieved self-sufficiency for its oil requirements.

FOUNDING CNOOC IN 1982

The year 1979 also marked the launch of the country's economic reform policies, led by Deng Xiaoping. The oil industry was among the first to seek out foreign investment. In 1979, the president of the country's oil company, then known as the China National Oil and Gas Exploration and Development Corporation, traveled to the United States, the United Kingdom, and Brazil, signing exploration and oil production partnership agreements with many of the world's leading oil companies, including Arco, British Petroleum (BP), Exxon, Mobil, Santa Fe, and Texaco.

In the early 1980s, the government took the decision to split up its oil and gas exploration operations into a number of government-owned corporate entities. Among these was China National Offshore Oil Corporation, or CNOOC, established in order to take over the exclusive rights to explore and develop the country's offshore oilfields. CNOOC was formally established in 1982. CNOOC took over all contracts and agreements between the Chinese government and the foreign oil corporations. At the same time, the company launched its first call for bids for contracts to develop blocks in the Pearl River Mouth Basin of the South China Sea, as well as the southern area of the Yellow Sea.

In 1983, CNOOC oversaw the creation of a number of new companies assigned to explore specific regions of the Chinese coastal waters. These included China Offshore Oil Nanhuanghai Corporation, headquartered in Shanghai, which took over the exploration rights in the Yellow and East China seas. For the South China Sea, CNOOC also created two companies, China Offshore Oil Nanhai East and China Offshore Oil Nanhai West. The former, headquartered in Guangzhou, took over the exploration of the eastern part of the South China Sea, while the latter, based in Zhanjiang, became responsible for the western part.

In May 1983, CNOOC awarded its first round of new contracts, to BP, Australia's BHP, Brazil's Petrobras, and Canada's Ranger. The success of this first bidding round led to a new round in 1984. In addition to the Pearl River Mouth basin and the South Yellow Sea basin, the company opened up part of the Ying Ge Hai Basin for bidding. The company awarded 22 blocks, covering an area of more than 108,000 square kilometers. A third round followed in 1989, this time for seven blocks spanning 32,000 square kilometers. In the meantime, CNOOC's own oil exploration operations had succeeded in locating the Suizhong 36-1 oilfield, with a proven reserve of 300 million tons.

KEY DATES

1957: Chinese government launches its first offshore oil exploration operations.

1967: China's first offshore oil well enters production.

1979: Chinese government begins pursuing exploration and development contracts with foreign companies.

1982: The China National Offshore Oil Corp. (CNOOC) is formed to oversee the development of China's offshore oil exploration and production sector.

1994: CNOOC acquires its first overseas oil exploration and production interests, in Indonesia.

1999: CNOOC regroups its oil exploration and production operations into CNOOC Ltd., which then goes public.

2005: CNOOC fails in its bid to acquire Unocal in the United States.

2010: CNOOC and Turkish Petroleum Company acquire offshore oil production rights in Iraq.

OIL IMPORTER FROM 1993

By 1990, China's offshore crude oil production neared 1.5 million tons per year. The country's rapid industrialization, as China emerged as a major global manufacturing center, quickly exceeded its output. By 1993, China had become a net oil importer. CNOOC had begun to respond to this transition, pursuing a multipart strategy. The first part of this strategy involved the continued expansion of the country's offshore exploration and drilling operations. In 1992, the company awarded a contract to the 25,000-square-kilometer Wan An Bei-21 block.

This was followed by the launch of a fourth round of bidding, now for a 72,800-square-kilometer area in northern and southern parts of the East China Sea. Bidding closed in 1994, leading to more than 18 partnership contracts between CNOOC and 15 foreign oil companies. The subsequent exploration rights covered an area of nearly 63,000 square kilometers.

CNOOC also began to position itself beyond its upstream operations toward becoming a fully integrated oil company. Toward this end, in 1991, the company launched a feasibility study for the construction of a petrochemicals complex in Nanhai. Partners in this study included Royal Dutch Shell, as well as China Petrochemicals Corporation and China National Petroleum Corporation. The Nanhai Petrochemical complex was formally launched in 1998, with Shell holding 50 percent, and CNOOC 40 percent.

In the meantime, CNOOC had also made progress on developing a third prong of its strategy. In 1994, the company reached an agreement to acquire Arco's 32.58 percent of the drilling and production rights to Indonesia's Malacca Strait. This investment made CNOOC the largest shareholder in that operation, which had already launched production. In this way, CNOOC completed its first oil shipment, of 30,000 tons, from Indonesia to China in 1995.

Lastly, CNOOC expanded its range of operations in 1995 with the launch of the Ninth Five-Year Plan, which called for the company to develop offshore gas exploration and production operations in parallel with its oil business. The company acted quickly on this, launching gas production at the Yacheng 13-1 gas field in Yinggehai Basin in 1996, and then in the Pinghu oil and gas field in 1999. The former began delivering gas to the Hong Kong market, while the latter supplied oil and gas to Shanghai.

RESTRUCTURING IN 1999

CNOOC's oil production grew steadily through the 1990s, backed by a string of successful oil discoveries. By 1996, the company's total production had topped 10 million tons for the year. By 1998, the company had raised its total production to more than 16 million tons. CNOOC then announced plans to raise its production to 30 million tons by as early as 2005.

The expansion of CNOOC's production levels came at a high cost, especially following the collapse of global oil prices in 1998. The company found itself burdened by high production costs. By the end of the decade, the company's cost per barrel nearly doubled the average production costs in Southeast Asia, while far outpacing the cost of producing oil in the North Sea as well. Only the company's position as a state-owned enterprise permitted it to operate at such inefficient levels.

Nonetheless, the Chinese government took steps to restructure its offshore oil operation in order to develop more efficient operations and boost its profit levels. This led to a major reorganization of the various companies that had developed under CNOOC since its founding in 1982. In 1999, the company created a new subsidiary, CNOOC Ltd., regrouping all of its oil exploration and production operations. CNOOC Ltd. was then listed on the Hong Kong and New York stock exchanges.

CNOOC regrouped its various support operations into dedicated subsidiaries as well. These included China Oilfield Services Ltd. (COSL), which listed on the Hong Kong Stock Exchange in 2002. The company added China Offshore Oil Marine Engineering in 1999, and a fertilizer production unit, CNOOC Chemical Ltd., in 2000.

INTERNATIONAL COMPETITOR FROM 2002

China emerged as the world's fastest-growing and one of the world's most powerful economies at the beginning of the century. The rapid growth of the country's industrial sector, and the concurrent expansion of a large-scale middle-class population continued to stimulate demand for oil. By the middle of the decade, China's oil consumption had come to rival the world's leading oil consumer, the United States.

While China's vast coal reserves and existing output helped meet some of its energy needs, the country had come to rely on oil imports for a significant and growing proportion of its oil supply. In order to reduce its dependence on foreign purchases, which exposed the country to the often extreme fluctuations in oil prices, CNOOC set out to build its own array of international oilfield assets.

CNOOC scored several early successes in this effort. In 2002, the company paid $585 million to acquire the Indonesian offshore oilfield assets of Repsol-YPF. The company followed up this purchase several months later with an agreement to pay $320 million to buy a 5 percent stake in the North West Shelf gas project in Australia. The company also launched an exploration partnership with Taiwan's Chinese Petroleum Corp. in the Taiwan Straits' Tainan Basin. Back at home, CNOOC completed a production partnership with Husky Corp., which had succeeded in developing a 60,000-barrel-per-day well in Wenchang field in the Pearl River Mouth basin. The company returned to Indonesia in 2003, acquiring a stake in that country's liquefied natural gas (LNG) project in Tangguh.

CNOOC's expanding international scope increasingly placed it in the company of the world's traditional oil leaders. In 2003, for example, the company paid $615 million to acquire 8.3 percent of the North Caspian Sea oil and gas project, which also featured Exxon Mobil and Shell as major shareholders. The deal signaled a shift in the global oil market. As one analyst explained to *Business Week*: "Chinese companies have come of age."

ENTERING IRAQ IN 2010

CNOOC's growing ambitions ran into a hurdle in 2005, however, when the company launched a surprise bid to acquire Unocal of the United States. CNOOC's bid, topping a rival bid from Chevron by $1 billion, quickly collapsed into a major controversy, as the U.S. government balked at allowing the Chinese government-controlled company to gain control of part of the U.S. oil industry, despite the fact that BP had already acquired two other U.S. oil companies, Amoco and Arco, without incident. In the end, CNOOC was forced to drop its bid for Unocal.

The company quickly found more willing markets elsewhere. In 2006, for example, CNOOC paid $2.27 billion to acquire 45 percent of a major oil and gas field off the coast of Nigeria. In 2009, the company reportedly bid $17 billion to acquire a majority stake in Repsol YPF from its Spanish parent. Repsol denied having received an offer, however.

Instead, in 2010, CNOOC announced two new deals. The first involved buying out one of its partners in the Panyu field in the South China Sea, raising its stake in that field to 75.5 percent, at a cost of $515 million. In May 2010, the company announced a successful bid to acquire the development and production contracts for the Missan Oil Fields, off the coast of Iraq, in partnership with Turkish Petroleum Corporation. The companies then announced plans to expand production of the field to as much as 450,000 barrels per day by 2016.

Soon after, the company announced that it had made a new oil discovery, in the Penglal PL9 field in the eastern part of Bohai Bay. CNOOC remained an integral component in the Chinese government's efforts to meet the country's ever-growing oil needs in the early 21st century.

M. L. Cohen

PRINCIPAL SUBSIDIARIES

China BlueChemical Limited; China Offshore Oil & Gas Development & Utilization Company; CNOOC Gas & Power Group; CNOOC Limited; CNOOC Marketing Company; CNOOC Oil & Petrochemicals Co., Ltd.

PRINCIPAL DIVISIONS

Upstream; Midstream & Downstream; Technical & Logistics Services; Financial Services; Other.

PRINCIPAL COMPETITORS

Arabian Fal Company for Trading and Contracting; China National Petroleum Corporation; China Petroleum & Chemical Corporation; Emirates National Oil Company Ltd.; ENI S.p.A.; Exxon Mobil Corporation; Gazprom Dobycha Yamburg Ltd.; Royal Dutch Shell PLC; Saudi Arabian Oil Co.; Uzbekneftegaz State Holding Co.

FURTHER READING

Beckman, Jeremy, "CNOOC Has Discovered Further Oil in the Eastern Part of Bohai Bay, Offshore China," *Offshore*, June 2010, p. 16.

"China's CNOOC and Turkish Petroleum Corp. Bag Oil Field Deal in Iraq," *Information Company*, May 18, 2010.

"China's CNOOC to Own Majority of Inorganics Company," *Chemical Week*, September 15, 2008, p. 9.

"CNOOC Meets Objection in Expansion to Upstream Operations," *China Chemical Reporter*, January 16, 2006, p. 8.

"CNOOC Regroups Refineries in Shandong," *China Chemical Reporter*, April 16, 2008, p. 6.

"CNOOC to Acquire Devon Energy's Stake in Panyu Field for $515 Million," *Information Company*, May 4, 2010.

Engardio, Pete, and Dexter Roberts, "Growing Up Fast," *Business Week*, March 31, 2003, p. 52.

Forney, Matthew, "Quest for Crude," *Time*, November 22, 2004, p. A14.

Leahy, Chris, "CNOOC Keeps Buying Abroad," *Euromoney*, February 2006, p. 47.

"Lending a Helping Hand," *Newsweek*, July 18, 2005, p. 46.

Maurer, Harry, and Cristina Linblad, "Hunting Black Gold," *Business Week*, August 24, 2009, p. 11.

Sloan, Allan, "Deals: Don't Count 'Baby CNOOC' Out," *Newsweek*, August 2005, p. 9.

Walt, Vivienne, "China's African Safari," *Fortune*, February 20, 2006, p. 41.

Chubu Electric Power Company Inc.

1, Higashi-shincho
Higashi-ku
Nagoya, 461-8680
Japan
Telephone: (+81 052) 951 8211
Fax: (+81 052) 962 4624
Web site: http://www.chuden.co.jp

Public Company
Incorporated: 1951
Employees: 28,611
Sales: ¥2.24 trillion ($25.26 billion) (2009)
Stock Exchanges: Tokyo Nagoya
Ticker Symbol: 9502
NAICS: 221122 Electric Power Distribution

■ ■ ■

Chubu Electric Power Company Inc. is Japan's third-largest electric power generation and distribution company. The company services the Chubu region in central Japan, including Aichi, Gifu, Mie, Shizuoka, and Nagano prefectures, a population of more than 16 million. As a result, Chubu's operations cover nearly 13 percent of Japan's entire population and 15 percent of the country's total electricity market. The Chubu region is also one of Japan's major industrial centers. Chubu Electric Power has positioned itself as a multi-energy services group, with nuclear, thermal, and hydroelectric power generation plants. The company's Hamaoka Nuclear Power Station has a generating capacity of around 5,000 megawatts (MW), while its network of 11 primarily liquefied natural gas (LNG)-power thermal plants add nearly 22,500 MW. The company also operates more than 180 smaller hydroelectric plants, adding more than 5,200 MW. In 2009, the company delivered nearly 123 terawatt hours of electricity.

In addition to its electric power generation, Chubu has developed a vertically integrated organization, providing transmission and distribution services, as well as on-site power generation for a number of its industrial customers. The company also operates construction and maintenance subsidiaries, as well as manufacturing operations for part of its machinery and materials supply. Chubu Electric Power is listed on the Tokyo, Nagoya, and Osaka stock exchanges and is led by Fumio Kawaguchi. The company reported revenues of ¥2.24 trillion ($25.26 billion) in 2009.

COMPANY ORIGINS IN THE FIFTIES

Chubu Electric was established in May 1951, a few months before the Japanese Constitution was promulgated and the year before the U.S. occupation ended. It was one of nine companies formed at the same time as part of the restructuring of Japan's energy industry after World War II. In addition to these nine companies, Okinawa Electric Power acted as a regional supplier to Okinawa prefecture. Except for Okinawa, the power systems of these companies were interconnected to ensure stable and efficient service for the entire country. In recognition of the public nature of electric power utilities, rates and other important factors were under the supervision of the Ministry of

COMPANY PERSPECTIVES

Chubu Electric Power Company strives to maintain the foundations of our business through continuing dedication to our customers in creating a future together by further developing the environmental and international awareness of the local community, expanding cooperation and understanding through our activities as a corporate citizen, and creating fresh vitality for the future whilst focusing on flexibility as well as the importance of self-responsibility.

International Trade and Industry (MITI), although the industry itself was private.

At the time of its formation, Chubu Electric was given responsibility for supplying electricity to Aichi, Gifu, Mie, and Nagano prefectures, as well as that portion of Shizuoka prefecture west of the Fuji River. Its shareholders' equity was ¥29.4 billion, and its generating capacity was 1.03 million kilowatts (kW). It soon emerged, however, that this capacity was inadequate. Because of the age of the company's equipment, which it had inherited from the restructuring, its actual generating capacity was in fact only 600,000 to 700,000 kW. To make matters worse, the Korean War created a sudden surge in demand for electric power as Japan became a rear-base for the U.S. Army. In order to tackle this problem the company adopted a dual approach by conducting a publicity campaign for energy savings and by constructing new power plants, both hydroelectric and coal-fired. Construction of the Hiraoka hydroelectric plant in 1952 was followed by the construction of the Oigawa hydroelectric plant and the Mie and Shin-Nagoya coal-fired plants. By the latter half of the 1950s, supply and demand finally balanced out. This expansion of Chubu Electric's generating power required spending ¥210 billion over 10 years, which was mainly covered with financing from the Japan Development Bank and with foreign capital.

In September 1959, a typhoon struck Chubu Electric's operating region, badly damaging one of the company's plants and flooding another on the coast for several months. Using the slogan "Electric power is the generator of recovery," the company responded with an all-out restoration effort. The efforts of the company to cope with this disaster earned it an award from the Disaster Committee Headquarters, the only award of this kind given to a private-sector company, and formed the basis of its approach to future disasters.

MEETING INCREASED DEMAND IN THE SIXTIES

The 1960s were a period of marked economic growth in Japan, highlighted by the 1964 Tokyo Olympics and the improvement of the country's infrastructure with the opening of the Tokaido bullet train and the Tomei and Meishin highways, which linked up major industrial areas in central Japan with Tokyo. Because it occupied part of the Pacific coast belt, the Chubu region attracted the heavy chemicals industry and demand for electric power increased by more than 10 percent per annum. For several years, the growth rate in this area was one of the highest in Japan.

To meet the increasing demand, the company introduced a large volume of new oil-fired generating capacity. In 1960, fossil-fuel-fired plants contributed more than half of the company's electricity output for the first time, and subsequently new coal-fired plants with capacities of over four million kW were built around Ise Bay, in Yokkaichi, Owashi, Chita, Nishi Nagoya, and Atsumi. At the same time this base was supplemented with hydroelectric plants, Hatanagi Unit 1 and Takane Unit 1, to meet peak demand.

In addition to developing new electricity sources, the company expanded its grid, constructing a 270,000 volt transmission line around Ise Bay and strengthening its links with other utilities. Because oil prices remained stable during this period of rapid economic growth, the company did not need to revise its rates between 1954 and 1964.

In the 1970s, problems stemming from the period of high economic growth began to emerge. Environmental pollution had been a growing problem in Japan since the late 1950s, when people began to suffer from mysterious and horrific diseases. Because the symptoms of those affected became so widespread, developing "Citizens' Movements" (Shimin-Undo) were able to coerce the government and industry into tackling the problem. In response to the pollution problem, Chubu Electric promoted dual measures, for fuel and plant, concerning atmospheric pollution, noise, and wastewater. These included reducing the sulfur content of its fuel. As with the later oil crises, Japan managed to turn adversity to advantage with the pollution problem and was to become one of the world's leading nations in terms of pollution control.

DIVERSIFICATION AMID OIL CRISES IN THE SEVENTIES

The first oil crisis hit in October 1973, a product of the fourth Arab-Israeli War. The price of crude oil rose above $10 a barrel, and after the second oil crisis in

KEY DATES
■

1951: Chubu Electric is established as Japan's energy industry restructures.

1952: Hiraoka hydroelectric plant is constructed.

1976: Firm's first nuclear plant, Hamaoka Unit 1, becomes operational.

1992: Firm partners with Italy-based Ente Nazionale per L'Energia Electricia.

1999: Chubu begins laying fiber-optic cable for household use.

2000: Retail sector of Japan's electric power industry begins to deregulate; subsidiary LNG Chubu Co. Ltd. is established.

2005: Chubu announces a 25-year liquefied natural gas (LNG) supply contract with Chevron.

2010: Chubu agrees to purchase two million metric tons of LNG from Indonesia.

1979, above $30. Chubu Electric revised its rates three times and largely managed to overcome the difficult times. A three-tiered rate system was introduced for household use, and a special rate for industrial users was introduced as the company promoted the concept of energy saving.

The oil crises proved a major turning point in Japan's economic development. The industrial emphasis moved from heavy chemicals to manufacturing, assembly, and knowledge-intensive industries. The rate of growth in demand for electric power, which had been 10 percent per annum, steadily increased. In response, Chubu Electric adopted what was called a "positive management" policy aimed at restructuring its business. Subsequent stabilization and decline in oil prices and the appreciation of the yen, reducing fuel costs further, meant that with little pressure on its balance of revenues and expenditures the company was able to reduce its rates four times up until April 1989, following the recommendations of MITI's Electricity Utility Industry Council.

In the early 1970s, the company began promoting diversification of its energy sources, mainly into nuclear power and liquefied natural gas (LNG). The promotion of these power generation methods was perceived by the company to reduce environmental pollution, especially carbon dioxide emissions. Its first nuclear power plant, Hamaoka Unit 1, started operation in March 1976, five years after construction began. Construction of Units 2, 3, and 4 followed. In December 1973, at the height of

the oil crisis, Chubu Electric entered into a contract with Indonesia for long-term supplies of LNG, and in March 1978 it commenced operation of two exclusively LNG-fired plants, Chita Units 5 and 6. It also promoted switches to LNG at Chita Units 1 to 4, Yokkaichi and Kawagoe. As a result, LNG's share of power generation reached 33 percent in 1989.

During the 1970s and 1980s, customer needs grew more sophisticated. Chubu Electric met the demand with various measures to introduce new technology and reduce costs. Measures included construction of a second 500,000 kilovolt (kV) transmission line, the introduction of super-high voltage lines for urban areas, enhancement of protection against lightning, the introduction of optical communications, improvement of information capabilities, and automation of facilities. In addition, the thermal efficiency of Yokkaichi Unit 4 and Kawagoe Unit 1, which started in 1989 using the latest technology, was raised to over 40 percent, compared with an industry average for the nine companies of 38.8 percent, within a year.

To meet increasingly varying customer needs, Chubu Electric promoted equipment for late-night consumption of electricity, heat pumps, 200-volt household appliances, office building air conditioning, zone heating and cooling, and electric heat for industrial use and institutional kitchens.

CHALLENGE PROGRAM IN 1984

In conjunction with these measures, Chubu Electric inaugurated a Challenge program in 1984 aimed at rationing and quality control, supported by Action Challenge Circles, information-and finance-gathering organizations set up abroad to facilitate these two functions. It established offices in Washington, D.C., in 1982 and London in 1985, and diversified its activities, principally into telecommunications and heat supply. In 1988, the company embarked on a program to update its corporate image and prepare itself for the 21st century.

Chubu Electric also continued to implement antipollution measures at its thermal power plants. Greater use of low-sulfur fuel oils, flue-gas de-sulfurizers, and LNG reduced sulfur-oxide pollution. Flue-gas denitrification, use of low-nitrogen fuels, and boiler modification greatly suppressed generation of nitrogen oxides. Also, all company power plants became equipped with electrostatic precipitators that remove soot from flue gases with a high collection efficiency of 90 percent or more. Measures being adopted to prevent water pollution by power plants included the purification of discharge water by such methods as coagulating sediment, neutralization, and filtration.

To deal with noise and vibration problems, consideration was given to the use of low noise apparatus and the installation of noise suppression devices. Also, where necessary, installation of machinery was confined to indoor or underground sites. In addition, the grounds of power plant sites were landscaped with greenery. The amount spent on thermal power protection in fiscal 1990 came to ¥40.8 billion ($258.2 million). However, Chubu Electric's overall policy on environmental protection focused on a rational balance between environmental protection and the stable supply of energy necessary for sustained economic growth.

DIVERSIFYING POWER SOURCES IN THE NINETIES

Chubu Electric also continued to diversify power sources, improve overall energy efficiency, and develop carbon dioxide removal techniques. Due to rising crude oil prices and the depreciation of the yen in the early 1990s, power generation costs were rising. To maintain the current level of rates charged to consumers, the company began to implement radical cost reduction measures by upgrading operations.

During this period, Chubu set forth several strategic goals. Between 1991 and 2000, Chubu Electric planned to reach a capacity of 10.86 million kW. Of this, 10.3 million kW was to come from sources developed by Chubu Electric: 2.24 million kW from nuclear power, 6.1 million kW from coal, 700,000 kW from LNG, and 1.26 million kW from hydroelectric sources. These numbers changed through the years, however, as demand increased.

Chubu Electric also believed that nuclear power generation was needed to ensure adequate power supplies and a sufficient diversity of sources. In addition to the 1.137 million kW Unit 4 reactor under construction at Hamaoka, the Units 1 and 2 at Ashihama, each with a planned output capacity of 1.1 million kW, were expected to provide power for the early 21st century. Plans for the Ashihama nuclear power plant, however, were later dropped due to residential protests.

Active development of thermal power, also considered necessary, centered primarily on coal. In addition to the Unit 1 to 3 generators under construction in the early 1990s at Hekinan, each with an output of 700,000 kW, plans for the Unit 1 and 2 generators at Shimizu, each with a capacity of one million kW, were also implemented.

With a view to fully exploiting indigenous Japanese energy resources, construction work on hydroelectric plants was proceeding at six sites with a combined total capacity of 1.095 million kW. As for existing hydroelectric plants, remodeling or improvement plans were also in operation.

EXPANDING SUPPLY CAPACITY IN THE EARLY NINETIES

Power supply was to be stabilized in relation to demand over the next 10 years, with the prospect of maintaining an additional 8 to 9 percent of demand in reserve capacity. The proportion of power supplied by nuclear power plants was expected to increase from 18 percent recorded in 1990, to 22 percent by 2000, while oil-fired power was expected to decrease from 40 to 24 percent during the same period, in accordance with an accelerated trend toward reduced dependence on petroleum.

Chubu Electric also planned to make improvements to supply reliability. In 1990, the Chubu trunk transmission line system was composed primarily of 500 kV lines, and electricity was distributed around the load centers, or high-consumption areas, of Nagoya. Power transmission facilities began to be expanded to cope with factors such as increasing power demand, progress in development of new power sources, and growing urbanization.

In the early 1990s, developments included the installation of a second 500 kV outer loop line. In addition, the 275 kV system within the city of Nagoya was being expanded. Specific measures to improve reliability included further lightning protection for transmission lines and reinforcement of lines linking substations, as well as automation of troubleshooting and service restoration procedures. The funds required for the implementation of the above-mentioned projects were set to total ¥618 billion during fiscal 1991 and ¥649 billion in 1992.

PARTNERSHIPS FROM 1992

While Chubu was focused on improving operations in the early 1990s, it was also gearing up for the partial deregulation of electric utilities in Japan. The company began to forge partnerships with international firms, including a 1992 joint venture with Italy's public electric utility Ente Nazionale per L'Energia Electricia. As part of the deal, both companies shared personnel as well as information about the electric power industry in each country.

Weakening demand from its industrial customers and a slowing of the Japanese economy during 1992, however, resulted in lackluster sales growth. In fact, in 1992 the company's growth levels were the lowest they had been since 1982. Sales and profits continued to fall in 1993 due to a cooler than usual summer, increased depreciation costs for its nuclear power plants, and the continuing economic slowdown. In 1994, however, a heat wave bolstered demand and despite continued rate cuts, Chubu's revenues surpassed ¥2 trillion for the first time in its history.

While sales continued to rise, the firm's profits did not fare as well because of increased facility repair costs. In 1995, the company reported a drop in profits of 6.7 percent. Nevertheless, Chubu was determined to prepare for its future. In 1996, the company adopted a new set of business policies that were designed to ensure its arrival into the 21st century as an electric power enterprise. Included in the new strategy was a focus on Chubu's customer relationships and its environmental practices.

PARTIAL DEREGULATION IN JAPAN IN THE MID-NINETIES

During this time, the electricity industry in Japan was undergoing major changes. In 1995, changes in the Electricity Utilities Industry Law allowed competition to enter into the electricity generation and supply market. Then, in 1996, a wholesale electric power bidding system enabled non-electric power companies to sell electricity to electric power companies. Finally, in March 2000, retail sales of electricity were partially deregulated, allowing large-lot customers (those demanding large amounts of electricity) to choose their power supplier.

The intent of deregulation was to foster competition, which in turn would lower the electricity costs in the country. The deregulation was slow to change the Japanese industry, however, and during 2001 Chubu and the nine other regional companies still controlled 99 percent of the market. In fact, only six Japanese-based companies, other than the original 10, supplied power to large customers, including retail stores and office buildings. This accounted for a 0.2 percent share of the overall market.

Amid the deregulation, Chubu continued to solidify its position in the Japanese market. In late 1999, the company announced plans to lay fiber-optic cable that would connect over three million households in Nagoya and other cities in the Chubu region (the company was the first Japanese utility to install fiber-optic cable for household use). Chubu then planned to lease these cables to telecommunications firms looking to use the lines for cable television and Internet applications. During 2000, the firm partnered with Iwatani International Corp. to form LNG Chubu Co. Ltd. The new venture was created to withstand increased

competition expected from further deregulation in the industry.

FIRST INTERNATIONAL VENTURE IN 2001

Another strategic alliance was formed in 2001 with Toyota Tsusho Corp. Both companies, along with Tomen Corp., planned to build and operate a coal-fired facility in Thailand, which was slated to be the largest such facility operated by an independent power provider. The deal also marked the first time that Chubu became involved in an international power generation venture.

Meanwhile, Chubu's nuclear power program faced a setback in 2000 when it was forced to abandon plans, in the works for nearly 40 years, to build its second nuclear power plant in Mie prefecture. The company also experienced a drop in demand as the Japanese economy slowed amid an international recession. As such, Chubu stopped operations at two of its thermal power plants and began to implement a cost-cutting program that would shave off nearly 20 percent of its expenses related to power generation and distribution by 2005.

Japan continued to make progress toward full deregulation of its electric power market. In 2002, the government adopted new legislation allowing multiple power producers to supply a major company. Chubu jumped at the chance, launching a supply partnership with Marubeni to provide the electricity to supermarket operator Uny Co. Chubu also introduced new cost-cutting measures in 2003, designed to shave off another 20 percent of its expenses. In this way, the company hoped to enhance its competitiveness ahead of the full deregulation of the market.

The company's nuclear power profile suffered, however, amid a scandal in 2002. In that year, Tokyo Electric Power Co., Chubu's largest competitor, admitted to falsifying its safety inspections at three of its nuclear power plants. Chubu Electric became caught up in the scandal as well, when it was forced to admit that it had failed to report a number of safety breaches, including a leak of radioactive water from one of its turbine valves.

EARTHQUAKE SHUTDOWN IN 2009

With prospects for future nuclear power plants in Japan dimming, Chubu continued to build its international profile through the decade. In 2004, for example, the company teamed with Mitsui and IPP Calpine to build a thermal power plant in Mexico. Two years later, Chubu and Mitsui agreed to buy out Calpine's 45 percent share of that plant. In addition to its existing Thailand operations, Chubu also extended into Qatar during the decade.

The company's research and development efforts also marked a number of achievements. In 2003, the company unveiled a refining process capable of converting super-heavy crude oil into a lower viscosity, low sulfur oil. This offered the prospect of reducing the global reliance on the Middle East oil reserves, with the exploitation of major super-heavy crude oil reserves in Venezuela and Canada. In 2004, the company's research and development program, working in partnership with Mitsubishi Heavy Industries, also announced that it had succeeded in developing a new type of stronger plastic through the combination of fly ash and polypropylene.

Through the end of the decade, Chubu also focused on ensuring the fuel supply for its thermal power plants. In 2005, the company signed an LNG supply contract with Chevron from its Gorgon project then under construction in Australia.

By December 2009, the two companies had refined the supply agreement, which called for Chevron to ship 1.44 million metric tons per year of LNG to Chubu for 25 years. Chubu also purchased a small equity stake in the Gorgon project as part of that agreement.

By then, the company had also reached an agreement to buy 500,000 metric tons of LNG per year from Sakhalin Energy group, for a 15-year period, starting in 2006. The company then carried out an expansion of its LNG terminal in Aichi, Japan, in 2007. In March 2010, Chubu added a new supply contract to acquire a total of two million metric tons of LNG from the Tangguh Block in Indonesia between 2011 and 2015.

The importance of ensuring its thermal power capacity had by then been underlined for Chubu after an earthquake in Suruga Bay forced the company to take its Hamaoka nuclear power plant offline in 2009. As a result, the company found itself obliged to purchase part of its power requirements, while also ramping up production at its own thermal power plants. Despite this setback, Chubu remained committed to nuclear power. In July 2010, the company joined with power producers Tokyo Electric and Kansai Electric, as well as with Toshiba, Hitachi, and Mitsubishi Heavy Industries, to form a partnership marketing Japan's nuclear power technologies to the international market.

Julian James Kinsley
Updated, Christina M. Stansell; M. L. Cohen

PRINCIPAL SUBSIDIARIES

Chuden Kogyo Co. Ltd.; Eiraku Development Co. Ltd.; Eiraku Auto Service Co. Ltd.; Chuden Bldg. Co. Inc.; Chubu Plant Service Co. Ltd.; C-Tech Corporation; Techno Chubu Company Ltd.; Chita LNG Co. Ltd.; Chubu Telecommunications Company Inc.; CTI Co. Ltd.; Toenec Corporation; Aichi Electric Co. Ltd.

PRINCIPAL DIVISIONS

Electric Power Business.

PRINCIPAL OPERATING UNITS

Construction; Energy; Manufacturing; Other Businesses; Real Estate Management; Service/Other; Transportation.

PRINCIPAL COMPETITORS

Chubu Electric Power Company Inc.; The Chugoku Electric Power Company Inc.; IHI Corporation; Kansai Electric Power Company Inc.; Kyushu Electric Power Company Inc.; Tohoku Electric Power Company Inc.; Tokyo Electric Power Company Inc.

FURTHER READING

"Anti-Nuke Vote Sends Gov't on Defensive," *Mainichi Daily News*, November 20, 2001.

"Chevron Signs 25 Year Gas Supply Deal with Japan's Chubu Electric," *Information Company*, December 17, 2009.

"Chubu Elec, Toyota Tsusho to Join Thai Power Plant Project," *AsiaPulse News*, August 17, 2001.

"Chubu Electric Signs Contract to Acquire Two Million Metric Tons of LNG," *International Resource News*, March 9, 2010.

"Chubu Electric Starts Generating Power at No. 4 Reactor at Hamaoka," *International Resource News*, September 17, 2009.

"Chubu Electric to Shift Coal Procurement to Own Trading Unit," *International Resource News*, March 9, 2010.

"Japanese Utilities Chill-Out with Eco-Ice," *Petroleum Times Energy Report*, September 1, 1997, p. 7.

"Japan's Chubu Electric Aims to Cut Costs 20% by FY05," *AsiaPulse News*, April 24, 2001.

"Japan's Chubu Electric Scraps Nuclear Power Plant Plan," *AsiaPulse News*, February 23, 2000.

"Japan's Chubu Power to Lay Fiber Optics for 3.4 Min Households," *AsiaPulse News*, December 22, 1999.

"Leaky Reactor—Shaky System," *Mainichi Daily News*, November 15, 2001.

Mullen, Theo, "Government and Market Pressures Cut Prices in Japan," *Electrical World*, July 1997, p. 37.

"Six Japan Firms Team Up to Sell Nuclear Power Technology," *TendersInfo*, July 6, 2010.

Wehrfritz, George, Amy Webb, and Hideko Takayama, "Breach of Faith," *Newsweek International*, September 30, 2002, p. 42.

Yamamoto, Daisuke, "Profile: Japan's Electric Power Industry," *AsiaPulse News*, November 2, 2001.

Complete Production
Services, Inc.

11700 Old Katy Road, Suite 300
Houston, Texas 77079
U.S.A.
Telephone: (281) 372-2300
Fax: (281) 372-2301
Web site: http://www.completeproduction.com

Public Company
Incorporated: 2005
Employees: 5,235
Sales: $1.05 billion (2009)
Stock Exchanges: New York
Ticker Symbol: CPX
NAICS: 213112 Support Activities for Oil and Gas
     Operations

■ ■ ■

Listed on the New York Stock Exchange, Complete Production Services, Inc., (CPS) is a Houston, Texas-based provider of specialized oilfield services that can be used individually or packaged in a sequence of operations that run the gamut of the oil and gas exploration production cycle, from field development and drilling to stimulation and production. CPS divides its activities among three segments: Completion and Production Services, Drilling Services; and Product Sales.

CPS focuses on unconventional oil and gas plays in North America where producers are pressed to save time and reduce costs and hire CPS to take advantage of its local knowledge and breadth of expertise. These plays

include the Barnett Shale of North Texas, the Haynesville Shale in North Louisiana, the Marcellus Shale in Pennsylvania, the Bakken Shale in North Dakota, the Fayetteville Shale in Arkansas, the Woodford Shale in Oklahoma, and some important Rocky Mountain basins. Thus, CPS maintains offices in Oklahoma, Texas, Arkansas, North Dakota, Montana, Wyoming, Colorado, Louisiana, Pennsylvania, Utah, and Alberta, Canada. The company also has an operation in Singapore.

PRIVATE EQUITY FIRM ROOTS

The man behind the creation of Complete Production Services was Laurence E. "L. E." Simmons, whose private equity firm, SCF Partners, cobbled together the assets that formed the company's foundation. He was raised in Kaysville, Utah, where his father started as a bank teller and became chairman of Salt Lake City's Zions Bancorporation. His sons all became interested in finance and would receive M.B.A.s from Harvard University. L. E. Simmons also studied economics at the London School of Economics. After earning his M.B.A. in 1972, he went to work at The First National Bank of Chicago and helped to establish a finance department that focused on the offshore oil and gas industry.

In the aftermath of the energy crisis, he moved to Houston in 1974 to start Simmons and Company, an investment banking firm that focused on the oilfield service industry in Texas, Louisiana, and Alaska as well as the North Sea. The Simmons brothers survived the steep downturn in the energy market in the early 1980s, and L. E. Simmons soon decided to make a change of direction. Rather than investment banking he wanted to become involved in equity ownership. Thus, in 1989 he formed SCF Partners and began investing in energy service and equipment companies.

By 2000 SCF had begun to look at oilfield service companies that focused on the completion and production phase of the natural gas exploration and production cycle. In May 2001 SCF formed a company called Saber that acquired a pair of Louisiana oilfield services companies. Next, in July 2002, SCF acquired a majority interest in a production enhancement company, Integrated Production Services, Ltd., which operated in Canada. It had been formed in April 2000, the result of a merger between OTATCO Inc. and Reliance Services Group. Based in Alberta, the wellbore services company expanded rapidly through a series of acquisitions and expansions while gaining a listing on the Toronto Stock Exchange.

Saber acquired Integrated Production Services in September 2002 and changed its name to Integrated Production Services, Inc. (IPS). Further acquisitions and organic growth ensued. To participate in the Barnett Shale play of north Texas, SCF formed Complete Energy Services, Inc., in November 2003. This enterprise as well was expanded both organically and through acquisitions stretching into the mid-continent and U.S. Rocky Mountain regions. In the summer of 2004, SCF formed another company, I.E. Miller Services (IEM), to acquire I.E. Miller of Eunice (Texas) No. 2, L.L.C., which provided rig logistics in Texas and Louisiana.

Also during 2004 both IPS and IEM launched independent operations in the Barnett Shale and the U.S. Rocky Mountain regions. Additionally, the SCF group in September 2004 acquired Hyland Enterprises, Inc., a Wyoming-based fluid-handling and oilfield equipment rental company. A month later, Hamm and Phillips Service Company, an Oklahoma-based fluid-handling, well-servicing, and oilfield equipment rental company, was added to serve the U.S. mid-continent region. Another SCF-funded acquisition followed in February 2005 with the purchase of Parchman Energy

Group, Inc. Operating in Texas, Louisiana, and Mexico, Parchman was a provider of intervention services and such downhole services as coiled tubing, production testing, and wireline services.

FORMATION OF CPS: 2005

In September 2005, SCF brought together IPS, CES, and IEM to create Complete Production Services, Inc., in which SCF held a 70 percent interest. Andy Waite of SCF Partners served as chairman of the company. Acting as president and CEO was Joseph C. Winkler, who brought a wealth of experience in oilfield services. After earning a degree from Louisiana State University, he worked for several units of Baker Hughes Incorporated, including Eastman/Teleco and Milkpark Drilling Fluids. He became chief financial officer of Baker Hughes IN-TEQ, and in 1993 was named CFO of D.O.S., Ltd., which provided solids control equipment and services and coil tubing equipment to the oil and gas industry. After Varco International, Inc., acquired D.O.S. in 1996, he became Varco's CFO and executive vice president. In 2003 he was named Varco's president and chief operating officer.

Two months after the combination, CPS acquired the Big Mac Group of companies, including Big Mac Transports, LLC; Big Mac Tank Trucks, LLC, and Fugo Services, LLC. Based in Oklahoma, Big Mac provided fluid handling services and allowed CPS to become involved in the eastern Oklahoma market and the new Fayetteville Shale play in Arkansas. When 2005 came to a close, CPS reported revenues of about $630 million and net income of $53.9 million. Also in 2005 CPS filed to raise funds through an initial public offering (IPO) of stock. Underwritten by Credit Suisse Securities, UBS Securities, Banc of America Securities, and Jefferies & Company, the offering was completed in April 2006. Oversubscribed, it raised $718 million, much of which went to SCF and other shareholders who took some profit, leaving CPS with $293 million, funds earmarked for further growth. CPS shares then began trading on the New York Stock Exchange under the CPX ticker symbol.

EXTERNAL GROWTH: 2006

CPS tapped into its cash to complete several acquisitions in 2006. The Arkoma group of companies were purchased in June for $18 million. These companies helped CPS build upon its assets in the Fayetteville Shale play and Arkoma Basin, providing rental tools, machining, and a wellsite service known as fishing. A month later CPS paid $54.3 million for the Turner group of companies providing well service rigs and

KEY DATES

2002: SCF Partners acquires Integrated Production Services.
2003: SCF forms Complete Energy Services.
2004: SCF acquires I.E. Miller.
2005: SCF combines assets to create Complete Production Services, Inc. (CPS).
2006: CPS is taken public.

wellsite services in the Texas panhandle region. In August 2006, CPS acquired most of the assets of a Tolar, Texas-based drilling company, Pinnacle Drilling Co., L.L.C., for $32.8 million. Another $36 million was used to buy the Femco group of companies in October 2006. These Lindsay, Oklahoma-based businesses provided fluid handling, frac tank rental, propane distribution, and fluid disposal services in central Oklahoma. Finally, in November 2006, CPS paid $144.6 million in cash and stock to acquire Pumpco Services, Inc., a Gainesville, Texas-based provider of well stimulation, pressure pumping, and cementing services.

CPS made some smaller acquisitions as well and divested some Canadian assets. All told, CPS spent $420 million on acquisitions in 2006 and another $304 million in capital expenditures to create organic growth opportunities. Also of note in 2006, the company completed a private offering of $650 million in 10-year, senior notes to restructure its debt and set the stage for sustained growth.

CPS recorded revenues of nearly $1.1 billion in 2006 and net income of $138.5 million. Late in the year management sensed a softening in demand for its services, and as a result elected to slow the pace of acquisitions in 2007 in order to preserve its position and strengthen its balance sheet. Nevertheless, CPS completed seven small yet strategic acquisitions and deployed $373 million in capital. These additions included a LaSalle, Colorado, provider of frac tank rental and freshwater hauling services; a Greeley, Colorado, provider of fluid handling and disposal services; a Rangely, Colorado, company that offered rig workover and roustabout services; and a Borger, Texas, company that provided fluid handling and disposal services.

WAITE STEPS DOWN: 2007

In March 2007, Waite stepped down as chairman, and Winkler assumed this post while continuing to act as

president and CEO. Although it achieved limited growth from acquisitions in 2007, CPS enjoyed a significant increase in revenues to nearly $1.5 billion. Net income increased to $157.9 million.

Because of an anticipated drop in natural gas prices, CPS made plans to reduce spending on acquisitions and capital expenditures in 2008. When the market instead showed signs of improvement, CPS proved nimble enough to change tack. Taking advantage of opportunities, it spent about $180 million on four acquisitions. In February 2008, it bought Rangely, Colorado-based KR Fishing & Rental, Inc. Two months later CPS added Frac Sources Services, a Texas company that provided pressure pumping services in the Barnett Shale play. In October 2008, a pair of acquisitions were completed: TSWS Well Services LLC, an Arkansas provider of well servicing and heavy haul services in northern Louisiana, east Texas, and southern Arkansas; and Shelocta, Pennsylvania-based Appalachian Wells Services, Inc., and its subsidiary, providers of pressure pumping, e-line, and coiled tubing services in the Appalachian region. These additions helped to drive revenues to $1.83 billion in 2008.

PLUMMETING GAS PRICES: 2008

Business conditions deteriorated rapidly in late 2008. Natural gas prices fell and as a result there was a sharp decline in the utilization of CPS assets early in 2009. From a peak in 2008, U.S. drilling activity decreased 55 percent. CPS was again decisive and the company quickly moved to lower capital expenditures and cut its cost structure. For the year, revenues fell to $1.6 billion and the company posted a net loss of $181.7 million.

Conditions began to improve in 2010, leading to a 23 percent increase in revenues in the first quarter of 2010 over the fourth quarter of 2009. The number of operating drilling rigs increased sharply, although still significantly lower than the rig count at its peak in 2008. Regardless, business was picking up for CPS, with every major service offering reporting improved performance. Moreover, the long-term outlook for the North American plays served by CPS appeared to be bright. The energy industry remained volatile and conditions could easily change, but CPS, despite its brief history, had proven itself adept at adapting quickly and had established itself as a stable service provider that customers could count on for years to come.

Ed Dinger

PRINCIPAL BUSINESS SEGMENTS

Completion and Production Services; Drilling Services; Product Sales.

PRINCIPAL COMPETITORS

Baker Hughes Incorporated; Schlumberger Limited; Weatherford International Ltd.

FURTHER READING

"Complete Production Names Winkler as Board Chairman," *Houston Business Journal*, March 26, 2007.

"Complete Production Sets $600M Private Offering," *Houston Business Journal*, November 15, 2006.

"Current Research on Complete Production Services, Inc.," *Europe Intelligence Wire*, April 11, 2007.

"Integrated Production Services LTD," *Alberta Report*, March 5, 2001, p. 57.

"L.E. Simmons: Rising High, Digging Deep," *HBS Bulletin Online*, October 1997.

"Positioning Strategy Pays Off Well for Complete Production," *Houston Business Journal*, April 25, 2007.

Toal, Brian A., "Service-Side IPOs," *Oil and Gas Investor*, October 2006, p. 75.

Concord Music Group, Inc.

---■---

100 North Crescent Drive
Beverly Hills, California 90210
U.S.A.
Telephone: (310) 385-4455
Fax: (310) 385-4466
Web site: http://www.concordmusicgroup.com

Wholly Owned Subsidiary of Village Roadshow Entertainment Group
Incorporated: 1973 as Concord Jazz, Inc.
Employees: 160
Sales: $100 million (2010 est.)
NAICS: 512210 Record Production

■ ■ ■

Concord Music Group, Inc., is one of the leading independent record companies in the United States. The firm's offerings cover a broad swath of the musical spectrum, with a significant portion of sales coming from a catalog of over 13,000 master recordings that includes such labels as Stax, Prestige, Fantasy, Specialty, Telarc, and Rounder. These give it the largest library of jazz in the world, as well as significant collections of folk, blues, classical, and world music. Concord maintains an active new release schedule as well, and issues albums by high-profile artists including Paul McCartney through Hear Music, a joint venture with Starbucks. In 2010 the firm took over worldwide marketing of the ex-Beatle's solo catalog through a licensing deal with his MPL Communications.

BEGINNINGS

Concord Music Group traces its roots to a record label called Concord Jazz, which was founded in 1973 by Carl Jefferson. Born in California in 1920, Jefferson had served in World War II and Korea before returning to his home state to prospect for gold. When it proved a bust he began selling used jeeps at a Berkeley gas station, and then in 1958 opened a Lincoln-Mercury dealership in the nearby city of Concord, which would go on to make him wealthy.

Jefferson had been a fan of jazz since childhood, when he listened to live big band music on the radio, and in 1969 he helped the city of Concord launch an outdoor jazz festival, which was an instant success. Several years later legendary guitarists Herb Ellis and Joe Pass asked for help putting out a record, which he financed, and in 1973 Jefferson established Concord Jazz, Inc., to serve the many older artists who were being neglected by the industry as new styles came to dominate the marketplace. It would be headquartered in a former seafood restaurant next door to his car dealership.

At about this same time, Jefferson persuaded the city of Concord to build a $4.2 million, 8,500-seat pavilion on the outskirts of town, but festival attendance dropped after it was moved there from a downtown park. He subsequently turned over booking to jazz promoter George Wein and San Francisco rock

Part of CMG's mission statement proclaims the company shall "enrich lives by providing music of timeless appeal in innovative ways." This commitment to the music-loving public is why we continue to focus on music of quality and long-term appeal, while being cognizant of the changes in the way that consumers find and experience music. Examples of how we're implementing this mission include the revival of the classic Stax label, home to the finest in R&B and soul music, and Hear Music, a joint venture with Starbucks that makes music more readily accessible to fans.

impresario Bill Graham, and focused his energy on the label.

CONCORD PICANTE LAUNCHES IN 1980

During the 1970s Concord's output grew steadily as Jefferson oversaw the recording of albums by legends Dave Brubeck, Stan Getz, Rosemary Clooney, Mel Tormé, and Art Blakey. In 1980 he sold his car dealership to concentrate full time on the label, and also launched offshoot Concord Picante to record such Latin Jazz artists as Tito Puente.

By 1990 Concord Records had issued more than 450 albums and its annual revenues had grown to $5 million. About 40 percent of sales were made overseas, where American jazz artists were often accorded more respect than in their home country. U.S. and Japanese discs were manufactured in the United States, while the firm's catalog was licensed to a German company for manufacturing and distribution in Europe. Jefferson's commitment to his artists was strong, and he shared profits with them as well as keeping every release in print.

In 1994 Jefferson, who was suffering from emphysema, sold Concord to rapidly growing music distributor Alliance Entertainment Corporation for $6 million, although he stayed on to run it. He died a year later at the age of 75, having anointed Alliance executive and fellow jazz lover Glen A. Barros to succeed him.

In 1997 Concord joined forces with Stretch Records, which had been founded in 1994 by popular pianist/composer/producer Chick Corea. Barros was a

fan of the more commercial jazz-rock fusion style he represented, and although it was a departure from Concord's original mission, Barros had discussed taking the label in new directions with Jefferson, who reportedly did not object.

ACT III COMMUNICATIONS BUYS FIRM IN 1999

In 1999 the now bankrupt Alliance's creditors took ownership of Concord, which they subsequently sold to Act III Communications, owned by famed television producer Norman Lear and entertainment industry executive Hal Gaba. The 24-employee Concord had been losing money due to distribution problems caused by its parent's bankruptcy, but it was soon restored to profitability.

In 2000 a sales alliance was formed with Peak Records, which had recently ended its association with a larger company. The first release under the deal was an album by the Rippingtons, a smooth jazz unit whose guitarist Russ Freeman co-owned Peak. The move represented a further drift into commercial waters, and the label expanded its horizons again in 2001 by signing pop vocalist Barry Manilow and forming a joint label venture with Hugh Hefner's Playboy Enterprises.

In the spring of 2002 Concord moved from the San Francisco Bay Area to Beverly Hills, putting it closer to the center of the record industry. Most of the company's 39 employees chose to relocate to the firm's new 6,000-square-foot facility, which was situated next to Act III's headquarters. Concord now had revenues close to $20 million, with a fourth of sales coming from older titles. New signings ranged from popular 20-year-old jazz vocalist/pianist Peter Cincotti to Latin jazz/hip-hop act Ozomatli.

In 2003 Concord Records celebrated its 30th year in business. The firm's catalog had grown to 1,000 titles, and it had won a total of 14 Grammy Awards. Anniversary celebrations included concerts and special rereleases of older material.

The summer of 2004 saw Concord achieve breakout success with Ray Charles's *Genius Loves Company,* a collection of celebrity duets released in conjunction with coffee chain Starbucks, which pushed the release via in-store play and counter displays. The legendary vocalist's final album (he had died just before its release) would go on to sell more than 3.2 million copies in the United States and win eight Grammys. During the year Concord also switched from Alliance's Innovative Distribution to Universal Music & Video Distribution, an affiliate of the record industry's largest label.

KEY DATES

1973: Carl Jefferson founds Concord Jazz in California.
1994: Jefferson sells company to Alliance Entertainment.
1999: Norman Lear and Hal Gaba's Act III Communications buys Concord.
2004: Fantasy catalog is acquired; firm is renamed Concord Music Group.
2007: Company forms partnership with Starbucks to launch Hear Music label.
2008: Concord becomes part of Village Roadshow Entertainment Group.
2010: Firm buys Rounder Records; begins marketing Paul McCartney's catalog.

ACQUISITION OF FANTASY IN 2004

In December 2004 Concord purchased Fantasy, Inc., of Berkeley, California, a 55-year-old record label whose output had ranged from jazz pianist Dave Brubeck to million-selling rockers Creedence Clearwater Revival. Over the years Fantasy had acquired a number of other important labels including Prestige, Riverside, Contemporary, Debut, Pablo, and Milestone (jazz); Stax/Volt (Memphis soul); Specialty (gospel/blues/R&B); and Takoma (folk/blues). Fantasy also owned numerous music copyrights. After the sale some operations would remain in the Bay Area, including Fantasy Recording Studios, while others were moved to Beverly Hills.

The $83 million purchase was financed by Tailwind Capital Partners, which would take a minority stake, although Gaba and Lear remained in control. The merged companies, which would become known as Concord Music Group, Inc., had combined revenues of more than $40 million. Concord was now the top jazz record company in the world, owning key albums by legends Miles Davis, John Coltrane, and Thelonious Monk, as well as boasting such important current artists as Nnenna Freelon and Patti Austin.

In 2005 Norman Lear and Hal Gaba joined with Clarity Partners to buy 50 percent of Village Roadshow Pictures Group, an Australian movie firm that was a unit of Village Roadshow Ltd. Later that same year Concord acquired Cleveland-based Telarc International, which had a catalog of more than 1,000 jazz, classical,

and blues albums, some on the fusion/world music label Heads Up. The 28-year-old Telarc had annual revenues of approximately $10 million. Cofounder Bob Woods would continue to run its operations from Cleveland.

During the year Concord also signed Creedence Clearwater Revival vocalist/songwriter John Fogerty, who had left Fantasy more than three decades earlier in a bitter dispute over royalties. A first-time career retrospective would be released, as well as new material. A deal was also cut during the year with AG Interactive to distribute Concord music through online and mobile platforms.

In 2006 Concord extended its pact with Universal Music Group to include international distribution. The company also partnered with XM Satellite Radio to release co-branded compilation CDs, the first of which would feature artists heard on XM's jazz channel. Concord was now issuing approximately 150 albums per year, half of which were rereleases of older titles.

HEAR MUSIC LABEL: 2007

In 2007 Concord and Starbucks expanded their relationship by forming the record label Hear Music, named after an imprint Starbucks had used since 1999 for compilation CDs sold in its stores. Starbucks' entertainment unit would handle the recording and packaging of Hear Music releases, with Concord responsible for marketing and distribution outside of the coffeehouse giant's 13,000 locations.

In the summer the first Hear Music project, Paul McCartney's *Memory Almost Full,* was released. McCartney had recently left EMI, the label he had spent the bulk of his career with, because he felt there was not enough promotional push behind his work. *Memory Almost Full* would prove his most successful release in a decade, with nearly half of copies sold in Starbucks cafes. The label subsequently released new albums from other major names including Joni Mitchell, James Taylor, and Kenny G.

The year 2007 also saw the 50th anniversary of the founding of Stax, which was celebrated with a campaign of reissues and concerts, as well as the reactivation of the label. Several performers were signed, including talented young vocalist Angie Stone and Isaac Hayes, the cowriter of many Stax classics and a star in his own right with hits including "Theme from Shaft" for Stax imprint Enterprise. During the year Fantasy Studios was also sold to Wareham Development, which licensed the name for continued use.

MERGER WITH VILLAGE ROADSHOW PICTURES IN 2008

In early 2008 Concord was merged with Village Roadshow Pictures Group to form Village Roadshow Entertainment Group, after which the record company would continue to function as a separate entity. Its ownership would now be split between Lear and Gaba's Act III Entertainment, Tailwind Capitol, Clarity Partners, Lambert Entertainment, and Village Roadshow Ltd. of Australia.

Facing a declining profit margin, in the spring of 2008 Starbucks announced it was pulling back from Hear Music and turning over operation of the label to Concord. The president of Starbucks Entertainment stepped down, and the sudden changes left some high-profile artists unhappy, including Carly Simon, who sued Starbucks.

Although sales of recorded music had been steadily shrinking for nearly a decade, as illegal file-sharing and a precipitous drop in the number of bricks-and-mortar record stores took their toll, Concord was still managing to turn a profit. The firm's success was due to several factors, including its focus on serving an older demographic, one which still valued possessing a physical object over a computer file. Although it was selling increasing numbers of downloads via such outlets as iTunes, these also tended to be for full albums, rather than the less profitable single tracks popular with younger buyers. Unlike the major record companies, which were seeking blockbuster hits, Concord planned for most of its releases to turn a profit, which it could achieve on sales of as few as 5,000 copies.

ROUNDER RECORDS AND MCCARTNEY CATALOG PURCHASES: 2010

In the spring of 2010 Concord added another important name to its holdings, buying 40-year-old Cambridge, Massachusetts-based Rounder Records, famed for its library of folk, blues, Cajun, and other roots music. Rounder had 3,000 albums in its catalog and a roster of artists that included Willie Nelson, children's star Raffi, and the duo of Robert Plant and Alison Krauss, whose 2009 *Raising Sand* album had sold two million copies and won five Grammys. Label founders Ken Irwin, Bill Nowlin, and Marian Leighton-Levy would remain in charge. Concord's revenues were expected to grow to $100 million after the purchase.

The company scored another major coup during the year when it secured worldwide rights to the post-Beatle catalog of Paul McCartney, who had defected from financially strapped EMI and had released a new live CD/DVD package on Concord the year before. Deluxe reissues would begin in August with the 1973 classic *Band on the Run*. Like many artists who joined the Concord family, the former Beatle stated that he was delighted to be involved with an organization that was run by people who truly loved music.

After nearly four decades in business, Concord Music Group remained focused on producing quality music for an adult audience. With a catalog that included deep veins of classic American jazz and roots music, as well as a roster of current artists and musical icons, the company was in a strong position for continuing success.

Frank Uhle

PRINCIPAL SUBSIDIARIES

StarCon LLC (50%).

PRINCIPAL COMPETITORS

Ace Records, Ltd.; EMI Group, Ltd.; Sony Music Entertainment, Inc.; Universal Music Group; Warner Music Group Corp.; Welk Music Group.

FURTHER READING

Amicone, Michael, "All That Concord Jazz," *Billboard*, May 31, 2003, p. 20.

Ben-Yahuda, Ayala, "Starbucks, Concord Music Group Form Label," *Billboard.biz*, March 12, 2007.

Brown, Joel, "Rounder Records Sold to Calif. Company," *Boston Globe*, April 15, 2010, p. B7.

Bulbeck, Pip, "Concord, Roadshow Link Arms," *Hollywood Reporter*, September 4, 2007.

Gallo, Phil, "Starbucks Serves Label to Concord," *Daily Variety*, April 24, 2008.

Hamlin, Jesse, "Carl Jefferson, 75—Jazz Producer," *San Francisco Chronicle*, March 31, 1995, p. D8.

Hildebrand, Lee, "He Used His Gold to Mine Jazz," *San Francisco Chronicle*, August 14, 1988, p. 35.

Mehr, Bob, "Stax Kicks Off Golden Celebration," *Commercial Appeal*, January 21, 2007, p. A1.

Morris, Chris, "Concord Buys Classic Telarc," *Hollywood Reporter*, December 19, 2005.

———, "McCartney Inks Licensing Deal with Concord," *Daily Variety*, April 20, 2010.

Ouellette, Dan, "Beyond Genius," *Billboard*, May 14, 2005.

Plambeck, Joseph, "An Indie That Believes in CDs," *New York Times*, May 10, 2010, p. B1.

Said, Carolyn, "Farewell to Fantasy," *San Francisco Chronicle*, December 4, 2004, p. C1.

Vrabel, Jeff, "McCartney to Anchor New Starbucks Label," *Billboard*, March 21, 2007.

Consumers' Association

2 Marylebone Road
London, NW1 4DF
United Kingdom
Telephone: (+44-20) 7770-7000
Fax: (+44-20) 7770-7600
Web site: http://www.which.co.uk

Nonprofit Organization
Incorporated: 1957
Employees: 431
Operating Revenues: £66.9 million (2009)
NAICS: 813319 Other Social Advocacy Organizations

■ ■ ■

Based in London, Consumers' Association (CA) is the largest consumer rights organization in Europe with more than 700,000 members. Operating as Which?, it tests and reviews a wide variety of consumer goods and services, makes recommendations, and bestows the coveted Which? Best Buy award. The organization's findings are published in *Which?* magazine and subject-specific titles: *Which? Money, Which? Computing, Which? Gardening,* and *Which? Holiday.* Online and mobile digital services include Which? Online as well as iPhone apps that make Which? reviews and recommendations available to consumers on the move. Which? also publishes how-to guides and books on consumer rights. Additionally, Which? campaigns for consumer rights and lobbies the government on the behalf of consumers. For an annual fee, consumers can gain access to the organization's attorneys through Which? Legal Service.

A registered charity, Which? receives no government support, nor does it accept advertising.

FOUNDER BORN IN 1915

Consumers' Association was founded in 1957 by a group of people headed by noted gadfly Michael Dunlop Young, who would later in life receive a peerage and become known as Lord Young of Dartington. Young was born in 1915 in Manchester, England, the child of an Irish actress and painter and an Australian violinist. He spent much of his early years in Australia but after a split between his parents he returned to England at the age of eight where he struggled to square his bohemian upbringing with traditional education. After leaving four schools, he was fortunate at the age of 14 to find his way to a new progressive school in Devon called Dartington Hall. It was founded and run by a wealthy couple who would take him on visits to the United States. Young thrived at Dartington and went on to earn a degree in economics at London University. In 1939 he became a barrister.

Unable to serve in the military during World War II due to asthma, he headed a think tank, Political and Economic Planning, and before the age of 30 was named director of research for England's Labour Party. He made his mark with the party in 1945 by writing the Labour manifesto, a quixotic affair, much of which was rejected by Labour's own candidate. It did, however, reveal an iconoclastic streak that would fully flower in the years to come.

During the war, Young had become interested in sociology, so much so that when he returned to the

COMPANY PERSPECTIVES

With over 50 years experience, Which? has your consumer interests at heart. We campaign to protect your consumer rights, review products and offer independent advice on a wealth of subjects.

London School of Economics to complete his doctorate, he switched his thesis research from political voting to housing conditions in London's East End. He quickly came to realize that Labour leaders were not adequately representing these constituents, and in 1952 he established the Institute of Community Studies. It served as an incubator for his ideas, which would include early morning educational television programming, the Open University, and the National Extension College, which provided long-distance learning.

FORMATION OF CONSUMERS' ASSOCIATION: 1957

Before World War II Young had read about U.S. consumer unions, such as Consumers Union, the publisher of *Consumer Reports*, founded in 1936. It was not until 1957, though, that he was ready to establish a British counterpart. He enlisted some cofounders to establish Consumers' Association, and set up shop in a converted garage in Bethnal Green in London's East End where washing machines and refrigerators were initially tested. The results were then published in a magazine called *Which?* Because of England's strict libel laws, which he was told would sink any attempt to publish unvarnished product reviews, he included his own name in the masthead to provide a measure of insulation. It was not until 1964 that the magazine for the first time would be sued for libel, an effort that ultimately failed.

Which? found a ready audience in Great Britain, tapping into the concerns of a postwar consumer society. In the first months 10,000 people enrolled in the organization to receive the magazine, published quarterly. That number reached 100,000 by 1958. A year later, as membership increased to 150,000, the magazine began to be published on a monthly basis. The 250,000 mark was reached in 1961. In that same year Which? moved its headquarters to a new site in London at 14 Buckingham Street. Young had also helped to found the International Organization of Consumer Unions, later renamed Consumers International.

The success of *Which?* led to satellite publications. In 1962 Which? launched the *Car Supplement*, which three years later was rebranded as *Motoring Which?*, and a medical publication that would in time evolve into the *Drug and Therapeutics Bulletin*. The organization also turned to advocacy during this period. In 1964 it made use of *Which?* to campaign against the use of lead-based paints on toys and faulty electric blankets.

NEW DIRECTOR: 1964

Which? was only one iron Michael Young had in the fire. In 1964 Peter Goldman took over as the director of the organization and a year later Young resigned from the governing council. Goldman had been a rising political star in the Conservative Party, but in a shocking development in 1962 lost what had been considered a safe seat. He gave up politics to run Which?, but he did not forfeit his political skills, which served the organization well over the years. It was Goldman who made Which? into an effective consumer advocate, one that by the 1970s politicians ignored at their own peril.

In 1971 the organization's efforts led to enactment of The Unsolicited Goods and Services Act, which made it an offense to send unordered goods to people, who were now free to keep the goods without paying. A year later the British government was persuaded to appoint its first Minister of Consumer Affairs. Moreover, Goldman and Which? played a key role in the 1972 creation of the Office of Consumer Unions, which lobbied the European Union on behalf of consumers. Other legislative achievements in the 1970s included the Consumer Safety Act, passed in 1978, and a year later The Sale of Goods Act, which regulated contracts for the buying and selling of goods.

TESTING LAB OPENS: 1970

Under Goldman, Which? expanded on a number of other fronts as well, broadening the organization's embrace to include health and lifestyle issues. Which? opened a market research survey unit and its own testing laboratory in 1970. It also expanded its publishing efforts. A second satellite magazine, *Money Which?*, was launched in 1968. *Handyman Which?* followed in 1971, and *Holiday Which?* in 1974. The organization's book publishing efforts were expanded in 1977 with the launch of the "Which? Way" series. Which? published paperbacks on such subjects as buying homes, insurance, secondhand goods, health products, and funerals, as well as overviews on consumer law and advice on planning pregnancies.

Which? continued to advocate on behalf of consumers in the 1980s. The organization's campaign

KEY DATES

1957: Consumers' Association (CA) is founded by Michael Young.
1964: Peter Goldman is named director.
1970: CA opens testing laboratory.
2004: CA is granted super-complaint powers by Britain's Department of Trade and Industry.

on competition led to the 1980 Competition Act, which defined anticompetitive practices. While the act did not prohibit the practices, it set the stage for tougher future legislation. In the early 1980s Which? began campaigning for the mandatory use of seat belts. After a decade of work on the issue, the British government in 1994 made seat belts compulsory for vehicles carrying children.

On the publishing side of the ledger, the organization launched *Gardening Which?* in 1982. A year later the flagship publication, *Which?*, was reintroduced as a full-color magazine in which *Handyman Which?*, *Money Which?*, and *Motoring Which?* were now incorporated. In 1986 Which? acquired *Self Health*, which would later be rechristened *Health Which?*

DWINDLING MEMBERSHIP

Which? membership peaked at one million in 1987, a year that was memorable for other reasons. Which? received charity status for the research aspect of its work, a long-harbored goal of Peter Goldman, who also died in 1987 at the age of 62. Shortly before his passing he achieved a personal distinction with his appointment as the director-general of the International Organization of Consumer Unions. Memberships, and in turn subscriptions to *Which?*, began to decline after 1987. In essence, Which? was a victim of its own success. The organization's advocacy efforts had resulted in consumer protection laws that greatly improved the quality of goods, much of which had also become less expensive and more reliable. As a result, consumers felt less need to thoroughly research their purchases. Moreover, alternative publications sprang up to review specific products, so that it was cheaper for consumers to purchase one of these titles instead.

Subscriptions for *Which?* slipped to 593,000 by 1997 and the subscription to satellite publications fell to 443,000. Which? attempted to reinvigorate itself and develop new sources of revenue with the adoption of the Internet. Which? Online was launched in 1996 and at-

tracted 3,000 subscribers by the end of the following year, a number that would increase steadily to 24,000 by the end of the decade. Other online ventures did not fare as well, however.

Taxcal, Which? was a fee-based service to help people with their taxes, but was the unfortunate victim of a hacker, who obtained customers' credit card information, creating a wealth of unwanted publicity. Another service, Which? Web Trader, helped consumers in the selection of Web trading sites, but it proved too expensive to perform the task and was shut down. The organization's Carbuster.com was designed to help consumers save money by purchasing cars online, an outgrowth of its work in exposing the overpriced car market in the United Kingdom. The site was sold and immediately shut down, in the process depriving some 2,000 customers of their deposits. To maintain its reputation, the organization, which had no legal liability, paid back the customers, resulting in a loss of £700,000.

NEW CENTURY REBUILDING EFFORT

Which? changed with the times in other ways, too. Under the leadership of Dame Sheila McKechnie, who took over as director in 1995, Which? found new issues to address, including the financial services industry and genetically modified foods. In 1997 the organization succeeded in persuading the government to establish an Independent Food Standards Agency. Nevertheless, the membership ranks continued to decline as the new century began, falling to 511,000 in 2003. Subscribers of Which? Online, on the other hand, increased to 68,000. Which? went "back to its knitting," in the words of Dame McKechnie, and rebuilt lost membership to the 700,000 level, helped in part by the introduction of a new look to its magazines in 2006. A year later it relaunched *Which? Money*. It also introduced a new series of consumer-based books in 2006 under the Which? Essential Guides banner.

Which? remained current in the early 2000s as well by taking up the challenge of new concerns, such as identity fraud, file theft, and the banking crisis. The continued importance of Which? was reflected in 2004 when Britain's Department of Trade and Industry granted it official super-complaint powers that allowed it to petition government agencies on behalf of consumers. With no shortage of consumer concerns, Which? and its mission remained relevant for the foreseeable future.

Ed Dinger

PRINCIPAL SUBSIDIARIES
Which? Ltd.

FURTHER READING

Ashley, Jackie, "The Fine Art of Being a Social Entrepreneur," *New Statesman*, December 18, 2000, p. 33.

Dean, Malcolm, "Lord Young of Dartington," *Guardian* (London), January 2002.

Dench, Geoff, "Young at Eighty: The Prolific Life of Michael Young," *Journal of the Market Research Society*, January 1996, p. 73.

Hilton, Matthew, "Which Is Which?" *History Today*, September 2004, p. 37.

Wedd, George, "British Consumerism Examined," *Contemporary Review*, October 2004, p. 241.

"Which Way Not?" *Management Today*, November 3, 2003, p. 52.

Consumers Union

—■—

101 Truman Avenue
Yonkers, New York 10703-1057
U.S.A.
Telephone: (914) 378-2000
Fax: (914) 378-2900
Web site: http://www.consumerreports.org

Nonprofit Company
Incorporated: 1936
Employees: 652
Sales: $248 million (2010 est.)
NAICS: 511120 Periodical Publishers; 541380 Testing
Laboratories

■ ■ ■

Consumers Union is the nonprofit organization that publishes the monthly magazine *Consumer Reports*, dedicated to providing consumers with information and advice on a wide range of consumer issues, including product safety, health care provision, financial services, and food production. Over the years, *Consumer Reports* magazine has garnered an extensive and loyal following of approximately 20 million readers, largely due to its reputation for impartiality. Before each issue of the magazine is published, more than 100 experts work in 47 labs to test, analyze, evaluate, and rate the performance, safety, reliability, and value of products made by companies throughout the world. Consumers Union does not accept any fees for product samples, and refuses to grant permission for the commercial use of its name on any test results for a product it has evaluated.

In addition to a national testing and research center in Yonkers, New York, and an auto testing facility in East Haddam, Connecticut, Consumers Union staffs advocacy offices in Washington, D.C.; Austin, Texas; and San Francisco for the purpose of testifying before state and federal regulatory agencies and filing lawsuits on behalf of consumers. Consumers Union has also established The Consumer Policy Institute to conduct research and implement education programs in the areas of toxic air pollution, community right-to-know laws, pesticides, and biotechnology issues.

EARLY HISTORY

Consumers Union was the outgrowth of a book titled *Your Money's Worth*, written by F. J. Schlink and Stuart Chase. When the book first appeared in 1927, it quickly became a best seller, since it was the first of its kind to describe in detail the fraud and manipulation surrounding the manufacture of food, medicine, cosmetics, automobiles, and household appliances. The popularity of the book can also be seen as an indication of the growth of the modern consumer movement within the United States during the 1920s. Authors such as Upton Sinclair had exposed the problems within the food industry, and President Herbert Hoover, himself an engineer, had encouraged the formation of groups such as the American Standards Association, and given more authority to the National Bureau of Standards to prescribe a standardization system for testing foods, textiles, and other products that the U.S. government was likely to purchase.

Schlink, a former staff member of the National Bureau of Standards, employed its work and findings as

COMPANY PERSPECTIVES

Test, Inform, Protect. Consumers Union, publisher of Consumer Reports, is a nonprofit [501(c)3] organization established to provide consumers with information and advice on goods, services, health, and personal finance, and to initiate and cooperate with individual and group efforts to maintain and enhance the quality of life of consumers.

a model for testing products that were used by consumers. After the publication of his book, Schlink used his membership in a White Plains, New York, men's club to summarize the experiences the members of the club had with certain products. Assembling his findings into the *Consumer Club Commodity List*, he began to sell mimeographed copies of the listings for one dollar each. By 1929, Schlink had received such an enthusiastic response from the general public that he formed Consumers' Research, an organization incorporated as a nonprofit consumer testing firm, the first such organization of its type in the world. Schlink opened an office in New York City and renamed his mimeographed list the *Consumers' Research Bulletin*. By 1933, there were over 42,000 subscribers.

In 1933, Schlink decided to relocate his operation from New York City to the rural village of Washington, New Jersey. However, after a short period, the engineers and journalist that formed the core of his staff grew disenchanted with country life and the long hours and low pay Schlink had imposed. When employees asked for a raise, their request was summarily rejected. When three employees attempted to form a union within Consumers' Research, Schlink fired them. His action precipitated a strike, however, and the demand that the fired workers not only be reinstated but all employees given a raise. Schlink retaliated with strikebreakers and private detectives, refusing mediation or arbitration, and described the strikers as communists.

In February 1936, the strikers from Consumers' Research decided to form an organization of their own in New York City. Named Consumers Union, the new organization brought together journalists, engineers, academics, and scientists committed to testing products used by consumers. Arthur Kallet, an engineer and former director at Consumers' Research who joined the strikers against Schlink, was appointed the first director of the organization. By May of the same year, *Consumers Union Reports* appeared, with detailed articles evaluating

and rating milk, soap, stockings, breakfast cereal, credit unions, and Alka-Seltzer. With little money and a circulation of only 4,000, the organization in its early reports was forced to concentrate on inexpensive items such as hot water bottles, radios, and fans. The reports were so successful, however, that by the end of 1936 circulation had increased dramatically to over 37,000 subscribers.

During the late 1930s, Consumers Union and its reports garnered a large amount of hostility from traditional magazine publishers. More than 60 publications refused to provide advertising space for Consumers Union because it had an explicit policy of criticizing products by name. In addition, during the late 1930s with the Great Depression still affecting most Americans, not many people were buying the reports because they were not buying large amounts of consumer products. Despite these challenges the organization and its magazine continued to grow. By 1939, *Consumers Union Reports* numbered over 85,000 subscribers.

The advent of World War II changed everything. Because the focus of manufacturing was on the production of tanks, guns, airplanes, trucks, and military uniforms, rather than on radios, refrigerators, and automobiles, the staff at Consumers Union did not have enough products to test and evaluate. When rationing was imposed, the staff at the organization found it even more difficult to procure items that it normally tested, such as shoes and soap. In 1942, Consumers Union changed the name of its magazine from *Consumers Union Reports* to *Consumer Reports* in order to indicate that it provided a service to all consumers, not just union members. However, during the same year circulation dropped to half the level of 1939, and the main office in New York City was forced to cut its staff.

THE POSTWAR ERA

When the war ended in 1945, Consumers Union and its magazine were poised for rapid growth: After nearly five years of getting by on the necessities of life, people across the United States were ready to embark on a buying spree. Fortunately for Consumers Union, the American public turned to its magazine for advice on what to buy. In 1946, the circulation of *Consumer Reports* numbered 100,000, but had increased to 400,000 by 1950. In 1952, *Consumer Reports* published the first automobile frequency-of-repair table. In 1953 the magazine published the first of a series of articles and tables on the tar and nicotine content of cigarettes, and the dangers of smoking. The following year, *Consumer Reports* issued its first tests and ratings on color television sets.

One of the most important turning points for Consumers Union also occurred in 1954 when the organization had become financially successful enough to expand and improve its laboratory and testing facilities. Consumers Union moved from New York City to Mt. Vernon, New York, in order to take advantage of larger space for its administrative office and laboratory facility.

Along with the move to a new location, Consumers Union decided not only to test and rate the quality of consumer products but to advocate on behalf of consumer interests. Staff personnel and board members of the organization began to testify on a regular basis before federal and state committees on a wide range of issues, including watered ham, the price-fixing of drugs, and automobile safety. At the same time, due to the increased revenues from growing subscriptions, Consumers Union began to provide financial assistance to various other consumer groups such as the American Council on Consumer Interests and Ralph Nader's Center for Auto Safety. By the end of the 1950s, Consumers Union had grown large and influential enough to start building a worldwide consumer movement, providing funding and advice to newly formed organizations such as the International Organization of Consumers Unions, and the British-based Consumer's Association. When the founding director, Arthur Kallet, retired in 1957 after 21 years of devoted service, Consumers Union had grown to become the largest and most influential organization promoting consumer interests.

GROWTH AND INFLUENCE

Consumer Reports continued to enhance its reputation as an impartial judge of consumer products in the 1960s. In 1962, the magazine issued its first report on automobile insurance and discovered that reform was needed due to rates that varied by hundreds of dollars for the same level of insurance. In 1965, *Consumer Reports* rated the Toyota Corona particularly favorable for "long-distance driving." By 1975, the Corona was the number one import in the U.S. automobile market. After Nader published his famous book *Unsafe at Any Speed* in 1965, Consumers Union asked the author to serve as a board member for the organization, and dedicated itself to providing even more information on the cars and trucks made within the automobile industry.

During the 1970s, Consumers Union's influence as an advocate for consumer interests increased significantly. Due to the years of product ratings provided by *Consumer Reports*, the U.S. government established the National Commission on Product Safety. In 1972, Consumers Union opened an office in Washington, D.C., to further impress on government officials the importance of its work and the changes needed for issues surrounding consumer confidence. Regional offices were later opened in San Francisco, California, and Austin, Texas, for the same purpose. In 1974, *Consumer Reports* published a series on the extent of pollution in the waterways throughout the United States, with detailed recommendations for cleaning them up. The series was regarded so highly that it won the National Magazine Award, the first of three given to *Consumer Reports*.

In the 1980s, *Consumer Reports* initiated a television section, and also a magazine for children called *Penny Power* (later renamed *Zillions*). In 1983, the magazine implemented a phone-in service for consumers to check automobile prices and the cost of repairs. Since the organization, especially under the earlier influence of Nader, continued to develop its methods for testing and rating automobiles, in 1986 the board of directors voted to purchase a drag strip in East Haddam, Connecticut, to renovate and construct a state-of-the-art evaluation facility for cars, trucks, and the growing market for recreational vehicles. Based on tests conducted at this facility, *Consumer Reports* discovered that the Suzuki Samurai easily rolled over, and rated it "Not Acceptable." By this time, the reputation and influence of *Consumer Reports* had become so great that sales of the Suzuki Samurai dropped precipitously.

MOVING INTO THE 21ST CENTURY

By 1995, paid circulation for *Consumer Reports* reached over 4.7 million readers, placing the periodical on the top 10 list for paid subscriptions. By the end of 1996, the publishing industry estimated that *Consumer Reports* had a total readership of over 18 million, including library subscribers and an estimated four readers per copy pass-along factor. One of the most popular magazines in the United States, *Consumer Reports* showed no sign of decreasing readership, especially with its decision to move toward multimedia publishing in the mid-1990s. This resulted in an expansion of Consumers Union's role in providing consumers with detailed evaluations and ratings of products, and included a radio program, a newspaper column, television programming, additional newsletters, and CD-ROM products. In 1997, Consumers Union launched its first Web site, ConsumerReports.org.

Faster and greater changes were in store for *Consumer Reports* with the dawn of the new century. In 2001, Rhoda Karpatkin retired as president of Consumers Union, and James A. Guest, who chaired the board of directors for the company from 1980 to 2000 became the sixth president of the company. Guest became president during a virtual media explosion. Within one year of his presidency, ConsumerReports.org hit the one million subscriber mark, becoming one of the most popular and most successful subscription-based Web sites in the world.

Understanding the remarkable capabilities that the online edition offered the company, Consumers Union quickly launched more Web sites, with a special emphasis on grassroots activism. On Earth Day 2005, GreenerChoices.org was opened, with the purpose of informing and empowering consumers on ways to be more environmentally friendly. Other Web sites followed, including HearUsNow.org, which worked to enable consumers to achieve better and more affordable media and communication lines, and Prescription ForChange.org, which promoted consumer awareness of issues surrounding health care. As this Web site suggested, Consumers Union began to focus heavily on health care issues, especially with the launch of its new subscription-based Web site, ConsumerReportsHealth.org. Also a subscription-based Web site, ConsumerReportsHealth.org centered on a variety of health issues, ranging from products to hospitals and even to conditions and their varying treatment options. Consumers Union also paired with the Stop Hospital Infections Campaign, and helped compare hospital compliance in each state with federal standards.

In 2006, the company bought the popular Web log (or "blog") Consumerist.com. The blog, which gave short, snappy, and honest reviews of products to an estimated 1.8 million people each month, remained a free Web site for its users. Also in 2006, Consumers Union began publishing *ShopSmart*, a shopping magazine aimed at women over 30.

In 2007, Consumers Union started an advertising stint that, by 2008 included four major runs of ads, including full-page ads in *USA Today*, as well as on popular auto Web sites such as CarandDriver.com and Edmunds.com. The ads decried extended warranties on cars. Other ads covered items such as gift cards. Previously, Consumers Union had done little advertising, but according to a March 18, 2008 interview on American Public Media's *Marketplace*, Vice President Kenneth Wiene said that the ads were primarily just an attempt to "'advance [their] mission through a means that is untraditional for Consumers Union."

However, neither these rapid changes in social media nor over 70 years of experience could have softened the blow that hit the company after a faulty product review. In February 2007, *Consumer Reports* published a study of 12 of the top-selling infant car seats on the market at the time. The car seats had been tested in both front-impact and side-impact collisions, and a remarkable 10 had been found to be inadequate. The results were immediately questioned and within two weeks were retracted by Consumers Union. The company later blamed miscommunication with the independent laboratory that was hired to do the testing for the fault, and noted that appropriate experts were not involved in any part of the testing. Although no lawsuits were leveled against Consumers Union, the company did correct its mistake in a subsequent magazine and tightened standards for research done at outside laboratories.

CONSUMERS UNION AND THE FUTURE

Nearly 80 years after its inception, Consumers Union remained an influential organization for most of the consumer market. Its rapid expansion into the social media worlds of the 21st century certainly aided its growth, but the company already had one highly desirable trait: name recognition. Consumers Union inspired in the minds of most consumers fair and balanced judgment, so much so that in 2010 the company could still cause major corporations such as Toyota to halt production of entire lines of vehicles. In this instance, Toyota ceased producing the Lexus GX 460 after *Consumer Reports* labeled it unsafe. By 2010, the company boasted combined Web and print subscriptions of 7.3 million.

Nevertheless, in order to continue its success in the 21st century, the company would have to continue to maintain a firm grasp on consumer trends. The *Wall Street Journal* article "Meet the Sticklers" noted that the company had begun to reprioritize the items it tested, replacing power washers, for example, with digital cameras. These changes denoted an increasing sensitivity to the changing needs of consumers. The company also had begun reviewing fewer products in greater depth. Such business-savvy choices, combined with a near legendary reputation for accurate reporting, would propel Consumers Union into the future.

Thomas Derdak
Updated, Laura Rydberg

PRINCIPAL COMPETITORS

Consumers Digest; Council of Better Business Bureaus, Inc.; J.D. Power and Associates; Underwriters Laboratories, Inc.

FURTHER READING

Bounds, Gwendolyn, "Meet the Sticklers—New Demands Test Consumer Reports; Flying in Cat Fur," *Wall Street Journal*, May 5, 2010, p. D1.

Clifford, Stephanie, "Consumers Union to Buy Gawker Blog Consumerist," *New York Times*, December 30, 2008, p. B3.

"Consumers Union Reports," *Consumers Union Publication*, May 1936.

"The Early Years Remembered," *Consumers Union Consumer Reports Publications*, 1996.

Horrigan, Jeremiah, "Consumer Reports: Tops in Testing," *Times Herald Record*, March 22, 1997, pp. 19–21.

Linn, Virginia, "Health Council Rates Magazines for Nutritional Value," *Atlanta Constitution*, April 16, 1998, p. 26.

Patton, Phil, "The Product Police," *Audacity*, Spring 1996, pp. 21–23.

Perez-Peña, Richard, "Bearer of Bad News Decides to Advertise It," *New York Times*, March 17, 2008.

Rouvalis, Cristina, "Consumer Reports Testers Give Products a Pounding," *Pittsburgh Post-Gazette*, July 27, 1998, pp. E1–E3.

Seelye, Katherine Q., "Magazine Will Begin Consulting with Experts," *New York Times*, March 21, 2007.

Warne, Colston E., "Consumers Union's Contribution to the Consumer Movement," in *Consumer Activists: They Make A Difference*, edited by Erma Angevine, Mount Vernon, NY: Consumers Union Foundation, 1982, pp. 85–110.

White, John R., "Who Are Those Guys at Consumer Reports?" *Boston Globe*, April 5, 1997, p. D1.

Wiene, Kenneth, Interview by Dan Grech, *Marketplace*, American Public Media, March 18, 2008.

Woller, Barbara, "Consumer Champion," *Gannett Newspapers*, June 28, 1998, pp. 3A–3E.

Daily Mail and General Trust PLC

Northcliffe House
2 Derry Street
London, W8 5TT
United Kingdom
Telephone: (+44 20) 7938 6000
Fax: (+44 20) 7938 4626
Web site: http://www.dmgt.co.uk

Public Company
Incorporated: 1922
Employees: 16,000
Sales: £2.11 billion ($3.37 billion) (2009)
Stock Exchanges: London
Ticker Symbol: DGMT
NAICS: 511110 Newspaper Publishers

■ ■ ■

Daily Mail and General Trust PLC (DMGT) is one of the largest media companies in the world. Headquartered in London, England, the company owns and operates several newspapers, including its namesake *Daily Mail*, as well as an increasing number of electronic media products, a risk assessment and management firm, Australian radio stations, and an events planning and staging group. The A&N Media umbrella holds the company's newspapers, including the well-known Associated Newspapers, Northcliffe Media, and Euromoney publications. Still family owned and operated, DMGT is led by Chairman Jonathan Harmsworth, Viscount Rothermere IV.

EARLY HISTORY

The founder of the *Daily Mail*, Alfred Harmsworth, was born in 1866 near the beginning of what was later to be called the Golden Age of British journalism. Harmsworth's interest in publishing was encouraged by his father, who purchased a printing set for the boy's seventh birthday. Although young Harmsworth was a sports enthusiast and interested in a great many pursuits, he was enthralled with the world of publishing.

After Harmsworth graduated from college, he decided to become a newspaper publisher. There were numerous "halfpenny" papers published throughout Britain on cheap paper and written in a dull manner, providing little information for a public growing more literate and hungry for knowledge. With a clear vision and untold amounts of energy, Harmsworth formed a partnership with his brother Harold, later the first Viscount Rothermere, and began working on a bold and radical newspaper, the *Daily Mail*.

On a spring morning in early May 1896, Harmsworth shut himself up in his office at 2 Carmelite Street and worked nonstop for the next two days and nights to write, edit, and produce the first paper aimed at bringing essential information to the working class on a daily basis. Initial circulation was estimated at 100,000, but by the time news vendors sold the final copy, the *Daily Mail* had sold out of 397,215 copies.

From the very first page, the reading public was enthralled with the *Daily Mail*. One of the most popular innovations of the new upstart was the inclusion of a daily women's page, which attracted intense

COMPANY PERSPECTIVES

■

Empowering people through information since brothers Alfred and Harold Harmsworth established the *Daily Mail* in 1896, DMGT is a publicly listed company quoted on the London Stock Exchange. Operating in over 40 countries, DMGT produces high-quality content, information, analytics, and events for both businesses and consumers.

derision from other publications that regarded female readers as beneath journalistic consideration.

Harmsworth is widely regarded as one of the progenitors of modern journalism. He had an uncanny instinct for news and an ability to see a story's potential even before events fully unraveled. He also displayed an intuitive gift for anticipating public opinion and, in many instances, knew what the public wanted to read. One of the best examples of this talent was a persistence in bringing the truth about the Boer War to the people of Britain.

WAR COVERAGE FOR THE PEOPLE: 1899–1910

By the beginning of the second Boer War conflict in the late 1890s, circulation of the *Daily Mail* had risen to over one million, higher than any other newspaper in the Western world. Harmsworth sent a team of journalists to cover the events and battles between British soldiers and Dutch Afrikaners in South Africa. Dispatches from the first female war correspondent, Lady Sarah Wilson (aunt of Winston Churchill), from the besieged town of Mafeking, described the plight of British soldiers facing almost insurmountable odds.

The British government, however, insisted all dispatches from South Africa undergo censorship due to the harmful effect military losses might have on public support for the war. Harmsworth was adamant the truth should not be hidden or repressed simply because it was unpleasant. The government, forced to listen to the mounting outcry of public opinion, finally relented and agreed to allow one newspaper the right to print uncensored news from the battlefront. After a hotly contested and bitter fight with other papers, the *Daily Mail* began bringing uncensored news from South Africa. Much to the dismay of the government, the *Daily Mail* published reports that His Majesty's government had been denying for many months.

In 1902 at the conclusion of the hostilities, the *Daily Mail* published the peace treaty terms as a world exclusive, even before the announcement was made by the British government. From that point onward, the *Daily Mail's* reputation for exclusive and reliable news, and its championing of the ordinary citizen, was unquestioned throughout the United Kingdom.

From the earliest days of the *Daily Mail*, Harmsworth advocated technological advances in the British newspaper industry. Taking advantage of worldwide communications, the paper established direct telegraphic contact between its London and New York offices and from 1905 onward was printed in Paris to be on breakfast tables 10 hours earlier than British papers transported across the English Channel. In addition, its offices were the first in Britain to install equipment enabling the development of pictures.

WORLD WAR I ERA THROUGH 1929

During the years immediately before World War I, Harmsworth began to use the *Daily Mail* to warn the British public about the growing militarization of Germany and the threat it posed to peace in Europe. Harmsworth and the *Daily Mail* were not only dismissed but roundly portrayed as engaging in "warmongering." When Harmsworth's predictions came true in August 1914, however, the *Daily Mail* devoted its pages to the trials and tribulations of common soldiers on the front line.

By 1915 the *Daily Mail* was reporting that British soldiers were being butchered by the thousands in France, and that one of the reasons for the appalling attrition rate was inferior weapons and inadequate ammunition. The Shell Crisis, as it came to be called, gave rise to an intense confrontation between the government and the British national press.

Harmsworth was hanged in effigy in front of the *Daily Mail* offices, copies of the paper were burned by a crowd at the London Stock Exchange, and circulation declined by a million copies in one day. Harmsworth nonetheless held his ground and by the time all of the facts were made public, the Asquith government was forced to resign. A subsequent coalition government and war prosecutions extended Harmsworth's influence to the halls of Parliament.

When Harmsworth died in 1922 at the height of his fame, he had been dubbed Lord Northcliffe by the king of England. As tributes poured in from around the world, Harmsworth was remembered for his innovative approach to publishing. Upon Harmsworth's death, brother Harold, Lord Rothermere, took control of the *Daily Mail* and incorporated its operations.

```
┌─────────────────────────────────────────────┐
│                                               │
│              KEY DATES                        │
│                   ■                           │
├───────────────────────────────────────────────┤
│  1896:  Alfred Harmsworth writes, edits, and  │
│         publishes the first edition of the    │
│         Daily Mail.                           │
│  1922:  Alfred Harmsworth dies and brother    │
│         Harold, Lord Rothermere, takes over.  │
│  1969:  Euromoney Publications is formed.     │
│  1971:  Viscount Rothermere II, great-nephew  │
│         of the paper's founders, takes over   │
│         operations.                           │
│  1978:  Viscount Rothermere III, Vere         │
│         Harmsworth, becomes chairman upon     │
│         his father's death.                   │
│  1988:  Newspaper moves its operations to     │
│         Northcliffe House in Kensington.      │
│  1998:  Jonathan Harmsworth, Viscount         │
│         Rothermere IV, is installed as        │
│         chairman.                             │
│  1999:  Free commuter paper Metro begins      │
│         publication.                          │
│  2009:  Company sells half of its Australian  │
│         radio subsidiary to Lachlan Murdoch.  │
│                                               │
└───────────────────────────────────────────────┘
```

BEFORE AND AFTER WORLD WAR II

Lord Rothermere continued his brother's traditions during the 1930s, trying to warn the public about the danger of Adolf Hitler's rise to power. As the *Daily Mail* began to champion Winston Churchill as the one to lead Britain's government in the possible event of a second world war, the newspaper began to increase its circulation dramatically.

When war was declared in September 1939 the *Daily Mail* strongly supported British military aviation and the creation of the Bristol Blenheim, then the most powerful bomber ever made. The bomber played a significant role in the Battle of Britain and the fight against Germany's Luftwaffe and was the first bomber to sink both German and Japanese submarines.

When World War II ended in 1945, the *Daily Mail*'s circulation continued to rise. Having garnered a sterling reputation for reporting reliable and trustworthy information during both world wars, the *Daily Mail* renewed its commitment to portraying momentous events with a journalistic flair.

One of the newspaper's great foreign correspondents, Noel Barber, became renowned for his elegant anecdotal reports on such topics as the Soviet invasion of Hungary in 1956, where he held a woman who died in his arms facing Russian tanks; his visit to the South Pole, where he was the first Englishman to make the trip since Captain Scott; and his coverage of

Sir Edmund Hillary's trek up the Himalayas. Throughout the 1950s and 1960s the *Daily Mail* set a standard and defined a style of reporting that legions of young reporters tried to emulate worldwide.

EXPANSION AND CONSOLIDATION: SIXTIES THROUGH EIGHTIES

Over the years the *Daily Mail* and its subsidiary, Associated Newspapers, had grown dramatically. In 1969 a new financially themed business-to-business unit called Euromoney was created while the company continued to buy and sell numerous London and regional publications. To centralize operations and standardize publishing procedures, the *Daily Mail* was relaunched in tabloid format in 1971 as it celebrated 75 years in business.

The publishing firm was also under new leadership as Viscount Rothermere II, great-nephew of the paper's founders, began running the company. Editor Sir David English, who later became chairman of the company's Associated Newspapers subsidiary, propelled the revised *Daily Mail* to numerous awards, more than any other newspaper.

In 1978 Esmond Harmsworth died and son Vere, the third Viscount Rothermere, took over duties in the boardroom. The venerated paper continued to earn accolades worldwide and in 1983 received a special British Press Award for its "relentless campaign against the malignant practices of Reverend Sun Myung Moon's Unification Church." The *Daily Mail* helped expose the brainwashing techniques of the Moonies and as a result of its coverage was sued for libel, ultimately leading to the longest libel action in British legal history. In the end, the paper was vindicated and, as a consequence of the evidence made public at the trial, Moon's activities were reviewed by the British government and severely curtailed.

In 1988, DMGT left its headquarters at Carmelite House on Fleet Street, the traditional site of British publishers for hundreds of years, relocating to Northcliffe House in Kensington, West London. As the newspaper moved to Kensington, the printing works moved eight miles away to a 12-acre parcel of land in London's Docklands. The state-of-the-art printing and distribution facility completed the company's modernization program. The distance separating the editorial, advertising, printing, and distribution offices was linked by a highly sophisticated electronic communications systems considered one of the best in the world.

THE AGE OF ELECTRONIC MEDIA

In the early 1990s the company expanded into educational and financial publishing, as well as radio and television. The age of electronic media completely changed the British publishing industry, although the *Daily Mail* stayed apace with various ventures including its expanding Euromoney financial unit. Harmsworth Publishing, the company's information publisher, created College-View, an innovative software program for colleges and universities to market themselves to thousands of high schools in the United States.

In association with the College-View program, two CD titles were released covering scholarship and career opportunities. Additionally, the company's rapid expansion into television and radio led to cable news, arts, and film channels; a controlling interest in the Broadcast Media Group, an Australian firm with regional radio stations; majority stake in Klassiska Hits, a radio station in Sweden; and Classic FM, a national classical music station in Britain.

Back in the print world, the average daily circulation of the *Daily Mail* surpassed two million in its centenary year, while the regional publications throughout Britain under the auspices of Associated Newspapers continued to grow. In spite of its success in traditional print journalism, the *Daily Mail* continued to explore new media.

Rothermere died suddenly in 1998 and was succeeded by 30-year-old son Jonathan Harmsworth (Viscount Rothermere IV). The new chairman pushed into electronic media in 1999 and also introduced *Metro*, a free commuter paper modeled after a daily rag in Stockholm, Sweden. Rothermere also continued buying and developing various Web sites and e-commerce portals. In the same year, Euromoney changed its name to Euromoney Institutional Investor, as the media giant pondered a bid for rival *Daily Express*. In 2000 DMGT lost out on the *Express* but consoled itself by selling part of its radio holdings to GWR Group for a higher (27 percent) stake in the company.

The following year DMGT continued to diversify, buying several consumer-themed online businesses, but turned once again to print with the purchase of regional and local papers in 2001. Over the next few years DMGT's revenues climbed steadily from $3 billion in fiscal 2002 to $3.8 billion in 2004, yet net income declined from 2002's $129.3 million to $111 million in 2004. As electronic media continued to supplant print, DMGT launched www.dailymail.co.uk and considered selling Northcliffe Newspapers. Although the unit accounted for more than a third of its operating profit, the newspaper unit had been experiencing weak ad sales.

AN UNCERTAIN PRINT FUTURE: 2005 AND BEYOND

In the end DMGT held on to the historic Northcliffe, merged it with Associated Newspapers, restructured the unit into regional divisions, then sold off underperformers. The company surprised the newspaper industry in 2006 with the purchase of former Communist paper *Pravda*, then went on to celebrate a phenomenal fiscal year with revenues of nearly $4.1 billion and net income soaring to 11 percent or $449 million, although the jubilance did not last.

In 2007 revenues still climbed to $4.6 billion, but income fell to 4.8 percent at $219 million and marked a spectacular fall from grace: DMGT had dropped out of Britain's leading industry index, the FTSE 100. The demotion was both a major corporate blow and a personal one as well for Rothermere, who many had believed incapable of leading the media empire like his forebears. To shore up its bottom line, DMGT announced it would sell a majority stake in the *Evening Standard*, one of its more than 200 subsidiaries. Former KGB agent and Russian billionaire Alexander Lebedev, along with former Prime Minister Mikhail Gorbachev, won the bidding war, although it did little to help as DMGT managed to bring in $4.2 billion in 2008 revenues but no profit. Worse was yet to come as revenues slid to £2.11 billion ($3.37 billion) and the company suffered losses of £301.88 million ($483 million), along with stock prices hitting an all-time low of £2.05 ($3.28) during the 2009 fiscal year. The year also saw the sale of half of DMG Radio Australia to a private investment firm owned by Lachlan Murdoch, the eldest son of media tycoon Rupert Murdoch.

To shake off its losses and prepare for an electronic future, DMGT launched dozens of new sites tied to its regional newspapers, bringing its Web site ownership total to more than 150. As industry analysts and seemingly everyone weighed in on the future of print media, DMGT released its first-quarter 2010 results, with better than expected numbers, although still a decline, in its newspaper division. It was nevertheless an improvement over the previous year and an indicator that DMGT's other operating units were gaining considerable ground, enough to support the conglomerate's overall goals. In July DMGT combined its national and regional newspapers under the new banner of A&N Media.

While many within the industry believed that the power and majesty of the print newspaper were long gone and legendary reporters such as Noel Barber extinct as "writers" blogged, tweeted, and texted, few believed print would disappear altogether. In the case of DMGT, the company continued to diversify its operations. Its newspaper division, perhaps representing the last bastion of British publishing royalty, would not, one hoped, go gentle into that good night.

Thomas Derdak
Updated, Nelson Rhodes

PRINCIPAL SUBSIDIARIES

A&N Media (Associated Newspapers Ltd. and Northcliffe Media Ltd.); DMG Events; DMG Information; DMG Radio; DMGT Pensions; Euromoney Institutional Investor PLC; Risk Management Solutions.

PRINCIPAL COMPETITORS

Axel Springer AG; Dow Jones; Guardian Media Group PLC; Informa PLC; Lagardere SCA; News Corporation; Pearson PLC; Telegraph Media Group Limited; Thomson Reuters Corporation.

FURTHER READING

Alarcon, Camille, "Northcliffe to Launch 45 New Websites," *Marketing Week*, September 11, 2008, p. 59.

Carlisle, Cristina, "The Media Business: What They're Buying in Nine Countries," *New York Times*, May 27, 1996, p. 32.

"Daily Mail Gets Stake in British TV Operation," *New York Times*, April 23, 1996, p. D6.

Darby, Ian, "Daily Mail & General Trust," *Campaign*, July 31, 2010.

"DMGT Reports Q1 Improvement," *PrintWeek*, February 19, 2010, p. 8.

Fernandez, J., "DMGT in Management Restructure," *Marketing Week*, September 18, 2008, p. 44.

Johnson, Mark, "Daily Mail Buys Former Communist Mouthpiece," *Campaign*, September 8, 2006.

"Multimedia's No-Man's Land," *Economist*, July 22, 1995, p. 57.

"A Press Lord's Progress," *Economist*, June 10, 2006, p. 66.

Reid, A., "Northcliffe Newspapers for Sale," *Campaign*, December 9, 2005, p. 8.

DANISCO

Danisco A/S

Langebrogade 1
P.O. Box 17
Copenhagen K, 1001
Denmark
Telephone: (+45) 32 66 20 00
Fax: (+45) 32 66 21 75
Web site: http://www.danisco.com

Public Company
Incorporated: 1989
Employees: 6,876
Sales: DKK 13.71 billion ($2.61 billion) (2010)
Stock Exchanges: Copenhagen
Ticker Symbol: DCO
NAICS: 325199 All Other Basic Organic Chemical
   Manufacturing; 325613 Surface Active Agent
   Manufacturing

■ ■ ■

Danisco A/S is one of the world's leading manufacturers of food ingredients. The company focuses on high-value-added ingredients such as emulsifiers, gums, cultures, and natural sweeteners, producing such food ingredients for the world's leading makers of dairy, baking, and confectionery products, ice cream, beverages, dietary supplements, and chewing gum. In addition, Danisco owns Genencor, a leading global biotechnology firm that ranks as the second-largest producer of industrial enzymes in the world. Such enzymes are used in a wide array of industries, including animal nutrition, detergents, bioethanol, textile treatment, carbohydrate processing, and foods and beverages. Based in Denmark with operations in about 50 countries around the world, Danisco generates about 37 percent of its revenue in Europe, 30 percent in North America, 18 percent in the Asia-Pacific region, and 10 percent in Latin America.

EARLY HISTORY OF DANSKE SUKKERFABRIKKER

Among the oldest of the companies involved in the 1989 merger was Danske Sukkerfabrikker. This company had been established in 1872 by financier C. F. Tietgen, who also owned Privatbanken. Tietgen invested some five million rix-dollars in equity to start his own sugar production company. Developments since the middle of the 19th century had enabled the production of sugar from beets, a crop more easily grown in Denmark and the rest of Europe than sugarcane. Tietgen's company began operations by acquiring two existing sugar refineries in Copenhagen, while starting construction on new refineries, including one in Odense, which began construction in 1872. Tietgen's investment capital also went to ensuring a supply of raw beets, supplementing farmers who wished to convert their production to beets. Danske Sukker also began experimenting with breeding and developing its own beet seed, but without success. Instead, the Danish beet market relied on international imports for its seeds.

Tietgen's Odense refinery began operations in 1873. By the end of that decade, De Danske Sukkerfabrikker had added other refineries, including one in Lolland in 1880, originally built by the Frederiksen brothers, Erhard and Johan, who had been among the first

---

COMPANY PERSPECTIVES

Mission: To help our customers increase their competitiveness through innovative, sustainable and bio-based ingredient solutions that meet market demand for healthier and safer products.

Danes to begin sugar beet farming. Danske Sukkerfabrikker was by then one of the country's leading sugar refiners. Beet sugar production grew in importance throughout the rest of the century. Danske Sukkerfabrikker continued to build a prominent position in the Danish market. By the 1880s the company's production warranted the creation of a dedicated railway network linking beet farmers to refineries.

Danske Sukker's production grew steadily and by 1910 the company was capable of meeting the sugar demand for all of Denmark. The outbreak of World War I presented the company with a number of difficulties, most notably the inability to import beet seeds. Danske Sukker had dropped its own breeding program in 1903. During the war years, the company turned once again to development of its own seeds. By 1920, the company's seed production had grown sufficiently to create a dedicated subsidiary, which later became known as Danisco Seed. For much of that company's history, however, it was more closely identified with its first major product success, the Maribo-N beet variety introduced in 1928. The company's research and development efforts quickly paid off again in 1930 with the development of the world's first polyploid sugar beet, a tetraploid beet seed that was finally launched in 1950 as Maribo-P. The following decade, Danske Sukker invested more than DKK 100 million to convert its operations from split sugar manufacturing and sugar refinery facilities into a network of plants capable of producing finished product through a single combined production process. This development eliminated the need for transporting the raw sugar, which led to the closing of the company's railway system by the middle of the 1960s.

EARLY HISTORIES OF DANSKE SPIRITFABRIKKER AND GRINDSTEDVAERKET

Danske Sukker founder Tietgen's interests extended beyond that industry. In 1881 Tietgen and partner C. A. Olesen founded a new company, De Danske Spiritfabrikker, uniting several small-scale distillers to form a single company for the production of Danish national drink aquavit, or "water of life," a clear alcoholic beverage similar to gin. De Danske Spirit led a consolidation of the entire Danish distillery sector. At one time the country counted more than 2,500 small independent distillery companies. By 1923, that number had been reduced to just one, as Danske Spiritfabrikker became the sole distiller in all of Denmark. In 1924 the company went even further, receiving a monopoly for the production of yeast and all distilled spirits in the country. The company was to hold that monopoly until the early 1970s, when Denmark's entry into the European Community brought the spirits monopoly to an end.

The third major part of the "new" Danisco became part of the "old" Danisco at the end of the 1930s. Grindstedvaerket had been founded in the town of Grindsted in 1924 as a producer of organic chemicals. The company extended its range through the 1930s and gradually came to focus on various food ingredients, such as emulsifiers (useful for preserving the texture of bread, ice cream, and other foods), flavoring agents, and enzymes for processing foods. Danisco took over Grindstedvaerket in 1939, but the food ingredients arm became Danisco's major operation, responsible for the majority of its sales.

Those sales were boosted after World War II with the launch of the company's Cremodan brand of emulsifiers and hydrocolloids, used for the production of ice cream, in 1948. In the 1950s, Danisco began to spread beyond Denmark and the Scandinavian market, establishing a sales subsidiary in Germany. The following decade, Danisco launched another successful product line, Dimodan monoglycerides.

By the late 1970s, industrial production of processed foods had successfully lured vast numbers of the world's consumers with an ever expanding range of prepared foods. The prepared foods industry's growth was propelled by revolutionary shifts in the workforce, as women abandoned traditional roles to pursue careers outside the home. The growing number of working households left less time for the preparation of meals, and food companies stepped into that breach with new varieties of ready-to-eat foods. Ingredients concerns such as Danisco formed the backbone of the growing processed foods industry, supplying the additives and ingredients that promoted food preservation and enhanced flavor, as well as texturing and color agents to enhance products' appeal to the consumer. The increasingly global scope of the food industry encouraged Danisco to boost its own international activity. A step toward this goal was the renaming of its main Grindst-

KEY DATES

1872: C. F. Tietgen creates De Danske Sukkerfabrikker to produce beet sugar in Denmark.
1881: Tietgen and C. A. Olesen found De Danske Spiritfabrikker as a leading aquavit distiller and exporter.
1920: Danske Sukker begins research and development in beet sugar seeds and forms future Danisco Seed.
1924: I/S Grindstedvaerket is founded as an organic chemicals concern.
1939: Danisco takes over Grindsted, which is then expanded into food ingredients production and becomes Danisco's main subsidiary.
1989: Merger among Danske Sukker, Danisco, and Danske Spirit creates "new" Danisco.
1999: Danisco merges with Finland's Cultor, creating one of the world's largest food ingredients companies.
2005: Company acquires full control of Genencor, a biotechnology firm specializing in industrial enzymes.
2009: After selling its sugar division, Danisco is focused solely on food ingredients and industrial enzymes.

edvaerket to the more international Grindsted Food Products in 1980.

That name change accompanied Danisco's entry into the world's primary market for processed foods, the United States, with the construction of a factory in Kansas. The company reinforced its North American presence with the opening of a factory for the production of pectin, a thickening agent, in Mexico. Over the next several years, Danisco's operations spread around the world. In 1983 the company bought a production facility in France, followed by the purchase of a new plant in Spain in 1985. The company built its own Brazilian operation, an emulsifier plant, in 1986. Another emulsifier facility was constructed in Malaysia in 1990.

DEVELOPMENTS SURROUNDING THE 1989 MERGER

Despite the loss of its monopoly in 1973, De Danske Spiritfabrikker remained Denmark's dominant distiller throughout the 1980s. De Danske Sukkerfabrikker had

also secured the dominant position in the country's sugar industry, both as producer and as distributor, extending its control of the domestic market in 1989, when it acquired the country's last remaining independent sugar refinery, Sukkerfabrikken Nykobing.

A number of other key elements of the "new" Danisco also had been undergoing rapid development. One of these was the later Danisco Sweeteners, which had been founded originally in 1976 as a joint venture between Finnsugar, later known as Cultor, and pharmaceuticals maker Hoffmann-La Roche to produce the new artificial sweetener Xylitol. This product, which proved to have antitartar properties as well, became a widely used ingredient in sugar-free foods and candies, such as chewing gum. Cultor itself was to become a major part of the "new" Danisco; the company was quickly establishing itself as one of Scandinavia's leading food ingredients groups, particularly with such acquisitions as the food ingredients operations of U.S. pharmaceutical giant Pfizer Inc.

Cultor also brought with it a 50 percent interest in another U.S.-based company, Genencor, founded in 1982, which had built a growing business around its genetically manipulated biotechnology products. Meanwhile, Danisco Seed also had been working in the biotechnology sector during the 1980s. In 1990 the subsidiary's research resulted in the first outdoor planting of a genetically manipulated beet plant.

The 1989 merger of De Danske Spiritfabrikker, De Danske Sukkerfabrikker, and Danisco was one of the largest ever carried out in Denmark and created one of the company's largest industrial groups. The company's core businesses complemented each other well, creating so-called cluster competencies. The three components continued to pursue developments in their own sectors, however, now under the umbrella name of Danisco.

Danisco Sugar proved to be one of the fastest-growing components of the new Danisco. After establishing itself as the single remaining sugar producer in Denmark in 1989, the division started its drive to become one of the dominant players in the European sugar market. In 1991 the company acquired eight refineries in what was now the eastern part of the reunified Germany. The following year, the company took over the entire sugar industry of Sweden, making it the fourth-largest sugar company in Europe. Later in the decade, Danisco Sugar continued to expand in its core European market, such as with the 1998 purchases of stakes in sugar refineries in Poland and Lithuania.

The Grindsted Food Products unit changed its name to Danisco Ingredients in 1995, at the same time that it acquired a new pectin plant in the Czech Republic. The company continued to add to its operations through the end of the decade, notably with the acquisition of an emulsifier factory in Sweden in 1996 and the purchase of U.K.-based flavorings manufacturer Borthwicks in 1997. The company in 1998 added another flavorings producer, the U.S.-based Beck Flavors, as well as companies in Germany and Malaysia.

The year 1999 marked a new turning point for Danisco. In that year the company merged with Finland's Cultor, creating one of the world's largest food ingredients groups. As part of the merger, Danisco's ingredients arm took on a new name, Danisco Cultor. The company created the new Sugar and Sweeteners Division, merging Danisco's sugar production with Cultor's sugar arm, Sucros Oy, and its Xylitol and other artificial sweeteners operations. At the same time, Danisco took over Cultor's stake in Genencor, leading the two companies to develop a cooperation agreement in 2000, calling for the development of new biotechnology products for the food ingredients sector.

FOCUSING ON FOOD INGREDIENTS AND GENENCOR: EARLY 21ST CENTURY

Following the Cultor merger, Danisco moved to reorganize its operations, focusing on a new core of ingredients, sugar, and sweeteners. The company began selling off its now noncore operations, including Danske Spirit and the company's former frozen foods and other foods subsidiaries, which were jettisoned in favor of the higher-margin ingredients sector. The company also had begun to build up a packaging arm, most notably with the acquisition of Sidlay, the second-largest flexible packaging company in the United Kingdom. By 2001, however, Danisco had decided to abandon that sector to focus on its more closely related operations.

Although sugar and sweeteners remained an important part of Danisco's operations, representing, together with Danisco Seed, some 28 percent of the company's sales, food ingredients were claiming a rising share of Danisco's revenues, reaching 25 percent by the end of fiscal 2000. This unit saw significant developments at the start of the new century, such as the beginning of flavorings production in India and the 2001 acquisition one month later of Florida Flavors, a U.S.-based fruit flavorings supplier to the fruit juice industry. In August 2001 the company paid $100 million for the Germantown division of Australia's Goodman Fielder, giving the company a leading position in the worldwide texture agents market. At the same time, Danisco announced its intention to step up its activities in China and the rest of Asia, forecasting that these markets held the strongest promise for future growth.

By 2003, Danisco's global strength as a food ingredients supplier was evident in the fact that one out of every four loaves of bread eaten worldwide included one of the company's ingredients. That year, Danisco entered the xanthan gum market by acquiring majority control of a Chinese company. This business became part of Danisco's textural ingredients division, a major consumer of xanthan gum, a thickening and suspension agent. Danisco completed a much more significant deal in May 2004 when it acquired the food ingredients business of the French firm Rhodia for DKK 2.27 billion ($373 million). Among this business's products were cultures, textural ingredients, enzymes, and food safety ingredients. Annual cost savings of about DKK 150 million ($25 million) were realized in the integration of the Rhodia business into Danisco's existing food ingredients operations.

Less than a year later, in April 2005, Danisco completed its largest deal since its 1999 takeover of Cultor when it acquired the 58 percent of Genencor it did not already own for DKK 3.53 billion ($620 million). Included in the buyout was Eastman Chemical Company's 42 percent stake in Genencor as well as the shares held by others. Having secured full control of Genencor, Danisco ranked as one of the two largest producers of industrial enzymes in the world. Danisco and another Danish firm, Novozymes A/S, controlled about 63 percent of the global industrial enzyme market. These enzymes were used in such areas as grain processing, ethanol, detergents, and personal care products, as well as foods and beverages.

SMALLER WITH A PURPOSE

Danisco's transition from predominantly a sugar producer to one of the world's largest manufacturers of food ingredients and enzymes was led by Alf Duch-Pedersen, who served as CEO from 1997 to mid-2006. Following his retirement, Duch-Pedersen was succeeded by Tom Knutzen, who had previously headed NKT Holding A/S, a Danish industrial conglomerate best known as a producer of power cables and cleaning machines. The new leader further narrowed the company's focus by selling its flavors division to Firmenich SA, a privately held firm based in Switzerland, for DKK 3.36 billion ($615 million) in July 2007. An even more dramatic divestment was completed in February 2009 when Danisco sold its sugar unit to Germany's Nordzucker AG in a transaction valued at DKK 6.8 billion ($1.15 billion).

Although these divestments left Danisco a much smaller company, with revenue dropping from DKK 20.91 billion in 2006 to DKK 13.71 billion in 2010, they also created a company with globally strong positions in two key areas, food ingredients and industrial enzymes. Danisco was also a more profitable company, as evidenced by the improvement in its operating profit margin from 10.3 percent to 12.3 percent over this same period. As it moved into the second decade of the 21st century, Danisco was maintaining its heavy investments in research and development in order to continue producing innovative new products, while it was also involved in a cutting-edge joint venture with du Pont attempting to create an enzyme capable of producing a second-generation version of bioethanol based on agricultural residues such as corncobs and switchgrass. Through such initiatives, Danisco aimed to retain its position among the world leaders in its chosen fields.

PRINCIPAL SUBSIDIARIES

A/S Syntetic; Danisco Australia Pty Limited; Danisco Austria GmbH; Danisco Brazil Ltda.; Danisco (Beijing) Culture Co., Ltd. (China); Danisco (China) Co. Ltd.; Danisco (Zhangjiagang) Textural Ingredients Co. Ltd. (China); Danisco Ingredients (Shanghai) Co. Ltd. (China); Danisco Sweeteners (Anyang) Co., Ltd. (China; 54%); Genencor (Wuxi) Bio-products Co., Ltd. (China); Danisco Czech Republic, a.s.; Danisco Sweeteners Oy (Finland); Danisco France SAS; Danisco Deutschland GmbH (Germany); Danisco India Pvt. Ltd.; Danisco Italy S.p.A.; Danisco Japan Limited; Danisco Malaysia Sdn. Bhd.; Danisco Mexicana S.A. de C.V. (Mexico); Genencor International, B.V. (Netherlands); Danisco New Zealand Limited; Danisco Norway AS; Danisco Poland Sp. z.o.o.; Danisco Portugal, Industrias de Alfarroba Lda.; Danisco Romania S.R.L.; ZAO Danisco (Russia); Danisco Singapore Pte. Ltd.; Innovation Ingredients (Proprietary) Limited (South Africa); Danisco Cultor Espana S.A (Spain); Danisco Cultor (Switzerland) AG; Danisco Switzerland AG; Danisco Dis Ticarat Limited Sirketi (Turkey); Broadland Foods Ltd. (UK); Danisco Beaminster Ltd. (UK); Danisco Northampton Ltd. (UK); Danisco UK Ltd.; Agtech Products Inc. (USA); Danisco US Inc.; Danisco USA Inc.; Danisco (China) Holding Co. Ltd.; Cultor OY (Finland); Danisco Finland Oy; Danisco

Holding France S.A.S.; Danisco Beteiligunggesellschaft mbH (Germany); Danisco Ingredients Beteiligungsgesellschaft mbH (Germany); Danisco Holding Holland B.V. (Netherlands); Danisco South Africa (Pty.) Ltd.; Danisco Cultor Sweden AB; Danisco Holdings (UK) Ltd.; Danisco Holding USA Inc.

M. L. Cohen
Updated, David E. Salamie

PRINCIPAL DIVISIONS

Cultures; Emulsifiers; Genencor; Gums & Systems; Sweeteners.

PRINCIPAL COMPETITORS

Associated British Foods plc; Cargill, Incorporated; Chr. Hansen A/S; Cognis GmbH; J.M. Huber Corporation; Kerry Group plc; Novozymes A/S; Royal DSM N.V.; Tate & Lyle PLC.

FURTHER READING

Cortzen, Jan, *Merchants and Mergers: The Story of Danisco,* Copenhagen, Denmark: Børsen, 1997, 373 p.

"Danisco Buys Eastman's Stake in Genencor," *Chemical Market Reporter,* January 31, 2005, p. 2.

"Danisco: Cluster Buster," *Economist,* April 15, 2000.

Landau, Peter, "Danisco Acquisition Creates a Food Ingredients Giant," *Chemical Market Reporter,* April 5, 1999, p. 39.

———, "Danisco Inches Up Flavor Ladder with Its Acquisition of Beck," *Chemical Market Reporter,* October 19, 1998, p. 13.

Racanelli, Vito J., "Danisco Faces Not-So-Sweet Future," *Barron's,* August 22, 2005, p. M7.

Seewald, Nancy, "Danisco to Acquire Full Ownership of Genencor," *Chemical Week,* February 2, 2005, p. 10.

Walsh, Kerri, "Danisco to Restructure Ingredients Business," *Chemical Week,* September 27, 2006, p. 51.

Walsh, Kerri, and Esther D'Amico, "Danisco to Buy U.K. Emulsifier Maker," *Chemical Week,* January 28, 2008, p. 29.

Zwirn, Ed, "Danisco to Divest Flavors for $611m," *ICIS Chemical Business Americas,* May 7–13, 2007, p. 6.

Delmarva Power & Light Company

800 King Street
Wilmington, Delaware 19801
U.S.A.
Telephone: (302) 451-5500
Fax: (302) 283-6090
Web site: http://www.delmarva.com

Subsidiary of Pepco Holdings, Inc.
Incorporated: 1909 as American Power Company
Employees: 5,000
Sales: $1.54 billion (2009)
NAICS: 221122 Electric Power Distribution

■ ■ ■

Delmarva Power & Light Company is a Wilmington, Delaware-based subsidiary of Pepco Holdings, Inc., a Washington, D.C.-based electricity and natural gas distribution holding company. A regulated utility, Delmarva provides electricity to nearly 500,000 commercial and residential customers in the Delmarva Peninsula that includes Delaware and parts of Maryland and Virginia. Sixty percent of its customers are located in Delaware. The company also delivers natural gas to about 125,000 customers in northern Delaware.

19TH-CENTURY ROOTS

A variety of small electric and gas companies were brought together to create Delmarva Power & Light. The oldest was Wilmington Coal Gas Company, formed in 1851. The first to offer electricity was the Arnoux City Electric-Light Company chartered in Delaware in 1882 to illuminate the streets of Wilmington with arc-light, soon to be replaced by Edison's new incandescent lighting system. In 1886 a new company was formed to succeed Arnoux and was named Wilmington Electric-Light Company. It provided street lighting as well as power to the Wilmington City Railway Company.

Wilmington Electric-Light became known as Wilmington Light and Power, and along with Wilmington City Electric fell under the control of Philadelphia, Pennsylvania, financier Thomas Dolan, who would also cobble together a massive holding company, the United Gas Improvement Company. In 1928 the Wilmington companies along with two other United Gas subsidiaries operating near Wilmington, Newcastle Electric and the American Power Company, were brought together to form Delaware Power and Light Company. Because the company's corporate lineage was traced through American Power Company and its founding date of 1909, Delmarva Power would consider 1909 as its date of birth as well. Delaware Power became part of United Gas Improvement in 1930.

Despite its name, Delaware Power and Light did not serve all of Delaware until 1943. In September of that year the company merged with Eastern Shore Public Service Company and extended its operations to Delaware's Kent and Sussex Counties. Eastern Shore also served the Maryland and Virginia portions of the Delmarva Peninsula. The deal was completed through the sale of $15 million in bonds as well as a new issue of stock, the proceeds of which retired the publicly held debt and preferred stocks of Delaware Power and Eastern Shore. A year later Delaware Power was spun off from United Gas Improvement, as required by utility holding company legislation passed in the 1930s, and became an independent company.

POSTWAR GROWTH

Following World War II, Delaware, like the rest of the country, enjoyed strong economic growth, and Delaware Power expanded its operations to keep pace with the growing demand for electricity. In 1951 the utility opened the Edge Moor Power Plant with two steam stations. It was one of the first power plants to include a fully centralized control system, which improved efficiency as well as safety. A third unit was added in 1954, and a fourth unit in 1966.

It was also in 1966 that Delaware Power changed its name to the more expansive Delmarva Power & Light Company. A secondary offering of stock was conducted in that year to fund further growth. The Delaware City generating station opened in 1968 as did the diesel generating stations of the Crisfield, Maryland, plant.

A gas turbine operation opened in Tasley, Virginia, in 1972, and a year later the Christiana generating station near Wilmington began generating electricity from a pair of combustion turbines powered by low-sulfur diesel. A fifth unit also opened at the Edge Moor facility in 1973. Additionally, Delmarva maintained a supply of reserve power by participating in what was known as the "Philadelphia Electric Group," a power sharing arrangement between Delmarva Power, Philadelphia Electric Company, and Atlantic City Electric Company. Concerns about adequate power supplies lessened in the early 1980s when demand for electricity fell. As a result, the company postponed the completion of a $1 billion oil-fired power plant in the fall of 1982.

NEW LEGISLATION CHANGES INDUSTRY

Despite expansion over the years, Delmarva Power remained a relatively small utility. It looked to gain scale in 1985 by merging with Atlantic City, New Jersey-based Atlantic Energy Inc., another small player, but after some study the two sides opted to remain independent. Business conditions would soon change, however. In 1992 the U.S. Congress passed the Energy Policy Act that opened up competition in the bulk power market. Two years later Delmarva Power sought to take advantage of new opportunities by acquiring the Conowingo Power Company, a Maryland retail electric subsidiary of Philadelphia's Peco Energy Company.

Further deregulation of the energy industry took place in 1996, resulting in a wave of utility mergers. A mid-size utility, Delmarva Power found itself in what was likely to become an increasingly difficult position. Atlantic Energy, an even smaller player, was vulnerable as well. Thus, in 1996 the two companies renewed the merger talks of a decade earlier and agreed to what was in effect a marriage of convenience. The combined company would serve about one million customers and generate revenues of $2 billion. It also looked to take advantage of the opening of new casinos in Atlantic City to grow further. In addition to size, the company hoped to consolidate operations to cut overhead and save an estimated $500 million over the next 10 years.

FORMATION OF CONECTIV: 1998

To complete the merger of Delmarva Power and Atlantic Energy, a new holding company called Conectiv was formed. The merger itself would be delayed as approval had to be received at both the state and federal levels. It was not until the first quarter of 1998 that the merger was consummated. In the meantime, Delmarva Power had taken steps to develop non-regulated energy businesses. In the third quarter of 1996 the company launched an energy trading unit, which set up shop in Newark, Delaware. Early in 1997 it signed its first deal with Tosco Corporation, a refining and marketing company, charged with improving pipeline margins. In addition, Delmarva Power reached an agreement in late 1996 to provide comprehensive utility management services to Happy Harry's Drug Stores and W.L. Gore & Associates. It also diversified by acquiring heating, ventilation, and air-conditioning repair companies, a move that failed to succeed, as did an effort to market electricity sales in Pennsylvania. Following the Delmarva Power and Atlantic Energy merger, the trading unit forged a joint venture with CNE Energy Services in Connecticut to offer retail gas services.

Conectiv also formed a market research unit called MANIAC and took advantage of 600 miles of fiber cable used for internal communications to spin off an unregulated business called Conectiv Communications, an incipient regional telephone company. Capacity on the network was also being sold to local exchange carriers, competitive local exchange carriers, and interex-

KEY DATES

1909: American Power Company is founded.
1928: Merger creates Delaware Power and Light Company.
1966: Delmarva Power & Light Company name is adopted.
1998: Delmarva Power merges with Atlantic Energy to form Conectiv.
2005: Delmarva Power name is re-adopted.

change carriers. The hope was that in less than five years, Conectiv Holdings would generate half of its earnings from these unregulated businesses. In the meantime, Conectiv was selling off some of its noncore power plants. Rather than maintain round-the-clock power plants, the company now preferred to build plants that ran on a spot basis that cost less to operate and generated higher returns.

PEPCO ACQUIRES CONECTIV: 2001

Even as the Conectiv brand was taking shape, industry observers maintained that the company was still too small for the industry and a likely target for a larger player. Moreover, the four states in which it operated had opened up electricity sales to outside competition, or were about to, and Conectiv would be hard pressed to fend them off. With the price of its stock falling, making it vulnerable to takeover, the company put itself up for sale in 2000. Another regional utility in need of growing larger was Potomac Electric Power Company, a Washington, D.C.-based utility. It had already scuttled a two-year effort to merge with Baltimore Gas & Electric Co. in a $3 billion deal because of the restrictions imposed by regulators. In 2000 Pepco Holdings, Inc., was formed as a holding company for the assets of the utility, and a year later Conectiv agreed to be acquired by Pepco in a $2.2 billion cash and stock deal brokered by Credit Suisse First Boston. In addition to their complementary energy businesses, both companies offered telecommunications assets. Pepco provided telecommunications services in Washington through Starpower Communications Inc., half owned by Princeton, New Jersey's RCN Corp.

The Delmarva Power & Light brand emerged again in 2005, as Pepco elected to take advantage of the historic brand name. As a result, Delmarva Power served its traditional Delmarva Peninsula market, while

Atlantic City Electric served the needs of southern New Jersey and PEPCO served Washington, D.C., and Maryland's Montgomery and Prince George's counties. A fourth unit, Pepco Energy Services, served a broad section of the United States, offering a variety of energy services, including energy performance contracting and renewable energy generation. Another unit, Conectiv Energy, was dedicated to power generation, which continued to grow. New units opened at the Edge Moor Power–Hay Road Power Complex in 2002 and 2003. A solar photovoltaic system opened in Vineland, New Jersey, as did a new 100-megawatt generating station in Millville, New Jersey.

NEW RELIABLE ENERGY REQUIREMENTS

Delmarva Power was required by legislation passed by the state of Delaware in April 2006 to seek bids for long-term contracts for cost-effective power, this in the light of significant rate increases that had accompanied deregulation, which had promised lower prices to consumers. Moreover, new laws required the new demand be met with energy-efficient, renewable sources of energy before fossil fuel generation could be considered. Delmarva Power was also required to have 20 percent of its electricity supply come from renewable sources by 2019.

Delmarva Power received bids from NRG Energy, which proposed converting a power plant in Indiana River, Delaware, to coal gasification to add 400 megawatts of power; and New Jersey-based Bluewater Wind, which proposed a 600-megawatt wind park in the Atlantic Ocean some 12 miles off the coast of Delaware's Rehoboth Beach. In 2007 Delmarva Power recommended a bid from sister company Conectiv Energy, while ranking the wind park as its second choice. The former was deemed more reliable, according to the company, while the later was regarded highly for its environmental benefits.

The Delaware Public Service Commission and three other state agencies in May 2007 disregarded the recommendation of Delmarva Power and instructed it to negotiate a purchase power agreement with Bluewater, which would result in the United States' first offshore wind park. Bluewater had reached a similar agreement with the Delaware Municipal Electricity Corporation, Inc., to supply about 100,000 Delaware residents in areas not served by Delmarva Power, but it was contingent upon a deal with Delmarva Power. Negotiations were far from smooth, but finally in June 2008 a 25-year power agreement was reached, the first for an offshore wind park in the United States.

The proposed wind park struggled to find financial backing, due in large part to the low price Delmarva Power had negotiated. The situation grew worse when Bluewater's owner, Australia's Babcock & Brown, went bankrupt. Bluewater was then acquired by NRG and the project was back on track. It remained to be seen whether the project would meet a target launch date of 2012 or become the first operational offshore wind park in the United States. Nonetheless, it figured to be a major supplier in Delmarva Power's future. Delmarva Power would lose its close ties to Conectiv Energy, on the other hand. In July 2010 Pepco Holdings sold Conectiv Energy for $1.63 billion, essentially repositioning itself as a regulated transmission and distribution company.

Ed Dinger

PRINCIPAL COMPETITORS

Allegheny Energy, Inc.; FirstEnergy Corp.; Public Service Enterprise Group Incorporated.

FURTHER READING

Burr, Michael T., "Conectiv Bets Future on Competition," *Electric Light & Power*, June 1999, p. 1.

House-Layton, Kate, "Renewable Power Agreement Could Be Reached by December," *Delaware State News*, September 24, 2007.

Keough, W. F., "Atlantic Energy, Delaware Firm Plan to Merge Operations," *Press of Atlantic City*, August 13, 1996, p. A1.

"Power Merger for Wilmington," *New York Times*, October 30, 1928.

Richter, M. J., "Conectiv Objective," *Telephony*, July 19, 1999.

"Stock Split Is Proposed by Delaware Power Co.," *New York Times*, December 24, 1965.

Ulman, Danielle, "Rehoboth Wind Farm Project Moves Closer with Delmarva Power Deal," *Baltimore (MD) Daily Record*, June 24, 2008.

Willis, David P., "Mid-Atlantic Electric Utility Makes Bid for Delaware-Based Conectiv," *Asbury Park Press*, February 13, 2001.

Yingling, Bill, "A Mad Dash toward Deregulation," *Philadelphia Business Journal*, January 3, 1997, p. 12.

Dobbies
GARDEN CENTRES
it's in our nature
www.dobbies.com

Dobbies Garden Centres plc

Melville Nursery
Lasswade, Midlothian EH18 1AZ
United Kingdom
Telephone: (44 0131) 663 6778
Fax: (44 0131) 654 2548
Web site: http://www.dobbies.com

Subsidiary of Tesco PLC
Founded: 1865
Employees: 1,780
Sales: $130.9 million (2007)
NAICS: 444220 Nursery and Garden Centers

■ ■ ■

Based near Edinburgh, Scotland, Dobbies Garden Centres plc is a major U.K. retailer of gardening supplies, operating about 25 nurseries and garden centers as well as a Web site that offers merchandise around the clock. In addition to plants, which come with a five-year guarantee, Dobbies sells gardening tools, gardening apparel, fertilizers, gardening books, greenhouses, and outdoor furniture. The centers include restaurants and catering services as well as meeting facilities where gardening classes and other events are held. Dobbies also rents heavy equipment for gardening and landscaping as well as general construction work. The company is a subsidiary of Tesco PLC, a giant U.K. grocery retailer.

19TH-CENTURY ROOTS

The man behind the Dobbies name was James Dobbie. Born in Gordon, Berwickshire, Scotland, around 1817,

he was an amateur gardener who like many others in Great Britain during the Industrial Revolution made use of the new greenhouses to dabble in the cultivation of exotic plants. He did not turn his hobby into a business until 1865. He was in his early 20s in 1840 when he first became interested in growing flowers and was soon doing well in local flower shows. In 1850 he established his name among the top ranks of the horticultural field when he won two first place honors in the open competition, as well as two top prizes in the amateur competition, at a major show held by the Highland and Agricultural Society.

Dobbie moved to Renfrew, Scotland, where he was employed as chief constable and continued to pursue his gardening interests. He achieved acclaim for his leeks, onions, pansies, phlox, and marigolds, as well as other flowers and vegetables. Along the way, he saved the strains of his award-winning varieties. The demand by other gardeners for seeds became so great that he decided to start a business for his son, who was well trained for the endeavor. Dobbie's first commercially viable offering were seeds from a prized leek. In 1865 (some sources say 1862) Dobbie and his son marketed the seeds as "Dobbies Champion." In a matter of just two days, the entire stock was sold out.

When his son died, Dobbie resigned from his post as chief constable in 1866 and devoted all of his time to running the seed business, providing competitors and exhibitors with seeds from his select strains of flowers and vegetable. In order to expand the business he moved in 1875 to Rothesay, Scotland. Four years later he hired William Cuthbertson as his assistant. In 1887 Dobbie retired and sold the business to Cuthbertson, who took on a partner, Robert Fife. They were later joined by Archibald M. Burnie. Dobbie continued to garden in his retirement and lived until the age of 88, passing away in 1905.

ROYAL WARRANT: 1894

Cuthbertson and Fife adopted the Dobbie & Co. name for the business. For his part, Fife established a new award-winning strain. In 1894 several acres of additional land were acquired in Orpinton, Kent, to increase the company's seed production. It was also in that year that Dobbie & Co. was awarded a Royal Warrant, issued by Great Britain's royal family. While not a stamp of quality, the warrant was issued only to companies and people who had provided goods or services to the royal family for at least five years. As such, it was a highly coveted distinction and helped to increase the visibility of the Dobbie name. By the start of the 20th century, the company was mailing its seed catalog to more than 50,000 recipients in the United Kingdom and Europe.

Dobbie's seed farm was moved from Orpinton to Marks Tey, Essex, in 1904, where the company would produce seeds for the next half-century. The headquarters was moved to the outskirts of Edinburgh in 1910. By the early 1920s Cuthbertson's son and three sons of Fife had become involved in Dobbie & Co., and the Fife brothers now shared ownership. The company was primarily known for its International Prize leeks and Gold Medal sweet peas. Another move of the operation was made in 1934 when the business was relocated to Melville, the company's present-day headquarters. It was here that Dobbie & Co. developed into an international concern.

Deaths in the Fife family led to changes at the helm, and finally the company was sold in 1969 to Waterers, a Surrey nursery company. Although Dobbie was able to expand its marketing reach throughout Scotland and England, it remained a nursery business until Waterers' former managing director, David Barnes, acquired the company in 1984. He recognized a grow-

ing need for one-stop gardening centers and shifted the company in this direction. His son, James, bought him out in 1994 and took over as chief executive officer. Under his leadership, Dobbie was by the end of the 1990s operating five garden centers in Scotland, located at the original nursery in Melville, as well as Ardencaple in Helensburgh, Dalgety Bay in Fife, Chatelherault Country Park in Hamilton, and Westerwood in Cumbernauld.

GOING PUBLIC TO FUND EXPANSION: 1997

Dobbie continued to grow in the 1990s when it encroached on northeast England. By 1997 the chain of garden centers totaled eight units. To fund further expansion the company went public in 1997 as Dobbies Garden Centres plc, the proceeds used to purchase a site in Edinburgh for a new garden center and to provide working capital. The shares were listed on the Alternate Investment Market, a sub-market of the London Stock Exchange that allowed smaller companies to float their shares in the equity market.

After the stock offering James Barnes remained CEO. Dobbie upgraded its garden centers in 1999 when it opened a new "destination" center, offering numerous departments, restaurants, and other features such as water gardens and mazes to encourage customers to pay extended visits. New and renovated centers, ranging in size between 40,000 and 50,000 square feet, opened so that by 2001 Dobbies was the United Kingdom's second-largest garden center chain with 10 sites in Scotland and another five in England. Although plants still accounted for one-third of all sales, the chain was seeing a greater demand for lifestyle offerings, including garden furniture and structural garden features as well as grills, chinaware, and glass.

As the new century progressed, Dobbies continued to add stores and evolve its concept. New products, such as water garden equipment and ornamental fish, were added. In early 2004 the chain began tacking on what it called "farm shops" to the sites. They were essentially markets where farmers could sell their produce directly to consumers, who in recent years had become increasingly interested in the source of their food.

ACQUISITION SPURS E-COMMERCE: 2006

In addition to garden centers, Dobbies looked to the Internet to grow revenues. In the summer of 2006 it acquired Grovelands Garden Centre, which had developed an e-commerce business. Dobbies used it as a platform for its own enlarged Web-based business. The company was faring well, due in large part to an aging population that fueled a growing popularity with gardening, but Dobbies was lagging behind the category leader, Wyevale, which was operating 130 garden centers. It was a consolidating sector, making Dobbies a highly valued property.

In 2007 grocer Tesco PLC made a bid to acquire Dobbies, which was now operating 21 garden centers. For Tesco, Dobbies presented an opportunity to not only take advantage of a growing interest in gardening but to also take advantage of the garden centers to sell a slate of "green" merchandise, including insulation, solar panels, rain barrels, and wind turbines. Not everyone was pleased with the union between Dobbies and Tesco, however. Sir Tom Hunter, the billionaire majority owner of Wyevale, and a smaller chain called Blooms, was a Dobbies shareholder and not about to give Tesco an easy opportunity to become a threat to his own garden center chain.

Just hours after Tesco announced its takeover bid for Dobbies, Hunter doubled his interest in the company to 20 percent, paying a premium in the process. Subsequent purchases increased that amount to more than 29 percent. As a result, Hunter held a large enough stake to prevent Tesco from taking Dobbies private, and with Dobbies remaining a listed company he would be in a position to frustrate Tesco's expansion plans for Dobbies, plans that would pose a threat to Wyevale. It was not surprising, therefore, that he would refuse to sell his shares in Dobbies for the £15 per share the other shareholders accepted.

NEW SHARE OFFERING: 2008

Hunter and Tesco, which had its own wealthy aristocratic owner in Sir Terry Leahy, maneuvered for control of Dobbies for the next year. On Tesco's side was James Barnes, who used his own shares in Dobbies to back Tesco's position. As a result, Tesco was able to use its majority position to force Hunter to eventually capitulate. In April 2008 Leahy tried a new tack. Dobbies announced a plan to raise £150 million to reduce its £105 million debt load and fund a major expansion program to grow revenues well beyond the £83.5 million Dobbies generated in fiscal 2007, resulting in net income of £8.9 million. The funds were to be raised through a new issue of stock. Shareholders could purchase six of the new shares at £12 apiece for every six shares they already owned. Hunter was now placed in a difficult position. To protect his position he would have to raise £44 million. If he chose not to, Tesco would purchase enough new shares to dilute Hunter's share below 25 percent. With more than 75 percent control of Dobbies, Tesco would then be able to delist Dobbies and Hunter would be relegated to a passive investor with no power to influence Dobbies' operations.

Hunter took to the courts to block the offer of shares, accusing the Tesco-affiliated members of the Dobbies board of engineering a takeover of the company, but he found himself in an untenable position. On the one hand, he insisted that he was committed to Dobbies' long-term growth, despite his ties to the company's chief competitor, and on the other he was arguing against raising the funds Dobbies needed to achieve that growth. The judge in the matter was not persuaded by Hunter's arguments, and the new issue of stock went forward. Rather than contribute £44 million to prevent Tesco from delisting Dobbies, he elected to cut his losses. He sold his stake in Dobbies at £12 per share, far less than he would have received if he had accepted the buyout a year earlier.

At the end of the Hunter affair in May 2008, Tesco owned nearly 95 percent in Dobbies and delisted the company. Dobbies found itself with £150 million in cash. The funds were earmarked to help the company pursue an aggressive expansion plan. Over the next decade, Dobbies hoped to increase the number of garden centers to 100 and grow annual revenues to the £1 billion mark. It was more than likely that along the way it would clash again with its chief rival, Wyevale, and Sir Tom Hunter.

Ed Dinger

PRINCIPAL SUBSIDIARIES

Dobbies Garden Club.

PRINCIPAL COMPETITORS

Grafton Group plc; Travis Perkins plc; Wyevale Garden Centres Limited.

FURTHER READING

Blackwell, David, "Dobbies Displays Gift for Growth," *Financial Times*, February 15, 2001, p. 28.

———, "Dobbies Pushes Sales with New Farm Shops," *Financial Times*, February 11, 2004, p. 26.

Braithwaite, Tom, "Hunter Asks Court to Block Dobbies Issue," *Financial Times*, May 10, 2008, p. 15.

Finch, Julia, "Tesco Puts Down Roots in Garden Centre Market," *Guardian*, June 9, 2007, p. 39.

"Flourishing from Strong Roots," *Glasgow Herald*, March 24, 1989.

Gray, Alistair, "Tesco Wins Dobbies Court Case," *FT.com*, May 15, 2008.

Kollewe, Julia, "Garden Centre Chain Plans £150m Expansion," *Guardian*, April 10, 2008.

"Obituary: James Dobbie," *Gardeners' Chronicle*, October 21, 1905.

Ebro Foods S.A.

———————— ■ ————————

Paseo de la Castellana 20
Madrid, E-28046
Spain
Telephone: (+34 91) 724 52 50
Fax: (+34 91) 724 53 41
Web site: http://www.ebropuleva.com

Public Company
Founded: 1905
Incorporated: 2001 as Ebro Puleva
Employees: 6,000
Sales: EUR 2.2 billion ($3.08 billion) (2009)
Stock Exchanges: Madrid
Ticker Symbol: EVA
NAICS: 311212 Rice Milling; 311423 Dried and Dehydrated Food Manufacturing

■ ■ ■

Ebro Foods S.A. is Spain's largest foods group. The company is also the world's leading rice company and second-largest pasta producer. Ebro's Rice division generated 38 percent of the group's 2009 revenues of EUR 2.2 billion ($3.08 billion). Ebro's Pasta Division added 42 percent of the group's revenues in 2009. Altogether, the company owns nearly 60 brands covering 26 markets. Ebro also operates a small Biotech division focused on the development of so-called nutraceuticals as well as the production of biofuels. In March 2010, the company agreed to sell its Dairy division, including the Puleva and other brands, to France's Lactalis for EUR 630 million. That division accounted for 20 percent of group sales in 2009. Previously, the company had also divested its sugar division, to Associated British Foods, for EUR 385 million. Ebro Foods is listed on the Madrid Stock Exchange and is led by Chairman and CEO Antonio Hernández Callejas.

SUGAR ORIGINS IN 1903

Ebro Foods had its origins in Spain's late 19th-century sugar industry. Sugar grew to become an increasingly important commodity in Spain and elsewhere in Europe during the 19th century. The need to import sugar from the European colonies in South America, the Caribbean, Africa, and other sugarcane-growing regions limited the supply and kept sugar prices high, however.

Attention turned toward developing new sources of sugars from plants capable of growing in Europe's climate. Beets in particular proved a promising source of sugar. The invention of the first extraction methods for beet sugar in the late 19th century sparked a surge in sugar beet planting and the development of a sugar refining industry. In Spain, the first sugar refining factories began to appear in the early 1880s.

The sugar sector grew rapidly, as more and more farmers converted their production to beet sugar. This led in turn to the appearance of a large number of sugar factories throughout the country. In the years following World War I, Spain counted more than 60 sugar factories.

By then, a number of efforts had been taken in an attempt to regulate the somewhat chaotic growth of the sugar industry. In 1890, beet growers and sugar producers worked out an agreement in a first attempt to regulate prices in the sector. This effort failed to stop the proliferation of sugar factories, however. By 1900, the sugar sector remained highly fragmented, with too many factories competing for the market. In order to provide some order to the industry, a new company formed in 1903, called Sociedad General Azucarera de España (Spanish General Sugar Company, SGA), launching an initial consolidation phase. SGA formed the earliest component of the future Ebro Foods.

This period was also accompanied by the Spanish government's introduction of the first legislation overseeing the sugar industry in Spain in 1907. As a result, a new wave of larger companies began to appear. At the same time, the sugar industry, initially concentrated in the western Andalucia region, had begun to shift its focus to the Ebro Basin region. This led to the creation of a number of new sugar companies, most notably Compañía de Industrias Agrícolas, S.A., (CIA) and Compañía Anónima Azucarera del Ebro (Ebro), both founded in 1911. CIA's operations included the factories operated by Azucarera del Jalón, founded in 1904.

DISTILLERIES IN THE TWENTIES

Ebro, like CIA and SGA, expanded into the operation of distilleries during the 1920s. Ebro's extension into this area came at the end of 1928, when it acquired Bilbao-based Compañía de Alcoholes. Following that acquisition, Ebro changed its name, becoming Ebro Compañía de Azúcares y Alcoholes, S.A. Over the next decades, Ebro built a network of six distilleries. SGA's and CIA's distillery businesses included three and five distilleries, respectively.

All three companies also expanded into other complementary businesses, both before and after the Spanish civil war. The companies each entered the production of yeast for the bakery industry. Both Ebro and SGA operated three yeast factories, while CIA had a single plant. CIA moved into feed production, and at one point operated six feed factories. CIA also launched the production of glutamic acid, and Ebro opened a

citric acid factory. The companies later invested in another important staple in Spanish cuisine, rice.

Ebro, CIA, and SGA also developed a long history of partnerships, both among themselves and with third-party sugar producers. SGA and CIA teamed up to create Compañía Azucarera Peninsular in 1920. In the 1930s, the two companies joined together to establish Sociedad Azucarera Ibérica and Azucarera De La Bañeza. In 1953 Ebro joined CIA and SGA to create Azucareras Castellanas. This was followed by Azucarera Del Guadiana, founded by the three producers in 1967.

Ebro expanded on its own in 1968, taking over Sociedad Industrial Castellana. The company then joined with SGA to acquire Hijos de Carlos Eugui, S.A., in 1971. Through the middle of the 1980s, the companies added several more partnerships, including a yeast joint venture, Compañía General De Levadura, between SGA and CIA.

MERGERS IN THE NINETIES

The 1980s marked a new phase in the development of the Spanish sugar industry. The collapse of the Franco regime following Francisco Franco's death in the mid-1970s permitted Spain to apply for membership in the European Union (EU). In order to comply with the rules for EU membership, Spain launched a massive overhaul of its financial, industrial, and agricultural sectors. The sugar industry launched its own reorganization, in order to meet European productivity and quality standards. This sparked a wave of consolidation as the industry moved to focus on a smaller number of larger factories.

As major players in the Spanish sugar market, Ebro, CIA, and SGA took a leading role in this consolidation, taking over a number of smaller companies in the late 1980s. These included a 60 percent stake in Herba, a major Spanish rice brand. In 1990, CIA and Ebro announced their decision to merge and form Ebro Agrícolas, Compañía de Alimentación, which became one of Spain's leading sugar producers and food companies. The new Ebro now set in motion a restructuring strategy, shutting down a number of its sugar factories to focus on just 10 larger and modernized factories.

By the late 1990s, Ebro emerged as one of Spain's two largest sugar companies, the other being SGA. In 1998, the two companies agreed to merge together to form the undisputed Spanish leader, commanding 78 percent of the domestic sugar market. The larger company adopted a new name, Azucarera Ebro Agrícolas. In addition to its sugar operations, Ebro, through Herba, had also became a major player in the Spanish rice sector, controlling 41 percent of that market.

KEY DATES

1903: Sociedad General Azucarera de España (SGA) is founded to produce beet sugar in Spain.

1910: Future Puleva is founded as a wine producers partnership.

1911: Sugar companies Compañía de Industrias Agrícolas, S.A., (CIA) and Compañía Anónima Azucarera del Ebro (Ebro) are founded.

1958: Wine partnership, known as Uniasa, enters dairy production.

1976: Uniasa, later known as Puleva, goes public.

1990: Ebro and CIA merge their operations, becoming Ebro Agrícolas, Compañía de Alimentación.

1998: Ebro and SGA merge as Azucarera Ebro Agrícolas.

2001: Company acquires Puleva, becoming Ebro Puleva.

2003: Ebro Puleva begins acquiring international rice and pasta brands.

2008: Ebro Puleva sells its sugar business to Associated British Foods.

2010: Company sells its dairy division to Lactalis and becomes Ebro Foods.

ADDING PULEVA IN 2001

Ebro started out with 14 sugar factories, 4 distilleries, 5 feed plants, and 2 research and development laboratories. In 1999, the company appointed a new chairman, Vicente de la Calle, described as being close to the Spanish government. Calle laid out a new industrialization strategy for the company. At the same time, he sought to streamline the company, shedding a number of non-core operations, including feed production.

Calle soon ran afoul of the company's shareholders, which included two prominent savings banks. By 2000, Calle had been forced to resign from the company. José Manuel Fernández Norniella, a former secretary of state for trade, took Calle's place. Norniella led Ebro on a new strategy of becoming a leading and diversified foods company.

To this end Ebro completed its most ambitious acquisition to date, buying Spanish dairy products leader Puleva in a deal announced in 2000 and completed in 2001. Puleva had originated in 1910 as a

wine producing partnership in Granada, before diversifying into other agricultural products. The company, which became known as Uniasa in 1954, entered the dairy sector four years later, helping to pioneer the packaged milk sector in Spain. The company's initial dairy production reached 20,000 liters per day.

Through the 1960s, Uniasa expanded its production to include butter, powdered milk, sterilized milk, and flavored milkshakes. Expansions to its plant helped it reach a capacity of 200,000 liters per day by the beginning of the 1970s. In 1975, the company added a new dairy plant, with an initial production capacity of 400,000 liters per day. Over the next decades, the company continued to expand that facility, reaching one million liters per day of capacity.

Uniasa went public in 1976. In 1982 the company added an infant nutrition division, acquiring Compañía de Dietéticos y Alimentación S.A. Uniasa had also been developing its brand names, especially Puleva. The success of that dairy brand led the company to adopt it as its own name. Puleva continued to diversify through the 1980s, launching cheese production as well as entering the livestock sector in order to build its own dairy herds. Through the 1990s, dairy products became the group's major focus. The acquisition of two dairy groups, Leyma-Ram and Granjas Castello, in 1999, made Puleva the Spanish leader, with a market share of roughly 27 percent.

ACQUISITION DRIVE IN 2003

Ebro paid EUR 600 million to acquire Puleva, forming Spain's largest foods company, Ebro Puleva S.A. The company then restructured its operations into seven divisions, including sugar, dairy products, and rice, as well as more recently added operations including olive and other vegetable oils, biofuels, and an Internet business.

Ebro's focus began to shift, however, following the acquisition of Denmark's Danrice and Danpasta brands, for EUR 18.7 million ($22.5 million) in 2003. The acquisition marked the company's increasing focus on the rice and pasta sectors, and the beginning of its internationalization strategy. Over the next several years, Ebro completed a flurry of acquisitions, spending more than EUR 1 billion to build up a portfolio of nearly 60 rice and pasta brands in 26 countries.

In 2004, the company formed a joint venture with Riviana Foods, based in Texas, to enter the United Kingdom. The new company, S&B Herba Foods, then acquired Vogan & Co., a major producer of rice, lentils, and other dry goods for the U.K. market. This partnership soon led Ebro Puleva to buy Riviana itself, making the Spanish company one of the leading rice companies in the United States. Riviana's brand family included such popular brands as Carolina, Success, and Mahatma, and also gave the company a foothold in Puerto Rico and the South American market.

Ebro Puleva then turned its attention toward reinforcing its position in the European market. In March 2005, the company completed its next major acquisition, paying EUR 639 million to acquire France's Panzani, the leading producer of pasta and sauces for that market. In September of that year, the company bought Tarantella, a producer of pasta, sauces, and pulses (legumes) in the United Kingdom.

RICE AND PASTA LEADER IN 2010

Ebro Puleva continued to build its range of pasta and rice brands in the second half of the decade. The company paid EUR 284 million ($360 million) to acquire New World Pasta in the United States, doubling its U.S. revenues. The acquisition also positioned Ebro as the world's second-largest pasta company, after Barilla in Italy. Soon after, the company acquired another major brand, buying Minute Rice from Kraft Foods Global Inc. for $280 million. The following year, the company extended its operations to Germany, where it acquired leading pasta group Birkel Teigwaren and its Birkel, 3 Glocken, Schuele, Nudel Up, and other brands. The purchase also gave the company a presence in the Baltic region and Russia.

By the end of the decade, Ebro Puleva had become the world's leading rice company and its second-largest pasta producer. The transformation of the company's focus from its original sugar, and then dairy operations, had been motivated in part because of developments in the EU's legislation governing these sectors. The new changes, including the elimination of import tariffs and subsidies, promised a new competitive era for the European sugar and dairy markets.

Instead, Ebro Puleva decided to refocus itself around its core pasta and rice divisions at the end of the decade. At the end of 2008, the company announced its agreement to sell its sugar business, Azucarera Ebro, to Associated British Foods, owner of the British Sugar brand, for EUR 385 million ($519 million). This deal was completed in 2009. By then, the company had also begun looking for a buyer for its Puleva dairy business. This led to a new sale agreement, with France's Lactalis, which paid EUR 630 million for Puleva in May 2010. Following that sale, the company announced a change in name, becoming Ebro Foods S.A. in July 2010. Ebro Foods had successfully transformed itself from a Spanish

sugar company to a global player in the international rice and pasta markets.

M. L. Cohen

PRINCIPAL SUBSIDIARIES

Arrozeíras Mundiarroz, S.A. (Portugal); Biocarburantes de C. y León, S.A. (50%); Boost Nutrition C. V. (Belgium); Bosto Poland, S.L.; Danrice A.S. (Denmark); Euryza (Germany); Fallera Nutrición, S. L.; Herba Hellas, S.A. (Greece; 75%); Lustucru Frais (France; 99.8%); Mahatma Foods Ltd (Australia); Mundi Riso S.R.L. (Italy); Mundi Riz, S.A. (Morocco); Panzani, SAS (France); Puleva Biotech, S.A.; Riceland Magyarorszag (Hungary); Risella OY (Finland); Riviana Foods Inc. (USA); Riviana Puerto Rico; Rizerie Franco Americaine et Col. (France); S&B Herba Foods Ltd. (UK).

PRINCIPAL DIVISIONS

Rice; Pasta; Other Businesses.

PRINCIPAL OPERATING UNITS

Panzani; Ronzoni; Minute Rice; Lustucru; Taureau Ailé; Skinner; American Beauty; Danrice; La Cigala; Catelli.

PRINCIPAL COMPETITORS

Associated British Foods PLC; Barilla Holding S.p.A.; CSM N.V.; Groupe Danone; Grupo A J Vierci; Kraft Foods Inc.; Mars Inc.; MasterFoods USA Inc.; Nestlé Espana S.A.

FURTHER READING

"ABF Acquires Ebro Puleva's Sugar Unit," *just-food.com*, December 17, 2008.

Castano, Ivan, "Ebro Profits Slump as Costs Mount," *just-food. com*, February 27, 2008.

———, "Ebro Puleva 'Mulling Divestures,'" *just-food.com*, January 22, 2010.

———, "Puleva Sees US Profits up on Restructuring," *just-food.com*, September 21, 2009.

"Competitive Landscape," *Spain Food & Drink Report*, March 2010, p. 47.

"Ebro Puleva Buys Pasta Firm Birkel," *just-food.com*, July 13, 2007.

"Ebro Puleva H1 Gains Attributed to Acquisition Strategy," *just-food.com*, July 20, 2006.

"Ebro Puleva Invests 1 Bn Euros to Become Europe's Fifth Largest Food Group," *Europe Intelligence Wire*, March 14, 2005.

"Ebro Puleva S.A. Is Paying Approximately $280 Million in Acquiring the Minute Rice Brand and Assets in the US and Canada from Kraft Foods Global Inc.," *Prepared Foods*, September 2006, p. 35.

"Ebro Puleva to Change Name to Ebro Foods on Tuesday," *ADP News Spain*, May 31, 2010.

"Executive Summary," *Spain Food & Drink Report*, May 2010, p. 7.

Robinson, Simon, "Ebro Puleva Adds to Spain's Biofuel Push," *ICIS Chemical Business*, April 10, 2006, p. 8.

Edeka Zentrale AG and Company KG

New-York-Ring 6
Hamburg, D-22297
Germany
Telephone: (+49 040) 63 77 0
Fax: (+49 040) 63 77 22 31
Web site: http://www.edeka.de

Cooperative Company
Founded: 1908
Incorporated: 1918
Employees: 280,000
Sales: EUR 42.06 billion ($58.8 billion) (2009)
NAICS: 445110 Supermarkets and Other Grocery
(Except Convenience) Stores; 452910 Warehouse
Clubs and Superstores; 424410 General Line
Grocery Merchant Wholesalers

■ ■ ■

Edeka Zentrale AG and Company KG is the leading operator of supermarkets and discount grocery stores in Germany. The Hamburg-based cooperative oversees an empire of more than 12,000 stores owned and operated by more than 4,500 independent entrepreneurs. Edeka is organized into seven regional operating companies, which also operate a number of stores directly. Edeka's supermarket brands include EDEKA Center; EDEKA Neukauf; and EDEKA Aktiv markt. The company also controls the fast-growing deep-discount chain Netto Marken-Discount, which acquired 2,300 Plus Marken Discount stores from rival Tengelmann Group in 2008.

The company also operates cash-and-carry chain EDEKA C+C Grossmarkt.

THE RISE OF FOOD CO-OPS IN GERMANY IN 1907

Edeka's direct predecessor was established in October 1907 with only 800 marks in capital, at a time when co-ops were a new idea. Fritz Borrmann and Karl Biller were its first managers. This company, the Association of German Retail Co-ops, was soon joined by other co-ops all over the country. At a meeting in May 1908, a statute was presented to 80 representatives of 23 organizations, and Edeka itself was formally born.

From its first year, Edeka (EdK) was financially successful, and by 1910 it was able to establish an advertising division. EdK did not at first have its own brands, but in 1911 it purchased several famous brands. However, the young company soon felt the strength of its competitors, the industry's big retailers. The large retailers pressured suppliers not to sell Edeka goods at a discount, arguing that EdK was too small to receive the discounts big retailers were given. As a result, 44 supply companies boycotted EdK.

In its first years, EdK was very careful about giving loans and credits to its members, making all money transfers in cash rather than using credit. It was soon clear, however, that the co-op needed a bank. After long and intense discussion, the Genossenschaftsbank Edeka (Edeka Co-op Bank) was founded to provide loans to Edeka's small retailers.

During the months before World War I, the German economy was in a state of chaos. The government

COMPANY PERSPECTIVES

With foresight: entrepreneurs take the lead. EDEKA is the largest food retailer in Germany. The secret to our success is that we think and act with an entrepreneurial mindset. Traditionally, most of our full-range stores are managed by self-employed merchants. The 4,500 EDEKA entrepreneurs know their customers well, have a commitment to their regions and like taking fresh approaches. A model with a future: Each year we shepherd about 100 young merchants towards self-employment. And we all have one thing in common: our passion for food.

partially restricted free trade, and city and county administrations were ordered to confiscate goods if necessary. People rushed into shops and bought as much food as they could. As a co-op, Edeka's local, decentralized structure meant that it handled the crisis in a steady and reliable fashion. For this, the organization earned a strong reputation among consumers, and within the next several years, many Edeka shops were founded. Local administrations sought Edeka's cooperation, and some city governments even tried, unsuccessfully, to unify all small retailers into a single co-op.

LEGAL RECOGNITION IN 1918

Finally, in 1918 EdK gained legal recognition as a co-op and as a trader that bought large quantities of goods and, therefore, was entitled to discounts. With this legal status, there was no question any more about its official place in the German economy.

After World War I, while free trade was still restricted, EdK's members increased from 194 in 1918 to 578 by 1923. As terrible inflation wrought economic havoc, Edeka had to come up with ways to lessen its impact. One way was to issue 20-mark "saving coupons," to strengthen the company's financial base. Edeka suggested that each co-op member purchase at least one coupon each week, and it promised to pay 6 percent interest. Edeka also made a call for solidarity in 1923, when it needed a new office and a warehouse and asked each retailer to contribute 20 marks. Edeka, like many other companies, also began to issue its own money in another effort to combat inflation. EdK retailers were obliged to accept EdK money, which they could use to buy supplies from the central organization. This measure helped ensure that people would be able to shop at Edeka.

In 1924, EdK introduced several new policies for members. Each member store was required to use the name "Edeka" and to post an Edeka sign prominently. Shops also were required to sell Edeka brands. In its continuing effort to cope with inflation, in 1925 Edeka restricted its loans to not more than 5,000 reichsmarks per shop, and limited the liability of each shop to 7,500 reichsmarks. A year later, in 1926, new regulations required that all financial transactions be conducted in cash. This was an advantage for Edeka, since immediate payment, in cash, reduced its financial risk. By this time, EdK supplied a wide range of goods aside from food, including soap, floor wax, candles, and other products.

In a concerted effort to help small retailers, who often lacked experience as well as financial resources, EdK sent trained managers to member stores in trouble. During the Great Depression, customers trusted Edeka because of their experience during and after World War I, when Edeka's special role as a co-op ensured a stable and reliable market.

GOVERNMENT REGULATION DURING THE NAZI YEARS: 1933–45

After Adolf Hitler came to power in 1933, the whole economy was restructured and the government tried to organize institutions to regulate all sections of the economy. This effort was not entirely successful with EdK because of its decentralized organization.

After March 1934 it became illegal to import goods from foreign companies that were not part of a German company. To cope with this regulation, EdK was eventually forced to establish branches in Italy, Greece, and Turkey. Edeka also formed a subsidiary, Edeka Import and Export, a co-op with limited financial liability.

During the first years of Nazi rule, the large retailers once again tried to persuade the government to prevent Edeka from enjoying the discount and other advantages of larger companies. Between 1936 and 1939 Edeka was confronted with intense regulations and controlled prices. At this time Edeka added cigarettes to its goods, which then included some 400 items. Despite huge losses, EdK proved to be a stable company, even when in 1943 its Berlin headquarters office was bombed and burned down. At a time when thousands of companies failed, Edeka was able to stay in business, and its food stamps remained valid until February 1945, when Germany's food industry collapsed.

POSTWAR RECOVERY: 1945–60

After the war, the partition of Germany cut off almost all communication between the eastern and western

KEY DATES

1907: Fritz Borrmann and Karl Biller form the Association of German Retail Co-ops.
1918: Edeka gains legal recognition as a co-op.
1978: Edeka enters into an agreement with Horten to rent shop space in department stores.
1993: The Single European Market goes into effect.
2003: Company begins refocusing on the German market.
2005: Edeka acquires the Netto discount grocery chain.
2008: Edeka acquires more than 2,000 Plus discount stores.
2010: Edeka posts revenues of more than EUR 42 billion.

zones. The situation in Berlin was especially confusing, leading Edeka to establish a second headquarters in Hamburg.

A new generation of managers met in Bad Godesberg in 1945 to reestablish an active Edeka. Their first effort failed, but a second meeting in March 1946 in Göttingen made it clear that Edeka would continue to operate. The company's first annual report, for 1945, was written by both headquarters, in Berlin and Hamburg.

Of the 524 co-ops that existed before World War II, 201 in West Germany and 125 in East Germany survived the war. In 1952, however, the East German state brought an end to all Edeka co-ops in East Germany when it forbade governmental companies to deliver to the private sector. However, the situation in the West improved: In 1950 the central office counted 225 co-ops with total sales of DEM 15 million. Each co-op encompassed an average of 124 small retailers.

The 1950s, the years of the economic miracle, were a time of tremendous growth for all sectors of the economy. During this time more than 20 percent of all small retailers were part of Edeka, and the co-op expanded vigorously, constructing warehouses in Braunschweig for tins and vegetables, in Cuxhaven for fish, and in Kempten for cheese.

Edeka also continued to introduce new ideas and systems to customers and small retailers: Edeka stores were among the first to introduce self-service, since new packing machines enabled EdK to sell packaged goods. By 1958, 7,000 of 40,500 stores offered self-service.

Frozen food and fruits were introduced in 1955, and special diet and health foods were introduced in 1957.

PRODUCT INNOVATIONS, CORPORATE RESTRUCTURING IN THE SIXTIES

EdK did not stop its modernization. Shops continued to change to self-service. In 1962 delegations of the co-op traveled to the United States to compare the Edeka system to similar U.S. companies. Meanwhile, Europe took its first steps toward the Common Market. Edeka joined the Union of Food Coops (UGAL) in Brussels. From the foundation of UGAL in 1963, EdK helped lobby for co-op interests in the European market.

In its ongoing effort to sell a greater variety of goods, EdK started to sell meat in 1963. The wider range of EdK's goods enabled the co-op to survive in smaller villages and towns, since it meant that neighborhoods could buy all of their necessary food, such as bakery products, fruits, frozen food, and dairy products, from an Edeka store. In 1968 Edeka for the first time began to sell general household goods such as can openers and pens.

Competition was fierce, especially in the early 1960s, and many smaller retailers failed. To survive, EdK had to improve its weak points. Restructuring the stocking system through the use of rolling shelf containers helped retailers stock a wider variety of goods in the same space, helping mitigate rising rents. By 1965 regional computer centers were established to simplify communication among small retailers and Edeka's head office. Another important initiative to compete with other companies was education. EdK established a training center and started an international educational program in cooperation with Swiss and Austrian retailers in 1965.

Two years later two new subsidiaries were founded to help with the real estate problems of small retailers, especially retailers located in downtown areas. All of these organizational and educational steps, however, could not prevent the failure of 2,500 small retailers between 1968 and 1970.

REGIONAL OFFICES IN 1970

Edeka decided to tighten its organizational structure. Five regional offices were created, in Hamburg, Cologne, Frankfurt, Stuttgart, and Munich. Since 1970 each regional office was financed equally by the Edeka bank and the co-ops. Despite this change, however, Edeka was heavily criticized by the department of monopolies, which saw the size of the organization as proof of its monopolistic hold on the retail industry.

Edeka claimed that it simply represented small retailers and did not, as state officials assumed, dominate them.

In the economic turmoil that followed the oil shock in 1973, small retailers had a particularly hard time in Germany. Public opinion turned away from Edeka and from co-ops in general, which were seen as old-fashioned. Edeka began to concentrate more on public relations, and it recruited employees through workshops and cooperation with local schools. By 1975, 6,000 trainees worked in shops all over Germany. Three of every four EdK shops were remodeled between 1965 and 1975.

In 1978, Edeka entered an agreement with the department store Horten in which Edeka rented space in 58 department stores and set up food shops. The agreement came at a time when almost no Edeka stores had survived in the rapidly changing downtown areas. The EdK-Horten arrangement helped many retailers to survive, since renting one section of a department store was much less expensive than the rent for a separate street-level shop.

At the beginning of the 1980s, EdK was the largest independent group of small retailers in Europe, with 18,200 small retailers who owned 20,300 shops. By the end of 1988, Edeka had 11,000 members who operated a total of 13,150 stores and had total sales of more than DEM 20 billion. Some of this drop could be accounted for by the trend toward fewer, larger stores in the retail industry.

By the end of the 1980s each member was part of a regional co-op. Together, these regional co-ops ran 22 wholesale businesses for the individual stores, and each was a member of Edeka Zentrale, the holding company. The regional co-ops were also members of Edekabank, which handled both credit and insurance for Edeka members. In addition to supplying individual retailers and operating their own meat processing facilities, Edeka wholesale businesses supplied hotels and large restaurants.

EUROPEAN UNIFICATION: THE NINETIES

The formation of the Single European Market in 1993 had an understandably profound effect on the German food industry. In addition to exposing retailers to increased competition from rivals in neighboring countries, the opening of national borders also forced companies to comply with a host of new laws, which were enforced by the newly centralized governing body of the European Union. Since the integrated economy required an enormous degree of standardization to be effective, such areas as procurement, distribution, and food quality became subject to increased regulation.

To prosper in this highly competitive climate, Edeka was compelled to undergo its own transformation during the 1990s. The company recognized three keys to maintaining its role as a leading food retailer in Germany. The first key to Edeka's future success lay in the implementation of new technologies into its retail business model. In 1997 the company introduced an electronic pricing information system in its Baden-Württemberg outlet. The success of the venture led the company to launch the system in five additional stores the following year. In anticipation of the arrival of a single European currency in 1999, the system was designed to scan prices in both deutsche marks and euros.

Edeka also made its official entrance into the world of e-commerce in 2000, when it joined the WorldWide Retail Exchange, an extensive Internet resource geared toward establishing an online marketplace for distributors and retailers around the globe. As a way of providing new incentives to its customers, Edeka introduced a computerized card for its shoppers in 2001, allowing them to accumulate bonus points with their purchases.

The second key to Edeka's success involved expansion of its market reach. The company made a number of strategic acquisitions in the late 1990s, most notably in 1998, when its retail division enjoyed overall growth of 19.2 percent. In 1999 the company began merger negotiations with retail group Tengelmann Warenhandelsgesellschaft OHG. The fifth-largest food seller in Germany, Tengelmann had not done well in the unified economy, suffering losses of more than DEM 200 million in its supermarket operations. The merger fell through, however, after the two companies failed to reach an agreement. Edeka consoled itself, however, with the purchase of 110 of Tengelmann's supermarkets in 2001.

FOCUS ON GERMANY FROM 2003

Amid a new economic recession, Edeka began restructuring its organization as part of an overall cost-cutting effort. As a result, the company reduced the number of its regional companies to just seven in 2001. The company, which by then oversaw a network of more than 10,000 stores, also announced plans to close as many as 300 stores. In this way, Edeka hoped to increase operating profits by up to DEM 500 million annually.

During the new decade, Edeka decided to abandon its international operations. This process started in 2003, when the company sold off its 44-store chain of Ed Maxi Discounter stores in France. Edeka also sold 27 of its stores in the Czech Republic to the United

Kingdom's Tesco. By 2006, the company had completed its exit from that market, selling its remaining Czech stores to Pramen CZ. The company began selling off its supermarkets in Austria that year.

Instead, Edeka focused on expanding its position in the German market. This led the company to acquire 54.3 percent in one of its major rivals, AVA Allgemeine Handelsgesellschaft der Verbraucher, in 2002. The following year, Edeka raised its stake in AVA to 72.5 percent, and in 2006 gained full control of the company. This acquisition added 400 hypermarkets to Edeka's operations, as well as a chain of do-it-yourself stores and a Moscow shopping center, subsequently sold to Rewe and Metro Group, respectively.

BUILDING A DISCOUNT GIANT IN 2008

Edeka's interest increasingly turned to the discount grocery sector, which grew to account for 50 percent of Germany's total supermarket industry during the decade. Edeka decided to move into this market in earnest in the middle of the decade, becoming a major challenger to the segment's two giants, Aldi and Lidl. Edeka's first step came in 2005, when the company reached an agreement with France's ITM Enterprises to take over its 1,000-store Netto discount chain. By the end of 2007, Edeka's discount operations accounted for 15 percent of the group's total revenues, which passed EUR 30 billion that year. The discount division was also the company's fastest growing.

Edeka continued searching for opportunities to gain scale in its discount sector. This led the company to agree to merge its Netto chain with the larger Plus chain of more than 2,300 discount stores operated by Tengelmann. The original agreement called for Edeka to own 70 percent of the combined company compared to Tengelmann's 30 percent. That agreement ran afoul of Germany's competition authorities, however. Instead, Tengelmann agreed in 2008 to sell Edeka the Plus chain, in a deal worth EUR 11 billion.

Edeka now became Germany's largest food retailer, and the third-largest player in the fast-growing discount grocery sector. The company began the process of converting the Plus chain to its own banners, including 800 stores to its City-Markt banner. Edeka also announced plans to open as many as 1,000 new stores by 2010, in a bid to raise its total market share to 30 percent. In the meantime, the growth of its discount operations fueled Edeka's own growth. By 2010, the discount division represented 29 percent of the group's

total, which topped EUR 42 billion ($59 billion) for the year.

Updated, Steve Meyer; M. L. Cohen

PRINCIPAL SUBSIDIARIES

EDEKA Handelsgesellschaft Hessenring mbH; EDEKA Handelsgesellschaft Nord mbH; EDEKA Handelsgesellschaft Nordbayern-Sachsen-Thüringen mbH; EDEKA Handelsgesellschaft Rhein-Ruhr mbH; EDEKA Handelsgesellschaft Südbayern mbH; EDEKA Handelsgesellschaft Südwest mbH; EDEKA Minden-Hannover Holding GmbH; Marktkauf Holding GmbH Fuggerstraße 11; Netto Marken-Discount GmbH & Co. oHG; SPAR Handelsgesellschaft mbH.

PRINCIPAL DIVISIONS

EDEKA North; EDEKA Minden-Hannover; EDEKA Rhine-Ruhr; EDEKA Hessenring; EDEKA Northern Bavaria-Saxony-Thuringia; EDEKA South-West; EDEKA Southern Bavaria.

PRINCIPAL OPERATING UNITS

EDEKA Center; EDEKA Neukauf; EDEKA Aktiv markt; Marktkauf; Netto Marken-Discount; Plus Marken Discount; EDEKA C+C Grossmarkt.

PRINCIPAL COMPETITORS

Lidl Stiftung and Company KG; METRO AG; REWE-Zentral AG; Tengelmann Warenhandelsgesellschaft OHG.

FURTHER READING

"Discounter Edeka Is Set to Create 8,000 New Jobs in Germany This Year, following the Retailers' Acquisition of Plus," *Grocer*, January 17, 2009, p. 9.

Durchslag, Adam, "The Supermarket Discount Wars," *Acquisitions Monthly*, September 2008, p. S28.

"Edeka Details Discount Expansion," *just-food.com*, July 2, 2009.

"Edeka Poised for Radical Restructuring," *Global News Wire* (abstracted from *Die Welt*), May 23, 2001, p. 14.

Edeka: 75 Jahre immer in Aktion, Hamburg: Edeka Zentrale AG and Company KG, 1982.

"Edeka Thinks Future Mergers Make Sense," *Global News Wire* (abstracted from *Frankfurter Allgemeine Zeitung*), May 18, 1999, p. 21.

"Grocers 'Foolish' to Go Cool on Supermarkets," *just-food.com*, July 6, 2009.

FARMERS COOP SOCIETY

Farmers Cooperative Society

317 3rd Street NW
Sioux Center, Iowa 51250
U.S.A.
Telephone: (712) 722-2671
Fax: (712) 722-2674
Web site: http://www.farmerscoopsociety.com

Cooperative
Incorporated: 1907 as Farmers Mutual Incorporated Cooperative
Employees: 200
Sales: $150 million (2006 est.)
NAICS: 424510 Grain and Field Bean Merchant Wholesalers; 424910 Farm Supplies Merchant Wholesalers; 444190 Other Building Material Dealers

∎ ∎ ∎

Farmers Cooperative Society (FCS) is an agricultural organization that provides a variety of services to its farmer-members from seven centers located in northwest Iowa. In addition to its main office in Sioux Center, FCS maintains branches in Boyden, Ireton, Little Rock, Melvin, Ritter, and Sanborn, Iowa. The organization's Agronomy Division provides farmers with site-specific services, including seed sales, nutrient plans, and crop protection. The Grain Division markets the corn and soybeans of its members, while the Feed Division maintains four mills to produce custom livestock feed. FCS also operates the How-To Building Center (also known as the How-To Store) in Sioux Center offering lumber, paint, building supplies, hardware, and appliances for the construction of agricultural buildings as well as new home construction and remodeling projects.

FARMERS UNITING IN 1907

Disenchantment with privately owned grain elevators, which employed untrustworthy scales and charged hefty fees for grain marketing and other services, led farmers in the Sioux Center area to band together in 1907. In February of that year they formed the Farmers Mutual Incorporated Cooperative. Funds were raised through long-term notes as well as the sale of stock to farmers, and soon a new 2,500 bushel elevator was constructed at a cost of $5,525. In addition to storing and marketing grain for its members, the cooperative sold livestock and provided farmers with a variety of commodities, including coal, flour, and twine.

The society's initial growth was not to the satisfaction of its members and just two years after its launch a committee was formed to raise more money. A new manager was also installed, and in 1911 the cooperative was able to pay its first dividend. A year later Farmers Mutual stockholders voted to start a lumberyard, and funds were allocated to purchase an existing lumberyard and inventory in Sioux Center for $7,800. Other changes soon followed. In 1916 the society abandoned stock ownership for a mutual cooperative organization, and in 1919 the name was shortened to Farmers Cooperative Society.

The 1920s saw FCS pay off the notes incurred during its origins. The society also bought the Atlas Elevator in 1920, built a new scale and stockyards, and

COMPANY PERSPECTIVES

We accept a second century's new challenges invigorated by the innovative spirit alive in today's agriculture.

bought its first delivery truck. The first feed mill was also constructed, and in 1929 the Farmers Mixed Feeds name was adopted for the feed products it offered. The Black Hawk Feeds brand was coined a few years later.

FCS WEATHERS DEPRESSION

The close of the 1920s brought a stock market crash that had a ripple effect on the nation's economy, ushering in the Great Depression that spanned the 1930s. Although it was a challenging time, compounded by a period of severe drought, FCS fared better than most cooperatives and even had the wherewithal to launch the Progressive Farmers Coop Commission Firm in Sioux City to better market members' livestock. The same could not be said for the community in general, as many farmworkers left in search of work elsewhere.

World War II drained the area's labor force further, but the increased use of mechanized harvesting lessened the need for laborers as well as changed agriculture in other ways. The introduction of pull-type combines led to the cultivation of soybeans in Sioux County for the first time in the 1940s. Previously, farmers had shied away from the crop because it was difficult and time consuming to harvest soybeans with threshing machines. During this period, hybrid seed corn gained in popularity in the area, due in large part to the FCS staff that promoted its advantages to members. The war also made flax a popular crop, because of military demand for linseed oil and linseed oil-based paint products. In 1942 FCS bought a flax cleaner to accommodate this important new crop.

While some things in Sioux Center returned to normal after World War II came to an end in 1945, FCS continued to expand its operations. In the final years of the decade, the society added a new 55-foot scale, a new lumberyard office, and purchased land where government corn would be stored for the next decade. In the 1950s FCS purchased an oats de-huller and roller, followed by a new feed and mixing plant. These additions led to the hiring of a nutritionist and the 1957 opening of a feed formulation department that made available many new feed formulas to member-farmers. It was also during the 1950s that the society's

annual revenues first reached the $1 million mark.

FCS MERGES WITH IRETON COOP

Further expansion continued in the 1960s. The society merged with the Ireton Farmers' Cooperative Association in 1963. Like FCS, the cooperative was founded in 1907, again the result of dissatisfaction with private elevators. It was able to operate independently for the next half-century but by the early 1960s faced increasing competition, leading to the merger with FCS. The timing proved fortuitous because in 1964 the Ireton elevator, which was fully insured, was destroyed by fire. While a new elevator was constructed, Ireton members were able to make use of the Sioux Center elevator. A year after Ireton's new elevator opened in 1965, Sioux Center suffered its own share of misfortune when the elevator in town along with the feed mill were also destroyed by fire. The Ireton elevator and feed mill filled the void until new facilities could be built in Sioux Center.

FCS closed the 1960s with its first $10 million year. Low interest rates in the 1970s led many farmers to expand their operations in order to raise more crops and livestock. FCS expanded as well, opening a new lumberyard and the How-To Store in Sioux Center in the late 1970s to take advantage of the need for new farm buildings. Moreover, the community was enjoying a growth spurt. At the time, about 100 new homes were being constructed in the area each year and the new FCS enterprises served the needs of area builders and do-it-yourself customers. It was also in the 1970s that FCS installed its first computers, which provided a significant improvement to bookkeeping, a painstaking task that had been done by hand for 70 years.

Conditions soon deteriorated, however. In the early 1980s interest rates soared while commodity prices plummeted, so that by the mid-1980s FCS had to contend with a large amount of bad debt. It also had difficulty in marketing corn, due to the oversupply of commodities. New home construction also fell from 120 in 1983 to just 20 a year later, adversely impacting the lumberyard. To weather the tough times, FCS in 1984 froze the pay of hourly employees while implementing a 5 percent cut in the salaries of the management staff. Nevertheless, FCS posted a loss in 1984, and a year later the deficit widened to $600,000, the worst year in the company's history.

RETURN TO PROFITABILITY: 1986

A new general manager, Mary Richardson, was installed in 1986 and further cost-reduction steps were taken.

```
┌─────────────────────────────────────────────┐
│                                               │
│              KEY DATES                        │
│                   ■                           │
│  ─────────────────────────────────────────   │
│                                               │
│  1907:  Farmers Mutual Incorporated Cooperative is │
│         founded.                              │
│  1919:  Name is changed to Farmers Cooperative │
│         Society (FCS).                        │
│  1963:  FCS merges with Ireton Farmers'       │
│         Cooperative.                          │
│  1991:  Little Rock, Iowa, elevator is acquired. │
│  2002:  FCS merges with Siouxland Coop.       │
│                                               │
└─────────────────────────────────────────────┘
```

New credit and income policies were also implemented to help return FCS to profitability in 1986 when a profit of $47,000 was recorded. FCS was hardly enjoying flush times, however. Austerity measures continued and there was some discussion of merger with other cooperatives, although nothing came of it. In 1988 FCS also considered selling the lumberyard and the How-To Store, but in the end elected to keep both.

Better times for FCS and its members lay ahead in the 1990s. FCS forged alliances with both Land O'Lakes and Farmland Industries. FCS contracted with the latter for cattle feed and with the former for hog and poultry feed. In 1991 the society acquired an elevator and fertilizer plant in Little Rock, Iowa, from Langels' Inc. The elevator, now used by FCS to source grain, had started out as a private elevator in 1903. FCS also expanded through an alliance with other cooperatives in the mid-1990s. It was one of the early organizers of North Dakota-based Northern Plains Premium Beef, a cattle packing operation. In 1995 FCS joined with 13 other coops to form Cooperative Credit Corporation to provide member farmers with input financing. FCS expanded on other fronts as well. Sioux Center's Our Own Hardware store was acquired and folded into the How-To Store, and the Sioux Center feed mill automated its operations. Consideration was also given to the establishment of an ethanol plant to take advantage of the area's corn production. This effort eventually led to the creation of a separate cooperative, the Siouxland Energy and Livestock Corp.

A major factor in the prosperity of hog farmers in the mid-1990s was the growth of Asian markets. In the summer of 1997, however, a financial crisis struck Asia, resulting in a sudden drop in demand at a time of peak production for hog farmers as well as corn growers. To make matters worse, new competition emerged from Argentina and China. FCS was adversely impacted in 1998 when a deal fell through to supply $13,000 worth of grain a day to a proposed hog-feeding operation in

Wyoming when the Japanese backers of the venture were unable to provide the necessary financing. The cattle business of FCS members also suffered because of low beef prices and South Korea's reduced need for hides, which were used to make purses and baseball gloves.

MERGER WITH SIOUXLAND COOP: 2002

Unlike many cooperatives, FCS entered the new century relatively healthy. It added 500 new producers to its 2,250 membership ranks in 2002 with the merger with Siouxland Coop. Siouxland had formed in 1997 through the merger of the Farmers Coop Association of Boyden, Sanborn Coop Grain, and Ritter Farmers Elevator, all three of which were formed in the early 1900s. Sanborn brought with it an elevator in Melvin, Iowa. Siouxland expanded further in 1999 with the acquisition of the Melvin fertilizer plant. Talks were launched with FCS about a possible merger during this period, but there was not enough interest among membership to bring the idea to completion. The lines of communication remained open, however, leading to a change of heart in the early 2000s.

As the first decade of the 2000s progressed, FCS continued to grow. It formed Northwest Iowa Agronomy LLC in 2005, bringing together a regional coop and four local coops to establish a large fertilizer plant in Alton, Iowa. Increased corn and bean crops led to the construction of two steel 500,000 bushel bins in Sanborn, followed by a one million bushel wooden bunker. Sales topped the $150 million mark in 2006, while net income exceeded $2.5 million. In that same year, FCS considered a merger with Midwest Cooperative, but members of both organizations voted down the measure and elected to remain independent. FCS celebrated its 100th anniversary a year later. To remain vital, FCS renovated its confinement feedlot in 2009 and spent $100,000 on repairs to the feed mill. There was every reason to expect FCS to remain committed to fulfilling the needs of its members for years to come.

Ed Dinger

PRINCIPAL DIVISIONS

Agronomy; Feed; Feedlot; Grain; How-To Store.

PRINCIPAL COMPETITORS

AGRI Industries, Inc.; Gold-Eagle Cooperative; West Central Cooperative.

FURTHER READING

Bakker, Heidi K., *Century with Purpose, 1907–2007: Farmers Coop Society*, Sioux Center, IA: Farmers Coop Society, 2007.

Campbell, Dan, "High Society: Sioux Center Farmers Co-op Society Ties Future to NW Iowa Livestock Industry," *Rural Cooperatives*, September–October 2002, p. 4.

Fee, Rod, "Can New Cattle Co-op Packers Compete?" *Successful Farming*, December 1996, p. 34.

Wysocki, Bernard, Jr., "Farmers Are Hurt by Asian Crisis, Too," *Wall Street Journal*, July 20, 1998, p. A1.

FremantleMedia Ltd.

---

1 Stephen Street
London, W1T 1AL
United Kingdom
Telephone: (+44 20) 7691 6000
Fax: (+44 20) 7691 6100
Web site: http://www.fremantlemedia.com

Wholly Owned Subsidiary of RTL Group, a Unit of Bertelsmann AG
Incorporated: 1994 as Pearson Television
Employees: 1,700
Sales: EUR 1.18 billion (2009)
NAICS: 512110 Motion Picture and Video Production; 512120 Motion Picture and Video Distribution; 533110 Lessors of Nonfinancial Intangible Assets (Except Copyrighted Works)

■ ■ ■

FremantleMedia Ltd. is one of the top television production companies in the world. Its properties include internationally franchised reality hits *Idol*, *Got Talent*, *The X Factor*, and *The Farmer Wants a Wife*; popular game shows *The Price Is Right*, *Hole in the Wall*, and *Family Feud*; soap operas *Neighbors* and *Gute Zeiten, Schlechte Zeiten*; and such prime-time dramas as Britain's *The Bill*. The firm's programs are seen in more than 40 countries around the world, and it has production units in about half that number. Licensing, distribution, and sales are handled via FremantleMedia Enterprises, which also represents select outside firms such as Paramount. The company is owned by RTL Group, a division of German media conglomerate Bertelsmann AG.

ROOTS

FremantleMedia's beginnings date to the early 1990s, when Pearson plc, a 150-year-old British company with diverse interests in publishing, manufacturing, and oil, formed a television unit. In April 1994 the company paid £99 million to acquire Thames Television, an independent production company that had been founded in 1968. Thames had long produced shows for the Independent Television (ITV) network and exported some, including *The Benny Hill Show*, abroad. It had recently lost its bid to work with ITV, however, and after Pearson took control it was reconstituted as Britain's largest independent TV studio. Pearson soon also began purchasing minority stakes in broadcasting firms such as BSkyB and Channel 5.

In mid-1995 the company bought Australia's leading television studio, Grundy Worldwide Ltd., for $279 million. Grundy's programming was distributed in Asia and Europe, and its output included the long-running Australian/British soap opera *Neighbors* and numerous game shows. In the fall Pearson paid $40 million to buy six-year-old Los Angeles TV movie production/distribution firm ACI, and in 1996 it purchased U.K. production company SelecTV, whose units included Alomo Productions.

During the fall of 1997 Pearson made its largest acquisition to date with the purchase of All American Communications, Inc., for $515 million. All American had been founded in 1981 as an offshoot of the successful Scotti Brothers record company, and in 1991 it had begun production (with partner LBS Communications, which it would later acquire) of a recently canceled NBC action-drama called *Baywatch*, which was soon syndicated to local TV stations across the United States.

Led by tan, swimsuit-clad Pamela Anderson and David Hasselhoff, *Baywatch* became a huge hit worldwide, giving All American the cash to fund the 1994 acquisition of international game show distributor Fremantle Group, the 1995 purchase of Mark Goodson Productions (owner of Fremantle-distributed hits *The Price Is Right* and *Family Feud*), and the 1996 purchase of talk show distributor Orbis Entertainment.

By 1998 Pearson had studio operations in 16 territories worldwide, and produced and/or distributed about half the game shows seen around the world, as well as numerous TV movies and a few syndicated dramas such as *Baywatch*. The company's acquisitions continued during that year with the purchases of EVA Entertainment and Regent Productions of the United Kingdom, Mastrofilm of Italy, and Cape Waterfront Television of South Africa. A German unit called team-Worx was also established, and in 1999 Pearson bought Cologne-Sitcom of Germany and Vihde of Finland.

PEARSON MERGES WITH CLT-UFA IN 2000

In 2000 Pearson Television merged with CLT-UFA, a broadcasting company with 22 television channels and 18 radio stations that was owned by the RTL Group. Ownership of RTL would be split between Bertelsmann AG (30 percent), Groupe Bruxelles Lambert (30 percent), Pearson (22 percent), and WAZ (7 percent), with the remaining 11 percent traded publicly. Pearson and CLT-UFA would together hold 65 percent of Britain's Channel 5, as well as owning several joint ventures in Germany. The company's production capabilities would be used to supply CLT-UFA's

broadcast outlets with content, with the latter in turn providing work for Pearson.

Pearson Television now had 160 programs in production that were seen in 35 countries, which helped make RTL Group the largest content producer and broadcaster in Europe. Soon after the merger, Pearson also bought Talkback Productions of the United Kingdom, the nearly 20-year-old producer of *Da Ali G Show* and *Smack the Pony*, among others.

In early 2001 Bertelsmann bought Groupe Bruxelles Lambert's 30 percent stake in RTL, giving it controlling interest (it later also bought the portions owned by Pearson and WAZ), and in the summer it was announced that Pearson Television's production operations would be rebranded as FremantleMedia, Ltd. The company also revived the Thames Television name, which had been unused since the early 1990s (subsequently merging it with Talkback to form talk-backThames), and changed the names of other Pearson-branded units as part of an overall restructuring. FremantleMedia had by now absorbed several former CLT-UFA assets including Germany's leading TV/film studio UFA, whose history dated to 1917 and included the production of such classic silent movies as Fritz Lang's *Metropolis*, as well as a period working for the Nazis and postwar nationalization.

LAUNCH OF *POP IDOL* IN OCTOBER 2001

In October 2001 a new prime-time music show, coproduced by FremantleMedia and 19 Television, debuted on Britain's ITV network. Created by onetime Spice Girls manager Simon Fuller and Bertelsmann Music Group (BMG) record executive Simon Cowell, *Pop Idol* featured amateur singers competing to win a recording contract, with four judges (including the acerbic Cowell) critiquing their performances and audience members voting to choose the winner by phone or online. The program became a sensation. After it ended all three of the top finalists had number one U.K. hits for FremantleMedia sister company BMG.

At the same time the U.S. television syndication market had grown bleak due to falling advertising rates and audience fragmentation, and in 2001 FremantleMedia North America formed an alliance with Tribune Co., which would take over distribution of game shows including *Family Feud*, as well as coproducing others. Tribune had stakes in several broadcasting companies, which provided guaranteed outlets for the programs. FremantleMedia also began trying to sell versions of its foreign hits to the major U.S. networks and cable channels. Because these would be funded by clients,

```
┌────────────────────────────────────────────────────┐
│                                                      │
│                  KEY DATES                           │
│                      ■                               │
│  ──────────────────────────────────────────────     │
│  1994:  Pearson plc buys Thames Television.          │
│  1995:  Pearson acquires Grundy Worldwide, produc-   │
│         ers of soap opera *Neighbors*.               │
│  1997:  Company purchases All American Com-          │
│         munications, home to *Baywatch* and *Price Is│
│         Right*.                                      │
│  2000:  Merger with CLT-UFA makes firm a part of     │
│         RTL Group/Bertelsmann.                       │
│  2001:  Pearson Television is rebranded as Fremantle-│
│         Media Ltd.; *Pop Idol* debuts in Britain.    │
│  2006:  *America's Got Talent* is launched.          │
│                                                      │
└────────────────────────────────────────────────────┘
```

rather than internally (as with syndicated shows), there was less financial risk.

The first to be sold was a spin-off of *Pop Idol*, which was rechristened *American Idol—The Search for a Superstar* (producers of a similar New Zealand show called *Popstars* had threatened a lawsuit over the name). It was considered a somewhat risky concept in the United States, where music programs had fallen out of favor, and was rejected by several networks before being picked up by Fox, which slated it for summer, when the competition was mostly reruns. The panel of three judges would again include Cowell, with a scheduled run of 13 weeks from June to early September 2002.

Although it began with relatively little fanfare, *American Idol* quickly connected with viewers, spurred in part by the growing interest in reality-based programs and the recent popularity of prime-time game shows including *Who Wants to Be a Millionaire*. The finale was watched by a staggering 23 million viewers, and after the competition ended winner Kelly Clarkson had a number one album for BMG-owned RCA Records. A second U.S. season was quickly scheduled for early the next year as the firm scrambled to create versions in other markets.

IDOL GOES INTERNATIONAL IN 2003

By mid-2003 FremantleMedia had launched the show in 20 different territories, including South Africa, Australia, and Lebanon, and at year's end a competition between 11 international winners, *World Idol*, was broadcast. The company was now signing a broad range of licensing deals for clothing, games, fragrances, karaoke products, trading cards, and more, and the show's finalists were filling stadiums on successful concert tours. Although

voting in the United States was through toll-free phone numbers, in most countries the calls were charged to audience members, with FremantleMedia receiving a cut.

More franchised versions were added in 2004, when *Idol's* worldwide audience topped 100 million viewers, with some 700 million votes cast overall. The show was the most popular on American television, and dominated the ratings in many other countries as well. In North America alone, licensed goods worth more than $50 million had been sold, and the Fox network had paid the company an estimated $75 million for broadcast rights.

To ensure the quality of the many different editions of *Idol*, and its other franchised shows, FremantleMedia used a staff of England-based "fliers" who visited foreign production units, although in a few markets, such as Iceland and Kazakhstan, locals were given complete control. Occasionally new ideas, such as the American concept of judges choosing a "wild card" contestant, or the lighting design developed in Germany, were adopted franchise-wide. In addition to *Idol*, which dominated the ratings in virtually every market it had entered, the firm was having success with other reality-based series including *Wife Swap*, *How Clean Is Your House*, *The Farmer Wants a Wife*, and *The Swan*, and it also continued to produce a slate of soap operas, game shows, and dramas. FremantleMedia had recently been appointed by Mark Burnett Productions to create franchised versions of its U.S. hit *The Apprentice* in foreign markets as well.

X FACTOR REPLACES *POP IDOL* IN 2004

In England *Pop Idol* was replaced after its second competition by the similar Simon Cowell-produced *X Factor*, which was a huge hit when broadcast in the late summer and fall of 2004. Cowell had promoted the switch so that he could take greater control of the program (and its profits) through his Syco company, but *Idol* co-creator 19 Television filed suit. It was later settled out of court with 19 taking partial ownership of the show and Cowell agreeing to five more seasons as a judge on *American Idol*, while also reportedly taking a small stake in it.

FremantleMedia's success was spawning continued expansion, which included the December 2003 purchase of Crackerjack, an Australian producer of comedies, game shows, and reality-based programs, and the June 2004 acquisition of production company Blue Circle from RTL/Holland Media Group. In September the company also formed a joint venture in Japan with programming firm Vogue Planet. FremantleMedia now had revenues of nearly $1 billion.

In 2004 the company consolidated its interactive and licensing operations to better integrate them in each territory, and also sold theatrical film rights to the now dormant *Baywatch* to DreamWorks SKG. In the first half of 2005 FremantleMedia signed so-called first-look deals with several prominent reality show producers; formed a joint venture with Stuart Krasnow Productions, creators of the hit *The Weakest Link*; bought three-fourths of Danish production firm Blu Entertainment; took an equity stake in film/TV producer Peace Arch Entertainment Group; won worldwide rights to the fashion design show *Project Runway*; and founded a division to develop content for new media platforms.

In November Fox Broadcasting agreed to pay $18 million more for *American Idol 5* than had been originally contracted, receiving in return a guarantee of up to six additional series, which would themselves be produced at a similar or higher fee structure. Simon Cowell also signed a separate agreement guaranteeing his participation.

AMERICA'S GOT TALENT DEBUTS IN 2006

In early 2006 FremantleMedia began syndicating *American Idol Rewind*, a reedited version of early entries in the series, and in the summer launched *America's Got Talent*, a variation on *Idol* produced with Cowell that featured dancers, musicians, and other performance styles. The Regis Philbin-hosted show proved a sizable hit, and after a U.K. version was launched the following year, *Got Talent* editions subsequently appeared in more than two-dozen countries, with ratings that approached those of *Idol*.

In July 2006 *Latin American Idol* began airing in 24 Central and South American countries. The coproduction with Sony Entertainment Television featured competitors from around the region. During the year FremantleMedia also created an on-demand video service that offered some 200 hours of comedy from talkbackThames; launched the Simon Cowell-produced *American Inventor* competition program and *Live from Abbey Road*; consolidated the Grundy and Crackerjack units as FremantleMedia Australia to create the largest independent production house in that country; and released the company's first theatrical film, *Mischief Night*, as a joint venture with U.K.-based Verve Pictures.

In 2007 FremantleMedia's U.S. slate grew again with the debuts of prime-time game show *Million Dollar Password*, hosted by Regis Philbin for CBS, and *Temptation*, a reworking of catalog title *Sale of the*

Century, on Fox-affiliated MyNetworkTV. The company also sold *Farmer Wants a Wife* to The CW network and launched *Idol* offshoots *The Search for the Next Great American Band* on Fox and *Can You Duet* on CMT. Elsewhere the firm partnered with @radical.media to distribute marketing-infused "branded entertainment" programs in several regions, boosted its presence in Asia, expanded operations in France and Spain, and began negotiations to start a subsidiary unit in Russia. A $58 million fund was also started to finance production deals with established performers/producers. During 2007 FremantleMedia produced over 10,000 hours of programming worldwide.

Other streams of revenue for the firm included product placement, in which companies such as Ford and Cingular paid to have their wares visible in programs; sales of *Idol* performances via Apple's iTunes store the day after they were broadcast; an *Idol*-themed summer camp for children; and an attraction at Walt Disney World in Florida that featured daily *Idol*-inspired singing contests whose winners would be able to compete for future slots on the actual show.

JAPANESE JOINT VENTURE: 2008

In the spring of 2008 FremantleMedia formed a partnership with TV Man Union, one of Japan's top production companies. Although successful around the world, the firm had not been able to make significant headway in that country, and it was hoped that a strong local partner could give it a better foothold. New shows of the year included *Love Race*, a dating competition that used social networking Web sites; a variety program starring Ozzy and Sharon Osbourne; and a licensed adaptation of the "Brain Wall" segment of Japan's Fuji TV show *Minasan no Okage deshita*, which was retitled *Hole in the Wall*. It quickly connected with audiences and was soon being adapted for more than three-dozen markets.

The firm's distribution arm, FremantleMedia Enterprises, was also busy, securing worldwide rights to four NBC-TV programs including *Shark Taggers* and *America's Toughest Jobs*; selling the second season of *Live from Abbey Road* in 60 territories; and cutting a deal to produce the first authorized filmed biography of Brazilian soccer legend Pelé.

In 2008 the company also launched UFA Cinema, a German production unit that was expected to produce 10 feature films per year; bought a 20 percent stake in Australian TV/film production company Beyond International; boosted its production deal with Toronto-based Insight Production Co.; cut a number of mobile-content deals; signed a coproduction agreement with the

Spike cable network; and signed a contract to make exclusive programs for YouTube.com, with which it would split proceeds.

PURCHASE OF ORIGINAL PRODUCTIONS IN 2009

In February 2009 FremantleMedia purchased 75 percent of Thom Beers's Original Productions, creator of such hit reality shows as *Ice Road Truckers* and *Deadliest Catch*. The firm also bought small stakes in Canadian video-game maker Ludia, which it had worked with for some time, and Wide-Eyed Entertainment, a computer animation producer. Other deals were cut with producers of scripted television dramas and publisher Liquid Comics, while a production unit was also established in India. An *Idol* iPhone application was released during the year, as well, which allowed purchasers to view clips from the program and track their favorites.

In March 2009 a class-action lawsuit was initiated in California against FremantleMedia and several affiliates that alleged the firm overworked its employees and falsified time cards to avoid paying overtime. Earlier, several dozen *American Idol* employees had filed claims against FremantleMedia North America before the California Division of Labor Standards Enforcement, claiming they had been forced to work long hours without overtime pay, breaks, or health insurance, while the firm's Hollywood coproduction of *Temptation* had been picketed by the Writers Guild of America after writers walked off because they were working without a contract.

In April the company cut a belated deal with YouTube to run discreet ads under clips from *Britain's Got Talent*, including one of contestant Susan Boyle that had become an online phenomenon with more than 100 million views. Fall saw the formation of a family and children's entertainment division, while FremantleMedia Enterprises cut deals to market Paramount-branded merchandise internationally and distribute National Geographic Home Entertainment content in the United Kingdom and Ireland. Sales for the year were just under EUR 1.2 billion, with net earnings of EUR 155 million. The firm produced or sold some 9,500 hours of programming during the year, which aired in 57 countries.

In the U.S. the *Idol* franchise was starting to show its age as original judge Paula Abdul quit and was replaced by comedian Ellen DeGeneres, and Simon Cowell announced he would leave at the end of the 2010 season to focus on *X Factor*. During that year the company also acquired the remaining 25 percent of Danish production firm Blu, which was renamed FremantleMedia Sweden.

In the nearly two decades since its founding as Pearson Television, FremantleMedia Ltd. had grown into an international production powerhouse. Hugely popular reality-based franchises including *Idol*, *Got Talent*, and *The Farmer Wants a Wife*, and game shows including *The Price Is Right*, *Hole in the Wall*, and *Family Feud*, could be seen in many countries around the world. The firm also had a stable of long-running hits such as *Neighbors* and *The Bill* that were extremely popular in specific markets. With extensive global production, licensing, and distribution infrastructure firmly established, the company's future looked bright.

Frank Uhle

PRINCIPAL SUBSIDIARIES

FremantleMedia North America (USA); Fremantle UFA (Germany); talkbackTHAMES (UK); FremantleMedia Australia; FremantleMedia Group Ltd. (UK); FremantleMedia Asia Pte Ltd. (Singapore); FremantleMedia Operations B.V. (Netherlands); Fremantle Productions Latin (USA); FremantleMedia Sverige AB (Sweden).

PRINCIPAL DIVISIONS

FremantleMedia; FremantleMedia Enterprises.

PRINCIPAL COMPETITORS

BBC Worldwide Productions; Banijay Entertainment; Endemol B.V.; Eyeworks Holding B.V.; Mark Burnett Productions, Inc.; Shine, Ltd.; Sony Pictures Television International; Zodiak Entertainment.

FURTHER READING

Brennan, Steve, "Pearson Becoming Fremantle," *Hollywood Reporter*, August 21, 2001, p. 8.

Consoli, John, "*Idol*'s Cowell Back on Fox for Five Years," *Mediaweek*, November 30, 2005.

"FremantleMedia Pushes RTL Formats Stateside," *Television Business International*, June 1, 2002.

Hibberd, James, "'American Idol' Producer Hit with Lawsuit," *Hollywood Reporter*, March 19, 2009.

"Pearson TV and Euro Giants Link in #12bn Merger," *Evening Standard*, April 7, 2000.

Ryan, Leslie, "FremantleMedia Reinvents Itself," *Television Week*, March 15, 2004, p. 30.

Schneider, Michael, and John Hopewell, "FremantleMedia Stepping into Drama," *Daily Variety*, March 29, 2009.

Sexton, Paul, "It's Already a Global TV Hit Format—But the Show Must Go On," *Financial Times*, May 4, 2004, p. 10.

Sloan, Paul, "The Reality Factory," *Business 2.0*, August 1, 2004, p. 74.

Spring, Greg, "Pearson Maneuvering Its Game Pieces,"

Electronic Media, January 5, 1998, p. 1.

Turner, Mimi, "Fremantle Out to Build Shows, Brand," *Hollywood Reporter*, October 9, 2007.

Gateway Group One

———————— ■ ————————

604-608 Market Street
Newark, New Jersey 07105
U.S.A.
Telephone: (973) 465-8006
Fax: (973) 465-9389
Web site: http://www.gatewaygroupone.com

Private Company
Incorporated: 1979 as Gateway Security
Employees: 3,500
Sales: $76.4 million (2009)
NAICS: 561612 Security Guards and Patrol Services

■ ■ ■

Gateway Group One is a Newark, New Jersey-based privately held company offering security-related services. The flagship division, Gateway Security Services, provides security guards as well as such services as security assessments, integrated security solutions, disaster recovery planning, human resources management services, incident reporting, and around-the-clock dispatch center and Emergency Security Officer Response Teams. Gateway Frontline Services provides customer service personnel to airports, including all three New York City airports, other transportation hubs, hospitals, stadiums, and malls. In addition to its New Jersey headquarters, Gateway operates offices in Los Angeles and India. The company's chairman is its founder, Louis Dell'Ermo. Serving as chief executive officer is Kurus Elavia, who started out as a security guard at Gateway.

ORIGINATING WITH PRUDENTIAL'S GATEWAY CENTER: 1979

A native of Newark, New Jersey, Louis Dell'Ermo was well familiar with both the community and law enforcement. He was a 23-year veteran of the Newark police department, serving both as a homicide detective and a narcotics officer. He was also well known in Newark because of his work with such civic groups as the Police Athletic League and the Boys Club. It was due to his local knowledge and ties that he was asked in 1979 by Prudential Insurance Company to consider providing unarmed security for the company's Gateway Center, a major office-and-hotel complex in Newark. "They felt that the people that had to do security in an area like Newark had to know the demographics and respond to the site-specific needs," Dell'Ermo explained in a 1999 interview with *Inc.* magazine.

He enlisted help from his wife, Vivian, who became the company treasurer, and their son, James. It was his son, just out of high school, who submitted the successful bid for the Prudential contract. The family then set up an office in the complex and drew on its name for the new business, calling it Gateway Security. Another son, Gregory, would also come to work for the company and eventually become vice president of finance. A high school friend of James Dell'Ermo, Michael Marini, played an important role in the growth of the company as well and would one day become vice president of business development.

Dell'Ermo took advantage of his local connections in the hiring of his first employees. He used off-duty and retired police officers, firefighters, teachers, and even some of the former players on the Police Athletic League football team he coached. As the demand for Gateway's services grew, he looked to the graduates of security-training programs, but he continued to focus on local residents. "They can tell by the noise of traffic what's happening. They know what to expect." Dell'Ermo's understanding of Newark also influenced other decisions. When one of his clients wanted to use dogs as a security measure at a downtown site, Dell'Ermo advised against the police-state approach because it would remind too many people of the riots the city had endured in the 1960s when the police had used dogs on minorities. Instead, Dell'Ermo adopted the soft look, unarmed guards wearing blazers, that would become a trademark of Gateway Security. The way employees represented the company was so important that applicants were asked to demonstrate their smiles. "We can always teach employees the skills needed to succeed in their job," Louis Dell'Ermo told *New Jersey Monthly*, "but we can never teach them how to smile."

ELAVIA JOINS COMPANY: 1988

Dell'Ermo's local edge allowed Gateway to compete against national security firms, but it was still very much a small business in 1988 when Kurus Elavia joined the company. Born in India, Elavia earned a degree in accounting and business from the University of Mumbai. He was also athletic, primarily playing volleyball before turning to martial arts as a way to maintain his fitness. This interest led to trips to Bangkok, Thailand, where he learned several disciplines, including tae kwon do, judo, and weapons. After a brief stint teaching martial arts to police officers in India, he came to the United States in 1987 when he was given an opportunity to teach martial arts on a summer appointment at a YMCA in Cleveland, Ohio. He was offered a full-time position and decided to stay in the country as an immigrant. When the teaching position did not work out and he had just $30 left in his pockets, he hitch-hiked to New York where he had a friend. He quickly found that his business degree from India was of little

use and he accepted the only work he could find. He sold newspapers in the Bronx and lottery tickets at candy stores. Because of the large Indian community in Newark he settled there and began selling newspapers in Newark's Pennsylvania Station.

A friend suggested that Elavia apply for work at Gateway Security. He was initially told to leave because the lady at the desk was too busy, but he persevered and was hired in 1988, becoming the company's 54th employee. Paid $6.50 per hour he served as a loading dock security guard at a parking lot across from the Prudential Center in Newark, working from 6 a.m. until 2 p.m. He then began to work his way up through the ranks of Gateway Security as the company grew. He became a guard, assistant manager, manager, and began to serve as a troubleshooter, dispatched to any site where there were customer service issues. He also played an important role in persuading Home Depot to award its security services to Gateway.

The demand for security services had increased steadily over the years. According to *Nation's Business*, there were some 300,000 private security guards employed in 1981. Ten years later that number increased to 500,000 and was on pace to top 750,000 by the end of the century. Thus, relying solely on organic growth, Gateway was able to increase sales to about $5 million in 1993 and more than $10 million just five years later.

CHANGE IN DIRECTION: 1998

After Elavia had been with Gateway for a decade, the Dell'Ermo family considered selling the business. Elavia left to work as a securities broker, but grew disenchanted after just two months. Over the years he had grown close to the Dell'Ermo family, especially James. Together they developed a new business plan, and over a breakfast meeting in 1998 they presented it to Lou Dell'Ermo. Elavia asked for a chance to run the company, promising that he could double revenues in a matter of three years. He maintained that Gateway Security had been providing a wonderful service for 20 years and had developed what he called a "subconscious brand." His vision was to build that brand and take Gateway beyond physical security to customer service, providing personnel to work concierge and help desks and similar posts in office buildings and public facilities. Lou Dell'Ermo was won over, and in 1999 Elavia was named Gateway's chief operating officer.

At the time of Elavia's ascension to the company's management team, Gateway employed about 500 people and was generating $11 million in annual sales. He was able to grow that amount by landing some

KEY DATES

1979: Company is founded.
1998: New growth plan is developed.
1999: "Red Jacket" program is launched at Newark International Airport.
2006: Kurus Elavia becomes chief executive officer.
2007: Gateway Group One name is adopted.

major corporate clients, including Ikea, Lucent, and Pfizer. The company also made a conscious effort to develop a more diverse workforce. Because of the varied demographics of Newark, the company had achieved a high level of diversity without conscious effort, but now Gateway looked to leverage that diversity in order to supply personnel for increased customer service capabilities. It also became bilingual before others in the security field embraced the idea.

TESTING THE RED JACKET PROGRAM: 1999

A major break for Gateway soon came when the Port Authority of New York and New Jersey, which operated the area airports, asked Gateway to develop a "red jacket" pilot program at Newark International Airport. The goal was to make roving customer service people available to assist passengers. The program proved successful and Gateway used it to develop an airport business at a measured pace. Given an opportunity to bid on the security contracts for Continental Airlines, for example, Gateway opted to focus only on wheelchair service. In time, however, Gateway would take on other services and eventually won contracts at all three Port Authority airports and was involved in all terminal operations.

The September 11, 2001, terrorist attacks on the United States brought changes to airport security, and the security industry in general. There was an immediate surge in demand for Gateway's services. The attacks also brought changes to airport security. Because the company's focus had been on customer service, it was not adversely effected when the Transportation Security Administration took control of checkpoint security. Gateway was able to continue the organic growth of its airport business, winning contracts with the major airlines to provide skycaps, baggage handlers, and parking management personnel.

Rather than doubling sales in three years, Gateway tripled them. With revenues of $38 million, the

company made *Inc.* magazine's list of the fastest-growing companies in urban areas in 2004. In the meantime, James Dell'Ermo succeeded his father as chief executive officer. Revenues improved to $70 million by 2006 and employment approached 4,000. In October of that year, the Dell'Ermo family named Elavia Gateway's chief executive officer. It was the harbinger for further changes at the company.

Gateway had always provided training to its employees, but a business opportunity was created with the passage of the New Jersey Security Officer Regulation Act, which required 24 hours of training for security personnel. In 2007 Gateway took advantage of its expertise to form Frontline Academy LLC and offer an expanded slate of courses as well as certification to Gateway personnel and others. Gateway also formed Frontline Services for its customer care personnel. Having clearly outgrown its Gateway Security name, the company changed it in November 2007 to Gateway Group One, an umbrella under which its three services (security personnel, customer care personnel, and training) could be offered in something of a one-stop shop.

LOS ANGELES OFFICE OPENS: 2008

Gateway opened a West Coast branch in Los Angeles in October 2008 after winning a contract to provide security and customer care personnel to the Los Angeles International Airport. In April 2009, the new office secured further Los Angeles-area clients in Air Pacific and The Kyoto Grand Hotels and Gardens. The mandate of the regional office was to solicit business west of the Mississippi River. Elavia also used his ties in India to start a branch of the company there. As the reputation of Gateway continued to grow, it appeared the company had only begun to scratch the surface of its potential, both in the United States and abroad.

Ed Dinger

PRINCIPAL SUBSIDIARIES

Frontline Academy LLC; Gateway Frontline Services; Gateway Security Services.

PRINCIPAL COMPETITORS

Command Security Corporation; Guardsmark, LLC; Wackenhut Services, Incorporated.

FURTHER READING

Barker, Emily, "The Old Neighborhood," *Inc.*, May 1999, p. 65.

DeNise, Antoinette, "Keeping It in the Family," *New Jersey Monthly*, November 1, 2004.

"Gateway Wants to Make the City a Safer Place," *Business News New Jersey*, May 3, 1999, p. 11.

Grossman, Naomi, "Kurus Elavia: Security Superstar," *IndUS Business Journal*, November 15, 2006.

Perone, Joseph R., "CEO Always Keeps the Future in Mind," *Star-Ledger* (Newark, NJ), March 12, 2009, p. 42.

Verdon, Joan, "Onetime $6.50 Guard Now Runs the Business," *Record* (Bergen County, NJ), August 19, 2009, p. B3.

Geox S.p.A.

Via Feltrino Centro 16
Biadene di Montebelluna, I-31030
Italy
Telephone: (+39 0423) 2822
Fax: (+39 0423) 282125
Web site: http://www.geox.it

Public Company
Founded: 1995
Incorporated: 2004
Employees: 2,408
Sales: EUR 865.01 million ($1.3 billion) (2009)
Stock Exchanges: Borsa Italiana
Ticker Symbol: GEO
NAICS: 316211 Rubber and Plastics Footwear Manufacturing; 316213 Men's Footwear (Except Athletic) Manufacturing; 316214 Women's Footwear (Except Athletic) Manufacturing; 316219 Other Footwear Manufacturing

■ ■ ■

Geox S.p.A. is one of the fastest-growing footwear and apparel brands in the world. The company is the number one selling footwear brand in Italy, and claims the global number two position in the "lifestyle casual footwear" segment. Geox is most well-known for its "breathable" footwear technology. The company's footwear line is based on a patented system of micropores and specialized fabrics that enable shoes to dissipate heat and perspiration, while remaining waterproof. Geox has also extended its technology into its own range of clothing, especially outerwear. Known for its classic and casual footwear lines, the company has also taken on such giants as Nike and adidas, launching its own line of sports shoes, also featuring its breathable technology. Geox markets its products through a global network of more than 10,000 multi-brand resellers, as well as through its own network of directly operated or franchised Geox Shops.

Each year the company sells 20 million pairs of shoes and two million articles of clothing in more than 100 countries. Geox operates two small factories in Italy, turning to manufacturers in China, Mexico, Romania, and elsewhere for most of its production. In 2009, the company posted revenues of EUR 865 million ($1.3 billion). The company is led by founder and Chairman Mario Moretti Polegato and CEO Diego Bolzonello.

HOLEY INSPIRATION IN 1989

Born in 1952, Mario Moretti Polegato initially set out to join the Villa Sandi winery in Montebelluna, in Treviso, Italy, owned and operated by his family. Polegato received degrees in wine making and law, then spent 15 years as the head of the winery. In 1989, Polegato traveled to the United States to represent the winery at a conference. Polegato went on a hiking trip, during which his perspiring feet gave him the inspiration to develop a new shoe design based on a perforated sole.

There are several variations of Polegato's "eureka" moment. In one version, reported by *Footwear News*, Polegato was visiting New Mexico, and had gone for a hike in the Grand Canyon, and used a sharp rock to poke holes in his shoes. In other versions, Polegato had attended a vintners convention in Reno, Nevada, and had stopped off in Colorado to hike before returning to Italy. Instead of a rock, Polegato used a pocket knife—borrowed, according to *Business 2.0*, from a gas station—in order to cut large holes in the soles.

In another version, Polegato's inspiration came to him while in Reno. As he told *Newsweek*: "I remember, I took from my luggage sneakers with a rubber-bottomed sole. As soon as I took these shoes in my hand I asked myself, 'Why is it that every time I need to use a rubber-bottomed sole, I have a problem with my feet: perspiration?' And, with a pocket knife, I cut holes in the bottom of the sole."

In any event, Polegato sought to refine the concept of a perforated sole. If simple holes in the soles were adequate enough for dry conditions, the shoes were not suitable for more humid climates. Polegato set out to solve the technical problem of providing ventilation to allow the heat and perspiration vapors to escape, while maintaining the sole's impermeability.

PATENTED TECHNOLOGY IN 1994

Polegato enlisted the help of chemical engineers at the University of Padua, visited the Space Museum in Houston to research NASA's space suit materials, then hired five employees to help him develop a prototype shoe at a small ski-boot factory owned by his family. Polegato soon succeeded in developing a two-part system composed of a perforated sole and a microporous inner membrane. The sole contained thousands of tiny holes, positioned around the ball of the foot where most of the foot's perspiration is produced. The holes were too small to allow water droplets to pass through, but small enough to allow heat and water vapor (from perspiration) to escape.

By 1994, Polegato had successfully obtained the worldwide patent for what he called the "breathable shoe." Polegato initially intended to license or sell the

technology to existing footwear companies, shopping the idea to Nike, adidas, and Puma, among others. When these companies declined to take up Polegato's technology, he decided to launch his own company in 1995, backed by a $500,000 bank loan. Polegato chose the name Geox for his shoes: "geo" evoked earth and nature, while the "x" reflected the company's focus on technology. As Polegato explained, as reported by *WWD*: "Geox is not a shoe brand—there are so many of those. ... This is a technological company, where projects and technology are applied to the shoe. We solve a common foot problem, but we are the only ones to have this technology."

Geox initially produced a line of children's shoes in order to test-market the product. The choice of the children's shoe segment came because of its relatively short life-cycle, given the rapid growth of children's feet. The shortened buying cycles in turn helped the company limit the early risks of a young start-up company. The rapid success of the company's first children's line encouraged the company to expand into full-scale production of an extended range of women's and men's footwear as well. For this, Geox differentiated itself from other "comfort" shoe brands, matching its micropore technology with stylish footwear designs.

DIPPING A TOE IN THE UNITED STATES IN 2000

Geox achieved impressive growth in its first five years. By 1999, the company had grown into Italy's leading footwear brand. The company had also launched its international expansion, becoming a strong seller in France, Germany, Spain, Sweden, Norway, and other European markets, as well as in Japan, Australia, Chile, and Russia. For the most part, Geox's early growth was driven by its wholesale division, supplying the multibrand retail channel.

Toward the end of the decade, however, Geox began developing its own retail store format, called Geox Shop. The company also supported its retail sales with heavy investments in marketing, spending as much as 10 percent of its revenues on advertising. By the end of the 1990s, Geox had sold more than 16 million pairs of shoes.

Geox began targeting the U.S. market in 1999, signing up its first customers in 2000. Sales subsidiary Geox North America initially introduced the company's men's and women's footwear lines. The introduction of the group's children's shoe range soon after drove most of the company's early U.S. growth. By 2002 the segment had come to account for 65 percent of the company's North American sales. Part of this success

KEY DATES

1995: Mario Polegato founds Geox to produce "breathable" footwear.
2003: Geox launches an apparel line.
2004: Company goes public.
2008: Geox enters the sports shoes sector.
2010: Geox unveils its new "breathable" store format.

was attributed to the company's aggressive pricing strategy, positioning the Geox line as a lower-priced alternative to other, more expensive European brands. The company also succeeded in placing its shoes with a number of major retailers, including national chain Stride Rite. In 2002, the company rolled out its entire range to the 90-strong Nordstrom department store group.

Nonetheless, the North American market remained only a small part of Geox's overall business. By 2001, Geox's sales had grown to $204 million, a leap of 55 percent over the previous year. Exports by then accounted for 25 percent of revenues. The company was also strongly profitable. These profits came in part through Geox's decision to shift some of its production to two company-owned factories in Romania and Slovakia, while outsourcing the remainder to low-cost producers in Asia and Mexico.

ADDING APPAREL IN 2003

Geox remained committed to its technology-driven identity. In 2001, the company developed a new patented process for waterproofing leather. Whereas the group's early technology enabled rubber to breathe similar to leather, the group's new patents provided for a process through which leather soles achieved the impermeability of leather. The addition of leather-soled shoes also enabled the company to expand its footwear range into the "classic" segment.

Geox had also begun tackling similar perspiration-related issues related to clothing designs. In 1999, the company patented a new clothing design, essentially placing its micropore material in the shoulder. The company rolled out its first apparel items, focusing on outwear, to the Italian market in 2003.

Polegato moved to capitalize on the impressive growth achieved by the company. By 2004, the company's own retail network had topped 200 stores, at

the same time as it had gained a presence in more than 50 countries. The company by then ranked as the top among Italy's fastest-growing fashion brands, posting average growth rates of more than 30 percent. The company was also the most profitable, beating out its luxury brand rivals with net margins of 16 percent.

These figures backed the company's successful listing on the Borsa Italiana in December 2004. Polegato sold 29 percent of the company, in a listing that was oversubscribed by seven times. Polegato, who had invested $1.2 million of his family's money to launch the company, now found his stake worth $1.7 billion.

NEW YORK FLAGSHIP IN 2005

By 2005, Geox's international operations had expanded to 68 countries, through more than 500 company-owned stores, as well a growing network of 10,000 multi-brand retailers. By the end of the year, Geox's sales volume had jumped to 13 million pairs of shoes, generating annual revenues of nearly $575 million. This placed the company at the number three position in the comfort shoe segment, behind the Clarks and Ecco brands. In 2005, Geox set out to raise its U.S. profile, opening a new 600-square-meter flagship store on New York City's Madison Avenue. The company's fortunes now took off in the United States, driven in part by the rise in obesity, and the resulting surge in interest in comfort shoes.

Geox also prepared to roll out its apparel line to the international market. The company had achieved strong success with its line of jackets in Italy. Based on just that market, apparel sales represented 5 percent of the group's total revenues. In 2007, the company launched its apparel line on a worldwide basis, both in its Geox Shop chain and in its multi-brand retailer network. By the end of 2009, the company's apparel division accounted for nearly 11.5 percent of total sales. Geox expected this figure to rise to as much as 50 percent in the coming years.

In the meantime, Geox began seeking out other expansion avenues. During its first decade, Geox had focused on the classic and casual footwear categories, avoiding direct competition with sportswear-oriented footwear giants such as Nike and adidas. Following its initial public offering, however, Geox launched a new research and development effort in order to develop its own sports shoe technologies. By 2008, the company had succeeded in patenting what it called its Net System, transforming the entire shoe into a breathable membrane.

"BREATHABLE" STORE IN 2010

Rather than take on Nike and adidas head-to-head in the performance segment of the sports shoe market, Geox remained focused on the comfort aspects of its shoe designs to boost its marketing appeal. The company sought to develop its sports shoe line first among its existing customer base, before targeting the high-performance sports segment proper. As part of this effort, however, Geox developed its own line of golf shoes in 2009.

Geox continued to invest strongly in its expansion despite the economic downturn at the end of the decade. In 2009 alone, the company opened a net total of 100 new Geox Shops. Geox also planned to add another 80 stores through 2010. These included the company's latest store format, the "Breathable" store, an eco-friendly design opened in Milan. The company expected to roll out the store format, which featured technology designed to reduce energy expenditures, to its stores in New York, Rome, Toronto, and elsewhere. At the same time, after nearly 15 years of steady growth, Geox was forced to take a breather, as its sales dropped more than 3 percent, to EUR 865.01 million ($1.3 billion) in 2009. Geox nevertheless had given itself a sure footing as one of the world's leading comfort shoe brands.

M. L. Cohen

PRINCIPAL SUBSIDIARIES

Breathing Concept Inc. (USA); Geox Asia Pacific Ltd. (Hong Kong); Geox Canada Inc.; Geox Deutschland Gmbh (Germany); Geox do Brasil Participacoes Ltda (Brazil); Geox France Sarl; Geox Hellas S.A. (Greece); Geox Holland B.V.; Geox International Holding B.V. (Netherlands); Geox Japan K.K.; Geox Manufacturing Italia S.r.l.; Geox Respira SL (Spain); Geox Retail Czech Sro (Czech Republic); Geox Retail France Sarl; Geox Retail S.r.l.; Geox Retail Slovakia Sro; Geox Suisse SA (Switzerland); Geox Sweden AB; Geox UK Ltd.; Notech N.H. Kft (Hungary); S&A Distribution Inc. (USA);

S&A Retail Inc. (USA); Technic Development Slovakia Sro.

PRINCIPAL DIVISIONS

Footwear; Apparel.

PRINCIPAL OPERATING UNITS

EU Trading Companies; Non-EU Trading Companies; Technical Production Companies.

PRINCIPAL COMPETITORS

adidas AG; Asics Corporation; Fila Holding S.p.A.; Freudenberg und Co.; Grendene S.A.; Nike Inc.; PUMA AG Rudolf Dassler Sport; Sketchers U.S.A. Inc.

FURTHER READING

"Blessed Relief for Sweaty Feet," *Business Week*, March 22, 2004, p. 28.

Carr, Debra, "Waiting to Exhale," *Footwear News*, October 11, 1999, p. 31.

Cass, Meghan, "Geox Overhauls US Plan," *Footwear News*, July 20, 2009, p. 6.

"Geox Distribution Deal Confirmed," *just-style.com*, September 12, 2008.

"Geox Merges Manufacturing Unit," *just-style.com*, October 26, 2009.

Hoppough, Suzanne, "Flat-Footed," *Forbes Global*, November 29, 2004, p. 46.

Kuchment, Anna, "Holes in Your Soles," *Newsweek*, April 14, 2008, p. 6.

Moin, David, "Geox Two Step," *WWD*, March 4, 2008, p. 22.

Morais, Richard C., "Very Sweaty Equity," *Forbes Global*, September 19, 2005, p. 42.

Schenker, Jennifer L., "Geox Takes on the Goliaths of Sport," *Business Week*, April 14, 2008, p. 22.

Schubert, Siri, "Holey Innovation!" *Business 2.0*, August 2006, p. 54.

Woodard, Richard, "Geox Holds Nerve in Expansion Drive," *just-style.com*, November 13, 2009.

Zargani, Luisa, "Geox Opens 'Breathable' Store," *WWD*, March 30, 2010, p. 9.

Grupo Ferrovial S.A.

Principe de Vergara 135
Madrid, E-28002
Spain
Telephone: (+34 91) 586 25 65
Fax: (+34 91) 586 26 89
Web site: http://www.ferrovial.com

Public Company
Incorporated: 1952
Employees: 108,117
Sales: EUR 12.09 billion ($16.9 billion) (2009)
Stock Exchanges: Madrid
Ticker Symbol: FER
NAICS: 237310 Highway, Street, and Bridge Construction; 237110 Water and Sewer Line and Related Structures Construction; 327310 Cement Manufacturing; 515210 Cable and Other Subscription Programming; 517212 Cellular and Other Wireless Telecommunications; 541330 Engineering Services; 561720 Janitorial Services

■ ■ ■

Grupo Ferrovial S.A. is a diversified company with operations spanning public works and other large-scale construction projects; toll road and car parks construction and operation; airport operations; and services ranging from infrastructure maintenance to airport handling to municipal and waste treatment services. Grupo Ferrovial is also a globally operating company, with a presence in 45 countries and more than 108,000 employees. In Spain, Ferrovial is the country's leading construction company, and, through subsidiary Cintra, the country's largest operator of toll roads. Cintra is also one of the world's leading toll road operators, with more than 25 concessions in Canada, Chile, Greece, Ireland, Portugal, and the United States, including the Indiana Toll Road and the Chicago Skyway. Altogether, Cintra operates more than 2,900 kilometers of toll roads.

Other major components of the Ferrovial group include BAA, the United Kingdom's largest airport operator, with six airports including Heathrow, Stansted, Southampton, Glasgow, Edinburgh, and Aberdeen. Ferrovial also operates airports in Naples, Italy, and Antofagasta, Chile. Amey is a leading provider of infrastructure maintenance services in the United Kingdom. Swissport is the world's leading provider of airport handling services, with operations at nearly 180 airports in 38 countries. Ferrovial's Cespa provides municipal waste treatment services in Spain and Portugal. Ferrovial Agromán is the group's primary construction subsidiary, and counts the Guggenheim Museum in Bilbao as one of its major achievements. The group's Budimex subsidiary is the leading construction company in Poland, while U.S.-based Webber is a major road builder in the Texas market.

Spain accounts for just 35 percent of Ferrovial's total revenues of EUR 12.09 billion ($16.9 billion) in 2009. The United States and Canada generate 7 percent of revenues, while Poland accounts for 6 percent; the rest of Europe combines for another 14 percent of group revenues. Construction remains the company's largest division, with 37 percent of revenues, followed by Services (30.5 percent) and Airports (25.6 percent). Grupo Ferrovial is listed on the Madrid Stock Exchange, and is led by Chairman Rafael del Pino and CEO Íñigo Meirás. The founding Del Pino family remains the company's largest shareholder, with 44 percent of its shares.

WORKING ON THE SPANISH RAILROAD IN THE FIFTIES

Born in 1920, Rafael del Pino y Morena became one of Spain's leading industrialists. At the conclusion of the Spanish civil war, del Pino entered the country's prestigious Universitaria de Ingenieria de Caminos, Canales y Puertos (Road, Canal, and Port Engineering), receiving a doctorate in 1947. Del Pino's university career was also to help him establish important political contacts that became essential for the company he was to found. Upon completing his doctorate, Del Pino joined Vias y Construcciones S.A., where, within a short time, he rose to a director's position.

Del Pino left Vias y Construcciones in 1952 to spend the summer traveling across Europe and plotting out his next career move. Returning to Spain, del Pino launched his own construction company. Called Ferrovial (literally, "railroad"), del Pino's company initially specialized in construction of railroad ties but quickly extended itself to the construction of railroads themselves. Del Pino's initial holding in his company was just 50 percent, with the remainder held by members of his family. Through the 1950s, however, del Pino steadily bought out the other family members' shares, gaining 100 percent control by the beginning of the 1960s.

Del Pino's political connections helped his company secure a number of important railroad construction contracts. The company also branched out in the early 1960s into other public works projects, notably with the construction of the Salto 2 hydroelectric plant on the Sil River. International operations were also an early feature of Ferrovial, such as the award for the contract for Libya's Hedjaz railroad in the early 1960s.

Government contracts remained the most important source of revenues for the fast-growing Ferrovial. The beginning of massive infrastructure investments by the Spanish government under Francisco Franco marked a period of strong growth for Ferrovial as the company extended its operations to include highway and roadway construction. The inauguration of the National Toll Highway Program in the mid-1960s gave Ferrovial a number of important contracts to build the country's toll road system. The company also joined with Europistas to win the concession to operate Bilbao-Behobia toll road in 1968.

BRANCHING OUT IN THE SEVENTIES

Into the 1970s, Ferrovial began to branch out, creating a number of new subsidiaries to operate its diversifying interests. By 1975, the company had created its Ibervial S.A. real estate subsidiary, which later was to become Ferrovial Immobiliaria. The company also established Cadagua S.A. as it entered public services operations, such as waste management and street cleaning services. Ferrovial's expanding interests in concessions led it to form Eurovias, which was granted the concession to operate the highway between Burgos and Arminon. Del Pino himself was gaining prominence among Spain's industrial community. In 1972, he was named president of the management committee overseeing the Empresa Nacional del Gas (National Gas Company), charged with creating the new Enagas company. Del Pino subsequently was named president of Enagas, a position he held until 1974. The Enagas position helped del Pino win new friends among Spain's energy industry, such as Claudius Boada, who later was to become president of the American Hispanic Bank.

In 1976, Ferrovial began construction of its first large-scale housing development, the Covibar development in Madrid. That development, which was to reach more than 4,400 homes, gave the company an important boost toward becoming a leader in the Spanish residential development sector. Meanwhile, as the Spanish construction market entered a slump following the death of Franco, Ferrovial found an increasing heavy construction clientele in such countries as Libya, Mexico, Paraguay, and Kuwait. As the Spanish construction crisis deepened, international contracts came to represent a larger proportion of the company's revenues. At the height of the slump, which lasted from 1979 to 1984, more than a third of Ferrovial's construction revenues came from its foreign operations.

CONSTRUCTION BOOM IN THE EIGHTIES

Joining del Pino in 1981 was eldest son Rafael del Pino y Calvo-Sotelo, a fellow graduate of the Ingenieria de Caminos, Canales y Puertos University, who also received an M.B.A. from the Massachusetts Institute of Technology. The younger del Pino started his career at the company's Libyan operations, learning the business from the ground up, before taking on increasingly central positions in the company in the late 1980s.

The Spanish construction industry entered a new boom phase in the middle of the 1980s and Ferrovial's Spanish construction operations once again generated the largest share of its growing business. By then, the company had begun to formulate its strategy for becoming one of Spain's leading construction companies. After winning the concession for the Sant-Cugat-Terrassa-Manresa highway, Ferrovial captured a strong share of the building boom sparked by the approach of Barcelona's hosting of the 1992 Olympic Games.

If Spain had long been Western Europe's poor cousin, the beginning of the 1990s marked a period of new economic growth for that country. Ferrovial was by then in primary place to capture a strong share of the booming construction market. The privatization of much of Spain's industrial base also presented a variety of opportunities for the company in the early 1990s.

During this first half of the decade, Ferrovial established several new subsidiaries as it again began to diversify its operations. Ferrovial Conservacion S.A. was established to spearhead the company's entry into infrastructure and facility maintenance and conservation services. The company coupled the creation of Ferrovial Immobiliaria with the launch of its first foreign real estate developments, notably in neighboring Portugal. Ferrovial also played a major role in the construction of Spain's high-speed train railroad network.

ACQUIRING AGROMÁN IN 1995

In 1995, Ferrovial took a giant step forward in its quest to become Spain's leading construction firm when it acquired a majority shareholding in struggling, publicly traded rival Agromán S.A. While Ferrovial itself had long resisted a public offering, preferring to maintain its family-owned status, the Agromán acquisition was to lead to a public offering by Ferrovial in 1999 as the company moved to acquire the remaining shares of Agromán. The Agromán acquisition helped Ferrovial's sales jump to nearly EUR 1.6 billion in 1996. The company's strong growth through the second half of the decade was to enable it to nearly double its revenues in less than five years.

After merging its own construction operations with those of Agromán's to form the new subsidiary Ferrovial Agromán Internacional S.A., Ferrovial continued to boost its other operations. In 1996, the company turned to the South American market, where it was awarded highway concessions in Chile. That year, the company also completed construction of the headquarters building for Compania de Telecomunicaciones de Chile (CT), the country's tallest building and one of the tallest on the South American continent.

Another high-prestige Ferrovial project was completed the following year, when the Guggenheim Museum in Bilbao became one of the decade's architectural highlights. Meanwhile, Ferrovial continued to build up its concessions operations, acquiring urban services group Ferogasa in 1997. By 1998, Ferrovial tagged its concessions operations for further growth, creating a new subsidiary, Cintra, to hold its operations in that sector. Cintra immediately began its own expansion, launching into airports facilities ownership and management with the acquisition of nine airports in Mexico. Cintra also stepped into the car park market with a number of key acquisitions, including those of Dornier, Reinrod, Fernet, and ESSA. By the end of 1999, the company's parking concessions topped 110,000 spaces.

PUBLIC OFFERING IN 1999

Ferrovial went public in 1999, selling nearly 35 percent of its shares in what was Spain's largest public offering to date. The del Pino family nonetheless retained their majority control of the company, with more than 57 percent of outstanding shares. The public offering enabled the company to make a number of new moves, notably in the concessions market. By 2000, it had increased its number of airport concessions to 12, including the purchases of the Bristol Airport in England, and the winning of concessions contracts for the Cerromoreno Airport in Antofagasta, Chile, and a 99-year contract to operate the Niagara Falls airport. The company also achieved a number of new highway concessions contracts, including the H-407 toll road in Canada.

Rafael del Pino y Moreno retired from the company he had founded, giving up his chairman's position to son Rafael del Pino y Calvo-Sotelo. The younger del Pino had been one of the driving forces behind the company's diversification during the 1990s. As chairman, the younger del Pino led the company on a new drive to raise its diversified operations to account for at least 50 percent of total sales by 2004.

INTERNATIONAL DIVERSIFICATION DRIVE

The new millennium marked a major new phase in Ferrovial's development. By the end of the decade, the company not only succeeded in reducing its exposure to the cooling Spanish infrastructure market, it also established itself as one of the world's fastest-growing and most diversified infrastructure and services companies, with operations spanning 45 countries.

In 2001, Ferrovial moved into Eastern Europe, buying up 58.5 percent of Budimex, the leading construction company in Poland. The company also boosted its stake in Autopistas del Sol to 75 percent, then, through Cintra, acquired its first toll road concession, the N4/N6 Motorway, in Ireland in 2002.

The acquisition of Amey Plc in the United Kingdom added a new dimension to Ferrovial's growing services division in 2003. Amey was a leading provider of maintenance and other services to the road, rail, and underground railway sectors in the United Kingdom, as well as a provider of facility management services. Amey also owned a 33 percent stake in Tube Lines, which held a 30-year maintenance contract for three London Underground lines. Ferrovial increased its stake in Tube Lines to 66 percent in 2004.

By then, Cintra had successfully bid for its first major toll road contract in the United States, winning the concession for the Chicago Skyway in 2004. In 2005, Cintra added a number of contracts as part of the Trans-Texas Corridor project, then acquired leading Texas infrastructure group Webber that year. The company then added a 75-year concession for the Indiana Toll Road in 2006. Other Cintra successes during the decade included a 55-year contract to design, build, and operate a 59-kilometer toll road between Cremona and Mantua in northern Italy. Also in 2006, the group entered Greece, with the contract to build and operate the Ionian toll road.

ACQUIRING BAA IN 2006

Ferrovial's growing airport operations took a major step forward in 2006, when the company outbid Goldman Sachs to acquire BAA for £16 billion ($29.7 billion). BAA was the United Kingdom's and the world's largest airport operator, with a portfolio including seven airports, most notably London Heathrow. The purchase allowed Ferrovial to become one of the world's leading infrastructure and services companies. Following the BAA acquisition, Ferrovial restructured its operations, establishing five core divisions, including a new Airports division. By the end of the decade, this division had become the group's third-largest revenue generator, behind its Construction and Services divisions.

The BAA acquisition hit a snag, however, when the United Kingdom's competition authorities demanded that Ferrovial sell off part of the company's U.K. airports holdings. As a result, Ferrovial was forced to sell off Gatwick Airport during the economic downturn, raising just £1.5 billion at the end of 2009. This sale nonetheless helped the company, which had become highly leveraged in debt in order to pay for BAA. By then, the company mourned the death of its founder, Rafael del Pino y Moreno, who died in 2008 at the age of 87.

Ferrovial continued to add to its range of contracts into the end of the decade. The company gained two new toll road contracts in Poland, for the A1 and A4 highways, and emerged as the preferred bidder for a £2.7 billion contract to build a highway in Birmingham, England, in 2009. In that year, Ferrovial also declared its intention to buy out the minority shareholders in Cintra. Ferrovial hoped to take advantage of Cintra's strong cash flow. This had become increasingly necessary as the company struggled with the effects of the global recession. By the end of 2009, the company's revenues, which had peaked at EUR 14.6 billion in 2007, had slipped back to less than EUR 12.1 billion.

Nonetheless, Ferrovial's diversification drive had successfully shielded the company from the difficulties besetting the Spanish construction market. After years of explosive growth, this market hit a wall at the end of the decade, collapsing into what many analysts considered to become a long-lasting slump. By 2010, however, Ferrovial had reduced its exposure to the Spanish market to just 35 percent of its revenues. The company continued to seek out new international expansion opportunities. In July 2010, for example, the company boosted its U.K. infrastructure operations with the purchase of WYG Engineering, the railroad consultancy operations of WIG Plc. Grupo Ferrovial remained committed to its status as a world-leading infrastructure and services company.

M. L. Cohen

PRINCIPAL SUBSIDIARIES

Amey Plc (UK); BAA Plc (UK; 55.87%); Budimex, S.A. (Poland; 59.06%); Cespa, S.A.; Cintra, S.A. (66.88%); Ferrovial Agromán, S.A.; Ferrovial Servicios, S.A.; Grupisa, S.A.; Swissport Group; The Webber Group (USA); Tube Lines, Ltd (UK).

PRINCIPAL DIVISIONS

Construction; Toll Roads and Car Parks; Airports; Services.

PRINCIPAL OPERATING UNITS

Ferrovial; Webber; Amey; BAA; Budimex; Cespa; Cintra.

PRINCIPAL COMPETITORS

Acciona S.A.; ACS Actividades de Construccion y Servicios S.A.; Bouygues S.A.; Fomento de Construcciones y Contratas S.A.; Hochtief AG; Landesbank Baden-Wurttemberg AG; RWE AG; Skanska AB; VINCI S.A.

FURTHER READING

Arnold, Martin, "BAA's Duty Free Stores Are Sold," *Financial Times*, March 10, 2008, p. 15.

Clark, Pilita, "Forced Sale of Gatwick Airport Contributes to Heavy BAA Losses," *Financial Times*, February 23, 2010, p. 19.

"Construction Lifts Ferrovial Profits," *Financial Times*, November 3, 2000.

"Ferrovial Buys Canadian Highway Concession," *Reuters*, May 11, 1999.

"Grupo Ferrovial Does Not Rule Out Growth through Acquisitions," *AFX Europe*, April 19, 1999.

Kozlowski, Pawel, "Ferrovial Wants Budimext to Diversify into Telecoms," *Reuters*, May 31, 2000.

Mulligan, Mark, "Diversification Sees Group Take to the Skies," *Financial Times*, June 21, 2007, p. 4.

———, "Ferrovial Faces Revolt over Cintra Move," *Financial Times*, March 11, 2009, p. 24.

———, "Ferrovial Founder Dies, Aged 87," *Financial Times*, June 16, 2008, p. 15.

———, "Meiras Named as Successor to Ferrovial Chief," *Financial Times*, May 1, 2009, p. 16.

———, "Spanish Steps to Nightmare of Airport Security," *Financial Times*, June 30, 2007, p. 9.

Parsons, Claudia, "Ferrovial Rises after Spain's Biggest Private IPO," *Reuters*, May 5, 1999.

"Spanish Ferrovial Takes Railway Consultancy from UK WYG," *M&A Navigator*, July 9, 2010.

Tarzian, Joan, "Ferrovial: Building a New Future," *Business Week Online*, June 28, 2006.

Guararapes Confecções S.A.

———— ■ ————

Rodovia RN 160, KM 3
Natal, Rio Grande do Norte 59115-900
Brazil
Telephone: (55 84) 3204-1100
Fax: (55 84) 3227-2337
Web site: http://www.guararapes.ind.br

Public Company
Founded: 1956
Employees: 34,196
Sales: BRL 3.06 billion ($1.76 billion) (2009)
Stock Exchanges: São Paulo
Ticker Symbol: GUAR
NAICS: 313210 Broadwoven Fabric Mills; 315221
Men's and Boys' Cut and Sew Underwear and
Nightwear Manufacturing; 315223 Men's and
Boys' Cut and Sew Shirt (Except Work Shirt)
Manufacturing; 315224 Men's and Boys' Cut and
Sew Trouser, Slack, and Jean Manufacturing;
442299 All Other Home Furnishings Stores;
448110 Men's Clothing Stores; 448120 Women's
Clothing Stores; 448130 Children's and Infants'
Clothing Stores; 452111 Department Stores
(Except Discount Department Stores); 522210
Credit Card Issuing; 522220 Sales Financing;
522291 Consumer Lending

■ ■ ■

Guararapes Confecções S.A. is both a leading Brazilian
manufacturer and retailer of apparel. The company
claims that its factories turn out more product each year
than any other in Latin America, chiefly for its
subsidiary Lojas Riachuelo S.A. Riachuelo is one of the
three largest department store chains in Brazil that
specialize in selling clothing.

RETAIL AND MANUFACTURING: 1947–83

Nevaldo Rocha arrived in Natal, the state capital of Rio
Grande do Norte, at the age of 12 as a refugee from a
drought that was searing the interior of Brazil's
impoverished northeast. He opened, in 1947, a small
fabric store for apparel that he named "The Capital."
Four years later, the enterprise opened a small clothing
plant in Recife, the capital of the state of Pernambuco.
It also acquired various points of sale for this clothing.
In 1956 Nevaldo and his brother Newton founded
Guararapes in Recife. Two years later, they moved its
headquarters to Natal, where they opened the
company's first true clothing factory. Guararapes made
its initial public offering (IPO) of stock in 1970. The
company established clothing factories in 1976 in Fortaleza, Ceará, and Mossoró, Rio Grande do Sul. In the
same year it established its first retail chain, Super G.

The combination of manufacturing and retail added
synergy to Guararapes. In 1979 the company opened
another textile factory in Natal (where it remained for
18 years) and acquired two more retail chains in which
to sell its clothing, Riachuelo and Wolens. Riachuelo
absorbed Wolens and another chain, Setra, in 1983.

SURVIVING AND PROSPERING AGAIN: 1987–96

Guararapes, in 1987, decided to make Riachuelo the
exclusive channel of distribution for one of its clothing

KEY DATES

1956: Nevaldo Rocha and his brother establish Guararapes Confecções.

1979: Company acquires a small retail clothing chain, Lojas Riachuelo.

1990: Guararapes avoids liquidation by stretching out its debt payments.

2003: Company decides to integrate production and retail sales more closely.

2009: Lojas Riachuelo has 107 stores in 21 Brazilian states.

lines. This action proved a mistake, because delays in getting the apparel to the stores resulted in the enterprise borrowing money at high interest rates. When customers failed to respond to the offerings, the company had to lower its prices. By the end of 1990, Lojas Riachuelo was a chain of 103 stores, with 6,800 employees and $220 million in annual revenue. However, it was on its way to losing nearly $7 million that year. Meanwhile, the clothing factories had lost ground to Chinese competitors. Guararapes, $40 million in debt, was teetering on the brink of liquidation. Guararapes filed for bankruptcy protection and restructured its operations. Its creditors agreed to stretch out payments on its debts over eight years.

During the next two years the number of Riachuelo's stores and employees fell by about half, and its revenues dropped by about the same proportion. The chain was still losing money, but a much smaller amount. Riachuelo, which in the mid-1980s had received at least 70 percent of its merchandise from the Guararapes factories, now was working with 500 suppliers, most of them offering lower prices and many of them Chinese themselves. This enabled the store chain to reduce its own prices by 20 percent and win back customers.

Lojas Riachuelo soon settled on a different clientele, however: one focused more on quality than price. The chain placed its emphasis on fashion, and particularly on stylish accessories. It began to position its stores in the shopping centers of Brazil's largest cities while closing smaller units in smaller cities.

For the Guararapes textile and clothing factories, the outlook seemed dim. The retail outlets had originally been established to market their production, but they could no longer count on Riachuelo to support the wares. The number of factories fell from seven to four, and the number of workers from 22,000 to 7,000. However, Nevaldo Rocha refused to separate the store chain from the manufacturing plants or to sell off the latter. He saw no reason to do so, since the combined enterprise was doing well. In 1996, for example, it reached almost $400 million in sales and earned a profit of $43 million.

FASHION FOR THE MASSES: 1999–2002

Lojas Riachuelo continued to lead the way into the 21st century as one of the three main Brazilian department store chains specializing in apparel. Its annual sales grew from BRL 552 million ($303 million) to BRL 903 million (only $309 million, reflecting the fall of the currency against the U.S. dollar) between 1999 and 2002, and the number of its stores increased from 64 to 72. Riachuelo and its two rivals, C&A and Lojas Renner, were attempting the seemingly impossible: to deliver fashionable apparel to a mass market at low prices.

C&A, the largest of the three chains, signed supermodel Gisele Bündchen to promote its wares. Riachuelo sponsored São Paulo Fashion Week, Brazil's major fashion event, and a contest that attracted 300,000 hopefuls seeking a modeling contract with a major agency. It also made available in its stores a small book of fashion tips. All three spent freely on advertising. In 2000 Riachuelo opened a distribution center in Natal and earmarked BRL 40 million ($22 million) to build another one at Guaralhos, in the São Paulo metropolitan area. That center opened in 2002.

Lojas Riachuelo was also paring the ranks of its suppliers from 600 to 400 in this period. The best of them, from the chain's point of view, worked closely with management, conferring with headquarters almost on a daily basis. Because they had access to privileged information, they were, in general, barred from working for Riachuelo's principal competitors.

FAST FASHION FROM THE FACTORIES TO THE SALES FLOOR: 2003–10

Persuaded that the two Guararupes branches, manufacturing and retail, needed to be integrated again, Nevaldo Rocha, in 2003, ordered a major strategic change. The 180-day period between production in the factories and sales in the store was to be reduced radically: a concept that came to be called "fast fashion." In this way there would be less likelihood that the merchandise would fall victim to changes in public taste. By late 2005 this cycle had been reduced to 40 days, with the objective of reducing it further.

By 2005 Guararapes had sales of more than BRL 2.5 billion ($1 billion), with Riachuelo responsible for some 80 percent of the total. Also in that year, the company opened Midway Mall in Natal. Some 240,000 square meters in size, it became the largest shopping center in Brazil. The three-floor structure included 13 anchor stores, a food court, a seven-screen movie multiplex, and a concert hall to be completed in 2010.

The Guararapes apparel factories in 2007 were furnishing about 10,000 retailers as well as Lojas Riachuelo with basic items, including jeans, T-shirts, dress shirts, and socks. The following year, however, its production was earmarked principally for the retail chain. Some 300 assorted models of clothing began being turned out for Riachuelo, but in smaller lots than in the past.

The immediate effects were negative for the bottom line, mainly because the change in the rhythm of production required a 50 percent increase in employment. However, the great variety of goods available was popular with customers, and they tended to choose the items with higher profit margins. Moreover, the merchandise was changed every month to keep it up to date. The company's profits rose by 56 percent in 2009 although revenues climbed by only 13 percent. By 2010, 90 percent of the goods sold by Lojas Riachuelo came from the Guararapes factories.

GUARARAPES IN 2009–10

Guararapes had three plants in Fortaleza, Ceará, producing denim cloth and shirts, woven shirts, trousers, shorts, and jeans. Another three in Extremoz, near Natal, were turning out fabrics, shirts, trousers, and sportswear. Guararapes claimed to be the largest clothing producer in Latin America in 2009, with 200,000 articles produced each day by more than 6,000 workers. (Revenue figures for Brazilian textile and apparel manufacturers indicated, however, that it did not rank in the top five.) More than 80 percent of its production went to Lojas Riachuelo.

Lojas Riachuelo accounted for 90 percent of the parent company's sales in 2009. Of the 107 Riachuelo stores in 21 states at the end of 2009, 46 were located on properties owned by Guararapes and 67 were in malls. The 15.7 million credit cards issued by the chain accounted for 57.5 percent of its sales. Beginning in 2010, customers had the option to exchange these cards for Visa and Mastercard. Guararapes had operational contracts with both.

The process of deciding which merchandise to display started with an awareness of the latest tendencies in fashion as exemplified in national and international collections. Among the factors studied were particular articles of clothing and colors favored by influential designers. Nevertheless, however trendy, any style had to be measured against day-to-day Brazilian life and economic reality. For example, 60 percent of the sales of Lojas Riachuelo were in the tropical north and northeast, the poorest parts of the nation as well as the warmest.

Lojas Riachuelo's style department was divided into three teams, located in São Paulo, Fortaleza, and Natal. As the fashion center, São Paulo was the fastest to pick up on new trends abroad. The information was passed on to designers in Fortaleza and Natal, who created small samples and worked closely with executives at the Guararapes factories. In all, the process, from initiation to the delivery of goods, took six months to a year.

Pool, a label created in 1982 and associated with the early career of motor racer Ayrton Senna, remained the company's brand for youth. For young men, this came in the form of Pool College, Pool Atitude, and Pool Black; for older men, Pool Originals, Pool Work, and Pool Casual. For young women there was Pool Atitude, Pool Trendy, and Pool Glam. Guararapes was spending almost one-third of its marketing budget on Pool. For young women, the singer Ivette Sangalo had become the face of Pool, with a line of clothing, shoes, and lingerie bearing her name. The opening of Pool stores was foreseen by the end of 2011.

Lojas Riachuelo was selling apparel for infants and small children, men and boys, and women and girls. It was also selling home furnishings. Established in 2008, Midway Financiera, a subsidiary of Lojas Riachuelo, was the financial agent for the Guararapes group. In addition to issuing the store credit card, it offered other options for financing consumer sales, personal credit, and other financial products and services, and it was thought to be the nucleus of a future Banco Riachuelo. Transporadora Casa Verde was the group's logistics company.

The emphasis on fashion did not mean that Guararapes was planning to go upscale. To the contrary, Lojas Riachuelo had its sights on the emerging middle and lower middle class in a nation that was experiencing rapid economic growth. Their purchasing power remained rather modest, however. Roughly 80 percent of the chain's cardholders were earning less than BRL 1,000 (about $570).

Investors were impressed by Guararapes' plans for the future, which included the opening of 12 Lojas Riachuelo stores in 2010 and 14 in 2011. The company's stock rose by 320 percent in 2009, better than that of any other listed retail company. During the year it received a loan of BRL 443 million ($255 million) from Brazil's official development bank, Banco do Desenvolvimento Econômico e Social (BNDES).

Nevaldo Rocha, now more than 80 years old, was still president of Guararapes in 2010. His son Flávio was president of Lojas Riachuelo. Most of the company shares were in family hands and about one-fourth were "free float": that is, purchased and traded on the stock exchange.

Robert Halasz

PRINCIPAL SUBSIDIARIES

Lojas Riachuelo, S.A.; Midway Financiera S.A. – Crédito Financiamento e Investimento; Riachuelo Participações Ltda.; Transportadora Casa Verde S.A.

PRINCIPAL COMPETITORS

C&A Mode KG; Lojas Renner S.A.

FURTHER READING

Carvalho, Denise, "A inspiração veio da Espanha," *Exame*, April 7, 2010, pp. 66, 68.

"De peça em peça para ser a maior do mundo," *Diário do Comércio*, September 21, 2009.

Facchini, Claudia, "Com vendas en alta no fim do ano, varejistas despontam na bolsa," *Valor Econômico*, January 7, 2010.

Mano, Cristiane, "A ditadura da moda," *Exame*, October 16, 2002, pp. 50–52.

Onaga, Marcelo, "Ele quer ser a Zara brasileira," *Exame*, October 26, 2005, pp. 66–67.

Scheller, Fernando, "Riachuelo muda e se aproxima da Renner," *O Estado de São Paulo*, May 17, 2010.

Vassallo, Cláudia, "A batalha de Guararapes," *Exame*, June 4, 1997, pp. 61–62.

"A vitrine está mais iluminada," *Exame*, April 14, 1993, p. 52.

Harry & David Holdings, Inc.

2500 South Pacific Highway
Medford, Oregon 97501
U.S.A.
Telephone: (541) 864-2362
Toll Free: (800) 345-5655
Fax: (541) 864-2742
Web site: http://www.hndcorp.com

Private Company
Incorporated: 1972 as Bear Creek Corporation
Employees: 1,168
Sales: $489.59 million (2009)
NAICS: 454110 Electronic Shopping and Mail-Order
Houses; 111339 Other Non-Citrus Fruit Farming

■ ■ ■

Harry & David Holdings, Inc., is a multichannel
retailer of branded, premium fruit and gourmet food
products. Harry & David Holdings grows, manufactures, and packages its products, using acreage in
Oregon and two distribution centers to serve its customers. The company's retail business consists of 136
stores in 35 states. Its products are marketed through its
stores, Web site, and popular catalog under a variety of
brand names, including Royal Riviera, Tower of Treats,
Cushman, and Moose Munch.

BEAR CREEK ORCHARDS: 1910

The story of family-run Harry & David can be traced
back to Sam Rosenberg, a prosperous clothier and hotel
owner, who built the luxury Seattle Hotel Sorrento in
Seattle in the early 1900s and traded it in 1910 for 240
acres of pear trees in southern Oregon's Rogue River
Valley. The tract, named Bear Creek Orchards, cost
$300,000. The pears were Doyenne du Cornice, a thin-
skinned, easily bruised fruit hybridized in France in the
1700s and renowned for their fine texture and flavor.
The Rogue Valley, with its rich volcanic soils and sunny
microclimate free of frost, proved better suited to the
Cornice pear than its birthplace in France. Under
Rosenberg's management, the pears took first place
twice at the annual New York pear show.

After Rosenberg died in 1916, his sons, David and
Harry, 27 and 26, who had studied agriculture at Cornell University, took over the family business. Bear
Creek Orchards flourished. The Rosenberg growers were
able to raise larger-than-average pears, weighing approximately one pound apiece. They sold their pears,
renamed Royal Riviera to set them apart from similar
varieties grown in Oregon, California, and France, to
the grand hotels and restaurants of Europe. Their
harvesters were migrant workers, who lived in tents in
the orchards and drove carts pulled by mules. Local
women labored as packers. They were hired seasonally to
fill wooden boxes with fruit and ice. The boxes were
then transported by rail to San Francisco, as well as the
East Coast and, ultimately, to Europe.

Throughout the 1920s, the fame of the Royal Riviera pear grew. Harry and David increased their land
holdings and planted more pear trees. They built the
first cold storage warehouse in their river valley in 1924
to reduce fruit spoilage and extend the selling season.
After the stock market crash in 1929, however, and the

COMPANY PERSPECTIVES

We've been listening to our customers for over 70 years now. And after all that time in the gifting and entertaining business, we take considerable pride in our ability to help make every event a celebration. Here are just a few of the ways we make sure our quality is Cream-of-the-Crop: We grow and select the fruit from our own orchards here in Medford, Oregon. We bake the cakes and cookies, make the chocolates and confections. We pack each gift by hand and ship it in its own specially designed, protective box. We create the "Harry and David difference" in everything we do, and back it with the Strongest Guarantee in the Business. Our customers and their lucky friends will be delighted, we promise.

subsequent worldwide depression, the brothers' business slumped. However, when other pear growers in the region began to rip out their Cornice orchards in favor of more mainstream crops such as apples, corn, and potatoes, Harry and David Rosenberg, instead, took samples of their pears to business acquaintances in Seattle and San Francisco. They hoped to offset the loss of their export business with increased sales closer to home.

By 1934, the brothers were enjoying a modest success with their fruit baskets, mailed "right from the orchard," and Harry set off for New York City with 15 boxes of his prized pears. He checked into the Waldorf-Astoria, but after one week had sold nothing. Not certain what to do with his ripening pears, he consulted an advertising executive, G. Lynn Sumner, who wrote out 15 letters from Harry and David Rosenberg on hotel stationery and sent each one, accompanied by a box of pears, to a top Manhattan business executive. Recipients included Walter Chrysler, David Sarnoff, and Alfred Sloan. This first direct-mail effort yielded orders for 489 boxes of pears.

LAUNCHING A MAIL-ORDER BUSINESS: 1934–38

Back home, the brothers worked up a four-page flyer, which they themselves mailed. Their strategy worked and, all in all, the business sold 6,000 boxes of pears in 1934. By 1935, shipments surpassed 15,000 boxes. In May 1936, David Rosenberg traveled to New York to discuss further marketing plans with Sumner. This trip

produced a full-page ad in *Fortune* magazine, which played on the theme of making a "royal" delicacy available to the common man. The award-winning ad set the tone that identified Harry and David for years to come: "Imagine Harry and me advertising our pears in *Fortune*!" read the headline for the ad, which went on to say, "Out here on the ranch we don't know much about advertising, and maybe we're foolish to spend the price of a tractor on this space, but ... we believe you folks who read *Fortune* are the kind of folks who'd like to know ... our story."

With similar ads in *National Geographic, Time,* the *New York Times,* and other publications, Harry and David reached a broad consumer base, and sales took off. To satisfy the flood of mail orders, Harry and David had to increase pear production, and enlarge their storage and order-processing facilities. In 1937, they began construction of a large, modern packing plant. In 1938, they bought the Hollywood Orchard, nearly doubling their acreage. That year, the brothers also started their Fruit-of-the Month Club, which soon became their best-known offering. For $14.95, customers could sign up to send or receive a different fruit gift six times a year: pears in December, apples in January, preserves in April, nectarines in August, peaches in September, and grapes in October. The response to the club yielded a further increase in business. Orders shot up to 87,000 in 1938.

Business remained surprisingly strong throughout World War II. However, it was a challenge to find the labor to harvest the hundreds of acres of pears each October, and Harry and David, themselves the target of anti-Semitism, decided to change their last name to Holmes to hide their identity as Jews. One year, Harry and David persuaded congressional and military authorities to allow 600 soldiers from nearby Camp White to bring in the crop. Another year, they relied upon the help of German prisoners of war to pick the fruit. Women and children also became part of the wartime labor force.

POST-WORLD WAR II EXPANSION

Following the war, business blossomed. The brothers built a new warehouse, packing house, cold storage, and office, and invested in IBM's latest data-processing technology, the punch card, to handle mail orders, mailing lists, and the payroll. The company expanded its product offerings as sales continued to climb, and fruit cakes, fruit preserves, ceramic candy-filled Santas, miniature Christmas trees, dried flowers, and holly came to grace the pages of the Harry and David catalog.

The company's attention to quality and detail became a well-publicized part of the business. Glenn

KEY DATES

1910: Samuel Rosenberg purchases Bear Creek Orchards.
1916: Samuel Rosenberg's sons, Harry and David, take over the family business.
1938: The brothers debut Harry & David's Fruit-of-the Month Club.
1966: Bear Creek Orchards acquires Jackson & Perkins, the nation's first mail-order rose nursery.
1972: Company forms Bear Creek Corporation.
1986: Shaklee Corporation acquires Bear Creek.
1989: Yamanouchi Pharmaceutical Co., Ltd., acquires Shaklee Corporation.
1991: Harry & David opens its first outlet store in Oregon.
2004: Bear Creek Corporation becomes Harry & David Holdings.
2008: One year after selling Jackson & Perkins, Harry & David Holdings acquires Wolferman's and Cushman Fruit Co.

Harrison, later executive vice president, "would look for things," according to one company publication, "like crooked labels or the square knots on ribbons. If they weren't right, he'd rip them out. ... They did not want fingerprints on the [preserve] jars, so we all learned to handle them by the lids," said one retiree. When express shipping charges climbed to prohibitive amounts in 1947, the firm began a system of loading straight cars for a given city, then delivering the packages directly to the post office to avoid delays en route.

JACKSON & PERKINS ACQUISITION: 1966

Glenn Harrison took over the day-to-day decision making for the $5 million business, along with David Holmes Jr., in 1953, after Harry Holmes withdrew from active participation in the business because of a heart condition. David Holmes had died in a fatal car accident in 1950. When David Holmes Jr. assumed leadership of the company in 1959, he shifted corporate headquarters to Newport Beach, California, where he cultivated an entrpreneurial bent, creating a number of subsidiaries (selling jewelry, toys, clothing, travel trailers) which met with only modest success.

However, the company's core business continued growing. By 1961, the company was bringing in $8 million. Two years later it had its own fleet of refriger-

ated cars and trucks to carry Harry and David fruit packages to 39 mailing points throughout the United States.

In 1966 Bear Creek Corporation acquired Jackson & Perkins, one of the world's largest suppliers of new rose varieties. A. E. Jackson and Charles Perkins had begun their business in Newark in 1872, wholesaling strawberry and grape plants. The duo also sold directly to customers who stopped by their farm. Later the partners also began growing roses and, by the early 20th century, roses had become Jackson & Perkins' main product.

Jackson & Perkins, like Bear Creek Corporation, was a family-run business, and, in the early days, Charles Perkins himself sold and personally guaranteed all his roses. In time, the company ventured into breeding new roses, and in 1901, it introduced its first hybrid, the Dorothy Perkins Climber. Under the continuing direction of hybridizer Dr. J. H. Nicolas and, later, Eugene Boerner, Jackson & Perkins became one of the foremost producers of new roses worldwide. Boerner especially gained a reputation for hybridizing many of the early varieties in the class of floribunda, so named by a cousin of Charles.

In 1939, quite by accident, Jackson & Perkins became the world's first mail-order rose nursery. At that year's New York World's Fair, the company set up a garden display called "A Parade of Modern Roses." When a number of out-of-state visitors wanted to buy roses, but did not want to carry the plants home themselves, Jackson & Perkins agreed to mail them the plants. The following season, the same customers and others returned to order more roses by mail. Over the next several years, the mail-order portion of the company grew so much that Jackson & Perkins began publishing a spring catalog of roses.

GEOGRAPHIC AND MANAGERIAL MOVES: 1961–68

By the early 1960s, the very successful company had outgrown its New York location. It headed west, relocating its growing fields first to Pleasanton, California, for the long growing season, and then, in 1966, to the San Joaquin Valley of California where the loamy soil, abundant water, and 262-day growing season made it ideal for rose cultivation. The company's headquarters relocated to Medford, Oregon, so that the company's storage, packaging, and order-processing facilities could be shared with Bear Creek Orchards. Jackson & Perkins' research facility was also moved to California, where hybridizers William Warriner and then Keith Zary continued to manufacture new varieties of roses.

In 1968, David Holmes Jr. stepped down from active management of Harry and David and John Holmes, Harry Holmes's son, took over the business. He formed Bear Creek Corporation in 1972 as an umbrella organization for the company's several functions. In 1976, he took the corporation public. Although considered a "reluctant" president, according to company literature, John Holmes led his company through a time of exponential growth. He invested in completely computerizing Bear Creek, not only for processing orders and bookkeeping, but to develop the practice of direct mail.

Throughout the 1980s, Harry and David continued to publish its "honest-to-gosh" full color catalogs. The company still had a country store, produce stand, and flower market at its compound gate, but within those gates the business was very much of its time. Under the direction of John Holmes, Harry and David now transported its food to major cities in temperature-controlled trucks and railway cars. Jackson & Perkins dominated U.S. rose production with its approximately 24 million roses per year.

OWNERSHIP CHANGES: 1984–89

As a result of its success, Bear Creek began to attract offers from interested buyers, and in January 1984, R.J. Reynolds Development Corporation acquired Bear Creek Corporation for $74 million as part of its own effort to generate growth through acquisition. Nearly three years later, in November 1986, Shaklee Corporation, a vitamin, household goods, and personal care products company, purchased Bear Creek from R.J. Reynolds for $123 million. Bear Creek earned between $12 million and $13 million in 1986, and $11.4 million in 1987, helping out the stalled Shaklee. In 1988, Shaklee named William B. Williams president and chief executive officer of Bear Creek Corporation and senior vice president of the parent corporation. Williams brought with him nearly 20 years of general retailing and mail-order experience at Neiman Marcus, Inc. He remained in charge of Bear Creek when, in 1989, Yamanouchi Pharmaceutical Co., Ltd., acquired Shaklee Corporation.

During Williams's early years at Bear Creek, the company achieved growth through the acquisition of related businesses. In 1988 Jackson & Perkins merged with Armstrong Roses and the wholesale operations of both companies were combined into a single marketing, sales, and administrative unit called Bear Creek Gardens. In 1989 Bear Creek Corporation acquired Orchids Only Inc., a Portland, Oregon-based direct marketer of orchids and other floral gifts. Williams viewed this acquisition as part of Bear Creek's commitment to expand the company's direct-marketing business.

FIRST RETAIL OUTLET OPENS: 1991

The 1990s spawned new ventures from within at Bear Creek. In 1991 the company opened its first Harry and David outlet store near Medford, Oregon, featuring catalog items plus frozen foods and picnic and kitchen accessories. By 1994 the company's store division oversaw 11 outlet stores. In 1993 Bear Creek founded a separate business, Northwest Express, a catalog company offering apparel, lifestyle accessories, and home accessories "in the spirit of the outdoors" with golf-themed items, fishing accessories, and decorative items featuring the flora and fauna of the Pacific Northwest.

The family-run business had grown into a sophisticated operation. By 1997 Harry and David achieved $300 million in sales. By 1998 that number had reached $325 million. Gone were the original pear trees, replaced with dwarf Cornice stock, easier to spray, prune, and harvest. Harry and David stores numbered 50 and had achieved a national presence, and Harry and David's award-winning Web site was chosen by *Catalog Age* for its first Gold Award. Bear Creek's other ventures were successful as well. In 1998 Jackson & Perkins won top prize in international rose competitions in England, Germany, and the Netherlands. The business in Medford was still fronted by a fruit stand and the fruitcake recipe was still the 1957 original, but behind all this stood a hangar-sized packing house, a huge cold-storage facility, a network of kitchens, machines shops, and offices, and several hundred acres of orchards.

True to its homespun beginnings, Bear Creek Corporation still engaged in little traditional advertising, relying on its award-winning catalogs to spur sales, but the company had developed a knack for capturing media moments by designing products that were "newsworthy," for example, the Jackson & Perkins' Veterans' Honor Hybrid Tea Rose, unveiled at Arlington National Cemetery in 1999, or the Princess Diana Memorial Rose, promoted in 1997, a few months after the princess's death. When the *Wall Street Journal* picked Harry and David's truffle heart as the best Valentine's Day box of chocolates, the company sold its entire supply of hearts on the day that story appeared in print.

ONLINE PRESENCE DEVELOPS: 1996–2000

Building on more than a half century of direct-marketing experience, the move to the Internet was a natural extension of the company's catalog sales, although Bear Creek waited until 1996 to go on the Web. In 1999 e-commerce sales topped $25 million, and the company created a new Internet division. The company's Web site offered services in addition to products: gift reminder services and electronic gift certificates as well as gift suggestions, an online gift registry, real-time inventory, verification of shipment, and package tracking.

The Internet also introduced Bear Creek Corporation to a younger customer base and posed the challenge of "jazzing up" the company's brand appeal, according to the editorial director of *Catalog Age*. By 2000, with an expected $400 million in sales, Bear Creek was looking to add "an element of fashion," according to CEO Williams, overhauling its catalog to include more appetizing shots of prepared foods. Looking to the future, it aimed to make a quarter of its sales online by 2005, and was opening stores at the rate of about 75 a year.

FROM BEAR CREEK TO HARRY & DAVID HOLDINGS: 2004

Profound changes occurred as Bear Creek Corporation navigated its way through the first decade of the 21st century. Revenue growth during the period remained essentially flat, but there were advances on other fronts that told a more dynamic tale. In March 2004 Bear Creek Holdings, Inc., was formed to acquire Bear Creek Corporation, a transaction that was concluded in June 2004, when Bear Creek Corporation was acquired from Yamanouchi. Concurrent with the sale, Beer Creek Holdings changed its name to Harry & David Holdings, Inc., the new corporate banner for the Harry & David and Jackson & Perkins businesses. In conjunction with the acquisition, Wasserstein & Company, LP and Highfields Capital Management LP took equity stakes in Harry & David Holdings. By the end of the decade, Wasserstein owned 66 percent of Harry & David Holdings and Highfields owned 34 percent of the company.

Annual revenues reached $565 million when the corporate name occurred, a total that would rise and fall in succeeding years as management acquired and divested assets. Before Williams struck his deals, Harry & David Holdings made moves in other areas, most notably by creating a wholesale business early in the decade. Although representing only a small percentage of the company's overall volume, the wholesale business, which primarily supplied confectionery products to department stores, grew rapidly, serving more than 2,500 locations by 2005. In 2007 the company completed a $16 million expansion of its Hebron, Ohio, facility, its largest distribution center. Roughly 45,000 square feet was added to the facility, which gave Harry

& David Holdings the ability to produce nearly 60 percent of its product line at the facility.

CUSHMAN AND WOLFERMAN'S PURCHASES: 2008

Divestitures and acquisitions occurred next, as the company severed long-standing relationships and fleshed out its product line. In 2007 Harry & David Holdings sold Jackson & Perkins, bidding farewell to a business it had owned for four decades. The sale of Jackson & Perkins, along with some Southern California land holdings, gave the company $49 million it used to complete two acquisitions the following year. First, in early 2008, the company paid $23 million for Wolferman's, a Kansas-based marketer of premium gift breakfast products. Wolferman's generated $27 million in revenue in 2007.

Next, Harry & David Holdings purchased West Palm Beach, Florida-based Cushman Fruit Co. in August 2008. Cushman, which generated $19 million in sales in 2007, was best known for its HoneyBells, a rare natural hybrid of Dancy Tangerine and Duncan Grapefruit. Financial figures for the Cushman acquisition were not disclosed, but Harry & David Holdings was believed to have paid less for Cushman than it did for Wolferman's.

The end of the decade represented a tortuous period for companies of all types, as a global economic crisis forced business leaders to shelve plans for growth and focus instead on survival. Harry & David Holdings felt the pain delivered by the harsh economic conditions. In November 2009, the company reported a $21.7 million loss for the previous fiscal quarter, one year after it reported a $15.1 million loss for the same quarter. "We're in an uncertain period," Williams acknowledged in the November 6, 2009 edition of the *Mail Tribune*. "The sales challenges that emerged last year have not been reversed. If you use last year as a base line, there is more chance to be under last year than above last year. We are responding by reducing expenses wherever possible."

Williams made substantial cuts in the company's inventory, offering far fewer items in the Harry & David catalog. He closed eight stores, leaving the company with 136 retail locations. His actions bore fruit, enabling Harry & David Holdings to record increasing earnings during the first half of 2010 despite a decline in revenue. Further challenges remained to be overcome as the company plotted its future, but assuming Harry & David Holdings withstood its greatest test, the years ahead promised to witness the continued growth of one of the premier mail-order businesses in the United States.

Carrie Rothburd
Updated, Jeffrey L. Covell

PRINCIPAL SUBSIDIARIES

Harry & David Operations Corp.

PRINCIPAL COMPETITORS

Houdini Inc.; Lindt & Sprungli (Australia) Pty. Ltd.; 1-800-FLOWERS.COM, Inc.

FURTHER READING

Alley, Bill, "Story of a Century: 1935–1939," *Southern Oregon Historical Society*, July 15, 1999, p. B2.

Aronovich, Hanna, "Fruit of Labor," *Food and Drink*, July–August 2005, p. 96.

Horovitz, Bruce, "Selling Pears at $5 a Pound," *USA Today*, December 3, 1999, p. 1B.

Preszler, David, "Marketer Gains Worldwide Attention with Catalogs Aimed at Media," *Associated Press*, August 7, 1999.

Shaw, Diana, "Have Pears, Will Ship," *USA Weekend*, December 1, 1991, p. 20.

Stiles, Greg, "Harry and David Holdings May Be in for a Slow Christmas This Year," *Mail Tribune*, November 6, 2009.

Streeper, Dick, "A Picture of U.S. Rose Industry Is Gradually Coming into Focus," *San Diego Union-Tribune*, November 5, 1989, p. F31.

Haworth, Inc.

One Haworth Center
Holland, Michigan 49423-9576
U.S.A.
Telephone: (616) 393-3000
Fax: (616) 393-1570
Web site: http://www.haworth.com

Private Company
Incorporated: 1948 as Modern Products Inc.
Employees: 7,000
Sales: $1.11 billion (2009)
NAICS: 337214 Office Furniture (Except Wood) Manufacturing; 337211 Wood Office Furniture Manufacturing; 337127 Institutional Furniture Manufacturing; 337215 Showcase, Partition, Shelving, and Locker Manufacturing; 337121 Upholstered Household Furniture Manufacturing

∎ ∎ ∎

Haworth, Inc., is a global provider and one of the leading North American manufacturers of office furniture and workplace systems. Known for its innovative design, which has pushed the envelope on ergonomics, sustainability, and adaptability in furniture, Haworth offers full lines of workspace furniture that feature cabling systems, chairs, desks, files, lighting, movable walls, raised floors, storage units, tables, and wood and metal casegoods. Some of its major brands include Monaco, Moxie, Patterns, PLACES, and X9. Haworth's innovation in design is reflected in the more than 250 patents it has achieved, and its commitment to the environment and

sustainable furnishings is reflected in dozens of industry awards. Haworth has about 60 showrooms throughout the world and services contract furniture markets through approximately 600 dealers in 120 countries.

FROM HOBBY TO BUSINESS: FORTIES AND FIFTIES

Haworth began as a hobby for its founder, Gerrard W. Haworth, a graduate of Western Michigan University and the University of Michigan who began teaching industrial arts in a Holland, Michigan, high school in 1938. Hoping eventually to help finance college educations for his children, Haworth sought to supplement his income by beginning a part-time woodworking business out of his garage. Over the next 10 years, his craftsmanship was recognized, and the number of orders he received for wood products grew.

Hoping to turn his passion for woodworking into a full-time profession, Haworth approached a local bank for a loan in 1948. Having had no prior business experience, however, he was rejected as too great a risk. Undaunted, Haworth mortgaged his home and accepted a $10,000 loan from his father, and, once obtaining the money he needed to begin business, he quit his teaching position, purchased secondhand shop equipment, and founded Modern Products. During its first two years, the company employed six woodworkers at a small plant in Holland and received orders for a wide variety of products. Then, in 1951, Modern Products won a contract that would determine the course of its business.

That year Haworth was approached by an architect who had designed an office partition to be used at the

COMPANY PERSPECTIVES

Using our products, services, and knowledge, our mission is to provide each of our customers with a tailored interior that enhances their business, stirs their spirit, and sustains the planet. All Haworth products are characterized by global trend developments and reflect a constant endeavor to continue developing. Haworth has created a company culture that stands for absolute customer satisfaction, technical advancement, and innovative design as well as living a clear sense of responsibility for the environment. Haworth products can be constantly adapted to perfectly suit the perpetually changing external conditions in which they are used; the customer can therefore be sure that the products will enjoy long-term use.

new United Auto Workers (UAW) union headquarters in Detroit. Haworth accepted the job of producing the partitions, and he set about planning the prototype. Referred to as a "bank partition," the product measured 66 inches high, consisting of 43 inches of wood and 12 inches at the top made of glass. The prebuilt partitions were well received at the UAW headquarters, and, speculating that other companies might also be interested in them, Haworth decided to focus his business on their production.

GROWTH AND DEVELOPMENT OF PANEL BUSINESS: SIXTIES AND SEVENTIES

Business boomed over the next 10 years, growing 30 to 40 percent annually. In 1959, Modern Products became a national manufacturing concern. In 1961, the company moved to larger facilities. During this period, Haworth's teenage son Richard began working at Modern Products, sweeping floors and operating some of the machinery. In 1964, having graduated from Western Michigan University with a bachelor's degree in business, Richard became an assistant sales manager at Modern Products, working at a plant in his hometown of Holland. Within two years, he was promoted to vice president for research and development, but he soon was obliged to leave the company for service in the U.S. Army. When Richard returned to Modern Products in 1969, his father relied on him to help develop a new type of office furniture product.

During the 1960s, competitor Herman Miller, Inc., of Zeeland, Michigan, had introduced the innovative Action Office System, consisting of movable panels, shelves, cabinets, and desktops that could be rearranged to create workstations and open spaces to accommodate a variety of floor plans. Richard countered with the development of a unique movable panel insulated with carpeting to reduce noise and help ensure privacy. Modern Products began manufacturing these new panels in 1971, and the following year the company's sales were estimated at $6 million.

Over the next few years, Richard Haworth became increasingly interested in panel design. Christopher Palmeri, in an article in *Forbes*, stated that Richard's colleagues remembered him "anonymously visiting competitors' showrooms and taking their furniture apart" to learn more about panel construction. During this time, he devised a method of installing electrical wiring inside panels that would exert a tremendous influence on the industry. Modern Products' prewired panels, introduced and patented by Richard Haworth in 1975, could be easily snapped together and eliminated the client's need to pay extra for electricians to wire office spaces. The new line of these panels, called Uni-Group, was a huge success, and sales in 1975 increased sharply to around $10 million, while the number of people employed at Modern Products grew to 136.

The company's name was also changed in 1975 to Haworth, Inc., and a new corporate headquarters was established in Holland. In 1976, G. W. Haworth stepped aside, becoming chairperson and naming his son president. Richard Haworth oversaw subsequent years of phenomenal growth at Haworth.

RAPID GROWTH OF PROFITS, EXPANSION OF BUSINESS: EIGHTIES

Not only did the office systems and furniture industry as a whole become more profitable in the 1980s, but Haworth consistently grew at a rate more than two times the industry average. In 1980, Haworth set up a European division after reportedly spending nearly $30 million to acquire the West German chair manufacturing company Comforto GmbH. By 1986, Haworth had become the country's third-largest office furniture manufacturer. Its sales exceeded $300 million, and its staff of 2,600 was producing office chairs, filing cabinets, and fabrics, in addition to the popular panels. Three years later, the company opened a showroom in London and estimated that nearly 10 percent of its sales were generated in foreign countries.

During its expansion, Haworth became involved in a legal dispute with industry giant Steelcase Inc. that

KEY DATES

1948: Company is founded by Gerrard Haworth.
1976: Company's name is changed to Haworth, Inc.; prewired office panels are introduced.
1986: Haworth becomes the third-largest company in the U.S. office furniture industry.
1997: Company wins more than $200 million in a patent infringement case against Steelcase.
2008: Haworth opens its new global headquarters on its 60th anniversary.

would last more than 15 years. Steelcase had begun marketing a panel similar to Haworth's prewired panel in the late 1970s. Claiming that Steelcase had infringed on his patent, Richard Haworth sought compensation from the company in the early 1980s. Steelcase argued, however, that its prewired systems were developed by its own staff and brought into question Haworth's right to the patent. In November 1985, Haworth filed a civil lawsuit against Steelcase. The case was tried in a Michigan court, and in May 1988 a U.S. District Court judge ruled in favor of Steelcase. In January 1989, however, the decision was overturned by the U.S. Court of Appeals, which found several errors in the Michigan court's interpretation of the case and ruled that Haworth's rights as patent holder had been infringed upon.

The case was not definitively settled until 1997, when the U.S. District Court for western Michigan ordered Steelcase to pay Haworth damages of $211.5 million. This was deemed one of the largest patent litigation judgments in U.S. history. Richard Haworth filed a similar suit against Herman Miller, Inc., in 1992, declaring in *Forbes* that, although litigation leads to bad will between the companies, "we believe we have to protect what we invest in."

The late 1980s was a difficult time for the office systems industry. Aggressive discounting and the increased sale of used office equipment led to a shakeout of the industry's smaller companies and to decreased earnings for Steelcase, Herman Miller, and Haworth. Nevertheless, Haworth continued to gain market share, and in 1990 it purchased the Mueller Furniture Company, a Holland-based manufacturer of wooden tables and chairs. In December of that year *Industry Week* magazine compared Haworth to an "overachieving younger sibling, who's content not just to catch up, but to overtake big brother's lead."

During this time, Haworth's unique corporate philosophy attracted attention in the business community. Referring to employees as "members," Haworth espoused a participative management style in which all members were required to spend one hour per week brainstorming ways in which Haworth could better serve the customer. During busy periods, the company paid members overtime for this one-hour commitment. Characterizing its approach as "customer-driven," Haworth produced a creed for its members that, in the words of Richard Haworth, "put profit last on purpose because we believe profits are a result of doing the right thing, focusing on quality, our customers, and giving our employees freedom to do what's right."

NEW PRODUCTS AND ACQUISITIONS IN THE EARLY NINETIES

In response to customer needs for a more open, interactive workspace than the paneled workstations provided, Haworth introduced new products in the 1990s. Conference tables were developed that could be easily rearranged to form circles, U-shapes, or individual tables, as were panels of lower heights made of transparent materials. Furthermore, Haworth made available adjustable-height work surfaces. The Trakker adjustable table, for example, contained a computer memory that could be programmed to adjust the table to as many as 19 different heights. The computer could be set to periodically remind users to adjust the table in order to lessen their chances of stress injuries.

Haworth had begun a run of acquisitions with its purchase of Comforto in the 1980s. The 1990s saw a marked increase in Haworth's size, as it bought office and business furniture makers across the world. It concentrated on low- to middle-priced office furniture manufacturers, buying or investing in a dozen companies between the late 1980s and 1993. Some of the companies it bought included Mueller Furniture Company, Kinetics, and Lunstead, all acquired in 1990. In 1993, Haworth purchased Globe Business Furniture, a domestic manufacturer of seating, institutional furniture, and ready-to-assemble office furniture. Globe was headquartered in Hendersonville, Tennessee, and had estimated sales of more than $100 million for 1992. It sold its products through catalogs, warehouse clubs, and office superstores, and so it gave Haworth entry into these mass-market distribution channels.

Haworth picked up GSP Manufacturing in 1994, a maker of upholstered wood office furniture located in Tijuana, Mexico. Then in 1995, Haworth purchased Office Group America, of Leeds, Alabama. Office Group had sales of $150 million for 1995 and consisted of two units, Anderson Hickey and United Chair. All of the added subsidiaries pushed Haworth's total sales up to $1.2 billion by 1995. That year it did better than its close rival Herman Miller, Inc., giving Haworth the number two ranking in the office furniture industry.

Gerald Johanneson, who joined the company as executive vice president of marketing and sales in 1986 and then became chief operating officer in 1988, was named company president in 1994. Johanneson was the first president of the company to come from outside the Haworth family. Three years later, Johanneson was named CEO.

By 1995, Haworth was deriving about 30 percent of its sales from overseas and hoping to push that figure to 50 percent by the end of the decade. Foreign acquisitions were key to Haworth's growth strategy. The company realized that many of its major customers operated globally. It had contracts with such firms as Motorola and Sun Microsystems, and these companies were likely to want Haworth to work with them in overseas locations. Richard Haworth developed a lengthy process of getting to know possible acquisition targets. He explained his system in an article he authored for the January–February 1995 *Mergers & Acquisitions*, detailing how his firm worked for five or six years sometimes with companies it hoped to buy, moving cautiously toward formal acquisition talks. However, for Haworth, the long period of getting to know the target company paid off.

RISING REVENUES, INNOVATIVE PRODUCTS, AND EUROPEAN EXPANSION

By 1996, Haworth boasted rapidly accelerated revenues, which had almost doubled in five years while the furniture market itself saw an increase of only 30 percent. Haworth's operating margins were also better than those of its close competitors. Haworth had margins of 10 percent, versus 8 percent for Herman Miller and 6 percent for Steelcase. The slew of acquisitions had given Haworth a complete line of office furniture across all price ranges, but it had a good concentration of low- to medium-priced lines. The company worked hard to keep manufacturing prices down, to be able to continue to keep prices below its competitors. Although Haworth almost quadrupled in size over the early 1990s, the percentage it spent on sales, administrative, and other expenses went down significantly. The company also was known for lowering its prices in order to undercut competitors. A New York furniture distributor quoted in a May 1996 *Forbes* article described Haworth's policy thus: "If Miller and Knoll are offering 65% off on a project, Haworth says

71%." By 1996 Haworth boasted that it won 65 percent of all new contracts it bid on.

In the late 1990s and into the next decade, Haworth worked on developing innovative products. It established a research and development group in the late 1990s to work on ergonomically designed furniture and office space. Haworth not only looked to design more comfortable chairs and desks, but strived to design work spaces that helped workers concentrate and reduced stress. Haworth also invested in new computer software, using a system that enabled customers to view virtual workspaces on the screen so that changes could be previewed. The system also tallied estimated costs.

The company closed the decade boosting its European presence. In 1999, Haworth broadened its global operations by acquiring several companies: Art Collection, dyes, Nestler, and Roder from DWL AG in Germany and Kemen in Spain. The five European furniture makers brought a combined $121 million in annual sales to Haworth. With the acquisitions, Haworth became the third-largest European furniture maker. In addition, the four German companies combined with Haworth's Comforto brand made the company an industry leader in Germany.

CANADIAN ACQUISITIONS, JOB CUTS, AND FLEXIBLE FURNITURE

Haworth's acquisitions did not slacken as the company moved into the 21st century. In 2000, Haworth acquired a majority interest in a Canadian maker of laminate office furniture, Group Lacasse. Haworth also bought another Canadian company that year, Smed International. Smed, a Calgary-based manufacturer of office interiors sold under the brand Constructive Solutions, had sales in Canadian dollars of $192 million and agreed to be bought by Haworth rather than accept another hostile offer. The Smed acquisition was expected to boost Haworth's sales so that it would surpass its rival Herman Miller for the number two spot in the office furniture industry with $1.54 billion in sales, compared to the leader in the office furniture industry, Steelcase, with $2.76 billion in 1998 sales. The Canadian brands Lacasse and Avenue complemented the company's own Haworth, Anderson Hickey, Globe, and United Chair brands and contributed to a sizable laminate casegoods portfolio of products.

In 2001, Haworth acquired a leading Swiss manufacturer of office furniture, Elan Florian Weber AG. Haworth that same year was forced to cut its workforce for the first time in its history due to global recessionary conditions and an industry slump. The company closed a plant in the state of Washington, eliminating

250 jobs, and trimmed executive positions around the country. Slacking sales in 2002 produced additional reduction in employees. In 2003, Haworth slashed another 250 jobs at Michigan factories and reduced workweeks for other workers to just three days.

Haworth had already won numerous awards for its environmentally friendly designs and production processes. During the early 2000s, the company increasingly geared its product lines to adaptability and sustainability, as well as ergonomic concerns. Haworth focused on making its furniture adaptable to customers' needs and touted that adaptability, like sustainability, need not ignore style. Major product lines early in the decade included Tutti, a furniture group with four "atmospheres" that included desks, storage units, and technology components with compatible families of products: Spaceware, freestanding ceilings and screens, and Workwear, work tools and lighting. In 2003, Haworth also launched the freeform Moxie with translucent appearances and partial space dividers that empowered the customer with choices to create the style that fit the required utility.

Robert Krasa was named president and CEO of Haworth in 2003, succeeding the retiring Gerald Johanneson. Krasa had joined Haworth in 2001, after 27 years with Dow Corning Corporation, and had previously served as Haworth's president of the North America Contract Furniture unit. Krasa, however, resigned 18 months later, citing need for family time, and Richard Haworth, company chairman, assumed the additional CEO title.

MANUFACTURING CONSOLIDATION, A NEW COMPETITOR, AND INNOVATIVE DESIGNS

In October 2003, Haworth acquired the assets of Michigan-based Interface Architectural Resources, a producer of raised-access flooring. The purchase enhanced Haworth's lines of movable walls, raised-access flooring, and electrical-module cabling. Prompted by a continuing slump in the office furniture industry, Haworth consolidated manufacturing activities in 2004. Factories in Texas, North Carolina, Arkansas, and Pennsylvania were closed and production relocated at three Michigan facilities.

Meanwhile, Hon Industries (later renamed HNI Corporation) of Muscatine, Iowa, in 2004 passed both Herman Miller and Haworth, becoming North America's second-largest office furniture manufacturer. Hon's aggressive acquisition campaign early in the decade substantially boosted Hon's revenues, ending the long-standing battle between Haworth and Herman Miller for second place within the office furniture industry.

In 2004, Haworth's Chicago showroom was stripped down to its shell and rebuilt using Haworth's full range of interior products and furnishings, resulting in three Best Large Showroom Awards from the International Interior Design Association in five years. The showroom also earned Gold Certification (second only to Platinum) from LEED, the green building certification program that encouraged sustainable building practices. In 2005, Franco Bianchi, the former head of Haworth's Italian operations, became president and CEO of the corporation.

While Haworth had its own European furniture design teams, the company often worked with well-respected designers and design firms. These included José Serrano who designed SE04 modular lounge seating and collaborated with Haworth on the award-winning Planes conference system. Other European designers who contributed to Haworth's furnishings included Mario Ruiz who, in 2005, designed the well-received K22 office furniture series. In 2006, the German designer Martin Ballendat created the exclusive sled-base chair, the "b_sit," for Haworth. That same year, Michael Welsh as lead designer collaborated with Germany's ITO Design to create the Zody task chair, the industry's first chair to win the Gold MBDC Cradle to Cradle score. The chair also earned a 2006 IDEA Ecodesign award for sustainable design. Two years later, Welsh led the design and creation of the Very seating line that became an award winner. Wolfgang C. R. Mezger also designed three Haworth product lines: gemini, tanis, and m_sit, the latter which took home the iF 2006 product design award.

NEW WORLD HEADQUARTERS AND RECESSION-COUNTERING STRATEGIES

In 2008, the company celebrated its 60th anniversary and opened its new corporate headquarters at One Haworth Center. The new headquarters was designed to reflect the values of the company, including sustainability and adaptability. Within the new global headquarters, Material ConneXion, an international materials consultancy with a library of sustainable materials, established its first Innovation Lab. The lab was built with Haworth's business aims and product design concerns in mind and placed more than 4,500 materials at the company's disposal.

Haworth was forced to undertake facility closings and staff cuts because of a worsening global recession.

As a result, in December 2008, Haworth announced plans to cut 350 manufacturing positions through the closing of a Michigan seat factory and by encouraging early retirement through the offer of enhanced retirement packages. In August 2009, the company began consolidating its Calgary, Canada production, laying off 600 employees there and relocating operations to west Michigan where Haworth received a $20 million tax credit to create new jobs. The changes were prompted by an excess capacity of furniture and a poor sales environment. Haworth also planned to divest its 767,000-square-foot Calgary manufacturing facility and relocate its Calgary showroom. By the end of the decade, Haworth's Canadian operations had been pared down to Quebec manufacturing facilities.

As companies shuttered their doors because of the continuing recession, the demand for office furniture continued to diminish. To generate new sales, Haworth promoted its furniture lines to noncorporate markets: schools, government agencies, and hospitals. The company also expanded the range of its product lines beyond office space and acquired in 2009 the Minnesota-based Tuohy Furniture Corporation that designed and manufactured storage units and reception-area and conference furniture.

By the end of 2009, Haworth's revenues had fallen to a decade low of $1.11 billion, and its workforce since 2001 had been sliced from 10,000 to 7,000. As it entered the next decade, the company was clearly feeling the effects of a poor global economy. The success of its expanded marketing strategy was not immediately certain. The strength of its furniture lines appeared less dependent upon specific industry trends than on the larger economic climate.

Tina Grant
Updated, A. Woodward; Roger Rouland

PRINCIPAL SUBSIDIARIES

Haworth UK Ltd.; Haworth Schweiz AG (Switzerland); Haworth Spain; Haworth Portugal; Haworth Benelux B.V. (Netherlands); Haworth SpA (Italy); Haworth Ireland; Haworth Hungary; Haworth GmbH (Germany); Haworth France; Haworth Czech s.r.o.; Haworth Benelux B.V. (Belgium); Haworth Australia Pty Limited – Melbourne; Haworth Australia Pty Limited – Sydney; Haworth Brisbane; Haworth Beijing (China); Haworth Chengdu (China); Haworth Hong Kong L.L.C.; Haworth Furniture (Shanghai) Co. Ltd.; Haworth Pune, Ishanya (India); Haworth India Pvt. Ltd; Haworth India Pvt. Ltd – Chennai; Haworth India Pvt. Ltd – Hyderabad; Haworth India Pvt. Ltd – Mum-bai; Haworth India Pvt. Ltd – Delhi; Heyworth Tokyo (Japan); Timsdeco Limited (South Korea); Haworth Malaysia; Cornersteel Systems Corporation (Philippines); Haworth Singapore Pte Ltd; Network International Co. (Taiwan); Creative Office Solutions Co. Ltd. (Thailand); Groupe Lacasse, LLC (Canada).

PRINCIPAL DIVISIONS

Haworth North America; Haworth Europe; Haworth Asia; Haworth Middle East & Africa.

PRINCIPAL COMPETITORS

ABCO Office Furniture; Commercial Furniture Group; Global Upholstery Co. Inc.; Herman Miller, Inc.; HNI Corporation; Inscape Corporation; Kimball International, Inc.; Knoll, Inc.; Krueger International, Inc.; Neutral Posture, Inc.; Norstar Office Products, Inc.; Steelcase Inc.; Teknion Corporation; Trendway Corporation; Virco Mfg. Corporation.

FURTHER READING

Benson, Tracy E., "America's Unsung Heroes," *Industry Week*, December 3, 1990, pp. 12–22.

Brandsen, Ken, "Renovating for the Future: Michigan Furniture Manufacturer Stakes Its Claim to Sustainability with a New, World-Class Headquarters," *Environmental Design & Construction*, June 2008, pp. 79+.

Brown, Christie, "You Say 65% Off, They Say 71%," *Forbes*, May 20, 1996, p. 164.

Cowan, Coleman, "Is There a Better Way to Court a Company?" *Business Week*, July 23, 2007, p. 55.

Davidsen, Judith, "Contract with the Planet," *Interior Design*, March 1, 2008, p. 139.

Galadza, Sofia, "Showcasing Ideas: The New Haworth Is About Workspaces, Not Workstations," *Contract*, December 2004, pp. 34+.

Girard, Kim, "Want to See That Desk in 3-D?" *Computerworld*, April 6, 1998, p. 55.

Grahl, Christine L., "Breaking the Sustainable Product Barrier," *Environmental Design & Construction*, September 28, 2001.

"Green and Growing," *Contract*, July 2006, p. 16.

Haworth, Richard, "The Mid-Sized Firm as a Global Acquirer: Haworth Inc.," *Mergers & Acquisitions*, January–February 1995, p. 31.

"Haworth's International Initiative," *Industry Week*, February 15, 1993, p. 26.

"Hon Leaps Past Herman Miller & Haworth in Sales," *Wood & Wood Products*, May 2004, p. 18.

Knudson, Brooke, "Turner Is Walking the Talk: Turner Construction Co. Is Overseeing the Transformation of Haworth's Corporate Headquarters," *Construction Today*,

October 2008, pp. 147+.

McClenahen, John S., "Global Citizen: Commitment to People and Community," *Industry Week*, January 4, 1993, pp. 31, 34.

Palmeri, Christopher, "Smart Boy," *Forbes*, May 11, 1992, p. 146.

"A Shape-Shifter in the Office," *Business Week*, June 7, 1999, p. 104.

"Sweet Justice," *Forbes*, January 27, 1997, p. 14.

Ward, Jill, "Green and Gorgeous: Haworth's 'Natural' Chicago Showroom Proves Sustainable Design Is Good Design," *Environmental Design & Construction*, June 2005, pp. 20+.

Weeks, Katie, "Full of Moxie: Designed to Enhance Performance and Corporate Culture, Haworth's Moxie Capitalizes on Flexibility and Scalability with a Sense of Fun," *Contract*, June 2003, pp. 52+.

Holland & Barrett Retail Limited

Vitality House
6th Avenue, Centrum 100
Burton-upon-Trent, DE14 2WP
United Kingdom
Telephone: (+44-1283) 560-000
Fax: (+44-870) 606-6606
Web site: http://www.hollandandbarrett.com

Subsidiary of NBTY, Inc.
Incorporated: 1920 as Heath & Heather
Employees: 3,529
Sales: $443.9 million (2009)
NAICS: 445299 All Other Specialty Food Stores

■ ■ ■

Holland & Barrett Retail Limited is a U.K. retailer of vitamins, minerals, herbal supplements, toiletries, diet products, and body building and sports nutrition supplements. It is also the largest health food retailer in the United Kingdom, offering a variety of dried fruit, nuts, seeds, and mixes. Holland & Barrett operates more than 550 stores in the United Kingdom and Ireland and also sells its wares online. An additional 10 franchised stores operate in South Africa. In the Netherlands Holland & Barrett stores operate under the De Tuinen banner. The company is owned by NBTY, Inc., a major U.S. manufacturer and marketer of nutritional supplements. NBTY also operates the Julian Graves chain of about 335 health food stores in the United Kingdom.

19TH-CENTURY LINEAGE

The men who provided Holland & Barrett with its name were Alfred Slapps Barrett and Major William Holland. In 1870 they went into business together in London and acquired the three-year-old Dodd & Burls grocery shop, which also sold men's and women's clothing. Barrett and Holland sold both food and clothing until the early 1900s when the clothing department was moved to a nearby location. After Holland's death in 1915, Barrett operated both shops. In the 1920s he sold the grocery business to Messrs Alfred Button & Sons, who continued to operate the store under the well-known Holland & Barrett name until the 1970s when Booker, McConnell Ltd. bought out the family. At this stage, the grocery store took the name Budgens, which would also adorn a Booker-owned chain of convenience stores, and the clothing shop's name was shortened to Barrett's because Booker had reserved the Holland & Barrett name for a chain of health food stores it had cobbled together.

Booker had been established in 1834 in Guyana by merchant brothers Josias, George, and Richard Booker, who operated sugar plantations and trading companies and were heavily involved in the sugar and rum trade. The company was taken public in 1920 and was listed on the London Stock Exchange. In 1968 the company was renamed Booker, McConnell Ltd. By this time, political unrest in Guyana led the company to diversify into such areas as supermarkets. It also took advantage of a tax loophole that made it advantageous to acquire author's copyrights at a flat rate and then collect royalties. Among the authors that became associated with Booker were mystery writer Agatha Christie and

COMPANY PERSPECTIVES

Holland & Barrett has the benefit of over 80 years of experience in the health supplement industry. We offer one of the most extensive staff-training programmes in the retail industry, an unparalleled range of natural health food products, as well as an intense commitment to quality goods at exceptional values.

the creator of James Bond, Ian Fleming. It was Fleming who suggested that the company fund a literary prize, which in time became the highly coveted Booker Prize.

ACQUISITION OF HEATH & HEATHER: 1970

Booker efforts at diversification also brought involvement in organic food production, and vitamin and nutritional supplement manufacturing. In 1970 the company added the Heath & Heather chain of herbal remedy shops, which would then take the Holland & Barrett name Booker had acquired. Heath & Heather had its own ties to another well-known prize: golf's Ryder Cup, awarded to the winner of a biennial contest between teams of professional golfers from the United States and Europe. The man behind the Ryder cup as well as Heath & Heather was Samuel Ryder.

Ryder was born in Lancashire, England, in 1858. His father, among other endeavors, was a seed merchant. Ryder worked for him until a falling out, upon which he moved to London to start a competing seed business. He made his mark in the 1890s with the mail-order sale of penny seed packets, a business that thrived and allowed him to launch a separate mail-order herbal remedy business under the Heath & Heather name with his brother James in 1920. It is this date that today's Holland & Barrett marks as its birth and this shop it considers its birthplace.

Heath & Heather prospered, due in part to the use of golf sponsorships in its marketing. Samuel Ryder had taken up golf late in life as a way to get fresh air and became an enthusiast of the game. In 1923 Heath & Heather sponsored a match-play tournament for professional golfers, and the following year sponsored a match-play tournament that pitted a pair of American professionals golfers against a pair of British professionals. To spur the growth of British professional golfers, who lacked the wealthy patrons of their American counterparts, Ryder donated a cup to be

awarded for a team competition. The trophy was first presented in 1927. Samuel Ryder died in 1936, but his name would be forever linked to golf through the Ryder Cup.

Heath & Heather moved its mail-order operations in 1924 to a former hat factory, 24,000 square feet in size. The company then added retail outlets and by 1946 there were 46 shops in the chain. In 1968 Heath & Heather was acquired by Associated Health Foods, a company formed in 1957 to market polyunsaturated foods. In the two years before Booker acquired Heath & Heather, the chain expanded its product mix to include vitamins, supplements, and health foods.

HEATH & HEATHER ADOPTS HOLLAND & BARRETT NAME

In 1970 Booker married the Heath & Heather chain with the Holland & Barrett name and developed a successful formula of diverse selection and low prices. Booker continued to invest in health foods into the 1980s, its holdings including a major French health food company, organic food producers, and vitamin and nutritional supplement manufacturers in both the United States and the United Kingdom. The Heath & Heather chain was expanded as well, increasing to more than 180 outlets by the early 1990s, as annual sales approached £50 million. In the late 1980s, however, Booker had begun to focus on the wholesale food distribution business and looked to divest noncore holdings. The French health food assets were sold in 1989 and the British interests soon followed.

Lloyds Chemists plc acquired Holland & Barrett in 1991. Lloyds Chemists had been founded in 1973 by Allen Lloyd, a recently qualified pharmacist, who bought his first shop that year. He began acquiring more pharmacies, topping the 100 mark in 1986 when Lloyd took the company public. More acquisitions followed so that by the early 1990s Lloyds Chemists was the second-largest owner of pharmacies in the United Kingdom. A downturn in drugstore sales soon resulted in a change in direction, however, and approximately 100 of the Lloyds Chemists shops were closed. A number of others were converted to other uses: 180 outlets adopted a new health and beauty format and 30 outlets made the shift to the Holland & Barrett format. Lloyds Chemists opened additional Holland & Barrett outlets as well. In 1996 the chain added its 400th store.

NEW OWNER: 1997

The mid-1990s brought new competition to Holland & Barrett as well as a new corporate parent. In 1996,

KEY DATES

1870: Holland & Barrett retail store opens.
1920: Heath & Heather is founded.
1970: Heath & Heather adopts Holland & Barrett name.
1991: Lloyds Chemists plc acquires Holland & Barrett.
1997: NBTY, Inc., acquires Holland & Barrett.

GNC Corporation, the United States' giant nutritional supplement retail chain, entered the U.K. market with the acquisition of Health & Diet Group. Lloyds Chemists, in the meantime, found itself the object of a takeover battle. GNC was one of the contenders, as were venture capitalists. In the end, Gehe, a German drug distributor, bought Lloyds Chemists in early 1997 for its pharmacy business and elected to put the Holland & Barrett chain and other acquired assets up for sale. Later in the year Holland & Barrett was sold to a New York-based firm, NBTY, Inc.

NBTY grew out of Arco Pharmaceuticals, a company established in Bohemia, New York in 1960 by Arthur Rudolph. In 1970 it formed a subsidiary, Nature's Bounty, Inc., which produced vitamins and food supplements. Spun off as a public company in 1972, Nature's Bounty enjoyed strong growth over the next 20 years, but it also courted controversy because of the expansive health claims made in its advertising. In light of the negative publicity it received in the early 1990s when it settled claims by the Federal Trade Commission, Nature's Bounty changed its name in 1995, adopting its stock symbol, NBTY. After some disappointing years, the company posted record earnings of $13.4 million on sales of $194.4 million in fiscal 1996, setting the stage for the $168.8 million purchase of Holland & Barrett, which in a single stroke made NBTY the largest retailer of vitamins and health foods in the United Kingdom while adding another $145 million in sales to the balance sheet.

Taking advantage of the financial resources of its new corporate parent, Holland & Barrett tripled its advertising budget in late 1997, primarily to promote the chain's private-label products. NBTY also helped Holland & Barrett to fund the opening of new stores. In 2003 NBTY acquired GNC's wholesale and retail U.K. operations, and many of those GNC stores were rebranded as Holland & Barrett outlets. Also in 2003 NBTY acquired the De Tuinen ("The Garden") chain of 65 natural products stores in the Netherlands from Dutch supermarket giant Ahold NV, paying $16.6 million. While the operation was folded into Holland & Barrett, it retained the established De Tuinen name. The deal also provided NBTY with an important foothold in continental Europe and set the stage for Holland & Barrett to pursue international expansion. To support that effort, the chain hired its first marketing director in February 2003. A month later the company added to its presence in the Netherlands by acquiring the Health & Diet Group from Dutch food group Royal Numico. Health & Diet operated about 56 GNC stores as well as a wholesale operation that mostly supplied health stores in the United Kingdom.

Holland & Barrett reached 500 units in size and enjoyed strong sales growth as the decade unfolded. In the fall of 2006 Holland & Barrett was named England's most profitable main street chain, boasting an operating margin of more than 30 percent. The River Island fashion chain, which ranked second, had an operating margin of just 22.8 percent. In order to maintain its performance, Holland & Barrett pursued a new marketing strategy in 2007, one that sought to communicate to a wider audience for its health care products.

EXPANSION PLAN: 2007

Due to poor economic conditions Holland & Barrett experienced sluggish sales in 2007. The chain had developed a plan to open 100 new stores in the next year, and while that did not bear fruit, Holland & Barrett's group, NBTY Europe, was able to grow through external means. In the fall of 2008 it acquired the 350-outlet Julian Graves chain of health food shops for $25 million. Because Julian Graves and Holland & Barrett were competitors, an antitrust investigation was launched by U.K. regulators. The matter was not settled until September 2009 when approval for the deal was granted. While Holland & Barrett and Julian Graves would be operated independently, their combination still provided economies of scale and other benefits.

Holland & Barrett evolved further as the decade came to an end. It launched the Dr. Organic private label for personal care products. The initial slate of 68 products included lotions, bodywashes, shampoos, and toothpastes, and positioned Holland & Barrett to compete more directly with The Body Shop. The chain also began carrying fresh fruit in some stores and severed ties with the agents it had used to find sites for new stores. Instead, the company brought that responsibility in-house. About 30 stores were expected to open in 2010, and there was every reason that more outlets were to follow in the ensuing years.

Ed Dinger

PRINCIPAL SUBSIDIARIES
De Tuinen BV (Netherlands).

PRINCIPAL COMPETITORS
Alliance Boots GmbH; Co-operative Group (CWS) Ltd; Superdrug Stores Plc.

FURTHER READING

"Boardmans-Bishop's Stortford and Thorley," http://www. stortfordhistory.co.uk.

Clews, Mary-Louise, "Holland & Barrett Launches Body Shop Challenger Range," *Marketing Week*, June 4, 2009, p. 6.

Hall, James, "Profile Peter Aldis Chief Executive, Holland & Barrett Proof That Vitamins Really Work," *Daily Telegraph*, December 8, 2008, p. 4.

Harrison, Keely, "A New Breed of Store," *Super Marketing*, February 28, 1992, p. 35.

"Holland & Barrett Rejig Installs First Marketing Chief," *Marketing*, February 27, 2003, p. 4.

"NBTY Back on Acquisition Trail with Purchase of Netherland's De Tuinen," *Nutraceuticals International*, January 2003.

Sandher, Hardeep, "Holland & Barrett Embarks on Healthy Expansion Plan," *Property Week*, November 27, 2009, p. 63.

Husky Energy Inc.

707 8th Avenue Southwest
Calgary, Alberta T2P 3G7
Canada
Telephone: (403) 298-6111
Fax: (403) 298-7464
Web site: http://www.huskyenergy.ca

Public Company
Incorporated: 1938 as Husky Refining Co.
Employees: 4,272
Sales: CAD 15.07 billion (2009)
Stock Exchanges: Toronto
Ticker Symbol: HSE
NAICS: 211111 Crude Petroleum and Natural Gas
    Extraction; 213112 Support Activities for Oil and
    Gas Operations; 324110 Petroleum Refineries

■ ■ ■

Husky Energy Inc. is the third-largest integrated oil and
natural gas concern in Canada, carrying out extraction,
transport, storage, upgrading, marketing, and retail
operations. Husky conducts its business in three primary
sectors: upstream, midstream, and downstream. The
company's upstream assets, devoted to the exploration,
development, and production of crude oil, natural gas,
and natural gas liquids, are located in western Canada,
offshore eastern Canada, offshore Greenland, the United
States, offshore China, and offshore Indonesia. The
company's midstream activities consist of transporting
and processing refined petroleum products. Husky's
downstream business encompasses refining and marketing petroleum products such as gasoline, diesel, and
ethanol blended fuels through its network of Husky's
retail locations. The company's chain of service stations,
located primarily in western Canada, comprises nearly
600 locations.

THE NIELSON ERA: 1938–78

Husky Energy's roots are in Wyoming. It was there that
Glenn Nielson, a rancher from Cardston, Alberta,
persuaded a farm supply cooperative and a Montana
contractor to join him in purchasing two heavy oil
refiners. The facilities were organized into the Husky
Refining Co. on January 1, 1938, with headquarters in
the small town of Cody. The company expanded slowly
in the prewar years, with annual revenues in the
hundreds of thousands of dollars. Husky Refining
gradually acquired tracts of oil-rich land, waiting to
develop them until it had enough revenue to proceed
without debt. By 1940 the company's assets also
included a small chain of gas stations and a trucking
line.

The demand for heavy oil skyrocketed during
World War II, allowing the young company to attain
financial stability for the first time. When the war had
run its course, Nielson's Canadian background reas-
serted itself, and in 1946 he moved one of his refineries
to Alberta. Husky Oil and Refining Ltd. was
incorporated in Canada the following year as a wholly
owned subsidiary of the U.S. company. With
headquarters in Calgary, the Canadian company
processed heavy oil, producing bunker fuel for railroads
and asphalt for highways. In 1953 the Canadian branch

COMPANY PERSPECTIVES

Husky's strategy is to build a solid foundation for profitable growth by expanding and developing an integrated portfolio of assets. The company looks for synergistic opportunities to enhance shareholder value. Our focus on strategic sourcing, contracting and solid business based execution is designed to create long term benefits for Husky and suppliers.

separated from its U.S. parent and was renamed Husky Oil Ltd. Both companies went public independently. Operations in Canada gradually outpaced activities south of the border until, in 1960, the Canadian company bought all shares of the U.S. unit.

During the 1960s Husky Oil Ltd. grew into a true integrated company, with producing, refining, and marketing divisions. About CAD 35 million was invested in the development of heavy oil operations and reserves in the Lloydminster area, and Husky also began exploring for conventional oil. By the end of the decade the company was a major regional presence, with annual revenues in 1970 of about CAD 175 million. A few years later the Organization of Petroleum Exporting Companies oil embargo pushed oil prices higher and made further expansion possible. Husky bought the marketing and refining assets of Union Oil Company in 1976, an acquisition that included a retail network in western Canada and a refinery in Prince George, British Colombia. Profits that year reached CAD 30 million on revenues of CAD 522 million. In the late 1970s Husky began considering a major new undertaking: the construction of an expensive upgrader that could convert heavy oil into synthetic light oil. The company began looking for partners who, like Husky, desired a new outlet for their heavy oil production.

BOB BLAIR BUYOUT: 1978

As the company entered 1978, the Nielson family expected to lead Husky comfortably into its fifth decade. By the end of the year, though, an outside entrepreneur seized control after a month of whirlwind takeover bids. At the beginning of June 1978, Glenn Nielson was chairman of Husky, while his son Jim acted as CEO. The two owned only about 20 percent of the company, but ran it like a private family firm. Then, on June 9, they received a message that Wilbert Hopper, president of the state oil and gas company Petro-Canada, wished to meet with them. He offered to buy

out the Nielsons at a CAD 9 premium over the last recorded trading price. The Nielsons refused. Notwithstanding the huge tax liability after such a deal, they did not want the independent Husky absorbed by a concocted state conglomerate. Acting quickly, they turned to Dr. Armand Hammer, chairman of the Los Angeles-based multinational Occidental Petroleum Corporation. Occidental arranged a higher counterbid and also structured the deal to reduce tax consequences for the Nielsons. Both Occidental and Petro-Canada made formal offers and waited for shareholders to accept.

In the end, control of Husky went to an outsider: Bob Blair, CEO of Alberta Gas Trunk Line Co. Ltd., a company dealing in natural gas pipelines and petrochemicals. Blair had a reputation as a nationalist, progressive oilman with ties to the Liberal Party. He had been buying shares in Husky since early in 1978, and managed to acquire a controlling 37 percent stake by the end of June. The two major contenders were forced to abandon their bidding war. Under Blair's ownership, the Nielsons stayed on as consultants. However, soon dissatisfied with their reduced role at Husky, they sold out their share and moved back to Wyoming to concentrate on other enterprises.

TURBULENT EXPANSION: 1979–91

By May 1979, Alberta Gas Trunk Line held 68 percent of Husky. Blair renamed AGTL "Nova Corp." in 1980. That year Marathon Oil Corporation made an offer for Husky, but the transaction was abandoned at the request of U.S. Steel, which was engaged in a friendly takeover of Marathon. Nova began pouring money into Husky, which in 1982 ranked 13th in Canadian oil production. Husky acquired a small producing company, Candel Oil Ltd., built a new refinery at Lloydminster, and moved into an elegant new office complex in downtown Calgary. Exploration began in North Africa, Indonesia, Australia, and offshore Newfoundland. Bigger was better throughout the 1980s. Husky did, however, get rid of its Denver-based U.S. subsidiary in 1984. The unit's oil and gas production operations were sold to Marathon Oil and the downstream operations, to a group of investors that included three former Husky executives. The transaction helped reduce Husky's growing debt.

Husky's expansion policy began to appear ill-advised in the second half of the decade, when Arab nations flooded the world market with cheap oil. Husky recorded its first year-end loss in 1986, and the share price plummeted. Soon Husky was looking for a private partner to prop up the company's finances. The company found a willing investor in Li Ka-shing, a

KEY DATES

1938: Glenn Nielson founds Husky Refining Co. in Cody, Wyoming.

1946: Nielson moves some Husky operations to Alberta, Canada.

1953: The U.S. and Canadian companies separate and go public.

1960: Canadian Husky Oil Ltd. acquires all shares of the U.S. unit.

1991: Hong Kong investor Li Ka-shing acquires all but 5 percent of Husky and installs new management.

1998: Husky invests heavily in acquisition and development of properties offshore Newfoundland.

2000: Husky merges with Renaissance Energy and goes public.

2007: Refinery in Lima, Ohio, is acquired for $1.9 billion.

2010: Lau is replaced as CEO by Asim Ghosh.

Hong Kong billionaire with holdings in Canada and a friendly business relationship with Blair. In a deal worth about CAD 855 million, Li bought a 43 percent stake in Husky Oil through his Hutchison Whampoa trading company. Li's family acquired another 9 percent, and 5 percent was purchased by the Canadian Imperial Bank of Commerce. Nova was left with a 43 percent stake. Husky was delisted from the stock market, but Blair continued to run the company. With restored optimism, Husky looked for good returns in the coming decade.

Continued expansion and low oil prices, however, prevented Husky from attaining financial prosperity. In particular, the Lloydminster Bi-Provincial Upgrader project, initiated in 1988, was a financial black hole for many years. In theory, the upgrader was to make a profit on the differential between the prices of heavy and light oil. If the differential was wide enough and the upgrading process fairly efficient, Husky could make money converting heavy oil into light. However, both the high cost of the project and the uncertainty of oil prices discouraged potential industry partners from joining Husky on the project. Consequently, Husky President Art Price turned to the government. Early in 1984 he succeeded in persuading the Liberal-controlled federal government to provide financing, but the deal fell through when the Progressive Conservatives gained control in the fall elections.

After negotiating for several more years and trimming the price of construction, Husky finally won a deal. In 1988 the provincial governments of Alberta and Saskatchewan, together with the federal government, agreed to fund 75 percent of the estimated CAD 1.2 billion cost of constructing an upgrader. Even though Husky provided only one-quarter of the equity for the deal, it was to receive half of the profits. Blair insisted that the jobs and tax revenue generated by the upgrader would make the deal worthwhile for all parties. The upgrader would process 46,000 barrels per day of heavy crude, a welcome development in a market that was oversupplied with heavy oil. Husky commenced construction of the upgrader, persevering over the next few years despite about CAD 300 million in cost overruns.

Expansion continued into the 1990s amid poor performance. In 1988, Husky carried out a takeover of Canterra Energy Ltd., a large Calgary-based conventional oil company, in a deal that made Husky one of the 10 largest oil and gas producers in Canada. The company also built a gas-processing plant north of Calgary, but lost out on a potentially lucrative supplier for the plant. In 1990 Shell Canada Ltd. and Husky were battling over who would develop a major gas discovery near the town of Caroline, a village 100 miles northwest of Calgary. Once partners, the two companies now had competing proposals for development. The town of Caroline favored Shell's proposal, which would build a new gas plant nearby. Husky, on the other hand, wanted to transport the gas 35 miles by pipeline to its Ram River gas plant. Shell's plan won approval that fall from the Alberta Resources Conservation Board.

HONG KONG TAKING CHARGE: 1992

By 1992, it was clear that Blair's aggressive expansion had only pulled Husky further into debt. The company lost CAD 315 billion in 1991. Once again, Li stepped in with an offer from his Hutchison Whampoa holding company. He negotiated a deal late in 1991 to buy Nova's remaining 43 percent stake in Husky for approximately CAD 325 million. Li then took a stronger hand in management of the company. He sent John Chin-Sung Lau to Husky in 1992 as vice president. Although Lau had no experience in the oil industry, he had successfully turned around some of Li's other businesses with a strict focus on efficiency and profits.

Lau's first years at Husky were rocky, and employees felt that Lau and President Art Price were competing for their loyalty. Price eventually resigned in mid-1993, and Lau became CEO. Now the undisputed leader, he set about ridding the company of useless undeveloped properties, laid off hundreds of employees, and scrapped the company's "quality work environment" initiative. *Canadian Business* wrote that Husky was gaining a reputation as a bad place to work, marred by reports of sexual harassment and disrespect toward female employees. A former employee was quoted as saying, "Lau was very hardnosed, all teeth and claws. He was very abrasive." Nevertheless, by 1996 Husky was performing better and Lau was declaring himself willing to give employees more access to management. The company made a CAD 35 million profit in 1996 on revenues of CAD 2.11 billion.

The Lloydminster upgrader was also emerging from years of dismal performance. The upgrader began operation in 1992 and lost CAD 140 million in the first three years of operation, due to the fact that the cost of upgrading was higher than the heavy oil-light oil price differential. The federal and provincial Alberta governments sold their stakes in the project in 1994, but Husky and the Saskatchewan government held on to 50 percent stakes in the hopes that the facility would eventually turn a profit. Eventually the upgrader reorganized to operate more efficiently, the price differential improved, and the upgrader made a combined CAD 26 million in 1996 and 1997. Saskatchewan managed to recover all the money it had put into the project and sold its interest to Husky for CAD 310 million in 1998.

LOOKING EASTWARD: 1998–99

With a financial situation that looked fairly secure in the short term, Husky began to focus more attention on projects that held promise for long-term profits. The Canadian oil industry began extensively developing properties off the east coast of Canada by the late 1990s. Husky had a minority interest in the second project in the area, Terra Nova, and was the operator and majority holder for a third project, White Rose. Both properties were located in the Jeanne d'Arc Basin offshore of Newfoundland. Husky had been exploring in the east coast area since 1982 and then invested heavily there in 1998 and 1999.

Extensive work at Terra Nova began in mid-1998, when a floating production and storage system was constructed. Production commenced there in January 2002 after delays. The White Rose project was in an earlier stage of development. Husky, working with partner Petro-Canada, struck oil on the site in 1999, but subsequent drilling in 2000 was less promising. After carefully reconsidering the prospects at White Rose, Husky announced in March 2002 that it would move ahead with development.

The company was also looking even farther east, working on projects in China. In April 1998 Husky began testing production from wells in the Pucheng oilfield in Henan Province, in a joint venture with China National Petroleum Corporation. In late 2000 the company also signed an agreement to develop two fields in the South China Sea with the China National Offshore Oil Corporation. Other expansion included the purchase of Mohawk Canada Limited for CAD 102 million in July 1998. The acquisition added about 300 gas stations and an ethanol plant to Husky's assets. Profits were rising steadily after 1998, with net earnings in 1999 reaching CAD 43 million on revenues of CAD 2.79 billion.

PUBLIC DEBUT AT THE MILLENNIUM

In the summer of 2000 Husky took a step that catapulted it into the leading ranks of Canada's oil and gas producers. The company merged with a smaller public oil concern, Renaissance Energy Ltd., for approximately CAD 3.02 million. The combined company, renamed Husky Energy Inc., took over Renaissance Energy's listing on the Toronto Stock Exchange. When the deal was announced, there was some negative reaction to the idea of a large private company swallowing a small public company, and Husky tried to build trust by releasing an unprecedented amount of information about its finances and operations. When the deal went through, Li and his family controlled about 70 percent of the new public company. Husky's leadership said that Renaissance, which worked primarily with small low-risk oil pools in western Canada, would provide steady income to finance capital development at the offshore Newfoundland fields, expand retail stations in Canada, and work with oil sands in Alberta.

Husky sparkled during its first decade in the public spotlight, distributing more than CAD 6 billion in dividends and achieving a total shareholder return of 490 percent between 2000 and 2009. Revenue soared during the decade, increasing threefold to more than CAD 15 billion. Profits climbed at a greater pace, swelling from CAD 400 million to CAD 1.4 billion. The decade confirmed Lau's legacy as an astute leader, marking the end of an 18-year tenure at Husky that saw the company's financial totals increase exponentially.

FAST-PACED EXPANSION: 2003–09

The growth during the period came from Lau's bold moves on the expansion front. In 2003 Husky paid $588 million to acquire assets owned by Marathon Canada Limited, a subsidiary of U.S.-based Marathon

Oil Corporation. The purchase added proven reserves of 39.8 million barrels of oil equivalent (boe) and daily production of 27,000 boe, 28 percent of which the company immediately sold to Houston, Texas-based EOG Resources Inc. for $320 million. After the transaction, Lau vowed to complete further deals, saying he was searching for acquisitions ranging in price from $1 billion to $2 billion.

Progress with the White Rose project provided the next highlight of the decade, as years of planning, construction, and considerable investment began to bear fruit. Production at the property began in November 2005 and the first shipment of crude oil, 600,000 barrels, occurred one month later. By May 2006, after the completion of a fourth production well, the company had achieved daily production of 100,000 barrels at White Rose. As daily production climbed at the White Rose site, another development project reached fruition. After two years of construction, the company completed work on the Tucker Oil Sands project in mid-2006, a property with an expected life span of 35 years. Husky anticipated extracting approximately 350 million barrels of bitumen from the Tucker property.

A major acquisition followed the success of the first steam injections at the Tucker site, one that strengthened the company's presence in the United States. In 2007 Husky acquired a refinery in Lima, Ohio, from Valero Energy Corp. The company paid Valero $1.9 billion for the refinery, which had a daily capacity of 165,000 barrels. The refinery supplied gasoline to the company's service stations in Ontario, the number of which quadrupled after Husky acquired 98 stations from Suncor Energy in late 2009.

NEW LEADERSHIP: 2010

Shortly after purchasing the service stations, Husky announced its capital improvement budget for 2010. The company earmarked $3.1 billion to spend on its development projects in Canada and Southeast Asia, a 20 percent increase over the budget for 2009. The responsibility for determining the allocation of the fund fell to a new CEO. In February 2010, Lau announced his retirement as president and CEO, revealing his plans to move to Hong Kong where he planned to lead the development of Husky's businesses in the Asia-Pacific region. His replacement was announced in May 2010,

signaling the start of a new era for Husky. Asim Ghosh, who had joined Husky's board of directors in May 2009, took the helm. Formerly the CEO of India's Vodafone Essar Limited, Ghosh built the cellular phone company into one of the largest in the world, realizing impressive success he hoped to emulate at Husky.

Sarah Ruth Lorenz
Updated, Jeffrey L. Covell

PRINCIPAL SUBSIDIARIES

Husky Oil Operations Limited; Husky Oil Limited Partnership; Husky Terra Nova Partnership; Husky Downstream General Partnership; Husky Energy Marketing Partnership; Sunrise Oil Sands Partnership (50%); BP Husky Refining LLC (50%); Lima Refining Company; Husky Marketing and Supply Company.

PRINCIPAL COMPETITORS

Imperial Oil Limited; Shell Canada Limited; Suncor Energy Inc.

FURTHER READING

Burton, Brian, "Making the Grade: Husky Oil Steps Boldly Where the Multinationals Wouldn't Go," *Oilweek*, November 16, 1992, p. 20.

Carlisle, Tamsin, "Husky Oil Agrees to $2.06 Billion Plan to Purchase Renaissance Energy Ltd.," *Wall Street Journal*, June 20, 2000, p. C21.

"Husky Energy Appoints New President & Chief Executive Officer," *Marketwire Canada*, May 21, 2010.

Hutchinson, Brian, "Energy Roughneck," *Canadian Business*, August 1996, pp. 20–23.

"A Joint Venture of Canada's Husky Oil and China National Petroleum Corp.," *Oil and Gas Journal*, April 6, 1998, p. 3.

McMurdy, Deirdre, "A Billionaire's Bargain," *Maclean's*, November 4, 1991, p. 48.

Sharpe, Sydney, "Scratching at the Door," *Financial Post*, March 29, 1997, p. 12.

"Takeover Dogfight," *Canadian Business*, September 1988, p. 158.

Warn, Ken, "Husky in Talks with Chinese Oil Group," *Financial Times*, February 20, 2002, p. 33.

Westell, Dan, "Husky Energy Acquires Marathon Assets," *Financial Times*, August 21, 2003, p. 16.

International Youth Hostel Federation

2nd Floor, Gate House
Fretherne Road
Welwyn Garden City, Hertfordshire AL8 6RD
United Kingdom
Telephone: (+44 17 07) 324-170
Fax: (+44 17 07) 323-980
Web site: http://www.hihostels.com

Nonprofit Organization
Founded: 1909
Employees: 19
NAICS: 721199 All Other Traveler Accommodations

■ ■ ■

International Youth Hostel Federation is a nonprofit organization that oversees the operation of affiliated youth hostel associations worldwide. Operating under the brand name Hostelling International, the organization sets standards that members must comply with, including matters related to cleanliness, security, and privacy. Each year 35 million overnight stays are recorded at the more than 4,000 hostels in 80 countries governed by the organization. International Youth Hostel Federation hosts an annual conference for member organizations as part of its efforts to promote and to support national and regional youth hostel associations.

RICHARD SCHIRRMANN'S VISION

A century before the hostel industry generated more than $1 billion in annual revenue, the concept for the worldwide movement was born. Generations of travelers looking to save money on lodging were indebted to the groundwork laid by Richard Schirrmann, who conceived the idea of student hostels while he was working as a teacher in the Westphalia region of Prussia. His vision inspired an international movement, fanning the development of national associations whose roots could be traced to August 26, 1909, to the night of Schirrmann's epiphany.

Born in Prussia in 1874, Schirrmann followed in the footsteps of his father, earning his teacher's certification in 1895. He was sent to Altena, Westphalia, in 1903, where his teaching philosophy took shape, an ideology centered on the adverse effect industrialization had on students. As often as he could, he escaped to the countryside, taking his students along with him, creating what he termed a "wandering school" that placed an emphasis on learning by direct observation. Schirrmann's excursions and hiking trips frequently lasted several days, which introduced him to the need that youth hostels would fulfill.

On August 26, 1909, a thunderstorm forced Schirrmann's group of students to search for shelter in the Bröl Valley. Caught in a downpour, the group found refuge in a school building, where they were offered a night's stay in a classroom by the school's headmaster and straw bedding and milk by a local farmer. While his students slept and the storm raged on, Schirrmann thought about his predicament—not the first time he had been forced to bivouac in the countryside—and he developed a solution. He envisioned using schools to provide lodging during holidays, turning vacated buildings into youth hostels, or *Volksschülerherbergen*, that

Our Mission: To promote the education of all young people of all nations, but especially young people of limited means, by encouraging in them a greater knowledge, love and care of the countryside and an appreciation of the cultural values of towns and cities in all parts of the world, and as ancillary thereto, to provide hostels or other accommodation in which there shall be no distinctions of race, nationality, colour, religion, sex, class or political opinions and thereby to develop a better understanding of their fellow men, both at home and abroad.

would provide safe, inexpensive housing for students traveling from village to village.

FIRST HOSTEL OPENED: 1912

Schirrmann wrote an essay about his ideas for *Volksschülerherbergen* in 1910. The publication of the article attracted immediate support for his proposal, giving him the resources to realize his vision, although the idea of using schools as hostels was abandoned from the start. Schirrmann established his first, full-fledged hostel in Altena, using the donations he had received to restore a dilapidated castle in the town and remodel according to his design. In 1912 the Altena hostel opened, featuring dormitories for male and female students with triple-tier bunks, a kitchen, washrooms, and a shower bath.

Once the first youth hostel was opened, observers of Schirrmann's concept wasted little time before following suit. Although Schirrmann was an active proponent of *Volksschülerherbergen*, the strides achieved by the hostelling movement eclipsed the efforts of a single individual. The adoption of the concept spread with the speed of a wildfire. One year after the Altena hostel opened, there were 83 youth hostels in operation, providing 21,000 overnight stays during the year. By 1921, the number of overnight stays had soared to 500,000, as other countries formed regional associations of youth hostels. Although they had used Schirrmann's concept as their blueprint, the other European countries that had begun opening hostels did so independently, rarely communicating with each other or with Schirrmann.

Fiefdoms of hostel organizations developed throughout Europe, creating a patchwork of autonomous entities that gradually developed into national bodies. By 1931 there were 12 national associations of

youth hostels existing in Europe, together governing the operation of 2,600 hostels. Schirrmann's idea had proven to be immensely popular: More hostels were opened in the first 20 years of the movement than were opened in the next 80 years. By the early 1930s, as the number of hostels proliferated, there was a need to lend cohesion to the sprawling growth, setting the stage for the creation of the International Youth Hostel Federation.

HOSTELS UNITE: 1932

The leaders of the hostel movement met for the first time in a hotel. In October 1932 the first international conference of the hostel movement was held in Amsterdam. In attendance were the representatives from 11 national associations: Belgium, Czechoslovakia, Denmark, England and Wales, France, Germany, Ireland, Netherlands, Norway, Poland, and Switzerland. Schirrmann, representing the German association, attended the gathering and, befitting his contributions to the movement, was elected president of the newly formed International Youth Hostelling Federation. For the first time, hostels were unified under one organizational umbrella that determined standards, controlled membership, and provided support to member organizations. The formation of a central body, necessary in the early 1930s in Europe, became critical as the popularity of the movement spread, exporting Schirrmann's vision to Africa, Asia, North and South America, Australia, and New Zealand.

The establishment of an international governing body created a framework for international expansion. Attendees at the second international meeting in 1933 included Americans Isabel and Monroe Smith, who returned home and began organizing a national association to oversee the operation of hostels in the United States. They opened the first U.S. youth hostel in Northfield, Massachusetts, in 1934, an event that marked the birth of American Youth Hostels. As had occurred 20 years earlier in Germany, the opening of the first hostel in the United States quickly led to the establishment of other hostels. Within a year of its formation, American Youth Hostels comprised a network of more than 30 hostels scattered throughout New England, drawing widespread support and the backing of the country's president, Franklin D. Roosevelt, who served as American Youth Hostel's honorary president in 1936.

GROWTH CHECKED BY WORLD WAR II

On both sides of the Atlantic Ocean, the network of hostels affiliated with the International Youth Hostel Federation was expanding. Drawing support from

KEY DATES

1909: Richard Schirrmann envisions using vacated school buildings as hostels.

1912: First full-time hostel opens in a renovated castle.

1932: Hostel operators from 11 nations gather in Amsterdam and form the International Youth Hostel Federation.

1945: Rebuilding efforts begin after the hostel movement's decline during World War II.

1974: At the 30th International Youth Hostel Federation Conference, 49 nations are represented.

2009: International Youth Hostel Federation celebrates its centennial.

recreational clubs, individual supporters, and corporate sponsors, the International Youth Hostel Federation flourished during its first decade, but the organization's efforts to extend its reach were derailed before it could celebrate its 10th anniversary. War clouds were gathering in Europe and soon hostilities would spread throughout the world, stalling the growth of the hostelling movement. Schirrmann was the first to experience the effects of Adolf Hitler's rise to power on hostelling. In 1936 the National Socialist government led by Hitler removed Schirrmann from his post as president of the International Youth Hostel Federation. Elsewhere, as nations readied for war, the push to open new hostels lost momentum. In 1940, the first full year of the war, there were only 91 overnight stays at hostels by those traveling to another country, with roughly one-quarter of all rooms occupied by soldiers.

The end of World War II marked the beginning of a rebuilding period for the International Youth Hostel Federation. Schirrmann, no longer constrained by the toppled Nazi government, began reestablishing the German youth hostel system, a monumental task that would fill his days until his death in 1961. In the United States, the American Youth Hostel organization resumed where it had left off at the start of the war. The International Youth Hostel Federation affiliate incorporated as a nonprofit organization in 1949 and opened its first association-owned hostel in Indiana in 1954. New hostel associations in other parts of the world made their debut during the period as well.

In 1957 the Kenya Youth Hostel Association was formed, giving the International Youth Hostel Federa-

tion a presence in Africa that soon led to the formation of national associations in Egypt, Sudan, Ghana, and a handful of other African nations. The movement spread to Asia as well during the post-World War II era, before moving south and securing a foothold in Australia and New Zealand. By the beginning of the jet age, the International Youth Hostel Federation stood as a truly global force, holding sway as one of the world's largest travel organizations.

CHARACTERISTICS OF
HOSTELLING EVOLVE: 1970–99

As rebuilding efforts gave way to robust expansion, several factors worked to hostelling's advantage. Commercial air travel and the advent of jet airplanes reduced the time and the cost required to travel great distances. Additionally, baby boomers came of age, creating a surge in the number of young adults and adults that traveled. For many, staying at inexpensive hostels became a popular lodging option, evinced by the growing stature of the International Youth Hostel Federation. At the organization's 30th conference in 1974, 185 delegates and guests attended, representing hostel associations in 49 countries.

In the decades to follow, the formation of new national and regional youth hostel associations expanded the network the International Youth Hostel Federation governed. The organization reinvested the revenue it generated from its activities into the network, which enabled hostels in remote locations to share in the proceeds produced by the most popular hostels. The International Youth Hostel Federation's operating surpluses also were used to stimulate the hostelling ethic through promotional efforts that raised awareness of its member associations.

The years from the 1980s to the beginning of the 21st century witnessed significant changes in the types of hostels in operation and in their clientele. Nearly a century after Schirrmann had envisioned providing inexpensive, dormitory lodging for German school students, hostels had evolved considerably. Although large dormitories continued to exist, particularly in massive, 600-bed urban hostels (something Schirrmann would have viewed as an abomination of *Volksschülerherbergen*), private and semiprivate rooms began to appear in hostels. Other changes in the characteristics defining the hostelling movement emerged as well. Students no longer represented the International Youth Hostel Federation's sole target audience, as adults, families, and senior citizens began using hostels frequently. The broadening of its customer base led the International Youth Hostel Federation to adopt Hostelling International as the brand name for the organization in the mid-1990s, a name that reflected the universal appeal of hostels.

The International Youth Hostel Federation continued to expand and exert its influence over its member associations in the 21st century. On the expansion front, the notable event during the period was the inclusion of China as a member in 2006. Although hostels existed in China prior to its acceptance by the International Youth Hostel Federation, the facilities did not meet the standards demanded by the organization. As the organization began ensuring that its affiliated hostels in China reached its standards, it began introducing a new set of criteria for the more than 4,000 other hostels it governed.

The organization began augmenting the "Assured Standards" program that had been in place for years with what it called "HI-Q, the HI Quality Management System," which focused on hostel management and operations. The worldwide implementation of the HI-Q program was underway as the organization celebrated its 100th anniversary in 2009, recognizing its birth as the night Schirrmann listened to a thunderstorm while pioneering the concept of hostels.

Jeffrey L. Covell

PRINCIPAL COMPETITORS

A&O Hotels and Hostels; Hostelworld.com Ltd.; Meininger City Hostels; St. Christopher's Inns.

FURTHER READING

"Chinese Hostels Join International Federation," *Business Daily Update*, July 25, 2006.

Fuller, Sharon, "Groups Aim to Appreciate the World through Hostelling," *St. Louis Post-Dispatch*, August 9, 2001, p. 18.

Ordaz, Daniel Garcia, "Hostelling 101," *Valley Morning Star*, January 23, 2006.

Petersen, Scott, "Hostels Going Upscale for Sophisticated Crowd," *Winnipeg Free Press*, July 8, 2006, p. E8.

"Step into Hostel Terrain with New Options," *Boston Herald*, December 21, 1997, p. 82.

Irving Oil Limited

201 Crown Street
Saint John, New Brunswick E2L 5E5
Canada
Telephone: (506) 202-2000
Fax: (506) 202-3868
Web site: http://www.irvingoil.com

Private Company
Founded: 1924
Employees: 7,000
Sales: $6.14 billion (2009)
NAICS: 324110 Petroleum Refineries; 324191 Petroleum Lubricating Oil and Grease Manufacturing; 424720 Petroleum and Petroleum Products Merchant Wholesalers (Except Bulk Stations and Terminals); 424710 Petroleum Bulk Stations and Terminals; 447110 Gasoline Stations with Convenience Stores

■ ■ ■

Irving Oil Limited is a vertically integrated energy company involved in the processing, transportation, and sale of petroleum products. Irving Oil operates the largest refinery in Canada, a facility that produces more than 300,000 barrels of finished energy products per day, including gasoline, jet fuel, home heating fuel, ultra-low-sulfur gasoline, and diesel. The company owns 13 marine terminals, a delivery fleet of tractor-trailers, and a fleet of tankers. Irving Oil's retail operations comprise more than 700 service stations. The company, owned and managed by the Irving family, operates throughout eastern Canada and in the northeastern United States.

THE IRVING PATRIARCHS

There was no bigger name in New Brunswick than the Irving name, representing a family dynasty that dominated the province's commerce for more than a century. The influence of the family spread throughout Atlantic Canada and into the northeastern United States, extending its reach into shipbuilding, forestry, trucking, media, and consumer products businesses. An estimated CAD 7 billion filled the family's coffers, the fortune amassed by four generations of Irving family members who built on the foundation laid by James Durgavel (J. D.) Irving in the late 19th century.

The son of Scottish immigrants, J. D. Irving established the epicenter of the Irving empire in Bouctouche, New Brunswick, a rural community located on the province's east coast. In 1882, he purchased a small sawmill in Bouctouche, the start of an enterprise that would grow to include a gristmill for grain refining, a carding mill for textile manufacturing, a general store, and three farms. The businesses became part of J. D. Irving, Ltd., a company transformed into a conglomerate by J. D. Irving's son, Kenneth Colin (K. C.) Irving, who also started the family's most profitable business, Irving Oil.

Born in Bouctouche in 1899, K. C. Irving figured as one of Canada's most accomplished business leaders. Prone to schoolyard fights in his youth, K. C. Irving attempted to enlist in the Canadian Expeditionary Force at the start of World War I, but his father intervened,

COMPANY PERSPECTIVES

Our purpose is to be the regional market leader in processing, transporting and marketing finished energy products, as well as offering complementary products and services, to consumers. We will work together to achieve our purpose by focusing on our core competencies of customer service and supply chain management. We will succeed by consistently adding value to our knowledge and physical assets, creating mutual value with our human resources, and for our customers. We are a principled organization in which all stakeholder relationships appreciate over the long-term. We are distinguished by our belief in the worth of an individual and in the meaning of a promise.

demanding he enroll at Acadia University instead. K. C. Irving followed his father's orders and attended the Nova Scotia-based institution, but he left before completing his studies. He embarked on a cross-country trip, heading west to British Columbia, and when he returned he succeeded in joining the war effort. K. C. Irving entered the Royal Flying Corps as a fighter pilot, but hostilities ended before he saw any action. When he returned to Bouctouche following the war, his entrepreneurial zeal was unleashed.

FORMATION OF IRVING OIL: 1924

K. C. Irving began operating a small service station and garage, setting out on his own rather than joining his father's company. The station, opened in 1924, served as a Ford sub-dealership and sold Esso gasoline, but Irving soon became irritated with Esso's parent company, Imperial Oil, and expressed his independent inclinations again. When Imperial Oil set up another Esso dealer in Bouctouche, Irving promptly stopped selling gasoline under the Esso name and began using his own brand, Primrose.

As an aviator, Irving fully understood the importance of fuel quality to an engine's performance. For Primrose, he used gasoline that was blended with a higher octane level than the Esso-branded fuel, which made the hand-cranked engines of the era easier to start. His industriousness, his skills as a mechanic, and his ability to relate to customers distinguished Irving further, giving him advantages over competitors that drove his business forward. A second service station opened in 1925, as Irving began to tighten his hold on

the Bouctouche market, but soon his hometown success led him to larger pastures.

RETAIL NETWORK GROWS: 1931–51

In 1931 Irving was offered the Ford dealership franchise in Saint John, the largest city in New Brunswick. Saint John became the new hub of the Irving family businesses, home to Irving Oil and, after Irving's father's death in 1933, home to J. D. Irving, Ltd. Although the 1930s presented Irving with a harsh economic climate, the decade saw the ambitious entrepreneur realize his first significant burst of growth. He opened a lubricants packaging and blending plant in Saint John that heralded the launch of a line of Irving-branded motor oils. He also began turning his retail operation into a chain. The dirt roads of New Brunswick and in neighboring provinces were being paved during the 1930s, increasing the flow of traffic just as Irving began opening new service stations. In selecting sites for new Irving Oil units, he favored locations at a town's entrance, putting up signs that read, "Follow the Irving signs and you can't go wrong."

After expanding throughout New Brunswick, Irving extended the reach of his retail operations into adjoining provinces. The Irving Oil chain stretched into Nova Scotia and made its first move out of the Maritime provinces during the early 1940s when new service stations began appearing in Quebec. When Newfoundland became the 10th Canadian province in 1949, Irving Oil established a presence on the island, widening the scope of its operations during the postwar economic boom period. K. C. Irving's sons joined him at Irving Oil just as the economic climate brightened. Arthur Irving joined the company in 1951 and his brother Jack Irving followed a year later. Under their father's guidance, the second generation of Irving Oil's leadership took on particular duties at the company. Arthur Irving spearheaded the expansion of the company's retail operations, recruiting managers for new service stations and converting acquired service stations to the Irving Oil brand. Jack Irving oversaw the company's construction and engineering projects, devoting his time to strengthening Irving Oil's infrastructure.

REFINERY BEGINS OPERATION: 1960

By the mid-1950s Irving Oil was a formidable force in Atlantic Canada. The company operated terminals stretching from Montreal, Quebec, to St. John's, Newfoundland, facilities used with increasing frequency by

KEY DATES

1924: Kenneth Colin (K. C.) Irving opens his first service station.

1960: To supply its chain of service stations, Irving Oil builds its own refinery.

1972: Entry into the United States is gained by opening a service station in Bangor, Maine.

1997: Irving Oil spends CAD 1.5 billion to upgrade its Saint John refinery.

2009: After announcing plans to build a second refinery, Irving Oil cancels the project.

tankers transporting petroleum products from South America and refineries located in the U.S. Gulf Coast. Major oil companies had taken note of Irving Oil, which gave K. C. Irving the opportunity to hatch plans for his most ambitious undertaking. He wanted to build his own refinery, a massive project that required the assistance of a major oil company. Irving succeeded in finding a partner, signing an agreement with Chevron that entailed selling 49 percent of Irving Oil to the oil giant in exchange for the financial and technical help required to build a refinery.

In 1960, a momentous juncture in Irving Oil's history, the refinery began operating with an initial capacity of 40,000 barrels per day (b/d). During the first half-century of its operation, the Saint John refinery produced enough gasoline to drive across Canada 128 million times, enough jet fuel to fly a Boeing 747 around the world 28,000 times, and enough home heating fuel to heat 150,000 homes for 150 winters.

As a refiner with the ability to process the petroleum products it sold, Irving Oil became a decidedly more powerful and profitable enterprise after 1960. The company gained greater ability to compete alongside far bigger rivals such as BP, Gulf, Fina, Texaco, Shell, and Esso, and the profits generated by entry into the refining business enabled K. C. Irving and his two sons to become more ambitious in their growth plans. In 1970 the company had the financial power to build the Irving Canaport, the first deepwater terminal in the Western Hemisphere, a facility located at the entrance to Saint John Harbour that gave Irving Oil the ability to accommodate ultra-large crude carriers. The following year the company expanded the capacity of its refinery, increasing production to 160,000 b/d, which enabled Irving Oil to produce jet fuel, asphalt, and bunker fuel.

REFINERY UPGRADE AND U.S. EXPANSION: 1971–74

A new era in Irving Oil's history began when K. C. Irving retired in 1972. Arthur Irving, 42 years old at the time, became president of Irving Oil and his brother Jack Irving assumed the duties of executive vice president. Arthur Irving incorporated a convenience store concept into the company's retail operations during the decade, unveiling stores that operated under the name "Maritime Product Bar." Jack Irving, concentrating on Irving Oil's infrastructure, also made strides in the 1970s, overseeing the expansion of the refinery in 1974 that increased production to 250,000 b/d and ordering the construction of four new tankers, which increased the size of Irving Oil's fleet to 10 vessels.

The flurry of activity in the early 1970s included a major expansion southward. The company entered the U.S. market in 1972 when it opened a service station in Bangor, Maine. From Bangor, Irving Oil began to spread its presence throughout New England, using a marketing office in Portsmouth, New Hampshire, to oversee its growth in the world's largest gasoline market. The company's U.S. business was owned entirely by the Irving family, which necessitated a separate Irving Oil logo to distinguish the stores from the Canadian stores owned partly by Chevron. In 1986 the company's U.S. operations secured a quick injection of growth with the acquisition of D. W. Small, a company that operated a chain of stores called "Maineway." The chain was rebranded, eventually adopting the name "Mainway."

The separate branding of Irving service stations in the United States and Canada ended during the late 1980s. In 1988, after Chevron and Irving Oil decided to pursue different business strategies, Irving Oil acquired all of the shares purchased by Chevron in the late 1950s. The transaction left the Irving family in full control of its sprawling enterprise.

During the 1980s a new facet of Irving Oil's business appeared, but the venture failed to find a permanent place in the company's operations. PRO-CARE service centers began appearing during the decade, a retail concept that featured four service bays and large inventories of car parts. Each unit was staffed with certified mechanics, but changes in engine technology caused the service market to shrink just as Irving Oil stepped up its expansion efforts in the sector. As business slowed, the company began replacing its PRO-CARE service centers with units that carried convenience store items such as beverages, dairy products, and groceries.

AN ENORMOUS UNDERTAKING: 1997–2001

The 1990s witnessed the greatest single capital investment in Irving Oil's history. The Saint John refinery, which had been last upgraded in 1974, became a hub of activity starting in 1997 when the company began "The King of Cats" project. Irving Oil spent CAD 1.5 billion during the four-year project that employed 3,500 workers at its peak. The upgrade, completed in 2001, increased the refinery's capacity to refine heavier, more acidic crude oil, and increased production to 300,000 b/d, or nearly eight times the daily production of the original facility. The project also enabled Irving Oil to produce ultra-low-sulfur gasoline and to meet California's strict environmental standards for gasoline years before mandated by governmental regulation. The company became a major supplier to the California market and in 2003 became the first oil company to receive a Clean Air Excellence Award from the U.S. Environmental Protection Agency.

During the first decade of the 21st century, Irving Oil represented a powerful force in the petroleum industry. The company was responsible for 64 percent of Canada's petroleum product exports to the United States, 55 percent of New Brunswick's foreign exports, and it accounted for nearly one-fifth of gasoline imports to the United States. Another indication of the company's stature emerged in 2006, when the Saint John refinery processed the two billionth barrel of crude oil in its history. Reaching the milestone should have been the news of the year for Irving Oil, but an announcement late in the year rivaled its significance.

PLANS FOR SECOND REFINERY: 2006–09

In October 2006 reports surfaced that Irving Oil was contemplating building a second refinery. In January 2007 the rumors were confirmed when the company started the regulatory process for constructing a new refinery by applying for environmental permits from authorities in Ottawa and New Brunswick. Irving Oil began moving forward on the project, planning to build a CAD 7 billion refinery in Saint John with a production capacity of 300,000 b/d.

In March 2008 Irving Oil formed a partnership with a major oil company much like it had with Chevron in the late 1950s. British oil giant BP and Irving Oil entered into a memorandum of understanding to jointly work on the engineering, design, and feasibility of the mammoth project, a phase in the refinery's development that was expected to take between 12 and 15 months and cost more than $100 million. Once both parties agreed to commit to the project, construction would begin in 2011, possibly taking as long as eight years to complete.

As Irving Oil and BP scrutinized the details of the project, economic conditions deteriorated rapidly. A global economic crisis at the end of the decade derailed plans for a second refinery, with BP and Irving Oil announcing in July 2009 that they would not proceed with the project. Although the aborted project represented a disappointment to Irving Oil, the company stood on solid ground, well equipped to weather the uncertain economic times. A CAD 220 million investment in the Saint John refinery in late 2009 reflected the long-term confidence of the company. Preparing for better times ahead, the Irving family appeared destined to leave an indelible mark on Canadian business for years to come.

Jeffrey L. Covell

PRINCIPAL SUBSIDIARIES

Irving Oil Corporation; Irving Oil Inc.; Irving Oil Marketing Limited.

PRINCIPAL COMPETITORS

Getty Petroleum Marketing Inc.; Imperial Oil Limited; Suncor Energy Inc.

FURTHER READING

Goodwin, Daniel, "$1-Billion Upgrade Prepares Canadian Refinery for Future Specs," *Oil and Gas Journal*, March 27, 2000, p. 45.

"Irving Oil and BP Will Not Proceed with Proposed Second Refinery," *CNW Group*, July 24, 2009.

"Irving Oil's Saint John Refinery Reaches Two Billion Barrel Milestone," *CNW Group*, March 1, 2006.

"Irving Passes on Most Acquisitions, but Eyes $20 Million New England C-Store Expansion," *Oil Express*, July 14, 2003, p. 5.

"2004 Refiner of the Year—Irving Oil," *World Refining*, April 2004, p. 36.

J. D. Irving, Limited

300 Union Street
Saint John, New Brunswick E2L 4M3
Canada
Telephone: (506) 632-7777
Fax: (506) 648-2205
Web site: http://www.jdirving.com

Private Company
Founded: 1882
Employees: 15,000
NAICS: 115310 Support Activities for Forestry; 236115 Single Family Housing Construction; 321113 Sawmills; 322299 All Other Converted Paper Product Manufacturing; 324110 Petroleum Refineries; 423860 Transportation Equipment and Supplies (Except Motor Vehicles) Merchant Wholesalers; 444110 Home Centers; 444190 Other Building Material Dealers; 447190 Other Gasoline Stations

■ ■ ■

J. D. Irving, Limited, (JDI) is a family-owned conglomerate that dominates several industries in the Canadian Maritimes. JDI, managed by the Irving family, ranks as Canada's second-largest privately owned pulp and paper producer. The company owns four shipyards, three trucking companies, a railroad, vast tracts of timberlands, and numerous newspapers and radio stations. JDI also controls several consumer products, distribution, industrial equipment, and construction companies, as well as a chain of home improvement stores. The Irving family's holdings also include Irving Oil Limited, a gasoline, oil, and natural gas producer and exporter. JDI operates throughout Canada and maintains a substantial presence in Maine and New York.

19TH-CENTURY ORIGINS

The sprawling business empire owned and managed by the Irving family traced its roots to the entrepreneurial efforts of James Durgavel (J. D.) Irving. The son of Scottish immigrants, J. D. Irving started his namesake business in Bouctouche, New Brunswick, a rural community located on the province's east coast. In 1882, when he was 22 years old, Irving purchased a small sawmill in Bouctouche, establishing a business foundation that his descendants would develop into an influential, dominant force. "You used to hear about there being company towns," a professor at the University of New Brunswick said in the October 18, 2008 edition of the *Hamilton Spectator*. "We have a company province."

The rise of one of Canada's most powerful families began with the Bouctouche sawmill. Irving expanded the business in subsequent years, adding a gristmill for grinding grain, a carding mill for manufacturing textiles, a general store, and three farms. His efforts turned Bouctouche into a company town, a community whose economy was controlled by and dependent upon JDI. The leap in stature from a local to a provincial force was completed by his son, Kenneth Colin (K. C.) Irving, regarded as one of the greatest figures in Canadian business history.

COMPANY PERSPECTIVES

Our growth is driven by a set of consistent fundamental values through the years: uncompromising quality in making our products and committed service to our valued customers; an unwavering focus on continuous improvement and innovation in our diverse businesses; and a responsibility to make a positive difference in our communities, where we are proud to live and work, as well as to the health of the land, air and water that sustains our world.

SECOND GENERATION LED BY K. C. IRVING

Born in Bouctouche in 1899, K. C. Irving lived until the age of 93, devoting his life to making JDI one of the most powerful conglomerates in North America. His contributions to expanding the family business were enormous and demonstrated his insatiable appetite for diversification. Prone to schoolyard fights in his youth, K. C. Irving attempted to enlist in the Canadian Expeditionary Force at the start of World War I, but his father intervened, demanding he enroll at Acadia University instead. K. C. Irving followed his father's orders and attended the Nova Scotia-based institution, but he left before completing his studies. He embarked on a cross-country trip, heading west to British Columbia, and when he returned he succeeded in joining the war effort. K. C. Irving entered the Royal Flying Corps as a fighter pilot, but hostilities ended before he saw any action. When he returned to Bouctouche following the war, his entrepreneurial zeal was unleashed.

Arguably, K. C. Irving's single greatest achievement during his lengthy professional career was one of his first moves on the business front. In 1924, when he was 25 years old, Irving formed Irving Oil Limited, establishing his first retail location in Bouctouche. The foray into the energy sector, destined to be the family's most profitable business nearly a century later, proved to be instrumental to Irving's diversification efforts in the years to follow. The profits generated by Irving Oil's gas and oil business provided the seed money for JDI's expansion into the transportation, construction, industrial, and retail sectors, giving Irving the financial fuel to drive JDI's growth.

Irving left Bouctouche in 1931, drawn from his hometown to open a Ford dealership and a lubricants plant in New Brunswick's largest city, Saint John. JDI's main offices soon made the move as well, as control of the family business passed from one generation to the next. J. D. Irving died in 1933, leaving K. C. Irving in command. K. C. Irving expanded into other sectors of the forestry business and diversified into retail food processing in the years leading up to World War II, as he established a presence throughout the Maritime provinces of New Brunswick, Nova Scotia, and Prince Edward Island.

THE IRVING EMPIRE TAKES SHAPE: 1933–69

The expansion and diversification completed during the 1930s was just the start for K. C. Irving. His most ambitious efforts were realized following World War II, when his three sons joined the family business and helped their father secure a stranglehold on economies in the Maritimes and across the border in Maine. The eldest of the third generation was James (J. K.) Irving, who gravitated toward the forestry interests controlled by JDI. Arthur Irving, born in 1931, was two years younger than J. K. Irving, the only member of the publicity-shy Irving family who could be described as a socialite. Arthur Irving found his niche in the family business by involving himself in operation of Irving Oil and JDI's other energy-related assets. The youngest of K. C. Irving's sons, John (Jack) Irving, was born in 1932. Jack Irving's specialty became overseeing the family's real estate holdings.

JDI's pace of growth was frenetic during the postwar years, moving in numerous directions. In the 1950s the company acquired pulp mills in Saint John and sawmills throughout New Brunswick, using the properties as a base to expand south into upstate New York, where JDI established a presence in the timber processing business. The decade also saw JDI purchase a shipyard in Saint John, launch several of its own trucking companies, and form heavy industry companies such as Irving Equipment.

The original focus of JDI, the forestry business, was expanded extensively during the 1960s, as K. C. Irving and his son J. K. assumed a near monopoly over the timber business in their region. JDI quickly became the largest forestry concern in the Maritimes and northern Maine through the acquisition of timberland, logging operations, and processing mills. The company also became the region's largest industrial competitor, establishing JDI subsidiaries involved in steel fabrication and prefabricated concrete. JDI delved into producing fertilizer and providing agricultural services through Cavendish Agri-Services, manufacturing personal care products such as tissue and paper towels under the brand names Majesta and Royale, and marketing frozen food through Cavendish Farms.

KEY DATES

■

1882: J. D. Irving purchases a sawmill in Bouctouche, New Brunswick.
1933: K. C. Irving takes control of the family business after his father's death.
1950s: J.D. Irving, Ltd., diversifies into shipbuilding, trucking, and manufacturing.
1970s: New businesses in retail, home construction, and communications broaden the scope of the company.
1992: Following K. C. Irving's death, control of the company passes to the third generation of the Irving family.
2007: J. D. Irving, Ltd., celebrates its 125th anniversary.

DIVERSIFICATION: 1970–79

The roster of JDI businesses expanded with each passing year. The company secured a foothold in marine towing and dredging through Atlantic Towing. It entered the railroad business through the purchase of New Brunswick Southern Railway. It began constructing modular homes through Kent Homes and it built a chain of home improvement stores that operated under the name Kent Building Supplies. The company's involvement in the trucking business intensified with the formation of Scot Trucks, as did its involvement in the shipbuilding business with the purchase of shipyards in Halifax, Pictou, Liverpool, Shelburne, and Georgetown, which made JDI the largest shipbuilder in Canada. The company also pushed headlong into the media business, purchasing more than two dozen newspapers and several radio and television stations. The spreading sprawl of JDI made the Irvings one of the most powerful families in Canada, a family that easily brushed aside any competitive threat in its region and a family that enjoyed a multibillion-dollar fortune.

Although his sons contributed to the growth of the company, K. C. Irving was credited with turning his father's forestry company into a business empire. JDI become one of the largest, privately owned family businesses in the world, and his death in 1992 marked a momentous juncture in the history of JDI. Control of the company passed to his three sons, with each taking control of broadly defined segments of JDI's diversified, vertically integrated business. J. K. Irving, the eldest son, inherited the forestry business. Next in line, Arthur Irving, took control of the energy business. The youngest

heir, Jack Irving, assumed responsibility for the family's activities in real estate, a far smaller segment of JDI's business than the two massive energy and forestry segments.

EXPANSION: 1990–99

As the third generation of leadership took hold of the reins of command, JDI continued to add to its influence. During the early 1990s, the company ranked as the second-largest privately owned pulp and paper producer in Canada, owning tissue, pulp, and newsprint mills in Saint John, a corrugated medium mill in St. George, New Brunswick, a tissue-converting plant in Dieppe, New Brunswick, and logging operations throughout the province. After acquiring one million acres of timberland in Maine in 1998, JDI became the largest private landowner in the state. Elsewhere in the Irving empire, the formidable presence of the company was spread across diverse industries, holding sway in diaper production, communications, construction, real estate, and retail. Estimates by the end of the 1990s put one in 12 New Brunswickers under the employ of JDI and its subsidiaries.

FOURTH GENERATION TAKES THE HELM AT THE MILLENNIUM

As JDI entered the 21st century, the fourth generation of the Irving family rose in prominence. Each of K. C. Irving's three sons began to give day-to-day control over the family business to their children. Jim Irving Jr., the oldest son of J. K. Irving, followed in his father's footsteps, taking over operational control of JDI's forestry business, assuming responsibilities that soon led to his appointment as president and CEO of JDI. His younger brother, Robert Irving, oversaw the company's Moncton branch operations, which ranged from trucking companies to diaper producers.

Kenneth Irving, the oldest son of Arthur Irving, ran the operations side of the family's energy business, putting him in a position to launch ambitious and lucrative projects such as expanding Irving Oil's liquid natural gas business. Kenneth Irving's younger brother, Arthur Leigh Irving, served as an executive in JDI's marketing department. The only son of Jack Irving employed by JDI was John Irving Jr., who worked in the company's real estate division.

After more than 125 years of growth, JDI stood as a towering competitor in its region. Decades of expansion and diversification created a corporate behemoth and a fortune for the Irving family that *Forbes* magazine estimated at CAD 6.7 billion. The years ahead promised to witness the continued dominance of JDI and the Irving family in the Maritimes, as New Brunswick's most powerful family looked to the great-grandchildren of J. D. Irving to perpetuate the dynasty. The first member of the fifth generation of the family to rise to prominence was Jamie Irving, the son of Jim Irving Jr., who at age 27 was named publisher of the *Saint John Telegraph-Journal*. Roughly two dozen more of Jamie Irving's generation were coming of age by the end of the first decade of the 2000s, giving the family ample managerial resources to ensure its legacy in the decades ahead.

Jeffrey L. Covell

PRINCIPAL DIVISIONS

Forestry & Forest Products; Transportation; Shipbuilding & Industrial Fabrication; Retail and Distribution; Consumer Products; Industrial Equipment & Construction; Specialty Printing.

PRINCIPAL COMPETITORS

Canfor Corporation; Tidewater Inc.; Weyerhaeuser Company.

FURTHER READING

"Bowater Sells Timberlands to Irving," *Pulp & Paper*, December 1998, p. 23.

El Akkad, Omar, "The Irving Family Tree," *Globe & Mail*, November 22, 2007, p. A5.

Woodard, Colin, "If It's Not Irving, It's Not New Brunswick," *Hamilton Spectator*, October 18, 2008, p. WR04.

Jacques Vert Plc

———————————■———————————

46 Colebrook Row
London, N1 8AF
United Kingdom
Telephone: (+44 870) 034-5688
Web site: http://www.jacques-vert-plc.co.uk

Public Company
Incorporated: 1972 as Matthew Royce Manufacturing
   Limited
Employees: 1,283
Sales: £115.3 million (2010)
Stock Exchanges: London
Ticker Symbol: JQV
NAICS: 315234 Women's and Girls' Cut and Sew Suit,
   Coat, Tailored Jacket, and Skirt Manufacturing;
   448120 Women's Clothing Stores

■ ■ ■

Jacques Vert Plc is a U.K.-based women's fashion design company and retailer. The London Stock Exchange-listed company maintains four womenswear brands. The Jacques Vert label focuses on elegant "occasion wear" and offers dresses, skirts, blouses, trousers, and jackets as well as coordinated accessories, such as hats, shoes, scarves, bags, and jewelry. The Planet label caters to the professional woman and includes a corporate wear collection. Windsmoor branded apparel focuses on classic styling and luxury fabrics to produce a so-called eternal look. Finally, the Precis Petite line offers collections to flatter women five-feet, three-inches and under.

Jacques Vert sells its wares online and through nearly 1,000 retail outlets, including freestanding stores but mostly in-store concessions in department stores in the United Kingdom, Ireland, and Canada, including Debenhams and House of Fraser. The company maintains two home offices. Department heads and designers are based in Islington, North London, while support services are provided by an operation in Seaham, England.

BEGINNINGS IN 1972

Jacques Vert was founded as Matthew Royce Manufacturing Limited by a pair of London tailors, Jack Cynamon and Alan Green. The partners took turns serving as managing director and chairman of the women's apparel manufacturer. In 1977 they introduced a new coordinated line of suits and separates aimed at the discerning woman. In keeping with the sophisticated styling, they coined a French name for the brand, Jacques Vert, a play on their names: "Jacques" for Jack and "Vert," French for "green." The brand, distributed through department stores and high-end specialty shops in the United Kingdom, proved so successful that the company adopted its name, and Matthew Royce Manufacturing Limited became Jacques Vert.

By the mid-1980s, Jacques Vert was operating three shops under its own name and production was handled by a pair of adjoining factories, supplemented by production from the Far East. By fiscal 1985 the company was generating annual sales of £8.5 million, a fourfold increase in four years. In late 1985 Jacques Vert went public on the unlisted securities market, raising

COMPANY PERSPECTIVES

At Jacques Vert Plc our customer is at the centre of everything we do and we understand that whatever the occasion she is shopping for, her experience begins with us!

funds to further its expansion plans, which included entering the U.S. market as well as Canada.

FOUNDERS SHARE TITLE: 1988

In January 1988 Cynamon and Green became joint chairmen of Jacques Vert because the alternating chairman and managing director titles had caused confusion in their dealings with people outside the company. Otherwise, business was thriving. A new plant had recently opened in Devon and the number of company-owned shops increased to 11. To keep up with growing demand Jacques Vert in September 1988 paid £500,000 to pursue Maitland Womenswear, a maker of women's jackets and skirts. While the company did not purchase the Maitland label, it added machinery, a plant in Upton, Yorkshire, and 180 skilled employees. While sales of its apparel were strong, the same could not be said of Jacques Vert's fashion jewelry business, Connections. In late 1989 the business was sold to its management team for £275,000.

At the start of the 1990s Jacques Vert was operating 18 shops in the United Kingdom, and two in Canada. In February 1990, a store was opened in Newport Beach, Rhode Island, soon followed by other stores in the Los Angeles area and Sherman Oaks, California. To appeal to a wider market in the United States, the company introduced a more casual and youthful weekend line under the Alain Cannelle label. Neither the label nor the U.S. stores would prove to have staying power, however.

In 1994 Cynamon retired from the company at the age of 60, although he remained as a nonexecutive director. Green stayed on as executive chairman for a while, but in 1995 turned over day-to-day control of the business to a new chief executive, David Tiedeman. He would last little more than a year at the post, as Jacques Vert encountered manifold problems, some of them unavoidable and some the result of its own mistakes. The company had always done well by appealing to older women, 50 years and older, outfitting them for weddings and other special occasions. Jacques Vert attempted to attract a younger demographic but its new

designs failed to win over these women and also displeased the line's core customers. To make matters worse, difficulties in installing a new computer system hindered distribution and service to wholesale customers, and the late delivery of fabric from suppliers prevented the company from delivering its apparel, resulting in the loss of wholesale customers.

Replacing Tiedeman was Bill Reid, who became executive chairman in May 1996. He was familiar with the business, having served as a nonexecutive director since 1993. Problems with the new computer system and suppliers were redressed, but Reid faced other hurdles in his effort to turn around Jacques Vert, which over the next year issued several profit warnings that sent the price of its stock tumbling. To cut costs, he outsourced manufacturing to Hong Kong, Morocco, and Portugal, and closed the company's British plants, eliminating 450 jobs in the process.

The company also exited wholesaling, selling its Grace Collection wholesale brand, and closed its House of Fraser concession operations. At the same time, the company added other department store concessions and increased its own chain of Jacques Vert shops to 22. The stores were also upgraded and new designers were brought in to reinvigorate the Jacques Vert line. After three years in the wilderness, Jacques Vert returned to profitability in late 1998.

SECONDARY STOCK OFFERING: 2001

Jacques Vert posted mixed results at the start of the new century. Nevertheless, the company was able to make a secondary offering of stock in 2001 to fund the expansion of its retail outlets, relying mostly on department store concessions. Jacques Vert enjoyed better success in the fiscal year ending in April 2002, when sales totaled £29.6 million due to a strong second half. The company was also able to save money by moving its head office to a smaller location, helping it to reverse a pretax loss of £95,000 in fiscal 2001 into a pretax profit of £879,000 in fiscal 2002.

With Jacques Vert's finances in good shape, Reid was able to engineer a major acquisition in the fall of 2002, offering £18 million for another publicly traded apparel company, William Baird, which was twice as large as Jacques Vert. Baird was an old-guard firm that when it was founded in 1893 had been involved in coal and iron production before turning to textile manufacturing and eventually clothing retailing. By 2000 Baird had fallen on difficult times when it lost a major contract with British retailer Marks & Spencer after a 30-year relationship. Baird unsuccessfully sued its former customer for the unexpected termination and was forced to close 16 factories. A new chief executive was installed in August 2001, but Baird continued to struggle.

Reid proposed a stock swap between Jacques Vert and Baird, one that in the end would leave Baird shareholders with 53 percent of the enlarged Jacques Vert. The idea was backed by investors, who agreed with Reid that the two companies made a good fit. Three of Baird's womenswear brands would mesh neatly with Jacques Vert: Planet, Windsmoor, and Precis Petite. Over the years, Baird had lost touch with its older, core customers, making the same mistake as Jacques Vert: trying to appeal to a younger market. Thus, Jacques Vert had experience in rectifying such an error in judgment and possessed a keen sense of the target market. Baird's clothing was already available at Jacques Vert's retail outlets, but Baird was also sold in many other outlets that would now become open to selling the Jacques Vert line. In addition, there were obvious opportunities to realize savings on overhead by consolidating backroom operations.

BAIRD ACQUISITION: 2002

Baird held out for six weeks but finally relented when Reid sweetened his offer, promising Baird shareholders 70 percent of the combined business. The deal was accomplished by Vert issuing nine new shares for eight Baird shares instead of the one-for-one swap originally proposed. A major reason why Reid revised the offer was Baird's successful sale of its outdoor brand Lowe Alpine for £13.5 million. There were other assets slated for sale as well, including some engineering and manufacturing facilities. The company also planned to sell a pair of menswear European wholesale brands: Melka, a 60-year-old shirt and trouser line, and Tenson, an outdoor clothing label. A review of the businesses, however, indicated that the brands had received little attention from Baird's management. They were retained with the belief that they held global appeal that could be successfully exploited.

Reid took charge of the enlarged Jacques Vert after the acquisition of Baird was completed, but he would have little opportunity to mesh the two operations. In April 2003 the 65-year-old Reid underwent surgery and died in hospital from complications. His finance director and chief aide in turning around Jacques Vert, Paul Allen, was named acting chief executive. The position became permanent a month later, when a nonexecutive chairman was also elected.

With the loss of Reid, Jacques Vert was hampered as it assimilated the Baird acquisition. Baird's European wholesaling division was restructured, leading to charges taken and a pretax loss in fiscal 2004 on sales of £157.2 million. Another change that resulted from the addition of Baird was the switch from in-house manufacturing to outsourcing much of the apparel to the Far East. The company did, however, retain a plant in Sri Lanka that also performed contract work for other major apparel companies. In addition, Jacques Vert began the task of revitalizing the three Baird brands it retained. In the case of Planet, a more fundamental change was in store. It had always been a workwear department store brand, but did not keep pace with the way women now dressed for work. Hence, Jacques Vert's designers sought to make the line more fashionable.

RESTRUCTURING EFFORT: 2006

For the time being the Melka and Tenson brands remained in the fold, and in 2006 another restructuring effort was launched. By the end of the year, Jacques Vert elected to divest the menswear brands that comprised the wholesale division and focus on its core retail business and four womenswear brands. In December 2006 the wholesale unit was sold to a Swedish concern, Lagrummet, for £6.25 million.

Baird brought a legacy problem that also adversely impacted Jacques Vert's balance sheet. The cost of Baird's pension plan had spiraled out of control, forcing Jacques Vert to engineer an equitable solution with the fund trustees. In the summer of 2006, after six months of negotiations, the company agreed to make a one-time contribution of £5 million to end its obligation. Members of the plan were now given the choice of a lump sum or transferring to a new defined benefit pension plan sponsored by Jacques Vert. The company, for its part, gained future cost certainty.

In January 2008 Jacques Vert sold its Sri Lanka plant and became completely focused on its retail operations. Difficult market conditions led to a loss of £2.9 million on sales of £110.9 million in fiscal 2009, but a year later the company enjoyed a strong rebound. Revenues increased to £115.3 million and operating profits totaled £5.3 million. For the first time in 15 years Jacques Vert was able to pay shareholders a dividend. During the year, the company closed some of its department store concessions that were deemed not profitable enough. On the other hand, Jacques Vert was investing in its online business, which was performing well. After several years of adjustment, the company appeared well positioned for ongoing growth.

Ed Dinger

PRINCIPAL COMPETITORS

Alexson Group PLC; French Connection Group PLC; J.P. Boden & Co. Limited.

FURTHER READING

Cope, Nigel, "Jacques Vert Chief Resigns as Group Dives into Red," *Independent* (London), March 29, 1996, p. 25.

"Jacques Vert Chairman Bill Reid Dies," *Europe Intelligence Wire*, April 3, 2003.

Johnson, Andrew, "Wall Street Jacques Vert Keen to Stitch Up Baird Deal," *Daily Express*, October 17, 2002, p. 65.

Joseph, Joe, "High Expectations at Jacques Vert," *Times* (London), January 18, 1988.

Stewart, Heather, "Clothing Baird Drags Jacques Vert into Red," *Guardian* (London), July 7, 2004, p. 18.

Tomkins, Richard, "Jacques Vert Coming to USM," *Financial Times*, December 7, 1985, p. 10.

Townsend, Abigail, "Jacques Vert Profits from Refocus on the Older Woman after Dropping Officewear Experiment," *Yorkshire Post*, June 26, 2002.

Walsh, Fiona, "William Baird Bows to a New Bid from Jacques Vert," *Evening Standard*, November 28, 2002.

White, Constance C. R., "Jacques Vert Takes Aim at U.S. Weekends," *WWD*, January 3, 1990, p. 1.

"Womenswear Starts to Pay Dividends for Fashion House Jacques Vert," *Times* (London), July 2, 2010.

James Fisher and Sons Public Limited Company

———————— ■ ————————

P.O. Box 4, Fisher House
Barrow-in-Furness, Cumbria LA14 1HR
United Kingdom
Telephone: (+44 1229) 615-400
Fax: (+44 1229) 836-761
Web site: http://www.james-fisher.co.uk

Public Company
Founded: 1847 as James Fisher and Sons
Incorporated: 1926 as James Fisher and Sons Public Limited Company
Employees: 1,428
Sales: £249.59 million (2009)
Stock Exchanges: London
Ticker Symbol: FSJ
NAICS: 483111 Deep Sea Freight Transportation; 483113 Coastal and Great Lakes Freight Transportation; 488330 Navigational Services to Shipping; 488390 Other Support Activities for Water Transportation

■ ■ ■

Established as a shipowner in Cumbria, England, in the 1840s, James Fisher and Sons Public Limited Company has aptly transformed itself when many similar, now defunct shipping firms failed to do so. James Fisher today is the leading provider of marine services in the United Kingdom and a specialist-technical supplier of engineering services to the nuclear decommissioning and marine industries both at home and abroad. The company delivers its services through five business segments. Defence Services supplies rescue services and submarine equipment to government agencies on an international basis and support services for ships involved in defense activities. Marine Oil Services transports refined petroleum products in northwest Europe. Offshore Oil Services, based in Scotland and Norway, supplies specialist equipment and engineering services to the international offshore oil and gas industry, with a focus on the North Sea. Specialist Technical Services provides nuclear decommissioning industry services, global offshore ship-to-ship transfer services, the sale and rental of pneumatic fenders, and the design and manufacturing of electrical penetrators used in the offshore oil industry. Shipping Services offers an extensive suite of ship-management services.

ORIGINS AND EARLY YEARS

James Fisher and Sons was founded in 1847 to develop a fleet of ships to transport iron-laden hematite from the hills of Cumbria, near the company's home base of Barrow-in-Furness. The iron was in great demand because of growing industrialization in the country, and Hematite-filled iron ore was plentiful along the Barrow peninsula. The company's early growth was fueled by exports of this hematite product, which was of interest to one of the company's early customers, the Barrow Haematite Iron and Steel Company, a major international hematite-iron exporter.

James Fisher's initial focus was on the management and owning of ships that transported local ore to smelters in south Wales and other locations. In the 1850s, in order to limit the company's risk in the owning of ships,

COMPANY PERSPECTIVES

Since our beginnings in 1847, the company has developed from a ship-owner into a provider of marine and specialist technical services of the highest quality, building on the experience and expertise gained over more than 150 years of operating in the marine environment.

which were subject to numerous types of hazards, James Fisher began selling shares of its newly constructed ships to Barrow-area investors, while keeping a small stake in each for itself.

The company during its first few decades used the local AB Gowan as its preferred shipbuilder. By the end of the 1850s, James Fisher was the largest customer of the Berwick shipyard controlled by Gowan, a status the company maintained for the next 20 years. Between the 1850s and the 1870s, Gowan built more than two dozen vessels, primarily schooners, for James Fisher. These vessels ranged widely in size, from the small 91-ton schooner *Economist* to the 208-ton brig *Buccleuch*.

By 1868, James Fisher owned 70 ships, and by the 1870s, James Fisher had the largest coasting fleet, or fleet of vessels to haul freight, in the United Kingdom. James Fisher employed this fleet while serving as a shipping agent for a major iron industry firm, Schneider and Company, and transported ore, iron, and steel rails on British and European coastal and sea routes. On return trips, bulk products such as grain and timber were often brought back to Barrow. Along with short-sea journeys and coastal trading, some ships were involved in longer, more dangerous, deep-sea journeys and trading.

In 1870, James Fisher and Sons acquired the Furness Shipbuilding Company but only built one ship itself, the *Ellie Park*. By the late 1870s, the shipbuilding industry was changing. In 1877, the final ship built from AB Gowan was added to the Fisher fleet before the Gowan shipyard closed. Subsequently, larger vessels made of iron were exchanged for the older ships made mostly of wood. As steamers were added to the fleet, wooden sailing ships were gradually phased out.

INCORPORATION, GOING PUBLIC, AND LAST YEARS AS A FAMILY BUSINESS

As it entered a new century, the company controlled a fleet that was a mix of cargo steamers and sailing ships.

In 1926, the firm was incorporated and became a public limited company. Operated by three successive generations of Fishers, James Fisher and Sons through a century of operations was a family-run business controlled by immediate family. However, in the third generation, one son died in his youth and the other married late and had no children. As a result, plans were made for a nephew, lured into the company prior to World War II, to take control of the firm, but he died in 1959 while still in his early 40s.

During the 1950s, James Fisher underwent significant changes. In 1952, it became a public company, and James Fisher was listed on the London Stock Exchange for the first time. The firm also began operating ships that traversed the Irish Sea as well as the English Channel.

Beginning in the 1960s, James Fisher became increasingly controlled by nonfamily directors who managed the company. During this period, traditional bulk loads became less profitable and increasingly less available, and the company developed a reputation for hauling especially heavy and irregular cargo. In this way, James Fisher and Sons developed a lucrative niche business, transporting heavy equipment, even railroad locomotives, across the sea. The firm also adopted a method of unitized loads: freight calculated on the basis of steel pallets on ships that could transport up to 15 tons. Along with its heavy-load business, the company had other profitable businesses provided by its coastal tankers and port operations. In addition, in 1965, James Fisher developed its first vessel to haul irradiated, or spent, nuclear fuel.

DEVELOPMENT OF NEW NICHE BUSINESS

Beginning in the 1980s, James Fisher pared down its traditional fleet but added ships during the remaining years of the decade that specialized in particular marine services: cable laying, subsea excavation, and underwater engineering. By the early 1990s, the company had taken on substantial debt. In 1993, David Cobb became chairman. He oversaw the sales of unneeded vessels and the slashing of unnecessary overhead costs. By 1994, the company had sailed from a £5.63 million loss to a pre-tax profit of £2.28 million, with the sales of ships buoying the company's cash surplus. By the mid-1990s, James Fisher operated 15 of its own vessels while managing six nuclear fuel transport ships owned by the state-reprocessing firm British Nuclear Fuels plc (BNFL).

In 1997, James Fisher more than doubled the size of its tanker fleet with the acquisition of P&O Tank-

KEY DATES

1847: Company is founded by James Fisher to develop a fleet of ships to transport hematite from Cumbria.

1926: Business is incorporated as a public limited company.

1952: James Fisher and Sons goes public and is listed on the London Stock Exchange.

2005: Company has what Chairman Tim Harris calls "a year of transformation," transitioning from ship ownership to a focus on marine support services.

2007: Firm's annual revenues leap from £118 million to £182 million as earnings climb above £20 million for the first time.

ships and its 17 oil-product tankers. With the addition of the P&O business, James Fisher gained a significant presence in European markets and became the largest group in Britain transporting clean petroleum products. That same year, the company's research and development department created for underwater excavation what was called a Hydro-Digger, which the firm expected would replace traditional means of dredging. Using a water-driven jet propeller, the Hydro-Digger was designed to be environmentally friendly. To complement its underwater excavation operations, James Fisher in 1998 acquired Underwater Engineering Services, a unit of North Sea Assets, PLC.

By 2000, James Fisher's three cable-laying ships, working for telecommunications companies, provided nearly half of the company's gross profits. The company's fleet by this time was varied. It included tankships, heavy-lift roll-on/roll-off vessels for transporting vehicles, nuclear fuel carriers, a dive-support vessel, as well as cable-laying ships. In September 2001, P&O executive Tim Harris jumped ship, leaving the James Fisher competitor where he had been chief executive, and was soon expected to become company chairman. Harris joined James Fisher as a board member, but in 2002, he became company chairman. Harris and his newly appointed chief executive, Angus Buchanan, quickly set in motion a series of sales and acquisitions to fully transform the 150-year-old company from a shipowner to a provider of marine specialty services.

By 2002, the company's major support services included hauling nuclear waste for BNFL and managing British Ministry of Defence transport vessels. The company also operated a substantial fleet of tankers that carried petroleum products off the U.K. shores, but this business was dependent upon weather and global economic factors. In 2002, company management concluded that its shipping business was too cyclical to guarantee future growth, which would have to come from marine-support services. In March 2002, James Fisher sold the remaining two vessels from its fleet of dry-cargo ships, which had become an unprofitable line.

To bolster its support offerings, and to offset a fall-off in cable-laying work, James Fisher began actively seeking acquisitions with higher profit margins. In August 2002, the company hired finance boutique executive Hambro Rabben specifically to locate acquisitions to expand the company's marine services. He succeeded, and a flurry of acquisitions ensued.

TRANSFORMATION OF THE COMPANY: RAPID EXPANSION OF MARINE SERVICES

In late 2002, James Fisher acquired Scan Tech Holdings of Norway, a provider of offshore equipment rental and engineering-support services for the oil and gas industry. The acquisition complemented the company's existing underwater engineering services in Aberdeen, Scotland, those of Seafloor Dynamex which had designed the Hydro-Digger and which provided different equipment than Scan Tech. In 2002, Fisher also acquired Rumic, a provider of offshore personnel services that operated submarine rescue services for the British Royal Navy, and Ocean Fleets Ltd., a marine consultancy and engineering design services provider. By the end of the year, Chairman Harris proclaimed that "we intend our marine-support services division—our least capital-intensive activity—to become the largest and most profitable business in the group, providing good quality, reliable earnings and cash flow. Our aim is simple—to be the UK's leading provider of marine services; this will enable James Fisher to continue its exceptional and proven cash generating ability and earnings growth in the coming years."

In 2003, Buchanan left the company and was succeeded as chief executive by Nick Henry, another former P&O executive. To expand its marine support services, James Fisher in 2003 acquired two small firms, a maintenance service provider for the Royal Navy and a supplier of engineering support services for large air compressors used in the oil industry. In December 2004, James Fisher acquired three companies: Remote Marine Systems Limited (RMS), a producer of Remote Handling Equipment for oil and nuclear industries; Nuclear Decommissioning Limited, an engineering support service provider for the nuclear industry; and Reanco Team AS, a Haugesund-based provider of offshore living-quarters installation services.

By the end of 2004, marine support services were generating 40 percent of the firm's income, while the company's once mainstay tankship business continued to generate a sizable share of profits through long-term contracts, which earned income for the company whether the ships were in use or not. The company increasingly had diversified, with business spread between ship management, marine services, subsea excavation, cable-laying, and nuclear fuel transportation, along with tankship operations.

In 2005, James Fisher's Rumic, which operated the Royal Navy Submarine rescue service, successfully saved seven Russian sailors trapped in a Russian submarine 625 feet below the surface of the Pacific Ocean. The sailors were retrieved with less than 10 hours of air remaining in their craft by personnel from Rumic, which volunteered its Scorpio 45 submersible to achieve the rescue.

COMPLETING THE TRANSITION FROM SHIPOWNER TO MARINE SERVICES FIRM

In January 2005, James Fisher established a new division, Defence Services, uniting the defense activities of Rumic and James Fisher. The firm continued expansion of its support services in 2005 with more acquisitions, including Monyana Engineering Services, a supplier involved in the design, refurbishing, and provision of hydraulic winches to the oilfield services industry; and Harsh Environment Systems Limited, a provider of custom-made solutions for nuclear decommissioning monitoring. Additionally, in its largest marine services purchase to date, James Fisher acquired FenderCare Marine, a leading international supplier of anticollision pneumatic fenders and the largest global ship-to-shore provider with 19 bases worldwide, with more than half of its income generated from global defense industries. By the end of 2005, James Fisher's expanded marine support services were generating a full half of the firm's profits, during a period that Harris called "a year of transformation."

After writing down the value of one cable-laying ship, selling a second, and relegating the other to dry dock and discontinued operation, James Fisher in 2006 sold its remaining cable-laying vessel. The company had transitioned from a concentration on ship ownership, dating to the early days of James Fisher and Sons, to a focus on marine services in the defense, specialist-technical, and offshore oil service sectors. These sectors, as well as oil tankship operations, represented the

company's four divisions: Oil Tankship (later renamed Marine Oil Services); Defence, which was providing submarine rescue services; Offshore Oil, which rented oil industry equipment; and Specialist-Technical, whose most significant asset was FenderCare's mooring operations.

In 2006, the firm formed Fisher Offshore Limited to provide offshore and seabed construction and equipment services. Scan Tech UK and Monyana Engineering Services were merged in the process. The company that year also acquired businesses that helped flesh out its marine services for the future. James Fisher acquired U.K.-based Strainstall Group Limited, a provider of custom safety and productivity monitoring products for subsea environs, including hostile and potentially explosive areas. Next, it created the new firm James Fisher Inspection & Measurement Services to provide acoustic, optical, and x-ray technology services to defense, nuclear, and offshore industries.

James Fisher that same year acquired Gjerde Lofteteknikk AS, a Norwegian marine lifting-equipment supplier, and the James Fisher Defence (JFD) subsidiary purchased the U.K. submarine rescue service from the Defence Sales Agency so it could offer submarine rescue services to other countries. In December 2006, JFD won its first contract as a James Fisher business: a £10 million award to provide the Republic of Korea Navy with a submarine rescue vehicle.

In January 2007, James Fisher acquired rival tanker operator FT Everard for £350 million, forming the largest U.K.-owned shipping and marine services group. Everard operated 11 small-product tankers, had four new-build ships expected to enter service that year, and owned Cattedown Wharves in Plymouth. With the acquisition, James Fisher had a fleet of about 30 vessels and entered the year focusing on integrating its existing ships with that of the Everard fleet. That same year, the company acquired Pump Tools, a downhole tools and systems manufacturer, and NDT Inspection and Testing Ltd, a provider of testing services to nuclear and aerospace industries. James Fisher also sold its marine electronics subsidiary Ships Electronic Services (SES), in an SES management buyout, and sold three product tankers but agreed to lease those back for 10 years.

REALIZING THE REWARDS OF A NEW FOCUS

While Harris heralded 2005 as "a year of transformation" for the company, 2007 was the year in which James Fisher's revenues and earnings were fully realized by its marine services development. In 2007, the company boosted its revenues to £182 million, up from £118 million a year prior. Earnings also blossomed, rising to more than £20 million for the first time.

In 2008, JFD joined with Singapore Technologies Marine Ltd to form the 50-50 joint venture First Response Marine Pte Ltd. The venture was created to provide the Republic of Singapore navy with comprehensive submarine rescue service, including a mother ship, submarine rescue system, and necessary maintenance services. For its part, JFD agreed to design and supply the submarine rescue service, including a new rescue submersible, and operate and maintain the rescue assets for the 20-year life of the contract. James Fisher in 2008 also acquired JCM Scotload, a producer of load measurement devices for the offshore oil industry.

James Fisher in 2009 orchestrated a strategic merger of its Remote Marine Services and its Pumptools to create the new subsidiary RMSpumptools Ltd. within its Offshore Oil division. That same year, the company acquired MB Faber Ltd (Faber), an engineering services provider to the nuclear and aerospace industries, and integrated Faber with the firm's existing nuclear decommissioning operations.

In 2010, James Fisher's FenderCare purchased Australian Commercial Marine Pty Ltd of Perth, Australia, a regional provider of marine equipment to port, shipping, and offshore industries, which Fender-Care planned to help expand in Australia. Early the same year, the company purchased GMC Produkt, a Norway-based producer and wholesaler of winches, cranes, and fire safety equipment. Clearly, as it entered its second decade of the 21st century, James Fisher picked up where it left off in the first decade: expanding its marine services businesses. The company had proven that its marine service operations could stand on its own and maintain a profitable company even in the face of a global economic downturn.

As it looked to the future, James Fisher also eyed expansion of its more traditional area of business, its coastal oil tanker fleet, which by 2010 was able to transport eight million tons of refined product annually. This line of business, however, was the one most exposed to cyclical and economic downturns, but organic growth in its high-margin niche marine service lines more than made up for any profit losses from global economic conditions in the oil transportation business. Moreover, the company's well-seasoned management did not appear ready to sink an anchor and moor itself. As it began a new decade, James

Fisher's future appeared to be one of continued growth and profitability.

Roger Rouland

PRINCIPAL SUBSIDIARIES

Buchan Technical Services Limited; Fender Care Marine Services Group Limited; Fender Care Marine Solutions Limited; Fender Care Naval Solutions Limited; James Fisher Everard Limited; James Fisher Inspection and Measurement Services Limited; James Fisher Mimic Limited; James Fisher Nuclear Limited; James Fisher Offshore Limited; James Fisher Rumic Limited; James Fisher (Shipping Services) Limited; James Fisher Tankships Holdings Limited; JF Faber Limited; JF Nuclear Limited; RMSpumptools Limited; Scan Tech Air Supply UK Limited; Scan Tech AS (Norway); Strainstall Group Limited; First Response Marine Pte Ltd (Singapore; 50%); Foreland Holdings Limited (25%).

PRINCIPAL DIVISIONS

Defence Services; Marine Oil Services; Offshore Oil Services; Specialist Technical Services.

PRINCIPAL COMPETITORS

A.P. Møller-Mærsk A/S; Frontline Ltd.; Teekay Corporation.

FURTHER READING

Armstrong, John, "(Review): *Around the Coast and across the Seas: The Story of James Fisher and Sons,*" *Journal of Transport History,* March 2001.

Around the Coast and across the Seas: The Story of James Fisher and Sons, Leyburn, England, St. Matthew's Press, 2000.

Block, Lawrence, "Shipping Firm Gets Back on Even Keel," *Sunday Times* (London), January 18, 1998, p. 12.

"Fisher Plots a Steady Course," *Mail on Sunday* (London), November 2, 2003, p. 13.

Hall, William, and Ruth Sullivan, "Change at the Top for James Fisher," *Financial Times,* December 7, 2004, p. 28.

"International Cooperation Saves Trapped Submariners," *Maritime Journal: Insight for European Commercial Industries,* September 1, 2005.

"James Fisher Acquires FenderCare," *Maritime Journal Online,* April 1, 2005.

"James Fisher & Sons," *Investors Chronicle,* September 8, 2006.

"James Fisher Buys Everard," *Maritime Journal,* January 1, 2007.

MacIsaac, Mary, "With a Fair Wind Blowing, There Are Profits to Be Made on the High Seas," *BusinessScottsman.com*, April 6, 2003.

"Marine Services Arm Is a Boost for Fisher," *Mail on Sunday* (London), December 22, 2002, p. 8.

"Marine Services Merger Could Herald Wave of New Aberdeen Jobs," *Europe Intelligence Wire*, December 16, 2002.

White, Garry, "James Fisher Rides a Steady Wave," *Daily Telegraph Online* (London), August 15, 2009.

John Simon Guggenheim Memorial Foundation

———————■———————

90 Park Avenue
New York, New York 10016
U.S.A.
Telephone: (212) 687-4470
Fax: (212) 697-3248
Web site: http://www.gf.org

Nonprofit Organization
Incorporated: 1925
Total Assets: $237.24 million (2008)
NAICS: 813211 Grantmaking Foundations

■ ■ ■

John Simon Guggenheim Memorial Foundation is a prestigious nonprofit organization that since 1926 has awarded numerous fellowships to members of the American Academy of Arts and Sciences as well as Nobel Prize winners, poets laureate, and others in specialized disciplines. The annual Guggenheim fellowship competitions provide 6- to 12-month stipends for advanced professionals, those who have shown exceptional capacity for productivity or creative ability as writers, scientists, scholars, artists, playwrights, filmmakers, photographers, or composers in the United States, Canada, Latin America, or the Caribbean. The foundation receives roughly 4,000 applications each year and names approximately 200 fellows. It sets no specific quotas for the allocation of fellowships among fields of endeavor or requirements as to the expenditure of funds by its fellows.

THE GUGGENHEIMS
MEMORIALIZE THEIR SON: 1925

In 1925, Simon Guggenheim, an industrialist and a senator from Colorado from 1907 to 1913, and his wife, Olga, a philanthropist and art patron, established the John Simon Guggenheim Foundation in memory of their son. John Simon Guggenheim had died of pneumonia and mastoiditis at 17 on April 26, 1922, while attending Phillips Exeter Academy.

Guggenheim's grandfather, Meyer Guggenheim, had made a fortune in mining, and his father was one of seven brothers who controlled a mining and smelting empire in North and South America, M. Guggenheim's Sons. Senator Guggenheim worked as the chief ore buyer for his family's mining and smelting operation before moving to Denver, Colorado. Originally from Switzerland, the Guggenheims were Jewish and strongly committed to overcoming the legal and social obstacles of the Old World.

Senator Guggenheim decided in 1924 to form a foundation that would support educational purposes similar to the Rhodes Scholarship, but of greater breadth. He engaged 30-year-old Henry Allen Moe, a Rhodes scholar from 1920 to 1923, to head the foundation's offices. The plan was to make the first public announcement about foundation funds early in 1925 and to appoint the first fellows by the fall of that year.

Moe envisioned the fellowship program as "a big, statesmanlike idea." He toured the country during the summer and early fall of 1925 interviewing the presidents of 12 colleges and universities to solicit their input and support for the Guggenheim fellowships. A second trip to New England colleges and universities lined up distinguished scholars to serve on the foundation's Educational Advisory Board. Moe also wrote to the heads of universities abroad, asking for their cooperation should fellows wish to undertake research at their institutions.

In its *Outline of Purposes*, distributed in early 1925, the foundation described four types of awards to individuals, grants to supplement sabbatical salaries, research fellowships for advanced scholars, renewals of awards for recipients who needed more time, and publication subsidies for work produced during the fellowship. On the cover of the *Outline*, a paragraph identified the fellowship's overall purpose: "To improve the quality of education and the practice of the arts and professions in the United States, to foster research, and to provide for the cause of better international understanding, the John Simon Guggenheim Memorial Foundation Fellowships for Advanced Study Abroad offer to young men and women opportunities under the freest possible conditions to carry on advanced study and research in any field of knowledge or opportunities for the development of unusual talent in any of the fine arts, including music."

THE FOUNDATION'S FIRST 10 YEARS: 1925–35

In 1925, a news story titled "John Simon Guggenheim Memorial to Supplement Rhodes Scholarships," announced Senator Guggenheim's $3 million gift to the new foundation. Candidates were to be chosen "without distinction on account of race, color or creed." The original age guidelines for fellows were flexible, judging accomplishment in relation to age rather than imposing strict age limits. New York Governor Alfred E. Smith signed into law an act incorporating the Guggenheim Foundation that year.

Although the first regular competition was held in 1926, a limited number of applications were considered for 1925, and 15 individuals were chosen to become the first class of Guggenheim fellows, among them Aaron Copland, a young composer from New York. Thirteen of the fellows received awards of $2,500. The other two received awards of $1,500. The following April, the Committee of Selection, drawn from the larger Educational Advisory Board, chose 39 candidates for fellowships from among the nearly 900 applicants and recommended five of the 1925 fellows for second fellowships for a total gift of $99,600.

In 1928, the foundation considered applications in the fine arts for the first time. In 1929, it moved its offices to larger quarters a few blocks away on Fifth Avenue at 45th Street, where it expanded in square footage for the next 37 years. "Henry Moe saw to it," according to the official foundation history, "that not a thin dime was spent unnecessarily. He believed ... that nothing should be wasted on ostentatious headquarters. ... The Foundation established a reputation new in New York, or elsewhere, of Spartan simplicity." By the end of 1929, the foundation's assets totaled nearly $5 million with the addition of another $1 million gift from the Guggenheims. The following year, the foundation adopted its "exchange" program in Mexico, and nominated two Mexican men for fellowships.

The foundation's fellowship program was extended to Cuba, Argentina, and Chile in 1931 with plans to extend to Puerto Rico in 1932. The program was also expanding into new fields as well. Martha Graham became the first Guggenheim fellow in choreography in 1932, the first year that the number of applicants topped 1,000. (Five years later, photography made its appearance in 1937 with Edward Weston, then filmmaking with Maya Deren in 1946.) By 1933, of the nearly 500 fellows, 54 had been artists. All but two of these took part in an exhibition of 136 works at the Whitney Museum of American Art that year. By 1936, 165 of the 360 fellows to that date were artists; fellows ranged in age from 22 to 65 at the time of their fellowship; 22 percent had no college degree; and 36 percent were unaffiliated with an educational or research institution.

On the foundation's 10th anniversary in 1935, the Guggenheims gave a third donation of securities worth $781,875. Six years later, when George Denver Guggenheim, the philanthropists' other son, then 32, committed suicide, the couple added his trust fund of $1.11 million to the foundation's endowment, increasing its assets to $8 million.

THE FORTIES: OLGA GUGGENHEIM BECOMES FOUNDATION PRESIDENT

Brazil, Peru, and Uruguay joined the Latin American program, and Canada joined the U.S. competition beginning with the competition of 1940. The last few years of the 1940s saw the fellowship program expand to include all the Latin American republics, and in the 1950s, the foundation began to extend its reach to the European colonial possessions in the Western Hemisphere. Beginning with the 1941 competition, there were no geographical restrictions on the awards, expanding upon a 1934 competition decision that allowed some U.S. fellows not to spend their fellowship periods abroad. A similar decision was made in 1965 regarding fellows from Central and South America, who were no longer required to visit the United States.

After Simon Guggenheim died of pneumonia, two months shy of his 74th birthday in 1941, Olga Guggenheim became president of the foundation in 1942. She oversaw the introduction of several new types of fellowships stipends concurrent with the war effort. Fellows could postpone their fellowship period because of war service, or align their work with work that the government wanted them to do. Additional fellowships to assist war-related emergency work were also added. The foundation also offered "post-service" awards "to be granted to scholars and creative workers who [were] serving the nation's war effort in the Armed or other Governmental Services" upon their release from wartime duty. During 1944, 1945, and 1946, 152 post-service fellowships were awarded.

At the end of 1946, by which time about $3.25 million had been awarded to some 1,450 fellows, the foundation's assets had reached $24.3 million. The foundation itself received an award in 1946 from the National Association for American Composers and Conductors: the Henry Hadley Medal for its services to the world of music.

THE FIFTIES AND SIXTIES: THE COX COMMITTEE AND THE IRS

During the first half of the 1950s, the foundation faced repeated involvement by the U.S. government. In 1951, the U.S. Commissioner of Internal Revenue, reversing a policy that had been in effect for a quarter-century, argued that fellowships were "compensation for personal services" to be included in the recipients' taxable gross incomes beginning in 1950. The foundation initially furnished additional gifts of up to 20 percent of their original grants to fellows who had received payments in 1950 and 1951 to cover tax expenses. In 1954, under the new tax law, fellowship recipients could deduct amounts spent for travel, research, clerical help, or equipment incident to their fellowship work.

The following year, the House of Representative's Cox Committee claimed that the Guggenheim was using its resources for "un-American and subversive activities," disseminating "radicalism throughout the country to an extent not excelled by any other foundation." Moe appeared before the Cox Committee to explain the foundation's aims and procedures, saying, "We have no lines that we desire to develop. We have only one line, which is concerned with people. We aim to train people to do better what they are fitted to do and want to do. That is our program." However, the foundation began to check the names of fellowship nominees against the lists published by the House Committee on Un-American Activities. Moe assured his readers that the foundation's policies had not been affected: "So far as concerns this Foundation, we expressly dissociate ourselves from such talk. We have not been intimidated; and our giving is not timid."

Olga Guggenheim announced her retirement as president in 1961 "to clear the way for the reorganization of our corporate offices." Following changes in the constitution and by-laws, Dale E. Sharp became chairman of the board and Henry Allen Moe president, while Olga Guggenheim was named president emeritus. She remained in that position until 1970 when she died at 92, bequeathing to the foundation $41.49 million and increasing the value of the foundation's assets to $115 million by the end of 1972.

Other administrative changes also occurred during the early 1960s. In 1963, Henry Allen Moe retired, two days before his 69th birthday, and Gordon Ray, who had been professor of English and provost at the University of Illinois in Urbana (and a holder of four Guggenheim fellowships), became the foundation's president, the second chief executive officer in its 38-year history. *Time*, in its July 12 issue, took note of Moe's retirement, calling him the "wise, undisputed dean" of the foundation world who "gave 'Guggie' fellowships the status of a U.S. intellectual knighthood." The foundation's offices moved permanently to 90 Park Avenue in 1965.

The Tax Reform Act of 1969 formalized changes instituted by the Internal Revenue Service in 1951. It allowed grants to individuals as long as the purpose of the grant was "to achieve a specific objective, produce a report or other similar product, or improve or enhance the literary, artistic, musical, scientific, teaching, or other similar capacity, skill, or talent of the grantee." However, the individuals had to show that they had used their grants in the ways specified in the law. As a result, the foundation began to ask fellows to submit brief statements at the conclusion of their fellowship periods. In 1987, the Tax Reform Act of 1986 made fellowship grants part of recipients' taxable income. Fellowship holders could still deduct from taxable income any portions of their grants used for professional expenses, just as they could deduct such expenses from any other category of taxable income.

THE SEVENTIES AND EIGHTIES: FINANCIAL PRESSURES

In 1975, Moe died at the age of 81, having become the first chairman of the National Endowment for the Humanities after leaving the Guggenheim Foundation. To mark the foundation's 50th anniversary that year, a *Directory of Fellows: 1925–1974*, recording the names of 8,395 fellows, was published.

During the 1970s, the number of fellowships awarded each year peaked (at 394 in 1972) and then declined in order to maintain their average monetary value. Inflation was not the only problem. The Tax Reform Act of 1969 required a variable payout that reached nearly 8 percent and an excise tax of 4 percent, and the stock market decline of 1973–74 reduced the endowment from $115 million to $79 million.

Gordon Ray died at the age of 71, less than 16 months after his retirement from the foundation in 1985. Joel Conarroe, the Thomas S. Gates Professor of English and dean of the School of Arts and Sciences at the University of Pennsylvania and a 1977 fellow, suc-

ceeded him as chief executive officer. Under Conarroe, the foundation began to cut expenditures by lowering overhead, reducing the annual fellowship budget to the minimum payout required by law in 1989, engaging in more aggressive investing, and implementing a fundraising campaign. The campaign was begun with letters written by prominent fellows to all previous fellowship holders in their fields in 1990, and by 2000, the number of contributing fellows amounted to nearly 1,400.

The 1989 budget for fellowships was cut by about 15 percent or $1 million. In 1990, it was cut by another $1.7 million. Over the two-year period from 1989 to 1990, the number of fellowship awards dropped by almost half from 290 in 1988 to 165 in 1990. These actions allowed a steady upward movement both in the number of awards and in their average monetary value. Between 1990 and 1999, the amount allocated to fellowships rose from $4.32 million to $7.15 million, and the number of awards increased from 165 in 1990 to 213 in 1999. During this period the foundation's assets rose from about $123.6 million to about $210.6 million.

2000 AND BEYOND: AN AMERICAN INSTITUTION

In 2002 Joel Conarroe retired, and Edward Hirsch, a poet, essayist, and University of Houston professor, replaced him as president. Three years later, an "all-star" reading at Cooper Union's Great Hall took place, celebrating the foundation's "generosity." Otherwise, except for notices of awards to individuals, the Guggenheim was not much in the news during the first decade of the new century. By 2010, the annual pool of applicants in the United States and Canada numbered 3,000, from which 180 fellows were chosen. Another 37 fellows were chosen from Latin America and the Caribbean. Despite having adapted to harder financial times, the Guggenheim Memorial Foundation was an established part of the scholarly and artistic landscape in the Western Hemisphere.

Carrie Rothburd

FURTHER READING

"Farewell Groves of Academe," *Time*, July 12, 1963, p. 80.

Gussow, Mel, "Poet Will Take Over Presidency of Guggenheim Foundation," *New York Times*, September 3, 2002, p. 3.

Kaufmann, David, "Gazing at the Guggenheims," *Forward*, December 17, 2004, p. 11.

Tanselle, G. Thomas, and Peter Franklin Kardon, *John Simon Guggenheim Memorial Foundation, 1925–2000: A Seventy-*

Fifth Anniversary Record, New York: John Simon Guggenheim Memorial Foundation, 2001.

Unger, Debi, and Irwin Unger, *The Guggenheims: A Family History*, New York: HarperCollins, 2005.

Kaman Corporation

———■———

1332 Blue Hills Avenue
Bloomfield, Connecticut 06002
U.S.A.
Telephone: (860) 243-7100
Fax: (860) 243-6365
Web site: http://www.kaman.com

Public Company
Incorporated: 1945 as Kaman Aircraft
Employees: 4,032
Sales: $1.15 billion (2009)
Stock Exchanges: NASDAQ GS
Ticker Symbol: KAMN
NAICS: 423830 Industrial Machinery and Equipment
Merchant Wholesalers; 332912 Fluid Power Valve
and Hose Fitting Manufacturing; 336411 Aircraft
Manufacturing; 336412 Aircraft Engine and Engine
Parts Manufacturing; 336413 Other Aircraft Parts
and Auxiliary Equipment Manufacturing; 423840
Industrial Supplies Merchant Wholesalers; 332993
Ammunition (Except Small Arms) Manufacturing;
423610 Electrical Apparatus and Equipment, Wir-
ing Supplies, and Related Equipment Merchant
Wholesalers; 333922 Conveyor and Conveying
Equipment Manufacturing; 334511 Search, Detec-
tion, Navigation, Guidance, Aeronautical, and
Nautical System and Instrument Manufacturing;
334513 Instruments and Related Products
Manufacturing for Measuring, Displaying, and
Controlling Industrial Process Variables; 423990
Other Miscellaneous Durable Goods Merchant
Wholesalers

■ ■ ■

Kaman Corporation is a diversified company operating
in two business segments: industrial distribution and
aerospace manufacturing. Kaman is North America's
third-largest distributor of power transmission and motion control products and offers more than two million
industrial components for distribution. The company's
Aerospace unit manufactures company-branded bearings
and components and metallic and composite aerostructures for defense, commercial, and foreign governmental
markets. Aerospace subsidiaries also produce arming,
safing, and fuzing devices for bomb and missile systems
for the U.S. military and its allies, subcontract
helicopter development work, and provide support
services for Kaman's SH-2G Super Seasprite and
K-MAX helicopters.

Kaman's primary customers include the U.S.
military, Boeing, Lockheed Martin, Raytheon, Sikorsky
Aircraft Corporation, and Airbus. Kaman's operations
include about 200 branches, distribution centers, and
call centers in the United States, Canada, and Mexico.
Manufacturing facilities are located in North America,
the United Kingdom, and Germany, which, along with
Australia and New Zealand, are the principal geographic
areas served by the company.

FOUNDER'S EARLY LOVE OF AVIATION

Kaman is the progeny of U.S. paragon Charles H. Kaman, an inventor, entrepreneur, musician, humanitarian,

and visionary. He was born in 1919 and raised in Washington, D.C. His father, a German immigrant, was a construction supervisor who managed work on the Supreme Court building and Union Station in Washington, D.C. Charles Kaman demonstrated an early interest in aviation design. During the 1930s, he competed in the city's model airplane design contests held at a local playground. He also showed an enthusiasm for music. Kaman became an accomplished guitar player as a teenager and even turned down an offer to play with the Tommy Dorsey band for an alluring $75 per week.

Kaman continued to pursue his interest in aviation during college. For a contest held in Washington, D.C., he made a model plane, which took more than 100 hours to build and was made of balsa wood, covered with an ultra-thin film, and driven by a rubber band. Kaman wound the propeller 1,500 times and asked the judge to clock his warm-up flight. After setting an unofficial record for time aloft, Kaman became determined to surpass his own record. He decided to wind the propeller 3,500 times, using an eggbeater. At about 3,000 turns the band snapped and the plane imploded. Nevertheless, the episode cemented his desire to become an innovator in the burgeoning aviation field.

Kaman graduated magna cum laude with a bachelor of aeronautical engineering degree in 1940 from Washington's Catholic University. Although he had dreamed since childhood of becoming a professional pilot, a severe infection following a tonsillectomy that left him deaf in one ear made that an impossibility. Instead of piloting flying machines, Kaman decided to build them. After college, he accepted a position with aviation pioneer United Aircraft (the forerunner of United Technologies Corporation, later a Kaman Corporation competitor). He went to work in the company's helicopter division, Hamilton Standard, which was marshaled by renowned inventor Igor Sikorsky. Kaman was told to help design propellers.

The chief dilemma facing helicopter engineers during the industry's early years was stability and control. Engineers were challenged to figure out how to devise a machine that could be easily maneuvered and landed, particularly in high winds. Aside from stability and control, helicopters in the early 1940s suffered from several problems. Vibration was a major obstacle. Because of the way in which the rotor was controlled from its hub, the entire aircraft would vibrate, putting stress on the machine that reduced its durability and dependability.

Kaman's contributions were quickly recognized at United. By 1943, he had become head of aerodynamics. Despite his success at United, Kaman became frustrated by the company's lack of attention to his ideas. Specifically, Kaman suggested an improvement that might increase the stability of United's helicopters. He wanted to put flaps on the main rotor and scrap the tail rotor altogether to improve control. On his own time, Kaman built a homemade rig to test his theories. He fashioned the contraption in his mother's garage using junk parts, including an engine from a 1933 Pontiac, the rear end of an old Dodge, and a bathroom scale.

When tested, Kaman's initial designs failed. However, after several weeks of experimenting, he was able to build a device that incorporated his revolutionary servo-flap rotor control system. The new design significantly reduced vibration. It also required much less force by the pilot to maneuver the aircraft, thus improving stability and control. Excited by his discovery, Kaman approached the manager of engineering at United and even demonstrated his rotor blade test rig. "Charlie, we have our inventor at United Aircraft," explained his supervisor. "His name is Igor Sikorsky. We don't need another one."

GOING IT ALONE: THE FORTIES

Because United was not interested in his ideas, Kaman decided to go to work for an employer who would put his theories into practice: himself. With $2,000 and some rudimentary laboratory equipment, Kaman in 1945 started a company that would become a multimillion-dollar corporation, a leader in aviation technology, and, among other accomplishments, a guitar supplier for rock stars. Kaman shaped his new enterprise around the contraption that he made in his mother's garage. He raised funds to develop his company, Kaman Aircraft, by holding weekend flying shows with his homemade aircraft, the K-125, at Bradley Field in Connecticut, where he solicited observers to invest in his idea.

Kaman was able to generate enough capital to build a new helicopter, the K-190, by 1948. It incorporated a

```
┌─────────────────────────────────────────────────┐
│                                                   │
│              KEY DATES                            │
│            ────────■────────                      │
│                                                   │
│  1945: Kaman Aircraft is established.             │
│  1948: Kaman introduces the K-190 helicopter.     │
│  1963: Kaman's UH-2 utility helicopter is         │
│         introduced into the U.S. Navy.            │
│  1994: Kaman's new K-MAX "aerial truck"           │
│         helicopter is certified by the Federal    │
│         Aviation Administration.                  │
│  2007: Kaman sells its music business to Fender   │
│         Musical Instruments in order to focus     │
│         operations on aerospace and industrial    │
│         distribution.                             │
│                                                   │
└─────────────────────────────────────────────────┘
```

dual-rotor system (but no tail rotor) and was touted as the most stable, easy-to-fly helicopter ever built. To reinforce his claim of stability, Kaman conducted a public relations coup in November 1948 at Bradley Field. Ann Griffin, a young housewife with virtually no flying experience, jumped into the cockpit of the exotic machine and flew it for 10 minutes before an astonished audience. The stunt was widely publicized and resulted in an infusion of capital into Kaman's company. Most importantly, the staged event helped Kaman to get his first helicopter orders.

Kaman, like many of his helicopter industry contemporaries, had grand visions for his flying machines. Many engineers believed that the helicopter would eventually replace the automobile as the vehicle of choice for families. Each family would have a helicopter in its backyard or on its roof. People would zip to work, to the grocery store, or even to vacation destinations in a matter of minutes or hours. Unfortunately, physical realities emerged that made the concept unfeasible given 20th-century technology. Thus, Kaman decided that the immediate future of his company was in the commercial and defense markets.

INNOVATIONS IN HELICOPTER DEVELOPMENT: FIFTIES AND SIXTIES

Kaman achieved important technical breakthroughs during the late 1940s and 1950s. In 1951, for instance, he designed the world's first gas-turbine powered helicopter. The innovation became a major industry influence on the design of helicopter power systems through the mid-1990s. Despite such advances, Kaman Aircraft realized spotty financial success. Kaman was unsuccessful at marketing his K-225 (the successor to the K-125) as a crop duster. In addition, although

descendants of the K-190 and K-225 models were purchased for use in search and rescue missions in the 1950s, his servo-flap design never found a mass market.

Kaman's helicopters, which became known as synchropters, had many advantages over other machines. Their chief drawback, however, was slowness. As the military increased its emphasis on speed during the 1950s and 1960s, synchropters lost favor to speedier designs that were more appropriate for battle. Kaman's machines still found demand in a variety of military applications, however, that required improved control and stability (search and rescue operations and heavy lifting jobs, for example), particularly during the Korean War.

One of Kaman Aircraft's crowning achievements in the helicopter industry was its creation of the UH-2 utility helicopter. Kaman won the contract to design the machine in a contest. The project posed a formidable challenge because of the extremely demanding requirements set forth by the U.S. Navy. It wanted a vehicle that could fly at night for several hundred miles with no external navigation. It also had to be able to pick up downed pilots at sea under icy conditions and then return to a different location. Because of the complexity of the instrumentation, Kaman found that the machine also had to have less than one-tenth of a G of vibration to make the display panel readable for the pilot. Kaman's UH-2 met the requirements and was introduced into service in 1963.

In addition to the UH-2, other successful Kaman helicopter designs included the H-43 Husky and the SH-2. The former was used during the Vietnam War to rescue downed pilots and was the first helicopter to perform with no loss of life or accidents attributable to the aircraft. The SH-2, an antisubmarine aircraft, still was being used by the U.S. Navy in the early 1990s.

Throughout the 1950s and early 1960s, Kaman Aircraft's inventions relating to airplanes, rotors, drones, and other technologies made pivotal contributions to the field of aviation. Among its most notable innovations were the servo-controlled rotor, gas-turbine helicopter, twin-turbine helicopter, all-composite rotor blade, and remotely controlled helicopter. Kaman also set numerous records related to time-to-climb, altitude, and other factors.

Although Kaman managed to show a profit every year during the 1950s and early 1960s, its sales fluctuated because of its dependence on military contracts. In the early 1960s, President John F. Kennedy's administration ordered 220 Seasprite helicopters from Kaman. Five days later, however, Kennedy was assassinated. President Lyndon Johnson rescinded the order, and Kaman's helicopter division was devastated.

INITIAL DIVERSIFICATION: SIXTIES

The detrimental impact of the loss of the large Pentagon contract was diminished by Kaman's other operations. Since the late 1950s, Kaman had been trying to reduce its dependence on defense contracts, particularly related to helicopters. The company board of directors determined that Kaman should operate in three basic business segments: defense, industrial, and commercial. Over time, they decided, each division would be built to approximately one-third of company sales. In the 1950s, Kaman began expanding into aerospace parts manufacturing, aerodynamics subcontracting, and advanced nuclear research, among other defense and industry-related activities. As a result of its diversification, Kaman continued to post profits throughout the 1960s and 1970s.

One of Kaman's most intriguing ventures away from the helicopter business involved musical instruments. In part because of his own interest in playing the guitar, Charles Kaman had long been interested in the music business. In the early 1960s, he set out to develop his own guitar. He sought help from Martin, a Pennsylvania-based manufacturer of acoustic guitars. Kaman was surprised at the primitive methods that Martin and other companies were still using to produce the instruments. He believed that he could improve both the guitars and the production process by incorporating modern manufacturing techniques and aerospace technology.

The owners of Martin refused to sell their company, so Kaman started his own operation. He drew on his knowledge of harmonics, which he gleaned from building helicopter rotors, to build a guitar with composites that still had a natural sound. "In a helicopter, you take vibration out," Kaman explained in the July 26, 1993 *Business Week.* "In a guitar you put it in." The end result of Kaman's early efforts was the Ovation guitar, a top industry seller distinguished by its round-back design. Kaman Music Corporation met with success during the late 1960s and particularly beginning in the 1970s by developing new products and acquiring other manufacturers. In 1974, Kaman's son, C. William Kaman II, started his career making guitars at Kaman Music Corporation. He became president of that division in 1986.

ACQUISITIONS AND EXPANSION: SEVENTIES AND EIGHTIES

Kaman continued to build its consumer and defense-related businesses throughout the 1960s and 1970s. In addition, it expanded into several industrial segments through merger and acquisition beginning in 1971. In that year, Kaman purchased three industrial distribution businesses, launching a buying spree that would propel Kaman Corporation into the *Fortune* 500 by the 1980s. Kaman purchased more than 30 industrial companies during the 1970s and 1980s, helping to make its Kaman Bearing and Supply subsidiary the third-largest U.S. industrial distributor. By 1989 that division accounted for roughly half of Kaman Corporation's revenues, had 156 offices in the United States and Canada, and supplied more than 750,000 different parts to every major industry.

Charles Kaman had success integrating the companies that he acquired into a cohesive whole. When appraising buyout candidates, Kaman looked for situations in which both companies stood to gain from each other's competencies. A musical instrument manufacturer, for example, might benefit from Kaman's marketing and distribution channels while Kaman would get access to new production facilities or patented processes or products. In addition, he applied years of experience in determining the integrity and substance of the candidate. "After 45 years, I just walk through, and I've got it in about 10 minutes, maybe half-an-hour," Kaman told *Enterprise.* "You can read it. ... When we visit a military base I can tell you what the base commander is like by the attitude of the sentry at the guard house—are we greeted with smiles, does he know what's going on?"

At his home office, Kaman set the leadership example that permeated his organization. Kaman was his company's major stockholder, but unlike most executives, he had purchased all of his stock on the open market rather than receiving it as compensation, reflecting his faith in the company. In addition, he paid himself a relatively low salary compared with other chief executive officers of companies of similar size, and much of that was tied to the company's performance. Kaman believed in direct communication and candor and advocated empowering workers and recognizing their contributions. "There's no politicking, no vying for power around here," stated Kaman in *Enterprise.* "It's just straight-arrow stuff." Kaman Corporation was recognized for its acute management team and fruitful working environment.

Kaman continued to diversify into new markets and expand its defense, industrial, and consumer divisions during the 1970s and 1980s. Significantly, Kaman reopened its helicopter production line in 1981. It began manufacturing an updated version of its old Seasprite helicopter called the SH-2F, or LAMPS (Light Airborne Multi-purpose System) for the U.S. Navy, which wanted to use LAMPS as a submarine hunter and utility craft. The SH-2F had Kaman's original servo-flap system as well as a tail rotor. Renewed interest in the servo-flap design was partially a result of new technology and materials that made it more feasible for integration into new helicopters.

As Kaman expanded into new markets and revived its activities in old ones, its revenues continued to swell during the 1980s. Sales topped $380 million in 1983, about $6.4 million of which was net income. Receipts increased to $556 million by 1985 and then past $760 million in 1988 as net earnings rose past the $25 million mark. Kaman's workforce likewise increased, from 4,800 in the early 1980s to nearly 6,500 by 1989. Although sales of musical instruments languished, defense-related work boomed. Kaman continued to especially be a powerful influence in the high-tech defense arena. One of the company's projects in 1986 was an $8.5 million contract to build an electromagnetic coil gun, a high-tech cannon that used synchronized magnetic waves to fire projectiles at a velocity of 2.5 miles per second.

ONGOING HUMANITARIAN INITIATIVES AND A NEW KAMAN PRESIDENT

Besides his lauded achievements in aviation and technology, Charles Kaman was also well known for another of his passions, breeding guide dogs for the blind. When a blind boyhood friend had his life improved by a guide dog, Kaman became interested in the animals. To improve blind people's access to the dogs, Kaman and his wife in 1960 launched the Fieldco Guide Dog Foundation, a nonprofit foundation that bred and trained dogs for the blind.

Kaman handled his dog breeding operation in the same way he managed his business affairs. He applied rigorous breeding standards and was able to gradually weed out genetic defects, particularly susceptibility to certain disease strains that traditionally plagued guide dogs. The Kamans opened their own school in 1981 to match dogs with owners. During the early 1990s, the school provided dogs to recipients for $150, a mere fraction of the $17,500 training cost. In 1990, Fieldco launched an initiative to begin matching 100 owner and dog teams annually over the next decade.

At the age of 71, Charles Kaman stepped aside as president of Kaman Corporation in 1990 but remained chief executive and chairman of the board. He was succeeded by Harvey S. Levenson. Levenson took the reins just as the company was slipping into a downturn. After doubling its sales between 1980 and 1989, Kaman suffered setbacks, primarily attributable to defense industry

cutbacks. Several of its contracts expired and new federal defense spending programs were capped in the wake of the post-Cold War military transition. Net earnings dropped to $8.7 million in 1989, and the rampant revenue growth achieved during much of the 1980s waned.

ADAPTING TO DEFENSE SPENDING CUTBACKS IN THE NINETIES

Kaman's strong performance in its industrial technologies, distribution, and music businesses allowed it to remain profitable between 1990 and 1992. However, as defense dollars ebbed, Kaman made adjustments to the new environment by restructuring and cutting its workforce to about 5,300 employees by 1993. That year, the company posted a disappointing loss, mostly as a result of restructuring costs, and total revenues remained below $800 million. Nevertheless, the company held a strong technological edge in its core markets and was solidly positioned for future growth. Virtually every mass-produced aircraft in the world already used Kaman parts, which secured the company's dominant market presence.

Kaman Music became the largest independent distributor of musical instruments in the United States with more than 13,000 products when it acquired Hamer Guitars, a $100 million guitar manufacturer, in the early 1990s. Boosting the music segment's credibility was a long list of star performers who were using Kaman's guitars (and other equipment), including Glen Campbell, Richie Sambora of Bon Jovi, and Phil Collins. In 1993, Kaman himself was recognized by the Music Distributors Association, which presented him with a Music Industry Leadership Award. By that year, music and consumer products constituted about 20 percent of Kaman's total sales. Industrial products and distribution activities represented about 43 percent, and defense-related goods and services constituted the remainder of sales.

Kaman offset its defense-related losses by repositioning its helicopter products for use in commercial markets. In 1994, the company's breakthrough K-MAX helicopter was certified by the Federal Aviation Administration. The K-MAX was touted as an "aerial truck" and was designed specifically for repetitive heavy lifting. The K-MAX could lift three tons, more than its weight, and was particularly suited to logging in environmentally sensitive forests, firefighting, construction work, heavy equipment transportation, and a variety of other specialty and industrial uses. The helicopter sold for $3.5 million or could be leased for $1 million per thousand hours of use. By the end of

1995, the K-MAX was operating in the United States as well as Canadian, European, and South American markets.

AWARDS AND SUCCESS IN THE LATE NINETIES

At the end of 1995, the company's president and chief operating officer, Harvey Levenson, retired. Charles Kaman, who still held the positions of CEO and chairman, reassumed the office of president that he had vacated just five years earlier. The second half of the 1990s was marked by a series of honors and awards for the company leader. In 1995, the Department of Defense awarded him its Distinguished Public Service Medal. In 1996 he was inducted into the Naval Aviation Hall of Honor and awarded the National Medal of Technology. During the following two years, Kaman received the National Aeronautic Association's Wright Brothers Memorial Trophy and was awarded the Spirit of St. Louis Medal by the American Society of Mechanical Engineers.

As the 1990s progressed, Kaman Corporation continued to focus on building smaller, lightweight aircraft that could nonetheless carry heavy loads. One of its most notable successes was the refurbishment of its SH-2 Seasprite helicopters for marketing to overseas navies. The company took the original SH-2s, which the U.S. Navy had ceased to purchase, and retrofitted them with new avionics, engines, and cockpits. In 1996 and 1997, Kaman won $1 billion in orders for the refurbished Seasprites from Egypt, Australia, and New Zealand. The contracts helped boost Kaman's income substantially, allowing it in 1997 to top $1 billion in annual revenue for the first time in company history.

Another major source of the record revenue for fiscal 1997 was the company's sale of its 40-year-old Kaman Sciences subsidiary. Kaman sold the subsidiary, which provided software support and research to government agencies, to ITT Industries for $135 million.

CHANGING OF THE GUARD AT THE END OF THE 20TH CENTURY

By 1998, Charles Kaman was nearing 80. Speculation about who would replace him was pervasive, but the company was offering no information on its succession plan. In August 1998, one possible successor, Kaman's son C. William Kaman II, retired from his position as head of the company's music division, announcing that he would no longer be involved in the day-to-day operations of the business. That same month, the elder Ka-

man suffered a mild stroke and spent the remainder of the year convalescing. In December 1998, the company announced that it would begin searching for a new CEO. Charles Kaman continued to serve as CEO while the search was conducted.

In July 1999, the company announced that Paul R. Kuhn would become Kaman Corporation's new CEO. Kuhn had served previously as senior vice president of operations for the aerospace engine businesses of Coltec Industries.

Kaman relinquished his seat as CEO but kept his position as chairman of the board. However, Charles Kaman's health soon became an issue again for the company. In June 2000, the 81-year-old was hospitalized with pneumonia. In August, his condition led the company to transfer his majority voting power to two committees, which included Kaman family members. In March 2001, the company announced that its founder and leader for more than half a century would not be seeking reelection to its board of directors. Kuhn was elected chairman of the board.

MAJOR CONTRACTS AND ACQUISITIONS: EARLY 21ST CENTURY

After receiving a U.S. Marine Corps contract in 1999 to design a remote-piloting system and install it in a K-MAX, Kaman in 2000 earned another Marine contract for the development of a remotely piloted K-MAX helicopter that could eventually undertake unmanned troop resupply missions. That same year, Kaman Aerospace earned a $75 million contract to supply rotor blade systems to MD Helicopters, Inc., for their MD Explorer aircraft. Kaman Aerospace's shipbuilding team also was chosen by Litton Ingalls Shipbuilding to design electric propulsion motors and drive electronics for an industry competition for the U.S. Navy's DD-21 destroyer. The company earned other major contracts early in the decade.

In 2002, the Electromagnetics Development Center of Kaman Aerospace was chosen as part of a Northrop Grumman-led team to design advanced propulsion engines for the U.S. Navy's next generation of destroyer in a contract worth about $50 million. Kaman also became part of Northrop Grumman's U.S. Navy-selected team developing the Rapid Airborne Mine Clearance System. In addition, Kaman in 2002 won a major structural components contract for the Boeing C-17 military transport aircraft. Other contracts included a $35 million joint award to Kaman's Electro-Optics Development Center and the University of Arizona to develop a 6.5-meter aperture collimator for the Steward Observatory Mirror Lab, and a contract with Boeing Commercial Airplanes to supply aircraft subassemblies for Boeing planes.

Early in the new century, Kaman sold its K-MAX to European customers, Wucher Helicopters in Austria and Heli-Air Zagel Lufttransport AG in Germany, the latter for use in forestry and construction applications. Kaman also had multiyear contracts, stemming from the previous decade and ending in the early 2000s, to provide refurbished Seasprite helicopters to the Royal Australian Navy and the Royal New Zealand Navy. During the same period, the company sold K-MAX external-lift helicopters for the U.S. State Department's counter-drug efforts in Peru. Despite recessionary conditions, Kaman expanded its aerospace and industrial distribution operations through acquisitions.

The company in 2001 purchased the distribution network of A-C Supply, Inc., of Milwaukee, Wisconsin, a wholesaler and manufacturer of industrial products that increased Kaman's presence in the upper Midwest. The acquisition became part of Kaman Industrial Technologies Corporation (KIT). Kaman also purchased the Wichita, Kansas-based Plastic Fabricating Company, a producer of plastic structural components for aircraft markets. In 2002, Kaman secured a majority interest in Delamac S.A. de C. V., a leading industrial products wholesaler in Mexico which made new markets accessible to Kaman's customers operating south of the border. Kaman also increased its footprint in the European aircraft market, acquiring the German-based RWG Frankenjura-Industrie Flugwerklager, a manufacturer of aerospace ball bearings that supplemented Kamatics bearings operations and expanded Kaman's European aerospace business.

In addition, the company purchased the Florida-based Dayron, a bomb fuze manufacturer which boosted Kaman into the ranks of leading fuze suppliers for precision guided U.S. Army and Navy weapons. In 2003, Kaman broadened its operations in southeastern states by acquiring the Alabama-based Industrial Supplies, Inc., an industrial products distributor. With the acquisition, Kaman was in more than two-thirds of the top 100 U.S. industrial markets.

Kaman Music expanded its product range early in the decade. The music division took over global sales and marketing for Fred Gretsch Enterprises, including the top-of-the-line Gretsch-branded drum products that complemented the company's entry-level drum products. The company also added Sabian cymbals and percussion items in 2002. That same year, Kaman Music acquired Latin Percussion, Inc., an international distributor of Latin percussion instruments that supplemented Kaman's healthy line of popular percus-

sion brands and instruments. To enhance its distribution, Kaman Music consolidated its two Texas warehouses into one state-of-the-art California facility in 2002, and the Currier Piano division doubled its manufacturing capacity by opening a new North Carolina facility.

FINANCIAL HURDLES

After topping $1 billion in sales in 1997, the next three years the company sustained that level of revenue. In 2001, however, there was a global economic downturn, and Kaman's revenues fell to $877 million. Earnings, meanwhile, had dropped from a 1997 high of $70.5 million to roughly half that amount in 2000 and just $11.7 million in 2001. Tough economic times continued into 2002, and a decline in helicopter contracts led the company to phase out a Kaman Aerospace plant in Connecticut, resulting in the eventual layoff of about 400 personnel. While Kaman's sales were essentially flat in 2002, the company posted a net loss of $33.6 million, largely attributable to pretax charges, write-downs, and write-offs. Revenues rose slightly in 2003, but more importantly, the company was back in the black, reporting earnings of $19.4 million.

In 2004, Kaman Dayron began manufacturing what was considered the fuze of the future, the advanced FMU-152A/B Joint Programmable Fuze, for the U.S. Air Force (USAF). The fuze's advantage was that it could be reprogrammed by pilots in flight to accommodate tactical situation changes. The following year, Kaman Aerospace landed a contract worth a potential $100 million from Sikorsky Aircraft to produce cockpits for Sikorsky's UH-60 Black Hawk helicopter.

A CHANGING COMPANY

During the second half of the decade, Kaman was a company in transition, readying itself to become both more attractive to investors and in the process become a sleeker more focused firm. A significant move occurred in 2005 when Kaman Corporation's stock was recapitalized to create a single one-share, one-vote common stock. The two-class stock structure had been devised by Charles Kaman during the early years of his corporation when he was very much in need of capital but concerned about forfeiting control of his nascent business. The 2005 change was expected to please investors because companies with multiple classes of stock were often viewed as unconcerned with accountability to shareholders.

Kaman's innovative history in helicopter development again was on display in 2006. In April the company conducted a test-flight demonstration of what it then called its BURRO+ (short for Broad-Area Unmanned Responsive Resupply Operations), based on the initial award from the U.S. Marines in 1999 to develop a remotely piloted K-MAX. After developing a piloted demonstration model from that contract, separate demonstrations for the military followed in 2003 and 2005. In 2006, the converted K-MAX demonstration included a 12-hour flight, which was a simulated mission without refueling, illustrating what Kaman believed was unprecedented in terms of an unmanned helicopter's endurance. The 2006 trial flight demonstrated the craft was ready for the next step in development, and Kaman joined with Lockheed Martin in 2007 to design and produce a more advanced model.

In a changing of the guard, Neal J. Keating became president of Kaman Corporation in 2007 and assumed the added role of chief executive officer and chairman of the board the following year. Keating succeeded the retiring Paul Kuhn as chairman. A veteran executive in both aerospace and industrial distribution businesses, Keating was a former senior-level manager at Rockwell International.

Two significant developments at Kaman Music suggested the subsidiary was preparing for a new phase of growth. Kaman Music at mid-decade acquired MBT Holding Corporation, a wholesaler of musical instruments and accessories that was second only to Kaman Music in terms of business size. In July 2007, Edward Miller, a 35-year company man, was named president of Kaman Music, succeeding the retiring Robert Saunders. Miller's tenure at the top of the subsidiary was short-lived. In a surprise to the industry, Kaman Corporation, after nearly 40 years in the music business, sold Kaman Music Corporation to Fender Musical Instruments Corporation in early 2008 for $120 million. Kaman's new management believed the company was more attractive to investors as a strictly aerospace enterprise.

ACQUISITIONS, CONTRACT AWARDS, AND IMPROVED CASH FLOW

In 2008, Kaman made a trio of acquisitions. The KIT subsidiary acquired the Virginia-based Industrial Supply Corp. (ISC). Adding to Kaman's distribution business, which included North America's third-largest power transmission and motion-control products operation, the 75-year-old ISC was a supplier of power transmission, material handling, fluid power, and industrial supply products with $55 million in annual sales. KIT also acquired the Puerto Rico-based Industrial Rubber and Mechanics, Incorporated, a fluid-power products

wholesaler that complemented the company's distribution operations. That same year, Kaman Aerospace Group, Inc., spent $85.1 million to acquired U.K.-based Brookhouse Holdings, Limited, a manufacturer of aerospace engineering equipment and tools.

Substantial contracts for the company during the period included Kaman Aerospace Corporation's award to produce Black Hawk helicopter cockpits for Sikorsky Aircraft Corporation through 2012. The agreement called for an initial guaranteed order of $74 million with the opportunity for Kaman to earn nearly $200 million if Sikorsky exercised all contract options. In 2009, Kaman received a $53 million USAF contract for joint-programmable fuzes valued at $53 million. In a second military award that year, Kaman Aerospace received a U.S. Marine Corps contract to demonstrate the capacity of its Unmanned K-MAX helicopter to transport cargo to soldiers stationed at high altitudes and in extreme environs. Lockheed was subcontracted to integrate the unmanned aerial system, focusing on conversion of the K-Max to a completely autonomous craft designed for resupply assignments. Kaman in 2009 landed a five-year contract with Bell Helicopters for composite helicopter blade skins and skin core assemblies.

REORGANIZATION OF KAMAN

In 2009, Kaman Aerospace International Corporation was merged into Kaman Aerospace Corporation, and Industrial Supply Corporation was merged into Kaman Industrial Technologies Corporation. The reorganization effectively placed Kaman operations in two large market segments: industrial distribution and aerospace products. The Industrial Distribution group provided power transmission and motion-control products. The Aerospace group produced bearings and other aircraft components as well as metallic and composite aerostructures for fixed- and rotary-wing aircraft. It also supplied arming, fuzing, and safety mechanisms for bomb and missile systems, subcontracted helicopter work, and provided support for its existing helicopters in operation. That same year, Kaman debuted its own brand, ReliaMark, for bearings, oil seals, roller chains, and shaft collars.

Kaman closed the decade earning $32.65 million on revenues of $1.15 billion. Both figures were down slightly, from $35.6 million in profit on sales of $1.25 billion in 2008. The company attributed the dip in revenues to a modest falloff in distribution sales, which was largely offset by growth in the Aerospace Group and sales from the three companies that Kaman acquired in 2008. In large measure, Kaman weathered fairly well the economic storms related to recessionary conditions at the end of the decade. While suffering a slight drop in sales in 2009, of about 9 percent, the company's diverse product line and loyal customer base kept the company's profit margins from nose-diving.

2010 AND BEYOND: BUILDING ON ITS STRENGTHS

In early 2010, the subsidiary KIT made a trio of acquisitions. It acquired Fawick de Mexico SA de CV, a distributor of fluid power and lubrication products. The company bought the Oklahoma-based Allied Bearings Supply Co. Inc., a wholesaler of bearings, material handling, power transmission, and industrial products. Additionally, the company acquired Minarik Corporation, a California-based distributor of automation and motion control products. KIT also inked a North American distribution deal with Bison Gear and Engineering allowing the company to distribute Bison's gears, expanding Kaman's ability to address the electrical needs of its clients.

Following the divestment of Kaman Music and the elevation of Keating to the company's top three seats, Kaman Corporation quickly made a series of acquisitions, as if to show investors it was serious about further developing its two-pronged focus. While Kuhn had vowed to keep the company together, Keating clearly planned to develop the industrial distribution and aerospace business, seeing those as the future of the company. Meanwhile, the company once again was active in helicopter innovation, as it worked with Lockheed Martin to develop an unmanned K-MAX resupply craft.

While Kaman's profits were likely to stem from its two-million-plus products offered through its industrial distribution unit (which in 2009 accounted for 60 percent of all sales), bearings, precision products, and aerostructures for aerospace markets were also expected to continue to play a large role. Big-ticket contracts such as the one Kaman had with Boeing running through 2013 to provide wing-control surfaces for the USAF A-10 fleet, were certainly expected to help the company's bottom line. Likewise, successful development and military approval of an unmanned K-MAX could prove a new boon to Kaman's reputation and a bow to the company's roots in helicopter development.

Dave Mote
Updated, Shawna Brynildssen; Roger Rouland

PRINCIPAL SUBSIDIARIES

Kaman Aerospace Group, Inc.; Kaman Aerospace Corporation; Kaman X Corporation; Kamatics Corporation; Kaman Aerostructures Group - Wichita, Inc.; Kaman Precision Products, Inc.; RWG Frankenjura-Industrie Flugwerklager GmbH (Germany); Kaman UK Holdings Limited; Brookhouse Holdings Limited (UK); Brookhouse Group Holdings Limited (UK); Brookhouse 2004 Limited (UK); Brookhouse Tooling Limited (UK); Brookhouse Composites Limited (UK); Brookhouse Aerospace Limited (UK); Brookhouse (SPD) Tool Company Limited (UK); Brookhouse Automotive Limited (UK); Brookhouse IM Limited (UK); Kaman Industrial Technologies Corporation; Kaman Industrial Technologies, Ltd. (Canada); Delamac de Mexico, S.A. de C.V.; Industrial Rubber & Mechanics, Inc. (Puerto Rico).

PRINCIPAL OPERATING UNITS

Aerospace; Industrial Distribution.

PRINCIPAL COMPETITORS

Agusta Aerospace Corporation; Alliant Techsystems Inc.; Applied Industrial Technologies, Inc.; GKN plc; Goodrich Corporation; Kaydon Corporation; Kellstrom Aerospace LLC; Motion Industries, Inc.; MSC Industrial Direct Co., Inc.; Spirit AeroSystems Holdings, Inc.; Textron Inc.; Triumph Aerostructures - Vought Aircraft Division; United Technologies Corporation; WESCO International, Inc.; W.W. Grainger, Inc.

FURTHER READING

"Big Sales Gains at Kaman Music," *Music Trades*, December 2000, p. 31.

Birchard, Bill, "The Art of Acquisition," *Enterprise*, Fall 1989, p. 9.

"Charges Hurt Kaman Net, Strong Quarter for Music," *Music Trades*, October 2002, pp. 41+.

"Deal Snapshot: US Kaman to Buy Allied Bearings Supply," *M & A Navigator*, March 1, 2010.

"Fender Buys Kaman: Acquisition Creates $700 Million Player with Extensive Brand Stable," *Music Trades*, December 2007, pp. 18+.

"Kaman Aerospace Corporation: Pushing the Envelope of Helicopter Technology," *Rotor & Wing*, January 15, 2006.

"Kaman Buys Latin Percussion; Purchase Vaults Kaman to Forefront of Hand Percussion Market," *Music Trades*, December 2002, p. 22.

"Kaman Buys MBT/Musicorp Creating $220 Mil. Megadistributor," *Music Trades*, September 2005, pp. 26+.

"Kaman Corp. Eliminates Non-voting Stock," *Music Trades*, July 2005, p. 73.

"LockMart and Kaman Aerospace Team Up for Manned and Unmanned Helicopter Systems Worldwide," *Space Daily*,

March 9, 2007.

Rose, Peter, "Kaman Industries Goes High-Tech," *Idaho Business Review*, May 2, 1994, p. A10.

Smart, Tim, "What Do Dogs, Guitars, and Choppers Have in Common?" *Business Week*, July 26, 1993.

"Unmanned Aerial System Tested for Logistics Resupply Missions," *Army Logistician*, January–February 2009, pp. 56+.

"US Kaman Inks Deal to Buy Fawick de Mexico," *M & A Navigator*, February 25, 2010.

Kayem Foods Incorporated

75 Arlington Street
Chelsea, Massachusetts 02150
U.S.A.
Telephone: (617) 889-1600
Toll Free: (800) 426-6100
Fax: (617) 889-5478
Web site: http://www.kayem.com

Private Company
Founded: 1909
Employees: 500
Sales: $145 million (2009 est.)
NAICS: 311611 Animal (Except Poultry) Slaughtering;
311612 Meat Processed from Carcasses

∎ ∎ ∎

Kayem Foods Incorporated is the largest privately owned meat processor in New England. Kayem makes Kayem Franks, the top-selling brand of frankfurters in New England and al fresco chicken sausage, the top-selling brand of chicken sausage in the United States, two of roughly 500 products sold by the company under a dozen brand names. Prominent Kayem brands include Schonland's, Meisterchef, Old Tyme, and Triple M. The company's selection of sausages and hot dogs are complemented by a range of deli meats that include corned beef, ham, pastrami, roast beef, bologna, turkey, and chicken. Kayem sells its products to retail and food-service customers, relying on two Massachusetts-based production facilities in Chelsea and Woburn. The company is owned by the Monkiewicz family.

HUMBLE BEGINNINGS IN 1909

A century of sausage making by the Monkiewicz family began modestly. Kazimierz Monkiewicz, a Polish immigrant, established the profession for generations of his descendants when he opened a small shop in Chelsea, Massachusetts, across the Mystic River from Boston. Monkiewicz opened his store in 1909, the year he and his wife emigrated from Poland.

Monkiewicz sold handmade kielbasa from his storefront, using a recipe that would be marketed under the name "Kayem Old Tyme Natural Casing Frankfurts." In the early days of his business, before Monkiewicz and his family turned to brand names, marketing, and advertising slogans to excite interest in their traditional Polish sausages, Monkiewicz looked to his neighbors to support his business, building his reputation one customer at a time. His cachet as a butcher and sausage maker grew, and so did the scope of his business. Monkiewicz used his profits to buy a wagon and a team of horses and began making deliveries outside his neighborhood to nearby communities, beginning the gradual expansion of his business from a storefront operation to regional purveyor of sausages and other meats.

The evolution from a neighborhood business to a regional company of note took time. The transition was made with the help of Monkiewicz's four sons, Romould, Frank, Anthony, and Walter, the generation that established sausage making as a family business and orchestrated its development toward an iconic stature within New England. After the family business grew beyond its storefront roots, it was known to Chelsea residents as K. Monkiewicz, Inc., an era in the company's history when the "Kayem" brand name was used as a label sold by K. Monkiewicz, Inc. Eventually, Kayem, derived from the initials of the founder, became the name of the company, the name that would become well known to New Englanders and familiar in markets far removed from the northeastern United States.

ACQUISITIONS FUEL EXPANSION:
1987–97

Methodical growth described Kayem's progress for more than a half-century. The founder's four sons expanded the family business throughout Massachusetts and into selected markets in neighboring states, but they purposefully drew rein on Kayem's geographic march, never embracing the growth-oriented strategy espoused later in the company's history. The turning point in Kayem's corporate strategy occurred once the third generation of the family began directing the course of the company, a generation led by Kazimierz Monkiewicz's grandson Ray Monkiewicz.

To accelerate the pace of expansion, the third generation turned to external means of growth. Kayem, for the first time in its history, began to acquire other companies. Acceptance of the new corporate strategy met with some resistance. "Some of my uncles didn't like the idea," Ray Monkiewicz recalled in the May 30, 2008 issue of the *Boston Business Journal*. "They thought it would change the culture, but we had to grow." Kayem began acquiring other companies in the late 1980s, implementing an expansion campaign that saw the company purchase Massachusetts-based competitors such as the DeCosta Sausage Co. and New Hampshire-based Schonland's.

As Kayem extended its geographic reach, the Monkiewicz family was forced to make changes to ensure the company successfully transitioned to the next level of

competitiveness. Seasoned executives were hired from major, international consumer products companies such as Sara Lee and Procter & Gamble, giving the company professionals to scale up its operations. "We had to bring in outside talent," Ray Monkiewicz said in the May 30, 2008 issue of the *Boston Business Journal*.

After roughly a decade of expansion, Kayem had begun to transform itself into a formidable competitor in the Northeast. Annual sales reached the $100 million plateau in 1996, a total derived from hundreds of products sold under labels such as DeCosta, Triple M, Meisterchef, and the company's flagship brand, Old Tyme.

PRODUCTION PLANT
EXPANSION: 1997

The company, nearing its 80th anniversary, had successfully penetrated markets in New Hampshire, Vermont, Maine, Rhode Island, and Connecticut. Kayem stood as a regional force, holding sway in New England, but it had also begun to carve out a presence in international markets. By 1997, the company was generating one-quarter of its revenue from overseas sales, enjoying a bustling export business that supplied meat products to Russia and neighboring Eastern European countries. "There is such a demand in Europe for low-cost protein products," Ray Monkiewicz said in the August 6, 1997 edition of the *Boston Herald*.

The Monkiewicz family moved forward on increasing both its domestic and international business by expanding its Arlington Street production plant beginning in 1997. Plans were developed to add 35,000 square feet to Kayem's 140,000-square-foot facility, an addition that was expected to double its daily production of frankfurters and add 60 to 75 positions to the 400 employees on its payroll. The expansion was projected to cost nearly $10 million, funds that the privately owned company secured by turning to municipal and state agencies. Tax-exempt bonds issued through the Massachusetts Development Finance Agency helped financed the expansion project, as did other governmental allowances. Chelsea, targeted by the state for economic development, offered Kayem a reduction in property taxes for a 10-year period. Massachusetts also offered the company a one-time corporate income tax credit of 5 percent.

The third generation of the Monkiewicz family pressed ahead with expansion plans as the company entered the 21st century. In New England, Kayem ranked as the largest producer of natural casing frankfurters and the leading brand of frankfurters in both the deli and meat section of supermarkets. The

KEY DATES

1909: Kazimierz Monkiewicz begins selling handmade sausages from a storefront in Chelsea, Massachusetts.

1980s: Kayem begins acquiring competitors.

1997: Expansion of the company's plant in Chelsea doubles daily production.

2002: Kayem launches its first television advertising campaign.

2009: Kayem Franks become the official hot dog of the Boston Red Sox during the company's centennial.

company also collected a substantial stream of revenue from foodservice customers, courting both retail and institutional customers. At its Arlington Street plant, Kayem produced nearly one million frankfurters each day. At another production facility in Woburn, Massachusetts, which the company had gained through the 1997 acquisition of Genoa Sausage Co., the company processed deli meat, producing ham, turkey breast, cured Italian specialty products, corned beef, pastrami, and bologna. The entire operation yielded more than 500 products marketed under eight separate brands.

FROM REGIONAL TO NATIONAL BRAND: 2002–08

Having secured a dominant position in New England, the Monkiewicz family set its sights on turning Kayem into a national force. By the first years of the decade, the company shipped its products to the Chicago area, the Carolinas, New York, New Jersey, and Florida, but Ray Monkiewicz wanted Kayem to become a genuine national company with distribution stretching from coast to coast. Toward this end, the company launched its first television advertising campaign in 2002, spending $400,000 to air commercials during prime time on the major television networks. "It is, by far, the largest allocation this company has ever made toward advertising," Kayem's vice president of sales and marketing said in the July 5, 2002 issue of the *Boston Business Journal*.

The leap toward national prominence was expected to take years, as Kayem contended with numerous challenges, notably establishing a distribution network capable of serving customers from California to Maine. As the company pursued its objective, several significant

events stood out in the years leading up to its centennial celebrations.

A change in leadership occurred in 2008. Ralph O. Smith was named president and CEO in 2008 when Ray Monkiewicz assumed the responsibilities of chairman. At the time of Smith's appointment, there were more than a dozen Monkiewicz family members working for the company, including Matt Monkiewicz, vice president of marketing, and Peter Monkiewicz, vice president of manufacturing.

NEW LEADERSHIP AND SPONSORSHIP DEALS: 2008–10

Smith took over day-to-day control of the company in November 2008, not long after Kayem had made a major acquisition. In April the company completed a deal with Arkansas-based Tyson Foods, Inc., purchasing the Jordan's, Deutschmacher, Kirschner, Essem, Tasty Bite, and Williams of Vermont brands. "Kayem Foods is a worthy steward for these important brands and the traditions they have created," Ray Monkiewicz said in a May 20, 2008 release of *Internet Wire*. "Like Kayem, these brands began as corner meat markets and matured into providers of delicious authentic meat products using the highest quality standards."

Kayem's centennial celebrations in 2009 marked not only the founding of the business but 100 years since the Monkiewicz family arrived in the United States. The small shop opened in 1909 by Kazimierz Monkiewicz had developed into an iconic brand in New England, one that earned Kayem Foods a coveted contract during its anniversary year. In April the company signed a contract with Major League Baseball's Boston Red Sox that represented a multiyear sponsorship deal with the famed baseball club. Under the terms of the agreement, Kayem was given the license to manufacture and distribute the Fenway Franks line of hot dogs. The licensing agreement also made Kayem the "Official Hot Dog of the Boston Red Sox" and the "Official Hot Dog of Fenway Park," where the Boston Red Sox played their home games.

As Kayem began its second century of business, the company continued in its efforts to make a name for itself on the national stage. As the largest meat processor in New England and the owner of the top-selling brand of frankfurters in the region, the company possessed a solid foundation to make its leap to the national level. Evidence of the company's recognition outside of New England was found in April 2010, when Major League Baseball's Tampa Bay Rays made Kayem Franks the "Official Hot Dog and Sausage of the Tampa Bay Rays" and the team's home ballpark, Tropicana Field. In the years ahead, further exposure promised to accelerate Kayem's evolution into a national company.

Jeffrey L. Covell

PRINCIPAL COMPETITORS

Hormel Foods Corporation; Kraft Foods Inc.; Sara Lee North American Retail.

FURTHER READING

Gambon, Jill, "Expanding Kayem Foods Keeps Links with Family Roots," *Boston Business Journal*, May 30, 2008.

"Kayem Foods Acquires Jordan's, Deutschmacher, Kirschner and Essem Brands from Tyson Foods," *Internet Wire*, May 20, 2008.

"Kayem to Beef Up Production," *Boston Herald*, August 6, 1997, p. 30.

Qualters, Sheri, "Hot Dog! Kayem Foods Launches Its First TV Campaign," *Boston Business Journal*, July 5, 2002.

Keds, LLC

191 Spring Street
Lexington, Massachusetts 02420
U.S.A.
Telephone: (617) 824-6000
Toll Free: (800) 680-0966
Fax: (800) 446-1339
Web site: http://www.keds.com

Subsidiary of Collective Brands, Inc.
Founded: 1916
Employees: 500
NAICS: 316211 Rubber and Plastics Footwear Manufacturing

■ ■ ■

Keds, LLC, competes in the casual segment of the footwear industry, marketing product lines for women, men, and children. Regarded as the first mass producer of sneakers, the company sells its shoes under the "Keds," "Keds Collective," and "PRO-Keds" labels. Keds operates primarily as a wholesaler, selling its merchandise to retail customers and online to consumers. Keds is a subsidiary of Collective Brands, Inc., a $3.3 billion, Topeka, Kansas-based holding company that owns a portfolio of footwear brands.

THE FIRST SNEAKER: 1916

Keds sprang from the sprawling operations of U.S. Rubber Company, one of the original 12 companies tracked by the Dow Jones Industrial Average. An amalgamation of nine rubber companies, U.S. Rubber was formed in 1892. The company was supported by numerous divisions, including a rubber footwear division. U.S. Rubber manufactured its footwear under 30 different brands, operating with a decentralized structure for roughly 25 years until it consolidated its footwear activities under a single brand. Keds became the new banner for U.S. Rubber's footwear business in 1916, heralding the birth of what quickly became a brand of iconic stature.

The first product released under the Keds brand was the first canvas shoe with a soft rubber sole, the Champion. One year later, in 1917, Henry Nelson McKinney, an agent for an advertising firm named N.W. Ayer & Son, applied a descriptive word to Champions that made Keds a part of fashion history. As early as 1887, Boston schoolchildren had used the word *sneakers* to describe their tennis shoes, but when McKinney used the term to refer to Keds' soft, noiseless rubber soles, Champions became the first mass-marketed shoe line advertised as sneakers.

U.S. Rubber's footwear division blossomed under the aegis of Keds. By the early 1920s, the brand had become the preferred footwear for professional tennis players. In 1924, for instance, the company was able to claim 11 national championships and two world championships had been "Won on Keds," according to newspaper advertisements from the year. Other athletes followed suit, marking the appearance of Keds on professional basketball players and Olympic soccer players.

Keds enjoyed the best of both worlds during its formative decades. The brand became a fashion statement, worn by Greta Garbo and later generations of celebrities such as Audrey Hepburn, Marilyn Monroe, and Jacqueline Kennedy Onassis. It also secured a presence in the athletic world, becoming a visible label that aided its development into becoming a fixture of classic U.S. style. The company paid tribute to its ability to thrive in both realms with the introduction of the Triumph in 1926. Combining fashion and athletics, the shoe featured a tweed, ankle-high upper and the brand's trademark rubber sole.

The Triumph aside, Keds approached its two distinct markets separately. In 1938, the company launched a line exclusively designed for women, its primary customer. Dubbed Kedettes, the line featured the first high-heel shoe with a shock-absorbing rubber sole. A decade later, in 1949, the company addressed its popularity in the athletic market with the creation of PRO-Keds, a product line geared for serious athletes. PRO-Keds debuted with the Classic Royal, which cemented Keds' reputation on the basketball court. In later year, basketball stars such as Jo Jo White, Kareem Abdul-Jabbar, and Pete Maravich wore Keds, favoring the PRO-Keds Royal Master.

PURCHASE BY STRIDE RITE: 1979

The first half-century of Keds' existence represented the brand's heyday, setting a precedent that would be hard to match in later decades. The responsibility of overseeing the brand's success fell to new hands in the 1970s, as Uniroyal, which earlier had purchased U.S. Rubber, cut its ties to the footwear business. In 1979 Lexington, Massachusetts-based Stride Rite Corporation, a footwear company founded 80 years earlier, purchased Keds for $18 million, taking ownership of the brand that had been losing money for Uniroyal. Under Stride Rite's direction, the brand effected a quick recovery, regaining its lost luster by 1982.

Once Keds began to shine under Stride Rite's control, it enjoyed robust growth, demonstrating impressive financial performance during the 1980s. It greatest gains came after the 1987 release of *Dirty Dancing*, which featured Jennifer Grey dancing in a pair of

Keds. Sales tripled during a three-year period after the film's debut, giving the brand a level of cachet in the fashion world that had not existed for decades.

As Keds entered the 1990s, the brand began to suffer, particularly as the pace of change in the footwear industry escalated. The company's Champion Oxford, a white canvas women's sneaker with a blue-labeled heel, continued to fare well in the casual footwear market. However, the product was seasonal, designed primarily for only warm-weather wear. Furthermore, over the years the brand had found little success in attracting younger customers. Aside from the boon provided by *Dirty Dancing*, Keds had struggled to win the affection of 18- to 25-year-old women. The brand's typical customer was a 43-year-old woman, giving Keds a narrow demographic target that limited its potential in the footwear market.

The fundamental flaws of the Keds brand became more pronounced as the years progressed. The company, belatedly, entered the e-commerce race in 1999, developing a Web site capable of taking online orders, but a presence on the Internet did not correct the problems of the stagnating brand.

REVAMPING KEDS: 2000–05

More aggressive action aimed at revitalizing the Keds brand took place as the company entered the 21st century. The efforts to find the right approach were ongoing, occupying management's attention for most of the decade ahead. In 2000 the company tried to fix the problem of Keds' seasonality by expanding the brand's product line, launching an advertising campaign that featured various styles and colors, which were touted as casual footwear built for comfort. "People are going to take notice that we're not just the white sneaker with the blue label," the company's vice president of marketing said in the February 28, 2000 issue of *Advertising Age*. "We can become more fashion-relevant and try to get into a 365-days-a-year opportunity."

In 2001 the company introduced a new label, Keds Kids, which was developed for children between the ages of five and eight. The debut of Keds Kids was followed by the release of a collection designed for children between the ages of eight and 12, a line called Keds Between. The company also revamped its Keds All Baby line, a collection targeted for the youngest Keds customers.

After operating exclusively as a wholesaler for 85 years, Keds entered the retail sector in mid-2001, opening its first Keds store. The first unit opened in suburban Atlanta, Georgia, marking the beginning of

KEY DATES

1916: Keds is created to unify the footwear brands marketed by U.S. Rubber Co.
1949: The PRO-Keds line debuts.
1979: Stride Rite Corporation acquires Keds for $18 million.
2001: Keds opens its first retail store.
2007: Payless ShoeSource acquires Stride Rite and changes its name to Collective Brands, Inc.

the company's bid to raise the visibility of its brand and reposition it with a wider and younger demographic. Another unit opened in suburban Atlanta followed by three store openings in Florida and a sixth in Ohio. Half of the stores stocked merchandise for women and children, while the remainder catered exclusively to women, with each store averaging roughly 1,200 square feet. "We don't even want to call it a shoe store," a Keds executive said in the June 29, 2001 issue of *Boston Business Journal.* "It's a lifestyle store to us. It allows Keds to come across as a lifestyle brand. Today, people aspire to purchase brands and what a brand strives for. Down the road, these stores could be the launching point for licensing in these other categories."

MANAGERIAL CHANGES: 2002–04

Shifts occurred in the way Keds conducted its business and in its management, both prompted by the company's drive to secure a more profitable future. In January 2002 Dan Friedman, who had joined Keds as president in 1999, resigned his post amid numerous other executive changes throughout Stride Rite. The departure of Friedman, filled temporarily by Stride Rite's chairman and CEO, David Chamberlain, signaled the start of a major brand overhaul, one the company hoped would staunch declining market share and a pattern of financial losses.

In May, five months after Friedman resigned, Gerrald Silverman took the helm. Previously the president of Stride Rite's children's group, Silverman aimed his efforts at injecting life into what he perceived to be a stale brand. "Frankly," he said in the May 27, 2002 issue of *Footwear News,* "our customer is just waiting for us to come in and excite her and tap again into the emotional connections she has with the brand with something relevant and surprising."

Silverman's attempts to breathe new life into the Keds brand failed to produce their desired result. His stay at Keds was brief, ending in January 2004, a year-and-a-half after it had begun. Stride Rite's president, Rick Thornton, took charge temporarily as a search for a new leader began. Midway through the year Shawn Neville, the former president and CEO of Footstar's athletic division, was appointed as Keds' new chief. Neville assessed his predecessor's tactic and criticized the attempt to diversify into casual sandals as driving toward "a future they didn't have permission to create," according to the January 31, 2005 issue of *Footwear News.*

NEVILLE'S STRATEGY: 2005–07

Neville took on his responsibilities at a time when Keds was experiencing difficulty in distinguishing itself in an increasingly competitive casual footwear market. Sales stood at less than $200 million, the company was reeling from a decade of declines in average selling price, and the prospects of an aging customer base provided little confidence for a healthy financial future. Keds was undergoing its second major overhaul in three years, unable to find its footing in a market in which it had once thrived. For a solution to the profound problems hobbling the company, Neville looked to Keds' heyday. "We've got to rebuild our bridge from the past," he said in the January 31, 2005 issue of *Footwear News.*

Neville focused on reconnecting with Keds' heritage as a maker of youthful, athletic-leisure sneakers. The company's advertising budget doubled, nearly reaching an estimated $10 million as Neville sought to make Keds an aspirational brand for young, fashion-conscious consumers. In an attempt to relive the boom years following the release of *Dirty Dancing,* Neville negotiated a sponsorship deal with the makers of *The Aviator,* a film starring Leonardo DiCaprio whose portrayal of Howard Hughes included wearing a pair of Triumphs. Although the efforts to reposition the brand failed to deliver financial returns, Neville saw progress, believing his more immediate goals to be rejuvenating brand awareness and increasing Keds' market share in the premium and specialty segments of the footwear market.

The end of the decade witnessed a change in ownership that gave Keds a new parent company to support its progress in the years ahead. In 2007 Payless ShoeSource acquired Stride Rite for roughly $800 million, making it part of its Brands Performance + Style Group. Payless ShoeSource, based in Topeka, Kansas, operated more than 4,000 retail stores, generating $2.7 billion in sales at the time it completed the deal. Subsequent to the acquisition, Payless ShoeSource changed its name to Collective Brands, Inc., the holding company that controlled Keds as it neared its centennial and looked to rekindle the vitality once shown by the first sneaker maker in the United States.

Jeffrey L. Covell

PRINCIPAL COMPETITORS

Converse Inc.; Skechers U.S.A., Inc.; Vans, Inc.

FURTHER READING

Bowers, Katherine, "Rewinding Fashion," *Footwear News*, January 31, 2005, p. 20.

Cardona, Mercedes M., "Keds Tries on Comfort Positioning," *Advertising Age*, February 28, 2000, p. 38.

Goodison, Donna L., "Stride Rite Steps into the 'Lifestyle' Market with Keds," *Boston Business Journal*, June 29, 2001, p. 15.

Lenetz, Dana, "Keds Taps Silverman as President," *Footwear News*, May 27, 2002, p. 2.

Lustigman, Alyssa, "Keds Apparel Targets Lifestyle Customer," *Sporting Goods Business*, January 1992, p. 14.

K12 Inc.

2300 Corporate Park Drive
Herndon, Virginia 20171
U.S.A.
Telephone: (866) 283-0300
Fax: (703) 483-7330
Web site: http://www.k12.com

Public Company
Incorporated: 1999
Employees: 993
Sales: $315.6 million (2009)
Stock Exchanges: New York (Arca)
Ticker Symbol: LRN
NAICS: 611110 Elementary and Secondary Schools;
611630 Language Schools; 611710 Educational
Support Services

■ ■ ■

In the relatively new market of online education, K12 Inc. has quickly proven itself both pioneering forerunner and leader. This publicly held company creates the curriculum for students, the training for teachers, and the assessment tools for both, allowing K12 to innovatively combine these often fractured sections of the educational spectrum. Furthermore, in addition to traditional subjects of reading, writing, and arithmetic, K12 takes a keen interest in specialized subjects and foreign languages. As early as elementary school, students using K12 can take classes in Spanish, French, German, Chinese, or Latin. High schoolers also benefit from the wide array of Advanced Placement (AP) courses and elective courses such as personal finance or oceanography. The company markets its vast curriculum to public charter schools, "hybrid" schools, online private schools, and for parents who homeschool their children.

FILLING AN EDUCATIONAL NEED

Founder Ron Packard conceived the idea for K12 as an answer to a difficult problem. Packard held a B.A. in economics and mechanical engineering from the University of California, Berkeley, and an M.B.A. (with honors) from the University of Chicago. After working both on Wall Street and in South America, Packard was hired by investor Michael Milken to direct Milken's Knowledge Universe Learning Center, as well as strategize its investments. Nine months later, Knowledge Universe acquired a private preschool chain, of which Packard was made CEO, in addition to his already specified duties.

On top of this, Packard sought to be a devoted father. One night, while helping his daughter with her math homework, he found himself dissatisfied with the material she was studying. Packard determined that his own background should have been sufficient enough to teach his daughter math, and so began looking online for curriculum. He did not have much luck. According to an interview in the December 2008 issue of *Washington Smart CEO*, Packard said that he could not find a true curriculum, only supplemental education sites. "Nowhere was there a site that explained, 'this is first-grade math,' or 'This is second-grade math and if your child passes this test, they're on par with the best kids in the world.'"

At K12, our mission has remained steadfast: To provide any child access to exceptional curriculum and tools that enable him or her to maximize his or her success in life, regardless of geographic, financial, or demographic circumstance.

We have become a leader in providing individualized, one-to-one learning solutions to students from kindergarten through high school across the country. These solutions have literally changed lives and opened up possibility for many children. Our biggest fans continue to be parents who are seeking to tap into their children's unique potential and who have seen what can happen when children can work at the right pace and with the tools, approaches, and content that make learning come alive.

This conundrum started Packard thinking. He recalled his own foray into self-paced learning: a course in astronomy at Berkeley. For that course, Packard had been responsible for reading a book and coming in weekly to take a test over the material he had covered. Packard admitted that such a course design was far from interactive, and recent developments in CD-ROM curriculum had done little to solve that problem. Nevertheless, Packard had two reasons to follow his desire to create a better system for his daughter: He believed that other parents would be interested in the product and that the phenomenon of the Internet had the power to bring a high level of interactivity to self-paced learning.

Packard's dream quickly expanded into the creation of an entire curriculum. In 2000, he wrote a business plan and presented it to former Secretary of Education Bill Bennett. Both Bennett and Packard's boss, Milken, were convinced by the plan, and Packard received an initial $10 million in capital from Milken and Oracle CEO Larry Ellison. It was determined that lower start-up costs, in addition to a tech-friendly environment and potential educational networks, could be found in Virginia rather than tech-savvy California. Soon after this decision was reached, the company was incorporated and moved to Virginia.

A DIFFICULT TASK

Packard knew that the nationwide rate of homeschoolers was rising, and that homeschooling could easily prove a viable market for the company. Nevertheless, Packard envisioned a different sort of approach to self-paced learning, with a heavy emphasis on interactivity. For that reason, his first focus was on creating an online public school. As with any public school, K12 would have to operate within the framework of standardized tests, certified teachers, and state-approved curriculum, each customized to the particular state, or even school district, from which a student might come.

There was an immense task ahead, and knowing that he needed help, Packard hired John Holdren, the well-connected head of a Virginia-based curriculum provider. Packard, Holdren, and a staff of 110 people began work in the spring of 2001 with an enormous goal: to create a curriculum for every grade, every class from kindergarten to grade two, as well as to create the system through which each lesson would be taught. It was "grueling" according to Packard's interview with *Washington Smart CEO*: "everyone we had [was] working seven days a week, day and night. ... We had people sleeping in the office."

If the work load was not enough, Packard also knew that he needed to raise a very large amount of money, $40 million to be precise. Much to Packard's delight, the money came through, primarily from private donors. When asked by *Washington Smart CEO* why so many people were so eager to work for and donate to a pre-revenue start-up Internet company, so soon after the burst of the Internet bubble in California, Packard had only one response: "K12 was an idea in which people believed."

The hard work paid off. Packard presented his company to U.S. Undersecretary of Education Eugene Hickok and to the governor of Pennsylvania, Tom Ridge. Both men were impressed by the company, and Pennsylvania signed on to become the first state to accept the virtual charter school. Not too long after Pennsylvania signed on, Governor Bill Owens of Colorado joined as well. With two states confident in the prospects of K12, Packard and the company could breathe a sigh of relief. Classes for the two states began in September 2001, with approximately 900 students enrolled.

A VIABLE ALTERNATIVE

Packard's plan for creating an online charter school could not have come at a better time. K12 was founded alongside the passage of the No Child Left Behind (NCLB) Act of 2001. The act, which was signed into law by President George W. Bush, sought to bring broad gains in student achievement. K12 chose to see passage of the law as an opportunity to reflect upon its own goals for education. K12's 2009 annual report stated that by the convergence of concerns found between its own goals and that of the NCLB Act, the company had "the opportunity to make a significant impact."

Furthermore, charter schools were growing in popularity at the time of the incorporation of K12. Charter schools began in 1988 as an alternative to traditional public schools. By 2008, more than 1.3 million students were enrolled in charter schools in 40 states and the District of Columbia. Charter schools had been a controversial subject since their inception. K12's innovative foray into the world of virtual charter schools raised even more eyebrows. Nonetheless, Packard was convinced that the K12 package cost taxpayers less than traditional schools. He told *Washington Smart CEO*, "We might be getting 70 percent of the funding a traditional school gets."

A nationwide interest in higher student standards, combined with an increasing movement toward charter schools opened the door for K12 to many interested parents, but marketing proved to be harder than perhaps Packard had envisioned. Packard ran targeted ads in newspapers. He also hosted "open houses" in hotel lobbies for parents. He discovered these face-to-face open houses to be critical for the development and growth of the company, since they both marketed the company and earned valuable consumer trust. Packard told *Washington Smart CEO* that often the first response from parents was that the program was "too good to be true."

Although the K12 model may have been hard to believe in for some, it was a relatively simple procedure for a student to start. For a typical student, participation in a K12 online, public charter school started first with enrollment. After enrollment, the student received in the mail not only his entire curriculum for the semester, but also a laptop computer. Internet access was paid for by the state or district. Next, a K12 teacher in the area affiliated with the school district contacted the student to schedule a meeting with the student and his parents, as well as to conduct a placement test (K12 found that

most students operated at different levels of math and reading skills). Thereafter, the student logged into the school web site every weekday, and followed a schedule for each traditional subject he would study in a normal public school. Throughout the course of the day, the teacher was able to see how the student was progressing, and keep even minute-to-minute tabs on the student. Parents were also able to see how and what their student was learning. K12 was also careful to plan in social events for its students. Once a month students in kindergarten through eighth grade were told to meet for a field trip. Combined, each of these facets served as the K12 experience.

As for accreditation, K12 became an AdvancED accredited corporation. AdvancED served 27,000 public and private schools throughout the United States, as well as in 65 countries worldwide.

CONTINUING GROWTH

As the company expanded it added curriculum and systems for grades three through five. It also signed three new states: Ohio, California, and Idaho. By 2008, its seventh year of operation, K12 had seen remarkable growth. Twenty-one states and the District of Columbia had signed charters with K12, and the company was serving over 50,000 full-time students.

More importantly, the company had also expanded enough to include other schooling options. Because the World Wide Web, and thus school, could be taken anywhere with K12, the company also appealed to students looking for different educational options. For instance, as the company grew, it worked out opportunities for its curriculum, or even single courses, to be available to homeschooling families. The same option was open to students who were high-performing athletes or artists, and who had less time to devote to formal schooling due to intense training schedules. Military families also found K12 to be an alternative to traditional education, since K12 could grant U.S. diplomas to students overseas. An online private virtual academy was also established, to serve as a less expensive, but still premium, private education. Finally, K12 worked with school districts to create what would be called "hybrid" schools, schools in which students spent two to three days a week in traditional classrooms, and the rest of the school week working from home, using the online K12 curriculum.

Fiscally, the company took an important leap in 2007 when it went public on the New York Stock Exchange. Although most public school systems struggled for fiscal support, K12 was fortunate in its unique position as a corporation, and sales remained strong throughout its first few years on the market.

CURRICULUM EXPANSION

An important step for the company began in 2007 with the acquisition of Power Glide Language Solutions, a provider of online world language courseware. K12, along with teachers and administrators across the nation, were finding that it was crucial for students to speak more than one language. As one teacher told *Education Week*, "The demand for an internationally educated student even before he or she goes to college seems to be recognized … but can't often be made by school districts." PowerspeaK12, as Power Glide's name was changed to, reflected the growing desire for foreign language classes at all educational levels. According to K12, powerspeaK12 was especially unique since it was tailored specifically to children and adolescents. By 2010, classes offered through powerspeaK12 included Spanish, French, German, Latin, and Chinese.

K12's interest in foreign language expanded into adult education as well. In 2009, K12 signed a five-year agreement with Cengage Learning. The agreement granted its Gale brand the exclusive right to distribute K12's adult language curriculum to public libraries across the United States. Furthermore, K12 bridged the gap between elementary and adult foreign language education by signing a contract with Middlebury College, the well-known liberal arts college in Vermont, in 2010. The agreement launched the creation of Middlebury Interactive Languages, a series of courses in French and Spanish for high school students. According to *Education Week*, K12 hoped that by working with Middlebury College, it would be able to take the "best of both worlds," the flexibility of an online curriculum combined with collegiate standards.

K12 also began to take a keen interest in providing courses that, because of expense or any other reason, might not be available to the typical high school student as an elective. By 2010, K12 offered over 30 AP courses in five subjects, as well as electives in less popular courses such as oceanography or entrepreneurship. The company also offered summer school courses to students who either needed to review, or retake, certain subjects.

MIXED REVIEWS

K12's hard work was highly lauded. In 2007, Packard received the James P. Boyle Entrepreneurial Leadership Award from the Education Industry Association. In 2009, the Association of Educational Publishers also awarded the Distinguished Achievement Award to K12 for its algebra curriculum. Additionally, the United States Distance Learning Association had presented K12 with several different awards for its work in distance learning, including the prestigious 21st Century Best Practices Award in 2010.

Even the success stories on a smaller, more personal scale, seemed to speak well of K12. June 2010 saw the first graduation of students from the Youth Connection Charter School, Virtual High School. This school, powered by K12 and based out of Chicago, was founded to provide online courses to Chicago students, ages 18 to 31, who had dropped out of school and needed fewer than seven credits to graduate. Many graduates of the program asserted that had it not been for the school and K12, they would not have been able to go back and earn their diplomas, according to an article in *Education Business Weekly*.

Nevertheless, critics of the program remained ambivalent. An article in the journal *School Administrator* questioned the credibility of online education, wondering if virtual reality could ever replace face-to-face instruction. The article challenged schools to determine if a hands-on science experiment could ever really be replaced by "a hands-on keyboard experience." Furthermore, the issue of authenticity also became more prevalent when the student was outside the classroom. "Who really is doing all those assignments?" it queried.

Finally, states themselves had their own uncertainties about online education. One of the most prevalent problems centered on teacher accreditation. Because online teachers were not bound by state lines, accreditation differences among states became vague. This, and other facets of online education would be subjects for legislators to discuss for many years to come, according to *School Administrator*.

THE POTENTIAL FOR A STRONG FUTURE

Despite these criticisms and fears, K12 seemed unruffled. The company, which continued to grow steadily, operated in 25 states and the District of Columbia (Oregon, South Carolina, Indiana, and Hawaii were signed onto K12 in 2009). From 2006 to 2009, average enrollment of students increased by 40 percent. K12 also opened its doors to an entirely new arena when its first International Academy was established in Dubai for the 2008–09 school year.

Financially, the company was also thriving. From 2006 to 2009, net income increased from $1.4 million to $12.3 million. According to *Washington Smart CEO*, the market, and presumably profitability along with it, would continue to grow. Researchers predicted that the virtual school industry could produce annual revenue of

$5.5 billion to $11 billion. Fiscally, K12 was poised to take its mission well into the future, and thus far, its consumers were eager to go along.

Laura Rydberg

PRINCIPAL COMPETITORS

Apollo Group, Inc.; Blackboard Inc.; DeVry Inc.

FURTHER READING

Ash, Katie, "Vt. College, K12 Inc. Forge Language-Learning Partnership," *Education Week*, May 19, 2010.

Glass, Gene V., "Potholes in the Road to Virtual Schooling," *School Administrator*, April 2010.

"Grade Expectations: Adding Seats to the Virtual Classroom," *Washington Smart CEO*, December 2008.

"60 Chicago Students Graduate from Youth Connection Charter School Virtual High School, Powered by K12: Chicago's First Online Dropout Recovery Program," *Education Business Weekly*, June 30, 2010.

CPAs, Consultants & Advisors

LarsonAllen, LLP

———▪———

220 South 6th Street, Suite 300
Minneapolis, Minnesota 55402
U.S.A.
Telephone: (612) 376-4500
Fax: (612) 376-4850
Web site: http://www.larsonallen.com

Private Company
Incorporated: 1953 as Larson & Allen
Employees: 1,400
Sales: $225 million (2009 est.)
NAICS: 541219 Other Accounting Services

■ ■ ■

Based in Minneapolis, Minnesota, LarsonAllen, LLP, is among the United States' top 20 accounting firms, employing 1,400 people in regional offices located in Arizona, Florida, Illinois, Massachusetts, Missouri, North Carolina, Pennsylvania, Texas, Washington, D.C., and Wisconsin. The firm is organized along industry and service lines. Some of those industries include agribusiness, construction and real estate, finance, government, health care, hospitality, manufacturing, and trucking and transportation.

In addition to traditional accounting and auditing services, LarsonAllen provides benefit services, executive search services, information security, tax help, and valuation and forensic services as well as industry-specific services. LarsonAllen Financial, LLC, offers such financial services as asset management, estate and financial planning, pension design and consulting,

investment consulting, and employee education. To serve clients outside the United States, LarsonAllen maintains an affiliation with Nexia International.

POST-WORLD WAR II ORIGINS

LarsonAllen was founded in 1953 by the firm's longtime chief executive officer, Rholan Larson, and John Allen. The two had met while studying accounting at the University of Minnesota in 1946. After graduation a year later they both went to work for an accounting firm in Iowa. They then returned to Minnesota and went to work for separate firms, but remained close, nurturing an idea of one day starting their own accounting business. Finally in 1953 they decided to strike out on their own. Because they were both family men, they took a measured approach. One of them would open a new office while the other would keep his old job. If necessary, they could combine their incomes to help both families make ends meet. On the basis of a coin flip, it was Larson who quit his job, and in October 1953 he opened an accounting practice in a suite of offices leased by a group of attorneys located over a drugstore in the Miracle Mile Shopping Center in the Minneapolis suburb of St. Louis Park. It was little more than a cubbyhole, but at $50 a month to rent, which included light secretarial service, it was affordable.

Allen would never be called upon to share his salary with Larson. The new practice found steady work, and precisely one year later, in October 1954, Allen joined Larson at what was now known as Larson & Allen. They soon took on a third partner, Robert Weishair, an Army veteran who had worked in the Army finance

COMPANY PERSPECTIVES

LarsonAllen is organized along industry and service lines, yet we are not a firm of individual practices. Our groups are interdependent and recognize that together, by pooling our talents, experience, and knowledge, we can provide better service to clients.

division in St. Louis. After his discharge in 1949 he became a certified public accountant and launched a solo practice, renting an office in the same suite of offices as Larson & Allen. Because of their proximity the three men got to know one another and eventually decided they should join forces. Thus, in August 1957 the firm Larson, Allen, Weishair & Co., LLP was formed.

Larson served as chief executive of the firm, which mostly catered to small businesses. From the start, the firm's principals sought to offer more than the typical accounting, audit, and tax services. Because of the nature of its small business clientele, it was also called on to provide these ancillary services, all in the cause of helping clients succeed in their own businesses. Larson Allen provided manual bookkeeping services in the days before computers and prepared financial statements and tax returns. It also provided consulting services. This inclusive approach would one day evolve into a "total client service" business model.

NEW CEO: 1989

Larson served as CEO until the end of 1986. In 1989 he was succeeded by Gordon A. Viere, whose tenure in the top post would extend beyond 20 years. It was also during the 1980s that the firm built up its staff and expanded the types of services it could offer clients. It became involved in mergers and acquisitions, employee benefits analysis and planning, staffing, valuations, and risk management. The firm also established Lawco Financial to serve as a securities broker and dealer. Having assembled a slate of core competencies, the firm sought the best way to leverage them and decided to focus on specific industries. "Beginning in the 1990s," Viere told *Accounting Today*, "we no longer called ourselves an accounting firm with specialized services, but a consulting and financial services firm that has a very significant core competency in account services."

The 1990s brought expansion to Larson Allen on a number of fronts. It added capabilities to become a one-

stop shop for its industry-specific clients, while also extending its reach across the United States. Early in 1990 Larson Allen began with a local step, merging with a pair of small accounting firms to create a 50-person office in neighboring St. Paul, Minnesota. This came at a time when the Big Six accounting firms were electing to exit St. Paul. The participants were the six-person Calof and Calof, and the 38-employee Sands Rust and Co. Later in 1990 Larson Allen acquired an area human resource consulting firm, Andrews Co., to provide bookkeeping and accounting placement, management search, and human resource consulting.

HCC PURCHASE: 1995

Following a recovery from the recession of the early 1990s, Larson Allen resumed growth through acquisitions in the mid-1990s. St. Louis, Missouri-based health care consulting firm Health Capital Consultants (HCC) was added in August 1995. Not only did HCC build up Larson Allen's health care practice, it brought branch offices in Atlanta; Chicago; New York; Oxnard, California; and Columbus, Ohio. In January 1996 Larson Allen acquired Epic USA, allowing the firm to offer integrated telecommunications and information systems consulting services to its clients. Based in Bloomington, Minnesota, Epic maintained branch offices in Boston, Detroit, and New York, and project offices in Toledo, Ohio, and Brussels, Belgium. It also served health care organizations as well as financial institutions, manufacturers, utilities, schools, and government facilities.

In March 1997 Larson Allen supplemented its health care practice with the acquisition of M.G. Verly & Associates, which brought 30 hospitals as clients, and Matthews Claeys, CPA, a specialist in regulatory matters. While extending its reach, Larson Allen did not lose sight of its home market. In April 1996, Larson Allen acquired its chief competitor in St. Cloud, Minnesota: McMahon, Hartmann, Amundson & Co., a 40-person operation that generated $2.5 million in annual revenues. In November 1997, Larson Allen acquired St. Louis-based St. John, Mersmann & Co., a firm that focused on health care as well as construction, manufacturing, retail, real estate, and nonprofit corporations.

By 1998 Larson Allen had increased annual revenues to $43 million and was well entrenched as the largest accounting firm headquartered in Minnesota. As the decade came to a close it continued to add to its scale and capabilities. Early in 1999 it launched Larson-Allen Technology Solutions, LLC. While an information technology solutions provider, the new unit focused on financial system planning and electronic commerce and a limited range of industries that included health care,

KEY DATES

1953: Rholan Larson and John Allen form accounting firm.
1957: Robert Weishair joins company.
1986: Rholan Larson retires as CEO.
1999: LarsonAllen Technology Solutions is formed.
2007: LarsonAllen, LLP name is adopted.

construction, manufacturing, and wholesale/retail distribution. Also in an effort to meet the needs of its clients, Larson Allen replaced its eight quarterly newsletters in 1999 with a glossy magazine, *Effect*. The firm also continued to pursue external growth opportunities. In June 1999 LarsonAllen Manufacturing Group acquired Tennessen Associates, Inc., a national company providing facility management, warehouse design, manufacturing process planning, and administrative process planning to midsize manufacturing and distribution companies. Late in 1999 Larson Allen added to its St. Louis presence with the acquisition of Curry Lenhardt & Co., an 18-person practice that mostly represented midwestern auto dealerships.

PHILADELPHIA EXPANSION: 2000–01

Larson Allen was a $75 million a year firm employing 700 people across the country at the start of the new century. It was both a time of contraction and expansion for the firm. Schiffman Hughes Brown, of Philadelphia, Pennsylvania, was acquired in February 2000. A year later, Larson Allen acquired another Philadelphia accounting firm, Mathieson Aitken Jemison, which now absorbed Larson Allen's other Philadelphia units but operated under the LarsonAllen banner. The combined branch was now well positioned to better serve East Coast-based clients and attract new business.

A month later Larson Allen added to its St. Louis office by acquiring Citerman & Tumbarello of nearby Clayton, Missouri, and followed that transaction with the purchase of the five-person accounting firm Warmbrodt & Associates along with its Integra Asset money management practice. In its home market, in the meantime, Larson Allen closed the St. Paul branch in early 2001 and consolidated its operation into the main office in Minneapolis.

Because of some major corporate scandals, in particular the exploits of Enron, accounting firms were no longer permitted to do both auditing and consulting

work for a company. These changes opened up opportunities for second-tier accounting firms such as Larson Allen, which also benefited from the demise of scandal-ridden Arthur Andersen, one of the Big Six accounting firms. Larson Allen grew annual revenues to the $100 million level in 2003. It then strengthened its position in the mid-Atlantic region in 2004 by acquiring Charlotte, North Carolina-based Bullard, Blanchard John PLLC. The 13-person practice was combined with the 47 employees of Larson Allen's Charlotte branch. Because of Larson Allen's expanding client base, the firm outgrew its Austin, Minnesota, office that served as a hub for several regional offices and added more space in 2005.

ADOPTION OF LARSONALLEN NAME: 2007

Over the years the fusion of the Larson and Allen names to create the LarsonAllen brand had been applied to several subsidiaries. In 2007 the company took the logical step of supporting the brand by changing the corporate name from Larson, Allen, Weishair & Co., LLP to LarsonAllen, LLP. As such, the firm continued to grow as the first decade of the new century closed. After having established itself in the Washington, D.C., market in 2006 with the acquisition of Langan Associates, LarsonAllen expanded its presence with the June 2008 acquisition of Schreiner, Legge & Company, an addition that was especially helpful in growing the firm's credit union practice while also bolstering its East Coast presence.

In August 2009 LarsonAllen turned its attention to the Midwest, acquiring Belleville, Illinois-based Ganim, Meder, Childers & Hoering, P.C., a specialist in accounting, tax, and consulting services for financial institutions, health care clients, construction, real estate, and other industries. Early in 2010 LarsonAllen acquired Philadelphia-based Third Age, Inc., which specialized in planning, research, management, and marketing services for the senior housing market and senior care providers throughout the country. Also in January 2010, LarsonAllen acquired Chicago-based Africk Chez P.C., a firm that served clients in several industries, providing accounting, tax, and business advisory services. LarsonAllen now employed 1,400 people and generated annual revenues of $225 million. There was every reason to believe that firm would continue to grow its business across the United States in the coming years.

Ed Dinger

PRINCIPAL SUBSIDIARIES

LarsonAllen Financial, LLC; LarsonAllen Search LLC.

PRINCIPAL COMPETITORS

Baker Tilly Virchow Krause, LLP; BKD, LLP; Plante & Moran, PLLC.

FURTHER READING

Barshay, Jill J., "Accounting Firm Absorbs St. Cloud Competitor," *Minneapolis Star Tribune*, March 20, 1997, p. 3D.

Franta, Michelle, "Let's Flip for It: The History of Larson-Allen," *Effect*, Fall 2003, p. 27.

Johnson, Brian, "Minneapolis-Based Larson Allen Is a Firm That Construction Companies Can Count On," *Finance and Commerce Daily Newspaper*, September 11, 2001.

"Larson Allen Consolidating Offices," *St. Paul Pioneer Press*, January 31, 2001, p. 2C.

"Magazine Replacing a Firm's Newsletters," *Practical Accountant*, June 1999.

Miller, Tracey L., "Deft, Cool Lawco Charts Solid Growth," *Accounting Today*, January 19, 1998.

Peters, Dave, "Merger to Join 3 Firms," *St. Paul Pioneer Press*, January 9, 1990, p. 5C.

Legendary Pictures Films, LLC

—————————————————————

4000 Warner Boulevard, Building 76
Burbank, California 91522
U.S.A.
Telephone: (818) 954-1940
Fax: (818) 954-3884
Web site: http://www.legendarypictures.com

Private Company
Incorporated: 2004
NAICS: 512110 Motion Picture and Video Production

■ ■ ■

An independent film production company funded by a consortium of private investors, Legendary Pictures Films, LLC, makes a range of movies for kids and adults. Focusing on action, adventure, science fiction, and fantasy, Legendary has established itself in the film industry by creating a portfolio of box-office successes and working with strong directors. Five of its films have each grossed over $350 million worldwide: *The Hangover, The Dark Knight, 300, Batman Begins,* and *Superman Returns.* Under a partnership deal with Warner Brothers Pictures, the two companies split production costs and profits 50/50.

VENTURING INTO HOLLYWOOD: 2004

Legendary Pictures was founded by Thomas Tull in 2004 as a film production company funded by private equity. Tull's idea for the company came in 2003 over dinner conversation with an executive at Metro-Goldwyn-Mayer who complained about the difficulties surrounding film financing. Having been interested in Hollywood from an early age (as a child he had often watched two or three VHS movies a day in Binghamton, New York), Tull began investing in Hollywood business opportunities.

At 35, Tull's career had skirted the edges of the entertainment industry for almost 10 years. After college, he had abandoned plans to become a lawyer. Instead, he got his start in business buying and selling a small chain of laundromats in upstate New York and later a chain of car-repair centers. Tull's first foray into the entertainment world came in 1996 when he ran a North Carolina-based investment fund launched during the dot-com boom. In that position, he helped craft a deal that created Red Storm Entertainment, which designed games based on Tom Clancy books. Later, he became president and director of a media and entertainment investment company, the Convex Group, where he oversaw projects such as the purchasing of the Web site howstuffworks.com.

Spurred by his love of movies, in 2004 Tull quit his job at Convex. Relying on his experience as a venture capitalist, he spent the next 18 months on the road raising money to start Legendary Pictures. He raised $500 million in the form of committed capital to be invested in a portfolio of films to be produced over several years. He also worked on crafting a lucrative arrangement with Warner Brothers Pictures, a unit of Time Warner. In a November 2005 *Variety* article, he described the fund-raising process as "long" and "arduous."

COMPANY PERSPECTIVES

Legendary Pictures is an independent production company founded in 2004 to create, develop, co-produce and co-finance major motion pictures. The company currently enjoys a unique strategic partnership with Warner Brothers. Legendary develops its own projects in-house in addition to selectively partnering on the development and production of Warner Bros. initiated projects. Productions to date include *Where the Wild Things Are, The Hangover, The Dark Knight, 300, Superman Returns,* and *Watchmen.*

By early 2005, Legendary was up and running, backed by a consortium of Wall Street hedge funds, including ABRY Partners, AIG Direct Investments, Banc of America Capital Investors, Columbia Capital, Falcon Investment Advisors, and M/C Venture Partners. Legendary's management team hailed from the entertainment industry. Its president, Chris Lee, had been a production chief at Columbia Pictures/TriStar, having worked on blockbuster films such as *Jerry Maguire* and *Philadelphia* during his career.

With the goal of building a library of commercial movies in the fantasy, science fiction, action, and adventure genres, Tull and his management team selected a logo based on the Celtic "shield knot." Dating back to Ireland, circa 5000 B.C.E., the logo harkened to an ancient age, symbolizing the strength and power of many of Legendary Pictures' future film heroes and warriors.

PARTNERING WITH WARNER BROTHERS PICTURES: 2005

After months of negotiations, in June 2005 Warner Brothers Pictures announced a multiyear, 25-picture agreement with Legendary. Each company immediately benefited from the partnership in distinct ways. Legendary and its non-Hollywood investors gained industry cachet by associating with A-list directors while Warner Brothers received a $500 million boost to its film financing coffers. The deal came at a critical time for the studio. According to an October 2005 article in *Daily Variety*, it was looking to trim costs and institute possible layoffs in early 2006 in anticipation of a revenue slowdown. However, the partnership enabled Warner Brothers to share the risk of big-ticket films such as *Superman Returns* and display fiscal responsibility to its investors.

The partnership agreement was a rare one in Hollywood, a 50/50 production and distribution split. This enabled Legendary to lure a new source of capital into the industry: private equity. Despite plenty of doubters, several cash-rich investors were inspired to venture into the dicey world of film finance. In a January 2006 *Investment Dealers' Digest* article, Tull said: "We specifically built a movie studio, but essentially we built one attractive to private equity, and that's never been done before." Another reason Legendary was attractive to investors was that there were several possible exit options, including selling equity stakes after five years to Warner Brothers or other firms. There was also talk of a Legendary initial public offering at some point.

With its offices located on the Warner Brothers lot, Legendary aimed to work on five to six films per year as part of the 25-picture deal. Considering itself an active investor, it involved itself in all stages of the moviemaking process, including casting, budgeting, green-lighting, merchandising, and marketing. In the same *Investment Dealers' Digest* article, Tull said of the relationship with Warner Brothers: "It's wrong for people to think of the $500 million as a 'fund.' Rather, Legendary is an operating company. … The way we approach it is very simple. We each put up half the money. We each work to produce the film. After the studio recoups costs, our nickel sits next to their nickel, and we share all revenue streams."

In addition to being a partner on Warner Brothers-produced projects, Legendary also planned to develop its own movies. Given the constantly shifting nature of content distribution channels, the company's goal was to build a portfolio of proprietary content. John Watkins, a Legendary investor, told *Investment Dealers' Digest*: "We believe that owning proprietary content is a good place to be … in a digital world, owning proprietary content is king." Focusing on action, adventure, fantasy, and science fiction, Tull pushed for the company to take a hands-on approach to its movies, actively reviewing scripts and consulting with directors. In a February 2009 *Wall Street Journal* article, he said: "We treat each film like a start-up."

EARLY UPS AND DOWNS: 2006

In October 2005, just a few months after Legendary and Warner Brothers had struck their deal, the two companies announced four coproductions. Although the slate of movies appeared promising, the partnership suffered some early setbacks. When *Superman Returns* was released in 2006, it underperformed. Then, two more flops were released back-to-back: *The Ant Bully* and *Lady in the Water*. The one early success, *Batman Begins*, eventually earned more than $370 million worldwide.

KEY DATES

2004: Legendary Pictures is founded by Thomas Tull.

2005: Company signs partnership agreement with Warner Brothers.

2007: Legendary and Warner Brothers sign a new, $1 billion agreement extending for five years.

2008: *The Dark Knight* grosses more than $500 million at the box office, making it the third-highest-grossing film ever in the United States.

2010: *Inception* earns record box-office receipts during its opening weeks.

Legendary's luck made a comeback in 2006 when director Zack Snyder pitched Frank Miller's graphic novel *300* to Tull. The novel was a violent historical fiction about the last stand of a band of Spartans against Persian invaders, a retelling of the Battle of Thermopylae. Snyder had shopped the idea all over Hollywood. Dozens of studios had declined, saying they had similar projects in the pipeline or that "sword-and-sandal" flicks were passé. However, Tull was a huge fan of Miller's graphic novels, and he did not hesitate to sign on immediately. The film went on to gross nearly $500 million worldwide and had one of the biggest openings of 2007.

In the wake of the success of *300*, Snyder approached Tull about making *Watchmen*, a story based on a character in a DC Comics series. The story had been tossed around various studios since 1986, and Tull was skeptical at first. Eventually he gave the project a green light, but in 2008, 20th Century Fox sued to block the film's release, claiming that it owned the film rights. By 2009, the lawsuit was settled and the film was released. That year, the film went on to gross more than $185 million worldwide.

A STRING OF RECORD SUCCESSES: 2007–09

By June 2007 Legendary and Warner Brothers were satisfied with the results of their arrangement. Although their partnership had included some flops, it had also produced some blockbusters. Extending their 2005 partnership an additional five years to 2012, Legendary committed to investing $1 billion in a portfolio of 45 films coproduced by Warner Brothers. The size of the new investment reflected the ambitious financial goals of the company's investors. Movies that were part of the deal included *Where the Wild Things Are* and *The Losers*.

The new partnership agreement got off to a good start. One year later, in July 2008 *The Dark Knight* earned record numbers at the box office with more than $300 million in ticket sales in the first 10 days, making it the second-biggest movie of the year. By 2009, the movie had grossed more than $500 million at the box office, making it the third-highest-grossing film ever in the United States. The studios set another record that year when *The Hangover* opened, which ended up earning more than $277 million domestically and adding another $190 million internationally. Its total earnings made it the top-grossing R-rated comedy ever by topping the 16-year-old, $234 million record set by *Beverly Hills Cop*.

In an October 2009 *Wired Magazine* article, Tull attributed Legendary's success in part to its focus on famous directors: "[Legendary is] a very director-driven company. ... Look at who we've had the privilege of working with. Bryan Singer, Spike Jonze, Chris Nolan. ... We're working on our third movie with Nolan right now, *Inception*. Zack Snyder—we're on our third movie with him too. Look at *The Hangover*, which has been a tremendous success for us. You could have dismissed it and said, 'Ah, another Vegas comedy.' But in Todd Phillips' hands? That's what got us really excited about it."

TAKING RISKS AND INNOVATING: 2010

In July 2010, *Inception* opened. Based on an innovative idea, the movie starred Leonardo DiCaprio as an agent who invades people's dreams. The complex action-thriller represented a gamble. At the time, Hollywood shunned releasing big summer movies based on novel ideas. Original movies rarely earned the $100-million-plus openings that guaranteed blockbuster success. Adding to the risk, there was no video game or product tie-ins that could help Warner and Legendary generate revenue beyond ticket sales and DVDs. However, those involved in the film believed it would succeed. Insiders claimed that its director, Christopher Nolan, was about to become as common a household name as Steven Spielberg, James Cameron, and Peter Jackson. Warner executives often compared *Inception* to *The Matrix*.

The gamble paid off. In its first weekend, *Inception* earned more than $60 million and another $43 million the following weekend. By the end of July, *Inception* was on track to gross more than $300 million domestically and become the second-most-popular release of the summer. Having spent $160 million on the production,

Warner and Legendary were positioned to make a hefty profit.

Although the economy was still faltering in 2010, Legendary appeared unfazed. Plans for future movie productions included *Gears of War*, based on the Epic Games franchise; a film adaptation of Blizzard Interactive's *Warcraft* universe; and a remake of *Clash of the Titans*. In addition, Tull aimed to branch out with a digital department for Web ventures. There were also plans to become more involved in video games.

Carrie Rothburd

PRINCIPAL COMPETITORS

Canal+ SA; DreamWorks Animation SKG Inc; Focus Features; Fox Searchlight Pictures Inc.; Paramount Vantage; The Weinstein Company LLC; Sony Pictures Classics.

FURTHER READING

Baker, Chris, "Thomas Tull's Legendary Pictures Goes 'All In' for Geek Movies," *Wired Magazine Online*, August 2010, http://www.wired.com/underwire/2009/10/thomas-tull/all/1.

Barnes, Brook, "Billion-Dollar Deal to Be a Partner in Some Warner Films," *New York Times*, June 26, 2007, p. C2.

Brophy-Warren, Jamin, "A Producer of Superheroes," *Wall Street Journal*, February 27, 2009, p. W1.

Fritz, Ben, "Company Town: Warner Gambles on Untested Commodity," *Los Angeles Times*, July 13, 2010, p. 1.

Holson, Laura M., "Warner Venture with Investors," *New York Times*, June 22, 2005, p. C7.

McClintock, Pamela, "Legendary Soups Up Pic Presence," *Daily Variety*, October 31, 2005, p. 1.

———, "A Tull Order to Fill," *Variety*, November 21, 2005, p. 6.

O'Connor, Colleen Marie, "Private Equity Comes to the Big Screen," *Investment Dealers' Digest*, January 16, 2006, p. 1.

Leo A Daly Company

—■—

8600 Indian Hills Drive
Omaha, Nebraska 68114-4039
U.S.A.
Telephone: (402) 391-8111
Fax: (402) 391-8564
Web site: http://www.leoadaly.com

Private Company
Incorporated: 1915
Employees: 1,145
Sales: $198.4 million (2009)
NAICS: 541310 Architectural Services; 541330
  Engineering Services

■ ■ ■

Omaha, Nebraska-based Leo A Daly Company is a well-respected international architecture, planning, engineering, interior design, and program management firm. It maintains more than 20 offices around the world, employing in excess of 1,100 design and engineering professionals. It also offers relocation and post-construction services. Daly has completed projects in all 50 states and about 80 countries. Dallas-based subsidiary Lockwood, Andrews & Newman, Inc., also maintains a dozen offices in Texas, Chicago, Miami, Phoenix, and Sacramento, providing engineering, infrastructure, and program management services. Known for its multidisciplinary approach, the firm is led by Chairman and CEO Leo A. Daly III, a grandson of the founder.

OMAHA ROOTS: 1915

Leo A Daly Company was founded in 1915 by a young architect, Leo Anthony Daly Sr., an Omaha native born in 1890. His practice first gained prominence in 1922 when he developed the master plan for Omaha's Boys Town home for transient young men. Immigrant Irish priest Father Edward J. Flanagan had started the effort in 1917 by renting a boardinghouse in Omaha, and in 1921 borrowed money to purchase Overlook Farm outside of the city. With Daly's planning skills it became the Village of Boys Town. Daly remained involved with the organization and his firm helped to expand Boys Town over the years. Flanagan also received acclaim, becoming the subject of the 1938 film *Boys Town*, his role played by Spencer Tracy, who received an Academy Award for his performance.

Daly maintained his practice until his death in 1952. Before World War II he became involved in the higher-education market when in 1929 his firm was responsible for the construction of the Creighton University Administration Building. Another major prewar project was the Woodmen of the World Insurance building in Omaha. The war then proved to be a turning point in the history of the firm. Contributing to the war effort, Daly was involved in projects that required a team approach. After the war, the firm pursued the idea further, organizing projects around a multidisciplinary team that included architects, engineers, planners, and interior designers. What would one day become commonplace was at the time considered a radical departure in the way buildings were constructed.

SECOND GENERATION TAKES HELM: 1953

Playing a key role in the development of the team concept was Leo Daly's son, Leo A. Daly Jr. He was born in 1917 and attended Creighton University before graduating with a degree in architecture from the Catholic University of America in 1939. He immediately joined his father's firm as a draftsman and made partner two years later. In 1948 he was named vice president, and in 1952 became president following the death of his father. He took over a firm with 50 employees.

Under Leo Daly's leadership, the firm expanded into a number of sectors. It became involved in the health care sector for the first time in 1955 with the construction of the Clarkson Hospital in Omaha. The company also took advantage of its location to support the Strategic Air Command (SAC). Following World War II, Omaha's Offutt Air Force Base became the home for SAC because it was out of range of the bombers and missiles of the Soviet Union. As the Cold War intensified, SAC's role in U.S. defense intensified, leading to expansion of the Omaha facilities. In 1956 Daly won a contract to construct a new command headquarters, an especially challenging assignment for both Daly's architects and engineers because it was built underground to withstand nuclear attack.

Having proven itself to the military, Daly sought further government contracts. To help in this endeavor, the firm opened an office in Washington, D.C., in 1964. Not only did this office help Daly to secure domestic government work, it became the home for the firm's international operations. A year after opening the office, Daly won contracts to build U.S. embassies in India and Pakistan. These projects then became calling cards for further international work. In 1967 Daly opened its first foreign office, located in Hong Kong. Moreover, it was one of the first international offices to be opened by any U.S. architectural firm. An office in Saudi Arabia would follow and the firm developed a thriving business in the Middle East.

Although Daly was now developing a global reputation, it did not overlook its home market, continuing to win major contracts in Omaha, including those with repeat customers. The firm furthered its relationship with Woodmen of the World Insurance in 1965 with the construction of a new building, the Woodmen of the World Tower. The project was also significant because it was Daly's first high-rise and paved the way for additional work in the future. Another significant Omaha construction project was also subterranean. In 1977 Daly completed an addition for insurer Mutual of Omaha, most of which was underground in an effort to reduce energy consumption. The innovative design included ground-level skylights. Two years later, Daly demonstrated further skill in designing energy-efficient buildings when it constructed a new facility for Lockheed Martin that received awards for energy efficiency as well as a novel design that permitted quick interior space reconfigurations.

LEO DALY JR. DIES: 1981

Daly's focus in the 1950s and 1960s was on high-technology defense projects. The firm shifted its focus again in the 1970s, devoting more resources to health, education, and research projects. By now, the third generation of the Daly family was heavily involved in the business. Like his father, Leo A. Daly III studied architecture at Catholic University of America, graduating in 1967. He was well seasoned by 1981 when his father died suddenly from a heart attack at the age of 63. At the time, the younger Daly was senior vice president and director of international operations, based in Riyadh, Saudi Arabia. He returned home to Omaha to take over as chairman and president. As the head of the firm, he dropped the "III" from his name to become the new Leo A. Daly and continue the evolution of his grandfather's practice.

Leo Daly expanded the firm both at home and abroad in the 1980s, and as a result traveled extensively, mostly splitting his time between Omaha, Washington, D.C., and Los Angeles. Nevertheless, he continued to consider Omaha his home and gave no thought to moving the firm's headquarters from middle America. He also strengthened the company's domestic operations, launching a six-year reorganization effort that transformed outposts to full-service offices in Atlanta, Honolulu, Los Angeles, San Francisco, Seattle, and St. Louis. In this way, Leo A Daly Company was able to respond quickly to opportunities in these markets. In 1988 Daly opened a new full-service office in Chantilly, Virginia, near Dulles International Airport, while keeping its Washington, D.C., office.

KEY DATES

1915: Leo A. Daly Sr. founds company in Omaha.
1922: Master plan is developed for Boys Town.
1952: Daly dies, succeeded by Leo A. Daly Jr.
1981: Leo A. Daly III becomes president and chairman.
1991: Lockwood, Andrews & Newman Inc. is acquired.

Overseas, in the meantime, Daly was forced to shift its focus from the Middle East. In some ways, Daly was the victim of its own success. Over the years the firm had provided advance training to a large number of Saudi Arabian architects and engineers, so that by the early 1980s they were able to handle projects themselves and squeezed out Daly and other Western firms. Turning more attention to Asia, Daly in 1982 forged an agreement with Japan's Nihon Architects, Engineers & Consultants Inc. to pursue joint ventures in both the Far East and the United States. In addition to an office in Tokyo, Daly added branches in Singapore and Taipei, Taiwan. The firm also opened an office in Madrid, Spain, to pursue more projects in Europe.

TEXAS ACQUISITION: 1991

Organic growth gave way to external expansion in the 1990s. Daly acquired a major Texas engineering and architectural firm, Lockwood, Andrews & Newman Inc. (LAN), in November 1991. To supplement its Houston headquarters, Lockwood maintained branch offices in four other Texas cities, and brought with it expertise in transportation, infrastructure, and the environment. The two firms were a good fit, in large measure because they had both designed major aviation projects, Daly in San Francisco and Los Angeles, and LAN in Houston, where it designed hangars, maintenance facilities, runways, and taxiways. Later in the 1990s Daly would win airport contracts in Honolulu and in Washington, D.C., at Ronald Reagan Airport. LAN also brought welcome expertise in environmental and civil engineering and opened up new opportunities for Daly in Texas as well as Mexico.

Daly enjoyed success in several sectors in the 1990s. The Phoenix office during this time developed a new source of projects. The focus of the office had always been on office buildings, restaurants, banks, retail structures, and hotels. The Phoenix branch also did some work in Las Vegas. When the state of Arizona

began approving Indian gaming facilities in 1993, Daly used its modest track record in the casino business to pursue gaming contracts in Arizona. This success led to Indian casino projects in other states and Canada. Because each new casino sought to outshine the last, the projects increased in scale and budget, much to the benefit of Daly's balance sheet.

The final years of the century brought other significant projects to Daly. In 1995 the firm completed the Cheung Kong Center in Hong Kong. The project was especially noteworthy because for the first time the firm made use of computers to regularly trade working drawings between the international office in Washington, D.C., and Hong Kong. In 1997 Daly enjoyed a pair of successes. The firm assembled the winning design team for the National World War II Memorial in Washington, D.C. Construction would not begin until 2001 and the memorial finally opened to the public in 2004. Also in Washington, Daly in 1997 began work on the Pope John Paul II Cultural Center. The unique combination museum, library, and resource center was dedicated in 2000 and began serving the needs of theologians from around the world.

The new century brought further growth and accolades to Daly. The firm won a major airport contract at Atlanta's Hartfield International Airport, hired to design a new international terminal. In 2002 the award-winning, 40-story Daly-designed First National Tower became the tallest building in Omaha as well as the tallest between the Missouri River and the Rocky Mountains. Daly used its expertise later in the decade to design its first high-rise project in the People's Republic of China, the Information Technology Center in Shanghai. The firm, as well, established a reputation for environmentally responsible projects with the Carl T. Curtis, Midwest Regional Headquarters Buildings for the U.S. Department of the Interior's National Parks Service. The Omaha structure was the first in the state to receive Gold LEED Certification as an environmentally friendly project, and only the 44th building in the United States and 48th in the world to achieve this distinction.

FURTHER ACQUISITIONS

In the early 2000s Daly completed a pair of acquisitions. In 2003 it purchased Minneapolis-based Setter Leach and Lindstrom, a 90-employee, full-service architectural and engineering company. Founded in 1917 Setter allowed Daly to reenter the federal government market from which it had shied away in recent years. In 2009 Daly added West Palm Beach, Florida-based Schwab, Twitty & Hanser Architectural Group, an architectural and planning firm that included an office in Tampa and provided a nice complement to Daly's

Miami office. It was not likely to be the last effort to expand Daly by external means in the years to come.

Ed Dinger

PRINCIPAL SUBSIDIARIES

Lockwood, Andrews & Newman Inc.; Setter Leach & Lindstrom Inc.

PRINCIPAL COMPETITORS

HOK Group, Inc.; Skidmore, Owings & Merrill LLP; SmithGroup Companies, Inc.

FURTHER READING

"Daly Co. Acquires Florida Group," *Omaha World-Herald*, February 14, 2009, p. 1D.

"Daly Looks to Pacific for Growth," *Omaha World-Herald*, September 6, 1987.

Johnson, Brian, "Omaha-Based Architectural Firm Merges with Minneapolis Firm," *Finance and Commerce Daily Newspaper*, March 4, 2003.

Jordon, Steve, "Daly Company Adds Large Houston Firm," *Omaha World-Herald*, November 13, 1991, p. 23sf.

———, "Management by Flying Around," *Omaha World-Herald*, December 18, 1988, p. 1m.

"Leo A Daly: Building from Technical Skills," *Architectural Record*, August 1998, p. 61.

Lions Gate Entertainment Corporation

2700 Colorado Avenue
Santa Monica, California 90404
U.S.A.
Telephone: (310) 449-9200
Fax: (310) 255-3870
Web site: http://www.lionsgate-ent.com

Public Company
Incorporated: 1997
Employees: 497
Sales: $1.6 billion (2010)
Stock Exchanges: New York Toronto
Ticker Symbol: LGF
NAICS: 512110 Motion Picture and Video Production; 512120 Motion Picture and Video Distribution; 512191 Teleproduction and Other Postproduction Services

∎ ∎ ∎

Lions Gate Entertainment Corporation is a leading independent film and television production company, the largest surviving firm of its kind not owned by any Hollywood studio. Jon Feltheimer, chief executive, and Michael Burns, vice chairman, have forged the largest vertically integrated competitor to the major studios. Lions Gate manages a production facility, television unit, foreign sales arm, and an outsized library, which collects titles for the home entertainment market and generates nearly half of the company's revenues.

ORIGINS IN 1997

Lions Gate Entertainment Corporation was founded by financier Frank Giustra in the summer of 1997. Giustra, the son of a Sudbury, Ontario, nickel miner, had served previously as CEO of Yorkton Securities, Inc., an investment bank that specialized in funding mining ventures. During his years as a banker, he also had been involved in the financing of a half-dozen films. A lifelong movie fan, Giustra had decided that he wanted to enter the entertainment business when he reached the age of 40. Leaving Yorkton in December 1996, he set out to assemble a Canadian film company that could compete with Hollywood on its own terms.

To fund the new venture he put up $16 million of his own money and used his banking connections to arrange for $40 million in financing from investors, including Yorkton. Giustra then obtained $64 million when Lions Gate merged with Toronto Stock Exchange listee Beringer Gold Corp. to became a public company. Beringer's mining assets were quickly sold off, and the newly christened Lions Gate Entertainment set out to purchase several existing Canadian film businesses with its new war chest.

One of Lions Gate's first purchases was Cinepix Film Properties, a Montreal-based producer and distributor that had been founded in 1962 by John Dunning and Andre Link, who both still ran the company. Cinepix released both English- and French-language films, and it was one of Canada's leading independent motion picture companies. Cinepix also had a U.S. distribution arm based in New York. The company produced 10 to 12 modestly budgeted titles

COMPANY PERSPECTIVES

Lions Gate is the leading independent producer and distributor of motion pictures, television programming, home entertainment, family entertainment, video-on-demand and digitally delivered content. Its prestigious and prolific library of nearly 12,000 motion picture titles and television episodes is a stable source of recurring revenue and is a foundation for the growth of the Company's core businesses. The Lionsgate brand name is synonymous with original, daring, quality entertainment in markets around the globe.

annually and also distributed edgy art-house fare such as grunge rock documentary *Hype*, Vincent Gallo's offbeat *Buffalo 66*, and *Sick: The Life & Death of Bob Flanagan, Supermasochist*. In addition, Cinepix owned 56 percent of Cine-Groupe, a Montreal-based animated film and production company. Giustra renamed Cinepix Lions Gate Films after the acquisition, but kept its leadership intact. An offshoot, Lions Gate International, was later formed in Los Angeles to serve as a worldwide distribution branch.

Lions Gate also bought North Shore Studios, located in Giustra's home base of Vancouver, British Columbia. North Shore (subsequently renamed Lions Gate Studios) was Canada's largest film production facility, with six busy sound stages. Because it was less expensive to work there, many U.S. production companies chose Vancouver to shoot their movies and TV shows. The series *The X Files* was shot at North Shore for its first five seasons, and other U.S. shows such as *Millennium* used the studio as well.

Another branch of Lions Gate was Mandalay Television, a California-based producer of made-for-TV movies. Mandalay was acquired in a deal with Hollywood mogul Peter Guber, who was given 4 percent ownership of Lions Gate. Guber was a controversial figure in the film world, with a string of hit movies such as *Batman* and *Midnight Express* to his credit, but also a reputation for profligate spending. He had run Columbia Pictures for five years starting in 1989, but the company had been forced to write down $510 million in lawsuit and contract settlement expenses following his departure.

GAMBLING ON GUBER IN 1998

In early 1998 Lions Gate announced a second, larger deal with Guber to form Mandalay Pictures, which would produce feature films costing between $15 million and $75 million each. Guber and his partners Paul Schaeffer and Adam Platnick would own 55 percent of Mandalay, and Lions Gate would own the rest. The complicated financial arrangement called for Giustra's company to put up $80 million, with more than $700 million coming from Paramount Pictures and other companies who would share distribution rights. Lions Gate would not earn anything from the deal until after the distributors had recouped their costs. Noting Guber's reputation, Lions Gate declared that it had protective measures in place that would guard against excessive spending. A total of 20 films was to be produced in a five-year period, with the first due in 2000.

In June 1998, Lions Gate completed another purchase picking up a bankrupt film distributor called International Movie Group, Inc. (IMG). Ten years earlier IMG had received $14 million in financing from Frank Giustra and Yorktown Securities, but the company had gone belly up in 1996. IMG's main asset was its film library, which included such titles as Jean-Claude Van Damme's *Kickboxer*. IMG's holdings were integrated into Lions Gate's other operations, and its former CEO, Peter Strauss, was named president of newly formed Lions Gate Entertainment, Inc., which would become the U.S. parent company for Lions Gate's U.S. interests. Strauss had put in many years in the movie business, going back to Allied Artists Pictures Corp., where he had overseen production of such classic films as *Cabaret* and *The Man Who Would Be King*. Strauss had been instrumental in bringing Giustra and Guber together.

Lions Gate's newly allied divisions were now beginning to bring home contracts and make production plans. Mandalay Television announced that it would be shooting TV series for ABC (*Cupid*), Lifetime (*Oh Baby*), UPN (*Mercy Point*), and Showtime (*Rude Awakening*). Lions Gate Films also picked up distribution deals for Paul Schrader's *Affliction* and several other projects. Another new subsidiary, Lions Gate Media, was formed at this time to explore additional television production possibilities.

Lions Gate also was drawing attention for two controversial projects with which it was involved. One was the Adrian Lyne-directed remake of Vladimir Nabokov's *Lolita*, which was slated to be released uncut in Canada through Lions Gate Films. The portrait of an obsessive pedophile had received a great deal of negative prerelease publicity, as well as a few critical raves. It eventually was released for a limited run before being broadcast on cable television. A much larger controversy involved the company's plans to film Bret Easton Ellis's novel *American Psycho*, which depicted a stockbroker

KEY DATES

1997: Lions Gate is formed; company purchases Cinepix, North Shore Studios, and Mandalay TV.
1998: Deal is signed to co-fund Mandalay feature films; company is listed on the American Stock Exchange.
1999: Company receives first Oscars for *Affliction* and *Gods and Monsters*.
2000: Founder Frank Giustra steps down as CEO; company purchases Trimark Holdings.
2002: Lions Gate sells its equity interest in Mandalay Pictures.
2003: Company purchases Artisan Entertainment, Inc.
2009: Company acquires TV Guide Network.
2010: Carl Icahn battles for control of the company.

who was also a sexual sadist. The company was wooing Leonardo DiCaprio for the lead, his first role after the blockbuster *Titanic*. Despite the offer of a reported $21 million, DiCaprio turned the project down, possibly because his fan base of teenage girls would be unable to view the anticipated R to NC-17 rated film. The company continued with its production plans after DiCaprio dropped out, however, and signed Christian Bale for the role.

ASSESSING THE FIRST YEAR'S RESULTS

At the end of the company's first year in business, a loss of $397,000 on revenues of $42.2 million was reported. Lions Gate's stock also had fallen to a low of $1.40 a share. The annual loss was far from unexpected for a new company, but the slipping share price was bothersome, as it reduced the company's ability to make acquisitions. Purchase of an U.S. reality-based television company, Termite Art Productions, could be made only with the issuance of three convertible promissory notes, rather than a stock swap, because of the low price. The $2.75 million deal brought Lions Gate the maker of a wide spectrum of programs that ranged from History Channel documentaries to tabloid-style fare such as *Busted on the Job*.

Concern about the low share price finally led Giustra to call a shareholders' meeting for October 30, where a vote was made to list Lions Gate on the American Stock Exchange (AMEX). A two-for-one stock consolidation was effected to bring the share price up to the AMEX minimum. It was hoped that the greater exposure of an AMEX listing would boost the stock's value.

In January 1999 the company named Roman Doroniuk, formerly with competitor Alliance Communications, to the posts of president and chief operating officer. Giustra remained Lions Gate Entertainment's CEO and chairman. Meanwhile, Lions Gate Films was scoring kudos for the films *Affliction* and *Gods and Monsters*, which were now in theaters, while hockey comedy *Les Boys 2* was breaking box-office records in French Canada. Cine-Groupe also signed a deal to produce 26 half-hour episodes of a cartoon series called *Mega Babies*, to premiere on Fox Family TV in the fall of 1999. The previous year Fox Family had purchased a 20 percent stake in Cine-Groupe. A new infusion of $16.5 million also was received when 5.4 million shares of Lions Gate stock were sold on a "bought-deal" basis.

In March, the company received its first Academy Awards when James Coburn won an Oscar for best supporting actor in *Affliction* and *Gods and Monsters* was honored for Bill Condon's adapted screenplay. Lions Gate had reportedly spent $500,000 in a public relations campaign to promote the two films, which were nominated for a total of five awards.

Controversy over *American Psycho* continued to mount in Toronto, where scenes for the movie were being shot. Several antiviolence and victim's rights groups were protesting the film's production, although city officials ultimately issued a permit allowing location shooting. Many Canadians were up in arms about the project because notorious Ontario sex killer Paul Bernardo was found to have a copy of the book at his bedside.

MORE NEW PROJECTS IN 1999

In April 1999 the company moved its financial operations to Toronto, where new president Doroniuk's offices were located. Giustra and the corporate headquarters remained in Vancouver. New projects on which company divisions were working included TV movies *The First Daughter* and *The Linda McCartney Story*, TV series *Hope Island* and *Cliffhangers*, and animated feature *Heavy Metal 2000*, produced for Columbia Tri-Star.

When the company released its figures for the second fiscal year, it reported losses of $9.3 million on revenues of $78.3 million. The studio and film divisions were the healthiest, with video sales to the United States via new subsidiary Avalanche Films and half-owned

Sterling Home Entertainment particularly strong. The biggest chunk of red ink was attributable to the investment in Mandalay Pictures. Because of "accounting rules," in the words of president Doroniuk, Lions Gate was picking up 100 percent of Mandalay's losses. In the summer the company put its 13.8-acre Vancouver studio complex up for sale. The asking price was $28 million, but there were no immediate takers. The company's television division also had been restructured to emphasize hour-long non-network series over the production of more financially risky network shows.

In the summer Lions Gate scored a hit in theaters when the Canadian-produced drama *The Red Violin* took in nearly $10 million on the art-house circuit. The Samuel Jackson-starring film was made by a French- and English-Canadian team and was financed and shot internationally. In the fall the company announced two more major deals. Lions Gate Television was to produce a miniseries based on author Dean Koontz's novel *Sole Survivor*, and Lions Gate Films would distribute a new low-budget film starring and coproduced by Kevin Spacey titled *The Big Kahuna*. Spacey reportedly took Lions Gate's $1.5 million offer over several larger ones because he was impressed with the company's track record and its marketing savvy.

Late in the year Lions Gate was seeking still more capital, arranging for a $13.4 million line of credit and filing a preliminary prospectus to sell $30 million in preferred stock shares and common stock purchase warrants. In December the first release from Mandalay Pictures also reached theater screens. *Sleepy Hollow*, directed by Tim Burton, grossed $30 million in its opening weekend despite mixed reviews. Lions Gate also began distributing *Dogma*, which was directed by Kevin Smith and was the company's widest release to date. The film grossed $8.7 million on its opening weekend, and it was expected to earn triple that amount over time. *Dogma* was another controversial project, a satire of Catholicism whose distribution had been switched from Disney-owned Miramax to Lions Gate because of the subject matter.

In January 2000 a $33.1 million influx of cash was obtained from a group of investors that included Microsoft cofounder Paul Allen, former Sony executive Jon Feltheimer, German broadcasting company Tele-Munchen, and SBS Broadcasting SA. The money was earmarked to fund more acquisitions.

RAPID GROWTH UNDER NEW CEO FELTHEIMER

The new financing was quickly followed by dramatic management shifts at the company. Jon Feltheimer took over Giustra's job as CEO, with the founder retaining only his board chairman duties. A short time later President Doroniuk made his own exit, apparently frustrated at having been passed over for Giustra's job. While the dust was clearing, Lions Gate took home its third and fourth Oscars when *The Red Violin* garnered a statuette for best original score and *Sleepy Hollow* won for art direction.

Quickly grabbing the reins, industry vet Feltheimer announced an increase in filmmaking activity, with 15 movies budgeted at $5 million to $20 million to be made annually. In addition, the Avalanche video subsidiary would soon start production on several $1 million genre films to help expand its catalog. Acquisition of another independent film company and a film library were also on Lions Gate's agenda. In June the company accomplished the latter, purchasing low-budget film and video distributor Trimark for an estimated $50 million in stock and cash, plus assumption of $36 million in debt. The 10-year-old company specialized in action and genre films and had a 650-title library. Trimark also owned a Web site, CinemaNow, which offered broadband streaming capabilities. Lions Gate was expected to begin featuring its own products on the site, which showcased independent films, some available exclusively over the Internet.

After only three short years in business, Lions Gate Entertainment had seen many changes and was still growing rapidly. The company was expanding on its strengths as a producer and distributor of independent films, while at the same time growing its home video and television production divisions in an effort to establish itself as a permanent part of the movie industry. Revenues continued to grow (from $74 million in 1999 to $177 million in 2001), yet losses piled up through 2001 despite improved margins in the television and film divisions and ramped-up motion picture production.

One of Lions Gate's major issues was that it remained relatively unknown on Wall Street. Even after reaping awards for *Monster's Ball* in 2001 and turning a profit, its stock did not trade. Still the company continued on its path of producing edgy, unconventional movies that received critical acclaim. Beginning with *Monster's Ball*, it launched its new record label, Lions Gate records, to release select sound tracks. It sold its share in Mandalay Pictures to focus on its own core businesses in 2002. In 2003 it purchased Artisan Entertainment, Inc., a diversified motion picture, family, and home entertainment company with a large film library, to become Hollywood's largest independent studio. By 2004, it was releasing approximately 15 motion pictures and 150 hours of television programming a year.

ATTRACTING INVESTORS, EXPANDING THROUGH ACQUISITION

Finally, in 2004, Lions Gate began to attract investors' attention, among them Paul Allen of Microsoft, James L. Dimon of Bank One, and Mark Cuban, an Internet billionaire and owner of the Dallas Mavericks basketball team, who was also a part of the Weinstein Co. Its shares increased 251 percent from 2003 to 2004. "We have no desire to be No. 1 when we release a picture," Feltheimer was quoted in the *New York Times* in February 2004, although he did predict generating a cash flow in the following fiscal year so that he did not have to "pray for a film to succeed." The company's film library meanwhile gave it some stability.

After the company released Michael Moore's *Fahrenheit 9/11* in 2004, it headed to Hollywood in 2005, selling its eight sound stages and production offices in Canada in 2006. Moore's film, which had proved too controversial for mainstream U.S. movie companies, became Lions Gate's highest-grossing film.

For the next four years, Lions Gate continued to gobble up other companies, purchasing Redbus Film Distribution Ltd. and Redbus Pictures in 2005, Debmar-Mercury in 2006, Mandate Pictures and Canada-based Maple Pictures Corp. in 2007, and TV Guide Network in 2009. In its annual report for 2009, it announced that it had released approximately 18 to 20 motion pictures theatrically per year over the last three years, which included films it had developed and produced in-house, as well as films that it had acquired from third parties.

CARL ICAHN BATTLES FOR CONTROL: 2010

In March 2010, Carl Icahn, who, with almost 19 percent of Lions Gate's shares, was the company's second-largest shareholder, began a battle to gain control of the entire company after Lions Gate expressed interest in acquiring Metro-Goldwyn-Mayer and its library of titles. In late May, after Icahn denounced the board publicly for putting aside $16 million for potential golden parachutes for top executives, he extended his tender offer for the third time. In June, Icahn announced he would wage a proxy war at the company's annual meeting in September.

Meanwhile the company continued its business as usual. It intended to release 10 to 12 motion pictures

theatrically in 2010 and to produce approximately 70 hours of television programming. (It had produced approximately 69 hours of television programming for each of the preceding three years, primarily prime time television series for the cable and broadcast networks.) It would also distribute its library of approximately 8,000 motion picture titles and approximately 4,000 television episodes and programs directly to retailers, video rental stores, and pay and free television channels in the United States, Canada, the United Kingdom, and Ireland, through various digital media platforms, and indirectly to other international markets through its subsidiaries, third parties, and through its newest platforms, TV Guide Network and TV Guide Online.

Although it had reported operating and net losses for fiscal years 2004, 2008, and 2009, Lions Gate continued to be an active contributor in the motion picture industry and, with its large film library, one of the last of the vertically integrated independents.

Frank Uhle
Updated, Carrie Rothburd

PRINCIPAL SUBSIDIARIES

Avalanche Films; Cinepix Animation, Inc.; Cinepix Films, Inc.; LG Pictures, Inc.; Lions Gate Entertainment Inc.; Lions Gate Films Corp.; Lions Gate Films Inc.; Lions Gate Media Corp.; Lions Gate Media Inc.; Lions Gate Television; Trimark Holdings; Distribution International Cine-Groupe J.P. Inc. (56%); Sterling Home Entertainment (50%).

PRINCIPAL COMPETITORS

Alliance Atlantis Communications, Inc.; Artisan Entertainment, Inc.; Bertelsmann AG; DreamWorks SKG; Metro-Goldwyn-Mayer, Inc.; The News Corporation Ltd.; Overseas Filmgroup, Inc.; Sony Pictures Entertainment; Time Warner, Inc.; Unapix Entertainment, Inc.; Universal Studios, Inc.; Viacom, Inc.; The Walt Disney Company; The Weinstein Company.

FURTHER READING

Bond, Paul, and Etan Vlessing, "Lions Gate Gets New Partners in $33.1 Mil Deal," *Hollywood Reporter*, January 5, 2000, p. 1.

Bouw, Brenda, "Lions Gate Founder Steps Down as Chief Executive: Frank Giustra to Be Replaced by Jon Feltheimer," *National Post*, March 22, 2000, p. C1.

———, "Two Lions Gate Films Up for Five Oscars," *National Post*, February 11, 1999, p. C8.

Craig, Susan, "Lions Gate Loses Senior Executive," *Globe and Mail*, April 7, 2000, p. B2.

Dash, Eric, "Taking Big Risks Out of Small Films," *New York Times*, February 29, 2004, p. 6.

Dunkley, Cathy, "Roaring Growth for Lions Gate," *Hollywood Reporter*, May 12, 2000, p. 1.

Fritz, Ben, and Claudia Eller, "Company Town: Lions Gate Tender Offer Extended; Investor Carl Icahn Continues His Battle to Seize Control of the Santa Monica Studio," *Los Angeles Times*, May 22, 2010, p. 3.

———, "Company Town: Icahn to Launch Proxy Fight for Control of Lions Gate; The Activist Investor Has Been Critical of the Film and Television Studio's Management," *Los Angeles Times*, June 2, 2010, p. 1.

Harris, Dana, "Trimark Fits Plate of Prowling Lions Gate," *Variety*, June 12, 2000, p. 8.

Johnson, Ross, "The Movie Midas," *New York Times*, March 7, 2005.

Lyons, Charles, "Lions Gate-Keepers," *Variety*, March 27, 2000, p. 8.

Steinberg, Brian, "Lions Gate Finds Own Territory in Hollywood Jungle: Yet to Roar on Wall Street: 'Mini-Major' Movie Studio Values Its Independent Status," *National Post*, July 30, 2002, p. IN3.

M.D.C. Holdings, Inc.

———— ∎ ————

4350 South Monaco Street, Suite 500
Denver, Colorado 80237
U.S.A.
Telephone: (303) 773-1100
Fax: (303) 741-4134
Web site: http://www.richmondamerican.com

Public Company
Incorporated: 1972 as Mizel Development Corporation
Employees: 1,089
Sales: $898.3 million (2009)
Stock Exchanges: New York
Ticker Symbol: MDC
NAICS: 236117 New Housing Operative Builders;
522292 Real Estate Credit; 523920 Portfolio
Management; 551112 Offices of Other Holding
Companies

∎ ∎ ∎

M.D.C. Holdings, Inc. (MDC), builds homes under the name "Richmond American Homes," ranking as one of the 10 largest homebuilders in the United States. MDC purchases finished lots for the construction of single-family, detached homes. The company operates in Arizona, California, Nevada, Colorado, Utah, Maryland, Virginia, Florida, and the Delaware Valley region that includes parts of Pennsylvania, Delaware, and New Jersey. MDC also offers financial services to its customers, originating mortgage loans through HomeAmerican Mortgage Corporation, selling homeowners' insurance through American Home Insurance Agency, Inc., and providing title-agency services through American Home Title and Escrow Company.

FOUNDER'S BACKGROUND

The guiding force behind MDC during its first four decades of business was Larry Mizel, whose shrewdness earned him a fortune estimated to exceed $100 million. Mizel built a homebuilding empire that ranked among the largest construction companies in the United States, an achievement that would have surprised few of his peers 40 years earlier. After earning a bachelor's degree in business administration from the University of Oklahoma in 1964, Mizel studied law at the University of Denver, where he began to demonstrate his penchant for deal making. "He was always an entrepreneurial person," a fellow student recollected in the July 2004 issue of *ColoradoBiz*. "While we were all studying, he was putting deals together in law school."

Mizel completed his first major real estate deal in 1966. One year before completing his studies, he used part of a $20,000 inheritance from his grandfather to finance the construction of an apartment building in Denver. Mizel invested $18,000 in the $180,000 project, but his involvement ran deeper than his 10 percent stake. "I was one of a group of people and I was an investor versus the syndicator," he said in a rare interview in the July 2004 issue of *ColoradoBiz*. "By starting in that form I learned the business because I became an active investor. I learned how to build, finance. I was the first manager of the project. I lived there. I did the payroll by hand." The 10-story De-Medici Apartments was Mizel's first project, the first of thousands to follow in the decades ahead.

COMPANY PERSPECTIVES

We may be among the biggest builders in the nation, but being the biggest is not our ultimate goal. We're more concerned with being the best. From the quality craftsmanship to the responsive customer service, every aspect of our business is focused on one target: the pursuit of operational excellence. We want everyone who comes in contact with our company—whether it's a customer, vendor or potential employee—to immediately notice our professionalism on every level.

TAKING ROOT IN DENVER: 1972

Although Mizel got his start with an apartment building, he would spend his career building single-family homes. That segment of the construction industry became the focus of MDC's direct predecessor, Mizel Development Corporation, which Mizel founded in 1972 and immediately took public. Based in Denver, the company established itself as a real estate developer and homebuilder during its first decade of business, forming a foundation its 29-year-old founder would use to begin his climb toward national prominence.

During its first decade of business, MDC built a reputation that reflected the character of its founder. Mizel worked tirelessly, scrutinized the Denver housing market, and avoided risk. In 1977 he created Richmond Homes Limited as a subsidiary to pave his entry into the Colorado homebuilding market, marking the birth of the "Richmond American Homes" banner that MDC used to sell its homes. Revenues grew steadily, eclipsing $60 million annually by the time the company celebrated its 10th anniversary. From that point, MDC's financial stature began growing rapidly, as Mizel broadened the scope and extended the reach of his operations.

MDC made the leap from a regional to a multistate homebuilder during the 1980s, as Mizel took his first steps beyond Colorado's borders into neighboring states. The company's financial growth reflected the push into new markets. Between 1982 and 1985, annual revenues leaped sixfold, reaching $375 million, making Mizel's operation a rising force in the homebuilding industry. MDC's volume of business, already growing energetically, was about to expand more rapidly as Mizel began acquiring rivals and realized the immediate growth delivered by orchestrating an acquisition campaign. In 1985 the company completed one of its first major transactions, acquiring Denver-based Wood Bros., a homebuilder that generated $250 million in annual revenue.

The 1980s also saw MDC develop into a more comprehensive participant in the housing market. The company stepped up its land development activities, but more ambitious was its diversification into the mortgage banking business. Through several subsidiaries, most notably HomeAmerican Mortgage Corp., the company provided loans for customers who purchased its homes. MDC also managed the day-to-day operations of Asset Investors Corp., a publicly traded real estate investment trust, giving it an additional stream of revenue and profits.

CRISIS: 1987–92

MDC flourished as it delved into new business areas and unleashed its homebuilding activities. By 1986, revenues had skyrocketed to $963 million, from which the company posted a $35.7 million profit. Encouraged by his success, Mizel attempted to steer MDC far afield, making an unsuccessful, $94 million bid to acquire Vicorp Restaurants Inc., operator of the Village Inn and Baker's Square family-restaurant chains, in 1987. As it turned out, the failed takeover of a restaurant company would be the least of Mizel's concerns during the last years of the decade. For the first time in his career, Mizel had to contend with a crisis, as MDC's loping stride turned into a limp.

Unfortunately for Mizel and his team of executives, the revenue total recorded in 1986 was an amount they would not equal for years to come. By 1988, revenues had slipped to $840 million, but far more worrisome was the $31.3 million loss posted for the year, only two years after the company had registered a profit of $35.7 million. Mizel restructured his operations after the company began losing money, selling homebuilding and mortgage operations in Texas, Florida, Georgia, Arizona, and Colorado. Mizel also scaled back his involvement in several metropolitan markets, including Dallas, Phoenix, and Denver. MDC, struggling to find its balance, omitted dividend payments on its stock in the fourth quarter of 1988 and indefinitely suspended future dividend payments.

MDC's financial difficulties stripped the company of the vitality it had displayed since its formation, but an anemic balance sheet was not the only problem Mizel faced. The U.S. Securities and Exchange Commission (SEC) began investigating MDC in late 1987 for possible violations of securities laws. In the early 1990s, federal law-enforcement officials indicted MDC and President and co-CEO David Mandarich for making

KEY DATES

1972: Larry Mizel founds Mizel Development Corporation (MDC).
1977: Mizel enters the Colorado homebuilding market.
2005: Revenues reach a record high of $4.8 billion.
2009: Reeling from adverse market conditions, MDC generates $898 million in revenue and posts a $107 million loss.

fraudulent campaign contributions. According to SEC documents, MDC reimbursed subcontractors for contributions they made to politicians and political causes favored by MDC's leadership. The company pleaded guilty to the charges and paid a $220,400 fine, which resolved the matter, but still left Mizel and Mandarich with the daunting task of restoring their company's luster.

TURNAROUND YEARS: 1995–99

From the debacle of the late 1980s and early 1990s, Mizel and his chief deputy executed a remarkable comeback. Mizel was vague in his description of how MDC effected its turnaround. "We focused on what was necessary to be successful, and we worked really hard every day," he said in a July 2004 interview with *ColoradoBiz.* "We met all of our obligations and as the economy improved our business improved."

By the time MDC celebrated its 25th anniversary in 1997, it had fully recovered from its problems earlier in the decade. The company ranked as the seventh-largest homebuilder in the country, having eclipsed its sales peak in 1986 to begin a new era in which each year brought record high financial totals. MDC surpassed $1 billion in annual revenue for the first time in 1998 and ended the decade with more than $1.5 billion in revenue and homebuilding operations in six states: Colorado, California, Arizona, Nevada, Virginia, and Maryland. Aside from a failed foray into secondary mortgage lending during the late 1990s, the company ended the decade excelling on all fronts.

MDC entered the 21st century flush with success. Aided by lower interest rates, the company was posting record high totals in home orders, home closings, profits, and revenues. It expanded its financial services business to include title-agency services, a business conducted through American Home Title and Escrow Co., and homeowners' insurance through American

Home Insurance Agency. The company strengthened its homebuilding operations through internal expansion and external expansion, acquiring companies that gave it a dominant position in key markets. The acquisition of KE&G Homes in 2001 made MDC the largest homebuilder in the Tucson, Arizona, market. The purchase of W.L. Homes in 2002 made MDC the third-largest homebuilder in Las Vegas and paved the company's entry into the Salt Lake City, Utah, market. By 2004, when revenues flirted with the $4 billion mark, MDC had homebuilding operations in 10 states, having recorded record sales and profit totals for each of the previous five years.

A PRECIPITOUS FALL: 2007–09

A notoriously capricious business, the homebuilding industry demonstrated its cyclical behavior during the second half of the decade. MDC generated a staggering $4.8 billion in revenue in 2005, but, just as in 1986, the total proved difficult to equal for many years to come. "After a record-setting six-year run," *Investor's Business Daily* noted in its February 24, 2005 issue, "even the most optimistic analysts see home construction and sales easing this year and next." The National Association of Home Builders forecast an 8 percent decline in home construction for the next several years, predicting a similar decline for new- and existing-home sales, but the national trade association could not have foreseen how disastrous the future would be for homebuilders such as MDC. Economic conditions deteriorated rapidly in the last years of the decade, creating a business climate that drew comparison with the Great Depression.

Financial figures posted by MDC during the period showed a company in distress. The plunge in financial totals was sudden and profound. The $4.7 billion in revenue generated in 2006 plummeted to $2.7 billion in 2007, a period that saw a $333 million profit transmogrify into a $756 million loss. Orders for new homes dropped from 10,229 to 6,504 during the period and the number of home orders recorded as backlog, which had hovered at 6,500 during the company's mid-decade peak, fell to 1,947. From there, the tale told by the financial figures became grimmer. In 2008 revenues continued to fall, sliding to $1.3 billion, a year that also produced a $382 million loss. In 2009 MDC lost another $107 million while generating $898 million in revenue, roughly the same total it had generated in the 1980s.

The housing market felt the full sting of the historic economic conditions, and MDC showed it was not immune to the perniciousness of the times. Nonetheless Mizel, along with President and COO

Mandarich, had extricated MDC from adverse circumstances before. As the company prepared for the future, Mizel and Mandarich faced the most daunting challenge of their careers.

Jeffrey L. Covell

PRINCIPAL SUBSIDIARIES

AHT Reinsurance, Inc.; Allegiant Insurance Company, Inc.; American Home Insurance Agency, Inc.; American Home Title and Escrow Company; ASFC-W, Inc.; ASW Finance Company; HomeAmerican Mortgage Corporation; MDC.com, Inc.; M.D.C. Home Finance Corporation; M.D.C. Land Corporation; M.D.C. Residual Holdings, Inc.; MDC/Wood, Inc.; Monaco Street Financial I, Inc.; Monaco Street Financial II, Inc.; RAH of Florida, Inc.; RAH of Texas, LP; RAH Holdings, LLC; Richmond American Construction, Inc.; Richmond American Homes Corporation; Richmond Realty, Inc.; StarAmerican Insurance Ltd.; Yosemite Financial, Inc.

PRINCIPAL COMPETITORS

D.R. Horton, Inc.; KB Home; PulteGroup, Inc.

FURTHER READING

Arellano, Kristi, "One of Denver's Largest Homebuilders Expands in Utah, Nevada," *Denver Post*, April 5, 2002.

Elliott, Alan R., "MDC Holdings Inc., Denver, Colorado; Builder Looks to Lay a Sturdier Foundation," *Investor's Business Daily*, February 24, 2005, p. A4.

Maynard, R., "Tops in Tucson," *Builder*, March 2001, p. 15.

Titus, Stephen, "King of Home Builders: Larry Mizel Gives Back Plenty—but He Doesn't Look Back," *ColoradoBiz*, July 2004, p. 18.

"Vicorp Defense Thwarts M.D.C.'s Takeover Try," *Nation's Restaurant News*, May 25, 1987, p. 3.

The Manitowoc Company, Inc.

———————————■———————————

2400 South 44th Street
Post Office Box 66
Manitowoc, Wisconsin 54221-0066
U.S.A.
Telephone: (920) 684-4410
Fax: (920) 652-9778
Web site: http://www.manitowoc.com

Public Company
Founded: 1902 as Manitowoc Dry Dock Company
Employees: 13,100
Sales: $3.78 billion (2009)
Stock Exchanges: New York
Ticker Symbol: MTW
NAICS: 333120 Construction Machinery Manufacturing; 333294 Food Product Machinery Manufacturing; 333319 Other Commercial and Service Industry Machinery Manufacturing; 333415 Air-Conditioning and Warm Air Heating Equipment and Commercial and Industrial Refrigeration Equipment Manufacturing; 333923 Overhead Traveling Crane, Hoist, and Monorail System Manufacturing

■ ■ ■

The Manitowoc Company, Inc., is a manufacturer specializing in two areas: cranes and foodservice equipment. Its cranes operations, which contribute about 60 percent of overall sales and which serve the heavy construction, energy, infrastructure, and other industries, lead the world in lattice-boom cranes, tower cranes, rough-terrain cranes, truck-mounted cranes, and boom trucks. Manitowoc also ranks second worldwide in all-terrain cranes. Its crane brands include Manitowoc, Grove, Potain, and National. The foodservice group, accounting for about 40 percent of revenues, produces a wide range of foodservice equipment for the restaurant, convenience store, lodging and hospitality, health care, and institutional foodservice sectors, as well as for commercial beverage and bottling applications. Among the 35 brands included within this group are such industry-leading makes as Manitowoc commercial ice-making machines, Kolpak walk-in refrigerators and freezers, Servend combination ice/beverage dispensers, Frymaster gas and electric fryers, Cleveland steam cooking equipment, and Garland commercial ranges, grills, and induction units.

EARLY HISTORY

The founders of Manitowoc Company, Charles C. West and Elias Gunnell, originally worked for the Chicago Ship Building Company in Chicago, Illinois. In 1899, however, when Chicago Ship Building was purchased by American Shipbuilding, a company based in Cleveland, Ohio, the former firm was subsumed under the latter and lost its decision-making authority and engineering autonomy. Disappointed with the results of the purchase, West and Gunnell decided to buy a shipyard of their own. West, a marine engineer and naval architect, and Gunnell, an experienced shipbuilder, designer, and mechanic, reached the conclusion that their shipyard would build steel ships rather than the wooden ships commonly built at that time. However, after consulting their acquaintances within the

COMPANY PERSPECTIVES

Our mission is to continuously improve economic value for our shareholders. The centerpiece of our efforts will continue to be high-quality, customer-focused products and support services. Research, marketing, resources, manufacturing, support services, and all related elements will generally be product oriented. The company will apply this focus in evaluating and guiding its business units.

shipbuilding industry, the two entrepreneurs were convinced that the best plan of action was first to purchase a yard where wooden ship repairs could be done. This would provide them with financial stability, and then, in due time, they could buy and install the necessary equipment for building steel ships.

The only shipyard for sale on the shores of Lake Michigan was located in Manitowoc, Wisconsin. Owned by brothers Henry and George Burger, the Manitowoc operation had grown large and lucrative from its extensive wooden ship repair business. Having found an acquisition that ideally suited their purposes, West and Gunnell bought the Burger and Burger shipyard in 1902 for $110,000. Gunnell assumed the position of president and West became the general manager of the new Manitowoc Dry Dock Company. The first vessel launched by Manitowoc Dry Dock was the *Cheguamegon*, a wooden passenger steamer under construction at the time of the purchase. By 1903, however, the company had contracted its first steel ship repair job, and by 1905 the firm had launched the passenger steamer *Maywood*, the first steel vessel built in the Manitowoc shipyard.

In 1904 Gunnell, West, and L. E. Geer, the secretary and treasurer of Manitowoc, had created a separate tool company to manufacture marine engines and other types of machinery necessary to outfit a ship. In 1905 Manitowoc purchased this company and incorporated it within its shipbuilding operations. In 1908 Manitowoc purchased Manitowoc Steam Boiler Works, a major manufacturer of marine boilers, pulp digesters, dryers, furnaces, ladles, vulcanizers, kilns, buoys, buckets, creosoting retorts, and tanks. These two acquisitions gave Manitowoc not only the ability to build new steel vessels but also the capability to completely equip them for operational service. With sales increasing and financial stability assured, to reflect a more modern image management decided to change

the name of the firm, first to Manitowoc Shipbuilding and Dry Dock Company, in 1910, and then to simply Manitowoc Shipbuilding Company, in 1916.

During World War I the company grew dramatically. Although the war had started in 1914, the United States did not enter the hostilities in Europe until 1917. When Congress declared war on Germany in April 1917, however, the entire operations of Manitowoc were subsumed under the authority of the U.S. Shipping Board Emergency Fleet Corporation. The board immediately placed a large contract with Manitowoc for 3,500-ton freighters, and the company embarked on an extensive expansion program to fill this order. During the course of the war, West was recruited by the U.S. Navy Bureau of Construction to supervise the construction of a Ford Motor Company shipbuilding plant in River Rouge, Michigan, near Ford's headquarters. For more than 18 months, West commuted between Manitowoc and Detroit to fulfill his duties to both companies. Before the war, Manitowoc turned out an average of six ships per year. By the time the war ended in 1918, the company was capable of turning out 18 ships annually and had built 33 3,500-ton freighters used during the war effort.

DIVERSIFYING, INCLUDING INTO CRANES

Unfortunately, when World War I ended the U.S. government canceled the remaining freighter contracts with Manitowoc. This loss of wartime revenue led to a postwar depression, not only for Manitowoc but also for the entire shipbuilding industry in the Great Lakes region. With its expanded capacity for shipbuilding, and numerous employees hired for the wartime production effort, West and Gunnell searched for new business that would compensate for the disappearance of government contracts. Luckily, the two men arranged for the company's shipbuilding plant to be converted into a railroad locomotive maintenance and repair shop. This kept the company barely solvent, with funds enough to pay employee wages, but it was clear that Manitowoc would have to undergo a transformation to survive.

In 1920 West and Gunnell came to a sharp disagreement as to the direction of the company. West was convinced that Manitowoc could survive only by implementing a broadly based diversification strategy. Gunnell, on the other hand, maintained that the company should continue to emphasize its shipbuilding capacity. Unable to reach a point of mutual agreement, the company was put up for sale. Interestingly enough, West made the only offer to purchase the firm. For a total of $410,000, West and Geer bought the company and renamed it Manitowoc Shipbuilding Corporation.

KEY DATES

1902: Charles C. West and Elias Gunnell purchase the Burger and Burger shipyard in Manitowoc, Wisconsin, and rename it Manitowoc Dry Dock Company.

1920: West buys out the original shareholders and renames the company Manitowoc Shipbuilding Corporation.

1925: Manitowoc enters the crane business through an agreement to manufacture Moore Speedcranes.

1945: Foodservice equipment enters the mix when Manitowoc begins manufacturing freezers.

1952: The increasingly diverse firm is renamed The Manitowoc Company, Inc.

1971: Company goes public and is listed on the NASDAQ.

1993: Company stock is shifted to the New York Stock Exchange.

2008: British commercial cooking equipment supplier Enodis plc is acquired for $2.1 billion; Manitowoc's marine group, its founding business, is divested.

An immediate policy of diversification was established, including an expansion of the boiler works and new products for the machine shop. Because marine boilers were losing their popularity, the boiler works diversified into the manufacture of paper mill equipment; dryers for coal, rock, and clay; brewery tanks; air nozzles; and heating boilers. In 1925 the machine shop reached an agreement to manufacture Moore Speedcranes under the Moore patents. By 1928, Manitowoc had taken over the manufacture and sale of all of the crane models produced by the Roy and Charles Moore Crane Company. The diversification program did not mean that shipbuilding at the company was interrupted. During the 1920s, Manitowoc constructed its first self-unloading vessel, two car ferries, five tugboats, four deck barges, two dipper dredges, two dump scows, two derrick scows, a floating dry dock, and the largest suction dredge in the world at the time.

THE GREAT DEPRESSION AND WORLD WAR II

With the stock market crash of 1929, the era of the Great Depression began in the United States. Manitowoc, like many other businesses during the time, was hard hit by the downward trend in business. Sales dropped precipitously from more than $4 million in 1931 to less than $500,000 by 1933. During the middle of the decade, the company operated at a net loss for four years in a row. Many employees were laid off, and those that remained were forced to take a reduction in their salaries. The company's shipbuilding business was severely affected by the Depression, and management was forced to rely more heavily on the crane business (now producing models under the Manitowoc name). During the 1930s, Manitowoc introduced an improved version of the Speedcrane and began a maintenance service to repair and keep cranes in first-class condition. Manitowoc cranes soon garnered a reputation for high quality within the industry and were purchased to help construct the Senate Office Building, the National Gallery of Art, the National Archives, and the Jefferson Memorial, all located in Washington, D.C.

In 1940, as the start of another world war became more evident to U.S. government officials, the Navy contracted Manitowoc to build 10 submarines and provided the company with funds to make the necessary plant improvements and expansion. Although West hesitated because of his previous experience with U.S. government contracts, which left the company in dire financial straits after World War I, he reluctantly decided to engage in a comprehensive plant conversion. The increased capacity soon proved itself useful. Just one week after Pearl Harbor had been attacked by the Japanese, which initiated U.S. involvement in World War II, the company received an order from the U.S. Navy for immediate delivery of six cranes for use in salvaging operations in the harbor. More than 58 cranes were made by the company for the Navy's Floating Dry Docks during the war, and 79 cranes and shovels were delivered to the U.S. Army.

Besides a huge order for submarine construction during the war, Manitowoc also built landing craft for use in both the Pacific and European theaters of operation. Extensive testing was conducted along the shores of Lake Michigan by company engineers, and design changes were made before actual production was begun. Manitowoc built a total of 1,465 landing craft and received a presidential citation for the vehicle's performance during the Normandy landing in June 1944. In addition, by the end of the war the company had constructed 28 submarines for the U.S. Navy and had received the Navy "E" for excellence in production five times.

THE POSTWAR YEARS

The immediate period after World War II brought the same problems that had confronted the company after

World War I: the necessary reorganization of the company and its manufacturing facilities to a peacetime economy. Unlike what happened the previous time, however, the U.S. Navy reimbursed Manitowoc for its wartime expenses and helped it to dismantle the Navy's portion of its shipbuilding operations. West, still in control of the company's direction, decided once again that diversification was the answer.

Looking for products to manufacture that did not require significant capital investment, Manitowoc started making dry-cleaning units and, in addition, freezers for Firestone and Westinghouse (production of the latter beginning in 1945). Soon the firm was making commercial frozen-food cabinets used in supermarkets and restaurants. By 1950, more than 50 percent of Manitowoc's equipment works was devoted to this business. In 1952 Manitowoc Shipbuilding Company was reorganized. To reflect its increasingly diverse operations, the company name was changed to The Manitowoc Company, Inc. Two chief units were made into subsidiaries, Manitowoc Shipbuilding, Inc., and Manitowoc Engineering Corporation (the cranes operation). A third, Manitowoc Equipment Works, became a division.

Manitowoc's shipbuilding operation was plagued by union strikes throughout the late 1940s. With the end of the postwar recession in the marine industry, the firm reclaimed its role as a major shipbuilder and repair facility in the Great Lakes region. During the early 1950s, the company constructed the prototype of Nautilus, the country's first nuclear submarine. In addition, numerous commercial vessels were built during the decade, including the largest self-unloader on the Great Lakes, a coal hauler, the first diesel-powered car ferry, and five crane barges. West was particularly pleased to see his company survive the difficulties of the postwar period. When he died in 1957, he left behind what was considered to be a thriving firm with great potential for the future. The founder's son, John D. West, took over as president.

During the 1960s, Manitowoc continued to grow. The manufacture of dry-cleaning units was expanded, as well as the production of freezers and frozen-food cabinets. In 1966 the company introduced the Manitowoc Ice Dispenser, which quickly became very popular in both the hospital and lodging industries. Because shipbuilding at the time consisted mostly of smaller vessels such as dump scows and crane barges, management decided to combine its operations with another Great Lakes shipbuilding firm and relocate Manitowoc's shipbuilding operation to Sturgeon Bay, Wisconsin. In 1968 Manitowoc purchased all of the assets of the Sturgeon Bay Shipbuilding and Dry Dock Company and subsequently renamed its reorganized business the Bay Shipbuilding Corporation. This combination of

both resources and facilities resulted in major contracts during the 1970s, including the first 1,000-foot ship, built to haul coal for Detroit Edison.

GROWTH AND TRANSFORMATION DURING THE SEVENTIES AND EIGHTIES

During the early 1970s the company relocated and reorganized its shipbuilding operation. It also was listed on the NASDAQ in 1971 through an initial public offering. The company divested its dry-cleaning operation and sold off its freezer and frozen-food cabinet business.

The most successful and profitable product made by the company after World War II was its custom-built cranes. From the mid-1920s to 1945, management regarded the sale of its cranes as a fortuitous product of a necessary diversification program started after World War I. After World War II, the demand for the company's cranes began to increase dramatically. During the 1950s and 1960s, Manitowoc was at the forefront of developing technological innovations to increase the quality of its cranes. The company was the first manufacturer to use T-1 high-strength steel in booms, design a controlled-torque converter for crane applications, and develop extendible crawlers. In 1967 Manitowoc engineers designed an assembly called the Ringer that doubled the lift capacity of any basic crane.

By 1977, sales for Manitowoc cranes were reported at $146.5 million, whereas shipbuilding and repair revenues amounted to $73 million and ice cube maker sales totaled $14.4 million. In the late 1970s the company spent $35 million to build new manufacturing facilities for the Manitowoc Engineering and Manitowoc Equipment Works operations on a 100-acre site called SouthWorks located southwest of downtown Manitowoc.

John West remained CEO of Manitowoc through 1986 and chairman for most of the decade, but it was Ralph Helm who increasingly led the company during the 1980s, first as president and COO (1981–86) and then as president and CEO (1986–90). Helm had previously spent two decades at the Manitowoc Engineering crane subsidiary, helping increase sales there from $18 million in 1962 to more than $143 million by 1980.

During the 1980s, Manitowoc rode an economic roller coaster. The recession of the early 1980s, and the collapse of the petroleum boom, led to a dramatic plunge in Manitowoc's sales. The company's crane business fell flat, especially in the areas of large lift cranes used in the construction and offshore oil industries. The company's manufacture of ice-making machines for the foodservice, health care, and convenience store markets also took a nosedive, and shipbuilding at the Sturgeon Bay facility had to be abandoned altogether.

By the end of the decade, conditions at Manitowoc had improved slightly. Manitowoc's crane business had benefited from the revival of offshore drilling in the Gulf of Mexico, and the company claimed that it was the only manufacturer of large lift cranes left in the United States. All of the firm's competitors had either sold their holdings to foreign interests or gone out of business. The company's ice-machine business replaced the crane business as Manitowoc's most profitable operation during the middle and late 1980s, and the Sturgeon Bay facility reported that it was one of only three remaining Great Lakes shipping repair and maintenance shops for the country's largest iron-ore carriers.

SHIFTING TO MORE MODERN CORPORATE MANAGEMENT

In 1990 Fred M. Butler was named company president and CEO. Butler was a relative outsider, having joined the company as manager of administration only in 1988. Starting as an engineer, Butler had spent more than three decades moving up the ranks of a South San Francisco-based construction firm called Guy F. Atkinson Company. His perspective as an outsider is credited with shaking up a relatively moribund company and injecting it with a more modern operating philosophy.

During the early 1990s, Butler implemented a comprehensive cost-cutting and reorganization strategy, including a revamped marketing program that significantly enhanced Manitowoc's presence across the United States and in Europe. Modernization at the firm's large crane and boom-truck facilities increased production, and the introduction of new crane designs, especially the Model 888 crane with a 220-ton lift capacity, gained immediate market acceptance. At the same time, Bay Shipbuilding cut back on its shipbuilding operations but expanded its ship repair business to include two additional locations in the Great Lakes region (in Toledo and Cleveland, Ohio). By the mid-1990s, the unit operated more than 60 percent of all dry-dock footage on the Great Lakes.

On the ice-machine front, as part of Butler's drive to expand in the Asia-Pacific region, Manitowoc in 1994 entered into a joint venture to build ice machines with the Hangzhou Household Electric Appliance Industrial Corporation. The venture was based in the large city of Hangzhou, located about 100 miles southwest of Shanghai, China. Meantime, in 1993, Manitowoc's stock was shifted to the New York Stock Exchange to secure the broader exposure offered by that market.

Butler's most important move, however, was to persuade the company's traditionally conservative board of directors to direct some of Manitowoc's hoard of cash toward acquisitions. The company's first major acquisition came in November 1995, when The Shannon Group, Inc., a major manufacturer of commercial refrigeration equipment, particularly walk-in refrigerators and freezers, was purchased for $126 million. The purchase of Shannon turned Manitowoc into the largest supplier of commercial ice-cube machines and walk-in refrigerators in the world. The company now derived more than half of its revenues from foodservice equipment, with cranes and related products contributing 39 percent and shipbuilding/ship repair only 7 percent.

In 1996, when company sales surpassed the half-billion-dollar mark, Bay Shipbuilding lived up to its name for the first time in years when it completed construction of *Integrity*, a 460-foot integrated tug/barge. This was the first new Great Lakes vessel built since 1982. In 1997 the Equipment Works subsidiary, which specialized in ice-making machines, changed its name to the more descriptive Manitowoc Ice, Inc. This subsidiary was bolstered in October of that year through the $73 million purchase of Sellersburg, Indiana-based SerVend International, Inc., the third-largest maker of ice and beverage dispensers in the United States. SerVend's major customers included fast-food restaurants, convenience stores, and soft-drink bottlers.

ACQUISITIONS TO CENTER STAGE IN LATE 20TH CENTURY

A key figure in these two major foodservice acquisitions was Terry D. Growcock, who had joined the company in 1994 as head of Manitowoc's ice-machine subsidiary. Having previously served in management positions at a variety of manufacturing companies, Growcock was soon promoted to head of Manitowoc's foodservice group in March 1995. When Butler retired as president and CEO in July 1998, Growcock was selected to succeed him, becoming the first company president to come through the foodservice side. Under his leadership, Manitowoc nearly tripled its 1997 revenues of $545.9 million by the year 2002, when sales hit $1.41 billion. Driving this growth was a string of acquisitions that Growcock engineered.

In 1998 Manitowoc gained a manufacturing presence in Europe with the acquisition of a 50 percent interest in Fabbrica Apparecchiature per la Produzione del Ghiaccio, S.r.l. (F.A.G.), an ice-machine firm based in Milan, Italy. The company also entered into a license agreement with Blue Star, an Indian company, to manufacture Kolpak walk-in refrigerators for sale in the Middle East and Asia. During 2000 Manitowoc purchased full control of its Chinese joint venture and also paid $21.2 million for Harford Duracool, LLC, a maker of walk-in refrigerators and freezers serving the U.S. East Coast.

The cranes business expanded as well. In November 1998 U.S. Truck Crane, Inc., (USTC) was bought for $51.5 million. Based in York, Pennsylvania, USTC produced boom trucks, rough-terrain forklifts, and other materials handling equipment. After another boom truck manufacturer, Pioneer Holdings LLC, was acquired in 2000, the company's three boom truck lines (the other being Manitex) were consolidated under a new brand, Manitowoc Boom Trucks. That same year, Manitowoc introduced the most popular crane in its history, the Model 999 lattice-boom crane, which could lift 275 tons. More than 80 of the units were sold within seven months of introduction.

Manitowoc's marine group nearly tripled its revenues through the $66.7 million purchase of Marinette Marine Corporation in November 2000. Based in Marinette, Wisconsin (just across Green Bay from Bay Shipbuilding's facility in Sturgeon Bay), the purchased shipyard, which specialized more in midsized research and military (particularly U.S. Coast Guard and U.S. Navy) vessels, was a good fit with Manitowoc's existing shipyards, which focused on commercial vessels. Manitowoc now operated more than 60 percent of the U.S. dry docks in the Great Lakes.

TWO KEY CRANE ACQUISITIONS: POTAIN AND GROVE

With the company's appetite for growth increasing, Manitowoc next completed what at the time were the two largest acquisitions in company history, both of crane companies. In May 2001 the firm offered $307 million in cash and assumed $138.8 million in debt for Potain S.A. (later renamed Potain SAS). At the time a subsidiary of Groupe Legris Industries SA, Potain was headquartered near Lyon, France, and was a global leader in tower cranes for the building and construction industry. With annual sales of about $300 million, Potain operated eight manufacturing facilities in France, Germany, Italy, Portugal, and China and distributed its cranes to more than 50 nations. The addition of Potain helped push Manitowoc's revenues past the $1 billion mark for the first time in 2001.

In August 2002 Manitowoc acquired Grove Worldwide for about $278 million. Grove, which had just emerged from bankruptcy, was one of the world's leading makers of mobile telescopic cranes. Its headquarters were in Shady Grove, Pennsylvania, and it had other plants in Germany and France. Grove also owned National Crane Corporation, a maker of boom trucks that competed directly with Manitowoc Boom Trucks. As a condition of approving the purchase of Grove, the U.S. Department of Justice stipulated that Manitowoc had to sell one of the two boom truck makers. The company elected to divest Manitowoc Boom Trucks, which was sold to Quantum Heavy Equipment LLC in early 2003. In another 2002 acquisition, Manitowoc purchased full control of its F.A.G. ice-machine venture in Italy, which subsequently began operating as Manitowoc Foodservice Europe, S.r.l.

The two crane purchases significantly expanded Manitowoc's presence overseas, with sales outside North America increasing from less than 6 percent in 2000 to more than 21 percent two years later. Nevertheless, this acquisition spree did not come without a price. Manitowoc posted a net loss of $20.5 million in 2002 thanks to $74 million in special charges, including costs incurred restructuring some of the crane and foodservice operations. The substantial expansion of the crane business, which now generated more than 60 percent of overall revenues, left Manitowoc dependent once again on a more cyclical business just as the global economy was struggling mightily. Difficult market conditions and heightened competition translated into depressed earnings for both 2003 and 2004.

PERIOD OF RAPID GROWTH

The more robust global economy of the middle years of the decade featured a major worldwide boom in infrastructure and commercial construction spending that lifted demand for Manitowoc cranes and sent the company's profits into an upward trajectory starting in 2005. By 2007 Manitowoc had achieved what was by far its best year ever, posting profits of $333.6 million on revenues of $4.01 billion. The profit figure was double that of the previous year, while sales had increased 36 percent.

Acquisitions and global expansion remained key strategies for growth during this period, and both strategies were evident in the company's July 2007 purchase of the Indian firm Shirke Construction Equipments Pvt. Ltd. for $64.5 million. Shirke was a market leader in India's tower crane sector and had served as Potain's Indian manufacturing partner and distributor since 1982. Another key market for global expansion was China. In 2005 Manitowoc's foodservice group opened a new, 190,000-square-foot manufacturing facility in Hangzhou for the production of ice machines. A year later, the firm opened a new, 805,000-square-foot crane manufacturing plant in Zhangjiagang, China, a move that solidified Manitowoc's position as the leading producer of cranes in one of the world's fastest-growing construction markets. Manitowoc also opened a new tower crane manufacturing plant in Slovakia to serve the growing markets of Eastern Europe.

At the same time, Manitowoc was driving growth through product innovation. Among the more than 50 new foodservice products introduced in 2005 and 2006 were a flaked ice dispenser for the health care market, a residential ice machine, and a number of energy-saving ice machines. One of the introductions in 2007 was the FlexTower self-service beverage dispenser, which could dispense up to 16 noncarbonated beverages in a compact design appropriate for convenience stores. Also in 2007, the company debuted an entirely new type of crane that included features of crawler, tower, and mobile telescopic cranes. The Grove GTK1100 offered a combination of a high degree of mobility and exceptional lifting capacity that was particularly suited for refineries and wind power applications.

ENODIS ACQUISITION AND RESULTING BALANCE BETWEEN CRANES AND FOODSERVICE EQUIPMENT

The next major turning point in Manitowoc's history came in 2008 when the firm acquired Enodis plc. Manitowoc had taken a run at purchasing the British commercial cooking equipment supplier two years earlier for $1.7 billion, but the two companies ended takeover talks amid concerns that a merger might not pass regulatory muster. Manitowoc renewed its pursuit of Enodis in the spring of 2008 with an offer of $1.87 billion, but Illinois Tool Works Inc. stepped in with a competing offer, setting off a months-long takeover battle. Manitowoc emerged victorious from a one-round auction overseen by the United Kingdom's Takeover Panel late in June. The company closed its acquisition of Enodis in October 2008 with a reported purchase price of $2.1 billion in cash. This was by far Manitowoc's largest acquisition in its history.

The takeover diversified Manitowoc's foodservice equipment lines by adding Enodis's restaurant fryers and other hot-food equipment to Manitowoc's strong array of ice machines, refrigeration equipment, and beverage dispensers. Enodis had a portfolio of about 30 brands, including Frymaster gas and electric fryers, Cleveland steam cooking equipment, and Garland commercial ranges and grills. Although another key aspect of the takeover was the boost it gave to Manitowoc's hitherto modest presence in the European market, Enodis was

well entrenched in North America, where it generated more than 70 percent of its sales.

To gain regulatory approval for the deal, Manitowoc agreed to divest Enodis's global ice-machine business, and this operation was sold to a private-equity firm in May 2009 for $160 million. In the meantime, in December 2008 Manitowoc sold its marine group to Italian shipbuilder Fincantieri Marine Group Holdings Inc. for $120 million. Through the sale of its founding business and the acquisition of Enodis, Manitowoc positioned itself to operate two globally powerful businesses manufacturing cranes and foodservice equipment.

Although the former remained the firm's largest unit, its share of overall revenues was much reduced, from about 80 percent to around 60 percent. Manitowoc's more balanced portfolio proved almost instantly valuable when the global economy turned down sharply right around the time of the Enodis deal's consummation. Slumping construction markets around the world resulted in a deep drop in crane demand. Manitowoc's crane group consequently suffered a drop in sales of more than 40 percent in 2009, which sent overall sales down 16 percent, to $3.78 billion. The company's 2009 net loss of $704.2 million was deepened by hefty goodwill and intangible asset impairment charges as well as $39.6 million in restructuring expenses. Early in 2009, Manitowoc had slashed its crane group workforce by 22 percent, or about 2,100 jobs, and the company also shut down two foodservice facilities as part of its integration of Enodis.

Through the first six months of 2010, as the crane group continued to struggle in a global economy far from fully recovered, Manitowoc posted a small net loss and saw overall sales fall about 22 percent. Again, however, the results would have been much worse had the company not acquired Enodis. Sales for the crane group plummeted 39 percent compared to the same period in 2009, but the foodservice group's revenues of $780 million represented an increase of about 6 percent and comprised nearly half of Manitowoc's overall total. The acquisition of Enodis had thus mitigated the effects of an inevitable downturn in the company's boom-and-bust crane business.

Thomas Derdak
Updated, David E. Salamie

PRINCIPAL SUBSIDIARIES

Cleveland Range LLC; Convotherm Ltd. (UK); The Delfield Company LLC; Enodis Corporation; Enodis Group Ltd. (UK); Frymaster LLC; Garland Commercial Industries LLC; Grove Cranes Ltd. (UK); Grove U.S. L.L.C.; Jackson MSC LLC; Kysor Industrial Corporation; Lincoln Foodservice Products LLC; Manitowoc Beverage Systems Ltd. (UK); Manitowoc Crane Companies, LLC; Manitowoc Crane Equipment (China) Co., Ltd.; Manitowoc Crane Group (UK) Limited; Manitowoc Crane Group France SAS; Manitowoc Crane Group Germany GmbH; Manitowoc Crane Group Mexico SRL de CV; Manitowoc Cranes, LLC; Manitowoc Foodservice Companies, LLC; Manitowoc France SAS (France); Manitowoc Potain Ltd. (UK); Merrychef Ltd. (UK); Multiplex GmbH (Germany); Potain GmbH (Germany).

PRINCIPAL DIVISIONS

Manitowoc Crane Group; Manitowoc Foodservice.

PRINCIPAL COMPETITORS

Ali S.p.A.; Changsha Zoomlion Heavy Industry Science & Technology Development Co., Ltd.; AB Electrolux; The Furukawa Electric Co., Ltd.; Hitachi Sumitomo Heavy Industries Construction Crane Co., Ltd.; Hoshizaki Electric Co., Ltd.; Illinois Tool Works Inc.; Kobelco Construction Machinery Co., Ltd.; Liebherr-International AG; Sumitomo Corporation; Tadano, Ltd.; Terex Corporation.

FURTHER READING

Barrett, Rick, "Manitowoc Co. Trimming 2,100 Jobs in Crane Division," *Milwaukee Journal Sentinel*, January 30, 2009.

———, "Manitowoc Co. Wins Enodis," *Milwaukee Journal Sentinel*, July 1, 2008.

———, "Manitowoc Shares Slip After Sale of Marine Group," *Milwaukee Journal Sentinel*, August 5, 2008.

Buck, Jonathan, "Manitowoc to Purchase Enodis," *Wall Street Journal*, April 15, 2008, p. B3.

Content, Thomas, "Manitowoc Picks Up Crane Maker," *Milwaukee Journal Sentinel*, March 19, 2002.

Gallun, Alby, "New CEO Cultivates Manitowoc Growth Plan," *Business Journal-Milwaukee*, December 4, 1998, pp. 26+.

Higgins, Terry, "Strategy Shows Upside for Manitowoc," *Business Journal-Milwaukee*, November 16, 1996, pp. 21+.

"Hoisting Job," *Forbes*, April 19, 1999, p. 152.

Manitowoc: 75 Years of Growth and Diversification, 1902–1977, Manitowoc, WI: The Manitowoc Company, 1977, 44 p.

Prestegard, Steve, "Manitowoc Steers toward Ice," *Marketplace Magazine* (Appleton, WI), April 30, 1996, p. 12.

Vallely, Ian, "The Preacher and the Profit," *Cranes Today*, June 2005, pp. 25–26.

Voyage of Vision: The Manitowoc Company, A Century of Extraordinary Growth, Manitowoc, WI: The Manitowoc Company, 2002, 176 p.

Manufacture Prelle & Cie

—————■—————

7 rue Barodet
Lyon, 69004
France
Telephone: (+33 472) 10 11 40
Fax: (+33 472) 10 11 41
Web site: http://www.prelle.com

Private Company
Founded: 1752
Incorporated: 1927
Employees: 40
NAICS: 313312 Textile and Fabric Finishing (Except Broadwoven Fabric) Mills; 541490 Other Specialized Design Services

■ ■ ■

Manufacture Prelle & Cie is the oldest and one of the last of the great Lyon silk houses. Founded in 1752, Prelle also possesses the largest French archive of fabric designs and patterns, as well as fabrics and weaving techniques, which enables the company to re-create antique silk tapestry and upholstery for the restoration of royal palaces, historical residences, and museums, among other projects. Most of Prelle's production, however, is for the private sector, furnishing the homes of the world's wealthy. Fabric prices range from EUR 500 per meter to up to EUR 20,000 per meter and more. Exports form the bulk of the company's sales. Some 80 percent of the group's sales volume comes directly from outside of France. In addition, another 10

percent of Prelle's fabric reaches the export market through a number of Prelle's clients.

Prelle continues to operate from its original workshop on Lyon's Croix Rousse hill, the historic heart of the once mighty Lyon silk industry. Because of the intricate nature of much of the company's fabrics, traditional hand-looms form an essential part of Prelle's production equipment. The company's hand-loom workshop includes five velvet looms, four figured fabric looms, and four looms used for creating sample fabrics. Prelle nonetheless operates a range of computer-driven powered looms, as well as a number of shuttle and rapier looms. Prelle supports its production through sales offices in Paris and New York. The company is led by CEO Guillaume Verzier, a descendant of Aimé Prelle, who took over the silk workshop in 1927.

ORIGINS OF THE LYON SILK INDUSTRY

Lyon's position as the center of France's silk industry stemmed from a royal decree of King Louis XI (1423–1483), calling for the creation of a silk workshop, known as a *manufacture*, in Lyon. The southern city also became a major thoroughfare for the more established Italian silk producers of the period. Over the next century, Lyon's silk markets came to control much of the kingdom's silk trade.

Silk manufacturing in the city took off especially after the arrival of two Italian silk merchants, Naris and Turchetti (who later adopted the French name of Étienne Turquet). Naris and Turchetti established their own silk *manufacture* in Lyon in 1536. Importantly, they also

COMPANY PERSPECTIVES

Thanks to the continued use of draw looms and encouraged by decorators who order reweavings of antique silks, the *manufacture* is able to consecrate year after year a certain portion of its time to official restoration projects. We use antique fabrics to create a product that restores a past brilliance to royal palaces, luxurious historical residences and museums. Strengthened by an extensive collection of archives and up to date technology, the *manufacture* is increasingly capable of responding to increasing demands of accuracy and authenticity that come from the world of curators and interior decorators. This recent activity is just as prestigious as that of the past.

founded a training school, bringing silk spinners and winders from Italy to teach their craft to the local populace. This growing group of skilled workers, coupled with the city's established silk markets and manufacturers, led King François I to give the monopoly for silk manufacturing to the city of Lyon in 1540. In addition, all silks arriving from outside of France, including Italian silks but also silks from Thailand, China, and other silk producing centers in the Far East, were required to enter through Lyon.

Lyon's own silk weavers, known as *canuts*, made increasing strides in their own technique, establishing the reputation of their silks as among the finest in the world. This reputation grew especially after improvements made to the traditional Italian loom construction by master weaver Claude Dangon. The improved looms helped raise the quality of the city's silk fabrics, further stimulating demand. More and more weavers joined the trade, and by 1620 the city counted more than 10,000 looms. These were originally housed in the old city center, known as Vieux Lyon, where the buildings featured ceilings high enough to accommodate the large looms.

SILK ARCHIVES FROM 1752

Lyon's silk industry experienced a number of ups and downs over the next century. Under the reign of Louis XIV, and his finance minister, Colbert, the city's silk manufacturing and trade were regulated for the first time. Many of the silk weavers were French Huguenots. The Revocation of the Edict of Nantes, which had granted religious freedom, in 1685, sparked a wave of

emigration. The Huguenots brought their weaving skills to such markets as the Netherlands, Switzerland, Italy, Germany, and the United Kingdom, which developed their own silk centers to rival that of Lyon. With the end of Louis XIV's reign, France sank into an extended period of conflict, resulting in a drop in orders for silk.

The reign of Louis XVI represented a new period of growth for the Lyon silk industry. The royal court placed large orders for tapestries and other furnishings for King Louis and his wife Marie Antoinette, helping to stimulate a new boom period for the city. Manufacture Prelle & Cie dated its own origins from this period, with the creation of a silk workshop in 1752. By then, the city's silk industry had adopted its dual nature, composed on the one hand of the *manufactures*, who owned their own looms, generally operating from their own homes, and were responsible for the actual production of the fabrics.

On the other hand were the designers, or *dessinateurs*, who were responsible for creating the patterns and fabric designs. These designs, along with samples of the resulting fabrics and instructions for the method behind their production, constituted a silk workshop's "archives." The possession of these archives formed a major part of a silk producers' capital. Through various mergers and acquisitions, these archives were passed down from workshop to workshop. In this way Prelle, which was only formally established in 1927, traced its own history back to the mid-18th century and to the earliest fabric designs in its archives.

Among the names associated with Prelle's archives were Marie-Olivier Desfarges, a prominent supplier of fabrics to Louis XVI and Marie Antoinette, founded in 1774. Another name associated with Prelle was Pierre-Toussaint Déchazelle, born in 1752 and who later became head of the prestigious Lyon's École Gratuité de Peinture, founded in 1756 in order to train designers for the silk industry. Déchazelle gained renown during the late 18th century for his tapestries as well as for his clothing textiles designs, produced in partnership with the Germain *manufacture*. The end of the 18th century also corresponded with a new peak in the Lyon silk industry. By 1786 the number of looms in the city had grown to 15,000.

SILK FACTORY IN 1881

Lyon's silk industry suffered a new setback with the French Revolution in 1798. The silk producers' association with France's aristocracy placed them on the front lines of peasant anger. Thousands of people involved in the silk trade were executed, while many more were forced to flee the country. By the end of the century,

KEY DATES

1752: Silk workshop is established in Lyon.
1881: Lamy & Giraud founds a workshop on Lyon's Croix Rousse, with Eugène Prelle as chief designer.
1927: Aimé Prelle acquires the company and renames it Prelle & Cie.
1955: Prelle begins restoration project for Louis XIV's apartment in the Palace of Versailles.
1994: Prelle adds CAD software and equipment for the first time.
2007: Prelle is given status as an "Entreprise de Patrimoine Vivant."

Lyon had lost some 90 percent of its silk industry. The period also saw destruction of much of the industry's archives, making the surviving fragments all the more valuable.

The silk trade once again began building during the reconstruction period, especially after the visit to the city by Napoleon Bonaparte and his wife Josephine in 1802. By then, too, Joseph Marie Jacquard had invented his mechanical loom. The Jacquard loom helped to revolutionize the French silk weaving industry at the beginning of the 19th century. During this period, also, the silk industry moved to new quarters on the Croix Rousse, a hilly quarter in Lyon, which became the new heart of the Lyon silk trade.

Movement toward the creation of the future Prelle also took place during the first half of the century. A number of names associated with the company reached prominence during this time. These included designer Jean-François Bony, who had inherited the Desfarges archives and then became a highly regarded designer in his own right. Bony joined with another prominent manufacturer, Bissardon. In 1818, the archives and workshops of both Bony and Bissardon were acquired by another house, Chuard. This silk house was in turn merged into Corderier & Lemire in the 1830s. That house's founder, Charles Corderier, had also come to control the Déchazelle archives. Corderier & Lemire remained a major silk house until 1865, when it was acquired by Lamy & Giraud, established by Antoine Lamy.

Throughout much of the 19th century, Lyon's silk sector resembled more of a cottage industry, with production largely carried out in workers' own homes. The arrival of new mass-producer fabrics in the latter half of the century, however, forced the Lyon houses to respond by developing the first true silk factories. Lamy & Giraud took part in this trend. In 1881, Lamy regrouped all of its various workshops into a new and larger workshop on the Croix Rousse. This site was to remain home to the silk workshop, later known as Prelle, through the 20th century and into the 21st century.

BECOMING PRELLE IN 1927

Despite the increasing competition amid the industrialization of the silk industry in the late 19th century, Lamy & Giraud remained among the most prominent of Lyon's silk *manufactures*. The company remained a principal supplier to the royal houses and other prestigious institutions in France and throughout Europe. The company also received an increasing number of orders from the United States. At the same time, a new type of customer had begun to emerge with the appearance of a wealthy class of industrialists and entrepreneurs.

The Prelle name became associated with Lamy & Giraud when Eugène Prelle, himself a descendant of silk producers, joined the company. By 1880, Prelle had become the company's chief designer and earned widespread recognition for his fabric designs. Lamy & Giraud changed its name to Lamy & Gauthier in 1900. Soon after World War I, Aimé Prelle, son of Eugène, bought the company. In 1927, the company changed its name, to Manufacture Prelle & Cie, or more simply Prelle & Cie.

The Lyon silk industry enjoyed a new heyday during the Art Deco era. By the end of World War II, however, the sector had gone into a decline, as tastes changed and new fabrics and production methods appeared. Prelle hung on, however, while most of its rivals disappeared, in part because of its control of the city's most extensive archives.

ADDING CAD IN 1994

In the postwar era, Prelle picked up new business as a major producer of fabrics and tapestries for the many restoration projects put into place in France and around the world. In 1955, for example, the company was asked to re-create the fabrics for Louis XIV's apartments in the Palace of Versailles. Prelle agreed, launching a project that would take nearly 30 years to complete. For this project, the company built a new loom based on the original design. The weaving of the fabric, a gold and silver brocade, proved highly labor intensive, with an output of just three centimeters per day.

Prelle had become the largest of the remaining Lyon silk houses. The company continued to operate nine traditional hand-looms, enabling the company to produce a wide range of fabrics and textiles that could not be manufactured otherwise. With the decline of European royalty, and a slowdown in restoration orders from the French state in the 1980s, the company's client base shifted more firmly to the private sector.

In 1989, Guillaume Versier, representing the fifth generation of the Prelle family to lead the company, took over as the company's CEO. Versier then reoriented the company's sales strategy to target the ultra-luxury segment, and especially the export market. By the end of the 1990s, exports grew to represent more than 80 percent of the group's sales.

Versier acquired the company in 1993 through a leveraged buyout, in which he acquired the shares in the company held by other family members. Versier launched a new series of investments designed to help the company keep pace with the times. In 1994, for example, the company purchased new computer-aided design, or CAD-driven, machinery. These modern looms operated alongside the group's traditional hand-looms, which remained necessary for the production of most of the company's traditional fabrics and designs.

Near the end of the decade, Prelle invested FRF 900,000 (approximately $130,000) to refurbish its Paris showroom. The company also joined with four other Lyon businesses to open a showroom in New York City in 1998. At the same time, Prelle invested FRF 2.5 million ($350,000) to carry out a further modernization of its production equipment.

HERITAGE COMPANY IN 2007

Prelle appeared ready to end its long history in Lyon. In 1998, Versier announced that he was considering moving the company to Italy, to take advantage of lower wages and less restrictive labor laws. As Versier told *Les Echos* at the time: "A hand-crafted company like ours has less and less of a future in France."

In the end, however, Prelle remained faithful to its Lyon base, and to its workshop on the Croix Rousse hill. This fidelity was rewarded in 2007, when the company was granted the label of Entreprise du Patrimoine Vivant ("Living Heritage Enterprise"), confirming the company's status as a part of France's corporate and cultural heritage. Despite suffering the effects of the economic recession in 2009, which saw new orders come to a virtual standstill, Prelle & Cie remained the living testament to 500 years of French silk tradition.

M. L. Cohen

PRINCIPAL OPERATING UNITS

Workshop and Headquarters; New York Showroom; Paris Showroom.

PRINCIPAL COMPETITORS

Huzhou Dachang Silk Factory; Jiangsu Chunhua Silk Group; Jiangsu Wujiang Silk Group Company Ltd.; Moscow Silk Joint Stock Co.; SunflagLtd.; Wujiang Silk Company Limited; Xinjiang Hetian Area Silk Factory.

FURTHER READING

Blanc, Odile, "Le Goût de la Soie," http://www.plumart.com/vf4903/html/body_6049soie.html, November 2003.

Depagneux, Marie-Annick, "La Manufacture de Soierie Prelle fête Ses 250 Ans," *Les Echos*, August 9, 2002, p. 15.

———, "La Manufacture Prelle Envisage une Délocalisation en Italie," *Les Echos*, December 21, 1998, p. 22.

"Made of Silk," *B There Mag*, July 7, 2008.

"Prelle Company, or the Weaving of Old Fabrics," http://www.pointcarre.com/Tribune/imarticles/Brocatelle/GB_general.html.

"Prelle Fortifie Ses Racines pour Faire de la Resistance," *Journal du Textile*, May 12, 2009, p. 43.

Rafferty, Jean Bond, "Dream Weavings," *Town & Country*, November 2002, p. 212.

Sultan, Mylène, "Le Fleuron de la Soierie Lyonnaise," *L'Express*, October 19, 2006.

Van Hooff, Dorothée, "Aristocratische Zijde," *Residence*, October 2008, p. 148.

MDVIP, Inc.

6001 Broken Sound Parkway Northwest, Suite 100
Boca Raton, Florida 33487
U.S.A.
Telephone: (561) 886-1486
Toll Free: (866) 696-3847
Fax: (561) 892-4684
Web site: http://www.mdvip.com

Wholly Owned Subsidiary of The Procter & Gamble
Company
Incorporated: 2001
Employees: 200
Sales: $84.3 million (2008)
NAICS: 621111 Offices of Physicians

■ ■ ■

The leading U.S. concierge medicine business, MDVIP, Inc., operates a national network of physicians providing personalized and preventive health care. The company's focus on preventive care includes risk factor identification through EKG and specific screenings, laboratory tests, medication review, and other means. In exchange for an annual membership fee, patients receive, along with diagnostic services, a wellness plan and their doctor's phone number for 24-hour access. MDVIP provides its physicians with services that include market and demographic analysis, regulatory review, insurance support, marketing support, electronic medical records systems, and billing and collection of membership fees. As of 2010, MDVIP served more than 125,000 patients through 365 company-affiliated physicians in 28 states

and the District of Columbia. In February 2010, MD-VIP became a wholly owned subsidiary of The Procter & Gamble Company.

ORIGINS

The initial idea for MDVIP came from Boca Raton, Florida, physicians Dr. Robert Colton and Dr. Bernard Kaminetsky who were overburdened by their patient load of about 3,000 people each. The two physicians sought out Dr. Edward Goldman, an entrepreneur/ physician who in the 1990s had founded the Boca Raton-based medical information firm Cybear and was also involved in the founding of two health care physician management and consulting firms. Goldman agreed to help coordinate the financing and organization of the new venture, and in 2000 in Boca Raton, Goldman and Steve Geller, former president of Arco Toys, cofounded MDVIP. Geller became chairman and Goldman chief executive of the new firm, whose latter three letters stood for "Value in Prevention." Doctors Goldman and Colton donated most of the initial seed money for the company, totaling about $5 million.

MDVIP was not the first concierge medicine company. It followed one pioneer in the United States, the Seattle-based MD2 company formed in 1996. At that time, MD2 charged an annual individual retainer fee of $13,200 and a family fee of $20,000. A year before MDVIP launched, the Institute of Medicine, an independent arm of the National Academy of Sciences, issued an eyebrow-raising report about health care in the United States. The report addressed issues related to medical errors, patient safety, and physician integrity

COMPANY PERSPECTIVES

Our goal at MDVIP is to literally change the delivery of primary care in America. We will do this by creating a partnership between doctors and patients, built on exceptional personalized and preventive care. Every day we aim to improve the lives of physicians by enabling them to focus on prevention and wellness and improve the lives of patients by empowering them to live their best life possible.

and called for further inquiry into exam room care. Such issues were important to Colton and Kaminetsky, who wanted to turn to concierge medicine because they believed patient care was compromised by demands placed on them by HMOs, PPOs, and other institutional constraints and by the high number of patients that doctors were forced to see.

MDVIP's philosophy of "value in prevention" was to be carried out by the physician with a manageable patient portfolio that allowed for more personalized care for the patient. To guarantee such care, the company limited the size of each affiliate physician's practice to no more than 600 patients to allow for personal attention during office visits. Preventive care involved various methods of risk-factor identification tests conducted in order to provide the patient with a detailed, personalized wellness plan that was designed to prevent illness and disease. Because the company's membership fee was designed to help the patient prevent, and not treat, illness and disease, MDVIP physicians could continue to accept insurance plans after transitioning to concierge practice.

To bring physicians into the fold, MDVIP established a sales team that drew from leads secured from local medical professionals, contacted and set up individual dinner meetings with prospective physicians, and then made sales pitches, presenting MDVIP as an alternative to traditional insurance-reimbursement-based practices that required doctors to sometimes maintain a portfolio of thousands of patients. Before becoming affiliated with MDVIP, a doctor had to agree to limit practice size, close the existing practice, make arrangements for patients who did not want to become MDVIP members, and became an independent contractor for MDVIP. To receive services, a patient paid a $1,500 annual membership fee, of which the physician kept two-thirds while the company earned the remaining third.

CONTROVERSY OVER CONCIERGE MEDICINE

Goldman himself initially lined up a handful of local physicians in the Boca Raton area to launch the company, and in March 2001, MDVIP opened for business. Its first two affiliate doctors were Colton and Kaminetsky. By the end of 2001, MDVIP had a half-dozen physicians under contract and 2,000 patient-members. In early 2002, MDVIP hired iBX Group, Inc., to provide a turnkey technology package of services for MDVIP, including online medical records management. By June 2002, MDVIP had about 3,500 members and eight physicians in Palm Beach County, Florida, as well as one newly signed doctor in Boston.

Almost immediately upon opening for business, MDVIP became the center of controversy surrounding the nature of concierge or what was sometimes called "boutique-styled" medical practices. Some patients of doctors who switched to MDVIP claimed that concierge medicine was really "wealth care," the beginning of a two-tiered health care system. One of the company's and concierge medicine's earliest and most vocal critics on the national stage was Florida Senator Bill Nelson, who claimed MDVIP should not be able to collect both a membership fee and bill Medicare for services. MDVIP's response throughout the controversy was that it was simply responding to a need within the health care market and that its practices were legal: It billed Medicare only for services not covered by MDVIP's membership fee.

Despite MDVIP's response, in March 2002, U.S. Representative Henry Waxman along with three other Congress members asked Department of Health and Human Services (HHS) Secretary Tommy Thompson and Inspector General Janet Rehnquist to investigate MDVIP for possible Medicare violations. Then, in early 2003, U.S. Representative Ben Cardin of Maryland introduced a bill in the House of Representatives that would prohibit membership-fee charging physicians from participating in Medicare. About the same time, Nelson introduced a similar bill in the Senate. The growing firestorm of attention MDVIP was receiving sparked the American Medical Association (AMA) to review, for the first time, concierge practices. In a preliminary finding, the AMA announced that concierge and "boutique-style" physician arrangements appeared to be legal but further investigation was necessary to determine whether they were in fact ethical. At about the same time early legislation on concierge medicine was being introduced in Congress, the AMA found "no evidence that special physician-patient contracts … adversely impact the quality of patients' care or the access of any group of patients to care."

KEY DATES

2000: MDVIP is founded.
2001: MDVIP's first affiliated physicians begin practice.
2005: Company receives its first outside investment, a $6 million minority outlay from a private equity firm.
2007: Procter & Gamble (P&G) buys a 48 percent stake in MDVIP.
2010: P&G acquires complete control of MDVIP, which becomes a wholly owned P&G subsidiary.

Findings from government agencies and other professional agencies were likewise favorable in various ways to MDVIP's cause. The Centers for Medicare and Medicaid in 2002 stated that physicians could enter into retainer contracts with patients as long as those contracts did not violate Medicare guidelines. In 2003, HHS ruled concierge medical practices were not illegal. The federal government in essence took a hands-off approach to concierge medicine. Meanwhile, evidence was building that the typical physician did in fact face constraints that impacted the quality of care patients received in the examining room, an unfortunate fact that concierge medicine was designed to ameliorate by limiting a physician's practice size. In 2003, the American College of Physicians agreed that doctors have to struggle to balance professionalism with pressures from their practice. In 2004, a Harvard University study revealed 55 percent of respondents were dissatisfied with their health care and that 40 percent of those who were dissatisfied believed the quality of health care had deteriorated in the previous five years.

ATTAINING MARKET-LEADING STATUS

With findings and rulings in its favor mounting, in December 2003, MDVIP launched a concerted effort to grow beyond its Florida base via a three-month advertising blitz in Boston. The effort was part of a larger campaign to introduce MDVIP to the public in East Coast states. Print ads in the *Boston Globe* presented traditional medicine in the form of an exhausted patient pictured in a crowed waiting room, a condition the ad suggested was not present in an MDVIP waiting room. Television spots appearing on cable news channels linked MDVIP to The New England Medical Center in Boston, which was part of the company's referral program. This referral group later became known by what MDVIP called its Medical Centers of Excellence (MCE), a program whereby MDVIP partnered with nationally ranked providers of specialty care and testing.

MDVIP expended little capital on lobbying during its initial years, but in 2004, the company invested $120,000 on lobbyists to ensure concierge medicine was portrayed in a positive light. That same year, the U.S. Government Accountability Office concluded concierge medicine posed no threat to patient access to physicians. By this time, the AMA had ruled on concierge medicine's ethics, suggesting concierge businesses were ethical if doctors made arrangements for their former patients who elected not to participate in concierge care. The company also released findings related to its own care. A preliminary study of MDVIP physician practices revealed health care quality measurements exceeding national averages and documenting that MDVIP patients experienced a 30 percent reduction in hospitalization stays and length of stays compared to other patients.

To increase its lobbying efforts and enhance its reputation, MDVIP hired in July 2005 the legal and lobbying firm Akin Gump, whose partners included former HHS Secretary Tommy Thompson, who had left his government post in December 2004 and joined Akin Gump. Under Thompson, HHS had ruled that concierge practices could charge or exclude Medicare patients so long as fees charged for services were not covered by Medicare. MDVIP hired Gump to in part retain Thompson to promote concierge medicine to big business and serve as chairman of its Committee on Cost Reduction through Preventive Healthcare. MDVIP charged the former HHS secretary with directing its own company program that would devise and address how best to employ policies on the use of preventive care in reducing national health care costs.

By 2005, MDVIP was clearly the largest player on the national stage in the concierge market with over 60 physicians serving about 20,000 members in 13 states. MDVIP that year accepted its first outside investment, a $6 million minority outlay from private equity and venture capital firm Summit Partners, which helped expand the company's sales force and enhance its electronic medical records system to include individual Web pages for each patient. That same year, the company was listed as number 30 on *Inc.* magazine's list of the fastest-growing U.S. companies, having recorded revenue growth of more than 1,840 percent over a three-year period en route to 2004 revenues of $16.3 million.

UNDER THE PROCTER & GAMBLE UMBRELLA

In 2006, MDVIP expanded into Illinois, its 15th state, and expanded its affiliation to more than 130 physicians serving 40,000 patients in 21 major U.S. markets, including New York, Chicago, Los Angeles, Atlanta, Boston, Philadelphia, Miami, Baltimore, San Francisco, and Washington, D.C. To chart its expansion, the company identified major metropolitan markets that represented the highest potential growth areas and set a target of eventually enrolling 6,000 to 10,000 physicians as affiliates by adding 80 to 150 doctors a year. With approximately 280,000 primary care physicians in the United States, the company viewed its growth strategy as realistic. While competition was gradually increasing in the concierge medicine field, the company saw competition as a good sign: The concierge model for health care was increasingly being both marketed and accepted by private individuals and corporate customers. Moreover, MDVIP had as advantages its industry-leading size, five years of experience in the field, and competitive membership fees compared to other higher-end concierge services. The company's services were getting high marks from patients, too, based on an annual membership renewal rate of 95 percent.

MDVIP's success did not go unnoticed. After studying MDVIP for a year, Procter & Gamble (P&G), in January 2007, acquired a 48 percent stake in MDVIP. MDVIP viewed the new arrangement as an opportunity to benefit from the large-scale research and marketing arms of P&G. In 2007, MDVIP signed a deal with Avalon Healthcare, Inc., a new Florida statewide health plan which agreed to count the cost of MDVIP's annual membership toward its own premium for those who enrolled in health plans with a $3,000 or more deductible. That same year, MDVIP expanded into California, Connecticut, Massachusetts, and New York and hired Winsper, an independent strategy and marketing firm, to develop a multimedia approach to reach potential patients and physicians.

In 2008, MDVIP Chairman and cofounder Steve Geller and CEO and cofounder Dr. Edward Goldman were named co-winners of the Ernst & Young Florida Entrepreneur of the Year Award. MDVIP also received recognition as having one of the more effective Web sites in the health care industry, as *Health Executive* listed the company's site in its Top 10 Health Information Technology Innovators list. The company, which during its early years was criticized as offering "wealth care," also received positive press for its participation in pilot programs to provide services gratis through its Project Access for patients with chronic conditions. MDVIP vowed to expand Project Access to 20 ad-ditional communities in markets the company served. The company also continued to expand its MCE group. By 2008, MCE included about a dozen nationally ranked providers of specialty care and testing. By the end of the year, it was serving a record 100,000 patients through more than 265 affiliate physicians in 23 states and Washington, D.C.

In 2009, MDVIP expanded into Colorado, Delaware, Kansas, and Oklahoma, giving the company offices in 28 states. In February of that year, Bret Jorgensen was named MDVIP's chief executive officer, assuming the role founder Goldman had held since the company's inception. Jorgensen brought 20 years of executive health care-related experience to the job but had little time to employ his experience running the company. Ten months after he became CEO, P&G announced it was acquiring complete control of MDVIP. Before the decade closed, the Federal Trade Commission approved the deal, and in February 2010, MDVIP became a wholly owned P&G subsidiary. P&G appointed Daniel Hecht as MDVIP's chief executive, while Jorgensen remained on the company board along with cofounder Dr. Edward Goldman. Former Chairman and cofounder Steve Geller retired.

FUTURE PROSPECTS

Some industry observers thought P&G had wisely placed itself ahead of a curve, that many disgruntled and overworked physicians were chomping at the bit to reduce the size of their practices, and that MDVIP was thereby likely to expand its number of physician affiliates accordingly. "Procter & Gamble is a pretty smart company because the future of primary care is in direct practices like ours," said Thomas LaGrelius, board chairman of the Society for Innovative Medical Practice Design (formerly the American Society of Concierge Physicians) at the time of the acquisition. "Right now there are about 300,000 primary-care doctors, and all are dying on the vine except for those doing direct practice. Procter & Gamble can see the writing on the wall and wants to invest in this business."

To invest in concierge medicine, P&G brought to bear its business unit Future Works, which the company defined as an "entrepreneurial new-business generator transforming fledgling businesses currently serving new market businesses into businesses that can scale to serve the mass market." Future Works looked for businesses with which P&G was or could be strategically aligned and saw an opportunity in MDVIP "for cross pollination," a company spokesman said. In choosing to invest in concierge medicine, P&G selected MDVIP for its name recognition, profitability, and leadership in the field.

Some industry observers suggested that 10,000 to 20,000 doctors would move to private or concierge care within a few years of the P&G acquisition of MDVIP. Whether the industry would grow that fast, and whether the consumer products giant P&G could help propel MDVIP's growth remained uncertain. About half of MDVIP's patients were retirement age, and P&G's health care line of products were increasingly marketed to an aging baby-boomer population interested in wellness and longevity. Whether that sharing of clientele would result in a profitable "cross-pollination" for MD-VIP was also uncertain. While the MDVIP placard was the dominant one in the market as of 2010, some industry observers predicted it might have to lower its membership fee to generate patients and to attract the thousands of doctors expected to transition to concierge care.

Roger Rouland

PRINCIPAL COMPETITORS

The Direct Care Group; EliteHealth.MD LLC; MD2 International; ModernMed, Inc.; Signature MD.

FURTHER READING

Andrews, Michelle, "An Experiment with Concierge Medical Care," *U.S. News & World Report Online*, May 8, 2008.

Craver, Martha Lynn, "Elite Doctors' Offices: Another Sign of Trouble," *Kiplinger Business Forecasts*, February 6, 2003.

"The Doctor Will Really See You Now," *Business Week*, July 9, 2001, p. 10.

"$1,500 Fee Opens Door to Doctors; Service May Expand to Bay Area," *Tampa Tribune*, August 25, 2001, p. 7.

Galewitz, Phil, "'Boutique' Doctor Practices Require Further Study, AMA Panel Says," *Palm Beach Post*, June 19, 2002.

———, "P&G Buys into Boca Firm," *Palm Beach Post*, January 7, 2007, p. 9B.

Gray, Patricia B., "Deluxe Doctors," *Fortune Small Business*, July 1, 2004.

Hawryluk, Markian, "Boutique Medicine May Run Afoul of Medicare Rules: Letter from Congressmen Asks Administration to Investigate 'Concierge' Physician Practices That Charge a Membership Fee," *American Medical News*, April 8, 2002, p. 5.

Kavilanz, Parija B., "Doctors' Orders: Avoid Insurance: Many Physicians, Fed Up with Patient Overload and Filing Claims, Are Minimizing Insurance-Based Coverage and Offering Round-the-Clock Service for a Retainer," *Fortune Small Business*, August 17, 2009.

Lasalandra, Michael, "Boutique Care Lures Doc from Regular Hub Practice," *Boston Herald*, June 1, 2002.

LeClaire, Jennifer, "Is There a Doctor in the House? Edward Goldman Thinks Patients Will Pay a Premium for Personalized Preventive Health Care through Membership in MD-VIP," *South Florida CEO*, March 2006, p. 20.

"Major Companies Increasing Their Healthcare Presence," *Modern Physician Online*, January 11, 2010.

"Procter & Gamble Buys Full Stake in MDVIP," *Business Courier of Cincinnati*, February 4, 2010.

Reiss, Cory, "'Concierge' Doctors Seen as Threat to Other Systems," *Sarasota Herald Tribune*, August 29, 2005.

Rutter, Callie, "A Brief History of Concierge Medicine," *American Academy of Private Physicians*, 2010.

Silverman, Jennifer, "MDVIP: Internists Find It Pays to Offer Boutique Care," *Internal Medicine News*, November 1, 2001, p. 33.

Versel, Neil, "Do VIP Practices Upcharge Medicare?" *Modern Physician*, May 1, 2002, p. 6.

Wahlgren, Eric, "Concierge Medicine: Patients Pay Up for a Doctor's Undivided Attention," *HealthTechnologyReview.com*, February 15, 2010.

Williams, David E., "Boutique Medicine: When Wealth Buys Health," *CNN.com*, October 20, 2006.

Menasha Corporation

1645 Bergstrom Road
Post Office Box 367
Neenah, Wisconsin 54957-0367
U.S.A.
Telephone: (920) 751-1000
Fax: (920) 751-1075
Web site: http://www.menasha.com

Private Company
Founded: 1849
Incorporated: 1875 as Menasha Wooden Ware Company
Employees: 3,200
Sales: $1 billion (2009 est.)
NAICS: 322211 Corrugated and Solid Fiber Box Manufacturing; 322212 Folding Paperboard Box Manufacturing; 322299 All Other Converted Paper Product Manufacturing; 323119 Other Commercial Printing; 326199 All Other Plastics Product Manufacturing

■ ■ ■

One of the oldest privately held manufacturing companies in the United States, Menasha Corporation is a holding company with three main subsidiaries: Menasha Packaging Company, LLC, ORBIS Corporation, and LeveragePoint Media Corporation. Neenah, Wisconsin-based Menasha Packaging, the largest and oldest of the company's businesses, produces corrugated packaging, protective interior packaging, point-of-purchase displays, and folding cartons. It operates about 20 manufacturing plants and other facilities in the United States, mainly in the Midwest and mid-Atlantic regions. Also part of Menasha Packaging is Cortegra Group, Inc., a leading U.S.-based provider of packaging and labeling services and anti-counterfeiting solutions for the pharmaceutical industry. Headquartered in Oconomowoc, Wisconsin, ORBIS is a producer of plastic returnable and reusable packaging that is used by a variety of customers to move products and materials through the supply chain. LeveragePoint Media, based in Hoffman Estates, Illinois, is a major national provider of in-store marketing materials and services for pharmaceutical and consumer product firms.

From its 19th-century origins in woodenware production, Menasha shifted to paper-based packaging and material handling products in the 1920s and 1930s, earning its reputation as a "box maker." From the 1970s onward, active acquisitions resulted in rapid growth and diversification, carrying Menasha well beyond its original scope of interests in packaging and woodenware. By the beginning of the second decade of the 21st century, the company employed approximately 3,200 workers in about 50 locations in the United States, Canada, Mexico, Belgium, and China. Menasha remains majority owned by descendants of its founder, Elisha D. Smith, after more than 160 years of operation.

EARLY HISTORY: FROM PAILS TO FOREST PRODUCTS

Menasha's origins date back to entrepreneurial efforts of woodenware manufacturers in the mid-19th-century Midwest. In 1849 a pail factory was founded in Menasha, Wisconsin. The undercapitalized venture, which was simply called the Pail Factory, was then sold to Elisha D. Smith for $1,200 in 1852. Under Smith's leadership, the venture survived the Panic of 1857, an economic crisis that bankrupted thousands of U.S. businesses, and expanded smartly during the Civil War, supplying pails and other wooden storage and shipping containers to the Union forces. By 1871 the Pail Factory had become the largest woodenware maker in the Midwest, with 250 employees manufacturing products ranging from pails to tubs, churns, measures, butter tubs, fish kits, kannikins, keelers, and clothespins.

Just one year later, however, post-Civil War inflation sent costs soaring faster than the factory's revenues, forcing the Pail Factory into receivership, $250,000 in debt. Smith's father-in-law, Spencer Mowry, provided the venture with an infusion of cash and reorganized it as Menasha Wooden Ware Company. It was incorporated under that same name on May 24, 1875. The original pail factory was destroyed by fire in 1878. Twelve years later, in 1890, the entire company was devastated by another fire, with only the Cooperage Shop escaping destruction. Quick reconstruction was followed by further expansion. In 1894 the founder's son, Charles R. Smith, merged the broom handle and barrel factory that he had founded with the Menasha Wooden Ware Company, creating the world's largest manufacturer of turned woodenware. By 1899, when the company founder died at age 72, Menasha Wooden Ware had annual revenues of $1 million and 1,000 people on the company payroll. Charles R. Smith was named to succeed his father, although he had in fact been running the company for nearly a decade.

To provide vital raw materials as the company grew over time, Menasha began purchasing timberlands and related operations, first in Wisconsin, in 1900, and then in the Pacific Northwest, in 1903. By 1915, Menasha supplied 27 million feet of timber annually and was the nation's foremost producer of wooden food packaging in bulk. In 1929, at its plant in Tacoma, Washington, the company began production of wood flour, a powder made from spruce shavings that was used in explosives,

plastic wood, and other products. In 1969 lumber products were further expanded as Menasha merged with the John Strange Paper Company, creating the Appleton Manufacturing Division and a majority interest in the Wisconsin Container Corporation, later to become Menasha's Solid Fibre Division.

By 1980, wood fiber production, which was used primarily as industrial fillers and extenders in products such as plywood and molded plastics, had increased enough to warrant an additional wood fiber plant in Centralia, Washington, and the 1987 purchase of another plant in Marysville, Washington. Over time, Menasha would form its Forest Products Group specifically to develop its timber interests. By the early 1990s, its Land & Timber Division managed the corporation's 100,000 acres of timberlands in the Pacific Northwest alone, meeting worldwide timber needs. In addition, the Wood Fibre Division produced organic-based wood flours.

SHIFTING TO CORRUGATED CONTAINERS

While timber development provided raw materials for woodenware and wood packaging, its uses changed to paper production as Menasha moved into production of corrugated containers. In 1926 Menasha Wooden Ware was split into two separate but affiliated companies, the Menasha Wooden Ware Company, which owned a portfolio of stocks, and the Menasha Wooden Ware Corporation, which continued the manufacturing and marketing operations. (This arrangement lasted until 1981, when the investment company and the operating company were merged back together.) Accommodating changes in packaging technology, the latter organization produced Menasha's first corrugated containers in 1927. By 1935, corrugated containers had supplanted their wooden predecessors, and Menasha discontinued its line of barrels, converting woodworking plants to the manufacture of toys and juvenile furniture, a product line that continued only until 1952.

To supply its growing corrugated business with necessary raw materials, the corporation in 1939 acquired a 60 percent interest in the Otsego Falls Paper Company in Michigan. Full ownership was gained 16 years later. The Otsego Falls mill formed the basis for Menasha's Paperboard Division. Its paper machines produced corrugating medium for several markets: the production of corrugated containers at Menasha's own container plants, outside sales, and trading in exchange for additional types of paperboard used but not manufactured by Menasha.

From the postwar era into the early 1960s, Menasha focused on expansion of its core business in corrugated containers and timber, acquiring and developing new facilities for corrugated medium, containers, plywood, wood fiber, and lumber. Major investments in the G.B. Lewis Company of Watertown, Wisconsin, led to Menasha's funding of that company's reorganization and Menasha's subsequent entry into plastic handling containers and other plastic products. With diminishing emphasis on woodenware products and increased diversity in the field of plastics, Menasha Wooden Ware Corporation changed its name to Menasha Corporation in 1962.

EMPHASIZING COMMUNITY SERVICES

Corporate growth occasioned new emphasis on community services. In 1953 the Charles R. Smith Foundation, which was later renamed Menasha Corporation Foundation, was formed as an independent philanthropic organization funded by 1 percent of Menasha's pretax earnings. By the 1990s, the foundation provided substantial support for charitable, educational, health and welfare, cultural, and environmental projects and programs. In education, the foundation contributed to a wide variety of colleges and universities, in addition to sponsoring scholarship programs for its employees and other qualified students. At the University of Wisconsin-Stout and Oregon State University, the foundation also sponsored fellowships for select students studying packaging or forestry. Beneficiaries of health and welfare allocations included the United Way campaigns in communities where Menasha had plants, and various chapters of Special Olympics, hospitals, workshops for children with developmental disabilities, mental health centers, medical research appeals, and other concerns.

The foundation also contributed to various cultural organizations, including the New Dramatists in New York City, Wisconsin Public Broadcasting, the Bergstrom-Mahler Museum in Neenah, Wisconsin, and the Oregon Coast Music Festival in Coos Bay, Oregon. Starting in the 1980s, the foundation increased contributions to environmental groups, including the Nature Conservancy, the Sigurd Olson Environmental Institute, the Ruffed Grouse Society, and the International Crane Foundation.

In the 1960s Menasha began a move toward packaging innovation and diversification that would position it as a main industry player by the 1990s. As part of a strategy to increase its share of the Midwest's corrugated market, the company in 1966 purchased a plant in Coloma, Michigan, from Twin Cities Container Corporation. In addition to expansion of existing container plants and paperboard operations, Menasha began production of multicolor corrugated containers, foreshadowing future advances in graphics that would figure strongly a decade later. In 1967 new corporate offices were established in the town of Neenah, Wisconsin, replacing the former headquarters that had been destroyed by fire in 1964. Then, in 1968, the company purchased Vanant Packaging Corporation and developed its Sus-Rap Packaging operation, custom engineering and manufacturing interior protective packaging items to meet specific end-use requirements. Primary products of that line included Sus-Rap, Menasha Pads, and SuperFlute protective packaging. In 1969 a new wood-flour plant was opened in Grants Pass, Oregon, and in 1972 the Hartford Container Company, of Hartford, Wisconsin, operator of a corrugated box plant, was acquired. Further expansion in packaging included the 1977 purchase of a plant in Mt. Pleasant, Tennessee, and the 1989 purchase of Colonial Container Company of Green Lake, Wisconsin, another producer of corrugated boxes.

DIVERSIFYING INTO PLASTICS

Just as changing packaging technologies had introduced corrugated containers to the woodenware arena in the

1930s, so the rise of plastics in the 1950s pushed Menasha to innovate and diversify in various areas of plastic manufacturing. In 1955 Menasha purchased a 51 percent interest in G.B. Lewis Company of Watertown, Wisconsin, which like Menasha had gotten its start in the 19th century as a woodenware maker and was in the midst of a shift in focus. Menasha's investment in the Lewis Company helped fund the latter's reorganization into a plastics company and introduced Menasha to the field of plastic material handling containers for the first time. The Lewis Company and plastics in general would become keys to long-term growth and diversification. In 1973 Menasha Corporation assisted in the construction of two new G.B. Lewis company plants in Monticello and Manchester, Iowa. By 1975, G.B. Lewis had been fully acquired, and Menasha formed the LEWISystems and Molded Products Divisions of its Plastics Group. Success of LEWISystems prompted the 1980 purchase of Dare Pafco Products Company of Urbana, Ohio, to increase that division's capacity.

In 1971, meantime, Menasha strengthened its profile in plastics by acquiring a one-third interest in Poly Hi Inc. of Fort Wayne, Indiana, a leading manufacturer of ultra-high-density polyethylene extruded products. Menasha gradually increased its investment in Poly Hi, taking full ownership of the company in 1977. As was the case with G.B. Lewis, the growth pattern at Poly Hi called for increased manufacturing capabilities, prompting the 1981 acquisition of Scranton Plastics Laminating Corporation of Scranton, Pennsylvania. Menasha's plastics operations expanded into reusable plastic and metal products with the 1984 acquisition of Traex Corporation of Dane, Wisconsin, specializing in such items as serving trays, dispensers for straws and condiments, tumblers, bus boxes, and ware-washing racks used in the foodservice industry worldwide.

Menasha's Plastics Group went international in 1985, when the corporation launched its first foreign joint venture with the Japanese firm of Tsutsunaka Plastic Industry Co. Ltd. for the production of ultra-high-density polyethylene products. The joint venture's capital was set at ¥15 million, with projected sales of ¥1 billion for 1988. In 1987 Poly-Hi operations extended operations to Europe, with construction of a plant in Scunsthorpe, England. The following year, a precision injection molder of thermoplastics and engineered resins, Thermotech, was added to the Plastics Group. That division produced high-performance plastic components for various applications including automotive, electrical/electronic appliances, and medical equipment.

VENTURING INTO PROMOTIONAL GRAPHICS

Menasha's developments in packaging and plastics were paralleled, and often supplemented, by innovations in graphics and promotional labeling. In 1977 the corporation acquired a graphics container plant in Roselle, New Jersey, which it then moved to South Brunswick, New Jersey. In 1982 Vinland Web-Print, a producer of web-printed paper and plastic film products, was also acquired. Construction of an additional graphics container plant was completed two years later, in Olive Branch, Mississippi. Expanding into identification and merchandising tags and labels, the corporation acquired Mid America Tag & Label Co. in 1985, followed by its 1986 acquisition of Murfin, Inc., a Columbus, Ohio, web-fed screen printer of label and identity products.

With the 1987 acquisition of Neenah Printing, the corporation extended its graphics operations to a full range of printing services in commercial, business forms, and packaging applications, ranging from sample booklets to high-image-quality lithographic brochures. In 1989 the corporation added Labelcraft Corporation of Farmingdale, New Jersey, to its Mid America division, specializing in custom-designed tags and pressure-sensitive labels. Production capacity for those items was further augmented by the 1990 purchase of Denney-Reyburn Co. of West Chester, Pennsylvania, and Tempe, Arizona. These investments quickly paid off, winning valuable accounts in the early 1990s. In 1991 a division of Mid America that served industrial customers was combined with the Denney-Reyburn plant in Arizona to form the Printed Systems Division.

Over the course of its business expansion, Menasha also developed a Material Handling Division to manufacture reusable plastic container systems including recycling containers, food handling products, small parts bins, work-in-process containers, Stack-N-Nest containers, distribution containers, and transport trays, among other products. In 1986 the corporation's Molded Products Division introduced plastic pallets designed to maximize warehouse inventory stacking and reduce work-in-progress inventories by virtue of their uniform weight. Their wooden predecessors had not only been costly to maintain, but could vary by several pounds in weight, resulting in inventory error of up to thousands of parts in lightweight merchandise. In 1991 similar plastic pallets, marketed as Convoy Opte-Packs, were combined with reusable corrugated sidewalls to maximize carrying volume and strength.

Meanwhile, Menasha struggled throughout the 1970s to find a way to unlock some of the value of the company for its shareholders. The company paid very little in the way of a regular dividend, and because its stock was not publicly traded, shareholders could not easily sell their stock. One solution was to take the company public, an idea proposed several times in the early 1970s but not acted on. Menasha also pursued a number of mergers with other companies in the mid-1970s, including with Fibreboard Corporation, a leading West Coast paperboard producer, but the deals all fell apart for one reason or another.

At this point, revenues were growing steadily, advancing for instance from $138 million in 1975 to $240 million in 1979, but earnings had stagnated at about $11 million. The company therefore found itself at the crossroads, and in the late 1970s considered a number of strategic courses. The one it settled on called for the company to remain privately held and to adopt a more aggressive growth strategy for its existing businesses. In part to provide the shareholders with some liquidity, Menasha engineered the sale of its North Bend, Oregon, paper mill; its Anaheim, California, box plant; and secondary fiber facilities in Portland and Eugene, Oregon, to Weyerhaeuser Company for $68 million in stock. Menasha shareholders now held stock in Weyerhaeuser, a public company, which they could sell to raise cash if they so desired.

In response to heightened environmental concerns of the 1980s, Menasha took initiatives to literally clean up its act, along with its surroundings. In its "Environmental Mission Statement," the corporation noted that "environmental and industrial hygiene goals can and should be consistent with economic health." In 1989 negotiations were made with several discounters, including Wal-Mart Stores, Inc., to provide products such as unbleached cellulose packing material that could replace bubble wrap; other products included recyclable shipping boxes, video cases, and other ecological alternatives.

CONSOLIDATING AND EXPANDING FURTHER

In 1991 Menasha Corporation consolidated its developed industries into six primary business groups: Forest Products, Packaging, Promotional Graphics, Information Graphics, Plastics, and Material Handling. The Forest Products Group consisted of the Land and Timber division, Menasha Development, and Wood Fibre. The Promotional Information Graphics Group consisted of Mid America, Murfin, Neenah Printing, and Printed Systems. The Packaging Group was made up of Menasha Packaging, Paperboard, and Color divisions; the Material Handling Group included Convoy, LEWISystems, and Special Products; and the Plastics Group combined Appleton Manufacturing, Molded Products, Thermotech, Traex, and Poly Hi. Such an operating structure divided the various divisions into working groups while permitting them to interrelate as working parts of an ever more diverse organization.

Menasha continued to grow in the early to mid-1990s. In 1991 Menasha Packaging was bolstered through the acquisition of North Star Container, Inc., which operated a box plant in Brooklyn Park, Minnesota. The following year a point-of-sale business was formed to sell promotional products produced by the Mid America, Neenah Printing, and Color Divisions (the latter division changed its name to DisplayOne in 1994 to reflect an increasing focus on point-of-purchase displays). Robert D. Bero, who had been vice president of the plastics group, was named president and CEO in 1993.

Also that year, Menasha acquired New Jersey Packaging Company, a producer of pressure-sensitive and heat-seal labels for the pharmaceutical and health care industries. In another 1993 acquisition, Menasha took over the U.S. operations of Solidur Deutschland GmbH, the leading European producer of ultra-high molecular weight (UHMW) polyethylene. These operations were merged into Poly Hi to form Poly Hi Solidur. Four years later Solidur Deutschland itself was purchased and amalgamated with Poly Hi Solidur, which became the world's leading producer of UHMW.

The Material Handling Group was a particular focus for expansion in the mid-1990s. In 1993 Dura-PAK was established as a supplier of reusable protective interior packaging, particularly for the automotive and electronics industries. LEWISystems expanded the following year through the opening of a new plant in Urbana, Ohio. Next, in 1995, Menasha acquired Donray Company of Mentor, Ohio, a producer of foam-cushioned packaging, including corrugated boxes with cushion inserts. Then in 1996, the company acquired Madison Heights, Michigan-based WolPac, Inc., which specialized in designing and engineering material handling systems for the automotive industry. This growth spurt was consolidated that same year with the creation of ORBIS, which combined the operations of LEWISystems, Convoy Plastic Pallets, DuraPAK, Donray, and WolPac, thereby providing customers with a one-stop source for plastic returnable and reusable packaging products and services. ORBIS further expanded its product portfolio via the 1997 introduction of the BulkPak line of plastic bulk containers for a wide variety of applications. A consolidation similar to the one that formed ORBIS occurred within Menasha's promotional materials operations. In 1996 America Tag & Label, DisplayOne, and the point-of-purchase business were merged to form Promo Edge.

In the meantime, Menasha Packaging continued its decades-long expansion. In 1995 Mid South Packaging of Cullman, Alabama, and Southwest Container Corporation of Phoenix, Arizona, both of which were operators of corrugated container businesses, were acquired. During 1996 operations began at a corrugated sheet plant in Erie, Pennsylvania, and Middlefield Container Corporation of Middlefield, Ohio, was acquired. There was also one divestment of a noncore business by Menasha Corporation during this period. The Molded Products Division, which made such custom-molded products as plastic shells for lawnmowers and parts for buses, was sold to a private investment group.

DECENTRALIZING AND RESTRUCTURING

In 1999 Menasha's board of directors made a strategic decision to further decentralize the company's structure. Differences over how this fundamental shift should be implemented led to Bero's departure from the company. Thomas J. Prosser, the board chairman, was named CEO on an interim basis, until the October 2000 appointment of Harold R. Smethills Jr. to the position of president and CEO. Smethills, who had a background as a lawyer, banker, and corporate turnaround specialist, was brought onboard to implement the restructuring.

One of the first steps in the multiyear restructuring was the reorganization of the Material Handling Group into a wholly owned subsidiary called Menasha Material Handling Corporation. This subsidiary, created in 2000, comprised ORBIS, a division called Menasha Services that offered complete returnable packaging solutions to companies who elected to outsource this function, and subsidiary operations in Canada, Mexico, and Brazil. Menasha Packaging enlarged itself in 2000 through two acquisitions: Pittsburgh-based Package Products, Inc., and Pennsylvania Container Corporation, based in Latrobe, Pennsylvania. The former firm produced packaging and folding cartons used in supermarket in-store delis and bakeries, while the latter manufactured corrugated boards, sheets, and containers.

A major change in the company's portfolio of businesses occurred in 2001 when the forest products business of Menasha was spun off into a separate company, Menasha Forest Products Corporation. The descendants of Menasha Corporation's founder maintained majority control of both companies. Also in 2001, Menasha Material Handling was renamed ORBIS Corporation. Completing the restructuring, Menasha Corporation began operating in 2001 as a holding company with four main subsidiaries (Menasha Packaging Company, ORBIS, Poly Hi Solidur, Inc., and Promo Edge

Company) and several investment companies either wholly or majority owned by Menasha: New Jersey Packaging, Menasha Printed Systems, Stratecom Graphics, Thermotech, and Traex. Menasha had thus shifted from a very centralized organizational structure to a decentralized one, with the holding company consisting of just a small staff focusing on overall strategic issues, and each subsidiary operating independently, better able to respond quickly to the needs of its particular market. Smethills hired a director for mergers and acquisitions to take the lead in seeking further growth opportunities for the subsidiaries. In addition, the company set up Menasha University to address its shortage of leaders, a heritage of the former centralized structure. This initiative offered a range of leadership and management training programs and courses to selected Menasha employees.

In the immediate aftermath of the restructuring, Menasha tightened its focus by divesting four of the businesses that had been placed into the "investment" category: Traex was sold to Libbey Inc. in December 2002, Menasha Printed Systems was sold to Kay Toledo Tag in August 2003, Stratecom Graphics was sold to Cypress Multigraphics, Inc., in September 2003, and Thermotech was sold to private-equity group Audax Management Co. LLC in December 2003. Another private-equity firm, Dunsirn Partners L.L.C., acquired the laminating division of Menasha Packaging late in 2003.

STRENGTHENING CORE NICHE AREAS

Menasha also strengthened the remaining core through strategic, "bolt-on" acquisitions. ORBIS gained a plastic pallet manufacturer, Cookson Plastic Molding of Latham, New York, in October 2001, and then the following year, Nucon Corporation, which specialized in plastic pallets for the beverage industry, serving the U.S., European, and Mexican markets. Menasha Packaging bolstered its position in consumer packaging and point-of-purchase displays through two acquisitions: Philadelphia-based Triangle Container Corporation in December 2002 and United Packaging of Schaumburg, Illinois, in March 2003.

Early in 2004, Menasha implemented a temporary leadership structure in which the president of each of the company's main units reported directly to a member of the board of directors. This change coincided with Smethills's resignation as the corporation's president and CEO. He was credited with not only shepherding Menasha through its major restructuring but also guiding the firm through a period when the manufacturing economy suffered a major downturn. In mid-2004

Prosser retired from his position as board chairman and was succeeded by Donald C. Shepard III, a fifth-generation descendant of the company's founder.

In July 2004 the Promo Edge office in Hoffman Estates, Illinois, was turned into a new subsidiary named LeveragePoint Media Corporation with a focus on providing in-store marketing materials and services for consumer product companies. The remaining Promo Edge facility, a plant in Neenah specializing in the label, sweepstakes, and gaming portions of the printing industry, was sold a month later to WS Packaging Group, Inc.

Menasha's period of operating without a chief executive ended in May 2005 when Arthur W. Huge was named president and CEO, becoming the 12th CEO in the company's history and the eighth from outside the founding family. Huge had joined Menasha in March 2001 as CFO. The new leader quickly carried out a key divestment that tightened the company's focus on its packaging businesses. In August 2005 Menasha sold Poly Hi Solidur to the Swiss firm Quadrant AG for $85 million. Later, in 2006, the company sold its last mill operation, the Otsego Falls paperboard mill, after determining that costs could be lowered by contracting for the paper it needed for its corrugated box and display converting operations.

In 2006 Menasha expanded its pharmaceutical packaging business by acquiring Creative Press of Evansville, Indiana, producer of such pharmaceutical packaging items as folding cartons, pressure-sensitive labels, inserts, product manuals, and brochures. New Jersey Packaging, Menasha's existing operation in this same field, expanded in 2006 by opening a new manufacturing facility in Raleigh, North Carolina. These operations were then combined in 2007 under a new subsidiary called Cortegra Group, Inc., which operated under the umbrella of Menasha Packaging. In December of that year, Cortegra purchased Capital Printing & Graphics of Fairfield, New Jersey, a provider of packaging for the generic pharmaceutical and neutraceutical markets. Keeping pace with the growing pharmaceutical industry, Cortegra in 2008 opened a new, 62,000-square-foot manufacturing plant in Evansville.

MAJOR ACQUISITIONS

In the meantime, ORBIS in December 2006 acquired the North American material handling business of the U.K. firm LINPAC Group Limited. Although the terms of the deal were not disclosed, Menasha called it the largest acquisition in the company's history. The acquired business was the leading producer and distribu-

tor of collapsible bulk containers and pallets, serving the automotive, food and beverage, and general industrial markets. The transaction included two plants in Kentucky and a facility in Shanghai, China. In October 2008 ORBIS completed an even larger deal when it acquired Norseman Plastics Holdings Limited. Based in Toronto, Norseman produced plastic reusable containers, trays, bins, and pallets used in a variety of applications, including bakery, beverage, dairy, recycled material, and waste collection. The firm operated manufacturing and warehousing facilities in Toronto; Howell, Michigan; Osage City, Kansas; and Kissimmee, Florida.

In the midst of contending with the severe economic downturn that began in the later months of 2008, Menasha again changed its top leadership following Huge's retirement in May 2009. After a three-month period of interim leadership, James M. Kotek was named the corporation's president and CEO. He had been president of ORBIS. By this time, after more than 160 years as a privately held manufacturer, Menasha Corporation was a $1 billion company with a handful of strong subsidiary businesses. The company was still majority owned by descendants of Elisha D. Smith, but the top executives had all been nonfamily members since the early 1960s.

Kerstan Cohen
Updated, David E. Salamie

PRINCIPAL SUBSIDIARIES

Menasha Packaging Company, LLC; Cortegra Group, Inc.; ORBIS Corporation; LeveragePoint Media Corporation.

PRINCIPAL COMPETITORS

Graphic Packaging Holding Company; International Paper Company; Longview Fibre Company; Rock-Tenn Company; Shorewood Packaging Corporation; Smurfit-Stone Container Corporation; Sonoco Products Company.

FURTHER READING

Blodgett, Richard, *Menasha Corporation: An Odyssey of Five Generations*, Lyme, CT: Greenwich Publishing Group, 1999, 168 p.

Dresang, Joel, "Huge Named to Run Menasha Corp.," *Milwaukee Journal Sentinel*, May 10, 2005, p. D3.

———, "Menasha Board Dismisses CEO in Restructuring," *Milwaukee Journal Sentinel*, January 23, 2004, p. D1.

———, "Menasha Chief Quits over Split with Board on Strategy," *Milwaukee Journal Sentinel*, July 13, 1999.

———, "Menasha Corp. to Sell Unit for $85 Million," *Milwaukee Journal Sentinel*, June 28, 2005, p. D3.

———, "New Leader Is on a Mission at Menasha Corp.," *Milwaukee Journal Sentinel*, July 29, 2001, p. 1D.

Pryweller, Joseph, "Menasha Sells Thermotech to Private Equity Firm Audax," *Plastics News*, January 26, 2004, p. 3.

Whitehead, Sandra, "On the Prowl for Growth Opportunities," *Corporate Report Wisconsin*, January 1991, sec. 1, p. 10.

METRO Group

———————— ◼ ————————

Schluterstrasse 1
Düsseldorf, 40235
Germany
Telephone: (+49 180) 5638760
Fax: (+49 180) 5780500
Web site: http://www.metro.de

Public Company
Founded: 1879
Incorporated: 2002
Employees: 300,000
Sales: EUR 65.53 billion ($91.74 billion) (2009)
Stock Exchanges: Frankfurt
Ticker Symbol: MEO
NAICS: 452111 Department Stores (Except Discount Department Stores); 444130 Hardware Stores; 445110 Supermarkets and Other Grocery (Except Convenience) Stores

◼ ◼ ◼

METRO Group (Metro) is one of the world's leading retail companies, ranking third behind Wal-Mart and Carrefour. Metro Group operates more than 2,100 stores across 34 countries, and employs more than 300,000 people. The company posted total revenues of EUR 65.53 billion ($91.74 billion) in 2009. Metro operates through four primary sales divisions. Metro Cash & Carry is the world's leading wholesale cash-and-carry supplier, with 668 stores in 30 countries, and sales of EUR 30.6 billion. Real is Metro's hypermarket division, operating 441 stores in Germany, Poland,

Romania, Russia, Turkey, and Ukraine. Real generated revenues of EUR 11.3 billion for Metro Group in 2009. The company's Media Markt and Saturn stores combine to form the largest consumer electronics retail business in Europe, with 818 stores in 16 countries and annual revenues of EUR 19.7 billion. Lastly, Metro Group controls the Galeria Kaufhof and Inno department store chains, in Germany and Belgium, with 141 stores producing sales of EUR 3.5 billion. Metro Group also operates a fifth division, Metro Group Asset Management, which oversees the company's real estate development and management operations in 32 countries. Metro Group is listed on the Frankfurt Stock Exchange and is led by CEO Eckhard Cordes.

BEISHEIM FOUNDS METRO CASH & CARRY: 1964–95

Metro's global retail/wholesale empire began as Metro SB-Grossmarkte, a cash-and-carry business that German entrepreneur Otto Beisheim founded in 1964 in Mulheim. Popularized in the United States, cash-and-carry operations departed from traditional wholesale models by allowing commercial customers to pick and purchase goods at distribution centers, then haul them away in their own vehicles. Benefits included lower prices, larger product selection, extended business hours, and immediate possession of merchandise. Operating under the name Metro Cash & Carry, the company received financial backing in 1967 from the Franz Haniel & Cie. industrial dynasty and the Schmidt-Ruthenbeck family, also wholesalers. Beisheim and his new partners each controlled one-third of the shares in the company.

The infusion of capital enabled Beisheim and his partners to expand cash-and-carry outlets within and beyond German borders. In 1968, Metro joined with Dutch conglomerate Steenkolen Handelsvereniging NV (SHV) and established a company in the Netherlands operating as Makro Cash & Carry. Nine Western European countries became home to Metro and Makro wholesale outlets by 1972. Expansion into retailing soon followed. In the early 1980s, Metro and Union Bank of Switzerland made a major acquisition, German department store chain Kaufhof AG. As Metro gained controlling interest in the company, it steered Kaufhof toward converting some stores into specialized fashion and shoe outlets, and investing in consumer electronics (Media Markt and Saturn) and computer businesses. In late 1992, the Metro added another retail conglomerate to its portfolio, buying a majority stake in the German holding company Asko Deutsche Kaufhaus. Asko's properties included retail and wholesale grocery networks, furniture stores, and Praktiker home-improvement centers.

By 1993, privately held Metro had controlling stakes in Kaufhof, Asko, and Asko's subsidiary Deutsche SB-Kauf, all companies listed on European stock exchanges. The holdings not only left Metro with a dominant market share in the German food-retailing sector, but elevated it to one of the largest retailing groups in the world. Metro had an estimated 180 companies under its management, including brand-name businesses such as SB-Kauf supermarkets, Massa discount stores, computer chain Vobis, office supply group Pelikan, Adler clothing stores, and AVA department stores. Along the way Metro had become Metro Holding, with its headquarters and leader, Beisheim,

locating in Baar, Switzerland. Entering his 70s, reclusive billionaire Beisheim retired from active management of the company in 1994. He turned over the reins to close associate Erwin Conradi, who had joined Metro in 1970. Conradi would dominate the company management over the next five years.

BECOMING EUROPE'S LARGEST RETAIL GROUP: 1995–98

Conradi announced in October 1995 that Metro Holding planned to establish a new company, Metro AG, by merging its four largest German operations: Kaufhof, Asko, SB-Kauf, and Metro Cash & Carry. The merger was largely driven by Europe's sluggish consumer spending and crowded retail sector. "Consumer confidence over the coming years looks likely to remain weak," Conradi explained in a March 1996 interview with the *Daily Telegraph*. "Price will become even more important and for companies that means cost savings will be more vital than ever." Consolidation allowed the new group to cut costs while boosting sales and creating a platform for global expansion. Conradi estimated sales would rise to DEM 76.4 billion ($52 billion) in 1998, more than 22 percent above the group's 1995 total. He added that net profits would double over the period from DEM 719 million to DEM 1.47 billion.

In May 1996, shareholders for publicly traded Kaufhof, Asko, and SB-Kauf approved a share-swapping plan and merger backdated to the beginning of the year. With an estimated value of $10 billion, Metro AG was headquartered in Düsseldorf/Cologne. Overnight it became the largest retailer in Europe and among the top five in the world. The company was listed on the German DAX stock index for the first time on July 25, 1996. Under a complex ownership arrangement, privately held Metro Holding retained a 60 percent stake in the company, a stake controlled by Beisheim and the Haniel and Schmidt-Ruthenbeck families via another holding company. First year net sales for the new company came in at DEM 55 billion ($35.4 billion) and net profit at DEM 717 million ($393 million). The company had just over 130,000 employees.

Following the consolidation, Metro embarked on a series of acquisitions and divestitures designed to strengthen core businesses and move ahead with expansion. In 1997 it added 59 Wirichs home-improvement centers to complement the Praktiker chain. It bought computer and restaurant holdings, and disposed of fashion, furniture, and some retail and wholesale grocery outlets. Foreign sales grew 50 percent as five chains (Real, Media Markt, Praktiker, Adler, and

KEY DATES

1964: Otto Beisheim founds Metro SB-Grossmarkte, a wholesale business that becomes Metro Cash & Carry.

1967: Haniel and Schmidt-Ruthenbeck families become Beisheim's partners.

1968: Metro Cash & Carry expands to the Netherlands, opening Makro Cash & Carry stores.

1993: Company acquires a majority interest in Asko Deutsche Kaufhaus.

1994: Beisheim retires from active management of Metro and Erwin Conradi is appointed president of Metro Holding board.

1996: Metro Holding merges Asko, Metro Cash & Carry, Kaufhof, and Deutsche SB-Kauf to create Metro AG.

1998: Metro purchases Makro Cash & Carry and Allkauf and Kreigbaum hypermarket chains.

2002: Metro AG changes its name to Metro Group.

2006: Metro acquires Wal-Mart's 85 hypermarkets in Germany and the Géant hypermarket chain in Poland.

2010: Metro expects to open its first Media Markt in Shanghai, China, and six cash-and-carry stores in Punjab, India.

Vobis) launched operations in other European countries. Metro Cash & Carry, already in 15 countries, opened its first stores in Romania and China. However, 1997 proved to be a disappointing year for shareholders. Sales increased to DEM 56.8 billion ($31.7 billion), but net profit fell from DEM 717 million ($393 million) in 1996 to DEM 623 million ($309 million). Even with added expansion costs, the profit figures weighed in lower than management expected.

The buying and selling continued into 1998. Metro fortified its profitable European cash-and-carry operations by purchasing 196 Makro Cash & Carry stores from SHV Makro NV of the Netherlands for $2.7 billion. Metro later bought out the remaining interest that the parent company Metro Holding held in SHV Makro, a move made to guarantee investors full profits from the businesses. Metro also added to its portfolio the well-known Allkauf and Kreigbaum "hypermarkets," known as combination grocery/department stores.

FOCUSING ON CORE BUSINESSES: 1998

Entering 1998, investors and industry analysts still lacked confidence Metro was on the right track. Many criticized the retail giant for being overly diversified, without a coherent strategy, and subject to mysterious ownership. Shareholders also had concerns about the company's low profit margins.

Metro was indeed diversified. It had 13 independent operating divisions at the end of 1997. The glut of companies included wholesale food outlets, three department store chains, hypermarkets, food stores, discount stores, consumer electronics centers, home-improvement centers, three computer centers, fashion centers, shoe stores, restaurant and catering services, and real estate and support companies. The concerns over the company's structure and strategy compelled Metro to embark on a DEM 5 billion ($2.7 billion) reorganization program in the fall of 1998. Hans-Joachim Korber replaced Klaus Wiegandt as management board chairman, and Korber pushed forward a plan to concentrate on just four core businesses.

The program also called for Metro systematically to shed noncore business chains through a new subsidiary, Divaco (initially Divag). Metro invested DEM 350 million in Divaco and retained a 49 percent stake. A group of investors led by Deutsche Bank managed it. In December, Metro transferred to Divaco companies generating sales of DEM 16 billion ($9.6 billion) and employing 34,000 workers. The banished businesses included 813 Vobis computer stores, 143 Kaufhalle and 25 unprofitable Kaufhof department stores, fashion and shoe stores, Tip discount stores, and Kaufhalle's real estate business. Divaco sold 165 Tip stores to Berman retailer Tengelmann for DEM 375 million in late 1998. A year later, trying to raise cash for expansion, Metro disposed of additional assets by selling and leasing back its retail real estate. In a joint venture with Westdeutsche Landesbank that raised DEM 5.4 billion, Metro sold the ground under 290 retail outlets in Germany, Turkey, Greece, Hungary, and Luxembourg.

Metro's financial numbers for 1998 finished strong. The Makro acquisition drove six months' sales up 62 percent, with year-end figures hitting DEM 91.7 billion ($54.7 billion, EUR 46.8 billion). Net income jumped 19 percent to DEM 735 million (EUR 579 million). The company was one of the strongest performers on the German DAX. International expansion also moved smartly ahead, with foreign business contributing 35.2 percent to total sales in 1998 and company payroll climbing above 181,000.

MERGER SPECULATION: 1999

Investor confidence was short-lived, however. From an all-time high of DEM 153 (EUR 78.5) in January 1999, company stock dropped 20 points on the DAX by the end of March and hovered there the rest of the year. Sales dipped to DEM 85.7 billion ($44.1 billion, EUR 43.8 billion) and net income dropped to DEM 713 billion (EUR 305 billion). Metro added another 73 foreign outlets, and introduced a customer loyalty program "Payback" at the Real and Kaufhof chains. It also launched its first Internet business activities with the Kaufhof and Metro Cash & Carry units.

Merger and acquisition rumors dominated Metro's press coverage as stiff competition and stagnant growth in European retailing drove companies to look for partners to secure market share. The entrance of U.S.-based Wal-Mart onto the scene exacerbated the pressures. During 1998, Wal-Mart had acquired nearly 100 German hypermarkets with annual sales of $3.1 billion. In early 1999 reports surfaced that the world's largest retailer had an interest in buying all or part of Metro. A Metro official responded by saying a merger "would not be a congenial get-together." However, speculation persisted.

Analysts identified the Netherlands' largest retailer, Ahold, and British retail group Tesco, as possible merger or acquisition candidates for Metro. In January 2000 reports surfaced that management for Metro and the U.K.-based retailer Kingfisher were having preliminary discussions. Metro continued to deny any interest in merging. "Of course people call us, of course we talk to them," said Metro Supervisory Board Chairman Conradi in the January 26, 2000 *Financial Times*. "But we have not actively been pursuing any deal and neither should we, as our competitive position is not at risk." Industry insiders thought otherwise. Several believed some or all of the three original partners wanted to sell their shares to Wal-Mart in order to invest in non-retail interests. The partners were bound to act together under agreement in effect until 2003.

Merger rumors peaked in July 2000 when German newspaper *Welt am Sonntag* reported that Metro would transfer its Real chain of hypermarkets and Extra grocery chain to Wal-Mart, which wanted to continue to expand in Germany. Metro would in turn acquire around 1,000 of Wal-Mart's Sam's Club warehouse outlets. Metro's original partners this time issued a formal statement denying an interest in selling the company. They also asserted that they planned to maintain their cooperation for an indefinite period and sustain their commitment to Metro. At the same time, the partners announced that Conradi would resign. Some industry observers viewed Conradi's resignation as a dismissal for the supervisory board chairman's failed negotiations with Wal-Mart and French retailer Carrefour, which later acquired the French group Promode and replaced Metro as Europe's largest retailer. Others contended that Metro Executive Board Chairman Korber had threatened to leave if Conradi stayed. Korber and management board members reportedly felt Conradi blocked management decisions, which in turn delayed restructuring and expansion, specifically the acquisition of SHV Makro's additional cash-and-carry stores in Asia and Latin America.

KORBER TAKES CHARGE IN 2000

By September 2000, there were several new faces on the Metro management board. To streamline the strategic decision-making process, Metro had reduced seats on the board from five to four. Korber retained the chairmanship along with his CEO title. In charge of balancing the family members demands with increasing Metro shareholder value, Korber reaffirmed Metro's commitment to international expansion, especially with the cash-and-carry business in Europe and Asia. However, he resisted recommendations that Metro attempt to boost its share price by divesting poorly performing food retail and home-improvement chains and focusing on profitable cash-and-carry and electronics stores. The company's four-part divisional makeup consisting of cash-and-carry (Metro, Makro), food retail (Real, Extra), nonfood specialty (Media Markt, Saturn, Praktiker), and department stores (Galeria Kaufhof) was "optimal," according to Korber.

In an effort to become more visible to investors, the company began to draw up its consolidated annual financial statements according to the International Accounting Standards (IAS). To promote entrepreneurial thinking within Metro, Korber introduced the control and management tool EVA (Economic Value Added) and benchmarking. The company also instigated incentives ranging from stock options for managers to merit pay for shop employees. Metro continued its advance into e-commerce and in June 2000 acquired controlling interest in Cologne-based Internet service company Primus-Online.

PURSUING PROFITABILITY: 2001–02

Metro's 2000 sales numbers met most analysts' expectations for Europe's restrained retail market. Fueled by growth in the cash-and-carry business, sales for 2000 grew to EUR 46.9 billion (DEM 91.8 billion, $44.1 billion), up over 7 percent from EUR 43.8 billion previous year. Pretax profit climbed 10.7 percent to

EUR 754 million. Sales abroad climbed to 42.2 percent of all sales. Kaufhof, the struggling department store division Metro had considered selling, registered a pretax profit of 7.2 percent after adopting the "Galeria" concept that appealed to upper-income, ethnically diverse urban consumers.

Metro opened another 80 retail outlets in 2001, bringing the store count up to 2,249. Cash-and-carry stores were opened for the first time in Russia and Croatia. Metro continued to push retail operations to develop high-brand recognition and store concepts. Sales figures rose 5.5 percent to EUR 49.5 billion ($44.2 billion) for 2001, slightly lower than the 6 percent predicted number. Foreign sales rose to 44.4 percent of total sales. However, pretax profits dropped 10.7 percent to EUR 673 million. Based on 2001 sales, Metro ranked first in Germany, third in Europe, and fifth in the world among retailers. Korber had little interest in rankings, however. "We do not build an empire but rather develop our company to be profitable in the long run," said Korber in a September interview in the German business magazine *Focus Money*.

At the end of the first quarter of 2002, Korber predicted Metro group sales would hurdle the EUR 52 billion mark by year-end. By 2003 he expected sales figures for outlets outside Germany to exceed those within its borders. The company's ongoing expansion resulted in its first cash-and-carry stores in Vietnam in March 2002.

Under Korber, Metro moved ahead on a strategy based on internationalizing core retail operations, enhancing shareholder value, and creating brand awareness among consumers for retail outlets. Expansion efforts continued to focus on developing new stores organically and without incurring the costs and risks of acquisitions. Cash-and-carry operations, with 384 stores in 22 countries, remained the largest revenue producer in the group, accounting for 45 percent of the group's sales, or EUR 22.7 billion in 2001. Metro management remained committed to setting profitability targets for each of its independent sales divisions.

METRO GROUP IN 2002

In recognition of its increasingly international profile, Metro changed its name in 2002, becoming Metro Group. By 2003, Metro Group laid claim to being the third-largest retailer in Europe and the fifth largest in the world, with sales of EUR 54 billion ($67 billion). The company also revealed itself as one of the most forward thinking, with the opening of its so-called Future Store in 2003. This store, based at one of the company's Extra supermarkets in Germany, was designed as a testing ground for new retailing technologies, including electronic shelf labels, self-scanners, and RFID (radio-frequency identification) capabilities. The company opened a second Future Store in Toenisvorst in 2008.

Metro Group continued exploring new international markets, opening its first store in Japan in 2002. The following year, Metro opened its first stores in India and in Ukraine. Much of the company's growth came through the expansion of its Metro Cash & Carry and Media Markt/Saturn consumer electronics chains, with new stores opening in Greece in 2005 and in Sweden and Russia in 2006. Metro's Cash & Carry business also expanded strongly in the Chinese market, opening its 22nd outlet in Harbin in 2005, with plans to open up to 50 more stores in China by 2010.

Metro Group also worked on building its Real hypermarket chain. The company opened its first Real in Moscow in 2005, then launched the banner in Romania in 2006. In that year, Metro completed two significant acquisitions to boost its hypermarket division. In August of that year, the company acquired Wal-Mart's 85 stores in Germany after the U.S. retail giant, following nine years of losses, threw in the towel on its operations there. This purchase was followed by the takeover of the Polish operations of the French Géant hypermarket chain.

FOCUSING ON INDIA AND CHINA IN 2010

By 2007, Metro's revenues had passed EUR 64 billion ($90 billion). The company also brought in a new CEO that year, Eckhard Cordes, who also served as CEO of Franz Haniel & Cie. Cordes promptly launched Metro on a new strategic initiative, called Shape 2012. The plan was designed to cut costs and simplify the company's structure in order to boost Metro's operating efficiency. Under the maxim "as decentrally as possible, as centrally as necessary," the company reorganized its operations into four core sales divisions, as well as a fifth division to oversee its real estate and development operations.

As a result, Metro sold off its Extra supermarket chain in 2008. In February 2009, the company also sold its Adler clothing store operations. At the same time, Metro continued expanding its international operations. The company responded to the success of its Russian operations by opening a dedicated distribution center for that country in Noginsk.

Metro's attention also turned increasingly toward the fast-growing markets in India and China. In 2009, the company announced that it had reached a partnership with Foxconn Technology Group to roll out its Media Markt consumer electronics chain in China. In June 2010, the partnership announced that it had settled on the site of its first location, in Shanghai, slated to be opened in October of that year. By then, Metro had also announced plans to invest up to $180 million to open six new cash-and-carry stores in the state of Punjab, India, through 2010.

With sales of EUR 65.53 billion ($91.74 billion) in 2009, Metro had grown into the number three retailer in the world, behind Wal-Mart and Carrefour. The company had also begun to reap the benefits of the Shape 2012 program. By mid-2010, the company had seen its first profits growth since 2008. As Cordes explained to *MMR*: "With this program, we are also unfolding the full strength of our company. Shape 2012 will give a new profile to our company." With a presence in 34 markets worldwide, Metro Group expected to continue to play a role in shaping the global retail sector.

Douglas Cooley
Updated, M. L. Cohen

PRINCIPAL SUBSIDIARIES

GALERIA Kaufhof GmbH; INNOVATION S.A. (Belgium); Makro Autoservicio Mayorista S. A. U. (Spain); MAKRO Cash & Carry Belgium NV; MAKRO Cash & Carry CR s.r.o. (Czech Republic); Makro Cash & Carry UK Holding Limited; Makro Cash and Carry Polska S.A.; Mediamarket S. p. A. (Italy); Media-Saturn-Holding GmbH; METRO AG; METRO Cash & Carry France S.A.S.; METRO Cash & Carry International GmbH; METRO Cash & Carry International Holding GmbH (Austria); METRO Cash & Carry OOO (Russia); METRO Cash & Carry ROMANIA SRL; METRO Distributie Nederland B.V.; METRO Groß- und Lebensmitteleinzelhandel Holding GmbH; METRO Großhandelsgesellschaft mbH Düsseldorf; METRO Italia Cash and Carry S. p. A.; METRO Jinjiang Cash & Carry Co., Ltd. (China); METRO Kaufhaus und Fachmarkt Holding GmbH; real,- SB-Warenhaus GmbH.

PRINCIPAL DIVISIONS

Metro Cash & Carry; Real; Media Markt and Saturn; Galeria Kaufhof; Real Estate.

PRINCIPAL COMPETITORS

Arcandor AG; Baur Kaufhaus Gmbh; Galeria Kaufhof GmbH; Globus Holding GmbH and Company KG;

Marktkauf Holding GmbH; REAL SB-Warenhaus GmbH.

FURTHER READING

Benoit, Bertrand, "Aiming for More Cash Than Carry," *Financial Times* (London), December 20, 2000, p. 20.

———, "Price War Puts Metro Independence in Question," *Financial Times* (London), January 26, 2000, p. 30.

Benoit, Bertrand, Richard Rivlin, and Susanna Voyle, "Metro Must Win Family Holders," *Financial Times* (London), January 22, 2000, p. 16.

Brasier, Mary, "German Giant on Retail Stage," *Daily Telegraph*, March 15, 1996, p. 26.

Dempsey, Judy, "Metro Sees Sharp Rise after Merger," *Financial Times* (London), March 15, 1996, p. 27.

"Eckhard Cordes, CEO—Metro AG," *MMR*, June 14, 2010, p. 130.

Garry, Michael, "Metro Group Backtracks," *Supermarket News*, November 15, 2004, p. 67.

"Metro AG: Weary of Food Fights," *Agri-Food News from Germany*, December 2000, http://www.atn-riae.agr.ca.

"Metro Changes Name," *MMR*, December 9, 2002, p. 21.

"Metro Confirms to Sell Divaco Stake by Year-End, Denies to List Real Estate Unit," *FT.com Financial Times*, March 19, 2002, http://www.news.ft.com.

"Metro Group Has Announced Plan to Enter and Rapidly Expand in China with a Chain of Electronics Stores," *Grocer*, March 28, 2009, p. 9.

"Metro Looks Abroad for 2001," *CNN*, May 10, 2000, http://www.cnn.com.

"Metro Plans to Set Up Real Hypermarket Chain in Moscow," *FT.com Financial Times*, April 3, 2002, http://www.news.ft.com.

"Metro Sees 2002 Sales, Profit Growth," *CNN*, March 26, 2002, http://www.cnn.com.

"Metro Splits Business," *MMR*, April 19, 2010, p. 15.

"Metro to Bring Format to China," *MMR*, June 14, 2010, p. 65.

"Tapping a New Mass Market," *Business Week*, November 18, 2002, p. 41.

Waller, David, "German Retailer Plans Hive-off," *Financial Times* (London), January 3, 1993, p. 22.

———, "Secretive Retailer Extends Its Tangled Web of Interests," *Financial Times* (London), December 8, 1992, p. 21.

Wood, John, "Giant's Local Touch," *Grocer*, August 16, 2003, p. 15.

Young, Vicki M., "Metro Group CEO Steps Down," *WWD*, September 21, 2007, p. 18.

Zweibach, Elliot, "Metro Buys Quebec Independent," *Supermarket News*, September 7, 2009.

———, "Metro Eyes Potential Acquisition Opportunities," *Supermarket News*, March 13, 2006, p. 24.

Minera Alumbrera Ltd.

4139 Distrito de Hualfín
Belén, Catamarca
Argentina
Telephone: (54 038) 3548-5100
Fax: (54 11) 4316-8399
Web site: http://www.alumbrera.com.ar

Private Company
Incorporated: 1993
Employees: 1,200
Sales: $1.26 billion (2009)
NAICS: 212221 Gold Ore Mining; 212234 Copper Ore and Nickel Ore Mining

■ ■ ■

Minera Alumbrera Ltd. is the company that operates the largest mine in Argentina. Located in the Andes Mountains, this mine yields both copper and gold. After being processed on-site from mined ore and sent by pipeline to a filtration plant, the mineral concentrates are transported by rail to a port for export abroad. Minera Alumbrera is managed by a Swiss company and owned by this company and two Canadian companies. It is the only producer of copper in Argentina and is the second-largest producer of gold.

PREPARING TO MINE DEPOSITS OF COPPER AND GOLD

The Bajo de la Alumbrera area, in the province of Catamarca, has long been known for its veins of copper and gold, in addition to alum (*alumbre*), a common ore composed of potassium aluminum sulfate and ammonium aluminum sulfate. There were small-scale mining activities in the late 19th and early 20th centuries. By 1969 a government body named Yacimientos Mineros de Agua de Dionisio (YMAD) had been established to study the possibilities of exploiting this large deposit. Catamarca held a 60 percent stake in this body. The national government and the National University of Tucumán held 20 percent each.

The project did not get underway, however, until a 1993 reform of Argentina's laws attracted investment from the joint venture that established Minera Alumbrera Ltd. This law authorized a concession to operate the mine and established a 3 percent royalty, payable to the provincial government, on the value of production at the pit head. The tax level was to remain in force for 30 years. The new mining law also provided for accelerated depreciation on mining equipment and allowed mine operators advance rebates on value-added tax on their goods and services. Minera Alumbrera and YMAD signed a contract in 1994 that granted the latter a 20 percent share of the profits generated by the project.

M.I.M. Holdings Ltd., an Australian company, took a half-share in the consortium. North Ltd., another Australian company, and Rio Algom Ltd., a Canadian company, split the remainder equally. In 1994 Minera Alumbrera completed the drilling of 20 holes concentrated on the south side of the mineral deposit and determined the area it was going to exploit in the next five years. Bajo de la Alumbrera became Argentina's largest mining project. It was predicted that by 2000, it would be the world's ninth-largest copper mine and 14th-largest gold mine.

Some $1.2 billion was invested, with financing for the projects by banks in six countries and risk insurance covered by governments in seven countries. About 6,000 jobs were created, not only in the open-pit mine and processing plant but also for construction of a power line and a pipeline to carry the ore to a filtration plant, from where the treated concentrate would be shipped by rail to a port for export abroad. Underway by 1997, it was the world's largest start-up mining project involving base metal extraction.

THE FIRST FEW YEARS OF OPERATIONS: 1997–99

The ore was extracted, crushed, and treated by conventional grinding, milling and flotation processes at the mine, located 2,600 meters (about 8,500 feet) above sea level. This concentrate was then mixed with water and pumped through the world's longest slurry pipeline, 317 kilometers (193 miles), to a filtration plant at Cruz del Norte in the neighboring province of Tucumán. A 202-kilometer (125-mile) high-voltage power line was built to transport electricity for the mine from El Bracho, Tucumán.

After removing the water, the concentrate was transported 830 kilometers (516 miles) by 40-car trains owned by the company to the Paraná River port of General San Martín, near Rosario, Santa Fe. From there the material, fully subscribed in advance, was shipped to smelters in eight countries: Brazil, Canada, Finland, Germany, India, Japan, South Korea, and Spain. By 2005 China and Bulgaria were also important customers, and Poland was also taking a small share of the mine's concentrate.

Extensive measures were taken to lessen the environmental impact of the project. Tailings were stored behind a dam created to collect most of the water needed by the mill that was processing the ore. During construction, which included the power line and pipeline, there was extensive monitoring of water, air quality, and acid drainage at all sites and nearby villages. All animals were protected, and several hundred cactuses estimated to be between 300 and 400 years old were relocated during construction of the tailings area.

In spite of these measures and the certification and recertification of Minera Alumbrera's environmental management in accord with the norms of ISO 14001: 2004, the company did not escape dozens of accusations of environmental abuse. These included possible contamination of the artificial canal by the filtration plant; the alleged presence of strontium, a radioactive material; alleged spills of toxic materials from the slurry pipeline; and allegations of air pollution, radiation emitted from the power line, and invasion of indigenous cemeteries. The company was also accused of illegal export of its minerals. None of these charges was sustained in the courts, however.

Minera Alumbrera's mine and mill reached commercial rates of production in February 1998. By the end of 1999 the massive project was removing 340,000 metric tons of ore and waste rock from the mine each day. The open pit was expected to eventually reach about a mile in diameter and more than a quarter mile in depth.

OWNERSHIP AND OTHER CHANGES: 2003–07

In 2003 Minera Alumbrera produced 34.2 million metric tons of ore, 198,500 metric tons of copper in concentrate, and 710,000 troy ounces of gold, mostly in concentrate. The following year its revenues came to more than $1 billion. Between 2002 and 2005 exports from the mine brought in $2.58 billion.

There were major changes in the ownership of Minera Alumbrera during 2003 and the following years. Xstrata plc, a Swiss company, acquired M.I.M. Holdings in 2003 and its half-share in the mine. It then assumed management responsibility for Minera Alumbrera. The quarter-share formerly held by North was sold to Wheaton River Materials Ltd., a Canadian company. Wheaton River also purchased half of the quarter-share held by Rio Algon. The other half was sold to Northern Orion Resources Inc., another Canadian company. In 2005 Wheaton River sold its holding in Minera Alumbrera to Goldcorp Inc., another Canadian company. Two years later, Yamana Gold Inc., also Canadian, acquired Northern Orion Resources.

KEY DATES

1993: Minera Alumbrera is founded by a consortium of three companies.

1997: Operations begin at the mine and other facilities after $1.2 billion in investment.

2003: Xstrata plc assumes half-ownership and management of Minera Alumbrera.

2007: Minera Alumbrera begins extracting molybdenum from its mine.

2009: Minera Alumbrera's exports since 2002 have reached almost $31 billion.

Xstrata announced an upgrade in the metal content of the mine in 2004. A drilling program confirmed the existence of 80 million tons of additional reserves, amounting to an additional 350,000 tons of contained copper and 1.2 million ounces of gold over the life of the mine. The lifetime of the mine, previously estimated at 20 years and later downgraded to 17 years, was thereby extended by 2.5 years, assuring metal production until mid-2015. Extraction of molybdenum from the ore began in 2007, when an added concentration plant for the metal was built. Some 450 metric tons had been extracted by the end of 2008.

CONTRIBUTIONS TO THE NATION: 2008–09

By 2010 Minera Alumbrera had fulfilled its potential to Argentina. Its exports between 2002 and 2009 came to $30.93 billion. During the previous year its exports constituted 42 percent of the nation's mining exports. Its goods and services with Argentina contributed ARS 1.13 billion ($305 million) to the national economy in 2009. Taking into consideration taxes and royalties paid in 2009, plus salaries, contributions to social security, purchases of goods, and national services, the sum came to ARS $3.06 billion ($825 million). For each person directly employed by Minera Alumbrera, an estimated

8.2 workers owed their jobs indirectly to the project.

In 2009 Minera Alumbrera paid ARS 622.7 million ($167.8 million) in taxes on its profits. It also paid royalties of ARS 106.6 million ($28.7 million) to Catamarca, accounting for more than 70 percent of the province's revenues. Between 2004 and 2009 Catamara distributed ARS 278 million (about $90 million) from these royalties to municipalities in the province. Minera Alumbrera's distribution of profits to YMAD in 2009 came to ARS 398.9 million ($107.5 million). YMAD received almost ARS 1.6 billion (over $500 million) in the years between 2006 and 2008. Minera Alumbrera had operating profit of $449 million in 2009.

During 2008, Minera Alumbrera treated 37 million metric tons of ore in order to produce 156,893 tons of copper in concentrate and 504,403 ounces of gold, mostly in concentrate. Asia was the principal destination for Minera Alumbrera's exports, with 54 percent of the total. Europe accounted for more than 40 percent. The main importing nations were Brazil, Canada, China, Finland, Germany, India, Japan, the Philippines, South Korea, and Spain. There were no suitable refineries in Argentina because of its distance from the world's leading consumers of copper and gold.

Robert Halasz

FURTHER READING

"Alumbrera: Newest Copper-Gold Producer for Rio Algom," *Canadian Mining Journal*, February 2000, pp. 18–21.

The Argentine Economy, Buenos Aires: Julio Moyano Comunicaciónes, 1997, p. 374.

"Responsible de 44% de las exportaciones del sector," *Mercado*, April 2010, pp. 58–59.

Seselovksy, Alejandro, "Y pensar que algunos creen que son el sexo débil," *Revista Gente*, May 31, 2005, pp. 92–94, 96.

Warn, Ken, "Prospects Transformed," *Financial Times*, July 1, 1997, p. 6.

———, "Success of Argentine Mining on Test," *Financial Times*, January 8, 1999, p. 24.

"Xstrata Upgrades Alumbrera Reserves," *Engineering and Mining Journal*, September 2004, pp. 23–24.

New York Life Insurance Company

51 Madison Avenue
New York, New York 10010
U.S.A.
Telephone: (212) 576-7000
Toll Free: (800) 710-7945
Fax: (212) 576-8145
Web site: http://www.newyorklife.com

Mutual Company
Incorporated: 1845 as Nautilus Insurance Company
Employees: 17,500
Total Assets: $208.15 billion (2009)
NAICS: 524113 Direct Life Insurance Carriers

■ ■ ■

New York Life Insurance Company is the leading mutual life insurance company in the United States and one of the largest life insurance companies in the world. New York Life is also one of the largest asset-management firms in the country, with more than $250 billion in assets under management. The company has nearly 12,000 domestic sales agents and about 8,000 international agents operating in developing countries in Asia and Latin America, including Mexico, China, Hong Kong, India, South Korea, Taiwan, and Thailand. The company also sells life insurance policies through AARP and other professional associations and affiliated groups. Along with life insurance, New York Life provides a diverse range of other products and services, including retirement plans, long-term care insurance, institutional asset management and trust services, and

securities services and products including retail and institutional mutual funds such as 401(k) products. The company boasts the highest possible financial strength, as ranked by the four major credit rating agencies, and it is a *Fortune*100 firm.

BUILDING THE BUSINESS: MID-19TH CENTURY

Life insurance was an infant industry when New York Life's predecessor, Nautilus Insurance Company, began operations in the 1840s. Marine and fire insurance were important, but people hesitated to assign a cash value to human life and often associated life insurance with gambling. As the economy became more industrial and the population more mobile, society recognized the need to secure a family's welfare against the loss of the breadwinner. In 1840, New York State passed a law allowing a married woman to insure her husband's life with immunity from having the benefits seized by his creditors. Such legislation recognized the use of life insurance in a developing industrial economy and widened life insurance's potential market beyond wealthy speculators.

New York Life has its origins in a charter granted by the New York state legislature to Nautilus Insurance Company in 1841 for the sale of fire and marine insurance. The company began issuing policies in April 1845 and soon decided to jettison its fire and marine business in order to concentrate on life insurance. By 1849, the company was so securely established in this new business that it petitioned the state legislature and had its name changed to New-York Life Insurance

COMPANY PERSPECTIVES

New York Life is #1 in life insurance sales and #1 in customer satisfaction in the U.S. New York Life's sales force is recognized as one of the best trained in the industry, which makes our agents among the most qualified for understanding and addressing each customer's individual needs. Simply put, we're not a public company. This means unlike publicly traded companies that manage their business for the short-term benefit of shareholders, we are guided by the longer-term needs and expectations of our policyholders. This makes New York Life, essentially, a partner in helping achieve your long-term goals and means we will be around for you and your family for years to come. When you consider all these factors, it is easy to see why New York Life is the Company You Keep.

Company. In 1917 or 1918, the company dropped the hyphen from its name.

The company's early operations coincided with the development of U.S. life insurance. Policies issued by New-York Life were usually limited to short periods of time and placed a variety of restrictions on their owners. Policyholders in the 1840s could not travel south of Virginia and Kentucky during the summer because the company considered the southern climate a health risk. Southerners applying for policies faced higher premiums and restrictions on their travel as well. Before 1850, the company considered overland travel to California too dangerous for policyholders to undertake without paying an extra premium. Epidemic diseases were of great concern to the company in its early years, too. Outbreaks of cholera and yellow fever often threatened the company's security and temporarily forced it to restrict new business to Manhattan and Brooklyn in 1849.

Despite such natural threats, the company grew quickly and established an adequate reserve for paying out dividends and benefits to policyholders. This success was in large part due to the company's most innovative contribution to the young industry, the use of agents to sell policies. Previously, insurance sales had centered on a home office that served local merchants and elites wealthy enough to protect their property and lives. New-York Life's use of agents to seek out new business greatly expanded the market, and the company soon

established agencies in New England, the southern states, and as far west as California.

CIVIL WAR RISKS AND POSTWAR EXPANSION

The Civil War presented the company with its first major crisis, since it had developed a sizable southern business. President Abraham Lincoln's prohibition of commerce with the Confederate states during the war cut off communication between the home office and its southern policyholders, creating a host of problems, including lapsed payments and unpaid claims. The company compensated for these losses, however, by issuing policies to soldiers and civilians involved in combat. One of the few companies to take on such war risks, New-York Life managed continued growth despite its southern losses. In fact, the company sold more than half of the 6,500 new life insurance policies issued in New York City in 1862.

After the war, New-York Life expanded quickly with the nation's booming economy. The company recovered its southern business by paying benefits on death claims left unsettled during the war and by allowing former customers to renew their lapsed policies. As the nation pushed westward, so did the company, establishing agencies in Utah, Montana, and Nevada in 1869 and in San Francisco in 1870. New-York Life also became an international name during this era, opening offices in Canada in 1868, Great Britain in 1870, Paris in 1884, Berlin in 1885, Vienna in 1887, Amsterdam in 1891, and Budapest in 1894.

Intense competition marked the insurance industry in the last two decades of the 19th century, and it was during this time that the company emerged as one of the largest mutual insurance companies in the nation. Competition was fueled in part by the introduction of tontine policies, a type of life insurance in which a number of policyholders would forgo their annual dividends and award the money to the last survivor of the group. The winner enjoyed a considerable payoff for his or her longevity. New-York Life began selling tontine policies in 1871, and by 1900, its growth in sales made it one of the nation's three largest mutual insurance companies, along with Mutual Life Insurance Company and Equitable Life Assurance Society.

Reorganization of the company's agency system also promoted its growth. In 1892, President John A. McCall implemented the branch office system, a structure that would serve the company well. The home office opened branch offices throughout the United States to act as liaisons between the company's New York operations and its agents in the field. The result was improved

KEY DATES

1845: Firm begins doing business as Nautilus Insurance Company.
1984: New York Life enters the financial services market.
1988: Company enters the international life insurance market.
2000: Company brings all asset management businesses under one roof.
2007: Company receives a superior rating from all four major credit rating firms.

communications, which allowed for more effective administration of the agency force. In addition, sales incentives and professional training were provided to agents.

WORLD CONDITIONS CREATING VOLATILE ENVIRONMENT: EARLY TO MID-20TH CENTURY

The boom of the 1880s and the 1890s did not go unchecked. New-York Life entered the 20th Century at odds with progressive reformers, who accused rapidly growing insurance companies of mismanagement and malfeasance. In 1905, the New York State Legislature convened an investigative committee under the leadership of William W. Armstrong to examine the state's insurance companies and make recommendations for regulatory reform. With the legal assistance of future U.S. Supreme Court Chief Justice Charles Evans Hughes, the Armstrong Committee heard testimony from the industry's most powerful executives, including John A. McCall.

The Armstrong Committee found New-York Life free from many of the abuses common in other companies, but it also recommended curbing the practices that had pushed the industry's expansion since the Civil War. In 1906, New York outlawed the sale of tontine policies, prohibited excessive commissions for agents, and limited the amount of new business a company could do each year. Company officers actively lobbied for revision of these laws. Under the vocal leadership of Darwin Kingsley, who had become president in 1907, the company achieved some success in having its new business ceiling increased and agent incentives reinstated later in the decade.

New-York Life prepared early for World War I, selling securities and borrowing in order to increase cash

reserves and meet wartime obligations. During the war, the company also issued war-risk policies. The war's greatest challenges came in its aftershocks. The worldwide influenza epidemic of 1918 and 1919 hit the United States with unexpected ferocity: Death claims resulted in a $10 million loss for the company, almost twice the cost of benefits paid during the war.

During the Russian Revolution of 1917, the company's assets in Moscow were seized. Soon afterward, New York Life began its withdrawal from Europe, a reaction to unfriendly regulation and a volatile world economy.

The company's assets were not involved in the stock market crash in October 1929 because state regulation and conservative planning had kept New York Life investments out of common stocks and in more secure government bonds and real estate. New York Life moved into its current corporate headquarters on Madison Avenue in New York City in 1929. The move represented the company's entry into a modern era of closer ties to the nation's economy and diversification into new financial markets. The company weathered the Great Depression and became an important source of capital in the cash-short economy. Its greatest losses during the Depression were in the form of lapsed payments and canceled policies, a trend finally reversed by the booming wartime economy of the 1940s.

INDUSTRY ON THE RISE: FIFTIES TO SEVENTIES

Wartime production and the postwar baby boom revived the insurance industry, and New York Life tailored its products and investments to take advantage of these economic and demographic changes. With the development of group insurance in the first half of the 20th century and the passage of the federal Social Security Act in 1935, people began to buy insurance less for its one-time benefit to surviving family members and more for its lifelong investment security. New York Life introduced its first group insurance policies in 1951 and expanded its coverage in group and personal policies to include accidents and sickness as well as death. Two years later, it offered the employee protection plan, a combination of individual life and group sickness coverage designed for small businesses. The success of its group plans sustained New York Life's remarkable growth in the decades following World War II.

Recognizing the need for housing in the postwar nation, New York Life began moving its assets out of wartime government securities and into real estate development in the late 1940s. The company established a mortgage-loan program for veterans in 1946 and also invested in residential housing developments in Queens and Manhattan, New York, as well as in Chicago and Princeton, New Jersey, during the 1940s and 1950s. In 1969, it established the Nautilus Realty Corporation to handle its commercial and residential real estate operations, which proved to be of increasing importance as inflation in the 1970s and 1980s made other investments less desirable.

In the 1960s, New York Life introduced the family insurance plan, a policy of comprehensive family coverage. When economic recession and inflation caused the lapse rate on new policies to increase in the early 1970s, the company created an insurance conservation office to study ways of better serving, and thus keeping, customers. The introduction of its Series 78 policies in 1978 made conversion between short-term and life policies more flexible for investment purposes and reduced premiums for women, who were buying an increasing percentage of the company's personal policies. Further innovations included a widening variety of annuities, cost-of-living adjustments in benefits, and the sale of mutual funds. New York Life also expanded its business offerings in the 1970s. In 1974, the company created a pension department and began selling employee protection insurance, a policy plan popular with small businesses. In the 1970s alone, New York Life's group insurance sales increased by 152 percent.

DIVERSIFICATION AND INTERNATIONAL EXPANSION: EIGHTIES

Inflation and high interest rates in the early 1980s hurt New York Life's new business sales and reduced its reserves, as policyholders borrowed against their policies for cheap credit. The company quickly adapted to these circumstances by taking advantage of deregulation in the financial services industry. In early 1984, it acquired MacKay-Shields Financial Corporation, and two years later the company began marketing its own MainStay mutual funds through this new subsidiary. The company also expanded its annuity business through its subsidiary New York Life Insurance and Annuity Corporation. In 1986, the company introduced NYLIFE as a new brand name for its financial products, differentiating this growing business from its traditional life insurance policies.

Another major growth area for New York Life during the 1980s was health care. The spiraling cost of medical care in the 1970s and 1980s strengthened the appeal of insurance as a security against long-term illness. In 1987, New York Life purchased controlling interest in Sanus Corporation Health Systems, one of the largest health care companies in the nation. At the time, New York Life's greatest concern in the health care field was AIDS. In the late 1980s, New York Life became one of the most visible promoters of AIDS awareness in New York City as well as a generous supporter of the American Foundation for AIDS Research. The company opposed anti-testing laws introduced in various states, arguing that testing for the AIDS virus was a necessary step in assessing the risks involved in new policies.

New York Life's diversification into real estate development, mutual funds, partnership investments, annuities and pensions, and health care preserved its consistent market position and prepared the firm to take advantage of expanding demand for these new products in the decade to come. The company also entered the international life insurance field in 1988 under the name New York Life Worldwide Ltd., incorporated in Bermuda and established in Hong Kong after the company acquired a life insurance firm there. New York Life Worldwide ultimately became a subsidiary of New York Life International, LLC, the international arm of New York Life.

REACTING TO CHANGING MARKETPLACES: NINETIES

New York Life expanded its international footprint in Asia in 1992. The company established the joint venture New York Life Insurance Ltd. (later wholly owned) in South Korea and also set up New York Life Insurance Taiwan Corporation. The latter firm was expanded to include more than 30 offices and became one of the leading international subsidiaries for New York Life.

New York Life also reorganized its management structure in 1992. As a result, a team of specialists from areas such as actuarial, legal, marketing, and service led by a product manager could move new offerings through the pipeline and out into the market more quickly than in the past. In 1993, New York Life rolled out a variable annuity policy and in 1994 its first variable universal life policy. To tap into a market of more conservative investors, the company began selling a variable annuity product through the banking system in 1995. Bank sales channels had grabbed 25 percent of the annuity market, and New York Life deviated from its traditional agent sales system to take advantage of the trend.

New York Life merged its group health division with its managed care provider (Sanus) to create NYL-Care in 1995. The consolidation brought together a mixture of health care products, including indemnity coverage and preferred-provider and health maintenance organization (HMO) plans. An estimated 3.5 million people, through a network of about 175,000 physicians and more than 2,200 hospitals, were expected to be served.

Problems with the company's limited partnerships prompted New York Life to exit that business in 1996. A majority of its holdings were involved in poorly performing oil and gas deals. The company decided to fully reimburse all investors as part of a class-action lawsuit settlement.

CHANGES IN MANAGEMENT AND EVOLUTION OF THE INDUSTRY AT CENTURY'S END

Sy Sternberg moved up to chairman and chief executive officer in 1997, succeeding Harry G. Hohn. A 40-year veteran with the company, Hohn had led New York Life since 1990. Sternberg said in a March 1997 press release, "Under Harry Hohn's direction, New York Life has successfully diversified and grown into a *Fortune* 100 company with over $18 billion in annual revenues. In addition to his legacy of financial strength, he has left a company with a reputation for integrity and for putting the customer first. He has left a solid foundation upon which we can build with confidence."

New York Life sold its NYLCare Health Plans subsidiary in 1998. Aetna Inc. purchased the operation for $1.05 billion in cash, money which New York Life planned to use to bolster its core life insurance, annuities, and asset management segments. The company planned to purchase established businesses both at home and abroad. At the time, New York Life was the fourth-largest U.S. life insurance company, as ranked by assets, and the second-largest writer of new life insurance premiums. Holding $17 billion in assets under management, the company's MainStay Funds ranked among the top 50 fund families.

Two major decisions about the company's long-term future arose early in Sternberg's tenure. In the late 1990s, New York Life became one of several life insurance carriers that backed legislation which would have allowed insurance companies to demutualize into a corporate structure dubbed a mutual holding company (MHC). The bill was defeated, but at the time, Sternberg was a strong advocate of its passage. Ultimately, several major insurers demutualized and went public, coveting the revenue-raising potential such a move would bring, especially at a time of industry consolidation. After he backed the MHC bill, Sternberg and the company took an about-face and decided that the company's mutualization was a strength, and New York Life actively began marketing its mutuality to differentiate the company from firms going public.

Moreover, New York Life had a well-recognized brand, was strongly capitalized, and had a well-seasoned career agency insurance delivery system, all characteristics which differentiated it from some other firms looking to benefit from demutualization.

New York Life also faced the question of how best to expand its cash flow and grow the company while maintaining its mutuality. Ultimately, while it would broaden its product line for the domestic market, the company decided to pursue an international expansion strategy. That stratagem focused initially on select markets in Asia and Latin America, markets within developing economies with underdeveloped insurance industries in locales where profit margins could be higher than in the United States.

OPENING THE 21ST CENTURY: INTERNATIONAL EXPANSION AND REORGANIZATION OF ASSETS

New York Life opened the new century with its first major thrust into the emerging Latin American market and with further expansion into Asia. New York Life acquired, for about $570 million, the Mexico-based Seguros Monterrey Aetna, the third-largest life insurer in Mexico at the time. Seguros held 23 percent of the individual life market in its territory, but less than 2 percent of the Mexican population purchased life insurance products, leaving room for market development. The acquisition was combined with the company's fledgling south-of-the-border life insurance operation to form Seguros Monterrey New York Life, S.A., a firm that soon became Mexico's leading life insurance sales agency. New York Life entered Thailand in 2000 through acquisition of the sizable Siam Commercial Life Assurance Company. The firm was renamed Siam Commercial New York Life and ultimately expanded to include 27 branches.

New York Life aligned all of its assets managed under one roof in 2000 through the creation of the subsidiary New York Life Asset Management. The reorganization brought $130 million in assets together from several company businesses: MacKay Shields LLC; Madison Square Advisors LLC; MainStay Management LLC; New York Life Benefit Services LLC; Stable Value; and New York Life's real estate and securities operations. New York Life followed a trend in the insurance industry, distancing its financial products from traditional insurance products, in order to improve its competitive strength. The move also protected the parent company from financial liabilities and in turn gave the smaller operation more flexibility.

New York Life reached a record net income of $1.2 billion in 2000. The strong showing translated to the largest ever dividend distribution for policyholders to that time, an estimated $1.46 billion slated for 2001. The international business more than doubled operating revenue to $1.2 billion.

LEGAL ISSUES, MAJOR CLAIMS, AND MARKET DEVELOPMENT

In 2001, 10 of its former agents sued New York Life, claiming the company defrauded 10,000 agents of their health insurance and retirement benefits and wrongfully fired 1,300 employees in order to dodge federal retirement laws. A federal judge quickly dismissed the suit's federal racketeering charges but ruled the trial could go ahead with other claims. That same year, a matter related to the company's long-dissolved European operation was finally resolved. New York Life settled claims with the survivors of ethnic Armenians killed by Turkish soldiers during World War I. A 1999 class-action lawsuit led to legislation allowing Armenians living in California to pursue claims against insurers for unpaid benefits.

Not much later, New York Life faced an onslaught of life insurance claims related to an act of terrorism: the destruction of the World Trade Center in New York on September 11, 2001. The nation's insurers, including New York Life, relaxed claims processing procedures in light of the absence of death certificates for those still missing in the rubble. Testifying before the House Financial Services Committee, Sternberg said, "This is a time for the insurance industry to be visible. This is a time for us to be charitable. And this is a time for us to stand as a pillar of stability in a none-too-stable world." He also acknowledged that the insurance industry, a major investor in U.S. businesses, could be negatively affected by any long-term economic downturn brought on by the terrorist attacks.

On the domestic front, Sternberg cut costs in the main life insurance and annuity line but also added new products such as long-term care. In late 2001, New York Life launched a large-scale internal Web project designed to create a virtual library and database for New York Life's agents and other employees. As New York Life pumped capital and resources into overseas operations during the early 2000s, it enhanced its agent sales activities as well, supplementing its career agency system with a system of brokers acting as independent agents and selling to high-end corporate clients.

However, New York Life's clear push in the early 2000s was to further expand its footprint overseas. The company entered India in 2001 through the joint venture Max New York Life Insurance Company, Ltd., formed with Max India Ltd. Max New York Life opened concurrently in eight cities, becoming the first newly government licensed private insurer to operate nationally in India. New York Life entered China in 2002 through a joint venture operation, the Shanghai-based Haier New York Life. The venture also set up representative offices in Beijing, Chengdu, and Guangzhou. By 2002, New York Life had moved into not only Hong Kong, Taiwan, South Korea, Mexico, Thailand, and India, but also China and Argentina. In the process, New York Life had spent $800 million over four years to build operations in Asia and Latin America.

RECORD PROFITS AND LEGAL SETTLEMENTS

New York Life continued to post record numbers in 2002 despite recessionary conditions on its home turf. Domestic sales of life insurance jumped more than 40 percent (the largest leap in written premiums by any life insurer that year) as net income rose nearly 25 percent to $1 billion. International sales nearly kept pace, rising more than 30 percent in the first year New York Life's international business earned a profit.

New York Life management did not expect such phenomenal growth on an ongoing basis. For one, the traditional domestic life industry because of demutualization was consolidating and projected by some analysts to shrink. The company also had to closely monitor overseas operations as political and economic changes could occur quickly and affect the bottom line. For example, New York Life in the early 2000s pulled back on Taiwan activities because low interest rates there kept profit margins low. Nonetheless, Sternberg was dedicated to the international business, believing that domestic growth rates would level off and that true double-digit long-term growth would have to come from select markets overseas in Asia and Latin America. To help fund international expansion, New York Life in 2002 generated $1 billion through surplus notes, bringing the company's statutory capital to more than $10 billion by 2003.

In 2003, the company's asset-management arm, New York Life Investment Management (NYLIM, formerly New York Life Asset Management), launched two hedge funds, a global macro fund and a long/short equity fund with as much as $50 million dedicated to each. The equity hedge fund was run by Q.E.D. Investments Group and the fixed income fund by MacKay Shields, both arms of NYLIM. In 2003, sales roles more than 250 percent to $292 million, up from $115 million a year earlier.

New York Life settled two costly legal disputes in 2004. The company agreed to make benefits available to agents who had in 2001 claimed they were denied benefits (stemming from their 2001 lawsuit), cut the agents' tax burden, and paid benefits through a tax-qualified program as well as contribute upward of $16 million (the final settlement was $14 million) to a fund for pension benefits of 3,000 former agents. The company also settled a dispute with African-American policyholders related to a period from 1920 through 1948. African Americans had claimed that New York Life charged them higher premiums than white policyholders. The company apologized for what it claimed was standard practice of the time and agreed to refund as much as $10 million to policyholders and their families who were owners of endowment policies. Endowment polices, later eliminated by the company, were a type of life contract that repaid premiums plus interest at the end of policy terms.

POPULARITY OF CONSUMER WEB SITE AND ANNUITY PRODUCT

New York Life's Web site became the consumer's favorite in late 2004, as tracked quarterly by Dalbar, Inc. By 2005, the company's site had solidified that top spot after putting together several consecutive quarters of first-place rankings. The Web site's popularity was due in part to its ease of use and an improved agent-locator utility, as well as a user quiz and video testimonials. Subsequent developments to the Web site included user options to provide feedback in real time and rate the site's information. The site late in the decade was also made visually-impaired accessible, able to read aloud Web content at the push of a button.

A New York Life attorney resigned in 2006 after it was learned he never had been licensed to practice law. The employee, Michael Watson, had been with the firm since 1996. He had been promoted in 2005 to first vice president and deputy general counsel in the legal department concerned with acquisitions, investments, and mergers.

In 2006, New York Life launched a retirement annuity under the brand name Guaranteed Lifetime Income, which soon made the company the leading seller of such a product. That same year, the insurer conducted a mock test of its asset evaluation and cash surplus. This was done to test its cash flow resilience in the event of three catastrophic situations: a pandemic, a drop of 40 percent in the stock market, and a low interest rate lasting a decade or more. Company analysis of the test revealed New York Life had more than adequate liquidity and surplus to withstand any or all of the catastrophes simultaneously and still have solid capital levels.

FISCAL DISCIPLINE, MANAGEMENT CHANGES, AND SUPERIOR CREDIT RATINGS

In February 2007, New York Life made a timely change in its investment strategy just before the global economy began to sour and the related credit crisis became evident to the general populace. Believing that the markets reflected irrational activity, New York Life transferred much of its cash flow into more dependable U.S. Treasury bonds. The transfer occurred just before mortgage defaults became endemic and the company's competitors' cash flow began to dry up. New York Life's move to Treasury bonds proved to be one of foresight. In August 2007, Standard & Poor's upped New York Life's financial strength rating one level to AAA, the highest possible rating, and also upgraded New York Life Insurance and Annuity's rating to the same level. The upgrade meant that cumulatively the company held the highest possible ranking from all four major credit rating agencies, a status matched only by two other life insurance firms. The Standard & Poor's upgrade was based in part on the fact that the company had $14.7 billion in surplus and asset reserves and that 2006 annual earnings had jumped 17 percent to $1.1 billion based on double-digit growth of revenues, rising to $12.3 billion.

Management changes at the top of New York Life in 2007 and 2008 left a young Theodore (Ted) Mathas clearly at the helm. In 2007, Frederick J. Sievert, who had been president of the company since 2002, retired and was succeeded by Mathas. In 2008, Sternberg retired, and Mathas became New York Life chief executive, as well as chairman, while retaining his post as president. Mathas, at the age of 40, became the youngest CEO of a major financial services firm. Before serving as president, Mathas headed asset management and brokerage arms of New York Life and helped lead the U.S. insurance operations. Sternberg's retirement came after he had steered New York Life for 11 years to a position of unprecedented financial strength (growing the company's surplus from $6.5 billion to $14 billion) and navigated the insurer through decisions over demutualization and international expansion as well as through legal hurdles and the recession beginning midyear and stretching through the end of the decade. The company had become, said Sternberg at the time of his retirement, "a domestic company with international operations, not an international company with domestic operations. You won't see us trying to become another AIG."

In 2009, A.M. Best Company revised New York Life's credit outlook from stable to negative based on losses related to equity investments and fixed-income credit in addition to the potential for future losses on company investments. New York Life continued to maintain its superior rating in terms of its financial strength. A.M. Best observed the company's very solid market position, its creditworthiness, and its capitalization, as well as its consistent strong revenue growth and earnings.

New York Life closed the decade earning $1.22 billion on revenues of $14.38 billion in 2009; it also recorded $286.9 billion of assets under management. New York Life continued to maintain its superior ratings from the four major credit rating agencies. In addition, *Fortune* magazine in early 2010 rated New York Life the leading life insurer in the United States and the most admired insurance company in the world, the latter as ranked by industry analysts, directors, and executives. The company was also ranked 64th on the *Fortune* 500. New York Life's continued profitability and favorable recognition from the industry came at a time when other insurers found their credit ratings and sales falling.

GROWING INTERNATIONALLY AND LEADING THE U.S. INDUSTRY

Despite the global recession at the end of the first decade, New York Life had made market-share inroads in most of its international locations by the end of the decade. International business accounted for about 25 percent of the company's new sales and about 10 percent of total revenues. However, because of the cost of doing business abroad, international business accounted for only about 2 percent of New York Life earnings. Company projections, however, suggested international revenues could grow to as much as 25 percent of all company sales during the oncoming decade and 15 percent of total earnings within the first five years of that decade. To enhance sales in India, in May 2010, New York Life Max and one of India's largest banks, Axis Bank, signed a deal in which Axis would market New York Life products for a 10-year period. Axis Bank became one of several international distribution channels used by the company. The company was also selling life insurance through the leading Thailand bank, job sites in Mexico, and telemarketing channels in Taiwan.

Just as the company's principal product line continued to be life insurance, the company continued to tout its mutuality as the best structure for a life insurance company, given that it owed nothing to shareholders and worked for policyholders alone. New York Life viewed its mutuality as a long-term benefit for the company and its customers. It believed its capital

structure was strong and could afford to remain a mutual company. While Sternberg looked to international sales as the source of future revenue growth for the company, Mathas believed that there existed substantial opportunities for annuity sales to aging domestic customers desiring new sources of income. Both would likely prove to be substantial revenue sources in the 2010s.

As it moved into the new decade, New York Life appeared well positioned to weather further global economic downturns. The company's decade-old international business was taking advantage of local distribution channels and making a profit, and New York Life was targeting as it had in the past current markets, as in retirement annuities, to generate revenues. The company's strength continued to be its well-funded cash surplus, which had consistently grown throughout the previous decade.

Timothy J. Shannon
Updated, Kathleen Peippo; Roger Rouland

PRINCIPAL SUBSIDIARIES

New York Life International, LLC; NYLife Securities LLC; New York Life Investment Management LLC; Seguros Monterrey New York Life, S.A. (Mexico); Haier New York Life (China); New York Life Insurance Worldwide Ltd. (Hong Kong); Max New York Life Insurance Company Ltd. (India); New York Life Insurance Ltd. (South Korea); New York Life Insurance Taiwan Corporation; Siam Commercial New York Life Insurance Public Company Limited.

PRINCIPAL COMPETITORS

Massachusetts Mutual Life Insurance Company; MetLife, Inc.; The Northwestern Mutual Life Insurance Company; Prudential Financial, Inc.; TIAA-CREF.

FURTHER READING

Abbott, Lawrence F., *The Story of NYLIC*, New York: New York Life Insurance Company, 1930.

Ackermann, Matt, "New York Life Gets Top Grade from S&P," *American Banker*, August 20, 2007, p. 6.

————, "N.Y. Life Relaunches Asset Unit," *American Banker*, October 26, 2000, p. 7.

"A.M. Best Revises Outlook to Negative for Issuer Credit Ratings of New York Life; Affirms Financial Strength Rating," *Health & Beauty Close-Up*, June 15, 2009.

"Bringing Innovation to Insurance," *Baseline*, July 30, 2008.

Cardona, Mercedes M., "NYLife Modernizes Image; First National Spots in Years Highlight Insurer's New Role in Financial Services," *Crain's New York Business*, March 27, 2000, p. 4.

De Paula, Matthew, "A Building of Trust at Just the Right Time: New York Life's Latest Marketing Effort Breaks a Yearlong Advertising Silence, Putting the Company Back on the Scene Just When Its Message Matters Most to Consumers," *US Banker*, November 1, 2002, p. 28.

Duffy, Shannon P., "New York Life Paying $14 Mil. to End ERISA Suit," *Legal Intelligencer*, March 11, 2008.

Elstein, Aaron, "Keeping Good Company; Young New York Life Veteran Takes Over CEO Post While Insurer's Flying High," *Crain's New York Business*, June 30, 2008, p. 29.

Fraser, Katharine, "N.Y. Life Selling Annuity through Banks," *American Banker*, November 8, 1995, p. 11.

Fritz, Michael, "Thrifty Insurance Companies Plan to Start Their Own Banking Units; Setting Up Thrifts Easier, Cheaper Than Acquiring Commercial Banks," *Crain's New York Business*, March 20, 2000, p. 27.

Hudnut, James M., *Semi-centennial History of the New-York Life Insurance Company*, New York: New-York Life Insurance Company, 1895.

Moore, Kim, "A Global Manifesto: Unlike Most of His Rivals, Sy Sternberg, Chief Executive Officer of New York Life, Is Seeking Long-Term Growth Globally Rather Than by Diversifying into Banking and Securities," *Reactions*, December 23, 2003, p. 18.

"New York Life Gets Vietnam License; AIG Promised General Insurance License," *Reactions* (UK), July 25, 2005, p. 8.

"New York Life Says It's Well-Prepared for a Pandemic," *Health & Beauty Close-Up*, July 12, 2009.

Vardi, Nathan, "Settling a Case—After 85 Years," *Forbes*, May 14, 2001, p. 120.

Wipperfurth, Heike, "Mutually Exclusive; As Rivals Go Public, NY Life Stands Pat; Daring to Give Wall Street the Brush-Off," *Crain's New York Business*, May 7, 2001, p. 1.

The Northwestern Mutual Life Insurance Company

———————————— ■ ————————————

720 East Wisconsin Avenue
Milwaukee, Wisconsin 53202-4797
U.S.A.
Telephone: (414) 271-1444
Fax: (414) 299-7022
Web site: http://www.northwesternmutual.com

Mutual Company
Incorporated: 1857 as Mutual Life Insurance Company
   of the State of Wisconsin
Employees: 7,000
Total Assets: $167.18 billion (2009)
NAICS: 524113 Direct Life Insurance Carrier

■ ■ ■

The Northwestern Mutual Life Insurance Company (NML) is the largest direct provider of individual life insurance in the United States. NML offers life, disability, and long-term care insurance as well as employee benefits and retirement products. The company has $1.2 trillion worth of life insurance protection in force, from which it derives approximately 80 percent of its premium production. With $167 billion in assets, NML supplies various forms of insurance to nearly four million policy owners.

GAINING A CHARTER: 1857

NML began as the entrepreneurial vision of "General" John C. Johnston, of Catskill, New York, who earned his rank as head of the local state militia. In 1850, at age 68, Johnston and his son moved to New York City,

where they became agents in the employ of the Mutual Life Insurance Company of New York. Within three years of their arrival, the Johnstons were operating the company's most successful agency.

In 1854, at age 72, General Johnston sold his interest in the company and moved with his grandson, John H. Johnston, to a 3,000-acre farm near Janesville, Wisconsin. He soon determined that the area would benefit from low-cost, mutual life insurance. Consequently, with a petition signed by 36 of the area's leading citizens as the first board of trustees, the state legislature chartered the Mutual Life Insurance Company of the State of Wisconsin on March 2, 1857. Explicitly modeled on the New York company, it was to be headquartered in Janesville and to limit its investments to mortgages on Wisconsin real estate and government bonds. Its first policy contracts were issued on November 25, 1858. Johnston never served as president but was a general agent.

When many of the original trustees left the company, their places were taken by men from Milwaukee, Wisconsin, eager to obtain control of the company. Following the legislature's revocation of the provision requiring a Janesville headquarters, the trustees voted on March 7, 1859, to move the company to Milwaukee. Johnston had lost control of the company and terminated his association as an agent on March 11, 1859.

The Milwaukee group elected as president Samuel S. Daggett, formerly of the Milwaukee Mutual Fire Insurance Company. The company's only full-time employee was the secretary, Amherst W. Kellogg. Since

COMPANY PERSPECTIVES

Northwestern Mutual's mission is to develop life-long relationships with clients founded on sound guidance and expert solutions, backed by the company's exceptional financial strength and the promise we make to be there for policyowners when their financial security is put to the test. As a mutual company with no shareholders, Northwestern Mutual seeks to share its gains with policyowners and deliver consistent, long-term value to clients.

trustees met quarterly and the officers were part time, the trustees established an executive committee of five trustees in June 1859, including the president and vice president as ex officio members. This step marked the beginning of the committee system which, despite some recent modifications, became the most conspicuous feature of the company's managerial organization.

FIRST GEOGRAPHIC EXPANSION: 1859

Like any fledgling insurance company, there was a need to increase sales, and a sales force was established under a general agency system. In 1859, when the first out-of-state contract was made in Minnesota's St. Paul-Minneapolis area, the company began to expand beyond Wisconsin. In 1860, the first out-of-state local agency was appointed, in Iowa. By 1867, the company had expanded its mortgage holdings beyond Wisconsin, although its principal holdings were still Wisconsin, primarily Milwaukee, real estate. To reflect the fact that the company was becoming a regional institution, it changed its name in 1865 to Northwestern Mutual Life Insurance Company. At that time, "Northwest" described the states now in the Midwest. When Samuel Daggett died in 1868, the company he helped nurture had passed through its formative years.

The search for a successor to Daggett led to the most serious power struggle in NML's history. The pivotal figure was Heber Smith, the superintendent of agents. By collecting proxies from the policyholders, Smith helped elect Lester Sexton as the new president in 1869. When Sexton died after two months in office, John H. Van Dyke, a young lawyer, was elected to replace him. Smith, who was elected vice president, believed that individuals seeking loans had to purchase policies. The issue was trusteeship, whether funds should be invested on a criterion other than that of obtaining

the highest yield consistent with safety. After the Panic of 1873, the board of trustees wanted to exercise its judgment over loans, and in 1874, Henry L. Palmer, a lawyer and one of the original group of Milwaukee investors, was elected president. Palmer would remain president for 34 years.

The agents were not left voiceless. An association of agents had been created in 1868, but was inactive for several years. It was revived in 1877 and served as a forum unique to the life insurance industry at which field agents discussed problems of mutual interest and maintained communication with the home office. A year later the company hired salaried loan agents, effectively separating the selling of insurance from the lending of funds. In 1887 a finance committee was established to focus exclusively on financial and investment questions. It was created to ease the burden on the executive committee, but its membership duplicated most of the important personnel.

NML AND ITS INDUSTRY MATURE: 1881–1915

In 1881 NML created the insurance and agency committee with general responsibility for all phases of the insurance program. From that point until 1900, the life insurance industry was one of the fastest-growing industries in the United States. Many new types of contracts were introduced by companies aggressively competing for sales. NML approached most of these new developments with its traditional conservatism.

NML established an inquiry department in 1878 to cope with a problem inherent in insurance sales, "moral hazard," namely, that persons most likely to submit claims would be those most likely to demand policies. Health examinations and character checks were required for each applicant. The company restricted itself only to the "healthiest" regions of the country, those that did not have high mortality rates. By 1907, the company's sales agencies were closely integrated with Northwestern's overall management policies. Management also attempted to be more responsive to the policyholders by establishing a policyholders examining committee in 1907 which annually evaluated everything from the company's accounting practices to managerial performance.

The growth of sales and development of new types of policies led to abuses in the industry. The 1905 Armstrong Committee investigation in New York, aimed at the three largest companies in that state, provoked a similar investigation by the Wisconsin legislature targeting NML. While the Armstrong hearings discovered considerable concentration of control at the top, NML

standards, simplicity of operation, and conservative investments.

A FOCUS ON LIFE INSURANCE: 1910–29

When Palmer stepped down in 1908, he had established a managerial succession that made George C. Markham the obvious choice. In the wake of the Armstrong investigation, insurance markets began to change. Group insurance and disability and double indemnity clauses were started at this time, but NML's management refused to adopt any of these innovations. Markham's administration was not market-oriented. It was preoccupied with investment problems. Many disability clauses were later proved unsound. In 1909, the company took the lead in the new field of business life insurance for partners and for key personnel. Nevertheless, agent dissatisfaction developed because the company would not enter new areas such as disability and group insurance. NML found itself developing into a specialty company by limiting its policies to individual life insurance.

When NML moved to Milwaukee, it occupied offices near the corner of Broadway and Wisconsin. It had outgrown several offices since then, but its new ones were never more than a block away. In 1910, it purchased a city block at the east end of Wisconsin, four blocks away. True to its conservatism, NML built a "Roman temple" in an age of skyscrapers. When the new building was occupied in 1914, the company became more compartmentalized. The sense of personalism that had characterized the days when executive and clerk worked side-by-side were gone. The fact that the new cafeteria offered free lunch on a daily basis was little compensation. During World War I, NML followed the practice of the insurance industry in adding a "war-risk" clause to policies, resulting in increased premium costs for servicemen. At the same time, the federal government provided life insurance policies to men in service.

William D. Van Dyke, whose father had been president in the 1870s, replaced Markham in 1919. Van Dyke, a lawyer, was an investment specialist, an important talent during the 13 years he served as president. By 1919, NML was the sixth-largest U.S. life insurance company and the leading farm mortgage lender among life companies. Since farm conditions were poor in the 1920s, the company began to explore other possibilities. NML led the field in the move toward larger loans, and, after 1925, increased its urban loans. In spite of a decline in the value of its large holdings of railroad securities and its hesitancy to invest in

was found to have a relatively large group of self-perpetuating managers.

The rivalries that existed between the heads of the New York companies led to such practices as twisting (use of misrepresentation to have someone end one life insurance policy and buy another) and rebating (return of part of a premium payment) in the attempt to increase sales. Even though NML condemned and canceled agents found guilty of these practices, the legislature found examples. Similarly, the Armstrong investigation strongly criticized deferred dividend policies. NML dropped these policies before that investigation was underway, but the Wisconsin legislature echoed the New York findings.

Lastly, the Armstrong investigation was concerned that the sales of the New York companies were too large to be absorbed by the mortgage market. On the other hand, the Wisconsin legislature found NML's conservative financial policies to be excellent. What was disappointing to the legislature was the relatively small portion of the company's portfolio invested in its home state. The largest state for investment was Illinois, where the growing Chicago real estate market absorbed over a third of the company's loans until 1907, and a quarter of the loans thereafter. The Wisconsin investigation led to an attempt to legislate the principle of trusteeship that NML tried to follow. Many of the unworkable laws were repealed or amended in 1915. NML came through this difficult period relatively unscathed because of the three principles its president, Henry Palmer, instilled into the corporate character: conservative underwriting

the expanding utility field, NML's rate of earnings was superior to that of other life companies.

During the 1920s the companies with the greatest sales growth were those with two or more lines of contracts, such as group and ordinary life or life and health insurance. NML made only modest changes in policy contracts and investment plans, and continued to grow. Its expanding operations required the construction of an addition to the home office in 1932.

The absence of diversification led to agent unhappiness. While the sales department was in the vanguard of the industry in preparing agents to sell to the needs of prospects, there was little effective coordination between the underwriting and sales departments. Michael Cleary, vice president since 1919, moved to improve the company's relations with agents.

THE GREAT DEPRESSION AND WORLD WAR II

With the Great Depression in 1929, the problems facing the company's investment and operations policies became as grave as those facing the underwriting and marketing programs. Shortly after the stock market crash, NML acquired a large amount of real estate due to foreclosures on farms and railroads.

As the Depression worsened, policyholders began to demand cash. In response to the outflow of funds, NML made several changes to its products to improve their marketability. In 1933, women were accepted as risks for the first time in 58 years, but they were limited to half the insurance a man could purchase. Age limits were generally lowered, and a new family-income plan was adopted.

Van Dyke died in 1932, and the company was without a president for four months until Michael Cleary was selected. Cleary's good relations with those in the field soon expanded to include those in the home office. He helped maintain morale during a difficult time for the life insurance industry. The need for additional personnel to help with these tasks meant that the agency force increased between 1929 and 1933.

In 1938 the federal government began another investigation of the insurance industry. The Temporary National Economic Committee called numerous executives to Washington, then echoed many of the complaints of the Armstrong Committee. NML emerged with an enhanced reputation for corporate ethics, service to its policyholders, and honesty in its policies and practices.

With the advent of World War II, the war-risk clause was added to policies sold after October 1940.

The clause went into effect two weeks after the bombing of Pearl Harbor on December 7, 1941.

Cleary suffered a fatal heart attack in 1947 and was replaced by Edmund Fitzgerald, who had first joined NML in 1932 as a part-time employee. Fitzgerald's name would later be borne by one of the company's largest and most famous investments, the Great Lakes freighter that sank in Lake Superior in 1975.

FALLING BEHIND: 1945–65

Home office expenses rose to double premium income between 1946 and 1954. Under Fitzgerald, an administrative restructuring with additional specialized service and research functions was completed by 1955. NML began to computerize its operations in the late 1950s, cutting costs, improving service, and delaying the need for a new building. Fitzgerald needed to increase the yield on NML's portfolio. In 1933 NML had the second-largest mortgage account among the major firms. It was the second lowest by 1947. NML had the smallest stocks and bonds portfolio in 1933, and the third largest by 1947. By 1955, the company ranked fifth in mortgage holdings, and its holdings of private securities had increased relative to the public bonds it purchased during World War II.

By not diversifying, NML had not kept up with its rivals, and its relative position within the industry was falling. The decision to remain an individual, select-risk insurer, however, was made to maximize safety. NML attempted to meet the market conditions of the postwar era with the same methods which had proved successful in the past. The agency system was improved. A "short course" for agents had been introduced in 1935, and sophisticated agent training commenced following the war.

More advanced training was left to various Chartered Life Underwriter (CLU) programs, and NML had the highest proportion of CLUs on its staff of all the major companies. The CLU designation was granted by the American College of Life Underwriters to individuals who had successfully completed the college's battery of courses on economics and insurance. Recruitment was difficult in the postwar years. Although agent income was high due to postwar prosperity, alternative employment outside the life insurance industry provided a great deal of competition.

Fitzgerald led the company into a greater involvement with national organizations and national issues, ending the company's historical isolation. NML became more involved in its home city, Milwaukee. When Fitzgerald retired in 1958, his successors, Donald Slichter, who became president that year, and Robert Dineen, who followed him in 1965, continued on the path of stable growth and selective change.

Competition forced NML to introduce products that it had resisted for years. In 1956 it took on some substandard risks. These risks occurred in a population less healthy than those included in the actuarial calculations for insurance premiums. Because substandard risks were excluded from the calculations for normal premiums, persons in the less-healthy group had to pay an additional premium. The company's version of double indemnity was introduced in 1959. Another area pursued was the pension trust business. Initiated by agents in 1938, these trusts involved large numbers of individual policies for employees of corporations. Such trusts were costly to service, cumbersome to administer, difficult to protect from the competition, and similar to group insurance. Eventually, this business was lost because of the company's refusal to rewrite them as a single group policy. On the other hand, the insurance service account introduced to the industry in 1962 was a particularly effective innovation. Customers with multiple policies could remit a monthly payment covering all policies rather than receive an annual bill for each policy.

DIVERSIFICATION AND REORGANIZATION: 1967–81

In 1967, Francis Ferguson was elected president of "the sleeping giant," as the company was described in the industry, "the most stubbornly traditional of the top ten" companies, according to John Gunda's *The Quiet Company*. A corporate reorganization from vertical to horizontal was accomplished by 1968, with departments realigned by groups. Ferguson introduced the concept of strategic planning, which, in the 1980s, turned NML from a product- to a market-driven company. He introduced extra ordinary life in 1968, which replaced whole life as the company's most popular product within a year, because it helped counter the negative effect of inflation on whole life policies.

As the Depression-era employees began to give way to those from the baby boom generation, a desire to grow and to innovate was felt within the company. Bonuses were introduced as an incentive to agency growth, and, finally, NML decided to market its products more aggressively. It purchased a share of the commercial time on the broadcasts of the 1972 Olympic Games and introduced its corporate slogan, "The Quiet Company." The sleeping giant had awakened.

The company's investments also became more visible, particularly in the form of the Great Lakes freighter the *Edmund Fitzgerald*. Other notable investments included major real estate ventures and energy exploration. An addition to the home office, Northwestern Mutual Place, was completed in 1981.

In 1980, Ferguson became chairman of the board and Donald Schuenke was elected president. Together they presided over a transformation of NML. The company, shifting from its historic specialist role, began to diversify. All previous product innovations had been risk-based on individual lives. In 1982, NML made its initial move in the direction of group and health insurance by acquiring Standard of America Life Insurance Company. That same year, non-annuity investment products and fee-based services were added when NML acquired Robert W. Baird & Company, Wisconsin's largest investment-banking organization.

NML STICKS TO ITS GUNS: 1981–89

The 1980s brought a number of challenges for insurance companies in general. The federal government, contemplating a tax on the cash value of life insurance policies, prompted insurers to spend more time and money fighting such proposals. Interest rates climbed, in the early 1980s, reducing the appeal of their fixed return policies. In addition, the nation was hit by the AIDS crisis and its related costs and controversies.

Even as the 1980s brought significant change, much remained familiar, including free lunches in the company's cafeteria, a tradition since 1915. Despite diversification, NML's primary attention remained largely on its traditional individual life policies. "The Quiet Company," NML's corporate slogan, emphasized that it put the policyholder first. It ranked first in dividend performance more often between 1940 and 1990 than any other company.

The belief in the equal treatment of all policyholders, fiscal conservatism, an insistence on efficiency, and the adherence to excellence continued to guide NML as competitors launched newer, flashier products. A case in point was universal life, a product offered in response to plummeting whole-life sales during the early 1980s interest rate hike. NML refused to offer it, believing the product was not in the long-term interests of customers or the company. "Though Northwestern Mutual agents were eaten alive by the competition, they held tight for almost six years before the company released a new product that could compete with universal life without sacrificing the company's values," wrote Leslie Werstein Hann for *Best's Review*. Some universal life sellers were later sued when the product did not perform as promised.

By the end of the decade, NML's policyholders numbered more than two million. Its $28.5 billion in assets ranked it as the nation's 10th-largest life insurance company, with over $200 billion insurance in force, 7,000 agents associated with over 100 general agencies, and almost 300 district agencies representing the company in every state of the union. Investment operations were conducted out of the home office and 13 real estate investment field offices located throughout the country. Schuenke became chairman, and James Ericson was elected NML's 15th president in 1989.

MARKETING ADJUSTMENTS: 1991–99

An investment made back in the mid-1980s began reaping rewards as the new decade began. In 1985, NML put $250 million into MGIC Investment Corp., a mortgage insurance company hit hard by defaults in the oil-producing states. The company continued to bleed over the next several years, and NML began to sweat a bit. Finally, in 1989, MGIC turned a profit, and two years later NML reduced its holdings to 68 percent from 95 percent through an eight million share stock offering. A second offering followed in 1992, and MGIC stock split two-for-one in 1993. MGIC's 1994 net income hit $159 million, and the business ranked second among mortgage insurers in terms of market share. By 1995 NML had pared its holdings down to 20 percent and planned to sell an additional 10 percent. Ultimately, the initial $250 million investment deal produced more than $1 billion for NML.

While the MGIC investment proved to be stellar, NML had some flies in the ointment. Disability income insurance, their worst-performing product, needed to be turned around. NML got caught up in a "benefits escalating arms race," according to William C. Koenig, an NML executive quoted in *Best's Review*. Moreover, the company had not kept close enough tabs on the costs related to the product line, thus compounding the problem. In 1998, NML revamped the department, raised prices, lowered benefit amounts, and tightened underwriting.

NML's experience with disability insurance prompted some operational changes when the company began developing a long-term care product in 1997. A separate subsidiary was formed and the administration of the product was outsourced, allowing NML to easily evaluate costs, react quickly to regulatory changes, and, if needed, fund growth through issuance of bonds. On January 1, 1999, NML broadened its investment business with the purchase of Frank Russell Co., a privately owned Tacoma, Washington-based investment management and advisory firm.

Frank Russell, operating in more than 30 countries, held approximately $40 billion in assets under management and provided consulting services for more than $1 trillion in client assets. Institutional investors held the 63-year-old company in high regard, and the Russell 2000 was the most widely used benchmark for small cap stocks. The sale, estimated to exceed $1 billion, was considered mutually beneficial. Frank Russell would retain a great deal of independence, while NML would gain a foothold internationally.

DISPLAYING STRENGTH AT THE MILLENNIUM

NML's reputation in its core insurance segment remained solid: named "Most Admired" in its industry for 16 years, according to *Fortune* magazine rankings. An important factor in the company's success was its sales force, considered among the best in the industry. While others in the insurance business had widened their distribution systems, NML stayed the course and emphasized sales force growth and development.

Hann wrote for *Best's Review*, "Northwestern Mutual's agents are among the most productive and financially successful in the life insurance industry." The agents, who based on four-year retention rates stayed with the company longer than average, received no company subsidies or base salaries but relied solely on commissions.

Stock-based ownership was another industry trend NML was loath to follow. Mutual insurance companies Prudential, Metropolitan, and John Hancock were moving toward public ownership. Ericson, president and CEO, told *Best's Review* in 1999 that NML would remain a policyholder owned company unless regulatory requirements or taxation changes forced the move. With that in mind, NML had lobbied the state of Wisconsin to pass legislation allowing mutual insurance companies to convert to a mutual holding company structure.

NML laid the groundwork for a trust company in 2000. True to form, NML continued to take measured steps as other insurance companies raced to expand their services. A loosening of federal regulations had prompted some insurance companies to move quickly into not only trust services but toward full banking capability. NML planned to market its trust services to its own affluent client base and through Frank Russell.

ZORE TAKES THE HELM: 2001

In May 2001, NML President Edward J. Zore stepped up as CEO. His 10-year plan for NML included doubling company assets to $200 billion and increasing personal life's market share to 10 percent from 7.5 percent. He projected Frank Russell Co.'s assets would grow to $400 billion from the existing $66 billion.

Tragically, Zore and other insurance executives soon had to factor in new scenarios as they made their projections for the future. Insurance companies were hard hit by the terrorist attacks against the United States on September 11, 2001. NML was expected to process $150 million in life claims related to the destruction of New York's World Trade Center. NML, like other insurers, did not invoke war-risk exclusions, calling the events an act of terrorism. The company eventually paid $125 million in death benefits to the 157 NML policy owners killed during the attacks.

Under Zore's leadership, NML demonstrated particular strength during its 15th decade of business. In 2002 construction began on the initial phase of an NML campus in Franklin, Wisconsin, a Milwaukee suburb. Corporate headquarters remained in downtown Milwaukee, but to accommodate the company's growing payroll, further space was needed. The first phase of the project included a five-story, 500,000-square-foot office building and a 40,000-square-foot computer data center, a $125 million expansion that was scheduled to be completed in 2004. Long-range plans called for the project to include as many as four buildings with two million square feet of office space.

Zore and management team had ample reasons for the optimism reflected in the scope of the construction project. Of the 1,200 life insurance companies in the United States, NML ranked as the leader in personal life policies, controlling nearly 9 percent of the market. Less than 4 percent of its clients abandoned their policies, an attrition rate that was less than half the industry average. Further good news could be found in the company's diversified, $90 billion investment portfolio, which was steadily increasing in value. Dividends paid to policy owners were increasing as well, nearing $4 billion annually during the first half of the decade, which was far more than any other U.S.-based insurer.

NML TURNS 150: 2007

NML was firing on all cylinders as it progressed toward its 150th anniversary. In early 2007, several months before the occasion was observed by a three-day celebration, the company reached a plateau no other direct provider of life insurance had reached. NML's life insurance policies, which accounted for approximately 80 percent of its premium production, reached the $1 trillion mark. "Reaching $1 trillion is an extraordinary milestone for us, particularly as we prepare to mark our 150th year in business," Zore said in the February 8,

2007 release of *A.M. Best Newswire.*

Company representatives, staff, and family members flocked to Milwaukee for anniversary celebrations in mid-2007. Former U.S. Secretary of State Colin Powell and retired anchorman Dan Rather spoke before attendees. Comedian Jerry Seinfeld supplied the entertainment, joined by musician Sheryl Crow. The grandeur of the festivities befitted the legacy of one of the oldest companies in the United States, observing a tradition of success that continued in the years following NML's 150th anniversary.

In 2008 the company paid more than $5 billion in dividends to participating policy owners, a record high. Despite the economic turmoil that soon swept across the globe, NML continued to shine. Dividends paid to policy owners fell to $4.5 billion in 2009, but the company projected an increase in 2010 to $4.7 billion. The years ahead promised to see one of the titans of the insurance industry continue to add to its remarkable record of success.

Louis P. Cain
Updated, Kathleen Peippo; Jeffrey L. Covell

PRINCIPAL SUBSIDIARIES

Northwestern Long Term Care Insurance Company; Frank Russell Company; Northwestern Mutual Investment Services, LLC; Northwestern Mutual Wealth Management Company; Strategic Employee Benefit Services.

PRINCIPAL COMPETITORS

AIG American General Life Companies; New York Life Insurance Company; Prudential Financial, Inc.

FURTHER READING

De Martini, Thomas, "Northwestern Mutual Reaches $1 Trillion of Individual Life Insurance," *A.M. Best Newswire,* February 8, 2007.

Gallagher, Kathleen, "Milwaukee-Based Financial Company Issues More Shares," *Knight-Ridder/Tribune Business News,* April 11, 2001.

———, "New Chief of Milwaukee-Area Life Insurance Firm Wants to Double Firm's Assets," *Knight-Ridder/Tribune Business News,* July 25, 2001.

Geer, Carolyn T., "Where the CEO's Shop for Insurance: Northwestern's Secret? It's a Mutual," *Fortune,* March 1, 1999, pp. 264+.

Gores, Paul, "Agents to Hear Famous Voices: Rather, Vitale, Powell Help Northwestern Mutual Mark 150th," *Milwaukee Journal Sentinel,* July 23, 2007.

Gurda, John, *The Quiet Company: A Modern History of Northwestern Mutual Life,* Milwaukee: Northwestern Mutual Life Insurance Company, 1983.

Jones, Laflin C., *To Have Seen a Century,* Milwaukee: Northwestern Mutual Life Insurance Company, 1957.

Novozymes A/S

Krogshoejvej 36
Bagsværd, DK-2880
Denmark
Telephone: (+45) 44 46 00 00
Fax: (+45) 44 46 99 99
Web site: http://www.novozymes.com

Public Company
Incorporated: 2000
Employees: 4,993
Sales: DKK 8.49 billion ($1.49 billion) (2009)
Stock Exchanges: Copenhagen
Ticker Symbol: NZYM B
NAICS: 325188 All Other Inorganic Chemical Manu-
   facturing

■ ■ ■

Novozymes A/S is the world's leading producer of enzymes, used in the production of detergents, biofuels, sugars, and many other applications. Other company products include microorganisms, for use in wastewater processing and other cleaning purposes, and biopharmaceutical ingredients, including proteins. Enzymes, which are proteins used to catalyze biological and chemical processes, represented 92 percent of Novozymes' revenues of nearly DKK 8.5 billion ($1.5 billion) in 2009. The company produces detergent enzymes, used for laundry and dishwashing detergents; food enzymes, used in the production of beer, alcohol, bread, juice, and wine; and feed enzymes, used to boost the nutritional value of animal feeds. Novozymes, which was

spun off from Novo Nordisk in 2000, is listed on the Copenhagen Stock Exchange and is led by CEO Steen Riisgaard. The company is part of Novo Group, the holding company that controls both Novozymes and Novo Nordisk.

INSULIN ORIGINS IN THE TWENTIES

For most of its history, Novozymes operated as a small division of Novo Nordisk, a world-leading producer of insulin and other biomedical products. Novo Nordisk was founded as a basement laboratory, Novo Industri, by brothers Harald and Thorvald Pedersen in the early 1920s. By 1925, the Pedersens had succeeded in producing their first commercial-grade insulin, just four years after the discovery of the hormone created a revolution in diabetes care.

Novo expanded into larger production facilities in the 1930s, starting with the acquisition of a former dairy factory in Fuglebakken in 1931. The new quarters also provided the company with the space for developing its own research program, which in turn enabled the company to diversify its operations into a number of complementary areas. Among these was the production of enzymes, initially of trypsin, starting in 1941. Trypsin, like insulin, was found in the pancreas. The enzyme had come into demand for use by the tanning industry as part of the leather batting process. As a result, Novo found itself competing with the leather industry for the available animal pancreases. By becoming a supplier of trypsin to the leather industry, Novo was able to minimize the impact of this competition.

COMPANY PERSPECTIVES

Novozymes is the world leader in bio-innovations. Together with customers across a broad array of industries, we create tomorrow's industrial bio-solutions, which both improves our customers' business and the use of the planet's resources

Novo's expanding pharmaceutical business helped drive its enzymes business into the postwar period. The company developed an expertise in fermentation technologies as a part of a move into the production of penicillin and other antibiotics in the late 1940s and 1950s. Fermentation played a major part in the development of the modern enzymes market from the 1960s. In the meantime, the company had also launched the production of heparin, used for the treatment of blood clots. Trypsin was an important component of heparin, and in order to ensure its supply, Novo sought an alternative to animal pancreases.

Fermentation provided the key to the non-animal-based production of enzymes. This breakthrough allowed Novo to begin marketing its first enzyme produced through the new process, amylase, used by the textile industry, before the end of the 1950s. In 1963, the company reached a new breakthrough, launching alcalase. This was the first enzyme designed to be incorporated into laundry and dishwashing detergents. The enzymes were used to target the proteins in specific stains, causing a chemical reaction to break up the proteins and eliminate the stains.

PUBLIC OFFERING IN 1974

By the end of the 1960s, Novo had emerged as one of the world's leading enzymes producers. Enzymes themselves had become an increasingly important industrial component, used in a wide variety of industries. The food industry, for example, required enzymes for the production of a range of products, including the conversion of the starches in corn and wheat and other cereals into glucose, fructose, and other sugars. The production of alcohol and beer, as well as bread and other baked goods, also increasingly incorporated enzymes to speed up and stimulate the chemical reactions involved in their manufacture.

Novo responded by constructing a number of new enzymes factories. The company replaced the former dairy plant at Fuglebakken with a custom-built enzymes

and pharmaceuticals complex in 1967. In 1969, Novo added a second facility in Kalundborg, again producing both pharmaceuticals and enzymes. The company also expanded its fermentation capacity during this time.

Novo faced a major setback at the beginning of the 1970s, when the first in a long series of controversies arose concerning the possible health risks involved in the use of enzymes, particularly in the production of food additives such as high-fructose corn syrup. The result was a severe drop in enzyme sales. The U.S. National Academy of Sciences stepped in to refute the growing body of evidence of these dangers, permitting enzyme sales once again to soar. The United States proved a particularly lucrative market for Novo and other enzyme manufacturers during this time. Much of this growth was driven by the rising demand for high-fructose corn syrup, which began replacing sugars in soft drinks before becoming a nearly ubiquitous food additive. Novo responded to the growth in demand by building its first factory in the United States, in Franklin County, North Carolina, in 1977.

ENZYMES LEADER IN THE NINETIES

Production at the new facility started in 1979. By then, Novo had also expanded into the Latin American market, launching a sales office in Brazil. That office expanded into a full-fledged production subsidiary in 1989, in Araucária, Paraná. The late 1970s were also marked by Novo's first move into the Asian markets, starting with a partnership with Mitsui & Co. in Japan in 1977. Novo Industri Japan began operations that year, with Novo owning 90 percent of the new company.

Novo had also reorganized its ownership structure, placing the Pedersen family's shares in the company into a new shareholding vehicle, Novo Foundation. In this way, the Pedersen brothers were able to retire while also protecting the company against the threat of a takeover. The company created two classes of shares, placing the "A" shares, with a majority of voting rights, under the foundation's control. In 1974, the company launched a public offering of its "B" shares, on the Copenhagen Stock Exchange. In 1981, the company became the first in Scandinavia to list its shares on the New York Stock Exchange as well.

While Novo's enzymes sales continued their rise, the company's insulin and other biomedical products remained its major focus. This became particularly true following Novo's 1989 merger with smaller Danish rival Nordisk Gentofte A/S, becoming Novo Nordisk. The merger gave Novo Nordisk control of approximately 50 percent of the global insulin market.

KEY DATES

1925: Novo Industri produces commercial insulin.

1941: Novo launches its first enzymes production.

1963: Novo launches its first detergent enzymes.

1979: Novo adds its first U.S. enzyme factory, in North Carolina.

1989: Novo merges with Nordisk and becomes Novo Nordisk.

2000: Novozymes is spun off as a separate company from Novo Nordisk.

2010: Novozymes announces commercial production of new second-generation ethanol enzyme.

By the early 1990s, Novo Nordisk's enzymes division ranked among the world's leaders, especially in the market for detergent enzymes. The company continued to boost its production capacity. In 1992, for example, Novo spent $120 million on an expansion of its Franklin County, North Carolina, factory. The expansion tripled the company's U.S. production totals, adding new fermentation facilities, as well as a granulation tower and warehouse. In 1995, the company expanded the site again with the construction of a new office building, which became the company's sales and marketing headquarters in the United States.

NOVOZYMES IN 2000

By then, the company had also added a dedicated enzymes research and development (R&D) office for the U.S. market, which opened in California in 1992. The company also entered the Chinese market during the decade, beginning construction of a plant in Tianjin in 1994. That factory, with 160,000 square meters of production space, was completed in 1998. By then, the company had also added a regional headquarters in Beijing.

Leading the enzymes division in the late 1990s was Steen Riisgaard, described by *Time* as "a passionate environmentalist who went into business because he thought he could do good." Riisgaard led the division into the development of new "technical" enzymes, including enzymes used in the production of textiles, but especially those that could be used to convert plant matter into fuel. The company initially focused on developing enzymes that could be used to convert the sugars in corn and other cereals into biofuels. The division also formed a number of partnerships, notably with

Bayer for the production of textiles enzymes, and Roche, for the production of feed enzymes.

In 2000, Novo Nordisk carried out a reorganization of its operations, creating a new holding company, Novo A/S, controlled by the Novo Foundation. Novo Nordisk then spun off its enzymes operations into a new and separate company, Novozymes, in 2000. Riisgaard became the CEO of the new company, which then was listed on the Copenhagen Stock Exchange. Novozymes became not only the leading enzymes producer in the world, but one of the only "pure-play" companies in the sector. This allowed Novozymes to devote a greater proportion of its revenues, up to 16 percent, toward its R&D program.

ACQUISITIONS IN 2002

Novozymes' growth into the new century came both through its R&D effort and through the entry into a number of new markets. In 2002, for example, the company acquired a license to produce hyaluronic acid, a sugar-based molecule used in a number of applications, including contact lens cleaning solution and cosmetics. Also that year, the company acquired Sweden's BioGaia Fermentation, a producer of proteins, such as monoclonal antibodies, used in pharmaceutical production. Novozymes also added a microorganisms division that year, buying George A. Jeffreys, based in Salem, Virginia, which produced microorganisms and enzymes used in cleaning swimming pools, septic tanks, and other applications.

The company next formed a partnership with Denmark's Chr. Hansen to produce enzymes for the dairy industry, a market in which Novozymes had exited in the early 1990s. In 2003, Novozymes added another acquisition, buying Roots Inc., a producer of biological care products for turf and plants. Novozymes then entered a partnership with Australia's Meditech to help fund clinical trials testing hyaluronic acid as a treatment for intestinal cancer. Later in the decade, the company expanded its production of hyaluronic acid, launching construction of a new factory in Tianjin, China, in 2009.

Part of Novozymes' own R&D effort, however, focused on the creation of a new class of enzymes used for the production of so-called second-generation biofuels. The first generation of bioethanol had a number of drawbacks, most notably that it was highly expensive to produce, while at the same time causing a massive disruption of the global trade in corn and other cereals. The new generation, however, focused on converting cellulose to fuel. The new technology promised to use only agricultural waste by-products.

BIOFUEL BREAKTHROUGH IN 2010

Novozymes' R&D effort took off with a $14.8 million grant from the Department of Energy in 2001. The company received a second round of funding later in the decade, raising its total to nearly $30 million. The funding soon brought results. By 2005, the company announced its intention to introduce a commercially viable second-generation enzyme by 2010. In 2008, the company's confidence grew, and it announced plans to spend up to $100 million to build a new production plant for both first- and second-generation enzymes in Blair, Nebraska. In April 2009, the company raised its budget for the new facility to $200 million.

In February 2010, Novozymes unveiled its second-generation enzyme, dubbed Cellic Ctec2. The new enzyme would support production of ethanol for just $2 per gallon, making it a truly viable and renewable rival to petroleum-based fuel. The company expected to launch full-scale commercial production of the new enzymes early in 2011, and also expected the per-gallon production price of ethanol to drop sharply as manufacturers incorporated the new technology. These included China's Sinapec, which agreed in May 2010 to build an ethanol production demonstration factory based on the new Novozymes' enzyme and using corn stover as a feedstock.

Soon after, Novozymes announced another extension of its newly developing enzyme technology. In 2010, the company announced a partnership with Brazil's Braskem to co-develop enzyme technology to produce polypropylene from sugarcane and sugarcane waste. As a leader in the global enzymes market, Novozymes had positioned itself at the forefront of the drive to reduce the world's reliance on fossil fuels.

M. L. Cohen

PRINCIPAL SUBSIDIARIES

Novozymes Biopharma SE AB (Sweden); Novozymes (China) Biotechnology Co. Ltd.; Novozymes (China) Investment Co. Ltd.; Novozymes (Shenyang) Biologicals Co. Ltd.; Novozymes Australia Pty. Ltd.; Novozymes Austria GmbH; Novozymes Belgium BV; Novozymes Bioindustrial A/S; Novozymes Bioindustrial China A/S; Novozymes Bioindustrial Russia A/S; Novozymes Biologicals France S.A.; Novozymes Biologicals Japan Ltd.; Novozymes Biologicals, Inc. (USA); Novozymes Biopharma AU Ltd.; Novozymes Biopharma UK Ltd.; Novozymes Biopharma US, Inc.; Novozymes Biotech, Inc. (USA); Novozymes Deutschland GmbH (Germany); Novozymes Enzim Dis Ticaret Limited Sirketi (Turkey); Novozymes France S.A.; Novozymes Italia Srl. (Italy); Novozymes Japan Ltd.; Novozymes Korea Limited; Novozymes Latin America Ltda. (Brazil); Novozymes Malaysia Sdn. Bhd.; Novozymes Mexico, S.A. de C.V.; Novozymes Netherlands B.V.; Novozymes North America, Inc. (USA); Novozymes S.A. (Pty) Ltd.; Novozymes Singapore Pte. Ltd.; Novozymes South Asia Pvt. Ltd. (India); Novozymes Spain S.A.; Novozymes Switzerland AG; Novozymes US, Inc.

PRINCIPAL DIVISIONS

Enzyme Business; BioBusiness.

PRINCIPAL OPERATING UNITS

Detergent Enzymes; Technical Enzymes; Food Enzymes; Feed Enzymes; Microorganisms; Biopharmaceutical Ingredients.

PRINCIPAL COMPETITORS

Danisco A/S; Genencor International Inc.; Koninklijke DSM N.V.

FURTHER READING

Coons, Rebecca, "Novozymes Ramps Up Focus on Second-Generation Biofuels," *Chemical Week*, October 27, 2008, p. 30.

Kher, Unmesh, "Turning Waste into Fuel," *Time*, June 13, 2005, p. A12.

Milmo, Sean, "Novo to Spin Off Enzymes Unit in November," *Chemical Market Reporter*, September 11, 2000, p. 6.

"Novozymes: Agriculture and Bio-Based Industries Could Generate $230 Billion by 2020," *Manufacturing Close-Up*, July 2, 2010.

"Novozymes Breaks Ground on Enzyme Plant," *Feedstuffs*, April 6, 2009, p. 4.

"Novozymes Broadens Business Plans," *Industrial Bioprocessing*, February 9, 2001, p. 7.

"Novozymes Enzyme Business Depends on Innovation," *Industrial Bioprocessing*, August 19, 2005.

"Novozymes: New Enzymes Turn Waste into Fuel," *Health & Beauty Close-Up*, February 19, 2010.

Ramesh, Deepti, "Novozymes Breaks Ground in China for Hyaluronic Acid Unit," *Chemical Week*, May 11, 2009, p. 31.

Sissell, Kara, "Cleaning Up in the Enzymes Business," *Chemical Week*, February 28, 2001, p. 45.

Walsh, Kerri, "Novozymes Acquires US Enzymes Maker," *Chemical Week*, June 19, 2002, p. 14.

Nugget Market, Inc.

168 Court Street
Woodland, California 95695
U.S.A.
Telephone: (530) 669-3300
Fax: (530) 662-0929
Web site: http://www.nuggetmarket.com

Private Company
Incorporated: 1926
Employees: 1,500
Sales: $250 million (2010 est.)
NAICS: 445110 Supermarkets and Other Grocery (Except Convenience) Stores

■ ■ ■

Nugget Market, Inc., is a regional chain of grocery stores in northern California. Its stores include nine Nugget Market locations and three Food 4 Less units. The Nugget Market stores are full-line groceries, with a unique European marketplace design. The emphasis is on the freshest produce, fine meats, a large wine department, and high-quality prepared foods. The Food 4 Less stores offer national brand foods and fresh produce at prices set at least 10 percent below competitive area grocery stores. Although the company is relatively small, it is perceived as a leader in the grocery industry. As the grocery industry responded to the inroads of Wal-Mart and other large warehouse-type chains, Nugget emerged as a successful model. Nugget was able to make thriving stores in locations that other regional grocers had abandoned.

Its emphasis on dramatic architectural design and distinctive services including in-store chef's kitchens, while still remaining competitive in price, sets Nugget apart. The company has been praised by national grocery industry journals as well as honored by *Fortune* magazine as one of the nation's top companies to work for. Seen as a trailblazer in an era of change, the company has grown rapidly since 2000. Nugget Market, Inc., is owned and run by members of the founding Stille family.

BEGINNINGS AS A FAMILY GROCERY

Nugget Market began as a single store, opened by William Stille and his son Mack Stille in 1926 in Woodland, California. Woodland is about 15 miles from the state capital, Sacramento, in the midst of California's fertile agricultural valley. The name "Nugget" was taken as a reference to California's gold rush heritage, and the original store was adorned with gold pillars at its front entrance. The original store was small, at only 14 feet by 30 feet. The store did well, however, allowing the owners to remodel many times over.

The Stilles introduced innovations to the industry. Nugget Market had its own meat department, for example. When the chain started out, shoppers were used to buying their meat at a butcher shop. Nugget Market also installed refrigerated produce cases, another commonplace feature today that was a novelty in the early 20th century. William Stille built the store's first refrigerated cases himself. Nugget also led area groceries in installing powered belts to pull items toward the cashier.

Perhaps what stood out the most about Nugget Market in its early years was its commitment to fresh produce. Mack Stille made it his mission to bring the freshest available produce into his store. He traveled extensively through the West in order to compare quality. By the 1940s, Nugget Market had made an arrangement with produce distributor United Produce to take advantage of its wide selection of fresh fruits and vegetables. Early photos show the Nugget parking lot thronged with cars and the entryway packed with shoppers.

COMPETING ON PRICE

Leadership of the company passed to the younger founder, Mack Stille, and then in the 1950s to Mack's son Gene. From the 1950s to the 1970s, the single store continued to remodel and innovate. In 1968 it introduced a concept that was ahead of its time. Called everyday low pricing, or EDLP in industry shorthand, this was at the time a new strategy. The grocery industry was going through a period of sharp division between high- and low-price purveyors. The EDLP strategy let Nugget make a blanket promise to its shoppers, that they would get good value every time they shopped. This was in contrast to having to compete on price by offering drastic reductions or periodic specials. A concept so ingrained that modern consumers hardly think about it was nevertheless untested in the late 1960s. This set Nugget apart from its competition in the region. It also continued to nudge forward the company's trajectory as a trendsetter.

Nugget Market opened an in-store deli department in the 1970s. This offered prepared foods, shifting the shopping emphasis from ingredients to finished meals. While many other stores soon adopted some form of deli counter, Nugget Market went much further, and opened its own in-store Chinese kitchen in 1987. The Stille family had seen many Chinese restaurants in the area open with fanfare and then go out of business. They saw a demand for quality Chinese food, but the restaurant model seemed to have some difficulties. Consequently, they set up a Chinese restaurant kitchen inside Nugget, with its own chef, and offered freshly made Chinese entrées. Around this time, Nugget found a new produce distributor, Nor Cal Produce. Nor Cal was able to deliver a more extensive list of fresh fruits and vegetables, and it offered higher quality.

BRANCHING OUT

By the late 1980s, Nugget Market had developed a substantial track record of early adoption of trends and skillful adaptation to changing conditions. The company opened a second store in Davis, and then bought two defunct Alpha-Beta stores in Sacramento and converted these to Nugget units. In 1991, Nugget opened a new store under a different banner, Food 4 Less. The first Food 4 Less, in Vallejo, was what is known as a "price-impact" store, meaning its emphasis was on low price. This was of course spelled out in the new store's name. The Nugget Market units, too, were careful to keep their prices competitive, with an eye to the other regional chains such as Ralph's, Raley's, Albertsons, and Safeway.

Gene Stille's son Eric became chief executive of Nugget Market in 1996. Looking back on the company at that time, the *Sacramento Bee* described Nugget as "a nondescript 70-year-old grocery chain" (April 22, 2007). Although the company had been a leader in many of its practices, it was close enough to its competitors that it could be called mainstream or traditional. Nonetheless, the chain was on the brink of growth that would make it a different kind of grocery. Under Eric Stille's direction, the company carefully considered the challenges confronting small grocery chains. It acted creatively, using influences from other successful retailers. Always eager to try new things, Nugget forged a different pattern of grocery store over the next decade that soon attracted attention nationwide.

CHANGING COMPETITIVE LANDSCAPE

In the late 1990s and early 2000s, traditional grocery stores were faced with shrinking market share. Consumer demographics in Nugget's region also shifted, bringing new demands. The first challenge to such a small chain as Nugget was the burgeoning of non-grocery retailers who also sold food. Wholesale clubs including Costco and Sam's, as well as drugstores and dollar stores, took a bigger chunk of consumers' food spending in this era. Over a five-year period tracked in the late 1990s to early 2000s, the non-grocery retailer share of the overall grocery market climbed from just

```
┌─────────────────────────────────────────────┐
│                                               │
│              KEY DATES                        │
│                   ■                           │
│  ─────────────────────────────────────────   │
│  1926:  Father and son team open first Nugget │
│         Market in Woodland, California.       │
│  1968:  Company introduces everyday low pricing│
│         concept.                              │
│  1987:  Company opens Chinese kitchen in store.│
│  1996:  Eric Stille, representing the fourth  │
│         generation of family ownership,       │
│         becomes chief executive.              │
│  2000:  New model store debuts.               │
│                                               │
└─────────────────────────────────────────────┘
```

over 30 percent to almost 40 percent. Because consumers could pick up food at these other stores, the number of trips to traditional supermarkets fell. In 1998, consumers on average made 85 trips a year to supermarkets, according to a retail industry study cited in the *Sacramento Bee* (November 21, 2004). By 2003, shoppers were only making 72 trips on average.

Although this trend had been growing since the late 1990s, when Wal-Mart moved its large-format groceries into California in 2004, the pressure on traditional grocers increased visibly. Wal-Mart opened three of its so-called Supercenters in the state that year, with announced plans to open three dozen more by 2008. The giant retailer's planned locations included three in Nugget's territory: Woodland, Roseville, and Yuba City. The Supercenter format included all the housewares, hardware, clothing, and other departments of the typical Wal-Mart, plus a complete grocery store within the store. In other words, the Supercenter did not merely have an aisle where consumers could pick up crackers and juice. It offered a fully stocked grocery, including fresh produce, backed by Wal-Mart's deep pockets and extensive distribution network.

To survive against Wal-Mart, grocers needed to compete on price. Furthermore, to bring shoppers to Nugget instead of any other place shoppers could pick up food, the chain had to give consumers a good reason to choose it. Demographics in northern California influenced Nugget's strategy. Many people were moving out of the high-priced Bay Area and shifting into Nugget's territory. These sophisticated big-city shoppers were used to gourmet and specialty foods. Celebrity chefs were also popularizing new foods with widely viewed cable television shows.

Nugget, faced with competition on price and in the variety of places its customers could choose to shop, went with a new design concept that made a trip to Nugget something different. Eric Stille told the

Sacramento Bee in November 2004, "Coming here needs to be more of an event than a chore." Stille masterminded a dramatic redesign, while maintaining Nugget's commitment to EDLP.

NEW LOOK

Stille had already been experimenting with extra enticements to consumers before he launched the new Nugget in 2000. He had asked his merchandise buyers to search out unusual items, and had his staff chefs come up with intriguing menu items. The new stores had a dramatic new look that housed all Nugget's specialty departments in a seamless way. In 2000, the company remodeled two stores, one in Vacaville and one in Davis, to echo the look of a European marketplace. The Davis store, Nugget's second unit in that town, had housed three other groceries that had all failed. The building had been empty for two years when Nugget bought it. At Stille's first walk-through, he had to step over pigeons that had gotten trapped inside and died.

This decrepit spot became a lofty, light-filled grocery with over 400 varieties of produce arrayed in a two-story open atrium. The produce area was given the space and light of an outdoor street market, and themed with the name Fresh & Main. Stille's design team borrowed elements from retailers including the youth clothing chain Urban Outfitters and the shopping area in Caesars Palace in Las Vegas. Where the old Nugget had featured beige linoleum and white shelving, the new design used polished concrete flooring, warm earth tones, and many scenic elements such as canopies hung from the ceiling painted with clouds, huge baskets and bowls to hold fresh bread and vegetables, and hefty imported furniture as display stands.

The new format stores, at about 50,000 square feet, included bakeries, as many as three separate kitchens for prepared foods, a juice bar, an espresso bar, a wine cellar complete with wine steward, even a bath and body section with fresh ingredients displayed on shaved ice. A *Supermarket Business* profile in June 2000 claimed the new design gave the store "a feeling of almost total involvement for both the shopper and the store associate." It also brought the outdoors in, and exuded playfulness and novelty.

The company redesigned its existing four stores, and by 2008 had expanded to nine locations. The new stores could no longer be called nondescript or traditional. Nugget was clearly something different from the other chains in the area. Equally important, it did this without letting go of its stance on pricing. While it offered pricey gourmet items and bottles of wine costing hundreds of dollars, shoppers could still buy milk and cereal and such everyday items at prices typical of the area. Nugget also opened more Food 4 Less units, so that by 2008 it had three of these low-cost stores.

The chain's expansion was expensive, but seemed to have paid off. Opening a new store cost as much as $16 million. However, sales grew in double digits as the chain added new units and approached $250 million by the end of the decade. The Nugget chain had differentiated itself from its competition. It had become such a desirable retailer that nearby cities courted it.

The company also maintained itself as an agreeable place to work. It remained a family company, and while Eric Stille was at the helm, his father Gene chaired the board and was well known to employees throughout the chain. Nugget was exceedingly careful in whom it hired, and had a very high rate of employee retention. The enthusiasm and knowledge of store staff was part of the Nugget appeal. The company rewarded good work and good ideas, and maintained a free flow of information from bottom to top. The company appeared on *Fortune* magazine's list of the 100 best companies to work for in 2006. It came in at number 33. Over the next five years, the company steadily worked its way up the list. In 2010, it stood at number five.

BEYOND HOME GROUND

As Nugget emerged at the end of the decade a successful, lauded grocery firm, it faced the challenge of sustaining growth. It still faced pressure from Wal-Mart, and had abandoned one planned new store when it found that a Wal-Mart Supercenter was opening nearby. High-end groceries such as Whole Foods also pressured Nugget. It was still very small compared to other regional chains such as Save Mart. Save Mart, headquartered in Modesto, had sales of $5 billion, dwarfing Nugget's estimated $250 million. The company hoped to open more locations within a 100-mile radius of its headquarters, Woodland. It also

contemplated breaking that limit, looking at locations along California's famed scenic Highway 101.

The company announced no new store openings at the end of the decade, perhaps in response to the economic downturn that affected the U.S. economy as a whole. As it contemplated future moves, Nugget could look back on its long tradition of innovation and responsiveness to market conditions. The company was still privately owned, with several generations of the Stille family actively engaged in running the chain. Whatever changes the competitive grocery industry might bring, Nugget Market seemed prepared to move forward or to hold steady with its values in place.

A. Woodward

PRINCIPAL COMPETITORS

Raley's; Save Mart Supermarkets; Whole Foods Market, Inc.; Wal-Mart Stores, Inc.

FURTHER READING

Ingram, John, "At the Corner of Fresh & Main," *Supermarket Business*, June 15, 2000, p. 29.

Major, Meg, "Precious Mettle," *Progressive Grocer*, February 1, 2005, pp. 34–38.

———, "Striking Gold," *Progressive Grocer*, April 1, 2008, pp. 28–33.

Mellgren, James, "Retailer Profile Nugget Markets," *Gourmet Retailer*, September 2008, pp. 20–22.

Ortiz, Jon, "Making a Market: Nugget Thrives amid Big Grocery Competitors," *Sacramento Bee*, April 22, 2007.

———, "Sacramento, Calif.-Area Grocery Stores, Hit by New Rivals, Rethink Strategy," *Sacramento Bee*, November 21, 2004.

Turcsik, Richard, "Golden Nugget," *Progressive Grocer*, April 2001, p. 24.

Ohio National Financial Services, Inc.

One Financial Way
Cincinnati, Ohio 45242
U.S.A.
Telephone: (513) 794-6100
Toll Free: (800) 366-6654
Fax: (513) 794-4504
Web site: http://www.ohionational.com

Private Company
Founded: 1909 as The Ohio National Life Insurance
Company
Employees: 850
Total Assets: $21.85 billion (2009)
NAICS: 524113 Direct Life Insurance Carriers; 525110
Pension Funds

■ ■ ■

Cincinnati-based Ohio National Financial Services, Inc.,
is a leading provider of individual and group life insurance, annuities, mutual funds, pension plans, and more.
Through its Ohio National Life Insurance Company
and Ohio National Life Assurance Corporation affiliates,
the company does business in 47 states, the District of
Columbia, Puerto Rico, and Santiago, Chile. In addition to sales and broker associates, the company sells
financial services via banks and the Internet.

FORMATIVE YEARS

Ohio National traces its roots back to September 9,
1909, when the company was established as The Ohio

National Life Insurance Company. Initially doing business from a single-room office in downtown Cincinnati,
the company was led by Robert Palmer, Charles C.
Lemert, and Dr. John L. Davis. Growth began during
the company's first full year of operations. After issuing
its first policy in 1910, Ohio National acquired Toledo
Life and Seven States insurance companies.

In 1913 Ohio National named Albert Bettinger
president. The company's first general counsel, Bettinger
was a practicing Cincinnati lawyer for 46 years, and was
an authority on river transportation. He guided the
company until 1922, when he died at the age of 88.
That year, Ohio National's assets totaled approximately
$4 million. Bettinger was succeeded by Mooresville,
Missouri, native Troy W. Appleby, who had joined the
organization as an actuary eight years before and helped
further the growth of its sales force.

During the early 1920s Ohio National made its
foray into the participating whole life insurance market.
This development, which allowed policyholders to
obtain ownership interests in the company, laid the
groundwork for Ohio National's eventual transition into
a mutual insurance company. One final milestone during the 1920s was the installation of a punch-card
machine in 1928, which improved the efficiency of
record-keeping.

EARLY ACQUISITIONS

Ohio National began the 1930s with plans to acquire
Toledo, Ohio-based Toledo Travelers Life Insurance
Company. By this time the company was conducting
business in 15 states. The acquisition increased its insur-

ance in force to $85.25 million, and its assets to $13 million.

By 1931 negotiations were underway to acquire The United Life and Accident Insurance Company of Concord, New Hampshire. However, the deal was called off midway through the year by United Life's directors. Despite difficult economic conditions resulting from the Great Depression, the company was able to grow via a number of other successful acquisitions. In 1931 Ohio National acquired the American Old Lines and Omaha Life insurance companies, followed by Bankers Reserve Life Company of Omaha in April 1933.

Ohio National's assets continued growing during the first half of the 1930s, reaching $18.38 million in 1932 and $37 million in 1934, when the company celebrated a quarter century of operations. It also was in 1934 that Ohio National relocated its headquarters to an area north of downtown Cincinnati. The company occupied a larger facility that included features such as "silent" typewriters and indirect lighting.

Ohio National ushered in the 1940s by acquiring Rockford, Illinois-based Home Security Life Insurance Company, as well as Cincinnati-based Columbia Life Insurance Company. That year, the company's assets reached a record high of $55.3 million, and insurance levels reached $216.64 million. The following year Cleveland, Ohio-based Great Lakes Life Insurance Company was acquired.

LEADERSHIP CHANGES

Progress continued during the second half of the decade. In 1946 a Field Advisory Board was established to maintain and improve connections between corporate headquarters and general field agents regarding marketing, strategy, and products. The following year President Troy W. Appleby died at the age of 73, ending a 25-year run as company president. During his tenure, insurance in force had grown from $1 million to $325 million. He was succeeded by John H. Evans, who had been with the company since 1922.

Following Appleby's death in 1947, Ohio National bid farewell to Dr. Ben S. Leonard in 1949. Dr. Le-

onard, age 93, had served as a vice president since 1922. In addition, he had been a member of the company's board for 38 years. On a positive note, the company ended the decade with assets of $100 million.

By the early 1950s Ohio National's operations spanned 26 states, as well as the District of Columbia. In 1955 the company began selling group life insurance. A leadership change took place in 1956 when John Evans was named chairman and M. Reynolds Dodson, who had been with Ohio National since 1928, became president. During his tenure, Dodson made personal visits to nearly all of the company's field agents.

BECOMING A MUTUAL COMPANY

Ohio National ended the 1950s on a high note, celebrating 50 years of operations. In addition, the company completed its transformation into a mutual company. Ownership of Ohio National was now held by the company's policyholders. Another important milestone that took place in 1959 was the addition of an IBM computer, which allowed the company to automate a number of processes.

During the early 1960s Ohio National's assets totaled nearly $220 million. The company started off the decade by holding its first annual policyholders meeting in 1960. The following year Ohio National relocated to a new headquarters facility located at 237 William Howard Taft Road. Twice the size of its previous facility, the new location offered ample room for expansion. It also was in 1961 that the company began offering individual disability income insurance.

In 1967 Ohio National's assets totaled $324 million. The following year the company established a full-service retail broker/dealer enterprise named The O.N. Equity Sales Company (ONESCO). Ohio National ended the 1960s by organizing two mutual funds (Compass Growth and Compass Income) in partnership with New York-based Guardian Life Insurance Company, Equitable Life Insurance Company of Iowa, and Minnesota Mutual Life Insurance Company. It was in 1969 that the company sold its first $1 million life insurance policy.

Ohio National ushered in the 1970s by branching out into the variable annuity market in 1970. Several leadership changes occurred during the early part of the decade. In 1971 M. Reynolds Dodson was elevated to the role of chairman and CEO. At that time Paul E. Martin was named president. Martin held the role of president until the following year, when he became chairman and CEO. Burnell F. Saum succeeded Martin as president.

KEY DATES

1909: The Ohio National Life Insurance Company is established.

1910: Company issues its first policy and acquires Toledo Life and Seven States insurance companies.

1959: Ohio National celebrates 50 years of operations and completes its transformation into a mutual company.

1998: Company reorganizes as a mutual insurance holding company.

2009: Ohio National celebrates its 100th anniversary and 20 consecutive years of continuous life insurance sales growth.

By 1978 Ohio National's assets had reached the $600 million mark. To strengthen communication with the company's agents, it established the Agents Advisory Council. A new subsidiary named Ohio National Life Assurance Corporation was established in 1979. More leadership changes unfolded that year. In addition to retaining his role as president, Saum succeeded Martin as chairman and CEO.

75TH ANNIVERSARY

The 1980s included the introduction of several new products, including universal life insurance in 1982. Two years later the company celebrated 75 years of operation and its assets exceeded $1 billion. More leadership changes occurred at this time. In 1984 Bradley L. Warnemunde was named president and chief operating officer. The following year he remained president and succeeded Saum as chairman and CEO.

In 1985 Ohio National's life insurance in force exceeded $10 billion, up significantly from $5 billion only five years before. New product growth continued as the company introduced variable life insurance in 1987. That year, the nonprofit Ohio National Foundation also was established.

Ohio National ushered in the 1990s by acquiring the Pennsylvania National Life Insurance Company in 1993. That year, David B. O'Maley was named president and chief operating officer. The following year, O'Maley remained president, but assumed the additional roles of chairman and CEO.

In 1995 Ohio National's insurance in force totaled $24 billion, up from approximately $15 billion in 1991.

A flurry of significant changes began at this time. The company launched its first Web site in 1995, and adopted the Ohio National Financial Services trade name the following year. It also was in 1996 that Ohio National relocated to a massive new corporate headquarters complex in Montgomery, Ohio.

By 1997 Ohio National was preparing to address the issue of year 2000/Y2K compliance for its computer systems, ensuring that they would correctly recognize the year 2000 and not fail. To ensure its readiness, the company used tools from Compuware Corp. for testing purposes. More than four million lines of computer code, which the company had developed internally over the years, required conversion and testing. After forming a task force that involved weekly meetings with the CEO, Ohio National began providing Y2K-related updates to policyholders via its Web site.

REORGANIZATION

Pivotal developments continued to unfold in 1998. After securing approval from shareholders, the company reorganized as a mutual insurance holding company, becoming the first mutual company in Ohio to do so. The company's new structure, which was officially adopted on August 1, allowed it to secure access to capital via the stock market.

By 1998 Ohio National ranked as one of the nation's 25 largest mutual life insurance companies. That year the company chose the information technology (IT) services company CTG to serve as its strategic IT services provider. In addition, Ohio National was recognized as one of the nation's 100 best companies to work for by *Fortune* magazine.

In order to market variable annuities through banks and securities brokerage firms, Ohio National formed its Institutional Sales arm and acquired 51 percent of the Connecticut-based investment adviser Fiduciary Capital Management Inc. in 1998. Ohio National ended the 1990s with $38.7 billion of life insurance in force. In addition, the company generated revenues of $703 million in 1999.

INTERNATIONAL EXPANSION

Ohio National ushered in the millennium by acquiring the Santiago, Chile-based life insurance and annuity company BHIF America Seguros de Vide, which became Ohio National Seguros de Vida. As part of an effort to improve customer service, the company signed a $4.83 million, 10-year contract to license a work management system from Computer Sciences Corp.

During the early 2000s the company was focused on growing its life insurance and asset accumulation businesses. In keeping with this strategy, in 2001 Ohio National established an alliance that involved the sale of its group life and health insurance business to Canada Life Assurance Co. Midway through the year, National Security Life & Annuity Co. was established via a strategic alliance with Security Mutual Life Insurance Company of New York.

In 2002 Ohio National acquired a controlling stake in the New York-based institutional asset manager Suffolk Capital Management. Early the following year the company agreed to acquire Security Mutual Life Insurance Company of New York. Following the deal Security Mutual Life became a wholly owned Ohio National subsidiary.

TECHNOLOGY FOCUS

By 2005 Ohio National's information technology budget totaled approximately $16 million, and the company employed more than 100 IT workers. The company undertook a number of important IT initiatives, including the implementation of a new policy administration system, the development of a Web portal for brokers and dealers, and the rollout of a new enterprise content management system.

By 2006 Ohio National was marketing financial and insurance products in 47 states via some 50,000 representatives. More than 800 people were employed at the company's corporate headquarters. The company ended the year by naming Warren H. May to the newly created position of executive vice president and senior agency officer. Revenues increased 27.7 percent, reaching $3.1 billion, and assets under management grew more than 10 percent, reaching $22.5 billion.

Ohio National's strong performance continued into the end of the decade. In 2007 the company set an industry record for individual life insurance sales performance. In addition, its variable annuity sales increased more than 81 percent. The following year, pretax operating earnings skyrocketed more than 125 percent, reaching $386.1 million.

Several leadership changes took place during 2009. In March the company named Kristal Hambrick as senior vice president of life product management for its Ohio National Mutual Holdings Inc. business. In November, Gary T. "Doc" Huffman was named vice chairman and chief operating officer. He joined a four-person office of the chairman that also included Vice Chairman and Chief Risk Officer Ronald J. Dolan; Vice Chairman John J. Palmer; and Chairman, President, and CEO David B. O'Maley.

CENTENNIAL CELEBRATION

Other significant milestones in 2009 included a celebration of Ohio National's 100th anniversary. In addition, the company recorded its 20th consecutive year of continuous life insurance sales growth. Assets under management reached $26.5 billion, and total assets reached $21.85 billion. These milestones were especially significant considering the difficult economic climate.

Ohio National's heritage of technology leadership continued in 2010. At that time the company signed a 10-year contract with Computer Sciences Corp. Specifically, Ohio National committed to using new technology for business analytics, as well as the management of asset accumulation and disbursement.

Over a century of operations, Ohio National had demonstrated its ability to achieve remarkable growth. The company had succeeded through the practice of fiscal responsibility, sound leadership, and continued investment in technology. Moving forward, Ohio National appeared to have excellent prospects for continued success during the 21st century's second decade.

Paul R. Greenland

PRINCIPAL SUBSIDIARIES

The Ohio National Life Insurance Company; Ohio National Life Assurance Corporation; Ohio National Equities, Inc.; The O.N. Equity Sales Company; Ohio National Investments, Inc.

PRINCIPAL COMPETITORS

Great American Financial Resources, Inc.; MetLife, Inc.; Prudential Financial, Inc.

FURTHER READING

"Insurance Concerns Join; Ohio National Life Takes Over Bankers Reserve of Omaha," *New York Times*, April 23, 1933, p. N9.

"Life Companies to Merge; Ohio National Insurance Purchases Toledo Travelers," *New York Times*, February 6, 1930, p. 40.

"Ohio National to Buy Chilean Life & Annuity Company," *BestWire*, April 4, 2000.

"Ohio Nat'l Now a Mutual Holding Company," *National Underwriter, Life & Health/Financial Services Edition*, August 10, 1998, p. 38.

Panko, Ronald J., "Ohio National Names Vice Chairman, Chief Operating Officer," *BestWire*, November 11, 2009.

Woehr, Maria, "Growth Engine Al Bowen, SVP of Information Systems, Is Modernizing Ohio National Financial Services' Infrastructure to Support Agents' Use and Aggressive Business Growth," *Insurance & Technology*, November 2006, p. 26.

Old Dutch Foods, Inc.

—————————■—————————

2375 Terminal Road
Roseville, Minnesota 55113
U.S.A.
Telephone: (651) 633-8810
Fax: (651) 633-8894
Web site: http://www.olddutchfoods.com

Private Company
Incorporated: 1934 as Old Dutch Products Co.
Employees: 1,000
Sales: $264 million (2009 est.)
NAICS: 311919 Other Snack Food Manufacturing;
311911 Roasted Nuts and Peanut Butter Man-
ufacturing

■ ■ ■

Old Dutch Foods, Inc., is one of the largest regional producers of potato chips and other salty snacks in Canada as well as the upper Midwest of the United States. In addition to owning and operating business headquarters and manufacturing plants in Minneapolis and Roseville, Minnesota, Old Dutch Foods also operates Old Dutch Snack Foods, Ltd., based out of Winnipeg, Manitoba. The subsidiary boasts high sales in Canada, and uses plants in Airdie and Calgary, Alberta; Winnipeg; Lachine, Quebec; and Hartland, New Brunswick.

In 2001, the salty-food snack market was an $8 billion industry, primarily controlled by manufacturing giant Frito-Lay. Old Dutch, along with a few other regional potato chip companies, worked hard to displace

Frito-Lay within its region, focusing on the creation of a "premium" potato chip image as well as experimenting with different flavors and other snack food innovations. The company's success has placed it eighth overall in sales in 2010. Its products, including number-one seller Dill Pickle Potato Chips, continues to drive the company forward in the market battle for consumers.

EARLY OPPORTUNITIES

In 1934, Old Dutch Products Co. was founded by an undocumented man in St. Paul, Minnesota. The man would peel, slice, fry, and package the potatoes by hand, and would then sell them to retail locations from the back of his car. These humble beginnings were not enough to stop this anonymous opportunist, and by 1937 his business had grown large enough to require larger quarters. The company, along with its 25 employees, moved to a building on 3rd Street in Minneapolis. During World War II, the name was changed to Old Dutch Foods, primarily so that it would not be confused with the nationally advertised household cleaner Old Dutch Cleanser.

After the war, in 1951, Vern Aanenson, along with partner A. C. Eggert, bought Old Dutch Foods. Aanenson had been chief financial officer of D.W. Onan Co., a maker of electrical generators during the war. After the war he bought Old Dutch because, according to what his son Steve Aanenson told the *Minneapolis Star Tribune*, Vern recognized a good business opportunity.

Aanenson and Eggert continued to grow the company. In 1952, they purchased the potato chip division of Potato Products, Co. in East Grand Forks,

COMPANY PERSPECTIVES

To make and deliver premium, innovative, and delicious snack food products throughout Canada and the upper Midwest in the United States.

Minnesota. By 1954, the company opened trade with Canada. At that time, 200 dime-bags of chips were sent in four trucks to Thunder Bay, Ontario, across the border from Grand Portage, Minnesota. The venture into Canada succeeded, and in 1958, work began on a new Old Dutch plant on Sargent Avenue in Winnipeg, Manitoba.

PROFITS GO UP AS OLD DUTCH MOVES NORTH

Intrigued by the possibility of a strong Canadian trade, the company first tried to break into the Toronto salty snack market in 1959. The venture was unsuccessful, primarily due to the strong presence of Hostess Frito-Lay, the conglomeration of Canadian potato chip company Hostess and snack food giant Frito-Lay, in the Toronto area. Nevertheless, Old Dutch remained determined to break into the Canadian market, and so shifted its attention to central and western Canada. In 1965, Old Dutch Foods, Inc., became the parent entity to Old Dutch Snack Foods, Ltd., which based its operations out of Winnipeg. Aanenson continued to meet with success in western Canada, and opened plants in 1970 in Calgary, Alberta, and in 1980 in Airdie, Alberta.

Operations in the United States were fruitful, although growing at a slower pace than in Canada. In 1965, Aanenson bought out his partner Eggert, and moved the U.S. plant from Minneapolis to Roseville, Minnesota. By the 1980s, the factory in East Grand Forks, Minnesota, had closed, but Old Dutch had expanded its reach into a number of midwestern states, including Iowa, North Dakota, South Dakota, Wisconsin, and the Upper Peninsula of Michigan.

FREE PUBLICITY AND OTHER LEGAL PROCEEDINGS

In 1988, Nielsen data collected by the company showed that Old Dutch controlled just over 50 percent of the potato chip market from Thunder Bay, Ontario, to Vancouver, British Columbia. This news was especially heartening to the company, considering that Hostess

Frito-Lay controlled only around 27 percent of the market. Confident that a break into the Toronto market would now be possible, Old Dutch launched its products into retail stores across eastern Canada in 1991. However, soon after the products hit the shelves, Hostess Frito-Lay representatives began buying up the stock. The outcry that was soon leveled against Hostess Frito-Lay was instigated by consumers. According to an article written by Tony Kennedy of the *Star Tribune*, the public was made aware of the commotion when an aficionado of Old Dutch, pleased that his favorite potato chips were for sale, made a return trip to his neighborhood grocery store, only to find them gone. A store clerk, according to Kennedy, "told him that someone from Hostess Frito-Lay had cleaned out the inventory."

Furthermore, Hostess Frito-Lay was also accused of pressuring store owners to drop Old Dutch products, or else risk higher pricing on the Hostess Frito-Lay products than their "Old Dutch-free" competitors would receive. Throughout the melee, however, Old Dutch did not raise the alarm, nor even file a complaint. As Steve Aanenson told the *Star Tribune* in December 1991, "'we knew it was going on. ... I guess we figured that if we can't sell chips better than they can, maybe we don't belong in the market.'" Moreover, Aanenson noted that he believed that the conflict was not the fault of the top corporate management. Of course, the brouhaha did not hurt Old Dutch. Name recognition, as well as a sudden surge in popularity, solidified the company's presence in Toronto.

Old Dutch did alert the public, and the courts, however, on a popcorn price-fixing scheme in 1989. The lawsuit contended that Golden Valley Microwave Ellis Popcorn Co., Wyandot Inc., Weaver Popcorn Co., and Curtice-Burns Foods Inc., all conspired to fix prices on bulk popcorn, as well as to allocate customers and territories. In a July 1992 article in the *Star Tribune*, Steve Aanenson, then director of Special Projects for Old Dutch, said that the company had bought about 15 million pounds of popcorn within the 10 years covered by the suit. The legal proceeding was resolved in 1992, with the five distributors paying a combined $6.8 million to Old Dutch and other customers, but not admitting guilt, per agreement of the settlement.

EXPANDING THE PRODUCT WITHIN THE FAMILY

In 1998, Vern Aanenson died at the age of 82, leaving the business to his two sons, Steve and Eric. Steve would take over control of the company, to serve as the chief executive officer, and would co-own Old Dutch with his brother Eric, who would serve as chief operating officer.

The Aanenson brothers maintained the high-quality product that Old Dutch was known for, but they also began to focus on expanding the product line. The cut-throat and ever demanding consumer market required newer, bolder flavors and choices. As early as 1980 the first tortilla chip line was introduced in Canada. In 2004, Old Dutch released a new line of Mexican snack foods dubbed "Del Norte," with the dual aim of pleasing both the growing Hispanic population in the upper Midwest, as well as the increasingly sensitive palate of the average consumer. The line endeavored to feature more authentic salsas and tortilla chips than the present Old Dutch Restaurante line.

Old Dutch also went outside the confines of its product to support nonprofit organizations. From 2003 to 2007, Old Dutch donated $625,000 to Kidsport, a Canadian organization that worked to break down barriers that might prevent children from playing sports. In a public statement released on April 24, 2007, Old Dutch maintained that its involvement was a continuation of its support for active lifestyles, as it had not only been the first product in Canada to commit to a trans-fat free product line, but had also worked to create more healthful snack alternatives.

In 2005, 25 percent of the shares of Canadian snack company Humpty Dumpty Snack Foods Inc. were sold to Old Dutch for CAD 6 million. At first, three of Humpty Dumpty's major shareholders objected to the sale, and threatened to sue. Humpty Dumpty controlled about 12 percent of the snack market east of Manitoba, and also served as a producer of private-label snacks for retailers. The company had already been courted by a few different snack food companies, but each time the deal had been rejected by shareholders. This time the fracas was quelled quickly. By 2006 Old Dutch was able to purchase the remaining shares of Humpty Dumpty for CAD 26 million.

LOOKING TO THE FUTURE

Although Old Dutch had earned its name and reputation, its battle with giant Frito-Lay was far from over. The snack foods market was still primarily controlled by Frito-Lay. Other regional companies which also vied for recognition and market share included Utz Potato Chip Co. Inc., which was based in Pennsylvania and catered to the northeastern United States.

Part of Frito-Lay's success had been its ability to break into the market of "premium potato chips," a market once known exclusively to regional companies such as Old Dutch and Utz. Old Dutch managed to not only stand its ground, but also expand, by committing itself to a balance between innovation and tradition. In 2005, Old Dutch Snack Foods Ltd., introduced beef jerky and pepperoni jerky and by 2010 had also introduced a variety of roasted, salted, and flavored nuts and seeds. These joined the already popular snack choices of Bac'n Puffs, pretzels, Arriba-brand tortilla chips, and of course, potato chips, offered in Canada. By law, the snacks produced in Canada were unavailable for sale in the United States. Nevertheless, the products between the two countries were often highly similar. Old Dutch sold its potato chips, Baked Cheese Stix, and dips in the United States as well as Canada. The United States did have its own Restaurante line of tortilla chips and salsa as well as the specialty line of Dutch Crunch Kettle Chips.

Old Dutch's vast product line in both Canada and the United States was telling of a picky but voracious consumer market. According to the article "Worth Its Salt," featured in the July 2001 issue of *Prepared Foods*, the snack foods market was at the mercy of the increasingly finicky customer: "The challenge for snack developers is finding a new success, not a simple matter in an industry where nearly three quarters of launches fail." Prepackaged chips and dips, fat-free and "functional" (vitamin-loaded foods) foods, as well as organic foods represented the future of the industry. If Old Dutch wished to continue to succeed, it would need to quickly and deftly adapt to the ever-changing appetite of its customers.

Laura Rydberg

PRINCIPAL SUBSIDIARIES

Old Dutch Snack Foods, Ltd. (Canada); Humpty Dumpty Snack Foods Inc. (Canada).

PRINCIPAL COMPETITORS

Frito-Lay North America, Inc.; Snyder's of Hanover, Inc.; Utz Potato Chip Co., Inc.

FURTHER READING

Bloom, Richard, "Humpty Dumpty Holders Oppose Old Dutch Deal," *Globe and Mail*, February 4, 2005, p. B8.

Egerstorm, Lee, "Roseville, Minn., Firm Launches Tortilla Chip, Salsa Line Aimed at Hispanics," *Knight-Ridder/Tribune Business News*, June 26, 2004, p. 1.

Kennedy, Tony, "Plan to Resolve Popcorn Price-Fixing Suit Gets Preliminary Court Approval," *Minneapolis Star Tribune*, July 8, 1992, p. 1D.

——, "Snack Attack: Old Dutch Foods Is Ambushed by Hostess Frito-Lay in Toronto Stores," *Minneapolis Star Tribune*, December 23, 1991, p. 1D.

Roberts, William A., Jr., "Worth Its Salt," *Prepared Foods*, July 2001, pp. 19–21.

Shah, Allie, "Old Dutch Foods Owner and President Vernon Aanenson, 82, Dies," *Minneapolis Star Tribune*, August 13, 1998, p. 8B.

Silcoff, Sean, "Old Dutch Buys Humpty Dumpty: No. 2. Players in East, West Team Up to Fight Frito-Lay," *National Post*, March 22, 2006, p. FP1.

P.C. Richard & Son LLC

150 Price Parkway
Farmingdale, New York 11735
U.S.A.
Telephone: (631) 843-4300
Fax: (631) 843-4309
Web site: http://www.pcrichard.com

Private Company
Founded: 1909
Employees: 2,600
Sales: $1.55 billion (2010 est.)
NAICS: 443111 Household Appliance Stores; 443112
Radio, Television, and Other Electronics Stores

■ ■ ■

P.C. Richard & Son LLC is one of the largest major-appliance and consumer-electronics retailing chains in the fiercely competitive metropolitan New York area. The number of its stores increased from 11 in 1985, all in the city's borough of Queens and the two Long Island counties east of the city, to 38 in 1996, including outlets in New Jersey and Connecticut and four of the city's five boroughs. By 2010 the company had expanded to 55 locations. In addition to sales via brick-and-mortar locations, the company sells consumer-electronics via its Web site. P.C. Richard & Son is led by a fourth generation of the Richard family.

EARLY YEARS

A Dutch immigrant, Peter Christiaan (P. C.) Richard was working as a milkman in Brooklyn when he opened a hardware store in 1909 with his wife, Adelta. "We lived in the back like gypsies," P.C. Richard's only son, Alfred J. (A. J.), recalled in a *New York Times* interview. "[H]e had a little partition and he had a counter. And he fixed furnaces, replaced window glass. And that's how he accumulated inventory."

After three years the landlord told the Richards he was not going to renew their lease, so they moved to a building they bought in Queens. Their first electrical appliance was an iron that cost $4.95 in 1924. "People just wouldn't spend that," said A. J. Richard. "They were getting, some of them, only $2.75 a week," he noted. In order to stimulate business, the store began offering credit, accepting as little as 50 cents a week. P.C. Richard & Son later laid claim to being the oldest appliance store in New York, if not the entire country.

According to A. J. Richard's account, during the 1920s he persuaded housewives to abandon their washboards and buy ringer washers by offering $5 to try the machines in their homes. After a while, he said, he was selling more Westinghouse washing machines than anyone else. A. J. Richard also said he instituted deferred-payment plans and rebate programs, established the first roadside drive-in appliance showroom, and had 15 salesmen working different territories. He claimed to have founded the first nonmanufacturer's service department after beginning to sell tube radio sets in 1935 and realizing that he would sooner or later have to repair them.

A. J. Richard became president of the company in 1947, when his father retired. There was a second Queens store in 1952, when P.C. Richard opened a third in Bellmore, a community in Long Island's Nassau County. By now the company was selling television sets, according to A. J.'s son Gary Richard, as well as radios and a variety of home appliances. (In another interview, however, Gary Richard would recall that the company did not begin to sell TVs until the beginning of the 1980s.)

Give and take between P.C. Richard and its vendors was an important element in the company's success, according to Gary Richard, who credited the willingness of one manufacturer to defer payment with saving P.C. Richard from bankruptcy in the 1950s. As urban dwellers continued to fill the two Long Island counties east of New York City, P.C. Richard grew with them. Even so, sales volume was still a relatively modest $27 million in 1983.

MAJOR EXPANSION

In 1986, however, P.C. Richard had 16 stores, including five newly opened in Queens, and it ranked ninth among major appliance dealers in the United States, with sales volume of $96 million in these appliances alone. The company had sales in excess of $200 million in 1987 and was reportedly the largest General Electric dealership in the nation. Hundreds of appliances were on display in its stores, which averaged 10,000 to 11,000 square feet in size. By this time Gary Richard had succeeded his father as president. Corporate headquarters were in Hauppauge, Long Island.

P.C. Richard had sales volume of about $300 million in 1990, including about $130 million of electronics equipment and $110 million of appliances. The Richard chain also had been selling ready-to-assemble furniture since the mid-1970s. Among such items were entertainment centers, audio racks, and television and microwave-oven stands. The 21 stores, including five opened in Brooklyn during 1990 (the first in that borough since the original P.C. Richard store) were being fitted with a racetrack design to take customers on the perimeters of every department and encourage impulse buying. A sophisticated computer system linked billing and inventory throughout the chain, enabling a customer credit card to be approved in 15 seconds. The

company began adding home office equipment to its product mix just before Christmas 1993.

In a 1990 *HFD/Home Furnishings Daily* interview, Gary Richard said that in the 1980s "much of our competition walked away from the appliance business, which left room for us, so we stayed with it." Not mincing words, he went on to declare, "It was not logical for those retailers to be in the appliance business. You don't get rich in this business, especially if your advertising is devious, or if you bait and switch products." Interviewed by another trade journal in 1993, he emphasized the importance of satisfying the customer.

There were 28 to 30 P.C. Richard stores—five of them former Newmark & Lewis outlets—in the summer of 1993, ranging from 8,000 to 18,000 square feet in size. The company, long debt-free, was now willing to take on a sizable level of credit in order to open stores outside its Long Island base. The included three in New Jersey, three in Connecticut, and one on Staten Island. In addition, the company was building a new 600,000-square-foot warehouse in Farmingdale, Long Island, and expanding showrooms in Hauppauge, Plainview, Babylon, and Patchogue. P.C. Richard also had a 40,000-square-foot service center in Central Islip, Long Island.

HONESTY AND INTEGRITY

Gary Richard acknowledged that the company's $30 million expansion program had been prompted by the demise of competitors as a result of the 1990–91 recession, including the giant retailers Crazy Eddie Inc. and Newmark & Lewis Inc. and more than a dozen smaller operators. "We're strong enough to do it," said Richard, "and if we don't, we could be wounded later." Richard went on to say his company prided itself on honesty and integrity with vendors, customers, and employees and had built strong partnerships with its suppliers. "Some of our failed competitors were ruthless with the vendors," he claimed. "They had no mercy. Consequently, the vendors walked away from them when things began to go bad."

Among the practices Richard cited were selling gray-market merchandise (meant for sale overseas and usually lacking a U.S. warranty), baiting and switching (advertising an item at a very low price to pull in customers, then saying it was out of stock and offering a more expensive model instead), charging extra for accessories that were supposed to be included free (such as batteries), and not passing on the sales tax. Asked why these practices were rife in electronics retailing, Richard called it "a want, not a need, business. If I have five camcorders in the trunk of my car, I can go to any block, ring five doorbells, and sell them. It's not the

KEY DATES

1909: Dutch immigrant Peter Christiaan (P. C.) Richard establishes a hardware store.
1947: P. C. Richard's son, A. J. Richard, becomes president.
1986: President Gary Richard represents a third generation of family leadership.
1993: An initial public offering is planned, but the company ultimately decides to remain private.
2004: Gregg Richard is named president and A. J. Richard dies at age 95.
2009: P.C. Richard celebrates its 100th anniversary.

same with appliances. Nobody wants a refrigerator. They buy one because they need it, probably because their old one broke."

REMAINING PRIVATE

For a time P.C. Richard considered going public in order to finance its expansion. In connection with a public offering of common stock planned for August 1993, the company revealed that it had net sales of $314.6 million and net income in excess of $6 million in the 1992 fiscal year ended January 31, 1993. The company's long-term debt was only $500,000, but about $11 million of the proceeds from the proposed stock sale was earmarked to repay a note issued in May 1993, in lieu of a dividend, to a family holding company that was also leasing 17 locations to the company for $3.3 million a year. Another $24 million was to be used to enlarge, replace, and open new stores.

P.C. Richard ultimately decided to remain private. Interviewed in 1996 for *DM/Discount Merchandiser*, Gary Richard rhetorically asked, "What do we need underwriters, analysts, and the stock market telling us what to do, when we can do it ourselves when we want to do it? We generate all our own expansion money internally, and we are very successful at it."

Among the things outsiders were ready to tell the company to do was cut the payments to Gary Richard and his brother, Peter. In 1992 they shared total compensation of $2.8 million, or 15 percent of pretax profits, of which $2 million came in the form of bonuses. In the proposed public offering, the brothers' future bonuses were to be reduced to 7 percent of pretax profits.

GROWTH CONTINUES

P.C. Richard's mammoth new warehouse in Farmingdale, the size of 15 football fields and the largest on Long Island, was completed by the summer of 1995. Corporate headquarters also moved to the site. In 1996 P.C. Richard opened its first Manhattan store by taking a 20-year lease on a three-story building in the Union Square area. With the opening of this outlet the chain had 38 stores and owned 22 buildings. The typical showroom offered 5,000 items, including personal computers. P.C. Richard's 1995 fleet of 60 trucks and 35 trailers was averaging 1,000 deliveries a day.

One reason P.C. Richard had survived the retailing bloodletting of the early 1990s, according to industry observers, was its decision to avoid suicidal price-cutting. These observers said the chain had a reputation for keeping prices and margins higher than other operations in the metropolitan New York area. One reason it had been able to do so was its strong retail-support program and its reputation for reliability. According to Gary Richard, high employee morale was another reason. The salaries of its sales staff were based on commissions, but company executives were going to great lengths to convince these personnel that they could move up the ladder to managerial positions.

As long as the company remained private, however, it was clear that the top positions would be going to a fourth generation of Richards. Gary's son, Gregg, had by 1995 been chosen as his father's ultimate successor. Peter Richard Jr., son of Peter Richard Sr., Gary's brother, was scheduled to succeed his father as executive vice president. Four other children of Gary and the senior Peter were also involved in the company.

Heading into the late 1990s, P.C. Richard operated 38 locations. In December 1997 the company began reselling paging services when it named Paging Partners Corporation as its exclusive paging provider. It was around this time that the company established the P.C. Richard Foundation to support charities and noteworthy causes.

In 1999 P.C. Richard celebrated its 90th anniversary. That year the company began dabbling in e-commerce when it became a charter member of brandwise.com, an e-commerce comparison shopping site operated by brandwise LLC. P.C. Richard ended the decade with 40 retail stores in Brooklyn, Manhattan, Queens, Westchester, Bronx, Long Island, and New Jersey.

A NEW MILLENNIUM

In early 2000 P.C. Richard continued to expand its wireless communications lineup by offering Nextel phones at all of its locations. Later in the year the company began offering DISH Network satellite service from EchoStar Communications Corp. By 2002 P.C. Richard's sales totaled approximately $802 million. The company employed 2,137 employees who worked at 44 stores and a 650,000-square-foot distribution center. Other operations included a 150,000-square-foot distribution and training center in Whippany, New Jersey, as well as an 80,000-square-foot electronic service repair center and sales training facility in Farmingdale, New York.

Midway through 2002 P.C. Richard signed a 20-year lease for a 35,000-square-foot store in the Bronx. Early the following year the company spent $2.5 million to acquire land on Central Park Avenue, for the development of a 36,000-square-foot Yonkers store. It also was in 2003 that P.C. Richard acquired certain assets of the bankrupt chain, Nobody Beats the Wiz.

Additional entertainment options also were added for P.C. Richard customers in early 2003, when the company began selling DIRECTV satellite television equipment. An important leadership change took place in 2004 when Gregg Richard was named president. In December of that year the company mourned the loss of A. J. Richard, who died at the age of 95 from pneumonia.

In December 2006 P.C. Richard spent $21 million to acquire property for a new store (the company's 50th) in Staten Island, which opened its doors in mid-2007. In October 2007 a new, 50,000-square-foot store was established in the Riverhead area of Long Island. The company ended the year by establishing a partnership with Cablevision Systems Corp. that enabled consumers to sign up for cable television, Internet, and telephone service at P.C. Richard stores.

ACCELERATED GROWTH

Growth continued during the later years of the decade. In 2008 P.C. Richard celebrated the grand opening of its 51st store in Nanuet, New York. Early the following year the company announced plans to expand into Connecticut with a new store in Norwalk. The move was facilitated by the bankruptcy of Circuit City, which had vacated a 33,000-square-foot store on Connecticut Avenue.

In early 2009 P.C. Richard partnered with Verizon Wireless to establish store-within-a-store concepts, staffed by Verizon Wireless employees, in more than 30 of its showrooms. Around the same time the company announced plans to acquire four additional fomer Circuit City locations, including three central New Jersey stores, as well as a New York location in the College Point area of Queens. P.C. Richard also established a new 325,000-square-foot distribution and training facility in Carteret, New Jersey.

In mid-2009 the P.C. Richard & Son Theater opened in the New York City headquarters of Clear Channel Radio. By securing naming rights to the new 5,500-square-foot space, which was used to broadcast live performances, P.C. Richard was able to take advantage of promotional opportunities by reaching millions of listeners on a weekly basis. The company ended the year by celebrating its 100th anniversary in October.

P.C. Richard continued growing in 2010. In May the company opened its first Pennsylvania superstore, with a location in Philadelphia. At that time P.C. Richard announced it also would open up to five new Connecticut stores.

Throughout a century of operations, P.C. Richard had demonstrated its ability to thrive. The company's growth during the difficult economic conditions that prevailed beginning in late 2007 was especially noteworthy. Moving forward, P.C. Richard appeared to have excellent prospects for continued success during the 21st century's second decade.

Robert Halasz
Updated, Paul R. Greenland

PRINCIPAL COMPETITORS

Best Buy Co., Inc.; J & R Electronics Inc.; Sears, Roebuck and Co.

FURTHER READING

Becker, Maki, and Tracy Connor, "Pioneering Giant in the N.Y. Retail World, P.C. Richard & Son Legend A.J. Richard Dead at 95," *New York Daily News*, December 30, 2004, p. 20.

Bernstein, James, "Electronics Retailing Heats Up," *Newsday*, February 20, 1996, p. A27.

Fox, Bruce, "Seizing the Opportunity," *Chain Store Age Executive*, May 1993, pp. 51–52.

Johnson, Jay L., "P.C. Richard & Son: A Regional Survivor," *DM/Discount Merchandiser*, September 1996, pp. 20–21.

Julianelli, Jane, "6 in Family Moving P.C. Richard to the Future," *New York Times*, July 23, 1995, pp. 1, 9.

Miller, Stephen, "A. J. Richard, 95, Built Shop into an Appliance Giant," *New York Sun*, January 6, 2005, p. 5.

"P.C. Richard Marks 100th Anniversary," *TWICE*, October 12, 2009, p. 24.

Podsada, Janice, "P.C. Richard Expanding into State; Appliance Retailer Eyes Manchester, Newington Sites; Retail," *Hartford Courant*, May 11, 2010, p. A6.

Williams, Jasmin K., "A New York Institution," *New York Post*, October 11, 2005, p. 40.

Pampa Energía S.A.

Bouchard 547
Buenos Aires, C.F. C1106ABG
Argentina
Telephone: (54 11) 4510-9500
Fax: (54 11) 4510-9455
Web site: http://www.pampaenergia.com

Public Company
Incorporated: 1945 as Frigorífico La Pampa S.A.
Employees: 5,000
Sales: ARS 4.09 billion ($1.10 billion) (2009)
Stock Exchanges: Buenos Aires New York
Ticker Symbols: PAMP; PAM
NAICS: 221111 Hydroelectric Power Generation; 221112 Fossil Fuel Electric Power Generation; 221121 Electric Bulk Power Transmission and Control; 221122 Electric Power Distribution

∎ ∎ ∎

Pampa Energía S.A. is the largest fully integrated electricity company in Argentina. Its principal assets are divided among subsidiaries that generate, transmit, and distribute electricity. Many foreign investors sold their holdings in Argentina following the financial meltdown of the early years of the 21st century, but the Argentine entrepreneur Marcos Marcelo Mindlin assembled enough capital to buy several utilities cheaply and take an important position as an energy consolidator.

PRIVATIZING ARGENTINA'S ELECTRICAL SUPPLY IN THE NINETIES

Electricity first became available in Argentina in 1887, with the first public street lighting in Buenos Aires. The Argentine government began to involve itself in the electricity sector in 1946, when it established a directorate to construct and operate electricity generating plants. Concessions were granted in the 1960s to private companies to generate and distribute electricity. By 1990, however, the national government controlled virtually all of the electricity supply. In addition, several provinces operated their own electricity companies.

In 1991 the Argentine government undertook an extensive privatization program of all state-owned industries. Virtually all business activities carried out by Argentine state-owned enterprises in the electricity sector were privatized. Distribution and transmission activities were defined as monopolies requiring a concession and government regulation. Distributors were required to sign up new customers and meet any increased demand. Generation of electricity was also regulated by the government but was not deemed a monopoly activity, although the operation of existing hydroelectric power plants required concessions. Many of the provincial governments also privatized their electricity companies.

PURCHASING LA PAMPA IN 2005

At the end of 2001 and the beginning of 2002 Argentina experienced a financial crisis that virtually paralyzed the national economy through most of 2002.

COMPANY PERSPECTIVES

Mission: To pursue standards of excellence in the provision of energy generation, transmission, and distribution services, fulfilling our objective of contributing to the growth of the Company, its employees, and community at large.

Our Challenges: Toward our clients: to ensure a continuous provision of energy, reaching the highest service standards. Toward the communities where we operate: to promote sustainable development, reinforcing our commitment and respect for the environment. Toward our employees: to provide an ethical and challenging working environment, full of professional growth and improvement opportunities. Toward our shareholders: to achieve a higher return on investment, sustained in the long term. Toward the country: to contribute to the country's development and job creation, improving quality of life for Argentine people.

Although its unit of currency, the peso, was devalued against the U.S. dollar, the electricity companies were required to maintain existing peso prices and rates for transmitting and distributing electricity to their customers. This policy, combined with a high rate of inflation, resulted in a decline in revenues for the companies and the deferral of further investments. For the next three years Argentina's power grid was unable to attract any private investment. By 2005, however, the Argentine economy was booming and, as a result the electricity companies were operating at near full capacity to meet growing national energy demand. Prominent among those who saw opportunities for investment in this sector was Marcos Marcelo Mindlin, who had founded the investment group Grupo Dolphin S.A. in 1987. This group invested in many Argentine economic sectors, including agriculture, banking, electricity, energy, and real estate.

Pampa Energía was the continuation of a meatpacking company, Frigorífico La Pampa, S.A., established in 1945. This company operated a refrigerated warehouse in Puerto Madero, the port area of Buenos Aires. Argentina's economy fell into severe recession at the close of the 1990s, and Frigorífico La Pampa lost money in every year from fiscal 1999 through 2005. Its activities as a meatpacking plant were discontinued in 2002 and it became, in effect, a shell company.

In November 2005 Marcelo Mindlin's brother, Damián Mindlin, Gustavo Mariana, and Ricardo Torres acquired 83 percent of La Pampa in November 2005 for $1 million and renamed it Pampa Holding S.A. Marcelo Mindlin became president of Pampa Holding and moved up to chairman of the board shortly after.

GOING PUBLIC: 2006–07

At the end of fiscal 2006 (June 30, 2006), Pampa Holdings LLC owned three-quarters of the capital of Pampa Holding S.A. Based in Delaware, this limited liability company was controlled by another LLC that acted as its managing member. That company was in turn controlled by Uruguay-based Dolphin Fund Management S.A., which was controlled by Grupo Dolphin.

Pampa Holding made its initial public offering of shares on the Bolsa de Comercio de Buenos Aires in early 2006. It raised ARS 485 million ($157 million) in capital from new shareholders and about $240 million in subscription rights from existing ones. During 2007 Pampa Holding augmented its resources further by a new share offering in Buenos Aires and also in Luxembourg that raised ARS 1.36 billion ($435 million).

Investor interest in Pampa Holding was based on the judgment that the Argentine government had no choice but to allow electricity rates to rise so that the companies could deliver badly needed additional supplies to the public. As a result of the nation's economic recovery, energy demand rose 21 percent between 2001 and mid-2007. A government program adopted in 2006 included measures seeking to create incentives for generation plants to meet increasing energy needs by allowing them to sell new energy generation at unregulated market rates.

ACQUIRING GENERATING COMPANIES: 2006–09

The directors of Pampa Holding decided that the economic sector with the highest potential of capital appreciation in Argentina was electrical energy. Accordingly, in May 2006 the company purchased a majority stake in Inversora Nihuiles S.A., which owned 51 percent of Hidroeléctrica Nihuiles S.A., and Inversora Diamante S.A., which owned 59 percent of Hidroelétrica Diamante S.A. Nihuiles and Diamante controlled hydroelectricity generating complexes operating in the province of Mendoza under 30-year concessions established in 1994. The seller was EDF International S.A., a subsidiary of Electricité de France. The purchase price was $55 million.

Shortly before the end of 2006, Pampa Holding acquired a majority stake in Central Térmica Güemes for $16.7 million. This electricity generating plant, also in northern Argentina, privatized in 1992, was powered by steam and natural gas.

Pampa Holding acquired Central Termoeléctrica Loma de la Lata in 2007. This Patagonian generating plant, next to the largest natural gas field in Argentina, was powered by three gas turbines. The purchase price was $60 million. Soon after, Pampa Holding acquired Central Térmica Piedra Buena, a thermal generation plant in the province of Buenos Aires, for $85 million. This plant was powered by natural gas or fuel oil.

Pampa Holding had also taken a half-share in Inversora Ingentis S.A., a joint venture company that was building a gas-fired generation plant in the province of Chubut in Patagonia. This company became wholly owned by Pampa Holding in 2009.

TRANSMISSION AND DISTRIBUTION ACQUISITIONS: 2006–07

Pampa Holding entered the electricity transmission market in 2006–07, when it purchased nearly 90 percent of Transelec Argentina S.A. for $48.5 million. The rest of the shares were purchased by the Mindlin brothers and Gustavo Mariani in 2008 for about $12.3 million. Transelec owned half of Compañia Invesora en Tranmisión Eléctrica Citelec S.A., which in turn owned nearly 53 percent of Compañia de Transporte de Energía Eléctrica en Alta Tension Transener S.A.

Founded in 1992, Transener was the largest high-voltage electricity transmission company in Argentina, transporting 95 percent of the nation's electricity when it was privatized the following year. It was awarded an exclusive 95-year concession to provide high-voltage electricity transmission services throughout its network.

In 1997 Transener purchased the transmission assets of state-owned Empresa Social de Energía de Buenos Aires S.A. (Eseba) for $220.2 million. This acquisition became Transba S.A., which had been awarded an exclusive 95-year concession to operate the electricity transmission system of the province of Buenos Aires, Argentina's wealthiest and most populous province. In addition to holding 90 percent of Transba, Transener also was conducting service operations in Brazil and Paraguay. Following its purchase of Transener, Pampa Holding refinanced $220 million of the company's $289 million debt by means of a 10-year bond offering at an annual interest rate of almost 9 percent.

Pampa Holding entered the electricity distribution market in 2007 with the purchase of a majority interest in Empresa Distribuidora y Comercializadora Norte S.A. Edenor. Privatized in 1992, Edenor, the largest distributor of electricity in Argentina, held an exclusive 95-year concession to distribute electricity to the northern part of the province of Buenos Aires and the northern part of the city of Buenos Aires.

Edenor was owned in this period by a consortium composed of Argentine, French, Spanish, and North American partners. One of its chief concerns was dealing with theft of its power supplies, said to represent one-fifth of all power sold. Edenor successfully put into operation a fraud eradication plan consisting of one million individual inspections and normalizing service for 410,000 needy power users. However, like Transener, Edenor found itself in difficulty in the grave economic crisis of the first years of the 21st century and, in 2002, suspended payments on its debt, which eventually reached $534 million. The debt was restructured in 2006.

Pampa Holding paid for the acquisition of Edenor by transferring to the seller ARS 1.25 billion (about $400 million) worth of stock that it had issued on the Bolsa de Comercio de Buenos Aires. It was the largest such offering on the Bolsa in the previous 10 years.

PAMPA ENERGÍA: 2008–09

Pampa Holding changed its name to Pampa Energía in July 2008. The subsequent world financial crisis put a stop to further transactions for a while, but in October 2009 the company issued American Depositary Receipts, the equivalent of shares, on the New York Stock Exchange. Following this event, 80 percent of Pampa's common shares were in public hands. The other shares belonged to management, including Pampa

Holdings LLC and Grupo Dolphin S.A.

Also in 2009, Pampa Energía formed an alliance with Argentina's largest fossil-fuel producer, YPF S.A. It agreed to contribute $29 million to drill new gas wells in the area of Patagonia near the Loma de la Lata power plant. In return, YPF gave Pampa Energía title to half the gas produced in the area.

Distribution was the largest sector of Pampa Energía's business in 2009, accounting for 51 percent of its revenues. Generation amounted to 42 percent and transmission to 7 percent.

With increased demand for electricity due to Argentina's economic revival but no new supplies, the nation experienced shortages at peak times for consumption. In 2007 the government restricted supplies to large commercial and industrial consumers, and even households suffered sporadic power cuts. To stimulate further investment in public power, the government, in 2008, lifted the freeze it had imposed on electricity rates for residential and industrial consumers in the Buenos Aires metropolitan area. However, of Pampa Energía's net profit of ARS 214.74 million ($57.88 million) in 2009, about 70 percent was unrelated to energy but rather the result of financial investments and investments in real estate.

With shortages of natural gas and diesel oil reported, Pampa Energía's decision to seek new fuel sup- plies seemed farsighted. Argentina was dependent on natural gas for about half of its energy needs.

Robert Halasz

PRINCIPAL SUBSIDIARIES

Corporación Independiente de Energía S.A.; Electricidad Argentina, S.A.; Inversora Nihuiles S.A.

FURTHER READING

The Argentine Economy, Buenos Aires: Julio Moyano Com- munications, pp. 314–15, 396–97, 404–05.

"EDF's Argentinian Adventure," *Power Economics*, March 2001, p. 8.

"Marcelo Mindlin," *Banker*, November 2006, pp. 80–81.

"Pampa Powers Up," *LatinFinance*, July/August 2007, pp. 29–30.

Pineiro, José Luis, *Transmission & Distribution World*, May 2001, pp. 48+.

Platt, Gordon, "Argentine Electric Company Lists ADRs in New York," *Global Finance*, November 2009, p. 15.

"Power Privatization Programme Progresses Patchily," *Modern Power Systems*, February 1996, p. 5.

Quiroga, Carla, "Los 10 empresarios de 2009," *Apertura*, December 2009, p. 34.

Webber, Jude, "Political Risk Revisited," *LatinFinance*, February 2007, p. 22.

Peabody Energy Corporation

701 Market Street
St. Louis, Missouri 63101
U.S.A.
Telephone: (314) 342-3400
Fax: (314) 342-7799
Web site: http://www.peabodyenergy.com

Public Company
Incorporated: 1890 as Peabody Coal Company
Employees: 7,300
Sales: $6.01 billion (2009)
Stock Exchanges: New York
Ticker Symbol: BTU
NAICS: 212111 Bituminous Coal and Lignite Surface Mining; 212112 Bituminous Coal Underground Mining

■ ■ ■

Peabody Energy Corporation is the largest private-sector coal company in the world and the largest coal mining company in the United States. As a majority shareholder in 30 coal mining operations and with more than nine billion tons in coal reserves, Peabody Energy extracts more than 224 million tons of coal per year. Coal mining operations are located in Wyoming, Colorado, New Mexico, Arizona, Indiana, Illinois, Venezuela, and New South Wales and Queensland, Australia.

COALTRADE, the company's worldwide marketing, trading, and brokerage operations, has offices in St. Louis, London, Beijing, Mongolia, and in Newcastle, New South Wales. COALTRADE sells more than 244 million tons of coal per year to customers on six continents. Peabody coal powers 10 percent of electricity generation in the United States, and it supplies 2 percent of electricity generation worldwide. The company is involved in several power generation projects, including experimental low emissions power plants and the Prairie State Energy Campus, a fully integrated coal mining and power generation project in Illinois.

ORIGINS

Peabody Coal was founded in the 1880s by Francis S. Peabody. The son of a prominent Chicago attorney, Peabody graduated from Yale University with the intention of studying law in Chicago. Displaying little aptitude for the profession, however, he opted for a career in business, working at a bank for a brief period before embarking on a private retail venture in 1883. With a partner, $100 in start-up capital, a wagon, and two mules, the 24-year-old Peabody established Peabody, Daniels & Company, which sold and delivered coal purchased from established mines to homes and small businesses in the Chicago area. Capitalizing on the social and business relations cultivated by Peabody's father, the company attracted a large customer base and experienced success from the onset. As sales continued to increase, the company rose to prominence among the major coal retailers in Chicago.

During the late 1880s Peabody bought out his partner's share of the business, and in 1890 the company was incorporated in the state of Illinois under the name Peabody Coal Company. Five years later, in order to meet increasing customer demand, Peabody began its own mining operation, opening Mine No. 1 in the southern Illinois county of Williamson. This venture represented the first step in Peabody's transition from coal retailer to mining company.

At the beginning of the 20th century, coal-burning fireplaces and furnaces constituted the chief source of heat for both private residences and public buildings. Moreover, the railroad and shipping industries relied heavily on coal to power their steam engines. Over the next 10 years, however, the increasing popularity of alternative fuels (including natural gas, which had applications in home heating, and diesel fuel, which could be used to power locomotives) led to a greatly reduced demand for coal in what had been its primary markets. Nonetheless, coal became an important commodity for another developing industry during this time, as electricity was brought to homes and businesses in urban and eventually rural parts of the country. The operation of electrical utility plants demanded large amounts of coal. In 1913 Peabody Coal won a long-term contract to supply coal to a major electric utility, and, realizing the growing importance of this market, the company began focusing on obtaining similar high-volume, long-term supply contracts, while acquiring more mining and reserve property to meet expected demand.

Having anticipated and adapted to changes in the marketplace, Peabody Coal thrived. The company obtained a listing on the Midwest Stock Exchange in 1929 and became known as a coal producer rather than retailer. Despite adverse economic conditions during the Great Depression and disputes and strikes involving the unionization of mine workers, the company continued to realize profits and growth. In 1949 Peabody Coal was listed on the New York Stock Exchange. During this time, Francis S. Peabody retired and was succeeded as company president by his son, Stuyvesant (Jack) Peabody, who later ceded control to his own son, Stuyvesant Peabody Jr.

MERGER WITH SINCLAIR IN 1955

By the mid-1950s Peabody ranked eighth among the country's top coal producers. Dependent on under-

ground mines, however, the company lost market share to competitors engaged in surface mining, a less expensive process that yielded a higher volume of coal. Heavy losses at Peabody ensued in the early 1950s. The company engaged in merger talks with Sinclair Coal Company, the country's third-largest coal mining operation. Peabody management believed that Sinclair could offer the company access to greater financial resources and surface mining operations that would help it to remain competitive.

Like Peabody, Sinclair was founded in the late 19th century as a retail operation. Sinclair provided customers in the vicinity of Aurora, Missouri, with coal for heating their homes and businesses. During the 1920s, Sinclair President Grant Stauffer was approached by Russell Kelce, an ambitious coal miner who sought to put his years of practical experience to use in an executive capacity. Born into a long line of coal miners, Kelce had begun working in the mines of Pennsylvania while in his teens. He later moved to the Midwest, where his father had established a mining operation. Stauffer and Kelce reached an agreement in which Stauffer would be responsible for cultivating a large customer base and long-term contracts, and Kelce would oversee mining operations. By 1926 Kelce had purchased a significant share of Sinclair Coal Co., and he became president when Stauffer died in 1949.

Kelce was also named president of the new company that resulted when Sinclair and Peabody merged in 1955. That year, Sinclair acquired 95 percent of Peabody's stock and moved Peabody's headquarters to St. Louis. However, the Peabody name, familiar to investors due to its listing on the New York Stock Exchange, was retained. Under the leadership of Russell Kelce, and, later, his brothers Merl and Ted, Peabody doubled its production and sales by opening new mines and acquiring established mines in the western states, including Arizona, Colorado, and Montana. By the mid-1960s, the company had opened a mine in Queensland, Australia, its first venture outside North America.

THE LITIGIOUS SEVENTIES AND EIGHTIES

In 1968 Peabody's assets were acquired by Kennecott Copper Corporation. Although Peabody became the largest coal producer in the United States during this time, its position under Kennecott was made tenuous by an antitrust suit. The Federal Trade Commission (FTC) ruled that Kennecott's purchase of Peabody was in violation of the Clayton Act, a decision that Kennecott challenged. In 1976, after eight years of litigation, the FTC ordered Kennecott to divest Peabody Coal Company. Peabody Holding Company, Inc., was

KEY DATES

1883: Francis Peabody starts a retail coal venture.
1955: Peabody merges with Sinclair Coal.
1968: Kennecott Copper Corporation acquires Peabody.
1976: Federal Trade Commission orders Kennecott to sell Peabody; holding company is formed.
1990: Hanson PLC acquires Peabody.
1997: Hanson spins off Peabody into The Energy Group.
1998: Lehman Merchant buys Peabody.
2001: Company goes public as Peabody Energy Corporation.
2004: A $432 million acquisition includes a low-sulfur coal mine in Colorado and two mines in Australia.
2007: Peabody begins trading and brokering coal in Asia.

formed. The following year it bought Peabody Coal for $1.1 billion. Edwin R. Phelps presided over Peabody during these years of litigation, and in 1978 he was named the company's chairperson. The presidency was then transferred to Robert H. Quenon, a former executive in the coal division of Exxon.

Quenon met with several challenges at Peabody, including poor labor relationships, low employee morale, financial losses, and outdated plants and equipment. However, he later recalled in an interview for Peabody's *Pulse* magazine that he was encouraged by the fact that the company "had a very good management team. They understood coal, and made things happen." Quenon oversaw a reorganization of Peabody that resulted in separate divisions for sales, marketing, mine operations, resource management, and customer service. By selling off several of its properties, the company was able to finance more modern facilities and equipment. Moreover, Quenon was able to capitalize on the OPEC oil crisis by renegotiating longer term contracts with customers who feared that coal prices, like oil prices, would soon increase dramatically.

Although Peabody became more financially stable, it also faced union strikes and litigation over safety issues during the 1970s and 1980s. The longest strike took place from December 1977 through March 1978. It ended when mine workers throughout the country accepted a new three-year contract. The 110-day strike could have led to power shortages and industrial layoffs.

However, this threat to the nation's economy was avoided largely due to the stockpiling of coal that occurred before the strike commenced. Nevertheless, this strike and another in 1981 that lasted for 75 days proved costly to Peabody, and the company strove to improve its relations with its employees.

The safety of Peabody mines was called into question beginning in 1982, when the company was charged with tampering with the results of safety tests at its mine in Morganfield, Kentucky. The tests, made mandatory for all coal mines by the Mine Safety and Health Administration (MSHA), measured the amount of coal dust to which miners were exposed. Excessive amounts of the dust were linked to pneumoconiosis, commonly known as black lung disease. Peabody pleaded guilty to 13 charges of tampering with the test results in December 1982 and paid fines totaling $130,000. Also during this time, MSHA found the company's Eagle No. 2 mine in Illinois in violation of safety standards. Eagle No. 2 failed to provide adequate roof support beams, which resulted in the accidental death of a foreman.

Reacting to these and other similar disasters, Peabody focused its attention on safety, designating teams of engineers to design stronger roofs and better ventilation systems at its underground mines. In addition, the company patented its invention of a "flooded bed scrubber," which operated in conjunction with mining machinery to reduce the amount of coal dust in the mines.

In 1983 Quenon was made president and CEO of Peabody's parent company, Peabody Holding Co., and Wayne T. Ewing was named president of Peabody Coal. Two years later, when Ewing moved to the Peabody Development Company, another subsidiary of Peabody Holding, he was replaced at Peabody Coal by Howard W. Williams. Improved labor relations at Peabody were reflected in the successful negotiations of contracts with the United Mine Workers. The company and its miners avoided strikes in 1984 and 1988.

Growth in Peabody's operations continued. In 1984 the company acquired the West Virginia coal mines of Armco Inc. for $257 million, resulting in new contracts with northeastern utility companies. During this time, Peabody's headquarters were relocated in Henderson, Kentucky, which offered closer proximity to its central mines.

CLEARING THE AIR IN THE NINETIES

The passage of the Clean Air Act Amendments by Congress in the early 1990s forced many coal producers, including Peabody, to reassess their operations. Phase I of the act mandated that U.S. industries work to reduce the amount of sulfur dioxide emissions produced by their plants. Although the installation of scrubbers at coal-burning power plants would enable such companies to modify the effects of high-sulfur coal themselves, most customers preferred to switch to a low-sulfur coal product. As a result, Peabody's competitive status hinged on its ability to renegotiate customer contracts and provide a product lower in sulfur content.

Some Peabody mines, including Eagle No. 2, lost major contracts and were forced to close, whereas others were able to implement new equipment and procedures that produced low-sulfur coal. The prospect of the stricter clean air requirements outlined in Phase II of the act, scheduled to go into effect by 2000, prompted Peabody to invest heavily in technology, hoping to be better prepared for eventual shifts in demand.

Hanson PLC acquired Peabody Holding Company, Inc., in 1990, a year after the bidding process had been set in motion by Newmont Mining Corporation, a company in which Hanson had a 49 percent shareholding. Irl F. Engelhardt was named president of Peabody Group, while G. S. (Sam) Shiflett became Peabody Coal's 13th president.

In addition to the responsibilities of containing costs and implementing substantial changes in the company's Illinois Basin mines, Shiflett faced the threat of a strike by United Mine Workers during the first year of his presidency. Several developments in the coal industry contributed to dissatisfaction among mine workers. Technological advancements, including the computerization of some mining operations, led to reductions in the workforce. Moreover, new nonunion mining operations emerged, offering stiff competition through lower coal prices, which unionized miners feared would lead to wage cuts. Finally, as coal companies were increasingly acquired by large, international conglomerates, the lines of communication between labor and management became convoluted, and the potential for rifts increased.

The costly, extended strike and over a year of negotiations ended in December 1993, when the union agreed to a new four-year contract. The contract included provisions for an improved health care plan as well as the establishment of the Labor Management Positive Change Process (LMPCP). LMPCP, an effort to resolve future problems through cooperation rather than confrontation, invited employees to voice concerns regarding mine conditions and job security and suggest solutions. As chairperson of the Bituminous Coal Operators' Association, Peabody President Shiflett was instrumental in designing and negotiating the contract to resolve the strike.

In the mid-1990s, Peabody continued to rely on the utility industry as its primary customer base. With analysts predicting steady increases in the country's demand for coal in the 1990s and bolstered by rising demand at electric generation plants, Peabody Group looked forward to renewed profits and expansion throughout the 1990s.

CHANGING HANDS IN THE LATE NINETIES

Peabody and Eastern Group, a U.K. electricity distribution and generating company, were spun off by Hanson in March 1997 to create The Energy Group PLC. The new company planned to become an integrated electric company and immediately began buying U.S. power marketing companies such as Boston-based Citizens Lehman Power LLC. Renamed Citizens Power, this was eventually sold to Edison Mission Energy for about $110 million.

Within four months of listing on the London and New York stock exchanges, Energy Group attracted a takeover bid by Portland-based PacifiCorp. In May 1998, Lehman Merchant Banking Partners emerged as Peabody Group's new owner, paying Texas Utilities $2.3 billion. Texas Utilities had acquired Energy Group PLC for $7.4 billion and retained ownership of Eastern Group.

Peabody Coal raised its stake in Evansville, Indiana-based Black Beauty Coal Co. to 81.7 percent in February 1999. Peabody had owned 43.4 percent of Black Beauty and paid $150 million to buy 33.3 percent more from P&M Coal Mining Co. and 5 percent from a management group. Just before the purchase, Peabody had paid $1.3 million to settle a United Mine Workers claim related to the 1994 transfer of coal reserves to Black Beauty, a nonunion company.

Peabody announced a $1 billion, six-year contract to supply the Tennessee Valley Authority's Cumberland Generating Station in August 1999. The contract stipulated that two-thirds of the coal come from mines in Kentucky. Union and government officials were negotiating to keep those mines open beyond 2002, offering millions in incentives and concessions. Within a few months, Illinois Power would stop buying coal from Peabody's last Illinois mine, choosing lower-polluting Wyoming coal instead.

In late 2000, Peabody Coal's Black Mesa Mine in Arizona drew protests from members of the Hopi and Navajo tribes, which had leased Peabody the lands since the mid-1960s. The protesters took issue with the pumping of billions of gallons of water from the "N" aquifer to move pulverized coal along a 273-mile pipeline to the Mojave Generating Station in Laughlin, Nevada. A Peabody representative cited studies that the operations consumed less than 1 percent of the aquifer's water. (Members of the Hopi tribe would later sue Peabody for discrimination on the basis of national origin, alleging that the company hired only Navajos at its Kayenta and Black Mesa mines.)

P&L Coal Holdings Corporation, known commonly as Peabody Group, changed its name to Peabody Energy Corporation in April 2001. Peabody Energy netted $456 million in an initial public offering (IPO) held on May 22, 2001. The energy sector, stoked by California's recent power crisis, was hot again. The emphasis placed on coal by President George W. Bush and the Department of Energy made Peabody's pure play even more appealing. Lehman Merchant Banking Partners, a unit of Lehman Bros., retained a 59 percent stake in the company. Peabody was still left with $1 billion in debt after the IPO. Lehman had long placed a priority on reducing Peabody's debt. In January 2001, Peabody sold an Australian coal business to London's Rio Tinto PLC for about $450 million plus the assumption of $119 million in debt.

DOMESTIC AND INTERNATIONAL STRATEGY FOR THE 21ST CENTURY

Under the leadership of Irl Engelhardt, Peabody Energy sought to transform itself into a public company. In the United States, Peabody shifted from high-sulfur coal mining to primarily low-sulfur coal mining due to cost and environmental considerations. Also, the company invested in technology to reduce emissions at coal-fueled power generation stations. Internationally, Peabody prepared to supply growing Asian economies with coal. In particular, rapid economic development in China and India promised to sustain high demand for coal for decades to come.

In the western United States, Peabody purchased low-sulfur coal properties that would garner higher profit margins than its Appalachian operations. Peabody acquired mines in the Powder River Basin, an area rich in low-sulfur coal that overlapped Wyoming and Colorado. Peabody expanded the North Antelope-Rochelle coal mine in Wyoming, the largest coal mine worldwide. The acquisition placed Peabody among the largest coal producers worldwide.

In 2004 Peabody purchased the Twentymile Mine in Colorado, which produced more than seven million

tons of low-sulfur coal per year. It was one of the largest underground mines in the United States and one of the most productive. Installation of new equipment and the addition of 80 new employees resulted in a 40 percent increase in production.

The Twentymile Mine was part of a larger acquisition package that included two mines in Queensland, Australia. Peabody Energy purchased the three coal mines from RAG Coal International for $432 million. With annual production at seven million tons of coal, the Australian mines provided Peabody with a base of customers in growing Asian markets.

Although the company purchased a high-sulfur coal mine in southern Illinois and Indiana, it did so to retain its lead position in the southern Illinois energy market. In 2005 Peabody initiated development of a $2 billion electricity power plant adjacent to the mine, in Illinois. The Lively Grove Mine would supply coal to the 1,500 megawatt plant, which would use new technology for reducing carbon emissions from burning coal. Several municipal and cooperative utilities agreed to purchase an aggregate 47 percent interest in the project, called the Prairie State Energy Campus.

DIVESTMENTS, EXPANSION, AND IMPROVED PROFITABILITY

By early 2005, Peabody successfully made the transition to a profitable public company. The company divested its high-cost Appalachian assets, and expansion of the company's overall mining capacity occurred just as the market for coal began to explode due to higher costs for oil and natural gas. Revenue increased 29 percent in 2004, to $3.6 billion.

With George Boyce as chief operating officer, then chief executive officer, Peabody continued to develop international operations. Serving Asian markets involved developing sizable coal producing operations and opening new sales offices. The company opened an office in Beijing in the fall of 2005; established a relationship with Shenua Group, one of the largest coal producers in China, in April 2006; and began dealing in coal in early 2007. Joint ventures with established Chinese coal producers in 2009 further expanded Peabody's brokering and mining activities.

Peabody Energy accelerated mine development in Australia. The October 2006 acquisition of Excel Coal, Ltd., included 500 million tons of coal reserves. Construction of a coal export terminal in New South Wales, Australia, supported coal exports to China. In 2008 the company completed its acquisition of the Millennium Mine in Queensland and increased production capacity to three million tons annually. In the fall of

2009 Peabody Energy opened sales offices in Jakarta, Indonesia, and in Singapore.

Peabody planned to double coal production and exports by 2014. However, negotiations to acquire Macarthur Coal Ltd., the largest worldwide exporter of metallurgical coal, dissolved in the summer of 2010. Nevertheless, Peabody was well-positioned for growth, and Boyce considered the development of 100 gigawatts of clean electricity by 2025 to be a national security issue.

THE ENVIRONMENTAL FUTURE

As the coal industry sought to address public concern for carbon dioxide emissions at coal-fueled electricity generating plants, Peabody became interested in technologies for "clean coal." In 2007 Peabody joined the FutureGen Industrial Alliance, a collaboration with 12 energy companies and the U.S. Department of Energy, to develop a 275-megawatt power plant that reduced emissions more than 90 percent. FutureGen expected to open the power station using carbon capture technology in Mantoon, Illinois, in 2012.

However, Peabody and the coal industry faced opposition to the development and implementation of carbon capture and storage (CCS) technology from environmentalists. CCS involved a process of siphoning hydrogen from coal-burning emissions and using it to produce emission-free electricity. The remaining carbon dioxide would be stored underground, in geological formations. While this resolved the problem of air pollution, the safety of underground storage remained unproven.

Peabody obtained federal subsidies to invest in the development of clean coal technology. The company invested in technologies of other projects, such as China's GreenGen. In 2010 Peabody purchased a $15 million equity interest in Calera Corp. Calera developed CCS technology that recycled synthetic carbon monoxide into usable cement-like materials.

Tina Grant
Updated, Frederick C. Ingram; Mary Tradii

PRINCIPAL SUBSIDIARIES

Black Beauty Coal Company (81.7%); COAL TRADE LLC; Peabody Energy Australia Coal Pty, Ltd.

PRINCIPAL DIVISIONS

Western U.S. Mining; Midwestern U.S. Mining; Australian Mining; and Trading and Brokerage.

PRINCIPAL COMPETITORS

Arch Coal, Inc.; BHP Billiton Ltd.; CONSOL Energy Inc.; Kennecott Energy Co.; Massey Energy Company; Patriot Coal Corporation; Rio Tinto Ltd.

FURTHER READING

Brown, Mike, "Mine-Safety Chief Backs 'Judgment Call' in Note," *Louisville Courier-Journal*, September 23, 1986.

Dalin, Shera, "King Coal's Reign nears an End; Marissa Workers Ponder Life after Mining," *St. Louis Post-Dispatch*, November 15, 1998, p. E1.

Edwards, Greg, "Boyce Digs Peabody's Way to China," *St. Louis Business Journal*, April 23, 2010.

Eubanks, Ben, "Standing Up at Peabody," *St. Louis Business Journal*, January 14, 1985, pp. 1A, 13A.

Fanelli, Christa, "Peabody Energy Surges into IPO," *Buyouts*, June 4, 2001, p. 3.

Fiscor, Steve, "West Virginia's Largest Coal Company Trains for Positive Change," *Coal*, November 1994, pp. 25+.

Hudson, Repps, "Peabody Is Sold for $2.3 Billion; N.Y. Merchant Bankers May Sell It to the Public," *St. Louis Post-Dispatch*, May 20, 1998, p. C1.

Julian, Alan, "Peabody Ups Black Beauty Stake; $150 Million Deal Raises Union Questions," *Evansville Courier & Press*, February 16, 1999, p. B6.

Kammer, Jerry, "Tribes at Odds with Mine; An Unpleasant Water Fight Is Brewing," *Arizona Republic*, October 25, 2000, p. B1.

Lenhoff, Alyssa, "Miners Wonder What Coal Talks Will Produce," *Charleston Gazette*, January 5, 1988.

Lucas, John, "Peabody Gets $1 Billion Contract with TVA," *Evansville Courier & Press*, August 20, 1999, p. A1.

"Peabody Completes Buy of Three RAG Coal Mines," *St. Louis Business Journal*, April 15, 2004.

"Peabody Joins Effort to Build Near-Zero-Emissions Coal Plant," *St. Louis Business Journal*, September 13, 2005.

Schneider, Keith, "Coal Company Admits Safety Test Fraud," *New York Times*, January 19, 1991, p. 14.

Smothers, Ronald, "Union Prepares for Long Strike at Coal Mines," *New York Times*, February 6, 1993, p. 6.

Sprouls, Mark W., "Peabody's Roots Cling to Markets," *Coal*, November 1994, pp. 33+.

Symons, Emma-Kate, "Peabody Energy IPO Spotlights Resurgent Coal," *Pittsburgh Post-Gazette*, May 23, 2001, p. C4.

Tritto, Christopher, "Peabody Poised for Rebound as Reserves Soar," *St. Louis Business Journal*, January 5, 2007.

Willoughby, Jack, "Offerings in the Offing: Payday for King Coal," *Barron's*, May 7, 2001, p. 49.

Perrigo Company

515 Eastern Avenue
Allegan, Michigan 49010-9070
U.S.A.
Telephone: (269) 673-8451
Fax: (269) 673-7535
Web site: http://www.perrigo.com

Public Company
Founded: 1887
Incorporated: 1892
Employees: 7,700
Sales: $2.27 billion (2010)
Stock Exchanges: NASDAQ Tel Aviv
Ticker Symbol: PRGO
NAICS: 311514 Dry, Condensed, and Evaporated Dairy
   Product Manufacturing; 325411 Medicinal and
   Botanical Manufacturing; 325412 Pharmaceutical
   Preparation Manufacturing; 325413 In-Vitro
   Diagnostic Substance Manufacturing

■ ■ ■

Perrigo Company is the world's largest manufacturer of over-the-counter (OTC) pharmaceuticals, nutritional supplements, and infant formulas for store brands, producing more than 2,400 such products. The OTC pharmaceuticals include analgesics, cough and cold remedies, allergy and sinus medicines, and gastrointestinal and smoking cessation products. Nutritional products include vitamins and nutritional supplements. Perrigo supplies more than 800 different retailers with these products under the retailer's own label so that they can be promoted as house brands. The largest Perrigo customer by far is retailing giant Wal-Mart, which accounted for 23 percent of net sales for fiscal 2010. The company also markets certain products under its own brand name, Good Sense, although such products account for only a small percentage of sales. Perrigo manufactures and markets its OTC store-brand products primarily in the United States, the United Kingdom, Mexico, and Australia.

Perrigo also develops, manufactures, and markets generic prescription products, with about 300 such products in its portfolio. In addition, company plants in Israel and India manufacture active pharmaceutical ingredients for generic drug and branded pharmaceutical companies. Perrigo has enjoyed nearly continuous growth since the end of World War II. This growth can be partly attributed to the mass acceptance of generic and store-brand pharmaceutical products.

EARLY YEARS

The company was founded by Luther and Charles Perrigo in 1887. The Perrigo brothers had moved to Allegan County, Michigan, a few years earlier from New York. Once in Michigan the brothers established a modest business. Luther Perrigo ran a country general store and apple drying business, while Charles helped with sales. Luther decided to package generic home remedies and sell them to other small country stores like his own. The first packaging plant for these medicines was run out of Charles Perrigo's home, but Charles soon moved to Ohio, leaving the business entirely to his brother. Luther became president of the firm when it in-

COMPANY PERSPECTIVES

At Perrigo, our mission is clear—we seek to provide quality, affordable, healthcare products. An essential part of that mission, of course, is quality.

"Quality" is more than a concept at Perrigo, it is our most important priority. That is why we continually invest our time and resources in the quest to achieve ever higher levels of quality execution and quality products—for you, our own family members and everyone who uses our products.

corporated in 1892. Perrigo remained a family-owned business for 90 years. Five of the company's next seven presidents were descendants of Luther Perrigo, who died in 1902. His son Harry became president at that time, holding the position for the next 49 years.

During the 1920s the company turned to the private-label concept in order to build customer loyalty. Stores ordering a certain minimum number could have their own names imprinted on the labels. Products of the era that were the subject of such deals included aspirin, bay rum, Epsom salts, sweet oil, and zinc oxide. In the mid-1930s Perrigo gained its first major private-label customer, the K & W group, a buying organization that evolved into the People's Drug Store chain. The second such customer was Sam's, a major Detroit area drug chain. At the same time the company's customer base was shifting from small general stores to large regional and national drug chains.

POST-WORLD WAR II SHIFT FROM PACKAGER TO MANUFACTURER

Harry Perrigo turned over the reins to his brother Ray in 1951. It was in the 1950s, while still under the leadership of Ray Perrigo and William L. Tripp Sr., a future president, that the company made a crucial decision. Perrigo shifted its focus from that of a repackager of generic drugs to a manufacturer of quality drugs and beauty aids.

William L. Tripp, one of Luther Perrigo's grandchildren, became president in 1967. During Tripp's tenure as president the company began to reap the rewards of the change from repackager to manufacturer. The company's income and the number of Perrigo employees quadrupled. When Tripp died in 1969 his son Bill Tripp Jr. took over the presidency.

During the 1970s Perrigo's base of customers expanded with the addition of grocery chains and mass merchandisers to the core drugstore chains. By the time of Bill Tripp Jr.'s death in a boating accident in 1980 at the age of 45, Perrigo was the leading private-label manufacturer of health and beauty products in the United States. William C. Swaney had been named president of the company two years before the accident, becoming the first leader of the company who was not a member of the Perrigo family.

END OF FAMILY OWNERSHIP

Swaney's presidency lasted from 1978 until 1983. In those five years Perrigo sales tripled and the company became a much larger operation all around. Swaney acquired new companies, set up distribution centers in three states, and expanded and refurbished existing plants. Before leaving as president Swaney oversaw the sale of the company from the Perrigo family to the management. Almost 100 years of family ownership ended.

Michael Jandernoa, who had joined the company in 1979 as vice president for finance, became the seventh president of Perrigo in 1984, while Swaney took over as chairman of the board and CEO. Swaney instituted a style of management at Perrigo that his successor Jandernoa admitted he probably would have tried to block had he been in a position to do so at the time. However, Jandernoa came to appreciate the open style of administration that Swaney initiated. The company contended that the different disciplines interacted in the decision-making process much more than in traditional U.S. businesses.

GROW GROUP ERA

Jandernoa continued the policy of expansion started by Swaney. Perrigo acquired Bell Pharmacal Labs of South Carolina in 1984. Early in the Jandernoa presidency, however, the board of directors began entertaining offers from larger companies interested in acquiring Perrigo itself. In 1986 Perrigo became the largest single company in Grow Group, Inc., a publicly held group of 23 manufacturing companies that bought Perrigo for $45 million. Jandernoa was named CEO of Perrigo. He continued to serve as president. Perrigo represented about a third of Grow Group. As the largest component in a conglomerate with access to capital through the New York Stock Exchange, Perrigo was able to raise new funds for more expansion.

Perrigo celebrated the company's centenary with two ambitious building projects. It built a $1.5 million

KEY DATES

1887: Luther and Charles Perrigo begin packaging generic home remedies and selling them at their own store and to other general stores.

1892: Company is incorporated.

1986: Company is sold to Grow Group, Inc., for $45 million.

1988: Grow Group sells the company back to management for $106 million.

1991: Perrigo is taken public.

1997: Controlling stake in Mexican pharmaceutical firm Química y Farmacia, S.A. de C.V., is acquired.

1999: Personal care business is divested to focus the company on OTC drugs and nutritional products.

2001: Perrigo acquires Wrafton Laboratories Ltd., a U.K. maker of store-brand pharmaceuticals.

2005: Company acquires Israel-based Agis Industries Ltd.

2010: PBM Holdings, Inc., maker of store-brand infant formulas, is purchased.

plant for the manufacture of effervescent tablets and a $3.5 million graphic arts complex to house all of the company's printing needs. Because Perrigo supplied many different retailers with the same house-brand product, printing facilities were an important part of the firm's production system. The graphics and printing department employed about 290 people and produced almost 70 percent of the company's labels and 44 percent of its cartons in the early 1990s. The construction of the graphics department, coupled with other expenses, totaled approximately $12.6 million in outlays to the company's printing and graphics department since the Grow purchase in 1986.

BACK TO MANAGEMENT OWNERSHIP AND THEN TAKEN PUBLIC

After only two years as a part of Grow Group, however, Perrigo was sold back to its management in 1988 in a $106 million deal. That year the company posted sales of $146 million, but by 1994 company sales had ballooned to $669 million. Three years after the sale by Grow to Perrigo management, Jandernoa took the company public. The stock proved popular, although the value fell and rose significantly over time. The market value of the company in July 1994 based on a closing price of $14 a share was $1 billion, for instance. However, this price was down from a value of $32 a share in January 1994.

The drop in the value of Perrigo shares was attributed to a drop in sales growth. The company, in fact, had another year of record sales and continued to expand, but stock speculators felt that the market had overreacted to the Perrigo stock offering and had inflated the value beyond its true market worth. Some analysts predicted that the drop in growth was a sign that the national brands would win back bargain-hunting customers in a healthy economy.

Other problems that Perrigo faced in its competition with national brands in the early 1990s concerned finding the right price range for its products. While Perrigo had long wielded its ability to offer lower prices than national brand competitors, sometimes the price difference could be so dramatic (more than 50 percent in some cases) that it could have a reverse effect on the consumer. The consumer weighed the relative cost savings with a judgment on efficacy equivalence. If the price difference was too dramatic, some observers contended, the consumer became suspicious of the Perrigo brand and turned to the national brand. Perrigo therefore developed a system whereby some of the money that it saved from advertising was spent on market research to determine exactly how its products were accepted by the consumer, which products were worth developing, and which had limited potential because of brand allegiance.

One reason for Perrigo's enormous dominance over the store-brand market was its ability to work closely with retailers to promote consumer allegiance to store brands. Beginning in the 1980s Perrigo instituted a major campaign to help retailers design labels, manage inventory, and develop promotions. Perrigo used its house printing and graphics department to ensure accuracy and reliability in labeling and packaging, permitting rapid new product introductions. Perrigo also enjoyed an advantage over many of its competitors because retail stores had a real incentive to give Perrigo's products prominence on their shelves. Profit margins for store-brand products were considerably greater than for national brands. The store's public image could be enhanced as well, provided the product sold under their name was satisfactory.

Most of Perrigo's products were packaged to be readily identifiable with the national brand equivalents. There was a fine line between taking advantage of the competitor's advertising and carving out a niche that was independently recognized by the consumer. The *OTC Market Report* disclosed in 1995 that the company was threatened with lawsuits "once or twice a year," but the vast majority of them were settled in a short time. Most of the disputes focused on product dress rather than the actual content of the product. While Perrigo management had become accustomed to lawsuits from competitor companies, in July 1994 Perrigo found itself faced with a lawsuit from closer to home. Its former parent company, Grow Group, filed suit against the company. The Grow Group, valued at less than half of Perrigo, demanded the return of Perrigo stock or a sizable settlement in lieu thereof. Grow claimed that Perrigo management did not act in good faith at the time of the 1988 sale, particularly alleging that they did not reveal a pending agreement to supply products to Wal-Mart, and asked for $2 billion in actual damages and $2 billion in punitive damages. Perrigo contended that the suit was wholly without merit.

One of the company's strengths was that it faced little legitimate competition. In December 1994 the company purchased Vi-Jon Laboratories, Inc., a leading manufacturer of store-brand personal care products, thereby expanding Perrigo's sales and eliminating a potential competitor at the same time. The purchase price was about $33 million. A similar acquisition occurred earlier, in January 1992, when Cumberland-Swan, Inc., a Tennessee-based maker of store-brand personal care products and vitamins, was bought for $35 million.

As the patents on dozens of major prescription drugs began to run out in the mid-1990s, Perrigo began to aggressively go after these lucrative new sources of revenue. Once a prescription drug was reclassified as OTC, the patent holder had two years of exclusivity. At that point generic versions of brand-name OTC products could be produced. An example of this process was Tavist-D, a decongestant and antihistamine that switched from prescription-only to OTC status in 1992. Two years later, Perrigo reached an agreement with the drug's maker, Sandoz Pharmaceuticals Corp., to begin making a store-brand version of Tavist-D in 1995. In subsequent years, Perrigo increasingly turned to such joint ventures to develop new products.

Also in the mid-1990s, Perrigo began looking to the international market for growth, forming subsidiary Perrigo International, Inc., to lead this effort. Among the initially targeted countries were Canada, Japan, Mexico, and Russia.

LATE-CENTURY TRAVAILS

With the Grow Group lawsuit still pending, Perrigo received another legal headache in early 1995 when it was the subject of a class-action lawsuit initiated by

shareholders. The investors had purchased company stock through an October 1993 secondary offering, in which mostly shares held by company officials were sold. Only a few months later the stock price plunged after its stellar earnings growth began to fade. The plaintiffs claimed that company officials inflated the stock's offering price by withholding critical information indicating potential problems facing Perrigo. By the late 1990s, however, both this suit and the one brought by the Grow Group had been dismissed, but not before Perrigo had spent about $27 million defending itself against the suits, which also served as a major distraction.

Revenue growth slowed and profits fell in both fiscal 1995 and 1996 thanks to a number of factors: stiffer competition, including surging sales of the pain reliever Aleve, which switched to OTC status in 1994 and cut into Perrigo's analgesic sales; difficulties with the personal care product lines that had been acquired from Vi-Jon Laboratories; and two unusually weak cold and flu seasons in a row. Perrigo responded in June 1995 with a restructuring involving 180 job cuts, a reduction in distribution centers from seven to four, and a merger of sales and marketing functions across all of the company's product lines.

Results for fiscal 1997 were better with both revenues and profits on the upswing. Aiding this performance was the launch of additional store-brand products for former prescription drugs that had switched to OTC status. These included Aleve and the hair-restoration product Rogaine. In late 1997 Perrigo purchased an 88 percent stake in Química y Farmacia, S.A. de C.V. (Quífa), for $17 million. Based in Monterrey, Mexico, Quífa was a producer of both OTC and prescription products. The purchase provided Perrigo with its first manufacturing capacity outside the United States.

Perrigo also spent $14 million to acquire a minority stake in Sagmel, Inc., the largest distributor of pharmaceutical products in Russia and Ukraine, in 1997. This move soon turned disastrous, however, when the Russian economic crisis erupted, and the subsequent devaluation of the ruble cost the company millions, and ended its Russian venture. Compounding the company's difficulties was the continuing poor performance of its personal care business. In June 1998 Perrigo announced that it would sell this unit, which included baby care items, toothpaste, deodorants, and other products, in order to focus on its higher-margin OTC drug and nutritional product lines. Two plants in California and Missouri were closed, eliminating about 160 jobs from the workforce, and an $86.9 million restructuring charge was taken, resulting in a net loss for the year of $51.6 million.

More difficulties cropped up following the botched implementation of a new companywide computer system. Installation of the system began in September 1998, and it would take 18 months before all of the problems were ironed out. Perrigo suffered tens of millions of dollars in lost revenues because products could not be shipped to its customers. New product development was largely put on hold as company officials had to concentrate on the computer fiasco. The company did manage to sell its personal care business in August 1999 to a Nashville investor group calling itself Cumberland Swan Holdings Inc. A further cost-cutting move in 1999 involved the elimination of another 130 jobs from the company payroll, a measure aimed at saving as much as $6 million a year.

EFFECTING A TURNAROUND UNDER NEW LEADERSHIP

In May 2000 David T. Gibbons was brought onboard as president and CEO. Jandernoa remained chairman. Reputed to be a turnaround artist, Gibbons had more than three decades of experience at two major consumer goods companies, Minnesota Mining & Manufacturing Company and Rubbermaid Incorporated. Gibbons joined Perrigo at a particularly dark time. Stock prices had plummeted to just over $5 per share.

Within months of taking his post, the new leader had to grapple with two more challenges. In August 2000 the Food and Drug Administration (FDA) issued a warning letter to the company because it had mislabeled 500-milligram acetaminophen as 200-milligram ibuprofen. Perrigo voluntarily stopped production of the product, and the FDA said that it would not approve any new Perrigo products until the quality-control issue was fixed. Gibbons soon had 130 people working on this issue, and when the FDA revisited the plant in question in May 2001, it received a clean bill of health. The company was then able within the next couple of months to rush to market two new products, private-label versions of Pepcid AC, an acid reducer, and Advil Cold and Sinus. Perrigo was now placing an increasing emphasis on being the first to market, particularly with products switching from prescription to OTC status, because a new FDA incentive gave the first to market with such a "switch" drug a 180-day period of exclusivity before competitors could join the fray—a keen advantage. In the first years of the 21st century, Perrigo succeeded in being first to market on 80 percent of the switch products it sold. In fact, with one-third of such products, Perrigo remained the only supplier of a store-brand equivalent.

In November 2000, meanwhile, the FDA recommended that phenylpropanolamine (PPA), a key ingredient in many cough and cold remedies, no longer be considered safe because it was believed to cause hemorrhagic stroke. Perrigo used PPA in 10 of its product formulas, resulting in a huge recall that cost the company about $21 million. Despite these latest difficulties, Perrigo managed to achieve a profit of $27.7 million in fiscal 2001, which was a 43 percent increase over the prior year. In June 2001, at the end of that fiscal year, Perrigo paid $44 million to acquire Wrafton Laboratories Limited, a manufacturer of store-brand products for grocery and pharmacy retailers in the United Kingdom.

During fiscal 2002 and 2003 Perrigo achieved steadily increasing profits and made numerous new product introductions. In fiscal 2002 these included store-brand equivalents of Excedrin Migraine and Centrum Performance, a multivitamin. Perrigo that year began an expansion of its research and development lab in Allegan to bolster its ability to develop new products. In addition, the Mexican subsidiary Quifa, now wholly owned by Perrigo, was restructured in order to build its store-brand business and de-emphasize its prescription drug activities. In January 2003 Perrigo's recovery had proceeded to the point where it could count on ongoing cash flow, and could begin paying a dividend for the first time.

That same month, the company signed an agreement with Andrx Corporation whereby Andrx would manufacture and Perrigo would package and resell several versions of Claritin. A blockbuster as a prescription allergy drug, Claritin was the latest brand-name drug to make the switch to an OTC product, and it was potentially one of the most lucrative for Perrigo. In June 2003 the company began shipping a store-brand version of Claritin-D 24 Hour. Two months later, Gibbons was rewarded for his turnaround efforts by being named to the additional post of chairman. Jandernoa relinquished the post but remained on the board of directors.

A MOVE INTO GENERICS

A newly confident Perrigo invested about $5 million in internal research and development during fiscal 2004, as a first step into the rapidly growing generic prescription drug market. The company then accelerated its entrance into this sector in March 2005 by acquiring Israel-based Agis Industries Ltd. for about $841 million. Agis's generics business focused on topical, dermatological products. In addition, plants in Israel and Germany produced active pharmaceutical ingredients for generic drug and branded pharmaceutical companies. In association with its purchase of the publicly traded Agis, Perrigo was listed on the Tel Aviv Stock Exchange. Also in connection with the Agis acquisition, Perrigo took a $386.8 million write-off of in-process research and development acquired in the deal, leading to a net loss of $353 million for fiscal 2005.

During 2006, Perrigo shut down two production facilities in Michigan, located in Holland and Montague, as part of its integration of Agis. The company that year also contended with a large hit to its revenues stemming from new federal rules that placed restrictions on the purchases of OTC products containing the decongestant pseudoephedrine because this active ingredient was being misused to manufacture methamphetamine. Perrigo and other makers of cough and cold remedies worked quickly to develop new products not containing pseudoephedrine, with Perrigo debuting formulations featuring the generic decongestant phenylepherine.

In October 2006 Perrigo brought onboard Joseph Papa as its new president and CEO, succeeding Gibbons, who remained chairman for another year before Papa assumed that position as well. Papa was a veteran of the health care industry who had most recently served as chairman and CEO of the pharmaceutical and technologies services segment of Cardinal Health, Inc. Soon after Papa joined the company, Perrigo was forced to recall about 11 million bottles of acetaminophen caplets after discovering metal fragments had gotten into some batches because of premature wearing of the equipment used to make the pills. The recall cost the firm about $6.5 million.

Over the next few years, Perrigo continued to churn out new products, including OTC store-brand versions of two major heartburn medications, Prilosec OTC and Pepcid Complete, which were introduced in fiscal years 2008 and 2009, respectively. These debuts helped the company generate $328.1 million in net sales related to new products in fiscal 2009. This represented about 16 percent of Perrigo's total sales for the year of $2.01 billion.

BUILDING STRENGTH THROUGH ACQUISITIONS

At the same time, Perrigo completed a series of acquisitions to strengthen its existing product lines and expand into new ones, as well as extend its geographic reach. In March 2007 the company spent about $12 million for Qualis, Inc., a privately held manufacturer of store-brand head lice treatment products. Perrigo bolstered its overseas operations in January 2008 by acquiring Galpharm Healthcare Ltd., the leading producer of OTC store-brand pharmaceutical products in the United

Kingdom, for $83.3 million. In a September 2008 deal mainly designed to bolster the firm's manufacturing capacity, Perrigo paid $43.6 million for J.B. Laboratories, Inc., which produced OTC and nutrition products for leading drug firms. J.B. operated a 160,000-square-foot manufacturing plant and leased a 150,000-square-foot warehouse, both located in the vicinity of Holland, Michigan.

Perrigo expanded its operations south of the border in October 2008 by acquiring Laboratorios DIBA S.A. for $24.5 million. DIBA specialized in store-brand OTC and prescription pharmaceuticals, including antibiotics, hormonals, and ophthalmics. A month later, Perrigo purchased the leading U.S. manufacturer of store-brand pediatric electrolytes, enemas, and feminine-hygiene products, Lake Worth, Florida-based Unico Holdings, Inc., for $51.9 million.

In early 2010 Perrigo divested an Israel-based consumer products business that had been one of the assets acquired in the purchase of Agis. At the same time, Perrigo was in the process of restructuring the manufacturing operations of its active pharmaceutical ingredients division by shutting down a plant in Germany and constructing a new one in India. In a March 2010, $48.6 million deal, the company bought Orion Laboratories Pty Ltd., a firm based in Perth, Australia, that was a leading supplier of OTC store-brand pharmaceutical products in Australia and New Zealand.

A month later, Perrigo made a major move into a product category adjacent to its existing lines by acquiring PBM Holdings, Inc., for about $810 million. PBM, based in Gordonsville, Virginia, was the leading producer and distributor of store-brand infant formulas, pediatric nutritional products, and baby foods in the U.S. mass merchandising, warehouse club, grocery, and drugstore channels. Perrigo also gained a greater presence overseas through PBM's operations in Canada, Mexico, China, Saudi Arabia, and elsewhere. This deal was expected to add about $300 million to Perrigo's fiscal 2011 sales, after the firm had enjoyed its best year ever in 2010, when it reported net income of $222.5 million on sales of $2.27 billion.

Donald C. McManus and Hilary Gopnik
Updated, David E. Salamie

PRINCIPAL SUBSIDIARIES

L. Perrigo Company; Perrigo Company of South Carolina, Inc.; Perrigo New York, Inc.; Perrigo Holland, Inc.; Perrigo Florida, Inc.; PBM Holdings, Inc.; Perrigo Israel Pharmaceuticals Ltd.; Chemagis Ltd. (Israel);

Química y Farmacia, S.A. de C.V. (Mexico); Laboratorios DIBA S.A. (Mexico); Wrafton Laboratories Limited (UK); Brunel Pharma Limited (UK); Galpharm Healthcare Ltd. (UK); Orion Laboratories Pty Ltd. (Australia).

PRINCIPAL COMPETITORS

Aaron Industries, Inc.; Abbott Laboratories; Actavis Group hf.; Dr. Reddy's Laboratories Ltd.; E. Fougera & Co.; Glenmark Generics Inc.; International Vitamin Corporation; LNK International, Inc.; Mead Johnson Nutrition Company; NBTY, Inc.; Nestlé S.A.; Ohm Laboratories, Inc.; Sandoz International GmbH; Taro Pharmaceutical Industries Ltd.; Teva Pharmaceutical Industries Limited; TOLMAR Holding, Inc.; Triax Pharmaceuticals, LLC; Watson Pharmaceuticals, Inc.

FURTHER READING

Berman, Dennis K., "Perrigo to Buy Israeli Drug Maker Agis Industries," *Wall Street Journal*, November 15, 2004, p. B6.

Crawley, Nancy, "'It's Tough to Knock Us Off the Shelf,' Perrigo Shows," *Grand Rapids (MI) Press*, June 10, 2001, p. G1.

Emrich, Anne Bond, "Perrigo Welcomes New President, CEO," *Grand Rapids (MI) Business Journal*, October 16, 2006, p. 3.

Kirkbride, Rob, "Perrigo Counts on Prescriptions for Healthy Growth," *Grand Rapids (MI) Press*, August 12, 2003, p. A13.

Sabo, Mary Ann, "Perrigo Dumps Personal Care Business, Shuts Plants," *Grand Rapids (MI) Press*, June 30, 1998, p. B5.

Slowik, Elizabeth, "Newsmaker of the Year: Perrigo Surfs Recession with Strong Results from OTC Products," *Grand Rapids (MI) Business Journal*, January 25, 2010, p. 15.

Stern, Gabriella, "Cheap Imitation: Perrigo's Knockoffs of Name-Brand Drugs Turn into Big Sellers," *Wall Street Journal*, July 15, 1993, p. A1.

Wieland, Barbara, "No More Bitter Pills? New CEO Confident He Has Prescription for Turning Perrigo Around," *Grand Rapids (MI) Press*, October 1, 2000, p. B1.

Xu, Jodi, "Perrigo Plans to Buy Infant-Formula Maker," *Wall Street Journal*, March 24, 2010, p. B3.

Pixar Animation Studios, Inc.

1200 Park Avenue
Emeryville, California 94608
U.S.A.
Telephone: (510) 922-3000
Fax: (510) 922-3151
Web site: http://www.pixar.com

Wholly Owned Subsidiary of The Walt Disney Company
Incorporated: 1986
Employees: 850
NAICS: 512110 Motion Picture Production

■ ■ ■

Pixar Animation Studios, Inc., burst onto the big screen with the release of *Toy Story*, the first feature-length animated film created solely through computerized graphics. Nonetheless, Pixar's background is one of considerable pedigree, from roots at the University of Utah and the New York Institute of Technology before becoming part of George Lucas's Lucasfilm Ltd. of San Rafael, California. Purchased in 1986 by computer wunderkind Steven P. Jobs, cofounder of Apple Computer and NeXT Inc., the newly independent company was named after its primary product, the Pixar computer.

After several one-of-a-kind, award-winning computer graphics and animation software packages (including the patented RenderMan, Ringmaster, Marionette, and CAPS), Pixar's creative geniuses produced some memorable television commercials before joining forces with Walt Disney to design and produce feature-

length animated films. These works, *Toy Story* and its successor, *Toy Story 2*, as well as *A Bug's Life*, were huge hits for both Disney and Pixar, beloved by audiences and critics alike. Pixar's talent lineup has been the recipient of nine Academy Awards at the end of the first decade of the twenty-first century.

LAYING THE GROUNDWORK: THE SEVENTIES AND EIGHTIES

Pixar's tenuous evolution began in the 1970s when millionaire Alexander Schare, then president of the New York Institute of Technology (NYIT), was looking for someone to create an animated film from a sound recording of *Tubby the Tuba*. Enter a computer scientist named Ed Catmull with a Ph.D. from the University of Utah, who along with several others set up house (at Schare's expense) at NYIT's Long Island campus to work with computer graphics. Although *Tubby the Tuba* was never made, the team successfully produced video artwork. When creative mogul George Lucas proposed moving the team to the West Coast in 1979 as part of Lucasfilm Ltd., the breeding ground of the original *Star Wars* trilogy, Catmull and his colleagues agreed.

Over the next few years, Catmull and his ensemble created innovative graphics programs and equipment for Lucas, including an imaging computer called the "Pixar." The Pixar was then used to develop high-tech graphics and animation sequences for Lucasfilm projects. Unlike other computers, Pixar's software constructed high-resolution, three-dimensional (3D) color images of virtually anything, from buildings and cars to tornadoes and aliens. Remarkably, Pixar was also capable of helping medical professionals at Johns Hopkins diagnose

Pixar is an Academy Award-winning computer animation studio with the technical, creative and production capabilities to create a new generation of animated feature films, merchandise and other related products. Pixar's objective is to combine proprietary technology and world-class creative talent to develop computer-animated feature films with a new three-dimensional appearance, memorable characters and heartwarming stories that appeal to audiences of all ages.

diseases from 3D renderings of CAT scans and x-rays; giving weather technicians new images from satellites; and even helping prospectors locate oil from enhanced seismic readings, all at a speed some 200 times faster than previous computer programs.

In 1984, John Lasseter, who had met Catmull at a computer graphics conference and was employed by Walt Disney Studios, visited Lucasfilm for a monthlong stint. Lasseter, who had graduated from the California Institute of the Arts where he had won two Student Academy Awards for animated film, decided to stay. Meanwhile, after spinning off a joint venture called Droid Works, George Lucas started shopping around Pixar with hopes of a second spin-off. Pixar caught the interest of several companies, including EDS, then a division of General Motors; Philips N.V.; and computer whiz-kid Steve Jobs, cofounder and chairman of Apple Computer Inc. Unable to persuade Apple's board of directors to invest in or purchase the fledgling graphics company, Jobs reluctantly abandoned his hopes for owning Pixar.

However, circumstances changed drastically for Jobs in 1985. Stripped of his responsibilities and deposed from his Apple kingdom (at about the same time the first Pixar computer went on the market for $105,000), Jobs sold the majority of his Apple stock and started over. Plunging $12 million into a new computer enterprise named NeXT Inc., specializing in personal computers for colleges and universities, Jobs approached Lucas in 1986 and paid $10 million for the San Raphael-based Pixar and created an independent company. Although Catmull, Lasseter, and crew regarded Jobs as kin in their quest for high-tech fun and games given his laid-back reputation and status as a computer wonder boy, the new boss instructed them to put aside their dreams of animation and film and to instead concentrate on technical graphics they could sell.

HIGHS AND LOWS: LATE 1980s TO 1991

"If I knew in 1986 how much it was going to cost to keep Pixar going, I doubt if I would've bought the company," Jobs later told *Fortune* magazine. "The problem was, for many years the cost of the computers required to make animation we could sell was tremendously high." Luckily, Pixar's crew came up with several software innovations, which they used to create a myriad of products. In 1986 came the first of many Oscar nominations from the Academy of Motion Picture Arts and Sciences for a short animated film called *Luxo Jr.*

Next came *Red's Dream* in 1987, then the development of RenderMan, for which the company applied for and received a patent. A revolutionary graphics program that allowed computer artists to add color and create texture to onscreen 3D objects, RenderMan produced stunningly realistic photo images almost indistinguishable from actual photographs. RenderMan's brand of images paid off when *Tin Toy*, written and directed by Lasseter as the first computer-generated animation, won an Academy Award as Best Animated Short Film in 1988.

As CEO of Pixar, Jobs expanded the company's leading-edge graphics and animation capabilities by joining forces in July 1989 with the San Francisco-based Colossal Pictures, a live-action, animation, and special effects studio, for collaboration purposes and to broker Pixar for television commercials and promotional films. With Colossal's background and experience in broadcast media and Pixar's unique computer capabilities, the partnership was poised for tremendous success. By 1990 when more than a dozen RenderMan products were introduced, RenderMan licensing fees finally began to pay off. Not only were many hardware and software packagers incorporating the graphics program into their products, but RenderMan was endorsed by such industry heavyweights as Digital Equipment, IBM, Intel Corporation, and Sun Microsystems. In addition, Pixar created two commercials in its association with Colossal. The second commercial, for Life Savers "Holes" bite-size candies (which took 12 weeks to produce using RenderMan's software), aired in March and was a hit with audiences.

In April 1990 Pixar signed a letter of intent to sell its valuable yet stagnating hardware operations, including all proprietary hardware technology and imaging software, to Vicom Systems of Fremont, California. The move, which included the transfer of 18 of Pixar's 100 employees, was finalized several weeks later and allowed Pixar to devote the company's full energy to further development of its rendering capabilities. Before the end

```
┌─────────────────────────────────────────┐
│                                           │
│            KEY DATES                      │
│                 ■                         │
│                                           │
│  1979:  George Lucas brings Ed Catmull and associ-  │
│         ates from the New York Institute of Technol- │
│         ogy to the West Coast as part of Lucasfilm   │
│         Ltd.                              │
│  1986:  Lucas spins off Pixar computer graphics unit, │
│         which is bought and incorporated by Steve    │
│         Jobs.                             │
│  1988:  Company receives first Academy Award for     │
│         *Tin Toy.*                        │
│  1995:  *Toy Story* debuts and conquers box office;  │
│         company completes its initial public offering. │
│  1997:  *A Bug's Life* opens at the box office.      │
│  1999:  *Toy Story 2* debuts and breaks box-office   │
│         records; Pixar claims its ninth Academy      │
│         Award for Technical Achievement.             │
│  2000:  Company moves to new headquarters in Em-     │
│         eryville, California.             │
│  2006:  Company becomes a subsidiary of The Walt     │
│         Disney Company.                   │
│                                           │
└─────────────────────────────────────────┘
```

of the year, Pixar moved from San Rafael to new $15 million digs in the Point Richmond Tech Center of Richmond, California, and reached revenues of just under $3.4 million, although still not reporting a profit.

While Jobs's other company, NeXT Inc., seemed to prosper and was expected to reach $100 million in computer sales, Pixar still struggled to make ends meet in 1991. In February, 30 employees were laid off, including President Charles Kolstad. Jobs, sometimes criticized as a mercurial spinmeister with too little substance to back up his visions and words, was brought to task in the media for the shortcomings of both companies. Salvation came to Pixar in the name of *Toy Story*, the first full-length computer-animated feature film, as a collaboration between Pixar and Lasseter's old stomping grounds, Walt Disney Studios. Signing a contract to produce quality "digital entertainment," Pixar was responsible for the content and animation of three full-length films. Disney provided the funding for production and promotional costs, owning the marketing and licensing fees of the films and their characters. Although Disney retained the lion's share of revenue and profit, Pixar negotiated for a slice of the gross revenues from the box-office and subsequent video sales. At this juncture, neither Disney nor Pixar knew the potential of their alliance, one that proved successful beyond their wildest expectations.

THE RIGHT MIX OF MAGIC AND MASTERY: 1992–95

In 1992, the joint project between Pixar and Disney called CAPS (computer animated production system) was another stellar development, winning Pixar's second Academy Award (shared with Disney). The following year, Jobs's NeXT Inc., like Pixar before it, was forced to lay off workers and sell its hardware division to concentrate on software development and applications. Nonetheless, 1993 was a banner year for Pixar, with RenderMan winning the company's third Academy Award and a Gold Clio (for advertising excellence) for the funky animated Listerine "Arrows" commercial. The next year, Pixar won its second Gold Clio for the Lifesavers "Conga" commercial, a colorful romp with a contagious beat. Despite such heavy accolades from critics and peers, Pixar still had not managed a profit since its spin-off in 1986, and reported a loss of $2.4 million on revenues of $5.6 million for 1994.

The following year, in 1995, Pixar was wrapping up its work on *Toy Story* and everyone was anxious for the finished result to hit theaters in November. Tom Hanks, Tim Allen, Don Rickles, and Annie Potts had signed on to voice major characters, and Randy Newman was composing the film's musical score. By the end of the third quarter with more than 100,000 copies of Render-Man sold and a huge licensing deal with Bill Gates and Microsoft, Pixar announced its first profit ever—$3.1 million on revenues of $10.6 million.

For Pixar, 1995 was a string of accelerating successes: first came *Toy Story*'s pre-Thanksgiving release, grossing over $40 million its first weekend, with rave reviews from critics and families alike. Leading box-office receipts, both Disney and Pixar hoped *Toy Story* could best *Pochahontas*'s $140 million take earlier in the year. Next came Pixar's initial public offering (IPO) of 6.9 million shares in November on the NASDAQ. The market closed at $22 per share, up from its initial offering of $12 to $14 each, giving Pixar a market value of some $800 million. Jobs, who since his purchase of Pixar for $10 million had sunk an additional $50 million into the enterprise, recouped a handsome paper profit of more than $600 million for his 80 percent stake. The shares eventually hit a high of $45.50 on November 30.

Another boon came when *Toy Story* garnered several award nominations, including Randy Newman's score for two Golden Globes and an Oscar; an Oscar for Catmull and Thomas Porter, director of effects animation or digital scanning technology; and an additional Special Achievement Oscar for Lasseter's writing, direction, and technical wizardry for *Toy Story*.

MULTIPLE LIGHTNING STRIKES: 1996–99

After the release of *Toy Story*, while part of Pixar's crew worked on a CD-ROM game of the animated film, others were busy working on several Coca-Cola commercials for the Creative Arts Agency, hired by Michael Ovitz. Pixar was also immersed in its next Disney film, *A Bug's Life*, which was scheduled for release in two years. By February 1996, *Toy Story* had grossed over $177 million at the box office and in March Lasseter attended the Academy Awards to receive his Oscar. He brought along Woody and Buzz Lightyear, who were part of several sketches and fodder for running gags during the live telecast. Pixar completed the year with a huge leap in revenues, up to $38.2 million (from 1995's $12.1 million), extraordinary net income of $25.3 million, and stock prices hitting a high of $49 per share in the fourth quarter.

Although Bob Bennett of Autodesk, Inc., a client and competitor of Pixar, had said that Pixar was the best in the world at what it did, continued advances in computer and graphics technology brought considerable competition. Everyone it seemed, from Digital Domain and Industrial Light & Magic to Microsoft and Silicon Graphics, was trying their hand at graphics software development. After the stellar success of *Toy Story*, all the major motion picture studios were creating computerized animation, including DreamWorks SKG, Turner Broadcasting, Warner Bros., and even Disney.

Other developments surrounded Jobs, as Apple stumbled horribly and the company came close to financial ruin. Still attached to the company he had cofounded and brought to enormous success, Jobs came to its rescue in 1997 shortly after Apple bought his NeXT Inc. Few doubted Jobs's ability to juggle both Pixar and Apple, and they were right. Not only did Jobs bring Apple back to the forefront of the computer industry with the flashy iMac, but Pixar went on to rule the box office with *A Bug's Life*. During the magic holiday window of October, November, and December 1997, *A Bug's Life* was up against four animated films, including another insect-related story by DreamWorks SKG, titled *Antz*. DreamWorks had also released *The Prince of Egypt* and Nickelodeon brought *The Rugrats Movie* to the big screen as well. Even so, Pixar beat the pack and went on to ring up over $360 million in worldwide box-office receipts, even topping *Toy Story*.

Once again Pixar was nominated for and won big at the Academy Awards: two separate awards for Scientific and Technical Achievement (for the Marionette 3D Animation System, and for digital painting), as well as another for Best Animated Short Film (*Geri's Game*). Pixar also finally received a sizable financial boost in 1997, as revenues and net income reached $34.7 million and $22.1 million, respectively. The box-office and critical triumphs of both *Toy Story* and *A Bug's Life* also brought a new deal with Disney to produce an additional five pictures within the next 10 years, with both companies as equal partners. The agreement eclipsed the previous deal. The former's remaining two films became the first two of the new five-picture negotiation. Lastly, Pixar would sell Disney up to 5 percent of its common stock at $15 per share.

In early 1998 *A Bug's Life* was released on video and DVD simultaneously and Pixar's top guns worked feverishly on the sequel to *Toy Story*, slated for release in November. The sequel was a gamble, since only one animated feature film had ever spawned a theater-released follow-up, Disney's *The Rescuers Down Under*. Most sequels or prequels were released directly to video. Pixar was ready to buck the trend. Dollars from its venture with Disney continued to slowly trickle in and Pixar finished the year with $14.3 million in revenue and net earnings of $7.8 million.

The last year of the century brought more kudos for Pixar. David DiFrancesco won the company's ninth Academy Award (for Technical Achievement), *Toy Story 2* opened in November to sweeping box-office dominance (even higher receipts than *Star Wars: The Phantom Menace*'s first few weeks of release the year before), and the company celebrated its fifth-consecutive profitable year, with revenues of $121 million and earnings topping $50 million.

THE NEW CENTURY: RELEASING A STRING OF BOX-OFFICE HITS

Pixar was as busy as ever during the first months of the 21st century as the company prepared to move into its new 225,000-square-foot headquarters in Emeryville, California. It was also hard at work on its next full-length animated film in collaboration with Disney.

The new feature, released in 2001, was *Monsters, Inc.*, for which Pixar had developed a new version of its proprietary software. By then the company's revenues had skyrocketed more than 1,000 percent since 1998, and its three feature films comprised half of the top-grossing animated films of all time. (Although *Monsters, Inc.* brought in more than $500 million worldwide, DreamWorks' *Shrek* triumphed over *Monsters, Inc.* at the Oscars.) In fact, Pixar's annual revenues had been uneven over time because of the lull in sales between film releases. Merchandising, distribution, and marketing, managed by Disney, accounted for 95 percent of its revenues in 2000.

With the company's fifth film, *Finding Nemo*, in production in 2002, Pixar began work on the second phase of its Emeryville campus. The expansion would accommodate the 70 new employees the company had brought on board since 2001.

During the first half of 2003, Pixar began to explore separating from Disney and talked with Warner Brothers, Fox, and Sony about distribution. Jobs wanted an arrangement whereby Pixar financed and received the profits from its films while Disney distributed them for a 7 percent distribution fee, but Disney was not interested. "After 10 months of trying to strike a deal with Disney, we're moving on," Jobs said in a statement on the company's Web site in January 2004 after the two companies broke off talks.

By the end of 2003, Pixar's staff had reached 700 in number, and the company had two creative teams capable of producing a feature film a year. That year, Pixar released *Finding Nemo*, which became its fifth straight blockbuster. By year's end, the film had attained $340 million in box-office sales. Company revenues for 2003 were $262 million, up from $202 million for 2002.

MERGER WITH DISNEY: 2006

Pixar's film for 2004 was *The Incredibles*, another box-office hit, enjoying total box-office sales of $261 million. In 2005, it began to explore plans to reunite with Disney in a straight distribution-only agreement once Michael Eisner, Disney's chief executive and nemesis of Jobs, left that company in 2006. After months of discussion, Disney wound up buying Pixar, and installing Ed Catmull as president and John Lasseter as chief creative officer of the combined Pixar and Disney Animation Studios. Lasseter reported directly to Robert Iger, Disney's chief executive officer and president as of October 2005. Also in 2006, the Museum of Modern Art in New York celebrated Pixar in a show of more than 500 works of art from Pixar's studios called "Pixar: 20 Years of Animation".

In 2006, Pixar released its sixth blockbuster, *Cars*, and in 2007, *Ratatouille* hit box offices to general acclaim. The film ranked number one in 13 countries for its first three consecutive weekends. *Wall-E* followed in 2008 and *Up* in 2009. Noted *Newsweek* in a 2009 article, Pixar excelled at morality tales wrapped around adventure stories in which an individualist spirit struggled against the forces of conformity and mediocrity,

By 2009, Pixar had released eight films, all celebrated blockbusters with none earning less than $360 million. Despite a slow, financially difficult beginning, Pixar had landed on the fast track and was known throughout the world. Beginning with *Wall-E*, however,

reviewers began to see Pixar as falling victim to its own successful formula, just as Disney once had.

According to *Maclean's* in July 2008, "Pixar doesn't do adaptations." Instead the studio was known for giving its animation directors an unmatched degree of creative freedom to develop original stories. Brandon Neeld of the Pixar Planet Web site was quoted in the article as saying, "Pixar movies aren't held together by toilet humor and pop-culture references that bring in the kiddies for a big blockbuster weekend and then get cast aside."

However, Pixar's artistry, according to some, threatened to contribute to a decrease in its films' popularity. The studio responsible for technological breakthroughs and brilliantly crafted animated films still held true to the intention stated in its 1996 annual report: "Though Pixar is the pioneer of computer animation, the essence of our business is to create compelling stories and memorable characters. It is chiseled in stone at our studios that no amount of technology can turn a bad story into a good one." Even as Pixar continued to release box-office hits, such as *Up* in 2009 and *Toy Story 3* in 2010 (the latter had crossed the $1 billion mark in worldwide sales by the end of August), the type of computer animation most popular at the close of the first decade of the 21st century was the sort used in such new hits as DreamWorks' *Shrek* or Fox's *Ice Age*. There was a chance that Pixar in the decade to come might lose ground to studios that were less artful and more crassly commercial.

Nelson Rhodes
Updated, Carrie Rothburd

PRINCIPAL COMPETITORS

DreamWorks SKG; Fox Entertainment Group, Inc.; The Jim Henson Company, Inc., Lucasfilm, Ltd.; Warner Bros.

FURTHER READING

Baker, Molly, and Thomas R. King, "Pixar Share Offering, Hyped by *Toy Story*, Is Looking Good," *Wall Street Journal*, November 29, 1995, pp. C1, C2.

Deutschman, Alan, "Into Every Life a Little Rain," *Fortune*, May 6, 1991, p. 111.

Gelman, Eric, et al., "Showdown in Silicon Valley," *Newsweek*, September 30, 1985, pp. 46–50.

Giles, Jeff, and Corie Brown, "This Bug's for You," *Newsweek*, November 16, 1998, pp. 79–80.

"The Great Leap of Computer Graphics," *Fortune*, April 27, 1987, p. 7.

Kay, Jeremy, "Pixar Files for Divorce from Disney, Relationship to End in 2006," *Screen International*, January 30, 2004.

Krantz, Michael, "Animators, Sharpen Your Pixels," *Time*, November 30, 1998, pp. 109–10.

Lohr, Steve, "Woody and Buzz, the Untold Story," *New York Times*, February 24, 1997.

Lond, Harley W., "'Toy Story 3' Blasts Past $1 Billion Mark," http://insidemovies.moviefone.com/2010/08/29/toy-story-3-blasts-past-1-billion-mark/.

Markoff, John, "Apple Computer Co-Founder Strikes Gold with New Stock," *New York Times*, November 30, 1995, pp. A1, D7.

Reeves, Scott, "Pixar's Initial Offering Gives Investors a Chance to Bet on Animated Films," *Wall Street Journal*, November

3, 1995, p. A9E.

Schlender, Brent, "Steve Jobs' Amazing Movie Adventure," *Fortune*, September 18, 1995, pp. 154–72.

Schlender, Brent, and Steve Jobs, "The Three Faces of Steve Jobs," *Fortune*, November 9, 1998, p. 96.

Tracy, Eleanor John, "Droids for Sale," *Fortune*, August 5, 1985, pp. 63–64.

"Two Cheers for Apple," *Fortune*, February 17, 1986, p. 9.

Wallace-Wells, David, "High Times," *Newsweek*, May 25, 2009, p. 86.

Weinman, James J., "The Problem with Pixar," *Maclean's*, July 7–July 14, 2008, p. 76.

Wilson, Lizette, "Executive of the Year: Steve Jobs," *San Francisco Business Times*, December 26, 2003, p. 1.

Plains Exploration & Production Company

700 Milam Street, Suite 3100
Houston, Texas 77002
U.S.A.
Telephone: (713) 579-6000
Toll Free: (800) 934-6083
Fax: (713) 579-6611
Web site: http://www.pxp.com

Public Company
Incorporated: 2002
Employees: 808
Sales: $1.18 billion (2009)
Stock Exchanges: New York
Ticker Symbol: PXP
NAICS: 211111 Crude Petroleum and Natural Gas Extraction

∎ ∎ ∎

Plains Exploration & Production Company (PXP) is an oil and gas exploration company with assets in California, the Gulf Coast region, the Gulf of Mexico, Colorado, Wyoming, Texas, and Oklahoma. PXP has estimated proved reserves of 359.5 million barrels of oil equivalent, 60 percent of which is oil. The company also has an interest in an exploration block offshore of Vietnam.

HISTORY OF THE LOS ANGELES BASIN

Although PXP was formed as an independent company in 2002, it owed its existence to a momentous oil discovery made 122 years before its birth. In 1880 a predecessor of Puente Oil Co. discovered the Brea-

Olinda Oil Field near Los Angeles, touching off a rush for oil in an 875-square-mile region known as the Los Angeles Basin, an area that would become one of the most densely populated oil producing regions in the world. The frenzied search for other fields followed immediately, realizing particular success in the early 1920s when the Huntington Beach and Long Beach Oil Fields were discovered in the early 1920s and the Wilmington Oil Field was discovered in 1932. Characterized as "supergiants," the three fields contained 5.4 billion barrels of oil equivalent (boe), sufficient to make California responsible for producing one-fifth of the world's oil supply.

Exploration efforts continued in the decades to follow, achieving their last great success in 1976 with the discovery of the Beta Oil Field. The year also marked the birth of Plains Resources Inc., an independent energy company that would later spawn PXP. Plains Resources entered the Los Angeles Basin in 1992, by which time the practice of drilling into shallow reservoirs had given way to tapping into far deeper reservoirs. Plains Resources purchased assets from Chevron U.S.A. located in the Inglewood, East Beverley Hills, San Vincente, and South Salt Lake fields, securing properties that more than quadrupled its stature by increasing its oil reserves from 18 million barrels to 74 million barrels. The purchase also formed the basis of what would become PXP a decade later.

PLAINS RESOURCES SETS PXP FREE: 2002

Plains Resources added to its holdings in subsequent years, becoming an energy company involved in the

KEY DATES

1992: Plains Resources acquires assets in the Los Angeles Basin that form the foundation of a new subsidiary, Plains Exploration & Production (PXP).
2002: Plains Resources spins off PXP as a separate company.
2003: PXP acquires 3TEC Energy, gaining its first sizable natural gas properties.
2007: Acquisition of Pogo Producing Co. nearly doubles PXP's proven reserves.

exploration, production, and transportation of oil and natural gas. For strategic purposes, the company began to restructure itself as the 1990s progressed. In 1998, the company formed Plains All American Pipeline, L.P. to acquire pipelines and it spun the subsidiary off as a master limited partnership in an initial public offering (IPO) of stock. Although a separate company, Plains All American remained closely tied to Plains Resources, sharing the same CEO, Greg Armstrong, with its former parent company and having 54 percent of its stock owned by its former parent company. A similar arrangement would be made when Plains Resources decided to separate itself from its exploration and production activities, a decision that gave birth to PXP as an independent company.

When Plains Resources reduced its equity stake in Plains All American in 2001, Armstrong began devoting all his efforts to the development of Plains All American. Armstrong handed his responsibilities as Plains Resource's CEO to James C. Flores, a Louisiana native who made his fortune and built his reputation by developing an exploration and production firm named Ocean Energy. Ocean Energy became a thriving enterprise, eventually commanding a $5.3 billion price tag when Devon Energy acquired the company in 2003.

Flores left Ocean Energy before the sale, embarking on a career as a private investor in January 2001 that ended in May 2001 when he became chairman and CEO of Plains Resources. Like his predecessor, Flores sought to separate Plains Resources into separate companies to gain greater value for shareholders. Flores set his sights on the exploration and production efforts undertaken by a Plains Resources subsidiary, Plains Exploration & Production Company, L.P., the direct predecessor to PXP.

The original plan to set PXP free from Plains Resources entailed completing an IPO. In October 2002 PXP filed with the U.S. Securities and Exchange Commission (SEC) to sell five million shares to the public, an offering that was expected to raise nearly $59 million. Poor market conditions and flagging profits totals from PXP's drilling efforts in California and Illinois forced Flores to pursue a different course, however. The IPO was canceled and in December 2002 PXP was spun off, its stock distributed to Plains Resources shareholders in a tax-free transaction. PXP began the new, independent era of its existence with assets offshore California, in the Los Angeles Basin, and in the Illinois Basin in southern Illinois and Indiana. The company's daily production, nearly all oil, was roughly 25,000 boe, from which PXP generated $188 million in revenue in 2002.

With Flores presiding as president, CEO, and chairman, PXP set out on its own. Flores was committed to expanding PXP's role in the exploration and production segment of the energy industry, progress that could be measured by PXP's daily production totals, the size of its proved reserves, and by its geographic expansion. Growth was achieved through internal means (PXP spent $34 million in 2003 drilling 25 new wells in the Los Angeles Basin), but Flores primarily relied on external means to increase the company's stature.

ACQUISITIONS: 2003–04

PXP's first major acquisition was announced in February 2003. The company revealed it had agreed to purchase 3TEC Energy Corporation in a transaction valued at $432 million. The acquisition, completed in June 2003, gave PXP new operating areas in eastern Texas and southern Louisiana, but perhaps most important the addition of 3TEC substantially increased PXP's involvement in natural gas. Before the purchase of 3TEC, PXP relied on oil for 95 percent of its production. 3TEC, in contrast, derived 86 percent of its production from natural gas. "3TEC's high-quality, natural gas-oriented properties bring more balance to our reserve base and production mix and diversity to our risk portfolio," Flores said in the March 2003 issue of *Oil and Gas Investor*. Once 3TEC was absorbed, PXP's daily production climbed to 43,000 boe, 37 percent of which was natural gas.

Flores made his next move on the acquisition front one year later. In February 2004, he reached an agreement to acquire a crosstown rival, Houston-based Nuevo Energy Company, which owned substantial energy properties in California. PXP completed the deal, valued at $945 million, in May 2004, nearly doubling its oil reserves and daily output and giving it properties offshore California as well as in the San Joaquin Valley near Bakersfield, California. The addition of Nuevo made PXP the fourth-largest producer in the San Joaquin Valley, the second-largest producer in the Los Angeles Basin, and the fifth-largest producer in California. "In a nutshell," Flores said in the August 19, 2004 issue of *Investor's Business Daily*, "Nuevo put us in a dominant position in California."

PXP's proven reserves rose to 425 million boe and its daily production jumped to more than 70,000 boe after the Nuevo acquisition. Flores was ready to add to the totals, but before he completed his next move, he tended to other matters. He devoted considerable time during 2004 to dealing with finances. He amended bank lines and closed a private placement to improve PXP's balance sheet. PXP moved to new main offices in downtown Houston during the year and it severed the last of its administrative ties with Plains Resources. As executive chairman of Plains Resources, Flores helped take the company private, a conversion that was completed by selling the company to Vulcan Capital, a private-equity company run by Microsoft Corporation cofounder Paul Allen. Plains Resources emerged from the deal as a private company named Vulcan Energy Corporation, leaving Flores wholly focused on PXP.

PROPERTY SALES: 2005–06

A series of divestitures followed the Nuevo acquisition, as Flores trimmed away assets he deemed strategically irrelevant. PXP exited southern Texas and shed some offshore California properties in early 2005, selling $140 million worth of assets. In April 2005 the company agreed to sell 275 oil wells in Oklahoma and eastern Texas, a deal valued at $350 million. One year later, Flores was ready to complete another acquisition, announcing plans in April 2006 to pay $1.46 billion in stock for Louisiana-based Stone Energy, which owned assets primarily in the Gulf of Mexico, on the Gulf Coast, in the Rockies, and offshore China. The acquisition would have diversified PXP geographically, but the company's stock dropped 21 percent during the ensuing month, scuttling the deal.

Flores returned to divestitures after he failed to purchase Stone Energy, but it was not long before he made another attempt to launch PXP's expansion campaign. In August 2006 the company sold oil and gas assets that represented 45 million barrels of reserves and 8,900 boe of daily production. Occidental Petroleum Corporation agreed to pay $865 million for the assets. The following month, Flores agreed to sell working interests in two Gulf of Mexico discoveries and one deep-water exploration project, striking the deal with Norway's Statoil ASA for $700 million. After selling nearly $2 billion worth of assets since the purchase of Nuevo, Flores began spending substantial sums to bolster PXP's profile.

PXP DOUBLES IN SIZE: 2007

The three-year hiatus from acquisitions ended in 2007 with the completion of two major transactions. In April 2007 PXP agreed to pay $946 million to acquire the Piceance Basin assets owned by Laramie Energy. The basin, located in northwestern Colorado, contained five of the 50 largest gas fields in the United States. Proved reserves on the acreage acquired by PXP were estimated to be 386 billion cubic feet of gas. "To us," Flores said in the April 19, 2007 issue of *Oil Daily*, "it's the San Joaquin Valley of gas and the time is 50 years ago." Flores quickly followed the move into the Piceance Basin with the largest acquisition in PXP's history.

In July 2007 Flores revealed his plans to purchase another crosstown rival, Pogo Producing Co. The stock and cash deal, completed in November 2007, amounted to more than $3.8 billion. The massive merger added properties in the Permian Basin and the San Juan Basin in the southwestern United States and in Wyoming's Madden gas field, increasing proven, probable, and possible reserves to 1.4 billion boe. PXP's daily production nearly doubled and its proven reserves increased by 219 million boe to 635 million boe. When the deal was completed PXP shareholders owned 66 percent of the merged company and Pogo shareholders owned the remaining 34 percent.

After the Pogo merger, Flores, who remained in charge of the combined entity, returned to executing a divestiture program, ending the decade focused primarily on property sales. At the end of 2007 he announced definitive agreements to sell $1.7 billion worth of oil and gas assets to Occidental Petroleum and XTO Energy Inc. The divestiture included assets located in the Permian Basin and the Piceance Basin. In December 2008 another $1.2 billion of Permian Basin and Piceance Basin assets were sold to the same two parties. The one major acquisition completed during the period excited Flores and his management team as they prepared for the future. In July 2008 PXP acquired a 20 percent interest in Chesapeake Energy Corporation's Haynesville Shale property for $1.6 billion. The company spent $652 million on drilling activities on the property, which was expected to produce 125 million cubic feet of natural gas by the end of 2010.

Jeffrey L. Covell

PRINCIPAL SUBSIDIARIES

Arguello Inc.; Arroyo Grande Land Company LLC; Cane Rive Development LLC; Latigo Petroleum, Inc.; Lompoc Land Company LLC; Montebello Land Company LLC; Nuevo Energy Company; Plains Acquisition Corporation; Plains Resources Inc.; Plains Vietnam Ltd. (Cayman Islands); Pogo Alberta, ULC (Canada); Pogo Finance, ULC (Canada); Pogo New Zealand; Pogo New Zealand Holdings, LLC; Pogo Partners Inc.; Pogo Producing Company LLC; PXP Aircraft LLC; PXP Gulf Coast LLC; PXP Louisiana L.L.C.; PXP Louisiana Operations LLC.

PRINCIPAL COMPETITORS

Apache Corporation; Occidental Petroleum Corporation; Stone Energy Corporation.

FURTHER READING

Alva, Marilyn, "Plains Exploration & Prod.," *Investor's Business Daily*, August 19, 2004, p. A6.

Gosmano, Jeff, "Plains Takes Out Pogo for $3.6 Billion," *Oil Daily*, July 18, 2007.

Kelly, Andrew, "Plains Makes Big Move into Piceance Basin," *Oil Daily*, April 19, 2007.

Lonkevich, Dan, "EPL Makes Bid to Buy Stone," *Houston Chronicle*, May 26, 2006, p. 3.

Sullivan, John A., "Plains Exploration & Production Expands with $335 Million South Texas Acquisition," *Oil Daily*, March 4, 2008.

Westuski, Jodi, "Plains, 3Tec Combination Reduces Plains' Oil Weight," *Oil and Gas Investor*, March 2003, p. 83.

Williams, Peggy, "Urban Oil," *Oil and Gas Investor*, July 2004, p. 43.

Radio Flyer Inc.

6515 Grand Avenue
Chicago, Illinois 60707
U.S.A.
Telephone: (773) 637-7100
Toll Free: (800) 621-7613
Fax: (773) 637-8874
Web site: http://www.radioflyer.com

Private Company
Incorporated: 1923 as Liberty Coaster Wagon Company
Employees: 92
Sales: $90.3 million (2008)
NAICS: 339932 Game, Toy, and Children's Vehicle
    Manufacturing

■ ■ ■

Radio Flyer Inc. is the world's leading manufacturer of children's toy wagons, and the leading producer of wagons, spring horses, and tricycles in the United States. The company's principal product, the classic "little red wagon," is an icon of American childhood. It can be seen in advertisements, movies, parades, walk-a-thons, and children's hospitals, as well as around the parks and homes of families with children. The Radio Flyer, the company's most famous model, is trademarked due to its shape and red color. In addition to classic steel wagons, Radio Flyer manufactures wooden and plastic wagons. The company makes more than 50 wagons, including products sized for stuffed animals and miniatures used as key chains. Nostalgia for the Radio Flyer contributes to the company's success in making

and marketing other riding toys. These include a variety of scooters, tricycles, spring horses, push-pull toys, and self-propelled, ride-on toys.

EARLY YEARS

Radio Flyer Inc. was founded by Italian immigrant Antonio Pasin. Pasin's family had been fine woodworkers for generations, specializing in furniture and cabinetry, and he grew up working in wood as well. However, he longed to leave his small town outside of Venice and make a new start in the United States. His family backed his plan, selling their mule to raise money for Antonio's ticket. He arrived in Chicago in 1914. Pasin sought work as a cabinetmaker, but he could only find unskilled work, beginning as a water boy for a crew of sewer diggers. Eventually Pasin found a job that used his woodworking skills, finishing pianos in a piano factory.

After living in the United States for three years, he saved enough to buy his own woodworking tools and to rent one room to use as a shop. In the evenings Pasin worked alone, crafting children's wooden wagons. During the day, he walked the streets of Chicago peddling his samples. Pasin worked tirelessly and alone until 1923, when his wagon business had picked up enough that he was able to hire helpers. He incorporated his business as Liberty Coaster Wagon Company, fondly naming it after the Statue of Liberty that had greeted him when he arrived in his new country.

Although Pasin's background was in woodworking, he soon became enamored of a new technology, metal stamping. Henry Ford had used metal stamping in his automobile factories, where huge machines stamped identical pieces out of sheets of steel. Pasin believed the automotive method could be used for his wagons, enabling him to mass-produce an inexpensive, well-built product. Pasin consciously studied Ford's factory method. His aim was not only to adapt metal stamping to toy wagons, but to produce a quality product along efficient lines.

MASS PRODUCTION OF NEW CHILDHOOD ICON DURING THIRTIES

Pasin refitted his factory for metal stamping by the late 1920s, and Liberty Coaster began manufacturing stamped steel wagons. The company churned out thousands of identical red wagons in the same manner that Ford produced the Model T, and Pasin won for himself the nickname "Little Ford." By 1930 the company became the world's largest producer of children's coaster wagons. That year Liberty Coaster changed its name to Radio Steel & Manufacturing Company. This new name made note of both the new metal technology and the company's popular Radio Flyer model.

Introduced in 1927, the Radio Flyer set the standard for what a wagon should look like. Also, the name "Radio Flyer" captured the excitement of the era's burgeoning radio industry as well as public fascination with flight. The company's motto "For every boy. For every girl" resonated with consumers. The wagon represented a basic toy that provided years of fun for all kinds of kids, not a fad product or something that appealed only to a niche group.

Radio Steel's exhibit at the 1933 Chicago World's Fair forever established the company's "little red wagon" as a symbol of childhood fun. Pasin's exhibit featured a 45-foot statue of a boy riding a Radio Flyer wagon. Underneath the statue Pasin displayed miniature red wagons which he sold as souvenirs to visitors for 25 cents each. The exhibit represented a costly risk that returned great benefits, increasing sales for years to come.

Although the company made its mark with the simple red coaster wagon, it also made more sophisti-

cated products, such as the Streak-O-Lite of 1934, a wagon with control dials and working headlights. Another popular 1930s model was the Zep, which imitated the streamlined styling of the day's fancy automobiles.

While the Great Depression idled many other industries, Radio Steel worked at full capacity throughout the 1930s, manufacturing at least 1,500 wagons a day. The company became a major employer, and Pasin provided steady work to scores of people, mostly Italian Americans like himself. Pasin passed on his success to his workers, initiating generous programs such as English language tutoring within the factory. He also provided interest-free loans to his workers so they could build houses, contributing to the stability of the mostly Italian neighborhood around the factory on Chicago's West Side.

WORLD WAR II AND BEYOND

When the United States entered World War II, many industries converted to making wartime products. Radio Steel halted its production of wagons to manufacture so-called blitz cans. These were five-gallon containers used for either fuel or water, mounted on tanks, trucks, and jeeps. Radio Steel's blitz cans saw service in Europe, the Pacific, and Africa.

After the war the factory went back to making wagons and developed several new models in tune with the times. In the era of the station wagon, Radio Steel began producing its Radio Rancher Convertible, a high-capacity wagon with removable steel stake sides. Beginning in 1957 the company branched out into making garden carts. These were not toys, but metal carts designed to haul yard waste, perhaps a shrewd line extension in view of the growth of suburbia and suburban gardens. Soon the company also began making wheelbarrows.

Nonetheless, the classic little red wagon continued to be the company's mainstay. Radio Steel continued production unabated, even though the toy industry in the United States began to change. During the 1970s the industry consolidated, with many small, private firms being bought out by larger competitors. These large firms, including Mattel and Hasbro, made inroads into the wagon market with branded products of their own. By the 1980s the market had swayed away from simple, classic toys to increasingly high-tech items such as video games. Big toy companies also poured money into faddish toys and toys that could be marketed through licensing tie-ins to movies and television shows.

Despite these developments, Radio Steel plugged away in much the same way it always had. In 1977, the

```
┌─────────────────────────────────────────────┐
│                                               │
│            KEY DATES                          │
│              ──■──                            │
│                                               │
│  1917:  Italian immigrant Antonio Pasin begins │
│         producing and selling children's wooden │
│         wagons in Chicago.                     │
│  1923:  Pasin founds Liberty Coaster Wagon     │
│         Company.                               │
│  1933:  Exhibit at Chicago World's Fair establishes │
│         the Radio Flyer brand.                 │
│  1957:  Firm extends product lines beyond toys, to │
│         garden carts.                          │
│  1987:  Company adopts the name Radio Flyer Inc. │
│  2000–01: Retro Red Line of riding toys is     │
│         introduced.                            │
│                                               │
└─────────────────────────────────────────────┘
```

company improved its core product with several patented safety features. These included a new ball joint between the wagon handle and the undercarriage in which fingers could not get pinched, and a controlled turning radius to prevent accidental tipping. It also deployed new toys, such as the Fireball 2000, a 1970s children's car. The company also made bicycles and tricycles.

CHANGES IN THE NINETIES

In 1987 Radio Steel & Manufacturing changed its name for a third time, to Radio Flyer Inc. This name immediately brought to mind its most popular product. By this time the company was a distinct anomaly in the U.S. toy industry, because it had remained privately owned and was still run by the family of its founder. Mario Pasin had succeeded his father Antonio, and Mario's sons Robert and Paul also were involved in the firm. Larger companies still made competitive inroads in the wagon business. Rubbermaid, mostly known for its kitchenware, produced a line of plastic wagons through its Little Tikes division.

During the 1990s Radio Flyer worked to expand its product line and intensify marketing in order to maintain market share. It used the Radio Flyer name on toy bicycles, such as the Totally Rad Flyer Bicycle. Its name received wide press in 1992 with the release of a movie called *Radio Flyer*, the story of the imaginary journeys of two boys in their Radio Flyer wagon. The wagon image also was used extensively in advertising, and the Radio Flyer was featured in advertisement campaigns by car makers Porsche and Chevrolet and in ads for the insurance company Northwestern Mutual Life.

In 1996 Antonio Pasin's grandsons Robert and Paul took over management of the company from their father, with Robert succeeding as president and Paul as executive vice president. The third generation of the Pasin family moved aggressively to build new types of wagons. In addition to classic red tricycles and steel wagons of various sizes, the company unrolled plastic wagons with updated designs. In 1996 Radio Flyer introduced the Voyager wagon and the Trailblazer, two plastic wagons that retained the classic red color but were otherwise quite different from the company's standard product. The trailblazer was a very sturdy wagon, 10 percent larger than competitors' similar models, but with unique features that made it easy and compact to store. The Voyager was a wagon shaped more like a little car, with an asymmetrical body. It had two seats, one rear- and one front-facing, accessed by a hinged side door. The Voyager also featured a built-in storage compartment and an arched canopy roof. Radio Flyer acted to protect its new wagon features with patents.

In 1996 Little Tikes, the wagon division of Rubbermaid, challenged a patent issued to Radio Flyer for a storage system it used. Both companies had wagons with similar storage systems, but only Radio Flyer held a patent. In all, Radio Flyer held 30 patents on various aspects of wagon design, and it had even trademarked the shape of its classic Radio Flyer.

In 1997 Radio Flyer marked 80 years in the wagon business. For a promotional celebration, the company produced what it billed as the "World's Largest Wagon," a 27-foot-long, 15,000-pound behemoth that then visited cities across the United States.

Radio Flyer introduced a new model plastic wagon in 1999, which it called "the most innovative wagon ever created." This was its Quad Shock, a plastic vehicle shaped much like the classic Radio Flyer, but mounted on steel wheels served with four heavy-duty shock absorbers. The company followed the Quad Shock with a Radio Flyer Sport Utility Wagon, capitalizing on the popularity of the sport-utility vehicle among suburban families.

New marketing strategies involved licensing agreements with other toy makers. In partnership with Enesco, the company produced a series of Christmas ornaments featuring teddy bears and other animals seated in Radio Flyer wagons. Other products included train cars, key chains, and refrigerator magnets. In partnership with Danbury Mint the company produced miniature wagons to go with that company's line of collectible porcelain dolls. Radio Flyer also worked with Mattel, one of the two largest U.S. toy companies, licensing its name on the popular Hot Wheels brand of toy cars to make what appeared to be a souped-up race car-type wagon. Other licensed products included a toy Radio Flyer wagon that held a stuffed Curious George monkey, and another similar toy with a Gund brand stuffed bear.

NEW GENERATION OF PRODUCT DEVELOPMENT

Continuing to build on nostalgia for its brand image, Radio Flyer hired Kaleidoscope Imaging to design a line of riding toys. The Retro Red Line of 10 toys was reminiscent of mid-20th-century styles. For instance, the Retro Red Tricycle, introduced in 2000, featured chrome handlebars and plastic streamers hanging down from the rubber handles. In 2001 Radio Flyer launched retro-style scooters and bicycles, a foot-propelled red roadster, and a pedal race car, all in red and cream. Also, the company updated its wagon with seats that folded down when the wagon was used for hauling. The Pathfinder, launched in 2003, became the top-selling wagon worldwide.

Radio Flyer marked a number of milestones in 2003. That year company founder Antonio Pasin was inducted into the Toy Industry Hall of Fame. Also, Radio Flyer moved manufacturing from Chicago to China, due to lower materials costs and the need for specialized equipment for new products. Most significantly, the company established its own team of industrial designers and engineers led by Thomas Schlegel as vice president of product development.

The designers began a four-stage design process with 40 to 50 product ideas and built makeshift models from which to identify and resolve problems early. On-site lathe equipment allowed designers to manufacture prototypes at advanced stages in order to begin testing quickly. The least viable concepts were eliminated at each stage. At consumer focus groups, designers watched how children and parents used a prototype. When 15 to 20 product concepts remained, they were presented to mass merchant toy buyers.

Products that reached the fourth stage but were terminated underwent a process of analysis. For instance, Schlegel developed a prototype for the Fold 2 Go Wagon, a collapsible red wagon, based on a folding utility cart. Retail buyers loved the concept, but Pasin and Schlegel decided to forgo distribution due to concerns about children's safety. Ultimately, the Fold 2 Go Wagon was improved and released to the market in 2005. Also, it set the stage for development of the Twist Trike, which provided flexibility to grow with the child or to become a low-riding three-wheeler.

Minivans inspired the Ultimate Family Wagon which included more comfortable seat backs and cupholders for both children and adults. The design allowed for alternative use as a table for play or eating, or as a space for hauling. With a retail price of $136, the Ultimate Family Wagon competed with strollers as a way to transport children, such as when going to a park or zoo.

Radio Flyer developed other play riding products. In 2005 the company introduced a line of spring horses that became the company's top-selling product over the next three years. Scooter variations included a detachable handle to make a skateboard. The Cloud 9 Wagon, introduced in 2009, added luxury comforts such as padded seats and an iPod connection, and also included fold-out storage.

By 2008 the product development staff increased to 20 product designers in Chicago and another 10 in China. Together the teams developed approximately 20 new products per year. Radio Flyer's success with new products resulted in a nearly quadruple increase in revenues over the course of the decade, from about $25 million in 2000 to almost $100 million a decade later.

A. Woodward
Updated, Mary Tradii

PRINCIPAL COMPETITORS

Hasbro, Inc.; Mattel, Inc.; Newell Rubbermaid Inc.; Pacific Cycle, Inc.

FURTHER READING

Chiem, Phat X., "Blazing a New Wagon Trail," *Chicago Tribune*, February 15, 2000, pp. B1, B4.

Frankston, Janet, "Radio Flyer Inc., Little Tikes Co. in Toy Patent Dispute," *Knight-Ridder/Tribune Business News*, August 1, 1996.

Mannion, Annemarie, "Playing the Oldies—Radio Flyer Turns Back the Clock with Retro Red Line Trikes, Scooters, and Bikes," *Chicago Tribune*, April 8, 2001, p. 1.

Neville, Lee, "Toy Story," *U.S. News & World Report*, October 20, 1997, p. 12.

"Product Recalls," *Consumers' Research Magazine*, November 1992, p. 36.

"Radio Flyer Rolls Out New Wagons," *Playthings*, July 1996, p. 46.

Reinke, Jeff, "Rollin' with the Changes: How New Strategies Have Fed Design Innovation and Helped Radio Flyer Expand Its Offerings," *Product Design & Development*, 2008, p. 30.

Scanlon, Jessie, "Radio Flyer Learns from a Crash," *Business Week Online*, October 22, 2009.

Rakuten Inc.

Shinagawa Seaside Rakuten Tower
4-12-3 Higashishinagawa, Shinagawa-Ku
Tokyo, 140-0002
Japan
Telephone: (+81 3) 6387 1111
Web site: http://www.rakuten.co.jp

Public Company
Incorporated: 1997
Employees: 4,874
Sales: ¥298.25 billion ($3.27 billion) (2009)
Stock Exchanges: Tokyo
Ticker Symbol: 4755
NAICS: 541513 Computer Facilities Management
   Services

■ ■ ■

Rakuten Inc. is Japan's leading provider of online retailing services, through Rakuten Ichiba (market), an online department store that connects more than 33,000 merchants selling more than 50 million products with over 64 million registered members. Rakuten controls more than 26 percent of Japan's total online business to consumer trade market. The company has also developed a diversified range of other Internet-based services, including travel and hotel and other reservations services; online securities trading and brokerage services; and consumer credit, loans, and payment services. These operations generated more than ¥298 billion ($3.27 billion) in 2009.

While Japan forms Rakuten's largest market, the company has been taking steps to expand its operations onto a global level. The company has extended the Rakuten Ichiba platform to Taiwan and other Asian markets. The company has also begun building up a presence in Western markets, acquiring Linkshare and Buy.com in the United States, PriceMinister in France, and forming a B2B2C (business-to-business-to-consumer) partnership in China with Baidu Inc, a leading search provider in that country. The company is led by founder and CEO Hiroshi Mikitani and is listed on the Tokyo Stock Exchange.

INTERNET IDEA IN 1997

Rakuten was the brainchild of Hiroshi Mikitani, widely credited as one of the pioneering forces in Japan's e-commerce sector. Mikitani originally worked as an investment banker for the Industrial Bank of Japan. While there, Mikitani was sent to the United States, where he enrolled in Harvard Business School and earned an M.B.A. in 1993. This was not Mikitani's first trip to the United States. He had already spent two years there as a boy while his father taught economics at Yale University.

After receiving his M.B.A., Mikitani returned to Japan and his position in Industrial Bank of Japan. During his time at Harvard, however, Mikitani had been inspired to develop plans to launch his own business. Over the next two years, Mikitani saved his earnings, and by 1995 had gathered enough funds to form his first company, a consultancy providing advice on mergers and acquisitions to the growing Internet and technology sectors. Mikitani named his company

Crimson Group, after the Harvard school colors. Among Mikitani's early clients was Softbank, which later emerged as one of Japan's leading Internet and mobile communications players.

Crimson's success soon provided Mikitani with the resources to establish his own Internet company. In 1997, Mikitani founded MDM Inc. and his own online venture. The new service adapted the traditional marketplace format to the Internet era. Instead of developing its own retail offering directly, the company provided space and services for merchants to market their own products. Mikitani chose the name Rakuten Ichiba, adapting the name of Japan's first marketplace, the Rakuichi-Rakuza, formed in the 16th century.

Rakuten started out with just 13 virtual shops, all of which were opened by Mikitani's friends as a personal favor. The company attracted just 30 visitors in its first month, but nonetheless succeeded in generating more than $3,000 in revenues. Convincing Japan's traditionally conservative shopkeepers and business owners to establish a presence on the Internet initially proved difficult. To generate new customers, the company offered fixed fees as low as $500, vastly undercutting other merchant-hosting providers charging as high as $10,000 per year. In this way, the company slowly built up its range of merchants, topping more than 1,500 stores by 1999. In that year, the company changed its name to Rakuten Inc.

PUBLIC OFFERING IN 2000

Rakuten benefited from the surge in the booming growth of both Internet usage and online transactions among Japanese consumers. By the beginning of 2000, the company had signed up 2,000 stores, and topped 3,000 by the middle of the year. Rakuten had also added new services such as online auctions in 1998 and Rakuten Furima, an online flea market boasting more than 40,000 items per month, in 1999. The company also began selling advertising, again undercutting rival portals with an aggressive pricing strategy.

The company also provided merchants with a range of support services. The company initiated its "Rakuten University" training program in 2000, enabling clients and their shops to develop a strong online presence. In that year, the company launched a mobile version of Rakuten Ichiba, further expanding its total consumer base. The company added a merchant support center, and also provided software, called Rakuten Merchant Server, which enabled sellers to modify their store pages.

By 2000, Rakuten Ichiba generated more than 70 million page views each month, ranking it at number four in Japan. This strong growth also fueled the success of the company's initial public offering (IPO), completed in April 2000 through a listing on the Tokyo exchange's JASDAQ index. The offering raised $450 million. By June of that year, the company's market capitalization had soared to $6 billion.

The proceeds of Rakuten's IPO fueled an ambitious expansion effort. The company launched a hugely successful online book-selling joint venture with Nippon Shuppan Hanbai that year. The company also established a subsidiary in the United States. Acquisitions fueled much of Rakuten's expansion, however. These included the purchase of Infoseek Japan, operator of a popular web portal and search engine from its U.S. parent. The company quickly managed to turn around that money-losing business, expanding its range of services while boosting its advertising content.

By the beginning of 2002, Rakuten had completed the acquisition of 10 companies. These included Techmatrix Corporation, which specialized in developing network infrastructures; Lycos Japan, another search provider and Web portal, later merged into Infoseek; and Bizseek, which specialized in trading used items.

MOVING INTO TRAVEL IN 2003

Rakuten dropped its fixed-fee policy in 2002, adopting instead a variable system with a wider scale of monthly fees. Merchants also began paying Rakuten a percentage of their sales, with average rates of 2.6 percent. While the new system brought complaints from a number of merchants, the company continued to attract new merchants, topping 8,000 by 2002.

```
┌─────────────────────────────────────────────┐
│                                               │
│              KEY DATES                        │
│                    ■                          │
│  1995:  Hiroshi Mikitani establishes a        │
│         consultancy, Crimson Group.           │
│  1997:  Mikitani expands into Internet-based  │
│         commerce, founding MDM Inc. and       │
│         launching Rakuten Ichiba.             │
│  2000:  Renamed Rakuten, the company goes     │
│         public on the Tokyo JASDAQ index.     │
│  2003:  Rakuten diversifies its online        │
│         operations into travel, securities    │
│         trading, and other markets.           │
│  2005:  Rakuten acquires Linkshare in the     │
│         United States.                        │
│  2010:  Rakuten signs an agreement to develop │
│         an e-commerce mall in China with      │
│         Baidu; company acquires Buy.com in    │
│         the United States and PriceMinister   │
│         in France.                            │
│                                               │
└─────────────────────────────────────────────┘
```

In that year, Rakuten began to revise its business model from its focus on e-commerce to a broader strategy of becoming a provider of a broad range of Internet-based services. The company's first extension beyond its retailing site was the creation of Rakuten Travel in 2002. This business was quickly expanded with the purchase of MyTrip.net in 2003, which was then merged into Rakuten Travel in 2004. By then, Rakuten Travel had emerged as a leading player in Japan's online travel and reservations market.

Rakuten also moved into the online securities sector, buying DLJdirect SFG Securities in 2003. This company later took on the name of Rakuten Securities. At the same time, Rakuten entered the consumer finance sector in 2004, taking over Aozora Card in 2005. The following year, the company added its own credit card services as well, rebundling these operations under subsidiary Rakuten Credit. The company added other financial partners, adding a mortgage operation in partnership with Shinsei Bank and an online banking venture with Tokyo Tomin Bank, both in 2006. This division quickly became a major revenue generator for the company, accounting for one-third of its total by the end of that year.

By then, Rakuten had spun off its auction business into a joint venture with mobile telephone giant NTT Docomo, in 2005. In that year, the company signaled that it had entered Japan's big leagues when Rakuten was granted the right to create the first new professional baseball team in Japan in more than 50 years.

FIRST INTERNATIONAL STEPS IN 2005

Mikitani committed a rare blunder in 2007, however, when he became determined to expand Rakuten into the media market. Mikitani had hoped to expand his range of Internet services to include multimedia content. For this, the company launched a surprise takeover offer, still a rarity in Japan, for Tokyo Broadcasting System Inc. (TBS). Rakuten acquired 20 percent of TBS. The takeover attempt quickly turned hostile, however. After sparking a national controversy, Rakuten was forced to retreat.

Instead, Mikitani focused on developing another major part of the company's strategy, expanding beyond Japan. Rakuten took a first step in this direction in 2005 when it acquired U.S.-based Linkshare Corporation. Linkshare was a major provider of online marketing services, with clients including Avon, Dell, American Express, 1-800-Flowers, and J.C. Penney. Rakuten paid $425 million for Linkshare, which provided the backbone for Rakuten's future expansion in the United States.

Much of Rakuten's initial international expansion targeted markets closer to home. In 2006, the company targeted the Taiwanese market, teaming up with President Chain Store, which also held the 7-Eleven franchise for the Taiwan market. Rakuten then began developing a Taiwanese version of its Ichiba, which went live the following year.

Elsewhere, Rakuten initially attempted to deploy its travel and reservations subsidiary as its international spearhead. The company invested more than $100 million in Ctrip, a leading online travel site in mainland China, in 2006. The company also set up Rakuten Travel affiliates in South Korea, Guam, and Thailand. By 2007, however, the company had revised its international strategy to focus instead on expanding its Ichiba concept. The company sold off its Ctrip stake that same year.

TARGETING AMAZON IN 2010

Rakuten instead established a European subsidiary, based in Luxembourg, in 2008. This operation was meant to serve as the company's business hub for the region. At the same time, the company strengthened its logistics operations in Japan, creating a dedicated subsidiary for this division. The company then launched a borderless delivery service in 2008. In this way, Rakuten Ichiba merchants could now reach a global market.

The year 2010 marked Rakuten's own arrival onto the global stage. Founder Mikitani announced the company's intention to overtake e-commerce leader Amazon to become the world's largest e-commerce company in the new decade.

The company's strategy got off to a good start in February of that year, as the company announced its return to the mainland Chinese market. This time the company teamed up with Baidu Inc., China's leading online search provider, and announced plans to launch a new online mall to challenge that market's leader, Taobao. The new e-commerce site, to be developed with a total investment of $50 million, was expected to be operational by 2013.

In May 2010, Rakuten announced a new partnership, with PT Global Mediacom Tbk in Indonesia. The two companies agreed to develop a localized version of Rakuten Ichiba for the Indonesian market. The new site would give the company access to that country's more than 20 million Internet users.

Shortly after, Rakuten signaled its intention to go head-to-head with the global e-commerce leader, Amazon. At the beginning of June 2010, the company reached an agreement to acquire Buy.com, based in the United States, for $250 million. The deal added more than 14 million new customers to Rakuten's rolls, while expanding its total range of products to more than 60 million.

Rakuten's European subsidiary quickly followed up that announcement with news of its own. Less than two weeks later, Rakuten announced another major acquisition. This time, the company agreed to pay EUR 200 million ($250 million) to buy PriceMinister. This France-based company operated a leading business-to-consumer mall, similar to Rakuten Ichiba, in France, Spain, and England. PriceMinister's customer base spanned more than 23 million registered consumers. Soon after the purchase, Rakuten announced its intention to expand PriceMinister into Germany as well. Rakuten had become a major challenger for global e-commerce leader Amazon.

M. L. Cohen

PRINCIPAL SUBSIDIARIES

Cyber Brains (Shanghai) Consulting Co., Ltd. (China); LinkShare Corporation (USA); LinkShare Ltd. (UK); PriceMinister SA (France); Rakuten Auction, Inc.; Rakuten Baseball, Inc.; Rakuten Enterprise Inc.; Rakuten Europe S.a.r.l. (Luxembourg); Rakuten Securities, Inc.; RAKUTEN TRAVEL KOREA CO., LTD. (South Korea); Rakuten USA, Inc.; Signature Japan Co., Ltd.; Taiwan Rakuten Ichiba Inc.

PRINCIPAL DIVISIONS

Credit and Payment Business; E-Commerce Business; Portal and Media Business; Professional Sports Business; Securities Business; Telecommunications Business; Travel Business.

PRINCIPAL OPERATING UNITS

O-net, Inc.; Rakuten Books; Rakuten Card; Rakuten FX; Rakuten Golden Eagles; Rakuten Ichiba; Rakuten Travel.

PRINCIPAL COMPETITORS

AEON Company Ltd.; Amazon Inc.; Idemitsu Kosan Company Ltd.; Inabata and Company Ltd.; Isetan Company Ltd.; Ito-Yokado Company Ltd.; Kintetsu Department Store Company Ltd.; Kose Corp.; Mitsui Fudosan Company Ltd.; Seven and I Holdings Company Ltd.; Softbank Corporation; Uny Company Ltd.

FURTHER READING

"Baidu and Rakuten JV to Build Online B2B2C Mall for Chinese Internet Users," *Health & Beauty Close-up*, February 6, 2010.

Froggatt, Mike, "Softbank and Rakuten: The Growing E-Commerce Competition for Amazon in Asia," *Emarketer Blog*, June 29, 2010.

"Hiroshi Mikitani," *Business Week*, January 14, 2002, p. 76.

"Is This Man Building the Amazon.com of Asia?" *Business Week*, February 21, 2000, p. 148J.

Minami, Kiyoe, and Chana R. Schoenberger, "A Taste of What's in Store," *Forbes Global*, July 21, 2008, p. 104.

"Online Retailer Rakuten to Buy Marketer LinkShare for $425 Million," *InformationWeek*, September 6, 2005.

"PriceMinister Racheté par le Japonais Rakuten," *Challenges*, June 17, 2010.

"Rakuten Makes Major Global Expansion Move with Acquisition of Buy.com," *Investment Weekly News*, June 5, 2010, p. 282.

"Rakuten Set to Purchase PriceMinister," *Direct*, June 18, 2010.

Ryall, Julian, "Tokyo Battle Is One for the Books," *Hollywood Reporter*, June 7, 2007, p. 16.

Schilling, Mark, "TBS Web Stalls Mall," *Daily Variety*, September 10, 2007, p. 10.

Toto, Serkan, "Japan's Rakuten: Can the Biggest E-Commerce Site You Never Heard of Become a Threat for Amazon Globally?" *TechCrunch*, July 5, 2009.

Regional Express Holdings Limited

81-83 Baxter Road
Mascot, NSW 2020
Australia
Telephone: (+61 2) 9023 3555
Fax: (+61 2) 9023 3599
Web site: http://www.rex.com.au

Public Company
Incorporated: 2002 as Australiawide Airlines Limited
Employees: 600
Sales: AUD 250.96 million (2009)
Stock Exchanges: Australian
Ticker Symbol: REX
NAICS: 481111 Scheduled Passenger Air Transportation; 481211 Nonscheduled Chartered Passenger Air Transportation; 481212 Nonscheduled Chartered Freight Air Transportation; 621910 Ambulance Services; 488190 Other Support Activities for Air Transportation

■ ■ ■

Regional Express Holdings Limited is the holding company for Regional Express Pty. Limited (Rex), an airline serving mostly rural communities in Western Australia. It was formed in 2002 to take over Kendell and Hazelton, two feeder airlines, after the collapse of Ansett, which had been Australia's second-largest carrier. Rex flies out of South Australia hubs of Adelaide, Melbourne, and Sydney and in 2009 it started services within Queensland via a hub at Townsville.

Since 2003 the airline has been run by Singaporean businessman Lim Kin Hai, known for his emphasis on controlling costs. In its first few years the carrier survived industry-wide problems such as dismal economic conditions, drought, and fluctuations in currency values and fuel prices that grounded several other regional airlines in Australia. Although it faces no direct competition on most routes, its philosophy is to keep fares low to stimulate traffic, a policy embraced by the mostly rural communities it serves.

AFTER ANSETT

Sir Reginald Myles "Reg" Ansett launched his namesake airline in 1936, beginning with Melbourne-Hamilton service. It became Australia's second most powerful airline, behind Qantas (Queensland and Northern Territory Aerial Service), which had been launched in 1920.

The arrival of Richard Branson's Virgin Group to Australia's domestic market around 1999 provided the first threat to the status quo that had existed for decades. According to an August 2002 *Canberra Times* article, 11 Australian airlines disappeared between 2000 and 2002. Ansett was the largest casualty.

Ansett employed 17,000 people when it folded. In addition to its own brand, the airline operated smaller regional airlines Hazelton, Kendell, Skywest, and Aeropelican, all of which were grounded after the parent company collapsed under a multibillion-dollar debt in September 2001.

2002 RELAUNCH

Ansett lost AUD 378 million for the year. Kendell alone accounted for one-fifth of the deficit, noted the *Age*,

COMPANY PERSPECTIVES

We are committed to providing our customers with safe and reliable air transportation with heartfelt hospitality. As a regional carrier, we constantly strive to keep fares low through our commitment to simplicity, efficiency and good value. We are committed to treating our customers as individuals and will respond to all their comments and complaints.

posting a AUD 75 million loss on revenues of AUD 227 million. Finance costs and unfavorable exchange rates wiped out its AUD 38 million operating profit.

There nevertheless remained considerable demand for air service in Southwest Australia. Hazelton and Kendell had together carried a million passengers annually. The two airlines together had 950 employees. Under bankruptcy administration, Kendell employed 550 people and Hazelton 280.

Regional Express was formed in August 2002 as Australiawide Airlines Limited and bid for the two regional airlines. Australiawide beat out at least one other bidder, Inland Marketing Corporation, and was able to acquire Hazelton and Kendell, paying more than AUD 40 million for the pair.

Investors included four Canberra businessmen: Pawl Cubbin, builders Bob Winnell and John Sayers, and developer John Hindmarsh, the latter of whom became chairman. Cubbin, its executive director, also was co-manager and director of Kingston-based ZOO Communication Company, which supplied marketing support for the airline. He told the *Canberra Times* that he joined the consortium after being impressed by Kendell's friendly staff on a recent flight.

The transaction was complex. Each airline was being run by separate court-appointed administrators. The sale was not approved until five days before launch date.

FIRST YEAR

Regional Express, also known as Rex, began operations on August 6, 2002, with a Wagga Wagga-Sydney flight. Its initial route network included almost three-dozen destinations in New South Wales, Victoria, South Australia, and Tasmania. Headquartered in Sydney, Rex had its main operations base in Wagga Wagga and a call center in Orange.

The airline proposed to increase flight frequencies but within three months nearly halved the number of

daily flights on Melbourne-Canberra and Sydney-Canberra routes due to low passenger counts. It withdrew from Coffs Harbour, a resort near Rockhampton, New South Wales, in March 2003 after two rivals materialized there.

Rex started out with 623 employees. The fleet comprised 21 Saab 340 turboprop aircraft and eight of the smaller Fairchild Metroliners. It did not hold on to Kendell's Bombardier Canadair Regional Jets, which had been operating at a loss.

In addition to cutting staffing levels, Rex renegotiated aircraft lease rates and won reduced airport landing fees from dozens of regional councils in exchange for keeping fares low and boosting traffic. Rex typically served small towns with populations of 25,000 or less, and had no competition on most of its routes.

MANAGEMENT SHAKEUP

Rex lost AUD 30 million in its first 11 months, when it carried 612,403 passengers and had revenues of AUD 93 million for fiscal 2003. CEO Michael Jones and chairman John Hindmarsh resigned at the end of June 2003 and Lim Kin Hai took over the airline's management. He was among the group of eight Singapore investors who had in June 2002 invested in Rex's start-up. Although new to the aviation industry, Lim was an experienced investor and served as board chairman of Singapore companies Lynk Biotechnologies and WooWorld, an electronic games developer. He had studied electronics engineering in France and worked for Singapore's Department of Defence for 10 years before setting out in business.

He soon fired two-dozen senior managers and proceeded to run the airline himself largely from Singapore. Attention to detail was what led the carrier to its first monthly profits in October 2003. Lim scrutinized invoices, scaled back in-flight meals, and otherwise micromanaged. Under his austere regime Rex posted a profit of AUD 11.4 million in fiscal 2004.

Rex had been losing money on its Canberra-Sydney and Canberra-Melbourne routes in particular. In July 2003 the airline called out the Australian government for not considering its lower priced service for official travel. Although it managed to double its market share of public service traffic to 4 percent, Rex canceled Canberra service in December 2004.

2005 IPO

In September 2005 Rex bought an initial 50 percent stake in freight and charter operator Pel-Air Aviation Pty

KEY DATES

2002: Regional Express (Rex), originally called Australiawide Airlines Limited, is formed to take over Hazelton and Kendell following collapse of Australia's second-largest airline, Ansett.

2003: Singaporean businessman Lim Kin Hai takes over management of the airline following a boardroom shakeup.

2005: Rex acquires Air Link and initial stake in charter operator Pel-Air Aviation Pty Limited; company goes public.

2007: Rex acquires pilot-training academy to cope with enduring pilot shortage.

Limited for AUD 12 million, acquiring the remaining shares two years later. Pel-Air had 23 aircraft and chiefly flew night cargo runs. Several months later Rex acquired Air Link, which operated nine planes out of Dubbo, for AUD 3 million.

In contrast to much of the industry, Rex was thriving despite record high fuel prices. Instead of hedging, it was able to pass on cost increases through surcharges. The airline carried 1.2 million passengers in 2005 as profits rose more than tenfold to AUD 11.3 million.

The holding company, Australiawide Airlines, was renamed Regional Express Holdings Limited in September 2005. Rex had its initial public offering (IPO) soon after, offering about 30 percent of shares for AUD 35 million. The November 2005 IPO on the Australian Stock Exchange valued Rex at AUD 115 million. Net profits rose to AUD 15 million as revenues reached AUD 174 million in 2006.

In October 2006 Rex signed a leasing agreement to renew the fleet with 25 Saab 340B Plus aircraft over the next three years. These were an updated version of the 340As that had made up most of Rex's fleet, and offered greatly improved performance characteristics in hot weather as well as increased passenger comfort. Rex owned 15 of its 32 Saab aircraft at the beginning of 2007, noted *Orient Aviation*. Well funded at the beginning, it still carried virtually no debt and had AUD 20 million in cash.

Rex considered acquiring Queensland-based airline Sunshine Express, a 40-employee operation connecting seven cities to Brisbane, in 2006 after it was grounded after losing an aircraft to a maintenance mishap. Rex demurred but the next year attempted to expand into Queensland with a short-lived Brisbane-Maryborough

service. According to an August 14, 2009 *Australian* article, Brisbane proved an expensive base.

Managing Director Geoff Breust, tiring of his long commute, stepped down in December 2007. James Davis became managing director in May 2008. He had been with Rex since the early days when it acquired Hazelton, where he was chief pilot.

ANNUS HORRIBILIS I & II

A severe pilot shortage disproportionately affected fixed costs for operating Rex's small aircraft. In 2008 half of its pilots left to make more money flying jets at the big airlines. Although Rex had to cancel flights due to a lack of pilots, passenger count rose 5 percent to 1.5 million for the year.

In December 2007 Rex acquired the Australian Airline Pilot Academy at Mangalore Airport, north of Melbourne, complaining that larger airlines preferred to poach its pilots rather than train their own. Although the pilot shortage had eased somewhat by 2009, Rex continued to invest in pilot training.

The airline also had to deal with unprecedented rises in fuel prices. Even so, net profit rose 3 percent in fiscal 2008, which it called "Annus Horribilis" in its annual report. In the midst of a dismal economy due to the worldwide credit crunch, Rex nevertheless retained the title of Australia's most profitable airline.

Net profit slipped 5.6 percent to AUD 23 million as revenue fell 3.7 percent to AUD 251 million in 2009, or "Annus Horribilis II." Although passenger counts continued to drop, falling 12.8 percent during the year, the airline benefited from lower fuel costs and a stronger Australian dollar. It was able to raise its fares for the first time.

In December 2008 the AirLink subsidiary ended scheduled service. It continued to fly charters as well as offer aircraft maintenance. In April 2009 Rex launched a small business-aircraft leasing division in Sydney called RexJet Executive Charter.

Lower cargo volumes prompted a restructuring of Pel-Air's overnight freight business. The fleet was reduced to just three Saab 340A aircraft. The Pel-Air subsidiary was nevertheless diversifying with new mining and patient-transport contracts. One of these, for Barrick Gold's Osborne Mine, provided a foothold for Rex to launch a second bid for scheduled service in Queensland in October 2009, using Townsville as a base.

ON TOP IN 2010

Aviation Week rated Rex the best-performing regional airline in the world in 2009, an award *Air Transport*

World duplicated in 2010. Rex was still profitable despite the dismal global economic climate. By this time, noted the company's annual report, at least eight other regional carriers had failed. Qantas had been scaling back its regional operations for years. In April 2009 the pilot academy was relocated from Mangalore, Victoria, to Wagga Wagga. It was soon expanded with a new hangar and AUD 12 million training facility.

Frederick C. Ingram

PRINCIPAL SUBSIDIARIES

Regional Express Pty Limited; Rex Freight & Charter Pty Limited; Rex Investment Holdings Pty Limited; Air Link Pty Limited; Pel-Air Aviation Pty Limited; Australian Airline Pilot Academy Pty Limited.

PRINCIPAL COMPETITORS

Alliance Airlines Pty Ltd.; Jetstar Airways Pty Ltd; Qantas Airways Ltd.; Virgin Blue Airlines Pty Ltd.

FURTHER READING

Anderson, Charles, "Rex on a Roll," Orient Aviation, February 2007, pp. 50–51.

"Canberra's Airline Investors Enter the Lion's Den," Canberra Times, August 17, 2002, p. C3.

Clack, Peter, "Rex Investor Tells of Last-Minute 'Nightmare,'" Canberra Times, October 16, 2002, p. A20.

Cooke, Graham, "Canberra Entrepreneurs in Kendell-Hazelton Hot Seat," Canberra Times, May 14, 2002, p. 14.

Creedy, Steve, "Rex Flies against the Ill Winds," Australian, Finance Sec., August 27, 2009, p. 20.

———, "Rex to Spread Wings with $35m Float," Australian, Finance Sec., September 27, 2005, p. 22.

———, "Rex's Medical Pitch Hits Ill-Wind," Australian, Features Sec., August 28, 2009, p. 31.

———, "Rex's Second Tilt at Queensland," Australian, Features Sec., August 14, 2009, p. 32.

Easdown, Geoff, "New Airline's Profits Set for Take-Off," Adelaide Advertiser, November 24, 2003, p. 29.

Fullbrook, David, "An Extraordinary Success Story as Rex Rises from the Ansett Ashes," Orient Aviation, March 2006.

"Funding Punt Pays Off for Rex Boss," Australian, Finance Sec., September 23, 2009, p. 40.

Heinrichs, Paul, "Rex Seeks an Aerial Flock," Sunday Age, August 11, 2002, p. 10.

Lott, Steven, "Australia's Rex Looks to Save Sunshine Express by Acquisition," Aviation Daily, August 16, 2006, p. 6.

Peterson, Anthony, "Unveiling a Name to Fill the Hole in Our Skies; First Look at a Brand New Airline," Daily Telegraph (Sydney), August 5, 2002, p. 5.

Thomas, Geoffrey, "Rex Blames Rivals for Poaching Pilots as Regional Routes Shut Down," Australian, Features Sec., November 9, 2007, p. 40.

———, "T-Rex," ATW Online, May 1, 2009.

Wood, Leonie, "Kendell Airlines Bled Ansett to the Tune of $75m," Age, July 16, 2002, p. 2.

Rezidor Hotel Group AB

Box 6061, Hemvaernsgatan 15
Solna, SE-171 06
Sweden
Telephone: (+46 08) 506 88730
Web site: http://www.rezidor.com

Public Company
Founded: 1960 as SAS Royal Hotel Copenhagen
Incorporated: 1980 as SAS International Hotels
Employees: 5,007
Sales: EUR 677 million ($947.8 million) (2009)
Stock Exchanges: Stockholm
Ticker Symbol: REZT
NAICS: 721110 Hotels (Except Casino Hotels) and
　　Motels

■ ■ ■

Rezidor Hotel Group AB is one of the fastest-growing hotel operators in Europe, the Middle East, and Africa. At mid-2010, the company's portfolio of hotels neared 400, including approximately 100 hotels under construction, for a total of more than 84,000 beds. Rezidor operates its brands under a master-franchise agreement with Carlson Hotels, in place since 1994. Carlson has also acquired shares in Rezidor, becoming its majority shareholder with more than 50 percent in 2010.

Rezidor's hotel brands include: Radisson Blu, its flagship chain, focused on the upscale four-star hotel market, with 195 hotels in operation and another 45 under development in 2010; Park Inn, a mid-market brand with 87 hotels in operations and 51 hotels under development; and Hotel Missoni, a "designer" hotel concept, which opened its first hotel in Edinburgh in 2009, with plans to open four new hotels in 2010. In April 2010, Rezidor announced an agreement to sell its luxury hotel brand, Regent, to Taiwan's Formosa International Hotels Corporation. The company is also likely to phase out its Country Inn brand, which operates two limited-service economy hotels.

Rezidor has adopted an "asset-light" development strategy. This means that the company has been shifting its expansion strategy to focus on franchised or managed hotels, which require no capital investment on Rezidor's part. In 2010, 50 percent of the company's hotel portfolio operated as managed hotels and 23 percent as franchised hotels. The Nordic market (Rezidor originated as part of SAS Airlines) accounts for 20 percent of the group's total number of beds. The rest of Western Europe adds 47 percent, with Eastern Europe, including Russia and the CIS market accounting for 18 percent, and the Middle East and Africa for 15 percent. Kurt Ritter, who joined the company in 1976, remains Rezidor's president and CEO. Rezidor is listed on the Stockholm Stock Exchange and posted revenues of EUR 677 million ($948 million) in 2009.

AIRLINE OFFSHOOT IN 1960

The rise of the passenger airline industry in the 1960s inspired Sweden's SAS Airline to expand into hotel accommodations. The airline signed noted architect Arne Jacobsen, who developed the concept for the SAS Royal Hotel. This hotel opened in Copenhagen in

1960, becoming the world's first "designer" hotel. The hotel also featured many of Jacobsen's own furniture designs, including his famous Egg and Swan chairs.

The Royal originally operated as part of the airline's catering division. The success of this first hotel, which became a Copenhagen landmark, encouraged SAS to develop its hotel brand. The company opened a series of hotels, targeting cities and markets served by its airline routes. As SAS's hotel operations grew, the company restructured its catering division, which became SAS Catering and Hotels. In 1982, the Hotel division was spun off as a separate business unit within SAS.

By then, SAS Hotels had expanded outside of the Scandinavian market for the first time, opening a hotel in Kuwait in 1980. The growing international profile of the hotel operation led SAS to reorganize the division as a full-fledged subsidiary, SAS International Hotels (SIH), in 1985. The new company launched an expansion drive through the end of the decade. This led to the acquisition of a 40 percent stake in InterContinental Hotels in 1989. SIH then weathered a slump in the international hotel market, brought on by a global recession and the Persian Gulf War at the beginning of the 1990s. In response, the company sold off its share of InterContinental in 1992.

Leading SIH by then was Kurt Ritter, born in Switzerland in 1947. Ritter's family operated a hotel in Interlaken, and Ritter went on to earn a diploma at the École hôtelière de Lausanne, one of the world's most prestigious hotel and catering schools. Ritter began his career as an assistant manager at a Bern hotel, before joining Ramada International Hotels in 1970. In 1976,

Ritter became general manager of the SAS Lulea Hotel in Sweden, then moved to Kuwait to manage the company's first non-European hotel. Ritter joined SIH's management in 1984, and by 1989 had become the company's president and CEO. Soon after, Ritter transferred SIH's head office to Brussels, Belgium.

RADISSON SAS IN 1994

In the mid-1990s, SIH remained a moderately sized player in the international hotel market. Through the first half of the decade, the company's total portfolio stood at just 29 hotels. SIH went in search of a partner to back its further growth. In 1994, the company found this partner in the form of Carlson Hospitality Worldwide, operator of the Radisson brand name. Carlson and SIH signed a master-franchise agreement, giving SIH the exclusive right to develop the Radisson hotel brand for the Europe, Middle East, and Africa markets.

The franchise agreement called for Carlson and SAS to combine their brands for these markets, creating the Radisson SAS hotel chain. This chain, which incorporated a blue square into its logo, targeted the four-star "first-class" hotel market, below the luxury segment. SIH also changed its name, becoming Radisson SAS Hotels & Resorts. Radisson SAS at first targeted further expansion in Europe and the Middle East. In 1999, the company rolled out its first hotels in Africa as well. One year later, the company's portfolio had expanded to more than 100 hotels.

Radisson SAS remained a single-brand hotel company into the beginning of the new century. CEO Ritter had by then begun developing still more ambitious plans for the company and in 2000 the company adopted a new strategy targeting the expansion of its portfolio to include multiple brands covering several hotel market segments. As Ritter explained to *Travel Agent*: "We needed a multibrand strategy. To continue with just one brand wasn't good enough in the sense that the growth was too slow."

Radisson SAS made its first move in its new direction in 2000, when it formed a joint venture to acquire the franchise for the small Malmaison chain of boutique hotels in England. Malmaison operated hotels in Newcastle, Manchester, and Leeds in England, and in Edinburgh and Glasgow in Scotland. Soon after the acquisition, the company launched construction of two new Malmaison hotels, in London and Birmingham. The company then laid plans to open four to five new Malmaison hotels per year, and eyed the expansion of the boutique format to other markets, including Germany.

KEY DATES

1960: SAS Airlines opens its first hotel in Copenhagen, designed by Arne Jacobsen.

1985: SAS reorganizes its hotel division as subsidiary SAS International Hotels (SIH).

1994: SIH signs a master franchise agreement with Carlson, and changes its name to Radisson SAS.

2001: Company changes its name to Rezidor SAS Hospitality.

2006: Company goes public as Rezidor Hotel Group.

2010: Carlson raises its shareholding in Rezidor above 50 percent.

REZIDOR IN 2002

In any event, Radisson SAS remained the company's true growth driver. The company had launched a still more ambitious hotel opening program. This saw the company extend beyond its original core markets, specifically the Scandinavian countries and Germany. Radisson now began to target growth into the Benelux markets, the Baltic countries, and France. At the same time, Radisson SAS took aim at the Eastern European markets, adding its first properties in Poland and Russia. In 2001, the company added a total of 20 new Radisson SAS hotels, with 25 hotels scheduled to open in 2002. This expansion raised the company's portfolio to more than 150 hotels in 38 countries, including Egypt.

Radisson SAS signaled the launch of its multi-brand strategy in October 2001, when it changed its name to Rezidor SAS Hospitality. The new name was meant to evoke the words *reside* or *rest* and *door* as well as *or*, (or "d'or"), the French for "gold." Rezidor then revised its master franchise agreement with Carlson in September 2002. Under the terms of the new agreement, Rezidor now became the exclusive franchise holder for the Europe, Middle East, and Africa markets for Carlson's full portfolio of brands, including the mid-market Park Inn, the luxury Regent Hotel brand, and the economy brand Country Inn.

Of the three, Rezidor focused especially on building up the Park Inn brand. Park Inn became part of the group's Middle Eastern strategy, where the luxury and four-star hotel segments approached saturation levels. On the other hand, the mid-market segment in these markets remained relatively undeveloped. The addition of the new Carlson brands also brought an end to Rezidor's share in the Malmaison joint venture.

With the new franchise agreement, Rezidor entered a new phase of explosive growth. The company's revenues grew from EUR 390 million in 2002 to top EUR 587 million in 2005, then climbed again past EUR 707 million in 2006. By then, the company already had 225 hotels in operation, as well as nearly 55 under construction. The Radisson SAS accounted for the majority of the group's properties, at 189 of its total, while the Park Inn brand had also expanded strongly, 77 properties in operation or under development.

PUBLIC OFFERING IN 2006

By then, Rezidor and Carlson had deepened their relationship. In 2005, SAS agreed to sell a 25 percent stake in Rezidor to Carlson, highlighting Rezidor's importance to the global expansion of the Radisson brand. Also in 2005, Rezidor added a new brand to its portfolio, negotiating with the Missoni fashion house for the rights to develop its own "designer" hotel brand. The first Hotel Missoni opened only three years later, however.

In the meantime, Rezidor had marked a new milestone in its development, when it completed its public offering on the Stockholm Stock Exchange. As part of that offering, Carlson increased its holding in Rezidor to 35 percent. As part of the listing, Rezidor changed its name again, becoming Rezidor Hotel Group.

Into the second half of the decade, Rezidor emerged as one of the world's fastest-growing hotel groups. By the end of 2007, the company's total portfolio had topped 300 hotels in operation or under contract, generating revenues of EUR 785 million. Much of the company's growth was fueled by its "asset-lite" strategy, which favored managed or franchised hotel contracts, in which Rezidor itself held little to no equity. The company reduced its number of leased hotels to just 27 percent of its total through the end of the decade.

SAS continued to sell off its shares of Rezidor, exiting the company completely in 2007. In its place, Carlson increased its own holding in the company to 42 percent that year. Rezidor continued its strong expansion, notably in the Russia and CIS markets. The company opened hotels in Ukraine, Georgia, and elsewhere in the region, becoming one of the largest international hotel groups in these markets.

MAJORITY SHAREHOLDER IN 2010

Rezidor completed the break with SAS in 2009, when it rebranded the Radisson SAS hotel chain as Radisson Blu. The new brand took its name from the blue square that had long been part of its logo. Radisson Blu then set its sights on a number of new markets, including Saudi Arabia, where it opened its first hotel that year. In the meantime, Rezidor had finally succeeded in developing the design concept for its Hotel Missoni brand, and opened that chain's first hotel in Edinburgh in June 2009. The company had also developed several other contracts for the Missoni brand, including a hotel opened in Kuwait in 2009, and several more hotels slated to open in Cape Town, Oman, and Salvador, Brazil, in 2010.

Rezidor increasingly focused its other hotel operations on expanding the Radisson Blu and Park Inn brands. The company renamed the latter brand as Park Inn by Radisson in June 2010 to reflect its relationship with the larger Radisson brand. At the same time, the company and Carlson announced an agreement to sell the luxury hotel brand, Regent, which operated just two hotels, to Taiwan-based Formosa International Hotels Corporation in 2010. Rezidor also placed the Country Inn economy brand under review, suggesting plans to drop this brand as well.

These moves came amid a new milestone in Rezidor's long-standing partnership with Carlson. In June 2010, the companies announced that Carlson had acquired additional shares in Rezidor, becoming its majority shareholder with more than 50 percent of Rezidor's stock. The investment in Rezidor came as part of Carlson's strategy of building up its own hotel portfolio to more than 1,500 hotels by 2015. With nearly 400 hotels in operation or under construction, Rezidor promised to play a major role in achieving Carlson's ambitions and promoting the Radisson name as one of the world's leading hotel brands.

M. L. Cohen

PRINCIPAL SUBSIDIARIES

Al Quesir Hotel Company S.A.E. (Egypt); RC International Marketing Services, Inc. (USA); Rezidor Finance S.A. (Belgium); Rezidor Hotel Amsterdam B.V.; Rezidor Hotel Holdings AB; Rezidor Hotel Milan S.r.l.; Rezidor Hotels ApS (Denmark); Rezidor Hotels Deutschland GmbH; Rezidor Hotels France S.A.S.; Rezidor Hotels Norway AS; Rezidor Hotels UK Ltd.; Rezidor International Hotels Management A/S (Denmark); Rezidor Resort France S.A.S.; Rezidor Royal Hotel, Beijing, Co., Ltd. (China); Royal Viking Hotel AB; The Rezidor Hotel Group S.A. (Belgium).

PRINCIPAL DIVISIONS

Eastern Europe; Middle East, Africa & Others; Nordic Region; Rest of Western Europe.

PRINCIPAL OPERATING UNITS

Radisson Blu; Park Inn; Hotel Missoni; Regent; Country Inn.

PRINCIPAL COMPETITORS

ACCOR S.A.; Compass Group PLC; Harrah's Entertainment Inc.; Hilton Worldwide; Jardine Strategic Holdings Ltd.; Loews Corporation; Marriott International, Inc.; SABMiller PLC; Sammons Enterprises Inc.; Suntory Holdings Ltd.

FURTHER READING

"Carlson Becomes Majority Shareholder of The Rezidor Hotel Group," *Investment Weekly News*, June 5, 2010.

"Carlson Hotels Acquires 25% Stake in Partner Rezidor SAS Hospitality," *Hotels*, May 2005, p. 12.

"Carlson, Rezidor to Sell Regent Luxury Hotel Ops to Taiwan's Formosa Intl.," *M&A Navigator*, April 16, 2010.

Murray, Rupert, "The Rebirth of the Midmarket Hotel," *Travel Trade Gazette UK & Ireland*, February 6, 2009, p. 30.

"Rezidor Announces Park Inn in Dubai Airport," *Travel Business Review*, September 4, 2009.

"Rezidor Hotel," *AirGuide Business*, October 19, 2009.

"Rezidor Hotel Group Announces Three New Hotels in Nigeria," *Travel Business Review*, August 17, 2009.

"Rezidor Opens New Paris Hotel," *Travel Business Review*, May 21, 2009.

"Rezidor to Rename Hotel Brand Park Inn by Radisson," *M2 EquityBites*, June 2, 2010.

Sharkey, Gemma, "Rezidor Celebrates First Fruit from Its Tie-up with Missoni," *Caterer & Hotelkeeper*, June 5, 2009.

Webber, Sara Perez, "Marching through Europe," *Travel Agent*, February 11, 2002, p. 58.

Rock-Tenn Company

504 Thrasher Street
Norcross, Georgia 30071-1967
U.S.A.
Telephone: (770) 448-2193
Fax: (770) 263-3582
Web site: http://www.rocktenn.com

Public Company
Incorporated: 1973
Employees: 10,300
Sales: $2.81 billion (2009)
Stock Exchanges: New York
Ticker Symbol: RKT
NAICS: 322130 Paperboard Mills; 322211 Corrugated and Solid Fiber Boxes Manufacturing; 322212 Folding Paperboard Box Manufacturing; 322213 Setup Paperboard Box Manufacturing; 322226 Surface-Coated Paperboard Manufacturing; 322299 All Other Converted Paper Product Manufacturing

■ ■ ■

Rock-Tenn Company, or RockTenn as the firm began calling itself in 2008, is one of the largest U.S. manufacturers of 100 percent recycled paperboard, a product made from recovered wastepaper that the company also converts into packaging products. These converted products include folding cartons for food, paper goods, health and beauty items, clothing, and other products; solid-fiber partitions used in the interiors of packaging of such items as glass containers (through RTS Packaging, LLC, a venture 65 percent owned by RockTenn); and laminated paperboard for book covers, furniture, and other products.

RockTenn is also one of the leading North American producers of temporary and permanent point-of-purchase displays. In addition, the company produces linerboard and corrugated medium, corrugated sheets, corrugated packaging, and preprinted linerboard for industrial customers, manufacturers of consumer products, and makers of corrugated boxes. RockTenn operates 11 paperboard mills, one recycled containerboard mill, and one recycled corrugated medium mill. Its 100 facilities in all are located in 27 states (mainly in the East and Midwest), Canada, Mexico, Chile, and Argentina. Long a privately held company, RockTenn made its first public offering of stock in 1994.

BACKGROUND ON PREDECESSOR ROCK CITY

Rock-Tenn Company was formed in 1973, the product of a merger between Tennessee Paper Mills Inc. and Rock City Packaging, Inc. Its origins date back to 1898, when the Rock City Box Company of Nashville, Tennessee, was founded. Among its customers in the mid-1940s were a local boot factory, a local candy manufacturer, a hosiery company, and several shirt manufacturers. The owners, Joe McHenry and A. E. Saxon, who also operated several other business ventures, wanted to sell out and retire. Rock City was attractive to Arthur Newth Morris, owner of the Southern Box Company, not least for its bank account of $60,000. Morris purchased the company in 1944 for $200,000, making a cash down payment of $50,000.

With a low-cost position in the marketplace, Rock-Tenn commits every day to creating and delivering value with innovation that produces new product ideas, generates revenue gains, improves equipment effectiveness and increases the quality of our work force. A performance-based, data-driven culture also helps us continuously reduce costs and increase customer satisfaction.

The 25-year-old Morris had been a printer and part-time Presbyterian minister when he went to work in 1926 for Edwin J. Schoettle, a Philadelphia industrialist who owned a group of box and printing companies that bore his name. For a monthly salary of $350 Morris was expected to manage several hundred employees, some of them more than twice his age. He also traveled along the Eastern Seaboard, explaining to meatpackers his discovery that they could avoid shrinkage of their hot dogs by putting them in Schoettle's boxes instead of stringing them up like bananas.

By 1935 Morris was making a salary on which he could comfortably support his wife and four children, but he wanted to go into business for himself. Armed with life savings of $5,000 and a $7,500 investment by his boss, he moved to Baltimore. There he managed the J.E. Smith Box & Printing Co. during the day, while running the Southern Box Company, a company he founded in 1936, at night. Using Smith's presses, die-cutters, and other boxmaking equipment during the evening, Morris began servicing two anchor customers who knew him from his Philadelphia days.

Only six months after Morris had left Philadelphia, Schoettle came to Baltimore to offer him a promotion and a $25,000 salary. When Morris refused, Schoettle offered to sell Morris his own majority share of Southern Box for $25,000. A bank loan to Morris made the deal possible. He moved to new quarters for $200 a month, left day-to-day management to one of his employees, and devoted himself to finding new accounts. In its first year the company made a few thousand dollars on sales of $60,000.

By 1942 Morris was doing well enough to open a corrugated box plant and to buy another Baltimore enterprise, the King Folding Box Co., where he installed a corrugated sheet cutter. Morris sold corrugated partitions to major glass companies, which needed them to separate the bottles and glasses they shipped. The fol-

lowing year the name of his enterprise was changed to Newth Morris Box Company. In 1944 another branch was opened in Jacksonville, Florida, where the company produced cardboard antiradar devices for World War II U.S. troops and popcorn boxes for movie theater owners. Following Morris's purchase of Rock City Box that same year, he changed the name of Newth Morris Box Co. to Rock City Box Sales Company.

BACKGROUND ON PREDECESSOR TENNESSEE PAPER MILLS

Morris's purchase of Rock City Box put him in contact with one of its suppliers and his future merger partner: Tennessee Paper Mills. A. L. Tomlinson and John Stagmaier, two of Tennessee Paper's three founders, were Athens, Tennessee, businessmen who already owned box factories. The company's third founder was A. M. Sheperd of Vincennes, Indiana, a boxboard manufacturer. Tennessee Paper Mills was incorporated in 1917 with Stagmaier as president, Tomlinson as vice president, and Sheperd as general manager. With $300,000 raised from stock offerings, the three men established a paperboard factory in Chattanooga, where operations began in July 1918. By the end of the year the new company had made a handsome net profit of $23,367 on sales of $165,799.

Although the founders originally planned to make board from wheat straw, they turned instead to wastepaper as the primary raw material. Thus Tennessee Paper became the first recycled paperboard mill in the South. To reduce its electric bill, the company installed its own steam generating plant in 1926. Paperboard production averaged 20 tons a day in the early years, reaching an average of 56.77 tons in 1930, the same year that the company produced a record 15,557 tons of product. This figure would not be matched for some time because of the Great Depression. Production dropped to 11,995 tons in 1934. The company remained profitable, however, although only modestly so. As the nation's economy slowly recovered, Tennessee Paper's volume of business increased to meet renewed demand. During 1939 the factory operated at 85 percent capacity, compared with the industry average of 71 percent. In 1941 it operated a record 305 days. Sales volume exceeded $1.7 million in 1945. A second paper-making machine doubled the mill's capacity in 1949.

Beginning in 1954, however, Tennessee Paper began losing customers to companies manufacturing lower-cost folding cartons and corrugated and plastic containers. The trend in the business was toward vertical integration. Many paperboard companies acquired, or merged with, their customers. Typically profits were made at the mill level, by selling boxes virtually at cost.

KEY DATES

1898: Rock City Box Company is founded in Nashville, Tennessee.

1917: Three partners form Tennessee Paper Mills, Inc., establishing in Chattanooga the first recycled paperboard mill in the South.

1936: In Baltimore, Arthur Newth Morris founds Southern Box Company (later renamed Newth Morris Box Company).

1944: Morris purchases Rock City Box and changes the name of his other company to Rock City Box Sales Company.

1967: Various companies owned by Morris are consolidated into Rock City Packaging, Inc.

1973: Tennessee Paper Mills and Rock City Packaging merge to form Rock-Tenn Company, based in Norcross, Georgia.

1994: Alliance Display and Packaging, maker of corrugated displays, is purchased; Rock-Tenn goes public.

1997: Waldorf Corporation, producer of folding cartons and recycled paperboard, is acquired.

2005: Paperboard and packaging operations of Gulf States Paper Corporation are acquired.

2008: Rock-Tenn acquires Southern Container Corp.; company begins calling itself "Rock-Tenn," although the official corporate name remains Rock-Tenn Company.

The effect on boxmakers was so severe that by 1957 Tennessee Paper was extending credit and loans to its customers in order to keep their accounts.

One of these customers was Rock City. Its consumption of Tennessee Paper's board grew from about 1,000 tons in 1944 to about 37,000 tons in 1972, when it took 44 percent of Tennessee Paper's total boxboard production. Between 1965 and 1968 Tennessee Paper bought 29.5 percent of Rock City's common stock, preparing the way for the eventual merger of the two companies. By then Rock City owed Tennessee Paper more than $4 million in loans.

Morris's burgeoning industrial empire grew both by acquisitions and by establishing new companies. Among the former was the Parks Box & Printing Co., located on a leased 11-acre tract in Norcross, Georgia. This land was purchased in 1957 and gradually became the focal point for management of all the Morris companies. A new 30,000-square-foot warehouse was added to the Norcross facility in 1960.

Each of the Morris companies operated as a separate and virtually autonomous profit center. Rock City opened not only small set-up and folding carton plants but also facilities in Livingston and Milan, Tennessee, to meet the packaging needs of shirtmakers. A set-up box division was established in 1955. Rock City Waste Paper Co. collected, sorted, and baled wastepaper for sale to paper mills. Other Morris companies and plants sprouted throughout the South. Sales grew from $8 million in 1959 to $12.9 million in 1967, when all the companies were consolidated into Rock City Packaging, Inc. Morris became chairman of the board and a son-in-law, Worley Brown, became president. Sales volume reached $23 million in 1972.

Meanwhile, in order to keep up with the competition, Tennessee Paper began buying customers to assure continued markets for its paperboard products. In 1964 it acquired Knoxville Paper Box Co., Inc., a manufacturer of folding and set-up boxes, for about $1 million. In 1969 Tennessee Paper acquired wastepaper factories in Knoxville and Atlanta, and in 1972 it built another wastepaper plant in Chattanooga.

FORMATION OF ROCK-TENN IN 1973

The merger of Rock City Packaging and Tennessee Paper Mills in 1973 gave Morris, Brown, and others who held stock in the former companies a controlling interest in the new corporation, Rock-Tenn Company. Most Tennessee Paper common stockholders received preferred stock in the new company that earned them triple the dividends they had been receiving. Some shareholders, however, opted for cash instead. The president of Tennessee Paper, W. Max Finley, and his immediate family, received common stock in the new company. Finley was elected chairman of the board and Brown became president and CEO.

Reorganization did nothing to slow down expansion. The Crescent Box & Printing Co. of Tullahoma, Tennessee, was acquired in 1973 and Clevepak Corporation's Conway, Arkansas, folding carton plant in 1974. By 1976 the company had 29 divisions. Sales in 1974, the first fiscal year after the merger, reached $47.7 million. In 1978 Bradley Currey Jr., a veteran officer of the Trust Company of Georgia who had helped effect the merger, became president and COO of Rock-Tenn. Brown became chairman of the board while remaining CEO. Finley moved to senior chairman of the board. Morris remained chairman of the executive committee until his death in January 1985. Currey later became

Rock-Tenn's CEO (in 1989) and chairman (in 1993) as well as its president.

ACQUISITION-FUELED GROWTH

In 1982 Rock-Tenn's sales volume reached $133 million and its production of recycled paperboard peaked at 180,000 tons, most of which it used itself in the manufacture of folding cartons and containers and corrugated boxes. Its many customers included Coca-Cola, du Pont, and Kentucky Fried Chicken, which it serviced from facilities in Alabama, Arkansas, Georgia, Maryland, Massachusetts, North Carolina, Ohio, Tennessee, and Texas with a workforce of 1,700 people. In a 1983 *Atlanta Constitution* interview, Currey attributed the decade-old company's growth to "luck, chance, and circumstance ... but the success of any company depends on its people." He added that the company had gone to great lengths "to make sure the workers know that we care." For instance, a group of senior executives took a month each year to travel to each of the company's facilities in order to talk to employees and present service awards.

Rock-Tenn made its largest acquisition in 1983, when it paid $40 million to buy 11 Clevepak Corporation plants, seven of which were making partitions to protect glass and plastic containers. Currey said the acquisition would allow Rock-Tenn to capture about one-fourth of the partition market, raise annual revenue to more than $200 million, and increase production of recycled paperboard to 235,000 tons. By 1989 net sales had reached $515.9 million, while net income totaled $31.1 million. The following year the company dedicated to Finley a 33,000-square-foot office building behind its headquarters in Norcross.

In 1990 Rock-Tenn acquired Allforms Packaging Corp. of Long Island and Box Innards Inc. of Orange, California. The next year it purchased the former Specialty Paperboard Inc. mill in Sheldon Springs, Vermont, and Ellis Paperboard Products Inc. of Scarborough, Maine, a manufacturer of folding cartons and solid-fiber partitions. The Ellis purchase included its Canadian subsidiary, Dominion Paperboard Products Ltd. With these additions Rock-Tenn controlled 60 manufacturing and distribution operations, including eight mills with a total annual production capacity of 607,000 tons of recycled paperboard products. Rock-Tenn now ranked sixth among U.S. producers of recycled paperboard, with a market share of 5.7 percent.

Net sales rose from $564.1 million in the fiscal year ending in September 1991 to $655.5 million in 1992, but dipped to $650.7 million in 1993. Net income increased from $25 million in 1991 to $33.2 million in

1992 before dropping to $25.5 million in 1993. The 1993 figure included unusual after-tax expenses of $5.8 million. Production in 1994 was 700,000 tons of recycled paperboard, of which 182,000 tons was clay-coated recycled paperboard.

PUBLIC STOCK OFFERING AND FURTHER ACQUISITIONS

The first public offering of Rock-Tenn stock, amounting to about 14 percent of the shares outstanding, was made in March 1994. A handful of shareholders offered about 3.6 million shares of Class A common stock, while the company itself offered about 900,000 shares. An analysis in *Barron's* described Rock-Tenn's balance sheet as "attractive" and said the company was "more soundly financed than many in its field," noting that long-term debt of $51.6 million was only one year's cash flow. Although calling the offering somewhat pricey at $16.50 a share, it noted that "Rock-Tenn's emphasis on recycling makes it well-suited to customers wishing to appear environmentally responsible, and could also prove profitable if use of woodlands is restricted." Officers and directors of Rock-Tenn still controlled about 71 percent of the combined voting power of Class A and B common stock after the offering.

In December 1993 Rock-Tenn paid $35 million for Les Industries Ling, a Canadian company that used recycled paperboard to make folding cartons. The newly acquired plant, which was to serve as the principal supplier of recycled clay-coated paperboard for Rock-Tenn's Vermont mill, became the company's second-largest folding carton facility. A year later, Rock-Tenn agreed to acquire Olympic Packaging, an Illinois-based manufacturer of folding cartons, and Alliance Display and Packaging Co. of Winston-Salem, North Carolina, maker of corrugated displays. The purchases, which boosted Rock-Tenn's acquisitions of manufacturing operations to 17 in a decade, cost about $75 million.

By the middle of the 1990s, Rock-Tenn had 59 facilities in 19 states and Canada. Net sales reached $705.8 million during 1994, constituting an 11.8 percent compounded annual growth rate over the previous decade. Net income came to a record $37.5 million. Late in 1995 COO Jay Shuster was named president of Rock-Tenn, with Currey retaining the posts of chairman and CEO.

In January 1997 Rock-Tenn consummated its largest acquisition to that point, purchasing Waldorf Corporation for $239 million in cash and the assumption of $170 million in debt. Based in St. Paul, Minnesota, Waldorf operated six folding carton plants and three paperboard mills in Illinois, Massachusetts,

Michigan, Minnesota, North Carolina, and Wisconsin. The firm had revenues of $377 million during 1996. The acquisition propelled Rock-Tenn into the number two position among producers of folding cartons in North America and also made the company the leading manufacturer of recycled paperboard in the United States.

Rock-Tenn followed up with two smaller deals in mid-1997, adding Wright City, Missouri-based Rite Paper Products, Inc., a producer of laminated recycled paperboard products primarily for the furniture industry, and the Davey Company, a manufacturer of high-density recycled paperboard mainly used in book covers and binders that operated mills in Aurora, Illinois, and Jersey City, New Jersey. Also in 1997, Rock-Tenn and Sonoco Products Company created a fiber partition joint venture called RTS Packaging, LLC, with Rock-Tenn holding a 65 percent stake and Sonoco the remaining 35 percent. The venture combined Rock-Tenn's eight partition plants with the seven that had been owned by Sonoco.

Although the purchase of Waldorf pushed Rock-Tenn's revenues past the $1 billion mark for the first time in 1997, difficulties in the integration process resulted in a depressed profit figure of $16.1 million. Some of the profit shortfall was attributable to costs stemming from plant closings, and the company closed additional plants in the next two fiscal years as profit levels recovered somewhat.

INCREASING FOCUS ON PACKAGING AND MERCHANDISING DISPLAYS

In October 1999 Rock-Tenn went outside its ranks for a new CEO, hiring James A. Rubright, who had previously been the head of the pipeline group and energy services business of Sonat, Inc. Currey handed over the chairmanship to Rubright as well in January 2000. Later in 2000, Shuster, having been passed over for the CEO position, left the company. Rubright accelerated the pace of restructuring at Rock-Tenn through the closure of a number of underperforming plants. He also shifted the company's emphasis away from the slow-growing recycled paperboard side and toward the areas with higher growth potential: the folding carton business, as well as the burgeoning merchandising display operation, which by the first years of the 21st century was the U.S. leader in point-of-purchase displays.

During 2000, Rock-Tenn closed one laminated paperboard products plant and three folding carton plants, resulting in 550 employee terminations and charges of $61.1 million, as well as a net loss for the

year of $15.9 million. Seven more plants were shuttered over the next three years, resulting in the loss of 450 more jobs and an additional $19 million in charges. Meantime, in February 2000 the company formed a joint venture with Lafarge Corporation called Seven Hills Paperboard, LLC, which was charged with producing gypsum paperboard liner for the U.S. drywall manufacturing plants of Lafarge. Rock-Tenn owned 49 percent of the venture.

Rock-Tenn also beefed up its merchandising display business, its fastest-growing segment, through two acquisitions costing a total of $25.4 million. In November 2001 Advertising Display Company, a producer of both temporary and permanent point-of-purchase displays, was acquired. In March of the following year Rock-Tenn bought Athena Industries, Inc., a Burr Ridge, Illinois, manufacturer of permanent point-of-purchase displays, with an emphasis on wire displays.

Acquisition activity continued in 2003 with the purchase of Cartem Wilco Group Inc., a privately held Canadian maker of folding cartons and specialty packaging, for $65.3 million. The deal accelerated Rock-Tenn's expansion into the growing pharmaceutical and health and beauty packaging market. Cartem Wilco, which operated plants in Montreal and Quebec City, also produced folding cartons for food packaging and consumer products. In August 2003 Rock-Tenn paid about $16 million for Pacific Coast Packaging Corp., located in Kerman, California. Rock-Tenn secured its first folding carton operation on the West Coast through this acquisition, gaining a manufacturer of folding cartons for the fast-food, in-store deli, and gift box markets. In order to heighten the focus on its core paper packaging businesses, Rock-Tenn in October 2003 sold its plastic packaging operations to Pactiv Corporation for $59 million.

MAJOR ACQUISITIONS OF GULF STATES ASSETS AND SOUTHERN CONTAINER

In the first of two major acquisitions completed during Rubright's tenure at the helm, Rock-Tenn paid $552.2 million in 2005 for the paperboard and packaging operations of Gulf States Paper Corporation. The most important asset gained in this deal was a pulp and paperboard mill in Demopolis, Alabama, that had the capacity to produce 327,000 tons of bleached paperboard per year and 91,500 tons of southern bleached softwood kraft market pulp. This mill was one of the lowest-cost bleached paperboard mills in North America, and its addition to the portfolio was one key factor in the much larger profits that Rock-Tenn began reporting in 2007. That year, net income totaled $81.7

million on sales of $2.32 billion, in comparison to the profits of just $17.6 million on sales of $1.58 billion recorded for 2004.

Also gained through the Gulf States transaction were 11 folding carton plants that mainly served the food packaging, foodservice, pharmaceutical, and health and beauty markets. The addition of these plants made Rock-Tenn the second-largest producer of folding cartons in North America, trailing only Graphic Packaging Holding Company. Over the next couple of years following the deal, Rock-Tenn closed several folding carton plants as part of its efforts to integrate the Gulf States assets and achieve annual cost savings of more than $25 million. The facilities shuttered included plants in Waco, Texas; Marshville, North Carolina; Kerman, California; and Stone Mountain, Georgia.

The second major acquisition of this era followed the formula of the Gulf States deal but bolstered Rock-Tenn's corrugated and merchandising display businesses. In the largest acquisition in company history, Rock-Tenn in March 2008 spent $1.06 billion for Southern Container Corp., a privately held firm based in Hauppauge, New York. The centerpiece of this deal was Southern Container's Solvay recycled containerboard mill, located near Syracuse, New York. Similar to the Demopolis mill, the Solvay plant was one of the lowest-cost containerboard mills in North America. Its three containerboard machines, which had been installed in 1994, 1999, and 2002, had a combined annual capacity of 720,000 tons.

Rock-Tenn also gained Southern Container's eight corrugated box plants and two corrugated sheet plants, as well as four high-impact graphics facilities. Through the latter, Southern Container had been one of the largest preprint manufacturers in North America, and so Rock-Tenn was able to significantly bolster its merchandising display business. This acquisition was also geographically significant with the addition of Southern Container's plants in the Northeast to Rock-Tenn's facilities primarily located in the South and Midwest. In another development from 2008, the company began referring to itself as "RockTenn," although the official corporate name remained Rock-Tenn Company.

The acquisitions of the Gulf States assets and Southern Container made RockTenn a vastly more profitable enterprise. Despite the major economic recession that began in the later months of 2008, the company enjoyed its most profitable year ever in fiscal 2009. Net income was a record $222.3 million on sales of $2.81 billion, while earnings per share were a best-ever $5.75. By comparison, the earnings per share figure for fiscal 2004 was just $0.50. Strong cash flow enabled

RockTenn to slash its net debt by $287 million, to $1.33 billion, giving the company financial flexibility to pursue further acquisitions and make other investments. In July 2010, for instance, RockTenn announced plans to spend $25 million to build a new, state-of-the-art chip mill adjacent to its Demopolis plant to supply that plant with wood chips and bark.

Robert Halasz
Updated, David E. Salamie

PRINCIPAL SUBSIDIARIES

Alliance Display Company of Canada; Dominion Paperboard Products Ltd. (Canada); Ling Industries, Inc. (Canada); Ling Quebec, Inc. (Canada); PCPC, Inc.; Pro-Tec Partitions, Inc.; Rock-Tenn Astra, LLC; Rock-Tenn Canada Holdings, Inc.; Rock-Tenn Company of Canada; Rock-Tenn Company of Canada III; Rock-Tenn Company of Texas; Rock-Tenn Converting Company; Rock-Tenn Financial, Inc.; Rock-Tenn Leasing Company, LLC; Rock-Tenn Mill Company, LLC; Rock-Tenn Partition Company; Rock-Tenn Services Inc.; Rock-Tenn Shared Services, LLC; Rock-Tenn XL, LLC; RTS Packaging Canada Inc.; RTS Embalajes de Argentina; RTS Embalajes De Chile Limitada; RTS Empaques, S. De R.L. de CV (Mexico); RTS Packaging Foreign Holdings, LLC; Southern Container Corp.; TenCorr Containerboard Inc.; Preflex, LLC; Solvay Paperboard LLC; Waldorf Corporation; Wilco Inc. (Canada).

PRINCIPAL OPERATING UNITS

Consumer Packaging; Corrugated Packaging; Merchandising Displays; Specialty Paperboard Products.

PRINCIPAL COMPETITORS

Carauster Industries, Inc.; Chesapeake Corporation; Graphic Packaging Holding Company; International Paper Company; MeadWestvaco Corporation; Menasha Corporation; The Newark Group; Packaging Corporation of America; Shorewood Packaging Corporation; Smurfit-Stone Container Corporation; Sonoco Products Company.

FURTHER READING

Arzoumanian, Mark, "How RockTenn Stopped Floundering," *Official Boards Markets*, April 17, 2010, p. 6.
Cochran, Thomas N., "Offerings in the Offing," *Barron's*, February 21, 1994, p. 50.

Fernandez, Don, "Rock-Tenn Co. to Close Carton Plant in Norcross," *Atlanta Journal-Constitution*, April 29, 2000, p. J1.

Herndon, Keith, "Rock-Tenn Seeks Knockout Punch," *Atlanta Constitution*, July 11, 1983, p. C12.

Luke, Robert, "Riding a Profitable Wave: Rock-Tenn, a Norcross-Based Maker of Packaging Products, Is Basking in the Affection of Wall Street," *Atlanta-Journal Constitution*, March 22, 2007, p. C1.

Mies, Will, "RockTenn Grows in Packaging," *Pulp and Paper*, September 2008, pp. 23–24+.

Paul, Peralte C., "Package Maker Rock-Tenn to Pay $851 Million for N.Y. Company," *Atlanta Journal-Constitution*, January 12, 2008, p. C1.

"Rock-Tenn Agreement to Purchase Waldorf," *Pulp and Paper*, February 1997, p. 23.

The Rock-Tenn Story, Norcross, GA: Rock-Tenn Company, n.d.

"Rock-Tenn to Buy Gulf States Packaging Assets for $540 Million," *Pulp and Paper*, June 2005, p. 6.

Shaw, Monica, "Packaging Success," *Pulp and Paper*, February 2006, pp. 24–27.

San Miguel Corporation

40 San Miguel Avenue
Mandaluyong City, Metropolitan Manila 1550
Philippines
Telephone: (+63-2) 632-3000
Fax: (+63-2) 632-3099
Web site: http://www.sanmiguel.com.ph

Public Company
Founded: 1890 as La Fabrica de Cerveza de San Miguel
Incorporated: 1913
Employees: 27,259
Sales: PHP 174.2 billion ($3.77 billion) (2009)
Stock Exchanges: Philippine
Ticker Symbol: SMC
NAICS: 551112 Offices of Other Holding Companies; 312120 Breweries; 312140 Distilleries; 112111 Beef Cattle Ranching and Farming; 112210 Hog and Pig Farming; 112320 Broilers and Other Meat Type Chicken Production; 112340 Poultry Hatcheries; 311119 Other Animal Food Manufacturing; 311211 Flour Milling; 311223 Other Oilseed Processing; 311225 Fats and Oils Refining and Blending; 311421 Fruit and Vegetable Canning; 311512 Creamery Butter Manufacturing; 311513 Cheese Manufacturing; 311520 Ice Cream and Frozen Dessert Manufacturing; 311611 Animal (Except Poultry) Slaughtering; 311612 Meat Processed from Carcasses; 311615 Poultry Processing; 311920 Coffee and Tea Manufacturing; 322211 Corrugated and Solid Fiber Box Manufacturing; 326199 All Other Plastics Product Manufacturing; 327213 Glass Container Manufacturing; 332115 Crown and Closure Manufactur-

ing; 332431 Metal Can Manufacturing; 324110 Petroleum Refineries; 424720 Petroleum and Petroleum Products Merchant Wholesalers (Except Bulk Stations and Terminals); 447190 Other Gasoline Stations

■ ■ ■

Best known for its internationally distributed beer, San Miguel Corporation is a conglomerate that in the early 21st century has been diversifying its operations still further. Its founding business, San Miguel Brewery Inc., utterly dominates the Filipino beer market, with a market share of around 90 percent. Although San Miguel Brewery is listed on the Philippine Stock Exchange, San Miguel Corp. holds a 51 percent controlling stake in the brewery, with the Japanese beer maker Kirin Brewery Company, Limited holding another 48.4 percent. Other holdings include a 97 percent stake in the publicly traded San Miguel Pure Foods Company, Inc., the leading producer of fresh and processed meats, poultry, flour, and feed in the Philippines; and a stake of about 79 percent in the publicly traded Ginebra San Miguel, Inc., a producer of gin and other hard liquors. San Miguel Yamamura Packaging Corporation, a joint venture controlled by San Miguel Corp. (65%) and the Japanese firm Nihon Yamamura Glass Company, Ltd. (35%), is the largest food and beverage and packaging company in Southeast Asia.

In 2007 San Miguel Corp. began a diversification into heavy industry and infrastructure-related businesses, seeking the higher margins on offer compared to its

COMPANY PERSPECTIVES

San Miguel's strategy today is to strengthen its core businesses of food, beverage and packaging—maintaining and building upon the dominant market positions held in most of its product segments—while unlocking new engines of growth and boosting aggregate margins. This diversification should allow the company to grow faster and perform more consistently. Indeed, there has never been a more hopeful time than the present to participate in industries that can really contribute to our country's progress—businesses like power, oil refining, banking, property development, bulk water, telecoms, and even infrastructure.

Guided by our core values of integrity, passion for success, teamwork, respect for people, innovativeness, customer focus and social responsibility, we are today in the midst of an unprecedented expansion program that will weave our products and services even more tightly into the fabric of everyday life.

traditional business lines. Over the next few years, the company acquired majority control of Petron Corporation, the Philippines' largest oil refining and marketing concern; a significant minority stake in Manila Electric Company, the largest electricity utility company in the Philippines; and a 49 percent interest in Filipino telecommunications firm Liberty Telecom Holdings, Inc. By 2010 San Miguel had also bought a power plant, a coal mining company, and stakes in projects building a toll road and expanding an airport in the Philippines.

FOUNDATION ON SOUTHEAST ASIA'S FIRST BREWERY

Don Enrique Ma Barretto de Ycaza established the brewery, Southeast Asia's first, in 1890 as La Fabrica de Cerveza de San Miguel. He named the company after the section of Manila in which he lived and worked. He was soon joined by Don Pedro Pablo Roxas, who brought with him a German brewmaster. San Miguel's brew won its first major award at 1895's Philippines Regional Exposition and led its imported competitors by a five-to-one margin by the advent of the 20th century. The company was incorporated in 1913 following the death of Don Pedro Roxas.

By that time, San Miguel was exporting its namesake brew to Hong Kong, Shanghai, and Guam. Andrés Soriano y Roxas joined San Miguel in 1918, beginning a multigeneration (albeit interrupted) reign of Sorianos. In 1990 San Miguel's *Beer Bulletin* noted that "Beer was the heart of San Miguel's business, and the soul from which emanated all its other businesses." Andrés Soriano initiated the company's diversification, which proceeded rather logically via vertical integration.

The experience cultivating barley naturally evolved into other agricultural businesses, for example. San Miguel gathered steam in the 1920s, when the company expanded into nonalcoholic beverages with the creation of the Royal Soft Drinks Plant in 1922. San Miguel entered the frozen foods market in 1925 with the creation of the Magnolia Ice Cream Plant. Soriano created the first non-U.S. national Coca-Cola bottling and distribution franchise in 1927. The Philippine company owned 70 percent of the joint venture, which grew to become Coke's sixth-largest operation. San Miguel's involvement in packaging began in 1938 with the opening of a glass plant to produce bottles for the brewery.

Although World War II interrupted San Miguel's brewing business, the company got back on the growth track in the postwar era, acquiring production facilities in Hong Kong in 1948. The company also resumed its program of vertical integration, even building its own power plant so that it would not be dependent on the Philippines' notoriously poor infrastructure. San Miguel also built a liquid carbon dioxide plant, additional glass bottle manufacturing facilities, and a carton plant during the postwar period.

The company shortened its name to San Miguel Corporation in 1963, and Andrés Soriano Jr. advanced to the company's presidency upon his father's 1964 death. Credited with instituting modern management theory, including decentralization along product lines, Soriano Jr. continued to diversify the food business during the early 1980s. He expanded into poultry production in 1982, built an ice cream plant in 1983, and added shrimp processing and freezing in 1984.

Over the decades, San Miguel earned a formidable reputation as a fierce competitor. The company used all the tools at its disposal. When it could not beat a rival through traditional means, it acquired and intimidated upstarts into submission. The Filipino government's complicity did not hurt, either. Long protected by high tariffs, San Miguel encountered its first major competitor in the beer market in the late 1970s. That was when Asia Brewery entered the segment. The rivalry between Asia Brewery and San Miguel came to a head in 1988, when Asia Brewery cannily introduced a bargain-priced "brand" called, simply, "Beer."

KEY DATES

1890: Don Enrique Ma Barretto de Ycaza establishes a brewery in Manila called La Fabrica de Cerveza de San Miguel.
1913: Brewery is incorporated.
1938: Company enters the packaging sector with the opening of a glass plant.
1963: Company shortens its name to San Miguel Corporation.
2007: Company launches diversification into heavy industry and infrastructure-related businesses; packaging operations are transferred into a joint venture with Nihon Yamamura Glass Company, Ltd.
2009: After San Miguel Brewery Inc. is taken public the previous year, Kirin Brewery Company, Limited acquires a 48 percent stake in the San Miguel Corporation subsidiary.

The imported product looked and tasted like its primary competitor, playing upon the fact that in the Philippines, the San Miguel brand was synonymous with "beer." It was a creative counter to San Miguel's notoriously aggressive and sometimes cutthroat competitive strategy, which had reportedly included "attempts to sabotage [Asia Brewery's] sales network and smash its empty bottles." Asia Brewery, whose owner was reputedly connected to sympathizers of Filipino strongman Ferdinand Marcos, even hired away San Miguel's brewmaster.

POLITICAL MACHINATIONS

Although San Miguel enjoyed virtual monopolies in its markets, that status did not shield it from the political machinations of the Philippines. The dictatorial reign of Marcos brought this element into sharp focus in the 1980s, when an intrafamilial proxy fight at San Miguel turned political. The dispute was instigated in 1983 by Enrique Zobel, a wealthy cousin of the Sorianos who owned the Ayala banking and real estate group and sided with the Marcos government. Unable to execute a takeover on his own, Zobel sold his 19.5 percent stake to Eduardo Cojuangco Jr. (known in some circles as "the coconut king").

Although Cojuangco was a cousin of Marcos opponent Corazon Aquino, he too sided with Marcos. Cojuangco's Coconut Industry Investment Fund (also known as United Coconut Planters Bank) accumulated

an additional 31 percent of San Miguel, giving him effective control of the conglomerate and leaving the Soriano family with a mere 3 percent. Cojuangco scooped up the chairmanship in 1984, when Andrés Soriano Jr. died of cancer. However, his reign over San Miguel lasted only two years. When Marcos lost the 1986 election to Aquino amid the "people power" revolution, Cojuangco and many other Marcos backers fled the country. (In fact, Marcos and Cojuangco left in the same helicopter.)

Andrés Soriano III resumed San Miguel's chairmanship and launched a campaign to reclaim the family legacy that year. However, when the new chairman tried to buy back the abandoned shares, he was blocked by an unexpected agency. The Aquino administration's Presidential Commission on Good Government (PCGG) assumed control (but not legal ownership) of the 51.4 percent stake and refused to relinquish it. The government asserted that the stake had been illegally obtained. In the 1970s Marcos had imposed a tax on the production of coconuts, a major Philippine cash crop, with the proceeds supposed to fund that industry's development. It was alleged, however, that the money was funneled into the Cojuangco-controlled United Coconut Planters Bank, and that Cojuangco then used much of the funds to help him purchase his controlling stake in San Miguel. The controlling interest carried nine of San Miguel's 15 directors seats with it. The PCGG continued to tend its San Miguel stake into the early 1990s, but it acceded de facto control of the conglomerate to Andrés Soriano III via a management contract with his A. Soriano Corp.

Soriano III was characterized by *Business Week*'s Maria Shao as an "introverted, almost reclusive" leader. Schooled at the University of Pennsylvania's prestigious Wharton School, Soriano III had dabbled in investment banking in New York City before returning to the Philippines. Soriano tried everything from legal machinations to joint-venture buyout schemes to wrest control of San Miguel from the PCGG, but to no avail.

CENTENARY CELEBRATION: 1990

At the same time, Soriano III continued the company's program of expansion, acquiring majority control of La Tondeña Distillers, Inc., the leading producer of hard liquor in the Philippines, in 1987 and adding beef and pork production to the company's food operations in 1988. In 1990 San Miguel threw a five-month party to celebrate its centenary. President Corazon Aquino called San Miguel "the best showcase of a Filipino company, a shining example of creative management and commitment to its public." The *Economist* contrastingly called

San Miguel "a showcase for much that is wrong with business in the Philippines."

The latter assertion was substantiated that same year, when Cojuangco returned to the Philippines (the *Journal of Commerce* noted that he "sneaked back into the country [in 1990] despite a ban on his return") to lay claim to his holdings. Notwithstanding the circumstances of his repatriation, a November 1992 article in *Asian Business* noted that "Cojuangco [was] expected to win eventually." All the same, Soriano III continued to hold the chairmanship. (Cojuangco, meantime, unsuccessfully ran for the Philippine presidency in 1992.)

INTERNATIONAL EXPANSION

Soriano III led the company to a new era of dramatic growth based on internationalization. This move was motivated by a number of factors. First, San Miguel had developed its core Philippine and Hong Kong markets to maturity and was faced with relatively slow growth there. Soriano hoped to expand into other countries and thereby mitigate the effects of the Philippines' unstable economy. Finally, the leader wanted to head off encroaching competition from the world's largest breweries, namely Anheuser-Busch and Miller of the United States, Kirin of Japan, and BSN of France. In an interview with *Asian Business*'s Michael Selwyn, Francisco C. Eizmendi Jr., then president of San Miguel, said that "what we are aiming to do is be a David among the Goliaths of international business, without losing our grip on the local market."

Having determined that overseas growth was imperative, Soriano allocated $1 billion to a five-year strategic internationalization program that focused on shaping up domestic operations, then progressing to licensing and exporting, overseas production, and finally to distribution of non-beer products. San Miguel's plant modernization plan involved sweeping improvements, from computerization to quality circles. These efforts laid the groundwork that would enable the company to compete with the world's food and beverage multinationals. A subsequent decentralization created a holding company structure with the 18 non-beer operations positioned as subsidiaries. This corporate reorganization freed the spun-off businesses from the bureaucratic shackles of a large conglomerate. In the course of this multifaceted effort to attain optimum efficiency, San Miguel reduced its workforce by more than 16 percent, from a 1989 high of 39,138 to 32,832 by 1993. These programs helped increase profit per employee by 56 percent in 1991 alone.

With its domestic "ducks in a row," San Miguel turned to the next stage in its internationalization, beer licensing, and exporting initiative. Although the company had exported beer for most of its history, this effort was intensified dramatically in the late 1980s. San Miguel's beer exports grew by 150 percent from 1985 to 1989 alone, and the brand was soon exported to 24 countries, including all of Asia's key markets as well as the United States, Australia, and the Middle East. Once the core brand was established in a particular market, San Miguel would begin to create production facilities, sometimes on an independent basis and sometimes in concert with an indigenous joint-venture partner. By 1995, San Miguel had manufacturing plants in Hong Kong, China, Indonesia, Vietnam, Taiwan, and Guam.

Thus, in spite of the overarching quarrel regarding San Miguel's ownership (not to mention other problems endemic to operating in the Philippines), the company's sales quintupled from PHP 12.23 billion in 1986 to PHP 68.43 billion by 1994. Net income increased twice as fast, from PHP 1.11 billion to PHP 11.86 billion over the same period, although San Miguel's overseas operations (as a whole) were not yet profitable.

RESTRUCTURING, ECONOMIC CRISIS: 1995–97

In 1995 San Miguel completed an initial listing of the stock of La Tondeña Distillers on the Philippine Stock Exchange, although the parent company retained majority control. The following year San Miguel purchased full control of its Hong Kong arm, San Miguel Brewery Hong Kong Limited. In April 1997 San Miguel's domestic soft-drink bottling unit, Coca-Cola Bottlers Philippines, Inc., was merged into the Australia-based Coca-Cola Amatil Limited (CCA). In effect, San Miguel exchanged its 70 percent interest in a Philippine-only operation for a 25 percent stake in CCA, which had operations in 17 countries, both in the Asia-Pacific region and in Eastern Europe. CCA soon demerged the latter operations into a U.K.-based firm called Coca-Cola Beverages plc (resulting in a reduction of San Miguel's stake in CCA to 22 percent). Seeking to maintain its focus on the Asia-Pacific region, San Miguel sold its stake in the new U.K. entity in mid-1998.

From 1995 through 1997, San Miguel suffered from a downturn in its main domestic businesses, while overseas operations were still in the red. Profits plummeted. In response, a major restructuring of the company's loss-making food businesses was undertaken. San Miguel's ice cream and pasteurized milk business was merged with operations of Nestlé to form Nestlé Philippines, Inc., and late in 1998 San Miguel's stake in this business was sold off. San Miguel also exited from the ready-to-eat meal sector and curtailed the operations of its shrimp farming business.

By late 1997 the company was also beginning to feel the effects of the exploding Asian economic crisis. In addition, the price of its stock was declining. At this point, a Hong Kong-based conglomerate, First Pacific Company Limited, stepped into the picture, acquiring a 2 percent stake in San Miguel and entering into negotiations to pay as much as $1.3 billion for the two government-sequestered stakes that remained the subject of lengthy litigation. First Pacific abandoned its takeover bid early in 1998, however, when the negotiations ran afoul of Philippine election-year politics.

BEGINNING OF A NEW COJUANGCO ERA

In April 1998 the antigraft court handling the case of the disputed San Miguel stakes ruled that Cojuangco was entitled to vote 20 percent of the shares, although he was not given ownership of the shares. This enabled Cojuangco to install three new directors on the company board. Then in May, Joseph Estrada won the Philippine presidential election. Cojuangco had been the main financial backer of Estrada, a former movie actor who had been Cojuangco's vice presidential running mate during their unsuccessful 1992 campaign, and Cojuangco also became chairman of Estrada's political party following Estrada's electoral victory. By early July 1998, Soriano III had resigned from his position as chairman of San Miguel, and the board of directors, which included seven government-controlled (and hence Estrada-controlled) seats, voted to return Cojuangco to the chairmanship. This marked an amazing comeback for the once-disgraced Cojuangco, and also left many observers worried about a possible return to the crony capitalism of the Marcos era.

Cojuangco moved quickly to turn around the fortunes of the foundering company. Restructuring moves included a flattening of management layers to speed up decision making and make the company more responsive to the marketplace. Overseas, the international headquarters were moved from high-priced Hong Kong to low-priced Manila as part of a larger cost-cutting initiative. The company also raised its domestic beer prices to make up for revenue lost from higher taxes on beverages and liquor. San Miguel increased its share of the domestic bottled water market by acquiring Metro Bottled Water Corporation, maker of Wilkins Distilled Water, in July 1999. Later in 1999 San Miguel announced that it would sell its minority stake in CCA through a stock offering, but these plans were soon abandoned when CCA's stock price declined sharply. Income from operations for San Miguel rose slightly in 1998 before surging 63 percent in 1999.

Using a huge hoard of cash built through the recent asset sales, Cojuangco completed a series of acquisitions from 2000 to early 2002. During 2000, San Miguel purchased J. Boag & Son Limited, an Australian brewer, for about PHP 2.4 billion ($56 million), as well as Sugarland Multi-Food Corporation, a Philippine juice maker, for PHP 2.9 billion. The latter firm, renamed Sugarland Beverage Corporation, was jointly acquired by San Miguel and its majority-owned subsidiary, La Tondeña Distillers.

KEY ACQUISITIONS IN 2001

Two major acquisitions of Philippine firms were then completed in 2001. Pure Foods Corporation was acquired for PHP 7.02 billion. Renamed San Miguel Pure Foods Company, Inc., the acquired company was a market leader in both processed meats and flour. The deal thereby expanded San Miguel's processed meat portfolio and also marked its first foray into the flour industry. In July 2001 San Miguel joined forces with The Coca-Cola Company to reacquire Coca-Cola Bottlers Philippines Inc., with San Miguel taking a 65 percent stake and Coca-Cola the remaining 35 percent. As part of the deal, San Miguel sold its shares in CCA back to that company.

Later in 2001, San Miguel sold its bottled water and juice businesses, now amalgamated as Philippine Beverage Partners, Inc., to Coca-Cola Bottlers Philippines. Finally, in February 2002, San Miguel completed the acquisition of an 83 percent stake in Cosmos Bottling Corporation in a PHP 15 billion ($282 million) deal completed through Coca-Cola Bottlers Philippines. Cosmos specialized in low-priced soft drinks and held the number two position in the Philippine market. The combination of Coca-Cola Bottlers Philippines and Cosmos gave San Miguel control of more than 90 percent of the Philippine soft-drink industry.

During and following this period of acquisitiveness, the question of who owned San Miguel remained unresolved. Estrada became embroiled in a corruption scandal and was then forced from power in January 2001 in a popular uprising backed by the military. Replacing Estrada as president was Gloria Macapagal-Arroyo, who almost immediately began maneuvering to oust Cojuangco from the chairmanship of San Miguel as part of her campaign to rid the country of corruption. Arroyo sought to replace five directors appointed by Estrada, but a technicality prevented her from doing so prior to the May 2001 annual meeting. Cojuangco was thus able to retain his position as chairman.

Then in December 2001 the Philippine Supreme Court ruled that Arroyo could in fact replace the five directors. Simultaneously, however, Cojuangco arranged a deal with the Japanese brewer Kirin Brewery Company, Limited whereby Kirin would invest PHP 27.88 billion ($544 million) for a 15 percent stake in San Miguel. Kirin finalized its investment in February 2002, gaining two board seats that Cojuangco could now count on to help him remain in power. By this time, Cojuangco had also gained popularity among investors for turning around the company and making it one of the most profitable in the country, despite a prolonged economic downswing. The government recognized this support by reaching a deal with Cojuangco in early 2002. Cojuangco could remain in control of the conglomerate until the antigraft court determined the true ownership of the disputed shareholdings. In return the government gained representation on important management committees and on the boards of 13 company subsidiaries.

DEAL MAKING AND STRATEGY SHIFT

The middle years of the first decade of the 21st century saw a number of changes in San Miguel's profile as a conglomerate. In 2003 La Tondeña Distillers, the publicly traded hard-liquor subsidiary in which San Miguel maintained a stake of about 79 percent, was renamed Ginebra San Miguel, Inc. In 2005 San Miguel completed its largest takeover ever, purchasing National Foods Limited, the largest dairy company in Australia, for about AUD 1.9 billion ($1.5 billion).

The deal making during this period culminated in the event-filled year of 2007. Early in the year, San Miguel sold its 65 percent stake in Coca-Cola Bottlers Philippines to The Coca-Cola Company for $590 million. San Miguel also turned around and divested National Foods just two years after acquiring it, selling it to Kirin for $2.6 billion. The company also sold another Australian asset, J. Boag & Son, to Lion Nathan Limited around this same time. San Miguel's packaging business, which ranked as the largest food and beverage and packaging company in Southeast Asia, was placed into a joint venture with Japan's Nihon Yamamura Glass Company, Ltd., with the latter purchasing a stake of 35 percent. The joint venture was named San Miguel Yamamura Packaging Corporation.

The ownership of San Miguel was further clarified when the Filipino government's stake held through its state pension funds and social security system were sold off. The PCGG, however, continued to administer a stake of about 24 percent on behalf of the Coconut Industry Investment Fund.

The most significant news of 2007 came midyear when San Miguel launched what analysts called the big-

gest strategic shift in the firm's 117-year history. The company said it planned to diversify into heavy industry and infrastructure-related businesses that it envisioned as having prospects for more growth and larger profits than its core businesses in alcoholic beverages and food. To raise capital for investments in new sectors, San Miguel began selling additional assets. In 2008 the company took its beer subsidiary, San Miguel Brewery Inc., public through an initial public offering. The following year, Kirin sold its stake in San Miguel Corp. and then purchased a stake of more than 48 percent in San Miguel Brewery for $835.3 million. San Miguel Corp. retained a controlling 51 percent stake. San Miguel in 2010 was also attempting to sell a stake of 49 percent in its San Miguel Pure Foods subsidiary.

By 2010 San Miguel Corp. had made a string of investments in heavy industry and infrastructure. It acquired majority control of Petron Corporation, the Philippines' largest oil refining and marketing concern, and a significant minority stake in Manila Electric Company, the largest electricity utility company in the Philippines. In 2010 the company made the winning bid in the auction to take over management of the contracted capacity of the Ilijan natural gas power plant in Batangas from the Philippine government. Among other purchases, San Miguel bought a coal mining company, stakes in projects building a toll road and expanding an airport in the Philippines, and a 49 percent interest in Filipino telecommunications firm Liberty Telecom Holdings, Inc. San Miguel had also bought a concession for an iron ore mine, with plans to set up a smelter to serve the needs of steelmakers based in the Philippines.

April Dougal Gasbarre
Updated, David E. Salamie

PRINCIPAL SUBSIDIARIES

Ginebra San Miguel, Inc. (79.4%); Petron Corporation (51%); San Miguel Brewery Inc. (51%); San Miguel Properties, Inc. (99.7%); San Miguel Pure Foods Company, Inc. (97%); San Miguel Yamamura Packaging Corporation (65%).

PRINCIPAL COMPETITORS

Anheuser-Busch InBev SA/NV; Asia Pacific Breweries Limited; JG Summit Holdings, Inc.; Tsingtao Brewery Co., Ltd.

FURTHER READING

Arnold, Wayne, "Manila Decides It Can Get Along with a Marcos Ally," *New York Times*, February 27, 2002, p. W1.

Frank, Robert, "Teflon Tycoon—The Crony Capitalist," *Wall Street Journal*, August 30, 1999, pp. A1+.

Hookway, James, "San Miguel Snaps Up Deals in Slump," *Wall Street Journal*, April 9, 2009, p. B1.

Landingin, Roel, "Brewery Chief Savours Switch to the Hard Stuff," *Financial Times*, June 22, 2010, p. 18.

———, "San Miguel Switches Its Growth Focus," *Financial Times*, October 9, 2007, p. 28.

———, "Share Purchase Helps San Miguel," *Financial Times*, January 7, 2010, p. 16.

Larano, Cris, "San Miguel Diversifies: Food Company Buys Stake in Power Firm as It Expands Reach," *Wall Street Journal Asia*, October 28, 2008, p. 8.

———, "San Miguel Seeks $1 Billion from Asset Sales," *Wall Street Journal*, March 18, 2010, p. B4.

Moore, Hannah, "Battle for San Miguel Brewing in Philippines," *Journal of Commerce*, March 6, 1991, p. 3A.

Nakamoto, Michiyo, and Roel Landingin, "Kirin Sets Its Sights on 49% Stake in San Miguel," *Financial Times*, February 21, 2009, p. 16.

"Opéra Bouffe," *Economist*, April 28, 1990, pp. 72–73.

Reyes, Cid, *History in the Brewing: A Centennial Celebration of San Miguel Beer*, Manila: Larawan Books, 1994, 167 p.

Reyes, Rexie, "San Miguel Puts Cojuangco Back in Driver's Seat," *Asian Wall Street Journal*, July 8, 1998, p. 1.

Selwyn, Michael, "Honour Is the Watchword," *Asian Business*, November 1992, pp. 36–37.

———, "The Secrets of San Miguel's Sparkle," *Asian Business*, November 1992, pp. 28–30.

Shao, Maria, "Andrés Soriano's Battle for San Miguel," *Business Week*, September 28, 1987, p. 54.

"Strange Brew," *Economist*, May 16, 1998, pp. 64–65.

The Shaw Group, Inc.

4171 Essen Lane
Baton Rouge, Louisiana 70809
U.S.A.
Telephone: (225) 932-2500
Toll Free: (800) 747-3322
Fax: (225) 987-3328
Web site: http://www.shawgrp.com

Public Company
Incorporated: 1987
Employees: 28,000
Sales: $7.29 billion (2009)
Stock Exchanges: New York
Ticker Symbol: SHAW
NAICS: 332996 Fabricated Pipe and Pipe Fitting Manufacturing; 541620 Environmental Consulting Services; 237130 Power and Communication Transmission Line Construction; 237110 Water, Sewer, and Pipeline Construction

■ ■ ■

The Shaw Group, Inc., is a provider of engineering and construction services for the energy, chemical, and construction industries. The company builds facilities for the power generation industry, including both fossil fuel and nuclear power plants. Another major component of its business involves restoring contaminated sites such as uranium processing facilities, part of its environmental engineering and sciences arm. A vertically integrated company, Shaw offers its clients comprehensive services ranging from pipe fabrication to engineering and design services. The company maintains more than 150 offices worldwide.

BUILDING A PIPE FABRICATION COMPANY: 1987–94

James M. Bernhard Jr. founded The Shaw Group in 1987. After graduating from college in the early 1970s, he worked his way through the ranks of various Baton Rouge, Louisiana, pipe fabrication and contracting companies. This experience gave him an expert's education in the operations of the pipe fabrication industry.

The fabrication of complex piping systems for power generation facilities and process facilities, including petrochemical and chemical processing and petroleum refining, is complex and demanding. Materials such as steel, titanium, and aluminum are the raw materials of fabrication. These materials are formed into pipes with diameters as large as 72 inches and walls as thick as seven inches. Some of these pipes become parts of "critical piping systems" used in high-pressure, high-temperature, or corrosive applications. Such systems must withstand pressures up to 2,700 pounds per square inch and temperatures up to 1,020 degrees Fahrenheit. These critical systems are used in power generation.

By the mid-1980s, the U.S. pipe fabrication industry was experiencing significant difficulties. Power plant construction was at a low ebb domestically, as was refinery construction due to a decline in oil and gas exploration. At the same time, pipe fabrication was a craft performed by skilled welders brought to construction sites for that sole purpose. This handicraft approach kept piping prices high, and contributed to a large-scale exodus from the industry.

Bernhard believed that the industry could again become successful in the United States. He wanted to transform pipe fabrication from a craft industry to an industry that produced its product in factories using machinery to the extent possible. Such a change in fabrication practices, he believed, would reduce piping costs and allow the domestic pipe fabrication businesses to become profitable again.

To implement his ideas, Bernhard founded The Shaw Group in 1987 and purchased the Benjamin F. Shaw Company, a century-old pipe fabricator. In 1998, its first full year of operation, Shaw reported revenue of $29.3 million. By 1993 when the company went public, its revenue had increased to $120.7 million.

BECOMING A TOTAL PIPING RESOURCE: 1994–97

The company began an aggressive but focused acquisition strategy with the proceeds of its initial public offering. In 1994, Shaw adopted the goal of becoming a "total piping resource." In pursuit of this end, it began a major expansion of its technical capabilities. In April 1994 Shaw purchased Fronek Company to give it the nucleus of engineering and design capabilities. During the same month, it purchased a company that fabricated pipe supports. The company also began to purchase huge pipe-bending machines from the Danish company Cojafex.

Part of Bernhard's strategy was to substitute machinery for skilled humans. The Cojafex machine was an integral part of that strategy. Even when much of a custom-piping system was produced in a factory, the pipes themselves had to be shaped by expert pipe cutters and welders. The machine eliminated this human labor. This state-of-the-art piece of equipment could bend a

pipe as much as 16 inches in diameter with walls as thick as 2.5 inches to the specifications of the customer. Although the Cojafex bending technology was not the sole similar machine on the market, it was the most advanced. The deployment of this machine gave Shaw a competitive advantage over other pipe fabricators.

Until 1994, Shaw supplied international customers by fabricating piping systems in its U.S. facilities and shipping them to the foreign site. U.S. fabricators could compete with foreign ones because labor costs were lower in the United States than in Germany and Japan, the home nations of some of their major competitors. U.S. manufacturers benefited from the greater availability of raw materials to them. The exchange rate of the dollar also contributed to the lower cost of U.S. produced systems.

INTERNATIONAL EXPANSION BEGINS: 1993

International demand for pipe products, especially for use in the construction of power plants, continued to outstrip domestic demand in the early 1990s. Shaw, therefore, expanded internationally. Late in 1993, the company entered into a joint venture agreement to build and operate a pipe fabrication facility in Bahrain. From there, it could supply all Arab states of the Gulf Cooperation Council without paying tariffs. A year later, it purchased the 50 percent of a Venezuelan subsidiary it did not already own. This facility allowed Shaw to benefit from lower labor costs in competition for international projects.

Shaw continued its strategy of expanding its capabilities through focused acquisitions in 1996. In January it acquired a fabrication facility and other assets in Oklahoma. The company followed this in March with the purchase of Alloy Piping Products located in Shreveport, Louisiana. Alloy was a leading manufacturer of specialty pipe fittings, products such as elbows and caps that connect pipes or in some way modify them so they can be integrated into a system. Shaw also added pipe insulation manufacturing to its capabilities by purchasing Pipe Shields, Inc., of California.

In 1997 and 1998, Shaw made two acquisitions that significantly increased the company's pipe-bending resources. First, it acquired NAPTech, Inc., of Utah, a piping systems and module designer and fabricator. NAPTech had experienced financial difficulties, including increasing net losses and liquidity problems. Nevertheless, it possessed three Cojafex bending machines, one capable of bending pipes with a diameter of up to 66 inches and a wall thickness of up to five inches. Shaw purchased Cojafex as a whole in 1998,

KEY DATES

1987: The Shaw Group is incorporated.

1994: Shaw acquires Fronek Company.

1997: Shaw acquires NAPTech, Inc., of Utah, a piping systems and module designer and fabricator.

1998: Company purchases Cojafex, BV of Holland, a leading company of pipe fabrication technologies.

2000: Shaw buys Stone & Webster (S&W), a provider of engineering, procurement, and construction services to the power plant industry.

2002: Shaw purchases The IT Group, a leading environmental remediation firm.

2006: Shaw acquires 20 percent of Westinghouse Electric Company.

thus taking control of the development and sales of a crucial pipe fabrication technology. Shaw considered these machines crucial enough to the pipe fabrication process that it stopped selling them to some competitors.

The company continued its international expansion. In October 1997 it bought a U.K. pipe fabrication company. The next month, it purchased Prospect Industries PLC, also located in the United Kingdom. Prospect was deeply in debt, so purchase negotiations were not difficult. With this purchase, came piping systems fabrication subsidiaries in Virginia and the United Kingdom. It also established a base in the Asia-Pacific region with Prospect's subsidiary, Aiton Australia Pty. Ltd., a piping system, boiler refurbishment, and project management enterprise. Shaw expanded its Venezuelan operations early in 1998 by purchasing a construction company. These acquisitions gave the company a total of four pipe fabrication facilities in regions outside the United States, a significant competitive advantage.

BECOMING A POWER PLANT BUILDER: 1997–2000

The purchase in 1997 of two industrial construction and maintenance companies signaled the expansion of Shaw's business strategy to planning and constructing entire power and process plants. In pursuit of this expanded strategy, it acquired a construction and maintenance company specializing in offshore facilities in 1998.

This string of acquisitions greatly increased Shaw's financial resources and returns. Its current assets increased from $80.6 million in 1995 to $251 million in 1998. Sales increased from $113.2 million in 1994 to $506.1 million in 1998, while net income increased from $3.4 million to $19.2 million during the same period. In recognition of this growth, Shaw moved from the NASDAQ to the New York Stock Exchange in 1996.

By the end of its 1999 fiscal year, Shaw had become a major supplier of pipe systems both domestically and internationally. It had provided services to some of the world's foremost multinational conglomerates, including AlliedSignal, Chevron, Mitsubishi, Monsanto, Raytheon, Hitachi, and Toshiba. It had formed strategic alliances with ABB, Air Products and Chemicals, Alstrom, BASF, Bechtel, Dow, General Electric, Orion Refining Company, Parsons Corporation, and Praxair, Inc.

Moreover, the demand for power plants, always strong internationally, had increased in the United States. The decommissioning of some nuclear plants had decreased domestic electrical supply. Demand for electricity was increasing, and wholesale power markets had been deregulated. These events generated a surge in the construction of domestic power plants. Shaw benefited from this trend. Power generation projects amounted to only 30 percent of the company's backlog in 1997 and 1998. Such projects, some of them foreign, accounted for 64 percent of an $818.3 million backlog at the end of its 1999 fiscal year.

STONE & WEBSTER ACQUISITION BOLSTERS CAPABILITIES: 2000

Despite its success in pipe design, engineering, fabrication, and installation, Shaw had difficulties making the transition to providing engineering, procurement, and construction (EPC) services for entire power plants. In part, these difficulties resulted from Shaw's inexperience in power plant construction, especially when it competed with large, established EPC contractors. Chairman Bernhard told *ENR* in 2002 that there was an additional problem: Power plant engineers were reluctant to subcontract with Shaw to do engineering work on projects for which Shaw was the prime contractor, and Shaw lacked appropriate engineering capabilities of its own.

Shaw resolved this problem in 2000 by acquiring Stone & Webster (S&W), a century-old provider of EPC services to the power plant industry. S&W had experienced financial difficulties for much of the previous decade. In the mid-1990s, it completed a major downsizing resulting from a dependence on the nuclear power industry after construction of nuclear plants had virtually stopped and from losses generated by noncore assets, such as real estate.

By 1998 the company again experienced financial difficulties resulting in part from losses of Asian construction contracts when that region experienced a severe financial crisis. The company was experiencing such severe liquidity problems that it agreed in May 2000 to sell most of its assets to Jacobs Engineering Group. The agreement with Jacobs called for Jacobs to provide S&W with a $50 million credit line to allow S&W to resolve its immediate liquidity problems. It also called for S&W to enter into Chapter 11 bankruptcy proceedings, a move that would protect S&W from potential lawsuits or adverse actions by its creditors.

The bankruptcy process, however, required that S&W's assets be disposed of by means of an auction administered by the bankruptcy court. This opened the way for Shaw to attempt to win S&W's assets. In July, Shaw won these assets after 20 rounds of bids lasting 18 hours. Shaw's final cash and stock bid was equal to about $163 million.

Not only did S&W bring EPC capabilities to Shaw, but the acquisition placed Shaw among the foremost companies with experience in the decommissioning and decontamination (D&D) of nuclear plants. S&W had built 17 of the reactors constructed in the United States in the 1970s and 1980s. It had done various kinds of work on 99 of the 104 nuclear facilities in the nation. Immediately before its bankruptcy, it was doing D&D work. This particular project was terminated because of the company's financial difficulties, but this was another new area opened to Shaw.

Shaw also took over a number of public infrastructure and environmental remediation projects started by S&W. In the environmental area, projects included remediation for former nuclear weapons production facilities and work on various Superfund sites. In the infrastructure area, Shaw took over projects such as the construction and management of a water supply tunnel and the engineering and construction of a water treatment plant.

REVENUE TRIPLES AT THE MILLENNIUM

Financially, too, the S&W acquisition had a major effect on Shaw. Its current assets increased from $252.1 million in 1999 to $1.1 billion in 2001, the first full year it owned S&W. During the same period, its sales increased from $494 million to $1.5 billion, and its net income

increased from $18.1 million to $61 million. Its total backlog increased from $818.3 million to $4.5 billion. Shaw debuted as number 835 on the *Fortune* 1000 in 2002.

Shaw quickly put its new capabilities and financial strength to work. In September 2000, after three years of discussions, Shaw formed a 50-50 joint venture, EntergyShaw, with the electric utility Entergy, to design and construct standardized power plants that could meet Entergy's increasing power needs. The partners also hoped the projected 10 to 15 percent cost savings of the plants would make them attractive to other North American and European customers.

In February 2001, the company contracted with BASF to engineer and manage the construction of an ethylene plant in China. Shaw agreed, in turn, to contract the construction of the plant to an independent Chinese company. This project allowed Shaw to profitably use some process industry equipment left with S&W when a contract was canceled.

The next month, Shaw announced an agreement with PG&E's National Energy Group for the construction of four separately sited gas-fired power plants, capable of producing a total of 4,400 megawatts of electricity on completion. Work on two of them started in 2001. Shaw initiated or extended similar agreements with other power generators, including NRG Energy and FPL Energy.

BUSINESS SLOWS: 2002

The continuation of the boom in power plant construction that had fueled much of Shaw's growth during the late 1990s began to show signs of weakening by 2002. The California energy crisis and consequent bankruptcy of two of the largest utilities in the nation, threats of volatile power prices and even blackouts in other states, and the collapse of the energy trading industry all raised questions about the longevity of the energy deregulation trend. This policy had stimulated the construction boom domestically.

Internationally, too, power plant construction had declined. The Asian financial crisis of the late 1990s had terminated many projects, and construction in that area had not yet recovered. The generalized economic uncertainty of the early 21st century contributed to construction declines in other regions as well.

Shaw had enough backlog at the beginning of 2002 to keep it busy for about 18 months, but it faced the twin dangers that some of the projects it had on its books would be canceled and that future projects would be harder to find. This prospect came as no surprise to the company. After all, Shaw came into being in the mid-1980s, at a time when construction of domestic power plants was not robust. In fact, such construction had always been notoriously cyclical.

ACQUISITION OF THE IT GROUP: 2002

In an effort to diversify Shaw's business focus beyond the power plant sector and to provide it with a diversified mix of income opportunities, the company agreed in January 2002 to bring The IT Group out of bankruptcy. The IT Group was a leading domestic and international firm specializing in environmental remediation, serving the government, commercial engineering and construction, solid waste, real estate restoration, and consulting sectors. The IT Group was especially strong in the government market.

When combined with the environmental business Shaw had acquired with its previous year's purchase of S&W, this new acquisition, approved by the Bankruptcy Court in April, gave Shaw a strong position in the environmental remediation industry. Shaw gained two major advantages from this. First, the business cycles of the environmental industry did not correlate with the cycles of the power production industry, thus Shaw's revenue stream became somewhat protected from the cyclical nature of that industry. Second, many of the contracts that came with The IT Group purchase were governmental. Usually contracted on a cost-plus-fixed-fee basis, an arrangement that was not as profitable to the contractor as were other alternatives, these government contracts, nevertheless, provided the contractor with a steady, reliable source of income.

Vibrant revenue growth elevated Shaw's stature in the years following the acquisition of The IT Group. The company's annual volume swelled nearly fivefold between 2002 and 2009, driven upward by a wealth of new business and further acquisitions. Shaw's comprehensive capabilities served it well when the Federal Emergency Management Agency (FEMA) looked for assistance in dealing with the aftermath of hurricanes Katrina and Rita in 2005. FEMA awarded Shaw a contract to provide housing assistance for displaced residents, which represented a financial boon to the company. In one quarter, Shaw generated $1.25 billion in revenue, nearly equal to the total for all of 2002, and posted a profit of $747 million.

WESTINGHOUSE ELECTRIC ACQUISITION: 2006

Shaw's greatest gains during the decade were made after completing a massive acquisition. The company

reorganized in the fall of 2006, grouping its business into four segments: energy and chemical, environmental and infrastructure, power, and pipe fabrication and manufacturing. One month after changing its corporate structure, the company announced its intention to acquire Westinghouse Electric Company, a producer of atomic power plant equipment, in a joint venture agreement with Toshiba Corporation. Shaw paid $1.08 billion for a 20 percent stake in Westinghouse, completing the deal through an acquisition subsidiary named Nuclear Energy Holdings, L.L.C. The acquisition was completed in October 2006, giving Shaw access to Westinghouse technology, which formed the basis for 63 of 104 licensed reactors in the United States and approximately half of the reactors operating in the world.

The partnership with Toshiba quickly bore fruit. Before the end of 2006, Shaw announced its involvement in a $5 billion contract to build four nuclear power plants in China. Construction was scheduled to begin in 2009, with the first plant slated to become operational in 2013. The contract was signed in March 2007, one month before Shaw announced it had secured a $700 million deal to service nuclear power plants in three U.S. states and another contract to build a power plant in Virginia. Massive contracts followed, lifting Shaw's annual revenue total above $7 billion by the end of the decade. In July 2007 the company was awarded a $1.29 billion engineering, procurement, and construction contract for an 800 megawatt plant for Duke Energy Carolinas LLC. In 2009 Shaw was awarded a contract for an undisclosed value to build two nuclear power plants in Florida, plants that were to be built with Westinghouse technology.

Anne L. Potter
Updated, Jeffrey L. Covell

PRINCIPAL SUBSIDIARIES

ACL Piping, Inc.; Aiton & Co. Limited; American Eagle Communities Midwest, LLC; Arlington Avenue E Venture, LLC; Atlantic Contingency Constructors, LLC; Associated Valve, Inc.; Badger Technologies, L.L.C.; Benicia North Gateway II, L.L.C.; B.F. Shaw, Inc.; Camden Road Venture, LLC; C.B.P. Engineering Corp.; Chimento Wetlands, L.L.C.; Coastal Estuary Services, L.L.C.; Cojafex B.V.; Eagle Industries, Inc.; EDS Equipment Company, LLC; EMCON/OWT, Inc.; Envirogen, Inc.

PRINCIPAL COMPETITORS

Bechtel Group Inc.; Chicago Bridge & Iron Company; Fluor Corporation; URS Corporation.

FURTHER READING

Angelo, William J., "Stone & Webster Is Short on Cash," *ENR*, November 8, 1999, p. 13.

———, "Stone & Webster Lures New Retirees in Cost-Cut Measure to Stem Red Ink," *ENR*, November 23, 1998, p. 19.

Basta, Nicholas, "Engineering and Construction Market Begins to Thaw," *Chemical Week*, April 24, 2002, pp. S3–S6.

"Baton Rouge-Based Shaw Group, Westinghouse Awarded Florida Nuclear Contract," *New Orleans CityBusiness*, January 5, 2009.

Guarisco, Tom, "New Digs for Shaw," *Greater Baton Rouge Business Report*, January 15, 2002, pp. 31–32.

Sayre, Alan, "Shaw Group Paying $1.08 Billion for Stake in Group Buying Westinghouse Electric," *America's Intelligence Wire*, October 4, 2006.

"Shaw Group Inc: IT Group Inc.," *Market News Publishing*, April 24, 2002.

"Shaw Just Keeps on Building," *Greater Baton Rouge Business Report*, October 9, 2001, p. 10.

Smith, Rebecca, "Entergy Forms Venture with Shaw for New Plants," *Wall Street Journal*, June 2, 2000, p. A4.

Shine Ltd.

———— ■ ————

Primrose Studios
109 Regent's Park Road
London, NW1 8UR
United Kingdom
Telephone: (+44 20) 7985 7000
Fax: (+44 20) 7985 7001
Web site: http://www.shinegroup.tv

Private Company
Incorporated: 2001
Employees: 361
Sales: £265 million (2009 est.)
NAICS: 512110 Motion Picture and Video Production;
    512120 Motion Picture and Video Distribution;
    533110 Lessors of Nonfinancial Intangible Assets
    (Except Copyrighted Works)

■ ■ ■

Shine Ltd. owns the Shine Group of companies, which include the largest independent television production firm in the United Kingdom. With a significant presence in Europe, the United States, and Australia, Shine holds the rights to popular reality TV formats *Master-Chef* and *The Biggest Loser*, and also produces dramas (*Spooks* and *Ashes to Ashes*), comedies (*Ugly Betty* and the U.S. version of *The Office*), and franchised regional versions of such shows as *Idol*, *The Farmer Wants a Wife*, *Big Brother*, and *Jeopardy*. Subsidiary Shine International distributes the company's own programs and those of outside producers including Merv Griffin Entertainment and Magical Elves Productions to more than 150 countries around the world, while the Shinevu unit develops digital content. Founder and CEO Elisabeth Murdoch, a daughter of News Corp. owner Rupert Murdoch, owns controlling interest in the firm.

EARLY YEARS

Shine Television was founded in England in March 2001 by Elisabeth Murdoch, the second-eldest daughter of Australian media mogul Rupert Murdoch. The 32-year-old Vassar graduate had a decade of experience in the industry, most recently as managing director of BSkyB's Sky Networks unit. Shine's ownership would be split between CEO/Chairman Murdoch, with an 80 percent stake; British Lord Waheed Alli (cofounder of *Survivor* creator Planet 24), with 15 percent; and broadcast company BSkyB, which would take 5 percent. The largest shareholder of the latter was Rupert Murdoch. The company's mission would be to create television programming of all types for U.K. or international clients, as well as small- to medium-budget feature films.

Shine's first two contracts included a two-year, £10 million deal to produce film and TV projects for BSkyB, and another to create a daytime program format for IPC Media, publisher of such glossy women's magazines as *Family Circle*. The firm soon began hiring an impressive array of talent that included former BBC head of documentaries Paul Hamann as creative director for factual programs, award-winning *Royle Family* producer Kenton Allen as creative director for entertainment, and former BBC lifestyle/features deputy editor Sally Anne Howard as executive producer. Shine productions would be represented in the United States by the William Morris Agency.

In May Shine sold a 20 percent ownership stake to European venture capital firm 3i for £6 million, which would be used to build the firm's rights management operation. The company now had a staff of 15, and was looking to grow to 30. In October a joint venture was formed with MindShare, a unit of advertising/communications giant WPP Group, called Shine: M. It was charged with developing programming that was not overtly commercial but directly supported the vision of a sponsor, who would provide funding for production and distribution.

Shine entered the U.S. market in early 2003 with the sale of hypnosis-dating reality show *Spellbound* to Fox and drama *Sinchronicity* to HBO, which also bought a 90-minute documentary about female circumcision. During the year the firm formed a joint venture with STW Communications of Australia called Missing Link and signed a distribution deal with Television Corp. for territories outside the United Kingdom and United States, while Shine: M signed a "first look" deal for syndication with Twentieth-Century Fox.

Despite its initial promise, Shine was still finding it difficult to produce a hit, and many of its creative staff were departing. The output deal with BSkyB had ended with completion of only the short-lived *Sex and the City*-inspired series *Single Girls* and a few shopping programs, although the firm was now producing four shows for Channel 4, three for Channel 5, and one for the BBC. In May Shine hired a new creative director for entertainment, Steven D. Wright, who had commissioned game shows and programs about celebrities for Channel 4, but at year's end the company was late in filing its annual report and received a fine.

HEX PRODUCTION WITH SONY IN 2004

At year's end things began looking up when well-regarded Talkback factual entertainment head John Silver joined Shine in the same role, while a commission

was won to produce a six-part teen horror series called *Hex* with Sony Pictures Television International. Dubbed "the British *Buffy*," it debuted on the Sky One network in October 2004 and was popular enough to warrant a second 13-episode season. For 2004 Shine's revenues increased to £18 million from £10 million, and the company broke even for the first time.

In February 2005 Murdoch was reportedly in talks with *American Idol/Britain's Got Talent* judge Simon Cowell to create a "high-concept game show." A fan of the original *Pop Idol* program starring Cowell, Murdoch had called her father urging him to buy it for the U.S. Fox network, which put Cowell's career into overdrive and generated immense profits for Fox.

In June Sony Pictures Television International bought a 15 percent stake in Shine for £5 million. Sony would receive a three-year first look deal for all markets outside the United States, and would continue to co-produce series with the company. During the month Shine also won a commission to produce *Project Catwalk*, a version of the popular reality-based American fashion series *Project Runway* that would star British model Elizabeth Hurley.

In 2005 Shine scored a U.K. hit with *MasterChef Goes Large* for BBC2, a revised version of a cooking competition series that had originally aired from 1990 to 2001. Featuring amateur chefs who competed in various trials prior to creating a full meal, it ran in the early evening four nights per week for eight weeks. The popular show later produced spin-offs *Celebrity MasterChef*, *MasterChef: The Professionals*, and *Junior MasterChef*.

In April 2006 *Hex* was canceled after its second season due to declining ratings, although BBC America would air it in the United States starting in June. Late in the year a new Shine-produced live interactive program called *My Games Fever* began airing on 10 of Fox's new MyNetworkTV channels in the United States. The two-hour program, which ran commercial-free on weekday afternoons, allowed viewers to participate online or via text-messaging for small prizes. It was dropped the following April, however.

PURCHASE OF KUDOS, PRINCESS, AND FIREFLY: DECEMBER 2006

In December 2006 Shine expanded dramatically through the acquisition of three U.K.-based independent production firms. The largest was Kudos Film and Television, the makers of hit dramas *Spooks* and *Life on Mars*, for which Shine paid £35 million. Princess Productions, a producer of entertainment shows including *The Friday Night Project*, was purchased for

KEY DATES

2001: Elisabeth Murdoch founds Shine Entertainment to produce television programs.
2006: Shine buys Kudos, Princess, and Firefly (later Dragonfly) production firms.
2008: Top U.S. independent TV producer Reveille purchased for $150 million.
2009: Company buys Metronome of Sweden; company launches Shine Germany, France, and Australia.

£20 million, while Shine paid £10 million for Firefly Film and Television, the producer of reality-based *Anatomy for Beginners* and *Going Cold Turkey*. The principals of each firm would receive cash along with an equity stake in Shine, although Murdoch would continue to retain controlling interest. Shine also hired talkbackThames COO Alex Mahon to take the position of managing director beginning in January 2007.

Kudos soon began expanding its feature film production, starting with *Mrs. Pettigrew Lives for a Day* (starring Frances McDormand), with hopes to develop some of its TV projects into features. Revenues for 2007 nearly quadrupled on the earnings of the firm's new acquisitions to £92 million, with the company turning a profit of £729,000 after recording a nearly £2 million loss in 2006.

In February 2008 Shine closed a deal worth about $150 million to purchase Los Angeles-based production firm Reveille, which was ranked the largest independent in the United States. Reveille was owned by NBC Entertainment co-chairman Ben Silverman (who had once been Elisabeth Murdoch's agent), and had produced U.S. reality hits *The Biggest Loser* and *American Gladiator*, as well as popular comedies *The Office* and *Ugly Betty*. Its first look agreement with NBC would continue, while Shine would rebrand its distribution subsidiary as ShineReveille International.

In July 2008 Shine announced formation of a new feature film unit, Shine Pictures, in partnership with U.S.-based producer/distributor New Regency. It would be run by the management of Kudos. In February 2009 another joint venture was launched with ITV Studios to develop pilots for ITV and international broadcast clients. Recent Shine successes included the fantasy drama *Merlin*, game show *Moment of Truth*, and the U.K. version of *American Gladiator*. The firm was now ranked the second-largest independent TV production

company in the United Kingdom, with revenues jumping to £238 million for the most recent fiscal year and profits topping £14 million.

Early 2009 also saw Elisabeth Murdoch turn down an offer to join the board of her father's News Corp., although she would attend meetings as an observer. British TV regulations required that broadcasters spend 25 percent of their production budgets with independent firms, which would no longer be possible if she worked for News Corp. because of its stakes in BSkyB and other Sky and Fox broadcast outlets. The entrepreneurial Elisabeth Murdoch had long been less enthusiastic about joining the family business than some of her siblings, and clashed in other ways with her conservative father (owner of the Fox News network), including being an enthusiastic supporter of Barack Obama.

EXPANSION TO EUROPE, AUSTRALIA IN 2009

In the spring of 2009 Shine began efforts to gain a foothold in Europe, setting up Shine Germany to pursue development and/or acquisition opportunities there via offices in Munich and Cologne run by former RTL2 senior vice president Axel Kuehn. An offshoot was also being planned for Australia, where Shine scored a major coup by hiring away the chief executive and chief operating officer of top production house FremantleMedia Australia, brothers Carl and Mark Fennessy. They would serve as joint CEOs of Shine Australia, whose working territory would also include New Zealand.

In April Shine paid $88 million for Sweden's Metronome Film & Television AB, which owned 15 production companies in Sweden, Denmark, Norway, Finland, and the United States, and produced regional versions of hits *Idol*, *Big Brother*, and *Deal or No Deal* as well as originals including *Clash of the Choirs*. The purchase was financed by JPMorgan and private investors. In June a French unit was also established, headed by former Endemol France Chief Creative Officer Thierry Lachkar, and in August ShineReveille International shortened its name to Shine International as it absorbed the international sales units of Metronome.

New reality-based programs in production included PBS concert series *Live from the Artist's Den*; *I Can't Believe I'm Still Single*, a celebrity matchmaking show for Showtime; *Blood Sweat + Gears*, about bicyclists trying to enter the Tour de France for Sundance; dog training program *Underdog to Wonderdog* for Animal Planet; and *The Naked Office*, a reality series about office workers who engage in nude group therapy.

In September Shine set up a new subsidiary called Shinevu that was headed by Joanna Shields, ex-CEO of Bebo, to develop Internet-based content. The company's recent expansion had made it a more direct competitor of stakeholder Sony, and the larger firm had begun considering selling its 20 percent stake. BSkyB now owned 13 percent, while members of management had smaller shares and Elisabeth Murdoch held more than 60 percent.

In February 2010 Shine International formed a joint venture with former Reveille owner Ben Silverman called Electus Distribution, which would handle worldwide sales for Silverman's new Electus company and possibly co-fund projects. According to trade publication *Broadcast*, Shine was now the largest independent TV production firm in the United Kingdom. Nearly two-thirds of its revenues were derived from international sales.

MASTERCHEF'S AUSTRALIAN SUCCESS SPURS GLOBAL LAUNCH IN 2010

In 2009 Shine had debuted a reworked version of its popular British format *MasterChef* in prime-time on Australia's Network Ten in partnership with Fremantle-Media Australia, with the finale attracting the largest recorded TV audience there for a non-sports program. It quickly spawned several spin-offs and a best-selling cookbook, as well as a New Zealand edition. The second season was even bigger, with the finale topping the previous show's record and causing the rescheduling of a televised debate between the prime minister and opposition leader. The show was aired nine hours per week for 12 weeks, providing a huge advertising windfall.

In 2010 *MasterChef* was rolled out in a number of different markets including Norway, France, Greece, Belgium, Sweden, and the United States, with Finnish and Indian editions set for 2011. Taking the Australian version as its template, whose changes included filming the participants living together, the U.S. version began airing in late July on Fox to solid ratings, with British celebrity chef Gordon Ramsay heading the judges' panel. Shine was also reportedly planning to revise the U.K. version to match the more successful Australian pattern. Launched at the same time on NBC was *Breakthrough with Tony Robbins*, which featured the self-help guru coaching people to improve their lives.

In the summer Shine also acquired British TV comedy producer Brown Eyed Boy (*Little Miss Jocelyn*, *3 Non Blondes*) from Motive Television for approximately £400,000, and hired the president of Fox Television Studios, Emiliano Calemzuk, for the newly created posi-

tion of CEO of Shine Group Americas. He would oversee the firm's North American operations, which were expected to expand.

Less than a decade after its founding as a small TV production studio in England, Shine Ltd. had developed a sizable international footprint. Through its subsidiaries the firm had expertise with a wide range of formats that included drama, comedy, and reality-based programming, and with the global rollout of the successful *MasterChef* format just beginning, Shine looked set for continued growth.

Frank Uhle

PRINCIPAL SUBSIDIARIES

Brown Eyed Boy; Dragonfly Film and Television; Kudos Film and Television; Metronome Film & Television AB (Sweden); Princess Productions; Reveille Productions (USA); Shine Australia; Shine France; Shine Germany; Shine International; Shine Pictures; Shinevu.

PRINCIPAL COMPETITORS

All3Media; BBC Worldwide Productions; Endemol B.V.; Eyeworks Holding B.V.; FremantleMedia Ltd.; Shed Media Plc; Zodiak Entertainment.

FURTHER READING

"The Broadcast Interview: Liz Murdoch—A Leading Light in Television," *Broadcast*, March 19, 2010, p. 8.

Bulbeck, Pip, "'MasterChef Australia' Breaks Ratings Record," *Hollywood Reporter*, July 27, 2010.

Clarke, Steve, "Shine Aims for International Expansion," *Daily Variety*, March 27, 2009.

Fenton, Ben, "Liz Murdoch Takes a Shine to Independence," *Financial Times*, July 25, 2010.

Goldsmith, Charles, "Elisabeth Murdoch's Production Venture, Shine, Will Create Content for BSkyB," *Wall Street Journal*, March 23, 2001, p. B7.

Lockley, Nicholas, "Murdoch Wins £6m from 3i for Shine TV Venture," *Financial News*, May 14, 2001.

Martinson, Jane, "Sun Princess a Shining Star in Murdoch's Orbit," *Sydney Morning Herald*, March 23, 2010, p. 8.

Pasternak, Petra, "Old Pals Do 9-Figure Deal," *Recorder*, March 6, 2008, p. 4.

Robinson, James, "Media's First Daughter, an Independent Player," *Observer*, February 8, 2004, p. 7.

Ryan, Leslie, "U.S. Nets Take Shine to Murdoch Projects," *Electronic Media*, January 20, 2003, p. 6.

Teather, David, "Shine On—Elisabeth Murdoch Bounces Back," *Guardian*, March 24, 2001, p. 24.

Shine Ltd.

Thompson, Susan, "Shine in £65m Deal for Trio of Top Indies," *Broadcast*, December 15, 2006, p. 1.

Turner, Mimi, "Elisabeth Murdoch's Shine Goes Nordic," *Hollywood Reporter*, April 28, 2009.

———, "SPTI Takes 15% Stake in Shine," *Hollywood Reporter*, June 17, 2005.

SMA Solar Technology AG

Sonnenalle 1
Niestetal, 34266
Germany
Telephone: (+495 61) 9522 0
Fax: (+49 561) 9522 100
Web site: http://www.sma.de

Public Company
Founded: 1981 as SMA Regelsysteme GmbH
Employees: 4,231
Sales: EUR 934.3 million (2009)
Stock Exchanges: Frankfurt
Ticker Symbol: S92
NAICS: 334419 Other Electronic Component Manu-
    facturing

■ ■ ■

SMA Solar Technology AG is the global leader in the
design and manufacture of photovoltaic energy inverters
and related products for the solar energy industry. With
40 percent of the global market, SMA Solar Technology
is the only company to offer inverters that meet the
diverse needs of residential, commercial, and utility-scale
solar systems. SMA manufacturing plants include a five-
gigawatt facility in Kassel, Germany, and a one-gigawatt
manufacturing plant in Denver, Colorado. Thirteen
subsidiaries operate sales and service offices worldwide.

FOUNDERS' INTEREST IN
ELECTRICAL ENERGY SUPPLY

Founded in 1981 by four electrical engineers, SMA
Solar Technology AG began as SMA Regelsysteme

GmbH (Steuerungs- Mess- und Anlagentechnik,
translated as "control, measuring, and equipment
technology"). The founders shared a common interest in
developing energy supply technology, specifically in
micro-power applications. To the enterprise Gunther
Cramer brought innovative ideas on power electronics,
especially in the area of decentralized energy supply.
Peter Drews developed the hardware and software that
served as the operational foundation for supply systems.
Cofounder Reiner Wettlaufer, also an electrical engineer,
served as financial guide to SMA's engineering activities.

After a distinguished career in aerospace, cofounder
Dr. Werner Kleinkauf became professor for Electrical
Energy Supply Systems at University of Kassel. In addi-
tion to cofounding SMA, he founded the Institute for
Solar Energy Supply Technology (ISET) e.V. in 1988.
SMA originated from research being conducted at the
University of Kassel and the company frequently col-
laborated with ISET and other educational institutions
in developing state-of-the-art energy inversion
technology.

Roland Grebe, who joined the company in 1984,
contributed to the early success of SMA. Grebe
developed energy supply systems for railway coaches. In
1987 SMA formed the Railway Technology division,
which provided electricity supply systems to railway
companies throughout Europe.

Over time this background in railway power
technology contributed to SMA's involvement in photovoltaic inverter development. The energy supply on
moving trains required equipment that endured varying
extremes of outdoor temperatures, and temperature

variations affected the potential for power loss during inversion.

By the late 1980s SMA developed its first photovoltaic energy inverters. SMA gained needed capital when German glass products manufacturer FLABEG GmbH purchased a 50 percent interest in the company in 1987. The following year SMA introduced the PV-WR 1500, the first photovoltaic electricity inverter based on transistor technology. The use of transistors quickened the speed of the transition from direct current power to alternating current electricity, thus providing a steadier energy supply. Mass production of the PV-WR 1500 began in 1991.

As its solar inverter business became established, SMA formed the Photovoltaic division and developed the Sunny brand in 1994. The company's primary solar photovoltaic inverter was named Sunny Boy, and SMA housed the inverter in vibrant red casing.

TECHNOLOGICAL INNOVATIONS AND NEW PRODUCTS

Through product innovation, SMA gained industry recognition and leadership. In 1995 SMA launched the Sunny Boy 700, which used SMA's innovative string technology, which allowed a line of solar modules to be connected to one inverter. String technology significantly reduced the cost and eased the process of installation, as the Sunny Boy 700 required fewer cables. Designed for use in small and midsized solar systems, the Sunny Boy 700 garnered 94.4 percent energy yield efficiency. The product brought SMA recognition from the solar industry and won the Stiftung Warentest comparisons conducted by the German consumer organization of the same name.

Other innovative new products included the Sunny Boy 1500, the first transformerless inverter, launched in 1998. Without the technological requirement of the traditional transformer, this product featured a lighter weight and 96 percent efficiency. In 2002 SMA introduced the industry's first multi-string inverter, the Sunny Boy 5000TL. Multi-string technology redefined solar energy as a viable alternative, as it further eased system design and installation and lowered overall cost. Also, with three, independent maximum power point (MPP) trackers, the product increased energy yield to 96.2 percent.

SMA developed inversion technology for a wider variety of alternative energy situations. The Windy Boy inverter applied photovoltaic inversion to windmill generated power inversion requirements. Other new products included the Sunny Island inverter, a stand-alone product for off-grid solar power generation. The Sunny Central, introduced in 2003, accommodated large solar installations, such as ground-mounted utility plants.

Its solar inverter business solidly established, with sales exceeding EUR 100 million in 2004, SMA began to offer supplemental equipment. The Sunny Beam provided photovoltaic plant monitoring through radio-controlled communication. Sunny Backup, introduced in 2005, provided battery charging when the solar or utility power supply dwindled. The equipment instantly transferred the electrical system to battery power. The new Sunny Mini Central 8000TL, introduced in 2006, tested for 98 percent efficiency in energy conversion, a world record.

2000–07 INTERNATIONAL EXPANSION

International expansion began in 2000, with the formation of SMA America. The company opened a sales and service office in Rocklin, near Sacramento, California, to serve the growing California solar market. By 2004 that growth required SMA to open two new manufacturing plants in Germany. One plant produced the Sunny Central and the other the Sunny Island, both for export to the United States. SMA China initiated product distribution in Asia in 2003.

European market development accelerated with the formation of SMA Iberica (Spain) and SMA Italia in 2005, and SMA France and SMA Hellas (Greece) in 2007. Growth in Spain occurred at a particularly rapid pace, and the company opened service centers in Alicante, Barcelona, Huelva, Madrid, Talavera, and Granada. A warehouse near Barcelona was expanded in 2008. By that time the inverter installed capacity in

```
┌─────────────────────────────────────────┐
│                                           │
│            KEY DATES                      │
│                 ■                         │
│  ─────────────────────────────────       │
│                                           │
│  1988:  SMA introduces first photovoltaic power │
│         inverter to utilize transistor technology. │
│  1995:  Launch of Sunny brand coincides with │
│         introduction of string technology. │
│  2000:  Company begins international expansion. │
│  2009:  Growth of solar industry requires quadruple │
│         production increase, to 80,000 inverters per │
│         month.                            │
│                                           │
└─────────────────────────────────────────┘
```

Spain exceeded 450 megawatts. Along the Pacific Rim the company established SMA Korea in 2006 and SMA Australia in 2007.

2008–09: PREPARATIONS FOR FURTHER GROWTH

Rapid growth at SMA prompted the company to raise capital through an initial public offering (IPO) of stock. The company prepared for the IPO by repurchasing FLABEG's share of SMA stock. SMA spun off its Railway division into an independent subsidiary, and changed the company name to SMA Solar Technology, to reflect its primary business. SMA Solar offered 11.5 million shares of stock, including 4.5 million new shares, on the Frankfurt Stock Exchange in June 2008. The company raised EUR 150 million ($232.1 million) to be applied to meet the capital demands of rapid growth.

Upon completion of the stock offering, SMA Solar reorganized and expanded its management structure to better address the needs of the company's growing size. The supervisory board included Reiner Wettlaufer as deputy chairman of the supervisory board. On the managing board, Gunther Cramer took the position of chief executive officer, and Pete Drews, chief operating officer. A new executive position placed Roland Grebe as chief technology officer. In 2009 Pierre-Pacal Urbon succeeded Wettlaufer as chief financial officer, and Marko Werner became chief sales officer. A second level of management was expanded to 18 divisional positions in Germany. Thirteen managing directors covered international divisions.

2008–09: CHALLENGES OF HIGH DEMAND

During 2008 rapid growth in the U.S. solar market required SMA to expand production once again. In

March the company began construction of an 82,000-square-foot factory in Kassel, Germany. The plant would manufacture solar inverters designed for the U.S. solar market, including the latest series of Sunny Boy products. As demand for SMA inverters accelerated during 2009, the company expanded the project to 193,000 square feet. When the facility opened in April, it enabled SMA to increase production threefold.

By the time the Kassel factory, the largest inverter plant in the world, came online, growth at SMA required additional production space. The company's employees developed transitional measures to increase capacity to five-gigawatt capacity. To accommodate permanent production up to 10 gigawatts of inverter capacity, SMA acquired a 50-acre lot in the commercial area of Sanderhaeuser Berg, in Niestetal. The company planned to build a central warehouse and service center, as well as manufacturing plant at the site.

2009–10: SOLAR PRODUCT INNOVATIONS

SMA gained a new product line and a new base of technological information through the September 2009 acquisition of OKE-Services, a Dutch developer of microinverters that connected directly to each solar module. Because these small devices converted direct current to alternating current at the point of power generation, an entire solar energy system was not hindered by a single solar module with lower power output.

In early 2010 SMA introduced its landmark Opti-Trac Global Peak technology. The OptiTrac provided MPP efficiency during periods of shade or partial shade. By deriving maximum energy from the solar modules when shaded, the technology inverted a constant stream of power whereas conventional inverters produced a sudden jump. SMA offered OptiTrac Global Peak as a standard component of the Sunny Boy 3000TL, 4000 TL, and 5000TL inverters, with software upgrade available for older equipment.

NORTH AMERICAN EXPANSION IN 2010

Although electronic parts supply issues continued to stall production, a backlog of orders prompted SMA to continue its plans to increase manufacturing capacity. Growth in the North American market led the company to open a new plant in Denver, Colorado, in late spring 2010. By locating the plant in the United States, SMA expected to save on the cost of shipping and storage. The company's Denver location provided easy access to railway transportation, and SMA was drawn to the state for its qualified workforce. Chosen from among 10 cities, Denver supported SMA's $22 million investment with a $1 million fund for job creation and training during the company's first five years in operation. SMA benefited from state tax incentives as well.

SMA expected the plant to open in August 2010. The 180,000-square-foot facility initially employed 300 workers producing Sunny Boy, Sunny Central, and Sunny Island inverters. By the end of 2010 SMA expected the plant to operate at maximum capacity, at one gigawatt annually. The plant could readily accommodate additional growth in demand for the U.S. solar market and would potentially require 700 employees.

In anticipation of continued growth in the United States, SMA America relocated its marketing, sales, and training operations to a new office in Rocklin. SMA anticipated a twofold increase in staffing there. Existing space was converted to distribution and service operations.

In March 2010 SMA Solar established its Canadian subsidiary to serve the growing Ontario solar market. The subsidiary established a sales and service office and, in late 2010, planned to open a manufacturing facility capable of producing 500-megawatt inverters.

Mary Tradii

PRINCIPAL SUBSIDIARIES

SMA America Holdings LLC; SMA America Production LLC; SMA Benelux SPRL (Belgium); SMA Beijing Commercial Company Ltd. (China); SMA Czech Republic s.r.o.; SMA France S.A.S.; SMA Iberica Tecnologia Solar, S.L. (Spain); SMA Italia S.r.l. (Italy); SMA Middle East Ltd. (United Arab Emirates); SMA Railway Technology GmbH (Germany); SMA Solar Technology America LLC (USA).

PRINCIPAL OPERATING UNITS

Photovoltaics Technology; Railway Technology; Electronics Manufacturing.

PRINCIPAL COMPETITORS

Advanced Energy Industries, Inc.; Fronius International; Kaco New Energy GmbH; Power-One, Inc.; Sputnik Engineering AG.

FURTHER READING

"SMA Solar Cannot Raise Production as Planned—Report," *ADP News Germany*, June 14, 2010.

"SMA Solar Upbeat about Business in 2010—Report," *ADP Renewable Energy Track*, December 17, 2009.

"Solar Technology Leader Breaks Ground on Largest Inverter Factory on Earth," *Space Daily*, May 7, 2008.

Smith International, Inc.

1310 Rankin Road
Houston, Texas 77073-4802
U.S.A.
Telephone: (281) 443-3370
Toll Free: (800) 877-6484
Fax: (281) 233-5199
Web site: http://www.smith.com

Wholly Owned Subsidiary of Schlumberger Limited
Incorporated: 1937 as H.C. Smith Oil Tool Company
Employees: 21,931
Sales: $8.22 billion (2009)
NAICS: 213111 Drilling Oil and Gas Wells; 213112 Support Activities for Oil and Gas Operations; 333132 Oil and Gas Field Machinery and Equipment Manufacturing; 325998 All Other Miscellaneous Chemical Product and Preparation Manufacturing

∎ ∎ ∎

Smith International, Inc., is a leading global supplier of products and services for oil and gas producers, specifically during the drilling, completion, and production phases of their exploration and development activities. Smith International operates through three business units: M-I SWACO (51 percent of 2009 revenues), Smith Oilfield (27 percent), and Distribution (22 percent). M-I SWACO specializes in drilling fluids and systems as well as equipment used in drilling to control solids, manage pressure, and handle waste. This joint venture is 60 percent owned by Smith International and

40 percent by Schlumberger Limited. Smith Oilfield designs, manufactures, and markets highly engineered drill bits used to drill oil and natural gas wells and also offers a variety of drilling tools and services, including directional drilling, measurement-while-drilling, and logging-while-drilling services. The Distribution unit provides products and services to the energy, refining, petrochemical, power generation, and mining industries and also provides supply-chain management services within these fields.

These units operate from more than 40 major facilities and properties worldwide. About 60 percent of the company's revenues originate outside the United States. In February 2010 Smith International agreed to be acquired by Schlumberger in a deal initially valued at $11 billion.

EARLY HISTORY

The historical roots of Houston, Texas-based Smith International originate in Southern California, where the founder of the company, Herman C. Smith, resided and where the company maintained its corporate offices for most of the 20th century. The chain of events that led up to the creation of Smith International began in 1902, when Herman Smith opened a blacksmith shop in Whittier, California. Later that same year, oil was discovered in the area, a defining and auspicious discovery for Smith International and an event to be heralded by the 20-year-old Smith and his infant blacksmith shop. The arrival of oil rigs and attendant oil workers provided a welcome infusion of business for Smith's shop, keeping the young blacksmith busy

COMPANY PERSPECTIVES

Smith International is strongly committed to continually achieving world-class business performance through best-in-class people using premium equipment to deliver unparalleled solutions and impeccable service to our customer. SMITH will build a prominent global position in the oil and gas services industry based upon understanding our people, our customer and our investor. SMITH will conduct business worldwide with integrity in an unrivalled manner, becoming the preferred partner for our people and their families, our customer and their success, our investor and their trust.

Smith International … one world, one vision.

sharpening the oilmen's drill bits and providing a steady source of cash. For years, Smith kept the area's drill bits sharp and repaired other tools used in drilling for oil, developing a relationship with the oil drillers who frequented his shop that gradually led Smith in a new business direction and formed the foundation for Smith International.

By listening to oil drillers discuss the shortcomings of the tools of their trade and by eliciting their suggestions for improvements, Smith developed an expertise that set him apart from the typical blacksmith and, over time, distinguished his shop as a haven for oil drillers and their equipment. He began making unique adjustments to the tools brought into his shop and he began developing new tools. By the 1920s, Smith's business, which had been named H.C. Smith Manufacturing Company, subsisted on reworking fishtail bits and modifying oil tools as its mainstay business, having secured a place for itself in the California oil and gas industry by staying attuned to the peculiar needs of its customers.

The business of H.C. Smith Manufacturing, however, would not be inherited by Smith International, despite logical inferences to the contrary. In the history of Smith International, the three decades Smith spent in building H.C. Smith Manufacturing represented a proving ground for the establishment of the company that would eventually become one of the world's largest suppliers of drill bits and other oilfield products to the global oil and gas industry. For Smith International, the history of H.C. Smith Manufacturing was merely the

prelude to its distinct genesis and the decades of development to follow.

The cause for the interruption was attributable solely to Herman Smith, who, by the late 1920s, had decided it was time to retire. In 1929, at age 47, Smith sold the business he had created to Globe Oil Tools, then settled into retirement and ended his working days in the oil and gas industry. As it turned out, however, Smith's departure from the oil and gas industry did not mark the beginning of his retirement, but rather the start of a seven-year hiatus. Smith returned to action in the business world when he purchased Allen Brothers Oil Tools in 1936 and then the following year renamed the company H.C. Smith Oil Tool Company, the earliest predecessor to Smith International.

EMERGENCE OF SMITH INTERNATIONAL

Once back in business, Smith set to work building an enterprise that would make his name internationally recognized decades after his death, leaving a lasting vestige to his efforts in creating H.C. Smith Manufacturing Company and H.C. Smith Oil Tool Company. The H.C. Smith Oil Tool Company corporate title was retained until 1959, when the company went public and changed its name to Smith Tool Co. The following year a parent organization, Smith Industries International, Inc., was formed to facilitate expansion both domestically and abroad in the coming decade, which the company accomplished at a 15 percent rate during the 1960s.

By the end of the 1960s, another name change was in the offing, occurring in 1969 when "Industries" was dropped from the corporate title and Smith International, Inc., was adopted as the company's official name. As Smith International, Inc., the company would record its most prolific growth. Under the same corporate banner, the company also would struggle through its most tortuous years, teetering on the brink of failure.

By the beginning of the 1970s, Smith International had established itself as a leading manufacturer of drilling equipment for natural resource development, its broad line of drilling equipment used by companies involved in developing oil, gas, minerals, and water. Supported by a well-established overseas business, which generated nearly 40 percent of the company's total annual sales, Smith International had grown to become a roughly $100-million-a-year concern by the early 1970s, deriving three-quarters of its sales from its involvement in oil and gas markets. In the decade ahead, Smith International would register its most prodigious success,

KEY DATES

1902: Herman C. Smith opens a blacksmith shop in Whittier, California.

1929: Smith retires and sells his business to Globe Oil Tools.

1936: Smith comes out of retirement to acquire Allen Brothers Oil Tools.

1959: Company goes public as Smith Tool Co.

1960: Parent company Smith Industries International, Inc., is created.

1969: Company shortens its name to Smith International, Inc.

1986: A large patent infringement payment forces Smith International into Chapter 11 bankruptcy protection.

1987: Smith emerges from bankruptcy in December.

1989: Corporate headquarters are relocated from California to Houston, Texas.

1994: Smith acquires Dresser Industries, Inc.'s 64 percent interest in M-I Drilling Fluids Co.

1998: Company acquires Wilson Industries, Inc., distributor of oil and gas equipment, for $454 million in stock; buys Halliburton Company's 36 percent stake in M-I for $265 million.

2010: Company agrees to be acquired by Schlumberger.

outdistancing its competitors to leap to the top tier of its industry, ranking, by the beginning of the 1980s, as the second-largest drill-bit manufacturer in the world, trailing only Hughes Tool Company. Through internal growth, astute acquisitions, and international and domestic expansion, annual sales for the company soared exponentially, swelling to $1.2 billion by the beginning of the 1980s, while earnings followed suit, jumping to $133 million, more than the company had collected in sales a decade earlier.

NEAR-FATAL "TRIPLE WHAMMY"

Despite the impressive financial figures posted by the company, the early 1980s marked the beginning of what could have been the end for Smith International, as the demand for oil rigs shuddered to a halt in the face of declining oil prices. Heavily dependent on the fortunes of the oil and gas industry, Smith International began to suffer from the repercussive effects of anemic drilling

activity. This was not the first time the company's business had faltered in its nearly 50 years of existence in the frequently capricious oil market. Periods of market stagnation had pocked Smith International's financial performance throughout its history, but the effects of widespread depressed oil activity were exacerbated by other negative developments peculiar to Smith International, which would leave the company perilously close to complete collapse.

The first of the negative developments to compound the severity of pervasive depressed oil drilling activities was Smith International's ill-conceived, ill-timed attempt to take control of Gearhart Industries, Inc., an oilfield services company that specialized in sophisticated wireline, measurement-while-drilling services. In November 1983, as the oil industry continued its retrogressive slide, Smith International paid more than $100 million for General Electric Company's 23 percent stake in Gearhart, a move welcomed by Gearhart's founder, Marvin Gearhart, because it staved off General Electric's attempt to purchase his company. Marvin Gearhart's ire was raised, however, when Smith International increased its holding in Gearhart Industries to 33 percent, then announced it intended to acquire 56 percent of the wireline services firm. Marvin Gearhart vehemently opposed Smith International's tender offer and did everything in his power to thwart such a transaction from being completed, touching off a squabble between the two companies that, in the end, left Gearhart victorious in his attempt to keep his unwanted suitor at arm's length and saddled Smith International with enormous debt.

When the dust had settled from Smith International's failed attempt to acquire control of Gearhart Industries' sophisticated "downhole" measuring technology, the losses amounted to well over $150 million. Smith International withdrew its bid in March 1985, by which time the company had spent $165 million in trying to buy Gearhart Industries. The stock Smith International had acquired was sold for $80 million, but the company took an $85 million charge against working capital after selling its Gearhart Industries holdings, giving it a cumbersome burden to carry in the depressed economic times within the oil industry.

By mid-1985, the combined effects of a laggard economic climate and the losses incurred from the failed Gearhart Industries acquisition had thrust Smith International into a precarious position, forcing it to close plants, lay off more than half of its 14,000 employees, and cease production of certain products. Annual sales, which had stood at $1.2 billion in 1981, plummeted to $747 million in 1984. Earnings took a more precipitous plunge, dropping from $133 million in 1981 to a loss of $65 million in 1984. By all accounts, the early 1980s had been disastrous years for the company, but the worst was yet to come. The "St. Valentine's Day Massacre," as a Smith International chief financial officer dubbed it, was looming ahead, and its arrival would deliver a near-fatal blow to the company.

Smith International was still contending with the difficulties caused by its declining business and the Gearhart Industries imbroglio when, on February 14, 1986, the Federal District Court for the Central District of California issued a ruling that rocked the company. The judgment by the court marked the culmination of a lawsuit originally filed by Smith International against Hughes Tool in 1974, a lawsuit Smith International would later regret having filed. By the end of the protracted legal dispute over patents, Smith International was found to be the culprit and was ordered to pay what ended up being $205.4 million for its infringement upon Hughes Tool's patent for an "O-ring seal" rock bit.

Combined with Smith International's other losses, the ruling handed down by the court represented the third devastating strike incurred by the company, the meting of a "triple whammy" as one industry observer phrased it. Smith International reeled from the successive blows, leading a host of bankers and analysts to predict that Smith International would either be sold or forced into Chapter 11 bankruptcy.

INTO AND OUT OF BANKRUPTCY

On the heels of the judgment, immediate steps were taken to salvage the company, leading to what one analyst referred to as the company's "weekend bloodbath." Smith International laid off 32 vice presidents, consolidated several divisions, and announced it would lay off as many as 2,000 employees, but by the first week of March 1986 there was nothing left to do but seek protection under Chapter 11 of the U.S. Bankruptcy Code.

While under Chapter 11, Smith International divested its noncore businesses, retaining only its tool manufacturing and drilling divisions to carry the company forward. Its corporate office building in Newport Beach, California, was sold as well as a plant in Irvine, California, giving the company $46 million to go along with the $200 million raised through its divestiture of noncore businesses. The company also reached a settlement with Hughes Tool over the patent dispute, paying that firm $95 million. Smith International's headquarters were relocated to a one-story industrial building next to its primary plant in Irv-

ine, as consolidation and cost-cutting reigned during the company's nearly two-year-long battle to reorganize while in bankruptcy.

In December 1987 Smith International emerged from under the protective umbrella of bankruptcy, coming out of a year in which the company recorded $264.4 million in sales and registered a $26.1 million loss in earnings. Smith International was a shadow of its former self, but what remained was lean and, despite the loss recorded in 1987, capable of generating positive gains. Over the course of the following year, a vibrant company began to emerge, buoyed by its continued investment in research that provided Smith International with a range of new, high-technology drilling products. Net productivity per employee during 1988 stood at $126,000, an all-time high, fueling hopes that the company had begun to wrest free from the debilitating first half of the decade.

In 1989 Smith International closed its sprawling 638,000-square-foot Irvine, California, production facility, then consolidated all petroleum and mining-bit operations into its 169,000-square-foot manufacturing plant in Ponca City, Oklahoma. The company's headquarters moved as well, relocating from Irvine to Houston, Texas, where Smith International's management could superintend a company that had dramatically ameliorated its ability to compete as an oil and gas equipment and services firm. In March 1989 Doug Rock was named president and CEO. Rock, a chemist by training, had joined Smith in 1974 as a computer systems expert, working his way up through the ranks over the next 15 years.

EXITING DIRECTIONAL DRILLING

Smith International entered the 1990s as a company well-positioned in the high-technology drilling market, where demand was high for its heavy investment in products such as "steerable systems," or devices patterned after aerospace guidance systems that allowed oil workers to drill in different directions from a single site. In 1990 a proposed merger between Dresser Industries, Inc., and Smith International fell through when Dresser Industries backed out of the deal citing potential antitrust problems with the U.S. Justice Department.

The corporation faced more litigation when a federal lawsuit was filed accusing Smith International, Baker Hughes Incorporated (the product of the 1987 merger of Hughes Tool and Baker International Corporation), Camco International, and Dresser Industries of fixing prices of drill bits from 1986 through 1992. Although Smith vehemently denied any wrongdoing, it agreed to settle the suit in 1993 because the other three defendant companies had done so. Smith agreed to pay a $200,000 fine to settle the criminal suit and $19 million to settle a civil suit brought by customers.

By 1993 directional drilling technology was emerging as a key drilling innovation. Smith International's operations in this sector accounted for more than 40 percent of the company's revenues, but Smith was at a competitive disadvantage because two much larger firms, Halliburton Company and Baker Hughes, were furiously pumping money into their directional drilling units. Rock decided the time was right to exit the business, and in March 1993 he sold it to Halliburton for $270 million in Halliburton stock.

ACQUISITION SPREE BEGINNING WITH M-I IN 1994

The proceeds from this divestment were earmarked to develop a new niche for Smith International in the area of drilling fluids and other well-completion services and to restore some of the magnitude lost during the previous decade. On February 28, 1994, the company acquired Dresser's 64 percent interest in M-I Drilling Fluids Co. The $160 million acquisition ranked as the largest in company history. It also provided a tremendous boost to Smith International's stature as a competitor in the oil and gas equipment and services industry.

Houston-based M-I Drilling was a joint venture with Halliburton, which owned 36 percent of the venture. It specialized in drilling and completion fluids and systems, solids-control equipment, and waste management services for the oil and gas drilling industry. In drilling, fluids and muds were used for such procedures as cooling drill bits, lubricating drill pipes, flushing out rock cuttings, and balancing pressure in wells. Concurrent with the acquisition, Smith International reorganized into three operating divisions: Smith Drill Bits, Smith Drilling and Completion Services, and M-I Drilling Fluids. In the wake of the purchase of M-I Drilling, Smith International's revenues leaped to $653.9 million from the $220 million generated in 1993, while gross earnings doubled.

Over the next 10 years, Smith International completed more than 40 acquisitions to strengthen its existing operations and diversify into related areas. In June 1996 M-I became the largest firm in the worldwide drilling fluids industry by acquiring Anchor Drilling Fluids, A.S. from Norway's Transocean A.S. for $114.7 million in cash and assumed debt. Anchor was particularly attractive because of its strong presence in

the North Sea and Malaysia, where M-I had less of a presence. To pass antitrust muster with the U.S. Justice Department, M-I had to sell Anchor's U.S. operations, which were subsequently sold to Jordan Drilling Fluids.

Of the several other acquisitions completed by M-I from 1996 to 1998, two were especially noteworthy. In October 1997 M-I spent $17.3 million for Calgary-based Fleming Oilfield Services, Ltd., a provider of drilling fluid products and services to the Canadian oil and gas industry. Then in May 1998 Safeguard Disposal Systems, Inc., of Lafayette, Louisiana, was bought for $42.7 million in stock and cash. Safeguard specialized in the rental of waste management systems used in petroleum drilling. Meanwhile, Halliburton reached an agreement in early 1998 on a merger with Dresser Industries. To gain approval for this deal from the Justice Department, Halliburton had to divest its 36 percent stake in M-I. In August of that year, Halliburton sold the stake to Smith International for $265 million, giving Smith full control of M-I.

During this same period, Smith Drilling and Completion made its own string of acquisitions. Among these were the October 1996 purchase of The Red Baron (Oil Tools Rental) Ltd. for about $40.3 million and the April 1997 buyout of Tri-Tech Fishing Services, L.L.C., for approximately $20.4 million. Based in Aberdeen, Scotland, Red Baron supplied fishing and other downhole remedial products and services to oil and gas drillers in the North Sea, the Middle East, and Southeast Asia. Tri-Tech, operating out of Lafayette, Louisiana, had an operational profile similar to that of Red Baron, but it was active in the U.S. Gulf Coast region. The Smith Drilling and Completion unit was renamed simply Smith Services in August 1999.

1998 MERGER WITH WILSON INDUSTRIES

Smith International ventured into a new field in April 1998 through a merger with Wilson Industries, Inc., in a stock swap valued at about $454 million. Wilson, a private company based in Houston, was a distributor of pipe, valves, and other miscellaneous supplies to the oil and gas industry. Wilson became one of Smith International's main operating units.

Smith saw its revenues surge past the $2 billion mark in 1998 thanks to its string of acquisitions. However, the oil industry went into another cyclical downturn, leading to a net loss of $16.1 million in the final quarter of the year and full-year earnings of just $34.1 million, down from the 1997 total of $102.4 million. The company moved quickly to control costs, cutting its workforce from 9,100 in March 1998 to

6,300 in mid-1999. Revenues for 1999 fell about 15 percent, to $1.81 billion, but profits rebounded to $56.7 million.

In July 1999 Smith combined its M-I unit with the non-U.S. drilling fluid operations of Schlumberger's Dowell unit into a new M-I joint venture, 60 percent owned by Smith and 40 percent by its new partner. In addition to its contribution of assets, Schlumberger also paid Smith $280 million in cash. Just a couple of weeks after the deal's completion was announced, however, the U.S. Justice Department filed a petition in a U.S. district court accusing the two companies of a criminal violation of antitrust law. The government alleged that the new joint venture violated a 1994 consent decree that specifically barred Smith from combining M-I with the drilling fluid operations of Schlumberger and several other firms. In December 1999 a federal judge found Smith and Schlumberger guilty of criminal contempt, assessing each a fine of $750,000 and five years of probation. The firms also reached an agreement with the Justice Department whereby they would pay a $13.1 million civil penalty and would be able to continue operating the M-I joint venture.

With this legal distraction behind it, Smith International continued to seek growth via the acquisition route. Several deals involved M-I. In December 2000 M-I acquired Emerson's Sweco Division, a producer of specialty screen and separation equipment for oilfield applications, for $75 million. The oilfield and industrial screen operations of Madison Filter Belgium S.A. were acquired in October 2001 for $93.5 million. In January 2003 M-I paid about EUR 76 million for the oilfield chemical business of Finland-based Dynea International. Later in 2003, the M-I joint venture was renamed M-I SWACO. Wilson, meantime, was bolstered through the January 2001, $41.1 million acquisition of Van Leeuwen Pipe and Tube Corporation, a Houston-based distributor of pipe, valves, and fittings to the refining, petrochemical, and power generation industries.

Smith International posted record revenues and net income in 2001 of $3.55 billion and $152.1 million, respectively. Another cyclical downturn in exploration and production, however, hit the firm's results the following year. Revenues fell 11 percent and profits plunged 39 percent.

RECORD PERFORMANCE DURING EARLY 21ST-CENTURY BOOM PERIOD

This setback proved short-lived. Record global demand for energy, fueled in part by the rapid development of new global economic powers such as China, pushed energy prices into a sharply rising trajectory. The high energy prices encouraged oil companies to boost production, resulting in a concomitant increase in demand for oilfield services. From 2003 to 2008, Smith International enjoyed six straight years of rising revenues and profits. This historic boom period culminated with the record results for 2008 of $767.3 million in net income on revenues of $10.77 billion.

During this period, the company retained its position as one of the key players in the global oilfield products and services industry by continuing to introduce new products and completing a series of acquisitions to fill in gaps in its product and service offerings and to enlarge its geographic footprint. In August 2006, for example, M-I SWACO acquired the Scottish firm Specialised Petroleum Services Group Limited, a provider of clean-up products and engineering services for the removal of debris from well-bores to help increase well production. The purchase price was about $165.4 million in cash.

Smith International's largest acquisition by far during this boom period occurred in August 2008 when the company took over W-H Energy Services, Inc., for $3.03 billion in cash and stock. This deal propelled Smith International back into W-H Energy's specialty of directional drilling. The company's acquisition of W-H Energy, a firm also based in Houston, came at a time of consolidation in the oilfield services industry. Smith International and its competitors were under pressure to offer broader ranges of services in order to win contracts from the large, government-controlled oil companies of the Middle East and elsewhere, the operations of which were growing more rapidly than those of the major Western oil giants.

During the second half of 2008, the financial crisis and a slowing global economy quickly ended the boom times as crude oil prices plunged from their record midyear level of $145 per barrel down to below $40 a barrel by late in the year. The result was the most dramatic downturn in upstream activity since the mid-1980s. John Yearwood, who took over as Smith International CEO at the beginning of 2009, while Rock remained chairman, was thus faced with an immediate test of his executive leadership. In his first year at the helm the company suffered a drop in revenues of about 24 percent, down to $8.22 billion, and an 80 percent plunge in profits, down to just $148.5 million.

AGREEMENT ON ACQUISITION BY SCHLUMBERGER

Consolidation in the oilfield services industry continued in the downturn, with the largest deal involving Smith

International as acquiree rather than acquirer. In February 2010 the company agreed to be acquired by Schlumberger in an $11 billion, all-stock transaction.

By taking over Smith, Schlumberger would not only gain full control of M-I SWACO but also fill in one of the few holes in its oilfield offerings: the manufacturing of drill bits. Schlumberger also anticipated achieving more than $300 million in annual cost savings through merger synergies by 2012. In July 2010 regulators granted unconditional approval for the merger, and it was expected to be completed later in the year.

Jeffrey L. Covell
Updated, David E. Salamie

PRINCIPAL SUBSIDIARIES

CE Franklin Ltd. (Canada; 53%); Smith International Acquisition Corp.; Smith International Canada, Ltd.; Smith International (North Sea) Limited (UK); W-H Energy Services, LLC; Wilson International, Inc.

PRINCIPAL OPERATING UNITS

M-I SWACO (60%); Smith Oilfield; Distribution.

PRINCIPAL COMPETITORS

Baker Hughes Incorporated; Ferguson Enterprises, Inc.; Hagemeyer North America, Inc.; Halliburton Company; McJunkin Red Man Holding Corporation; National Oilwell Varco, Inc.; Newpark Resources, Inc.; Weatherford International Ltd.; W.W. Grainger, Inc.

FURTHER READING

Antosh, Nelson, "M-I Getting an Anchor in the Mud," *Houston Chronicle*, December 12, 1995.

Casselman, Ben, and Jeffrey McCracken, "Schlumberger Deal Widens Oil-Services Lead," *Wall Street Journal*, February 22, 2010, p. B3.

Davis, Michael, "Smith, Schlumberger Hit with Fines," *Houston Chronicle*, December 10, 1999.

De Rouffignac, Ann, "Rock on a Roll," *Houston Business Journal*, October 17, 1997, p. 12A.

Durgin, Hillary, "Purchase Puts Smith in New Fields: Wilson Industries Sold for $454 Million in Stock," *Houston Chronicle*, January 21, 1998.

————, "Smith Cut 900 Jobs in Quarter," *Houston Chronicle*, October 20, 1998.

Hatcher, Monica, "Is Energy Merger the First Domino? Deal between Schlumberger and Drill Bits Maker May Be a Catalyst for Diversification among Companies Here," *Houston Chronicle*, February 22, 2010.

Ivanovich, David, "Smith International's Choice to Swim against the Flow Proves to Be a Winning Strategy for Houston Drill Bit Company," *Houston Chronicle*, May 19, 1996.

Kardos, Donna, and Ben Casselman, "Smith International to Buy W-H Energy," *Wall Street Journal*, June 4, 2008, p. B6.

Pybus, Kenneth R., "Revenues Rise after Largest Buy in Smith International's History," *Houston Business Journal*, June 9, 1995, p. 22B.

Walsh, Jennifer, and L. M. Sixel, "Smith, Schlumberger Facing Charges," *Houston Chronicle*, July 28, 1999.

Sportif USA, Inc.

1415 Greg Street, Suite 101
Sparks, Nevada 89431
U.S.A.
Telephone: (775) 359-6400
Fax: (775) 353-3400
Web site: http://www.sportif.com

Private Company
Founded: 1965
Employees: 950
Sales: $120 million (2009 est.)
NAICS: 423910 Sporting and Recreational Goods and
　　Supplies Merchant Wholesalers

■ ■ ■

Sportif USA, Inc., a family-run apparel company, caters to active consumers who desire comfortable and durable sportswear. The firm's signature item, the Original 7-Pocket Stretch Short, has been a fundamental staple in the wardrobes of most outdoor enthusiasts since founder John Kirsch Sr. began his small business. The shorts have been duplicated and copied by apparel companies worldwide. Because of its commitment to customer satisfaction and staying current with trends in outdoor apparel, Sportif USA has grown from a one-person operation to a leading retailer of outdoor apparel.

A FAMILY AFFAIR: 1965–91

While John G. Kirsch was peddling his stylish and comfortable tennis shorts from the back of the family station wagon in 1965, he envisioned a company that would rival any of the leaders in the outdoor apparel industry. One innovation that started Kirsch moving in the right direction was the development of a new fabric. Using a Swiss material as a starting point, Kirsch worked with mills in Hong Kong and Japan to develop a new stretch, woven fabric. The comfortable, movable fabric eventually launched the design of Sportif's Original 7-Pocket Stretch short.

After developing and trademarking the new shorts, Kirsch entered into private-label contracts with other apparel retailers including L.L. Bean, Lands' End, and Eddie Bauer. These contracts provided a quick and relatively easy avenue for filling orders and staying solvent. Kirsch was so confident in the future of his endeavor that he moved his wife and four sons from Southern California to Nevada to expand his business.

For nearly two decades the company flourished in the private-label world and became innovators in using Gore-Tex and sun-protective fabric. In 1976 the waterproof and breathable Gore-Tex fabric was first used in rainwear and soon after was a popular fabric to use in boating apparel. Similarly, advances in using tightly woven, lightweight nylon or polyester fabric in dark colors offered greater ultraviolet (UV) protection for sun-intensive watersports and quickly changed the apparel business.

While Kirsch was dealing with the stress and strain that running the business had on his family, in March 1991 all involved were plunged into tragedy when Kirsch's twin-engine plane crashed into the San Bernardino Mountains. The founder's four children (ranging in age

COMPANY PERSPECTIVES

In 1965, Sportif USA began as a small business in southern California, headed by John G. Kirsch. In true entrepreneurial style, Kirsch sold tennis shorts from the back of the family's station wagon, gradually building a reputation for quality and comfort. As this reputation grew, so did the market for high-quality outdoor clothing. Tennis shorts led to hiking, which led to fishing and nautical apparel ... and so the Sportif brand took shape.

from teens to early 20s) were left with the legacy of realizing their father's dreams and business aspirations.

A LABEL OF ITS OWN: NINETIES

Upon the sudden death of his father, John Kirsch Jr., the eldest, became president of the company with brother Steven as vice president. Their mission to position Sportif as a leader in the outdoor apparel industry was nearly as steep as the mountains in which they lived. John Kirsch told Kathleen DesMarteau for a 1998 *Bobbin* magazine profile, "Those were the days when we created the problems in the morning and fixed them in the afternoon. ... In other words, it's when we started losing our hair and eyesight."

They persevered and eventually made a difficult and risky decision. For several years they gradually eased away from the private-label business and slowly increased apparel stamped with the Sportif USA label. In 1992 they started selling product through a mail-order catalog called *Waterfronts*.

By 1996 the company had experienced solid sales growth with more than 50 percent of its volume coming from private-label contracts. Feeling confident in their ability to produce quality clothing and successfully run a business, the Kirsch brothers decided it was time to cancel their private-label contracts and branch off into a style and label of their own.

The transition was rocky, but John Kirsch was willing to take a loss and invest in the future of a Sportif USA label. He explained to DesMarteau, "to develop a brand and an image—that's a long road, and it takes lots of time and dollars, but it also has a future." In order to counteract the loss of income from terminating contracts, Sportif reduced its workforce at the headquarters in Sparks, Nevada, from 75 to 38 employees. Initially sales volume took a massive hit, but recovery was imminent.

By 1998 John Kirsch Sr.'s dream finally had been realized. Only 2 percent of Sportif's production was for private-label contracts. The remaining 98 percent was in the Sportif USA label. As the company began to expand, it invested in new technology and also ventured into international trade.

BY LAND AND BY SEA

As the Sportif brand made a name for itself, the company faced stiff competition. The retailers the company had previously supplied with merchandise, namely L.L. Bean, Eddie Bauer, and Lands' End, were now rivals. In the early 2000s when e-commerce retail sales began to surpass traditional brick-and-mortar or catalog shopping, Sportif stayed in line with its successful competitors and developed a Web site that mirrored its *Waterfronts* print catalog. In a 2001 report, the U.S. Department of Commerce estimated a 67.1 percent increase in e-commerce retail sales from fourth-quarter 1999 to fourth-quarter 2000. In comparison, total retail sales rose 4.2 percent during that same period.

In addition to the company's classic 7-pocket stretch cargo shorts, the *Waterfronts* Web site and catalog offered a variety of nautically inspired clothing and accessories. Selections included various designs for shorts, shirts, long pants, watches, belts, sandals, shoes, and hats. Most clothing styles were offered in natural colors such as khaki, white, and indigo while graphic tees displayed fishing, boating, and island themes.

Even with the success of the company's online sales, competition remained fierce. The spring 2001 collection featured a new Tri-Tech fabric with UV protection. The quick-drying, lightweight fabric was durable and absorbed moisture away from the skin. Unfortunately, sales of the men's line had peaked in 1999 and remained relatively flat for the next several years. The company faced financial challenges and soon had to consider other means for survival.

DEBUT OF AVENTURA

As in the past, Sportif looked to consumer trends to spur future growth. In 2006 the company launched Aventura Clothing catalog and an apparel line for women on the go. When the new collection was announced, Vice President/General Manager Doug Moir told John Fischer of *Multichannel Merchant*, "We like to think of this new line as a tribute to the soccer mom who is going a million miles per hour every day."

In addition to simply offering comfortable clothing for active women, items were priced to encourage impulse catalog purchases. Ranging from $10 to about

KEY DATES

1965: John G. Kirsch starts a business by selling tennis shorts in Southern California.

1970: Kirsch relocates the family business to Nevada.

1991: Kirsch dies in a plane crash; eldest son John Kirsch Jr. and his three brothers manage the family business.

1992: Company begins selling clothing through catalogs.

1996: Focus moves away from private-label contracts and into expansion of the Sportif USA label.

2006: Sportif expands with the launch of Aventura, a line for women.

2009: Company broadens the scope of its eco-mission.

$55, sandals, skirts, tops, and shorts could be bought without customers feeling as though their purchases were an enormous investment. The no-nonsense clothing also featured organic cotton in support of Sportif's 2002 membership in the Organic Exchange whose mission was to promote the use of organic cotton.

The new women's line proved a successful endeavor, and four years after its inception, Aventura's eco-friendly alternatives had become its signature. The mission expressed on Aventura's catalog and Web site read, "Helping the earth … one garment at a time." By 2009 Aventura offered 100 styles in eco/sustainable textiles accounting for 80 percent of the total collection, sold to more than 650 retailers.

Following in Kirsch Sr.'s tradition for uniqueness and quality, Aventura merchandise was carefully designed and sold to individuals through the company Web site and to smaller boutique stores. In addition to organic cotton, Aventura clothing featured other fabrics such as hemp, bamboo, soy, and recycled polyesters. Concentrating on woven fabrics rather than knit (fabric primarily produced in the United States), Sportif ventured overseas to work directly with mills in China and India.

By eliminating the middleman, Aventura's fabrics and organic cottons could be sold at mid-market prices. In a *Retail Merchandiser* article, John Kirsch Jr. explained the value of selective marketing and sales: "We feel that when our clothes are in front of the customer, they tell the story about what makes Aventura products unique."

A COMMITMENT TO GREEN

The company's commitment to its green mission went beyond clothing. They recycled IT equipment, and its 30,000-square-foot offices were cooled by an earth-friendly air conditioning system that exchanged heated indoor air with cooler outdoor air. In comparison to traditional air conditioners, the exchange system greatly reduced the consumption of energy and natural resources.

Aventura's "eco-mission" was aimed at the 63 million consumers who valued "Lifestyles of Health and Sustainability" (LOHAS). In terms of customer satisfaction and corporate stability, Aventura claimed, "LOHAS describes a $228.9 billion U.S. marketplace for goods and services focused on health, the environment, clean technology and alternative energy, social justice, personal development and sustainable living." Aventura targeted women who shopped in the organic food aisles, committed a portion of their time and energy to nonprofit volunteering, and cared about the products they bought.

Combined with Sportif's original entrepreneurial spirit and commitment to customer satisfaction, Aventura Clothing provided a winning complement to the company's solid beginnings with its *Waterfronts* catalog and active wear. While maintaining Kirsch's legacy for quality, style, and function, Sportif USA had reached, and presumably would maintain, its goal of leadership within the outdoor apparel industry.

Jodi Essey-Stapleton

PRINCIPAL SUBSIDIARIES

Aventura Clothing; Waterfronts Clothing.

PRINCIPAL COMPETITORS

Columbia Sportswear Company; Eddie Bauer LLC; Lands' End, Inc.; L.L. Bean, Inc.; VF Outdoor, Inc. (North Face).

FURTHER READING

"Aventura Clothing," *Apparel Magazine*, May 2009.

DesMarteau, Kathleen, "On the Market or Coming Soon," *Apparel Magazine*, August 2005.

———, "Sportif's Brave New World," *Bobbin*, July 1998.

Fischer, John, "Sportif USA Launches Aventura Clothing," *Multichannel Merchant*, June 2005.

Griffin, Cara, "Tradetalk," *SGB: Sporting Goods Business*, November 10, 2000.

"Retail E-Commerce Sales in Fourth Quarter 2000," http://www2.census.gov/retail/releases/historical/ecomm/00Q4.pdf.

"Sportif USA/Aventura Clothing: New Direction," *Retail Merchandiser*, http://www.retail-merchandiser.com/supplier-reports/104-supplier-reports/1104-sportif-usaaventura-clothing-new-direction.html.

Syco Entertainment, Ltd.

9 Derry Street
Kensington
London, W8 5HY
United Kingdom
Telephone: (+44 20) 7361 8000
Web site: http://www.sonymusic.co.uk

Joint Venture of Simon Cowell and Sony Music Entertainment
Incorporated: 2002 as Syco Music
Employees: 28
Sales: $150 million (2010 est.)
NAICS: 512110 Motion Picture and Video Production; 512210 Record Production; 533110 Lessors of Nonfinancial Intangible Assets (Except Copyrighted Works)

■ ■ ■

Syco Entertainment, Ltd., is a joint venture between Simon Cowell and Sony Music Entertainment that develops and licenses television programs and music recordings. The firm owns Cowell's wildly popular *X Factor* and *Got Talent* reality competition formats, which are produced by FremantleMedia in numerous countries worldwide, and also coordinates the musical output of the programs' finalists and other Cowell-signed acts in partnership with Sony. The firm has offices in London and Los Angeles.

BEGINNINGS

Syco Entertainment is the brainchild of Simon Cowell, a record executive-turned media mogul best known as an opinionated judge on television's *American Idol* and *The X Factor*. Born in England on October 7, 1959, Cowell was the son of a property manager at music giant EMI. His mother was a socialite. He had little use for school and dropped out at 16. After several menial jobs, he ended up working in the mail room of EMI.

By the late 1970s Cowell had moved up to an executive position with EMI Music Publishing, and in 1981 he left to form an independent company called E&S Music with boss Ellis Rich. It folded within a year, however, and he returned to his former employer. In 1985 he struck out again to found Fanfare Records with promoter Iain Burton, which produced a number of top 10 hits in Britain. Four years later it, too, went under, and the now-broke Cowell was forced to move back in with his parents.

He was soon hired as an Artists and Repertory consultant with Bertelsmann Music Group (BMG), however, and over the next decade he signed a number of popular acts including vocalist Sinitta and groups 5ive and Westlife to his imprint S Records. Cowell also began to turn popular television properties into successful recordings, hitting the charts with records from the series *Teletubbies*, *Power Rangers*, and *WWF SmackDown*, as well as *Soldier Soldier* actors Robson & Jerome, whose version of the standard "Unchained Melody" was one of the 10 best-selling singles of the decade in the United Kingdom.

POP IDOL DEBUTS IN 2001

In 2000 Cowell was approached by the producers of a televised singing competition called *Popstars*, which had first aired in New Zealand, to appear as a judge in the forthcoming U.K. version. He turned the offer down, but when the show achieved modest success he vowed to best it with his own variation on the concept. The following year he partnered with Simon Fuller, owner of 19 Television and the manager of popular 1990s girl group The Spice Girls, to develop a show called *Pop Idol*. They quickly interested Simon Jones of Pearson Television (later to be known as FremantleMedia), who sold it to Britain's ITV network. Cowell, who had become attuned to television's power to sell music, claimed he was doing the show strictly to find promising new acts for his record label.

Pop Idol would start with auditions of singers and follow the process through to the selection of a winner, who (unlike *Popstars*) would be chosen by audience vote. Cowell was one of four judges who picked the initial group of 50 contestants from a large pool of hopefuls, and then critiqued each performance throughout the competition. Although the panel of music industry insiders frequently offered negative reviews, Cowell was particularly harsh, with such comments as, "If you sang like this 2,000 years ago, people would have stoned you," earning him the nickname of "Mr. Nasty" from the British tabloid press.

The program, which began airing in early October 2001 in a prime-time slot on Saturday nights, quickly became a ratings bonanza for ITV. At series' end the winner and top runner-up were signed to Cowell's S label and BMG, with Fuller's 19 Entertainment manag-

ing their careers. When the first release by Will Young came out in March 2002 it quickly sold 1.7 million copies, making it the fastest-selling single in U.K. history.

As with many popular new formats in the burgeoning reality-television genre, producer FremantleMedia began shopping the show overseas, selling it in Poland and South Africa while trying to place it with one of the major U.S. networks. Most expressed little interest, however, as two recent music-based reality shows (including an Americanized version of *Popstars*) had not done well in the ratings. The only positive response came from the smaller Fox network, which was considering buying it only if the producers would find sponsors themselves. Fortunately for Cowell and Fremantle, Fox owner Rupert Murdoch's daughter Elisabeth lived in England and was a big fan of *Pop Idol*, and she convinced him to pick it up.

AMERICAN IDOL MAKES COWELL A STAR IN THE UNITED STATES: 2002

In June 2002 *American Idol—The Search for a Superstar* debuted. The only English judge signed was Cowell, whom Fox had insisted on after viewing a tape of the U.K. version, with the other two (one less than in England) consisting of record producer Randy Jackson and singer Paula Abdul. The summer series, which was not heavily promoted and whose competition was mainly reruns, almost immediately developed a rabid following, and the finale was watched by an astonishing 23 million viewers. American viewers were especially fascinated with Cowell's unscripted, often caustic assessments of the contestants, while winner Kelly Clarkson's first release (on BMG-owned RCA, in partnership with S Records and 19 Recordings) validated the show's premise by hitting number one.

Cowell by this time had set up a new joint venture company in partnership with BMG, Simco Ltd. (commonly known as Syco Music), which would sign future *Idol* winners, and in 2003 he established an offshoot called Syco TV, which hired veteran television executive Nigel Hall to oversee its efforts. A Cowell-produced reality dating series called *Cupid* was launched in the United States during the summer, although it fared poorly with both critics and audiences.

American Idol (now shifted to a March through May season) continued to draw huge ratings, however, ranking as the number one program on U.S. television and appearing in sometimes equally popular FremantleMedia-produced versions in a growing number of countries around the world. In the United Kingdom,

KEY DATES

2002: Simon Cowell forms Syco Music to record acts from *Pop Idol*.

2004: Syco TV launches *The X Factor* on Britain's ITV network.

2005: Cowell sells his stake in Syco to Sony Music for $42 million.

2006: Syco-produced *America's Got Talent* debuts on NBC.

2009: Syco artist Susan Boyle has the fastest-selling debut album in history; Cowell and Sir Philip Green found Greenwell Entertainment.

2010: Syco Entertainment is created as a joint venture with Sony Music Entertainment; Cowell announces plan to quit *American Idol*, bring *X Factor* to United States in 2011.

Pop Idol's second season would be its last, in part because the latest winner had fared poorly on the record charts, but mainly because Cowell had decided to create a talent show of his own.

In the spring of 2004 Syco TV announced it would partner with FremantleMedia unit Thames Television to create a British singing competition called *The X Factor* for ITV. Cowell and two other judges (rock-star-wife-turned-reality TV star Sharon Osbourne and Irish pop group manager Louis Walsh) would mentor the aspiring singers until the final audience vote, with the winner getting a £1 million BMG/Syco record contract. Cowell, now worth a reported £45 million (£20 million derived from his work on *American Idol* alone), had also reportedly signed a £1.25 million, two-year exclusivity contract with ITV in the U.K.

X FACTOR A HIT IN 2004

Debuting in September, *X Factor* quickly proved a huge hit with the British public. Although it differed somewhat from *Pop Idol* in that it was open to both soloists and vocal groups, *Idol* co-creator Simon Fuller's 19 Television sued Syco and Cowell the week it debuted for breaches of contract and copyright.

When the show ended winner Steve Brookstein had a number one hit with a cover of a Phil Collins song (he would be dropped by Syco within three months after clashing with Cowell), and ITV quickly renewed the series for another fall run. Finalists would also tour concert halls under a management deal with Cowell associate Richard Griffiths's Modest! Management.

In the fall of 2004 a new vocal group, Il Divo, debuted on Syco/Sony BMG (the latter two firms having recently merged). Conceived, cast, and produced by Cowell, the group featured four attractive young male vocalists, three of whom had backgrounds in opera, the other in pop. Following Cowell's established pattern of recycling chart-tested older material, their album was a combination of classical pieces and chestnuts such as "My Way" and "You'll Never Walk Alone," plus a handful of new songs, which were sung in three different languages. Although it received scant radio play, Cowell targeted an enthusiastic, largely female audience by taking the group on TV shows such as *Oprah*, and by spring 2005 Il Divo was selling out large concert venues and starting to score chart hits worldwide. In the fall Syco TV also produced a documentary about the band Take That for its 10th anniversary, which received good ratings in Britain and helped sell 1.5 million albums.

In November an out-of-court settlement was reached in the lawsuit filed by 19 Television, with Cowell reportedly ceding one-fifth ownership of *X Factor* to 19, and also agreeing to continue to serve as a judge on the 19 coproduced *American Idol* for five more seasons, while taking a minority ownership stake in it. His fee for that program, for which he had been paid just $100,000 the first season, was now said to be $15 million per year, a figure that was soon expected to rise.

COWELL SELLS SYCO STAKE TO SONY IN 2005

Cowell also decided to sell his 50 percent stake in Simco Ltd./Syco Music to Sony BMG for a reported £45 million, which included his half ownership of *X Factor*. He signed separate five-year deals that gave Fox television in the United States "first look" at any Syco TV productions or Internet/mobile phone content, as well as giving Sony BMG rights to the recordings of artists from the shows. Fox also won Cowell's agreement not to produce *X Factor* in the United States for five years, fearing it would dilute the audience for *Idol*.

In June 2006 Cowell's empire added a potent new franchise when *America's Got Talent* began airing on NBC, after it had been passed on by Fox, which thought it too similar to *Idol* (a pilot had run in the United Kingdom in 2005, but gone no further there). The Syco TV/FremantleMedia coproduction, which was hosted by Regis Philbin and did not include Cowell as a judge, was open to any kind of act, the top prize being $1 million. It proved a sizable summer hit, averaging 12 million viewers, and the preteen winner (who, conveniently, was a singer) was signed to Syco and Sony

BMG unit Columbia. As had happened with *Idol*, the format was soon franchised to dozens of markets around the world via producing partner FremantleMedia.

American TV also saw two other Cowell-generated reality programs bow in 2006, *American Inventor* and *Celebrity Duets* (on ABC and Fox, respectively). Neither had staying power. A U.K. version of the latter was being prepared, as well, but was halted in court by the BBC, which had acquired a similar program. Despite the recent uptick in activity, Syco still had a staff of just eight, and its offices remained housed in the London headquarters of Sony BMG.

In late 2006 Syco hired former FremantleMedia managing director Simon Jones to serve as senior vice president of operations and international sales. He had helped sell the original *Pop Idol* and built its international franchise. Cowell also signed a new three-year, £20 million deal with ITV, which made him Britain's top-earning TV star. He was committed to three more *X Factor* series, as well as the forthcoming *Britain's Got Talent* and other programs yet to be announced. His take in the United States was now an estimated $45 million a year, second only to Oprah Winfrey for a TV performer.

At year's end the winner of the 2006 *X Factor* in the United Kingdom, Leona Lewis, was another huge success for Syco, with her debut release topping the crucial Christmas sales chart with "A Moment Like This," the same song *Idol* winner Kelly Clarkson had debuted with. By this time Syco artists recruited from *Idol* had sold 50 million records, while Il Divo's two albums had sold 11 million. Cowell claimed that Syco now accounted for 40 percent of Sony BMG's profits.

LAUNCH OF *BRITAIN'S GOT TALENT*: 2007

In the fall of 2007 *Britain's Got Talent* debuted, with Cowell on board as a judge, and it proved a major success for ITV. Cowell's other new ITV show, *Grease Is the Word*, which sought to cast the leads for a London production of the musical show, proved a disappointment, however, but the *X Factor* format was thriving, having been sold to 10 countries including Australia, Russia, and Spain. In October it was revealed that thousands of phoned-in votes for 2005 and 2006 *X Factor* shows in the United Kingdom had never been counted, and the callers were reimbursed for the charges accrued. Syco, FremantleMedia, and ITV had shared in the proceeds from the refunded calls, which were worth an estimated £900,000.

For 2007 Cowell earned an estimated $72 million, of which $45 million came from *Idol*, $15 million from the combination of *Britain's Got Talent* and *X Factor*, and another $12 million from recordings. He reportedly owned six lavish homes (two each in the United Kingdom, Los Angeles, and Barbados), an art collection that included several Picassos, and a small fleet of luxury autos that featured an Aston Martin, a Rolls-Royce, a custom Bentley limousine, and a $1.6 million Bugatti.

In early 2008 Leona Lewis became the first British female solo performer to have a number one hit in the United States in over two decades with "Bleeding Love," which also reached the top spot in 20 other countries. Although the top winner on *X Factor* was pledged a £1 million record contract, the British media had recently been reporting that this translated to a £150,000 advance, with the rest consumed by production costs and promotion. Post-show, the touring finalists were also reported to receive just £250 per appearance for concerts that typically filled large stadiums. Prior to the competition they had committed to these and other restrictions in an 80-page contract that also included a clause prohibiting them from criticizing Cowell publicly. He responded to the revelations by noting that the opportunity the show afforded was more than most performers could even dream of.

In June 2009 Cowell partnered with U.K. retail billionaire Philip Green to form a new company called Greenwell Entertainment, which would oversee Cowell's business interests. The two had become friendly in Barbados, where they both had homes. Also during the summer, tracks from several Syco artists were leaked online, allegedly after hackers had retrieved them from company computers. The firm sought help in identifying suspects from the police.

DISCOVERY OF SUSAN BOYLE: 2009

Cowell's success continued unabated in 2009 with the signing of Susan Boyle, a dowdy 48-year-old Scottish church volunteer who lived alone with a cat and had reportedly never been kissed, but who had a distinctive, powerful voice. In April a clip of her audition for *Britain's Got Talent*, which left the judges speechless, was viewed more than 100 million times on YouTube.com (where a delayed deal to include advertising caused Syco, ITV, and FremantleMedia to forfeit significant revenues).

Although she ultimately finished second to a dance troupe, in late November her first album became the fastest-selling debut in U.K. history and dominated the U.S. charts as well as those in 20 other countries. In the United States she was marketed via a special appearance on *America's Got Talent*, interviews with Oprah Winfrey and Larry King, and a TV Guide channel-aired Syco/talkbackThames coproduction, *I Dreamed a Dream: The Susan Boyle Story*, which also ran on ITV in the United Kingdom.

Although *Britain's Got Talent* had become a powerhouse, capturing some 50 percent of the viewing audience for the season finale, *American Idol* was beginning to show signs of age, with ratings dipping 15 percent below the previous year (nonetheless it remained the country's number one show). After Paula Abdul quit to be replaced by comedian Ellen DeGeneres (by then a fourth judge, singer-songwriter Kara DioGuardi, was part of the regular lineup), Cowell announced that the 2010 season would be his last. He planned to launch *X Factor* in the United States in the fall of 2011. The *X* format was now in 17 countries, while Syco's other major TV export, *Got Talent*, was in more than 40 where it was often the top-rated show. Cowell's long-expressed desire to create a music-related feature film had not yet materialized, but he was now reportedly in serious talks to remake the 1970s disco hit *Saturday Night Fever*, as well as considering a film about Boyle.

In October 2009 Cowell celebrated his 50th birthday with a lavish party that featured a host of A-list guests. He was ranked by *Forbes* as the highest-paid man on U.S. television, surpassing Donald Trump with estimated earnings of $75 million (*American Idol* host Ryan Seacrest placed third), and was declared the second highest-paid entertainer behind Oprah Winfrey.

At year's end a Facebook.com campaign to deny Cowell's latest *X Factor* winner the U.K. Christmas number one single succeeded, with a 1993 cut by Rage Against The Machine claiming that distinction via download only. Syco artists had held the highly sought-after spot every year since 2005, but this time Joe McElderry's cover of a Miley Cyrus song took second place. Susan Boyle took the edge off of any disappointment, however, with her album's sales of 8.3 million copies, making it the year's most popular disc worldwide.

FORMING SYCO ENTERTAINMENT JOINT VENTURE WITH SONY

In January 2010 it was announced that a new company called Syco Entertainment, Ltd., was being created as a joint venture between Sony Music Entertainment and Cowell. It would assume ownership of *X Factor*, *Got Talent*, and Syco's other TV formats, as well as the record contracts of Syco's musical acts. A five-year deal was also signed in which Sony would provide funding and get first refusal on all performers that were discovered on

the U.S. version of *X Factor*. Cowell (and minority shareholder Sir Philip Green) would reportedly split ownership 50-50 with Sony, although Cowell would have ultimate control, according to a Sony spokesperson. Publishing/media industry veteran Ellis Watson was named CEO in March, as the firm worked on plans to open an office in Los Angeles.

In February a Cowell-produced all-star cover of REM's "Everybody Hurts" was released in partnership with British tabloid the *Sun*, as a benefit for victims of the devastating earthquake in Haiti. In July it was announced that an *X Factor* magazine would be launched in the fall. In August, 19 Entertainment cut ties with Sony/Syco for *American Idol*, with recordings of future winners to be released by Universal Music.

In less than a decade Simon Cowell had gone from a comfortable position as a British record executive to heading a seemingly invincible worldwide multimedia empire, Syco Entertainment, Ltd., in a joint venture with Sony Music Entertainment. With his successful *X Factor* program set to launch in the United States in the fall of 2011, and the assistance of marketing expert Sir Philip Green, Cowell and Syco appeared to be on the cusp of even greater success.

Frank Uhle

PRINCIPAL DIVISIONS

Syco Music; Syco TV; Syco Film.

PRINCIPAL COMPETITORS

19 Entertainment Ltd.; 3Ball Productions; BBC Worldwide Productions; Bunim-Murray Productions; EMI Group, Ltd.; Magical Elves Productions; Mark Burnett Productions; Universal Music Group; Warner Music Group Corp.

FURTHER READING

Andreeva, Nellie, and James Hibberd, "Cowell Sets 'American Idol' Exit," *Hollywood Reporter*, January 11, 2010.

Arlidge, John, "The XX Factor: TV Star Simon Cowell Is Teaming Up with Sir Philip Green, King of the High Street," *Sunday Times*, June 28, 2009, p. 1.

Caesar, Ed, "Talent-Show Rivals End X Factor Spat with Deal to Split the Proceeds," *Independent*, November 30, 2005.

Carter, Bill, "Here Comes the Judge," *New York Times*, March 12, 2006, p. 1B.

———, "Will Simon Cowell Quit While He's So Far Ahead?" *New York Times*, April 21, 2009, p. 1C.

Cook, Stewart, "The Interview," *Observer*, December 9, 2007, p. 4.

Dunk, Marcus, "Xploitation," *Daily Mail*, January 27, 2009, p. 13.

Pomerantz, Dorothy, "Simon Cowell Got Rich by Appearing on America's Top-Rated TV Show; Can He Build a Business That Will Outlast His Own Fame?" *Forbes*, June 30, 2008, p. 90.

Robertson, Colin, "Interview—The Harshest Critic," *Broadcast*, July 23, 2004, p. 11.

Scott, Paul, "Simon's Xcess Factor," *Daily Mail*, December 23, 2006, pp. 18–19.

Sprague, David, "Judge Still Reigns on Hit Parade," *Daily Variety*, November 19, 2006.

Watts, Mark, "Pop Mogul Pockets £45m After Selling His *X Factor* Stake," *Express on Sunday*, March 26, 2006, p. 1.

Whitington, Paul, "Simon Makes It Simple," *Irish Independent*, December 12, 2009.

The Television Food Network, G.P.

1180 Avenue of the Americas, 11th Floor
New York, New York 10036
U.S.A.
Telephone: (212) 398-8836
Fax: (212) 736-7716
Web site: http://www.foodtv.com

Subsidiary of Scripps Networks Interactive, Inc.
Founded: 1993
Employees: 159
NAICS: 454111 Electronic Shopping; 515210 Cable
    and Other Subscription Programming; 511120
    Periodical Publishers

■ ■ ■

A cable channel that reaches nearly 100 million U.S. households, The Television Food Network, G.P. focuses on food-centered programming to fill its round-the-clock schedule. Shows produced for the network include "stand-and-stir" cooking demonstrations, world cuisine travel programs, chef and restaurateur biographies, and reality-based competitions. Trading on its stable of celebrity chefs, the Food Network has built a brand that includes a Web site, FoodTV.com, and magazine, *Food Network Magazine*. Popular shows include *Emeril Live*, *30-Minute Meals with Rachael Ray*, and *Iron Chef America*.

LAUNCHING A CABLE CHANNEL: 1993

In January 1993, Reese Schonfeld and Providence Journal Company announced a partnership to launch The Television Food Network in the fall. Schonfeld, the founding president and chief executive of CNN, and Providence, the cable arm of Colony Communications, were making a media savvy business move to stake an early claim in the upcoming cable industry boom. New federal regulations in 1992 had opened up the cable market. Cable operators planned to take advantage of subsequent industry changes by increasing their offerings by hundreds of channels.

From the start, the Food Network had a significant leg up on the competition. Providence's market position as a cable broadcaster enabled the network to avoid the biggest hurdle that faced most new cable networks: getting on the air. Among early investors in the Food Network were five major partners: Providence Journal Company, Tribune Broadcasting, Continental Cablevision, Scripps Howard Cable, and Landmark Communications.

In the early days, the Food Network's studio consisted of a one-bedroom apartment on New York's West 57th Street. Six employees worked out of the living room. The former food editor of *Ladies' Home Journal*, Sue Huffman, was vice president in charge of programming. The Food Network's target demographic was 24- to 55-year-old women. Because Food Network executives anticipated having a tough time filling the round-the-clock schedule, they planned to run the same eight hours of programming three times a day. Their 24-hour cycle consisted of six hours of original programming combined with two hours of existing cooking classics.

The new network's programming schedule included "stand-and-stir" cooking demonstrations, food news, and nutrition and fitness information. To entice viewers, many new programs featured hosts with national recognition. In a talk show, Robin Leach (of *Lifestyles of the Rich and Famous* fame) chatted with famous guests about food and took phone calls from viewers. In a cooking show, Jane Curtain (a former *Saturday Night Live* player) introduced vintage cooking programs hosted by famous chefs, including James Beard, Jacques Pepin, Dione Lucas, and Graham Kerr.

The Food Network also took chances with less recognizable talent. Emeril Lagasse, a New Orleans chef, starred in a series called *How to Boil Water*, which focused on cooking basics. *Food News and Views* gave viewers daily updates on foodie trends, government health initiatives, kitchen safety issues, and cookbook launches. While many shows on the network's programming schedule had been done before, the Food Network was unique in that it combined cooking shows with food and health programs all on one entertainment channel.

Because the Food Network was considered experimental media in the cable industry, it was difficult to sell advertising slots before launch. During the first five weeks there were almost no commercials scheduled. The only exception was Campbell Soup Company, which bought advertising at bargain-basement prices for hundreds (and not the usual thousands) of dollars for 30-second spots. The partnership was part of a formula that Food Network executives hoped would provide an alternative to the infomercials other small cable networks relied upon as a way to generate advertising revenue. Instead they opted to gamble running at a deficit for three to four years to build a more respectable brand.

If Food Network investors were thinking strategically from a cable industry business angle, they were also responding to cultural trends demonstrated by market

research. Surveys at the time indicated a growing public interest in cooking programs. In the early 1990s, the U.S. economy was in recession and more people were staying home to cook. Additionally, new concerns about healthy eating and dietary recommendations were raising cultural consciousness about food and food issues. Even the network's launch date was well timed. Food Network executives chose November 23, 1993, Thanksgiving Day. Julia Child, a respected and well-recognized chef, hosted holiday segments to underscore the network's cachet.

MODEST GROWTH: 1993–98

When Food Network launched, its executives projected moderate increases for the next few years. By 1996, the goal was to increase the network's subscriber base to a modest 18 million households and expand its programming from eight to 12 hours. Eighteen months later, in April 1995, the network was well on the way to reaching a subscriber base with 11 million households. Compared to the competition, though, this number was paltry. Moreover, at 0.3 the Food Network was barely a blip on the Nielsen ratings book. According to the data, more than 51 percent of its audience was working women, those 18 and older who worked more than 30 hours per week.

By the fall of 1996, the Food Network had exceeded its first goal, boasting a subscriber base of roughly 20 million. During its first few years, it also significantly increased in size from six to 160 employees. At the time, Emeril Lagasse's show was one of the network's biggest successes. Thanks to his nontraditional approach to cooking (which included yelping with joy and repeating catch phrases like "Bam!" and "Let's kick it up a notch!"), he had attracted a large audience. Network executives credited his popularity for being a large part of the Food Network's growth, along with the leadership of Erica Gruen, the Food Network's president and chief executive. A year later, in 1997, the network launched its Web site FoodTV.com.

Ownership changes at the Food Network in 1997 ushered in significant changes in the coming years. Newspaper publisher E.W. Scripps Company acquired majority control of the Food Network from A.H. Belo Corporation. Little more than a year later, in November 1998, Scripps stepped in and replaced Gruen with Eric Ober, a former Scripps employee and president of CBS. Insiders claimed the move was not a reflection on Gruen's leadership. Under Gruen, the Food Network's subscriber base had jumped from 16 million to 34 million, and its net advertising and Nielsen data had tripled. Instead, industry pundits interpreted Scripps' move as a sign of impatience. The network was still

KEY DATES

1993: Reese Schonfeld and Providence Journal Company launch The Television Food Network.

1995: The network is watched by 11 million U.S. households.

1997: E.W. Scripps Company acquires controlling interest; FoodTV.com is launched.

1999: The Food Network reaches 38.5 million homes; revenues hit $36 million.

2003: The network relocates to Chelsea Market.

2009: Hearst Magazines and Scripps launch *Food Network Magazine*.

2010: The network reaches 100 million homes.

waiting to turn a profit, and Scripps had not yet recouped its initial investment, which was estimated at $100 million to $125 million. While Scripps' business model for the network did not anticipate profitability until 2000 or 2001, Ober was expected to radically alter the Food Network's programming direction in an attempt to speed up the process.

Ober planned a mass-market approach to programming to broaden the network's focus and attract a more mainstream audience. New programs would be more story-oriented, including A&E-style biographies of famous chefs and restaurateurs, documentaries on the history of food, and travel programs that featured world cuisines. To support Ober's changes, Scripps doubled the production budget to $22.5 million and significantly increased the marketing and promotion budgets. Ober planned on making room for new programming by eliminating all reruns.

EXPANDING ITS AUDIENCE: 1999–2002

By March 1999, the Food Network had become a cult favorite, thanks in large part to Lagasse's popularity, as well as other programs such as *Two Fat Ladies* and *Too Hot Tamales*. It had expanded its reach to 38.5 million homes, and revenues had increased to $36 million. In addition to programming changes, the network was also attracting more viewers simply because of a larger market trend. Households had begun purchasing cable as a utility rather than as a luxury item. By mid-October, the network had launched nine additional original series, including a game show, a live cooking show, and a series of documentary specials, and had

debuted more than 1,000 hours of new programming.

Thanks to Ober's newly revamped mix of Hollywood-type entertainment and the network's relentless promotions, by the end of 1999, its revenue had jumped 60 percent and its subscriber base had grown to 43 million. However, it was still struggling to match the success of its competition. Networks such as USA and Home & Garden Television (which had also launched in 1993) boasted much higher subscriber numbers at 70 million and 60 million, respectively. The Food Network's recipe-centered programming still remained the network's backbone, but the style had shifted focus from directions and technique to the host's personality and celebrity. By 2001, Scripps had increased the programming budget by 67 percent, enabling Food Network executives to announce plans for airing 950 hours of original programming for the year. It would continue to diversify its lineup with shows geared toward general-interest audiences rather than foodies and industry professionals.

At its 10-year anniversary, in 2003, the Food Network boasted a considerable audience of more than 79 million subscribers from the United States to as far away as Polynesia. However, its viewership was still low. Nielsen Media Research reported it averaged 621,000 viewers. In comparison, Lifetime averaged 1.8 million and CBS had close to 11 million. It ranked 16th among basic-cable networks with weekly Nielsen ratings of 0.8 households (compared to 0.3 in 1995). Its Web site had about four million users with an archive of 25,000 recipes. The Food Network's reach had extended far beyond its initial 18-plus working female audience to college kids, singles, husbands and wives, and novice cooks and experts. It had tested more than 30,000 recipes and filmed 11,000 cooking shows.

That summer, it relocated its office, studios, and kitchen to the rapidly gentrifying Meat Packing District on New York's 75 Ninth Avenue. Appropriately situated in the West Village's Chelsea Market, which housed fresh food market vendors and fine restaurants, the 110,000-square-foot space was the former Nabisco cookie factory. The new digital/HD-ready facility featured studios, control rooms, audio and video post-production facilities, and included a fully functioning 3,500-square-foot support kitchen.

REDEFINING A GENRE: 2003–06

During its tenure, the Food Network had responded to changing U.S. values. More importantly, it had had an impact upon American culture. Perhaps more than any other media, the Food Network had changed the way Americans looked at the food industry and at chefs.

Shows such as *30-Minute Meals*, which featured a home-taught chef, Rachael Ray, had changed attitudes among viewers about their own ability to become cooks. It had also created the phenomenon of chef celebrities, including Mario Batali and Emeril Lagasse.

However, some industry insiders were not convinced that the radical changes the Food Network had implemented were positive. In a 2003 *Newsday* article, cookbook author and food writer James Villas characterized these changes: "To a certain extent, the network has been dumbed down." He was also bothered by the network's tendency toward "childishness," of which Lagasse was a prime example. However, former Food Network producer Rochelle Brown had a different take on the network's evolution: "They've really got it down to a balance of entertainment as well as being educational," she said in a 2003 *Newsday* article. The network's prime-time hours tended to be dominated by Lagasse and other light fare, while the daytime hours were filled with more traditional recipe shows.

In 2006, Food Network ownership was divided among the original partners: president/founder Reese Schonfeld, Colony Communications, Continental Cablevision, Landmark Communications, Scripps-Howard Cable Company, Tribune Broadcasting, Times Mirror Cable Television, Adelphia Communications, Cablevision Industries, and C-TEC Cable Systems. Scripps held 64 percent, Tribune held 29, and the minority stakeholders owned the remaining seven.

That year, the Food Network seemed to hit its stride with a diverse programming mix of lifestyle, personalities, and food. Its subscriber count topped 90 million. "Reinventing the cooking show is at the core of what has made the network so successful," said Bob Tuschman, Food Network senior vice president of programming, in a 2007 *Television Week* article. "We're a host-based network. People watch our shows because of the personalities." He credited Scripps' management changes in 2001 as the crucial turning point for the network's success: "That's when we launched *30-Minute Meals with Rachael Ray*. ... People instantly responded to her." Finding charismatic chefs was a key to the Food Network's success.

ATTRACTING A WIDER DEMOGRAPHIC: 2007–10

In 2007, the Food Network began undergoing a transformation. Having propelled food and chefs from low-key public television status to new celebrity heights, the network was trying to retain its revenue in the face of increasing competition. At the time, Food Network executives put a positive spin on the network's ratings,

boasting the average prime-time audience in 2007 was at 778,000 viewers, its highest ever. Additionally, its audiences were younger, which was especially attractive to advertisers. However, the network's total-day ratings had dipped to an average of 544,000 viewers, down from 580,000 in 2006. In addition, its signature weekend block of instructional programs, with an audience of 830,000 in 2006, had lost 15 percent of its audience. In December, it canceled *Emeril Live*, a show with an impressive 11-year run that was on the air every weeknight. Industry speculation was that it had become too expensive in light of softening ratings.

Slumping ratings were not the network's only obstacle. It was also attempting to take a broader stake in stars' outside activities. While the Food Network had been adept at creating celebrity chefs including Emeril Lagasse, Rachael Ray, and Paula Deen, it had not set up deals to share in their success beyond the network, such as outside merchandising. The network had begun insisting on a stake in book deals and licensing ventures, as well as control over outside activities. Although some stars accepted these changes, others balked and the network lost talent.

Meanwhile, the network's programming strategy had undergone changes, with a further broadening of the focus away from food itself. In a 2007 *New York Times* article, one of the network's former chefs, Mario Batali, opined: "They have decided they are mass market and they are going after the Wal-Mart crowd," which, he said, was "a smart business decision." While network executives did not view new programming the same way, they did admit that newly launched reality shows, including extreme cake building and extreme cooking shows, were a shift in network offerings.

In October 2008, Hearst Magazines and Scripps (now Scripps Networks Interactive) launched preview versions of *Food Network Magazine*, which officially debuted in May 2009. With tips on saving money at the grocery store and quick weekday recipes, the magazine aimed to appeal to every level of cook. One year after its launch, it was the second-largest foodie title on the market. Media industry pundits chalked its popularity up to its association with the Food Network as a recognizable brand and its stable of celebrity chefs.

By the end of 2009, *Food Network Magazine* had a circulation of one million. It seemed the broadened programming focus the Food Network had introduced in 2007 had started to have a significant impact on its subscribers, with much of the growth coming from younger audiences. Prime-time ratings were up 29 percent. The network's ratings spiked when it sidelined "stand-and-stir" cooking demonstrations from prime time in favor of such competitions as *The Next Food Network Star* and *The Next Iron Chef*. Programmers credited the increase in part to a recessionary trend toward home entertaining with the whole genre of home-focused cable shows benefiting.

By early 2010, Food Network reached almost 100 million U.S. households. Seventy percent of the network was owned by Scripps Networks Interactive with the remaining interest held by Tribune Company. The Web site was also expanding and included an online store that sold kitchenware and cookbooks and boasted an audience of more than 10 million users. It seemed that the Food Network's strategy to serve ever wider audiences would be the key to its continued success.

Carrie Rothburd

PRINCIPAL COMPETITORS

Bravo Company; Discovery Communications, Inc.; Public Broadcasting Service; A&E Television Networks, LLC; Allrecipes.com; America's Test Kitchen; E! Entertainment Television, Inc.; Oxygen Media, LLC; WE: Women's Entertainment LLC.

FURTHER READING

Block, Valerie, "All You Can Watch," *Crain's New York Business*, March 8, 1999, p. 1.

Carter, Bill, "Networks' New Cable Channels Get a Big Jump on the Competition," *New York Times*, March 14, 1994, p. 7.

Eddy, Kristin, "Chefs Right at Home: The Food Network, Now a Decade Old, Has Given Us Culinary Heroes and the Confidence to Star in Our Own Kitchens," *Newsday*, October 29, 2003, p. B6.

Jensen, Elizabeth, "Changing Courses at the Food Network," *New York Times*, December 17, 2007, p. 1.

Kaufman, Debra, "Food Network Grills, Chills, and Thrills; Cable Network Has Recipe for Success as It Reinvents the Cooking Show," *Television Week*, June 4, 2007, p. 14.

McAvoy, Kim, "Food Network," *Broadcasting Cable*, October 11, 1999, p. 42.

Menzie, Karol, "The Food Channel's Recipe for Success," *Sun*, November 21, 1993, p. 10J.

Robichaux, Mark, "They're Playing a Game of Chicken to Decide Who Rules the Roost," *Wall Street Journal*, January 15, 1993, p. B1.

Sagon, Candy, "All Talk, No Cooking; The Food Network Has Been Scrambling to Appeal to People Who Like Looking More Than Cooking," *Washington Post*, April 26, 2000, p. F1.

Texas Instruments
Incorporated

———■———

12500 TI Boulevard
Dallas, Texas 75266
U.S.A.
Telephone: (972) 995-3773
Toll Free: (800) 336-5236
Fax: (972) 927-6377
Web site: http://www.ti.com

Public Company
Incorporated: 1930 as Geophysical Service Inc.
Employees: 26,584
Sales: $10.42 billion (2009)
Stock Exchanges: New York
Ticker Symbol: TXN
NAICS: 334413 Semiconductor and Related Device
    Manufacturing; 335314 Relay and Industrial
    Control Manufacturing

■ ■ ■

Texas Instruments Incorporated (TI) is the fourth-largest semiconductor manufacturer in the world. TI develops and produces analog, digital signal processing, radio frequency, and digital light processing semiconductors, or chips, for consumer and industrial products. The company's products are designed to increase power efficiency and performance and to improve the mobility of electronics products. An important pioneer in the technology sector, TI operates worldwide, maintaining manufacturing facilities in Europe, Asia, South America, and North America.

ORIGINS

The history of Texas Instruments is intimately related to the history of the U.S. electronics industry. TI was one of the first companies to manufacture transistors, and it introduced the first commercial silicon transistors. It was a TI engineer, Jack Kilby, who developed the first semiconductor integrated circuit in 1958, and TI's semiconductor chips helped fuel the modern electronics revolution. (Kilby won a Nobel Prize in 2000 for his contributions.) After a disappointing performance in the 1980s, the corporation abandoned its long-helds but unfulfilled dream of becoming a consumer electronics powerhouse in favor of specialization in high-tech computer components.

TI's roots can be traced to Geophysical Service, a petroleum-exploration firm founded in 1930 by Dr. J. Clarence Karcher and Eugene McDermott. Headquartered in Dallas, Texas, Geophysical Service used a technique for oil exploration developed by Karcher. The technique, reflection seismology, used underground sound waves to find and map those areas most likely to yield oil. When Karcher and McDermott opened a research and equipment manufacturing office in Newark, New Jersey, to keep their research and their seismography equipment operations out of view of competitors, they hired J. Erik Jonsson, a mechanical engineer, to head it.

COMPANY PERSPECTIVES

Texas Instruments serves the world's most innovative electronics companies, helping them develop new ideas that change the way we live. By providing semiconductor technologies that promote greater power efficiency, enable more features, enhance performance and deliver more value, TI expands the possibilities every day for how we learn, connect, grow and discover.

FOCUS ON DEFENSE
CONTRACTS, ELECTRONICS:
1941–51

Toward the end of the 1930s, Geophysical Service began to change its business focus because of the erratic nature of the oil exploration business. The company was reorganized: an oil company, Coronado Corporation, was established in 1939 as the parent company, and a geophysical company, Geophysical Service Inc. (GSI), was formed as a subsidiary. McDermott and Jonsson, along with two other GSI employees, purchased GSI from Coronado in 1941. During World War II, oil exploration continued, and the company also looked for other business opportunities.

The skills GSI acquired producing seismic devices were put to use in the development and manufacture of electronic equipment for the armed services. This experience revealed marked similarities in design and performance requirements for the two kinds of equipment. Jonsson, encouraged by GSI's expansion during the war, helped make military manufacturing a major company focus. By 1942, GSI was working on military contracts for the U.S. Navy and the Army Signal Corps. This represented the beginning of the company's diversification into electronics unrelated to petroleum exploration.

After the war, Jonsson coaxed a young naval officer named Patrick E. Haggerty, a man of exceptional vision, to join GSI. At a time when many defense contractors had shifted their focus from military manufacturing to civilian markets, Haggerty and Jonsson firmly believed that defense contracts would help them establish GSI as a leading-edge electronics company. They won contracts to produce such military equipment as airborne magnetometers and complete radar systems. Haggerty, who was general manager of the Laboratory and Manufacturing (L&M) division, also set about turning GSI into a major electronics manufacturer. He and Jonsson soon

won approval from the board of directors to build a new plant to consolidate scattered operations into one unit. The new building opened in 1947.

By 1951, the L&M division was growing faster than GSI's Geophysical division. The company was reorganized again and renamed General Instruments Inc. Because its new name was already in use by another company, however, General Instruments became Texas Instruments that same year. Geophysical Service Inc. became a subsidiary of TI in the reorganization, which it remained until early 1988, when most of the company was sold to Halliburton Company.

The next major change came late in 1953, when Texas Instruments went public by merging with the almost-dormant Intercontinental Rubber Company. The merger brought TI new working capital and a listing on the New York Stock Exchange and helped fuel the company's subsequent growth. The postwar era was a heady time for Texas Instruments. In 1953 alone, TI acquired seven new companies. Sales skyrocketed from $6.4 million in 1949 to $20 million in 1952 to $92 million in 1958, establishing TI as a major electronics manufacturer.

DEVELOPMENT OF SILICON
TRANSISTOR: 1954

An important factor in TI's astronomical growth in the 1950s was the transistor. In 1952, TI paid $25,000 to Western Electric for a license to manufacture its newly patented germanium transistor. Within two years, TI was mass-producing high-frequency germanium transistors and had introduced the first commercial silicon transistor. The silicon transistor was based on research conducted by Gordon Teal, who had been hired from Bell Laboratories to head TI's research laboratories. Teal and his research team had developed a way to make transistors out of silicon rather than germanium in 1954. Silicon had many advantages over germanium, not least of which was its resistance to high temperatures. The silicon transistor was a critical breakthrough.

It was Patrick Haggerty who was convinced that there was a huge market for consumer products that used inexpensive transistors. In 1954, TI, together with the Regency division of Industrial Engineering Associates, Inc., produced the world's first small, inexpensive, portable radio using the germanium transistors TI had developed. The new Regency Radio was introduced in late 1954 and became the hot gift item of the 1954 Christmas season. The transistor soon usurped the place of vacuum tubes forever.

During all this, Haggerty and Mark Shepherd Jr., then manager of TI's Semiconductor Components divi-

KEY DATES

■

1930: Geophysical Service Inc. (GSI) is founded by J. Clarence Karcher and Eugene McDermott.

1939: Coronado Corporation is formed as a parent company for GSI.

1941: McDermott, J. Erik Jonsson, and two GSI employees purchase GSI from Coronado.

1951: Laboratory and Manufacturing (L&M) division is renamed Texas Instruments Inc. (TI).

1954: Industrial Engineering Associates and TI develop the world's first small portable radio.

1958: TI engineer Jack Kilby creates the first integrated circuit.

1967: TI engineers invent a handheld calculator.

1976: TI introduces an electronic digital watch that retails for $19.95.

1979: Firm begins selling home computers.

2001: Sales and profits drop dramatically due to a fallout in the semiconductor industry.

2009: After recovering from the downturn earlier in the decade, TI suffers from the onset of a global economic crisis.

sion and later chairman of TI, had been trying, with little success, to persuade IBM to make TI a supplier of transistors for its computers. However, Thomas Watson Jr., president and founder of IBM, was impressed with the Regency Radio, and in 1957 IBM signed an agreement that made TI a major component supplier for IBM computers. In 1958, Patrick Haggerty was named to succeed Jonsson as president.

From 1956 to 1958, Texas Instruments' annual sales doubled from $46 million to $92 million. In 1957, TI opened its first manufacturing facility outside the United States: a plant in Bedford, England, to supply semiconductors to Britain and Western Europe. In 1959, TI's merger with Metals and Controls Corporation, a maker of clad metals, control instruments, and nuclear fuel components and instrument cores, gave TI two U.S. plants as well as facilities in Mexico, Argentina, Italy, Holland, and Australia.

THE INTEGRATED CIRCUIT: 1958

One of Texas Instruments' most important breakthroughs occurred in 1958 when a newly hired employee, Jack S. Kilby, came up with the idea for the first integrated circuit. The integrated circuit was a pivotal innovation. Made of a single semiconductor material, it eliminated the need to solder components together. Without wiring and soldering, components could be miniaturized, which allowed for more compact circuitry and also meant huge numbers of components could be crowded onto a single chip.

To be sure, there were manufacturing problems to be overcome. The chips had to be produced in an entirely dust-free environment; an error-free method of "printing" the circuits onto the silicon chips had to be devised; and miniaturization itself made manufacturing difficult. Texas Instruments, however, realized the chip's potential and, after two years of development, the company's first commercial integrated circuits were made available in 1960. Although the electronics industry initially greeted the chip with skepticism, integrated circuits became the foundation of modern microelectronics. Smaller, lighter, faster, more dependable, and more powerful than its predecessors, the chip had many advantages. However, it was expensive, $100 for small quantities in 1962. Integrated circuits were nonetheless ideally suited for use in computers. Together, chips and computers experienced explosive growth.

Semiconductors quickly became a key element in space technology, too, and early interest by the military and the U.S. space program gave TI and its competitors the impetus to improve their semiconductor chips and refine their production techniques. Under Kilby, TI built the first computer to use silicon integrated circuits for the air force. Demonstrated in 1961, this 10-ounce, 600-part computer proved that integrated circuits were practical.

Chip prices fell to an average of $8 per unit by 1965, making the circuits affordable enough to use in consumer products. Another important breakthrough came in 1969, when IBM began using integrated circuits in all its computers. Soon the government was no longer TI's main customer, although defense electronics remained an important part of its business. Within 10 years of Kilby's discovery, semiconductors had become a multibillion-dollar industry. Early on, TI's management anticipated a huge worldwide demand for semiconductors, and in the 1960s the company built manufacturing plants in Europe, Latin America, and Asia. TI's early start in these markets gave the company an edge over its competitors.

In 1966, Haggerty was elected chairman of TI's board when Jonsson left to become mayor of Dallas. Haggerty had already challenged a team of engineers to develop a new product, the portable, pocket-sized calculator, to show that integrated circuits had a place in the consumer market. In 1967, TI engineers invented a prototype handheld calculator that weighed 45 ounces.

It was four years before the handheld calculator hit the stores, but once it did, it made history. Within a few years, the once-ubiquitous slide rule was obsolete.

FORAY INTO THE CONSUMER ELECTRONICS INDUSTRY: 1970

In 1970, TI invented the single-chip microprocessor, or microcomputer, which was introduced commercially the next year. It was this breakthrough chip that paved the way not only for small, inexpensive calculators but also for all sorts of computer-controlled appliances and devices. TI formally entered the consumer-electronics calculator market in 1972 with the introduction of a four-ounce portable calculator and two desktop models, which ranged in price from $85 to $120. Sales of calculators soared from about three million units in 1971 to 17 million in 1973, 28 million in 1974, and 45 million in 1975.

Despite this early success, TI was to learn many bitter lessons about marketing to the U.S. consumer. Even early success was hard won. Bowmar Instruments had been selling a calculator that used TI-made chips since 1971. In 1972, when TI entered the calculator market and tried to undercut Bowmar's price, Bowmar quickly matched TI and a price war ensued. TI subscribed to learning-curve pricing: Keep prices low (and profits small) in the early stages to build market share and develop manufacturing efficiencies, and then competitors who want to enter the market later will find it difficult or impossible to compete. After a few years, competitors did begin to make inroads into TI's business. By 1975, as increased competition in the market led to plummeting prices; the calculator market softened, leading to a $16 million loss for TI in the second quarter.

However, TI rebounded and again sent shockwaves through the consumer-electronics world in 1976 when it introduced an inexpensive, reliable electronic digital watch for a mere $19.95. Almost overnight, TI's watches grabbed a large share of the electronic watch market at the expense of long-established watch manufacturers. A little more than a year later, TI cut the price of its digital watch to $9.95.

A QUICK EXIT FROM WATCH PRODUCTION: 1981

When low-cost Asian imports flooded the market in 1978, however, TI began to lose its dominant position. TI also failed to capitalize on liquid crystal display (LCD) technology, for which it held the basic patent. It had not anticipated strong consumer demand for LCD

watches, which displayed the time continuously rather than requiring the user to push a button for a readout. When sales of LCD watches exploded, TI could not begin mass production quickly enough. The company's digital watch sales dropped dramatically in 1979. By the end of 1981 TI had left the digital watch business.

Meanwhile, in TI's mainstay business, semiconductor manufacturing, orders for chips became backlogged. TI had spread its resources thinly in order to compete in both the consumer and industrial markets, and worldwide chip demand had soared at the same time. Despite these problems, TI grew at a rapid rate during the 1970s. Defense electronics continued to be highly profitable and semiconductor demand remained strong, buoyed by the worldwide growth in consumer-electronics manufacturing. The company reached $1 billion in sales in 1973, $2 billion in 1977, and $3 billion in 1979.

Mark Shepherd was named chairman of the board upon Patrick Haggerty's retirement in 1976, and J. Fred Bucy, who had worked in almost all of TI's major business areas, was named president and remained chief operating officer. Haggerty continued as general director and honorary chairman until his death in 1980.

In 1978, TI introduced Speak & Spell, an educational device that used TI's new speech-synthesis technology, which proved quite popular. That same year, TI was held up as *Business Week*'s model for U.S. companies in the 1980s for its innovation, productivity gains, and phenomenal growth and earnings records.

ENTRY INTO PERSONAL COMPUTER MARKET: 1979

In mid-1979, TI introduced a home computer that reached the market in December. Priced at about $1,400, the machine sold more slowly at first than TI had predicted. In 1981, sales began to pick up, and a rebate program in 1982 kept sales, and sales predictions, very strong. In April 1983, TI shipped its one millionth home computer.

Suddenly, however, sales of the TI-99/4A fell off dramatically. By October, TI's overconfident projections and failure to predict the price competitiveness of the market had driven the company out of the home computer business altogether. By the time the 99/4A was withdrawn from the market, TI's usual competitive-pricing strategy had reduced the computer's retail price below the company's production cost, causing TI's first loss ever, $145 million, in 1983.

TI's consumer electronics never managed to become a consistent moneymaker. The company was often accused of arrogance, of trying to find mass markets for new TI inventions rather than adapting its product lines to accommodate customers' needs. In addition, TI's pursuit of both consumer and industrial markets often caused shortages of components resulting in backlogged or reduced shipments.

TRIMMING THE WORKFORCE: 1980–82

After experiencing its first loss, TI found regaining its footing difficult. A slump in semiconductor demand during the recession of the early 1980s made TI's heavy losses in home computers particularly painful. Cost-cutting became a high priority, and TI trimmed its workforce by 10,000 employees between 1980 and 1982. In addition, management decided that its matrix management structure was strangling the company and so began to modify the system to revive innovation. Although the company's engineers continued to lead the semiconductor field in innovations, increased competition both in the United States and overseas meant that technological superiority was no longer a guarantee of success. The company recorded another $100 million-plus loss in 1985.

TI President Fred Bucy was roundly criticized for being abrasive and autocratic, and the disappointments of the early 1980s hastened his departure. In May 1985, Bucy abruptly retired and Jerry Junkins was elected president and CEO. Junkins, a lifetime TI employee with a much cooler and more conciliatory management style, proved a popular chief executive.

TI's aggressive defense of its intellectual property rights highlighted activities in the late 1980s. In 1986, TI filed suit with the International Trade Commission against eight Japanese semiconductor manufacturers, and one Korean firm, who were selling dynamic random-access memories (DRAMs) in the United States without obtaining licenses to use technology that belonged to TI. TI reached out-of-court settlements with most of the companies but, more importantly, demonstrated that infringements on its patents would not be tolerated. Royalties from these decisions proved an important source of revenue (over $250 million annually) for TI.

TI COLLABORATES WITH HITACHI: 1988

In late 1988, Texas Instruments announced plans to join Japan's Hitachi, Ltd., in developing 16-megabit DRAM technology. Although this decision came as quite a surprise to the electronics industry, given TI's successful Japanese subsidiary and its manufacturing plant there, TI explained that the move was necessary to spread the mounting risks and costs involved in producing such an advanced chip.

Back in 1977, TI had boldly set itself a sales goal of $10 billion by 1989. Not long after, it upped the ante to $15 billion by 1990. The company actually entered the 1990s some $9 billion short of that extraordinary goal. After watching its share of the semiconductor market slide from 30 percent to a meager 5 percent over the course of the decade, Junkins took a decisive step. In 1989, the CEO inaugurated a strategic plan to radically reshape Texas Instruments, dubbed "TI 2000."

A key aspect of the plan was to loosen the corporation's traditionally tight corporate culture and encourage innovation. This fundamental change was intimately linked to a shift in manufacturing focus from low-cost, commodity-based computer chips to high-margin, custom-designed microprocessors and digital signal processors. For example, in 1989 TI embarked on a partnership with Sun Microsystems Inc. to design and manufacture microprocessors, sharing engineering personnel and proprietary technology in the process. TI garnered vital contracts with Sony Corporation, General Motors Corporation, and Swedish telecommunications powerhouse L.M. Ericsson.

The company promoted its repositioning with new business-to-business advertising. From 1988 to 1993, the specialty components segment increased from 25 percent of annual sales to nearly 50 percent. In 1993, Junkins told *Business Week* that TI was "looking for shared dependence" in these partnerships. He also hoped to parlay technological gains into mass sales.

REBOUNDING UNDER THE TI 2000 PLAN: 1990–99

Under Junkins, TI also increased its global manufacturing capacity through a number of joint ventures in Europe and Asia. A 1990 partnership with the Italian government allowed the shared construction expenses of a $1.2 billion plant. In 1991, the firm joined with Canon, Hewlett-Packard, and the Singapore government to construct a semiconductor facility in Singapore. By 1992, TI had forged alliances with Taiwanese manufacturer Acer, Kobe Steel in Japan, and a coterie of companies in Singapore. TI planned to invest $1 billion in Asian plants by the end of the decade. Joint ventures with Samsung Electronics Co., Ltd., and Hitachi, Ltd., in 1994 split the costs of building semiconductor plants in Portugal and the United States, respectively. TI 2000 also set a goal of increasing the company's high-margin software sales five times, to $1 billion, by the mid-1990s.

Although Texas Instruments recorded net losses in 1990 and 1991, the company's sales and profits rebounded in 1992 and 1993. Profitability, in terms of sales per employee, increased dramatically from $88,300 in 1989 to $143,240 in 1993. In 1992, the firm won the coveted Malcolm Baldrige National Quality Award in manufacturing and adopted the Baldrige criteria as its quality standards. Wall Street noticed the improved performance: TI's stock price more than doubled from 1991 to early 1993.

The firm continued to develop new products, invest in strategic alliances, and divest noncore, slow-growth businesses. In 1994, it launched the multimedia video processor, the first single chip processor to become available commercially that combined multiple parallel DSP and RISC chips. The following year, it won both the prestigious Singapore Quality Award and the European Quality Award. It was during this period that the company began to focus on DSP chips, which could convert analog signals into digital form in real time. Eyeballing the market as a lucrative growth avenue, TI invested heavily in this area. During the 1990s, DSP chips began to be used in such products as modems, cellular phones, personal computer (PC) market peripherals, and television sets. By 1997, TI controlled 45 percent of the market.

RESHAPING TI AT THE MILLENNIUM

While TI worked hard to get itself back on track in the 1990s, it continued to face hardships. During 1996, the price of its memory chips dropped by nearly 80 percent. Then, during an overseas business meeting in May, Junkins died suddenly of heart failure. Longtime TI employee Tom Engibous took over as president and CEO and stepped up the company's acquisition and divestiture plan. In 1997, several of the firm's business units were sold, including Defense Systems & Electronics, Mobile Computing, Software, MulTIpoint Systems, Inspection Equipment, the Mold Manufacturing businesses, the Chemical Operations department, the Telecommunications Systems division, and the Power semiconductor unit. The company also made several key acquisitions including Intersect Technologies, Amati Communications Corp., and GO DSP Corp.

When questioned about the company's rapid movements in a 1997 *Electronic Business* article, Engibous commented "a tragedy like that," referring to Junkins's death, "causes you to spend time reflecting. We concluded that what we were doing was in the right direction, but we thought we needed to do it at a much more rapid pace." As such, the company continued to acquire firms related to its DSP focus including Spec-

tron Microsystems, Adaptec Inc., Oasix Corp., and Arisix Corp. TI also sold its memory chip business to Micron Technologies Inc. for $880 million.

The acquisitions continued into the following year. TI added Butterfly VLSI Ltd., Integrated Sensor Solutions, Telogy Networks, ATL Research A/S, Libit Signal Processing Ltd., Unitrode Corp., and Power Trends to its arsenal. The firm continued to develop new products as well, including a DSP chip that facilitated high-speed Internet access. Along with leading the DSP market with a 48 percent share, TI held the top position in the analog semiconductor market for the second year in a row. All in all, TI launched 191 analog products in 1999, nearly seven times more than it developed in 1996.

TI entered the new millennium on solid ground. The company's financial performance appeared to be back on track with revenues of $11.8 billion and profits of $2.7 billion. During 2000, the firm purchased Toccata Technology ApS, Burr-Brown Corp., Alantro Communications, and Dot Wireless Inc. It also formed a partnership with Qualcomm Inc. in which both companies were allowed to supply integrated circuits for all wireless standards without infringing on patent rights. TI partnered with four China-based manufacturers to develop and distribute wireless handsets and consumer electronics. The company also teamed up with IMAX Corporation to develop digital projectors for movie theaters as well as IMAX theaters. Under the terms of the deal, IMAX became the exclusive licensee of TI's DLP Cinema technology.

The tide quickly changed, however, as 2001 became "the worst year in the semiconductor's history," according to the October 6, 2001 issue of *Business Week Online*. TI's sales plunged nearly 50 percent and the $3 billion the company recorded in net income in 2000 turned into a loss. TI cut costs to weather the storm and, importantly, maintained its research and development spending during the catastrophic start to the decade.

TEMPLETON TAKES CHARGE IN 2004

By the time leadership of the company was handed to Richard K. Templeton in 2004, TI had demonstrated remarkable resiliency. Templeton, who joined TI in 1980, rising to the post of chief operating officer in 2000, inherited control over a company exuding the same financial vibrancy that it had shown in the late 1990s. One month after his appointment as CEO, Templeton had the pleasure to announce a record high sales total of $3.2 billion for the preceding fiscal quarter and a more than threefold increase in net income to $441 million.

Intent on ensuring TI remained the third-largest chipmaker in the world, Templeton devised his strategy for the years ahead. For the first time since TI's exit from the PC in 1984, the company began to promote itself directly to consumers through a national marketing campaign in 2005. Aping Intel Corporation's effective "Intel Inside" advertising approach, TI paid for nationally broadcast commercials touting the picture quality of televisions using its proprietary digital light-processing (DLP) chips. The campaign was part of Templeton's broader strategy to make TI the premier supplier of chips and technology for a variety of consumer electronics products. "We see a world where every phone call is made across a TI chip, every picture is captured with a TI chip," Templeton said in the August 16, 2004 issue of *Business Week*. "If you weren't working on this 10 years ago, you're coming from way behind."

TI cast a wide net in its strategic plan for the first decade of the 21st century. The company chased numerous markets, leveraging its dominant position in the cellular phone market to develop chips for a broad range of consumer electronics market segments and for medical devices. Profits shot up to $2.3 billion in 2005, as the company used its expertise to distinguish itself in diverse markets. "With multiple customers in multiple markets, we have the advantage, because if one space isn't growing fast, the other is," Templeton said in the November 6, 2006 issue of *Business Week*.

The problem for TI was that by the end of the decade its multifaceted market strategy butted against a formidable barrier. Economic conditions worldwide deteriorated rapidly, stripping any and every semiconductor market of vitality. TI, beset by declining demand and increasing stockpiles of its products, experienced the same pain it had endured at the decade's start. Revenues slumped from $13.8 billion in 2007 to $10.4 billion in 2009. Profits fell as well, dropping from $2.6 billion to $1.4 billion during the period. TI's stature waned too, as the company was overtaken by Toshiba Corporation in 2008, when it dropped a position to become the fourth-largest semiconductor

company in the world. TI ended the decade with a smaller revenue volume than it had at the start of the decade, confronted with another crisis it had to endure to remain a leader in a dynamic, highly competitive industry.

Updated, April Dougal Gasbarre;
Christina M. Stansell; Jeffrey L. Covell

PRINCIPAL SUBSIDIARIES

Benchmarq Microelectronics Corporation of South Korea; Burr-Brown International Holding Corporation; Butterfly Communications Inc.; Integrated Circuit Designs, Inc.; Luminary Micro Asia Limited (Hong Kong); Luminary Micro Europe Limited (UK); Texas Instruments International (Overseas) Limited (UK); Texas Instruments Semiconductor Technologies (Shanghai) Co., Ltd. (China); Texas Instruments Semiconductores e Tecnologias Ltda. (Brazil); Texas Instruments Singapore (Pte) Ltd.; Texas Instruments Taiwan Ltd.; TI Europe Limited (UK) Texas Instruments Limited; Unitrode Corporation.

PRINCIPAL COMPETITORS

Intel Corporation; Samsung Electronics Co., Ltd.; ST-Microelectronics N.V.; Toshiba Corporation.

FURTHER READING

Boitano, Margaret, "Burn, Baby, Burn," *Fortune*, March 20, 2000, p. 254.

Josifovska, Svetlana, "Deep in the Heart of Texas Instruments," *Electronic Business*, October 2000, p. 116.

Kharif, Olga, "Texas Instruments' Long Road Back," *Business Week*, October 26, 2001.

Park, Andrew, "For Every Gizmo, a TI Chip," *Business Week*, August 16, 2004, p. 52.

Ristelhueber, Robert, "Texas Tornado," *Electronic Business*, December 1997, p. 35.

"TI, IMAX Partner," *Dallas Business Journal*, June 9, 2000, p. 20.

"To See Where Tech Is Headed, Watch TI," *Business Week*, November 6, 2006, p. 74.

Williams, Elisa, "Mixed Signals," *Forbes*, May 28, 2001, p. 80.

Thai Airways
International Public
Company Limited

—————— ■ ——————

89 Vibhavadi-Rangsit Road
Bangkok, 10900
Thailand
Telephone: (662) 545-1000
Toll Free: (800) 426-5204
Fax: (662) 545-3322
Web site: http://www.thaiairways.com

Public Company
Incorporated: 1947 as Thai Airways Company
Employees: 26,897
Sales: THB 163.88 billion (2009)
Stock Exchanges: Bangkok
Ticker Symbol: THAI
NAICS: 481111 Scheduled Passenger Air Transportation; 481112 Scheduled Freight Air Transportation; 481211 Nonscheduled Chartered Passenger Air Transportation

■ ■ ■

Thai Airways International Public Company Limited is Thailand's flag carrier, and one of its most influential companies. It is an example of the growing success and significance of Asian national carriers, which have carved a niche in ferrying industrial goods from the Far East to Western markets and in serving Western business and leisure travelers. Thailand's strategic location and enduring popularity as one of the most popular tourist destinations in the world ensure the carrier a central role in the Asian air travel market. Thai is a member of the Star Alliance and has code-share arrangements with dozens of airlines. The carrier flies more than 18 million passengers a year and has been eager to grow its relatively small air cargo operation.

ORIGINS

Airplanes were seen over the Thai capital of Bangkok as early as 1911, but it was not until 1947 that the government of Thailand established a national airline, Thai Airways Company. The country had recognized a need for such an airline network during post-World War II reconstruction. Until then, rivers and canals had been the traditional mode of transportation. The postwar years saw these replaced by highways and roads as main transport arteries, and the aviation industry developing worldwide at the time not surprisingly also had an impact on Thailand.

The original fleet of Thai Airways Company was a modest affair: three DC-6 prop-jets, each with 70 seats. Thai Airways' first head office in Bangkok was situated on New Road, directly across from the main post office. From these headquarters passengers could purchase tickets to nine domestic destinations, including the jungle resorts of Chiang Mai in the North, Lampang in the center of the country, and the pristine beaches of Hat Yai to the south.

In 1954 the Thai government identified 130 airfields throughout the country, 104 of which were functional. Thailand's main airport was Don Maung, outside Bangkok. Thai Airways expanded abroad in 1959 with the help of Scandinavian airline SAS, which assumed a 30 percent shareholding in a new subsidiary, Thai Airways International Ltd. SAS brought technical

COMPANY PERSPECTIVES

The new corporate vision statement, "The First Choice Carrier: Smooth As Silk. First Time. Every Time," is becoming a reality by establishing a common direction, cooperation, and sense of purpose throughout the company.

and managerial expertise and its old propeller planes to the fledgling national carrier. In return, SAS was awarded landing rights in Hong Kong.

Approximately 83,000 passengers were carried to nine Asian destinations in 1960, the first year of Thai's service. Routes included those from Bangkok to Calcutta, India, via Rangoon, Burma; Bangkok to Tokyo via Hong Kong and Taipei, Taiwan; and flights to Phnom Penh, Cambodia; Saigon, Vietnam; Kuala Lumpur, Malaysia; and Singapore. The airline's staff numbered 477. That year its pilots flew a total of 8,147 hours.

Thai owed much to its unique location. At the crossroads between East and West, North and South, Thailand was a sought-after stopover on numerous flights by airlines from around the world, a situation that afforded the airline considerable leverage in securing reciprocal landing rights in European and North American airports. Even into the 1990s, Thai remained in a strong bargaining position: long-range jumbo jets flying from Europe could skip India or the Middle East on their way to Australia, but they would need to refuel in either Bangkok or its rival Singapore.

In 1964 Thai added a Caravelle SE-210 jet aircraft to its fleet, which allowed the first scheduled service to Osaka, Japan; Kathmandu, Nepal; and Bali, Indonesia. The aircraft was able to fly between Bangkok and Hong Kong without refueling. It carried 72 passengers and had a takeoff weight of 48 tons.

ROMANCING TOURISTS

By the mid-1960s Thailand had become a tourist destination for Westerners traveling in Asia. The lure of the Orient was clear to Thai's founders. They recognized that the development of the company's regional route network would depend on access to tourist destinations both in Thailand and throughout Asia. The airline did its best to promote these locales, investing in advertising and public relations. Colorful pamphlets encouraged tour operators and travel writers to visit Asian resorts, and word of mouth in turn inspired other wayfarers to make the trip.

In 1969 the company entered the packaged holiday market with Royal Orchid Holidays, offering the flexibility of individually planned tour itineraries combined with the cost savings usually found only in large group tours. Thai did not, however, want to replace the travel agent, who traditionally sold tours to travelers; nor did it wish to replace tour operators in the field, who looked after travelers once they arrived at each of their tour destinations. Instead, Thai operated as the middleman, bringing travelers and tour operators together, thus putting more people on its planes. By 1972 Thai was ranked 44th among the world's international airlines, one place behind rival Philippine Airlines.

To emphasize the romance of the Orient, Thai's air hostesses began wearing traditional Thai silk costumes. Western airlines had been known to criticize their Asian counterparts for exploitation of their hostesses, who, it was charged, were required to maintain a submissive role (traditional in some Asian cultures) in order to offer what the airline perceived as first-rate cabin service. Although space limitations in cabins prohibited traditional costumes by the 1990s, by which time hostesses had switched to more comfortable two-piece silk uniforms, the philosophy persisted. In October 1991 airline President Kaset Rojananil announced a change in hiring policy at the airline: an applicant's physical beauty would be weighed before her educational qualifications. "Intelligent women tend not to be good-looking," he noted, according to *AsiaWeek*. Kaset, also a military general and member of the junta then ruling Thailand, maintained that applicants should be screened "the way beauty pageant judging panels select contestants."

COMPETING FOR MARKET SHARE

Beginning in the late 1960s, Thai also benefited greatly from Asians increasingly traveling to the West. Despite the twin oil shocks of the 1970s, the number of Asians traveling to the West grew by an average of 17 percent a year during the decade. The airline carried 1.31 million passengers to 26 destinations in 1976 alone. By the mid-1970s, Thai's staff had grown to 4,631, making the airline one of the nation's largest employers. Vacancies for cabin hostesses and stewards routinely elicited thousands of inquiries.

The 1981–82 world recession, however, had a dampening effect, bringing growth in passenger numbers down to 10 percent during those years. Passenger traffic to Asia was encouraged by the success of James Clavell's popular novel *Shogun* and the completion of the Tokyo Disneyland, which attracted six million visitors in its first six months of business, in 1981.

KEY DATES

1947: Thai Airways Company is established by government of Thailand.
1959: SAS acquires a strategic stake in new subsidiary, Thai Airways International Ltd.
1988: Thai International merges with Thai Airways.
1993: Thai International floats 10 percent of shares on the Bangkok Stock Exchange.
1997: Thai becomes fully privatized, joins Star Alliance.
2003: Government reduces shareholding to 67 percent after Thai posts record profits in midst of global aviation downturn.
2006: Suvarnabhumi International Airport opens in Bangkok.

As a state-owned airline, Thai was also charged with flying the national flag and acting as an overseas ambassador for Thailand. This included sponsoring leading Thai artists appearing overseas, including musicians and classical dance troupes. Beginning in the 1970s, the growing airline also began supporting community efforts in the region. In 1979, for example, the airline initiated the Asian SAE Write Awards to promote Asian literature.

Aside from establishing international goodwill, these efforts sent a message to Thai competitors that the airline would pursue every avenue to establish dominance in the region. U.S.-based airlines, such as Northwest Orient, Pan American, and United, also expanded into Asia in the 1970s. Regional rivals Singapore Airlines, Philippine Airlines, and Japan Air Lines Co., which were government-owned, were also competing ferociously for market share in the key corridor between London and Sydney and on the Bangkok-Tokyo route.

MODERNIZING AND DIVERSIFYING

Part of Thai's success was attributed to the quality of its in-flight meals. By the early 1990s Thai's flight kitchen at Don Maung Airport catered to 44 international airlines stopping over in Bangkok. In 1980 the airline established Air Lanka Catering Services Ltd., a 50-50 joint venture with Air Lanka to develop and operate a modern flight kitchen in Colombo, Sri Lanka. A decade later, Thai established Phuket Air Catering Co. Ltd., in which it held a 25 percent stake in partnership with the Phuket Pearl Hotel. The facility served 2,500 meals daily to flights moving through Phuket, in southern Thailand.

Another extension of the airline was its supply of aviation fuel. In 1983 Thai established Bangkok Aviation Fuel Services Ltd. (BAFS) at Don Maung Airport. The carrier took a 32 percent stake of BAFS, which operated from a depot near the airport housing storage tanks containing 51 million liters of jet fuel. Underground pipes from the depot to aircraft parking bays carried the fuel to customers. As an offshoot of BAFS, Thai in 1990 launched Fuel Pipeline Transportation Ltd. in partnership with Thailand's state-owned oil enterprises and various multinational oil companies. The aim of the new company was to improve fuel distribution by constructing a 68-kilometer pipeline from the oil refinery and depot at Bangchak and Chongnonsee, in Bangkok's dock area, to Don Maung Airport.

Thai also made inroads into the hotel business. In 1983 it obtained a 24 percent stake in the 775-room Royal Orchid K Hotel in central Bangkok. It also maintained a 40 percent stake in the 440-room Bangkok Airport Hotel, adjacent to Don Maung Airport.

Cargo was also another key element of the airline's business. In 1985 the carrier built a 14-acre "Cargo Village," in which goods scheduled for shipment to Europe, North America, and other parts of Asia were stored. Thai could carry up to 700 tons of cargo on flights to any of its 13 European destinations. The airline boasted that fresh orchids and popular tropical fruits such as rambutan and pineapple could be delivered to Don Maung Airport late in the afternoon and appear on store shelves in London or Paris the following afternoon. Cargo growth significantly fueled revenue for Thai. The airline recorded revenues of THB 12.6 million in 1981 and THB 23.8 million in 1986 before posting a record revenue base of THB 51.9 million in 1991.

Products for export (including textiles, VCRs, fashion products, and high-tech manufacturing tools) were also being increasingly shipped to global destinations, and promoted, by Thai Airway. The importance of such flights grew as companies worldwide adopted just-in-time inventory control.

LINGERING MILITARY INFLUENCE

In 1988 Chatichai Choonhavan's new administration installed air force generals at the top posts of the airline. This ushered in a period of corruption and diminished international stature that would be widely criticized in

Western media. In April, Thai International merged with Thai Airways, its onetime corporate parent.

By 1990 Thai was carrying just over 8.1 million passengers yearly and counted a staff of 18,272. The carrier's pilots flew 143,032 hours that year on 60 jet aircraft. The fleet included four 747-400 jets and six 747-200 jets. Thai Airways posted a profit of $139 million in fiscal 1990. However, the *Far Eastern Economic Review* reported that creative accounting disguised what was in fact the company's first loss in 20 years.

With an eye toward future growth, Bangkok planned to build a new airport at Don Maung scheduled to open in 2000, when more than 20 million travelers were expected. This venture prompted massive investment, including purchasing 27 new jet aircraft between 1992 and 1996. Thai's staff in this period was expected to increase from roughly 18,000 to 30,000 employees. To fund this expansion, the airline announced in January 1992 that it would list 20 percent ownership of the company on the Bangkok Stock Exchange. By turning to the private sector, Thai Airways International signaled a move away from full state control, a direction mirrored in the early 1990s across the airline industry as alliances and mergers between competing airlines proliferated.

In testament to its growing importance in Thai society, the airline began hosting a number of national events. In 1991 these included Bangkok's bicentennial celebrations, Visit Thailand Year, and Arts & Crafts Year. The following year saw Thai host Thailand's National Heritage Year. Among the sports events the company began sponsoring annually were the Professional Golf Association's Thai Open and Ladies' Open. The airline also continued to host a number of international tennis competitions.

CHANGES FOLLOWING COUP

In 1991, a military coup overthrew Chatichai Choonhavan. Military-sponsored candidates won their elections, and students were shot at subsequent pro-democracy protests in Bangkok in May. After five years of Thai Air Force control, a mostly civilian board was appointed in September 1992. Finance Ministry official Pandit Bunyapana replaced Gun Pimarnthip as chairman, while Chatrachai Bunyananta replaced as president another air force general, Air Chief Marshal Veera Kitchathorn, who had been implicated in the May killings. Chatrachai was a 20-year company veteran who had worked his way up the ranks and was credited with much of the airline's success in the mid-1980s. The new leadership effected a modest turnaround nearly immediately.

Chatrachai's work involved a complete restructuring in order to compete with the megacarriers venturing into Thai airspace. The airline needed to standardize its fleet; 18 different types were too many to maintain efficiently. Dispatch reliability proved a persistent problem due to the lack of cash for buying suitable equipment. The company's planes were typically only operated four or five hours per day, less than half the rates achieved by other airlines.

Some lackluster international routes, such as Seattle and Toronto, were dropped. The domestic market proved most unprofitable, thanks to impossibly low government-mandated fares. Years of nepotism had also helped swell the company's roster to 20,000, providing another target for cutbacks.

A PUBLIC COMPANY IN 1993

The company launched a successful initial public offering (IPO) in early 1993. Approximately 10 percent of the company's ownership went up for sale. Plans to offer another 10th of the shares were soon put into place, but they were quashed by profits that did not meet expectations. In fact, in July 1996, the government canceled the airline's refleeting program. Nonetheless, management persisted in lobbying for ways to reduce government ownership of the carrier. Nevertheless, upon the resignation of Amaret Sila-on in 1995, Air Chief Marshal Siripong Thongyai assumed command of the airline, which seemed to reverse the company's progression into professional management.

Thai International was again accepting aircraft deliveries in late 1997, necessitating more capital investments. The company finally became 100 percent publicly traded. In order to escape the crowded and expensive Bangkok International Airport, the company built a $120 million maintenance facility, the Thai Aircraft Engineering Service Co. Ltd., in the Gulf of Thailand.

After weathering coups, government meddling, and the other, less exotic factors that made managing airlines a challenge, Thai International managed to regain a measure of international prestige. An agreement between Thai International and Lufthansa developed into the powerful Star Alliance, which also included Air Canada, United Airlines, and SAS. In November 1998 the company was named one of the world's top 10 airlines by *Condé Nast*. It was not immune to tragedy, however, as one of the carrier's Airbus 310s crashed one month later, killing 101 people and injuring 45. The crash was attributed to severe weather and pilot disorientation. Singapore Airlines and Lufthansa planned to buy shares of Thai Airways in 1999, in order to counter the overtures of British Airways and Qantas into the Asian market.

Thai currency values collapsed in July 1997 at the beginning of the Asian financial crisis. However, the airline took in most of its revenues from foreign currencies. By 2000 Thai was expanding its network again.

PROFITABLE DESPITE SHORTCOMINGS

The carrier operated an unusually diverse fleet of 79 aircraft. According to press reports, commissions paid to purchasing officers had resulted in not just different makes of plane for the same mission, but multiple engines for individual aircraft types. Meanwhile, the carrier had neglected its computerized reservation systems and in-flight entertainment offerings, diminishing its product in the eyes of the lucrative business-class market.

To many observers, the payrolls seemed bloated, with 26,000 employees, for whom the company provided ample opportunities for overtime and even paid their income tax, a source told the *Asian Wall Street Journal*. The unions successfully prevented Thai Airways from selling off its maintenance and computer units in 1999.

Prime Minister Thaksin Shinawatra, who narrowly missed boarding a plane that had a deadly fire in March 2001, made some critical comments in the press. He installed new directors and named a new chairman. A succession of top executives followed over the next several years.

Thai was laden with debt of THB 151.6 billion and a debt to equity ratio of 11:1. The airline was nonetheless flying profitably in a period that grounded many weaker carriers worldwide. It made a profit of THB 1.9 billion in 2001 and in 2002 posted a record net profit of THB 10.18 billion ($238 million) on flat revenues of THB 129 billion as passenger count reached 18 million.

By the end of 2003 the company was paying dividends again, thanks in part to Thailand's improving national economy, fueled by a fast-growing automotive industry that saw the country as an alternative low-cost manufacturing base to China. While other airlines retrenched in the dismal aviation environment following the September 11, 2001, terrorist attacks on the United States, Thai used the opportunity to purchase used aircraft at low prices.

FURTHER PRIVATIZATION IN 2003

Thai posted a net profit of THB 12.5 billion ($301 million), another record, for the fiscal year ended September 30, 2003, a 22 percent increase despite the impact of SARS. Revenues were up to THB 134.5 billion. The airline carried 17 million passengers during the year. The Thai government reduced its holding from 93 percent to 67 percent in a November 2003 share sale. It had two years earlier decided to go without a strategic partner, that is, a strong foreign airline. Thai had been a member of the Star Alliance, a global airline group, since 1997.

Competition from budget airlines was beginning to eat into Thai's domestic market share. In June 2004 Thai launched its own low-cost carrier, Nok Air, by acquiring a 39 percent holding in its operating company Sky Asia for THB 195 million ($4.8 million). It began with three Boeing 737s leased from Thai.

Thai had in two years reduced the number of domestic routes, most of which were unprofitable to run, from 29 to 13. It had 61 international destinations. The tsunami of December 2004 impacted tourism but in 2005 the airline made an ambitious order for a half-dozen extended-range Boeing 777s worth $1 billion. It also rolled out a new identity program based on the themes High Trust, World Class, and Thai Touch and upgraded its business-class cabins on long-haul flights.

Bangkok's new Suvarnabhumi Airport opened in September 2006. Thai consolidated its international and domestic operations there, but soon returned the domestic services to the older, less expensive Don Muang, reported *Aviation Week & Space Technology*.

In 2006 the airline was expanding connections to India, aiming to grow religious-based travel to important Buddhist sites. Thai launched a nonstop Bangkok-Johannesburg service in 2007. However, the same year saw it retrenching from its nonstop service to Los Angeles and New York.

ADDRESSING CHALLENGES IN A GLOBAL MARKET

The increasingly liberalized world aviation market and new, longer range aircraft made the industry more globally oriented, with carriers such as Emirates poised to poach long-haul traffic, particularly the intercontinental crossings that used Bangkok or Singapore as mere refueling stops.

After posting profit of THB 4.43 billion in 2007, Thai lost THB 21.38 billion ($592.1 million) in 2008 during a global economic downturn, although revenues rose 1.6 percent to THB 200.1 billion. Among the factors making 2008 a disastrous year was a series of political demonstrations that shut down Bangkok airports for a week.

After instituting an emergency turnaround plan, Thai was able to post a THB 7.34 billion profit in 2009, although political disturbances continued into the spring and H1N1 outbreaks disrupted traffic. Revenues slipped 19 percent to THB 163.88 billion and expenses fell 31 percent, mainly due to lower fuel costs. (Thai had little protection from hedging but recovered its costs through fuel surcharges.) The airline carried 18.5 million passengers during the year. Cargo accounted for about one-fifth of revenues. It served 11 domestic and 61 international destinations with a fleet of 91 aircraft, including 6 at Nok Air.

Evidence of a turnaround continued into 2010, with passenger and cargo traffic both up. The airline was preparing to launch a joint venture with Tiger Airways, a low-cost affiliate of Singapore Airlines, in 2011.

Etan Vlessing
Updated, Frederick C. Ingram

PRINCIPAL SUBSIDIARIES

Thai-Amadeus Southeast Asia Co., Ltd. (55%); Donmuang International Airport Hotel Co., Ltd. (40%); Nok Air Co., Ltd. (39%); Suvarnabhumi Airport Hotel Col., Ltd. (30%); Phuket Air Catering Co., Ltd. (30%); Royal Orchid Hotel (Thailand) Plc. (24%); Bangkok Aviation Fuel Services Plc. (23%).

PRINCIPAL DIVISIONS

Passenger Transportation; THAI Cargo; THAI Maintenance; THAI Catering; THAI Ground Services; THAI Ground Support Equipment and Services; THAI Aviation Training; External Customer Services Training.

PRINCIPAL COMPETITORS

AirAsia Berhad; Bangkok Airways Co., Ltd.; Cathay Pacific Airways Limited; China Airlines Co., Ltd.; Emirates.

FURTHER READING

Crispin, Shawn W., "Thai Airways Goes It Alone: The Restructuring of Thailand's National Carrier Has Become a Test of Thai Nationalism; The Government Has Rejected a Foreign Partner but Analysts Think It's Only Postponing the Inevitable," *Far Eastern Economic Review*, July 26, 2001, p. 44.

Cumming-Bruce, Nick, and Umesh Pandey, "Thai Airways Directors Inherit Weakened Firm; Decade of Mismanagement Damaged Airline," *Asian Wall Street Journal*, October 8, 2001, p. 4.

Handley, Paul, "Change of Pilot," *Far Eastern Economic Review*, September 1992, p. 17.

"Have a Pleasant Flight," *AsiaWeek*, October 11, 1991.

Mathews, Neelam, "Matching Moves," *Aviation Week & Space Technology*, August 24, 2009, pp. 41+.

Pandey, Umesh, "Thai Airways Changes Partner Plans; Reversing Policy Seeking Foreign Investor Could Hurt Prospects for Reform," *Asian Wall Street Journal*, May 17, 2001, p. 1.

Perrett, Bradley, "Long-Haul Backtrack: Ultra-Long-Haul Services Aren't Working Out for Thai, and Competition in Australia Is Getting Too Hot," *Aviation Week & Space Technology*, January 22, 2007, p. 37.

Proctor, Paul, "New Chief Acts to End Woes at Thai Airways," *Aviation Week and Space Technology*, November 30, 1992, p. 41.

Putzger, Ian, "Opening Bangkok," *Air Cargo World*, December 2003, pp. 18–19.

Stanley, Bruce, "For Thai Airways, the Journey to Financial Gains May Be Rough," *Wall Street Journal Asia*, May 4, 2006, p. 19.

Tasker, Rodney, "Contrarian: While Other Airlines Are Hunkering Down, Thai Airways Moves Aggressively to Expand Its Fleet," *Far Eastern Economic Review*, April 3, 2003, p. 39.

Thai Airways International—32nd Anniversary, Bangkok: Thai Airways Public Relations, 1992.

Thomas, Geoffrey, "Asians Become Darlings of Alliance Investors," *Aviation Week and Space Technology*, May 4, 1998, pp. 24–25.

Tokyo Dome Corporation

—■—

1-3-61 Koraku
Bunkyo-ku
Tokyo, 112-8575
Japan
Telephone: (+81 03) 3811 2111
Fax: (+81 03) 3817 6066
Web site: http://www.tokyo-dome.co.jp

Public Company
Founded: 1936 as Korakuen Stadium Co., Ltd.
Incorporated: 1990
Employees: 1,925
Sales: ¥62.4 billion ($910.2 million) (2009)
Stock Exchanges: Tokyo
Ticker Symbol: 9681
NAICS: 713110 Amusement and Theme Parks; 713990
    All Other Amusement and Recreation Industries

■ ■ ■

Tokyo Dome Corporation operates one of Japan's larg-est and most iconic stadium, entertainment, and leisure complexes. The company oversees the Tokyo Dome baseball stadium, home to the Yomiuri Giants baseball team, and also Japan's largest concert hall with a capac-ity of 55,000 seats. The Tokyo Dome stadium is part of the larger Tokyo Dome City complex. Other attractions within Tokyo Dome City include the Geopolis indoor amusement park, the LaQua spa, the Meets Port garden and convention center, and the Tokyo Dome Hotel. Tokyo Dome Corporation also operates several restaurants and a bowling alley.

Other branches of Tokyo Dome Corporation include Korakuen Locomotive Co., which operates game centers, including batting cages; Matsudo Kousan Co., operator of the Matsudo KEIRIN bicycle racetrack; and Tokyo Dome Sports Co., Ltd., which operates sports clubs and spa facilities in the Tokyo Dome complex and elsewhere. The company also controls 50 percent of Australia's Terrey Hills Golf and Country Club. Tokyo Dome is listed on the Tokyo Stock Exchange and is led by President Shinji Kushiro. The company posted revenues of ¥62.4 billion ($910 million) in 2009.

TOKYO BASEBALL STADIUM IN THE THIRTIES

The Japanese love affair with the American sport of baseball predates World War II. The rising popularity of the game, and the formation of a number of profes-sional baseball teams led to the construction of a dedicated stadium for the sport in the Korakuen area of Tokyo's Suidobashi district. This was carried out by Ko-rakuen Stadium Co., Ltd., which started out with an initial capital of ¥2 billion in 1936. The company completed construction of the stadium the following year, becoming the first two-level stadium in Japan. Ko-rakuen Stadium initially had a capacity of 30,000, mak-ing it the largest stadium in Japan as well.

The stadium recorded a major milestone in the 1940s, when it played host to Japan's longest-ever baseball game, which ran for 28 innings. From its early days, however, the stadium served for more than just hosting baseball games. The Kinoshita Circus became a recurring guest, setting up a big tent with a capacity of

COMPANY PERSPECTIVES

We consider it our mission to expand the frontier of urban leisure entertainment to thrill and delight as many people as possible.

4,000. The stadium also played host to a ski-jumping competition, which required the transportation of snow from the mountains in Niigata. Into the end of the war the stadium also hosted Tokyo's Summer Sumo Tournament.

DIVERSIFYING IN THE FIFTIES

Korakuen Stadium Co. went public in 1949, listing its shares on the Tokyo and Osaka stock exchanges. The public offering helped fuel the group's expansion as it began adding to its range of operations by developing the site surrounding the stadium. This began in 1949 with the opening of a bicycle racing track, including bicycle rentals. This facility was also used to host soccer and American football games, as well as boxing matches and other sports events. The bicycle facility was operated by a subsidiary, Matsudo Kousan.

The success of the bicycle racetrack enabled the group to expand again, adding a second racing facility in Kagetsuen in 1950. That business was operated by another subsidiary, Kagetsuen Kanko Co. The following year, the company added an indoor ice skating rink, Korakuen Ice Palace, becoming the first in Tokyo to provide year-round ice skating. This facility also played host to ice revues and other skating events. The popularity of skating during this period also inspired the company to build a roller-skating park as part of the Korakuen complex, in 1954.

Korakuen Stadium Co. continued to respond to the growing U.S. influence on Japan's leisure and entertainment sectors. The company became the first in Japan to open a U.S.-style mechanized amusement park, in 1955. The site featured the country's first roller coaster, which became a major draw to the site, helping to reinforce the Suidobashi district as Tokyo's entertainment center.

HOTELS IN THE SIXTIES

The following decade, Korakuen expanded into another rapidly growing sport, opening the Korakuen Bowling Center in 1962. This facility featured 62 lanes and was also the first in Japan, and one of the first in the world,

to feature automatic pin-setting equipment. By then, Korakuen had also entered the resorts business, opening the Ishiuchi Korakuen Ski Resort in Joetsu in 1959. In 1965, the group opened the still more ambitious Atami Korakuen Hotel complex, located in the coastal town of Atami. In addition to hotel accommodations, the resort also featured its own amusement park and bowling alley. By then, the company had also added a third facility outside of Tokyo, an ice skating rink in Hakone.

Korakuen's expansion continued strongly through the 1970s and 1980s. In 1971, the company added a new subsidiary, Korakuen Locomotive, which opened a gaming center, including batting cages, and other amenities, such as the Amusement Machine Museum. When the city of Tokyo abolished bicycle racing, the company converted its bicycle racetrack into an indoor swimming complex.

In 1973, the company extended the stadium site with the opening of the Yellow Building, which added a new roller-skating rink, a new bowling alley, as well as an off-track betting parlor. That same year, the company added a presence in Sapporo, site of a popular snow festival, opening the Sapporo Korakuen Country Club.

In the meantime, the Korakuen stadium remained the primary income earner for the company. Korakuen continued to expand and modernize, adding another 10,000 seats in 1970. The company also spent ¥300 million to replace the stadium's fields with artificial grass, becoming the first in Japan to do so. The faster style of play helped spark a new surge in popularity for the sport, in turn driving up Korakuen's revenues and profits during the decade.

TOKYO DOME IN 1988

Korakuen continued in the 1980s to update the stadium. In 1981, for example, the company spent ¥1.12 billion to replace its scoreboard with a new scoreboard including a giant video screen. The new Aurora Vision screen played a part in Korakuen Stadium Co.'s efforts to diversify the range of events held at the stadium. The stadium hosted a mass held by Pope John Paul II in 1981. In 1987, Madonna played several sold-out shows as part of the Who's That Girl tour that established her as one of the world's top-selling recording artists.

The increasing diversity of the stadium's events, and the stadium's advancing age, convinced the company to undertake a major new project to replace Korakuen Stadium altogether. In its place, the company constructed the Tokyo Dome, the first baseball stadium in Japan to feature an all-weather dome. An air-supported structure, the dome was held in place by

KEY DATES

1936: Korakuen Stadium Co. is founded to build a baseball stadium in Tokyo, which opens in 1937.
1959: Company adds its first hotel and resorts operation, in Joetsu.
1988: Tokyo Dome replaces the former Korakuen Stadium.
1990: Company changes its name to Tokyo Dome Corporation.
2000: Company regroups its hotels and resorts into two separate subsidiaries.
2007: Tokyo Dome sells off its resorts and other operations outside of Tokyo.
2010: Tokyo Dome City unveils its newest attraction, Splash Garden.

slightly pressurizing the air inside the stadium. Completed in 1988, the Tokyo Dome quickly became one of Tokyo's iconic buildings, earning the nickname of the "Big Egg." The company embraced the nickname, developing the slogan "BIG Entertainments and Golden Games." The larger complex surrounding the stadium was renamed Big Egg City. One of the first events held at the new stadium was a heavyweight title fight between Mike Tyson and Tony Tubbs.

The new stadium also gave the company a new name, Tokyo Dome Corporation, in 1990. The company had, in the meantime, continued its own diversification. The company added a finance arm, Korakuen Finance Co., in 1980. This subsidiary became a major consumer lender in the Tokyo region, before being sold off by the company in 2006. The 1980s also witnessed the expansion of the company's hotel and resorts operations. The company opened the Osaka Korakuen Hotel in 1986, followed by the Sapporo Korakuen Hotel in 1988, and the Batoh Korakuen Golf Course and Hotel Resort in 1989. Also in 1989, Tokyo became a 50 percent partner in the Terrey Hills Golf and Country Club in Australia. Because of the limited room for new golf courses in Japan itself, Australia had become a popular destination for Japan's growing number of golfing enthusiasts.

HOTEL FLAGSHIP IN 2000

Tokyo Dome added other hotel properties in the 1990s, including the Mito Korakuen Country Club in 1996. In 1999, the company divided its hotel and resort holdings

into two dedicated subsidiaries, Tokyo Dome Hotel Corporation and Tokyo Dome Resort Operations Corporation. The following year, the company opened a new flagship hotel as part of the expanded Tokyo Dome complex.

The 43-story, 1,006-room hotel also featured three underground levels and came as part of the ongoing modernization of the former Korakuen leisure and entertainment site. Other new features included the Big Egg Plaza I and Prism Hall, completed in 1990, and Geopolis, an underground amusement park complex complete with roller coaster, opened in 1992. The company also built the Ski Dome, billed as the world's largest indoor ski slope, at a cost of $340 million, in 1994. These additions helped to raise the company's revenues to nearly $575 million by the middle of the decade.

LaQua spa was among the other attractions added. Built at a cost of $295 million, LaQua replaced the former Korakuen Amusement Park, torn down in 2001 after 50 years of operations. The new complex added a luxury spa, pool, and relaxation concept to the Tokyo Dome complex, as well as a shopping mall and several new amusement rides, including a roller coaster and a hubless ferris wheel. The LaQua facility opened for business in 2003.

By then, Tokyo Dome had become the center of some controversy when it was revealed the company and its predecessor had long provided free "gifts" to the Otowa-kai yakuza, one of the city's largest organized crime groups. These gifts amounted essentially to free tickets, worth as much as ¥78 million per year, and discounted access to other amenities in the Tokyo Dome concept. As company President Yuko Hayashi suggested in a news conference after the story broke: "There was a time when having an association with gangsters was all part and parcel of being a company in the entertainment industry." The company then claimed that it had put in place a monitoring system to abolish the practice.

NEW ATTRACTIONS IN 2009

In 2003, Tokyo Dome announced it planned to demolish the Ski Dome, which had experienced a sharp drop in business during the difficult economic period at the start of the century. In its place, the company began developing a new range of attractions, including the "Meets Port" garden and convention center complex opened in 2008. The following year, the company completed a major overhaul of the underground Geopolis amusement park, which reopened in April 2009.

By then, Tokyo Dome had completed something of an overhaul of its own operations. The company sold off its money-losing finance arm to U.S.-based investment firm Lone Star Group in 2006. Over the next year, Tokyo Dome Corporation shed most of its operations outside of Tokyo, including a number of golf courses, amusement parks, and country clubs. This streamlining also refocused the group's hotel portfolio around just five hotel properties.

The effort helped reduce Tokyo Dome Corporation's debt by more than ¥190 billion ($1.6 billion) through the beginning of 2010. By then, the company had begun to feel the effects of the global economic downturn. Ticket sales for the stadium's baseball and other sporting events dropped sharply, while the company attracted a reduced number of concerts to the stadium as well. The company's hotel operations suffered as well, with occupancy rates dropping below 80 percent through most of 2009.

Nevertheless, Tokyo Dome remained committed to expanding the array of attractions at Tokyo Dome City. In 2010, for example, the company debuted its new Splash Garden attraction. In this way, Tokyo Dome Corporation upheld the site's long tradition as the heart of Tokyo's entertainment and leisure sector.

M. L. Cohen

PRINCIPAL SUBSIDIARIES

Korakuen Locomotive Co., Ltd.; Matsudo Kousan Co., Ltd.; Sapporo Korakuen Hotel Co., Ltd.; Tokyo Dome Facilities Co., Ltd.; Tokyo Dome Hotel Corporation; Tokyo Dome Resort Operations Corp.; Tokyo Dome Sports Co., Ltd.

PRINCIPAL DIVISIONS

Tokyo Dome Stadium; Hotels.

PRINCIPAL OPERATING UNITS

Tokyo Dome City; Tokyo Dome Hotels; Geopolis; LaQua; MEETS PORT.

PRINCIPAL COMPETITORS

AEON Fantasy Company Ltd.; Joban Kosan Company Ltd.; Namco Bandai Holdings Inc.; Oriental Land Company Ltd.; Toei Animation Company Ltd.; Tokyotokeiba Company Ltd.; Toyo Construction Company Ltd.

FURTHER READING

"Lee's Japan's Next Biggest Thing," *Malay Mail*, April 21, 2006.

Sklarewitz, Norman, "Tokyo Dome Sees Record Year Despite Economic Recession," *Amusement Business*, November 1, 1992, p. 12.

"Tokyo Dome City to Add Spa, Rides," *Amusement Business*, March 19, 2001, p. 25.

"Tokyo Dome Corp. Showered Gangsters with Free Gifts," *Mainichi Daily News*, September 27, 2002.

"Tokyo Dome Slugged with 56% Net Profit Drop in Feb–Oct," *AsiaPulse News*, December 11, 2009.

"Tokyo Dome to Cut Debt Almost 40% by Selling Golf Course, Hotels," *AsiaPulse News*, October 16, 2006.

"The World's Largest Indoor Ski Slope, the Ski Dome in Tokyo, Japan, Is to Be Demolished," *Demolition & Recycling International*, September–October 2003, p. 4.

"Yakuza Feeding on Tokyo Dome," *Asahi Shinbun*, September 27, 2002.

Total S.A.

—■—

2 place Jean Millier, La Défense 6
Paris, 92078
France
Telephone: (+33 1) 47445853
Fax: (+33 1) 47445824
Web site: http://www.total.com

Public Company
Founded: 1924 as Compagnie Française des Pétroles
Employees: 96,387
Sales: EUR 131.33 billion ($183.86 billion) (2009)
Stock Exchanges: Paris New York
Ticker Symbols: 0000879764; TOT
NAICS: 211111 Crude Petroleum and Natural Gas Extraction; 324110 Petroleum Refineries; 324199 All Other Petroleum and Coal Products Manufacturing

■ ■ ■

Total S.A. is one of the world's largest integrated oil, gas, and petrochemicals companies, with operations spanning 130 countries and revenues of EUR 131.33 billion ($183.86 billion) in 2009. Total is also the largest publicly traded corporation in France and in the Euro zone, with a market capitalization of nearly EUR 106 billion. Total's oil production tops 2.28 million barrels of oil equivalent (boe) per day, and at the end of 2009 the company's proven reserves topped 10.5 billion boe. The company's Upstream division includes exploration and production operations in over 40 countries, with oil and gas production underway in 30 countries.

Total's Downstream division includes a total refining capacity of 3.6 million barrels per day. The company also operates a network of nearly 16,500 service stations under the Total, Elf, Elan, and AS 24 brands, making Total the leading refiner-marketer in the Western European and African markets. Total's Chemicals division focused on producing petrochemicals, fertilizers, and specialty chemicals. The company claims a 22 percent share of the total North American chemicals market, and 17 percent of the Asian chemicals market. Total is listed on the Euronext Paris stock exchange and is led by Chairman and CEO Christophe Margerie.

ROOTS IN WORLD WAR I FRENCH OIL CRISIS

The foundation of Total Fina Elf's initial company, Compagnie Française des Pétroles, France's oldest and, for most of its life, largest oil company, in 1924 came on the heels of France's realization that it needed secure energy supplies. In late 1917, France had come within three months of running out of fuel and seeing its World War I effort grind to a halt.

The United States and Russia, with their huge domestic resources, had supplied 90 percent of the world's oil needs. Since 1900, however, the British had developed a powerful presence through the activities of the Anglo-Persian Oil Company, which later became British Petroleum, and Royal Dutch Shell. The French found that the key to acquiring oil was the 25 percent stake in the fledgling Turkish Petroleum Company (TPC) held by Germany's Deutsche Bank.

TPC had been founded in 1911 to exploit the oilfields of Mesopotamia on either side of the German-built railway to Baghdad. The British-owned National Bank of Turkey had originally been TPC's major shareholder with 50 percent, but in 1914 the British government persuaded the bank to sell out to Anglo-Persian. An additional 25 percent was held by Royal Dutch Shell. In 1915, the 25 percent stake in TPC still held by Deutsche Bank was sequestered by the British.

ESTABLISHING CFP: 1924

Four years later, a new French government concluded that it was unacceptable that a foreign company should control the exploitation of France's oil rights in Mesopotamia, and the Compagnie Française des Pétroles (CFP) was established.

CFP's function was not limited to Mesopotamia. In the interests of developing an oil producing capacity "under French control," Chairman Ernest Mercier was charged with acquiring stakes in "any enterprise active in whatsoever oil producing region" of the world. CFP was to cooperate, with the support of the government, in "exploiting such oil wealth as may be discovered in France, her colonies, and her protectorates." The Compagnie Française des Pétroles was set up as a private, not a state-owned, firm.

On October 15, 1927, the Turkish Petroleum Company struck oil, a large find, at Baba Gurghur in Iraq. The discovery ended a debate among the TPC shareholders, some of whom wanted to receive dividends on their investments, others of whom wanted to be remunerated in crude oil. The French had favored crude, having no oilfields of their own. After Baba Gurghur they received it.

The TCP was restructured in 1928, with Anglo-Persian ceding half its stake to a consortium of five U.S. oil companies. The shareholders in the TPC signed a non-aggression pact known as the Red Line Agreement, circling a large area of the map of the Near and Middle East with red crayon. The area within the red line cor-

responded to the old Ottoman Empire at the end of World War I, encompassing Turkey, Syria, Saudi Arabia, Lebanon, Iraq, and Palestine. Within that region, the TPC shareholders, now including the U.S. giants Standard Oil of New York and Standard Oil of New Jersey, undertook not to compete with one another.

ENTERED REFINING IN 1929

Mercier came up against opposition from some of the company's shareholders to his cherished plans to delve into refining, but some of the oil distributors who backed CFP objected, not wanting to disrupt close ties with foreign refiners. A plan was developed for the French state to acquire a 25 percent stake in CFP and a 10 percent stake in a new refining subsidiary to be created by CFP, the Compagnie Française de Raffinage.

The Compagnie Française de Raffinage (CFR) was founded in April 1929. Its first refinery was opened at Normandy in 1933. The first shipment of CFP's own oil came from Iraq the following year when the pipeline from the wells to the Lebanese port of Tripoli went into operation. In the years up to World War II, CFR's refining capacity grew steadily, outstripping CFP's ability to supply it with crude. Further crude shipments came from Venezuela and the United States.

By 1929, all the Turkish Petroleum Company's oil came from Iraq under a concession awarded by the Iraqi monarch, King Feisal, installed by the British in 1921. TPC changed its name to Iraq Petroleum Company (IPC) in June 1929. By 1936, CFR was supplying nearly 20 percent of French demand for refined oil from two plants located at either end of the country, one in Normandy and the other in Provence.

ELF AQUITAINE'S BEGINNINGS

Elf Aquitaine, which became the substantial Elf portion of the Total Fina Elf name decades later, got its start before World War II as three small companies: RAP, SNPA, and BRP. The group was founded by the French government in 1939 as Regie Autonome des Pétroles (RAP) to exploit modest gas reserves discovered at Saint-Marcet in southwest France. However, the group's origins could be said to go back much further than that, to 1498 when Jacob Wimpfeling, a theologian from Alsace, was surprised to note mineral oil welling out of the ground at a place called Pechelbronn (fountain of pitch).

Almost 500 years later, in 1970, the Antar group, which then owned Pechelbronn, was taken over by Elf. A close historical connection might be perceived between the history of Elf and the history of France's energy policy as practiced by successive governments since World War II.

KEY DATES

1920: Petrofina (Compagnie Financière Belge des Pétroles) is founded by investors from Antwerp.
1924: Total is founded as Compagnie Française des Pétroles (CFP).
1954: Trademark "Total" is created and registered.
1985: CFP becomes Total-Compagnie Française des Pétroles.
1991: Company's name becomes Total S.A.
1995: Thierry Desmarest is made CEO of Total; Total is the first foreign oil company to produce in Iran since 1979.
1999: Total acquires Belgium's Petrofina and becomes Total Fina.
2000: Total Fina merges with Elf Aquitaine and becomes Total Fina Elf.
2003: Company changes its name to Total S.A. once again.
2006: Total spins off part of its chemicals operations as a separate company, Arkema.
2010: Total announces revenues of EUR 131 billion.

The discovery of gas at Saint-Marcet in the summer of 1939 was made by a small exploration syndicate set up with public funding earlier in the decade to prospect for oil and gas in the region. The Compagnie Française des Pétroles, Royal Dutch Shell, and Standard Oil of New Jersey could not be expected to plow much money into looking for oil or gas in France. The oil giants were wrong, but it was not until after the war that they were to discover it. The find at Saint-Marcet was modest, although it continued to produce gas until 1988. The RAP was immediately formed to exploit the new resource by extracting the gas and building a plant for its treatment near Boussens.

In 1941, CFP set up a new company, the second of Elf's forerunners, Société Nationale des Pétroles d'Aquitaine (SNPA), to look for oil and gas in the Aquitaine region, with the state owning 24 percent. CFP wound up owning 14 percent, along with the National Nitrogen Board, Saint Gobain, Pechiney, and Rhône-Poulenc. It was obvious that this project would include petrochemicals. Through the efforts of SNPA, Aquitaine was to become the oil and gas province of France. During the German occupation, the management of SNPA slacked off in its efforts to find oil. SN-PA's reluctance to help in the German war effort resulted in the deportation of the company's first chairman, Pierre Angot.

At the end of the war, President Charles de Gaulle was eager for the government to play an active role in restoring the country's control over its energy supplies. In 1945, he created the third of Elf's forerunners, the Bureau de Recherches de Pétrole (BRP), to help the process along. The role of this publicly funded venture was, according to its founding charter, to encourage oil and gas exploration in France, its colonies, and protectorates "in the exclusive interest of the nation." BRP was to identify and invest in exploration projects. It owned both the RAP and the government's share of SNPA.

AFRICAN EXPLORATION BEGINS AFTER WORLD WAR II

De Gaulle chose Pierre Guillaumat as the first chairman of BRP. Then 36 years old, Guillaumat was to prove the single most influential figure in the history of Elf Aquitaine, later retiring as chairman of Elf in 1977.

In the first years of its life, the most important investments made by BRP were in the French colony of Algeria and in equatorial Africa. Exploration operations in the Congo and Gabon were largely carried out through Société des Pétroles d'Afrique Equatoriale (SPAFE), a joint venture with various French banks. Consortia were formed between SPAFE, Mobil, and Shell. In Algeria, the beneficiary of BRP's funding was SN Repal, a joint venture with colonial government and the Compagnie Française des Pétroles. Also established was Compagnie de Recherche et d'Exploitation du Pétrole du Sahara (CREPS), a further oil exploration joint venture in Algeria between RAP with 65 percent and Royal Dutch/Shell with 35 percent.

BRP's failure to discover oil in the 1940s appeared to confirm the skepticism of those who doubted that oil would ever be discovered in the Algerian Sahara. Paradoxically, it was precisely this skepticism that had encouraged the French government to set up BRP in the first place. The privately owned oil companies, with shareholders' dividends to pay out, were not about to see large investments swallowed up by the sands of north Africa. In 1950, Guillaumat left BRP to become head of France's new Atomic Energy Commission.

TOTAL VERTICALLY INTEGRATED OIL COMPANY BY WORLD WAR II

Following Ernest Mercier's resignation in 1940, the new chairman Jules Meny entrusted the French interests in

IPC to Harold Sheets, the chairman of Standard Oil of New York. The rapid succession of chairmen at CFP during the war reflected the instability of those times. Mercier departed peacefully, but Meny was taken hostage by the Nazis in 1943 and deported to Dachau. Meny's successor, Marcel Champin, died in 1945, leaving the task of determining CFP's postwar strategy to his deputy, Victor de Metz, who was to serve as chairman for 25 years.

RAPID POSTWAR EXPANSION AT HOME AND ABROAD

The nationalization drive that affected so many French companies after the war did not engulf CFP. Its private shareholders were powerful and not worth alienating. More threatening for CFP in the long run was President de Gaulle's creation in 1945 of the BRP, which was much later to form one of the constituent parts of Elf Aquitaine. At its creation, however, BRP was charged exclusively with searching for oil in France, its colonies, and protectorates.

In the late 1940s and early 1950s, CFP expanded rapidly both at home and abroad. The company's annual supply of oil from the Middle East increased from 806,000 tons in 1945, to 1.61 million tons in 1950, to 8.824 million tons in 1953. The security of these supplies depended on the continuing stability of the region and its rulers' continuing respect for the oil companies' prewar concessions. Victor de Metz recognized that CFP needed to diversify its sources of supply.

After a fruitless venture in Venezuela from 1948 to 1951, CFP began exploration in Canada, then in French Equatorial Africa and Algeria. CFP's venture to develop the oil wealth of Algeria fared well. In 1946, the state-owned BRP had established, jointly with the French colonial government in Algeria, an oil exploration company, the Société Nationale de Recherche de Pétrole en Algerie (SN Repal). In 1947, CFP sent a geologist to Algeria to evaluate the region's prospects, teaming up in the 1950s with SN Repal to explore a huge promising region.

In 1956, a huge oilfield was discovered and an equally impressive gas field. CFP and SN Repal were able to organize a vast industrial complex that provided French engineers with the opportunity to gain priceless technological knowledge in all aspects of oil and gas exploration, production, transport, gas treatment, and maritime shipping.

MAJOR DISCOVERIES IN THE FIFTIES

The Lacq gas field, discovered by SNPA in southwest France in December 1951, was huge by French standards and impressive enough by any standards with reserves estimated at 250 billion cubic meters. Extracting the gas was to prove technically awkward on account of its highly toxic and corrosive impurities, notably hydrogen sulfate. In the longer term, however, SNPA was to turn these initial difficulties to its advantage. France became a net exporter of sulfates, and the expertise SNPA acquired in treating highly sulfurous natural gas also proved eminently exportable.

The other forerunners of Elf Aquitaine, RAP and SNPA, also struck oil in the Algerian desert at about the same time. In 1956, CREPS, the RAP and Shell joint venture, brought the Sahara's first marketable oil to the surface at Edjeleh. The following year, SNPA discovered oil at El Gassi. In 1956 and 1957, there were the first discoveries of oil in equatorial Africa, in Gabon, and in the Congo, and in the early 1960s, a very big discovery was made in the Gulf of Guinea.

However, the Compagnie Française des Pétroles was far from being a household name in France. CFP petrol stations did not cover the land, even though a large proportion of the fuel that the independent distributors sold had been refined at the plants of a CFP subsidiary. Distribution was not a particularly profitable activity, but a major oil producer without distribution facilities of its own risked being held for ransom by its distributors with the threat of losing their business. From 1946, Victor de Metz worked to remove this risk by creating the Compagnie Française de Distribution en Afrique to sell CFP's refined oil products in francophone Africa.

DEBUT OF TOTAL BRAND: 1954

CFP pursued the professionalization of petroleum marketing operations and the concentration of retail networks. The unveiling of the Total brand name occurred in 1954. The distributors of oil refined by CFR were now entitled to deck out their service stations in the Total colors and logo, giving them a stronger market identity. First tested in Africa and then brought to France in 1957, the plan was a success. In 1961, refineries belonging to CFP or working on its behalf treated 12 million tons of oil, seven million tons of which went on to be distributed under the Total brand name.

However, France's independent fuel distributors still were experiencing hard times, losing ground when competing with the big foreign oil companies. One by one they sold out, usually to CFP, as CFP expanded its market to Europe and Africa where it had begun marketing in 1968.

Because French authorities had urged CFP to gain a stake in the Sahara oilfields in the 1950s, and CFP refused, the French government withheld its approval when CFP considered taking over its partner's retail network. Instead, the government consolidated the foundations for the future Elf Group by establishing the Union Générale des Pétroles (UGP), that united RAP, SN Repal, SPAEF, and SNPA, all groups of which BRP was a driving force.

UGP thus gained the SNPA network in southwestern France, including French downstream assets owned by Caltex. These assets encompassed a refinery near Bordeaux, four oil tankers, and 1,400 service stations. In taking this step, the French government had set up a significant French company with assets in upstream, transport, downstream, and gas. The stage was set for vertical integration of the company.

While CFP was making strides in refining and selling its oil, the process of extracting it was becoming increasingly difficult. The model for a new relationship with the Middle Eastern governments was the 50-50 profit-sharing agreement signed by the Saudi government and the U.S. oil producers' consortium Aramco in 1950. In the same year, IPC struck a similar profit-sharing deal with the Iraqi government. The risks posed by nascent nationalism in the Middle East were made clear in 1951, when Muhammad Mussadegh came to power in Iran. He nationalized the assets of the Anglo-Iranian Oil Company, formerly the Anglo-Persian Oil Company and forerunner of British Petroleum, and an international embargo of Iranian crude failed to change his attitude.

More effective than either of these actions was a revolt linked to the British and U.S. intelligence services, which led to the restoration of the shah and Mussadegh's imprisonment in 1953. A year later, the oil companies and the Iranian government created an international consortium of oil companies led by Anglo-Iranian with a 40 percent share. CFP took a modest 6 percent stake in the venture.

INCREASED RELIANCE ON ALGERIAN OIL IN THE SIXTIES

Upheavals such as the one in Iran spurred the French effort to develop oil production in its Algerian colony. However, both CFP and BRP knew that any oil or gas discovered in Algeria would lie within the franc zone. The IPC installations in Iraq did not fall into this category and CFP had to fund its share of investment in the IPC in pounds sterling. In the late 1940s and early 1950s, when the franc was fast losing its purchasing power, this arrangement was not very satisfactory.

By 1962, the future Total and Elf groups realized that they needed to find resources other than those in Algeria, and to examine the political risks associated with their reserves. The French government revised its oil policy, making it vital that French oil companies be able to explore for oil beyond the borders of France and its former colonies.

CONSOLIDATION AND FORMATION OF ELF IN THE LATE SIXTIES

Large-scale nationalization took place in 1966, presided over by Pierre Guillaumat. BRP and RAP were transformed into ERAP. The majority stake in SNPA held by BRP thus passed to ERAP. Guillaumat became chairman both of the ERAP holding company and of its most dynamic subsidiary SNPA. The group was still receiving funds from the sales tax on petroleum products. These funds, known as support grants, increased as the government encouraged the group to diversify its oil supplies.

Government involvement in the oil industry was hardly unique in Continental Europe at the time. The Italians had created Ente Nazionale Idrocarburi (ENI) in 1953, and in 1965, the Spanish had restructured their oil industry, leading to the creation of Hispanoil.

Guillaumat and ERAP were more original in the deals they struck with oil-producing nations. ERAP's pioneering *contrats d'entreprise* were signed first with Iran in 1966 and two years later with Iraq. These were service contracts under which ERAP agreed to provide exploration and production skills in return for long-term crude supplies at preferential rates. The success of this arrangement in Iraq provided a framework for the amicable resolution of Franco-Iraqi differences when the Iraqi government nationalized the assets of the Compagnie Française des Pétroles, among others, in 1972. ERAP was also able to set up new operations in Nigeria (1962), Indonesia (1963), and Canada (1964), later launching a venture in Mexico.

ERAP and SNPA still lacked a recognizable brand name in France. This was remedied in 1967, when the Elf name and logo were unveiled at thousands of service stations around the country. The name "Elf" was chosen by a computer, according to corporate folklore, for its attractive connotations of nimbleness and sprightliness, and was not an acronym. Also significant was the partnership of BRP and RAP before the merger in an effort to expand oil and gas exploration and production in the British, Norwegian, and Dutch offshore zones in the North Sea.

Despite the Iraqi nationalization of the assets of Iraq Petroleum Company in 1971, CFP announced in its annual report that it would be maintained as before. On de Metz's retirement in 1971, the Compagnie

Française des Pétroles was one of the largest oil companies in the world; the company's oil production had risen at a rate 30 percent faster than global oil production in the 1960s.

ELF'S DIVERSIFICATION IN THE SEVENTIES

The oil and gas reserves of the future Total Group increased by 3.5 times between 1960 and 1971, to a total of 68 million metric tons. At the same time, those of the future Elf Group tripled to nearly 33 million metric tons. Both groups began searching for sites for new refineries. Total ultimately built at Dunkirk in northern France and at Vlissingen in the Netherlands. Elf took over the Antar Group, doubling its downstream sector, and inherited a stake in refineries in Alsace-Lorraine. During this time, SNPA kept its close ties with the major French chemical firms. However, none of the Elf component companies could envision the fast-growing demand for chemicals in France and Europe, not even CFP, which had diversified into chemicals in the late 1950s.

To make a greater commitment to chemicals, Total brought together as Total Chimie all the chemicals businesses run by CFP and CFR in 1968, also diversifying into polyethylene in partnership with German firms. The Group joined SNPA in founding the Compagnie de Petrochimie the following year. In 1971, the future Elf and Total formed Ato Chimie, which grouped all their chemical activities under one roof.

Following the oil crisis in 1973, Elf and Total cooperated in chemicals and upstream operations in the North Sea. Both companies had to learn to better handle risk, as oil prices were very unstable. The challenge for Elf at this time was to increase the proportion of oil in its resources and to expand its production base, which was primarily in the North Sea and West Africa. CFP, however, had widely dispersed production, with operations in Algeria, the Middle East, Indonesia, and the North Sea, as well as new operations in Yemen. It had also begun to explore in Argentina and Colombia.

The year 1975 found joint operations with ATO Chimie becoming increasingly difficult. Even so, the government encouraged the formation of Chloé Chimie in 1979, a second joint venture specializing in chloro-chemicals, with the assets coming from Rhône-Poulenc. Elf and Total held 80.5 percent of the newly established company's equity.

Because Total had been absorbed in consolidating its refining and marketing operations, its profitability in chemicals plunged. Total sold its stakes in Ato Chimie and Chloé Chimie in 1983, eliminating its chemical as-

sets by 1985. Elf was in better shape financially and wanted to build up a refining and marketing operation as well in the 1970s, and expanded its chemical operations, building a vast chemicals complex of base chemicals, specialty chemicals, and a hygiene-pharmaceuticals division.

In 1977, the year after the final merger between ERAP and SNPA to form the new Société Nationale Elf Aquitaine, Pierre Guillaumat retired. Albin Chalandon, who became chairman, raised Elf Aquitaine's profile in the United States through the acquisition in 1981 of Texas Gulf. The combination of Texas Gulf's strength as a producer of mined sulfur and Elf's existing production at Lacq made the group the world's largest producer of sulfur. Texas Gulf also had huge phosphate reserves and was one of the largest U.S. potassium-based fertilizer producers. The purchase tripled Elf's overall U.S. business at a stroke, and included interests in mining and oil exploration.

ELF AND TOTAL IN THE EIGHTIES

The oil crisis that extended into the 1980s forced both Total and Elf to reduce their refining capacities, sell off most of their tankers, and boost the productivity of their retail networks. The number of service stations owned by both was halved as supermarkets were gaining a foothold in the motor fuel market. Both groups began trading in both crude and refined products, launching aggressive market expansion programs aimed at Latin America, Southeast Asia, and Central Europe.

In 1985, the name by which CFP had come to be known universally was incorporated in its official title: CFP became Total CFP. At the same time the Compagnie Française de Raffinage and its distribution subsidiary, Total CFD, merged to become CRD Total France. By the end of the 1980s, CFP had an output of 520,000 barrels of oil equivalent per day (boe/d) over five zones. Now that it was known as Total, the company had also diversified into coal, nuclear power, and renewable energy sources. Total enlarged its portfolio rapidly in the early 1980s, doubling its overall chemicals revenues during the decade, even before gaining Petrofina assets.

In the meantime, the Elf Group carved out a position for itself in the U.S. market, taking over a division of American Can, Metal, and Thurmit Chemicals. In 1989, Atochem expanded into performance chemicals. In 1990, Elf swapped with Total, taking over the base chemicals division of Orkem in exchange for the paints company La Seigneurie. By this time, chemicals had become a major component of the Elf Group, as the company had the strongest commitment to chemicals of all the major oil companies.

Elf gained a vital foothold in Spain and eastern Germany, and was engaged in a modernization program while trying to reduce production costs, strengthening its brand image. By the end of the 1980s, Elf had made several major deep offshore discoveries in Africa and the Gulf of Mexico, and moved back into Iran where Total was already well established. The Elf Group had major assets and had gained considerable knowledge in medium and deep offshore operations.

Total had reduced excess refining capacity but continued to enter into new markets, divesting assets in the United States to make investments in China. The company also made its refining operations more efficient and tightened environmental standards. Total beefed up its presence in Africa and around the Mediterranean Basin, while planning growth in Southeast Asia. Total's merger with Petrofina strengthened the company's position as it added competitive refining operations and boosted market share in some European markets where Total lacked the critical mass for long-term profit.

In 1994, the French government sold all but 13 percent of its controlling interest in Elf, generating nearly $6 billion in the process. Ironically, the company suffered its first net loss ever, a $1 billion shortfall, that same year.

SERGE TCHURUK AN AGGRESSIVE LEADER FOR TOTAL IN THE EARLY NINETIES

Serge Tchuruk, Total's CEO, moved quickly to transform Total. By the early 1990s, the company had ceded its position as France's largest oil company to Elf Aquitaine. Tchuruk engineered Total's change from a bureaucratic, complex, sleepy firm into a sleeker, more modern, and more aggressive company. Two hundred subsidiaries were abolished and were replaced by a mere six profit centers. One-seventh of Total's service stations network closed in 1991. Finally, 6,500 jobs were eliminated. The company's marketing operations reached into new potentially more lucrative markets, as Total purchased interests in service station chains in Spain, Portugal, Czechoslovakia, Hungary, and Turkey.

On the production side, Tchuruk aimed to increase oil and gas production outside the Middle East by 50 percent by 1995. In 1991, a joint venture, 40 percent owned by Total, with British Petroleum (BP) and Triton Energy discovered an oilfield at Cusiana in Colombia,

while Total on its own discovered a significant gas field in Indonesia. In 1993, production began at a gas field in Thailand. By 1995, Tchuruk's emphasis on beefing up the company's gas business had made Total the world's third-largest gas producer, trailing only Royal Dutch/ Shell (Royal Dutch Petroleum Company) and Mobil Corporation.

In June 1991, the company changed its name to Total S.A., and soon began trading on the New York Stock Exchange for the first time. The French government reduced its direct shareholding in the company to 5.4 percent, increasing Total's independence and ability to act quickly and aggressively.

THIERRY DESMAREST COMES TO TOTAL IN THE LATE NINETIES

In 1995, Tchuruk was replaced by 15-year company veteran Thierry Desmarest, who almost immediately closed a $610 million deal to develop two offshore oilfields in Iran. Total thus became the first foreign oil company allowed back in Iran since the overthrow of the shah in 1979.

Because of Total's willingness to operate in controversial countries, it had fewer competitors for its projects and was able to make better deals, leading to exploration and development costs among the lowest in the industry. These lower costs contributed to steadily increasing profits, with net income rising from FRF 2.85 billion ($600 million) in 1992 to FRF 7.61 billion ($1.26 billion) in 1997.

In 1997, the company announced that it would invest $2 billion to develop an Iranian gas field. Prior to signing the deal, however, Desmarest got advance backing from the French government and the European Union (EU), lessening the possibility that U.S.-sponsored sanctions would threaten it. Total had just days before signing this Iranian deal completed its sale of Total Petroleum (North America) Ltd. to Ultramar Diamond Shamrock Corporation for an approximate 8 percent stake in Ultramar. Ultramar then assumed about $435 million in Total Petroleum debt.

Despite quite a large exposure to the Asian financial crisis that arose in 1997, Total's results for that year were extremely healthy: a 7.9 percent increase in sales to FRF 191.09 billion ($31.75 billion) and a 35 percent increase in profits to FRF 7.61 billion ($1.26 billion). Total's aggressive approach in the 1990s had turned the company into one of the most profitable in the industry as well as one of the most fearless in terms of controversial deal making.

TOTAL FINA BECOMES THIRD-LARGEST OIL COMPANY IN EUROPE

Total S.A. moved from being the second-largest oil company in France to the third-largest in Europe through its acquisition of Petrofina S.A., the Belgian oil and petrochemicals company. In a FRF 74 billion ($13 billion) deal, essentially a share swap, Total agreed with a group of shareholders to acquire a 41 percent stake in the company, beating out rivals Elf Aquitaine and ENI. Fina also had 2,500 service stations in the United States, most of which were in Texas, Arizona, and New Mexico.

A BRIEF OVERVIEW OF PETROFINA

Petrofina was a Belgium-based integrated oil company that had interests in oil and gas production, refining and marketing, and chemicals, principally in the United States and Europe. When it was established in 1920 as Compagnie Financière Belge des Pétroles (Belgian Petroleum Finance Company) by a group of Belgian financiers in Antwerp, the company's main strengths were refining and marketing, but chemicals became an important part of the company's business through production of polypropylene, polyethylene, and polystyrene. The company's upstream assets were in the United States, the United Kingdom, and Norway, and its refining assets were in the United States, Belgium, Italy, the Untied Kingdom, and Angola.

Starting out to extract and refine petroleum products, Petrofina had found oil in Romania through the Concordia Company. In the 1920s, with Pure Oil of Delaware, Petrofina founded Purfina, a distribution company in Belgium and Holland that became a wholly owned subsidiary of Petrofina in 1923. Purfina paraffin was produced at a warehouse in Antwerp and sold in bottles in grocery stores. The later purchase of the factory and a small refinery opened the way for car lubricants, medicinal oils, and products used in the preparation of foods. The Société Industrielle Belge des Pétroles (SIBP; Belgian Industrial Petroleum Company) was founded in Antwerp in 1949, beginning production in 1951. By the 1950s, the Congo, Angola, French Equatorial Africa, and Tunisia formed the African core of the group, with exploration, production, and distribution being developed in these areas. Major discoveries in Mexico, Canada, Angola, and Egypt followed.

Petrofina expanded throughout Europe, North America, and Africa, preparing for a boom in the car market. The company delved into chemistry in 1954, the beginning of the plastics age. At this time, Laurent

Wolters of Petrofina achieved his vision of "going to America" through the acquisition of Cosden Chemicals, marking Petrofina's entry into petrochemicals in the United States. The company also had crude oil and finished products cross the world in ships, and entered into the aircraft fuels market in 1960, establishing Belgo Chim at Feluy, Belgium's center region. Petrofina began a large-scale exploration of the North Sea, finding gas in 1966 in the British Sector.

In 1972, Petrofina diversified into paints. The group expanded under the leadership of Adolphe Demeure de Lespaul, with the profitable sale of the Canadian Petrofina, which helped Petrofina strengthen its assets in the United States in the midst of the 1970s oil crisis. Petrofina later bought back its shares in SIBP to focus on refining activities. In 1988, Fina Italia successfully launched exploration and production in Italy, and Fina Europe built a new high-tech factory for lubricants in 1991 at Ertvelde. In 1995, the refinery at Antwerp was equipped for deep conversion, which meant it could stay ahead of market developments and accomplish high levels of efficiency.

Wood Mackenzie Consultants Ltd. of Edinburgh stated in the *Oil and Gas Journal* that the merged Total Fina would have an estimated overall product market share of about 8 percent, which placed it fourth behind Shell (12.5 percent), BP-Mobil (11 percent), and Exxon (10 percent). The new company's market share of 25 percent in France and Belgium made it a market leader and put it ahead of rival Elf. The combined workforce of the two companies was about 69,100. The two companies combined had a processing capacity that exceeded crude production by more than 500,000 boe/d.

Total Fina's upstream division was based in Paris, with its refining, marketing, and petrochemicals division in Brussels. Total Chairman Thierry Desmarest was made chairman of Total Fina, while Petrofina CEO François Cornelis became vice-chairman of Total Fina's executive committee, over which Desmarest presided.

In February 1999, Elf Aquitaine and Eni of Italy signed a 10-year, $998 million contract to redevelop an Iranian oilfield. The two European oil companies and Tehran were to refurbish the Doroud offshore field near Kharg Island in the Gulf. This kind of foreign investment in Iran had been in opposition to U.S. policy to restrict far-reaching investment in Iran's strategic oil industry, although U.S. President Bill Clinton had waived these sanctions when Total also defied policy and with a $2 billion gas exploration contract in Iran in 1997. The United States had threatened sanctions against any country that invested more than $20 million in Iran or Libya. Clinton waived these potential sanctions if the EU would press Iran to stop encouraging international terrorism and developing nuclear weapons.

ACQUIRING ELF IN 2000

In July 1999, the newly named Total Fina launched a hostile bid for oil group Elf Aquitaine for $44 billion. Elf Aquitaine fought back, offering its own $53 billion cash and stock counterbid to acquire Total Fina. Ultimately, Total Fina acquired Elf Aquitaine for $54 billion, making the new Total Fina Elf the fourth-largest oil company in the world. Thierry Desmarest was to continue as chairman, while Elf Chairman Philippe Jaffre, who instigated the counteroffer in July, resigned.

Elf Aquitaine S.A., known simply as Elf, was one of France's largest oil companies and one of the world's top 10 petrochemical companies when it was acquired by Total Fina. Its more than 800 subsidiaries included hydrocarbon, chemical, and health care interests. At its core, Elf was a fully integrated oil and gas company, combining upstream production capacity from fields in more than a dozen countries worldwide with downstream operations encompassing five refineries and over 6,500 gas stations throughout Europe and West Africa, and churned out the equivalent of over one million barrels of oil a day (75 percent oil and 25 percent natural gas). Through its Elf Atochem subsidiary, the conglomerate also ranked among the world's top chemical companies, manufacturing both basic and specialty chemicals.

Total Fina and Elf had complementary strategies and would be able to strengthen their geographic presence in Africa and the Middle East. Total Fina had operations east of the Suez Canal, in Southeast Asia, and in Latin America, while Elf was a major presence in West Africa and the North Sea. This configuration apparently worked well, as Total Fina Elf's net income was up by 24 percent at the end of the first quarter of 2000.

TOTAL IN 2003

Desmarest stated that Total Fina Elf's plans were to expand its exposure in the Gulf of Mexico, and that lack of involvement in the United States was based on the lack of attractiveness of projects, not an aversion to the United States because of President George W. Bush's "axis of evil" speech about Iran and Iraq, where Total had extensive operations. Total's upstream strategy focused on four major projects, each of which provided more than 200,000 barrels of oil per day equivalent. The first was the $2.5 billion Elgin-Franklin development in the U.K. North Sea. The second was the $4.3 billion Sincor heavy oil project in Venezuela. The third

was the $2.6 billion Girassol field in Angola. The last project was the $2 billion South Pars gas development in Iran.

Desmarest quickly met the targets set at the time of the creation of Total Fina Elf. The company then launched a new set of goals in order to raise its oil and gas production. In May 2002, the company bought into the Russian Vankorskoye project in East Siberia through an agreement with the U.K.-registered Anglo Siberian Oil Company, making Total the operator and 52 percent owner of the 900 million barrels per day field through the deal with Anglo Siberian, which held a 59 percent interest.

The company's exploration efforts met with new success in June 2002, with a deepwater well in Campos Basin, off the coast of Brazil, in 2002. By the end of that year, Total Fina Elf had raised its total production to 2.4 million barrels per day. Also in June 2002, Atofina, the chemicals branch of Total Fina Elf, launched two major projects: the installation of an ethane cracker in Ras Laffan and a polyethylene plant in Mesaieed, both in Qatar.

Total Fina Elf moved to simplify its name in 2003, once again becoming Total S.A. The following year, the company announced a plan to spin off part of its chemicals operations in order to refocus its Chemicals division around the group's refinery and cracker output, petrochemicals, fertilizers, and specialty chemicals. As part of that effort, the company planned to regroup 150 subsidiaries, with 70 factories in 40 countries producing chlorochemicals, acrylics, fluorochemicals, intermediates, oxygenated products, and engineered polymers into a new company. The spin-off was completed in 2006, with the creation of Arkema SA.

RUSSIAN INVESTMENT IN 2004

In the meantime, Total had begun to catch up with larger rivals Exxon Mobil, BP, and Shell, while outpacing ChevronTexaco with a total daily production of 2.6 million barrels by 2004. This represented an increase of more than 400 percent in just one decade. Total was also among the most profitable in the industry, generating net profits of $9.8 billion in 2004.

Total emerged as one of the industry's most aggressive players as the company continued to seek to boost its oil reserves into the second half of the decade. In 2004, the company reached an agreement to acquire 25 percent of Russian gas producer Novatek, paying $1 billion. The following year, Total stepped up its presence on the African continent, buying Exxon Mobil's fuels and lubricants operations in 14 countries. The purchase included 500 service stations and 29 terminals in Chad,

Djibouti, Ethiopia, Eritrea, Ghana, Guinea, Liberia, Malawi, Mauritius, Mozambique, Sierra Leone, Togo, Zambia, and Zimbabwe.

Total next turned its attention to Europe, buying out Exxon Mobil's 30 percent stake in the Victoria gas field project in the Norwegian Sea in February 2006. Soon after, the company expanded its Middle Eastern presence, reaching a partnership agreement with Saudi Aramco to develop a 400,000 barrel per day refinery in Saudi Arabia. That plant was expected to begin production in 2011. By the end of the year, Total had also expanded its operations in Qatar, agreeing to acquire 16.7 percent of the Qatargas II liquefied natural gas (LNG) project in Qatar's Ras Laffan. Total also signed a 25-year contract to purchase 2.5 million metric tons of LNG per year from Qatargas II.

In 1998, Total expanded into the booming Nigerian offshore market. The company reached an agreement with PMEL Energy Nigeria and OMEL Exploration and Production Nigeria to acquire stakes in two deepwater offshore licenses. The first of these, a 25.67 percent stake in OPL 285, covered an area of 1,170 square meters near the Bonga fields. The second, a 14.5 percent stake in OPL 279, gave Total exploration rights to an area of 1,125 square kilometers 100 kilometers off the Nigerian coast.

TOP FIVE IN 2010

Christophe de Margerie, who had long led Total's exploration efforts, took over as the company's chairman and CEO at the end of the decade. De Margerie was soon put to the test when, with oil prices soaring and the first signs of a new global downturn appearing, Total announced a record profit of nearly EUR 14 billion ($20 billion) for 2008. When the company then announced plans to close one of its French factories, trimming more than 550 jobs, Total faced withering criticism.

Total had by then been transformed into one of the world's largest integrated oil and gas companies, with revenues topping EUR 131.33 billion ($183.86 billion) in 2009, and operations spanning more than 130 countries. While the company's net income dropped that year, to under EUR 7.8 billion, the company had also succeeded in maintaining its daily output at nearly 2.3 million barrels per day, and its proven reserves at 10.5 billion barrels. This was in spite of the rapid depletion of many of the world's oilfields and increasing difficulty of locating new large-scale reserves.

Total continued streamlining its chemicals operations in 2010. This led to the sale of its consumer specialty products division Mapa Spontex, a maker of

baby bottles and nipples, rubber gloves, sponges, and cleaning products, to Jarden Corp. for EUR 335 million ($449 million) in April 2010. By then, the company had also launched production at a new low-density polyethylene plant in Qatar in partnership with Qatofin. Total S.A. had grown from a relatively small, France-based petroleum group to become one of the world's top five integrated energy companies in the new century.

William Pitt
Updated, David E. Salamie;
Annette D. McCully; M. L. Cohen

PRINCIPAL SUBSIDIARIES

Total has operations in more than 130 countries.

PRINCIPAL DIVISIONS

Upstream; Downstream; Chemicals; Fertilizers, Specialties.

PRINCIPAL OPERATING UNITS

Oil; Natural Gas; Chemicals.

PRINCIPAL COMPETITORS

BP PLC; Chevron Corporation; China Petroleum and Chemical Corp.; ConocoPhillips; Exxon Mobil Corporation; Lukoil-Western Siberia Ltd.; Royal Dutch Shell PLC; Saudi Arabian Oil Co.

FURTHER READING

Bahree, Bhushan, and Thomas Kamm, "Total Seeks More Pacts with Iran, Despite U.S.," *Wall Street Journal*, March 17, 1998, p. A13.

Beacham, Will, "Qatar Is Vital to Total Plans," *ICIS Chemical Business*, January 18, 2010, p. 13.

Beckman, Jeremy, "Total Beginning Program of Global Expansion," *Offshore*, August 1993, pp. 126+.

———, "Total Takes on Victoria," *Offshore*, February 2006, p. 19.

"Costs Force Total Rethink on Iran," *MEED*, April 13, 2007, p. 8.

Davis, Nigel, "Total Is Left Holding a Strong Hand," *ICIS Chemical Business Weekly*, April 17, 2006, p. 18.

Fleming, Charles, and Bhushan Bahree, "France's Total Dismisses U.S.-Sanctions Threat," *Wall Street Journal*, September 30, 1997, pp. A18, A19.

George, Dev, "Total Focuses on Offshore and Gas," *Offshore*, August 1994, pp. 80+.

Gumbel, Peter, "Operation Total Makeover," *Time International*, December 8, 2003, p. 52.

Levine, Joshua, "The French Connection," *Forbes*, July 7, 2003, p. 37.

McNicoll, Tracy, "The Critics Can 'Go to Hell,'" *Newsweek International*, August 3, 2009.

Milmo, Sean, "Total Buys Petrofina in $13 Billion Deal," *Chemical Market Reporter*, December 7, 1998, p. 7.

Reed, Stanley, "Total Tries Harder," *Business Week*, October 25, 2004, p. 56.

Robinson, Simon, "Total to Spin Off Part of Chemicals," *EC-N–European Chemical News*, September 13, 2004, p. 8.

"Total Acquires Qatargas II," *MEED*, December 22, 2006, p. 9.

"Total Divests Consumer Specialties Business," *Chemical Week*, April 5, 2010, p. 7.

"Total Hits Oil Offshore Brazil," *Oil Daily*, June 18, 2002.

"Total Profits Fall 36% in Q1, Helped by Lack of US Exposure," *Oil Daily*, May 23, 2002.

"Total Reports Weaker Results, Plays Down US Acquisition Talk," *Oil Daily*, January 31, 2002.

"Total Sees Profits Double," *Oil Daily*, November 27, 2000.

Vielvoye, Roger, "Modern Management Style Brings New Look to Total," *Oil and Gas Journal*, February 25, 1991, pp. 15+.

Twitter, Inc.

---■---

795 Folsom Street, Suite 600
San Francisco, California 94107
U.S.A.
Telephone: (415) 896-2008
Fax: (415) 896-2115
Web site: http://twitter.com

Private Company
Incorporated: 2007
Employees: 141
NAICS: 517910 Other Telecommunications

■ ■ ■

Twitter, Inc., is a social networking service that enables subscribers to send and receive text-based messages called "tweets" of 140 characters or less. Subscribers can send and receive tweets through the Twitter Web site and with compatible mobile devices. Although registration is required to use Twitter, the service is free.

TWITTER'S FOUNDING TRIO

The birth of the concept underpinning Twitter could be traced to Jack Dorsey, who began his software development career at the age of 14. He started writing programming code for a dispatch company in his hometown of St. Louis, Missouri, developing a way for taxi drivers, limousine drivers, and couriers to communicate. Dorsey's fascination with dispatch software continued as he progressed through his teenage years and entered college. After transferring from Missouri University of Science and Technology, he began

working for one of the largest courier services in the country, DMS, while attending New York University.

Dorsey was a 10-year veteran in writing dispatch programs by the time he launched his career as an entrepreneur at the age of 24. In 2000 he started a company in Oakland, California, that dispatched couriers, taxis, and emergency services via the Internet. At around this time, Dorsey began exploring the idea of instant status communication, prompting him to tinker with fusing together dispatch software, instant messaging, and text messaging. His work in this area continued for several years, reaching fruition when he joined forces with the two other architects of Twitter's formation, Evan Williams and Isaac "Biz" Stone.

Before he gained fame in the technology sector, Evan Williams learned the nuances of civilization's oldest industry, agriculture. Williams grew up on a farm in Clarks, Nebraska, where he spent his summers irrigating crops. He enrolled at the University of Nebraska, but he left midway through his sophomore year, intent on entering the technology sector. He worked for several start-up firms in Texas and Florida before moving to California to work for O'Reilly Media, a technical book publisher focused on emerging technologies. Williams started at the company in a marketing position, but he soon began writing computer code, which led to freelance work with companies such as Intel Corporation and Hewlett-Packard Company.

In 1999, at the age of 27, Williams started his entrepreneurial career. He cofounded Pyra Labs, a start-up firm whose first product was a Web application that functioned as a project manager, contact manager, and a to-do list. An offshoot of the product became a Web application that created and managed Web logs, a product Williams dubbed "Blogger," giving the technology sector one of the most ubiquitously used words of the decade.

Pyra Labs survived the collapse of the technology sector at the millennium and showed enough promise to attract the attention of Google Inc. Google acquired the company in early 2003 and Williams went with the company, serving as a Google employee until October 2004, when he left to cofound a podcasting company, Odeo. Joining him in launching Odeo was Biz Stone, a Massachusetts native who helped Williams create Blogger. It was at Odeo's headquarters in San Francisco that Dorsey met Williams and Stone in 2006, a meeting that led to the creation of Twitter.

INITIAL RELEASE OF TWITTER: 2006

At Odeo's offices, Dorsey and Stone collaborated on the first Twitter prototype. The pair spent two weeks creating a program that would enable short messages to be shared among mobile devices. They launched the service in early 2006 for Odeo employees to communicate with one another. In July 2006 they released a full-scale version to the public. Referred to as "microblogging," Twitter limited its messages, called "tweets," to 140 characters, giving the public a new way to communicate that ignited frenzied use in staccato fragments. "We did a bunch of name-storming," Dorsey said in a February 18, 2009 interview with the *Los Angeles Times*, "and we came up with the word 'twitch' because the phone kind of vibrates when it moves. But 'twitch' is not a good

product name because it doesn't bring up the right imagery. So we looked in the dictionary for words around it, and we came across the word 'twitter,' and it was just perfect. The definition was 'a short burst of inconsequential information,' and 'chirps from birds.' And that's exactly what the product was."

Before Twitter began its exponential rise in popularity, its creators made several moves that affected which corporate entity controlled the new service. In October 2006, three months after launching Twitter to the public, Williams, Stone, Dorsey, and several other Odeo employees formed Obvious Corp. Through Obvious, the partners acquired all the assets of Odeo, including Twitter.com, from investors and other shareholders.

The moment when Twitter began to turn from being a novel communication service into a worldwide phenomenon could be traced to a particular time and place. At the nine-day South by Southwest music and digital conference in Austin, Texas, in March 2007, a team of Obvious employees set up a demonstration of Twitter that captured the crowd's interest. Next to the conference registration desk and in the hallway where attendees exited panel discussions, Obvious placed two 51-inch plasma screens that showed scrolling updates of tweets from bloggers attending the event, displaying information concerning the location of popular parties, restaurants, and which panel discussions were most memorable. Twitter usage increased from 20,000 tweets per day to 60,000 tweets per day during South by Southwest. "You would go into a panel room and 20 percent of the people would be staring at their phones, sending out or getting updates," an attendee said in the April 2, 2007 issue of *Business Week*.

TWITTER RANKS SWELL: 2007

One month after the South by Southwest festival, Williams, Dorsey, and Stone spun off Twitter as a separate company. Within a year of its creation, Twitter had shown that it could and needed to stand on its own, but the one pressing concern about its viability as an independent company was its business model. Twitter did not generate any revenue and its leaders had not articulated a way for the company to make money. Financially, the company remained afloat during its first years in business by relying on capital supplied by venture capital firms and investors. Early investors included Union Square Ventures, Internet pioneer Marc Andreessen, and Ron Conway, a venture capitalist who had been an early investor in Google, PayPal, and Ask Jeeves. Industry observers estimated that Twitter had $20 million at its disposal during its first year in business, although the company refused to divulge financial figures.

KEY DATES

2006: Twitter prototype is released to employees of Odeo.
2007: At the South by Southwest festival, the use of Twitter excites attendees.
2008: Number of messages posted per quarter reaches 100 million.
2009: Twitter signs its first sponsorship agreement with Microsoft Corporation.
2010: Number of messages posted per quarter reaches four billion.

For Williams, Dorsey and Stone, revenues and profits would have to wait. Initially, they were more concerned about improving Twitter's service and attracting a massive following. Once they had secured a significantly sized subscriber base, they would turn their attention toward developing a revenue-generating business model, they repeatedly informed the business press. Addressing their first objective, the trio achieved unmitigated success. The growth of the Twitter community was astounding. From 80,000 subscribers following the South by Southwest festival, the number of Twitter users eclipsed one million users one year later. Twitter had 500,000 tweets posted per quarter in 2007. By 2008 the number of tweets posted per quarter reached 100 million. Everyone from Britney Spears to the Dalai Lama "twittered," including presidential hopeful Barack Obama, whose tweets were sent to nearly 40,000 "followers," the third most popular Twitter account.

As the number of Twitter users mushroomed, so too did the size of what the founders referred to as the "Twitter Ecosystem." Twitter made its application programming interface (API) code freely available to the public, enabling third-party software developers to create applications for Twitter users. Applications such as TweetDeck and Seesmic, which let users segment and rearrange tweets on a computer screen, appeared. TwitPic enabled users to share photos. Twitterfeed gave users the ability to post messages to Twitter and to several other microblogging platforms at the same time. Twhirl enabled users to bring messages to their desktop without having to log onto the Twitter Web site.

Soon, there were several thousand applications that had registered with Twitter, and many more that had not registered, with an average of five new applications debuting per day. Most of the applications were offered for free, but there were some programs that charged a fee, representing the first trickle of revenue produced by Twitter, although the company itself did not receive any of the money.

FIRST REVENUES: 2009

The legions of Twitter users proliferated between 2008 and 2009. The number of tweets posted per quarter skyrocketed from 100 million to a staggering two billion. Corporations ranging from chemical giant Monsanto to coffee retailer Starbucks to airliner JetBlue used Twitter for everything from product testing to customer service to announcing sales. Politicians used Twitter, celebrities used Twitter, and, by 2009, more than seven million unique visitors accessed the company's Web site from personal computers each month, an increase of 1,382 percent from 2008.

"The question really becomes how do they take the next step?," an analyst asked in the March 24, 2009 issue of *Investor's Business Daily*. "Although it's wonderful to amass an audience like this, in the long-term their investors are going to be looking for a return on their investment, and that is where the rubber meets the road." The greater the rate of Twitter's growth became, the greater the urgency for a profit-making business model became, particularly and most vociferously from onlookers who salivated at the massive size of the Twitter community and wondered how to profit from the millions of Twitter users. The founders, in contrast, were reticent, at least publicly, to unveil a plan to make Twitter a commercial enterprise.

As the drumbeats for a financially viable business plan grew louder, reports emerged in 2009 of possible corporate partnerships and moneymaking strategies. Rumors, later confirmed, circulated that social-networking company Facebook offered to buy Twitter for $500 million in Facebook stock in March 2009, but negotiations collapsed over questions about the value of Facebook stock. Industry observers foresaw a partnership between Twitter and Google, envisioning a revenue-sharing agreement that would be based on Google placing advertisements in tweets. Stone sidestepped the question of whether Twitter and Google were linking up in an April 6, 2009 interview with *Investor's Business Daily*. "It should come as no surprise that Twitter engages in discussions with other companies regularly and on a variety of subjects," he said. "Our goal is to build a profitable, independent company and we're just getting started."

Twitter had begun to collect its first revenue shortly before Stone's comments. In March 2009 the company signed its first sponsorship agreement with Microsoft, inking a deal with the software giant to financially back "ExecTweets," a service designed to help businesspeople find and follow each other on Twitter. Although the sponsorship agreement did not represent a full-fledged, revenue-generating strategy, it did signal an important first toward a profitable future. By the end of the decade, much remained to be determined about Twitter's financial future, but there was little doubt about the popularity of Twitter. During its first four years of existence, more than 100 million subscribers signed up for the service, posting an astonishing four billion tweets during the first quarter of 2010, twice the total posted on a quarterly basis in 2009.

Jeffrey L. Covell

PRINCIPAL COMPETITORS

AOL Inc.; Facebook, Inc.; Google Inc.

FURTHER READING

Barlas, Pete, "Google-Twitter Reported Merger Talk Sparks Partnership Theories," *Investor's Business Daily*, April 6, 2009, p. A6.

———, "Twitter Seen Facing Challenges if Ads Part of Its Revenue Plans," *Investor's Business Daily*, March 24, 2009, p. A4.

Green, Heather, "Twitter: All Trivia, All the Time," *Business Week*, April 2, 2007, p. 40.

Sarno, David, "Twitter Creator Jack Dorsey Illuminates the Site's Founding Document," *Los Angeles Times*, February 18, 2009.

Walbridge

---

777 Woodward Avenue, Suite 300
Detroit, Michigan 48226
U.S.A.
Telephone: (313) 963-8000
Fax: (313) 963-8150
Web site: http://www.walbridge.com

Private Company
Incorporated: 1916
Employees: 1,000
Sales: $1.64 billion (2009 est.)
NAICS: 236210 Industrial Building Construction; 236220 Commercial and Institutional Building Construction; 237110 Water and Sewer Line and Related Structures Construction; 237310 Highway, Street, and Bridge Construction; 237990 Other Heavy and Civil Engineering Construction; 238110 Poured Concrete Foundation and Structure Contractors; 238290 Other Building Equipment Contractors; 238990 All Other Specialty Trade Contractors; 237130 Power and Communication Line and Related Structures Construction; 561210 Facilities and Support Services; 561720 Janitorial Services; 531390 Other Activities Related to Real Estate

■ ■ ■

Headquartered in Detroit, Michigan, privately held Walbridge is one of the nation's leading construction companies. The company is well-known for its work as an airport contractor, and its work in the area of manufacturing construction (especially steel and nonferrous metal plants). Walbridge also serves a variety of other markets, including commercial, power and energy, government, and infrastructure. The company's services include construction management, program management, general contracting, design-build and turnkey solutions, preconstruction, engineering management, decommissioning, equipment installation, and facilities management.

BEGINNINGS

Walbridge Aldinger was founded in 1916 by two Detroit, Michigan, contractors who sought to form a company that would be large enough to handle the many projects the growing city and its nascent auto industry were generating. George B. Walbridge had served as a colonel in the U.S. Army Corps of Engineers and had moved to Detroit in 1914 as vice president of the New York-based construction firm George F. Fuller Company. His partner, Albert H. Aldinger, was a banker of German extraction who had previously founded a Canadian construction firm.

The new company quickly began to take on major assignments. Early buildings included Detroit's Orchestra Hall (1920); the Women's Colony Club (1924); Ford's Dearborn plant (1925); Olympia Stadium (1927); and the United Artist Building (1928). The next few years saw the city's WWJ Broadcasting studios and the University of Michigan's women's dormitories completed, among many others. In 1945 Walbridge and Aldinger sold the company to 23-year-old John Rakolta and a partner.

Since Walbridge's founding in 1916, we have steadily grown to become one of the most successful construction companies in North America. With experience in diverse market segments, we adapt to fit our customers' unique project requirements.

Over the succeeding decades, the company came to concentrate on work for the automobile industry. One notable project was the Chevrolet Technology Center, completed in 1954. John Rakolta continued to run the company throughout these years, and as he grew older he began grooming his son to take over. John Jr. started working for the family business following completion of a degree in civil engineering, and in 1975 the 28-year-old began to take the reins from his father, assembling a new management team with John senior's blessings. He was named company president in 1979.

John Rakolta Jr. adopted a more aggressive approach than his father had, boosting revenues from $50 million in 1975 to $80 million in 1979. The company's earnings at this time were still primarily derived from contracts with carmakers. At the start of the 1980s, the expanding Walbridge Aldinger moved its headquarters from Detroit to the suburb of Livonia.

DIVERSIFICATION

One idea Rakolta had for growing the business was diversification into the commercial construction industry. Attempts to develop this area from within were made, but the key event came in 1984 when Walbridge Aldinger purchased a financially troubled Detroit-area commercial contractor named Darin & Armstrong. The acquisition more than doubled the company in size and also gave it a branch in Florida that operated throughout the southeastern United States.

Rakolta's eye was increasingly on cultivating clients outside of Michigan, with new projects soon under way in Florida, California, and elsewhere. Highlights of the 1980s included the Spaceship Earth building at the Epcot Center in Florida, the Ford Hermosillo Stamping Plant in Mexico, and Detroit's People Mover monorail system. The company also built three auto plants in Canada during the decade in partnership with Ellis-Don Ltd. of Toronto.

HEADING INTO THE NINETIES

In 1989 the company's headquarters were moved back to Detroit when a 100,000-square-foot building was acquired from U.S. Mutual Savings & Loan, after that company ran out of funds to complete a renovation of the structure. Walbridge Aldinger completed the work at a cost of some $9 million and moved 100 of its employees into the space. A parking structure also was built across the street for their use. The move was attributed in part to the company's desire to attract more minority employees, as African Americans made up a much larger percentage of Detroit's population than Livonia's. Another motive was simply that the company was investing in the city in which it had been founded.

John Rakolta Jr. was a strong booster of Detroit, which had seen its fortunes decline as economically advantaged residents fled to the suburbs and many once-proud buildings came to be abandoned in the downtown area. Rakolta and his wife, Terry, had earlier joined the Detroit Heritage Fund, a group of prominent local citizens who banded together in an attempt to revive the city's renowned London Chop House restaurant. The Rakoltas were active in conservative political causes as well, John as a fundraiser for the Republican Party and Terry with a campaign to protest the excessive doses of sex and violence on television. Her efforts to organize boycotts of advertisers garnered much national media attention.

AUTO INDUSTRY CONSTRUCTION

The 1990s started off well for the company, with Walbridge Aldinger completing the 44-story, $250 million One Detroit Center building in 1991. It was the city's first major new office structure since the five-tower Renaissance Center had been built in the mid-1970s. Work also was underway on the $700 million Chrysler Technology Center in Auburn Hills, Michigan. The company's docket consisted of approximately 60 percent auto industry-related construction, 30 percent commercial building, and 10 percent public projects. Walbridge Aldinger was now one of the top two contractors in the state of Michigan, second only to Barton Malow of Southfield. Annual revenues stood at $550 million, more than 10 times the 1975 figure.

The early 1990s saw a decline in revenues, however, as the economy slowed and building projects were scaled back. Walbridge Aldinger, again seeking to branch out, made its first bid on a Michigan Department of Transportation project, the $42 million Blue Water Bridge Plaza expansion in Port Huron. Before it could submit a bid, the company was required to undergo an

KEY DATES

1916: Company is founded in Detroit by George B. Walbridge and Albert H. Aldinger.

1945: John Rakolta and a partner acquire control of the company.

1975: John Rakolta Jr. begins to take over operations from his father.

1984: Acquisition of builder Darin & Armstrong doubles size of company.

1998: Company is first U.S. general contractor to receive ISO 9001 certification.

2003: Chairman-Emeritus John Rakolta dies at the age of 80.

2008: Company abbreviates its name, becoming Walbridge.

18-month certification process.

In 1993 Walbridge Aldinger was named the construction manager for Chrysler Corporation's newly announced world headquarters, which would be located near the automaker's Technology Center. In 1995 a strategic alliance was formed with Brown & Root, Inc., of Texas, called Walbridge Brown & Root International L.L.C. The new entity was charged with seeking international contracts for auto industry construction projects. Brown & Root, a subsidiary of Halliburton Co., operated internationally in the fields of engineering and construction, working for a wide range of clients, including governments, oil companies, and the chemical industry. The joint venture's first project was a Chrysler plant in Venezuela.

CONSTRUCTION BOOM

In 1997 Walbridge Aldinger won a contract with Toyota Motor Manufacturing of West Virginia to build a $400 million engine plant there. The project would require hiring some 700 workers, with completion scheduled for the following year. The U.S. construction industry was now returning to good health, with the Clinton era economic boom loosening up purse strings for new projects. Employment of construction workers also was up, and it was sometimes becoming difficult to find enough skilled workers for the many projects that were coming in.

Detroit had legalized casino gambling during the decade, and several major players in that industry began racing to complete lavish facilities in the downtown

area. The Detroit Lions and Detroit Tigers athletic teams also were making plans for new stadiums, and the company was involved with these projects as well. In the case of the Lions' stadium, Walbridge Aldinger and Perini Building Co. of Southfield were tapped initially to lay the groundwork for construction, but before actual work could commence they were dropped from the project, resulting in a severance payment to both companies.

In 1998 Walbridge Aldinger was rehired to work on the Lions' stadium, and the company also won a contract to demolish the landmark Hudson's department store building, an 88-year-old, 22-story structure that had been closed since 1983. A new Ford plant in India was completed during the year as well. Annual revenues reached a new high of $615 million.

ISO 9001 CERTIFICATION

The year 1998 also saw Walbridge Aldinger receive ISO 9001 certification. The International Organization of Standardization in Geneva, Switzerland, had issued the standards, which prescribed construction techniques that improved efficiency and productivity while reducing costs. Walbridge Aldinger put its employees through extensive training and the company underwent a 16-month assessment to receive the certification, which gave it an advantage in procuring contracts with major clients, including the big three automakers.

The following year Walbridge Aldinger won a $50 million bid to build portions of an access road to Detroit's Metro Airport. Since 1991 the company had performed $142 million worth of work at the site, building parking structures, roads, and a hangar. The new access road, which connected the southern end of the airport with two major public thoroughfares, would be three miles long when finished.

On May 15, 1999, the company performed the largest continuous concrete pour in history, using 150 concrete trucks carrying 2,333 separate loads. The 950-foot-long, 150-foot-wide section of concrete roadway was four feet thick. The decision to pour it continuously was dictated by the road's proximity to the airport's runways and the need to minimize disruption to travelers.

A NEW MILLENNIUM

The year 2000 saw the company once again off the Lions' stadium project because of a dispute with project manager Hammes Co. and clashes with the football team over costs. Co-contractor Barton Malow also withdrew. A major new assignment in Detroit was in the offing, however. Computer software and consulting giant Compuware was making plans to move from suburban Farmington Hills to the downtown area, and Walbridge Aldinger was brought in to manage the $550 million, 16-story project.

The company was hired by developer REDICO, which was to build the structure and then lease it to Compuware. In March 2000 REDICO's president died, however, and Compuware decided to fund the project itself. This resulted in a series of delays while the design underwent further development. Meanwhile, Compuware's stock value was falling precipitously, and some speculated that the project might be downsized if the slide was not reversed. Nonetheless, in the late fall of 2000 a tentative beginning was made at the building site in downtown Detroit. Completion was projected for June 2003.

In recognition for quality work at seven locations, in 2001 DaimlerChrysler picked Walbridge Aldinger from a group of 161 construction suppliers to receive a Commodity and Gold Award for ratings in the areas of quality, delivery, technology, and price. Midway through the following year Walbridge Aldinger formed a new business named Walbridge State after acquiring The State Group, which had operated as a subsidiary of Canada-based Bracknell Corp. The acquisition allowed the company to expand operations in southwest Ontario.

In September 2003 Walbridge Aldinger mourned the loss of Chairman-Emeritus John Rakolta, who died at the age of 80 following a battle with cancer. In December of that year a joint venture between the company and Detroit-based L.S. Brinker Co. was chosen to potentially renovate Detroit's Book Cadillac Hotel. Kimberly-Clark Corp. subsidiary Historic Hospitality Investments LLC and the City of Detroit were considering a $147 million renovation of the former historical landmark, shuttered since 1984, in time for Super Bowl XL in 2006.

PROGRESS CONTINUES

Progress continued in 2004 when Walbridge Aldinger served as the site preparation general contractor for a $2.1 billion expansion of DaimlerChrysler's Toledo Jeep Assembly plant in Ohio. The company ended the year with a sizable operations base. In addition to its Detroit headquarters, Walbridge Aldinger had offices in Aurora, Illinois; Kokomo, Indiana; Quad Cities, Iowa; Charlotte, North Carolina; Georgetown, Kentucky; Tampa, Florida; Mexico City, Mexico; Windsor, Ontario, Canada; and Sinaia and Bucharest, Romania. In addition, the formation of a new office in Shanghai,

China, was underway. By this time Walbridge Aldinger also owned the Romania-based diesel fuel injection equipment manufacturer Mefin Sinaia S.A., which employed 1,300 people.

Problems developed in mid-2005 when Walbridge Aldinger filed a $22 million lawsuit against the City of Detroit over cost disputes and delays connected with the renovation of a waste-treatment plant. Around the same time the company received first place in the 22nd Annual Thomas J. Reynolds Safety Awards for Excellence competition. The previous year, Walbridge Aldinger's employees worked 1.2 million safe man-hours with no lost time due to injury. The award was one of approximately 25 major safety recognitions the company had received since 2000.

In 2006 Walbridge Aldinger decided to sell a 515-acre parcel of land in Lyon Township, located at Grand River Avenue and Milford Road. The land, which the company had owned since 1984, was considered by some to be one of the most sought-after real estate parcels in the region. At one time Walbridge Aldinger had hoped to develop the land itself, but later decided such development did not fit within its strategy.

By 2005 Walbridge Aldinger employed a workforce of 1,200 people. The company's Belding Walbridge rigging subsidiary, which had grown to include 500 employees, generated revenues of approximately $170 million in 2006. Building on a project roster that included work for both NASA and the Vatican, the company was chosen to relocate the Bubble Chamber (used to record and research the collision of protons and neutrons) for Fermi National Accelerator Laboratory.

NAME CHANGE

In 2007 Walbridge Aldinger Construction Management, a joint venture with Detroit-based Jenkins Construction, was selected to manage the $158 million renovation of the Detroit Institute of Arts. In 2008 a major development took place when the company decided to abbreviate its name, becoming Walbridge. According to the company, the new name acknowledged its heritage "while also conveying innovation, precision and flexibility."

Following the renovation of Walbridge's world headquarters in 2009, the facility received Leadership in Energy and Environmental Design (LEED) Silver CI Certification from the U.S. Green Building Council, becoming Detroit's first commercial interiors project to receive the certification. Finally, in late 2009 Walbridge was awarded a $3.2 million contract to construct a fire station at the Volkswagen auto assembly plant in Chattanooga, Tennessee.

Walbridge had much to celebrate in 2010. In March the company's outstanding safety performance on military projects resulted in the Savannah District, U.S. Army Corps of Engineers' 2009 Large Military Contractor of the Year Award. The following month the company ranked first in the Associated General Contractors of America 2009 Construction Safety and Excellence Awards.

Midway through the year the company celebrated the opening of the new $318 million Northwest Florida Beaches International Airport. Walbridge served as general contractor for the many areas of the airport, including a 125,000-square-foot, seven-gate terminal and a 148-foot air traffic control tower. Finally, in June John Rakolta Jr. received an Ernst & Young Master Entrepreneur of the Year award. Throughout almost a century of operations, Walbridge had taken on some of the largest and most challenging construction projects in the Detroit area and beyond. Moving forward, the company appeared to have excellent prospects for continued success.

Frank Uhle
Updated, Paul R. Greenland

PRINCIPAL SUBSIDIARIES

Walbridge Canada; Walbridge Concrete Services; Walbridge de Mexico; Walbridge East; Walbridge Equipment Installation; Walbridge Facility Management; Walbridge Florida; Walbridge International; Walbridge Southeast; Walbridge West.

PRINCIPAL COMPETITORS

Barton Malow Company; EllisDon Corporation; The Turner Corporation.

FURTHER READING

Ankeny, Robert, "Firms Losing Stadium Work to Split $1.2M," *Crain's Detroit Business*, September 22, 1997, p. 7.

Barkholz, David, "Walbridge's Rakolta: Building on Success," *Crain's Detroit Business*, January 29, 1990, p. 1.

"Belding Walbridge Boasts a 'Tradition of Innovation,'" *Manufacturing Today*, November–December 2006, p. 156.

Fricker, Daniel G., "Compuware Redesign Hinders Its Detroit Site," *Detroit Free Press*, October 12, 2000.

Goodin, Michael, "Walbridge Gets Chrysler HQ Contract," *Crain's Detroit Business*, April 12, 1993, p. 1.

Grogan, Tim, and William J. Angelo, "Three Years of Double-Digit Growth Have General Builders Soaring," *Engineering News-Record*, May 31, 1999, p. 113.

"Walbridge," *Detroiter*, September 2009, p. 62.

Warrnambool Cheese and Butter Factory Company Holdings Limited

5331 Great Ocean Road
Allansford, Victoria 3277
Australia
Telephone: (+61-3) 5565-3200
Fax: (+61-3) 5563-2156
Web site: http://www.wcbf.com.au

Public Company
Incorporated: 1888
Employees: 397
Sales: $361.42 million (2009)
Stock Exchanges: Australian
Ticker Symbol: WCB
NAICS: 311513 Cheese Manufacturing; 311512 Creamery Butter Manufacturing; 311514 Dry, Condensed, and Evaporated Dairy Product Manufacturing

■ ■ ■

Warrnambool Cheese and Butter Factory Company Holdings Limited is Australia's oldest dairy processing company. The Australian Stock Exchange-listed business is based in Allansford, Victoria, where it maintains a plant that each year manufactures more than 80,000 tons of products supplied by some 600 operators in Victoria and South Australia. In addition to dairy products, the company manufactures whey protein concentrate and two value-added products: Enprocal, a high-protein supplement for the elderly and frail; and Pro10Active, a whey protein concentrate fortified with calcium, vitamin D, and other ingredients to help the elderly maintain

muscle and other body tissue. The company also operates Cheese World, a retail outlet near its plant that includes a museum, wine and cheese cellar, supermarket, and restaurant.

VICTORIA'S FIRST BUTTER FACTORY: 1888

Warrnambool was founded in 1888 by a group of farmers in the Allansford area, several miles from the city of Warrnambool. They had been producing butter on their farms and were now interested in starting a butter factory. John S. Weatherhead, who grew up on a farm and was educated in Warrnambool, was named manager of the newly formed Warrnambool Cheese and Butter Factory Company Limited. When the plant opened in November 1888 it became the first butter factory registered in the State of Victoria. In the first year, the company generated sales of £12,000 and posted a loss of £200. Under Weatherhead, Warrnambool was able to break even in the second year, and post a £1,000 profit in the third. At that point Weatherhead left to establish another enterprise, the Camperdown Cheese and Butter Factory Company Limited.

Cheese had been produced in the Allansford area since the mid-1800s, and in 1892 Warrnambool expanded into cheese production. By 1900 the company was producing about 350 tons of butter and 60 tons of cheese annually. The original wooden plant remained in operation until 1913 when it was destroyed by fire due to a boiler explosion. It was replaced by a new facility, but it too was destroyed by fire in February 1929. A third factory was constructed on the present-day site and expanded and renovated over the years.

PARTNERING WITH KRAFT BEGINNING IN 1934

A major turning point in the history of Warrnambool occurred in 1934 when the company asked U.S.-based Kraft Foods, then known as Kraft-Phenix Cheese Corporation, to lease its Australian plant. While some opposed the arrangement, characterizing it as a sellout, the relationship with Kraft that began in 1935 proved to be a boon for Warrnambool's supplier-shareholders. For its part, Kraft was able to develop a supply of quality bulk cheddar to adequately serve the Australian market. The plant, as a result, was upgraded by Kraft and became the most advanced operation in the country and the largest cheese producer in the Southern Hemisphere. Moreover, the Australian dairy industry benefited from Kraft's expertise, and standards in quality and consistency were raised in the country. Kraft also trained many future leaders of the Australian dairy industry.

Warrnambool was fortunate to develop a strong leader in its longtime Managing Director John McLean. He joined the company in 1956 as an intern when there were only 40 employees. Five years later he became production manager and in 1973 he was named managing director. At the time Warrnambool generated annual sales of AUD 16 million. The company enjoyed steady but hardly spectacular growth. In 1986 it added a revenue stream with the launch of Cheese World, which served as a retail outlet for the factory. The addition of a gift shop, general store, restaurant, and factory tours made Cheese World into a tourist attraction that helped promote the Warrnambool brand.

KRAFT NARROWS RELATIONSHIP: 1992

After a century in operation, Warrnambool did not experience radical change until the 1990s. In 1992 Kraft changed its relationship with Warrnambool. While it would continue to buy Warrnambool's cheese and market it under the Kraft label, it would no longer take responsibility for the running of the plant. A year later the management of the cheese factory was taken over by a joint venture with United Milk Tasmania. An AUD 35 million modernization of the cheese plant and the addition of a whey concentrate and drying plant followed, resulting in significant growth for Warrnambool in the 1990s.

The upgraded plant allowed Warrnambool to handle as much as one million liters of milk per day. Despite an increase in consumption of dairy products in Australia, Warrnambool's capacity was greater than the demand from Kraft. As a result, the company looked overseas and by necessity evolved into a global concern, selling cheese as well as whey (a by-product of cheesemaking), frozen cream, and other products in such markets as the United States, Canada, Japan, Korea, and the Middle East. In a matter of just two years, export sales increased 10-fold to more than AUD 30 million in 1994, about half of the company's total revenues.

Warrnambool's milk suppliers continued to increase their production, leading to further expansion of the Warrnambool facilities. A new automated milk drying plant, capable of producing 6.5 tons of powder per hour, was opened in 1998. Warrnambool was now more customer focused and looked to become more of an important player in the Southeast Asian market. At the same time, it also faced challenges presented by industry deregulation. In January 1999 its joint venture partner, United Milk Tasmania, was acquired by Bonlac Foods, creating Australia's largest supplier-owned dairy company. Uncomfortable working with Bonlac, Warrnambool decided it was better off operating the Allansford plant alone.

In the fall of 1999 the company asked its suppliers and investor shareholders to support a AUD 10 million capital restructuring plan. Annual sales at this stage approached the AUD 200 million level. When the sale of new stock was completed in early 2000, Warrnambool realized AUD 7.8 million. Because more than one-quarter of the suppliers rejected the idea, the share offer fell short of full subscription. Simultaneous with the share offer, the company completed negotiations to buy out Bonlac's interest in the Allansford manufacturing facilities, a right Warrnambool had received when Bonlac acquired United Milk Tasmania. Warrnambool also negotiated a 10-year cheese supply agreement with Dairy Farmers, which would market the cheddar cheese under its Coon brand. In addition, Warrnambool would continue to supply milk to a Dairy Farmer's plant that produced romano and parmesan-style cheeses.

OVERCOMING OPPOSITION TO GOING PUBLIC: 2003–04

Sales topped AUD 300 million in 2001 and Warrnambool opened an office in Tokyo, Japan. The company

KEY DATES

1888: Warrnambool Cheese and Butter Factory is established.
1935: Kraft takes over management of factory.
1973: John McLean is named managing director.
1992: Kraft's plant management ends.
2009: McLean is lured out of retirement.

looked to list its shares on the Australian Stock Exchange in 2003, a move in keeping with the capital restructuring plan of three years earlier when management promised shareholders that the stock would be marketable by 2003. The idea of listing the stock met with stiff opposition, however. Many of the supplier-shareholders were fearful that the suppliers, only half of whom were shareholders, would lose control of the company and that the short-term interests of equity shareholders would hold sway. Moreover, there was concern that Warrnambool would leave itself open to a hostile takeover, in which case the suppliers would lose all influence in the direction of the company. In June 2003 the bid to list Warrnambool's shares on the Australian Stock Exchange was defeated at a general meeting, narrowly failing to receive the requisite 75 percent approval. A second attempt was made in 2004 and succeeded. On May 27, 2004, Warrnambool made its debut on the Australian Stock Market.

Increasing demand for cheese and whey protein led Warrnambool to upgrade its plants in 2005. A year later the company completed a pair of acquisitions to expand its product offerings. The acquisition of Prime Nutrition brought the Enprocal product and other milk proteins, while the addition of Cheese Master, a maker of flavored, waxed, and packaged cheddar cheese, helped Warrnambool to increase its retail reach. The year 2006 was also noteworthy because John McLean retired after more than half a century with the company, 30 years of which he served as managing director and chief executive officer. He was succeeded by Neil Kearney, the former chief financial officer with National Foods who possessed a good deal of experience in the dairy industry in both Australia and international markets.

DAIRY PRICES PLUMMET: 2009

Kearney enjoyed a successful start as Warrnambool's new chief executive. Revenues increased to AUD 371.7 million in fiscal 2007 and AUD 525 million a year later. The company appeared to be on the threshold of a new

era in 2008 when Warrnambool negotiated a deal to join forces with National Foods to take joint ownership of the Australian Cheese Company. Declining milk and other dairy prices that collapsed in early 2009 scuttled the deal, however, and resulted in turmoil for Warrnambool.

Warrnambool attempted to deal with poor market conditions by slashing the prices it paid to suppliers in March 2009. The suppliers were furious, accusing management of siding with investor-shareholders over the needs of the supplier-shareholders who had built the company. Many of the farmers left Warrnambool for a rival concern, Murray Goulburn Cooperative. Although the payments were subsequently reinstated, Kearney was forced to resign in April 2009 and John McLean was persuaded to come out of retirement to take the helm and restore trust in management. While his return was welcomed by suppliers and many of the defectors returned to the fold, disgruntled farmers continued to press for the resignation of the company's chairman, David Karpin, who finally relented in May 2009.

Another victim of the supplier revolt was a new rights issue that would have funded the takeover of the Australian Cheese Company. The deal was subsequently terminated. Warrnambool soon had other concerns as well. Later in 2009 it became the target of unsolicited takeover bids from Murray Goulburn and Canadian dairy giant Saputo. The offers were rejected, but Murray Goulburn remained undeterred and presented a revised bid that was also spurned in February 2010. Murray Goulburn was content to bide its time, buying shares on the open market until it had accumulated a 10 percent position. According to the Warrnambool constitution adopted when it went public, no single shareholder could control more than 15 percent of the company until May 2011. In June 2010, McLean retired again, having at least stabilized the company, but given Murray Goulburn's continued interest in acquiring the business, the future of Warrnambool remained very much uncertain.

Ed Dinger

PRINCIPAL SUBSIDIARIES

Warrnambool Cheese & Butter Factory Company Limited; Australian Dairy Products Pty Ltd; Warrnambool Milk Products Pty Limited; Protein Technology Victoria Pty Ltd.

PRINCIPAL COMPETITORS

Danisco A/S; Fonterra Co-operative Group Limited; Goodman Fielder Limited.

FURTHER READING

Austin, Nigel, and Geoff Easdown, "Dairy Chief Walks after Milk Fiasco," *Herald Sun*, May 12, 2009.

Frith, Bryan, "Cheese Maker Battles with Two Competing Cultures," *Australian*, February 25, 2010.

Hopkins, Philip, "Dairy Firm Churns Out $8m in Capital," *Age*, February 7, 2000.

McNaught, Megan, "Big Cheese Signs Off," *Weekly Times*, August 23, 2006.

Pyle, Bill, "Dairy Stalwart an Example," *Weekly Times*, September 11, 2001.

"Resignation Turmoil at Warrnambool Cheese and Butter," *Foodweek*, May 15, 2009.

Smith, James, *The Cyclopedia of Victoria*, Melbourne, Australia: The Cyclopedia Company, 1904.

Williams, Ruth, "Churning Market Forces Dairy Boss' Comeback," *Age*, July 18, 2009.

The Weinstein Company LLC

———————————■———————————

345 Hudson Street, 13th Floor
New York, New York 10014
U.S.A.
Telephone: (646) 862-3400
Fax: (917) 368-7000
Web site: http://www.weinsteinco.com

Private Company
Incorporated: 2005
NAICS: 512110 Motion Picture and Video Production;
512120 Motion Picture and Video Distribution

■ ■ ■

The Weinstein Company LLC is in the business of movie production and distribution. It also produces the hit television show *Project Runway*, which airs on Lifetime. The company is owned by the Weinstein brothers, Harvey and Bob, who are known for changing the face of the independent motion picture industry with films including *Pulp Fiction, Shakespeare in Love, The English Patient, My Left Foot, Good Will Hunting*, and *The Piano*. Investors in The Weinstein Company, which also controls the Dimension Films label, include Goldman Sachs, French TV company TF1, and the advertising firm WPP Group.

LIFE AFTER MIRAMAX: 2005

In 2005, brothers Harvey and Bob Weinstein, generally considered two of the most innovative, intuitive, and combative players in the movie business, founded The Weinstein Company after The Walt Disney Company

bought them out as the heads of Miramax following the production of Michael Moore's antiwar *Fahrenheit 9/11*. The parting was not amicable, with Disney arguing that the Weinsteins had extracted more in bonuses than they had produced in profits. The duo left behind them the name of the independent studio they had founded (in memory of their parents Miriam and Max Weinstein) and its valuable film library. They ultimately retained ownership of the Dimension Films label and the publishing imprint Miramax Books.

With smart money gambling that the new company would become the most successful independent movie company in Hollywood, the Weinsteins did not fear for their future. They had already made a reputation for themselves as industry innovators with Harvey Weinstein overseeing such big-budget films as *Pulp Fiction, Shakespeare in Love, The English Patient, My Left Foot, Good Will Hunting*, and *The Piano*. Bob Weinstein had earned a name for himself on less-expensive, but extremely popular films, such as *Scream, Scary Movie*, and *Spy Kids*.

Almost immediately, the two brothers closed a financing deal that brought in close to $500 million in equity from investors that included Goldman Sachs, French television company TF1, luxury goods producer LVMH, SoftBank Corporation of Japan, advertising firm WPP Group, and Mark Cuban, owner of the Dallas Mavericks. The Weinsteins' backers were convinced that after 800 movies, 53 Oscars, and $4.5 billion in ticket sales at Miramax, the brothers could start all over again successfully. According to a 2005 *New York Times* article, these investors were gambling on Harvey Weinstein, "a singular force, a brawny, monomaniacal figure who has chewed his way through many industry conventions to become the rogue king of the movie business," and his appetite for revenge. With another $500 million in loan money, Harvey and Bob Weinstein were ready to show Disney its mistake with their newly formed entity, The Weinstein Company.

BAD TIMES IN HOLLYWOOD

Times were far from good for the movie industry in the second half of the decade. Box-office revenue was down 8 percent in 2005 from 2004. Hollywood was in a rut, and independent film studios were folding. In addition, without a film library, a primary source of profit to many studios at the time, the Weinsteins were at a disadvantage in generating income. At Disney they had enjoyed $700 million a year to invest in films. Instead The Weinstein Company's investors, who owned 49 percent of the company (the rest belonged to the Weinsteins), demanded that the brothers receive small salaries and no bonuses. They capped investment in any one movie at $40 million.

The plan for the new studio, which the brothers jointly chaired, was to release 25 films a year. Revenue was forecast at $500 million for year one and $1 billion for year two, with profits appearing in year three. The Weinstein Company would focus more on the sorts of low-budget films in which Bob Weinstein had specialized at Disney and less on Harvey Weinstein's "prestige pictures."

Surprisingly, The Weinstein Company's first box-office release, *Derailed*, produced in 2005 on a small budget, was far from a box-office success. Other less-than-usually profitable releases in 2005 included the offbeat comedy-drama *Transamerica*, the computer-animated family film *Hoodwinked*, the World War II-era comedy-drama *Mrs. Henderson Presents*, and the caper comedy *The Matador*. The years 2006 and 2007 also produced a string of non-hits.

CRITICAL ANALYSIS

The U.S. media began reporting that Harvey Weinstein had lost his ability to pick Oscar contenders. The *New York Times* ran an article in late 2007 headlined "More Misses Than Hits," claiming that The Weinstein Company's board was concerned by the company's poor box-office performance. The author commented that, "Now that the Weinsteins have what they want—independence—they can't seem to achieve what they keenly desire—success on their own terms."

In all, The Weinstein Company's domestic box-office tally for 2006 was $311 million. During the following year, through May, that figure had reached only $76.1 million. For Harvey Weinstein, however, the U.S. box office was no longer the measure of success that it had been, replaced by a new "universality of the [world] marketplace. ... Countries should not try to Westernize movies because they invariably don't work." In a 2007 *Independent Extra* article, Weinstein attributed the negative comments about his company, which had recently opened an office in Hong Kong, to envy: "The thing about my company is that it is the most written-about, the most envied. There are so many competitors and the one thing about us having been in this business for 27 years is that we have always been No. 1 or No. 2."

Numerous observers questioned what was going wrong at the company. Jeffrey Wells, editor of the Web site www.HollywoodElsewhere.com, was quoted in a 2008 *Sunday Telegraph* as saying, "The Weinsteins have suffered from the same pressures affecting the indie film sector that everyone else faces." For one thing, there was more competition than ever before. There were a dozen or more companies staffed by people who had been trained at Miramax that were now in competition with their former mentor. Brad Grey of Paramount, David Linde of Universal, Mark Gill of The Film Department, Chris McGurk of Overture, and Rick Sands of MGM were all schooled by the Weinsteins. All these companies contributed to a glut of product at the same time that there was a slowdown in the DVD market. In addition, margins at theaters had decreased, and the credit market had tightened.

A second factor mentioned in connection with The Weinstein Company's poor performance was lack of focus. In 2006, The Weinstein Company and co-investors Hubbard Media Group purchased Ovation TV, an arts-focused cable channel. The Weinsteins also purchased 70 percent of the video company Genius Products in 2006. In the spring of 2007, the company purchased the Halston designer label, and by the end of the year the company also owned the social networking site aSmallWorld.net, a 1,500-title library, and a $285 million Asia fund.

Harvey himself explained where he went wrong in an interview in an August 2009 *New York Times* article. "What happened was, I got more fascinated by these other businesses, and I figured, 'Making movies, I can do that in my sleep.' I kind of delegated the process of production and acquisitions. Yes, I had a say in it, but was I 100 percent concentrating? Absolutely not."

There was also the matter of Harvey's notorious bad temper. He had the reputation of being pugnacious, dubbed the "little Saddam Hussein of cinema" by Bernardo Bertolucci (recounted by Guy Adams in the *Independent*) and "Harvey Scissorhands" by directors for his penchant for heavily editing films himself (recorded by Kaleem Aftab in the *Independent*). People who only tolerated him when he was on top of his game now steered clear of working with him. "Harvey really cares about movies," was how Jeffrey Wells, of the Web site Hollywood Elsewhere, summed it up in a 2008 *Sunday Telegraph* article. "But fairly or unfairly, there are people who will not do business with the Weinsteins."

AIMING FOR PROFITABILITY: 2007–08

The Weinsteins engaged in a number of industry-related deals as well throughout 2006 and 2007. They announced a distribution pact with Metro-Goldwyn-Mayer (MGM) in February 2006, whereby MGM would distribute the product domestically in theaters, while The Weinstein Company retained long-term ownership of movies. In July 2006, the Weinsteins and Robert L. Johnson, founder of Black Entertainment Television, announced the creation of a joint venture studio titled Our Stories Films, which began to distribute African American-oriented films. In November 2006, a three-year deal with Blockbuster Video gave the video rental company exclusive rights for Weinstein films starting on January 1, 2007. On May 24, 2007, The Weinstein Company announced the launch of three new direct-to-video labels: The Miriam Collection, Kaleidoscope TWC, and Dimension Extreme. Weinstein Books also published its first book, *Bloodletting and Miraculous Cures*, on September 4, 2007.

The company continued its steps to become profitable in 2008. In a drive to find production partners, it entered into a seven-year deal to supply films to CBS's Showtime cable network. Detractors noted at the time the company's unusual advance bonus payment of $100 million to Showtime, claiming skepticism on the part of Showtime that the brothers would produce products as planned. On September 25, 2008, The Weinstein Company ended its three-year distribution pact with MGM three months before the December 31 end date, although this happened in part because of the output deal with Showtime.

The Weinstein Company also entered into a legal dispute over *Project Runway*, its most profitable venture to date in 2008. After the company transferred its hit show from NBC's Bravo channel to Lifetime, NBC filed a lawsuit claiming breach of contract. When the long and bitter litigation over the hit reality series ended in 2009, The Weinstein Company admitted to wrongdoing in not giving NBC the first right of refusal and paid NBC Universal an undisclosed sum.

These moves aside, much of The Weinstein Company's senior staff departed in 2008. By the end of 2008, the company had laid off 10 to 11 percent of its workforce. The CEO of Weinstein Books, Rob Weisbach, also resigned.

RESTRUCTURING

By 2009, The Weinstein Company had released about 70 films, but more than a quarter had failed to break the $1 million mark in box-office sales. Thirteen took in less than $100,000. Around this time, the company took on a bridge loan from Ziff Brothers Investment estimated at $75 million and hired financial adviser Miller Buckfire & Co. of New York to explore refinancing or restructuring options to help them, as they put it in a press release, "navigate through this economic climate."

At Miller Buckfire's suggestion, The Weinstein Company began to focus more heavily on marketing and distribution. Miller Buckfire urged the brothers to promote only 10 films per year. Thus, in late 2009, it closed its Hong Kong office and reduced staff by about 35 percent, bringing total staff numbers down to 90 from more than 150. Among those to depart was Tom Ortenberg, a Lions Gate veteran, who had come on board in January 2009 as president of theatrical films.

In September 2009, The Weinstein Company terminated its stake in Genius Products, which had served as its home video distributor since 2006, and gave its DVD business instead to Vivendi Entertainment. In October 2009, The Weinstein Company announced a joint venture with Perseus Book Group, whereby Perseus would be responsible for marketing, editing, publishing, and distribution of Weinstein Books releases.

TARANTINO TURNAROUND?

Box-office hopes for the company in late 2009 focused on the release of Quentin Tarantino's *Inglourious Basterds*, sales for which by late September were approaching $230 million. However, even normally upbeat Harvey Weinstein admitted publicly in an August 2009 *New York Times* article, "The ship's riding on the slate," and mused that if the movie were not successful, he and his brother would have to find employment elsewhere. In January 2010, The Weinstein Company announced more layoffs at the company after the box-office failure of *Nine*. Around this time, the company opted to wipe out its debt by turning over about 200 titles from its film catalog to Goldman Sachs as part of an arrangement with its insurance company.

The company, which had had negative cash flow for every year since its inception, was far from dried up, however. In February, The Weinstein Company made a deal with Sony Pictures Home Entertainment to release DVDs through Sony Pictures Worldwide Acquisitions Group. The Weinsteins also entered talks with Disney in 2010 to reacquire the Miramax name after Disney decided to close down the film imprint. In the end, negotiations were called off as a result of complications in financing and structuring the deal.

Meanwhile, the entire film industry kept watch on The Weinstein Company. Some posited that the Weinsteins had fallen victim to the bloated ways of Hollywood, gravitating toward more expensive, star-driven films. *Pulp Fiction*, an early Weinstein success, for example, cost $9 million to make. *Inglourious Basterds*, on the other hand, cost nearly $70 million.

Still there were those, such as director Kevin Smith, in an August 2009 *New York Times* article, who championed the Weinsteins as the only producers who cared about the quality and originality of their work. Sharon Waxman, founder of the movie news Web site www.TheWrap.com, opined in a June 2009 *Guardian* article, that the loss of The Weinstein Company "would be a terrible loss to those who love film." As of the summer of 2010, The Weinsteins were still making movies and The Weinstein Company was still battling to survive.

Carrie Rothburd

PRINCIPAL COMPETITORS

First Look Studios, Inc.; Focus Features; Fox Searchlight Pictures, Inc.; HBO Films; Imagine Entertainment; The Independent Film Channel LLC; Legendary Pictures Films LLC; Lions Gate Entertainment Corp.; Paramount Vantage; Rogue Arts; Sony Pictures Classics; Spyglass Entertainment Group LLC; Yari Film Group LLC.

FURTHER READING

Adams, Guy, "Drama in the Film Industry: Tough Times for Hollywood's Tough Guy," *Independent*, July 24, 2008.

Aftab, Kaleem, "Harvey Weinstein: Star Wars Fans Fight Back," *Independent*, April 7, 2008.

Carr, David, "Placing Bets on Miramax the Sequel," *New York Times*, October 31, 2005, p. 1.

———, "Weinsteins: More Misses Than Hits," *New York Times*, October 1, 2007, p. 1.

Carter, Bill, "Weinstein Strikes a Deal in 'Project Runway' Lawsuit," *New York Times*, April 2, 2009, p. 3.

Fritz, Ben, "Company Town: Weinstein Co. Raids Film Vault to Settle Debts," *Los Angeles Times*, June 25, 2010, p. 3.

Goldstein, Gregg, "Whither the Weinsteins?" *Hollywoodreporter.com*, July 21, 2008.

Goldstein, Greg, and Kimberly Nordyke, "Weinstein Co. Inks Deal with Showtime," *Hollywoodreporter.com*, July 15, 2008.

Harris, Paul, "International: Movie Moguls Bank on Tarantino to Save Fortunes of Ailing Studio," *Guardian*, June 2, 2009, p. 34.

Lauria, Peter, "Weinsteins' Splice—Harvey, Bob Cut Staff to Survive, Despite 'Basterds,'" *New York Post*, September 23, 2009, p. 35.

Segal, David, "The Brothers Grim," *New York Times*, August 16, 2009, p. 1.

Teodorcsuk, Tom, "Foreign Dispatch: Weinsteins' Star Begins to Fade," *Sunday Telegraph*, July 20, 2008, p. 5.

"There Are Plenty of Powerbrokers in Hollywood, and Few Come as Big, or as Boisterous as Harvey Weinstein," *Independent Extra*, November 5, 2007, p.2

Thompson, Anne, "An Unfair Target?" *Daily Variety*, May 28, 2007, p. 5.

Zeitchik, Steven, "Tom Ortenberg Exits the Weinstein Co.," *Hollywoodreporter.com*, September 26, 2009.

Wendy's/Arby's Group, Inc.

———■———

1155 Perimeter Center West, 12th Floor
Atlanta, Georgia 30338
U.S.A.
Telephone: (678) 514-4500
Toll Free: (888) 514-0924
Fax: (678) 514-5344
Web site: http://www.wendysarbys.com

Public Company
Founded: 1890 as Deisel-Wemmer Co.
Incorporated: 1929 as Deisel-Wemmer-Gilbert Corp.
Employees: 67,500
Sales: $3.58 billion (2009)
Stock Exchanges: New York
Ticker Symbol: WEN
NAICS: 722110 Full-Service Restaurants; 722211 Limited-Service Restaurants; 722213 Snack and Nonalcoholic Beverage Bars; 551112 Offices of Other Holding Companies

■ ■ ■

Wendy's/Arby's Group, Inc., is the third-largest quick-service restaurant company, trailing only McDonald's and Burger King. As the franchiser of two fast-food firms, Wendy's and Arby's, the company has more than 10,200 restaurant outlets worldwide, operating in 50 states and more than 20 countries. Wendy's, the third-largest burger chain in the world, has at least 6,500 restaurants operating in all states and in 20 countries. Arby's, specializing in roast beef sandwiches, is the third-largest sandwich company with more than 3,700

locations, dwarfed only by Subway and Quiznos. About 75 percent of Wendy's/Arby's outlets are franchises. About 20 percent of the company is owned by Nelson Peltz, chairman, and Peter May, vice chairman, through the investment company Trian Partners.

Wendy's/Arby's Group, Inc., traces its roots to three different companies: Wendy's, Arby's, and DWG Corporation, the latter a forerunner to Triarc Companies. DWG was founded in the last decade of the 19th century and became an investment company in the 1960s, the same decade both Wendy's and Arby's were founded. In the 1980s, Arby's was acquired by DWG, which under new ownership changed its name in 1994 to Triarc Companies. Triarc and Wendy's merged in 2008 and the combined company adopted the name Wendy's/Arby's Group, with both Wendy's and Arby's becoming separately run subsidiaries. The rich history of the Group also involves a trio of inventive entrepreneurs who became millionaires: Dave Thomas, who started Wendy's, and Leroy and Forrest Raffel, who founded Arby's. Another name, that of well-known corporate raider Victor Posner, also figures prominently.

DWG: FROM CIGAR SELLER TO CORPORATE RAIDER

Founded as an Ohio partnership in 1890, Deisel-Wemmer Co. began as an importer and manufacturer of cigars. In 1929, Deisel-Wemmer was acquired by an investment group, and its name was changed to Deisel-Wemmer-Gilbert. The company then began acquiring smaller competitors to maintain its share of an ever

COMPANY PERSPECTIVES

Our Vision: To continuously grow stakeholder value by leveraging the strengths of our vibrant, independent restaurant brands. Our purpose: Maintain aligned, people-driven culture and values. Attract, retain, and develop top talent. Offer performance-driven compensation and rewards. Support independent, relevant, and healthy brands focused on sales growth and profitability. Select and support excellent brand leadership. Set metrics for performance in sales and profits. Maintain a lean and efficient support organization. Provide strategies and resources for growth initiatives. Seek acquisitions of other brands and opportunities for growth. Establish metrics for creating shareholder value. Provide attractive franchisee value and competitive business models. Demonstrate community-minded citizenship and giving back by sharing the wealth.

shrinking market. In 1949, the company's name changed again, to DWG Cigar Corporation. During the 1950s, the cigar market shrank as smokers increasingly turned to cigarettes. Thus, in the early 1960s, DWG trimmed its product line and began looking for investment opportunities.

DWG acquired small stakes in other companies in the mid-1960s in order to diversify. After DWG was delisted by the New York Stock Exchange (NYSE) in 1965, it sold most of its assets and wrote off the rest in 1966. Concurrent with a November 1966 name change (to DWG Corporation) the company used capital from asset sales to acquire a 12 percent stake in National Propane Corporation. In less than one year, DWG had transitioned from a small cigar seller to an investment company.

POSNER'S POWER AT THE NEW DWG

While many of DWG's investors abandoned the firm after its NYSE delisting, Victor Posner viewed the company as an undervalued asset. His investment firm Security Management Company gobbled up DWG stock and began to dominate corporate governance, just as DWG was making a shift in business. As a result, DWG became a subsidiary of, and takeover vehicle for, Security Management.

Posner used his control over DWG to gain a stake in a utility maintenance and storage company and to acquire majority control of National Propane. During the 1970s, Posner expanded his empire and developed a reputation as a ruthless corporate raider. Posner's strategy was to look for undervalued companies, take control through stock acquisition, reduce overhead, and increase production and thereby profits. By 1976, Security Management controlled 67 percent of DWG, which in turn owned National Propane outright and 51 percent of Southeast Public Service Company and 42 percent of the shirt-maker Wilson Brothers.

ORIGINS OF ARBY'S

As fast food was becoming an American phenomenon in the 1960s, two brothers saw room for another player besides McDonald's and Burger King in the quick-serve industry. Leroy and Forrest Raffel, operating a foodservice equipment firm in Youngstown, Ohio, decided to open a new restaurant and, to separate themselves from the pack, create a place based on a menu of roast beef sandwiches. In 1964, the brothers opened their first restaurant, named R-B for Raffel Brothers (not "roast beef"). Along with "slow-cooked" roast beef sandwiches, the menu included extra-large iced tea and soft drinks.

R-B was a success, and in 1965, the Raffels opened five more restaurants. By 1970, the brothers had franchised the concept, and there were 500 restaurants. Meanwhile, they expanded their menu to include a variety of roast beef sandwiches and side items and changed the restaurant name from R-B to the near-homophone Arby's. To generate capital for further expansion, the Raffels decided to take Arby's public. However, the initial public offering (IPO) was aborted when market conditions turned sour. The Raffels, who were banking on IPO money to pay their bills, were forced to declare bankruptcy. Five months after filing for Chapter 11, though, Arby's was back in business. By 1975, Arby's again had 500 outlets throughout the United States.

Still looking for expansion capital, the brothers turned to another method: merger with a larger company. In 1976, the Raffels sold Arby's to Royal Crown Cola for $18 million but remained with the chain to manage Arby's operations. Between 1976 and 1979, Arby's added another 300 outlets, and the chain generated large profits. When Royal Crown Cola moved the franchise headquarters to Atlanta in 1979, the Raffels retired, having nurtured a fledgling firm into a national chain of more than 800 restaurants.

ARBY'S UNDER DWG CONTROL

Under its new management, Arby's lost sales and stature within the fast-food industry. In 1984, Royal Crown

KEY DATES

1929: Company's earliest predecessor, a forerunner of Triarc Companies, is incorporated as Deisel-Wemmer-Gilbert Corp., a name later shortened to DWG Corporation.

1964: The Raffel brothers open their first restaurant, named R-B.

1969: Dave Thomas establishes Wendy's.

1994: DWG is reincorporated as Triarc Companies, Inc.

2008: Triarc Companies, owner of Arby's, merges with Wendy's International, Inc.

Cola and its financially struggling Arby's subsidiary were acquired by DWG. Posner hired former Ralston-Purina fast-food division executive Leonard Roberts as Arby's new chief executive. Roberts retooled Arby's menu by eliminating items found in most fast-food restaurants and returning the menu's focus to roast beef and new specialty sandwiches. He also expanded Arby's search for new franchisees, initiated an aggressive advertising campaign, and pioneered new customer services such as acceptance of credit cards. Roberts's business strategy paid dividends. Sales increased, and the company opened up hundreds of restaurants in North America and a handful in Europe as well. By the end of the decade, Arby's had 2,100 restaurants which annually generated more than $1 billion, sales that made Arby's the 12th-leading fast-food business.

Meanwhile, Posner faced legal problems related to business dealings and disagreements with Roberts over how to run Arby's. Roberts was dissatisfied with how Posner managed Arby's finances, believing Posner was siphoning off its profits rather than reinvesting in Arby's growth and improvement. As a result, Roberts threw his support behind a group of franchisees who sought to acquire the Arby's chain. Posner rejected the offer and ultimately fired Roberts. In turn, executives fled the firm, and in 1991, just as Arby's was gearing up for international expansion, the company was missing key executives. Arby's floundered.

DWG itself was deeply in debt by the early 1990s and had sold its two shirt manufacturing firms and its citrus company. Posner too was in legal trouble related to charges of illegally trading stock to acquire one of his companies. Ultimately, Judge Thomas D. Lambros appointed three directors to sit on the DWG board. Lambros also ordered Posner to sell half of his common

shares and convert the other half to nonvoting preferred shares. With no control over his former takeover vehicle, Posner resigned as chairman in 1993 and pocketed $77 million from the sale of DWG stock. DWG stockholders, in return, agreed to drop all unresolved lawsuits that claimed Posner had looted his own company.

NINETIES: THE FIRST DECADE OF TRIARC COMPANIES, INC.

In 1993, DWG was acquired by Trian, an investment firm controlled by Nelson Peltz, who had gained his fame in the 1980s working with Michael Milken as a junk bond specialist, and Peter May. Upon taking control of DWG, Peltz became chairman and chief executive and May was named president and chief operating officer. To serve as Arby's chief executive, the partners hired Donald Pierce, who had previously run Taco Bell. Pierce ramped up Arby's expansion efforts and remodeled restaurants to reflect an Old West décor. By 1995, Arby's had 2,800 restaurants worldwide and annual revenues of more than $1.8 billion.

Triarc's new management moved quickly to give the company a focus. The firm sold disparate assets within its initial years to pare down to four areas of operation: fast food, soft drinks, liquefied petroleum gas, and textiles. Between 1995 and 1997, Triarc expanded its soft drinks line and acquired holdings that included the popular brands Stewart's Root Beer, Mistic, and Snapple. The latter two had suffered from brand mismanagement. Triarc soon restored Mistic and Snapple to profitability and in the process gained a positive reputation.

In its restaurant segment, Triarc decided to operate exclusively as franchiser and marketer of the Arby's brand. All company-owned units were sold, and Arby's enhanced its menu through co-brands, including T.J. Cinnamons' cinnamon rolls and premium coffees and Pasta Connection's pasta entrées. In July 1999, Arby's made its boldest international move to date, signing an overseas agreement with Sybra Restaurants Ltd. to develop more than 100 Arby's restaurants in the United Kingdom over a 10-year span.

After selling its textile operations, Triarc in 1999 sold its interest in National Propane, leaving the firm with interests in only beverages and franchise restaurants. Triarc entered the new century, then, as a slimmed down, focused company that had completely transformed itself since leaving the DWG name behind.

TRIARC: FOCUSING ON ARBY'S IN THE NEW CENTURY

Triarc had one more major move to make. In 2000, the company sold its beverage business, including Royal

Crown Company and Snapple Beverage Group, to Cadbury Schweppes plc. The sale left Triarc free to focus on marketing Arby's and selling franchises. By this time, the restaurant side of Triarc included Arby's franchisees in 49 states and nine countries. During the early 2000s, Arby's new product roll-out included its Market Fresh line of premium sandwiches, Market Fresh Salads line, and Market Fresh wrap sandwiches, in response to growing health concerns and interest in menu items low in carbohydrates.

Triarc diversified again in July 2004 with the acquisition of a 64 percent interest in Deerfield Capital Management LLC, an alternative asset management group for institutional investors with more than $8.5 billion of managed assets. The following year, the renamed Deerfield Triarc Capital Corp. went public, completing an IPO of 25 million shares on the NYSE.

By 2005, Arby's was the 10th-largest fast-food chain in the country, according to *Nation's Restaurant News*. In a reversal of strategy, Triarc that year acquired franchises, paying $175 million for the RTM Restaurant Group, Arby's largest franchisee, a 22-state, 775-restaurant operation. In 2006, Arby's launched its all-natural Chicken Naturals line that replaced the restaurant's entire line of chicken products. That same year, Arby's continued altering its menu for the health conscious and began a transition to French fries with no trans fat that eliminated the use of hydrogenated oil.

ORIGINS AND INITIAL SUCCESS OF WENDY'S

Wendy's was established by the self-made entrepreneur-turned-millionaire Dave Thomas. Born during the Great Depression and abandoned at birth, Thomas went to work at age 12, quit school and set out on his own at age 15, and earned $1.5 million as a Kentucky Fried Chicken franchisee and manager by age 35. In 1969, Thomas decided to launch his own restaurant, Wendy's, named after his daughter Melinda Lou, nicknamed Wendy. Established in Columbus, Ohio, Wendy's featured an intentionally small menu to save on labor expenses. It included made-to-order hamburgers with fresh beef, French fries, chili, soft drinks, and Frosty frozen dessert. Departing from the typical quick-serve restaurant decor with easy-to-clean tile and vinyl, Thomas installed carpeting, bentwood chairs, Tiffany-styled lamps, and tables decorated with vintage newspaper ads.

Wendy's was a success from the start, and Thomas opened a second restaurant in 1970 and began franchising in 1972. Wendy's also launched its first advertising campaign in 1972 with the slogan "Quality Is Our Recipe" and spots featuring a pigtailed, red-haired Wendy. The company's net earnings surpassed $1 million by 1974 on sales of nearly $25 million. Wendy's opened its 100th outlet and first Canadian restaurant in 1975 and went public the following year. The infusion of shareholder capital in turn spurred further company growth, and Wendy's operations grew fivefold in a year, with the 500th restaurant opened before the end of 1976.

Wendy's launched its inaugural national campaign in 1977, becoming the first restaurant chain with less than 1,000 outlets to broadcast national commercials. The initial "Hot 'n Juicy" spot garnered a Clio Award for creativity. Franchise numbers and company sales responded positively, with Wendy's opening its 1,000th restaurant and surpassing $1 billion in yearly sales by 1978. In the process, Wendy's became the first chain to pass the $1 billion sales plateau within its first 10 years and the fastest to reach 1,000 outlets. By the end of the decade, Wendy's had expanded not only into Canada but also Puerto Rico and Europe.

BURGER WARS, SLOWING GROWTH, AND FINANCIAL REBOUND

During the early 1980s, Wendy's growth slowed as a result of a recession and high beef prices. Thomas first appeared as Wendy's spokesperson in the television ad "Ain't No Reason (to go anyplace else)" in 1981 as the so-called burger wars fired up. The wars in part were fueled by Wendy's growth in the previous decade, and moves made by McDonald's and Burger King to stymie that growth. After introducing a salad bar, baked potatoes, and chicken breast sandwiches, Wendy's became the number three burger chain, in time for its 1983 debut of the Clio-winning "Where's the Beef?" commercials. Wendy's new menu items and the "Where's the Beef?" campaign propelled the company to record earnings of $76.2 million in 1985.

After failing at an attempt to serve breakfast, behind-the-scenes problems mounted for Wendy's. Absentee and new franchise owners contributed to a loss of $4.9 million in 1986, when 20 percent of franchises were close to failing and responded with a no-confidence vote presented to management. The dire situation brought Thomas out of retirement. Thomas named the new president and chief executive officer James W. Near, who had fashioned the Burger Boy Food-A-Rama chain and founded Sisters Chicken & Biscuits.

After Thomas hired him, Near fired top managers, cut 700 administrative jobs, eliminated failing franchises, and created a new restaurant design to lower franchise investment costs. For employees, programs were launched to give them a vested interest in Wendy's success: base pay was raised, benefits increased, bonuses were raised, and an employee stock option initiated, which made workers stakeholders. The changes helped Wendy's substantially reduce its employee turnover rate.

The recession of the late 1980s spawned a trend toward discount pricing. Wendy's kept pace with competitors and in 1989 introduced its Super Value Menu with 99-cent fare as well as new premium sandwiches appealing to big eaters. Thomas also took to the screen in new ads that received poor reviews from advertising critics but a positive response from consumers that revitalized sales, franchise expansion, and brand recognition.

WENDY'S REVITALIZED GROWTH IN THE NINETIES

Thanks to the restructuring engineered by Near, Wendy's rolled up consecutive years of 20 percent earnings increases between 1990 and 1993. Having guided Wendy's to a recovery, Near gave up his CEO chair in 1994 while remaining chairman. Gordon Teter, a senior vice president with 25 years of restaurant experience, became chief executive officer and established new primary objectives: taking market share from competitors and expanding internationally. While the company's domestic growth slowed during the mid-1990s, Wendy's expanded into Canada, Latin America, and the Far East.

In 1995, Wendy's acquired Canada's largest baked goods and coffee chain, Tim Hortons, with which Wendy's had previously opened more than a dozen dual-branded outlets. The acquisition provided Wendy's an opportunity to expedite co-branded openings, enter the Canadian breakfast market, and boost company revenues. During the mid-1990s, Wendy's expanded its operations in northern states, acquiring 125 existing fast-food outlets that were converted to a northeast foundation for Tim Hortons as well as new Wendy's outlets. Wendy's opened an average of 200 outlets a year between 1994 and 1997, surpassing a total of 5,000 Wendy's restaurants in 1997.

LATE NINETIES: MANAGEMENT CHANGES AND INTERNATIONAL CUTBACKS

In July 1997, James Near died, and Gordon Teter assumed the chairmanship of Wendy's while remaining CEO. Wendy's launched a series of pita sandwiches in 1997, but the menu addition did little to stem the ef-

fects of a downturn in the Asian economy. Moreover, Tim Hortons was not finding success outside of its home territory of Canada. Company net earnings slid downward in 1997, and Teter tried to stop the bleeding in 1998 by shuttering restaurants and easing back on expansion. The company turned to promoting recent consumer-oriented initiatives, including its health-conscious menu items and late-night hours of operation, introduced in 1996. Wendy's spent considerable capital promoting these extended hours. By 1999, 10 percent of all revenue was generated after 10 p.m. Systemwide revenues were nearly $6 billion by the end of the decade, and Tim Hortons sales surpassed $1 billion.

International operations continued to struggle. Wendy's could not compete with the larger McDonald's and Burger King. After withdrawing from South Korea, Wendy's closed most of its U.K. operations in 1999 and then shut down Hong Kong and Argentina outlets a year later. The closings effectively purged the company of all international operations save those in Canada.

In December 1999, Teter died of a heart attack and was succeeded by John T. "Jack" Schuessler, whose long association with Wendy's began in 1974 as a franchise manager trainee. Schuessler became president and chief executive in 2000 and chairman a year later. While the company had abandoned most of its international expansion plans, it maintained a North American expansion program entering the next century, mapping out plans to open 100 restaurants in Mexico over the next decade.

TRENDSETTING MENU INNOVATIONS AND A LOSS OF ITS FOUNDER

During the early 2000s, Wendy's was a trendsetter, establishing healthful eating options at quick-serve restaurants. In a 2002 national rollout, Wendy's launched its line of Garden Sensations salads, prepackaged salads that could be customized with various dressings and toppings. The rollout was accompanied by Wendy's largest advertising campaign to date. On the heels of its Garden Sensations launch, Wendy's in 2003 began promoting low-fat and nonfat Super Value Menu items as part of a national television campaign that emphasized eating smarter and saving money and carried the theme, "It's better here."

The year 2002 marked the passing of an era and expansion of Wendy's system of restaurants. Founder and company spokesman Dave Thomas, featured in more than 800 commercials, died in early 2002. Wendy's the same year acquired a 45 percent interest in Café Express, a 13-restaurant Texas-based upscale bistro chain, and the 169-restaurant chain Baja Fresh Mexican Grill.

Despite recessionary conditions, increased pressure from low-priced menus of competitors, and rising overhead costs, Wendy's experienced a nearly 5 percent rise in same-store sales in 2002, in part on the popularity of Garden Sensations. Meanwhile, McDonald's same-store sales fell by 1.5 percent and Jack in the Box by nearly 1 percent. By 2003, Wendy's, after introducing its alternative menu with salad bar, was winning the lunchtime fast-food fight over McDonald's. To regain lost ground, McDonald's and Jack in the Box launched their own salad lines in 2003.

STRUGGLING TO REPLACE FOUNDER'S VISION AND VOICE

In 2004, Wendy's continued expanding through acquisition and broadening its menu alternatives. The company acquired a majority interest in Café Express, and Tim Hortons acquired the bankrupt Bess Eaton with coffee shops throughout Connecticut, Massachusetts, and Rhode Island. Wendy's also revamped its line of chicken sandwiches and began providing consumers with an option of French fries for combo meals as well as milk for Kids' Meal drink choices and Mandarin oranges serving as a French fries alternative.

Despite increasing menu alternatives, Wendy's struggled after Dave Thomas died to find a successful growth and marketing strategy to keep its investors happy. Its first major advertising campaign after Thomas's death did not strike the right chord with consumers, and stores lost traffic when Wendy's raised its price on featured 99-cent specials (it lowered prices to 99 cents a year later). In addition, Wendy's faced increased competition from other firm's matching the company's health-conscious line of foods and poor public relations from a woman in 2005 who claimed to have found a finger in her chili (it was later discovered she planted it there, although the matter probably cost Wendy's millions). One cash-generating move Wendy's made was selling company-owned outlets to franchisees. This yielded nearly $170 million in 2005 with the sale of 175 units.

INVESTORS URGE WENDY'S TO MAKE CHANGES

With large investors urging Wendy's to make major changes by mid-2005, Nelson Peltz, who with his partner Peter May controlled Triarc Companies and the investment firm Trian, revealed in 2005 that Trian had acquired a 5.5 percent stake in Wendy's. Peltz urged Wendy's to make the company more competitive by shedding its smaller restaurant subsidiaries, threatened a proxy fight, and wrote a white paper criticizing Wendy's management and listing ways to restore the company to improve profits. In March 2006, Wendy's, feeling the pressure from Peltz, shareholders, franchisees, and competition, agreed to expand its board and add three members appointed by Peltz's Trian Fund Management. Wendy's also indicated it would divest Baja Fresh Mexican Grill and spin off Tim Hortons by year's end.

As the board room heated up, Schuessler in April 2006 abruptly retired as chairman and chief executive of Wendy's, and Kerrii Anderson, who had joined Wendy's in 2000 as chief financial officer, was named chief executive, and Director James V. Pickett was elected chairman. Under Anderson, Tim Hortons was spun off, Baja Fresh Mexican Grill was sold, and 355 management positions were slashed between mid-2006 and early 2007. Wendy's also launched a line of deli sandwiches to make the restaurant more competitive with sandwich chains. Most significantly, Wendy's announced it would entertain bids to acquire it or merge.

In mid-2006, Peltz disclosed that Trian's stake in Wendy's had grown to nearly 10 percent and it was interested in bidding for Wendy's. In order to view Wendy's confidential financial data, Peltz signed a one-year confidentiality agreement with Wendy's. Trian also agreed, for a period of one year, to not call for a merger nor launch a proxy battle and to keep its ownership stake in Wendy's below 10 percent.

TRIARC RESTRUCTURING AS PRELUDE TO MERGER WITH WENDY'S

As the year passed, Triarc Companies restructured. It sold its asset management group in April 2007, making it a pure play restaurant company as its sole line of business became Arby's. Triarc also cut executive staff, so the contracts of both Peltz and May were terminated although they remained on the corporate board as major stakeholders. The two together owned better than 34 percent of Triarc, and their Trian Management was retained to provide advice.

After two years of a tortured courtship, Wendy's International agreed in April 2008 to merge with Triarc Companies for $2.3 billion. The pact created one of the largest quick-serve food chains in the country with more than 10,000 outlets and $12.5 billion in annual sales. The combined company became known as Wendy's/Arby's Group, Inc. J. David Karam became president of the Wendy's subsidiary, succeeding Anderson, who had argued that a merger was unnecessary for Wendy's to be profitable. Roland Smith, successful in marketing the Arby's brand in the 1990s, was named president and chief executive of the Group and interim president of the Arby's subsidiary. Peltz and May continued to wield influence, serving as chairman and vice chairman, respectively.

In 2008 Wendy's announced plans to offer breakfast and snack items to more actively compete with McDonald's and Burger King. In 2009, Arby's launched its new Roastburger sandwiches and its Far East-flavored Sweet & Spicy Boneless Wings from 100 percent whole chicken breast. Arby's expanded geographically through an agreement to create 47 new restaurants in the United States and Canada via new and existing franchisees.

GEARING UP FOR EXPANSION IN THE NEXT DECADE

Expansion abroad also became a focus. In 2009, Wendy's reached an agreement with the Saudi-based Al Jammaz Group to construct 135 new co-branded Wendy's and Arby's restaurants in North Africa and the Middle East over a 10-year period. The deal represented the first international Wendy's-Arby's franchise agreement for a dual-branded restaurant. Wendy's also reinvested in Far East expansion, signing a pact with Kopitiam Investment Pte Ltd (Singapore's leading food-service management group) to develop 35 Wendy's restaurants in Singapore over a 10-year period. However, Wendy's allowed its Japanese franchise agreement to expire, resulting in the closing of 71 restaurants, although the company did not rule out returning to Japan later.

For its first full year as a consolidated company, the Group earned $5.06 million on revenues of $3.58 billion in 2009. At the end of the decade, the Group's marketing research revealed the potential for 8,000 additional restaurants beyond North America. The company also planned to remodel restaurants and expand its Wendy's breakfast program into more territory while broadening Arby's value menu. In the near term, the Group expected positive same-store sales for Wendy's and negative, but annually improving, same-store sales for Arby's.

April S. Dougal; John Simley; Dave Mote
Updated, Susan Windisch Brown;
David E. Salamie; Jeffrey L. Covell; Roger Rouland

PRINCIPAL SUBSIDIARIES

Wendy's/Arby's Restaurants, LLC; Arby's Restaurant Holdings, LLC; Wendy's International, Inc.

PRINCIPAL DIVISIONS

Wendy's; Arby's.

PRINCIPAL COMPETITORS

Burger King Holdings, Inc.; Chick-fil-A, Inc.; Doctor's Associates Inc.; McDonald's Corporation; Panera Bread Company; The Quiznos Master LLC; Yum! Brands, Inc.

FURTHER READING

Breckenridge, Tom, and Sandy Theis, "Wendy's Founder Dave Thomas Dies," *Cleveland Plain Dealer*, January 9, 2002, p. A1.

Campanella, Frank W., "Beefed-Up Menu: At Wendy's International, It's More Now Than Just Meat and Potatoes," *Barron's*, November 16, 1981, pp. 41+.

Carlino, Bill, "Wendy's Purchases Canada's Tim Hortons," *Nation's Restaurant News*, August 21, 1995.

"Dave's World," *Forbes*, January 3, 1994, p. 149.

Day, Sherri, "After Years at Top, McDonald's Strives to Regain Ground," *New York Times*, March 3, 2003.

De La Merced, Michael J., "Peltz Offer Is Accepted by Wendy's," *New York Times*, April 25, 2008.

Elliott, Stuart, "After Founder Dies, Wendy's Ponders New Ways to Pitch," *New York Times*, January 9, 2002, p. C1.

Feder, Barnaby, J., "Wendy's Gives Fund Three Seats," *New York Times*, March 3, 2006.

Higgins, Chester, Jr., "A Turnaround Plan That Includes Baconators," *New York Times*, November 24, 2007.

Ives, Nat, "Fast-Food Chains Are Adding Premium Salads to Their Menus After the Success of a Rival," *New York Times*, May 5, 2003.

Leung, Shirley, "Wendy's Sees Future Growth in Acquisitions and Ventures: Hamburger Chain Is Looking at Purchases of Other Food Concepts," *Wall Street Journal*, February 11, 2002, p. B4.

Papiernik, Richard L., "Wendy's Taps M&A Chief, Gears Up for Acquisitions," *Nation's Restaurant News*, September 17, 2001, pp. 1+.

Ruggless, Ron, "Café Express, Wendy's Take Fast-Casual Approach," *Nation's Restaurant News*, February 25, 2002, pp. 1+.

Sachdev, Ameet, "Wendy's Emerges as Rising Star among Fast Food Companies," *Chicago Tribune*, March 9, 2002.

Simon, Bernard, "Tim Hortons: Up from Doughnuts," *New York Times*, August 28, 2002.

Sorkin, Andrew Ross, "Investor Takes Aim at Wendy's," *New York Times*, December 13, 2005.

Warner, Melanie, "Diners Walk through One Door and Visit Two Restaurants," *New York Times*, July 11, 2005.

Westpac Banking Corporation

---■---

Level 2, 275 Kent Street
Sydney, NSW 2000
Australia
Telephone: (+61 2) 9374 7237
Fax: (+61 2) 8253 4128
Web site: http://www.westpac.com.au

Public Company
Founded: 1817 as Bank of New South Wales
Incorporated: 2002
Employees: 37,000
Total Assets: AUD 589.58 billion (2009)
Stock Exchanges: Australian New York
Ticker Symbols: WBC; WBK
NAICS: 522110 Commercial Banking; 523120 Securities Brokerage; 523920 Portfolio Management; 551111 Offices of Bank Holding Companies

■ ■ ■

Westpac Banking Corporation is Australia's oldest and one of its largest commercial banks, with total assets of nearly AUD 590 billion. The company serves more than 10 million customers across Australia and New Zealand, as well as in the near Pacific region. It also operates offices in London, New York, Hong Kong, Shanghai, and Singapore. In 2009, Westpac completed the acquisition of St. George Bank, the largest-ever banking merger in Australia. Westpac is listed on the Australian Stock Exchange and also trades on the New York Stock Exchange. The company is led by CEO Gail Kelly.

Westpac reported net profits of AUD 3.45 billion in 2009.

BANKING BACKGROUND

When Australia was settled, in the late 18th century, the colony's economy was based on a system of barter. A variety of foreign coins also circulated, but these usually found their way back overseas in exchange for the many imported goods the colony needed, so Australia had trouble keeping any form of currency in the colony. Governor Laughlan Macquarie was determined to solve his country's monetary problems. To help prevent currency from disappearing overseas, Macquarie had the center cut out of coins, creating a donut-shaped "holey dollar." The center piece, known as a "dump," was worth one quarter of a holey dollar. Nonetheless, currency and exchange problems continued to plague the Australian colonies.

In 1816, Governor Macquarie began to push for the establishment of a colonial bank, and a group of 46 subscribers formed a committee to organize the bank's operations. On April 8, 1817, Bank of New South Wales opened for business in a house in Macquarie Place. Edward Smith Hall was the cashier/secretary, and Robert Campbell Junior was the head accountant. The bank's first depositor was Sergeant Jeremiah Murphy, who entrusted £50 to the new bank.

Bank of New South Wales operated for five years under its original charter, granted by Governor Macquarie, and then for another five under a renewal issued by Governor Brisbane. In 1828, however, the British authorities declared the bank's charter invalid, claiming

COMPANY PERSPECTIVES

Our vision and values: Westpac's vision is to be the leading financial services company in Australia and New Zealand. Putting the customer at the centre of everything we do will help achieve this goal. We see our fundamental purpose as helping every customer achieve all their financial goals. Our ambition is to earn all of our customers' business by delighting them with the service and support that we provide and by serving them as a single team. Our strategy focuses on customers in our core markets of Australia, New Zealand and throughout the Pacific, and is based on: developing a deep understanding of our customers' needs; providing value-added solutions that seek to meet those needs; deepening and building long-term customer relationships; and dramatically improving the experience they have with us.

that colonial governors had no authority to issue such charters. Bank of New South Wales was then reorganized as a joint-stock company.

As trade expanded throughout the Australian colonies, Bank of New South Wales grew. In 1847, it employed the London Joint Stock Bank as its overseas agent in London. Foreign exchange was a growing area of the bank's activities. In 1850, the bank was incorporated by an act of the New South Wales Parliament and was allowed to establish branches. The first branch opened in the Moreton Bay area of what was soon to become the colony of Queensland. A year later gold fever struck Australia, and the bank soon sent its agents directly to the mining regions. Some branches were no more than a tent. Others were built with furnaces to smelt gold right on the premises. In 1853, the bank established an office to handle the colony's growing export trade.

The mid- to late 1800s saw widespread development of the country's resources. Bank branches were established at scattered points across the continent. Travel was difficult and often dangerous, as the story of Robert White, the "terror of the bushrangers" illustrates. In 1863, Robert White, an accountant at the Deniliquin branch of Bank of New South Wales was held up. After putting up a fight, he found himself bound and gagged, and the bank robbers headed out of town with £3,000 in gold and notes. The accountant managed to free himself, however, and was soon on the bandits' trail. He

successfully recovered the £3,000 and the bushrangers landed in jail. On another occasion, White was ambushed in Gympie while carrying a great deal of money. He drew his pistol and charged his adversaries, wounding two of them. After his banking career, White was elected to the New South Wales legislative assembly.

COMMERCIAL BANK OF AUSTRALIA OPENS: 1866

In 1866, Commercial Bank of Australia (CBA) opened in Melbourne. CBA focused on suburban and rural areas. In 1870, Henry Gyles Turner became general manager of CBA. Turner directed the bank for the next 30 years. By 1876, the bank was operating 34 offices and agencies throughout the Victoria territory. CBA expanded steadily across the rest of the continent and had offices in Sydney, Perth, Adelaide, and Brisbane by 1890.

In 1893, Australian banks faced a major crisis. Overvaluation of urban real estate and a sharp drop in wool prices precipitated a depression. Depositors panicked and scrambled to withdraw their funds. Fewer than half of the 28 conventional banks were able to continue operations without some interruption, but Bank of New South Wales was able to. Not until after 1900 did the economy fully recover. At that time, both Bank of New South Wales and CBA branched out further. CBA soon moved to Tasmania and New Zealand. "The Wales," as Bank of New South Wales had come to be known, ventured to Fiji, Papua New Guinea, and Samurai Island. Increased trade with the neighboring islands paralleled a general increase in foreign trade.

In 1914, World War I broke out. Many employees of both Bank of New South Wales and the CBA enlisted in the Australian Imperial Force. Of the 1,112 men from the two banks who volunteered, 186 were killed in action. In 1918, John Russell French, general manager of Bank of New South Wales, was knighted for his service in helping Australia finance the war effort.

Australia experienced the economic boom of the 1920s along with the rest of the world. In 1929, on the eve of the Depression, Bank of New South Wales appointed a new general manager. Alfred Charles Davidson took the helm at a time when Australian banking was undergoing many changes. Davidson introduced a travel department, which later became the largest in the Southern Hemisphere, and established the British and Foreign Department. The bank stepped up overseas operations in the early 1930s. In 1931, Alfred Davidson was instrumental in the Australian government's decision to devalue its currency, a move that improved

```
┌────────────────────────────────────────────┐
│                                              │
│              KEY DATES                       │
│                  ■                           │
│  ┌────────────────────────────────────────┐ │
│  │ 1817: Bank of New South Wales opens for  │ │
│  │       business.                          │ │
│  │ 1866: Commercial Bank of Australia (CBA) │ │
│  │       is established.                     │ │
│  │ 1982: Westpac is formed from the merger   │ │
│  │       of Bank of New South Wales and CBA.│ │
│  │ 1995: Westpac purchases Challenge Bank.   │ │
│  │ 1996: Firm merges with Trust Bank New     │ │
│  │       Zealand Limited.                    │ │
│  │ 1997: Westpac merges with Bank of         │ │
│  │       Melbourne.                          │ │
│  │ 1999: Merger talks with National Australia│ │
│  │       Bank Ltd. are called off.           │ │
│  │ 2009: Westpac completes the acquisition   │ │
│  │       of St. George Bank.                 │ │
│  └────────────────────────────────────────┘ │
└────────────────────────────────────────────┘
```

trade conditions for exporters. By the mid-1930s the economy was recovering from the Depression.

World War II brought about strict controls on Australian banking. Bank branches were closed to release workers for the war effort. The Japanese invasion of the Pacific threatened some of the branches of the CBA and "the Wales." Branches in New Guinea and elsewhere were closed. An air raid on the northern Queensland town of Darwin caused extensive damage to Bank of New South Wales branch there, and lesser damage to CBA's branch. During the war, Bank of New South Wales saw 3,330 (65 percent) of its male staff enlist.

FIGHTING NATIONALIZATION: LATE FORTIES

After the war, private Australian trading banks were soon entrenched in another conflict. On August 16, 1947, Prime Minister Ben Chifley announced that the banks would be nationalized. According to Chifley's plan, the Commonwealth Bank (Australia's central bank) would acquire the shares of the private banks and then appoint directors to run them as arms of the central bank. The private banks immediately challenged the constitutionality of nationalization and waged a political war to have the Labour Party ousted and eliminate the threat of other obnoxious legislation. The bankers were successful on both counts. The Australian High Court declared the Bank Act of 1947 unconstitutional because it interfered with the freedom of trade and commerce among the states guaranteed in section 92 of the Australian constitution. In 1949, the Labour Party was overwhelmingly defeated in the general

election. It was a major victory for Bank of New South Wales, CBA, and Australia's other private banks.

Throughout the 1950s, the Australian economy was in an upswing. Savings bank deposits were growing in popularity at this time. Before 1956, savings bank operations were conducted exclusively by the government-owned Commonwealth Bank. Bank of New South Wales entered the savings bank field in the late 1950s and competed aggressively for savings accounts. In compliance with government regulations, the bank earmarked a certain percentage of its savings bank deposits for housing construction loans. Demand for housing and durable goods was high in the 1950s and 1960s. In 1957, Bank of New South Wales purchased 40 percent of Australia's largest finance company, the Australian Guarantee Corporation Ltd. (AGC). AGC made loans to businesses as well as consumers and was active in investment and merchant banking as well as insurance.

In 1966, Australia switched from pounds to dollars. For the next two years, the public traded in its imperial currency (pounds, shillings, and pence) for new Australian dollars and cents. Banks had the difficult task of converting to the new decimal currency. Machinery had to be changed, staffs had to be retrained, and accounting had to be translated.

In the 1970s, Bank of New South Wales and CBA diversified both their services and their areas of operation. Both banks opened more branches overseas. At the same time each was busy acquiring different financial companies at home to expand upon the services they provided. Bank of New South Wales's holding in the Australian Guarantee Corporation increased to 54 percent by the early 1970s, while CBA operated a finance company, General Credit Ltd., as a wholly owned subsidiary. Both banks also became involved in merchant banking. Bank of New South Wales, for instance, owned a substantial number of shares in Partnership Pacific Ltd., Schroder Darling & Company, and Australian United Corporation. CBA held significant interests in the merchant banks Euro-Pacific Finance and International Pacific Corporation. In 1974, Australian banks entered the credit card field with Bankcard. Banks also got involved in insurance activities in the 1970s.

FORMATION OF WESTPAC: LATE SEVENTIES TO EARLY EIGHTIES

The mid-1970s saw the Australian continent in a severe recession. During these years the large amount of foreign investment in Australia's raw-commodities industries became a political hot potato. Australians felt that foreign investors had too much say in the allocation and development of their resources, particularly in petroleum and mining operations. The fact remained, however, that Australia lacked the capital to develop industry on its own. A debate over capital market regulations grew louder in the late 1970s. In 1979, growing pressure to deregulate the financial markets led to the appointment of a government committee to investigate the effects deregulation would have on the economy.

The committee, headed by Australian businessman Keith Campbell, reported its findings two years later, and deregulation soon followed. Foreign banks were allowed to set up shop in Australia, and many of the restrictions on the trading banks were removed. By 1982, it had become clear that competition from abroad and at home would be fierce in the future. Anticipating this inevitability, Bank of New South Wales and CBA decided to join forces to protect their position in the domestic market and strengthen their position overseas. Westpac was formed in October 1982, with Robert White as general manager. The merger was the largest in Australian history.

Robert White began his banking career at the age of 16 at Bank of New South Wales. He rose through the ranks, becoming general manager in 1978. White was determined to strengthen Westpac's position in world banking. The bank was a leader in the implementation of technology. Westpac's "handybank" automated teller machine network gave customers instant access to their accounts as early as 1980, and had developed substantially after 1982. In 1984, Westpac began work on its CS90 computerized banking system. Employing an IBM mainframe and computer-aided software engineering designed by the Canadian firm Netron, the bank revolutionized computerized banking. By 1988, Westpac officials were boasting the most advanced system in the world.

DIVERSIFICATION AND EXPANSION: MID- TO LATE EIGHTIES

Technological innovation was one of Westpac's key goals throughout the 1980s, and diversification was another. The bank stepped up operations in the euro-currency markets. It also opened new offices or branches in Jersey, Los Angeles, Seoul, Kuala Lumpur, and Taipei. Westpac's thrust was rewarded quickly: between 1982 and 1986, assets more than doubled.

In the late 1980s, Westpac took advantage of the deregulated financial markets around the world. In 1986, it took a greater stake in the gold-bullion markets

when it purchased part of the London dealer Johnson Matthey Bankers Ltd. In 1987, the bank acquired U.S. bond dealer William E. Pollock Government Securities. Westpac also continued to improve its branch network throughout the Pacific in the face of growing competition from Japanese banks.

Westpac's aggressive moves in the euromarkets and in technological development and application focused a great deal of attention on the bank. Its low exposure to Third World debt helped keep earnings healthy at a time when bad debt provisions were getting the best of many international banks.

On January 1, 1988, Stuart A. Fowler replaced Robert White as Westpac's managing director and CEO. Fowler continued the aggressive campaign begun by White. In 1988, the bank purchased the remaining shares of Australian Guarantee Corporation, making it a wholly owned subsidiary. As the 1980s closed, Westpac focused on bringing operating costs down through automation and elimination of redundant branch services. The bank's domestic footing was solid. Westpac controlled 25 percent of Australia's bank deposits.

GROWTH CONTINUES: NINETIES AND BEYOND

During the early 1990s, Australian banks saw profits dwindle as a result of increased exposure to bad loans. Westpac's expansion efforts were put on hold during this time period. By 1995, however, the industry recovered, and while Westpac was financially back on track, it had lost its leading position in the Australian banking industry.

In order to remain competitive, the company once again launched a growth program. It purchased Challenge Bank of Western Australia in 1995 in an AUD 684 million deal that enabled the bank to gain a leading position in the western region. The Challenge purchase was followed by a merger with Trust Bank New Zealand Limited in 1996. That year, the company secured profits of AUD 1.5 billion, an increase of 32 percent over the previous year. Then in 1997, Westpac acquired Bank of Melbourne. During 1998, the company began to offer online banking to its customers.

In 1999, CEO Robert Joss planned to increase Westpac's holdings even further and proposed a merger with National Australia Bank Ltd. (NAB). At the time, Australia had a "four pillar" policy, which discouraged mergers between the region's largest banks. NAB, however, wished to challenge the policy and announced the deal. Westpac's board, believing that it was a poor value for shareholders, turned down the deal. Joss resigned after the board's refusal and was replaced by David Morgan.

The new CEO immediately began a restructuring effort designed to reduce Westpac's cost-to-income ratio, which hovered at 58 percent due to its merger activity over the past three years. The ratio was the highest of the four leading banks. As part of the reorganization, the company announced that it would cut up to 3,000 jobs and focus on organic growth.

MAKING MERGER HISTORY IN 2009

Morgan sought new growth opportunities for Westpac into the new decade. In May 2000, the company paid AUD 1 billion ($578.5 million) to acquire a diversified financial portfolio from Standard Chartered Bank Australia Ltd. The company expanded into the Pacific market, acquiring 30 percent of Bank of Tonga and 42 percent of Pacific Commercial Bank.

In 2002, Westpac began a shift toward the higher-end banking sectors. As part of this effort, the company sold its consumer finance unit, Australian Guarantee Corporation, to GE Australia, for $1.65 billion. Instead, Westpac began beefing up its wealth management wing.

This was accomplished through three major acquisitions, all in 2002. In June, the company paid AUD 323 million to buy Rothschild Australia Asset Management Ltd. This business was then rebranded as Sagitta Wealth Management Ltd. In August, Westpac paid AUD 900 million to acquire most of BT Funds Management from Principal Financial Group. This business, including its New Zealand operations, was then renamed BT Financial Group. Lastly, the company acquired a 51 percent stake in Hastings Funds Management Ltd., paying AUD 36 million. The company later acquired the remainder of Hastings in 2005. Following these purchases, Westpac integrated its own wealth management operations into its new subsidiaries.

Westpac's growing asset management division allowed the company to post record profits of nearly AUD 2.2 billion in 2003. By the end of 2005, the company's net profit neared AUD 2.82 billion, and topped the AUD 3 billion mark in 2006. In that year, the company moved to restructure its New Zealand business, which had operated as a branch of the Australian bank throughout its 145-year history. In November 2006, Westpac incorporated this operation as Westpac New Zealand Limited. Westpac also expanded its overseas presence elsewhere, opening branch offices in Mumbai, India, and in Shanghai, China, in 2007.

David Morgan stepped down as Westpac's CEO that same year. In his place, Westpac named Gail Kelly as its chief executive. Kelly had previously served as CEO of another major Australian bank, St. George

Bank. By the end of Kelly's first year, Westpac's net profit had soared to AUD 3.86 billion.

Kelly's relationship with St. George helped smooth the way for Westpac's acquisition of that bank in 2009. The deal, worth AUD 12 billion, represented the largest-ever banking merger in Australia, and the second-largest corporate merger in the country's history. The combined company became one of Australia's top three banks, and its largest in terms of market capitalization, which reached AUD 83 billion in 2010. Following the merger, Westpac integrated St. George's own portfolio of wealth management brands into BT Financial Group. St. George, including its BankSA brand, continued to operate as an independent division.

The acquisition of St. George helped reduce the impact of the global recession on Westpac's balance sheet. Nonetheless, the company reported its first profit slip of the decade, with net profits dropping back to AUD 3.45 billion by the end of 2009. Westpac had begun looking forward, however. In February 2010, the company announced plans to launch Islamic banking products, in order to attract investments from Islamic institutions. As Australia's oldest bank, Westpac had also become one of its largest banks in the new century.

Updated, Christina M. Stansell; M. L. Cohen

PRINCIPAL SUBSIDIARIES

Asgard Capital Management Limited; Asgard Wealth Solutions Limited; Australia St.George Financial Services Limited; Beech Trust; BLE Capital Limited; BLE Holdings Pty Limited; Challenge Limited; Crusade Management Limited; Danaby Pty Limited; General Credit Holdings Pty Limited; Hastings Funds Management Limited; Hastings Management Pty Limited; Hitton Pty Limited; St.George Bank Limited.

PRINCIPAL DIVISIONS

Core Support; Group Treasury; Institutional; New Zealand Banking; Pacific Banking; Products and Operations; St. George Bank; Technology; Wealth; Westpac Retail & Business Banking.

PRINCIPAL OPERATING UNITS

Advance Investigate; Asgard; BT Financial Group; Hastings Fund Management; Rams Home Loans; Securitor; St. George Bank; Westpac; Westpac InstitutionalBank.

PRINCIPAL COMPETITORS

Australia and New Zealand Banking Group Ltd.; Bank of Queensland Ltd.; Bank of Western Australia Ltd.;

Commonwealth Bank of Australia; Macquarie Bank Ltd.; National Australia Bank Ltd.; Suncorp-Metway Ltd.

FURTHER READING

"Australian Banks Flex Their Muscles," *Banker*, January 1997, p. 13.

"Australian Consumer Sentiment Falls," *AsiaPulse News*, March 15, 2000.

"Australia's Westpac Restructuring to Involve 200 Job Cuts," *AsiaPulse News*, January 31, 2002.

From Holey Dollars to Plastic Cards: The Westpac Story, Sydney: Westpac Banking Corporation, 1987.

Taylor, Mike, "Westpac Reaps Fruits of Its Labour," *Money Management*, October 30, 2003.

"This Month: Westpac's China Gambit," *Banker*, July 1, 2007.

Westfield, Mark, "Win Some, Lose Some," *Banker*, December 1999, p. 56.

"Westpac Bank Reports Fiscal Results," *Global Banking News*, February 17, 2010.

"Westpac Banking Corporation," *Australian Banking & Finance*, November 28, 2003, p. 18.

"Westpac Banking Eyes Asia for Future Growth," *Bernama*, December 18, 2000.

"Westpac Branch Open in Shanghai," *Asia Today International*, February–March 2008, p. 8.

"Westpac Receives Approval to Form ADI," *Global Banking News*, February 12, 2010.

"Westpac to Offer Islamic Finance Product," *Global Banking News*, February 12, 2010.

Williams International Co., L.L.C.

2280 E. West Maple Road
P.O. Box 200
Commerce Township, Michigan 48390
U.S.A.
Telephone: (248) 624-5200
Toll Free: (800) 859-3544
Fax: (248) 669-1577
Web site: http://www.williams-int.com

Private Company
Incorporated: 1955 as Williams Research Corporation
Employees: 1,000
Sales: $250 million (2009 est.)
NAICS: 336412 Aircraft Engine and Engine Parts
Manufacturing; 336415 Guided Missile and Space
Vehicle Propulsion Unit and Propulsion Unit Parts
Manufacturing; 541710 Research and Development
in the Physical, Engineering, and Life Sciences

■ ■ ■

Williams International Co., L.L.C., is a leading manufacturer of small jet turbine engines. Founded by former Chrysler Corporation engineer Sam Williams, the company began by developing very small jet turbines for marine and automotive use. Williams specializes in smaller engines for business jets, rated at 1,400 to 3,400 pounds of thrust (by comparison, the Rolls-Royce BR700 engines on a Gulfstream G650 can each produce 16,000 pounds). The company's revolutionary engines have made new classes of passenger aircraft possible: light jets and very light jets.

The key to Williams's designs are simplicity, a greatly reduced number of parts, and novel production processes required to manufacture to watchmaker's tolerances. The company operates from two main locations: its headquarters and research center on the border of Commerce Township and Walled Lake, Michigan, and a manufacturing facility in Ogden, Utah.

HUMBLE BEGINNINGS IN MICHIGAN

Sam B. Williams earned a bachelor's degree in engineering from Purdue University in 1942 (an honorary doctorate was awarded 40 years later). After graduating he worked for Chrysler Corporation for 12 years, researching turboprop engines for naval aircraft during World War II and later working on small turbine engines for automotive use.

In 1955 Williams invested $3,500 to set up Williams Research Corporation in a warehouse in Birmingham, Michigan. He brought four other engineers with him. In 1959 the company moved 30 miles northwest of Detroit to a site on the edge of Walled Lake and Commerce Township.

The company's first engine, a turbojet called the WR1, weighed 23 pounds and only produced 60 pounds of thrust. It was originally developed as a boat motor for Outboard Marine Corporation. In 1964 a more powerful descendant called the WR2 appeared. Used to propel drones for reconnaissance or target practice, this was the company's first major success. Williams also supplied auxiliary power units (APUs), small

COMPANY PERSPECTIVES

Williams International is the leader in small gas turbine engine development, manufacture and field support. We took the lead through customer focus, vision, innovation, determination and perspiration.

turbine-driven generators used aboard aircraft, as well as industrial and marine turbines.

Williams was not the only firm working with small jet engines. France's Turboméca already had what would become, in its U.S.-built version, the engine for Cessna's T-37 military trainer of the 1970s. Other U.S. firms such as Garrett Corporation and Solar Aircraft Company were also active in the field. However, Williams's skill in miniaturizing more sophisticated jet engines would set it apart.

In 1967 Williams developed its first turbofan, called the WR19, which was twice as fuel-efficient as the company's earlier turbojets. Capable of developing 430 pounds of thrust, it was used in the Bell Flying Belt, an experimental flying backpack designed for infantrymen. Within a few years the company had also developed the Williams Aerial Systems Platform (WASP), a kind of jet-powered flying carpet.

LAUNCHING CRUISE MISSILES: 1973–92

The impact of the new engines extended far beyond such novelty applications. They were efficient enough to propel military payloads hundreds of miles at low altitudes. In the early 1970s Williams used its own funds to develop the F107, a 600-pound-thrust engine that, along with its F112 successor, propelled the U.S. arsenal of cruise missiles.

In 1974 the company bought a new 20,000-square-foot manufacturing plant in Ogden, Utah, for an estimated $350,000. First used to supply parts for jet engines, it cost $500,000 to equip the facility with modern precision manufacturing equipment.

Williams esteemed the local work ethic. The plant was also near Hill Air Force Base, a user of its products. The Ogden site began with about 30 employees and doubled within a few years. An additional, 48,000-square-foot facility was built four years later at a cost of $1.2 million, bringing total Ogden area employment to about 200 people.

Cruise missiles became an integral part of the U.S. arsenal during the Cold War. Antinuclear protestors picketed the Williams headquarters repeatedly in the 1980s. Williams supplied several thousand engines for the Air Force's Air-Launched Cruise Missile (ALCM) as well as Navy Tomahawks, hundreds of which were fired in the Persian Gulf Wars. By 1991, the company had built more than 12,000 engines in all. Up to then, only a handful of them had ever been used to transport people.

In the early 1990s Williams had about 1,100 employees, down from a Cold War peak of 2,000. The company had been renamed Williams International Corporation in 1981. A related limited liability corporation, Williams International Co., L.L.C., was formed in 1995.

INTRODUCTION OF FJ44: 1985

Williams had considered possibilities for commercial aircraft applications since the early 1970s. At the end of the decade the company began work on an engine known as the WR44 that would have powered the Foxjet 600, an early concept for personal business jets.

Around 1981, the company began developing its FJ44 program. Originally rated at 1,800 pounds of thrust, the engine was introduced to airframe designers in 1985. Within three years, it was incorporated into new light jet designs from Cessna, Swearingen Aircraft Corp., and Burt Rutan's famous experimental aircraft firm Scaled Composites.

It was Rutan's proof-of-concept Triumph jet that in 1988 provided the first human flight tests for the FJ44 engine. Swearingen's SJ30 project (later taken over by Emivest Aerospace Corp.) lingered in development for more than a decade. However, Cessna's FJ44-powered CitationJet, launched in 1992, became one of the most successful business jets ever, thanks to its very low price of $3 million. There were 100 of these in service by 1995 and 2,000 by 2004. In addition, a small industry emerged of retrofitting the FJ44 engine in earlier models of business aircraft.

As the first Williams engine designed to carry passengers, the FJ44 required certification with the Federal Aviation Administration, a tedious and expensive process. As a result, the company formed the Williams-Rolls, Inc., joint venture in 1989, in which esteemed engine manufacturer Rolls-Royce held a 15 percent interest and acted as a supplier for some components.

The company's miniaturization process typically followed three principles: simplifying the design, reducing the number of parts, and forging new production

KEY DATES

1955: Former Chrysler engineer Sam B. Williams launches Williams Research Corporation in Michigan to develop small turbine engines.

1974: Company opens a manufacturing plant in Ogden, Utah.

1981: Company is renamed Williams International.

1992: Cessna Aviation's highly successful CitationJet is first production passenger aircraft to use Williams engines.

2005: Williams-powered GlobalFlyer becomes the first jet to circumnavigate the globe without refueling.

techniques. The FJ44 had one-third the parts found in typical large business jet engines.

V-JETS: 1985–97

In 1985 Williams developed a full-scale mockup in collaboration with Scaled Composites that was designed to showcase the possibilities of light jets. Made of composite materials, the futuristic looking V-Jet featured a forward-swept wing (hence the V in the name) and both a tail and a canard. It was designed to seat four passengers and two crew members.

In 1996 the National Aeronautics and Space Administration (NASA) announced its General Aviation Propulsion program to revive the general aviation industry. Through it, NASA funded $39 million of the total $100 million cost to develop a very small jet engine from Williams called the FJX-2. Weighing just 85 pounds, it could generate 700 pounds of thrust for an unprecedented power-to-weight ratio.

The second of the V-Jets was designed as a flying demonstrator for the new FJX-2 engine. However, when the V-Jet II was first demonstrated at Oshkosh in 1997 it was powered with a pair of FJX-1 engines, derived from the F107 cruise-missile engine.

The new FJX-2 was small, weighing just 85 pounds, but capable of producing 700 pounds of thrust in a very tiny package. It had only a 10th as many parts as in a full-size jet engine. It was very fuel-efficient and quieter than any other turbofan on the market.

In 1998 the company began developing another engine, the FJ33. This was a much less radical design, described as a scaled-down FJ44. Williams delivered its 1,000th FJ44 engine in 1999. Successive evolutions

were more efficient and more powerful. The company had announced a higher-powered variant called the FJ44-2 in September 1995, rated at 2,300 pounds of thrust.

Crain's Detroit Business estimated revenues for the secretive, privately held company at $150 million in 1998. There were 800 employees, 500 of them at the headquarters and research facility in Walled Lake.

ECLIPSE: 1998–2002

Williams played a prominent role in the Eclipse 500 program, an ambitious attempt to revolutionize the business jet market by making a plane with a price of less than $1 million, or a third that of conventional jets. Eclipse Aviation Corporation was headed by Microsoft Corporation executive Vern Raburn and had backing from several industry titans. They hoped to revolutionize the general-aviation industry along the lines of a personal-computer industry paradigm.

The key to the project was the FJX-2 engine (called EJ-22 in its production version) still in development, which was a fraction of the weight of anything else available. However, its eventual installed weight reportedly grew to 200 pounds.

In November 2002, Eclipse Aviation severed the arrangement with Williams, saying its engine did not meet expectations for performance or reliability. Williams countered that the prototype plane weighed more than planned. Eclipse chose an alternate engine from Pratt & Whitney Canada Corporation (PWC), but ultimately folded five years later.

AFTER ECLIPSE: 2003–09

Williams was also adversely affected in January 2003 when Cessna selected a PWC engine for its new small business jet called the Mustang. (Williams remained the supplier for Cessna's CJ series of Citation business jet, however.) The emerging market for very light jets (VLJs) had attracted new aspirants such as the GE Honda Aero Engines LLC joint venture. Williams engines such as the new FJ33 were an obvious choice for designers of a long-sought-after class of planes called minijets, which were personal aircraft powered by just a single engine, rather than the two deemed necessary in light jets and VLJs.

Company founder Sam B. Williams died on June 22, 2009, in Indian Wells, California, at the age of 88. He was succeeded as chairman by one of his sons, company President and CEO Gregg G. Williams.

By this time the company's achievements had become an integral part of aviation history. There were

4,000 FJ44 engines in service by this time and production of the F107 cruise-missile engine had earned Sam Williams a Collier Trophy, the country's highest aviation honor. A single FJ44-2 engine powered the Virgin Atlantic GlobalFlyer on its historic around-the-world flight in 2005. It was the first jet to circumnavigate the globe without refueling.

By making engines smaller, Williams had also made them more efficient and quieter, while producing fewer emissions. In 2009 a unique project in Michigan applied a Williams turbine engine in a new, more overtly environmentally friendly way. Heat Transfer International (HTI), a spinoff of Thermocon Corp., used a Williams engine in a new biomass energy plant at a feed mill that used turkey litter as fuel.

Williams remained a closely held company and did not release annual reports. The dismal, credit-scarce economy had certainly dampened the business jet market, however. Consequently, Williams announced a round of layoffs at its Utah plant in early 2009.

Frederick C. Ingram

PRINCIPAL SUBSIDIARIES

Williams-Rolls Inc. (85%).

PRINCIPAL OPERATING UNITS

Commerce Township, Michigan; Ogden, Utah.

PRINCIPAL COMPETITORS

GE Honda Aero Engines LLC; Pratt & Whitney Canada Corp.

FURTHER READING

Daly, Pete, "HTI Builds 1st Biomass Energy Plant," *Grand Rapids Business Journal*, August 24, 2009, p. 1.

Esler, David, "FJ44 Turbofan Earns Its Stripes; Sam Williams' Miniscule FJ44 Turbofan Is Spawning New Classes of Business Jets," *Business & Commercial Aviation*, October 1, 1995, p. 56.

———, "Mighty Mite Trio; By Downsizing the Turbofan, a New Generation of Aircraft Is Taking Wing," *Business & Commercial Aviation*, January 1, 2005, p. 44.

Leyes, Richard A., II, and William A. Fleming, "Williams International," *The History of North American Small Gas Turbine Aircraft Engines*, Washington, DC: National Air and Space Museum; Reston, VA: American Institute of Aeronautics and Astronautics, 1999, pp. 383–432.

"Low-Cost GA Engines: Possibility or Pipe Dream? With Williams under NASA Contract to Build an Affordable Turbine Engine, Other OEMs Weigh a Competitive Response," *Business & Commercial Aviation*, April 1, 1998, p. 68.

McCracken, Jeffrey, "Secrets of Success; Williams Not Type Who Touts His Biz," *Crain's Detroit Business*, March 23, 1998, p. 1.

"Sam Williams, Light Jet Engine Innovator, Dies," *Weekly of Business Aviation*, June 29, 2009, p. 304.

Strong, Michael, "Williams Loses Jet Engine Deal; Eclipse Looks Elsewhere to Develop 'Miracle' Plane," *Crain's Detroit Business*, December 9, 2002, p. 1.

"Turbojet Firm to Open Plant in Industrial Park," *Ogden Standard-Examiner*, July 9, 1974, p. 1B.

Wolverine World Wide, Inc.

———————— ■ ————————

9341 Courtland Drive N.E.
Rockford, Michigan 49351-0001
U.S.A.
Telephone: (616) 866-5500
Toll Free: (800) 789-8586
Fax: (616) 866-0257
Web site: http://www.wolverineworldwide.com

Public Company
Founded: 1883 as Hirth-Krause Company
Incorporated: 1906
Employees: 4,018
Sales: $1.1 billion (2009)
Stock Exchanges: New York
Ticker Symbol: WWW
NAICS: 316213 Men's Footwear (Except Athletic) Manufacturing; 316214 Women's Footwear (Except Athletic) Manufacturing; 316219 Other Footwear Manufacturing; 316212 House Slipper Manufacturing; 316110 Leather and Hide Tanning and Finishing; 448210 Shoe Stores; 454111 Electronic Shopping; 533110 Lessors of Nonfinancial Intangible Assets (Except Copyrighted Works)

■ ■ ■

Wolverine World Wide, Inc., is one of the world's leading producers and marketers of nonathletic footwear, including casual, work, and outdoor shoes and boots as well as moccasins and slippers. The company sells around 43 million pairs of footwear per year, under such brands as Wolverine, Bates, HyTest, Merrell, Chaco, Sebago, Cushe, Soft Style, and the famous Hush Puppies. Wolverine produces additional lines under brands licensed from other firms, including Caterpillar, Harley-Davidson, and Patagonia. The company also produces Merrell, Sebago, and Wolverine brand apparel and accessories, and it licenses certain brands for use on non-footwear products produced by other companies, including Hush Puppies apparel, eyewear, watches, socks, handbags, and plush toys; and Wolverine eyewear and gloves.

The company's products are sold worldwide through department stores, footwear chains, specialty and independent retailers, and international licensees and distributors. Approximately 37 percent of sales originate outside the United States, with around 18 percent generated in Europe and 8 percent in Canada. While the company secures the vast majority of its sales from its footwear operations, other Wolverine businesses contribute about 10 percent of revenues. These include a pigskin tannery in the company's headquarters city of Rockford in west Michigan and a retailing business that operates more than 80 retail stores in North America and five in the United Kingdom under the names Hush Puppies, Hush Puppies and Family, Track 'n Trail, Rockford Footwear Depot, and Merrell. The company also maintains about two dozen Web sites selling its footwear directly to consumers. On the manufacturing side, 93 percent of the company's shoes are sourced via third-party manufacturers located in the Asia-Pacific region, South America, and India. The balance are produced at company-owned facilities in Michigan and the Dominican Republic.

THE FOUNDATION OF A FOOTWEAR EMPIRE

Wolverine was established in 1883 by G. A. Krause and his uncle, Fred Hirth, and named the Hirth-Krause Company. The son of Prussian immigrants, Krause brought a two-century heritage of leather tanning to the enterprise. The company originally sold leather, buttonhooks, lacing, and soles at wholesale, and purchased finished shoes for retail sale.

Krause began to consolidate vertically after 1900, placing his sons in independent, but related, shoemaking and leather tanning businesses. In 1903 he established a shoe manufacturing business in Rockford, Michigan. His eldest son, Otto, who had a degree in engineering from the University of Michigan, operated this arm of the family enterprise, which supplied finished footwear to the Hirth-Krause retail outlets. Five years later, G. A. and younger son Victor created the Wolverine Tanning Company, also based in Rockford, to supply leather to the shoemaking business.

Victor, whose postsecondary education had included apprenticeships in tanning, would be a driving force behind Wolverine's establishment as a premiere U.S. shoe company. In 1909 he traveled to Milwaukee, Wisconsin, to study a chrome tanning and retanning process developed by master tanner John Pfingsten. By 1914, Victor's own experiments had resulted in a tanning process for "shell horsehide," a cheap, durable, but heretofore unworkably stiff section of hide taken from the horse's rear. The company soon stopped using cowhide in favor of this unique new material.

Promoted as "1,000 mile shoes," the heavy-duty Wolverine boots boosted sales and helped increase corporate earnings almost 700 percent from 1916 to 1923. A centennial company history noted that "Wolverine boots and shoes became one of rural and small-town America's most popular brands."

In 1921 Hirth-Krause and the Rockford shoe factory, which had previously merged under the name Michigan Shoe Makers, were united with Wolverine to form Wolverine Shoe and Tanning Corporation. The company acquired a glovemaking business that same year and began manufacturing horsehide work gloves. Over the course of the decade, Wolverine built its first warehouse, created an employee profit-sharing plan, launched a nationwide advertising campaign, and erected its first consolidated headquarters.

INNOVATING DURING THE GREAT DEPRESSION AND WORLD WAR II

Although Wolverine survived the Great Depression intact, the accelerating transition from horse-drawn transportation to gasoline-powered transport severely diminished the need for horses in the United States. As a result, the company was compelled to turn to less reliable international markets for its hides.

When the United States entered World War II, the federal government's War Production Board assigned Wolverine to manufacture gloves for the troops and suggested that the company try pigskin as a raw material. It seemed like a fine idea until the company discovered the inadequacy of pigskinning methods, which were not satisfactory to either the tanners or the meat processors. Not only was it difficult to remove the skin without taking some of the flesh with it, but separating all the flesh from the skin often damaged the hide. Sometimes the only useful pieces were barely large enough to make a glove. A company history quoted one employee in the project who remarked, "It looked like these pigs didn't care to be skinned." Nevertheless, Wolverine did manage to manufacture enough gloves to keep the military happy and its books in the black throughout the war years.

PERFECTING PIGSKIN

When the global conflict ended, demand for pigskin gloves fizzled and Wolverine was forced to revert to cowhide, which was in steadier supply than horsehide and in more reliable condition than pigskin. Victor Krause, now serving as chairman, was convinced that pigskin could be a viable alternative to cowhide. It was softer than either cowhide or horsehide, widely available, woefully underused, breathable, and easy to dye and clean. He became so obsessed with "the pigskin processing dilemma" that he resigned Wolverine's chairmanship to dedicate his full attention to the question. His son, Adolph, advanced to corporate leadership.

Working as an unpaid consultant, Victor Krause assembled a team of engineers who spent two years designing a device that separated the pigskin from the

KEY DATES

∎

1883: G. A. Krause and his uncle, Fred Hirth, found Hirth-Krause Company, selling leather and shoe accessories at wholesale and purchasing finished shoes for retail sale.

1903: Krause establishes a shoe factory in nearby Rockford; Hirth-Krause and the shoe factory are later operated under the name Michigan Shoe Makers.

1908: Krause and younger son Victor create Wolverine Tanning Company, also based in Rockford, to supply leather to the shoemaking business.

1921: Michigan Shoe Makers and Wolverine Tanning are united to form Wolverine Shoe and Tanning Corporation.

1958: The Hush Puppies brand of casual shoes is launched nationally.

1965: Company goes public with a listing on the New York Stock Exchange.

1966: Company is renamed Wolverine World Wide, Inc.

1972: Leadership reign of the Krause family comes to an end.

Late 1980s: Company begins making hiking and outdoor boots under the Wolverine brand.

2003: Wolverine acquires Sebago Inc., maker of penny loafers and Docksides boat shoes.

2007: Company begins producing Patagonia brand footwear under a license agreement.

flesh without damaging either product. Wolverine patented the machine, which was created to fit neatly into the pig production process. By the early 1980s, Wolverine would have one of the world's largest pigskin tanneries.

When tanned, pigskin was soft and flexible, but it was not tough enough to be used in Wolverine's traditional work boots and shoes. In a radical departure from the company's historical emphasis, Krause designed a pair of casual shoes from the pigskin and presented them to Wolverine's board of directors. The board was not particularly enthusiastic about the new product, but decided that market research would determine whether and how to proceed.

According to corporate legend, the genesis of the Hush Puppies brand name came at a southern-style fish

fry where deep-fried nuggets of dough commonly known as "hush puppies" were served. When Jim Muir, a Wolverine sales manager, asked his host about the origins of the strange name, he was told that farmers used the treats "to quiet their barking dogs." That conversation reminded Muir of another colloquial meaning for "barking dogs": sore feet. It occurred to him that Wolverine's new shoes worked on sore feet just like hush puppies worked on yelping dogs, so he proposed the name as a new trademark. In 1957 Adolph Krause, the president of Wolverine and a son of Victor Krause, chose the canine name and basset hound logo from a field of 10 possibilities.

After a brief period of test marketing, the company launched a national advertising campaign in 1958 that was unprecedented in the shoe industry. Hush Puppies proved a timely innovation in footwear. With workers moving from farms to offices and from the countryside to the suburbs, Wolverine faced a decline in the sale of heavy-duty work shoes but looked forward to a boom in more casual shoes. Hush Puppies became the footwear phenomenon of the late 1950s and early 1960s. Wolverine took the brand international via licensing agreements, the first of which was sold to Canada's Greb Shoes, Ltd., in 1959. Renamed Wolverine World Wide, Inc., in 1966, the parent company's sales nearly quintupled from 1958 to 1965, when it made its initial public offering on the New York Stock Exchange.

DECLINING FORTUNES

Hush Puppies put Wolverine at the top of the casual shoe industry, but the branded shoes could not keep it there very long. Sales flattened in the late 1960s, as Hush Puppies' core market matured and the brand failed to win younger customers. The company attempted to diversify via acquisition during this period, acquiring Bates, Frolic, and Tru-Stitch shoes and slippers. In spite of these efforts, however, Wolverine World Wide's nearly 90 years of Krause family management came to an end after the company experienced a net loss in 1972. Wolverine appeared to recover in the later years of the decade, as sales increased from about $125 million in 1975 to about $250 million in 1980.

However, the new decade brought increased competition from imported and athletic shoes that seriously undermined the already weakened business. In 1981 the Reagan administration dropped import quotas in favor of freer trade, prompting a deluge of inexpensive shoes from Asia and Latin America. Half of the country's footwear manufacturers went bankrupt over the course of the 1980s, as the imports share of the U.S. market grew from 50 percent to 86 percent. During the same period, consumers began to turn from

Hush Puppy-type shoes to athletic shoes for casual wear, further eroding Wolverine's potential market.

Unlike so many of its compatriots, Wolverine survived the 1980s, but not without its share of fits and starts. Under the direction of Thomas Gleason from 1972 to 1992, the company struggled to meet the challenge by diversifying its footwear lineup, expanding its direct retail operation, leveraging the Hush Puppies brand via licensing, and moving some production overseas.

Wolverine World Wide had launched its own chain of "Little Red Shoe House" specialty stores, which emphasized children's shoes, in 1976. Acquisitions and internal growth expanded the company's retail operation to more than 100 stores by 1983. The well-known Hush Puppies logo was licensed to manufacturers of clothing, umbrellas, luggage, hats, and handbags, and could be found in 56 countries by 1987.

ENTERING THE ATHLETIC MARKET: 1981

From its well-established base in work shoes and "career casual" footwear, Wolverine diversified via acquisition and internal development. The company entered the athletic market with the 1981 purchase of Brooks Shoe Manufacturing Co., a struggling maker of running shoes. Wolverine acquired Town & Country and Viner Bros. shoes in 1982 and added Kaepa dual-laced, split-vamp specialty athletic shoes the following year. The company also developed its own new shoes, including the Body Shoe, which featured an ergonomic "comfort curve," and Cloud 10 shoes, with special cushioning for the ball of the foot. Wolverine hoped that its expanded line of comfortable yet fashionable footwear would attract more 30- to 45-year-olds to its stores.

In spite of these apparently well-thought-out efforts, Wolverine's bottom line continued to show signs of stress: Net income slid from $15.5 million in 1981 to $2.1 million in 1984. After a slight recovery in 1985, the company suffered a $12.6 million loss on sales of $341.7 million. The shortfall sparked a restructuring and reorganization that included the closure of five U.S. factories, the sale of two small retail chains and shuttering of 15 other outlets, the spin-off of Kaepa, and the divestment of a relatively new West German footwear manufacturing and 105-store retail operation. The domestic factory closings helped increase the proportion of Wolverine's shoes manufactured overseas to about 50 percent.

Analysts found plenty to blame at Wolverine. Some said that the company's new casual and career-oriented brands, including Town & Country, Harbor Town of Maine, and Wimzees Casuals, were cannibalizing Hush Puppies' sales. Among other criticisms were that top executives had lost direction, the company had grown too large to be efficiently managed, and that the firm had delved into wrongheaded diversification efforts.

REVITALIZING AMID PROBLEMS

In 1987 the company hired Geoffrey B. Bloom, a marketing and product development expert with 12 years of experience at Florsheim Shoe Co., as president and COO. In the waning years of the decade, Wolverine made another attempt at revitalization. The company leveraged its basic lines of work shoes and boots, dress shoes, and casual footwear to fit the multiple fashion and function demands of younger customers. For example, the company's 100-plus years of expertise in making durable work boots gave it insight into the development of hiking and outdoor boots. Wolverine used its own venerable brand and licensed the Coleman name for this new venture. The company hired new designers to update its athletic and casual shoes, and it even contracted with a Michigan State University laboratory for new footwear innovations.

Although Wolverine World Wide's net income rose to $7.7 million on sales of $324 million by 1988, other nagging problems stole the spotlight from this modest recovery. Most infamous of these was a 1989 lawsuit charging that Wolverine and Fred Goldston, a pigskin and cowhide broker, had conspired to steal cowhide from Southwest Hide Co. Goldston had been hired by Wolverine to raise the quantity and quality of pigskin rinds to supply the company's tannery.

Southwest originally accused Goldston of exchanging their high-grade cowhides with lower-quality skins, but when Goldston went bankrupt, the plaintiff added partner Wolverine to the suit. Faced with a jury verdict of more than $39.3 million, Wolverine elected to settle the suit for $8.5 million in cash and bonds in 1992. CEO Gleason continued to assert his company's innocence in spite of the settlement, claiming "We were just the deep pockets around." Wolverine was also plagued with quality-control and inventory problems in the late 1980s.

DRAMATIC RECOVERY

In the fall of 1990, Wolverine announced another restructuring, including plans to scale back its retail operations, shutter a manufacturing plant, and eliminate certain shoe lines. After multiple reorganizations, infrequent profitability, and sliding market share, the company elected to divest its Brooks athletic shoe division to Rokke Group, a U.S.-Norway joint venture, in 1992. The restructuring shrank Wolverine's overall revenues from more than $320 million in 1990 to $282.9 million in 1992, but allowed it to concentrate on its Wolverine and Hush Puppies brands, which made near-miraculous recoveries in the early 1990s.

Wolverine's revitalization after more than a decade of lackluster performance came about through a combination of rejuvenated designs, savvy marketing, strict cost controls, and a healthy dose of good luck. From 1990 to 1995, Geoffrey Bloom, who succeeded Thomas Gleason as CEO in 1993, closed more than 100 of the company's retail outlets, designating the remaining 60 as factory outlets. He also consolidated Wolverine's 16 divisions into five streamlined operating units, thereby increasing productivity (measured in revenue per employee) by nearly one-fourth from 1992 to 1994.

Taking a cue from fashion designer John Bartlett, newly hired designer Maggie Mercado revived 1950s-era styles such as the "Wayne" (nee Duke) oxford and "Earl" slip-on, offering the waterproof suede shoes in a rainbow of new colors such as Pepto-Bismol pink and Day-Glo green. Both Bartlett and designer Anna Sui featured the shoes in their 1995 collections. Hush Puppies soon began to turn up on the famous feet of stars such as Jim Carrey, Sharon Stone, David Bowie, Tom Hanks, and Sylvester Stallone. Hush Puppies also benefited from the trend toward dressing-down at work, filling the fashion gap between tennis shoes and dress shoes. Wolverine sent videotapes with tips for casual dressing at work to 200 businesses throughout the United States. In the ultimate retro coup, the company revived the "We invented casual" tagline that had launched Hush Puppies in 1958. By 1995, tony stores such as Barneys in New York and Pleasure Swell in California struggled to keep the shoes in stock.

BENEFITING FROM LICENSED BRANDS

While its Hush Puppies conquered the world of fashion, Wolverine World Wide's work boots and hikers tackled more mundane markets. In spite of steadily declining employment in U.S. construction and manufacturing sectors, sales of Wolverine work boots reached record levels in 1991. The high-tech, relatively lightweight footwear featured DuraShock shock absorbers and slip-resistant treads. Smart new ads told prospective customers that they could "hunt 'til hell freezes over." Coleman hiking boots gave Wolverine entrée into the mass market via distribution in Wal-Mart stores.

In 1994 Wolverine added another licensed brand to its stable when it acquired the worldwide license to market footwear under the Caterpillar name from Caterpillar Inc., the manufacturer of earthmoving equipment. Leveraging Caterpillar's rugged image, Wolverine promoted the new line as "walking machines, the toughest equipment on earth." Annual sales of the Caterpillar line reached nearly eight million pairs by 1997, eclipsing sales of the Wolverine brand, with sales being made in more than 100 countries. According to one Wolverine executive, the Caterpillar boots had become a trendy item with younger consumers looking for "funky" footwear.

A focus on international growth increased the geographic distribution of the company's sales to about 50 percent international by 1995. Wolverine was the only U.S. shoemaker to achieve a comprehensive contract in Russia. It had also established a Hush Puppies store in China, and its branded shoes were offered in more than 60 countries around the world. By 1995, Wolverine's turnaround was quite evident. Sales had risen by more than 46 percent from $282.9 million in 1992 to $414 million in 1995, and net income more than tripled from $4.7 million to $24.1 million during the same period.

EXPANDING THE BRAND PORTFOLIO

In 1996 Bloom was rewarded for his remarkable turnaround achievement by being named chairman. He also remained CEO but relinquished the presidency to Timothy O'Donovan, who was named COO as well the following year. O'Donovan had held a series of marketing, sales, and management positions since joining Wolverine in 1969, and as president of the Hush Puppies Company from 1992 to 1996, he played a key role in the turnaround led by Bloom.

Expansion was clearly still on the agenda for Bloom and O'Donovan in the later years of the 1990s. Wolverine paid $22.8 million in cash to the Florsheim Shoe Company in 1996 for the HyTest line of industrial work boots. That fall a line of Hush Puppies men's and women's slippers began reaching store shelves. The company's stable of outdoor footwear brands was augmented via the October 1997 acquisition of Merrell, a brand of performance footwear designed for backpacking, day hiking, and everyday use. Wolverine's aggressive drive into foreign markets continued in 1997 with the introduction of the Hush Puppies brand into Russia, China, France, and Scandinavia and the Caterpillar line into Russia, China, Brazil, and India.

During 1998 the company began producing a Harley-Davidson line of motorcycle, casual, fashion, and western footwear for men, women, and children under a license agreement with the Harley-Davidson Motor Company. The next year Wolverine launched its first full line of children's shoes and boots, including the Hush Puppies, Caterpillar, Harley-Davidson, and Coleman labels.

The growth initiatives helped revenues and profits increase smartly in 1996 and 1997, but the company managed only marginal increases in 1998 because of a weak fourth quarter. The economic crisis that erupted in Russia that year battered Wolverine's nascent moves into that market. The company took the difficult decision of closing down its Russian subsidiary, taking a $14 million charge in 1999 to do so, which in turn led to a decline in profits for the year.

RESTRUCTURING IN EARLY 21ST CENTURY

In April 2000 Bloom handed over the CEO reins to O'Donovan, with Bloom continuing as chairman. A month later Wolverine announced that it had entered into a license agreement with the Stanley Works, the famous U.S. toolmaker, to develop a line of Stanley brand work boots. In a first for Wolverine, the line, which was to be value priced at under $60 per pair, was to be sold through Payless ShoeSource, Inc., operator of the largest chain of shoe stores in the United States.

O'Donovan next faced the challenge of implementing a major restructuring of the company's global sourcing and manufacturing operations. Aiming to reduce operating costs by $10 million per year, Wolverine closed five of its manufacturing plants in New York, Missouri, Canada, Puerto Rico, and Costa Rica, shifting production to its remaining seven plants. Nearly 1,400 employees were cut from the payroll by the time the restructuring was complete in mid-2001, representing one-quarter of the workforce. In the end, the initiative substantially transferred more of the company's production outside the United States, a shift that many other U.S. footwear makers had made in the 1990s. Prior to the restructuring, 40 percent of Wolverine's shoes and boots were made in the United States, but by 2003 this figure was down to 5 percent.

Wolverine recorded $28 million in restructuring charges during 2000, resulting in a net income figure for the year of just $10.7 million. Revenues for the year, however, increased a respectable 6 percent thanks in large part to phenomenal sales of the Merrell brand. Wolverine sold nearly 4.5 million pairs of Merrell shoes in 2000, doubling the previous year's total, and the brand garnered sales in excess of $100 million, an increase of 80 percent. Driving these stellar results was Merrell's move beyond hiking boots.

In late 1998 Merrell invented a new footwear category when it began selling "aftersport" shoes, a line of comfortable moccasins or sandals with all-weather treads. As O'Donovan told the *Grand Rapids Business Journal* in 2001, "We found that after these hardcore users of Merrell products got off the ski slopes or mountain bikes, or finished trail running, we had an opportunity to sell them another pair of footwear they could wear after all those activities. That was the concept." In 2002 Wolverine sold more than seven million pairs of Merrell footwear, which was now distributed in more than 130 countries. Revenues for the brand reached $180 million.

Wolverine World Wide recorded its third straight year of record revenues in 2002, with sales increasing 14.9 percent that year, to $827.1 million. Profits increased 7.5 percent, reaching a record $47.9 million. That year Wolverine purchased the rights to the Track 'n Trail name, which had been the name of a shoe store chain before it declared bankruptcy in 2001. Wolverine's two existing mall-based retail outlets, which had been called UpFootgear, were rebranded Track 'n Trail. Wolverine also acquired its CAT (the Caterpillar line) and Merrell distribution businesses in Europe during 2002.

GROWING INTO A BILLION-DOLLAR BUSINESS

Continuing to seek new avenues for growth, Wolverine in November 2003 acquired Sebago, Inc., a privately held footwear maker based in Portland, Maine, for $16.8 million. This acquisition expanded Wolverine into more preppy footwear given Sebago's output of penny loafers and its flagship product, Docksides boat shoes. Sebago was known for the high quality of its shoes, which were handcrafted and handstitched. At the time Wolverine purchased it, Sebago made 75 percent of its shoes in two plants in Maine, and it prominently touted many of its brands as "Made in the USA." By April 2004, however, both plants had been shut down and production shifted to a Wolverine facility in the Dominican Republic.

Wolverine's only remaining domestic shoe-making plants, located in Michigan and Arkansas, continued to produce Bates military boots, a burgeoning business in the early 21st century because of U.S. involvement in wars in Iraq and Afghanistan. Wolverine's contract with the U.S. Department of Defense required that the boots be made in the United States.

In the meantime, workers at the Wolverine tannery in Rockford went on strike in July 2003, the first such action at the plant in 23 years. The workers were mainly concerned about their jobs being subcontracted out or shifted to China as the company wanted them to agree to contract language giving Wolverine just those rights. In mid-September, shortly after Wolverine hired "permanent replacement workers," the striking workers agreed to the company's terms. This did not end the acrimony as it was not until January 2004 that Wolverine agreed to give all the workers who had gone on strike their jobs back and to let the replacements go.

VENTURING BEYOND FOOTWEAR

Wolverine stepped outside its core business in mid-2004 to launch a line of Merrell packs, bags, and luggage. This venture beyond footwear presaged the company's later launch of apparel lines for the Merrell, Wolverine, and Sebago brands. Also in 2004, the Caterpillar and Harley-Davidson lines were placed within a newly created Heritage Brands Group. Sebago was transferred into this group as well a few years later.

In 2005 O'Donovan took on the additional title of board chairman, while Blake Krueger was named president and COO. Krueger had previously headed both the Caterpillar line and the Heritage Brands Group. That year, Wolverine World Wide enjoyed its best year ever, with record profits of $74.5 million and a milestone revenue figure over the $1 billion mark. Continuing to seek additional avenues for further growth, the company also reached a license agreement with Patagonia, Inc., a subsidiary of Lost Arrow Corporation, to begin producing Patagonia brand footwear. The plan was to create a new line of footwear in keeping with Patagonia's reputation as an environmentally conscious leader in premium, performance outdoor apparel. The Patagonia footwear line was placed within Wolverine's Outdoor Group alongside Merrell and made its debut in the spring of 2007.

Krueger was promoted to president and CEO in April 2007, while O'Donovan retained the board chairmanship. Wolverine enjoyed another year of strong growth in 2007, paced by robust Merrell sales, with that brand performing particularly well in Europe. Footwear orders from retailers fell sharply in the final months of 2008, however, amid the global financial crisis and the beginning of a lengthy and deep recession. As a result, Wolverine's profits for 2008 grew just 3.2 percent, while sales advanced only 1.8 percent.

While contending with the difficult economic climate, Wolverine in early 2009 launched a restructuring aimed at cutting annual costs by around $20 million. In a series of moves that slashed about 10 percent of the company workforce, or approximately 450 jobs, Wolverine shut down its Rockford tannery and shifted to the outsourcing of leather production for its Wolverine Leathers division; consolidated its U.S. footwear manufacturing operations into a single facility in Big Rapids, Michigan, resulting in the shutdown of its factory in Jonesboro, Arkansas; consolidated its North American distribution operations into existing warehouses in Michigan; and consolidated its European distribution arm into a single facility.

Restructuring costs of nearly $36 million shaved 2009 profits down to $61.9 million. Revenues for the year dropped about 10 percent, to $1.1 billion. Over the course of this difficult year, the company added two more brands to its portfolio: Cushe and Chaco. Based in the United Kingdom, Cushe was a line of fashion-forward footwear positioned as a youthful comfort brand. It became part of the Hush Puppies group. Chaco, placed into the Outdoor Group and based in Paonia, Colorado, specialized in technical performance sandals designed for water and outdoor use. Wolverine began touting Cushe and Chaco, along with Merrell and Sebago, as key drivers of its future growth. Other growth initiatives centered on expanding the firm's global footprint, increasing the number of company-owned stores, accelerating e-commerce activities, and boosting efforts to expand the company's brands beyond footwear into apparel and accessories. Early results from Wolverine's restructuring efforts coupled with a nascent economic recovery combined for a brighter 2010, when profits during the second fiscal quarter more than doubled to $17.2 million and sales increased nearly 5 percent to $258.2 million. At the beginning of 2010, meanwhile, Krueger assumed the duties of board chairman while remaining Wolverine president and CEO.

April Dougal Gasbarre
Updated, David E. Salamie

PRINCIPAL SUBSIDIARIES

BSI Shoes, Inc.; Chaco Outdoor, Inc.; Dominican Wolverine Shoe Company Limited (Cayman Islands); Hush Puppies Retail, Inc.; Hy-Test, Inc.; Sebago Dominican Limited (Cayman Islands); Sebago International Limited (Cayman Islands); Sebago Realty, LLC; Sebago USA, LLC; Spartan Shoe Company Limited (Cayman Islands); Supervision Design Ltd. (UK); Wolverine Colorado, Inc.; Wolverine Consulting Services (Zhuhai) Company Limited (China); Wolverine de Argentina, S.R.L.; Wolverine de Costa Rica, S.A.; Wolverine de Mexico S.A. de C.V.; Wolverine Design Center, Inc.; Wolverine Europe B.V. (Netherlands); Wolverine Europe Limited (UK); Wolverine Europe Retail B.V. (Netherlands); Wolverine Europe Retail

Limited (UK); Wolverine International GP, LLC; Wolverine International, L.P. (Cayman Islands); Wolverine International S.à.r.l. (Luxembourg); Wolverine International, S.L. (Spain); Wolverine Outdoors, Inc.; Wolverine Procurement, Inc.; Wolverine Slipper Group, Inc.; Wolverine Sourcing, Inc.; Wolverine Sourcing, Ltd. (Cayman Islands); Wolverine World Wide Canada, ULC; Wolverine World Wide Corporation, Inc. (Canada); Wolverine World Wide Europe Limited (UK); Wolverine World Wide HK Limited (Hong Kong).

PRINCIPAL DIVISIONS

The Heritage Brands Group; The Hush Puppies Company; Outdoor Group; Wolverine Footwear Group; The Wolverine Leathers Division.

PRINCIPAL COMPETITORS

adidas AG; Columbia Sportswear Company; Deckers Outdoor Corporation; LaCrosse Footwear, Inc.; L.L. Bean, Inc.; NIKE, Inc.; The North Face Apparel Corp.; Red Wing Shoe Company, Inc.; R. Griggs Group Ltd.; Rocky Brands, Inc.; Skechers U.S.A., Inc.; The Timberland Company.

FURTHER READING

Abel, Katie, "Passing the Torch: O'Donovan Hands Krueger CEO Spot," *Footwear News*, April 23, 2007, p. 1.

Daly, Pete, "Wolverine World Wide Has Been Just That for Decades," *Grand Rapids (MI) Business Journal*, May 11, 2009, p. 19.

———, "Wolverine's Merrell Brands Grows Strong in Europe," *Grand Rapids (MI) Business Journal*, June 25, 2007, p. B2.

Emrich, Anne Bond, "Wolverine Concentrates on Gaining Market Share," *Grand Rapids (MI) Business Journal*, October 13, 2003, p. 17.

———, "Wolverine Continues Building Global Brands," *Grand Rapids (MI) Business Journal*, February 5, 2001, p. 7.

———, "Wolverine World Wide Embraces Life after Realignment," *Grand Rapids (MI) Business Journal*, September 25, 2000, p. 7.

Knape, Chris, "Wolverine Buys Sebago, Docksides," *Grand Rapids (MI) Press*, July 25, 2003, p. A1.

Martinez, Shandra, "Wolverine Buckles Down to Weather Tough Times, *Grand Rapid (MI) Press*, February 5, 2009, p. A15.

———, "Wolverine World Wide Profits Drop," *Grand Rapids (MI) Press*, February 4, 2010, p. A10.

Murphy, Kevin, "Wolverine Tops $1B, Earnings Strong," *Grand Rapids (MI) Business Journal*, February 20, 2006, p. 7.

Newman, Eric, "Wolverine Inks Patagonia Deal," *Footwear News*, June 13, 2005, p. 20.

Plotkin, Amanda, "Fighting Back, WWW Shows Wall Street Its Sharpened Claws," *Footwear News*, December 20, 1999, p. 1.

Wieland, Barbara, "It's in the Shoes: Wolverine Soars on Success of Its Products," *Grand Rapids (MI) Press*, April 20, 2001, p. A5.

Wolverine Worldwide, Inc.: A Tradition of Success, Rockford, MI: Wolverine World Wide, Inc., 1983.

Woot, Inc.

4121 International Parkway
Carrollton, Texas 75007
U.S.A.
Telephone: (972) 417-3959
Fax: (972) 418-9245
Web site: http://www.woot.com

Private Company
Incorporated: 2004
Employees: 100
Sales: $163.53 million (2009)
NAICS: 454111 Electronic Shopping

■ ■ ■

Woot, Inc., is an online retailer operating under what it terms a "One Day, One Deal" business strategy. The company's flagship Web site, Woot.com, offers a limited quantity of one item per day, hosting daily sales that begin at 12:00 a.m. and end at 11:59 p.m. central time, or until the inventory is exhausted. Woot also operates other Web sites that offer one product at discounted prices. Shirt.Woot.com sells one designed T-shirt per day. Wine.Woot.com sells one selection of wine three days per week. Kids.Woot.com sells one children's item per day. Sellout.Woot.com offers a daily bargain recommended by manufacturers and retailers and one submitted by the public. Woot is led by its founder, Matt Rutledge.

FOUNDER'S FIRST COMPANY

Matt Rutledge built his career on exploiting the use of excess inventory. He used the detritus of manufacturers and retailers as the inventory for two companies, launching his entrepreneurial career while he was 23 years old with the founding of Dallas-based Synapse Micro, Inc., in 1994. Rutledge started the business as a distributorship that purchased computer components nearing the end of their ability to survive on retailers' shelves. He bought outdated motherboards and video cards and sold the merchandise to small, independent computer stores for bargain prices. Synapse Micro thrived in its niche, becoming a notable business in the Dallas area. By 2001, Rutledge's business had grown in scope, finding much larger customers for its inventory, profiting off sales to large retailers such as Fry's Electronics Inc.

The success of Synapse Micro spawned Woot, easily Rutledge's most successful entrepreneurial creation. Synapse Micro's volume of business grew to the point where the purveyor of excess inventory was producing its own steady stream of excess inventory. "We always had some kind of leftover stuff in our warehouse that our wholesale guys had given up on," Rutledge explained in the August 31, 2008 edition of the *Dallas Morning News*.

The surplus merchandise in Synapse Micro's warehouse did not serve as the only inspiration for Rutledge's second venture. When Rutledge and his employees were drinking beers one night after work, someone mentioned that the "Woot.com" Web address was available, which encouraged Rutledge to move

Woot.com is an online store and community that focuses on selling cool stuff cheap. It started as an employee-store slash market-testing type of place for an electronics distributor, but it's taken on a life of its own. We anticipate profitability by 2043—by then we should be retired; someone smarter might take over and jack up the prices. Until then, we're still the lovable scamps we've always been.

forward with launching a new business. "Woot," or "w00t," had entered the lexicon of the computer gaming world during the 1990s. Used by participants in role-playing games, the word was derived from the exclamation, "Wow, loot!" to celebrate discovering treasure within a game.

WOOT'S STRATEGY IS DEVELOPED: 2003–04

Rutledge adopted a quirky name for his company, but the most compelling peculiarity of Woot, Inc., was its business model. Rutledge defied many fundamental business precepts when he developed the idea for the venture, beginning with Woot's inventory. Instead of offering a vast selection of merchandise, Woot gave its customers the slimmest of choices, selling only one product each day. At midnight each day, a limited supply of a particular item was offered for sale, giving customers until 11:59 p.m. or until the supply was exhausted to purchase the item. Woot buyers scoured the globe, searching for bargain purchases in bulk from manufacturers and retailers, and offered their merchandise to visitors to Woot.com for heavily discounted prices. "That's where the power of this is, in the buying of inventory," Rutledge explained in the October 28, 2004 edition of the *New York Times*.

Rutledge bucked business convention in other ways, demonstrating an irreverent flair in his company's communication with customers. While the rest of the business world touted customer service, either genuinely or not, as a primary objective, Rutledge offered little hope of any help to Woot customers dissatisfied with their transaction. For those Woot customers who were looking for customer support, the company's Web site suggested "Googling" their queries, or consulting "a dating service, magic 8 ball, or Ouija board for general life questions." Another option given to disgruntled Woot customers was to sell their purchase on eBay. "It's likely

you'll make money doing this and save everyone a hassle," the company's Web site instructed customers. "If the item doesn't work, find out what you're doing wrong. Yes, we know you think the item is bad, but it's probably your fault."

Woot did not kowtow to its customers, but it did embrace them in ways atypical of conventional retailers. From the start, Rutledge wanted to make the Woot Web site a popular destination for bloggers, a stance that enabled Woot to benefit from the essentially free yet highly effective phenomenon of viral marketing. "We saw this as the right way to do buzz marketing," Rutledge said in a September 6, 2004 interview with *Advertising Age*. "There's a value here in actively building that community of consumers, the blogging community and our core demographic."

The approach added to the frank and candid nature of Woot.com. Next to whatever product was up for sale on a particular day were comments about the worth and value of the product, either excoriating, full of praise, or somewhere in between, posted by registered users of the Web site. Further revealing information was provided by the Web site, listing who purchased the first item, designated as "First Sucker," who purchased the last item, the "Wooter to Blame for the Sellout," and the percentage of sales per hour coupled with a geographic breakdown of "Woots by State," with each state shaded according to "Zero Wooters Wooting" and "Lots of Wooters Wooting." At the end of a day's sales, brought to a close by either time or supply, Woot.com revealed the number of items sold and, by deduction, its profit margin for the day.

WOOT.COM LAUNCHES: 2004

After purchasing the Woot.com address, Rutledge and a cadre of Synapse Micro employees spent a year developing the strategy for Woot. On July 15, 2004, the Web site launched, the latest entrant in a vast field vying for the estimated $66 billion spent by consumers online each year. Rutledge, 33 years old when Woot.com made its debut, hoped to attract 20,000 registered users by the end of the year, but his expectations were exceeded by far. More than 250,000 visitors flocked to the company's Web site during its first month online, as word of the bargains on Woot.com quickly spread throughout the blogging community. Blogs on Web sites such as engadget.com and fatwallet.com helped fan interest in Woot's unconventional approach to online retailing, requiring Rutledge to spend virtually nothing on marketing. By the end of the year, the number of registered users on Woot.com approached 100,000, with more than 50,000 visitors navigating to the Web site each day.

KEY DATES

2004: Woot.com Web site is launched.
2006: First of several Woot sister Web sites, Wine. Woot.com, is launched.
2007: Woot collaborates with Yahoo! to create Sellout.Woot.com.
2009: Kids.Woot.com Web site is launched.

People not only were registering and visiting the Web site, they were purchasing nearly everything Rutledge and his team of buyers put up for sale. They typically tried to purchase 1,000 items of whichever product they were selling and they typically exhausted their supply before the 24-hour sale ended, frequently selling out within hours of posting the item. Occasionally, Woot had surplus inventory, which was sold in a "Woot-Off," a sale that ended when the last item was sold, but the story of Woot's progress during its formative years was one of unmitigated success. "It went from something we thought would be a two- or three-person company with maybe some of the staff participating more like a hobby, to vastly outpacing the growth of Synapse, which is a Dallas 100 company itself," Rutledge explained in the January 1, 2005 edition of the *Dallas Morning News*.

Sales by the end of the company's first year reached $2.3 million, a total that would grow exponentially as more and more consumers learned of Woot.com. By October 2005 the number of registered Woot users had risen to 200,000, becoming an Internet phenomenon. As the company grew, the range of products posted daily grew as well. Initially, the company predominantly sold personal electronics items, including computers, computer peripherals, audio equipment, and televisions. The offerings soon represented a far more diverse selection, as household appliances, sporting goods, and other items were put up for sale.

CONCEPT EXPANDS: 2006–08

As Woot's merchandise mix broadened, so too did its scope. The company launched another site, Wine.Woot. com, in May 2006 after Rutledge and his managerial team discovered wine inventory was subject to the same overstock issues that enabled Woot.com to succeed in the electronics realm. Initially, the Web site offered one deal per week, but not long after its launch Wine.Woot. com offered a new selection of wine every Monday, Wednesday, and Friday. The next iteration of a Woot Web site appeared in July 2007, when Shirt.Woot.com

debuted. The Web site offered exclusive, original T-shirt designs for sale, primarily created by established artists, initially offering one new design per week before eventually increasing the frequency of the sales to a daily basis.

The next advancement in the evolution of Woot occurred not long after Rutledge's foray into selling T-shirts. In September 2007 the company announced it had formed a partnership with Yahoo!, an agreement revealed in a Woot press release titled, "Woot Sells Out!" Yahoo! approached Woot to improve the company's Yahoo! Shopping service, which led to the creation of Sellout.Woot.com, a site that could be accessed only through Yahoo! Shopping's front page at shopping.yahoo.com. For Woot, the deal with Yahoo! promised to enlarge its rapidly expanding customer base, giving the company, as the press release noted, "their gigunda audience of shoppers who've never met Woot."

Fast-paced growth elevated Woot's stature in the years that saw the company expand its reach. Annual sales increased 10-fold between 2004 and 2006, an increase fueled by the growing number of registered Wooters. By 2007, when the company signed its partnership agreement with Yahoo!, there were 700,000 registered users of Woot.com, enabling the company to generate $117 million in revenue. By 2008 the number of registered users, who could use their accounts to purchase items on sister Woot sites, had roughly doubled, nearing 1.5 million.

Rutledge enjoyed his greatest entrepreneurial success with Woot. In less than a decade, the company had emerged from the retailing chatter of the Internet and delivered its unique voice, distinguishing itself by its approach and its success in the e-commerce sector. Rutledge's concept continued to evolve as he prepared for the future. In 2009 he launched Kids.Woot.com, a Web site devoted to offering merchandise, on a daily basis, intended for children. In 2010 Sellout.Woot.com debuted, a Web site that offered bargains recommended by retailers and manufacturers alongside bargains discovered on the Internet by the Woot community. The years ahead would reveal the limitations or the limitlessness of Rutledge's e-commerce philosophy.

Jeffrey L. Covell

PRINCIPAL OPERATING UNITS

Woot.com; Shirts.Woot.com; Kids.Woot.com; Wine. Woot.com; Sellout.Woot.com.

PRINCIPAL COMPETITORS

eBay Inc.; Overstock.com, Inc.; Wal-Mart.com USA, LLC.

FURTHER READING

Bulik, Beth Snyder, "Woot Rolls Out New Online Retail Model," *Advertising Age*, September 6, 2004, p. 10.

Castelluccio, Michael, "Who Needs Rules?" *Strategic Finance*, July 2007, p. 57.

Godinez, Victor, "Carrollton, Texas-Based Woot.com Offers Goods One Deal at a Time," *Dallas Morning News*, January 1, 2005.

Metz, Rachel, "Deals from a Bargain Bin, One at a Time," *New York Times*, October 28, 2004.

Tiku, Nitasha, "Matt Rutledge: Woot," *Inc.*, September 2008, p. 200.

Wyeth

Wyeth, Inc.

———■———

500 Arcola Road
Collegeville, Pennsylvania 19426-3982
U.S.A.
Telephone: (610) 902-1200
Toll Free: (800) 999-9384
Fax: (610) 995-4668
Web site: http://www.wyeth.com; http://www.
pfizer.com

Wholly Owned Subsidiary of Pfizer, Inc.
Incorporated: 1926 as American Home Products
Employees: 42,000
NAICS: 325412 Pharmaceutical Preparation Manu- fac-
turing; 325414 Biological Product (Except
Diagnostic) Manufacturing; 541380 Testing La-
boratories

■ ■ ■

Wyeth, Inc., is a global pharmaceutical research and
manufacturing company. It develops and markets
traditional pharmaceuticals, vaccines, and biotechnology
products that serve both human and animal health care.
It has strong product lines in both prescription medications and in consumer health products, including over-
the-counter (OTC) medications and nutritional
supplements. Wyeth's brand name prescription drugs
include Premarin, to prevent postmenopausal osteoporosis; Enbrel, for rheumatoid arthritis; Tygacil, an
antibiotic; Lybrel, an oral contraceptive; Pristiq, an
antidepressant; Xyntha, which controls bleeding in cases
of Hemophilia A; and Prevenar 13, a vaccine for the
prevention of 13 different early childhood illnesses.
Popular OTC Wyeth products include Preparation H,
Chapstick, Centrum, Advil, Thermacare, Robitussin,
and Alavert. Wyeth markets its products in more than
140 countries, and has manufacturing facilities on five
continents.

1926–65: BIRTH AND DEVELOPMENT OF A CONGLOMERATE

Incorporated in 1926 as American Home Products
(AHP), the company came to be known as "Anonymous
Home Products" or the "withdrawn corporate giant."
Although the company marketed such popular products
as Black Flag insecticides, Easy-Off oven cleaner, Wool-
ite, and Chef Boyardee, as well as the familiar
pharmaceuticals Anacin, Advil, Dristan, Robitussin, and
Dimetapp, the corporate name never appeared on its
products' labels. Public relations was considered such a
low priority that switchboard operators answered the
phone with the company phone number instead of the
company name. Although executives at AHP made few
efforts to influence Wall Street analysts, the company's
many consecutive years of increased sales and earnings
made AHP shares a very popular investment.

AHP's unusual combination of anonymity and
financial success stemmed from its history of competent
management, product diversification through acquisition, and closefisted expenditures on virtually everything
except advertising. AHP managed to strike a balance
between the aggressive advertising of its consumer package goods and maintaining a reputable name within the
medical community.

and Sulphur, Kolynos dental cream, and Old English No Rubbing Floor Polish.

W. H. Kirn was named chairman of the new company in 1930 and served until 1935, when Alvin G. Brush, a salesman of Dr. Lyon's toothpaste, took over as president and chief executive officer, a position he held for the next 30 years. Brush's penchant for expansion through acquisition, while maintaining a sizable amount of cash in reserve, set the pattern for AHP's operating style. In his first eight years as president, Brush acquired 34 food and drug companies for a total of $25.6 million in cash and stock. One of AHP's earliest prizes was the acquisition of a sunburn oil in 1935 that the company transformed into Preparation H, which became one of the world's best-selling hemorrhoid treatments.

Other purchases included the 3-in-One Oil Company and Affiliated Products Inc., which made cosmetics and toiletries under such names as Outdoor Girl, Kissproof, and Neet. In 1938, AHP acquired Eff Laboratories, a manufacturer of commercial vitamin products, and S.M.A. Corporation, a producer of infant foods and vitamins. In 1939, Black Flag Company came under the AHP umbrella, followed in 1943 by G. Washington Coffee Refining Company, a manufacturer of grocery specialties. In 1946 another grocery specialties firm, Chef-Boy-Ar-Dee Quality Foods Inc., came aboard.

1965–83: EXPANSION THROUGH ADVERTISING

AHP's marketing genius transformed its newly acquired products into household names. Preparation H was a good example. By 1981 Preparation H had captured 64 percent of the hemorrhoid treatment market, and its success was attributable exclusively to the company's aggressive advertising. In 1968 AHP spent more than $2 million on radio spots and $6 million on television advertising for Preparation H. The figures became even more impressive when one realized that the radio code standards only readmitted the controversial advertisements for hemorrhoid medications in 1965 and that the National Association of Broadcasters continued to debate approval for television. AHP advocated a broadened scope of code approval even as it appropriated more funds for advertising on noncode television stations.

The struggle for an expanded consumer audience was fought not only over advertising codes for personal products. AHP's aggressive marketing style also brought investigations of the company's advertising copy. In 1967 the Federal Trade Commission (FTC) ordered AHP and three other companies to refrain from making

---

KEY DATES

1926: Company incorporates as American Home Products (AHP).
1930: AHP purchases the rights to manufacture the painkiller Anacin.
1932: AHP acquires pharmaceutical manufacturer Wyeth Chemical Company.
1994: AHP acquires American Cyanamid, including a majority interest in biotechnology firm Immunex.
1996–98: AHP disposes of its food businesses.
1997: AHP is forced to withdraw diet drugs Pondimin and Redux and faces a wave of lawsuits.
2001: AHP sells Immunex interest in exchange for an interest in biotechnology firm Amgen.
2002: AHP changes its name to Wyeth.
2009: Pfizer, Inc., completes its $68 billion acquisition of Wyeth.

AHP's strict management policy allowed for a minimal margin of error. If a product did not show promise before money was spent on promotion, it was dropped. If a division did not increase sales and earnings by 10 percent annually, a division president could be out of a job. Until the 1990s AHP found little reason to invest in research, preferring to wait for competitors to release innovative products, and then launch its own improved line. Alternatively, it would simply buy the competitor.

Expenditures were so closely monitored at AHP that, in 1983, employees at the Whitehall division paid $20 each to attend their own Christmas party. A journalist from *Business Week*, researching a rumor in 1970 that then-AHP Chairman and President William F. LaPorte had reduced the size of the toilet paper in the executive washrooms to save money, discovered that, in fact, the paper was 9/16-inch narrower than typical size. As late as 1980 LaPorte personally approved any expenditures more than $500, including anything from the purchase of a typewriter to a secretarial pay raise.

AHP's knack for acquiring little-known products and companies at a reduced price and turning them into moneymakers dated back to AHP's earliest years. In 1926 a group of executives associated with Sterling Products Inc. and Household Products Inc. consolidated several independent nostrum makers into a holding company. Its subsidiaries sold such medicinal products as Hill's Cascara Quinine, St. Jacob's Oil, Wyeth's Sage

false claims with regard to the therapeutic value of their hemorrhoid treatments. Citing the advertisements' unsubstantiated claims, the FTC prohibited any future misrepresentation.

Company executives were not intimidated by the FTC ruling. AHP, deeming the commission's findings "capricious" and "arbitrary," asked for a review before a federal appeals court. The company continued to run advertisements in more than 1,100 newspapers, 700 radio stations, and 100 television stations. In response, the FTC temporarily enjoined AHP from continuing to run the advertisements. The court finally upheld most of the commission's findings, and the advertising copy for Preparation H had to be permanently modified.

Throughout this controversy AHP executives remained characteristically unavailable for comment. This combination of persistent product promotion (at the risk of damaging company reputation) and a united but anonymous executive front came to the fore in the promotion of another AHP product. In 1930 the company had purchased the rights to manufacture a little-known painkiller called Anacin, previously promoted through samples to dentists. AHP's Anacin grew in popularity and became the nation's leading OTC analgesic. As with Preparation H, it took aggressive marketing to propel Anacin into this position.

By 1971 AHP spent more money on the promotion of Anacin than had any other analgesic manufacturer on a comparable product. Total costs for radio advertising reached $1.5 million, and costs for television advertising surpassed $25 million. In 1972 the FTC charged that AHP and two other analgesic manufacturers were promoting their products through misleading and unsubstantiated claims. Because no reliable scientific evidence existed as to the superiority of one brand over another, or the ability of analgesics to relieve nervous tension, the FTC disputed therapeutic claims and advertisements that did not identify generic ingredients such as aspirin and caffeine.

AHP and the other manufacturers refused to negotiate consent agreements, and so the FTC issued formal complaints and ordered hearings before an FTC administrative judge. The case was finally settled in 1981 and permanent limits were placed on misleading claims in Anacin advertisements. In 1982 a federal appeals court upheld the FTC ruling after AHP attempted to have it overturned.

During the hearings on aspirin advertisements, Johnson & Johnson's Tylenol made its market appearance. To maintain their market share, AHP and other aspirin manufacturers launched a campaign to promote aspirin's anti-inflammatory action. After several suits and countersuits between AHP and Johnson &

Johnson, a federal court judge in 1978 ordered the discontinuance of the advertising of Anacin's anti-inflammatory property as a claim of superiority over Tylenol.

Competition in the pain-reliever market was intensified by the introduction of ibuprofen. The drug was a non-steroidal anti-inflammatory agent that was as effective as aspirin and aspirin substitutes, but without the side effect of digestive tract irritation. AHP marketed its ibuprofen under the name Advil. Industry analysts suggested that ibuprofen could capture as much as 30 percent of the pain-reliever market.

The pattern of controversy and investigation established in the marketing for Preparation H and Anacin continued with several other AHP products. Easy-Off oven cleaner, Black Flag insecticide, Easy-On starch, and Aero Wax were all involved in an FTC investigation into deceptive advertising. Despite all of the controversy, no one could dispute AHP's success in capturing markets and acquiring products that became household staples.

AHP's advertising budget for 1985 was estimated at more than $412 million. Despite or perhaps because of this great expenditure, AHP gained a notorious reputation among advertising agencies as a demanding and uncompromising client. Paying the lowest possible commission rates, the company, nonetheless, demanded the best price for prime-time spots on television and expected promotion to be effective on strict budgets. In 1967 Ted Bates & Company, the fifth-largest advertising agency in the world at that time, resigned AHP's $20 million account because of "differences in business policy." This was not the first time an AHP account was abandoned by an agency. Grey Advertising Inc. and J. Walter Thompson similarly dropped the demanding company's account. The Bates agency was replaced with an in-house agency called the John F. Murray Company. At the time of the replacement, industry-owned agencies were rare.

By 1983 AHP grudgingly began to change its attitude toward promotion. The company hired world-renowned photographer Richard Avedon and actress Catherine Deneuve to promote its line of Youth Garde cosmetics. Despite this willingness to "upscale" its advertising, AHP was voted one of the 10 worst clients of 1983 by *Adweek*.

1932–94: DEVELOPMENT OF A PHARMACEUTICAL BUSINESS

The success of AHP's proprietary goods overshadowed the company's position as a leading manufacturer of ethical drugs. In 1932 AHP acquired Wyeth Chemical

Company (later Wyeth Laboratories), a pharmaceutical manufacturer with a long history, under unusual circumstances. Wyeth was run by family descendants until the death of Stuart Wyeth, a bachelor. He bequeathed the laboratory to Harvard, his alma mater, and the university in turn sold the company to AHP at a generous price. In the early 1940s AHP also acquired two other pharmaceutical laboratories, Ives and Ayerst.

AHP's prescription drugs and medical supplies accounted for 47 percent of sales and 62 percent of profits in 1983. The ethical drugs AHP produced included Ovral, a low-dosage oral contraceptive, and Inderal, a drug that reduced blood pressure and slowed the heartbeat. Inderal was introduced in 1968, and by 1983 supplied more than half of the U.S. market for beta-blocker drugs. The company also developed several new pharmaceuticals. AHP filed 21 new drug applications with the Food and Drug Administration (FDA) in 1985 alone.

In 1981, company President John W. Culligan was promoted to chairman and chief executive officer. LaPorte, who had been chairman since 1965, continued as chairman of the executive committee. Culligan, 64 years old at the time of the promotion, had been with the company since 1937. John R. Stafford, a lawyer recruited from Hoffmann-La Roche in 1970 as general counsel, was named company president on December 1, 1986. Some observers predicted that AHP's management changes would herald a modernization of LaPorte's highly centralized style of management and financial control, which contradicted contemporary theories of corporate management.

Nevertheless, this anachronistic approach guaranteed shareholders a handsome return on investment. In 1982 *Fortune* magazine's directory of the 500 largest U.S. industrial corporations ranked AHP 76th in sales and 24th in profits. The company had no long-term debt, and it paid out 60 percent of earnings in dividends. Despite a chronically low stock price in the late 1980s and early 1990s, AHP saw higher earnings and increased dividends every year from 1951 to 1993.

In 1983 AHP spent $425 million to buy Sherwood Medical Group. A manufacturer of medical supplies, Sherwood placed AHP in a competitive position to capture the lion's share of the growing medical-device market. That subsidiary was supplemented with the 1992 acquisition of Symbiosis Corp., a developer and manufacturer of disposable instruments for minimally invasive laparoscopic and endoscopic surgery.

Under Stafford's guidance in the late 1980s and early 1990s, AHP worked to transform itself into a health care company through acquisitions and divestments. In 1989, the firm divested its Boyle-Midway division and purchased A.H. Robins Co., an OTC drug manufacturer that complemented the White-hall laboratories subsidiary. In response to criticism of its low research and development (R&D) expenditures, AHP spent a record 11 percent of sales on R&D in 1990. The firm invested in Genetics Institute, Inc., a biotechnology firm specializing in blood cell regulation, bone repair, and immune system modulation, in 1992.

AHP's marketing of infant formula came under intense scrutiny and criticism in the late 1980s and early 1990s. Prior to 1988, infant formula was marketed strictly as a pharmaceutical product. Given historical product loyalty, formula makers offered their products free to pediatricians and hospitals in the hopes that the first formula a mother used would be the one she continued to purchase. According to a 1990 *Business Week* article, many doctors began to allege that hospitals promoted infant formula over breast-feeding, despite the inherent advantages of breast-feeding, because of the money and services received from manufacturers. When the federal government directed the states to purchase all formula from one manufacturer to garner lower prices, formula manufacturers were forced to compete directly for Women, Infants and Children (WIC) contracts, which constituted about 35 percent of state formula purchases. In June 1993, *Advertising Age* reported that the FTC had charged the top three formula marketers (divisions of Abbott Laboratories, Bristol-Myers Squibb Co., and AHP Corp.) with price-fixing in government nutrition programs.

Although food products received less attention in the 1990s, AHP did augment its Chef-Boy-Ar-Dee line with the 1992 purchase of Ro*Tel, the leading brand of canned tomatoes and green chilies in the Mexican food category. In 1993, the company added M. Polaner Inc., a jam maker, to the food products segment.

THE NINETIES: BECOMING A LEADING PHARMACEUTICAL AND BIOTECHNOLOGY FIRM

By 1993 over 60 percent of AHP's global revenues came from pharmaceuticals. The company was not yet a strong pharmaceutical manufacturer, though. In 1994, it reported only four products with patents extending beyond 1997. Its two lengthiest patents lasted until 2007. In an industry such as the brand name pharmaceutical industry, which depended on the profits derived from monopolies conferred by patent protections, AHP was not in a good competitive position. However, the company initiated a series of acquisitions and divestitures aimed at transforming itself into a major pharmaceutical company in 1994.

In that year, AHP spent about $9.7 billion to acquire American Cyanamid. This purchase expanded its product line to vaccines, cancer agents, and antibiotics. AHP also took a majority interest in Immunex Corp., a biotechnology firm. A major agricultural chemical business also came with the acquisition. Immunex rejected a 1995 attempt to purchase the remainder of the company. In 1996 AHP bought the remainder of Genetics Institute. In 1997 it purchased an animal health products company, and in 1998 a vitamin and nutritional supplement manufacturer.

To help pay for these purchases and to narrow its focus to human and animal pharmaceuticals, AHP sold many of its traditional product lines during these same years. It disposed of its oral-care products in 1995, its ophthalmic business in 1997, its medical-device business in 1998, its agricultural chemicals business in 2000, and its branded generic injectable products in 2002. Between 1996 and 1998, AHP also sold all of its food product businesses. In 2001, AHP sold its interest in Immunex to Amgen and acquired a 10 percent interest in that biotechnology company.

AHP's restructuring efforts encountered several challenges. During the 1990s, the pharmaceutical industry was undergoing a major consolidation through mergers and acquisitions. AHP tried unsuccessfully to join the trend. In 1998 AHP initiated separate merger negotiations with SmithKline Beecham and with Monsanto. Both of these proposed mergers failed. AHP followed this with an attempt to merge with Warner-Lambert in 1999. Although Pfizer eventually won Warner, AHP collected a $1.8 billion breakup fee in the transaction. Despite continued rumors that AHP was a suitor or target of takeover attempts, management denied such ambitions.

The company also confronted major legal problems. In 1996 studies implicated two of the company's weight-loss drugs, Redux and fenfluramine (Pondimin), in damage to users' heart valves, damage that might be fatal and sometimes required surgical replacement of the valve. At the FDA's request, AHP withdrew the drugs in 1997. Since 1992 millions of overweight Americans had used Pondimin in combination with phentermine, a combination known as fen/phen, to help them lose weight. Later, AHP introduced Redux for the same purpose. The 1996 findings unleashed a wave of product liability lawsuits. Eventually AHP spent over $13 billion defending itself and paid as much as $3.75 billion in settlements. As late as 2002 the company was not entirely sure of its total eventual liabilities. This uncertainty about its liability costs contributed greatly to AHP's inability to reach merger agreements during the 1990s.

Despite these problems, AHP, which changed its name to Wyeth in 2002, entered the 21st century with a strong pharmaceutical franchise. With strengths in vaccines, biotechnology, and traditional pharmaceuticals, Wyeth's products spanned a wide range of treatment areas. In addition, its pharmaceuticals on average had one of the longest remaining patent lives in the industry.

PHARMACEUTICAL DEVELOPMENT GAINS MOMENTUM FOR EARLY 21ST-CENTURY GROWTH

Wyeth began a major operational realignment in 2000, when the company purchased a new global headquarters and R&D facility in Collegeville, Pennsylvania. In addition to renovating laboratories and updating communications technology, Wyeth initiated construction on four new structures and leased nearby buildings to house training. Wyeth relocated several research laboratories to the Collegeville campus over the next three years. The company expected the consolidation of research departments with everyday business operations to facilitate the process of moving a product through the many steps between drug discovery and market distribution.

Research on several products came to fruition at this time. Prevenar, a vaccine for meningitis and other bacterium-based early childhood diseases, received FDA approval in early 2000. Wyeth quickly established worldwide distribution of the product. Other new products included Premarin, low-dosage estrogen used to prevent osteoporosis in postmenopausal women, and Enbrel, used to reduce effects of rheumatoid arthritis. Both were approved for market by the FDA in July 2003. Health care products included the Cypher coronary stent, shown to prevent blockages from reappearing in coronary arteries. In November 2005 Effexor XR, for the treatment of panic disorder, became available to the public.

In biopharmacology, the use of DNA proteins as the basis for drug development, Wyeth expanded its research capabilities at its Andover, Massachusetts, research facility. In October 2007 Wyeth further expanded its biotechnology capabilities through the acquisition of Haptogen, Ltd., based in Aberdeen, Scotland. An existing collaboration highlighted the complementary strengths of the two companies.

Wyeth became a recognized leader in pharmaceutical development, with nearly 500 products in various phases of research and regulatory approval. Wyeth was recognized by *R&D Directions* magazine as one of the top 10 companies involved in drug development for central nervous system disorders. Research included 11 substances for the treatment of Alzheimer's and another eight substances for treatment of depression, schizophrenia, acute stroke, and bipolar disorder.

Wyeth's product development gained momentum in 2007 and 2008, as the FDA approved several new drugs for marketing and distribution. These included Lybrel, a low-dose combination oral contraceptive, and Pristiq, a once-a-day serotonin-nonrepinephrine inhibitor for treatment of major depressive disorder in adults. Wyeth introduced Xyntha, a biopharmacological form of factor VIII protein used to compensate for the deficiency known to cause insufficient blood-clotting and bleeding in patients suffering from hemophilia A. In May 2008 Wyeth received approval for its Tygacil antibiotic to treat community-acquired pneumonia. Tygacil was previously approved for use in complicated intra-abdominal infections and complicated skin and skin structure infections.

Wyeth's success in pharmaceutical development attracted the attention of pharmaceutical giant Pfizer, Inc. Seven Wyeth product lines surpassed $1 billion in sales in 2007, and the biological basis of Wyeth pharmaceutical research complemented Pfizer's stream of product development. Pfizer emphasized large molecule drugs, while Wyeth's strength laid in small-molecule research, such as vaccines. Also, Pfizer's patent for Lipitor, the popular cholesterol-regulating drug, expired, so Pfizer needed new drugs in its development pipeline to compensate for the expected sales decline as generic forms of Lipitor entered the market.

Pfizer's acquisition of Wyeth began in 2008 and was completed in October 2009. The $68 billion transaction involved cash and a stock exchange. Regulatory approval for the acquisition obligated Pfizer to sell several animal health products. Pfizer's integration of Wyeth involved streamlining plant operations and reducing the number of substances under research by 25 percent.

Pfizer stood to benefit from Wyeth's new children's vaccine, Prevenar 13, in 2010. The vaccine was designed to prevent 13 different diseases common in early childhood, ages six weeks to six years old. The FDA approved Prevenar 13 in February, and Pfizer expected first year sales to exceed $3 billion.

Updated, April Dougal Gasbarre;
Anne L. Potter; Mary Tradii

PRINCIPAL OPERATING UNITS

Wyeth Pharmaceuticals; Wyeth Consumer Healthcare; Fort Dodge Animal Health.

PRINCIPAL COMPETITORS

Abbott Laboratories, Inc.; AstraZeneca plc; Bristol-Myers Squibb Company; Eli Lilly and Company; GlaxoSmithKline plc; Johnson & Johnson; Merck & Co.; Novartis International AG; Roche Holding AG; Sanofi-Aventis; Schering-Plough Corporation.

FURTHER READING

Barrett, Amy, "AHP-Warner: No Panacea, But," *Business Week*, November 15, 1999, p. 44.

Burton, Thomas M., and Scott Kilman, "Monsanto's Cost-Cutting Steps," *Wall Street Journal*, November 12, 1988, p. A4.

Golden, Frederic, "Who's to Blame for Redux and Fenfluramine?" *Time*, September 29, 1997, pp. 78–79.

Gopal, Kevin, "Life Science Living," *Pharmaceutical Executive*, July 1998, pp. 28–30.

Harris, Gardiner, "American Home, Warner-Lambert Post Earnings," *Wall Street Journal*, April 20, 2000, p. 15.

Hensley, Scott, "American Home Plans to Reduce Stake in Immunex," *Wall Street Journal*, August 10, 2000, p. A12.

"Immunex Corp.," *Wall Street Journal*, November 9, 1995, p. B6.

Koberstein, Wayne, "Executive Profile: Team AHP—Parting the Clouds," *Pharmaceutical Executive*, June 2000, pp. 46–62.

Levin, Gary, "Time for Bottle: Infant Formula Ads May Spurt," *Advertising Age*, June 7, 1993, pp. 3, 42.

Moore, Samuel K., "AHP Seeks a New Pharmaceutical March," *Chemical Week*, January 26, 2000, p. 16.

"More Megadeals Loom in the Drug Industry," *Mergers and Acquisitions*, April 2000, pp. 10–11.

Ono, Yumiko, "Colgate to Buy Oral Care Line in Latin America," *Wall Street Journal*, January 10, 1995, p. A3.

Papanikolaw, Jim, "BASF to Buy AHP-Cyanamid," *Chemical Market Reporter*, March 27, 2000, p. 1.

"Pfizer Exec: Wyeth Has Added Value to Drug Pipeline." *New London Day*, January 13, 2010.

Siler, Julia Flynn, "The Furor over Formula Is Coming to a Boil," *Business Week*, April 9, 1990, pp. 52–53.

Steinmetz, Greg, and Elyse Tanouye, "American Cyanamid Agrees to Takeover by American Home," *Wall Street Journal*, August 18, 1994, p. A3.

Wood, Andrew, "SmithKline, AHP Plan Merger," *Chemical Week*, January 28, 1998, p. 9.

Young's Market Company, LLC

—■—

2164 North Batavia Street
Orange, California 92865
U.S.A.
Telephone: (714) 283-4933
Toll Free: (800) 317-6150
Fax: (714) 283-6175
Web site: http://www.youngsmarket.com

Wholly Owned Subsidiary of Young's Holdings, Inc.
Incorporated: 1906
Employees: 2,130
Sales: $1.66 billion (2009)
NAICS: 424810 Beer and Ale Merchant Wholesalers;
424820 Wine and Distilled Alcoholic Beverage
Merchant Wholesalers

■ ■ ■

Young's Market Company, LLC, is one of the largest wholesalers and distributors of beer, wine, and distilled spirits in the United States. The company's market territory includes most of California, with a particularly strong presence in Los Angeles and Southern California. Young's Market operates in the state of Hawaii through its Better Brands subsidiary. The geographic range of Young's Market and its subsidiaries extends to Oregon, Washington, Alaska, Idaho, Montana, Wyoming, Utah, and Arizona. The company is the exclusive distributor of many well-known brands of wine and spirits, including several fine and rare wines. Young's Market Company is co-owned by brother and sister Vern Underwood Jr. and

Janet Smith, both descendants of the company's founders.

1888–1930: BUILDING A FOOD RETAIL EMPIRE

In 1888 John G. Young, founder of Young's Market Company, opened a small retail food store in downtown Los Angeles. When his fledgling business began to grow, Young's four younger brothers joined him in the venture. In 1906 the five Young brothers incorporated their business as Young's Market Company and opened their first joint store at 9th and Main Street in Los Angeles. Four years later, the company opened its first manufacturing plant to produce several of its own food lines, including salad dressings, mayonnaise, corned beef, and sausage products. It also established a facility in a nearby building for receiving fish and seafood.

In 1925 the Young brothers opened a luxurious new store on the corner of 7th Street and Union Avenue. The store, which also served as the Young's Market Company headquarters, became a landmark in downtown Los Angeles and an important part of the city's heritage. Built in an Italian Renaissance Revival style, the store's décor featured tile mosaics and friezes. Inside, affluent shoppers could find such gourmet offerings as chocolates made on-site, Young's own line of coffees, and a delicatessen that claimed to offer anything in the world. Young's Market quickly became the caterer of choice for Los Angeles. The company concocted elaborate wedding cakes for prominent area weddings and supplied William Randolph Hearst with food for his ranch. The company's delivery trucks made deliveries twice each day to many parts of the city.

COMPANY PERSPECTIVES

Young's Market Company is family owned and operated. The Underwood family have dedicated their lives to this industry and are committed to the company, our supplier partners and our customers. The Underwoods have helped shape the landscape of the beverage alcohol industry by operating with the utmost integrity and highest standards.

In 1925, with their flagship store thriving, the Young brothers began a chain of what they called "neighborhood" retail stores. The company spent the next several years growing its chain, expanding as far south as San Diego and as far north as Santa Maria. In 1934 Young's opened its first supermarket. The store, named Thriftimart Cash and Carry, was geared less toward the company's traditional gourmet fare and more toward standard grocery products. Four more Thriftimarts soon followed. In 1937, however, the Young brothers sold the five-store chain of supermarkets to Fitzsimmons Markets.

POST-PROHIBITION

While the Youngs were working on their Thriftimart chain, a momentous change was taking place in the United States. With the end of Prohibition in 1933, the federal government's ban on alcohol sales was lifted. Retailers immediately jumped into action, providing a thirsty public with drinks that had been illegal for 13 years. Young's Market was in the vanguard of the new liquor business that quickly formed. The company began wholesaling liquor, while at the same time maintaining its retail grocery business. In 1934 it turned its San Diego store into a combination wholesale and retail food and liquor operation.

As a liquor wholesaler, Young's took an approach slightly different from that of its competitors. At the time, wine and liquor brands were carried by several different distributors, usually with no territorial exclusivity. This meant that competing distributors often carried the same brands. Young's, however, sought exclusive rights to the labels it carried. The company also aligned itself closely with smaller, independent distillers. This approach led to several beneficial and long-lasting alliances with brands such as Bacardi rum and Christian Brothers brandy.

INTRODUCTION OF JOSÉ CUERVO

One of the company's most notable successes was the introduction of the José Cuervo tequila line in the United States. The José Cuervo relationship was established by one of Young's new salesmen, Vernon Underwood. At the time, most Americans were unfamiliar with the strange-tasting Mexican liquor. Underwood, who had become acquainted with the drink during his college years at the University of Arizona at Tucson, was sure that it could be a good seller in the United States. He managed to convince both Young and the head of the Cuervo distillery, and Young's obtained U.S. distribution rights from Cuervo.

Tequila might not have become as popular as it did without some further help from Underwood and Young's Market's advertising agency. The main obstacle to popularizing tequila was finding a way to drink it. In Mexico the traditional method of tequila drinking involved licking salt from the back of the hand, gulping the liquor, then sucking on a lime. It seemed unlikely that this routine was going to catch on in the United States, and sales of the drink were slow.

A Los Angeles restaurant suddenly started ordering five cases of tequila at a time, and Underwood decided to pay a visit to the restaurant's bar to investigate what was behind the increased sales. What he found was the margarita, a new tequila drink invented by the restaurant's head bartender. Young's ad agency used the drink as a springboard for a new tequila campaign, which proved very successful. Sales of Cuervo surged, eventually attaining such popularity that Young's sold the national distribution rights, retaining distribution only in its own territory.

The successful introduction of José Cuervo was to be only the first of Underwood's many contributions to Young's Market. Eventually, he married company founder John Young's daughter, Adrienne, and assumed an increasingly significant role in the business, becoming general manager and chief financial officer.

GROWING THE WHOLESALE BUSINESS

Since Young's began wholesaling liquor in the early 1930s, it had dealt with increasing conflict between the wholesale and retail sides of its business. Some of its wholesale customers were unhappy about doing business with a company that was competing directly against them on the retail level. In 1940, when Young's acquired a Dr Pepper franchise, it appeared that the time had come to choose between retail and wholesale. The company decided to give up its retail segment and

```
┌─────────────────────────────────────────────┐
│                                               │
│              KEY DATES                        │
│                 ■                             │
│                                               │
│   1888:  John Young opens his first retail    │
│          food store in downtown Los Angeles.  │
│                                               │
│   1906:  Young's Market Company is            │
│          incorporated.                        │
│                                               │
│   1925:  Young's Market opens its famous      │
│          headquarters store in Los Angeles.   │
│                                               │
│   1933:  Young's begins wholesaling wine      │
│          and spirits.                         │
│                                               │
│   1990:  The Underwood family buys out all    │
│          remaining stockholders of Young's    │
│          Market.                              │
│                                               │
│   1994:  Young's Market moves its             │
│          headquarters from Los Angeles to     │
│          Orange, California.                   │
│                                               │
│   2002:  Estate Group is established for      │
│          fine wine wholesale distribution.    │
│                                               │
│   2006:  Young's Market expands spirits       │
│          wholesaling with the formation of    │
│          Infinium Spirits.                    │
│                                               │
└─────────────────────────────────────────────┘
```

focus exclusively on wholesaling wine, spirits, and food. It quickly set about selling its chain of neighborhood stores, which by that time numbered 60. In May 1940, the company closed the doors of its famous headquarters store at 7th and Union.

With a newly defined focus, Young's Market expanded its liquor business in the 1950s, opening branch operations in Long Beach and Rialto, California. The company also built a new headquarters at 500 South Central Avenue in Los Angeles and moved its meat and food processing segments into a new facility just down the street.

In 1963 Young's Market President William G. Young died. He was replaced by Vernon Underwood, John Young's son-in-law and the company's general manager. One year later the company established its first subsidiary wine and spirits wholesale business, named the William George Company. The new subsidiary opened its first wholesale branch operation in Anaheim, California, in 1967.

Also in 1967, Young's Market made its first foray outside of California with the acquisition of two Hawaii-based liquor wholesale firms. The companies, Cereal and Fruit Products and Better Brands Ltd., were located in Honolulu. One year after the acquisition, the companies expanded their operations by opening a branch office in Kahului, Maui. A second Hawaii branch operation opened in 1972, in the community of Hilo. In 1975, Young's added a food wholesaling operation to its growing Hawaii liquor business. Based in Honolulu, Young's Meat and Provisions provided service to all of the islands.

BECOMING A VINTNER

In the meantime, Young's began exploring new domestic expansion and diversification possibilities. In 1968 the company became a vintner as well as a distributor when it purchased the Buena Vista Winery in Sonoma, California. A year later, Young's acquired 700 acres of land overlooking the San Francisco Bay to use as a new vineyard for the 100-year-old winery. Buena Vista's vineyard was a part of the Carneros viticultural region, characterized by shallow, dense soil, cool summers, and mild winters. The climate conditions in the Carneros region allowed for longer growing seasons and produced grapes with distinct flavors.

In 1976, with its vineyards thriving, Young's added a new, state-of-the-art fermenting winery to the Buena Vista Winery. Just three years later, the company sold the vineyards and winery to A. Racke GmbH & Co. of Germany, a family-owned wine and spirits business founded in 1855.

STEADY EXPANSION IN THE EIGHTIES

Young's started off the 1980s with more expansion. In 1980 the company's Hawaiian subsidiaries established a third wholesale branch, on the island of Kauai. Back home in Los Angeles, the company opened a warehouse operation in Orange County to service chain stores carrying liquor and wines. In addition, Young's Specialty Foods Division, which carried gourmet and natural food items, moved into an expanded space in Cerritos. The division moved to an even larger facility in just three years because of increasing business and a growing product line.

By the mid-1980s Young's distributorship covered virtually the southern two-thirds of California, stretching as far north as Santa Clara. In 1985, the company inched a bit farther north when it acquired a wholesale liquor distributorship in Union City and Santa Rosa. The distributorship, Rathjen Wines and Spirits, was absorbed into Young's and renamed Young's Market Company.

In 1988 Vernon Underwood retired from the business he had helped build for more than 50 years. Having served as the company's CEO and chairman of the board since 1974, he became chairman emeritus upon his retirement. His son, Vernon Underwood Jr., succeeded him as chairman and CEO. The younger Underwood, like his father, spent his entire career in the family business, starting as a warehouse worker in 1955. He served as the company's president since 1975.

UNDERWOOD BUYOUT: 1990

Although Young's Market had been controlled and managed by descendants of the founding Young brothers, the company acquired a handful of outside investors in its 100-plus years of existence. In 1990 the Underwood family bought out the other shareholders, purchasing 37,500 shares at $3,500 per share, and assumed full ownership.

After the buyout the Underwoods set about making some changes in the business. Most significantly, the company tightened its focus on the wine and spirits business, shedding its wholesale food distribution divisions. Young's meat distribution business, purchased by Con-Agra, and its seafood business, purchased by Hunt Bros., accounted for a combined $100 million in sales.

Another of the Underwoods' major changes involved the relocation of the company's headquarters. In 1994 Young's moved from downtown Los Angeles to a newly built, 210,000-square-foot facility in Orange, California. According to Underwood, the relocation put Young's closer to more customers and closer to one of its largest suppliers. Also in 1994, Young's Market reached $1 billion in sales.

In 1997 Young's Market entered into a strategic alliance with Sunbelt Beverage Corporation, a large liquor distributor with operations in Florida, Maryland, Arizona, Pennsylvania, and South Carolina. Affiliated companies were located in New York, Connecticut, and Washington, D.C. This alliance made Young's Market a part of the largest distribution network in the United States. Shortly after becoming a part of Sunbelt Beverage, Young's appointed Charles Andrews as its president and CEO. Andrews had served previously as the president and CEO of Sunbelt Beverage. However, the relationship with Sunbelt did not last, and family member Chris Underwood became CEO.

ADAPTING TO INDUSTRY CHANGES

Young's Market attempted to remake itself after the company posted only modest gains in sales during the late 1900s. Even with the 1997 acquisition of Wilson, Daniels, Ltd., a leading importer and wholesale distributor of wine and spirits with customers in every state and in Puerto Rico and Canada, sales remained relatively flat. Consumption of wines reached a peak and then hit a plateau during the 1980s, and sales of distilled spirits decreased for several years before finally stabilizing in the late 1990s.

To compensate for changes in wine and spirits consumption, Young's Market sought to expand its product offering and customer base. The company focused on western states where it conducted most of its business. In 2001 K&L Classic Wine Company, Young's western Washington distributor, and the Columbia Distributing Company, of Oregon, combined their wine distribution assets to form a joint venture, Young's-Columbia. As the largest wine distributor in the Pacific Northwest, the combination of Young's and Columbia's sales networks and their geographic range meant access to a wider selection of wines, the largest in North America. Prominent brands included Kendall Jackson, Vendage, Chateau Ste. Michelle, and Covey Run. Exclusive brands included Rosemount Estates, Sterling Vineyards, Cakebread Cellars, and Chateau St. Jean.

Another avenue of growth involved expanding the company's distribution of more expensive fine wines. Young's leveraged its experienced network of sales and customer service representatives into the establishment of a new division to handle fine wine, the Estate Group. In its first major contract, with Chalone Wine Group, Young's commenced distribution of products in California on July 1, 2002. Wine brands included red and white varietal wines from Napa Valley, such as Chalone Vineyard, Edna Valley, Carmenet, Acacia, Jade Mountain, Canoe Ridge, Dynamite, and Echelon. Another significant opportunity involved an exclusive distribution agreement signed with Castle Rock Winery, of Palos Verdes Estates, California, in September 2004.

Young's Market sought opportunities in specialized areas of spirits wholesale distribution. In 2005 the company purchased Seagram's Vodka from Pernod Ricard USA. Young's Market formed Infinium Spirits in 2006 to handle distribution of Seagram's Vodka as well as Pernod Ricard's brands of spirits, such as Corallejo Tequila. Infinium Spirits covered Alaska, Washington, Oregon, Idaho, Montana, Utah, and Wyoming. Also, Young's Market continued its distribution for Pernod Ricard's complete range of wine and spirits in California and Hawaii.

MAJOR NEW CONTRACTS

Young's Market signed major distribution contracts in 2009. The company became the exclusive distributor for Constellation Brands in Alaska, Oregon, and Washington. Already distributing about one million cases of wine and spirits annually for Constellation, Young's Market became the largest distributor by volume of wine and spirits in the Pacific Northwest through this multiyear agreement with Constellation.

In April Young's Market obtained the business of Don Sebastini & Sons and International Wine

Negociant. Young's Market signed a seven-year agreement to distribute Three Loose Screws wine in Alaska, Hawaii, California, Arizona, Washington, Oregon, Idaho, Utah, and Wyoming. The agreement covered Smoking Loon, Pepperwood Grove, SKN Napa Valley, Aquinas Napa Valley, B Side, and several other brands. The winemakers chose Young's Market for the alignment of values as another family-owned business, as well as for the quality of the company's distribution outlets.

In July 2010 Young's Market announced that Foley Family Wines decided to consolidate all of its distribution with Young's Market. A vintner of several distinctive brands of wine and spirits, the portfolio of fine wines included Kuleto, Merus, Altus, Three Rivers, Firestone, Lincourt, Sebastiani, and Wattle Creek. The distribution agreement also covered Boomerang Australian Vodka. The decision expanded a long-standing relationship with Young's Market that was instrumental in promoting widespread distribution of Firestone brand wines in California.

Shawna Brynildssen
Updated, Mary Tradii

PRINCIPAL SUBSIDIARIES

Better Brands Ltd.; Infinium Spirits; Wilson Daniels, Ltd.; Young's-Columbia (50%).

PRINCIPAL COMPETITORS

Charmer Sunbelt Group; Clare Rose, Inc.; Jay dor Corporation; Johnson Brothers Liquor Company; Liquid Investments Company, Inc.; National Distributing Company, Inc.; Paterno Imports Ltd.; Peerless Importers Inc.; Southern Wine & Spirits of America, Inc.; Wirtz Beverage Group LLC.

FURTHER READING

Britton, Charles, "Young's Market: Food Industry Innovator," *Southern California Business*, December 1, 1985, p. 7.

"K&L Classic Wine Co. and Columbia Distributing Company to Partner, Creating Premier Wine Distributor in the Northwest." *Business Wire*, December 21, 2001, p. 266.

Klayman, Gary, "In High Spirits: Family Firm Takes New Approach to Its Old Business," *Orange County Business Journal*, October 2, 1995, p. 1.

Wilson, Daniel, "A Fresh Look at Young's Market Co.," *Wines & Vines*, May 1, 1994, p. 37.

"Young's Market Company," *Beverage Dynamics*, July/August 2008, pp. S22+.

Cumulative Index to Companies

*Listings in this index are arranged in alphabetical order under the company name. Company names beginning with a letter or proper name such as Eli Lilly & Co. will be found under the first letter of the company name. Definite articles (The, Le, La) are ignored for alphabetical purposes as are forms of incorporation that precede the company name (AB, NV). Company names printed in **bold** type have full, historical essays on the page numbers appearing in bold. Updates to entries that appeared in earlier volumes are signified by the notation (**upd.**). This index is cumulative with volume numbers printed in bold type.*

Ambac Financial Group, Inc., 65 37–39

Ambassadors International, Inc., 68 16–18 (upd.)

AmBev *see* Companhia de Bebidas das Américas.

Amblin Entertainment, 21 23–27

AMC Entertainment Inc., 12 12–14; 35 27–29 (upd.); 114 17–21 (upd.)

AMCC *see* Applied Micro Circuits Corp.

AMCOL International Corporation, 59 29–33 (upd.)

AMCON Distributing Company, 99 27–30

Amcor Ltd., IV 248–50; 19 13–16 (upd.); 78 1–6 (upd.)

AMCORE Financial Inc., 44 22–26

AMD *see* Advanced Micro Devices, Inc.

Amdahl Corporation, III 109–11; 14 13–16 (upd.); 40 20–25 (upd.) *see also* Fujitsu Ltd.

Amdocs Ltd., 47 10–12

AMEC plc, 112 13–16

Amec Spie S.A., 57 28–31

Amedisys, Inc., 53 33–36; 106 34–37 (upd.)

Amer Group plc, 41 14–16

Amerada Hess Corporation, IV 365–67; 21 28–31 (upd.); 55 16–20 (upd.)

Amerchol Corporation *see* Union Carbide Corp.

AMERCO, 6 351–52; 67 11–14 (upd.)

Ameren Corporation, 60 23–27 (upd.)

Ameri-Kart Corp. *see* Myers Industries, Inc.

América Móvil, S.A. de C.V., 80 5–8

America Online, Inc., 10 56–58; 26 16–20 (upd.) *see also* CompuServe Interactive Services, Inc.; AOL Time Warner Inc.

America West Holdings Corporation, 6 72–74; 34 22–26 (upd.)

American & Efird, Inc., 82 5–9

American Airlines, I 89–91; 6 75–77 (upd.) *see also* AMR Corp.

American Apparel, Inc., 90 21–24

American Association of Retired Persons *see* AARP.

American Axle & Manufacturing Holdings, Inc., 67 15–17

American Ballet Theatre *see* Ballet Theatre Foundation, Inc.

American Banknote Corporation, 30 42–45

American Bar Association, 35 30–33

American Biltrite Inc., 16 16–18; 43 19–22 (upd.)

American Booksellers Association, Inc., 114 22–27

American Brands, Inc., V 395–97 *see also* Fortune Brands, Inc.

American Builders & Contractors Supply Co. *see* ABC Supply Co., Inc.

American Building Maintenance Industries, Inc., 6 17–19 *see also* ABM Industries Inc.

American Business Information, Inc., 18 21–25

American Business Interiors *see* American Furniture Company, Inc.

American Business Products, Inc., 20 15–17

American Campus Communities, Inc., 85 1–5

American Can Co. *see* Primerica Corp.

The American Cancer Society, 24 23–25

American Capital Strategies, Ltd., 91 21–24

American Cast Iron Pipe Company, 50 17–20

American City Business Journals, Inc., 110 18–21

American Civil Liberties Union (ACLU), 60 28–31

American Classic Voyages Company, 27 34–37

American Coin Merchandising, Inc., 28 15–17; 74 13–16 (upd.)

American Colloid Co., 13 32–35 *see* AMCOL International Corp.

American Commercial Lines Inc., 99 31–34

American Cotton Growers Association *see* Plains Cotton Cooperative Association.

American Crystal Sugar Company, 11 13–15; 32 29–33 (upd.)

American Cyanamid, I 300–02; 8 24–26 (upd.)

American Diabetes Association, 109 31–35

American Eagle Outfitters, Inc., 24 26–28; 55 21–24 (upd.)

American Ecology Corporation, 77 36–39

American Electric Power Company, V 546–49; 45 17–21 (upd.)

American Equipment Company, Inc., 104 14–17

American Express Company, II 395–99; 10 59–64 (upd.); 38 42–48 (upd.)

American Family Corporation, III 187–89 *see also* AFLAC Inc.

American Family Insurance Group, 116 25–30

American Financial Group Inc., III 190–92; 48 6–10 (upd.)

American Foods Group, 43 23–27

American Furniture Company, Inc., 21 32–34

American General Corporation, III 193–94; 10 65–67 (upd.); 46 20–23 (upd.)

American General Finance Corp., 11 16–17

American Girl, Inc., 69 16–19 (upd)

American Golf Corporation, 45 22–24

American Gramaphone LLC, 52 18–20

American Greetings Corporation, 7 23–25; 22 33–36 (upd.); 59 34–39 (upd.)

American Healthways, Inc., 65 40–42

American Heart Association, Inc., 114 28–31

American Home Mortgage Holdings, Inc., 46 24–26

American Home Products, I 622–24; 10 68–70 (upd.) *see also* Wyeth.

American Homestar Corporation, 18 26–29; 41 17–20 (upd.)

American Institute of Certified Public Accountants (AICPA), 44 27–30

American International Group Inc., III 195–98; 15 15–19 (upd.); 47 13–19 (upd.); 109 36–45 (upd.)

American Italian Pasta Company, 27 38–40; 76 18–21 (upd.)

American Kennel Club, Inc., 74 17–19

American Lawyer Media Holdings, Inc., 32 34–37

American Library Association, 86 15–19

American Licorice Company, 86 20–23

American Locker Group Incorporated, 34 19–21

American Lung Association, 48 11–14

American Machine and Metals *see* AMETEK, Inc.

American Maize-Products Co., 14 17–20

American Management Association, 76 22–25

American Management Systems, Inc., 11 18–20

American Media, Inc., 27 41–44; 82 10–15 (upd.)

American Medical Alert Corporation, 103 15–18

American Medical Association, 39 15–18

American Medical International, Inc., III 73–75

American Medical Response, Inc., 39 19–22

American Metals Corporation *see* Reliance Steel & Aluminum Co.

American Modern Insurance Group *see* The Midland Co.

American Motors Corp., I 135–37 *see also* DaimlerChrysler AG.

American MSI Corporation *see* Moldflow Corp.

American National Insurance Company, 8 27–29; 27 45–48 (upd.)

American Nurses Association Inc., 102 11–15

American Olean Tile Company *see* Armstrong Holdings, Inc.

American Oriental Bioengineering Inc., 93 45–48

American Pad & Paper Company, 20 18–21

American Pfauter *see* Gleason Corp.

American Pharmaceutical Partners, Inc., 69 20–22

American Physicians Service Group, Inc., 114 32–36

American Pop Corn Company, 59 40–43

American Power Conversion Corporation, 24 29–31; 67 18–20 (upd.)

American Premier Underwriters, Inc., 10 71–74

Armour *see* Tommy Armour Golf Co.

Armstrong Air Conditioning Inc. *see* Lennox International Inc.

Armstrong Holdings, Inc., III 422–24; 22 46–50 (upd.); 81 38–44 (upd.)

Army and Air Force Exchange Service, 39 27–29

Arnhold and S. Bleichroeder Advisers, LLC, 97 45–49

Arnold & Porter, 35 42–44

Arnold Clark Automobiles Ltd., 60 39–41

Arnoldo Mondadori Editore S.p.A., IV 585–88; 19 17–21 (upd.); 54 17–23 (upd.)

Arnott's Ltd., 66 10–12

Aro Corp. *see* Ingersoll-Rand Company Ltd.

Arotech Corporation, 93 53–56

ArQule, Inc., 68 31–34

ARRIS Group, Inc., 89 74–77

Arriva PLC, 69 42–44

Arrow Air Holdings Corporation, 55 28–30

Arrow Electronics, Inc., 10 112–14; 50 41–44 (upd.); 110 22–27 (upd.)

Arsenal Holdings PLC, 79 30–33

The Art Institute of Chicago, 29 36–38

Art Van Furniture, Inc., 28 31–33

Artesyn Technologies Inc., 46 35–38 (upd.)

ArthroCare Corporation, 73 31–33

Arthur Andersen & Company, Société Coopérative, 10 115–17 *see also* Andersen.

The Arthur C. Clarke Foundation, 92 9–12

Arthur D. Little, Inc., 35 45–48

Arthur J. Gallagher & Co., 73 34–36

Arthur Lundgren Tecidos S.A., 102 25–28

Arthur Murray International, Inc., 32 60–62

Artisan Confections Company, 103 23–27

Artisan Entertainment Inc., 32 63–66 (upd.)

Arts and Entertainment Network *see* A&E Television Networks.

Art's Way Manufacturing Co., Inc., 101 39–42

Artsana SpA, 92 13–16

Arval *see* PHH Arval.

ArvinMeritor, Inc., 8 37–40; 54 24–28 (upd.)

Aryzta AG, 112 25–29 (upd.)

AS Estonian Air, 71 38–40

Asahi Breweries, Ltd., I 220–21; 20 28–30 (upd.); 52 31–34 (upd.); 108 59–64 (upd.)

Asahi Denka Kogyo KK, 64 33–35

Asahi Glass Company, Ltd., III 666–68; 48 39–42 (upd.)

Asahi Komag Co., Ltd. *see* Komag, Inc.

Asahi National Broadcasting Company, Ltd., 9 29–31

Asahi Shimbun, 9 29–30

Asanté Technologies, Inc., 20 31–33

ASARCO Incorporated, IV 31–34; 40 220–22, 411

Asatsu-DK Inc, 82 16–20

Asbury Automotive Group Inc., 60 42–44

Asbury Carbons, Inc., 68 35–37

ASC, Inc., 55 31–34

ASCAP *see* The American Society of Composers, Authors and Publishers.

Ascend Communications, Inc., 24 47–51 *see also* Lucent Technologies Inc.

Ascendia Brands, Inc., 97 50–53

Ascension Health, 114 58–61

Ascent Media Corporation, 107 15–18

Ascential Software Corporation, 59 54–57

Ascom AG, 9 32–34

ASDA Group Ltd., II 611–12; 28 34–36 (upd.); 64 36–38 (upd.)

ASEA AB *see* ABB Ltd.

ASG *see* Allen Systems Group, Inc.

Ash Grove Cement Company, 94 41–44

Ashanti Goldfields Company Limited, 43 37–40

Ashdown *see* Repco Corporation Ltd.

Asher's Chocolates, Inc., 103 28–31

Ashland Inc., IV 372–74; 19 22–25; 50 45–50 (upd.); 115 26–33 (upd.)

Ashley Furniture Industries, Inc., 35 49–51

Ashtead Group plc, 34 41–43

Ashworth, Inc., 26 25–28

Asia Pacific Breweries Limited, 59 58–60

AsiaInfo Holdings, Inc., 43 41–44

Asiana Airlines, Inc., 46 39–42

ASICS Corporation, 57 52–55

ASIX Inc. *see* Manatron, Inc.

ASK Group, Inc., 9 35–37

Ask Jeeves, Inc., 65 50–52

ASML Holding N.V., 50 51–54

ASPCA *see* American Society for the Prevention of Cruelty to Animals (ASPCA).

Aspect Telecommunications Corporation, 22 51–53

Aspen Pharmacare Holdings Limited, 112 30–33

Aspen Publishers *see* Wolters Kluwer NV.

Aspen Skiing Company, 15 23–26

Asplundh Tree Expert Co., 20 34–36; 59 61–65 (upd.)

Assa Abloy AB, 112 34–37

Assicurazioni Generali S.p.A., 103 32–42 (upd.)

Assicurazioni Generali S.p.A., III 206–09; 15 27–31 (upd.); 103 32–42 (upd.)

Assisted Living Concepts, Inc., 43 45–47

Associated Banc-Corp, 116 52–55

Associated British Foods plc, II 465–66; 13 51–53 (upd.); 41 30–33 (upd.)

Associated British Ports Holdings Plc, 45 29–32

Associated Estates Realty Corporation, 25 23–25

Associated Grocers, Incorporated, 9 38–40; 31 22–26 (upd.)

Associated International Insurance Co. *see* Gryphon Holdings, Inc.

Associated Milk Producers, Inc., 11 24–26; 48 43–46 (upd.)

Associated Natural Gas Corporation, 11 27–28

Associated Newspapers Holdings P.L.C. *see* Daily Mail and General Trust plc.

The Associated Press, 13 54–56; 31 27–30 (upd.); 73 37–41 (upd.)

Association des Centres Distributeurs E. Leclerc, 37 19–21

Association of Junior Leagues International Inc., 60 45–47

Assurances Générales de France, 63 45–48

Assured Guaranty Ltd., 93 57–60

AST Research, Inc., 9 41–43

Astec Industries, Inc., 79 34–37

Astellas Pharma Inc., 97 54–58 (upd.)

AstenJohnson Inc., 90 31–34

ASTM SpA *see* Autostrada Torino-Milano S.p.A.

Aston Villa plc, 41 34–36

Astoria Financial Corporation, 44 31–34

Astra *see* PT Astra International Tbk.

AstraZeneca PLC, I 625–26; 20 37–40 (upd.); 50 55–60 (upd.)

Astronics Corporation, 35 52–54

Asur *see* Grupo Aeropuerto del Sureste, S.A. de C.V.

Asurion Corporation, 83 29–32

ASUSTeK Computer Inc., 107 19–23

ASV, Inc., 34 44–47; 66 13–15 (upd.)

ASX Limited, 115 34–39

AT&T Bell Laboratories, Inc., 13 57–59 *see also* Lucent Technologies Inc.

AT&T Corporation, V 259–64; 29 39–45 (upd.); 61 68 38–45 (upd.)

AT&T Istel Ltd., 14 35–36

AT&T Wireless Services, Inc., 54 29–32 (upd.)

At Home Corporation, 43 48–51

ATA Holdings Corporation, 82 21–25

Atalanta Corporation, 118 35–38

Atanor S.A., 62 19–22

Atari Corporation, 9 44–47; 23 23–26 (upd.); 66 16–20 (upd.)

ATC Healthcare Inc., 64 39–42

Atchison Casting Corporation, 39 30–32

ATE Investment *see* Atlantic Energy, Inc.

AtheroGenics Inc., 101 43–46

The Athlete's Foot Brands LLC, 84 17–20

The Athletics Investment Group, 62 23–26

ATI Technologies Inc., 79 38–41

Atkins Nutritionals, Inc., 58 8–10

Atkinson Candy Company, 87 39–42

Atlanta Bread Company International, Inc., 70 14–16

Atlanta Gas Light Company, 6 446–48; 23 27–30 (upd.)

Banner Aerospace, Inc., 14 42–44; 37 29–32 (upd.)

Banner Corporation, 106 54–57

Banorte *see* Grupo Financiero Banorte, S.A. de C.V.

Banque Nationale de Paris S.A., II 232–34 *see also* BNP Paribas Group.

Banta Corporation, 12 24–26; 32 73–77 (upd.); 79 50–56 (upd.)

Banyan Systems Inc., 25 50–52

Baptist Health Care Corporation, 82 37–40

Bar-S Foods Company, 76 39–41

Barbara's Bakery Inc., 88 21–24

Barclay Furniture Co. *see* LADD Furniture, Inc.

Barclays PLC, II 235–37; 20 57–60 (upd.); 64 46–50 (upd.)

BarclaysAmerican Mortgage Corporation, 11 29–30

Barco NV, 44 42–45

Barden Companies, Inc., 76 42–45

Bardwil Industries Inc., 98 15–18

Bare Escentuals, Inc., 91 48–52

Barilla G. e R. Fratelli S.p.A., 17 35–37; 50 77–80 (upd.)

Barings PLC, 14 45–47

Barloworld Ltd., I 422–24; 109 57–62 (upd.)

Barmag AG, 39 39–42

Barnes & Noble, Inc., 10 135–37; 30 67–71 (upd.); 75 50–55 (upd.)

Barnes & Noble College Booksellers, Inc., 115 44–46

Barnes Group, Inc., 13 72–74; 69 58–62 (upd.)

Barnett Banks, Inc., 9 58–60 *see also* Bank of America Corp.

Barnett Inc., 28 50–52

Barneys New York Inc., 28 53–55; 104 26–30 (upd.)

Baron de Ley S.A., 74 27–29

Baron Philippe de Rothschild S.A., 39 43–46

Barr *see* AG Barr plc.

Barr Pharmaceuticals, Inc., 26 29–31; 68 46–49 (upd.)

Barratt Developments plc, I 556–57; 56 31–33 (upd.)

Barrett Business Services, Inc., 16 48–50

Barrett-Jackson Auction Company L.L.C., 88 25–28

Barrick Gold Corporation, 34 62–65; 112 38–44 (upd.)

Barrière *see* Groupe Lucien Barrière S.A.S.

Barry Callebaut AG, 29 46–48; 71 46–49 (upd.)

Barry-Wehmiller Companies, Inc., 90 40–43

The Bartell Drug Company, 94 62–65

Barton Malow Company, 51 40–43

Barton Protective Services Inc., 53 56–58

The Baseball Club of Seattle, LP, 50 81–85

BASF SE, I 305–08; 18 47–51 (upd.); 50 86–92 (upd.); 108 85–94 (upd.)

Bashas' Inc., 33 62–64; 80 17–21 (upd.)

Basic Earth Science Systems, Inc., 101 65–68

Basin Electric Power Cooperative, 103 43–46

The Basketball Club of Seattle, LLC, 50 93–97

Basketville, Inc., 117 31–34

Bass PLC, I 222–24; 15 44–47 (upd.); 38 74–78 (upd.)

Bass Pro Shops, Inc., 42 27–30; 118 55–59 (upd.)

Bassett Furniture Industries, Inc., 18 52–55; 95 44–50 (upd.)

BAT Industries plc, I 425–27 *see also* British American Tobacco PLC.

Bata Ltd., 62 27–30

Bates Worldwide, Inc., 14 48–51; 33 65–69 (upd.)

Bath Iron Works Corporation, 12 27–29; 36 76–79 (upd.)

Battelle Memorial Institute, Inc., 10 138–40

Batten Barton Durstine & Osborn *see* Omnicom Group Inc.

Battle Mountain Gold Company, 23 40–42 *see also* Newmont Mining Corp.

Bauer Hockey, Inc., 104 31–34

Bauer Publishing Group, 7 42–43

Bauerly Companies, 61 31–33

Baugur Group hf, 81 45–49

Baumax AG, 75 56–58

Bausch & Lomb Inc., 7 44–47; 25 53–57 (upd.); 96 20–26 (upd.)

Bavaria S.A., 90 44–47

Baxi Group Ltd., 96 27–30

Baxter International Inc., I 627–29; 10 141–43 (upd.); 116 74–78 (upd.)

Baxters Food Group Ltd., 99 47–50

The Bay *see* The Hudson's Bay Co.

Bay State Gas Company, 38 79–82

Bayard SA, 49 46–49

BayBanks, Inc., 12 30–32

Bayer AG, I 309–11; 13 75–77 (upd.); 41 44–48 (upd.); 118 60–66 (upd.)

Bayerische Hypotheken- und Wechsel-Bank AG, II 238–40 *see also* HVB Group.

Bayerische Landesbank, 116 79–82

Bayerische Motoren Werke AG, I 138–40; 11 31–33 (upd.); 38 83–87 (upd.); 108 95–101 (upd.)

Bayerische Vereinsbank A.G., II 241–43 *see also* HVB Group.

Bayernwerk AG, V 555–58; 23 43–47 (upd.) *see also* E.On AG.

Bayou Steel Corporation, 31 47–49

BayWa AG, 112 45–49

BB&T Corporation, 79 57–61

BB Holdings Limited, 77 50–53

BBA *see* Bush Boake Allen Inc.

BBA Aviation plc, 90 48–52

BBAG Osterreichische Brau-Beteiligungs-AG, 38 88–90

BBC *see* British Broadcasting Corp.

BBDO Worldwide *see* Omnicom Group Inc.

BBGI *see* Beasley Broadcast Group, Inc.

BBN Corp., 19 39–42

BBVA *see* Banco Bilbao Vizcaya Argentaria S.A.

BCE, Inc., V 269–71; 44 46–50 (upd.)

Bci, 99 51–54

BDO Seidman LLP, 96 31–34

BE&K, Inc., 73 57–59

BEA *see* Bank of East Asia Ltd.

BEA Systems, Inc., 36 80–83

Beacon Roofing Supply, Inc., 75 59–61

Beall's, Inc., 113 37–40

Bear Creek Corporation, 38 91–94 *see also* Harry & David Holdings, Inc.

Bear Stearns Companies, Inc., II 400–01; 10 144–45 (upd.); 52 41–44 (upd.)

Bearings, Inc., 13 78–80

Beasley Broadcast Group, Inc., 51 44–46

Beate Uhse AG, 96 35–39

Beatrice Company, II 467–69 *see also* TLC Beatrice International Holdings, Inc.

BeautiControl Cosmetics, Inc., 21 49–52

Beazer Homes USA, Inc., 17 38–41

bebe stores, inc., 31 50–52; 103 47–51 (upd.)

Bechtel Corporation, I 558–59; 24 64–67 (upd.); 99 55–60 (upd.)

Beckett Papers, 23 48–50

Beckman Coulter, Inc., 22 74–77

Beckman Instruments, Inc., 14 52–54

Becton, Dickinson and Company, I 630–31; 11 34–36 (upd.); 36 84–89 (upd.); 101 69–77 (upd.)

Bed Bath & Beyond Inc., 13 81–83; 41 49–52 (upd.); 109 63–70 (upd.)

Beech Aircraft Corporation, 8 49–52 *see also* Raytheon Aircraft Holdings Inc.

Beech-Nut Nutrition Corporation, 21 53–56; 51 47–51 (upd.)

Beef O'Brady's *see* Family Sports Concepts, Inc.

Beer Nuts, Inc., 86 30–33

Beggars Group Ltd., 99 61–65

Behr GmbH & Co. KG, 72 22–25

Behr Process Corporation, 115 47–49

Behring Diagnostics *see* Dade Behring Holdings Inc.

BEI Technologies, Inc., 65 74–76

Beiersdorf AG, 29 49–53

Bekaert S.A./N.V., 90 53–57

Bekins Company, 15 48–50

Bel *see* Fromageries Bel.

Bel-Art Products Inc., 117 35–38

Bel Fuse, Inc., 53 59–62

Bel/Kaukauna USA, 76 46–48

Belco Oil & Gas Corp., 40 63–65

Belden CDT Inc., 19 43–45; 76 49–52 (upd.)

Belgacom, 6 302–04

Belk, Inc., V 12–13; 19 46–48 (upd.); 72 26–29 (upd.)

Bell and Howell Company, 9 61–64; 29 54–58 (upd.)

Dewberry, 78 83–86
Dewey Ballantine LLP, 48 136–39
Dex Media, Inc., 65 128–30
Dexia NV/SA, 42 111–13; 88 66–69 (upd.)
The Dexter Corporation, I 320–22; 12 102–04 (upd.) *see also* Invitrogen Corp.
DFS Group Ltd., 66 78–80
DG FastChannel, Inc., 111 91–94
DH Technology, Inc., 18 138–40
DHB Industries Inc., 85 89–92
DHL Worldwide Network S.A./N.V., 6 385–87; 24 133–36 (upd.); 69 121–25 (upd.)
Di Giorgio Corp., 12 105–07
Diadora SpA, 86 121–24
Diageo plc, 24 137–41 (upd.); 79 140–48 (upd.)
Diagnostic Products Corporation, 73 121–24
Diagnostic Ventures Inc. *see* DVI, Inc.
Dial-A-Mattress Operating Corporation, 46 136–39
The Dial Corporation, 8 144–46; 23 173–75 (upd.)
Dialogic Corporation, 18 141–43
Diamond of California, 64 108–11 (upd.)
Diamond Shamrock Corporation , IV 408–11 *see also* Ultramar Diamond Shamrock Corp.
DiamondCluster International, Inc., 51 98–101
Diana Shipping Inc., 95 126–29
Diavik Diamond Mines Inc., 85 93–96
Dibrell Brothers, Incorporated, 12 108–10
DIC Corporation, 115 174–77
dick clark productions, inc., 16 170–73
Dick Corporation, 64 112–14
Dick's Sporting Goods, Inc., 59 156–59
Dickten Masch Plastics LLC, 90 158–61
Dictaphone Healthcare Solutions, 78 87–92
Diebold, Incorporated, 7 144–46; 22 183–87 (upd.)
Diedrich Coffee, Inc., 40 152–54
Diehl Stiftung & Co. KG, 79 149–53
Dierbergs Markets Inc., 63 127–29
Diesel SpA, 40 155–57
D'Ieteren S.A./NV, 98 75–78
Dietrich & Cie *see* De Dietrich & Cie.
Dietsch Brothers Inc., 110 119–22
Dietz and Watson, Inc., 92 88–92
Digex, Inc., 46 140–43
Digi International Inc., 9 170–72
Digi-Key Corporation, 109 160–64
Digital Angel Corporation, 106 143–48
Digital Equipment Corporation, III 132–35; 6 233–36 (upd.) *see also* Compaq Computer Corp.
Digital River, Inc., 50 156–59
DigitalGlobe, Inc., 116 190–94
Digitas Inc., 81 107–10
Dillard Paper Company, 11 74–76 *see also* International Paper Co.

Dillard's Inc., V 45–47; 16 174–77 (upd.); 68 110–14 (upd.)
Dillingham Construction Corporation, 44 151–54 (upd.)
Dillingham Corp., I 565–66
Dillon Companies Inc., 12 111–13
Dime Savings Bank of New York, F.S.B., 9 173–74 *see also* Washington Mutual, Inc.
Dimension Data Holdings PLC, 69 126–28
DIMON Inc., 27 124–27
Dina *see* Consorcio G Grupo Dina, S.A. de C.V.
Diodes Incorporated, 81 111–14
Dionex Corporation, 46 144–46
Dior *see* Christian Dior S.A.
Dippin' Dots, Inc., 56 84–86
Direct Focus, Inc., 47 93–95
Direct Wines Ltd., 84 103–106
Directed Electronics, Inc., 87 131–135
Directorate General of Telecommunications, 7 147–49 *see also* Chunghwa Telecom Co., Ltd.
DIRECTV, Inc., 38 174–77; 75 128–32 (upd.)
Dirk Rossmann GmbH, 94 155–59
Disabled American Veterans, 114 159–62
Discount Auto Parts, Inc., 18 144–46
Discount Drug Mart, Inc., 14 172–73
Discount Tire Company Inc., 84 107–110
Discover Financial Services, 116 195–98
Discovery Communications, Inc., 42 114–17
Discovery Partners International, Inc., 58 93–95
Discreet Logic Inc., 20 185–87 *see also* Autodesk, Inc.
DISH Network Corporation, 112 149–55
Disney *see* The Walt Disney Co.
Disney/ABC Television Group, 106 149–54 (upd.)
Dispatch Printing Company, 100 140–44
Distillers Co. plc, I 239–41 *see also* Diageo PLC.
Distribución y Servicio D&S S.A., 71 123–26
Distrigaz S.A., 82 91–94
ditech.com, 93 181–84
The Dixie Group, Inc., 20 188–90; 80 88–92 (upd.)
Dixon Industries, Inc., 26 117–19
Dixon Ticonderoga Company, 12 114–16; 69 129–33 (upd.)
Dixons Group plc, V 48–50; 19 121–24 (upd.); 49 110–13 (upd.)
Djarum PT, 62 96–98
DKB *see* Dai-Ichi Kangyo Bank Ltd.
DKNY *see* Donna Karan International Inc.
DLA Piper, 106 155–58
DLJ *see* Donaldson, Lufkin & Jenrette.
DMB&B *see* D'Arcy Masius Benton & Bowles.

DMGT *see* Daily Mail and General Trust.
DMI Furniture, Inc., 46 147–50
Do it Best Corporation, 30 166–70; 104 113–19 (upd.)
Dobbies Garden Centres plc, 118 134–37
Dobrogea Grup S.A., 82 95–98
Dobson Communications Corporation, 63 130–32
Doctor's Associates Inc., 67 142–45 (upd.)
The Doctors' Company, 55 125–28
Doctors Without Borders *see* Médecins Sans Frontières.
Documentum, Inc., 46 151–53
Dodger Theatricals, Ltd., 108 214–17
DOF ASA, 110 123–26
Dofasco Inc., IV 73–74; 24 142–44 (upd.)
Dogan Sirketler Grubu Holding A.S., 83 107–110
Dogi International Fabrics S.A., 52 99–102
Dolan Media Company, 94 160–63
Dolby Laboratories Inc., 20 191–93
Dolce & Gabbana SpA, 62 99–101
Dole Food Company, Inc., 9 175–76; 31 167–70 (upd.); 68 115–19 (upd.)
Dollar Financial Corporation, 107 96–99
Dollar General Corporation, 106 159–62
Dollar Thrifty Automotive Group, Inc., 25 142–45; 115 178–84 (upd.)
Dollar Tree Stores, Inc., 23 176–78; 62 102–05 (upd.)
Dollywood Corporation *see* Herschend Family Entertainment Corp.
Doman Industries Limited, 59 160–62
Dominick & Dominick LLC, 92 93–96
Dominick's Finer Foods, Inc., 56 87–89
Dominion Homes, Inc., 19 125–27
Dominion Resources, Inc., V 596–99; 54 83–87 (upd.)
Dominion Textile Inc., 12 117–19
Domino Printing Sciences PLC, 87 136–139
Domino Sugar Corporation, 26 120–22
Domino's, Inc., 7 150–53; 21 177–81 (upd.); 63 133–39 (upd.)
Domtar Corporation, IV 271–73; 89 185–91 (upd.)
Don Massey Cadillac, Inc., 37 114–16
Donaldson Company, Inc., 16 178–81; 49 114–18 (upd.); 108 218–24 (upd.)
Donaldson, Lufkin & Jenrette, Inc., 22 188–91
Donatos Pizzeria Corporation, 58 96–98
Dongfeng Motor Corporation, 105 135–40
Donna Karan International Inc., 15 145–47; 56 90–93 (upd.)
Donnelly Corporation, 12 120–22; 35 147–50 (upd.)
Donnkenny, Inc., 17 136–38
Donruss Playoff L.P., 66 81–84
Dooney & Bourke Inc., 84 111–114

Environmental Power Corporation, 68 138–40

Environmental Systems Research Institute Inc. (ESRI), 62 121–24

Enzo Biochem, Inc., 41 153–55

EOG Resources, 106 174–77

Eon Labs, Inc., 67 172–74

E1 Entertainment Ltd., 111 112–16

EP Henry Corporation, 104 142–45

EPAM Systems Inc., 96 120–23

EPCOR Utilities Inc., 81 151–54

Epic Systems Corporation, 62 125–28

EPIQ Systems, Inc., 56 111–13

Equant N.V., 52 106–08

Equifax, Inc., 6 23–25; 28 117–21 (upd.); 90 177–83 (upd.)

Equistar Chemicals, LP, 71 148–50

Equitable Life Assurance Society of the United States, III 247–49 see also AXA Equitable Life Insurance Co.

Equitable Resources, Inc., 6 492–94; 54 95–98 (upd.)

Equity Bank Limited, 116 221–24

Equity Marketing, Inc., 26 136–38

Equity Office Properties Trust, 54 99–102

Equity Residential, 49 129–32

Equus Computer Systems, Inc., 49 133–35

Eram SA, 51 118–20

Eramet, 73 144–47

Ercros S.A., 80 102–05

eResearch Technology, Inc., 115 194–97

ERGO Versicherungsgruppe AG, 44 166–69

Ergon, Inc., 95 134–37

Erickson Retirement Communities, 57 127–30

Ericsson see Telefonaktiebolaget LM Ericsson.

Eridania Béghin-Say S.A., 36 185–88

Erie Indemnity Company, 35 167–69

ERLY Industries Inc., 17 161–62

Ermenegildo Zegna SpA, 63 149–52

Ernie Ball, Inc., 56 114–16

Ernst & Young Global Limited, 9 198–200; 29 174–77 (upd.); 108 246–53 (upd.)

Eroski see Grupo Eroski

Erste Bank der Osterreichischen Sparkassen AG, 69 155–57

ESCADA AG, 71 151–53

Escalade, Incorporated, 19 142–44

Eschelon Telecom, Inc., 72 119–22

ESCO Technologies Inc., 87 160–163

Eskimo Pie Corporation, 21 218–20

Espírito Santo Financial Group S.A., 79 158–63 (upd.)

ESPN, Inc., 56 117–22

Esporta plc, 35 170–72

Esprit de Corp., 8 169–72; 29 178–82 (upd.)

ESS Technology, Inc., 22 196–98

Essar Group Ltd., 79 164–67

Essef Corporation, 18 161–63 see also Pentair, Inc.

Essel Propack Limited, 115 198–201

Esselte, 64 119–21

Esselte Leitz GmbH & Co. KG, 48 152–55

Esselte Pendaflex Corporation, 11 100–01

Essence Communications, Inc., 24 153–55

Essex Corporation, 85 120–23

Essie Cosmetics, Ltd., 102 116–19

Essilor International, 21 221–23

The Estée Lauder Companies Inc., 9 201–04; 30 187–91 (upd.); 92199–207 (upd.)

Esterline Technologies Corp., 15 155–57

Estes Express Lines, Inc., 86 140–43

Etablissements Economiques du Casino Guichard, Perrachon et ie, S.C.A., 12 152–54 see also Casino Guichard-Perrachon S.A.

Etablissements Franz Colruyt N.V., 68 141–43

Établissements Jacquot and Cie S.A.S., 92 111–14

Etablissements Maurel & Prom S.A., 115 202–05

Etam Developpement SA, 44 170–72

ETBD see Europe Through the Back Door.

Eternal Word Television Network, Inc., 57 131–34

Ethan Allen Interiors, Inc., 12 155–57; 39 145–48 (upd.)

Ethicon, Inc., 23 188–90

Ethiopian Airlines, 81 155–58

Ethyl Corp., I 334–36; 10 289–91 (upd.)

Etienne Aigner AG, 52 109–12

Etihad Airways PJSC, 89 204–07

EToys, Inc., 37 128–30

ETS see Educational Testing Service.

Euralis see Groupe Euralis.

Eurazeo, 80 106–09

The Eureka Company, 12 158–60 see also White Consolidated Industries Inc.

Euro Disney S.C.A., 20 209–12; 58 113–16 (upd.)

Euro RSCG Worldwide S.A., 13 203–05

Eurocopter S.A., 80 110–13

Eurofins Scientific S.A., 70 88–90

Euromarket Designs Inc., 31 186–89 (upd.); 99 152–157 (upd.)

Euronet Worldwide, Inc., 83 143–146

Euronext N.V., 37 131–33; 89 208–11 (upd.)

Europcar Groupe S.A., 104 146–51

Europe Through the Back Door Inc., 65 135–38

European Aeronautic Defence and Space Company EADS N.V., 52 113–16 (upd.); 109 212–18 (upd.)

European Investment Bank, 66 109–11

Eurotunnel Group, 13 206–08; 37 134–38 (upd.)

Eutelsat S.A., 114 191–94

EVA Airways Corporation, 51 121–23

Evans & Sutherland Computer Corporation, 19 145–49; 78 98–103 (upd.)

Evans, Inc., 30 192–94

Everex Systems, Inc., 16 194–96

Evergreen Energy, Inc., 97 155–59

Evergreen International Aviation, Inc., 53 130–33

Evergreen Marine Corporation (Taiwan) Ltd., 13 209–11; 50 183–89 (upd.)

Evergreen Solar, Inc., 101 174–78

Everlast Worldwide Inc., 47 126–29

Evialis S.A., 100 156–59

EVN AG, 115 206–09

Evonik Industries AG, 111 117–27 (upd.)

Evraz Group S.A., 97 160–63

EWTN see Eternal Word Television Network, Inc.

Exabyte Corporation, 12 161–63; 40 178–81 (upd.)

Exacompta Clairefontaine S.A., 102 120–23

Exactech, Inc., 101 179–82

Exar Corp., 14 182–84

EXCEL Communications Inc., 18 164–67

Excel Technology, Inc., 65 139–42

Executive Jet, Inc., 36 189–91 see also NetJets Inc.

Executone Information Systems, Inc., 13 212–14; 15 195

Exel plc, 51 124–30 (upd.)

Exelon Corporation, 48 156–63 (upd.); 49 65

Exide Electronics Group, Inc., 20 213–15

Exito see Almacenes Exito S.A.

Expand SA, 48 164–66

Expedia, Inc., 58 117–21

Expeditors International of Washington Inc., 17 163–65; 78 104–08 (upd.)

Experian Information Solutions Inc., 45 152–55

Exponent, Inc., 95 138–41

Exportadora Bananera Noboa, S.A., 91 178–81

Express Scripts, Inc., 17 166–68; 44 173–76 (upd.); 109 219–24 (upd.)

Extended Stay America, Inc., 41 156–58

Extendicare Health Services, Inc., 6 181–83

Extreme Pizza see OOC Inc.

EXX Inc., 65 143–45

Exxaro Resources Ltd., 106 178–81

Exxon Mobil Corporation, IV 426–30; 7 169–73 (upd.); 32 175–82 (upd.); 67 175–86 (upd.)

Eye Care Centers of America, Inc., 69 158–60

Ezaki Glico Company Ltd., 72 123–25

EZchip Semiconductor Ltd., 106 182–85

EZCORP Inc., 43 159–61

F

F&W Publications, Inc., 71 154–56

F.A.O. Schwarz see FAO Schwarz

The F. Dohmen Co., 77 142–45

F. Hoffmann-La Roche & Co. A.G., I 642–44; 50 190–93 (upd.)

Marisol S.A., 107 260–64

Maritz Holdings Inc., 38 302–05; 110 305–09 (upd.)

Mark IV Industries, Inc., 7 296–98; 28 260–64 (upd.)

Mark T. Wendell Tea Company, 94 299–302

The Mark Travel Corporation, 80 232–35

Markel Corporation, 116 331–34

Märklin Holding GmbH, 70 163–66

Marks and Spencer p.l.c., V 124–26; 24 313–17 (upd.); 85 239–47 (upd.)

Marks Brothers Jewelers, Inc., 24 318–20 *see also* Whitehall Jewellers, Inc.

Marlin Business Services Corp., 89 317–19

The Marmon Group, Inc., IV 135–38; 16 354–57 (upd.); 70 167–72 (upd.)

Marquette Electronics, Inc., 13 326–28

Marriott International, Inc., III 102–03; 21 364–67 (upd.); 83 264–270 (upd.)

Mars, Incorporated, 7 299–301; 40 302–05 (upd.); 114 288–93 (upd.)

Mars Petcare US Inc., 96 269–72

Marsh & McLennan Companies, Inc., III 282–84; 45 263–67 (upd.)

Marsh Supermarkets, Inc., 17 300–02; 76 255–58 (upd.)

Marshall & Ilsley Corporation, 56 217–20

Marshall Amplification plc, 62 239–42

Marshall Field's, 63 254–63 *see also* Target Corp.

Marshalls Incorporated, 13 329–31

Martek Biosciences Corporation, 65 218–20

Martell and Company S.A., 82 213–16

Marten Transport, Ltd., 84 243–246

Martha Stewart Living Omnimedia, Inc., 24 321–23; 73 219–22 (upd.)

Martha White Foods Inc., 104 284–87

Martignetti Companies, 84 247–250

Martin-Baker Aircraft Company Limited, 61 195–97

Martin Franchises, Inc., 80 236–39

Martin Guitar Company *see* C.F. Martin & Co., Inc.

Martin Industries, Inc., 44 274–77

Martin Marietta Corporation, I 67–69 *see also* Lockheed Martin Corp.

Martini & Rossi SpA, 63 264–66

MartinLogan, Ltd., 85 248–51

Martins *see* Grupo Martins.

Martin's Super Markets, Inc., 101 330–33

Martz Group, 56 221–23

Marubeni Corporation, I 492–95; 24 324–27 (upd.); 104 288–93 (upd.)

Maruha Group Inc., 75 250–53 (upd.)

Marui Company Ltd., V 127; 62 243–45 (upd.)

Maruzen Company Ltd., 18 322–24; 104 294–97 (upd.)

Marvel Entertainment, Inc., 10 400–02; 78 212–19 (upd.)

Marvell Technology Group Ltd., 112 268–71

Marvelous Market Inc., 104 298–301

Marvin Lumber & Cedar Company, 22 345–47

Mary Kay Inc., 9 330–32; 30 306–09 (upd.); 84 251–256 (upd.)

Maryland & Virginia Milk Producers Cooperative Association, Inc., 80 240–43

Maryville Data Systems Inc., 96 273–76

Marzotto S.p.A., 20 356–58; 67 246–49 (upd.)

The Maschhoffs, Inc., 82 217–20

Masco Corporation, III 568–71; 20 359–63 (upd.); 39 263–68 (upd.); 111 295–303 (upd.)

Maserati *see* Officine Alfieri Maserati S.p.A.

Mashantucket Pequot Gaming Enterprise Inc., 35 282–85

Masland Corporation, 17 303–05 *see also* Lear Corp.

Mason & Hanger Group Inc., 110 310–14

Masonite International Corporation, 63 267–69

Massachusetts Mutual Life Insurance Company, III 285–87; 53 210–13 (upd.)

Massey Energy Company, 57 236–38

MasTec, Inc., 55 259–63 (upd.)

Mastellone Hermanos S.A., 101 334–37

Master Lock Company, 45 268–71

Master Spas Inc., 105 292–95

MasterBrand Cabinets, Inc., 71 216–18

MasterCard Worldwide, 9 333–35; 96 277–81 (upd.)

MasterCraft Boat Company, Inc., 90 290–93

Matador Records Inc., 113 247–51

Matalan PLC, 49 258–60

Match.com, LP, 87 308–311

Material Sciences Corporation, 63 270–73

The MathWorks, Inc., 80 244–47

Matra-Hachette S.A., 15 293–97 (upd.) *see also* European Aeronautic Defence and Space Company EADS N.V.

Matria Healthcare, Inc., 17 306–09

Matrix Essentials Inc., 90 294–97

Matrix Service Company, 65 221–23

Matrixx Initiatives, Inc., 74 177–79

Matsushita Electric Industrial Co., Ltd., II 55–56; 64 255–58 (upd.)

Matsushita Electric Works, Ltd., III 710–11; 7 302–03 (upd.)

Matsuzakaya Company Ltd., V 129–31; 64 259–62 (upd.)

Matt Prentice Restaurant Group, 70 173–76

Mattel, Inc., 7 304–07; 25 311–15 (upd.); 61 198–203 (upd.)

Matth. Hohner AG, 53 214–17

Matthews International Corporation, 29 304–06; 77 248–52 (upd.)

Mattress Giant Corporation, 103 254–57

Matussière et Forest SA, 58 220–22

Maui Land & Pineapple Company, Inc., 29 307–09; 100 273–77 (upd.)

Maui Wowi, Inc., 85 252–55

Mauna Loa Macadamia Nut Corporation, 64 263–65

Maurel & Prom *see* Etablissements Maurel & Prom S.A.

Maurices Inc., 95 255–58

Maus Frères SA, 48 277–79

Maverick Ranch Association, Inc., 88 253–56

Maverick Tube Corporation, 59 280–83

Maverik, Inc., 103 258–61

Max & Erma's Restaurants Inc., 19 258–60; 100 278–82 (upd.)

Maxco Inc., 17 310–11

Maxicare Health Plans, Inc., III 84–86; 25 316–19 (upd.)

The Maxim Group, 25 320–22

Maxim Integrated Products, Inc., 16 358–60

MAXIMUS, Inc., 43 277–80

Maxtor Corporation, 10 403–05 *see also* Seagate Technology, Inc.

Maxus Energy Corporation, 7 308–10

Maxwell Communication Corporation plc, IV 641–43; 7 311–13 (upd.)

Maxwell Shoe Company, Inc., 30 310–12 *see also* Jones Apparel Group, Inc.

MAXXAM Inc., 8 348–50

Maxxim Medical Inc., 12 325–27

The May Department Stores Company, V 132–35; 19 261–64 (upd.); 46 284–88 (upd.)

May Gurney Integrated Services PLC, 95 259–62

May International *see* George S. May International Co.

Mayer, Brown, Rowe & Maw, 47 230–32

Mayfield Dairy Farms, Inc., 74 180–82

Mayflower Group Inc., 6 409–11

Mayo Foundation for Medical Education and Research, 9 336–39; 34 265–69 (upd.); 115 298–303 (upd.)

Mayor's Jewelers, Inc., 41 254–57

Maytag Corporation, III 572–73; 22 348–51 (upd.); 82 221–25 (upd.)

Mazda Motor Corporation, 9 340–42; 23 338–41 (upd.); 63 274–79 (upd.)

Mazeikiu Nafta *see* Orlen Lietuva

Mazel Stores, Inc., 29 310–12

Mazzio's Corporation, 76 259–61

MBB *see* Messerschmitt-Bölkow-Blohm.

MBC Holding Company, 40 306–09

MBE *see* Mail Boxes Etc.

MBIA Inc., 73 223–26

MBK Industrie S.A., 94 303–06

MBNA Corporation, 12 328–30; 33 291–94 (upd.)

MC Sporting Goods *see* Michigan Sporting Goods Distributors Inc.

MCA Inc., II 143–45 *see also* Universal Studios.

McAfee Inc., 94 307–10

Milwaukee Brewers Baseball Club, 37 247–49
Mine Safety Appliances Company, 31 333–35
Minebea Co., Ltd., 90 298–302
The Miner Group International, 22 356–58
Minera Alumbrera Ltd., 118 300–02
Minera Escondida Ltda., 100 293–96
Minerals & Metals Trading Corporation of India Ltd., IV 143–44
Minerals Technologies Inc., 11 310–12; **52** 248–51 (upd.)
Minnesota Mining & Manufacturing Company, I 499–501; **8** 369–71 (upd.); **26** 296–99 (upd.) *see also* 3M Co.
Minnesota Power, Inc., 11 313–16; **34** 286–91 (upd.)
Minnesota Twins, 112 276–80
Minntech Corporation, 22 359–61
Minolta Co., Ltd., III 574–76; **18** 339–42 (upd.); **43** 281–85 (upd.)
The Minute Maid Company, 28 271–74
Minuteman International Inc., 46 292–95
Minyard Food Stores, Inc., 33 304–07; **86** 272–77 (upd.)
Miquel y Costas Miquel S.A., 68 256–58
Mirage Resorts, Incorporated, 6 209–12; **28** 275–79 (upd.) *see also* MGM MIRAGE.
Miramax Film Corporation, 64 282–85
Mirant Corporation, 98 243–47
Miroglio SpA, 86 278–81
Mirror Group Newspapers plc, 7 341–43; **23** 348–51 (upd.)
Misonix, Inc., 80 248–51
Mississippi Chemical Corporation, 39 280–83
Mississippi Power Company, 110 315–19
Misys PLC, 45 279–81; **46** 296–99
Mitchell Energy and Development Corporation, 7 344–46 *see also* Devon Energy Corp.
Mitchells & Butlers PLC, 59 296–99
Mitel Corporation, 18 343–46
MITRE Corporation, 26 300–02; **107** 269–72 (upd.)
MITROPA AG, 37 250–53
Mitsubishi Bank, Ltd., II 321–22 *see also* Bank of Tokyo-Mitsubishi Ltd.
Mitsubishi Chemical Corporation, I 363–64; **56** 236–38 (upd.)
Mitsubishi Corporation, I 502–04; **12** 340–43 (upd.); **116** 346–52 (upd.)
Mitsubishi Electric Corporation, II 57–59; **44** 283–87 (upd.); **117** 263–69 (upd.)
Mitsubishi Estate Company, Limited, IV 713–14; **61** 215–18 (upd.)
Mitsubishi Heavy Industries, Ltd., III 577–79; **7** 347–50 (upd.); **40** 324–28 (upd.)
Mitsubishi Materials Corporation, III 712–13

Mitsubishi Motors Corporation, 9 349–51; **23** 352–55 (upd.); **57** 245–49 (upd.)
Mitsubishi Oil Co., Ltd., IV 460–62 *see also* Nippon Mitsubishi Oil Corp.
Mitsubishi Rayon Co. Ltd., V 369–71
Mitsubishi Trust & Banking Corporation, II 323–24
Mitsubishi UFJ Financial Group, Inc., 99 291–296 (upd.)
Mitsui & Co., Ltd., I 505–08; **28** 280–85 (upd.); **110** 320–27 (upd.)
Mitsui Bank, Ltd., II 325–27 *see also* Sumitomo Mitsui Banking Corp.
Mitsui Marine and Fire Insurance Company, Limited, III 295–96
Mitsui Mining & Smelting Co., Ltd., IV 145–46; **102** 274–78 (upd.)
Mitsui Mining Company, Limited, IV 147–49
Mitsui Mutual Life Insurance Company, III 297–98; **39** 284–86 (upd.)
Mitsui O.S.K. Lines Ltd., V 473–76; **96** 282–87 (upd.)
Mitsui Petrochemical Industries, Ltd., 9 352–54
Mitsui Real Estate Development Co., Ltd., IV 715–16
Mitsui Trust & Banking Company, Ltd., II 328
Mitsukoshi Ltd., V 142–44; **56** 239–42 (upd.)
Mity Enterprises, Inc., 38 310–12
MIVA, Inc., 83 271–275
Mizuho Financial Group Inc., 25 344–46; **58** 229–36 (upd.)
MN Airlines LLC, 104 321–27
MNS, Ltd., 65 236–38
Mo och Domsjö AB, IV 317–19 *see also* Holmen AB
Mobil Corporation, IV 463–65; **7** 351–54 (upd.); **21** 376–80 (upd.) *see also* Exxon Mobil Corp.
Mobile Mini, Inc., 58 237–39
Mobile Telecommunications Technologies Corp., 18 347–49
Mobile TeleSystems OJSC, 59 300–03
Mocon, Inc., 76 275–77
Modell's Sporting Goods *see* Henry Modell & Company Inc.
Modern Times Group AB, 36 335–38
Modern Woodmen of America, 66 227–29
Modine Manufacturing Company, 8 372–75; **56** 243–47 (upd.)
MoDo *see* Mo och Domsjö AB.
Modtech Holdings, Inc., 77 284–87
Moelven Industrier ASA, 110 328–32
Moen Incorporated, 12 344–45; **106** 295–98 (upd.)
Moe's Southwest Grill *see* MSWG, LLC.
Moët-Hennessy, I 271–72 *see also* LVMH Moët Hennessy Louis Vuitton SA.
Mohawk Fine Papers, Inc., 108 353–57
Mohawk Industries, Inc., 19 274–76; **63** 298–301 (upd.)
Mohegan Tribal Gaming Authority, 37 254–57

Moksel *see* A. Moksel AG.
MOL *see* Mitsui O.S.K. Lines, Ltd.
MOL Rt, 70 192–95
Moldflow Corporation, 73 227–30
Molex Incorporated, 11 317–19; **14** 27; **54** 236–41 (upd.)
Moliflor Loisirs, 80 252–55
Molina Healthcare, Inc., 116 353–56
Molinos Río de la Plata S.A., 61 219–21
Molins plc, 51 249–51
The Molson Companies Limited, I 273–75; **26** 303–07 (upd.)
Molson Coors Brewing Company, 77 288–300 (upd.)
Monaco Coach Corporation, 31 336–38
Monadnock Paper Mills, Inc., 21 381–84
Monarch Casino & Resort, Inc., 65 239–41
The Monarch Cement Company, 72 231–33
Mondadori *see* Arnoldo Mondadori Editore S.p.A.
Mondragón Corporación Cooperativa, 101 347–51
MoneyGram International, Inc., 94 315–18
Monfort, Inc., 13 350–52
Monnaie de Paris, 62 246–48
Monnoyeur Group *see* Groupe Monnoyeur.
Monoprix S.A., 86 282–85
Monro Muffler Brake, Inc., 24 337–40
Monrovia Nursery Company, 70 196–98
Monsanto Company, I 365–67; **9** 355–57 (upd.); **29** 327–31 (upd.); **77** 301–07 (upd.)
Monsoon plc, 39 287–89
Monster Cable Products, Inc., 69 256–58
Monster Worldwide Inc., 74 194–97 (upd.)
Montana Coffee Traders, Inc., 60 208–10
The Montana Power Company, 11 320–22; **44** 288–92 (upd.)
Montblanc International GmbH, 82 240–44
Montedison S.p.A., I 368–69; **24** 341–44 (upd.)
Monterey Pasta Company, 58 240–43
Montgomery Ward & Co., Incorporated, V 145–48; **20** 374–79 (upd.)
Montres Rolex S.A., 13 353–55; **34** 292–95 (upd.)
Montupet S.A., 63 302–04
Moody's Corporation, 65 242–44
Moog Inc., 13 356–58
Moog Music, Inc., 75 261–64
Mooney Aerospace Group Ltd., 52 252–55
Moore Corporation Limited, IV 644–46 *see also* R.R. Donnelley & Sons Co.
Moore-Handley, Inc., 39 290–92
Moore Medical Corp., 17 331–33

ORIX Corporation, II 442–43; 44 324–26 (upd.); 104 354–58 (upd.)

Orkin, Inc., 104 359–62

Orkla ASA, 18 394–98; 82 259–64 (upd.)

Orleans Homebuilders, Inc., 62 260–62

Orlen Lietuva, 111 371–75

Ormat Technologies, Inc., 87 353–358

Ormet Corporation, 82 265–68

Orrick, Herrington and Sutcliffe LLP, 76 299–301

Orscheln Farm and Home LLC, 107 331–34

Orszagos Takarekpenztar es Kereskedelmi Bank Rt. (OTP Bank), 78 288–91

Orthodontic Centers of America, Inc., 35 323–26

Orthofix International NV, 72 260–62

OrthoSynetics Inc., 107 335–39 (upd.)

The Orvis Company, Inc., 28 336–39

Oryx Energy Company, 7 413–15

Osaka Gas Company, Ltd., V 679–81; 60 233–36 (upd.)

Oscar Mayer Foods Corp., 12 370–72 *see also* Kraft Foods Inc.

Oshawa Group Limited, II 649–50

OshKosh B'Gosh, Inc., 9 393–95; 42 266–70 (upd.)

Oshkosh Corporation, 7 416–18; 98 279–84 (upd.)

Oshman's Sporting Goods, Inc., 17 368–70 *see also* Gart Sports Co.

OSI Restaurant Partners, Inc., 88 286–91 (upd.)

Osmonics, Inc., 18 399–401

Osram GmbH, 86 312–16

Österreichische Bundesbahnen GmbH, 6 418–20

Österreichische Elektrizitätswirtschafts-AG, 85 307–10

Österreichische Post- und Telegraphenverwaltung, V 314–17

O'Sullivan Industries Holdings, Inc., 34 313–15

Otari Inc., 89 341–44

Otis Elevator Company, Inc., 13 384–86; 39 311–15 (upd.)

Otis Spunkmeyer, Inc., 28 340–42

Otor S.A., 77 326–29

OTP Bank *see* Orszagos Takarekpenztar es Kereskedelmi Bank Rt.

OTR Express, Inc., 25 368–70

Ottakar's plc, 64 302–04

Ottaway Newspapers, Inc., 15 335–37

Otter Tail Power Company, 18 402–05

Otto Bremer Foundation *see* Bremer Financial Corp.

Otto Fuchs KG, 100 310–14

Otto Group, 106 342–48 (upd.)

Otto Versand GmbH & Co., V 159–61; 15 338–40 (upd.); 34 324–28 (upd.)

Outback Steakhouse, Inc., 12 373–75; 34 329–32 (upd.) *see also* OSI Restaurant Partners, Inc.

Outboard Marine Corporation, III 597–600; 20 409–12 (upd.) *see also* Bombardier Inc.

Outdoor Research, Incorporated, 67 288–90

Outdoor Systems, Inc., 25 371–73 *see also* Infinity Broadcasting Corp.

Outlook Group Corporation, 37 294–96

Outokumpu Oyj, 38 335–37; 108 375–80 (upd.)

Outrigger Enterprises, Inc., 67 291–93

Outward Bound USA, 111 376–79

Overhead Door Corporation, 70 213–16

Overhill Corporation, 51 279–81

Overland Storage Inc., 100 315–20

Overnite Corporation, 14 371–73; 58 262–65 (upd.)

Overseas Shipholding Group, Inc., 11 376–77

Overstock.com, Inc., 75 307–09

Owens & Minor, Inc., 16 398–401; 68 282–85 (upd.)

Owens Corning, III 720–23; 20 413–17 (upd.); 98 285–91 (upd.)

Owens-Illinois, Inc., I 609–11; 26 350–53 (upd.); 85 311–18 (upd.)

Owosso Corporation, 29 366–68

Oxfam GB, 87 359–362

Oxford Health Plans, Inc., 16 402–04

Oxford Industries, Inc., 8 406–08; 84 290–296 (upd.)

P

P&C Foods Inc., 8 409–11

P & F Industries, Inc., 45 327–29

P&G *see* Procter & Gamble Co.

P&H *see* Palmer and Harvey Group PLC.

P.C. Richard & Son LLC, 23 372–74; 118 335–38 (upd.)

P.F. Chang's China Bistro, Inc., 37 297–99; 86 317–21 (upd.)

P.H. Glatfelter Company, 8 412–14; 30 349–52 (upd.); 83 291–297 (upd.)

P.W. Minor and Son, Inc., 100 321–24

PACCAR Inc., I 185–86; 26 354–56 (upd.); 111 380–84 (upd.)

Pacer International, Inc., 54 274–76

Pacer Technology, 40 347–49

Pacific Basin Shipping Ltd., 86 322–26

Pacific Clay Products Inc., 88 292–95

Pacific Coast Building Products, Inc., 94 338–41

Pacific Coast Feather Company, 67 294–96

Pacific Coast Restaurants, Inc., 90 318–21

Pacific Continental Corporation, 114 320–23

Pacific Dunlop Limited, 10 444–46 *see also* Ansell Ltd.

Pacific Enterprises, V 682–84 *see also* Sempra Energy.

Pacific Ethanol, Inc., 81 269–72

Pacific Gas and Electric Company, V 685–87 *see also* PG&E Corp.

Pacific Internet Limited, 87 363–366

Pacific Mutual Holding Company, 98 292–96

Pacific Sunwear of California, Inc., 28 343–45; 104 363–67 (upd.)

Pacific Telecom, Inc., 6 325–28

Pacific Telesis Group, V 318–20 *see also* SBC Communications.

PacifiCare Health Systems, Inc., 11 378–80

PacifiCorp, Inc., V 688–90; 26 357–60 (upd.)

Packaging Corporation of America, 12 376–78; 51 282–85 (upd.)

Packard Bell Electronics, Inc., 13 387–89

Packeteer, Inc., 81 273–76

PacketVideo Corporation, 112 303–06

Paddock Publications, Inc., 53 263–65

Paddy Power plc, 98 297–300

PagesJaunes Groupe SA, 79 306–09

Paging Network Inc., 11 381–83

Pagnossin S.p.A., 73 248–50

PaineWebber Group Inc., II 444–46; 22 404–07 (upd.) *see also* UBS AG.

Paiste AG, 115 379–82

Pakistan International Airlines Corporation, 46 323–26

Pakistan State Oil Company Ltd., 81 277–80

PAL *see* Philippine Airlines, Inc.

Palace Sports & Entertainment, Inc., 97 320–25

Palfinger AG, 100 325–28

PALIC *see* Pan-American Life Insurance Co.

Pall Corporation, 9 396–98; 72 263–66 (upd.)

Palm Breweries NV, 113 296–99

Palm Harbor Homes, Inc., 39 316–18

Palm, Inc., 36 355–57; 75 310–14 (upd.)

Palm Management Corporation, 71 265–68

Palmer & Cay, Inc., 69 285–87

Palmer and Harvey Group PLC, 114 324–28

Palmer Candy Company, 80 277–81

Palmer Co. *see* R. M. Palmer Co.

Paloma Industries Ltd., 71 269–71

Palomar Medical Technologies, Inc., 22 408–10

Pamida Holdings Corporation, 15 341–43

Pampa Energía S.A., 118 339–42

The Pampered Chef Ltd., 18 406–08; 78 292–96 (upd.)

Pamplin Corp. *see* R.B. Pamplin Corp.

Pan-American Life Insurance Company, 48 311–13

Pan American World Airways, Inc., I 115–16; 12 379–81 (upd.)

Panalpina World Transport (Holding) Ltd., 47 286–88

Panamerican Beverages, Inc., 47 289–91; 54 74

PanAmSat Corporation, 46 327–29

Panattoni Development Company, Inc., 99 327–330

Pentair, Inc., **7** 419–21; **26** 361–64 (upd.); **81** 281–87 (upd.)
Pentax Corporation, **78** 301–05
Pentech International, Inc., **29** 372–74
The Pentland Group plc, **20** 423–25; **100** 343–47 (upd.)
Penton Media, Inc., **27** 360–62
Penzeys Spices, Inc., **79** 314–16
People Express Airlines Inc., **I** 117–18
Peoples Energy Corporation, **6** 543–44
People's United Financial Inc. , **106** 349–52
PeopleSoft Inc., **14** 381–83; **33** 330–33 (upd.) *see also* Oracle Corp.
The Pep Boys—Manny, Moe & Jack, **11** 391–93; **36** 361–64 (upd.); **81** 288–94 (upd.)
PEPCO *see* Potomac Electric Power Co.
Pepco Holdings, Inc., **116** 382–85
Pepper *see* J. W. Pepper and Son Inc.
The Pepper Construction Group, LLC, **111** 385–88
Pepper Hamilton LLP, **43** 300–03
Pepperidge Farm, Incorporated, **81** 295–300
The Pepsi Bottling Group, Inc., **40** 350–53
PepsiAmericas, Inc., **67** 297–300 (upd.)
PepsiCo, Inc., **I** 276–79; **10** 450–54 (upd.); **38** 347–54 (upd.); **93** 333–44 (upd.)
Pequiven *see* Petroquímica de Venezuela S.A.
Perdigao SA, **52** 276–79
Perdue Farms Inc., **7** 422–24; **23** 375–78 (upd.)
Perfetti Van Melle S.p.A., **72** 270–73
Performance Food Group, **31** 359–62; **96** 329–34 (upd.)
Perini Corporation, **8** 418–21; **82** 274–79 (upd.)
PerkinElmer, Inc., **7** 425–27; **78** 306–10 (upd.)
Perkins & Marie Callender's Inc., **107** 345–51 (upd.)
Perkins Coie LLP, **56** 268–70
Perkins Family Restaurants, L.P., **22** 417–19
Perkins Foods Holdings Ltd., **87** 371–374
Perma-Fix Environmental Services, Inc., **99** 338–341
Pernod Ricard S.A., **I** 280–81; **21** 399–401 (upd.); **72** 274–77 (upd.)
Perot Systems Corporation, **29** 375–78
Perrigo Company, **12** 387–89; **59** 330–34 (upd.); **118** 349–55 (upd.)
Perry Ellis International Inc., **41** 291–94; **106** 353–58 (upd.)
Perry's Ice Cream Company Inc., **90** 326–29
The Perseus Books Group, **91** 375–78
Perstorp AB, **I** 385–87; **51** 289–92 (upd.)
Pertamina, **IV** 491–93; **56** 271–74 (upd.)
Perusahaan Otomobil Nasional Bhd., **62** 266–68

Pescanova S.A., **81** 301–04
Pet Incorporated, **7** 428–31
Petco Animal Supplies, Inc., **29** 379–81; **74** 231–34 (upd.)
Peter Kiewit Sons' Inc., **8** 422–24 *see also* Kiewit Corporation.
Peter Pan Bus Lines Inc., **106** 359–63
Peter Piper, Inc., **70** 217–19
Peterbilt Motors Company, **89** 354–57
Petersen Publishing Company, **21** 402–04
Peterson American Corporation, **55** 304–06
Pete's Brewing Company, **22** 420–22
Petit Bateau, **95** 327–31
Petland Inc., **110** 363–66
PetMed Express, Inc., **81** 305–08
Petrie Stores Corporation, **8** 425–27
Petro-Canada, **IV** 494–96; **99** 342–349 (upd.)
Petrobrás *see* Petróleo Brasileiro S.A.
Petrobras Energia Participaciones S.A., **72** 278–81
Petroecuador *see* Petróleos del Ecuador.
Petrof spol. S.R.O., **107** 352–56
Petrofac Ltd., **95** 332–35
PetroFina S.A., **IV** 497–500; **26** 365–69 (upd.)
Petrogal *see* Petróleos de Portugal.
Petrohawk Energy Corporation, **79** 317–20
Petróleo Brasileiro S.A., **IV** 501–03
Petróleos de Portugal S.A., **IV** 504–06
Petróleos de Venezuela S.A., **IV** 507–09; **74** 235–39 (upd.)
Petróleos del Ecuador, **IV** 510–11
Petróleos Mexicanos (PEMEX), **IV** 512–14; **19** 295–98 (upd.); **104** 373–78 (upd.)
Petroleum Development Oman LLC, **IV** 515–16; **98** 305–09 (upd.)
Petroleum Helicopters, Inc., **35** 334–36
Petroliam Nasional Bhd (PETRONAS), **56** 275–79 (upd.); **117** 305–11 (upd.)
Petrolite Corporation, **15** 350–52 *see also* Baker Hughes Inc.
Petromex *see* Petróleos de Mexico S.A.
Petron Corporation, **58** 270–72
Petronas, **IV** 517–20 *see also* Petroliam Nasional Bhd.
Petroplus Holdings AG, **108** 381–84
Petrossian Inc., **54** 287–89
Petry Media Corporation, **102** 326–29
PETsMART, Inc., **14** 384–86; **41** 295–98 (upd.)
Peugeot S.A., **I** 187–88 *see also* PSA Peugeot Citroen S.A.
The Pew Charitable Trusts, **35** 337–40
Pez Candy, Inc., **38** 355–57
The Pfaltzgraff Co. *see* Susquehanna Pfaltzgraff Co.
Pfizer Inc., **I** 661–63; **9** 402–05 (upd.); **38** 358–67 (upd.); **79** 321–33 (upd.)
PFSweb, Inc., **73** 254–56
PG&E Corporation, **26** 370–73 (upd.); **116** 386–90 (upd.)
PGA *see* The Professional Golfers' Association.

PGi, **115** 389–92
Phaidon Press Ltd., **98** 310–14
Phantom Fireworks *see* B.J. Alan Co., Inc.
Phar-Mor Inc., **12** 390–92
Pharmacia & Upjohn Inc., **I** 664–65; **25** 374–78 (upd.) *see also* Pfizer Inc.
Pharmion Corporation, **91** 379–82
Phat Fashions LLC, **49** 322–24
Phelps Dodge Corporation, **IV** 176–79; **28** 352–57 (upd.); **75** 319–25 (upd.)
PHH Arval, **V** 496–97; **53** 274–76 (upd.)
PHI, Inc., **80** 282–86 (upd.)
Philadelphia Eagles, **37** 305–08
Philadelphia Electric Company, **V** 695–97 *see also* Exelon Corp.
Philadelphia Gas Works Company, **92** 301–05
Philadelphia Media Holdings LLC, **92** 306–10
Philadelphia Suburban Corporation, **39** 326–29
Philharmonic-Symphony Society of New York, Inc. (New York Philharmonic), **69** 293–97
Philip Environmental Inc., **16** 414–16
Philip Morris Companies Inc., **V** 405–07; **18** 416–19 (upd.); **44** 338–43 (upd.) *see also* Altria Group Inc.
Philip Services Corp., **73** 257–60
Philipp Holzmann AG, **17** 374–77
Philippine Airlines, Inc., **6** 106–08; **23** 379–82 (upd.)
Philips Electronics N.V., **13** 400–03 (upd.) *see also* Koninklijke Philips Electronics N.V.
Philips Electronics North America Corp., **13** 396–99
N.V. Philips Gloeilampenfabriken, **II** 78–80 *see also* Philips Electronics N.V.
The Phillies, **106** 364–68
Phillips Foods, Inc., **63** 320–22; **90** 330–33 (upd.)
Phillips International, Inc., **78** 311–14
Phillips Lytle LLP, **102** 330–34
Phillips Petroleum Company, **IV** 521–23; **40** 354–59 (upd.) *see also* ConocoPhillips.
Phillips-Van Heusen Corporation, **24** 382–85
Phillips, de Pury & Luxembourg, **49** 325–27
Philly Pretzel Factory *see* Soft Pretzel Franchise Systems, Inc.
Phoenix AG, **68** 286–89
The Phoenix Companies, Inc., **115** 393–96
Phoenix Footwear Group, Inc., **70** 220–22
Phoenix Mecano AG, **61** 286–88
The Phoenix Media/Communications Group, **91** 383–87
Phones 4u Ltd., **85** 328–31
Photo-Me International Plc, **83** 302–306
PHP Healthcare Corporation, **22** 423–25

Rainbow Media Holdings LLC, 109 457–60

Rainforest Café, Inc., 25 386–88; 88 312–16 (upd.)

Rainier Brewing Company, 23 403–05

Raisio PLC, 99 354–357

Rakuten Inc., 118 370–73

Raleigh UK Ltd., 65 295–97

Raley's Inc., 14 396–98; 58 288–91 (upd.)

Rallye SA, 54 306–09

Rally's, 25 389–91; 68 313–16 (upd.)

Ralph Lauren *see* Polo/Ralph Lauren Corportion.

Ralphs Grocery Company, 35 368–70

Ralston Purina Company, II 561–63; 13 425–27 (upd.) *see also* Ralcorp Holdings, Inc.; Nestlé S.A.

Ramsay Youth Services, Inc., 41 322–24

Ramtron International Corporation, 89 365–68

Ranbaxy Laboratories Ltd., 70 247–49

RAND Corporation, 112 307–10

Rand McNally & Company, 28 378–81; 53 122

Randall's Food Markets, Inc., 40 364–67 *see also* Safeway Inc.

Random House Inc., 13 428–30; 31 375–80 (upd.); 106 388–98 (upd.)

Randon S.A. Implementos e Participações, 79 348–52

Randstad Holding nv, 16 420–22; 43 307–10 (upd.); 113 322–26 (upd.)

Range Resources Corporation, 45 353–55

The Rank Group plc, II 157–59; 14 399–402 (upd.); 64 317–21 (upd.)

Ranks Hovis McDougall Limited, II 564–65; 28 382–85 (upd.)

RAO Unified Energy System of Russia, 45 356–60

Rapala-Normark Group, Ltd., 30 368–71

Rare Hospitality International Inc., 19 340–42

RAS *see* Riunione Adriatica di Sicurtà SpA.

Rascal House *see* Jerry's Famous Deli Inc.

Rasmussen Group *see* K.A. Rasmussen AS.

Rathbone Brothers plc, 70 250–53

RathGibson Inc., 90 348–51

ratiopharm Group, 84 322–326

Ratner Companies, 72 294–96

Rautakirja Oy, 104 388–92

Rautaruukki Oyj, 115 407–10

Raven Industries, Inc., 33 359–61

Ravensburger AG, 64 322–26

Raving Brands, Inc., 64 327–29

Rawlings Sporting Goods Company, 24 402–04; 107 368–72 (upd.)

Raychem Corporation, 8 446–47

Raycom Media, Inc., 106 399–402

Raymarine plc, 104 393–96

Raymond James Financial Inc., 69 308–10

Raymond Ltd., 77 351–54

Rayonier Inc., 24 405–07

Rayovac Corporation, 13 431–34; 39 336–40 (upd.) *see also* Spectrum Brands.

Raytech Corporation, 61 306–09

Raytheon Aircraft Holdings Inc., 46 354–57

Raytheon Company, II 85–87; 11 411–14 (upd.); 38 372–77 (upd.); 105 352–59 (upd.)

Razorfish, Inc., 37 321–24

RCA Corporation, II 88–90

RCM Technologies, Inc., 34 371–74

RCN Corporation, 70 254–57

RCS MediaGroup S.p.A., 96 343–46

RDO Equipment Company, 33 362–65

RE/MAX International, Inc., 59 344–46

Read-Rite Corp., 10 463–64

The Reader's Digest Association, Inc., IV 663–64; 17 392–95 (upd.); 71 295–99 (upd.)

Reading International Inc., 70 258–60

The Real Good Food Company plc, 99 358–361

Real Madrid C.F., 73 274–76

Real Times, Inc., 66 261–65

Real Turismo, S.A. de C.V., 50 373–75

The Really Useful Group, 26 393–95

RealNetworks, Inc., 53 280–82; 109 461–68 (upd.)

Realogy Corporation, 112 311–14

Reckitt Benckiser plc, II 566–67; 42 302–06 (upd.); 91 392–99 (upd.)

Reckson Associates Realty Corp., 47 329–31

Recordati Industria Chimica e Farmaceutica S.p.A., 105 360–64

Recording for the Blind & Dyslexic, 51 312–14

Recoton Corp., 15 381–83

Recovery Engineering, Inc., 25 392–94

Recreational Equipment, Inc., 18 444–47; 71 300–03 (upd.)

Recycled Paper Greetings, Inc., 21 426–28

Red Apple Group, Inc., 23 406–08

Red Bull GmbH, 60 252–54

Red Hat, Inc., 45 361–64

Red McCombs Automotive Group, 91 400–03

Red Robin Gourmet Burgers, Inc., 56 294–96

Red Roof Inns, Inc., 18 448–49 *see also* Accor S.A.

Red Spot Paint & Varnish Company, Inc., 55 319–22; 112 315–19 (upd.)

Red Wing Pottery Sales, Inc., 52 294–96

Red Wing Shoe Company, Inc., 9 433–35; 30 372–75 (upd.); 83 315–321 (upd.)

Redback Networks, Inc., 92 319–22

Redcats S.A., 102 348–52

Reddy Ice Holdings, Inc., 80 304–07

Redflex Holdings Limited, 116 415–18

Redhook Ale Brewery, Inc., 31 381–84; 88 317–21 (upd.)

Redken Laboratories Inc., 84 327–330

Redland plc, III 734–36 *see also* Lafarge Cement UK.

Redlon & Johnson, Inc., 97 331–34

Redner's Markets Inc., 111 419–22

RedPeg Marketing, 73 277–79

RedPrairie Corporation, 74 257–60

Redrow Group plc, 31 385–87

Reebok International Ltd., V 375–77; 9 436–38 (upd.); 26 396–400 (upd.)

Reed & Barton Corporation, 67 322–24

Reed Elsevier plc, 31 388–94 (upd.)

Reed International PLC, IV 665–67; 17 396–99 (upd.)

Reed's, Inc., 103 351–54

Reeds Jewelers, Inc., 22 447–49

Reesnik *see* Koninklijke Reesink N.V.

Regal-Beloit Corporation, 18 450–53; 97 335–42 (upd.)

Regal Entertainment Group, 59 340–43

The Regence Group, 74 261–63

Regency Centers Corporation, 71 304–07

Regent Communications, Inc., 87 416–420

Regent Inns plc, 95 354–57

Régie Nationale des Usines Renault, I 189–91 *see also* Renault S.A.

Regional Express Holdings Limited, 118 374–77

Regions Financial Corporation, 106 403–07

Regis Corporation, 18 454–56; 70 261–65 (upd.)

RehabCare Group, Inc., 114 348–52

REI *see* Recreational Equipment, Inc.

Reichhold, Inc., 10 465–67; 112 320–23 (upd.)

Reiter Dairy, LLC, 94 361–64

Reitmans (Canada) Limited, 111 423–26

Rejuvenation, Inc., 91 404–07

Related Companies, L.P., 112 324–328

Reliance Electric Company, 9 439–42

Reliance Group Holdings, Inc., III 342–44

Reliance Industries Ltd., 81 332–36

Reliance Steel & Aluminum Company, 19 343–45; 70 266–70 (upd.)

Reliant Energy Inc., 44 368–73 (upd.)

Reliv International, Inc., 58 292–95

Remedy Corporation, 58 296–99

RemedyTemp, Inc., 20 448–50

Remington Arms Company, Inc., 12 415–17; 40 368–71 (upd.)

Remington Products Company, L.L.C., 42 307–10

Remington Rand *see* Unisys Corp.

Rémy Cointreau Group, 20 451–53; 80 308–12 (upd.)

Renaissance Learning, Inc., 39 341–43; 100 367–72 (upd.)

Renal Care Group, Inc., 72 297–99

Renault Argentina S.A., 67 325–27

Renault S.A., 26 401–04 (upd.); 74 264–68 (upd.)

The Renco Group, Inc., 114 353–56

Renfro Corporation, 99 362–365

Rengo Co., Ltd., IV 326

Southern Indiana Gas and Electric Company, 13 487–89 *see also* Vectren Corp.

Southern New England Telecommunications Corporation, 6 338–40

Southern Pacific Transportation Company, V 516–18 *see also* Union Pacific Corp.

Southern Peru Copper Corporation, 40 411–13

Southern Poverty Law Center, Inc., 74 312–15

Southern Progress Corporation, 102 388–92

Southern States Cooperative Incorporated, 36 440–42

Southern Sun Hotel Interest (Pty) Ltd., 106 435–39

Southern Union Company, 27 424–26

Southern Wine and Spirits of America, Inc., 84 371–375

The Southland Corporation, II 660–61; 7 490–92 (upd.) *see also* 7–Eleven, Inc.

Southtrust Corporation, 11 455–57 *see also* Wachovia Corp.

Southwest Airlines Co., 6 119–21; 24 452–55 (upd.); 71 343–47 (upd.)

Southwest Gas Corporation, 19 410–12

Southwest Water Company, 47 370–73

Southwestern Bell Corporation, V 328–30 *see also* SBC Communications Inc.

Southwestern Electric Power Co., 21 468–70

Southwestern Public Service Company, 6 579–81

Southwire Company, Inc., 8 478–80; 23 444–47 (upd.)

Souza Cruz S.A., 65 322–24

Sovereign Bancorp, Inc., 103 392–95

Sovran Self Storage, Inc., 66 299–301

SP Alpargatas *see* Sao Paulo Alpargatas S.A.

Spacehab, Inc., 37 364–66

Spacelabs Medical, Inc., 71 348–50

Spadel S.A./NV, 113 363–67

Spaghetti Warehouse, Inc., 25 436–38

Spago *see* The Wolfgang Puck Food Company, Inc.

Spangler Candy Company, 44 392–95

Spanish Broadcasting System, Inc., 41 383–86

Spansion Inc., 80 352–55

Spanx, Inc., 89 423–27

Spar Aerospace Limited, 32 435–37

Spar Handelsgesellschaft mbH, 35 398–401; 103 396–400 (upd.)

Spark Networks, Inc., 91 437–40

Spartan Motors Inc., 14 457–59

Spartan Stores Inc., 8 481–82; 66 302–05 (upd.)

Spartech Corporation, 19 413–15; 76 329–32 (upd.)

Sparton Corporation, 18 492–95

Spear & Jackson, Inc., 73 320–23

Spear, Leeds & Kellogg, 66 306–09

Special Broadcasting Service Corporation, 115 433–36

Special Olympics, Inc., 93 410–14

Specialist Computer Holdings Ltd., 80 356–59

Specialized Bicycle Components Inc., 50 445–48

Specialty Coatings Inc., 8 483–84

Specialty Equipment Companies, Inc., 25 439–42

Specialty Products & Insulation Co., 59 381–83

Spec's Music, Inc., 19 416–18 *see also* Camelot Music, Inc.

Specsavers Optical Group Ltd., 104 428–31

Spector Photo Group N.V., 82 344–47

Spectra Energy Corporation, 116 451–54

Spectrum Brands, Inc., 109 514–20 (upd.)

Spectrum Control, Inc., 67 355–57

Spectrum Organic Products, Inc., 68 346–49

Spee-Dee Delivery Service, Inc., 93 415–18

SpeeDee Oil Change and Tune-Up, 25 443–47

Speedway Motorsports, Inc., 32 438–41; 112 396–400 (upd.)

Speedy Hire plc, 84 376–379

Speidel Inc., 96 404–07

Speizman Industries, Inc., 44 396–98

Spelling Entertainment, 14 460–62; 35 402–04 (upd.)

Spencer Stuart and Associates, Inc., 14 463–65 *see also* SSI (U.S.), Inc.

Sperian Protection S.A., 104 432–36

Spherion Corporation, 52 316–18

Spicy Pickle Franchising, Inc., 105 434–37

Spie *see* Amec Spie S.A.

Spiegel, Inc., 10 489–91; 27 427–31 (upd.)

SPIEGEL-Verlag Rudolf Augstein GmbH & Co. KG, 44 399–402

Spin Master, Ltd., 61 335–38

Spinnaker Exploration Company, 72 334–36

Spirax-Sarco Engineering plc, 59 384–86

Spirit Airlines, Inc., 31 419–21

Sport Chalet, Inc., 16 454–56; 94 402–06 (upd.)

Sport Supply Group, Inc., 23 448–50; 106 440–45 (upd.)

Sportif USA, Inc., 118 418–20

Sportmart, Inc., 15 469–71 *see also* Gart Sports Co.

Sports & Recreation, Inc., 17 453–55

The Sports Authority, Inc., 16 457–59; 43 385–88 (upd.)

The Sports Club Company, 25 448–51

The Sportsman's Guide, Inc., 36 443–46

Springs Global US, Inc., V 378–79; 19 419–22 (upd.); 90 378–83 (upd.)

Sprint Nextel Corporation, 9 478–80; 46 373–76 (upd.); 110 427–33 (upd.)

SPS Technologies, Inc., 30 428–30

SPSS Inc., 64 360–63

SPX Corporation, 10 492–95; 47 374–79 (upd.); 103 401–09 (upd.)

Spyglass Entertainment Group, LLC, 91 441–44

SQM *see* Sociedad Química y Minera de Chile S.A.

Square D, 90 384–89

Square Enix Holdings Co., Ltd., 101 454–57

Squibb Corporation, I 695–97 *see also* Bristol-Myers Squibb Co.

SR Teleperformance S.A., 86 365–68

SRA International, Inc., 77 400–03

SRAM Corporation, 65 325–27

SRC Holdings Corporation, 67 358–60

SRI International, Inc., 57 333–36

SSA *see* Stevedoring Services of America Inc.

SSAB Svenskt Stål AB, 89 428–31

Ssangyong Cement Industrial Co., Ltd., III 747–50; 61 339–43 (upd.)

SSI (U.S.), Inc., 103 410–14 (upd.)

SSL International plc, 49 378–81

SSOE Inc., 76 333–35

St Ives plc, 34 393–95

St. *see under* Saint

St. James's Place Capital, plc, 71 324–26

The St. Joe Company, 31 422–25; 98 368–73 (upd.)

St. Joe Paper Company, 8 485–88

St. John Knits, Inc., 14 466–68

St. Jude Medical, Inc., 11 458–61; 43 347–52 (upd.); 97 350–58 (upd.)

St. Louis Music, Inc., 48 351–54

St. Luke's-Roosevelt Hospital Center *see* Continuum Health Partners, Inc.

St. Mary Land & Exploration Company, 63 345–47

St. Paul Bank for Cooperatives, 8 489–90

The St. Paul Travelers Companies, Inc., III 355–57; 22 492–95 (upd.); 79 362–69 (upd.)

STAAR Surgical Company, 57 337–39

The Stabler Companies Inc., 78 352–55

Stafford Group, 110 434–38

Stage Stores, Inc., 24 456–59; 82 348–52 (upd.)

Stagecoach Group plc, 30 431–33; 104 437–41 (upd.)

Stalaven *see* Groupe Stalaven S.A.

Stanadyne Automotive Corporation, 37 367–70

StanCorp Financial Group, Inc., 56 345–48

Standard Candy Company Inc., 86 369–72

Standard Chartered plc, II 357–59; 48 371–74 (upd.); 117 397–402 (upd.)

Standard Commercial Corporation, 13 490–92; 62 333–37 (upd.)

Standard Federal Bank, 9 481–83

Thermo Fisher Scientific Inc., 105
443–54 (upd.)

Thermo Instrument Systems Inc., 11
512–14

Thermo King Corporation, 13 505–07
see also Ingersoll-Rand Company Ltd.

Thermos Company, 16 486–88

Thermotech, 113 414–17

Things Remembered, Inc., 84 398–401

Thiokol Corporation, 9 500–02 (upd.);
22 504–07 (upd.)

Thistle Hotels PLC, 54 366–69

Thomas & Betts Corporation, 11
515–17; 54 370–74 (upd.); 114
442–48 (upd.)

Thomas & Howard Company, Inc., 90
409–12

Thomas Cook Travel Inc., 9 503–05; 33
394–96 (upd.)

Thomas Crosbie Holdings Limited, 81
384–87

Thomas H. Lee Co., 24 480–83

Thomas Industries Inc., 29 466–69

Thomas J. Lipton Company, 14 495–97

Thomas Nelson Inc., 14 498–99; 38
454–57 (upd.)

Thomas Publishing Company, 26
482–85

Thomaston Mills, Inc., 27 467–70

Thomasville Furniture Industries, Inc.,
12 474–76; 74 339–42 (upd.)

Thomsen Greenhouses and Garden
Center, Incorporated, 65 338–40

The Thomson Corporation, 8 525–28;
34 435–40 (upd.); 77 433–39 (upd.)

THOMSON multimedia S.A., II
116–17; 42 377–80 (upd.)

Thor Equities, LLC, 108 487–90

Thor Industries Inc., 39 391–94; 92
365–370 (upd.)

Thorn Apple Valley, Inc., 7 523–25; 22
508–11 (upd.)

Thorn EMI plc, I 531–32 *see also* EMI
plc; Thorn plc.

Thorn plc, 24 484–87

Thorntons plc, 46 424–26

Thos. Moser Cabinetmakers Inc., 117
403–06

ThoughtWorks Inc., 90 413–16

Thousand Trails Inc., 33 397–99; 113
418–22 (upd.)

THQ, Inc., 39 395–97; 92 371–375
(upd.)

Threadless.com *see* skinnyCorp, LLC.

365 Media Group plc, 89 441–44

3Com Corporation, 11 518–21; 34
441–45 (upd.); 106 465–72 (upd.)

The 3DO Company, 43 426–30

3i Group PLC, 73 338–40

3M Company, 61 365–70 (upd.)

Thrifty PayLess, Inc., 12 477–79 *see also*
Rite Aid Corp.

Thrivent Financial for Lutherans, 111
452–59 (upd.)

Thumann Inc., 104 442–45

ThyssenKrupp AG, IV 221–23; 28
452–60 (upd.); 87 425–438 (upd.)

TI Group plc, 17 480–83

TIAA-CREF *see* Teachers Insurance and
Annuity Association-College Retirement
Equities Fund.

Tianjin Flying Pigeon Bicycle Co., Ltd.,
95 421–24

Tibbett & Britten Group plc, 32
449–52

TIBCO Software Inc., 79 411–14

TIC Holdings Inc., 92 376–379

Ticketmaster, 13 508–10; 37 381–84
(upd.); 76 349–53 (upd.)

Tidewater Inc., 11 522–24; 37 385–88
(upd.)

Tieto Oyj, 117 407–11

Tiffany & Co., 14 500–03; 78 396–401
(upd.)

TIG Holdings, Inc., 26 486–88

Tiger Aspect Productions Ltd., 72
348–50

Tiger Brands Limited, 112 420–24

Tigre S.A. Tubos e Conexões, 104
446–49

Tilcon-Connecticut Inc., 80 373–76

Tilia Inc., 62 363–65

Tillamook County Creamery
Association, 111 460–63

Tilley Endurables, Inc., 67 364–66

Tillotson Corp., 15 488–90

TIM *see* Telecom Italia Mobile S.p.A.

Tim-Bar Corporation, 110 459–62

Tim Hortons Inc., 109 543–47 (upd.)

Timber Lodge Steakhouse, Inc., 73
341–43

The Timberland Company, 13 511–14;
54 375–79 (upd.); 111 464–70 (upd.)

Timberline Software Corporation, 15
491–93

TimberWest Forest Corp., 114 449–52

Time Out Group Ltd., 68 371–73

Time Warner Inc., IV 673–76; 7 526–30
(upd.) ; 109 548–58 (upd.)

The Times Mirror Company, IV
677–78; 17 484–86 (upd.) *see also*
Tribune Co.

TIMET *see* Titanium Metals Corp.

Timex Group B.V., 7 531–33; 25
479–82 (upd.); 111 471–77 (upd.)

The Timken Company, 8 529–31; 42
381–85 (upd.); 113 423–28 (upd.)

Tipiak S.A., 113 429–33

Tiscali SpA, 48 396–99

TISCO *see* Tata Iron & Steel Company
Ltd.

Tishman Construction Company, 112
425–28 (upd.)

Tishman Speyer Properties, L.P., 47
403–06; 112 429–34

Tissue Technologies, Inc. *see* Palomar
Medical Technologies, Inc.

Titan Cement Company S.A., 64
379–81

The Titan Corporation, 36 475–78

Titan International, Inc., 89 445–49

Titan Machinery Inc., 103 446–49

Titanium Metals Corporation, 21
489–92

TiVo Inc., 75 373–75

TJ International, Inc., 19 444–47

The TJX Companies, Inc., V 197–98;
19 448–50 (upd.); 57 366–69 (upd.)

TLC Beatrice International Holdings,
Inc., 22 512–15

TMP Worldwide Inc., 30 458–60 *see also*
Monster Worldwide Inc.

TNT Freightways Corporation, 14
504–06

TNT Limited, V 523–25

TNT Post Group N.V., 27 471–76
(upd.); 30 461–63 (upd.) *see also* TPG
N.V.

Tnuva Food Industries Ltd., 111
478–81

Tobu Railway Company Ltd., 6 430–32;
98 404–08 (upd.)

Today's Man, Inc., 20 484–87

TODCO, 87 439–442

The Todd-AO Corporation, 33 400–04
see also Liberty Livewire Corp.

Todd Shipyards Corporation, 14
507–09

Todhunter International, Inc., 27
477–79

Tofutti Brands, Inc., 64 382–84

Tohan Corporation, 84 402–405

Toho Co., Ltd., 28 461–63

Tohoku Electric Power Company, Inc.,
V 726–28

The Tokai Bank, Limited, II 373–74; 15
494–96 (upd.)

Tokheim Corporation, 21 493–95

Tokio Marine and Fire Insurance Co.,
Ltd., III 383–86 *see also* Millea
Holdings Inc.

Tokyo Dome Corporation, 118 445–48

Tokyo Electric Power Company, V
729–33; 74 343–48 (upd.)

Tokyo Gas Co., Ltd., V 734–36; 55
372–75 (upd.)

TOKYOPOP Inc., 79 415–18

Tokyu Corporation, V 526–28; 47
407–10 (upd.)

Tokyu Department Store Co., Ltd., V
199–202; 32 453–57 (upd.); 107
434–40 (upd.)

Tokyu Land Corporation, IV 728–29

Tolko Industries Ltd., 114 453–56

Toll Brothers Inc., 15 497–99; 70
323–26 (upd.)

Tollgrade Communications, Inc., 44
424–27

Tom Brown, Inc., 37 389–91

Tom Doherty Associates Inc., 25
483–86

Tombstone Pizza Corporation, 13
515–17 *see also* Kraft Foods Inc.

Tomen Corporation, IV 224–25; 24
488–91 (upd.)

Tomkins plc, 11 525–27; 44 428–31
(upd.)

Tommy Bahama Group, Inc., 108
491–95

Tommy Hilfiger Corporation, 20
488–90; 53 330–33 (upd.)

Tomra Systems ASA, 103 450–54

Tom's Foods Inc., 66 325–27

Tom's of Maine, Inc., 45 414–16

Třinecké Železárny A.S., 92 384–87
Trinity Industries, Incorporated, 7 540–41
Trinity Mirror plc, 49 404–10 (upd.)
TRINOVA Corporation, III 640–42
TriPath Imaging, Inc., 77 446–49
Triple Five Group Ltd., 49 411–15
Triple P N.V., 26 496–99
Tripwire, Inc., 97 433–36
TriQuint Semiconductor, Inc., 63 396–99
Trisko Jewelry Sculptures, Ltd., 57 388–90
Triton Energy Corporation, 11 537–39
Triumph-Adler see TA Triumph-Adler AG.
Triumph Group, Inc., 31 446–48
Triumph Motorcycles Ltd., 53 334–37
Trizec Corporation Ltd., 10 529–32
The TriZetto Group, Inc., 83 416–419
TRM Copy Centers Corporation, 18 526–28 see also Access to Money, Inc.
Tropicana Products, Inc., 28 473–77; 73 344–49 (upd.)
Troutman Sanders L.L.P., 79 427–30
True North Communications Inc., 23 478–80 see also Foote, Cone & Belding Worldwide.
True Religion Apparel, Inc., 79 431–34
True Temper Sports, Inc., 95 429–32
True Value Company, 74 353–57 (upd.)
TruFoods LLC, 114 457–60
Truman Arnold Companies, Inc., 114 461–64
Trump Organization, 23 481–84; 64 392–97 (upd.)
TRUMPF GmbH + Co. KG, 86 397–02
TruServ Corporation, 24 504–07 see True Value Co.
Trusthouse Forte PLC, III 104–06
Trustmark Corporation, 106 473–76
Truworths International Ltd., 107 451–54
TRW Automotive Holdings Corp., I 539–41; 11 540–42 (upd.); 14 510–13 (upd.); 75 376–82 (upd.)
TSA see Transaction Systems Architects, Inc.
Tsakos Energy Navigation Ltd., 91 483–86
TSB Group plc, 12 491–93
TSC see Tractor Supply Co.
Tsingtao Brewery Group, 49 416–20
TSMC see Taiwan Semiconductor Manufacturing Company Ltd.
TSYS see Total System Services, Inc.
TT electronics plc, 111 482–86
TTL see Taiwan Tobacco & Liquor Corp.
TTX Company, 6 436–37; 66 328–30 (upd.)
Tubby's, Inc., 53 338–40
Tubos de Acero de Mexico, S.A. (TAMSA), 41 404–06
Tucows Inc., 78 411–14
Tucson Electric Power Company, 6 588–91
Tuesday Morning Corporation, 18 529–31; 70 331–33 (upd.)

TUF see Thai Union Frozen Products PCL.
TUI see Touristik Union International GmbH. and Company K.G.
TUI Group GmbH, 42 283; 44 432–35
Tulikivi Corporation, 114 265–69
Tulip Ltd., 89 454–57
Tullow Oil plc, 83 420–423
Tully Construction Co. Inc., 114 470–73
Tully's Coffee Corporation, 51 384–86
Tultex Corporation, 13 531–33
Tumaro's Gourmet Tortillas, 85 430–33
Tumbleweed, Inc., 33 412–14; 80 377–81 (upd.)
Tumi, Inc., 112 439–42
Tunisair see Société Tunisienne de l'Air-Tunisair.
Tupolev Aviation and Scientific Technical Complex, 24 58–60
Tupperware Brands Corporation, 28 478–81; 78 415–20 (upd.)
Tupy S.A., 111 487–90
TurboChef Technologies, Inc., 83 424–427
Turbomeca S.A., 102 430–34
Turkish Airlines Inc. (Türk Hava Yollari A.O.), 72 351–53
Turkiye Is Bankasi A.S., 61 377–80
Türkiye Petrolleri Anonim Ortakliği, IV 562–64
Turner Broadcasting System, Inc., II 166–68; 6 171–73 (upd.); 66 331–34 (upd.)
Turner Construction Company, 66 335–38
The Turner Corporation, 8 538–40; 23 485–88 (upd.)
Turtle Wax, Inc., 15 506–09; 93 465–70 (upd.)
Tuscarora Inc., 29 483–85
The Tussauds Group, 55 376–78
Tutogen Medical, Inc., 68 378–80
Tuttle Publishing, 86 403–06
TV Azteca, S.A. de C.V., 39 398–401
TV Guide, Inc., 43 431–34 (upd.)
TVA see Tennessee Valley Authority.
TVE see Television Española, S.A.
TVI, Inc., 15 510–12; 99 462–465 see also Savers, Inc.
TW Services, Inc., II 679–80
TWA see Trans World Airlines.
TWC see The Weather Channel Cos.
Tweeter Home Entertainment Group, Inc., 30 464–66
Twentieth Century Fox Film Corporation, II 169–71; 25 490–94 (upd.)
24 Hour Fitness Worldwide, Inc., 71 363–65
24/7 Real Media, Inc., 49 421–24
Twin Disc, Inc., 21 502–04
Twinlab Corporation, 34 458–61
Twitter, Inc., 118 460–63
Ty Inc., 33 415–17; 86 407–11 (upd.)
Tyco International Ltd., III 643–46; 28 482–87 (upd.); 63 400–06 (upd.)

Tyco Toys, Inc., 12 494–97 see also Mattel, Inc.
Tyler Corporation, 23 489–91
The Tyler Perry Company, Inc., 111 491–95
Tyndale House Publishers, Inc., 57 391–94
Tyson Foods, Inc., II 584–85; 14 514–16 (upd.); 50 491–95 (upd.); 114 474–81 (upd.)

U

U.S. see also US.
U.S. Aggregates, Inc., 42 390–92
U.S. Army Corps of Engineers, 91 491–95
U.S. Bancorp, 14 527–29; 36 489–95 (upd.); 103 465–75 (upd.)
U.S. Borax, Inc., 42 393–96
U.S. Can Corporation, 30 474–76
U.S. Cellular Corporation, 31 449–52 (upd.); 88 408–13 (upd.)
U.S. Delivery Systems, Inc., 22 531–33 see also Velocity Express Corp.
U.S. Foodservice, 26 503–06
U.S. Healthcare, Inc., 6 194–96
U.S. Home Corporation, 8 541–43; 78 421–26 (upd.)
U.S. Music Corporation, 108 501–05
U.S. News & World Report Inc., 30 477–80; 89 458–63 (upd.)
U.S. Office Products Company, 25 500–02
U.S. Physical Therapy, Inc., 65 345–48
U.S. Premium Beef LLC, 91 487–90
U.S. Robotics Corporation, 9 514–15; 66 339–41 (upd.)
U.S. Satellite Broadcasting Company, Inc., 20 505–07 see also DIRECTV, Inc.
U.S. Silica Company, 104 455–58
U.S. Steel Corp see United States Steel Corp.
U.S. Timberlands Company, L.P., 42 397–400
U.S. Trust Corp., 17 496–98
U.S. Vision, Inc., 66 342–45
U S West, Inc., V 341–43; 25 495–99 (upd.)
UAB Koncernas MG Baltic, 117 418–22
UAL Corporation, 34 462–65 (upd.); 107 455–60 (upd.)
UAP see Union des Assurances de Paris.
UAW (International Union, United Automobile, Aerospace and Agricultural Implement Workers of America), 72 354–57
Ube Industries, Ltd., III 759–61; 38 463–67 (upd.); 111 496–502 (upd.)
Ubisoft Entertainment S.A., 41 407–09; 106 477–80 (upd.)
UBS AG, 52 352–59 (upd.)
UCB Pharma SA, 98 409–12
UFA TV & Film Produktion GmbH, 80 382–87
UGI Corporation, 12 498–500
Ugine S.A., 20 498–500

Wawa Inc., 17 535–37; 78 449–52 (upd.)
The Wawanesa Mutual Insurance Company, 68 399–401
WAXIE Sanitary Supply, 100 447–51
Waxman Industries, Inc., 9 542–44
WAZ Media Group, 82 419–24
WB *see* Warner Communications Inc.
WD-40 Company, 18 554–57; 87 455–460 (upd.)
We-No-Nah Canoe, Inc., 98 460–63
WE: Women's Entertainment LLC, 114 506–10
Weather Central Inc., 100 452–55
The Weather Channel Companies, 52 401–04 *see also* Landmark Communications, Inc.
Weather Shield Manufacturing, Inc., 102 444–47
Weatherford International, Inc., 39 416–18
Weaver Popcorn Company, Inc., 89 491–93
Webasto Roof Systems Inc., 97 449–52
Webber Oil Company, 61 384–86
Weber et Broutin France, 66 363–65
Weber-Stephen Products Co., 40 458–60
WebEx Communications, Inc., 81 419–23
WebMD Corporation, 65 357–60
Webster Financial Corporation, 106 486–89
Weeres Industries Corporation, 52 405–07
Weetabix Limited, 61 387–89
Weg S.A., 78 453–56
Wegener NV, 53 360–62
Wegmans Food Markets, Inc., 9 545–46; 41 416–18 (upd.); 105 488–92 (upd.)
Weider Nutrition International, Inc., 29 498–501
Weight Watchers International Inc., 12 530–32; 33 446–49 (upd.); 73 379–83 (upd.)
Weil, Gotshal & Manges LLP, 55 385–87
Weiner's Stores, Inc., 33 450–53
Weingarten Realty Investors, 95 442–45
The Weinstein Company LLC, 118 473–76
The Weir Group PLC, 85 450–53
Weirton Steel Corporation, IV 236–38; 26 527–30 (upd.)
Weis Markets, Inc., 15 531–33; 84 422–426 (upd.)
The Weitz Company, Inc., 42 431–34
Welbilt Corp., 19 492–94; *see also* Enodis plc.
Welch Foods Inc., 104 470–73
Welcome Wagon International Inc., 82 425–28
Weleda AG, 78 457–61
The Welk Group, Inc., 78 462–66
Wella AG, III 68–70; 48 420–23 (upd.)
WellCare Health Plans, Inc., 101 487–90

WellChoice, Inc., 67 388–91 (upd.)
Wellco Enterprises, Inc., 84 427–430
Wellcome Foundation Ltd., I 713–15 *see also* GlaxoSmithKline plc.
Wellman, Inc., 8 561–62; 52 408–11 (upd.)
WellPoint, Inc., 25 525–29; 103 505–14 (upd.)
Wells' Dairy, Inc., 36 511–13
Wells Fargo & Company, II 380–84; 12 533–37 (upd.); 38 483–92 (upd.); 97 453–67
Wells-Gardner Electronics Corporation, 43 458–61
Wells Rich Greene BDDP, 6 50–52
Welsh Rugby Union Limited, 115 484–87
Wendell *see* Mark T. Wendell Tea Co.
Wendy's/Arby's Group, Inc., 8 563–65; 23 504–07 (upd.); 47 439–44 (upd.); 118 477–83 (upd.)
Wenner Bread Products Inc., 80 411–15
Wenner Media, Inc., 32 506–09
Werhahn *see* Wilh. Werhahn KG.
Werner Enterprises, Inc., 26 531–33
Weru Aktiengesellschaft, 18 558–61
WESCO International, Inc., 116 459–62
Wesfarmers Limited, 109 591–95
Wessanen *see* Koninklijke Wessanen nv.
West Bend Co., 14 546–48
West Coast Entertainment Corporation, 29 502–04
West Corporation, 42 435–37
West Fraser Timber Co. Ltd., 17 538–40; 91 512–18 (upd.)
West Group, 34 502–06 (upd.)
West Linn Paper Company, 91 519–22
West Marine, Inc., 17 541–43; 90 438–42 (upd.)
West One Bancorp, 11 552–55 *see also* U.S. Bancorp.
West Pharmaceutical Services, Inc., 42 438–41
West Point-Pepperell, Inc., 8 566–69 *see also* WestPoint Stevens Inc.; JPS Textile Group, Inc.
West Publishing Co., 7 579–81
Westaff Inc., 33 454–57
Westamerica Bancorporation, 17 544–47
Westar Energy, Inc., 57 404–07 (upd.)
WestCoast Hospitality Corporation, 59 410–13
Westcon Group, Inc., 67 392–94
Westdeutsche Landesbank Girozentrale, II 385–87; 46 458–61 (upd.)
Westell Technologies, Inc., 57 408–10
Western Atlas Inc., 12 538–40
Western Beef, Inc., 22 548–50
Western Company of North America, 15 534–36
Western Digital Corporation, 25 530–32; 92 411–15 (upd.)
Western Gas Resources, Inc., 45 435–37
Western Oil Sands Inc., 85 454–57
Western Publishing Group, Inc., 13 559–61 *see also* Thomson Corp.

Western Refining Inc., 109 596–99
Western Resources, Inc., 12 541–43
The WesterN SizzliN Corporation, 60 335–37
Western Union Company, 54 413–16; 112 492–96 (upd.)
Western Wireless Corporation, 36 514–16
Westfield Group, 69 366–69
Westin Hotels and Resorts Worldwide, 9 547–49; 29 505–08 (upd.)
Westinghouse Air Brake Technologies Corporation, 116 463–66
Westinghouse Electric Corporation, II 120–22; 12 544–47 (upd.) *see also* CBS Radio Group.
WestJet Airlines Ltd., 38 493–95; 115 488–92 (upd.)
Westmoreland Coal Company, 7 582–85
Weston Foods Inc. *see* George Weston Ltd.
Westpac Banking Corporation, II 388–90; 48 424–27 (upd.); 118 484–89 (upd.)
WestPoint Stevens Inc., 16 533–36 *see also* JPS Textile Group, Inc.
Westport Resources Corporation, 63 439–41
Westvaco Corporation, IV 351–54; 19 495–99 (upd.) *see also* MeadWestvaco Corp.
Westwood One Inc., 23 508–11; 106 490–96 (upd.)
The Wet Seal, Inc., 18 562–64; 70 353–57 (upd.)
Wetterau Incorporated, II 681–82 *see also* Supervalu Inc.
Weyco Group, Incorporated, 32 510–13
Weyerhaeuser Company, IV 355–56; 9 550–52 (upd.); 28 514–17 (upd.); 83 454–461 (upd.)
WFS Financial Inc., 70 358–60
WFSC *see* World Fuel Services Corp.
WGBH Educational Foundation, 66 366–68
WH Smith PLC, 42 442–47 (upd.)
Wham-O, Inc., 61 390–93
Whataburger Restaurants LP, 105 493–97
Whatman plc, 46 462–65
Wheaton Industries, 8 570–73
Wheaton Science Products, 60 338–42 (upd.)
Wheelabrator Technologies, Inc., 6 599–600; 60 343–45 (upd.)
Wheeling-Pittsburgh Corporation, 7 586–88; 58 360–64 (upd.)
Wheels Inc., 96 458–61
Wherehouse Entertainment Incorporated, 11 556–58
Which? Ltd. *see* Consumers' Association
Whirlpool Corporation, III 653–55; 12 548–50 (upd.); 59 414–19 (upd.)
Whitbread PLC, I 293–94; 20 519–22 (upd.); 52 412–17 (upd.); 97 468–76 (upd.)
White & Case LLP, 35 466–69

Index to Industries

Accounting

American Institute of Certified Public
    Accountants (AICPA), 44
Andersen, 29 (upd.); 68 (upd.)
Automatic Data Processing, Inc., III; 9
    (upd.); 47 (upd.)
BDO Seidman LLP, 96
BKD LLP, 96
CPP International, LLC, 103
CROSSMARK, 79
Deloitte Touche Tohmatsu International,
    9; 29 (upd.)
Ernst & Young Global Limited, 9; 29
    (upd.); 108 (upd.)
FTI Consulting, Inc., 77
Grant Thornton International, 57
Huron Consulting Group Inc., 87
JKH Holding Co. LLC, 105
KPMG International, 33 (upd.); 108
    (upd.)
L.S. Starrett Co., 13
LarsonAllen, LLP, 118
McLane Company, Inc., 13
NCO Group, Inc., 42
Paychex, Inc., 15; 46 (upd.)
PKF International, 78
Plante & Moran, LLP, 71
PRG-Schultz International, Inc., 73
PricewaterhouseCoopers International
    Limited, 9; 29 (upd.); 111 (upd.)
Resources Connection, Inc., 81
Robert Wood Johnson Foundation, 35
RSM McGladrey Business Services Inc.,
    98
Saffery Champness, 80
Sanders\Wingo, 99
Schenck Business Solutions, 88
StarTek, Inc., 79

Travelzoo Inc., 79
Univision Communications Inc., 24; 83
    (upd.)

Advertising & Business Services

ABM Industries Incorporated, 25 (upd.)
Abt Associates Inc., 95
Accenture Ltd., 108 (upd.)
AchieveGlobal Inc., 90
Ackerley Communications, Inc., 9
ACNielsen Corporation, 13; 38 (upd.)
Acosta Sales and Marketing Company,
    Inc., 77
Acsys, Inc., 44
Adecco S.A., 36 (upd.); 116 (upd.)
Adelman Travel Group, 105
Adia S.A., 6
Administaff, Inc., 52
The Advertising Council, Inc., 76
The Advisory Board Company, 80
Advo, Inc., 6; 53 (upd.)
Aegis Group plc, 6
Affiliated Computer Services, Inc., 61
AHL Services, Inc., 27
Allegis Group, Inc., 95
Alloy, Inc., 55
Amdocs Ltd., 47
American Building Maintenance
    Industries, Inc., 6
Amey Plc, 47
Analysts International Corporation, 36
aQuantive, Inc., 81
The Arbitron Company, 38
Ariba, Inc., 57
Armor Holdings, Inc., 27
Asatsu-DK Inc., 82
Ashtead Group plc, 34

Avalon Correctional Services, Inc., 75
Bain & Company, 55
Barrett Business Services, Inc., 16
Barton Protective Services Inc., 53
Bates Worldwide, Inc., 14; 33 (upd.)
Bearings, Inc., 13
Berlitz International, Inc., 13; 39 (upd.)
Bernard Hodes Group Inc., 86
Bernstein-Rein, 92
Big Flower Press Holdings, Inc., 21
Billing Concepts, Inc., 26; 72 (upd.)
Billing Services Group Ltd., 102
The BISYS Group, Inc., 73
Booz Allen Hamilton Inc., 10; 101 (upd.)
Boron, LePore & Associates, Inc., 45
The Boston Consulting Group, 58
BrandPartners Group, Inc., 58
Bright Horizons Family Solutions, Inc., 31
Broadcast Music Inc., 23; 90 (upd.)
Bronner Display & Sign Advertising, Inc.,
    82
Buck Consultants, Inc., 55
Bureau Veritas SA, 55
Burke, Inc., 88
Burns International Services Corporation,
    13; 41 (upd.)
Cambridge Technology Partners, Inc., 36
Campbell-Ewald Advertising, 86
Campbell-Mithun-Esty, Inc., 16
Cannon Design, 63
Capario, 104
Capita Group PLC, 69
Cardtronics, Inc., 93
Carmichael Lynch Inc., 28
Cash Systems, Inc., 93
Cazenove Group plc, 72
CCC Information Services Group Inc., 74
CDI Corporation, 6; 54 (upd.)

Aerospace

Automotive

Bio-Technology

Chemicals

Conglomerates

Construction

Viatech Continental Can Company, Inc., 25 (upd.)
Vidrala S.A., 67
Vitro Corporativo S.A. de C.V., 34

Drugs & Pharmaceuticals

A.L. Pharma Inc., 12
A. Nelson & Co. Ltd., 75
Abbott Laboratories, I; 11 (upd.); 40 (upd.); 93 (upd.)
Aché Laboratórios Farmacéuticas S.A., 105
Actavis Group hf., 103
Actelion Ltd., 83
Adolor Corporation, 101
Akorn, Inc., 32
Albany Molecular Research, Inc., 77
Alfresa Holdings Corporation, 108
Allergan, Inc., 77 (upd.)
Alpharma Inc., 35 (upd.)
ALZA Corporation, 10; 36 (upd.)
American Home Products, I; 10 (upd.)
American Oriental Bioengineering Inc., 93
American Pharmaceutical Partners, Inc., 69
AmerisourceBergen Corporation, 64 (upd.)
Amersham PLC, 50
Amgen, Inc., 10; 89 (upd.)
Amylin Pharmaceuticals, Inc., 67
Andrx Corporation, 55
Angelini SpA, 100
Aspen Pharmacare Holdings Limited, 112
Astellas Pharma Inc., 97 (upd.)
AstraZeneca PLC, I; 20 (upd.); 50 (upd.)
AtheroGenics Inc., 101
Axcan Pharma Inc., 85
Barr Pharmaceuticals, Inc., 26; 68 (upd.)
Bayer AG, I; 13 (upd.); 41 (upd.); 118 (upd.)
Berlex Laboratories, Inc., 66
Biovail Corporation, 47
Block Drug Company, Inc., 8
Boiron S.A., 73
Bristol-Myers Squibb Company, III; 9 (upd.); 37 (upd.); 111 (upd.)
BTG Plc, 87
C.H. Boehringer Sohn, 39
Cahill May Roberts Group Ltd., 112
Caremark Rx, Inc., 10; 54 (upd.)
Carter-Wallace, Inc., 8; 38 (upd.)
Celgene Corporation, 67
Cephalon Technology, Inc, 45; 115 (upd.)
Chiron Corporation, 10
Chugai Pharmaceutical Co., Ltd., 50
Ciba-Geigy Ltd., I; 8 (upd.)
CSL Limited, 112
D&K Wholesale Drug, Inc., 14
Discovery Partners International, Inc., 58
Dr. Reddy's Laboratories Ltd., 59
Egis Gyogyszergyar Nyrt, 104
Eisai Co., Ltd., 101
Elan Corporation PLC, 63
Eli Lilly and Company, I; 11 (upd.); 47 (upd.); 109 (upd.)
Endo Pharmaceuticals Holdings Inc., 71
Eon Labs, Inc., 67
Express Scripts Inc., 44 (upd.)
F. Hoffmann-La Roche Ltd., I; 50 (upd.)

Fisons plc, 9; 23 (upd.)
Forest Laboratories, Inc., 52 (upd.); 114 (upd.)
FoxMeyer Health Corporation, 16
Fujisawa Pharmaceutical Company, Ltd., I; 58 (upd.)
G.D. Searle & Co., I; 12 (upd.); 34 (upd.)
Galenica AG, 84
GEHE AG, 27
Genentech, Inc., I; 8 (upd.); 75 (upd.)
Genetics Institute, Inc., 8
Genzyme Corporation, 13, 77 (upd.)
Glaxo Holdings PLC, I; 9 (upd.)
GlaxoSmithKline plc, 46 (upd.)
Groupe Fournier SA, 44
Groupe Léa Nature, 88
H. Lundbeck A/S, 44
Hauser, Inc., 46
Heska Corporation, 39
Hexal AG, 69
Hikma Pharmaceuticals Ltd., 102
Hospira, Inc., 71
Huntingdon Life Sciences Group plc, 42
ICN Pharmaceuticals, Inc., 52
ICU Medical, Inc., 106
Immucor, Inc., 81
Integrated BioPharma, Inc., 83
IVAX Corporation, 55 (upd.)
Janssen Pharmaceutica N.V., 80
Johnson & Johnson, III; 8 (upd.)
Jones Medical Industries, Inc., 24
Judge Group, Inc., The, 51
King Pharmaceuticals, Inc., 54
Kinray Inc., 85
Kos Pharmaceuticals, Inc., 63
Kyowa Hakko Kogyo Co., Ltd., 48 (upd.)
Laboratoires Arkopharma S.A., 75
Laboratoires Pierre Fabre S.A., 100
Leiner Health Products Inc., 34
Ligand Pharmaceuticals Incorporated, 47
MannKind Corporation, 87
Marion Merrell Dow, Inc., I; 9 (upd.)
Matrixx Initiatives, Inc., 74
McKesson Corporation, 12; 47 (upd.)
Medco Health Solutions, Inc., 116
Medicis Pharmaceutical Corporation, 59
MedImmune, Inc., 35
Merck & Co., Inc., I; 11 (upd.); 34 (upd.); 95 (upd.)
Merck KGaA, 111
Merial Ltd., 102
Merz Group, 81
Miles Laboratories, I
Millennium Pharmaceuticals, Inc., 47
Monsanto Company, 29 (upd.), 77 (upd.)
Moore Medical Corp., 17
Murdock Madaus Schwabe, 26
Mylan Laboratories Inc., I; 20 (upd.); 59 (upd.)
Myriad Genetics, Inc., 95
Nadro S.A. de C.V., 86
Nastech Pharmaceutical Company Inc., 79
National Patent Development Corporation, 13
Natrol, Inc., 49
Natural Alternatives International, Inc., 49
Nektar Therapeutics, 91

Novartis AG, 39 (upd.); 105 (upd.)
Noven Pharmaceuticals, Inc., 55
Novo Nordisk A/S, I; 61 (upd.)
Obagi Medical Products, Inc., 95
Omnicare, Inc., 49
Omrix Biopharmaceuticals, Inc., 95
Onyx Pharmaceuticals, Inc., 110
Par Pharmaceutical Companies, Inc., 65
PDL BioPharma, Inc., 90
Perrigo Company, 12; 59 (upd.); 118 (upd.)
Pfizer Inc., I; 9 (upd.); 38 (upd.); 79 (upd.)
Pharmacia & Upjohn Inc., I; 25 (upd.)
Pharmion Corporation, 91
PLIVA d.d., 70
PolyMedica Corporation, 77
POZEN Inc., 81
QLT Inc., 71
Quigley Corporation, The, 62
Quintiles Transnational Corporation, 21
R.P. Scherer, I
Ranbaxy Laboratories Ltd., 70
ratiopharm Group, 84
Reckitt Benckiser plc, II; 42 (upd.); 91 (upd.)
Recordati Industria Chimica e Farmaceutica S.p.A., 105
Roberts Pharmaceutical Corporation, 16
Roche Bioscience, 14 (upd.)
Roche Holding AG, 109
Rorer Group, I
Roussel Uclaf, I; 8 (upd.)
Salix Pharmaceuticals, Ltd., 93
Sandoz Ltd., I
Sankyo Company, Ltd., I; 56 (upd.)
Sanofi-Synthélabo Group, The, I; 49 (upd.)
Santarus, Inc., 105
Schering AG, I; 50 (upd.)
Schering-Plough Corporation, I; 14 (upd.); 49 (upd.); 99 (upd.)
Sepracor Inc., 45; 117 (upd.)
Serono S.A., 47
Shionogi & Co., Ltd., III; 17 (upd.); 98 (upd.)
Shire PLC, 109
Sigma-Aldrich Corporation, I; 36 (upd.); 93 (upd.)
SmithKline Beecham plc, I; 32 (upd.)
Solvay S.A., 61 (upd.)
Squibb Corporation, I
Sterling Drug, Inc., I
Stiefel Laboratories, Inc., 90
Sun Pharmaceutical Industries Ltd., 57
Sunrider Corporation, The, 26
Syntex Corporation, I
Takeda Pharmaceutical Company Limited, I; 115 (upd.)
Taro Pharmaceutical Industries Ltd., 65
Teva Pharmaceutical Industries Ltd., 22; 54 (upd.); 112 (upd.)
UCB Pharma SA, 98
Upjohn Company, The, I; 8 (upd.)
Vertex Pharmaceuticals Incorporated, 83
Virbac Corporation, 74
Vitacost.com Inc., 116
Vitalink Pharmacy Services, Inc., 15

Education & Training

Electrical & Electronics

Lynch Corporation, 43
Mackie Designs Inc., 33
MagneTek, Inc., 15; 41 (upd.)
Magneti Marelli Holding SpA, 90
Marconi plc, 33 (upd.)
Marquette Electronics, Inc., 13
Marshall Amplification plc, 62
Marvell Technology Group Ltd., 112
Matsushita Electric Industrial Co., Ltd.,
    II; 64 (upd.)
Maxim Integrated Products, Inc., 16
McDATA Corporation, 75
Measurement Specialties, Inc., 71
Medis Technologies Ltd., 77
MEMC Electronic Materials, Inc., 81
Merix Corporation, 36; 75 (upd.)
Methode Electronics, Inc., 13
Micrel, Incorporated, 77
Midway Games, Inc., 25; 102 (upd.)
Mitel Corporation, 18
MITRE Corporation, 26
Mitsubishi Electric Corporation, II; 44
    (upd.); 117 (upd.)
Molex Incorporated, 11; 54 (upd.)
Monster Cable Products, Inc., 69
Motorola, Inc., II; 11 (upd.); 34 (upd.);
    93 (upd.)
N.F. Smith & Associates LP, 70
Nam Tai Electronics, Inc., 61
National Instruments Corporation, 22
National Presto Industries, Inc., 16; 43
    (upd.)
National Semiconductor Corporation, II;
    26 (upd.); 69 (upd.)
NEC Corporation, II; 21 (upd.); 57
    (upd.)
Network Equipment Technologies Inc., 92
Nexans SA, 54
Nintendo Company, Ltd., III; 7 (upd.);
    28 (upd.); 67 (upd.)
Nokia Corporation, II; 17 (upd.); 38
    (upd.); 77 (upd.)
Nortel Networks Corporation, 36 (upd.)
Northrop Grumman Corporation, 45
    (upd.); 111 (upd.)
Oak Technology, Inc., 22
Océ N.V., 24; 91 (upd.)
Oki Electric Industry Company, Limited,
    II
Omnicell, Inc., 89
OMRON Corporation, II; 28 (upd.); 115
    (upd.)
Onvest Oy, 117
Oplink Communications, Inc., 106
OPTEK Technology Inc., 98
Orbit International Corp., 105
Orbotech Ltd., 75
Otari Inc., 89
Otter Tail Power Company, 18
Palm, Inc., 36; 75 (upd.)
Palomar Medical Technologies, Inc., 22
Parlex Corporation, 61
Peak Technologies Group, Inc., The, 14
Peavey Electronics Corporation, 16
Philips Electronics N.V., II; 13 (upd.)
Philips Electronics North America Corp.,
    13

Pioneer Electronic Corporation, III; 28
    (upd.)
Pioneer-Standard Electronics Inc., 19
Pitney Bowes Inc., III; 19 (upd.); 47
    (upd.)
Pittway Corporation, 9; 33 (upd.)
Pixelworks, Inc., 69
Planar Systems, Inc., 61
Plantronics, Inc., 106
Plessey Company, PLC, The, II
Plexus Corporation, 35; 80 (upd.)
Polaroid Corporation, III; 7 (upd.); 28
    (upd.); 93 (upd.)
Polk Audio, Inc., 34
Potter & Brumfield Inc., 11
Premier Industrial Corporation, 9
Protection One, Inc., 32
QUALCOMM Incorporated, 114 (upd.)
Quanta Computer Inc., 47; 79 (upd.);
    110 (upd.)
Racal Electronics PLC, II
RadioShack Corporation, 36 (upd.); 101
    (upd.)
Radius Inc., 16
RAE Systems Inc., 83
Ramtron International Corporation, 89
Raychem Corporation, 8
Raymarine plc, 104
Rayovac Corporation, 13; 39 (upd.)
Raytheon Company, II; 11 (upd.); 38
    (upd.); 105 (upd.)
RCA Corporation, II
Read-Rite Corp., 10
Redback Networks, Inc., 92
Reliance Electric Company, 9
Research in Motion Ltd., 54
Rexel, Inc., 15
Richardson Electronics, Ltd., 17
Ricoh Company, Ltd., III; 36 (upd.); 108
    (upd.)
Rimage Corp., 89
Rival Company, The, 19
Rockford Corporation, 43
Rogers Corporation, 61; 80 (upd.)
S&C Electric Company, 15
SAGEM S.A., 37
St. Louis Music, Inc., 48
Sam Ash Music Corporation, 30
Samsung Electronics Co., Ltd., 14; 41
    (upd.); 108 (upd.)
Sanmina-SCI Corporation, 109 (upd.)
SANYO Electric Co., Ltd., II; 36 (upd.);
    95 (upd.)
Sarnoff Corporation, 57
ScanSource, Inc., 29; 74 (upd.)
Schneider Electric SA, II; 18 (upd.); 108
    (upd.)
SCI Systems, Inc., 9
Scientific-Atlanta, Inc., 45 (upd.)
Scitex Corporation Ltd., 24
Seagate Technology, 8; 34 (upd.); 105
    (upd.)
SEGA Corporation, 73
Semitool, Inc., 79 (upd.)
Semtech Corporation, 32
Sennheiser Electronic GmbH & Co. KG,
    66
Sensormatic Electronics Corp., 11

Sensory Science Corporation, 37
SGI, 29 (upd.)
Sharp Corporation, II; 12 (upd.); 40
    (upd.); 114 (upd.)
Sheldahl Inc., 23
Shure Inc., 60
Siemens AG, II; 14 (upd.); 57 (upd.)
Sierra Nevada Corporation, 108
Silicon Graphics Incorporated, 9
Siltronic AG, 90
SL Industries, Inc., 77
Sling Media, Inc., 112
SMA Solar Technology AG, 118
SMART Modular Technologies, Inc., 86
Smiths Industries PLC, 25
Solectron Corporation, 12; 48 (upd.)
Sony Corporation, II; 12 (upd.); 40
    (upd.); 108 (upd.)
Spansion Inc., 80
Spectrum Control, Inc., 67
SPX Corporation, 10; 47 (upd.); 103
    (upd.)
Square D, 90
Sterling Electronics Corp., 18
STMicroelectronics NV, 52
Strix Ltd., 51
Stuart C. Irby Company, 58
Sumitomo Electric Industries, Ltd., II
Sun Microsystems, Inc., 7; 30 (upd.); 91
    (upd.)
Sunbeam-Oster Co., Inc., 9
SunPower Corporation, 91
Suntech Power Holdings Company Ltd.,
    89
Suntron Corporation, 107
SunWize Technologies, Inc., 114
Synaptics Incorporated, 95
Syneron Medical Ltd., 91
SYNNEX Corporation, 73
Synopsys, Inc., 11; 69 (upd.)
Syntax-Brillian Corporation, 102
Sypris Solutions, Inc., 85
SyQuest Technology, Inc., 18
Taiwan Semiconductor Manufacturing
    Company Ltd., 47
Tandy Corporation, II; 12 (upd.)
Tatung Co., 23
TDK Corporation, II; 17 (upd.); 49
    (upd.); 114 (upd.)
TEAC Corporation, 78
Technitrol, Inc., 29
Tech-Sym Corporation, 18
Tektronix, Inc., 8
Teledyne Technologies Inc., 62 (upd.)
Telxon Corporation, 10
Teradyne, Inc., 11; 98 (upd.)
Texas Instruments Incorporated, II; 11
    (upd.); 46 (upd.); 118 (upd.)
Thales S.A., 42
Thomas & Betts Corporation, 11; 54
    (upd.); 114 (upd.)
THOMSON multimedia S.A., II; 42
    (upd.)
THQ, Inc., 92 (upd.)
Titan Corporation, The, 36
TiVo Inc., 75
TomTom N.V., 81
Tops Appliance City, Inc., 17

Toromont Industries, Ltd., 21
Trans-Lux Corporation, 51
Trimble Navigation Limited, 40
TriQuint Semiconductor, Inc., 63
TT electronics plc, 111
Tweeter Home Entertainment Group, Inc., 30
Ultimate Electronics, Inc., 69 (upd.)
Ultrak Inc., 24
Uniden Corporation, 98
Unisys Corporation, 112 (upd.)
United Microelectronics Corporation, 98
Universal Electronics Inc., 39
Universal Security Instruments, Inc., 96
Varian, Inc., 12; 48 (upd.)
Veeco Instruments Inc., 32
VIASYS Healthcare, Inc., 52
Viasystems Group, Inc., 67
Vicon Industries, Inc., 44
Victor Company of Japan, Limited, II; 26 (upd.); 83 (upd.)
Vishay Intertechnology, Inc., 21; 80 (upd.)
Vitesse Semiconductor Corporation, 32
Vitro Corp., 10
Vizio, Inc., 100
VLSI Technology, Inc., 16
Vorwerk & Co. KG, 112 (upd.)
VTech Holdings Ltd., 77
Wells-Gardner Electronics Corporation, 43
WESCO International, Inc., 116
Westinghouse Electric Corporation, II; 12 (upd.)
Winbond Electronics Corporation, 74
Wincor Nixdorf Holding GmbH, 69 (upd.)
WuXi AppTec Company Ltd., 103
Wyle Electronics, 14
Xantrex Technology Inc., 97
Xerox Corporation, III; 6 (upd.); 26 (upd.); 69 (upd.)
Yageo Corporation, 16; 98 (upd.)
York Research Corporation, 35
Zenith Data Systems, Inc., 10
Zenith Electronics Corporation, II; 13 (upd.); 34 (upd.); 89 (upd.)
Zoom Telephonics, Inc., 18
Zoran Corporation, 77
Zumtobel AG, 50
Zytec Corporation, 19

Engineering & Management Services

AAON, Inc., 22
Aavid Thermal Technologies, Inc., 29
Acergy SA, 97
AECOM Technology Corporation, 79
Alliant Techsystems Inc., 30 (upd.)
Altran Technologies, 51
AMEC plc, 112
American Science & Engineering, Inc., 81
Amey Plc, 47
Analytic Sciences Corporation, 10
Arcadis NV, 26
Arthur D. Little, Inc., 35
Austin Company, The, 8; 72 (upd.)
Autostrada Torino-Milano S.p.A., 101

Babcock International Group PLC, 69
Balfour Beatty plc, 36 (upd.)
BE&K, Inc., 73
Bechtel Corporation, I; 24 (upd.); 99 (upd.)
Birse Group PLC, 77
Bowen Engineering Corporation, 105
Brock Group of Companies, The, 114
Brown & Root, Inc., 13
Bufete Industrial, S.A. de C.V., 34
C.H. Heist Corporation, 24
Camp Dresser & McKee Inc., 104
CDI Corporation, 6; 54 (upd.)
CH2M HILL Companies Ltd., 22; 96 (upd.)
Charles Stark Draper Laboratory, Inc., The, 35
Coflexip S.A., 25
CompuDyne Corporation, 51
Cornell Companies, Inc., 112
Corrections Corporation of America, 23
CRSS Inc., 6
Dames & Moore, Inc., 25
DAW Technologies, Inc., 25
Day & Zimmermann Inc., 9; 31 (upd.)
Donaldson Company, Inc., 16; 49 (upd.); 108 (upd.)
Doosan Heavy Industries and Construction Company Ltd., 108
Dycom Industries, Inc., 57
Edwards and Kelcey, 70
EG&G Incorporated, 8; 29 (upd.)
Eiffage S.A., 27; 117 (upd.)
Elliott-Lewis Corporation, 100
Essef Corporation, 18
Exponent, Inc., 95
FKI Plc, 57
Fluor Corporation, 34 (upd.); 112 (upd.)
Forest City Enterprises, Inc., 52 (upd.)
Foster Wheeler Ltd., 6; 23 (upd.); 76 (upd.)
Framatome SA, 19
Fraport AG Frankfurt Airport Services Worldwide, 90
Freese and Nichols, Inc., 107
Fugro N.V., 98
Gale International Llc, 93
Georg Fischer AG Schaffhausen, 61
Gilbane, Inc., 34
Great Lakes Dredge & Dock Company, 69
Grontmij N.V., 110
Grupo Dragados SA, 55
Halliburton Company, III; 25 (upd.); 55 (upd.)
Halma plc, 104
Harding Lawson Associates Group, Inc., 16
Harley Ellis Devereaux Corporation, 101
Harza Engineering Company, 14
HDR Inc., 48
Hittite Microwave Corporation, 106
HOK Group, Inc., 59
ICF Kaiser International, Inc., 28
IHC Caland N.V., 71
Invensys PLC, 50 (upd.)
Jacobs Engineering Group Inc., 6; 26 (upd.); 106 (upd.)

Jacques Whitford, 92
Jaiprakash Associates Limited, 101
James Fisher and Sons Public Limited Company, 118
Judge Group, Inc., The, 51
JWP Inc., 9
KBR Inc., 106 (upd.)
Keith Companies Inc., The, 54
Keller Group PLC, 95
Klöckner-Werke AG, 58 (upd.)
Kvaerner ASA, 36
Layne Christensen Company, 19
Leo A Daly Company, 118
Louis Berger Group, Inc., The, 104
MacNeal-Schwendler Corporation, The, 25
Malcolm Pirnie, Inc., 42
Mason & Hanger Group Inc., 110
McDermott International, Inc., III; 37 (upd.)
McKinsey & Company, Inc., 9
Mead & Hunt Inc., 113
Michael Baker Corporation, 51 (upd.)
Mota-Engil, SGPS, S.A., 97
MSE, Inc., 113
National Technical Systems, Inc., 111
NBBJ, 111
Nooter Corporation, 61
NTD Architecture, 101
Oceaneering International, Inc., 63
Odebrecht S.A., 73
Ogden Corporation, 6
Opus Corporation, 34; 101 (upd.)
PAREXEL International Corporation, 84
Parsons Brinckerhoff Inc., 34; 104 (upd.)
Parsons Corporation, The, 8; 56 (upd.)
PBSJ Corporation, The, 82
Petrofac Ltd., 95
Quanta Services, Inc., 79
RCM Technologies, Inc., 34
Renishaw plc, 46
Ricardo plc, 90
Rosemount Inc., 15
Roy F. Weston, Inc., 33
Royal Vopak NV, 41
Rust International Inc., 11
Sandia National Laboratories, 49
Sandvik AB, IV; 32 (upd.); 77 (upd.)
Sarnoff Corporation, 57
Science Applications International Corporation, 15; 109 (upd.)
SENTEL Corporation, 106
Serco Group plc, 47
The Shaw Group, Inc., 50; 118 (upd.)
Siegel & Gale, 64
Siemens AG, 57 (upd.)
SRI International, Inc., 57
SSOE Inc., 76
Stone & Webster, Inc., 13; 64 (upd.)
Sulzer Ltd., III; 68 (upd.)
Susquehanna Pfaltzgraff Company, 8
Sverdrup Corporation, 14
Technip, 78
Tech-Sym Corporation, 44 (upd.)
Teledyne Brown Engineering, Inc., 110
Tetra Tech, Inc., 29
ThyssenKrupp AG, IV; 28 (upd.); 87 (upd.)

Towers Perrin, 32
Tracor Inc., 17
TRC Companies, Inc., 32
U.S. Army Corps of Engineers, 91
Underwriters Laboratories, Inc., 30
United Dominion Industries Limited, 8;
  16 (upd.)
URS Corporation, 45; 80 (upd.)
VA TECH ELIN EBG GmbH, 49
VECO International, Inc., 7
Vinci, 43
Volkert and Associates, Inc., 98
VSE Corporation, 108
Weir Group PLC, The, 85
Willbros Group, Inc., 56
WS Atkins Plc, 45

Entertainment & Leisure

A&E Television Networks, 32
Aardman Animations Ltd., 61
ABC Family Worldwide, Inc., 52
Academy of Television Arts & Sciences,
  Inc., 55
Acclaim Entertainment Inc., 24
Activision, Inc., 32; 89 (upd.)
Acushnet Company, 64
Adams Golf, Inc., 37
Adelman Travel Group, 105
AEI Music Network Inc., 35
Affinity Group Holding Inc., 56
Airtours Plc, 27
Alaska Railroad Corporation, 60
Aldila Inc., 46
All American Communications Inc., 20
All England Lawn Tennis & Croquet
  Club, The, 54
Allen Organ Company, 33
Allgemeiner Deutscher Automobil-Club
  e.V., 100
Alliance Entertainment Corp., 17
Alternative Tentacles Records, 66
Alvin Ailey Dance Foundation, Inc., 52
Amblin Entertainment, 21
AMC Entertainment Inc., 12; 35 (upd.);
  114 (upd.)
Amer Group plc, 41
American Golf Corporation, 45
American Gramaphone LLC, 52
American Kennel Club, Inc., 74
American Skiing Company, 28
Ameristar Casinos, Inc., 33; 69 (upd.)
AMF Bowling, Inc., 40
Anaheim Angels Baseball Club, Inc., 53
Anchor Gaming, 24
AOL Time Warner Inc., 57 (upd.)
Apollo Theater Foundation, Inc., 109
Applause Inc., 24
Apple Corps Ltd., 87
Aprilia SpA, 17
Arena Leisure Plc, 99
Argosy Gaming Company, 21
Aristocrat Leisure Limited, 54
Arsenal Holdings PLC, 79
Art Institute of Chicago, The, 29
Arthur C. Clarke Foundation, The, 92
Arthur Murray International, Inc., 32
Artisan Entertainment Inc., 32 (upd.)

Asahi National Broadcasting Company,
  Ltd., 9
Aspen Skiing Company, 15
Aston Villa plc, 41
Athletics Investment Group, The, 62
Atlanta National League Baseball Club,
  Inc., 43
Atlantic Group, The, 23
Augusta National Inc., 115
Autotote Corporation, 20
Avedis Zildjian Co., 38
Aztar Corporation, 13
Bad Boy Worldwide Entertainment
  Group, 58
Baker & Taylor Corporation, 16; 43
  (upd.)
Baldwin Piano & Organ Company, 18
Ballet Theatre Foundation, Inc., 118
Bally Total Fitness Holding Corp., 25
Baltimore Orioles L.P., 66
Barden Companies, Inc., 76
Baseball Club of Seattle, LP, The, 50
Basketball Club of Seattle, LLC, The, 50
Beggars Group Ltd., 99
Bell Sports Corporation, 16; 44 (upd.)
BenQ Corporation, 67
Bertelsmann A.G., IV; 15 (upd.); 43
  (upd.); 91 (upd.)
Bertucci's Inc., 16
Big Fish Games, Inc., 108
Big Idea Productions, Inc., 49
BigBen Interactive S.A., 72
The Biltmore Company, 118
BioWare Corporation, 81
Black Diamond Equipment, Ltd., 62
Blockbuster Inc., 9; 31 (upd.); 76 (upd.)
Blue Note Label Group, 115
Boca Resorts, Inc., 37
Bonneville International Corporation, 29
Booth Creek Ski Holdings, Inc., 31
Boston Basketball Partners L.L.C., 14;
  115 (upd.)
Boston Professional Hockey Association
  Inc., 39
Boston Symphony Orchestra Inc., The, 93
Boy Scouts of America, The, 34
Boyne USA Resorts, 71
Brass Eagle Inc., 34
Bravo Company, 114
Brillstein-Grey Entertainment, 80
British Broadcasting Corporation Ltd., 7;
  21 (upd.); 89 (upd.)
British Film Institute, The, 80
British Museum, The, 71
British Sky Broadcasting Group plc, 20;
  60 (upd.)
Broadway Video Entertainment, 112
Brunswick Corporation, III; 22 (upd.); 77
  (upd.)
Burgett, Inc., 97
Burton Snowboards Inc., 22
Busch Entertainment Corporation, 73
C. Bechstein Pianofortefabrik AG, 96
C.F. Martin & Co., Inc., 42
Cablevision Systems Corporation, 7; 30
  (upd.); 109 (upd.)
California Sports, Inc., 56

Callaway Golf Company, 15; 45 (upd.);
  112 (upd.)
Camelot Group plc, 110
Canadian Broadcasting Corporation, 109
  (upd.)
Canlan Ice Sports Corp., 105
Canterbury Park Holding Corporation, 42
Capcom Company Ltd., 83
Capital Cities/ABC Inc., II
Capitol Records, Inc., 90
Carlson Companies, Inc., 6; 22 (upd.); 87
  (upd.)
Carlson Wagonlit Travel, 55
Carmike Cinemas, Inc., 14; 37 (upd.); 74
  (upd.)
Carnegie Hall Corporation, The, 101
Carnival Corporation, 6; 27 (upd.); 78
  (upd.)
Carrere Group S.A., 104
Carsey-Werner Company, L.L.C., The, 37
Carvin Corp., 89
CBS Inc., II; 6 (upd.)
Cedar Fair Entertainment Company, 22;
  98 (upd.)
Central European Media Enterprises Ltd.,
  61
Central Independent Television, 7; 23
  (upd.)
Century Casinos, Inc., 53
Century Theatres, Inc., 31
Championship Auto Racing Teams, Inc.,
  37
Channel Four Television Corporation, 93
Charles M. Schulz Creative Associates,
  114
Chello Zone Ltd., 93
Chelsea Ltd., 102
Chelsea Piers Management Inc., 86
Chicago Bears Football Club, Inc., 33
Chicago National League Ball Club, Inc.,
  66
Chicago Symphony Orchestra, 106
Chris-Craft Corporation, 9, 31 (upd.); 80
  (upd.)
Chrysalis Group plc, 40
Churchill Downs Incorporated, 29
Cinar Corporation, 40
Cinemark Holdings, Inc., 95
Cinemas de la República, S.A. de C.V., 83
Cineplex Odeon Corporation, 6; 23
  (upd.)
Cinram International, Inc., 43
Cirque du Soleil Inc., 29; 98 (upd.)
CKX, Inc., 102
Classic Vacation Group, Inc., 46
Cleveland Indians Baseball Company, Inc.,
  37; 115 (upd.)
Club Méditerranée S.A., 6; 21 (upd.); 91
  (upd.)
ClubCorp, Inc., 33
CMG Worldwide, Inc., 89
Cobra Golf Inc., 16
Codere S.A., 110
Coleman Company, Inc., The, 9; 30
  (upd.)
Colonial Williamsburg Foundation, 53
Colorado Baseball Management, Inc., 72
Columbia Pictures Entertainment, Inc., II

Jujamcyn Theaters Corporation, 112
Julius Blüthner Pianofortefabrik GmbH, 78
Jurys Doyle Hotel Group plc, 64
Juventus F.C. S.p.A, 53
Kaman Music Corporation, 68
Kampgrounds of America, Inc. (KOA), 33
Kawai Musical Instruments Mfg Co. Ltd.,, 78
Kayak.com, 108
Kerasotes ShowPlace Theaters LLC, 80
Kerzner International Limited, 69 (upd.)
King World Productions, Inc., 9; 30 (upd.)
Klasky Csupo Inc.,, 78
K'Nex Industries, Inc., 52
Knitting Factory Entertainment, 108
Knott's Berry Farm, 18
KTM Power Sports AG, 100
Kuoni Travel Holding Ltd., 40
Kushner-Locke Company, The, 25
Ladbroke Group PLC, II; 21 (upd.)
Lagardère SCA, 112
Lakes Entertainment, Inc., 51
Landmark Theatre Corporation, 70
Las Vegas Sands, Inc., 50
LaSiDo Inc., 58
Legendary Pictures Films, LLC, 118
Lego A/S, 13; 40 (upd.)
Liberty Livewire Corporation, 42
Liberty Media Corporation, 50; 111 (upd.)
Liberty Travel, Inc., 56
Life Time Fitness, Inc., 66
Lifetime Entertainment Services, 51
Lincoln Center for the Performing Arts, Inc., 69
Lionel L.L.C., 16; 99 (upd.)
Lions Gate Entertainment Corporation, 35; 118 (upd.)
LIVE Entertainment Inc., 20
Live Nation, Inc., 80 (upd.)
Liverpool Football Club and Athletic Grounds PLC, The, 105
LodgeNet Interactive Corporation, 28; 106 (upd.)
Los Angeles Turf Club Inc., 102
Lucasfilm Ltd., 12; 50 (upd.); 115 (upd.)
Luminar Plc, 40
MacGregor Golf Company, 68
Madison Square Garden, LP, 109
Majesco Entertainment Company, 85
Mammoth Mountain Ski Area, 101
Manchester United Football Club plc, 30
Mandalay Resort Group, 32 (upd.)
Maple Leaf Sports & Entertainment Ltd., 61
Marc Ecko Enterprises, Inc., 105
Marcus Corporation, The, 21
Marine Products Corporation, 75
Mark Travel Corporation, The, 80
Märklin Holding GmbH, 70
Martha Stewart Living Omnimedia, Inc., 73 (upd.)
MartinLogan, Ltd., 85
Mashantucket Pequot Gaming Enterprise Inc., 35
Matador Records Inc., 113

Matth. Hohner AG, 53
MCA Inc., II
McMenamins Pubs and Breweries, 65
Media General, Inc., 7
Mediaset SpA, 50
Mega Bloks, Inc., 61
Melco Crown Entertainment Limited, 103
Merlin Entertainments Group Ltd., 105
Metro-Goldwyn-Mayer Inc., 25 (upd.); 84 (upd.)
Metromedia Companies, 14
Métropole Télévision, 33
Métropole Télévision S.A., 76 (upd.)
Metropolitan Baseball Club Inc., 39
Metropolitan Museum of Art, The, 55; 115 (upd.)
Metropolitan Opera Association, Inc., 40; 115 (upd.)
MGM Grand Inc., 17
MGM/UA Communications Company, II
Midway Games, Inc., 25; 102 (upd.)
Mikohn Gaming Corporation, 39
Milan AC, S.p.A., 79
Milton Bradley Company, 21
Milwaukee Brewers Baseball Club, 37
Minnesota Twins, 112
Miramax Film Corporation, 64
Mizuno Corporation, 25
Mohegan Tribal Gaming Authority, 37
Moliflor Loisirs, 80
Monarch Casino & Resort, Inc., 65
Moog Music, Inc., 75
Motown Records Company L.P., 26
Movie Gallery, Inc., 31
Mr. Gatti's, LP, 87
MTR Gaming Group, Inc., 75
Multimedia Games, Inc., 41
Museum of Modern Art, 106
Muzak, Inc., 18
Namco Bandai Holdings Inc., 106 (upd.)
National Amusements Inc., 28
National Aquarium in Baltimore, Inc., 74
National Association for Stock Car Auto Racing, 32
National Broadcasting Company, Inc., II; 6 (upd.)
National CineMedia, Inc., 103
National Collegiate Athletic Association, 96
National Football League, 29; 115 (upd.)
National Hockey League, 35
National Public Radio, Inc., 19; 47 (upd.)
National Rifle Association of America, The, 37; 112 (upd.)
National Thoroughbred Racing Association, 58
Navarre Corporation, 24
Navigant International, Inc., 47
NBGS International, Inc., 73
NCL Corporation, 79
Nederlander Producing Company of America, Inc., 108
Netflix, Inc., 58; 115 (upd.)
New Jersey Devils, 84
New Line Cinema, Inc., 47
New Orleans Saints LP, 58
New York City Off-Track Betting Corporation, 51; 115 (upd.)

New York Shakespeare Festival Management, 93
New York Yacht Club, Inc., 103
News Corporation Limited, 46 (upd.)
NFL Films, 75
Nicklaus Companies, 45
19 Entertainment Limited, 112
Nintendo Company, Ltd., III; 7 (upd.); 28 (upd.); 67 (upd.)
Nordisk Film A/S, 80
O'Charley's Inc., 19
Old Town Canoe Company, 74
Old Vic Productions plc, 108
Orchard Enterprises, Inc., The, 103
Orion Pictures Corporation, 6
Outrigger Enterprises, Inc., 67
Palace Sports & Entertainment, Inc., 97
Paradise Music & Entertainment, Inc., 42
Paramount Pictures Corporation, II
Patch Products Inc., 105
Pathé SA, 29
Paul Reed Smith Guitar Company, 89
Paul-Son Gaming Corporation, 66
PDS Gaming Corporation, 44
Peace Arch Entertainment Group Inc., 51
Pearl Corporation, 78
Penn National Gaming, Inc., 33; 109 (upd.)
Petrof spol. S.R.O., 107
Philadelphia Eagles, 37
Philharmonic-Symphony Society of New York, Inc. (New York Philharmonic), 69
Phillies, The, 106
Pierre & Vacances SA, 48
Pittsburgh Steelers Sports, Inc., 66
Pixar Animation Studios, Inc., 34; 118 (upd.)
Platinum Entertainment, Inc., 35
Play by Play Toys & Novelties, Inc., 26
Players International, Inc., 22
Pleasant Holidays LLC, 62
Polaris Industries Inc., 12; 35 (upd.); 77 (upd.)
PolyGram N.V., 23
Poof-Slinky, Inc., 61
Pop Warner Little Scholars, Inc., 86
Portland Trail Blazers, 50
Powerhouse Technologies, Inc., 27
Premier Parks, Inc., 27
President Casinos, Inc., 22
Preussag AG, 42 (upd.)
Prince Sports Group, Inc., 15
Princess Cruise Lines, 22
Professional Bull Riders Inc., 55
Professional Golfers' Association of America, The, 41
Promus Companies, Inc., 9
ProSiebenSat.1 Media AG, 54
Publishing and Broadcasting Limited, 54
Putt-Putt Golf Courses of America, Inc., 23
QRS Music Technologies, Inc., 95
@radical.media, 103
Radio One, Inc., 67
Ragdoll Productions Ltd., 51
Raha-automaattiyhdistys (RAY), 110
Rainbow Media Holdings LLC, 109

Financial Services: Banks

Food Products

Health Care Services

Hotels

Information Technology

Andritz AG, 51
Applica Incorporated, 43 (upd.)
Applied Films Corporation, 48
Applied Materials, Inc., 10; 46 (upd.)
AptarGroup, Inc., 69
Arc International, 76
Arçelik A.S., 100
Arctic Cat Inc., 16; 40 (upd.); 96 (upd.)
AREVA NP, 90 (upd.)
Ariens Company, 48
Aristotle Corporation, The, 62
Armor All Products Corp., 16
Armstrong Holdings, Inc., III; 22 (upd.);
   81 (upd.)
Art's Way Manufacturing Co., Inc., 101
Ashley Furniture Industries, Inc., 35
Assa Abloy AB, 112
Atlantis Plastics, Inc., 85
Atlas Copco AB, III; 28 (upd.); 85 (upd.)
Atwood Mobil Products, 53
Austin Powder Company, 76
AZZ Incorporated, 93
B.J. Alan Co., Inc., 67
Babcock & Wilcox Company, The, 82
Badger Meter, Inc., 22
Baldor Electric Company, 21; 97 (upd.)
Baldwin Technology Company, Inc., 25;
   107 (upd.)
Ballantyne of Omaha, Inc., 27
Bally Manufacturing Corporation, III
Baltimore Aircoil Company, Inc., 66
Bandai Co., Ltd., 55
Barmag AG, 39
Barnes Group Inc., 13; 69 (upd.)
Barry-Wehmiller Companies, Inc., 90
Bassett Furniture Industries, Inc., 18; 95
   (upd.)
Bath Iron Works, 12; 36 (upd.)
Baxi Group Ltd., 96
Beckman Coulter, Inc., 22
Beckman Instruments, Inc., 14
Behr Process Corporation, 115
BEI Technologies, Inc., 65
Bekaert S.A./N.V., 90
Bel-Art Products Inc., 117
Belleek Pottery Ltd., 71
Benjamin Moore & Co., 13; 38 (upd.);
   115 (upd.)
Benninger AG, 107
Berger Bros Company, 62
Bernina Holding AG, 47
Berwick Offray, 70
Bianchi International (d/b/a Gregory
   Mountain Products), 76
BIC Corporation, 8; 23 (upd.)
Bing Group, The, 60
Binks Sames Corporation, 21
Binney & Smith Inc., 25
BISSELL Inc., 9; 30 (upd.)
Black & Decker Corporation, The, III; 20
   (upd.); 67 (upd.)
Blodgett Holdings, Inc., 61 (upd.)
Blount International, Inc., 12; 48 (upd.)
BLRT Grupp A.S., 117
Blyth, Inc., 18; 74 (upd.)
Bodum Design Group AG, 47
Bombril S.A., 111
Borrego Solar Systems, Inc., 111

Borroughs Corporation, 110
Boston Scientific Corporation, 37; 77
   (upd.)
Boyds Collection, Ltd., The, 29
BPB plc, 83
Bradley Corporation, 118
Brady Corporation, 78 (upd.)
Brammer PLC, 77
Breeze-Eastern Corporation, 95
Brenco, Inc., 104
Bridgeport Machines, Inc., 17
Briggs & Stratton Corporation, 8; 27
   (upd.)
BRIO AB, 24; 103 (upd.)
BRITA GmbH, 112
Broan-NuTone LLC, 104
Brother Industries, Ltd., 14
Brown & Sharpe Manufacturing Co., 23
Brown Jordan International Inc., 74
   (upd.)
Broyhill Furniture Industries, Inc., 10
Bruker Corporation, 113
BSH Bosch und Siemens Hausgeräte
   GmbH, 67
BTR Siebe plc, 27
Buck Knives Inc., 48
Buckeye Technologies, Inc., 42
Bulgari S.p.A., 20; 106 (upd.)
Bulova Corporation, 13; 41 (upd.)
Bundy Corporation, 17
Burelle S.A., 23
Bush Industries, Inc., 20
Butler Manufacturing Company, 12; 62
   (upd.)
California Cedar Products Company, 58
Cameron International Corporation, 110
Campbell Scientific, Inc., 51
Canam Group Inc., 114
Cannondale Corporation, 21
Capstone Turbine Corporation, 75
Caradon plc, 20 (upd.)
Carbide/Graphite Group, Inc., The, 40
Carbo PLC, 67 (upd.)
Cardo AB, 53
Carrier Corporation, 7; 69 (upd.)
Cascade Corporation, 65
Catalina Lighting, Inc., 43 (upd.)
Central Sprinkler Corporation, 29
Centuri Corporation, 54
Cepheid, 77
Champion Enterprises, Inc., 17
Charisma Brands LLC, 74
Charles Machine Works, Inc., The, 64
Chart Industries, Inc., 21; 96 (upd.)
Chemring Group plc, 113
Chittenden & Eastman Company, 58
Christian Dalloz SA, 40
Christofle SA, 40
Chromcraft Revington, Inc., 15
Cincinnati Lamb Inc., 72
Cincinnati Milacron Inc., 12
Cinemeccanica SpA, 78
Circon Corporation, 21
CIRCOR International, Inc., 115
Citizen Watch Co., Ltd., III; 21 (upd.);
   81 (upd.)
Clark Equipment Company, 8
Clopay Corporation, 100

Cloverdale Paint Inc., 115
Cognex Corporation, 76
Colfax Corporation, 58
Colt's Manufacturing Company, Inc., 12
Columbia Manufacturing, Inc., 114
Columbus McKinnon Corporation, 37
Compass Minerals International, Inc., 79
Concord Camera Corporation, 41
Congoleum Corporation, 18; 98 (upd.)
Controladora Mabe, S.A. de C.V., 82
Corrpro Companies, Inc., 20
Corticeira Amorim, Sociedade Gestora de
   Participaço es Sociais, S.A., 48
CPAC, Inc., 86
Craftmatic Organization Inc., 117
Crane Co., 8; 30 (upd.); 101 (upd.)
C-Tech Industries Inc., 90
Cuisinart Corporation, 24
Culligan Water Technologies, Inc., 12; 38
   (upd.)
CUNO Incorporated, 57
Curtiss-Wright Corporation, 10; 35 (upd.)
Cutera, Inc., 84
Cymer, Inc., 77
D. Swarovski & Co., 112 (upd.)
Daikin Industries, Ltd., III
Dalian Shide Group, 91
Danfoss A/S, 113
DCN S.A., 75
De Rigo S.p.A., 104
Dearborn Mid-West Conveyor Company,
   56
Deceuninck N.V., 84
Decora Industries, Inc., 31
Decorator Industries Inc., 68
Deere & Company, 113 (upd.)
Delachaux S.A., 76
De'Longhi S.p.A., 66
DEMCO, Inc., 60
Denby Group plc, 44
Denison International plc, 46
Department 56, Inc., 14
Derma Sciences Inc., 117
Detroit Diesel Corporation, 10; 74 (upd.)
Deutsche Babcock A.G., III
Deutsche Steinzeug Cremer & Breuer
   Aktiengesellschaft, 91
Deutz AG, 39
Dial-A-Mattress Operating Corporation,
   46
Diebold, Incorporated, 7; 22 (upd.)
Dixon Industries, Inc., 26
Dixon Ticonderoga Company, 12; 69
   (upd.)
Djarum PT, 62
DMI Furniture, Inc., 46
Dorel Industries Inc., 59
Dover Corporation, III; 28 (upd.); 90
   (upd.)
Dresser Industries, Inc., III
Drew Industries Inc., 28
Drexel Heritage Furnishings Inc., 12
Duncan Toys Company, 55
Dunn-Edwards Corporation, 56
Duracell International Inc., 9; 71 (upd.)
Durametallic, 21
Duriron Company Inc., 17
Dürkopp Adler AG, 65

Materials

Mining & Metals

Nonprofit & Philanthropic Organizations

West Fraser Timber Co. Ltd., 17; 91 (upd.)
West Linn Paper Company, 91
Westvaco Corporation, IV; 19 (upd.)
Weyerhaeuser Company, IV; 9 (upd.); 28 (upd.); 83 (upd.)
Wickes Inc., 25 (upd.)
Willamette Industries, Inc., IV; 31 (upd.)
WTD Industries, Inc., 20

Personal Services

Adelman Travel Group, 105
ADT Security Services, Inc., 12; 44 (upd.)
Alderwoods Group, Inc., 68 (upd.)
Ambassadors International, Inc., 68 (upd.)
American Retirement Corporation, 42
Ameriwood Industries International Corp., 17
Aquent, 96
Aurora Casket Company, Inc., 56
Bidvest Group Ltd., 106
Blackwater USA, 76
Bonhams 1793 Ltd., 72
Brickman Group, Ltd., The, 87
CareerBuilder, Inc., 93
Carriage Services, Inc., 37
CDI Corporation, 6; 54 (upd.)
Central Parking System, 18; 104 (upd.)
CeWe Color Holding AG, 76
Chemed Corporation, 13; 118 (upd.)
Chubb, PLC, 50
Correctional Services Corporation, 30
CUC International Inc., 16
Curves International, Inc., 54
eHarmony.com Inc., 71
Franklin Quest Co., 11
Gateway Group One, 118
Gold's Gym International, Inc., 71
Granite Industries of Vermont, Inc., 73
Greg Manning Auctions, Inc., 60
Gunnebo AB, 53
Hair Club For Men Ltd., 90
Herbalife Ltd., 17; 41 (upd.); 92 (upd.)
I Grandi Viaggi S.p.A., 105
Imperial Parking Corporation, 58
Initial Security, 64
Jazzercise, Inc., 45
Jostens, Inc., 7; 25 (upd.); 73 (upd.)
Kayak.com, 108
Kiva, 95
Lifetouch Inc., 86
Loewen Group Inc., The, 16; 40 (upd.)
Mace Security International, Inc., 57
Manpower, Inc., 9
Martin Franchises, Inc., 80
Match.com, LP, 87
Michael Anthony Jewelers, Inc., 24
Michael Page International plc, 45
OGF S.A., 113
Orkin, Inc., 104
PODS Enterprises Inc., 103
Prison Rehabilitative Industries and Diversified Enterprises, Inc. (PRIDE), 53
Randstad Holding nv, 113 (upd.)
Regis Corporation, 18; 70 (upd.)
Rollins, Inc., 11; 104 (upd.)
Rose Hills Company, 117

Rosenbluth International Inc., 14
Screen Actors Guild, 72
Segway LLC, 48
Service Corporation International, 6; 51 (upd.)
Shutterfly, Inc., 98
Snapfish, 83
SOS Staffing Services, 25
Spark Networks, Inc., 91
Stewart Enterprises, Inc., 20
Supercuts Inc., 26
Town & Country Corporation, 19
24 Hour Fitness Worldwide, Inc., 71
UAW (International Union, United Automobile, Aerospace and Agricultural Implement Workers of America), 72
Weight Watchers International Inc., 12; 33 (upd.); 73 (upd.)
Yak Pak, 108
York Group, Inc., The, 50
YTB International, Inc., 108

Petroleum

Abraxas Petroleum Corporation, 89
Abu Dhabi National Oil Company, IV; 45 (upd.); 114 (upd.)
Adani Enterprises Ltd., 97
Aegean Marine Petroleum Network Inc., 89
Agland, Inc., 110
Agway, Inc., 21 (upd.)
Alberta Energy Company Ltd., 16; 43 (upd.)
Alon Israel Oil Company Ltd., 104
Amerada Hess Corporation, IV; 21 (upd.); 55 (upd.)
Amoco Corporation, IV; 14 (upd.)
Anadarko Petroleum Corporation, 10; 52 (upd.); 106 (upd.)
ANR Pipeline Co., 17
Anschutz Corp., 12
Apache Corporation, 10; 32 (upd.); 89 (upd.)
Aral AG, 62
Arctic Slope Regional Corporation, 38
Arena Resources, Inc., 97
Ashland Inc., 19; 50 (upd.); 115 (upd.)
Ashland Oil, Inc., IV
Atlantic Richfield Company, IV; 31 (upd.)
Atwood Oceanics, Inc., 100
Aventine Renewable Energy Holdings, Inc., 89
Badger State Ethanol, LLC, 83
Baker Hughes Incorporated, 22 (upd.); 57 (upd.); 118 (upd.)
Basic Earth Science Systems, Inc., 101
Belco Oil & Gas Corp., 40
Benton Oil and Gas Company, 47
Berry Petroleum Company, 47
BG Products Inc., 96
Bharat Petroleum Corporation Limited, 109
BHP Billiton, 67 (upd.)
Bill Barrett Corporation, 71
BJ Services Company, 25
Blue Rhino Corporation, 56
Blue Sun Energy, Inc., 108
Boardwalk Pipeline Partners, LP, 87

Bolt Technology Corporation, 99
Boots & Coots International Well Control, Inc., 79
BP p.l.c., 45 (upd.); 103 (upd.)
Brigham Exploration Company, 75
British Petroleum Company plc, The, IV; 7 (upd.); 21 (upd.)
British-Borneo Oil & Gas PLC, 34
Broken Hill Proprietary Company Ltd., 22 (upd.)
Bronco Drilling Company, Inc., 89
Burlington Resources Inc., 10
Burmah Castrol PLC, IV; 30 (upd.)
Callon Petroleum Company, 47
Caltex Petroleum Corporation, 19
Calumet Specialty Products Partners, L.P., 106
CAMAC International Corporation, 106
Cano Petroleum Inc., 97
Carrizo Oil & Gas, Inc., 97
Chevron Corporation, IV; 19 (upd.); 47 (upd.); 103 (upd.)
Chiles Offshore Corporation, 9
The China National Offshore Oil Corp., 118
China National Petroleum Corporation, 46; 108 (upd.)
China Petroleum & Chemical Corporation (Sinopec Corp.), 109
Chinese Petroleum Corporation, IV; 31 (upd.)
Cimarex Energy Co., 81
CITGO Petroleum Corporation, IV; 31 (upd.)
Clayton Williams Energy, Inc., 87
Coastal Corporation, The, IV; 31 (upd.)
Compania Española de Petróleos S.A. (Cepsa), IV; 56 (upd.)
Complete Production Services, Inc., 118
Compton Petroleum Corporation, 103
Comstock Resources, Inc., 47
Conoco Inc., IV; 16 (upd.)
ConocoPhillips, 63 (upd.)
CONSOL Energy Inc., 59
Continental Resources, Inc., 89
Cooper Cameron Corporation, 20 (upd.); 58 (upd.)
Cosmo Oil Co., Ltd., IV; 53 (upd.)
CPC Corporation, Taiwan, 116
Crimson Exploration Inc., 116
Crown Central Petroleum Corporation, 7
Daniel Measurement and Control, Inc., 16; 74 (upd.)
Dead River Company, 117
DeepTech International Inc., 21
Den Norse Stats Oljeselskap AS, IV
Denbury Resources, Inc., 67
Deutsche BP Aktiengesellschaft, 7
Devon Energy Corporation, 61
Diamond Shamrock, Inc., IV
Distrigaz S.A., 82
DOF ASA, 110
Double Eagle Petroleum Co., 114
Dril-Quip, Inc., 81
Duvernay Oil Corp., 83
Dyneff S.A., 98
Dynegy Inc., 49 (upd.)
E.On AG, 50 (upd.)

Publishing & Printing

Real Estate

Retail & Wholesale

Volcom, Inc., 77
Von Maur Inc., 64
Vorwerk & Co. KG, 27; 112 (upd.)
W.B. Mason Company, 98
W.S. Badcock Corporation, 107
W.W. Grainger, Inc., V; 26 (upd.); 68 (upd.)
Waban Inc., 13
Wacoal Corp., 25
Waldenbooks, 17; 86 (upd.)
Walgreen Co., V; 20 (upd.); 65 (upd.)
Wall Drug Store, Inc., 40
Wal-Mart de Mexico, S.A. de C.V., 35 (upd.)
Wal-Mart Stores, Inc., V; 8 (upd.); 26 (upd.); 63 (upd.)
Walter E. Smithe Furniture, Inc., 105
Warners' Stellian Inc., 67
WAXIE Sanitary Supply, 100
Weiner's Stores, Inc., 33
West Marine, Inc., 17; 90 (upd.)
Wet Seal, Inc., The, 18; 70 (upd.)
Weyco Group, Incorporated, 32
WH Smith PLC, V; 42 (upd.)
White House, Inc., The, 60
Whitehall Jewellers, Inc., 82 (upd.)
Wickes Inc., V; 25 (upd.)
Wilco Farm Stores, 93
Wilkinson Hardware Stores Ltd., 80
Williams Scotsman, Inc., 65
Williams-Sonoma, Inc., 17; 44 (upd.); 103 (upd.)
Wilsons The Leather Experts Inc., 21; 58 (upd.)
Wilton Products, Inc., 97
Windstream Corporation, 83
Winmark Corporation, 74
Wolohan Lumber Co., 19
Wolverine World Wide, Inc., 59 (upd.)
Woolworth Corporation, V; 20 (upd.)
Woolworths Group plc, 83
Woot, Inc., 118
World Duty Free Americas, Inc., 29 (upd.)
Yamada Denki Co., Ltd., 85
Yankee Candle Company, Inc., The, 37
Yingli Green Energy Holding Company Limited, 103
Younkers, 76 (upd.)
Younkers, Inc., 19
Zale Corporation, 16; 40 (upd.); 91 (upd.)
Zany Brainy, Inc., 31
Zappos.com, Inc., 73
Zara International, Inc., 83
Ziebart International Corporation, 30
Zion's Cooperative Mercantile Institution, 33
Zipcar, Inc., 92
Zones, Inc., 67
Zumiez, Inc., 77

Rubber & Tires

Aeroquip Corporation, 16
AirBoss of America Corporation, 108
Avon Rubber p.l.c., 108
Bandag, Inc., 19
BFGoodrich Company, The, V

Bridgestone Corporation, V; 21 (upd.); 59 (upd.); 118 (upd.)
Canadian Tire Corporation, Limited, 71 (upd.)
Carlisle Companies Incorporated, 8
Compagnie Générale des Établissements Michelin, V; 42 (upd.); 117 (upd.)
Continental AG, V; 56 (upd.)
Continental General Tire Corp., 23
Cooper Tire & Rubber Company, 8; 23 (upd.)
Day International, Inc., 84
Elementis plc, 40 (upd.)
General Tire, Inc., 8
Goodyear Tire & Rubber Company, The, V; 20 (upd.); 75 (upd.)
Hankook Tire Company Ltd., 105
Kelly-Springfield Tire Company, The, 8
Kumho Tire Company Ltd., 105
Les Schwab Tire Centers, 50; 117 (upd.)
Myers Industries, Inc., 19; 96 (upd.)
Pirelli S.p.A., V; 15 (upd.)
Safeskin Corporation, 18
Sumitomo Rubber Industries, Ltd., V; 107 (upd.)
Tillotson Corp., 15
Treadco, Inc., 19
Trelleborg AB, 93
Ube Industries, Ltd., III; 38 (upd.)
Yokohama Rubber Company, Limited, The, V; 19 (upd.); 91 (upd.)

Telecommunications

A.S. Eesti Mobiltelefon, 117
A.H. Belo Corporation, 30 (upd.)
Abertis Infraestructuras, S.A., 65
Abril S.A., 95
Acme-Cleveland Corp., 13
ADC Telecommunications, Inc., 10; 89 (upd.)
Adelphia Communications Corporation, 17; 52 (upd.)
Adtran Inc., 22
Advanced Fibre Communications, Inc., 63
AEI Music Network Inc., 35
AirTouch Communications, 11
Alaska Communications Systems Group, Inc., 89
Albtelecom Sh. a, 111
Alcatel S.A., 36 (upd.)
Alcatel-Lucent, 109 (upd.)
Allbritton Communications Company, 105
Alliance Atlantis Communications Inc., 39
ALLTEL Corporation, 6; 46 (upd.)
América Móvil, S.A. de C.V., 80
American Tower Corporation, 33
Ameritech Corporation, V; 18 (upd.)
Amstrad plc, 48 (upd.)
AO VimpelCom, 48
AOL Time Warner Inc., 57 (upd.)
Arch Wireless, Inc., 39
ARD, 41
ARINC Inc., 98
ARRIS Group, Inc., 89
Ascent Media Corporation, 107
Ascom AG, 9

Aspect Telecommunications Corporation, 22
Asurion Corporation, 83
AT&T Bell Laboratories, Inc., 13
AT&T Corporation, V; 29 (upd.); 68 (upd.)
AT&T Wireless Services, Inc., 54 (upd.)
Avaya Inc., 104
Basin Electric Power Cooperative, 103
BCE Inc., V; 44 (upd.)
Beasley Broadcast Group, Inc., 51
Belgacom, 6
Bell Atlantic Corporation, V; 25 (upd.)
Bell Canada, 6
BellSouth Corporation, V; 29 (upd.)
Belo Corporation, 98 (upd.)
Bertelsmann A.G., IV; 15 (upd.); 43 (upd.); 91 (upd.)
BET Holdings, Inc., 18
Bharti Tele-Ventures Limited, 75
BHC Communications, Inc., 26
Blackfoot Telecommunications Group, 60
Bonneville International Corporation, 29
Bouygues S.A., I; 24 (upd.); 97 (upd.)
Brasil Telecom Participações S.A., 57
Brightpoint Inc., 18; 106 (upd.)
Brite Voice Systems, Inc., 20
British Broadcasting Corporation Ltd., 7; 21 (upd.); 89 (upd.)
British Columbia Telephone Company, 6
British Telecommunications plc, V; 15 (upd.)
Broadwing Corporation, 70
BT Group plc, 49 (upd.); 114 (upd.)
Cable & Wireless HKT, 30 (upd.)
Cable and Wireless plc, V; 25 (upd.)
Cablevision Systems Corporation, 7; 30 (upd.); 109 (upd.)
CalAmp Corp., 87
Canadian Broadcasting Corporation (CBC), The, 37
Canal Plus, 10; 34 (upd.)
CanWest Global Communications Corporation, 35
Capital Radio plc, 35
Carlton Communications PLC, 15; 50 (upd.)
Carolina Telephone and Telegraph Company, 10
Carphone Warehouse Group PLC, The, 83
Carrier Access Corporation, 44
CBS Corporation, 28 (upd.)
CBS Television Network, 66 (upd.)
C-COR.net Corp., 38
Centel Corporation, 6
Centennial Communications Corporation, 39
Central European Media Enterprises Ltd., 61
Century Communications Corp., 10
Century Telephone Enterprises, Inc., 9; 54 (upd.)
Cesky Telecom, a.s., 64
Chancellor Media Corporation, 24
Channel Four Television Corporation, 93
Charter Communications, Inc., 33; 116 (upd.)

Orange S.A., 84
Österreichische Post- und
  Telegraphenverwaltung, V
Pacific Internet Limited, 87
Pacific Telecom, Inc., 6
Pacific Telesis Group, V
Paging Network Inc., 11
PanAmSat Corporation, 46
Paxson Communications Corporation, 33
Petry Media Corporation, 102
PGi, 115
Phoenix Media/Communications Group,
  The, 91
PictureTel Corp., 10; 27 (upd.)
Portugal Telecom SGPS S.A., 69
Posti- ja Telelaitos, 6
Premiere Radio Networks, Inc., 102
Price Communications Corporation, 42
ProSiebenSat.1 Media AG, 54
PT Indosat Tbk, 93
Publishing and Broadcasting Limited, 54
Qatar Telecom QSA, 87
QUALCOMM Incorporated, 20; 47
  (upd.); 114 (upd.)
QVC Network Inc., 9
Qwest Communications International,
  Inc., 37; 116 (upd.)
Raycom Media, Inc., 106
RCN Corporation, 70
RealNetworks, Inc., 53; 109 (upd.)
Regent Communications, Inc., 87
Research in Motion Limited, 54; 106
  (upd.)
RMH Teleservices, Inc., 42
Rochester Telephone Corporation, 6
Rockwell Collins, 106
Rogers Communications Inc., 30 (upd.)
Rostelecom Joint Stock Co., 99
Royal KPN N.V., 30
Rural Cellular Corporation, 43
Safaricom Limited, 116
Saga Communications, Inc., 27
Salem Communications Corporation, 97
Sawtek Inc., 43 (upd.)
SBC Communications Inc., 32 (upd.)
Schweizerische Post-, Telefon- und
  Telegrafen-Betriebe, V
Scientific-Atlanta, Inc., 6; 45 (upd.)
Seat Pagine Gialle S.p.A., 47
Securicor Plc, 45
S4C International, 115
Shenandoah Telecommunications
  Company, 89
Sinclair Broadcast Group, Inc., 25; 109
  (upd.)
Singapore Telecommunications Limited,
  111
Sirius Satellite Radio, Inc., 69
Sirti S.p.A., 76
Skype Technologies S.A., 108
Società Finanziaria Telefonica per Azioni,
  V
Softbank Corporation, 77 (upd.)
Sonera Corporation, 50
Southern New England
  Telecommunications Corporation, 6
Southwestern Bell Corporation, V
Spanish Broadcasting System, Inc., 41

Special Broadcasting Service Corporation,
  115
Spelling Entertainment, 35 (upd.)
Sprint Nextel Corporation, 9; 46 (upd.);
  110 (upd.)
Starent Networks Corp., 106
StarHub Ltd., 77
StrataCom, Inc., 16
Swedish Telecom, V
Swisscom AG, 58
Sycamore Networks, Inc., 45
Syniverse Holdings Inc., 97
SynOptics Communications, Inc., 10
Talk America Holdings, Inc., 70
TDC A/S, 63
Tekelec, 83
Tele Norte Leste Participações S.A., 80
Telecom Argentina S.A., 63
Telecom Australia, 6
Telecom Corporation of New Zealand
  Limited, 54
Telecom Eireann, 7
Telecom Italia Mobile S.p.A., 63
Telecom Italia S.p.A., 43
Telefonaktiebolaget LM Ericsson, V; 46
  (upd.)
Telefónica de Argentina S.A., 61
Telefónica S.A., V; 46 (upd.); 108 (upd.)
Telefonos de Mexico S.A. de C.V., 14; 63
  (upd.)
Telekom Austria AG, 115 (upd.)
Telekom Malaysia Bhd, 76
Telekomunikacja Polska SA, 50
Telenor ASA, 69
Telephone and Data Systems, Inc., 9
Tele2 AB, 115 (upd.)
Télévision Française 1, 23
TeliaSonera AB, 57 (upd.)
Telkom S.A. Ltd., 106
Tellabs, Inc., 11; 40 (upd.)
Telstra Corporation Limited, 50
TELUS Corporation, 114 (upd.)
Terremark Worldwide, Inc., 99
Thomas Crosbie Holdings Limited, 81
Tiscali SpA, 48
Titan Corporation, The, 36
T-Netix, Inc., 46
Tollgrade Communications, Inc., 44
TV Azteca, S.A. de C.V., 39
Twitter, Inc., 118
U S West, Inc., V; 25 (upd.)
U.S. Cellular Corporation, 9; 31 (upd.);
  88 (upd.)
U.S. Satellite Broadcasting Company, Inc.,
  20
UFA TV & Film Produktion GmbH, 80
United Pan-Europe Communications NV,
  47
United Telecommunications, Inc., V
United Video Satellite Group, 18
Unitymedia GmbH, 115
Univision Communications Inc., 24; 83
  (upd.)
USA Interactive, Inc., 47 (upd.)
USA Mobility Inc., 97 (upd.)
UTStarcom, Inc., 77

Verizon Communications Inc. 43 (upd.);
  78 (upd.)
ViaSat, Inc., 54
Vivendi, 46 (upd.); 112 (upd.)
Vodacom Group Pty. Ltd., 106
Vodafone Group Plc, 11; 36 (upd.); 75
  (upd.)
voestalpine AG, 57 (upd.); 115 (upd.)
Vonage Holdings Corp., 81
Walt Disney Company, The, II; 6 (upd.);
  30 (upd.); 63 (upd.)
Wanadoo S.A., 75
Watkins-Johnson Company, 15
Weather Channel Companies, The, 52
West Corporation, 42
Western Union Financial Services, Inc., 54
Western Wireless Corporation, 36
Westwood One Inc., 23; 106 (upd.)
Williams Communications Group, Inc.,
  34
Williams Companies, Inc., The, 31 (upd.)
Wipro Limited, 43; 106 (upd.)
Wisconsin Bell, Inc., 14
Working Assets Funding Service, 43
Worldwide Pants Inc., 97
XM Satellite Radio Holdings, Inc., 69
Young Broadcasting Inc., 40
Zain, 102
Zed Group, 93
Zoom Technologies, Inc., 53 (upd.)

Textiles & Apparel

Acorn Products, Inc., 55
adidas Group AG, 14; 33 (upd.); 75
  (upd.)
Adolfo Dominguez S.A., 72
Aéropostale, Inc., 89
Albany International Corp., 8
Alba-Waldensian, Inc., 30
Alexandra plc, 88
Alexon Group PLC, 107
Algo Group Inc., 24
Allen-Edmonds Shoe Corporation, 61
Alpargatas S.A.I.C., 87
American & Efird, Inc., 82
American Apparel, Inc., 90
American Safety Razor Company, 20
Amoskeag Company, 8
Andin International, Inc., 100
Angelica Corporation, 15; 43 (upd.)
Annin & Co., 100
Anta Sports Products Ltd., 117
AR Accessories Group, Inc., 23
Aris Industries, Inc., 16
ASICS Corporation, 57
AstenJohnson Inc., 90
Athlete's Foot Brands LLC, The, 84
Authentic Fitness Corporation, 20; 51
  (upd.)
Avon Products, Inc., 109 (upd.)
Babolat VS, S.A., 97
Banana Republic Inc., 25
Bardwil Industries Inc., 98
Bata Ltd., 62
Bauer Hockey, Inc., 104
bebe stores, inc., 31; 103 (upd.)
Belleville Shoe Manufacturing Company,
  92

Utilities

New England Electric System, V
New Jersey Resources Corporation, 54
New York State Electric and Gas, 6
Neyveli Lignite Corporation Ltd., 65
Niagara Mohawk Holdings Inc., V; 45
   (upd.)
Nicor Inc., 6; 86 (upd.)
NIPSCO Industries, Inc., 6
NiSource Inc., 109 (upd.)
Norsk Hydro ASA, 10; 35 (upd.); 109
   (upd.)
North West Water Group plc, 11
Northeast Utilities, V; 48 (upd.)
Northern States Power Company, V; 20
   (upd.)
Northwest Natural Gas Company, 45
NorthWestern Corporation, 37
Nova Corporation of Alberta, V
NRG Energy, Inc., 79
NSTAR, 106 (upd.)
Oglethorpe Power Corporation, 6
Ohio Edison Company, V
Oklahoma Gas and Electric Company, 6
ONEOK Inc., 7; 116 (upd.)
Ontario Hydro Services Company, 6; 32
   (upd.)
Osaka Gas Company, Ltd., V; 60 (upd.)
Österreichische Elektrizitätswirtschafts-AG,
   85
Otter Tail Power Company, 18
Pacific Enterprises, V
Pacific Gas and Electric Company, V
PacifiCorp, V; 26 (upd.)
Paddy Power plc, 98
Pampa Energía S.A., 118
Panhandle Eastern Corporation, V
PECO Energy Company, 11
Pennon Group Plc, 45
Pennsylvania Power & Light Company, V
Peoples Energy Corporation, 6
Pepco Holdings, Inc., 116
PG&E Corporation, 26 (upd.); 116
   (upd.)
Philadelphia Electric Company, V
Philadelphia Gas Works Company, 92
Philadelphia Suburban Corporation, 39
Piedmont Natural Gas Company, Inc., 27;
   117 (upd.)
Pinnacle West Capital Corporation, 6; 54
   (upd.)
PJM Interconnection L.L.C., 116
Plains All American Pipeline, L.P., 108
PNM Resources Inc., 51 (upd.)
Portland General Corporation, 6
Potomac Electric Power Company, 6
Powergen PLC, 11; 50 (upd.)
Power-One, Inc., 79
PPL Corporation, 41 (upd.)
PreussenElektra Aktiengesellschaft, V
Progress Energy, Inc., 74
PSI Resources, 6
Public Service Company of Colorado, 6
Public Service Company of New
   Hampshire, 21; 55 (upd.)
Public Service Company of New Mexico,
   6
Public Service Enterprise Group Inc., V;
   44 (upd.)

Puerto Rico Electric Power Authority, 47
Puget Sound Energy Inc., 6; 50 (upd.)
Questar Corporation, 6; 26 (upd.)
RAO Unified Energy System of Russia, 45
Reliant Energy Inc., 44 (upd.)
Revere Electric Supply Company, 96
Rochester Gas and Electric Corporation, 6
Ruhrgas AG, V; 38 (upd.)
RWE AG, V; 50 (upd.)
Salt River Project, 19
San Diego Gas & Electric Company, V;
   107 (upd.)
SCANA Corporation, 6; 56 (upd.)
Scarborough Public Utilities Commission,
   9
SCEcorp, V
Scottish and Southern Energy plc, 66
   (upd.)
Scottish Hydro-Electric PLC, 13
Scottish Power plc, 19; 49 (upd.)
Seattle City Light, 50
SEMCO Energy, Inc., 44
Sempra Energy, 25 (upd.); 116 (upd.)
Severn Trent PLC, 12; 38 (upd.)
Shikoku Electric Power Company, Inc., V;
   60 (upd.)
SJW Corporation, 70
Sonat, Inc., 6
South Jersey Industries, Inc., 42
Southern Company, The, V; 38 (upd.)
Southern Connecticut Gas Company, 84
Southern Electric PLC, 13
Southern Indiana Gas and Electric
   Company, 13
Southern Union Company, 27
Southwest Gas Corporation, 19
Southwest Water Company, 47
Southwestern Electric Power Co., 21
Southwestern Public Service Company, 6
Spectra Energy Corporation, 116
State Grid Corporation of China, 108
Statnett SF, 110
Suez Lyonnaise des Eaux, 36 (upd.)
SUEZ-TRACTEBEL S.A., 97 (upd.)
TECO Energy, Inc., 6
Tennessee Valley Authority, 50
Tennet BV, 78
Texas Utilities Company, V; 25 (upd.)
Thames Water plc, 11; 90 (upd.)
Tohoku Electric Power Company, Inc., V
Tokyo Electric Power Company, The, V;
   74 (upd.)
Tokyo Gas Co., Ltd., V; 55 (upd.)
TransAlta Utilities Corporation, 6
TransCanada PipeLines Limited, V
Transco Energy Company, V
Trigen Energy Corporation, 42
Tri-State Generation and Transmission
   Association, Inc., 103
Tucson Electric Power Company, 6
UGI Corporation, 12
Unicom Corporation, 29 (upd.)
Union Electric Company, V
United Illuminating Company, The, 21
United Utilities PLC, 52 (upd.)
United Water Resources, Inc., 40
Unitil Corporation, 37
Utah Power and Light Company, 27

UtiliCorp United Inc., 6
Vattenfall AB, 57
Vectren Corporation, 98 (upd.)
Vereinigte Elektrizitätswerke Westfalen
   AG, V
VEW AG, 39
Viridian Group plc, 64
Warwick Valley Telephone Company, 55
Washington Gas Light Company, 19
Washington Natural Gas Company, 9
Washington Water Power Company, 6
Westar Energy, Inc., 57 (upd.)
Western Resources, Inc., 12
Wheelabrator Technologies, Inc., 6
Wisconsin Energy Corporation, 6; 54
   (upd.)
Wisconsin Public Service Corporation, 9
WPL Holdings, Inc., 6
WPS Resources Corporation, 53 (upd.)
Xcel Energy Inc., 73 (upd.)

Waste Services

Allied Waste Industries, Inc., 50
Allwaste, Inc., 18
American Ecology Corporation, 77
Appliance Recycling Centers of America,
   Inc., 42
Azcon Corporation, 23
Berliner Stadtreinigungsbetriebe, 58
Biffa plc, 92
Brambles Industries Limited, 42
Browning-Ferris Industries, Inc., V; 20
   (upd.)
Casella Waste Systems Inc., 102
Chemical Waste Management, Inc., 9
CHHJ Franchising LLC, 105
Clean Harbors, Inc., 73
Clean Venture, Inc., 104
Copart Inc., 23
Darling International Inc., 85
E.On AG, 50 (upd.)
Ecolab Inc., I; 13 (upd.); 34 (upd.); 85
   (upd.)
Ecology and Environment, Inc., 39
Empresas Públicas de Medellín S.A.E.S.P.,
   91
Fuel Tech, Inc., 85
Industrial Services of America, Inc., 46
Ionics, Incorporated, 52
ISS A/S, 49
Jani-King International, Inc., 85
Kelda Group plc, 45
McClain Industries, Inc., 51
MPW Industrial Services Group, Inc., 53
Newpark Resources, Inc., 63
Norcal Waste Systems, Inc., 60
Oakleaf Waste Management, LLC, 97
1-800-GOT-JUNK? LLC, 74
Onet S.A., 92
Pennon Group Plc, 45
Perma-Fix Environmental Services, Inc.,
   99
Philip Environmental Inc., 16
Philip Services Corp., 73
Republic Services, Inc., 92
Roto-Rooter, Inc., 15; 61 (upd.)

Geographic Index

Grupo Aeroportuario del Pacífico, S.A. de C.V., 85

Grupo Aeropuerto del Sureste, S.A. de C.V., 48

Grupo Ángeles Servicios de Salud, S.A. de C.V., 84

Grupo Carso, S.A. de C.V., 21; 107 (upd.)

Grupo Casa Saba, S.A. de C.V., 39

Grupo Comercial Chedraui S.A. de C.V., 86

Grupo Comex, 115

Grupo Corvi S.A. de C.V., 86

Grupo Cydsa, S.A. de C.V., 39

Grupo Elektra, S.A. de C.V., 39

Grupo Financiero Banamex S.A., 54

Grupo Financiero Banorte, S.A. de C.V., 51

Grupo Financiero BBVA Bancomer S.A., 54

Grupo Financiero Serfin, S.A., 19

Grupo Gigante, S.A. de C.V., 34

Grupo Herdez, S.A. de C.V., 35

Grupo IMSA, S.A. de C.V., 44

Grupo Industrial Bimbo, 19

Grupo Industrial Durango, S.A. de C.V., 37

Grupo Industrial Herradura, S.A. de C.V., 83

Grupo Industrial Lala, S.A. de C.V., 82

Grupo Industrial Saltillo, S.A. de C.V., 54

Grupo Mexico, S.A. de C.V., 40

Grupo Modelo, S.A. de C.V., 29

Grupo Omnilife S.A. de C.V., 88

Grupo Posadas, S.A. de C.V., 57

Grupo Sanborns, S.A. de C.V., 107 (upd.)

Grupo Televisa, S.A., 18; 54 (upd.)

Grupo TMM, S.A. de C.V., 50

Grupo Transportación Ferroviaria Mexicana, S.A. de C.V., 47

Grupo Viz, S.A. de C.V., 84

Hylsamex, S.A. de C.V., 39

Industrias Bachoco, S.A. de C.V., 39

Industrias Peñoles, S.A. de C.V., 22; 107 (upd.)

Internacional de Ceramica, S.A. de C.V., 53

Jugos del Valle, S.A. de C.V., 85

Kimberly-Clark de México, S.A. de C.V., 54

Mexichem, S.A.B. de C.V., 99

Nadro S.A. de C.V., 86

Organización Soriana S.A.B. de C.V., 35; 115 (upd.)

Petróleos Mexicanos (PEMEX), IV; 19 (upd.); 104 (upd.)

Proeza S.A. de C.V., 82

Pulsar Internacional S.A., 21

Real Turismo, S.A. de C.V., 50

Sanborn Hermanos, S.A., 20

SANLUIS Corporación, S.A.B. de C.V., 95

Sears Roebuck de México, S.A. de C.V., 20

Telefonos de Mexico S.A. de C.V., 14; 63 (upd.)

Tenedora Nemak, S.A. de C.V., 102

Tubos de Acero de Mexico, S.A. (TAMSA), 41

TV Azteca, S.A. de C.V., 39

Urbi Desarrollos Urbanos, S.A. de C.V., 81

Valores Industriales S.A., 19

Vitro Corporativo S.A. de C.V., 34

Wal-Mart de Mexico, S.A. de C.V., 35 (upd.)

Mongolia
Newcom, LLC, 104

Nepal
Royal Nepal Airline Corporation, 41

The Netherlands
ABN AMRO Holding, N.V., 50

AEGON N.V., III; 50 (upd.)

Akzo Nobel N.V., 13; 41 (upd.); 112 (upd.)

Algemene Bank Nederland N.V., II

Amsterdam-Rotterdam Bank N.V., II

Arcadis NV, 26

ASML Holding N.V., 50

Avantium Technologies BV 79

Baan Company, 25

Blokker Holding B.V., 84

Bols Distilleries NV, 74

Bolton Group B.V., 86

Buhrmann NV, 41

Campina Group, The, 78

Chicago Bridge & Iron Company N.V., 82 (upd.)

CNH Global N.V., 38 (upd.); 99 (upd.)

CSM N.V., 65

Deli Universal NV, 66

Drie Mollen Holding B.V., 99

DSM N.V., I; 56 (upd.)

Elsevier N.V., IV

Endemol Entertainment Holding NV, 46

Equant N.V., 52

Euronext N.V., 89 (upd.)

European Aeronautic Defence and Space Company EADS N.V., 52 (upd.); 109 (upd)

Friesland Coberco Dairy Foods Holding N.V., 59

Fugro N.V., 98

Getronics NV, 39

Granaria Holdings B.V., 66

Grand Hotel Krasnapolsky N.V., 23

Greenpeace International, 74

Grontmij N.V., 110

Gucci Group NV, 50; 115 (upd.)

Hagemeyer N.V., 39

Head N.V., 55

Heijmans N.V., 66

Heineken N.V., I; 13 (upd.); 34 (upd.); 90 (upd.)

HEMA B.V., 111

Holland Casino, 107

IHC Caland N.V., 71

IKEA Group, 94 (upd.)

Indigo NV, 26

ING Groep N.V., 108

Intres B.V., 82

Ispat International N.V., 30

KLM Royal Dutch Airlines, 104 (upd.)

Koninklijke Ahold N.V. (Royal Ahold), II; 16 (upd.)

Koninklijke Houthandel G Wijma & Zonen BV, 96

Koninklijke Luchtvaart Maatschappij, N.V. (KLM Royal Dutch Airlines), I; 28 (upd.)

Koninklijke Nederlandsche Hoogovens en Staalfabrieken NV, IV

Koninklijke Nedlloyd N.V., 6; 26 (upd.)

Koninklijke Philips Electronics N.V., 50 (upd.)

Koninklijke PTT Nederland NV, V

Koninklijke Reesink N.V., 104

Koninklijke Vendex KBB N.V. (Royal Vendex KBB N.V.), 62 (upd.)

Koninklijke Wessanen nv, II; 54 (upd.); 114 (upd.)

KPMG International, 10; 33 (upd.); 108 (upd.)

Laurus N.V., 65

LyondellBasell Industries Holdings N.V., 109 (upd.)

Mammoet Transport B.V., 26

MIH Limited, 31

N.V. AMEV, III

N.V. Holdingmaatschappij De Telegraaf, 23

N.V. Koninklijke Nederlandse Vliegtuigenfabriek Fokker, I; 28 (upd.)

N.V. Nederlandse Gasunie, V; 111 (upd.)

Nationale-Nederlanden N.V., III

New Holland N.V., 22

Nutreco Holding N.V., 56

Océ N.V., 24; 91 (upd.)

PCM Uitgevers NV, 53

Philips Electronics N.V., II; 13 (upd.)

PolyGram N.V., 23

Prada Holding B.V., 45

Qiagen N.V., 39

Rabobank Group, 116 (upd.)

Rabobank Group, 33

Randstad Holding nv, 16; 43 (upd.); 113 (upd.)

Rodamco N.V., 26

Royal Dutch Shell plc, IV; 49 (upd.); 108 (upd.)

Royal Grolsch NV, 54

Royal KPN N.V., 30

Royal Numico N.V., 37

Royal Packaging Industries Van Leer N.V., 30

Royal Ten Cate N.V., 68

Royal Vopak NV, 41

SHV Holdings N.V., 55

Telegraaf Media Groep N.V., 98 (upd.)

Tennet BV, 78

TNT Post Group N.V., V; 27 (upd.); 30 (upd.)

TomTom N.V., 81

Toolex International N.V., 26

TPG N.V., 64 (upd.)

Trader Classified Media N.V., 57

Triple P N.V., 26

Unilever N.V., II; 7 (upd.); 32 (upd.)

Constar International Inc., 64
Constellation Brands, Inc., 68 (upd.)
Constellation Energy Group, Inc., 116 (upd.)
Consumers Power Co., 14
Consumers Union, 26; 118 (upd.)
Consumers Water Company, 14
Container Store, The, 36
ContiGroup Companies, Inc., 43 (upd.)
Continental Airlines, Inc., I; 21 (upd.); 52 (upd.); 110 (upd.)
Continental Bank Corporation, II
Continental Cablevision, Inc., 7
Continental Can Co., Inc., 15
Continental Corporation, The, III
Continental General Tire Corp., 23
Continental Grain Company, 10; 13 (upd.)
Continental Graphics Corporation, 110
Continental Group Company, I
Continental Medical Systems, Inc., 10
Continental Resources, Inc., 89
Continucare Corporation, 101
Continuum Health Partners, Inc., 60
Control Data Corporation, III
Control Data Systems, Inc., 10
Converse Inc., 9; 31 (upd.)
Con-way Inc., 101
Cook Group Inc., 102
Cooker Restaurant Corporation, 20; 51 (upd.)
CoolSavings, Inc., 77
Cooper Cameron Corporation, 20 (upd.); 58 (upd.)
Cooper Companies, Inc., The, 39
Cooper Industries, Inc., II; 44 (upd.)
Cooper Tire & Rubber Company, 8; 23 (upd.)
Coopers & Lybrand, 9
Copart Inc., 23
Copley Press, Inc., The, 23
Copps Corporation, The, 32
Corbis Corporation, 31
Corcoran Group, Inc., The, 58
Cordis Corporation, 19; 46 (upd.); 112 (upd.)
CoreStates Financial Corp, 17
Corinthian Colleges, Inc., 39; 92 (upd.)
Corky McMillin Companies, The, 98
Corn Products International, Inc., 116
Cornell Companies, Inc., 112
Corning Inc., III; 44 (upd.); 90 (upd.)
Corporate Executive Board Company, The, 89
Corporate Express, Inc., 22; 47 (upd.)
Corporate Software Inc., 9
Corporation for Public Broadcasting, 14; 89 (upd.)
Correctional Services Corporation, 30
Corrections Corporation of America, 23
Corrpro Companies, Inc., 20
CORT Business Services Corporation, 26
Corus Bankshares, Inc., 75
Cosi, Inc., 53
Cosmair, Inc., 8
Cosmetic Center, Inc., The, 22
Cosmolab Inc., 96
Cost Plus, Inc., 27; 107 (upd.)

CoStar Group, Inc., 73
Costco Wholesale Corporation, V; 43 (upd.); 105 (upd.)
Cost-U-Less, Inc., 51
Cotter & Company, V
Cotton Incorporated, 46
Coty Inc., 36; 115 (upd.)
Coudert Brothers, 30
Council on International Educational Exchange Inc., 81
Country Kitchen International, Inc., 76
Countrywide Financial, 16; 100 (upd.)
County Seat Stores Inc., 9
Courier Corporation, 41
Cousins Properties Incorporated, 65
Covance Inc., 30; 98 (upd.)
Covanta Energy Corporation, 64 (upd.)
Coventry Health Care, Inc., 59
Covington & Burling, 40
Cowen Group, Inc., 92
Cowles Media Company, 23
Cox Enterprises, Inc., IV; 22 (upd.); 67 (upd.)
Cox Radio, Inc., 89
CPAC, Inc., 86
CPC International Inc., II
CPI Aerostructures, Inc., 75
CPI Corp., 38
CPP International, LLC, 103
CR England, Inc., 63
CRA International, Inc., 93
Cracker Barrel Old Country Store, Inc., 10
Craftmade International, Inc., 44
Craftmatic Organization Inc., 117
Craig Hospital, 99
craigslist, inc., 89
Crain Communications, Inc., 12; 35 (upd.)
Cramer, Berkowitz & Co., 34
Cramer-Krasselt Company, 104
Crane & Co., Inc., 26; 103 (upd.)
Crane Co., 8; 30 (upd.); 101 (upd.)
Cranium, Inc., 69
Crate and Barrel, 9
Cravath, Swaine & Moore, 43
Crawford & Company, 87
Cray Inc., 75 (upd.)
Cray Research, Inc., III; 16 (upd.)
Crayola LLC, 115 (upd.)
Creative Artists Agency LLC, 38
Credence Systems Corporation, 90
Credit Acceptance Corporation, 18
Cree Inc., 53
Crete Carrier Corporation, 95
Crimson Exploration Inc., 116
Crispin Porter + Bogusky, 83
Crocs, Inc., 80
Crompton Corporation, 9; 36 (upd.)
Croscill, Inc., 42
Crosman Corporation, 62
Cross Country Healthcare, Inc., 105
CROSSMARK 79
Crosstex Energy Inc., 107
Crowley Maritime Corporation, 6; 28 (upd.)
Crowley, Milner & Company, 19
Crown Books Corporation, 21

Crown Central Petroleum Corporation, 7
Crown Crafts, Inc., 16
Crown Equipment Corporation, 15; 93 (upd.)
Crown Holdings, Inc., 83 (upd.)
Crown Media Holdings, Inc., 45
Crown Vantage Inc., 29
Crown, Cork & Seal Company, Inc., I; 13; 32 (upd.)
CRSS Inc., 6
Cruise America Inc., 21
Crum & Forster Holdings Corporation, 104
CryoLife, Inc., 46
Crystal Brands, Inc., 9
CS First Boston Inc., II
CSG Systems International, Inc., 75
CSK Auto Corporation, 38
CSN Stores LLC, 116
CSS Industries, Inc., 35
CSX Corporation, V; 22 (upd.); 79 (upd.)
CTB International Corporation, 43 (upd.)
C-Tech Industries Inc., 90
CTG, Inc., 11
CTS Corporation, 39
Cubic Corporation, 19; 98 (upd.)
CUC International Inc., 16
Cuisinart Corporation, 24
Cuisine Solutions Inc., 84
Culbro Corporation, 15
CulinArt, Inc., 92
Cullen/Frost Bankers, Inc., 25; 111 (upd.)
Culligan Water Technologies, Inc., 12; 38 (upd.)
Culp, Inc., 29
Culver Franchising System, Inc., 58
Cumberland Farms, Inc., 17; 84 (upd.)
Cumberland Packing Corporation, 26
Cummins Engine Company, Inc., I; 12 (upd.); 40 (upd.)
Cumulus Media Inc., 37
CUNA Mutual Group, 62
Cunard Line Ltd., 23
CUNO Incorporated, 57
Current, Inc., 37
Curtice-Burns Foods, Inc., 7; 21 (upd.)
Curtiss-Wright Corporation, 10; 35 (upd.)
Curves International, Inc., 54
Cushman & Wakefield, Inc., 86
Custom Chrome, Inc., 16; 74 (upd.)
Cutera, Inc., 84
Cutter & Buck Inc., 27
CVR Energy Corporation, 116
CVS Caremark Corporation, 45 (upd.); 108 (upd.)
Cyan Worlds Inc., 101
Cybermedia, Inc., 25
Cyberonics, Inc. 79
Cybex International, Inc., 49
Cygne Designs, Inc., 25
Cygnus Business Media, Inc., 56
Cymer, Inc., 77
Cypress Semiconductor Corporation, 20; 48 (upd.)
Cyprus Amax Minerals Company, 21
Cyprus Minerals Company, 7
Cyrk Inc., 19
Cystic Fibrosis Foundation, 93

GEOGRAPHIC INDEX

NERCO, Inc., 7
NetApp, Inc., 116
NetCracker Technology Corporation, 98
Netezza Corporation, 69
Netflix, Inc., 58; 115 (upd.)
NETGEAR, Inc., 81
NetIQ Corporation 79
NetJets Inc., 96 (upd.)
Netscape Communications Corporation, 15; 35 (upd.)
Network Appliance, Inc., 58
Network Associates, Inc., 25
Network Equipment Technologies Inc., 92
Neuberger Berman Inc., 57
NeuStar, Inc., 81
Neutrogena Corporation, 17
Nevada Bell Telephone Company, 14
Nevada Power Company, 11
Nevamar Company, 82
New Balance Athletic Shoe, Inc., 25; 68 (upd.)
New Belgium Brewing Company, Inc., 68
New Brunswick Scientific Co., Inc., 45
New Chapter Inc., 96
New Dana Perfumes Company, 37
New England Business Service Inc., 18; 78 (upd.)
New England Confectionery Co., 15
New England Electric System, V
New England Mutual Life Insurance Company, III
New Enterprise Associates, 116
New Jersey Devils, 84
New Jersey Manufacturers Insurance Company, 96
New Jersey Resources Corporation, 54
New Line Cinema, Inc., 47
New Orleans Saints LP, 58
New Piper Aircraft, Inc., The, 44
New Plan Realty Trust, 11
New School, The, 103
New Seasons Market, 75
New Street Capital Inc., 8
New Times, Inc., 45
New Valley Corporation, 17
New World Pasta Company, 53
New World Restaurant Group, Inc., 44
New York & Company Inc., 113
New York City Health and Hospitals Corporation, 60
New York City Off-Track Betting Corporation, 51; 115 (upd.)
New York Community Bancorp Inc., 78
New York Daily News, 32
New York Health Care, Inc., 72
New York Life Insurance Company, III; 45 (upd.); 118 (upd.)
New York Restaurant Group, Inc., 32
New York Shakespeare Festival Management, 93
New York State Electric and Gas, 6
New York Stock Exchange, Inc., 9; 39 (upd.)
New York Times Company, The, IV; 19 (upd.); 61 (upd.)
New York Yacht Club, Inc., 103
Newark Group, Inc., The, 102
Neways Inc., 78

Newcor, Inc., 40
Newegg Inc., 107
Newell Rubbermaid Inc., 9; 52 (upd.)
Newfield Exploration Company, 65
Newhall Land and Farming Company, 14
Newly Weds Foods, Inc., 74
Newman's Own, Inc., 37
NewMarket Corporation, 116
Newmont Mining Corporation, 7; 94 (upd.)
Newpark Resources, Inc., 63
Newport Corporation, 71
Newport News Shipbuilding Inc., 13; 38 (upd.)
News America Publishing Inc., 12
News Communications, Inc., 103
News Corporation, 109 (upd.)
Newsday Media Group, 103
NewYork-Presbyterian Hospital, 59
Nexstar Broadcasting Group, Inc., 73
Nextel Communications, Inc., 10; 27 (upd.)
NextWave Wireless Inc., 112
NFL Films, 75
NFO Worldwide, Inc., 24
NGC Corporation, 18
Niagara Corporation, 28
Niagara Mohawk Holdings Inc., V; 45 (upd.)
Nichols Research Corporation, 18
Nicklaus Companies, 45
Nicole Miller, 98
Nicor Inc., 6; 86 (upd.)
Nielsen Business Media, Inc., 98
NIKE, Inc., V; 8 (upd.); 36 (upd.); 75 (upd.)
Nikken Global Inc., 32
Niman Ranch, Inc., 67
Nimbus CD International, Inc., 20
Nine West Group, Inc., 11; 39 (upd.)
99¢ Only Stores, 25; 100 (upd.)
NIPSCO Industries, Inc., 6
NiSource Inc., 109 (upd.)
Nitches, Inc., 53
NL Industries, Inc., 10
Nobel Learning Communities, Inc., 37; 76 (upd.)
Noble Affiliates, Inc., 11
Noble Roman's Inc., 14; 99 (upd.)
Noland Company, 35; 107 (upd.)
Nolo.com, Inc., 49
Noodle Kidoodle, 16
Noodles & Company, Inc., 55
Nooter Corporation, 61
Norcal Waste Systems, Inc., 60
NordicTrack, 22
Nordson Corporation, 11; 48 (upd.)
Nordstrom, Inc., V; 18 (upd.); 67 (upd.)
Norelco Consumer Products Co., 26
Norfolk Southern Corporation, V; 29 (upd.); 75 (upd.)
Norm Thompson Outfitters, Inc., 47
Norrell Corporation, 25
Norstan, Inc., 16
Nortek, Inc., 34
North American Galvanizing & Coatings, Inc., 99
North Atlantic Trading Company Inc., 65

North Face, Inc., The, 18; 78 (upd.)
North Fork Bancorporation, Inc., 46
North Pacific Group, Inc., 61
North Star Steel Company, 18
Northeast Utilities, V; 48 (upd.)
Northern States Power Company, V; 20 (upd.)
Northern Trust Corporation, 9; 101 (upd.)
Northland Cranberries, Inc., 38
Northrop Grumman Corporation, I; 11 (upd.); 45 (upd.); 111 (upd.)
Northwest Airlines Corporation, I; 6 (upd.); 26 (upd.); 74 (upd.)
Northwest Natural Gas Company, 45
NorthWestern Corporation, 37
The Northwestern Mutual Life Insurance Company, III; 45 (upd.); 118 (upd.)
Norton Company, 8
Norton McNaughton, 27
Norwood Promotional Products, Inc., 26
Notations, Inc., 110
NovaCare, Inc., 11
NovaStar Financial, Inc., 91
Novell, Inc., 6; 23 (upd.)
Novellus Systems, Inc., 18
Noven Pharmaceuticals, Inc., 55
NPC International, Inc., 40
NPD Group, Inc., The, 68
NRG Energy, Inc. 79
NRT Incorporated, 61
NSF International, 72
NSS Enterprises Inc., 78
NSTAR, 106 (upd.)
NTD Architecture, 101
NTK Holdings Inc., 107 (upd.)
NTN Buzztime, Inc., 86
Nu Skin Enterprises, Inc., 27; 76 (upd.)
Nucor Corporation, 7; 21 (upd.); 79 (upd.)
Nugget Market, Inc., 118
Nu-kote Holding, Inc., 18
NuStar Energy L.P., 111
Nutraceutical International Corporation, 37
NutraSweet Company, The, 8; 107 (upd.)
NutriSystem, Inc., 71
Nutrition for Life International Inc., 22
Nutrition 21 Inc., 97
NVIDIA Corporation, 54
NVR Inc., 8; 70 (upd.)
NYMAGIC, Inc., 41
NYNEX Corporation, V
Nypro, Inc., 101
O.C. Tanner Co., 69
Oak Harbor Freight Lines, Inc., 53
Oak Industries Inc., 21
Oak Technology, Inc., 22
Oakhurst Dairy, 60
Oakleaf Waste Management, LLC, 97
Oakley, Inc., 18; 49 (upd.); 111 (upd.)
Oaktree Capital Management, LLC, 71
Oakwood Homes Corporation, 15
Obagi Medical Products, Inc., 95
Oberto Sausage Company, Inc., 92
Obie Media Corporation, 56
Occidental Petroleum Corporation, IV; 25 (upd.); 71 (upd.)

United Defense Industries, Inc., 30; 66 (upd.)
United Dominion Industries Limited, 8; 16 (upd.)
United Dominion Realty Trust, Inc., 52
United Farm Workers of America, 88
United Foods, Inc., 21
United HealthCare Corporation, 9
United Illuminating Company, The, 21
United Industrial Corporation, 37
United Industries Corporation, 68
United Jewish Communities, 33
United Merchants & Manufacturers, Inc., 13
United National Group, Ltd., 63
United Nations International Children's Emergency Fund (UNICEF), 58
United Natural Foods, Inc., 32; 76 (upd.)
United Negro College Fund, Inc. 79
United Online, Inc., 71 (upd.)
United Parcel Service of America Inc., V; 17 (upd.)
United Parcel Service, Inc., 63; 94 (upd.)
United Press International, Inc., 25; 73 (upd.)
United Rentals, Inc., 34
United Retail Group Inc., 33
United Road Services, Inc., 69
United Service Organizations, 60
United Services Automobile Association, 109 (upd.)
United States Cellular Corporation, 9
United States Filter Corporation, 20
United States Pipe and Foundry Company, 62
United States Playing Card Company, 62
United States Postal Service, 14; 34 (upd.); 108 (upd.)
United States Shoe Corporation, The, V
United States Soccer Federation, 108
United States Steel Corporation, 50 (upd.); 114 (upd.)
United States Sugar Corporation, 115
United States Surgical Corporation, 10; 34 (upd.)
United States Tennis Association, 111
United Stationers Inc., 14; 117 (upd.)
United Talent Agency, Inc., 80
United Technologies Automotive Inc., 15
United Technologies Corporation, I; 10 (upd.); 34 (upd.); 105 (upd.)
United Telecommunications, Inc., V
United Video Satellite Group, 18
United Water Resources, Inc., 40
United Way of America, 36
United Way Worldwide, 112 (upd.)
UnitedHealth Group Incorporated, 103 (upd.)
Unitil Corporation, 37
Unitog Co., 19
Unitrin Inc., 16; 78 (upd.)
Univar Corporation, 9
Universal American Corp., 111
Universal Compression, Inc., 59
Universal Corporation, V; 48 (upd.)
Universal Electronics Inc., 39
Universal Foods Corporation, 7

Universal Forest Products, Inc., 10; 59 (upd.)
Universal Health Services, Inc., 6
Universal International, Inc., 25
Universal Manufacturing Company, 88
Universal Security Instruments, Inc., 96
Universal Stainless & Alloy Products, Inc., 75
Universal Studios, Inc., 33; 100 (upd.)
Universal Technical Institute, Inc., 81
Universal Truckload Services, Inc., 111
University of Chicago Press, The, 79
Univision Communications Inc., 24; 83 (upd.)
Uno Restaurant Corporation, 18
Uno Restaurant Holdings Corporation, 70 (upd.)
Unocal Corporation, IV; 24 (upd.); 71 (upd.)
UnumProvident Corporation, 13; 52 (upd.)
Upjohn Company, The, I; 8 (upd.)
Upper Deck Company, LLC, The, 105
Urban Engineers, Inc., 102
Urban Outfitters, Inc., 14; 74 (upd.)
URS Corporation, 45; 80 (upd.)
US Airways Group, Inc., I; 6 (upd.); 28 (upd.); 52 (upd.); 110 (upd.)
US 1 Industries, Inc., 89
USA Interactive, Inc., 47 (upd.)
USA Mobility Inc., 97 (upd.)
USA Truck, Inc., 42
USAA, 10; 62 (upd.)
USANA, Inc., 29
USF&G Corporation, III
USG Corporation, III; 26 (upd.); 81 (upd.)
UST Inc., 9; 50 (upd.)
USX Corporation, IV; 7 (upd.)
Utah Medical Products, Inc., 36
Utah Power and Light Company, 27
UTG Inc., 100
UtiliCorp United Inc., 6
UTStarcom, Inc., 77
Utz Quality Foods, Inc., 72
UUNET, 38
Uwajimaya, Inc., 60
Vail Resorts, Inc., 11; 43 (upd.)
Valassis Communications, Inc., 8; 37 (upd.); 76 (upd.)
Valero Energy Corporation, 7; 71 (upd.)
Valhi, Inc., 19; 94 (upd.)
Vallen Corporation, 45
Valley Media Inc., 35
Valley National Gases, Inc., 85
Valley Proteins, Inc., 91
ValleyCrest Companies, 81 (upd.)
Valmont Industries, Inc., 19
Valspar Corporation, The, 8; 32 (upd.); 77 (upd.)
Value City Department Stores, Inc., 38
Value Line, Inc., 16; 73 (upd.)
Value Merchants Inc., 13
ValueClick, Inc., 49
ValueVision International, Inc., 22
Valve Corporation, 101
Van Camp Seafood Company, Inc., 7
Vance Publishing Corporation, 64

Vanderbilt University Medical Center, 99
Vanguard Group, Inc., The, 14; 34 (upd.)
Vanguard Health Systems Inc., 70
Vann's Inc., 105
Van's Aircraft, Inc., 65
Vans, Inc., 16; 47 (upd.)
Varco International, Inc., 42
Varian, Inc., 12; 48 (upd.)
Variety Wholesalers, Inc., 73
Variflex, Inc., 51
Vari-Lite International, Inc., 35
Varlen Corporation, 16
Varsity Spirit Corp., 15
VASCO Data Security International, Inc. 79
Vastar Resources, Inc., 24
Vaughan Foods, Inc., 105
VCA Antech, Inc., 58
Vecellio Group, Inc., 113
VECO International, Inc., 7
Vector Group Ltd., 35 (upd.)
Vectren Corporation, 98 (upd.)
Veeco Instruments Inc., 32
Veit Companies, 43; 92 (upd.)
Velocity Express Corporation, 49; 94 (upd.)
Venator Group Inc., 35 (upd.)
Vencor, Inc., 16
Venetian Casino Resort, LLC, 47
Ventana Medical Systems, Inc., 75
Ventura Foods LLC, 90
Venture Stores Inc., 12
VeraSun Energy Corporation, 87
Verbatim Corporation, 14; 74 (upd.)
Veridian Corporation, 54
VeriFone Holdings, Inc., 18; 76 (upd.)
Verint Systems Inc., 73
VeriSign, Inc., 47
Veritas Software Corporation, 45
Verity Inc., 68
Verizon Communications, 43 (upd.); 78 (upd.)
Vermeer Manufacturing Company, 17
Vermont Country Store, The, 93
Vermont Pure Holdings, Ltd., 51
Vermont Teddy Bear Co., Inc., The, 36
Vertex Pharmaceuticals Incorporated, 83
Vertis Communications, 84
Vertrue Inc., 77
VF Corporation, V; 17 (upd.); 54 (upd.)
VHA Inc., 53
Viacom Inc., 7; 23 (upd.); 67 (upd.)
Viad Corp., 73
ViaSat, Inc., 54
Viasoft Inc., 27
VIASYS Healthcare, Inc., 52
Viasystems Group, Inc., 67
Viatech Continental Can Company, Inc., 25 (upd.)
Vicarious Visions, Inc., 108
Vicon Industries, Inc., 44
VICORP Restaurants, Inc., 12; 48 (upd.)
Victory Refrigeration, Inc., 82
Videojet Technologies, Inc., 90
Vienna Sausage Manufacturing Co., 14
Viewpoint International, Inc., 66
ViewSonic Corporation, 72
Viking Office Products, Inc., 10